CANADA

MINNESOTA

Duluth

St. Paul
Minneapolis

WISCONSIN

Lake Superior

Green Bay

MICHIGAN

Lake Huron

MAINE

Augusta

Burlington
Montpelier
VT NH
Concord
Manchester
Lowell
Portland

Boston

NEW YORK

Lake Ontario

Rochester
Syracuse
Albany

MA
Springfield
Providence

CT
Hartford
RI
New Haven

Buffalo

Madison
Milwaukee

Grand Rapids
Lansing
Detroit

Lake Erie

Erie

PENNSYLVANIA

Susquehanna River

Harrisburg

Newark
New York
Trenton

NEW JERSEY

IOWA

Cedar Rapids

Rockford
Chicago
Gary

Toledo
Cleveland
Akron

Wilmington

Des Moines

Davenport

ILLINOIS

Fort Wayne

OHIO

Wheeling

Pittsburgh

Philadelphia

Dover
DELAWARE

Baltimore
Washington, D.C.
Annapolis
MARYLAND

Omaha

Peoria

INDIANA

Columbus

WEST VIRGINIA

Springfield

Indianapolis

Cincinnati

Ohio River

Charleston

VIRGINIA

Richmond
Newport News

Kansas City

Missouri River

St. Louis

Louisville

Frankfort
Lexington

Huntington

James River

Norfolk

Topeka
Kansas City
Jefferson City

MISSOURI

KENTUCKY

Wichita

Springfield

Greensboro
Durham
Raleigh

NORTH CAROLINA

ATLANTIC OCEAN

Tulsa

Nashville
Knoxville

TENNESSEE

Tennessee River

Charlotte

Oklahoma City

ARKANSAS

Memphis

Greenville

SOUTH CAROLINA

Fort Smith
Little Rock

Huntsville

Columbia

Pine Bluff

Birmingham

Atlanta

Charleston

Dallas

Sabine River

Shreveport

LOUISIANA

MISSISSIPPI

Meridian
Jackson

ALABAMA

Montgomery

GEORGIA

Macon
Columbus

Alabama River

Savannah

THE UNITED STATES: POLITICAL

— International boundaries
— State boundaries
⊕ National capital
✸ State capital

0   100   200 Miles
0   100   200 Kilometers

Houston

Baton Rouge

New Orleans

Mobile

Biloxi

Tallahassee

Jacksonville

GULF OF MEXICO

Orlando
Tampa
St. Petersburg

FLORIDA

Fort Lauderdale
Miami

ATLANTIC OCEAN

PUERTO RICO   VIRGIN ISLANDS

GULF OF MEXICO

0   80 Miles
0   80 Kilometers

CUBA

Mississippi River

THE AMERICAN PAST

A Survey of American History

THE AMERICAN PAST

A Survey of American History

Volume I

ENHANCED EIGHTH EDITION

Joseph R. Conlin

THOMSON

WADSWORTH

Australia • Brazil • Canada • Mexico • Singapore • Spain • United Kingdom • United States

THOMSON
WADSWORTH

The American Past: A Survey of American History, Volume I:
To 1877, Enhanced Eighth Edition

Joseph R. Conlin

Publisher: Clark Baxter
Senior Acquisitions Editor: Ashley Dodge
Senior Development Editor: Margaret McAndrew Beasley
Assistant Editor: Ashley Spicer
Editorial Assistant: Heidi Kador
Associate Development Project Manager: Lee McCracken
Executive Marketing Manager: Diane Wenckebach
Marketing Assistant: Aimee Lewis
Lead Marketing Communications Manager: Tami Strang
Senior Production Manager: Michael Burggren
Senior Content Project Manager: Lauren Wheelock

Senior Art Director: Cate Rickard Barr
Manufacturing Manager: Marcia Locke
Senior Rights Acquistion Account
Manager, Text: Margaret Chamberlain-Gaston
Production Service: ICC Macmillan Inc.
Text Designer: Patricia McDermond and Dutton & Sherman Design
Photo Researcher: Lili Weiner
Cover Designer: Dutton & Sherman Design
Cover Image: © SSPL / The Image Works
Cover/Text Printer: Edwards Ann Arbor
Compositor: ICC Macmillan Inc.

Printed in the United States of America
1 2 3 4 5 6 7 11 10 09 08

For more information about our products, contact us at:
Thomson Learning Academic Resource Center
1-800-423-0563
For permission to use material from this text or product, submit a request online at
http://www.thomsonrights.com.
Any additional questions about permissions can be submitted by e-mail to
thomsonrights@thomson.com.

Thomson Higher Education
10 Davis Drive
Belmont, CA 94002-3098
USA

Library of Congress Control Number: 2007942230

ISBN-10: 0-495-56610-1
ISBN-13: 978-0-495-56610-6

To the memory of
J.R.C. (1917–1985)
L.V.C. (1920–2001)

Brief Contents

Table of Contents

List of Maps

How They Lived

Preface

TO THE PROFESSOR

I prepared this new edition because since the time I wrote its predecessor, recently published books (and some older ones that I read for the first time) convinced me that much of nineteenth-, eighteenth-, and seventeenth-century American history had changed. I have listed some of these areas below.

Because I wrote *The American Past* for young men and women who may be taking history only because it's a requirement, my overriding aspiration has been to produce a reading and learning experience that is pleasurable as well as illuminating. Narrative is the kind of prose that most people find enjoyable to read, so narrative is the way I do it. During the more than two decades that *The American Past* has been in print, I have heard from many professors—perhaps close to 200—who have assigned the text to their classes. It has been gratifying that even some of the annoyed correspondents closed their letters with a comment something like, "My students really like *The American Past*. They actually read it!"

NEW TO THIS EDITION

Topics on which I have focused or about which my understanding has been significantly altered since writing the seventh edition have received fresh treatment in this volume. These include:

- Pre-Columbian America
- The early slave trade in West Africa
- The conquest of Mexico
- Elizabethan era colonization ("the failed colonies")
- Witchcraft in colonial New England
- "The overlooked colonies," especially New Netherlands and New Jersey
- The Eastern Woodlands Indians
- New France and the Anglo-French rivalry
- The military history of the War for Independence
- Evangelical religion and denominations
- Fugitive slaves and the Underground Railroad
- Big city political machines
- Racism, Jim Crow segregation, and lynching
- The Civil Rights Movement in the courts
- Popular culture in the 1890s–1900s and 1950s
- The partisan upheaval of the late twentieth century

The treatment of the Revolutionary, Confederation, Federalist, and Jeffersonian eras, particularly of the great movers and shapers of the era, has been profoundly changed by recent scholarship. Since 1995 George Washington, Alexander Hamilton, John Adams, Thomas Jefferson, and James Madison have each been the subject of at least three biographical studies that range in quality from very good to superb (and there have been biographies of John Jay and Gouverneur Morris in the same league).

For the information of instructors who have previously assigned *The American Past,* chapters in this edition that have been written virtually from scratch or so substantially changed as to be new are Chapters 1, 2, 5, 6, 15, 17, 35, 46, 47, and 48. There are about ten **How They Lived** features new to this edition and several dozen new sidebars. I have discarded all the chapter bibliographies ("Further Reading") of the seventh edition and prepared new, more extensive ones with an emphasis on titles published since about 1980. The **Timelines,** lists of **Key Terms** (defined in an appendix), and the **Online Sources Guides** at the end of each chapter are new to this edition.

Where necessary, I have reorganized chapters for the sake of greater clarity and have polished the prose with an eye on making the book more appealing to survey course students. There are, I think, few paragraphs here that read word for word as they did in the seventh edition. I have added illustrative evidence new to me—data, facts, anecdotes—and fresh interpretations throughout the book.

ACKNOWLEDGMENTS

My publishers, as they prepared this new edition, asked history professors from every part of the country to read from one to three chapters of the book and to write critiques for my guidance during revision: What is done well? What is done not so well? What subjects are inadequately covered or could be better explained? Where are my interpretations dead wrong?

This time around all but a half-dozen of the chapter reviews were invaluable. I have not agreed with every criticism. Deadlines and space limitations prevented me from accommodating some suggestions for improvement with which I was and am in complete agreement. (I have filed them for future reference.) I am grateful for the extraordinary and, in my experience, unprecedented favors done me by the following professors of history and—it is a safe bet—teachers of the first order.

LIST OF REVIEWERS

George Alvergue, *Lane Community College*
Mary Ann Bodayla, *Southwest Tennessee Community College*
Scott Carter, *Shasta College*
Albert Churella, *Southern Polytechnic State University*
Craig R. Coenen, *Mercer County Community College*
Richard H. Condon, *University of Maine at Farmington*
Stacy A. Cordery, *Monmouth College*
Linda Cross, *Tyler Junior College*
Barry A. Crouch, *Gallaudet University*
Brian Dirck, *Anderson University*
William Marvin Dulaney, *College of Charleston*

Carla Falkner, *Northeast Mississippi Community College*
Francis Flavin, *University of Texas—Dallas*
George E. Frakes, *Santa Barbara City College*
Thomas M. Gaskin, *Everett Community College*
Joan E. Gittens, *Southwest State University*
Paula K. Hinton, *Tennessee Technological University*
John E. Hollitz, *Community College of Southern Nevada*
Robert R. Jones, *University of Southwestern Louisiana*
Martha Kirchmer, *Grand Valley State University*
Mary S. Lewis, *Jacksonville College*
Milton Madden, *Lane Community College*
Patricia L. Meador, *Louisiana State University, Shreveport*
Angelo Montante, *Glendale Community College*
Jack Oden, *Enterprise State Junior College*
Martin T. Olliff, *Troy University—Dothan Campus*
John S. Olszowka, *University of Maine—Farmington*
Emmett Panzella, *Point Park College*
Richard H. Peterson, *emeritus, San Diego State University*
Nancy L. Rachels, *Hillsborough Community College*
Michelle Riley, *Del Mar College*
Stephanie Abbot Roper, *West Texas A&M University*
Karen Rubin, *Florida State University*
William Scofield, *Yakima Valley Community College*
Richard S. Sorrell, *Brookdale Community College*
Amos St. Germain, *Wentworth Institute of Technology*
Ronald Story, *University of Massachusetts*
Ruth Suyama, *Los Angeles Mission College*
Daniel C. Vogt, *Jackson State University*
Pamela West, *Jefferson State Community College*
Loy Glenn Westfall, *Hillsborough Brandon Community College*
Donald W. Whisenhunt, *Western Washington University*
Lynn Willoughby, *Winthrop University*
Larry Wright, *Inver Hills Community College*

It has been my astonishingly good fortune to have as friends two remarkable librarians who were willing to put their expertise and time at my disposal.

Susan Kling of Bandon, Oregon organized and administered a massive, customized interlibrary loan program that put into my hands every book I requested of her, certainly more than a hundred over the last six months. The late Marilyn Murphy of Eureka, California did not know everything, as she enjoyed saying, but she knew where to find it out. I posed questions to her about the obscurest of data which, I was certain in many instances, simply did not exist. Instance after instance, often in hours, sometimes after a week with daily progress reports, she had the citation for me. Rest in peace, Marilyn.

For the third time now, Margaret McAndrew Beasley was the developmental editor of *The American Past*. Margaret coordinated me, the chapter reviewers, manuscript, photos, permissions, and a squadron of production people. Margaret remained calm and in control when I fell behind schedule or proclaimed an insurrection because of one or another editorial decision. If, in the end, she usually got her way, when the flare-ups were extinguished, I usually recognized that she had been right. There cannot be too many of Margaret's caliber in this business.

Finally, my thanks to those of the many people who had a hand in making this book whose names are known to me.

Clark Baxter, Publisher
Ashley Dodge, Senior Acquisitions Editor
Katy German, Production Project Manager
Rozi Harris and Merrill Peterson, Project Managers
Lili Weiner, Freelance Photo Researcher
Joohee Lee, Permissions Editor

TO THE STUDENT

"History" and "the past" are two different things. The past does not change, but *history* changes all the time because history is not an account of the past but the story of the past *as we understand it*. What we have in our heads is changeable indeed (or at least it should be).

Our understanding of what happened five hundred or even fifty years ago may change because of additions to the information available to us—the "sources," historians call them (speeches, letters, diaries, photographs, etc.)—or because of an alteration in the way we look at that information.

Documents thought lost forever are discovered, sometimes in far corners of farmhouse attics (it really does happen). Documents we never knew existed turn up, sometimes right in the archives where they belong but on the wrong shelf. The personal papers of important historical figures, sealed for twenty or thirty years by the terms of their last wills and testaments (usually to allow everyone mentioned in them to die off), are legally opened in a reading room crowded with historians. Governments, often grudgingly, eventually publish official documents that had been rubber-stamped "Top Secret."

History is also rewritten when sources of information that had been in full view all the time are suddenly understandable. During the short time (historically speaking) since the first edition of *The American Past* was published, the most momentous example of such a breakthrough was the deciphering of the written language of the ancient Maya. The innumerable carvings on the ruins of Mayan temples in Central America had long been admired for their artistry, and archaeologists knew they were more than decorations. When they were finally able to read most of the inscriptions, they not only revealed a portrait of Mayan civilization very different from what was in every textbook, they pushed back the date American history begins—for history is based on *written* sources—by a thousand years from that starting date known to everyone, 1492. Change indeed!

Technology changes history, too. The number-crunching capacity of the computer means that data that was always available but too vast to be approached—for example, the raw reports that census takers turned into the Census Bureau every ten years—becomes easily-accessible rich sources of social history. Baptismal and marriage registries moldering in thousands of churches, even the names and dates etched in stone in ancient graveyards, previously of interest only to genealogists and antiquarians, become historical goldmines.

Because history is changing all the time, history textbooks like this one are regularly revised. I have not prepared this eighth edition in order to keep *The American Past* up-to-date with coverage of events of the several years that have elapsed since the publication of the seventh. Fastidiously objective summaries of such "current events," at least as good as I could compile, are readily available in almanacs and news magazines.

All of this about the changeability of history will be old hat to research historians, history teachers, graduate students, and even history majors. However, *The American Past* was not written for people who already love history enough to have made it their profession. *The American Past* was written and revised for first- and second-year college students enrolled in United States history survey courses; majors in accounting, botany, mathematics, psychology, zoology, and a dozen other fields for whom the fact that history is always in flux may well be a fresh idea (and one worth knowing).

USING THE "DISCOVERY" SECTIONS IN THIS TEXTBOOK TO ANALYZE HISTORICAL SOURCES: DOCUMENTS, PHOTOS, AND MAPS

Astronomers investigate the universe through telescopes. Biologists study the natural world by collecting plants and animals in the field and then examining them with microscopes. Sociologists and psychologists study human behavior through observation and controlled laboratory experiments.

Historians study the past by examining historical "evidence" or "source" materials—government documents; the records of private institutions ranging from religious and charitable organizations to labor unions, corporations, and lobbying groups; letters, advertisements, paintings, music, literature, movies, and cartoons; buildings, clothing, farm implements, industrial machinery, and landscapes: anything and everything written or created by our ancestors that give clues about their lives and the times in which they lived.

Historians refer to written material as "documents." Brief excerpts of documents appear throughout the textbook—within the chapters and in the "Discovery" sections. Each chapter also includes many visual representations of the American past in the form of photographs of buildings, paintings, murals, individuals, cartoons, sculptures, and other kinds of historical evidence. As you read each chapter, the more you examine all this "evidence," the more you will understand the main ideas of this book and of the course you are taking. The better you become at reading evidence, the better historian you will become.

"Discovery" sections at the end of every chapter assist you in practicing these skills by taking a closer look at specific pieces of evidence—documents, images, or maps—which will help you to connect the various threads of American history and to excel in your course.

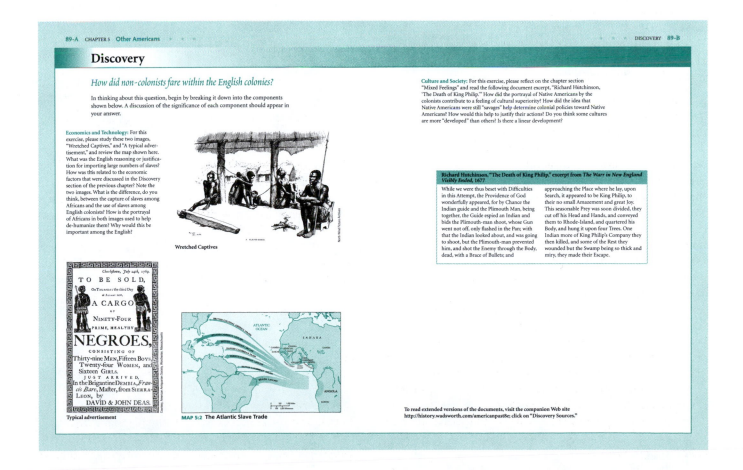

THE AMERICAN PAST

A Survey of American History

CHAPTER 1

Discoveries

Indians, Europeans, and the Americas About 15,000 B.C. to A.D. 1550

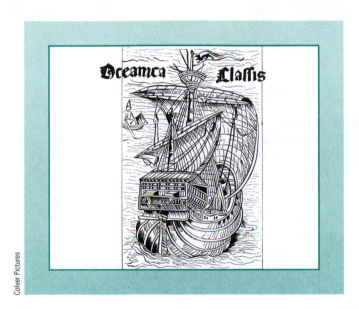

Colver Pictures

I feel a wonderful exultation of spirits when I converse with intelligent men who have returned from these regions. It is like an accession of wealth to a miser. Our minds, soiled and debased by the common concerns of life and the vices of society, become elevated and ameliorated by contemplating such glorious events.

Peter Martyr d'Anghiera

Broken spears lie in the roads;
We have torn our hair in our grief.
The houses are roofless now,
And their walls are red with blood. . . .
We are crushed to the ground;
We lie in ruins.
There is nothing but grief and suffering
in Mexico and Tlateloco.

Anonymous Aztec poet

From eastern Africa, their homeland, human beings colonized Asia and Europe but not, for geological epochs, the Americas. Even isolated Australia was peopled 20,000 years before a human being impressed a footprint in American mud.

Exactly when people discovered America is disputed, but the best bet is that, about 15,000 years ago, bands of stone age hunters began to cross from Siberia to Alaska on a "land bridge" that, for the last 10,000 years, has been drowned 180 feet beneath the frigid waters of the Bering Strait. Thus the name geologists have given the land bridge, **Beringia.** Beringia was high and dry 15,000 years ago because the earth was locked in an ice age. Much of the world's water was frozen in the polar ice caps and in glaciers larger than most

Distant Relations?

DNA research indicates that ancestors of the Ainu, a racial minority in northern Japan, were among the people who crossed Beringia. The Ainu share unique DNA with Blackfoot, Sioux, and Cherokee Indians. More difficult to make sense of, the Na-dene language of the Pacific Northwest shares cognates (words appearing to have the same origins) with the language of the Basques of the French-Spanish borderlands, and the languages of the Aleuts and Eskimos with Finnish. Unless it is coincidence, the "relationship" supports a few anthropologists who believe that Europeans emigrated to America by sea before the Beringians arrived.

The Incurious Explorer

Beringia is named for Vitus Bering, a Dane whom the Russian Czar sent east to determine whether Alaska was part of Siberia. Beginning in 1725, it took Bering and his party four years to cross Siberia and build seaworthy vessels. Bering sailed through the strait that now bears his name but saw no land to the east. Having a second go in 1741, he found Alaska, while his ship was anchored off Kayak Island, but Bering did not explore it. He never left his ship and the men he sent ashore for fresh water stayed all of ten hours.

nations today. Consequently, sea level was about 400 feet lower than it is now. Our beaches were miles inland from the surf. Vast tracts of what is now sea bottom were dry; Beringia was not really a bridge, it was a hundred miles wide.

The people who crossed to America had no idea they were discovering a "New World" empty of human beings. They were stone age nomads checking out the territory, as nomads do, following dinner—herds of caribou?—or fleeing enemies. In just a thousand years, however, these **Paleo-Indians** (old Indians, ancestors of American Indians) explored and colonized much of two continents. They advanced their frontier, on average, a mile a month.

THE FIRST COLONIZATION

The Paleo-Indians were prehistoric; that is, knowledge of them is beyond the compass of historians, who study the past in the written word. To learn about people who lived, loved, begat, hated, and died before there was writing, we must turn to archaeologists, linguists, and folklorists who sift particles of information, like gold dust from gravel, by analyzing artifacts (things people made), by studying the structure of language, and by analyzing tales passed through word of mouth from one generation to the next, and to the next.

The images these scholars sketch are fuzzier than the portraits historians can draw from written documents. As a Chinese saying has it, "the palest ink is clearer than the best memory." Still, fuzzy is better than blank. Without folklore and language analysis, without artifacts, the American past would not begin until A.D. 1492, when Europeans, who scribbled endlessly of their achievements and follies, made their discovery of the "New World," and inundated it with their numbers. Thanks to archaeology, linguistics, and folklore—and a few fragmentary written records by Indians only recently decoded—we can pencil in a more ancient past.

DIVERSITY

The Paleo-Indians knew no more of agriculture than of alphabets. When they crossed Beringia, there was not a farmer on the planet. Like all people of that day, the first Americans lived by hunting, fishing, and gathering. They took from nature the makings of their meals and clothing, shelter, tools, and weapons. They were nomads—they lived on the move, because, in all but environments that are the most lush, even a few hundred people soon exhaust the food that can be found in the neighborhood of their camps. Home, for Paleo-Indians, was where the food was. That, sooner or later, was somewhere else.

The Age of Exploration 1400–1550

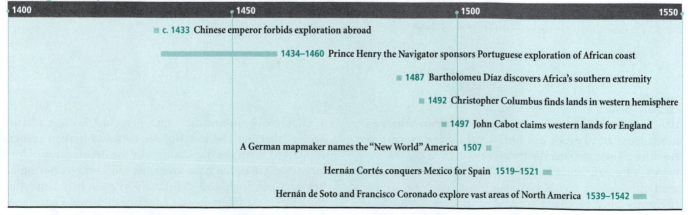

1400	1450	1500	1550

c. 1433 Chinese emperor forbids exploration abroad

1434–1460 Prince Henry the Navigator sponsors Portuguese exploration of African coast

1487 Bartholomeu Díaz discovers Africa's southern extremity

1492 Christopher Columbus finds lands in western hemisphere

1497 John Cabot claims western lands for England

A German mapmaker names the "New World" America 1507

Hernán Cortés conquers Mexico for Spain 1519–1521

Hernán de Soto and Francisco Coronado explore vast areas of North America 1539–1542

© Corbis

The Maya and Aztec built pyramid temples as awesome as Mesopotamian ziggurats. This is a smaller one but perfectly preserved. Some archaeologists believe that the "Mound Builders" of the Midwest were recalling Mesoamerican pyramids when they built their earthen monuments.

By the time the mysteries of agriculture were first unlocked in the Middle East about 8000 B.C., the Paleo-Indians had no contact with the "Old World," the Eurasian land mass. A global warming had melted the massive glaciers of the Ice Age and reduced the polar ice caps to a size close to their size today. Sea level rose, submerging Beringia. America was the whole world to the Paleo-Indians.

Cultures, ways of life, diversified rapidly. The Americas were uncrowded, to say the least. Wandering tribes found it easy—"natural"—to split up when their community grew too large for the range or when, human nature being what it is, bigwigs with a following had a falling out. Soon enough, the vastness of the Americas and the diversity of its climates and landforms isolated Paleo-Indian tribes from one another too. The result was a dizzying variety of cultures.

Languages, for example, probably once just a handful, multiplied until there were at least 500. Tribes living in harsh environments continued to survive precariously into historic times on what they could hunt, snare, net, gather, and grub. Other Indians learned how to farm. America is the only place besides the Middle East where agriculture was invented, and not learned from others. The greater abundance of food Paleo-Indian farmers produced made possible, in at least two places—**Mesoamerica** (meaning between the Americas: Mexico and Central America) and Peru—the creation of sophisticated civilizations.

Some Indians had mastered only primitive tool making when, after 1492, they were dazzled (and crushed) by European technology. Others perfected handicrafts to a degree of refinement not matched in Africa, Asia, and Europe. Some Indians sheltered in piles of brush. The Anasazi of present-day New Mexico built apartment houses five and six stories high.

Some Native Americans left no more mark on the land than the remains of campfires and garbage dumps that only space-age technology can locate. By way of contrast, about

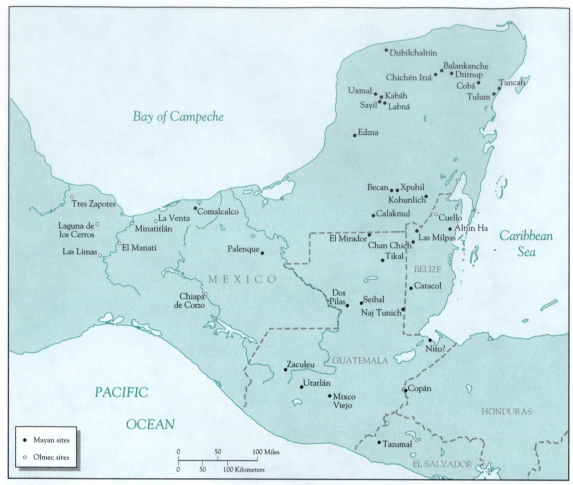

MAP 1:1 Mayan Cities. The Olmec, among whom Mesoamerican civilization originated, lived in southern Mexico. The Mayans, whose civilization peaked after Olmec civilization disintegrated, were centered in present-day Yucután, Guatemala, and Belize.

A.D. 1000, the "Mound Builders" of the North American heartland—our Midwest—were sufficiently numerous that they could heap up massive earthen structures that survive today. One mound complex near Cahokia, Illinois stretched over 5 square miles with a central platform 100 feet high and a sculpted bird 70 feet in height. In Ohio, two parallel "walls" extended 60 miles from Chillicothe to Newark.

The Indians' intimacy with nature made them canny in lore based on observation and trial-and-error experiment. Some prehistoric Americans understood the effects of more than 200 natural drugs and medicines in use today.

MESOAMERICAN CIVILIZATION

In Guatemala, Belize, and southern Mexico, a succession of peoples—Olmec, Maya, Aztec—farmed so productively they could congregate in large cities where some people specialized in work other than farming: urban life and the "division of labor" are two of the components of what historians call civilization. A third is a hierarchical social system; a small elite of soldiers and priests governed the Maya. A fourth component is a system of writing: as was developed in Mesopotamia

(Iraq), Egypt, Pakistan-India, and China, Mesoamericans invented such a system by which they carved records in stone and composed "books" on bark or processed strips of cactus fiber similar to Egypt's papyrus.

Alas for historians, after 1500 a zealous Spanish bishop, Diego de Landa, condemned these books as "superstition and lies of the devil" and destroyed all but a few. Only four Maya literary works survive. But inscribed rock was too much for the censors. Carved hieroglyphs are abundant in Mesoamerica and scholars have learned, only recently, to read many of them. They provide a chapter of the American past, mostly a chronicle of kings and their deeds, long thought unknowable.

At one time or another, about forty cities, several housing more than 20,000 people, dotted Mesoamerica. Teotihuacán, founded near present-day Mexico City about the time of Christ may have been home to 125,000 by A.D. 500. An aristocracy of priests and warriors governed these cities. They directed the construction of at least one pyramidal earth and stone temple in each. The pyramid at Chichén Itzá rose eighteen stories.

Locked in a Circle of Time

Another time it will be like this, another time things will be the same, same time, same place. What happened a long time ago, and which no longer happens, will be again. It will be done again as it was in far-off times; those who now live will live again.

Aztec Proverb

Maya priests were superb astronomers. Their solar calendar was almost perfect with 365 days in a year. With little seasonal change in temperature in Mesoamerica, however, and seasonal rains erratic and unpredictable, the solar year was less critical to the Maya than it was to calendar makers elsewhere who needed to know when the river would rise or when frost would kill crops still in the field. So, for reasons that no one has divined, the Maya devised other calendars unrelated to the movement of sun and moon.

Thus, they had a 13-day cycle of days and another of 260 days ($20 \times 13 = 260$; Mayan mathematics was based on 20 rather than 10). These cycles were tied in with the solar year in a manner best pictured as three cogwheels: a 13-toothed cog meshing with a 260-toothed cog also meshing with a 365-toothed wheel. (The Maya did not picture it this way. Like the Aztec, they had did not have wheels, let alone cogs.) Mathematically, however, they rotated the cogs one tooth each solar day. No single alignment of the cogs was repeated for 18,980 days—52 solar years on the button.

The complexity of the calculation illustrates the sophistication of Mayan mathematics. But, some scholars have

© Copyright The British Museum

suggested, the beauty of the math locked the Maya mind into a rigidly cyclical conception of history. The Maya seem to have believed that the events of each day were a repetition of the events of the day precisely 52 years earlier, and 104 years and 156 years earlier. Each 5,200 years (introducing the factor of 10!), the world was destroyed and created anew. Time passed, but there was no "progress" as western civilization would understand it, just repeated returns to where things had already been and would be again.

Such a view of history, the argument can be continued, was ill-suited for coping with the utterly unexpected. Hurricanes worried the Mayans as much because of their unpredictability as because of their destructiveness. How infinitely more troubling for their cultural heirs, the Aztecs, to cope with the arrival of huge seagoing canoes, white-skinned men with hairy faces in suits of iron, horses, dogs bigger than any Mexican animal, and cannons mowing down a dozen men from a hundred yards away? Mesoamerica's intellectual foundations may have been a Spanish ally that neither Aztec nor conquistador recognized.

The Maya were superb mathematicians and astronomers. They discovered the use of the zero, a breakthrough achieved in only one other world culture, India. They timed the earth's orbit around the sun as accurately as any other people of the time, applying their findings to an accurate calendar.

WAR AND RELIGION

The Maya did not build empires, an obsession of most Old World civilizations. Each city–state was an independent entity governing a rather limited hinterland. Not that the Maya and the others were peace-loving—far from it. They fought chronically with their neighbors. Their religion compelled war. Their gods (jaguar-like beings, eagles, serpents, the sun) thirsted for human blood.

In solemn public rituals, noblewomen made symbolic blood sacrifices by drawing strings of thorns through punctures in their tongues. Their brothers and husbands drew the barbs through their foreskins. Strips of fiber that were burned, dispatching the sacrifice in smoke to the heavens, sopped up the blood from these wounds.

But symbolic blood sacrifice was not enough for the Mesoamerican deities. They also demanded that priests throw young women into pits and drag men to the tops of the pyramids where, using razor-sharp stone knives, the priests tore their hearts, still beating when the operation was correctly performed, from their breasts. Thus the chronic war: the Mesoamericans needed captives to sacrifice.

CULTURAL CUL-DE-SAC?

Elsewhere in the world, states made war in order to exploit those they conquered. Along with the misery they caused, the wealth their conquests brought them made possible further breakthroughs in the evolution of civilization. The blood lust of the Mesoamerican gods, however, meant that the Maya and others made war for the unproductive purpose of rounding up people to kill. They expended vast resources in a direction that, in material and intellectual terms, led nowhere. Their genius and energy were devoted to staying on the right side of terrifying gods, to avoiding worse than that with which they had to contend when heaven was in a good mood. Mesoamerican culture was pathologically conservative.

Conservatism did not save them. Olmec culture disappeared abruptly about A.D. 900. The Maya also disintegrated dramatically. In one area, a population that had reached at least three million was, by 1500, down to 30,000. Once great cities—Tikal, Chichén-Itzá, Palenque—were overgrown by tropical vegetation, not to be rediscovered until 1840. By 1500, most Maya lived in villages. Some were still literate but in a less sophisticated language than their ancestors had used; they could read only fragments of the books and inscriptions that survived.

What happened? Recent research indicates a combination of factors. The Maya destroyed forests to have fuel for making the plaster with which they coated their temples. The result was soil erosion and a reduced food supply. A long period of serious droughts, beginning about A.D. 800, further devastated agriculture. And with widespread hunger came increased warfare and social collapse.

Mesoamerican civilization itself did not die. But by 500 its center was several hundred miles northwest of its Central America birthplace, in the valley of Mexico. The cultural heirs of the Olmec and Maya, the Aztec, were latecomers to Mesoamerica.

THE AZTEC

The Aztec (they called themselves "the Mexica," thus Mexico) had emigrated from the north during the 1200s. About 1325, they carved out an enclave on Lake Texcoco amongst longtime residents, most notably the Toltec and Texcocan. Primitive when they arrived, the Aztec embraced their neighbors' civilization and, during the early 1400s, defeated all of them in a series of wars. Aztec armies then struck east and west. They were triumphant from the Gulf of Mexico to the Pacific Ocean.

Their capital on Lake Texcoco, **Tenochtitlán,** was impregnable. Surrounded by water, it could be entered only on three narrow, easily defended causeways. If one of their subject peoples threatened them, the Aztec raised drawbridges spanning gaps in the viaducts. Combat was hand-to-hand; thirty-foot granite walls could not have made a city more secure.

The Aztec took no interest in the daily doings of the peoples they conquered. They left customs, religion, the making

MAP 1:2 Mexico Under the Aztec, 1519. The Aztec extorted tribute from peoples the breadth of Mexico but directly governed only Tenochtitlán and its hinterland.

and enforcement of laws, and the collection of taxes to native kings and nobles. All the Aztec wanted was submission and tribute. On appointed days (access to Tenochtitlán was closely regulated), each subject people was required to bring to the capital minutely prescribed quantities of bulk goods—maize, beans, salt, cloth, lumber—and jade, gold, and (as precious as gold in Mexico) feathers. They also brought people for sacrifice, for the Aztec adopted that Mesoamerican practice too. Failure to pay tribute on time meant an Aztec assault, without delay. The Aztec stationed military garrisons at key points among the subject peoples for just such occasions.

Tenochtitlán was among the world's grandest cities. Estimates of its population ranged from 60,000 to 250,000. By 1519 (the fatal year for the Aztec), much of the city was newly rebuilt. A disastrous flood in 1499 had destroyed thousands of buildings that were replaced in what can fairly be described as a massive urban renewal project. The dwellings of the poor were humble, of course, but better than the homes of Spain's lower classes, according to men who knew both. Nobles lived in large homes built, curiously, around a private courtyard as in Spain. The emperor's palace of 100 rooms covered 6 acres.

Tenochtitlán's streets, unlike streets in Europe, were quite clean. They were swept daily. Street life was lively with open-air markets, vendors selling tortillas and other "fast food," and fixed shops of many types. Thoroughfares were illuminated at night by glowing braziers (where passers-by could pause and warm their hands) and there were public toilets, even on roads (paths, more accurately, as the Aztec had no vehicles) outside the city. The pyramidal temples that were the emblem of Mesoamerican civilization rose in every quarter of Tenochtitlán. Each day began when, from their heights, priests blew conch shells and beat on drums.

BLOOD AND GORE

Tenochtitlán's main temple was huge—200 feet square at the base. Two dizzyingly steep staircases climbed to altars 200 feet above the street. The steps were black with the dried blood of sacrificial victims whose bodies, minus hearts, the priest threw down to be butchered; the Aztec practiced ritual cannibalism.

Aztec human sacrifice exceeded in scope anything that had gone before. Huitzilopochtli, a god who had accompanied the Aztec from the north, was said to demand 10,000 hearts in an ordinary year. In 1478, a year Huitzilopochtli was agitated, so the records say, priests dressed in cloaks of human skin and stinking of gore (they were forbidden to wash or cut their hair) sent 20,000 volunteers and captives to their doom in four days. The emperor Ahuitzotl, so it was said, slaughtered 80,000 to dedicate a new temple.

These astronomical figures are not to be taken as gospel fact. There is no ancient civilization that did not inflate its statistics into the realm of absurdity. But the point of the Aztec chroniclers who recorded the numbers is clear enough: lots of people were ritually slaughtered in ancient Mexico.

The number of victims was probably higher in the late 1400s and early 1500s than it had been earlier. The Aztec experienced a good many troubling years during that period. There was the flood of 1499, comets appeared in 1489 and 1506 (and worried people worldwide), and there was a total eclipse of the sun in 1496. There were several severe droughts within living memory. Common people and nobles alike repeated the story that female spirits were wandering the city at night, wailing in grief. In 1514, the king of neighboring Texcoco died; his last words were that Mexico would soon be ruled by strangers.

The Aztec were a people on edge in 1519 and none was edgier than Emperor **Moctezuma II,** whose reign began in 1502. It has been suggested that, psychologically, he was ready prey for enemies who devoted their lives and resources not just to staying on the right side of the gods, but to exploiting the new, strange, and vulnerable wherever they found it.

Other Discoverers

Columbus was not the first outsider to touch on America after the Paleo-Indians. Japanese fishermen may have survived being blown eastward across the Pacific. Some Japanese-like themes in Indian art tantalize archaeologists.

There are too many legendary pre-Columbian visitors to America to list. The Olmec told of black-skinned people in Central America; some have seen negroid features in the famous Olmec stone heads. A Chinese document of 200 B.C. tells of Hee Li, who visited a land to the East he called Fu-Sang. About

A.D. 700, Irish bards began to sing of St. Brendan, a monk who had sojourned far to the west of the Emerald Isle in a land "without grief, without sorrow, without death."

There is nothing legendary about Vikings from Greenland who, about A.D. 984, discovered Newfoundland and—they made about five voyages in all—probably sailed as far south as Nova Scotia. They called the region Vinland and built housing at L'Anse aux Meadows on Newfoundland's northwestern coast. They planned to stay; they had livestock and Vinland was at least more promising than Greenland. They traded with the local "skraelings" (wretches), cow's milk for furs.

But Vinland had a downside. It was too far from Scandinavia for trade. And Newfoundland's Indians grew hostile. Indeed, their attacks paralyzed the Vinlanders with fear. One skraeling assault was repulsed only when a pregnant woman, Freydis, disgusted by her trembling menfolk, seized a sword and chased the Indians away by slapping it on her breasts and, no doubt, having a word or two to say. Freydis had the cowards killed and she returned to Greenland with the survivors.

EUROPE: DRIVEN AND EXPANSIVE

On October 12, 1492, on a beach in the Bahamas, a thousand miles from Tenochtitlán, a group of rugged, ragged men, mostly Spaniards, rowed ashore from three small ships. They named their landfall San Salvador, Holy Savior. Their leader was a ruddy but graying Italian about forty. To his Spanish crew he was Cristóbal Colón, to us **Christopher Columbus.** To the Arawak, the Bahamians who welcomed him, he and his men were like nothing they had ever imagined.

CHRISTOPHER COLUMBUS

Falling to his knees, for he was as pious as any Aztec priest, Columbus proclaimed San Salvador the possession of the woman who had financed his voyage, **Queen Isabella** of Castille, and her husband, Ferdinand of Aragon, the first rulers of a unified Spain. Columbus would write them that the trees were "the most beautiful I have ever seen." He "found no human monstrosities, as many expected; on the contrary, among all these peoples good looks are esteemed." The Arawak were "very generous. They do not know what it is to be wicked, or to kill others, or to steal." He added that it would be easy to enslave them—without irony, for in Columbus's world owning slaves was one of the perquisites of the good life, being a slave just one of life's many misfortunes.

For the moment, Columbus enslaved no one. He enquired politely of the whereabouts of Japan and China. Those fabulous lands, not the balmy but poor Bahamas, were the places for which he was looking.

The evolution of the America we know—the history that runs traceably on a line to our own society and culture—began with Columbus's landing in the Bahamas. Our

Reproduced from the Collections of the Library of Congress

A charming, but fanciful, depiction of Columbus's landfall on the island he called San Salvador. There is no surf—the ocean is like a pond. Columbus was probably not bearded, but his costume rings true. The friar seated in the back of the boat is the artist's creation; there was no priest on Columbus's first voyage. The artist captured the character of the Arawaks well. They were an innocent, welcoming people. Columbus noted their docility, saying they would be easy to enslave.

historical legacy, whatever our genetic inheritance, lay not on the pyramids of Mexico but in the churches, state chambers, and counting houses of western Europe, a civilization that had already, by 1492, begun to impress people around the world.

MOTIVES

Columbus believed that San Salvador, and Cuba and Santo Domingo (Haiti and the Dominican Republic today), which

Prester John, Marco Polo, and Mansa Musa

Europe's fascination with Africa and Asia was fueled by *The Letter of Prester John*, which began to circulate about 1150. The ostensible author, John, a Christian king and priest, claimed to "reign supreme and to exceed in riches, virtue, and power all creatures who dwell under heaven." He wanted to form an alliance with Christian Europe in order to "wage war against and chastise" their common enemies, the Muslims.

At first, Europeans placed John in central Asia. But travelers found no Christians there; nor the red and green lions he mentioned in his letter, no ants that dug gold, or a pebble that made men invisible. Still, the prospect of a powerful Christian

friend with whom to catch the Muslims in a pincers (and from whom to buy the goods of the Indies) overcame skepticism.

The Voyages of Ser Marco Polo also included absurdities such as snakes wearing eyeglasses, but it was no hoax. Marco Polo of Venice lived in China for twenty years. His revelation that the Asian porcelains, silks, tapestries, and spices for which Europeans paid high prices cost a pittance in China was true. No document, more than Polo's *Voyages,* convinced the explorers of the fifteenth century that betting their lives on voyages to the East might mean fabulous riches.

The author of *The Letter of Prester John* probably got his idea from tales about the Christian king of Ethiopia who was, in fact,

bedeviled by Muslims (but was not all that rich). A number of Ethiopians visited Europe during the Middle Ages. In any case, in 1455, the pope authorized the Portuguese to form an alliance with the Ethiopian, John. A half century later, an embassy made an arduous but disappointing journey into that rugged country.

There was a fabulously rich king in the African interior but he was not a Christian. Mansa Musa was a Muslim who, in 1347, made a pilgrimage to Mecca from central west Africa accompanied by 500 slaves. He paid his way with (it was said) fifteen tons of gold. Mansa Musa was no more interested in fighting the Europeans than he was in making an impression on the Arabs and Turks. In Cairo, he could be bothered even to visit the sultan.

he visited after leaving El Salvador, were island fringes of "the Indies," the name Europeans gave collectively to mysterious, distant Cipango (Japan), Cathay (China), the Spice Islands (Indonesia), and India itself. Thus did Columbus bestow upon the Arawak and other Native Americas the name that has stuck to their descendants to this day—Indians.

A Versatile Word

India derives from the name of the Indus River, where Indian civilization was born. Europeans broadened the term as "the Indies" to refer all of southern and eastern Asia. Because Columbus thought that his landfall was in the western reaches of the Indies, West Indies has ever since been the collective term for the islands of the Caribbean, and the natives of all the Americas "Indians."

Nor does the word's misuse end there. The great British explorer of the eighteenth century, Captain James Cook, called the people of Australia, Hawaii, and two dozen other Pacific Islands he visited "Indians." But there, at last, the name did not stick.

Columbus had sailed from Spain to find a feasible sea lane to the Indies. In part, he was motivated by religion. A zealous Roman Catholic, Columbus believed God had selected him to carry the gospel of Christ to the lost souls of Asia. He had his worldly motives too. Columbus longed for personal glory. Like the artists and architects of the Renaissance, he craved recognition as a great individual. If obsession with self has become tawdry in our own time, individualism was once one of the forces that made Western civilization dynamic.

Another such force was greed. Columbus wanted wealth. He meant to get rich doing business with (or conquering) the peoples he encountered. Gold and silver were always in season. "Gold is most excellent," Columbus wrote, "He who has it does all he wants in the world, and can even lift souls up to Paradise." European gold and silver paid for the Asian gems and porcelains that rich Europeans coveted, the fine cotton cloth of Syria and silks of China, and tapestries and carpets that were beyond the craft of European weavers.

Then there were the exotic drugs, dyes, perfumes, and especially the spices of the Indies: cinnamon from Ceylon, Indonesian nutmeg and cloves, Chinese ginger, and cardamom and peppercorns (piper nigrum, black pepper, not chili peppers) from India. These were luxuries that made life more pleasant for the Europeans who could afford them, something more than a struggle for survival on earth and salvation after death.

HIGH OVERHEAD

The goods of the Indies had trickled into Europe since the Caesars ruled Rome. Over the centuries, Europeans learned from a few adventurers who traveled to east Asia that the silks and spices so expensive to them were dirt cheap in the Orient. Crusaders, knights who during the twelfth century ruled much of the Levant (present-day Syria, Lebanon, and Israel), enjoyed first hand the richer lifestyle of their enemies, the Muslim Arabs who had long enjoyed a regular trade with the Indies.

The Muslims drove the crusaders back to Europe but they brought back a taste for the luxuries of the East with them. The victorious Muslims were happy, as middlemen, to sell to them. They brought the textiles, gems, perfumes, and spices by ship via the Indian Ocean and Persian Gulf or Red Sea.

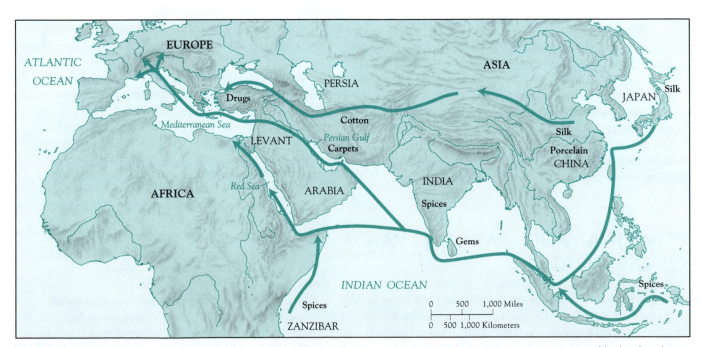

MAP 1:3 European Trade with Asia and Africa. Asian and East African goods—luxuries in Europe—were transported by land and sea as many as 8,000 miles.

Or, they bought them from central Asian caravaners who had carried them on the backs of donkeys to the Levant, Constantinople (now Istanbul), or the Black Sea. From these places, the goods were transported across the Mediterranean Sea in the vessels of Venice and Genoa, powerful Italian city–states. Italian merchants were the wholesale distributors who sold the spices and the rest to retailers from all over Europe.

By the time the goods of the Indies reached the castles of Spain and the market towns of France, they were expensive indeed. The cost of transport was prodigious. The silk that cloaked an English baron may have been carried 8,000 miles in a caravan. The routes passed through the domains of central Asian tribesmen who lived by preying on the trade. Caravaners paid tolls ("bribes") to pass safely, or they hired thugs to beat back the toll collectors. Either way, their operating expenses swelled. If the pepper and cloves that enlivened a German bishop's stew came by sea, Arab sailors had to deal with east African pirates, "tolls" again, or pay for expensive armed escorts. As always, all the costs were passed on to the consumers.

NOBODY LIKES A MIDDLEMAN

Then there was profit. The Levantines (or Genoese huddled in fortified trading posts on the Black Sea) were not in business for the glory of God and the service of humanity. The Italian wholesalers added their markup, shrugging off accusations they were gougers. Today, the magnificent Renaissance cathedrals and palaces the Italian merchant princes built are world treasures. In the time of Columbus, the glories of Italy were as likely to arouse bitter resentment among Europeans who paid extortionate "take it or leave it" prices for the Italians' Asian imports. Their money paid for the cathedrals and palazzi.

In western Europe, envy of Italian wealth fathered more than resentment. It fathered dreams of finding a route to the Indies that bypassed the eastern Mediterranean, which the Venetian navy, then the world's most powerful, pretty much controlled. Indeed, navigators from Genoa, which was gradually squeezed out of the trade by the Venetians, were major purveyors of the dream. Columbus was not the only Genoese who haunted the royal courts of western Europe with the message that the prince whose sailor found an ocean route to the Indies would stanch the flow of his country's wealth to Italy. Indeed, such a prince could imagine his subjects displacing the Venetians as Europe's wholesalers of Asian products.

PORTUGAL AND SPAIN: THE VAN OF EXPLORATION

Portugal was first to look for a new trade route. A glance at a map provides the first reason this should have been so. Portugal faces west, the Atlantic; its mountainous back is to Europe. Portugal's lifeblood was the ocean, fishing and trade with northern Europeans. Lisbon was a way station for Italian exports to Europe's north.

To the south of Portugal is Morocco, Portugal's ancient enemy, and south of Morocco the Sahara and a coast that was a mystery to everyone. Arab explorers had sailed as far south as Cape Bojador but their vessels, designed for the placid Mediterranean, were savaged by the constant, powerful winds of the cape. The Arabs called the Atlantic "the green sea of darkness" and wrote it off. They brought the slaves, gold, and ivory for sale in black Africa, across the Sahara on camels.

PORTUGUESE DISCOVERIES

A son and brother of Portuguese kings, Prince Henry, believed that the green sea of darkness could be mastered. Known to history as **Henry the Navigator** (although he personally made but one short sea voyage), Henry was fascinated by the Atlantic and by distant lands both real and imagined. He knew of the profits the Arabs enjoyed from their trans-Sahara trade and believed that African gold, ivory, and slaves could come Portugal's way by sea. He also thought that Prester John, a great Christian king who was looking for allies to fight against the Muslims, was a black African. (Prester John was a myth.) And Henry had learned from *The Voyages of Ser Marco Polo* (which, despite some fantastic moments, was not a myth) that in the Indies the trade goods that all Europe coveted cost little. Surely the Indies could be reached by rounding the southern tip of Africa.

Henry funded a kind of research and development center at Sagres in southern Portugal. He brought in mariners to share their experiences with mapmakers and scholars (many of them Genoese like Columbus) who poured over narratives written by ancient travelers in Asia. He organized fifteen expeditions to explore the African coast. Sailors blown out into the Atlantic by the troublesome winds that had turned the Arabs back discovered and colonized the island of Madeira, 350 miles from Africa, and the Azores, 900 miles west of Portugal.

Shipwrights at Sagres and Lisbon developed a vessel that could cope with ocean waves and winds, the caravel. Very sturdy, caravels could be rigged at sea with either the swiveling

Cheng Ho

Europe and Asia might easily have been brought together not by the Portuguese but by a Chinese Muslim almost a century earlier. Beginning in 1405, Cheng Ho (Zheng He) led six expeditions to the Indian Ocean. One of his fleets consisted of 62 vessels, some of them five-masted giants, one described as 400 feet long. He discovered (for China) Borneo, India and in Africa, Zanzibar and Kenya.

Cheng Ho wanted to round Africa from east to west. It is not far-fetched to imagine him reaching Europe (although, like European ships before the caravel, Cheng Ho's junks did not sail well against the wind). However, he died in 1433 and the emperor ordered his fleet disassembled and proclaimed the death penalty for Chinese who traveled abroad. The emperor had concluded there was nothing of value to China in distant lands.

triangular lateen sails of the Mediterranean for sailing into the wind or with the large square-rigged sheets of northern Europe that pushed a vessel at high speed when the wind was behind. Caravels had large, bulging holds but they required relatively small crews, so they could be provisioned for voyages far longer than any other craft of the era. An Italian in Prince Henry's service, Luigi da Cadamosto, described them as "the best ships in the world and able to sail anywhere." At a more homely level, Portuguese coopers improved casks to hold drinking water without constant leakage, something else that had discouraged long ocean voyages.

PORTUGAL'S ROUTE TO ASIA

Henry the Navigator died in 1460 but Portuguese exploration continued. Every few years, a ship mapped a more distant stretch of African coast, returning with slaves, gold, and ivory. Forts were built at strategic points, serving both as trading centers and rest stops for Portuguese explorers bound farther south. In 1488, one of these explorers, Bartholomeu Díaz, returned to Lisbon with the news that he had reached Africa's southern extremity. Díaz called it the Cape of Storms. The king promptly renamed it the Cape of Good Hope because, from there, surely, it would be clear sailing to the Indies.

Not for another decade would Vasco da Gama reach the Indian port of Calicut and return with profits twenty times the investment in his voyage. The Portuguese promptly extended their commercial empire—it was nothing in terms of territory—to east Africa as far north as Mombasa (in present-day Kenya), across the Indian Ocean in Goa (India), and as distant as Macau in China. In 1500, Pedro Cabral staked a Portuguese claim in South America when, bound for India, his ship was blown across the Atlantic to what is now Brazil.

The African and Asian trade enriched Portugal. Its merchants easily undersold the Venetians. Pepper in Lisbon sold for half the price charged in Venice and, at that, was ten to twenty times what the Portuguese had paid for it in India.

SPAIN GOES WEST

Columbus settled in Portugal in 1476 where he drew nautical charts and made a number of voyages, as far north as England, more significantly to the Canary Islands where he noted that the prevailing winds blew to the west, across the Atlantic. His "Enterprise of the Indies," which he asked King John II to finance in 1484, was based in part on this observation. By sailing before these winds, he said, he would make a short, speedy crossing of the Atlantic to the Indies. Japan was only 2,500 miles from Portugal.

Trying to reach the Indies by rounding Africa, as the Portuguese were doing, was a waste of resources. Portuguese navigators had explored far more than 2,500 miles of African coast and had no indication they were anywhere near its southern reach. (Díaz's discovery of the Cape of Good Hope was three years in the future.) Moreover, hugging the African coast meant struggling with adverse winds. Columbus would have easy sailing west and, a few degrees farther north, return to Portugal with the winds behind him.

Unfortunately for Columbus, the Portuguese were profiting richly buying African slaves, gold, and ivory. And advisors to John II told him that Japan was not 2,500 miles west

---

An "F" in Geography

School children were once taught that Columbus had to persuade Queen Isabella that the earth was round, a sphere. Not so—the shape of the earth was never an issue in Columbus's quest for funding. Ignorant landlubbers may have thought the world flat, that ships tumbled over the edge, but sailors knew better. The Portuguese routinely sailed to and from the Azores, 900 miles beyond the horizon. The well-educated Isabella knew better. The ancients, whom educated Europeans revered, had said the earth was a ball. Astronomers pointed out that, during lunar eclipses, the earth's shadow on the moon was round.

Columbus was, in fact, a poor geographer. He said that Japan lay 2,500 miles west; the actual distance is about 9,000 miles, just what Columbus's critics said. Had Columbus accepted this calculation, he would have had to scrap his dream and sign aboard a Portuguese ship coasting Africa. No vessel could be provisioned for a voyage of 9,000 miles. The fact that midway to Japan was an America teeming with provisions and fresh water did not, of course, feature in anybody's speculations.

On the Other Hand . . .

Columbus was a virtuoso navigator. He crossed the ocean in just four weeks, as well as anyone did it for centuries, and returned almost as quickly. If he was wrong about the size of the earth, he was a master of the currents and winds of the Atlantic.

As a colonizer, on the other hand, Columbus was the wrong man. He sited his first settlement, Isabella, in a malarial marsh three miles from fresh water! What was he thinking? As a governor, Columbus was worse. He proclaimed that Indians who failed to bring him gold each day would have their hands amputated, a law he could not enforce without destroying his colony. What was he thinking?

Having little gold to bring to Spain, Columbus brought enslaved Indians. This was another colossal blunder as church authorities promptly advised Queen Isabella that American Indians could not morally be enslaved. Columbus's captives, with whom he thought he would please the queen, were freed. One might lament that the great navigator spent his final years in disgrace, but Isabella had good reason to be sick of him.

but 9,000. (They were right.) And there was no string of Portuguese forts in which to take refuge and replenish supplies of food and water in the unknown Atlantic. Columbus, they said, would perish; any investment in his Enterprise would be a dead loss. The king agreed, calling Columbus "a big talker, full of fancy and imagination."

And so he took his scheme to Queen Isabella. Scholars from the University of Salamanca repeated what John II's advisors had told him: it was 9,000 miles across the Atlantic to Japan; no ship could be provisioned for such a voyage; the Enterprise of the Indies was "vain, impracticable, and resting on grounds too weak to merit the support of the government."

But Columbus had convinced influential men at Isabella's court. The queen paid Columbus a modest annuity just to keep him around. When, in 1492, she learned that Columbus had made his proposal to the kings of France and England, she decided to take a chance.

In fact, Isabella's financial risk was piddling. Outfitting Columbus cost no more than the annual salary of one of her many officials. The title Columbus demanded, "Admiral of the Ocean Sea," was an exalted one, but it did not cost the queen a ducat. Nor did the authority over any lands he might discover (another demand); nor a big cut of hypothetical profits. A town that owed the queen money and friends of Columbus picked up the cost of two caravels, the *Niña* and the *Pinta,* and the clumsy but larger *Santa Maria.*

FRUSTRATION

Four times Christopher Columbus crossed the Atlantic with letters from Isabella and Ferdinand addressed to the emperors of China and Japan. Four times he returned to Spain after his "Indians" told him that no, sorry, they had never heard of such illustrious persons. Four times, Columbus told Isabella and Ferdinand that, next time for sure, he would "give them as much gold as they need, . . . and I will also give them all the spices and cotton they need."

To the day he died in 1506, Columbus insisted he had reached some of the 7,448 islands that Marco Polo said ringed Asia. Sustained for half a lifetime by a vision, he could not admit what most knowing Spaniards understood by

Colver Pictures

The Santa Maria, *the largest of Columbus's vessels in 1492, and his flagship. Columbus did not like it because it was slow and difficult to handle. He preferred the* Niña *and the* Pinta.

1506, that his discoveries pointed to quite another conclusion: he had found lands previously unknown to Europe.

Until 1521, these lands had little value. Whereas the Portuguese were raking in huge profits from their African and Asian trade, only a few Spaniards lived comfortably on the two largest islands of the West Indies, Cuba and Santo Domingo, by exploiting Indian labor. Most of the Spanish

Why America? Why Not Columbia?

Why was the New World not named Columbia? In part, the fault was Columbus's. He never claimed that he had discovered a place that needed a name. He had visited "the Indies."

Amerigo Vespucci was an Italian who twice sailed to "the Indies." Whereas Columbus was a medieval man, Vespucci was a modern. He wrote of his voyages, "Rationally, let it be said in a whisper,

experience is worth more than theory"— this meaning the writings of the ancients, including the Bible. Marveling at American animals unknown in Europe, Vespucci noted: "So many species could not have entered Noah's ark," a heresy of which the pious Columbus was incapable.

It was Vespucci who first declared in print that it was a "New World" across the Atlantic. In 1507, a German cartographer, drawing the first map to show the Americas

separate from Asia, named this new world for Amerigo in the Latin form of his name, feminine—ending in "a"—because the Latin names for the continents of Europe, Africa, and Asia were of feminine gender.

In the late nineteenth century, a descendant of Amerigo, Signora America Vespucci, petitioned the United States Congress for compensation for 400 years unauthorized use of her name. She did not collect.

American Heritage Publishing

population, soldiers who had crossed the ocean to march on rich Asian cities, languished on the islands with "burnyng agues [fevers], . . . blysters, noysome sweates, aches in the body, byles, yellowe jaundyse, inflammations of the eyes."

No news from Cuba and Santo Domingo was good news. In 1513, Vasco Núñez de Balboa crossed the Isthmus of Panama and found another great ocean, the Pacific. The implication was painful: the real Indies were as distant as the scholars of Salamanca had said they were. In 1519, an expedition commanded by Ferdinand Magellan confirmed it. Sailing with five ships and 265 men, Magellan found an all-water route to the Pacific by rounding South America. But it was hardly a trade route. Magellan was killed. Only one of his vessels, the *Victoria*, commanded by Juan Sebastián de Elcaño, and just eighteen wretched seamen struggled back to Spain by sailing around the world.

The Spanish were barred from trading in the Indies anyway. In 1493, to avert a conflict between Spain and Portugal, the Pope, in **Inter Caetera,** divided the world's lands not "in the actual possession of any Christian king or prince" between the two nations. The line of demarcation ran from pole to pole a hundred leagues (about 300 miles) west of the Azores. The next year, in the Treaty of Tordesillas, the Portuguese persuaded Isabella and Ferdinand to move the line farther west (thus laying the legal grounds for Portuguese settlement of Brazil after its discovery in 1500). Either way, all Asia except the Philippines was off-limits to Spain.

THE SPANISH EMPIRE

In the same year Magellan set sail, a soldier commanding 11 ships led 508 soldiers, 200 Indians, and several Africans, with 7 cannon, 16 horses, and dozens of war dogs (gigantic mastiffs trained to kill) from Santo Domingo to Mexico. What Hernán Cortés found and did there ended Spain's envy of Portugal's commercial success.

CORTÉS IN MEXICO

Cortés was not the first Spaniard to set foot in Mexico. In 1511, Gonzalo Guerrero was shipwrecked on the Yucatán peninsula and actually became a military leader of the Maya. Another castaway who spoke Maya joined up with Cortés.

He worked as an interpreter in tandem with a girl, Malinche (Doña Marina, Cortés called her) who spoke both Mayan and Nahuatl, the Aztec language.

Cortés was an explorer who made a difference—overnight. He founded Vera Cruz in the spring of 1519. Learning of the riches of Tenochtitlán, he sent word to Cuba that he was marching there, hoping for a peaceable takeover of the Aztec, but prepared to conquer them. He called for reinforcements, tempting recruits with the fabulous stories he had been told of Aztec wealth.

The Tabascans, coastal Mexicans, attacked Cortés, but they were no match for cannon, horses, war dogs, and steel swords. The shrewd Cortés was a generous victor. He offered the Tabascans an alliance against the Aztec, whom, like virtually all Mexicans, the Tabascans resented because of the tribute the Aztec demanded. Cortés reprised this scenario—victory in battle, generous peace, alliance—several times on his long march to Tenochtitlán. Totomacs, Tlaxcalans, Tolucans, and Cholulans all joined him. By the time he reached the causeways over Lake Texcoco, Cortés commanded at least ten Indian warriors for each of his Spaniards.

The news of Cortés's progress (the Aztec intelligence network was superb) bewildered Moctezuma II. He rejected the advice of some of his nobles to attack the invaders outside the city. Moctezuma was troubled by the legend of Quetzalcoatl, a deity who—uncanny good luck for Cortés—was fair-skinned, had tried to forbid human sacrifice, and who had disappeared from Mexico in the direction from which Cortés came. To top things off, 1519 was Quetzalcoatl's year in the Aztec calendar. According to one of his advisors, the emperor "enjoyed no sleep, no food. . . . Whatsoever he did, it was as if he were in torment." Cortés did not have to battle his way over the causeways. On November 8, 1519, he and his huge army were welcomed into the city.

Within days, it was obvious that Cortés and his men were not gods. When soldiers stumbled on a store of jewels, silver, and gold in Moctezuma's palace, "as if they were monkeys, the Spanish lifted up the gold banners and gold necklaces. . . . Like hungry pigs they craved that gold." Always on top of developments, Cortés quickly made Moctezuma his hostage. He masterfully cultivated, cozened, and threatened him. Cortés thought he could have Mexico peacefully. For more than six months, Moctezuma did what he was told to do.

Bibliotheque Nationale, Paris

An Aztec artist drew this picture of Moctezuma II, Cortés, Malinche, and Spanish soldiers proceeding through Tenochtitlán. Curiously, a Spaniard altered the painting, depicting Cortés and Malinche in a European artistic style.

Outside the palace, however, Aztec nobles organized the increasingly hostile common people. Several times they refused to supply the huge quantities of food Moctezuma's "guests" consumed daily. In June 1520, a mob assaulted the palace. When Cortés marched Moctezuma out to quiet it, the emperor was struck by a rock and, shortly, died.

Conquistadora

Most of the women with Cortés were Mexicans, wives of Indian allies, bearers, and mistresses of the Spaniards. Doña Marina was Cortés's mistress as well as his translator and advisor. When Cortés was reinforced, a few Spanish women joined the expedition. On the *noche triste,* one of them, Maria de Estrada, quite unheard of by the Spanish, not only took up arms but impressed Cortés himself with her ferocity in battle.

CONQUEST

Tenochtitlán erupted behind the new emperor, Cuitláhuac and the Aztec came close to wiping out the Spaniards. Half of Cortés's men and perhaps 4,000 Tlaxcalans were killed on what the Spanish called *la noche triste,* the sad night, July 1, 1520. Nevertheless, even with their lives in the balance, the Spaniards insisted on carrying eight tons of gold and other treasure on their retreat. They really did suffer, as Cortés had told Moctezuma, "from a disease of the heart which can be cured only with gold."

But it was the Aztec, not the Spanish, who were doomed. Cortés mobilized his Indian allies and Spanish reinforcements. He returned to Tenochtitlán with 700 Spanish infantry, 120 crossbowmen, 90 cavalry, a "navy" of boats he had built to take control of the lake, and, so Cortés estimated, 50,000 Tlaxcalans and Texcocans. (Again, such figures are not to be taken too seriously.) For eighty days they assaulted a much smaller Aztec army led by yet another emperor, Cuauhtémoc. (Cuitláhuac had died of smallpox.) Cortés took Tenochtitlán, but hardly intact. When the battle ended on August 13, 1521, much of the city had been leveled.

Hernán Cortés had won a turnkey empire. He and his lieutenants inserted themselves at the top of Aztec society in place of the nobility they had effectively exterminated. (Fifteen thousand Aztec were killed on the final day of fighting.) They carved out great estates and lived off the labor of the masses as the Aztec nobles and priests had done. The traditional submissiveness of the common people made it possible for the Spaniards to rule with minimal resistance. Mexicans took quickly to the wheel, pulley, iron tools, and beasts of burden. Within 50 years, most had embraced the Roman Catholic religion while not abandoning many traditional practices.

THE CONQUISTADORES

The Spanish king—best known to history as Emperor Charles V—took little interest in his American empire. He spent the gold sent to him all right, but he never mentioned Mexico (now called New Spain) in his memoirs. Spanish adventurers, however, were electrified. There was a rush to the Americas by thousands of mostly young men who braved hideous conditions shipboard to search for Mexicos of their own. They called themselves **conquistadores**—conquerors. In a generation's lifespan, they subdued territory larger than Europe.

Rarely has history shaped a people for conquest as Spain's history shaped the conquistadores. Much of Spain is arid or mountainous; agriculture never attracted the ambitious. Because the Christian Spanish associated trade (business) with the despised Jews they had driven out of the country, the upper classes shunned commerce. The worldly role of the **hidalgo,** the Spanish male with pretensions to social standing, was to fight. He was a caballero, a knight. The bravery and fortitude of the conquistadors under daunting conditions awes us. The other side of their military character, their ruthlessness and cruelty, has also been remembered.

Spain's zealous Roman Catholicism factored into the conquistadors' achievement. Because the ancestral national enemy had been of another faith, Islam, Spanish nationalism and Roman Catholicism were of a piece. Like their Muslim foes, the Spaniards believed that a war even nominally for the purpose of spreading true religion was holy. Death in such a war was a first class ticket to paradise. It was a belief that made soldiers nonchalant about death and, for that, chillingly brave.

The Discoverer of the United States
The first European to visit what is now the United States was Juan Ponce de León. In 1513—at age 53, ancient for such gallivanting—Ponce sailed to Florida to find Bimini where, Indians said, there was "a particular spring which restores old men to youth"—the fountain of youth. In 1521, Ponce de León returned to Florida to live. Instead of paddling about in rejuvenating waters, he was killed by Indians.

EXPLORATION SOUTH AND NORTH

Spanish policy encouraged conquest by granting conquistadors the lion's share of the gold and silver they won. (The king got a fifth.) Conquistadors were granted land and *encomiendas,* the legal right to force the Indians who lived on their land to work for them. Peons (peasants) were not slaves—enslaving Indians was forbidden—but, in practice, the distinction was fine.

Only one conquistador's find rivaled that of Cortés. In 1531, an aging illiterate, Francisco Pizarro, led 168 soldiers and 62 horses high into the Andes Mountains of South America. There he found the empire of the Incas, 3,000 miles in extent, tied together by 12,000 miles of roads Pizarro called unmatched in Christendom. Inca highways were narrow. Like the Aztec, the Incas had no wheeled vehicles, so roads needed to accommodate only people on foot and llamas. Still, some stretches were magnificently engineered: one traversed a pass 16,700 feet above sea level; one of many cable bridges over gorges had a span of 250 feet.

Even bolder than Cortés, for reinforcement was out of the question, Pizarro was such an artist of deceit as to make Cortés look saintly. When he captured the Inca emperor, Athualpa, 80,000 Inca soldiers were paralyzed. For 8 months, they brought Pizarro a ransom of gold that filled a room 22 feet long by 17 feet wide. Then—so much for the honor of the caballero—Pizarro murdered Athualpa.

That was it for American treasure troves, although the search for them continued. In 1541, Francisco Orellana, commanding sixty men, searched for the mythical El Dorado, a king whom it was said was coated daily with gold dust that he washed off nightly in a pool. The pool may have been worth dredging. Orellana and forty-six survivors crossed tropical South America, 2,500 miles, on the Amazon River. Between 1539 and 1542, Hernando de Soto's army wandered what is now the southeastern United States in another fantasy-based search for riches. Viciously cruel with the Indians he battled, de Soto was buried in the Mississippi River. Only half the mourners at his funeral got back alive to the West Indies.

During the same years, Francisco Coronado trekked extraordinary distances in the Southwest. With about 300 conquistadors ("vicious young men with nothing to do"), a few blacks, and 800 Indians, Coronado was looking for the "Seven Cities of Cíbola," said to have been founded by seven Spanish bishops who, centuries earlier, had fled from the Moors to the "blessed Isles." One of these conurbations, according to an imaginative priest, Fray Marcos de Niza, was "the greatest city in the world . . . larger than the city of Mexico." Coronado's men found only dusty adobe villages. "Such were our curses that some hurled at Fray Marcos," wrote one soldier, "that I pray God may protect him."

SPANISH AMERICA

For more than a century Mexican and Peruvian gold and silver made Spain the richest and most powerful nation of Europe. By 1550, $4.5 million in precious metals crossed the Atlantic each year; by 1600, $12 million. Not for another century would the flow of riches dry to a trickle. American wealth financed the cultural blossoming of Spain and great armies to do the king's bidding.

By 1700, Spain's empire stretched from Florida and New Mexico to the Rio de la Plata in South America. In so vast a realm, economy and social structure varied immensely. Generally, however, the ownership of land in Spanish America was concentrated in the hands of a small group of *encomenderos* who lived off the labor of Indian peons and slaves from Africa.

Government was centralized in the hands of several viceroys (vice kings). The Roman Catholic Church exercised great power, generally for the good: many—not all—priests and friars took seriously their mission to protect the Indians from rapacious fellow Spaniards.

Priest-Ridden Land

No Catholic priest accompanied Columbus on his first voyage. On his second voyage, there were six priests and from there their numbers increased exponentially. Priests were everywhere in Spanish America, which was one small blessing on the Indians. Many, even most of the clerics regarded their mission as protecting the natives, and Spanish laymen had to tread warily in defying the powerful Church. The priests probably saved hundreds of thousands of lives.

When only a few hundred French or English had slept overnight on American beaches, Spanish America boasted 200 towns and cities, 20 printing presses, and 6 universities. The fate of the Indians, however, was not as bright a story. It has been estimated that there were at least 5 million Mexicans in 1500. In 1600, there were a million. In 1492, the Indian population of Santo Domingo was about 200,000; in 1508 it was 60,000; in 1514, 14,000. By 1570, only two small native villages survived.

THE BLACK LEGEND

It can seem a wonder that any Native Americans survived. Indeed, the horror they suffered was the lifetime message of priests who took up their cause. "I am the voice of Christ," Father Antonio de Montesinos told conquistadors who had come to church to doze, "saying that you are all in a state of mortal sin for your cruelty and oppression in your treatment of this innocent people."

A Dominican friar, Bartolomé de las Casas, devoted his life to lobbying the king for laws protecting the Indians. The Spaniards treated them, de las Casas said, "not as beasts, for beasts are treated properly at times, but like the excrement in a plaza." His scorching description of conquistador cruelty, *A Brief Relation of the Destruction of the Indians*, was overblown. De las Casas was a propagandist; propagandists exaggerate. But it was not fantasy; the *leyenda nera*, the "black legend" of Spanish cruelty, was true enough in its essence.

Still, the *encomenderos* must not be thought unique. In the context of the sixteenth century, the atrocities they perpetrated were close to routine. It was an era of indifference to suffering, and callousness was neither a Spanish nor a European monopoly. It was Asian, African, and Native American too, and exercised not only on those of different races. Warfare in Europe meant unmitigated horror for peasants caught in the paths of marauding armies. The bloodiness of Mesoamerican religion has been noted. Chinese techniques of torture were

By Permission of The Folger Shakespeare Library

■ *This portrayal of Native Americans, a woodcut, was carved in Germany about 1500, so the artist almost certainly never saw an Indian. Note the European facial features. Of all the tribes known to Europeans by 1500, only the Caribs of the West Indies ate human flesh.*

particularly exquisite. Africans needed no tutoring by outsiders in savagery.

Many more Indians died of pick and shovel than at sword point, and more died of disease than from labor.

THE COLUMBIAN EXCHANGE

Columbus's voyage established a biological pipeline between landmasses that had drifted apart 150 million years before human beings appeared on earth. Some species had flourished in both worlds: oaks, dogs, deer, mosquitoes, and the virus that causes the common cold. There were, however, many animals and plants in the Americas that were new to Europeans. And Europeans brought with them flora and fauna unknown to the Indians.

THE IMPACT ON AMERICA

Native American mammals were generally smaller and less suited for meat and draft than Old World livestock. The Aztec had only five domesticates: the turkey, Muscovy duck, dog, bee, and a cochineal insect. The Spanish were quick to import hogs, cattle, sheep, goats, and chickens along with European grasses to feed them (plus about 70 percent of the plants we call "weeds"). Indians soon depended on them. Even those native peoples who escaped Spanish conquest were glad to raid flocks and herds for food. The wool-weaving art identified with the Navajo of the American Southwest was refined when the Navajo adopted European sheep.

The sight of a man on horseback initially terrified the people of Mexico. It reinforced their briefly held delusion that the Spaniards were divine. Even after the Mexicans recognized that horses were ordinary beasts, the Spaniards' equestrian monopoly gave them an immense advantage in battle. Within two centuries, runaway horses gone feral had migrated as far as the Great Plains of North America. There they became the basis of several cultures that had never heard of Spain. The Sioux, Comanche, Pawnee, Nez Percé, Blackfoot, Crow, and other tribes of the plains, who had previously done their hunting on foot, captured mustangs and became peerless horsemen independent of European example.

Among the valuable "green immigrants" from the Old World were grains such as wheat and barley, citrus fruits, and sugar cane. Mexico was exporting wheat to the West Indies

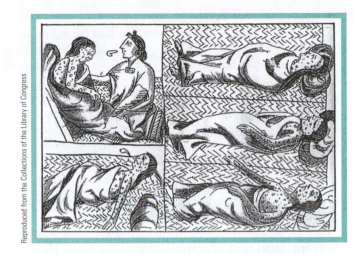

Reproduced from the Collections of the Library of Congress

An Aztec depiction of smallpox victims. The disease killed many Europeans and Africans, but it devastated Indian populations. Native Americans had inherited no resistance to it as Europeans and Africans had.

by 1535. It is difficult to imagine the West Indies without sugar cane, but it was an import. Columbus himself introduced lettuce, cauliflower, citrus fruits, figs, and pomegranates to America. Within a few decades of his death, bananas (from Asia) and watermelons (from west Africa) were being cultivated in the New World,

FEEDING THE WORLD

America contributed few food animals to world larders, but American plant foods revolutionized European, African, and Asian diets. Maize (Indian corn), an American native, astonished Europeans by the height of its stalks and the size of its grains. Cultivation of the crop spread to every continent, increasing the food supply and contributing to the runaway increase in population that characterizes the last five hundred years of human history.

The sweet potato became a staple in west Africa, where it was introduced by slave traders. (The yam, superficially similar, was already established there.) Beans, squash and pumpkins, peppers, strawberries (there was a European strawberry, but it was inferior to the American), vanilla and chocolate,

'Taters and Tomaters

Europeans took slowly to potatoes and tomatoes. Most believed that the former was an aphrodisiac and the latter poisonous. Some 300 years passed before the white potato became a staple in the country with which we most associate it—Ireland.

Tomatoes were grown in Europe as ornamentals by 1500. A Jesuit gourmet pronounced them excellent eating as early as 1590. Southern Italians were already growing them for their kitchens. By the eighteenth century, they were central to Mediterranean cuisine. In the United States, President Thomas Jefferson, a gourmet, served them at White House dinners, which is not to say that every guest partook.

Nonetheless, medical authorities warned so emphatically and tenaciously of the dire effects of eating tomatoes that, as late as 1820, Robert G. Johnson of Salem, New Jersey gathered a crowd hoping to seeing him collapse in agony when he announced he would consume a tomato on the steps of the courthouse.

VD

It has been suggested that syphilis was not carried from America to Europe, but was a mutation of yaws, a disease long endemic in hot climates in the Old World. If so, the timing and place of the mutation in Europe—1493 in Cadiz, the port to which Columbus returned—is a coincidence without rival. The case for an Old World origin of syphilis is next to no case at all. The only evidence for it is a similarity of the yaws microbe and the syphilis spirochete. The argument amounts to a case of, "it could have been."

The evidence for an American origin is mostly circumstantial—when and where syphilis first appeared in Europe—but powerfully so. And there is more than circumstance: Indians in Santo Domingo told de las Casas that the disease had been around long before Columbus. Signs of syphilis have been found in human bones in America dating to 4000 B.C., but none in African, Asian, and European bones before 1493.

wild rice, and tomatoes are American foods that were unknown in Europe, Africa, and Asia before 1492.

Of 640 food crops grown in Africa today, almost 600 of them originated in the Americas. Manioc (tapioca), also of American origin, is today a staple for 200 million people in the tropics. The white ("Irish") potato, a native of the Andes, provides basic subsistence for even greater numbers.

Many national cuisines depend on foods of American origin for their zest, notably the tomato and the extraordinary variety of chili peppers that have been developed from Mexican forebears. Think of Hungarian paprika and Italian sauces. These, as well as tobacco, were contributed to the Old World by the New.

DISEASE

The most tragic of the intercontinental transactions was in microscopic forms of life. Many diseases for which Europeans, Africans, and Asians had developed resistance, even immunity, were unknown to Native Americans before Columbus. Smallpox, measles, influenza, bubonic and pneumonic plagues, tuberculosis, typhoid fever, typhus, and cholera were as foreign to the Americas as horses and Spaniards. Biologically, the Indians had not learned "to live with" these killer diseases.

Why were they absent? Probably because all of these diseases first spread to human beings from domesticated animals—sheep, goats, cattle, pigs, and fowl. Native Americans had few such domesticates. The Indians of the Great Plains hunted herd animals—the bison—but they did not, like Europeans, Africans, and Asians, live in close daily proximity to them. The rarity of large cities in America also explains the absence of virulent epidemics in pre-Columbian America. Smallpox, measles, and the other terrible diseases Europeans brought on their ships are "crowd diseases." Highly infectious, once among dense populations, they rage and kill massively. If, before Columbus, similar afflictions appeared in the Americas, they died out for the lack of "crowds" in which to do their work.

Old World diseases were catastrophic in America. Transplanted Europeans and Africans suffered badly enough when, for example, smallpox swept through a population, but the Indians died in heartrending numbers.

America's microbic revenge was venereal disease. Europeans first identified syphilis as a new disease in 1493, in Cadiz, Spain, the port to which, in 1493, Columbus returned and dismissed his crew. Syphilis was next noticed in Naples, where several of Columbus's crewmen went as soldiers. It spread at terrifying speed throughout the world, following the trade routes. What better agents for spreading a sexually transmitted disease than seamen and the prostitutes who were their chief sexual partners?

Europeans, Africans, and Asians reacted to syphilis as Indians reacted to diseases previously unknown to them. Symptoms were severe and death came quickly. About ten million people died of syphilis within 15 years of Columbus's voyage. Only later did the disease take on the slower-acting form in which it is known today.

FURTHER READING

General D. W. Meinig, *Atlantic America 1492–1800,* volume 1 of *The Shaping of America: A Geographical Perspective on 500 Years of History,* 1986; Alvin M. Josephy Jr., *America in 1492: The World of the Indian People Before the Arrival of Columbus,* 1991.

Paleo-Indians Brian M. Fagan, *The Great Journey: the Peopling of Ancient America,* 1987 and *Ancient North America,* 2000; Stuart J. Fiedel, *Prehistory of the Americas,* 1991; Helen R. Sattler, *The Earliest Americans,* 1993; Francis Jennings, *Prehistory of America,* 1993.

Mesoamerican Civilization Norman Hammond, *Ancient Maya Civilization,* 1982; Linda Sechele and David Freidel, *A Forest of Kings: The Untold Story of the Ancient Maya,* 1990; Brian M. Fagan, *Kingdoms of Gold, Kingdoms of Jade: The Americas Before Columbus,* 1991; Linda Sechele and Mary Ellen Miller, *The Blood of Kings,* 1986; Jared Diamond, *Collapse: How Societies Choose to Fail or Succeed,* 2005.

European Exploration Daniel J. Boorstin, *The Discoverers: A History of Man's Search to Know His World and Himself,* 1985; Jared Diamond, *Guns, Germs, and Steel: The Fates of Human Societies,* 1997; Peter Russell, *Prince Henry "The Navigator": A Life,* 2000.

Columbus Samuel Eliot Morison, *Admiral of the Ocean Sea,* 1942; Kirkpatrick Sale, *The Conquest of Paradise,* 1990; William D. Phillips Jr. and Carla Rahn Phillips, *The Worlds of Christopher Columbus,* 1992.

Mexico and the Conquistadores William H. Prescott, *History of the Conquest of Mexico,* 1873; Hugh Thomas, *Conquest: Montezuma, Cortés, and the Fall of Old Mexico,* 1993; Leon Lopez-Portilla, *The Broken Spears,* 1962; Thomas C. Paterson, *The Inca Empire: The Formation and Disintegration of a Pre-Capitalist State,* 1991; John Logan Allen, *North American Exploration, vol. I,* 1997; J. C. H. King, *First Peoples, First Contacts: Native People of North America,* 1999; James Lockhart and Stuart B. Schwartz, *Early Latin America,* 1983;

Mark A. Burkhggolder and Lyman L. Johnson, *Colonial Latin America,* 1990; Donald J. Weber, *The Spanish Empire in North America,* 1990.

Biological Exchange Alfred E. Crosby, *The Columbian Exchange: Biological and Cultural Consequences of 1492,* 1972, and *Ecological Imperialism: The Biological Expansion of Europe,* 1986.

KEY TERMS

The following terms are covered in this chapter and can also be found in the list of Key Terms at the back of the book.

Amerigo Vespucci	**conquistadores**	**Inter Caetera**	**Paleo-Indians**
Beringia	**Henry the Navigator**	**Mesoamerica**	**Queen Isabella**
Christopher Columbus	**Hernán Cortés**	**Moctezuma II**	**Tenochtitlán**
Columbian Exchange	**hidalgo**		

 ## ONLINE SOURCES GUIDE

Use this listing to find online documents, images, interactive maps, simulations, and other resources related to this chapter:

American History Resource Center
http://history.wadsworth.com

Selected Document
Columbus's Letter to Gabriel Sanchez (1493)

Selected Images
Timucua people planting crops in sixteenth century
Caravans from the East

Artist's conception of Christopher Columbus
Plains Indian teepee
Sixteenth-century images depicting torture of Indians

Interactive Timeline (with online readings)
Discoveries: Indians, Europeans, and America
about 15,000 B.C. to A.D. 1550

Additional resources, exercises, and Internet links related to this chapter are available on *THE AMERICAN PAST* web site: http://history.wadsworth.com/americanpast8e

Discovery

How did the differences between the societies in the Americas and the ones in Europe lead to conflict and ultimately devastation for the cultures of the Americas?

In thinking about this question, begin by breaking it down into the components shown below. A discussion of the significance of each component should appear in your answer.

Religion and Philosophy: For this exercise, read the document excerpt, "Oral Tradition of the Origin of the Mide' Religion." How do you think religious differences led to cultural misunderstandings? Give specific examples. How might native religious practices have been viewed by the Spaniards as ungodly? Would this help to justify Spanish actions toward the Native Americans?

Oral Tradition of the Origin of the Mide' Religion

. . . When they arrived they found that the cousin had been dead four days, but the body had been kept so that they could see him.

The East manido' told his father and mother and their friends not to weep for the young man. Then the next morning he told the people to make a long lodge extending east and west, such as is now used for the Mide'. He showed them how to make it with the top open and the sides of birch bark and leaves, and he said that they must all bring tobacco and cooked food. In the center of the lodge he placed a Mide' pole, and told the Indians to sit in rows around the lodge; he also made a Mide' drum and rattles, such as are still used. . . .

Then the East manido' spoke to the parents of the dead man and to his own parents, saying, "I am about to leave you. I will be absent four days. You must stay here continuously and do every day as I have told you to do to-day." The old man promised to sing the Mide' songs and do everything as he had been told to do.

Then the East manido' took vermilion paint and also blue paint and made marks across the faces of the parents of the man and also his own parents—streaks across their foreheads, the lowest red, then blue and red alternately. Then he started away and said he would return on the morning of the fourth day. He went through the air toward the eastern sky. They could see him go. . . .

Culture and Society: For this exercise, read the document excerpt, "Bartolomé de Las Casas, 'Of the Island of Hispaniola'" and examine the illustration, "Portrayal of Native Americans." Keeping in mind that this illustration is a European view of how Native Americans might live, what image is the artist trying to portray? If this was your only knowledge of these people, how would you judge or describe them? Would you see this as "uncivilized" or "inhumane"? Compare this image to the descriptions of Spanish treatment of natives in the excerpt. Which is more "civilized" or "humane"? From the native viewpoint, is European civilization one that you would wish to adopt based on these interactions?

By Permission of The Folger Shakespeare Library

Portrayal of Native Americans

Bartolomé de Las Casas, "Of the Island of Hispaniola" (1542)

God has created all these numberless people to be quite the simplest, without malice or duplicity, most obedient, most faithful to their natural Lords, and to the Christians, whom they serve; the most humble, most patient, most peaceful and calm, without strife nor tumults; not wrangling, nor querulous, as free from uproar, hate and desire of revenge as any in the world. . . .

Among these gentle sheep, gifted by their Maker with the above qualities, the Spaniards entered as soon as they knew them, like wolves, tiger and lions which had been starving for many days, and since forty years they have done nothing else; nor do they afflict, torment, and destroy them with strange and new, and divers kinds of cruelty, never before seen, nor heard of, nor read of. . . .

The Christians, with their horses and swords and lances, began to slaughter and practice strange cruelty among them. They penetrated into the country and spared neither children nor the aged, nor pregnant women, nor those in child labour, all of whom they ran through the body and lacerated, as though they were assaulting so many lambs herded in their sheepfold.

To read extended versions of the documents, visit the companion Web site http://history.wadsworth.com/americanpast8e; click on "Discovery Sources."

CHAPTER 2

Settlements Across the Sea

The Reasons, the Failures, and a Success 1550–1624

North Wind Picture Archives

Where every wind that rises blows perfume, And every breath of air is like an incense.

Francis Beaumont and John Fletcher, English poets

The nature of the Country is such that it Causeth much sickness, and the scurvy and the bloody flux, and divers other diseases, which maketh the body very poor, and Weak. . . . We are in great danger, for our Plantation is very weak, by reason of the death, and sickness. . . . I have nothing to Comfort me, nor is there nothing to be gotten here but sickness, and death.

Richard Frethorne, early settler in Virginia

News of Columbus's discovery reached every European capital within months. Queen Isabella published his report even before she received Columbus in person. In Rome it was published in Latin, making it accessible to every educated European. By the time Columbus set sail on his second voyage to "the Indies" in September 1493, the story of the first was out in a half dozen editions.

King Henry VII of England (who had brushed off Columbus) funded an Italian navigator living in Bristol, John Cabot (Giovanni Caboto), who said that Columbus found no rich empires because he was too far to the south. Japan, Cabot pointed out, lay at nearly the same latitude as England. In 1497, he sailed due west, which, because winds and currents

were less favorable in the North Atlantic, made for a far more difficult crossing than Columbus's. Instead of reaching Japan, however, he found Nova Scotia. Like Columbus, Cabot insisted he had reached the Indies; Cape Breton Island was a thinly populated hinterland of China.

The French showed little interest in transatlantic exploration until 1523 when Jean Fleury captured three Spanish caravels. The cargo was most interesting: 500 pounds of gold dust and three large crates of gold ingots. It was Mexican booty Cortés had shipped to Spain. King Francis I then sent his hustling Italian navigator, Giovanni Verrazano, across the ocean. He cruised the North Carolina coast and infused new life into the belief that there was an easy sea route to the

© Corbis

Like Columbus, John Cabot believed that Asia could be reached by sailing west across the Atlantic. In 1497, he reached North America and claimed it for England. King Henry VII rewarded Cabot with an income of £20 a year for life—not much, and Cabot collected only once. He and his ship were lost on a second voyage in 1498.

Indies when he reported back home that only a narrow sandy spit separated the Atlantic from the "Indian Sea" or, as some mapmakers called it, "Verrazano's Sea." (Probably, Verrazano saw Pamlico Sound from across North Carolina's Outer Banks.) The pope scolded Francis I, reminding him that the world's non-Christian real estate had been divided between Portugal and Spain. Francis dipped his pen in sarcasm and asked to see the clause in Adam's will that authorized the pope to endow such gifts. (When a conquistador told a Cenú Indian what the pope had done, the Indian remarked, "The pope must have been drunk.")

THE ENGLISH REFORMATION

Drunk or sober, Adam's will or no, the Americas remained a Spanish (and Portuguese) monopoly for a half century. Other European nations might envy Aztec and Inca riches—they made the 1500s the **siglo de oro,** Spain's "golden century"—but they also feared the armies Spain's gold and

silver financed. The French made a half-hearted attempt to establish a base in Canada. In 1536, an Englishman, Richard Hore, sailed to Labrador with the harebrained plan of seizing an Indian to exhibit in London. A few French, English, and Dutch fishermen spent winters on Newfoundland and Nova Scotia, and even in New England to dry and salt the cod they had netted on the Grand Banks. But no nation made a serious attempt to found a permanent colony until late in the century.

EUROPE DIVIDED

The delay owed to more than fear of Spain. The sixteenth century was a time of turmoil in Europe, the era of the Protestant Reformation. When Cortés was shattering the Aztecs, a German monk, Martin Luther, was shattering the unity of western Christendom. When Coronado was searching for the seven cities of Cibola in the scorching Southwest, a French lawyer in rainy Geneva, John Calvin, was laying the foundations of a dynamic religious faith that would profoundly shape American history.

In 1517, Luther attacked several doctrines and practices of the Roman Catholic Church. Called to account by the Holy Roman Emperor Charles V (the selfsame king of Spain), Luther denied the pope's religious authority. The only source of God's word, he declared, was the Bible. In a short time, large parts of Germany and the Netherlands and all of Scandinavia embraced Lutheranism. Many ordinary folk had long been disgusted by the moral laxity common among Catholic priests. German princes, no paragons of morality themselves, were attracted to Lutheranism because, if they cut their ties to the Roman Church, they could seize church lands.

Spain, Portugal, Italy, and most of the French remained Catholic. In England, King Henry VIII condemned Luther in a book, *Defense of the Seven Sacraments,* which Pope Leo X so appreciated he named Henry "Defender of the Faith."

HENRY VIII

A few years later, the Defender attacked the Church. Henry had no quarrel with basic Catholic doctrine, or with Catholic rituals. His problem was his marriage of 20 years to a Spanish princess, Catherine of Aragon. After a history of babies dead in the womb or cradle, Catherine was at the end of her childbearing years. There was a daughter, Mary. But monarchs still rode with their soldiers on the battlefield. Henry believed that, if his Tudor dynasty were to be secure, he must have a son to succeed him, a king who could suit up in armor. For that he needed a new, young wife.

And there was Cupid, for Henry was a romantic. (He had been far more affectionate toward his wife, Catherine, than kings were expected to be.) Now he had fallen in love with a comely young flirt, Anne Boleyn. Anne wanted more than a mistress's pillow, she wanted a wedding ring.

The Roman Church forbade divorce—marriage was forever. However, when the rich and powerful had marital difficulties, bishops and popes were usually able to find grounds in the fine print for an **annulment;** that is, there never

Elizabeth Regina

Queen Elizabeth enjoyed a good time at banquets and balls. She was witty and enjoyed others who were witty. She had a romantic streak, but early on the politician in her decided she would not marry. A husband meant political complications. No sixteenth-century prince or nobleman would hover in the shadows as Elizabeth II's Prince Philip has done for fifty years. Elizabeth I flirted shamelessly with young men, and liked bawdy humor, but she really was a virgin queen. A pregnancy would have been the end of her.

She was vain, far from beautiful, and she was a sucker for flattery. Raleigh was just one of her "favorites" who knew there was no such thing as laying it on too thick. Portraits of the queen as an old woman (she died at age 69) show a grotesque clown-like face: no eyebrows—every hair had been plucked—her face starkly white, made up with lard dusted with chalk, then splotched with bright rouge. Her white hair was dyed a brilliant red.

But was the makeup nothing but vanity? With no eyebrows to arch involuntarily and her face encased in plaster, Elizabeth presented those who approached her throne with a face that could not be read. She betrayed no emotion from behind her mask—neither surprise, nor interest, nor approval, nor anger, no matter what a courtier or ambassador said.

had been a valid marriage in the eyes of God. Henry had a more plausible case for an annulment than others whom the Church had allowed to set their wives aside. But Pope Clement VII was in no position to be helpful. He was at odds with a far more powerful prince than Henry VIII, the Emperor Charles V, who was Catherine of Aragon's nephew. In 1527, the emperor's army had ravaged the city of Rome.

While the pope hemmed and hawed, Henry learned that Anne Boleyn was pregnant. If her son—for surely the child would be a boy—were to be king, he had to be legitimate. Henry directed his bishops to divorce him and Catherine and marry him to Anne. He directed Parliament to outlaw the pope's authority in England and to name him the head of the new Church of England. Henry then emulated the Lutheran German princes he had condemned; he dissolved England's 400 monasteries and nunneries and seized their lands. Beginning in 1538, Henry sold these prime properties to ambitious subjects. Simultaneously he filled his treasury and created a class of landowners whose wealth and social position depended on supporting the Church of England against the Church of Rome.

A HALF CENTURY OF INSTABILITY

Henry encouraged his subjects to vilify the papacy, of course, and he rejected the idea of monks and withdrawing into communities. But the king was personally comfortable with Catholic rituals and with episcopal church government—that is, the church was governed from above by bishops appointed by the king.

So, for ordinary Englishmen and women, the "English Reformation" meant little. The rhythms of their religious lives remained the same. Pope or king: what was the difference to a baker or a milkmaid? The now scattered monks and nuns: what were they but former landlords? Compared to the violence and psychic dislocations of the Reformation on the Continent, the English Reformation was easy not to notice.

However, as powerful people have discovered before and since, tinkering even a little with an established order of things can liberate a spirit of innovation. A true Protestantism germinated within the Church of England during the reign of Edward VI, Henry's son. Parish priests a bit too Catholic in their styles were dismissed. Churches were stripped of statues and other Catholic impedimenta, not least among them chalices and candleholders made of gold. The Protestant Book of Common Prayer, written in English, replaced Catholic devotionals in Latin.

Alas for the reformers around Edward, he died in 1553 when only 16. His successor, his half-sister Mary, was the intensely Catholic daughter of Catherine of Aragon. For two decades, Mary had seethed over her mother's humiliation and the break with Rome. Now queen, she repealed Edward's

The Background of English Colonization 1550–1603

	1550	1575	1600
1547–1553	Reign of Edward VI: Protestant reformers control Church of England		
1553–1558	Reign of Mary Tudor, a Catholic: peace with Spain; Protestants in exile in Geneva influenced by Calvinism		
Reign of Elizabeth I, 1558–1603	queen of England		
1570s	Ignoring official peace with Spain, "Sea Dogs" begin to raid Spanish ships and seaports		
Humphrey Gilbert and Walter Raleigh attempt to build colonies 1583–1591	in Newfoundland and on Roanoke Island, North Carolina		
Spanish Armada: Spain's attempt to invade England ends in disaster 1588			
Publication of Hakluyt's *Principal Navigations*, a persuasive argument for founding colonies in America 1598–1600			

Protestant reforms and appointed Catholics as bishops. Then she married Prince Philip of Spain, soon to be known as "His Most Catholic Majesty" because of his religious zeal. But even Philip was alarmed by the ardor with which Mary persecuted Protestants. Three hundred were executed during her reign, earning the queen the unattractive nickname, "Bloody Mary."

If Mary had been more sly than devout, if she had enjoyed a long life and delivered a son or daughter around whom English Catholics could have rallied, England might have been eased, over time, back into the Roman Church. Quite a few nobles and many of the gentry were still Catholic in their hearts. As always, a large proportion of people with wealth and social position at stake leaned in the direction the wind blew. The evidence implies that the common people in England (with the exception of those in London and southern England) were more Catholic than Protestant in their sentiments.

ELIZABETHAN ENGLAND: THE SEEDBED OF ENGLISH AMERICA

Mary was a fanatic; she would not dilly-dally when religious truth was at stake. She had only 5 years during which to swing her axe; she died childless in 1558.

Her successor, her half-sister, **Elizabeth,** had been raised a Protestant but she was no zealot. She did not, she said, care to make "windows into men's souls." She understood the real world of politics, as Mary had not. In a country divided religiously, Elizabeth had herself crowned in a hybrid ceremony, part Catholic, part Anglican.

She comforted Protestants by naming a Church of England man Archbishop of Canterbury and agreeing to bring back the Book of Common Prayer. But when the prayer book squeaked through Parliament by just three votes, Elizabeth backed off. She refused to persecute Catholics as Protestant

Until 1580, Queen Elizabeth responded to Spanish complaints about Francis Drake by saying that he acted without her permission. When, in 1580, Drake returned from his voyage around the world with his ship packed to the gunwales with Spanish treasure, the queen had to choose: she could return it and punish Drake, or she could accept responsibility for him, collect her royal share of his loot, and face the consequences of war with Spain. She boarded Drake's ship and knighted him.

Nasty Nationalism

English propagandists vilified Philip II and Spaniards in language that would cause shudders today. Scathing generalizations about other peoples were part and parcel of the intense nationalism that arose in western Europe during the 1500s.

Spain and Portugal were both Catholic, their histories parallel and their languages closely related. Nonetheless, Francis Xavier, a Spanish missionary in east Asia, wrote home of the Portuguese in China: "Their knowledge is restricted to the conjugation of the verb 'to steal' in which they show an amazing capacity for inventing new tenses and participles."

Spanish Virginia

The Spanish did not ignore America north of Florida. In 1526, about 500 colonists, including 100 slaves, began to build a town at the mouth of the Pee Dee River in what is now South Carolina. But the slaves rebelled and many escaped; only 150 Spaniards limped back to the Caribbean.

In 1571, Jesuit priests established a mission in Virginia, not far from where, thirty-five years later, the English founded Jamestown. They converted several high-ranking Powhatan to Catholicism, or so they thought. The Powhatan killed them.

Spain recognized England's rights to its North American colonies only in 1670.

advisors urged her to do. The emperor's envoy in England wrote home: "She has treated all religious questions with so much caution and incredible prudence that she seems both to protect the Catholic religion and at the same time not entirely to condemn or outwardly reject the new Reformation."

Elizabeth's Church of England, like her coronation, was a hybrid. Its rites were in English, which was enough for all but the most radical Protestants. But they were similar enough to Catholic rites that most tradition-minded Englishmen and women were comfortable with them. Elizabeth was a Protestant who was willing to wait. Indeed, during her reign, the numbers of steadfast English Catholics quietly evaporated.

THE SEA DOGS

Elizabeth was just as shrewd in foreign policy. Philip II tried to save Spain's alliance with England by proposing marriage to Elizabeth. It was out of the question. Elizabeth's courtiers were rabidly anti-Spanish; marrying Philip had been Bloody Mary's worst blunder. However, if Elizabeth insulted Philip with an abrupt refusal, it might mean a war that divided England could not win. So Elizabeth waffled; she hinted she might accept Philip's proposal, then avoided the Spanish king, killing time until Philip was worn down and left the country.

When Jean Ribaut, who had built a French Protestant fort in Florida, tried to buy supplies in England, Elizabeth threw him into prison for violating Spain's claim to Florida. But all the while she winked at a restless, swashbuckling fraternity of Spain-hating English sea captains (men much like Ribaut) who meant to "singe King Philip's beard" by raiding Spanish towns and seizing Spanish treasure ships.

The most daring and successful of these **sea dogs** (named for a shark common in English waters) was a slave trader who aspired to cleaner work, **Francis Drake.** In 1577, Drake set sail in the *Golden Hind,* rounded South America by the Strait of Magellan, and looted Spanish ports on the Pacific. It was a cakewalk. The ports were unfortified. No ship of any nation except Spain had ever plied those waters.

Drake correctly reckoned that Spanish warships awaited him in the Atlantic. Instead of returning to England the way he had come, Drake sailed north to California, reconditioned the *Golden Hind*—no one knows exactly where—and struck

west across the Pacific. His expedition was only the second to circumnavigate the globe.

While Drake was at sea, another sea dog, Martin Frobisher, sailed three times to Newfoundland. He was looking for a "northwest passage" through North America to Asia, but also for a likely site to plant a colony. Frobisher found what he thought was a gold mine. He forgot about colonies and northwest passages and carried a thousand tons of ore back to England. It turned out to be worthless rock. In 1578, Elizabeth licensed another sea dog, Sir Humphrey Gilbert, to establish a "plantation" in America on land "not in the actual possession of any Christian prince." Elizabeth was playing cute with Spain's claim to all of North America.

In 1580, Elizabeth abandoned discretion. Drake had returned, the *Golden Hind* so overloaded with Spanish treasure that it was close to capsizing. The profit on the voyage was

From the Collections of the Library of Congress

John White, later the governor of Roanoke, was an artist who painted the Indians of North Carolina so that Raleigh could use them when courting investors. In this watercolor White depicted a man and woman in the village of Secotan dining on boiled corn kernels. Indians boiled food by dropping heated rocks into watertight baskets. Understandably, they coveted the iron pots of the English, which could be set directly on a fire.

4,700 percent! As queen, Elizabeth was entitled to a share of the loot but that meant dropping the pretense of friendship with Spain. Elizabeth boarded the *Golden Hind* and knighted Drake.

SIR WALTER RALEIGH AND ROANOKE

In 1583, Gilbert sailed with 5 ships and 260 men. He headed first to Newfoundland where he knew there would be fishermen from whom he could buy provisions. There were plenty of them: 36 ships of a half dozen nations. The living was so good that Gilbert dawdled until winter. Then he headed south and was caught in a ferocious storm. Bold old dog to the end, Gilbert's last recorded words, shouted across the waves to another ship, were: "We are as near to heaven by sea as by land." He drowned.

Gilbert's half-brother, Walter Raleigh, inherited the license to found a colony and, quite on his own, he charmed his way into Queen Elizabeth's favor. She lavished properties and incomes on him, so much largesse that he did not dare risk it by going on a long voyage. Instead, in 1584, he sent an expedition to select a site for a colony. It returned singing the praises of the Chesapeake Bay and, a bit farther south, Roanoke Island in what is now North Carolina.

Roanoke appealed to Raleigh for several reasons. Manteo, an Indian who returned with the reconnaissance party, was from nearby Croatan Island. His tribe would be an ally. Also, Roanoke was closer to Spanish sea routes than the Chesapeake; Raleigh intended his colony to be a base for sea dogs raiding Spanish treasure ships. Moreover, a colony on Roanoke would not be easily seen from the Atlantic because its site was obscured by long barrier islands—huge sandbars, actually—now called the Outer Banks. (A Spanish ship later sent to destroy Roanoke came within two miles of the colony and never saw it.) Finally, Raleigh's maps showed him that "Verrazano's

Common Seamen

How They Lived

By our standards they were small men; few seamen of the age of discovery and colonization topped five and a half feet. Most were teenagers or men in their twenties; statistically, they were years younger than men who lived on land. In addition to the diseases that threatened everyone, seamen faced shipwreck, battle, and everyday hazards: they might be killed by a crewmate in a fight over a triviality. A seaman might die being punished. Discipline on the high seas was immediate and brutal. Floggings were as regular as rain. Keelhauling (dragging a man under water the length of the hull where, if he did not drown, his body was shredded by barnacles) was unusual but far from unknown. After a mutiny, Magellan beheaded one ringleader, quartered another alive, and marooned a third on a desert island. When he pardoned the other mutineers, they were so grateful that they became Magellan's most devoted followers.

Finally, the common seaman ran a high risk on long voyages of contracting scurvy, a vitamin C deficiency. Scurvy can be prevented and even reversed by a diet of fruits and vegetables. At sea, however, the menu did not include such foods because they were perishable. Meals consisted of salt beef, rock-hard biscuit called hardtack, water, and wine. Officers did better. The onions, garlic, and dried fruit in their larders doubtless explains the lower incidence of scurvy among them. Seventeenth-century ships that were not destroyed by enemies or by the sea had a life expectancy of ten years. It was about the same for the men who sailed them—those who were not drowned in a sinking, or killed, or captured by enemies.

A sailor's labor was heavy. Seamen hauled heavy canvas up and down masts, with pulleys as their only mechanical aid. Merely holding the ship on course was heavy work. The crude tiller pitted the seaman's strength against the forces of wind and ocean currents. Every ship leaked and had to be pumped constantly, by hand, during storms.

Ships on long voyages had to be serviced (or "refitted") regularly. Barnacles reproduced to a point where they were heavy enough to sink a vessel. If far from a friendly port, the crew sailed to a beach where at high tide, the ship was "careened," eased on its side. The men then scraped the barnacles—horrible work—and recaulked the hull with rope and pitch. If the captain decided that the sails needed to be rearranged (or "rerigged") seamen virtually rebuilt the ship above deck. On a good day, crews were kept hopping, repairing sails and lines, scrubbing the decks with vinegar and salt water. Officers knew that idleness and boredom were more likely to cause discontent than overwork. Criminals (the Portuguese called them *degredados*) were pardoned if they signed on for long voyages and survived.

Columbus's crew was rounded out with convicts, but most seamen of the age of discovery were volunteers. Most were born in ports and bred to the life. Their other options were not numerous. And, for all its dangers and discomforts, the sea offered a remote but alluring chance for social and economic advancement. Whereas some of the great captains of the era were, like Magellan, born into the upper classes, others, like Columbus, worked their way up from the bottom. Columbus first shipped out as a boy, perhaps only ten years old; he was illiterate until he was thirty. Yet he became an intimate of royalty. Many conquistadores first came to the New World as common seamen and lived to become wealthy landowners.

Sea"—free sailing to the Indies, so he thought—was somewhere in the neighborhood.

In 1585, Raleigh assembled five ships filled mostly with soldiers. Again, he stayed behind to protect his interests and, unfortunately, named a hothead (he may have been quite mad) to command the expedition. He made enemies of Indians living just a few miles from Roanoke by burning their village because of a petty theft. The soldiers left behind barely survived through winter. When Francis Drake (fresh from another round of robbing Spaniards) arrived with supplies, the colonists asked to be taken home. Drake took them.

In 1587, Raleigh sent ninety-one men, seventeen women, and nine children to found a colony on the Chesapeake. (He was spending a lot of money!) However, one of his captains (another ill-advised appointment) dumped the settlers on Roanoke. The governor of the colony, a talented artist named John White, was so ineffective as a leader he was virtually forced to return to England. Because White expected to return the following spring with supplies and more colonists, he left his daughter and granddaughter on the island.

Three years passed before White returned. He found Roanoke's buildings abandoned. The word "CROATOAN" was carved on one of the structures in "fayre Capitall letters." This was a good sign. White had instructed the colonists that, if they left the island, they were to leave the name of their destination in just such a way. If they were forced to leave for any reason, they were to punctuate their message by carving a cross. There was no cross "or signe of distress." Croatan Island made sense; it was Manteo's home, and he had been one of the colony's leaders.

But the settlers of Roanoke were never found. Many theories of what happened to them have been ventured, based on fleeting glimpses of Indians with blond hair or speaking Elizabethan English. None of the theories has been proved. It remains a mystery.

BEGINNINGS OF AN EMPIRE

Raleigh and White failed to resupply Roanoke on time because, in 1587, Queen Elizabeth proclaimed a "stay of shipping": no vessel could leave English ports without special license. Philip II had assembled a fleet of 130 ships with which to invade England as punishment for Drake's pillaging and to return the country to the Catholic Church. The queen wanted all her sea dogs at home.

THE SPANISH ARMADA

In the end, there was no invasion. The Invincible Armada of 1588 (the "Spanish Armada") was a disaster. Designed to transport 30,000 troops, its large galleons, galleasses, and galleys were harassed in the English Channel by small, quick English pinnaces. Regrouping in the harbor of Calais in France, the Armada was further disorganized by fire ships, old vessels the English lathered with tar, stuffed with gunpowder, and sailed aflame amidst the Spanish fleet. (The crews jumped off at the last minute to be rescued by speedy rowed boats.)

National Portrait Gallery, London

Sir Walter Raleigh was a "favorite" of Queen Elizabeth. That is, she kept him around for his conversation and favored him with property, paying positions at court . . . and a license to plant a colony. Artful flattery was a favorite's best tool. Raleigh named Virginia for Elizabeth, "the Virgin Queen."

The next year, returning home by rounding the British Isles to the north, the Armada was cursed by violent weather. Twenty ships were driven ashore in Ireland. Only half of the great fleet made it back to Spain, only a third of Philip's soldiers. The Elizabethans may be excused for assuming that God had lined up on their side. They called the storms that battered the Armada "the Protestant Wind" and told one another that "God himselfe hath stricken the stroke, and ye have but looked on." In truth, English cannon did not sink a single Spanish ship.

Whatever God's role in the affair, the Armada's debacle demonstrated that Spain was not invincible. As the *siglo de oro* drew to a close, England, France, and the Netherlands pondered the possibility of planting colonies in America.

PROMOTERS

The sea dogs showed that the English could challenge Spain. Some Elizabethan landlubbers promoted the idea that England should establish colonies as Spain had done. The most energetic of the propagandists was Richard Hakluyt, a bookish but by no means parochial minister of the Church of England. Hakluyt rummaged tirelessly through the libraries of Oxford and London, collecting hundreds of explorers' accounts of the geography, resources, and attractions of

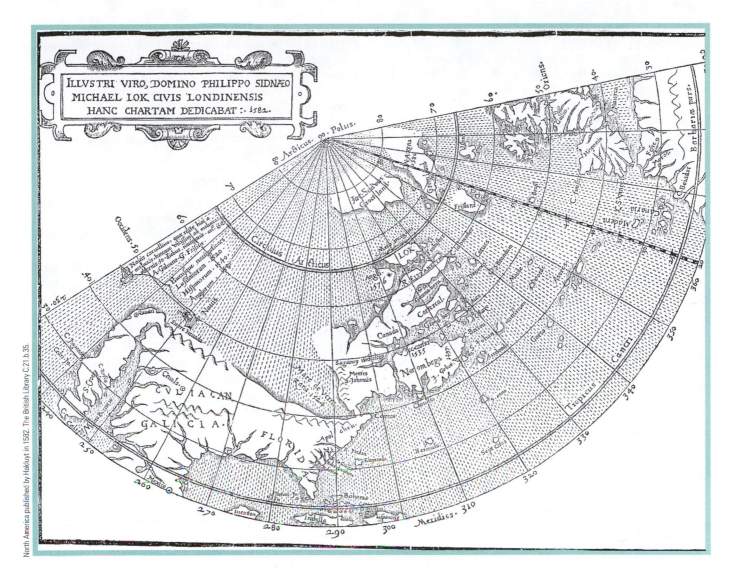

■ *A map of North America and the West Indies published by Richard Hakluyt in 1582. Canada, Bermuda, Florida, and Cuba (here called Isabella) are well-represented and accurately positioned. Most of North America, however, is pure imagination. Raleigh was drawn to Roanoke island on the North Carolina coast by, on this map, the proximity of "Verrazano's Sea" (Mare de Verrazana), which, as Verrazano said, was separated from the Atlantic by a narrow isthmus. What Verrazano probably saw was Pamlico Sound, which does not, however, provide the clear sailing to the Pacific and the East Indies shown here.*

America. His masterwork, *The Principal Navigations, Voyages, Traffiques, and Discoveries of the English Nation*, came out between 1598 and 1600.

In his books and in unnumbered conversations with men of money, Hakluyt argued that investment in American colonies would infallibly produce profit, add to England's prestige, and "enlarge the glory of the gospel." He lived until 1616, long enough to be a shareholder in the first successful English settlement in America.

Despite his setbacks, Raleigh continued to promote colonization. He told the queen he would make her "lord of more gold, and of a more beautiful empire, and of more cities and people, than either the King of Spain or the grand Turk." He had exhausted his own fortune on Roanoke Island and had to lobby other potential investors. But his day was over. Elizabeth's successor, James I, stripped Raleigh of everything Elizabeth had bestowed on him, then imprisoned him. Raleigh

spent a decade in the Tower of London. He emerged to have one last colonial adventure in South America, another failure, then returned to England and was beheaded.

The promoters, like advertisers of every era, played down the risks of living in America, puffed up the attractions beyond anything the Indians would have recognized, and simply lied through their teeth. Virginia, they said, rivaled "Tyrus for colours, Balsan for woods, Persia for oils, Arabia for spices, Spain for silks, Narcis for shipping, the Netherlands for fish, Pomona for fruit and by tillage, Babylon for corn, besides the abundance of mulberries, minerals, rubies, pearls, gems, grapes, deer."

HARD ECONOMIC FACTS

Every promoter of American colonies promised the possibility of finding gold, as was found in Mexico and Peru. Because the Spanish had not found the all-water passage to the

Indies, it had to be in the north, which the Spanish had hardly explored. Maps of the era showed "Verrazano's Sea" (his grandson claimed that just six miles of land separated it from the Atlantic) or the "Strait of the Three Brothers" (three Portuguese brothers claimed to have sailed through the passage west to east!). Belief in the existence of a "Northwest Passage"—a triumph of wishful thinking—would survive for more than 200 years. Promoters also envisioned colonies as havens from which sea dogs would sally forth to seize Spanish treasure ships. Hakluyt identified dozens of harbors and coves suitable to such enterprises.

Few English investors had moral qualms about stealing from the Spanish. After 1600, however, capturing treasure ships was much more difficult. The Spanish began to convoy them. It was expensive—twenty warships to defend twenty merchantmen—but it was effective.

More compelling for sober English capitalists, there were signs by 1600 that Spain's American gold and silver mines were not unmitigated blessings. Spain's fabulous wealth had enabled her grandees to purchase whatever they desired, to enjoy a style of life that was the envy of Europe, and to field huge **mercenary** armies that terrorized the continent. It was also evident, however, that the blizzard of riches blew out of Spain with as much force as it blew in. The Spanish purchased food abroad, impoverishing their farmers. Fisheries were neglected in favor of buying salted fish from others. The king's attempt to encourage the manufacture of textiles, leather, and iron goods was thwarted by the cheapness of imports. Even the majority of Spain's dreaded armies were German and Italian mercenaries who spent none of their wages in Spain.

Mexican and Peruvian gold and silver ended up in countries with no mines, but with a class of canny, grasping merchants and manufacturers. Other nations did the final count of the Spanish doubloons, including Spain's enemies, for the English and the Dutch were happy to make and transport whatever the Spanish would buy. These transactions left Spain poorer and her enemies richer. Hakluyt's projection of colonies buying English manufactures shipped by English merchants had more appeal to investors than the gold mines that might or might not lie under Virginia's forests.

SURPLUS POPULATION

The Crown (as the English called the government) took an interest in colonies because of the anxiety that there were just too many Englishmen and women. The population of England had soared during the 1500s, particularly the numbers of those with little or no means of feeding and sheltering themselves. Many people blamed the **enclosure movement.** That is, purchasers of monastery lands often expelled the peasants who had worked them as tenants and turned the fields into pastures for sheep, enclosing the fields with hedges. Areas that had grown crops that fed a hundred villagers plus some income for the landlord returned a much larger income when converted to wool production. But sheep provided work for a mere handful of shepherds.

Former tenants were sent on their way to wander the countryside in gangs, worrying villagers and gentry alike with their begging, bullying, and theft. The boldest and most desperate waylaid travelers on lonely stretches of highway. Most of the refugees flocked into the cities, especially London, to form a half-starved underclass that, like the poor of all ages, was a source of disease, disorder, and crime. "Yea many thousands of idle persons," Hakluyt wrote, "having no way to be set on work . . . often fall to pilfering and thieving and other lewdness, whereby all the prisons of the land are daily pestered and stuffed full of them."

His solution was the alchemy of a sea voyage. Colonies would be social safety valves. People who were economically superfluous and socially dangerous at home would become cheerful consumers of English manufactures, paying for them by producing the raw materials that England needed. "The fry of the wandering beggars of England, "that grow up idly, and hurtful and burdenous to this realm, may there be unladen, better bred up, and may people waste countries to the home and foreign benefit, and to their own more happy state."

The *"pestering poor": A beggar asks for alms from an elegantly dressed Elizabethan gentleman. Elizabethans believed that the growing number of destitute people unable to find work were a threat to domestic peace. They were a threat (note that the gentleman carries a sword with which to defend himself), but they were also a source of colonists to extend England's presence to North America.*

PRIVATE ENTERPRISE

The first colonies were financed and organized by private companies that were forerunners of the modern corporation. These **merchants-adventurers companies** ("adventurer" refers to the adventuring or risking of money) had developed as a response to the considerable expense and high risks involved in overseas trade.

That is, it was neither cheap nor a sure thing to send a ship laden with trade goods out to sea and bring other goods back to sell at home. Pirates, warships of hostile nations, and storms and shoals waited to do vessels in. A rich man betting a large part of his fortune on the fate of a single voyage was flirting with ruin. Instead, investors joined with others, each buying "shares" in the enterprise. The odds their ship would simply disappear were the same. But if it did, a dozen (or three dozen) shareholders shared the loss; nobody was

ruined. And some voyages in which they invested would return, often at considerable profit. Elizabethan capitalists did not get rich by being reckless. If a company could not offer something that looked like "sure, certayne, and present gayne," they took their money elsewhere.

Trading companies made themselves attractive to investors by winning privileges from the Crown. Thus, in 1555, the Muscovy Company agreed to enter the risky business of buying furs in semi-savage Russia in return for a monopoly on the sale of Russian furs in England. The biggest, most famous, and longest-lived of these privileged corporations was the East India Company. Chartered in 1600 to trade in India, its powers were so broad that it governed much of the Indian subcontinent for a century and a half.

When James I was persuaded that North American colonies would be beneficial to the nation, he issued two charters

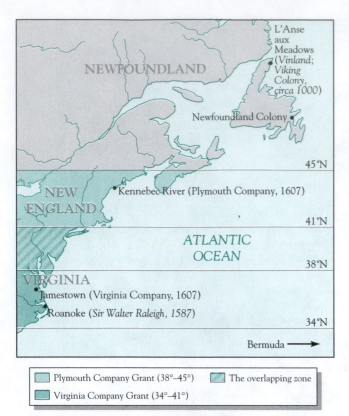

MAP 2:1 The Virginia and Plymouth Companies, 1607

The Virginia and Plymouth Companies both attempted to plant colonies in 1607. Only the London Company's Jamestown succeeded. Note the zone between 38 and 41 degrees north latitude. Both the Plymouth and Virginia companies were chartered to settle in that area. If one had settled there (neither did), the other company was obligated to build at least 100 miles away.

patterned on the charters of the Muscovy and East India companies. In 1606, the king authorized a company headquartered in the port of Plymouth to found a colony on the American coast between 38 and 45 degrees north latitude. The Virginia Company of London was granted the same privilege between 34 and 41 degrees.

The zones overlapped so as to hasten both companies along. Because they were forbidden to set up shop within a hundred miles of one another (so they would not compete in trading with the Indians), the first to get going had the pick of sites.

JAMESTOWN

Both companies sent expeditions in 1607. The Plymouth Company established Fort St. George on a bluff above Maine's Kennebec River. The forty-five settlers found the northern winter disagreeable but when Raleigh Gilbert arrived with a supply ship in the spring, he insisted that "all things were in great forwardness." Then, at summer's end, another relief ship informed Gilbert that his childless older

brother back in England had died; he had inherited the family fortune! Who needed Fort St. George? Everyone returned home with the happy heir.

THE FIRST FAMILIES OF VIRGINIA

The London Company had better luck in Virginia—if a decade of wholesale suffering and death may be called lucky. In May 1607, Captain Christopher Newport brought the *Susan Constant* and two other ships into Chesapeake Bay, landing his passengers on the James River (named for the king). Barely connected to the mainland, the site could be defended against Indians but the Spanish would discover its whereabouts only by accident. (Many people then believed that the Spanish had destroyed Roanoke.) Captain John Smith, a soldier who remained in Jamestown, as the fortified village they built was called, said that Newport's choice was "a verie fit place for the erecting of a great citie."

That was nonsense. Jamestown was surrounded by brackish swamp with little land suited to agriculture. Local Indians told the English the river water was undrinkable for several months each year. Two centuries later, when the town ceased to be Virginia's center of government, just about everyone who lived in the place moved out.

Jamestown's limited agricultural prospects were not important to Newport or the shareholders who employed him. The colonists were not expected to be self-sufficient; they would be regularly resupplied. Their job was to look for gold and to buy goods from the local Indians that would sell for a profit in England. Preposterously, several Polish glassmakers (probably Protestant refugees) set up a shop in which to practice their craft. The first Virginians arrived with some illusions about living in the wilderness.

SURVIVORS

Mere survival was soon in question. Captain Newport left Jamestown just enough food to scrape through the winter. So, when a fire in January 1608 destroyed the storehouse, the settlers took to the shallows, marshes, and forests to forage. The mysteries of hunting and gathering are not picked up in a day. The colonists were utterly ignorant of the local Indians' intimate knowledge of the country. Indeed, the Powhatan Indians may themselves have been so numerous as to be straining the range to its limits. They called Virginia Tsenahkommaka, "densely populated land." (Most estimates of the Powhatan population in 1607 are between 30,000 and 40,000. One historian believes there were 75,000; one recent account written on the subject estimates the number at 15,000.)

Hunger, John Smith wrote, forced many Jamestowners "to flee to the Savage Enemy." Smith, already on uneasy terms with the Powhatan, stayed with the others within the stockade. They died from starvation, amoebic dysentery, scurvy, typhoid fever, and enervating apathy. In 1607, the population of Jamestown was 144. When relief arrived in the spring of 1608, only 38 were alive. Somewhat more puzzling, the "starving times" continued for years. In 1608 and 1609, 500 new colonists arrived. In 1610, Jamestown's population

Thank You for Not Smoking

James I called smoking "a custom loathesome to the eye, harmful to the brain, dangerous to the lungs, and in the black stinking fume thereof, nearest resembling the Stygian smoke of the pit that is bottomless." Charles I felt the same way.

He said that smoking caused "enervation of the body and of courage."

Neither king was willing to take a cut in income in order to stifle the habit. When a big hike in the tobacco duty caused a sharp reduction in imports (and, therefore, taxes on tobacco), James I reduced the tax.

Two colonies enacted anti-smoking ordinances. Connecticut tried to license smokers; only those prescribed tobacco for reasons of health could apply. Massachusetts briefly forbade smoking out of doors, not for reasons of health or morality but to prevent fires.

was 60. Most of the survivors that spring were huddling near the water, living on little more than oysters.

The Powhatan may have tolerated Jamestown as long as they did because they expected nature to eliminate the newcomers for them.

AN UNPERMISSIVE SOCIETY

Smith credited his military discipline with saving the colony. In fact, his no-nonsense control—he executed one settler for making a dinner of his wife—did avert complete disintegration. But Smith was less than beloved. His successor as governor, George Percy, called him "an Ambitious unworthy and vayneglorious Fellowe."

Thomas West, Baron de la Warr, named governor in 1610, enforced an even more rigorous discipline. Intending to make the colony self-sufficient in food, de la Warr marched the settlers to the fields like soldiers. Troublemakers and the merely idle were punished swiftly and harshly. De la Warr's successor, Thomas Dale, may have been tougher. He prescribed the death penalty for dozens of offenses, including individual trading with the Indians and killing a domestic animal without permission. Virginians were whipped for throwing wash water into the streets or carrying out "the necessities of nature" within a quarter mile of the fort.

Authoritarian rule worked. Fields were expanded and adequate "earth-fast" houses (what we call pole buildings; no foundations) were erected. Virginia expanded along the banks of the James; outlying villages were constructed. But mortality remained high. Between 1610 and 1618, 3,000 new colonists arrived. In 1619, the population of Virginia was 1,000. Between 1619 and 1623, there were 4,000 newcomers. In 1624, the population of Virginia was 1,300.

Other emigrants died before they ever saw Virginia. In 1618, a ship that left England with 180 recruits managed to land only 50 of them alive. The Virginia Company was able to keep apace with the deaths only by throwing hordes of England's wretched poor into the American maw. Had the dying emigrants been people of substance, even artisans and freehold farmers, there would have been an uproar back home. But the Company found it difficult to recruit people a few rungs up the social ladder. The English were also colonizing conquered parts of Ireland, and those with a choice preferred the shorter voyage across the Irish Sea. In only a slight understatement, "none but those of the meanest quality and corruptest lives" went to Virginia.

THE "STINKING CUSTOM"

Had the Virginians not found a way to make money, the Company would surely have given up. But they did—in a native American plant that Columbus had brought back to Europe on his first voyage—tobacco.

Many Indians, including the Powhatan, cultivated tobacco, dried the leaves, and "drank" the smoke of the burning leaves for religious, social, and diplomatic reasons. (The custom of beginning negotiations by "smoking the peace pipe" was real.) Many were, no doubt, hooked on what was not yet identified as nicotine.

In the Old World, smoking got off to a bad start. The Spanish Inquisition jailed the first addict, Rodrigo de Jerez, for seven years because of his habit. James I loathed smoking, calling it a "stinking custom." The Russian Czar slit smokers' noses. The Turkish Sultan and the Shah of Persia decreed the death penalty for lighting up.

This was to no avail. Addictions are powerful adversaries. Inexorably, the smoking habit spread everywhere. (Before 1600, Russian explorers found the natives of remote northern Siberia smoking.) The lure of the exotic—the "trendy"–is always potent among the leisured classes, and others follow the trend, if they can afford it. Some European physicians seized on tobacco as a miracle drug, prescribing "the holy, healing herb" as "a sovereign remedy to all diseases." About 1580, Thomas Harriot said of regular smokers: "Their bodies are notably preserved in health, and know not many greevous diseases wherewithall wee in England are oftentimes afflicted."

At the time Jamestown was founded, the Spanish West Indies provided tobacco for just about everyone in Europe. John Rolfe, a smoker who arrived in Virginia in 1609, brought a pouch of West Indian seeds with him. This was a good thing, for he found the Powhatan's different species of tobacco to be "poore and weak and of a byting taste." Rolfe experimented in his garden in 1612. In 1614, he had more tobacco than he needed for his pipe and shipped four barrels to England. The reception was sensational. It sold quickly and at a huge profit. In 1617, Virginia exported 10 tons of tobacco at a profit of three shillings per pound! In 1618, the shipment reached 25 tons—and by 1628, 250 tons.

WHO SHALL TILL THE FIELDS?

Virginia had a reason to exist. Emigrants voluntarily crossed the Atlantic, some with money. They planted the very streets of Jamestown in tobacco. A colony recently starving now

When tobacco boomed in Virginia in the 1610s, the inhabitants of Jamestown planted every available square inch of the town in the crop.

North Wind Picture Archives

neglected grain and gardens in order to cultivate a weed to be burned. Company agents lamented that the settlers' "greediness after great quantities of tobacco causeth them [neither to] build good homes, fence their grounds, or plant any orchards." As late as 1632 in "An Acte for Tradesmen to Worke on Theire Trades," the Virginia Assembly commanded "gunsmiths and naylers, brickmakers, carpenters, joyners, sawyers and turners to worke at theire trades and not plant tobacco."

It was a losing effort. A carpenter could make a living in Jamestown. If he turned farmer he could tend a thousand tobacco plants plus four acres of maize, beans, and squash—enough to support a household of five. It did not require a gift for higher mathematics to calculate what the income would be from 10,000 tobacco plants.

But who would work for another? Land was endless. Who would work for a tobacco planter when a hike five or ten miles from Jamestown revealed lands that, planted in tobacco, could make a carpenter or brickmaker rich. The Jamestowners tried to enslave Indians but with little success. Indian captives disappeared into the forest at first opportunity.

One source of labor presented itself in 1619 when a Dutch ship with "20 and odd negars" aboard—they had probably been seized in the Spanish West Indies—tied up on the James.

The Virginians bought them with tobacco and ships' supplies. Periodically, other human cargos arrived. By 1660 there were 900 black Virginians in a total population of 25,000.

But blacks were a minority of the agricultural work force until after 1700. Most of Virginia's laborers were white Englishmen and women. They were not free. Some were convicts, sold to planters to serve out their sentences as servants. Other servants—not employees but bound by law to serve and obey their masters—were voluntary emigrants, poor people persuaded to sign "indentures." These documents bound them to work as servants for 4, 5, or 7 years in return for their passage to Virginia; and they had the chance, when their time was served, to set up as free men and women.

Virginia's **headright system,** instituted in 1618, used the abundant land to encourage planters to import servants. Each head of household who came to Virginia was granted 50 acres for each person whose transatlantic fare he paid. Thus, a family of five secured 250 acres upon disembarking. If the family had the means to bring ten indentured servants with them, they were granted another 500 acres. Thus was Virginia peopled, thus the tobacco grown, thus were the beginnings of a society in which some planters began to put together great estates.

Courtesy of John Carter Brown Library at Brown University

The Jamestown Massacre of 1622 was unexpected, sudden, terrifying, and devastating. Three hundred Virginians were killed, including several of the Africans who had been sold to tobacco growers three years earlier. The start of the massacre in Martin's Hundred probably looked much as this contemporary artist rendered it. Jamestown is in the distance, center.

THE MASSACRE OF 1622

For fifteen years the English and the Powhatan coexisted—uneasily. Most Virginians held the Indians in contempt, comparing them to the "savage Irish" whom the English had long disdained. Whites and Indians regularly skirmished although most incidents were more brawls than battles. The aging head of the Indian confederacy, Powhatan, did not much like the English, but he coveted the cloth, iron pots and pans, firearms, and novelties such as glass beads and mirrors that they offered in trade. In 1614, when John Rolfe married Powhatan's daughter, Pocahontas, something of a détente was inaugurated.

Then Powhatan died. His successor as chief was his brother Opechancanough. He grasped something that Powhatan never quite admitted. Opechancanough saw what many Indians after him were to learn: tiny, starving white enclaves grew in number and ceaselessly pushed into ancestral

hunting grounds, mowing down the trees, and chasing the game. By 1622, a number of Powhatan hamlets on the James and the Chickahominy Rivers had been forced to move to make room for tobacco.

In March 1622, Opechancanough and a large group of warriors entered Martin's Hundred, a village seven miles from Jamestown. They made as if to trade or chat when suddenly, they attacked, killing all seventy-five people there. They marched rapidly on Jamestown, wiping out other villages on the way. Had Jamestown not been warned they might well have destroyed it. In all, 347 Virginians were killed (including the founding father of the tobacco business, John Rolfe), about a third of Virginia's white and black population.

It was a catastrophe, but it was not enough when fortunes were being made. The survivors bandaged their wounds; the Virginia Company sent 1500 muskets and pistols, and, over two years, the Virginians gained the upper hand. Some called

Pocahontas

Shortly after landing in Virginia, John Smith was captured by the Powhatan. According to Smith—and he was more than capable of inventing a story—he was seconds away from having his skull crushed when Powhatan's 12-year-old daughter, Matoaka, also known as Pocahontas, "the playful one," begged the chief to spare Smith's life.

Pocahontas was playful. Naked, she visited Jamestown and turned cartwheels in the tracks that passed for streets. In 1614, Pocahontas became a Christian and married John Rolfe. She bore a son but both she and Rolfe died when he was still a lad—Pocahontas died in 1617 while visiting England, Rolfe in 1622 when Pocahontas's uncle attacked Jamestown.

for what we know as genocide: "a perpetuall warre without peace or truce [to] roote out from being any longer a people, so cursed a nation, ungratefull to all benefitte, and incapable of all goodnesse." About 200 Powhatan were invited to a peace parley and poisoned.

By 1625, the Powhatan had been reduced in number to as few as 5,000. Even then, they were able to launch another offensive in 1644 when they killed 500—one Virginian in twelve. What was left of the tribe was driven into the interior. In 1669, they numbered 2,000. By 1685, the Powhatan were extinct. The pattern of white–Indian relations that would be repeated for more than two and a half centuries had been drawn.

The Virginia Company was also a casualty of the Massacre of 1622. Although tobacco planters were prospering, the company never recorded a profit. In 1624, citing economic failure and the Massacre, James I revoked the company's charter and took direct control of Virginia. The House of Burgesses—a legislative assembly established in 1619, made up of twenty-two members elected by landowners—continued to meet. However, the Crown appointed a royal governor empowered to veto laws the Burgesses enacted.

MARYLAND: A SECOND TOBACCO COLONY

George Calvert was one of James I's most trusted advisors when Virginia was "royalized." He resigned the next year because he had become a Roman Catholic. James was having too much trouble with militant Protestants to have a Catholic in high office. Nevertheless, he liked Calvert and rewarded him by ennobling him as the first Lord Baltimore.

Calvert had long been interested in colonies. (He had owned shares in the Virginia Company.) Devoted to his new faith, he planned to establish a colony where English Catholics might find a refuge from the harassment and persecution that Calvert escaped because of his exalted status. He purchased land in Newfoundland but was dismayed by the bleak landscape and harsh winter. In 1628, he visited Virginia and liked what he saw; in 1632 he persuaded the new king, Charles I, to detach from Virginia the area north of the Potomac River and east of the Chesapeake and give it to him.

George Calvert died shortly after winning his charter but his son, Cecilius, the second Lord Baltimore, was also devoted to the idea of a refuge for Catholics. In 1634, he sent 200 settlers to the colony he called Maryland where they founded St. Mary's. Maryland prospered from growing tobacco but Baltimore's dream of a Catholic colony was dashed from the start. Catholics were never a majority of the population.

There were plantations there before it was Maryland. When Puritans, intensely hostile to Catholicism, poured into the colony, Calvert acted to prevent violent persecution of his co-religionists. His Act of Toleration of 1649 provided that "noe person or persons whatsoever within this province . . . professing to believe in Jesus Christ, shall from henceforth bee any waies troubled, Molested or discountenanced for or in respect of his or her religion." Reminiscent of "speech codes"

Courtesy of Maryland Department, Enoch Pratt Free Library, Baltimore

Cecilius Calvert, Lord Baltimore, hoped that Maryland would be a refuge for Catholics like himself. The Calverts and other Catholic nobles and gentry were immune from harassment because of their high social station; Catholics of humble social class were not. Many went to Maryland during the colony's early years, but they were outnumbered by Protestants, many of them fiercely anti-Catholic. After 1692, they could worship only privately in their homes.

in colleges today, Calvert even tried to outlaw verbal unpleasantness. He prescribed a whipping for "Persons reproaching any other within the Province by the Name or Denomination of Heretic, Schismatic, Idolater, Puritan, Independent, Presbyterian, Popish Priest, Jesuit, Jesuited Papist, Lutheran, Calvinist, Anabaptist, Brownist, Antinomian, Barrowist, Round-Head, Separatist, or any other Name or Term, in a reproachful Manner, relating to matters of Religion."

To no avail, Protestants repealed the Act of Toleration in 1654, inflicting double taxation and other disabilities on Roman Catholics. In 1689, John Coode led a successful rebellion of Protestants who, three years later, forbade Catholics to worship publicly. (Oddly, three of Coode's four lieutenants were married to Catholic women.)

OTHER BEGINNINGS

England was not the only European nation settling North American colonies. Except for the Dutch, however, the other enterprises were too far from the Chesapeake (and Plymouth in Massachusetts after 1620) to pose a threat to English dominance. Two French colonies were destroyed before they put a crop in.

THE FRENCH IN NORTH AMERICA

In 1562, Jean Ribault founded Charlesfort near what is now Port Royal, South Carolina. Like Roanoke, the colony simply evaporated. Two years later, René Goulaine de Laudonnière took 300 colonists to the St. John's River in Florida. Most of the settlers were **Huguenots,** French Protestants.

The colony was vexed by conflict with the Indians, the refusal of the self-proclaimed aristocrats among them to labor, and the desertion of men who stole the colony's boat in order to raid Spanish shipping. In 1565, Pedro Menéndez de Avilés led a small Spanish fleet to destroy the French colony. He was dismayed to discover five French warships anchored in the mouth of St. John's. It was a relief expedition commanded by Jean Ribaut. Menéndez withdrew a few miles to the south. When Ribaut's ships, bent on destroying Menéndez, were blown far beyond his camp and wrecked in a storm, Menéndez led 500 soldiers overland to Fort Caroline and easily captured it. With only one casualty, the Spaniards killed 142 during the attack. Learning that most of the survivors were Protestants, the Spanish murdered them.

French interest shifted north. In 1608, an extraordinary sailor (he made twelve voyages to the New World), Samuel de Champlain, founded Quebec on the St. Lawrence River. New France, the St. Lawrence river basin, grew slowly. In 1627, there were but 100 French there; in 1650, 657; and in 1663, 3,000. (There were 3,000 Europeans just in New Netherlands—New York—at that time; 50,000 whites and 2,000 blacks in the English colonies.) Rude as it was, Quebec was a religious and cultural, as well as administrative, center. A college was founded there in 1635 (a year before Harvard, the first English college in America) as well as an Ursuline convent school for Indian girls. But mostly, Quebec was a rude, uncomfortable trading post where Indians exchanged hides and furs for decorative trinkets, blankets, other textiles, iron tools and implements, guns, and brandy.

HISPANIC BEGINNINGS

In 1565, before marching on Fort Caroline, Pedro Menéndez de Avilés established St. Augustine, Florida between the Matanzas and San Sebastian Rivers. In 1586, Sir Francis Drake sacked the town, but St. Augustine recovered. By a full forty-two years, it is the oldest surviving European settlement in what is now the United States.

In 1609, two years after the founding of Jamestown, a party of Spaniards hiked the banks of the Rio Grande almost to its source in the Sangre de Cristo Mountains of New Mexico. There they founded Santa Fe, from which traders tapped the numerous Indians of the country for furs, hides, and small quantities of precious metals. Franciscan missionaries sallied out to win the Indians' souls. By 1630, the padres claimed to have baptized 86,000 mostly Pueblo (town dwelling) Indians.

Santa Fe is the oldest seat of government in the United States. (St. Augustine was administered from Cuba.) Its history, however, is not continuous. During the 1670s, the Pueblo Indians were ravaged by disease, hunger, and assaults by Apaches and Navajos, whom the small Spanish military garrison was unable to beat back. When some Pueblos reverted to their old religion, the Spanish hanged several and whipped dozens more.

In the summer of 1680, led by a chief whom the Spanish had imprisoned, Popé, nearly all the Pueblos around Santa Fe rebelled, killing half the priests in New Mexico and about 350 other Spaniards and Mexicans. The survivors fled south to El Paso. Popé's Rebellion was the Indians' most effective violent resistance to Europeans since the skraelings drove the Vikings out of Vinland. Only after ten years elapsed were the Spanish able to restore their power in Santa Fe. It remained the remotest European town of any size in North America, isolated by colossal distances from the imperial center of Mexico.

NEW NETHERLAND AND NEW SWEDEN

In 1624, the Dutch West India Company (organized much like the Virginia Company) established New Netherlands, claiming as its borders the Connecticut and the Delaware Rivers. Its capital was New Amsterdam, at the southern tip of Manhattan Island. New Amsterdam defended what the Dutch hoped would be both a fur-trading center and a colony of farmers. A fort where furs and hides were purchased from Indians was built at Fort Orange (Albany) on the upper Hudson River. Fort Orange was perfectly located to attract Indian traders from the east (present-day Connecticut), from the north, and via the Mohawk River from the west.

New Amsterdam grew slowly but steadily. It was a small but bustling commercial center. The colony exported more than 60,000 pelts during its first year. Annually thereafter, as many as a hundred Dutch ships tied up in the best harbor on the Atlantic seaboard.

Along the Hudson between New Amsterdam and Fort Orange, the West India Company tried to promote settlement

t' Fort nieúw Amsterdam op de Manhatans

Courtesy of the New-York Historical Society, New York City

This illustration depicts New Amsterdam, two or three years after its founding. The Dutch (and the English) always built a protective fort first, but the fort in New Amsterdam was far more formidable than the stockades around Jamestown and Plymouth. The artist makes it clear what the colony was all about—the fur trade. Indians are bringing furs by canoe; Dutch ships are waiting to haul them to Holland.

by granting huge "patroonships" to rich Hollanders. These were vast tracts of land with eighteen miles of river frontage. The patroon's part of the bargain was to transport and settle fifty families on his land, where they would be beholden to him almost as serfs. Only one patroonship succeeded, 700,000 acre Van Renssaelerwyck, just south of Fort Orange. Dutch immigrants preferred to find land in western Long Island, on Staten Island, and in what is now New Jersey. There they did not have to tip their hats to a patroon.

New Netherlands had trouble finding a good governor. The founder of New Amsterdam, Peter Minuit, who purchased Manhattan Island from the Indians for $25 (or so he thought) was quarrelsome, even defiant. Governor Willem Kieft was as incompetent an official who ever breathed American air. His soldiers slaughtered peaceful Indians who

had actually taken refuge with the Dutch. Several Algonkian tribes retaliated with results as devastating as the Jamestown Massacre, reducing the population of the colony to 700.

In 1638, Peter Minuit was back in New Netherlands but not with the West India Company's approval. Now employed by a Swedish colonial company, he founded a string of tiny settlements along the lower Delaware River and Delaware Bay, mostly on the western bank so as to avoid conflict with the Dutch. Only Christiana (in present-day Delaware) amounted to much. The Swedes and Finns (Finland was then part of Sweden) who emigrated spread out along the Delaware from the future site of Philadelphia to the southern end of the Bay. There were as many Dutch and English farmers eking out a living in New Sweden as there were Swedes and Finns.

FURTHER READING

General D. W. Meinig, *The Shaping of America: A Geographical Perspective on 500 Years of History,* Volume 1, and *Atlantic America 1492–1800,* 1986; Daniel Boorstin, *The Americans: The Colonial Experience,* 1958; Wesley F. Craven, *The Southern Colonies in the Seventeenth Century,* 1949; John E. Pomfret with Floyd Shumway,

Founding the American Colonies, 1970; Jack P. Greene and J. R. Pole, eds., *Colonial British America,* 1984.

English Background Keith Wright, *English Society, 1580–1680,* 1982; Peter Laslett, *The World We Have Lost,* 1965; Carl Bridenbaugh,

Vexed and Troubled Englishmen, 1968; A. L. Rowse, *Elizabethans and America*, 1959; Paul Johnson, *Elizabeth I*, 1974; James A. Williamson, *Sir Francis Drake*, 1975; Stephen J. Greenblatt, *Sir Walter Raleigh*; P. L. Barbour, *The Three Worlds of Captain John Smith*, 1964; Thomas E. Roche, *The Golden Hind*, 1973; Garrett Mattingly, *The Armada*, 1959.

Roanoke Karen Ordahl Kupperman, *Roanoke: The Abandoned Colony*, 1984; David B. Quinn, *Set Fair for Roanoke*, 1985; David Stick, *Roanoke Island: The Beginnings of English America*, 1983; Giles Milton, *Big Chief Elizabeth: The Adventures and Fate of the First English Colonists in America*, 2000.

Jamestown Carl Bridenbaugh, *Jamestown, 1544–1699*, 1980; Alden Vaughan, *Captain John Smith and the Founding of Virginia*, 1975; Thad W. Tate and David W. Ammerman, eds., *The Chesapeake in the Seventeenth Century*, 1979; the early chapters of R. Menard, *The Economy of British North America 1607–1789*, 1985; James Horn, *Adapting to a New World: English Society in the Seventeenth Century Chesapeake*, 1994; Peter Wood et al., *Powhatan's Mantle: Indians in the Colonial Southeast*, 1989; Helen L. Rountree, *The Powhatan Indians of Virginia*, 1988, 1990, and *Pocohontas, Powhatan,*

Opechancanough: Three Indian Lives Changed by Jamestown, 2005; Edmund S. Morgan, *American Slavery, American Freedom*, 1975.

Maryland Tate and Ammerman, *The Chesapeake and James Horn, Adapting to a New World* (above, "Jamestown"); John T. Ellis, *Catholics in Colonial America*, 1965; Lois Green Carr, ed., *Colonial Chesapeake Society*, 1988; Robert Cole, *World: Agriculture and Society in Early Maryland*, 1991.

Other Beginnings David J. Weber, *The Spanish Frontier in North America*, 1992; Jerald T. Milanich, *Florida Indians and the Invasion from Europe*, 1995; John T. McGrath, *The French in Early Florida: In the Eyes of the Hurricane*, 2000; Andrew L. Knaut, *The Pueblo Revolt of 1680: Conquest and Resistance in Seventeenth Century New Mexico*, 1997; W. C. Eccles, *France in America*, 1972; Bruce G. Trigger, *Natives and Newcomers: Canada's "Heroic Age" Reconsidered*, 1985; John Ferling, *Struggle for a Continent: The Wars of Early America*, 1993; Oliver A. Rink, *Holland on the Hudson: An Economic and Social History of Dutch New York*, 1986; Russell Shorto, *The Island at the Center of the World: The Epic Story of Dutch Manhattan and the Forgotten Colony that Shapes America*, 2004.

KEY TERMS

The following terms are covered in this chapter and can also be found in the list of Key Terms at the back of the book.

annulment	George Calvert	mercenary	sea dogs
Elizabeth	headright system	merchants-adventurers companies	siglo de oro
enclosure movement	Huguenots		
Francis Drake			

ONLINE SOURCES GUIDE

Use this listing to find online documents, images, interactive maps, simulations, and other resources related to this chapter:

American History Resource Center
http://history.wadsworth.com

Selected Documents
Richard Hakluyt, Discourse of Western Planting
Edward Haies, Sir Humphrey Gilbert's Voyage to Newfoundland
Charter to Sir Walter Raleigh
Letters Patent of the London Virginia Company (1606)
Letter on tobacco culture and the introduction of slavery (John Smith)
Samuel de Champlain's Voyages of Samuel de Champlain

Selected Images
Wood engraving of Ponce de Leon
Sir Francis Drake

Spanish soldiers committing atrocities in Florida
1624 engraving of adventures of John Smith
Pocahontas

Simulations
Colonial Expansion (Choose an identity as an Aztec, a Jamestown settler, or a Puritan in New England and make choices based on the circumstances and opportunities afforded.)

Interactive Timeline (with online readings)
Settlement Across the Sea: The Idea, the Failures, Success 1550–1624

Additional resources, exercises, and Internet links related to this chapter are available on *THE AMERICAN PAST* web site: http://history.wadsworth.com/americanpast8e

Discovery

What were the perceptions of migration to the New World as opposed to the realities?

In thinking about this question, begin by breaking it down into the components shown below. A discussion of the significance of each component should appear in your answer.

Economics and Technology: For this exercise, please read the excerpt from "John Hammond, 'Leah and Rachel'" and study the image entitled, "The 'Pestering Poor.'" What social problems can you identify in the illustration of the Old World that would make migration to the New World attractive? Would migration to the New World solve those problems? What does the document suggest are the positives of migration? Is the author being truthful? What agenda might the author have? What types of people might be attracted by such an offer?

The 'Pestering Poor'

John Hammond, "Leah and Rachel, or the Two Fruitfull Sisters, Virginia and Mary-Land" (1656)

John Hammond, a resident of Virginia, wrote this as a promotional tool to encourage more colonists to come from England. He discusses what life will be like for indentured servants, and for those with families.

Those servants that will be industrious may in their time of service gain a competent estate before their Freedomes, which is usually done by many, and they gain esteeme and assistance that appear so industrious: There is no Master almost but will allow his Servant a parcell of clear ground to plant some Tobacco in for himself, which he may husband at those many idle times he hath allowed him and not prejudice, but rejoyce his Master to see it, which in time of Shipping he may lay out for commodities, and in Summer sell them again with advantage, and get a Sow-Pig, or two, which anybody almost will give him, and his Master suffer him to keep them with his own,

which will be no charge to his Master, and with one years increase of them may purchase a Cow Calf or two, and by that time he is for himself; he may have Cattle, Hogs, and Tobacco of his own, and come to live gallantly; but this must be gained (as I said) by industry and affability, not by sloth nor churlish behaviour.

And whereas it is rumoured that Servants have no lodging other then on boards, or by the Fire side, it is contrary to reason to believe it: First, as we are Christians; next as people living under a law, which compels as well the Master as the Servant to perform his duty; nor can true labour be either expected or exacted without sufficient cloathing, diet, and lodging; all which both their Indentures (which must inviolably be observed) and the Justice of the Country requires.

Culture and Society: For this exercise, please read the excerpt from "Indian Massacre, 1622," and study the image entitled, "Jamestown Massacre of 1622." How is the Native American portrayed? How does this relate to what you learned in Chapter 1 about Spanish and Native American relations? Did the same problems exist in Spanish and English colonies in terms of their relationships with Native Americans? How did the Spanish treatment of Native Americans possibly create the problems in the 1622 massacre?

The Jamestown Massacre of 1622

Courtesy of John Carter Brown Library at Brown University

Indian Massacre, 1622 in Two Tragical Events, Anonymous

These accounts are William and Mary Professor Charles Edward Bishop's 1901 English translation of a 1707 Dutch translation of the original 1622 account.

. . . King Powhatan said that he would prefer seeing the country turned upside down rather than break a single article of the treaty, but, as will be proved later on, this conduct of the savages was nothing but hypocrisy and deceit, they only awaiting a favorable opportunity to kill out the English. . . .

On Friday before the day appointed by them for the attack they visited, entirely unarmed, some of our people in their dwellings, offering to exchange skins, fish and other things, while our people entirely ignorant of their plans received them in a friendly manner.

When the day appointed for the massacre had arrived, a number of the savages visited many of our people in their dwellings, and while partaking with them of their meal the savages, at a given signal, drew their weapons and fell upon us murdering and killing everybody they could reach sparing neither women nor children, as well inside as outside the dwellings. In this attack 347 of the English of both sexes and all ages were killed. Simply killing our people did not satisfy their inhuman nature, they dragged the dead bodies all over the country, tearing them limb from limb, and carrying the pieces in triumph around.

To read extended versions of the documents, visit the companion Web site http://history.wadsworth.com/americanpast8e; click on "Discovery Sources."

CHAPTER 3

Thirteen Colonies

England's American Empire 1620–1732

Culver Pictures

We must be knit together in this work as one man; we must entertain each other in brotherly affection; . . . we must uphold a familiar commerce together in all meekness, gentleness, patience and liberality; we must delight in each other, make others' conditions our own, rejoice together, mourn together, labor and suffer together.

John Winthrop

They differ from us in the manner of praying, for they winke [close their eyes] when they pray because they thinke themselves so perfect in the highe way to heaven that they can find it blindfold.

Thomas Morton

In 1608, 125 men, women, and children left the English village of Scrooby and made their way to the seaport of Hull. There they took ship to the "fair and beautifull citie" of Leiden in Holland where they intended to make their home.

They traveled furtively because they were breaking the law. Going abroad without the Crown's permission was illegal. The Scrooby villagers were willing to risk arrest because they were already being harassed for their religious beliefs. They belonged to a sect called "Separatists" because they believed that Christians who were "saved"—"saints" elected by God—should not worship together with the multitude. The doctrine guaranteed trouble. All Englishmen and women were expected to attend Church of England services and were fined—and worse—if they did not.

The Separatists are better known in history as the **Pilgrims.** One of their leaders, William Bradford, gave them the name because they wandered, as if on a pilgrimage, in search of a place where they could live godly lives, unmolested.

THE NEW ENGLAND COLONIES

The Pilgrims were not molested in Leiden. Religiously, the Dutch were divided—splintered. Most were Calvinists like the Pilgrims, but there were large minorities of Catholics, Lutherans, and Anabaptists. The rulers of the Netherlands, with serious political problems, thought that religious toleration was a better option than civil war.

Increasing and Multiplying

Nearly half of Plymouth's settlers died during the colony's first winter. Just two of the survivors more than made up for the loss within their own lifetimes. John Alden and Priscilla Mullins arrived on the *Mayflower* and married soon thereafter. (The wedding was immortalized two centuries later by Henry Wadsworth Longfellow.) Both lived into their eighties. They had 12 children of whom 10 survived to adulthood. Eight of the Aldens married and, together, had at least 68 children, more people than died in Plymouth in 1620–1621. Alden and Mullins's great-grandchildren, a few of whom they lived to see born, numbered 400, four times the original population of the colony.

Still, the Pilgrims were discontented. As English, they were notoriously strict with their children; Dutch parents were remarkably indulgent. The Pilgrims fretted that their off-spring were "getting the reins off their necks," picking up loose behavior from Dutch neighbors. And the Pilgrims were displeased, as foreigners living abroad often are, that their sons and daughters were growing up more Dutch than English. The Pilgrims may have fled the teachings of the Church of England, but they were still English to the core, and as ethnocentric as any Chinese, Ghanian, or Powhatan Indian.

PLYMOUTH PLANTATION

Some of the Pilgrims trickled back to England. Others, if less than content, stayed on until 1620 when a stroke of luck (God's intervention as far as the Pilgrims were concerned) provided a way out of their quandary. The old **Plymouth Company** had been reorganized as the Council for New England but was having problems recruiting settlers for a new colony. The tobacco boom in Virginia was attracting most English men and women willing to go to America. So, prominent shareholders in the company persuaded King James I to ignore the Pilgrims' religious practices if they relocated across the Atlantic.

The exiles in Leiden were delighted. In 1620, they returned to England just long enough to board two small America-bound ships, the *Mayflower* and the *Speedwell*. The *Speedwell* leaked so badly it turned back immediately. The *Mayflower* was none too seaworthy herself but, well-skippered, she survived a rough passage longer than that of Columbus a century earlier.

A hundred settlers, mostly Separatists, disembarked at the southern end of Massachusetts Bay. They built "Plimouth Plantation" on the site of Pawtuxet, an abandoned Wampanoag village. Pawtuxet had been wiped out three years earlier by disease introduced by English fishermen. To the Pilgrims, open fields ready to be plowed was a sign of God's approval. He had "cleared" the land of people (Wampanoag bones still littered the fields) to make room for his Saints.

God did not, however, see to it that the *Mayflower* left enough provisions behind and the winter of 1620–1621 was a hard one. Half of Plymouth's settlers died of malnutrition or disease before a relief ship arrived in the spring. God, having tested them—the Pilgrims saw God's hand at work at every turning—blessed them again. "A special instrument sent of God," Tisquantum, or Squanto, an Indian who spoke excellent English, joined them.

Squanto was a native of Pawtuxet. He had gone to England with fishermen in 1605, went in an English ship to Jamestown in 1614, and was captured by Spaniards and taken to Spain. He eventually escaped from Spain and made his way to England. Just six months before the Pilgrims arrived in Massachusetts, he had worked his way home on a fishing vessel and found Pawtuxet deserted.

A contemporary reconstruction of Plymouth when the settlement was several years old. "Streets" are wide enough for an ox or horse, but not a wagon. Dooryards were fenced not for privacy but to keep hogs out of gardens.

Samoset

Squanto was the second English-speaking Indian to greet the Pilgrims. The first was Samoset, a Penobscot from the Maine coast who walked into the village and shouted "Welcome!"

Samoset's English was rudimentary. He had picked it up from English fishermen. Squanto, who had lived in England for several years, was fluent and articulate. Unlike Squanto, who stayed in Plymouth,

Samoset returned to Maine. Like Squanto, however, he was smitten with English ways. He took the name John Somerset and lived in a mixed Indian and white village, Pemaquid.

The well-traveled Squanto was a good deal more cosmopolitan than any Pilgrim. When he adopted the newcomers as his tribe, he became, surely, the most valuable member of the community. He schooled the Pilgrims in Indian methods of hunting, fishing, and cultivation, and he guided them about the Massachusetts woods. According to William Bradford, now governor of the colony, Squanto asked for prayers so that "he might goe to the Englishmen's God in Heaven."

SELF-GOVERNMENT

Squanto was a better citizen than many who arrived on the *Mayflower*. Before stepping ashore, Bradford and other leaders worried that some of the "strangers" among them (non-Separatists) would defy their authority. Several had said as much; they meant to go their own way once off the ship. Because Plymouth Plantation lay outside the boundaries the company charter set for them, it was not clear that Bradford's and military commander Miles Standish's claims to authority had legal standing.

In order to assert it, forty-one passengers signed the "Mayflower Compact" while still aboard ship. The document began by asserting everyone's enduring loyalty to "our dread Sovereign Lord King James." The compact then bound the settlers together in a "Civil Body Politik" for the purpose of enacting and enforcing laws. The Mayflower Compact is memorable because of its implicit principle that a government's authority was based on the consent of those who are governed.

Not that the Pilgrims thought that they were creating a democracy. They would have shuddered. Democracy was a dirty word; in the seventeenth century it meant "mob rule." In practice, nevertheless, Plymouth was a rather democratic place. Almost every male Separatist head of household voted to elect the governor. (They reelected Bradford annually for thirty years.) Many community questions were resolved by vote. Women could not vote even if they were heads of household. Neither could adult unmarried males who owned no land, nor "strangers." Still, so broad a popular participation in government was found in few places elsewhere in the world.

SUBSISTENCE ECONOMY

The Pilgrims experienced little interference from England. The Crown took no interest in the colony after chartering a company to run it. The major shareholders in the Plymouth Company, who remained in England, would have dispatched reams of directives and a new governor (the Mayflower Compact meant nothing to them) had Plymouth come up with a moneymaker like Virginia's tobacco. But the Pilgrims never did. Furs and hides purchased from Indians provided some income with which to buy English goods. Fishing helped; there was a market for salted cod in Europe.

The English Colonies 1600–1700

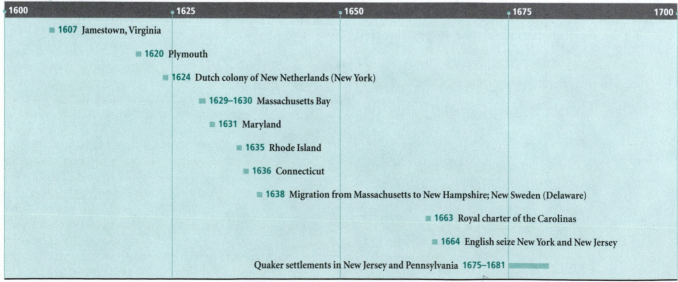

| 1600 | 1625 | 1650 | 1675 | 1700 |

■ 1607 Jamestown, Virginia

■ 1620 Plymouth

■ 1624 Dutch colony of New Netherlands (New York)

■ 1629–1630 Massachusetts Bay

■ 1631 Maryland

■ 1635 Rhode Island

■ 1636 Connecticut

■ 1638 Migration from Massachusetts to New Hampshire; New Sweden (Delaware)

■ 1663 Royal charter of the Carolinas

■ 1664 English seize New York and New Jersey

Quaker settlements in New Jersey and Pennsylvania 1675–1681 ■■■■■

Merrymount

"Merrymount" (later Quincy) was a few miles from Plymouth. In 1623, an unusual character named Thomas Morton persuaded several other immigrants to (in the words of Governor Bradford) found a town where they would be "free from service, and . . . trade, plante, & live togeather as equalls."

According to Bradford, Merrymount was riotous. The villagers were frequently drunk and "set up a May-pole, drinking and dancing aboute it many days togeather, inviting the Indean women, for their consorts, dancing and frisking together (like so many fairies, or furies rather), and worse practices."

Morton stole Indian trade from Plymouth by offering firearms in return for furs and hides. This worried Bradford because the

Indians were better hunters than the whites "by reason of ther swiftnes of foote, & nimblnes of body," and because their guns

might easily be turned against Plymouth. He sent Captain Miles Standish and a few soldiers to arrest Morton. There was no battle because, according to Bradford, Morton and his friends were too drunk to resist. The only casualty was a Merrymounter who staggered into a sword and split his nose.

Morton was put on an island to await the next ship bound for England. Indian friends brought him food and liquor and helped him escape, whence he returned to England on his own and denounced the Pilgrims. Neither he nor the Pilgrim Fathers were punished. If the authorities had been familiar with the phrase "can of worms," they would surely have applied it to the squabble.

But that was about it. Plymouth was largely a community of subsistence farmers. The Pilgrims raised enough food to feed themselves, but they were quite poor. When the governor of New Netherlands sent Governor Bradford "two Holland cheeses"—a rather modest gift, it would seem—Bradford had to apologize for "not having any thing to send you for the present that may be acceptable." Plymouth's population remained small. There was no repetition of the terrible mortality of the first winter, but epidemic disease was a regular visitor. In 1628, eighteen women arrived in Plymouth to find husbands; fourteen died within a year.

Plymouth's poverty discouraged the shareholders back in England. In 1627 they agreed to sell out to the colonists. Even then it took the Pilgrims fifteen years to pay them off. Nonetheless, the sale transferred legal control of Plymouth Plantation to its inhabitants. Plymouth was effectively a self-governing commonwealth until 1691 when it was absorbed into its younger but much larger neighbor to the north, Massachusetts Bay.

MASSACHUSETTS BAY

Self-government was half accidental in Plymouth. Had a plowman turned up a vein of gold ore in his cornfield, the Company would have exercised its charter prerogatives and the Crown might have royalized Plymouth as it did Virginia in 1624.

In Massachusetts Bay, by way of contrast, self-government was part of well-laid plans meticulously carried out. Massachusetts was a bigger and better-organized operation than Jamestown or Plymouth. The first wave of settlers in 1630 totaled a thousand people in seventeen ships. Such an operation required massive stores of provisions. There were no starving times in Massachusetts Bay (located about 40 miles north of Plymouth). The founders of the Bay Colony worked out the details before they weighed anchor. In just a few months, seven towns were under construction. And colonists kept coming. In the "Great Migration" of 1630–1640, 20,000 people arrived in Massachusetts.

They were a substantial lot. By design, the settlers were a fair cross section of English society. They were of both sexes, evenly divided. (The ratio of emigrants to Virginia was four men for each woman; in Spanish Mexico ten to one). They were of all age groups and social classes up to the rank of lady and gentleman. There was even one noblewoman in the first wave, but she had come just to have a look and returned to England. Most settlers were farmers and laborers, but there

"Dissenter"

The Pilgrims loathed the Roman Catholic Church but, oddly, the colony's military leader, 40-year-old Miles Standish, was from a Catholic family. Standish never joined the Pilgrims' church (although his children did). When Plymouth adopted a rule that all officials be church members, Standish and the governor simply ignored it. Standish held public office until his death in 1656.

Culver Pictures

The Beast

To the Puritans, the Roman Catholic Church was not just another Christian denomination. It was the Book of Revelations' "Whore of Babylon." The Pope was "the Beast." It has been suggested that, during the seventeenth century, the word *animal* replaced the word *beast* in everyday language referring to horses, cattle, sheep, and so on because, when a seventeenth-century Puritan heard the word "beast," he thought "pope." It was not fair to the animals.

were skilled artisans of many trades, and professionals, notably university-educated ministers.

The founders of Massachusetts Bay meant to create a *new* England, a society like one they had always known. Except in one particular: although they insisted that they were members of England's established church, the founders of Massachusetts abhorred the Church of England's structure and rituals, and none too politely. They called bishops "the excrement of Antichrist" and denounced church ceremonies as Catholic. England had embraced sinful ways; New England would be a truly godly commonwealth.

To ensure that they would shape their Zion without interference, the colonists brought the Massachusetts Bay Company charter with them. It provided the shareholders (all of them emigrants—shareholders who chose to remain in England sold out to those who went) with self-government. What took Plymouth twenty years to accomplish, Massachusetts Bay had from the start.

PURITAN BELIEFS

These cautious, prudent people were the **Puritans.** Like the Pilgrims, they were Calvinists. They believed that human nature was inherently depraved, that all men and women bore the stain of Adam and Eve's original sin. In the words of Massachusetts poet Anne Bradstreet, man was a "lump of wretchedness, of sin and sorrow."

It was a harsh doctrine: if God were just, and nothing more, every son and daughter of Eve would be damned to hell for eternity because of their sinful nature. God was all good; there was nothing a man or woman could do—no "good works," no act of charity, no sacrifice, no performance of a ritual, not even an act of faith—to earn salvation. Everybody deserved damnation.

Fortunately, God was not merely just, he was also loving and merciful. He chose some people—elected them—and bestowed grace upon them. They were his "Saints."

Having been so abundantly and undeservedly blessed—for they were as inherently sinful as anyone—the elect bound themselves in a covenant with God, a contract. They would enforce God's law in their community. They understood that if they failed to do so, if they tolerated sinning, God would punish their community as surely as he had punished his covenanted people of the Old Testament, the Hebrews, when they tolerated sin.

The Puritan covenant is central to understanding the society and culture of Massachusetts, which differs so significantly from our own that it can be difficult to realize that the Puritans are culturally our ancestors.

ERRAND IN THE WILDERNESS

Schoolchildren were once taught that the Puritans fled to America so that "they could worship as they pleased." Not really: unlike the handful of Pilgrims, the Puritans were numerous in old England, and they included quite a few people of high station. In regions where they were few, they were harassed. Where the major landowners, even nobles, were Puritans, they took over the Church of England parishes. Puritans were particularly powerful in England's eastern counties—Norfolk, Suffolk, Cambridgeshire, Lincolnshire—from which most of Massachusetts's settlers came. Massachusetts Bay's most prominent minister, John Cotton, had held the pulpit at St. Botolph's in old Boston, said to have been the largest parish church in England. He was a man of status and influence. Cotton did not hide in hedges to escape persecution. When Church authorities in London finally called him to task for his Calvinist preaching, he simply resigned, packed up, and went to Massachusetts.

Far from suffering because of their religious beliefs, most of the 20,000 Puritans who removed to Massachusetts in the "Great Migration" left England because they lacked the authority to prevent others from worshiping as they pleased. All around them they saw with dismay a "multitude of irreligious, lascivious, and popish persons." In tolerating this sinfulness, old England was flagrantly violating the covenant and courting God's wrath. "I am verily persuaded," wrote John Winthrop, who became governor of Massachusetts Bay, that "God will bring some heavy affliction upon this land"—England.

The Saints did not want to be around for the payoff. In Massachusetts, they would escape old England's punishment because their Church and colony would be purified of Catholic blasphemies (thus the name Puritan) and the covenant would be honored.

The Puritans said they were on an "errand into the wilderness." For many years, some of them nursed the illusion that old England would look across the ocean, see by the Puritans' example the error of their ways, and invite the Puritan fathers home to escort England into righteousness. "We shall be as a citty on a hill," Winthrop wrote, a beacon of inspiration visible from afar.

Guilt Trip

The early Puritans saw divine lessons in the most ordinary occurrences. When the Rev. Cotton Mather's small daughter fell into a fire and severely burned herself, Mather in painful anguish wrote in his journal: "Alas, for my sins the just God throws my child into the fire."

COMMUNITY

The Puritans believed in a community of a kind that little resembles what we mean by the word. Every member of the Puritan community was (in theory) bound to every other by a network of ties as intricate as a spider's web. People had rights, but their obligations to others—religious, economic, social—preoccupied the Puritans. In Winthrop's words, "every man might have need of [every] other, and from hence they might be knit more nearly together in the bond of brotherly affection."

The Puritans disapproved of individualism; they were uneasy with eccentricity. The covenant made it all-important to be ever on the lookout for sin and to punish it promptly. Even behavior that was mildly dubious attracted the notice of Puritan zealots, and a brotherly word or two. Judge Samuel Sewall heard that his cousin had taken to wearing a wig, then the height of fashion. The troubled judge crossed town to tell his kinsman that artificial hair was sinful; God had selected each person's hair; was one to question his choice? To the Puritans, Sewall was not a busybody. He was charitable; he was looking after his cousin's soul. The cousin liked his wig too well to give it up, but it never occurred to him to tell Sewall to mind his own business. He argued only as to whether wigs really were sinful.

Sin was solely an individual sinner's business only if others knew nothing of it. If the community was aware of a sin and failed to punish it, the entire community was subject to God's wrath. Simple people understood this principle so alien to us. In 1656, a teenager named Tryal Pore was caught in the sin of fornication; she told her congregation in her confession that "by this my sinn I have not only done what I can to Poull Judgement from the Lord on my selve but allso upon the place where I live."

BLUE LAWS

The statutes of Massachusetts (and other colonies) brimmed with regulations that would today be considered outrageous or ridiculous. And they applied to everyone, visitor as well as resident, the unregenerate as well as the elect, non-church members as well as church members.

God commanded that the Sabbath be devoted to him. Therefore, the Puritans forbade on Sundays activities that on Wednesday or Thursday were perfectly in order: working, tossing quoits or wrestling, whistling a tune, "idle chatter," "dancing and frisking," even "walking in a garden." Some

A few hours sitting in the stocks—public humiliation—was a common punishment for minor offenses in early New England. A variation was the pillory, in which the offender stood, head and hands similarly locked in place. Laughter and mockery on such occasions was tolerated; physical abuse of offenders was not.

things appropriate in private were forbidden in public. In 1659, a sea captain named Kemble returned from a three-year voyage and, not surprisingly, warmly kissed his wife while on the threshold to their home. He was sentenced to sit in the stocks for two hours for "lewd and unseemly behaviour."

A woman who was a "scold" (given to "Exorbitancy of the Tongue in Raling and Scolding") was humiliated on the ducking stool. She was strapped to a chair on a plank mounted like a seesaw, and dunked in a pond to her humiliation and everyone else's amusement. Church attendance was mandatory. In Maine (then part of Massachusetts) in 1682, Andrew Searle was fined five shillings "for not frequenting the publique worship of god" and for "wandering from place to place upon the Lords days." More serious offenders—thieves, arsonists, assaulters, wife beaters—were flogged, branded, or had their ears cropped or their nostrils slit.

However, so far as capital crimes were concerned, Massachusetts was positively liberal. In England during the seventeenth and eighteenth centuries, the number of capital crimes rose steadily until, in time, there were more than a hundred of them. A wretch could be hanged for snaring a rabbit on a gentleman's land. But the Puritans reserved hanging or burning at the stake for those offenses that were punished by death in the Bible: blasphemy, witchcraft, treason, murder, rape, adultery, incest, sodomy (homosexuality), and buggery (bestiality).

Never on Sunday

Husband and wife were not to have sexual intercourse on Sunday. Because a common superstition had it that a child was born on the same day of the week on which it was conceived, the parents of an infant delivered on Sunday (one in seven!) were at least the subject of gossip. The Rev. Israel Loring of Sudbury refused to baptize children born on Sunday. Then, one Sunday, his wife presented him with twins.

Puritan Names

Many Puritans named their children from the Old Testament, after the great figures, of course—Adam, Noah, Deborah, Judith—but also after obscure ones—Ahab, Zerubbabel, Abednego, and so on—whose names may have rung as discordantly in early Massachusetts as the names of people today who were named by "hippie" parents.

A few Puritans used their children's names to make a statement. Increase Mather, a prominent minister, was named from the Biblical injunction, "Increase, multiply, and subdue the earth." Records have not revealed anyone called Multiply or Subdue, but there was a Fight the Good Fight of Faith Wilson, a Be Courteous Cole, a Kill-Sin Pemble, and a Mene Mene Tekal Upharsin Pond. Other notable names: The Lord is Near, Fear-Not, Flee Fornication, and Job-Raked-Out-of-the-Ashes.

A couple named Cheeseman was told their infant would die during childbirth. Not knowing the child's sex, they baptized it Creature. Creature Cheeseman fooled the midwife and lived a long life with her unusual moniker.

Too much must not be made of these names. Only four percent of Puritans were saddled with them. Half of the girls in records of Massachusetts baptisms were bestowed just three rock-solid English names: Sarah, Elizabeth, and Mary. Almost as many boys were either John, Joseph, Samuel, or Josiah.

Even then, the Puritans were not bloodthirsty. Many people convicted of capital crimes were let off with lesser sentences. Between 1630 and 1660, fewer than twenty people were executed in Massachusetts: four murderers, two infanticides, three sexual offenders (including Thomas Granger, who coupled with "a mare, a cow, two goats, five sheep, two calves, and a turkey"), two witches, and four Quakers—members of a religious sect believed to "undermine & ruine" authority.

Cases of adultery during the sixty years the Puritans governed Massachusetts are beyond numbering, but there were only three executions for the crime. Most adulterers were let off with a whipping or branding or, although clearly guilty, they were acquitted by juries that did not want the offenders executed. Connecticut proclaimed the death penalty for a child who struck or cursed his parents, but the law was never enforced. When Joseph Porter was brought to court for calling his father "a thief, liar, and simple ape shittabed," his conviction was thrown out on appeal. New Haven made masturbation a capital offense but, although offenders were surely multitudinous, none was hanged.

It is important to understand about societies past that what their laws said does not necessarily tell us about everyday life. On paper, Massachusetts was a police state. But not every Puritan was a fanatic and the power of the authorities was not almighty. When two Quaker women were stripped to the waist and whipped until blood ran down their breasts, villagers were so disgusted that they mobbed the authorities and set the women free.

ASSUMPTIONS

Little as they approved of James I and Charles I, the Puritans assumed that monarchy was sacred. Democracy—known to them only in the abstract—was a horrifying concept. They were nationalists too; English customs, they believed, were superior to those of every other people. Children were born full of sin, "vipers and infinitely worse than vipers," and were to be rigorously "bent" to godliness and their parents' will. "Better whipped than damned." Wives were subordinate to their husbands, women to men, although not to male servants. (Once again, these were ideals: Puritans did not routinely brutalize their children, and many a wife, albeit privately, told her lord and master what he should do.)

The Puritans assumed that clear social distinctions were God's will. "Some must be rich, some poore," said John Winthrop, not some happen to be rich, some happen to be poor, as we might say. It was an offense when people dressed themselves in a way inappropriate to their social class. In Connecticut in 1675, thirty-eight women were arrested for wearing silk. Obviously, they could afford such finery; but their social standing did not entitle them to wear it. Another law forbade people of humble station—farmers, laborers—to wear silver buckles on their shoes. Silver was "fit" only for magistrates and ministers.

The magistrates who governed the New England colonies, which, at the start, legally owned all the land, closely regulated where people could acquire it. That is, a family could

Photograph by Wilfred French,
Courtesy of the Society for the Preservation of New England Antiquities

New Englanders did not build log cabins. Swedes and Finns living on the Delaware River introduced that durable American institution. New Englanders built framed houses sided with clapboards like this home constructed in Dedham, Massachusetts in 1637. Frame construction required a sawmill and skilled artisans, both of which the well-organized Puritans had from the start.

not pick up, move into the forest, select land for a farm, pay for it, and have a home. New arrivals and people of an overpopulated township for whom there was no land were, in groups of 50 to 100 families, allotted land for a new township usually abutting on an existing township at the edge of settlement. Within the new township, each family was assigned a homesite in a compact village, fields for tillage, a woodlot for fuel, and the right to keep livestock on the town common.

Social control enabled the Puritans to create the most literate population in the world. In 1642, Massachusetts required parents to teach their children how to read. In 1647, townships of fifty families were required to support an elementary school; towns of a thousand, a Latin (secondary) School (for boys only). A college to train ministers, Harvard in Cambridge, was founded in 1636.

This was a dangerous doctrine. Church members were a minority in Massachusetts. Williams's teaching threatened the Puritans' control of the commonwealth—the very reason they had come to America, to be in charge. If the majority of the people, the unregenerate as well as the Saints, made laws and elected officials, the covenant would soon lay in tatters and God would "surely break out in wrath" against the colony.

Williams also rattled the Winthrop oligarchy by preaching that their royal charter did not give them legal and moral ownership of the land. The Indians owned the land by right of occupation. Colonists must purchase it from the natives if they were to dwell on it. In fact, Massachusetts Bay did pay the Indians for much of the land they occupied. But when Williams called the Massachusetts charter "a solemn public lie," he was attacking a document that was sacrosanct. The charter was the foundation of Massachusetts's virtual independence.

RHODE ISLAND, CONNECTICUT, AND NEW HAMPSHIRE

In 1630, there were two colonies in New England: Plymouth and Massachusetts. Within ten years there were seven, four of which were to become states. The rapid multiplication of New England's colonies was a direct consequence of the Massachusetts Puritans' intolerance of diverse religious views and the General Court's (the governing assembly) tight control of land grants within the Colony.

TROUBLESOME ROGER WILLIAMS

Rhode Island and Providence Plantations (still the long official name of the smallest state) was founded by a brilliant but cranky minister named **Roger Williams** who had differences with the governors of Massachusetts from the start. Williams was a strict Puritan and impeccable in his personal behavior. But he came to conclusions at odds with Governor Winthrop, the General Court, and "establishment" ministers like John Cotton, and he insisted on expressing them.

Williams agreed that most people were damned, that God bestowed his grace on very few. But just who were the elect? Massachusetts ministers had procedures for determining who were "visible saints" and, therefore, who were admitted to church membership and had the right to vote. Williams insisted that no one could be sure of anyone's election but his own. To underscore his point, he said that while he prayed with his wife, he did not know for certain if she was truly saved. She knew and God knew; no one else knew.

Therefore, Williams concluded, religion and government—church and state in our terms—must be separate. If the elect could not be known, there must be no religious test, as in Massachusetts, to determine who could vote to choose magistrates; or, at a town meeting, who could vote whether to spend public money to bridge a stream or to keep it for an emergency. Every male head of household should have that right, Williams insisted.

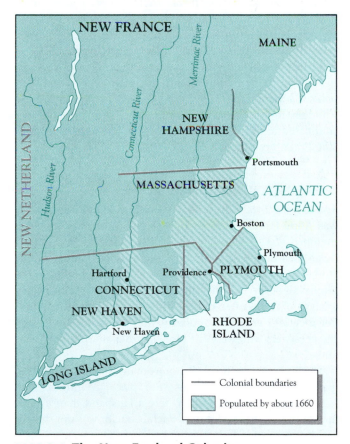

MAP 3:1 The New England Colonies

The Crown recognized seven colonial entities in New England: Plymouth (founded 1620), Massachusetts (1630), Connecticut (1636), Rhode Island (1636, chartered 1644), New Haven (1638), New Hampshire (chartered 1622, first real settlement 1638), and Maine (first settled 1623). Connecticut absorbed New Haven in 1622. Massachusetts acquired Maine in 1677. Plymouth was joined to Massachusetts in 1691. Eastern Long Island was settled by New Englanders but was incorporated into New York in 1664.

RHODE ISLAND: "THE SEWER OF NEW ENGLAND"

John Winthrop admired Roger Williams. He turned to him often for advice and assistance. But after several years of Williams's subversion, the top Puritans had their fill: Williams was ordered to return to England. Instead, he fled to the forest, spent the winter with the Narragansett Indians, and then established a farm and trading post, Providence, on Narragansett Bay, which was beyond the boundaries of both Massachusetts Bay and Plymouth. He soon had neighbors, Puritans who shared his beliefs or were attracted by the prime land on the bay.

Williams may have believed the king had no right to give away lands the Indians owned. However, he also knew that he needed the Crown's recognition of Rhode Island if the colony were to be secure from a takeover by Massachusetts Bay. In 1644, he sailed to London where he won a charter for his colony. Massachusetts, reverential toward its own charter, would not violate Rhode Island's.

In fact, the Massachusetts Puritans had good reasons to leave Rhode Island alone. It was useful as a place to which to banish dissenters. As long as problem settlers took their blasphemies beyond the colony's borders, the Puritan fathers did not have to fear God's anger. But shipping colonists back to England was risky: they might appeal to the Crown and win their case. Rhode Island was a better alternative—dissenters banished there were likely to stay there. The Puritans called Rhode Island the "sewer of New England." Quite like us, they shuddered to think about sewers. Quite like us, they understood their usefulness.

ANNE HUTCHINSON

The first important dissenter to be banished to Rhode Island was **Anne Hutchinson,** in 1638. Hutchinson was a devout member of the Massachusetts elite. (She was Winthrop's neighbor.) Taking seriously the admonition that saints should study the word of God, she invited people into her home on Sundays to discuss the morning's sermon. Hutchinson's analysis of it was often critical and sometimes acerbic. When her meetings grew in popularity, they raised the hackles of the preachers who were the targets of her sharp intelligence and wit.

They shook their heads that a woman should be a theologian. "You have stept out of your place," Winthrop told Hutchinson, "you have rather bine a Husband than a Wife and a preacher than a Hearer." Such behavior was not "fitting for your sex." Indeed, Winthrop believed that a woman jeopardized her mental balance by pondering difficult theological questions.

Had Hutchinson's offense been no greater than crowing, she might have gotten off with a reprimand. She had influential supporters. But Hutchinson taught that some people—her, for instance—were divinely inspired. This was *antinomianism,* a grave heresy. The word's two Greek roots mean *against* and *the law.* That is, antinomians believed that people specially blessed by God were above the rules and regulations

© Bettmann/Corbis

This representation of Anne Hutchinson being questioned by Governor Winthrop nicely captures the occasion. Records of the confrontation reveal that Hutchinson was confident, unyielding, and witty. She several times bested Winthrop but the governor had the power and Hutchinson was banished.

of human governments. As Winthrop put it, Hutchinson said that she was not "subject to controll of the rule of the Word or of the State."

To ensure that Anne Hutchinson was convicted, the General Court charged her with eighty heresies! They wanted a charge that would stick, and a good many did. She was banished to Rhode Island and some of her disciples followed her.

NEW HAMPSHIRE, MAINE, AND CONNECTICUT

As early as 1622, the Crown had given what are now the states of New Hampshire and Maine to two courtiers, granting them the same powers Lord Baltimore had in Maryland. John Mason and Fernando Gorges had no high-flown projects in mind, like Baltimore's Catholic refuge. They wanted to make money by selling land to settlers. Fishermen founded villages in Gorges's Maine and a few farmers drifted over the border from Massachusetts to Mason's New Hampshire. But not until a disciple of Anne Hutchinson, Rev. John Wheelwright, led a group north was there a noticeable English presence above Massachusetts.

Puritan Sunday

On Sunday morning, before sunrise in winter, Puritan families bundled up and walked to the meetinghouse. Few skipped services, even during a blizzard; absence meant a fine. The walk was usually short; most New Englanders lived in villages, their homes clustered together with the meetinghouse.

It was a meetinghouse, not a church. To call the simple, unpainted clapboard structure a church would have been "popish." The Puritans shunned every emblem hinting of the Church of Rome. There were no statues or other decorations such as adorned Catholic and Anglican churches. The meetinghouse was a place of preaching. If there was a steeple, it was crowned

by a weathercock, not a cross. It reminded the congregation that St. Peter denied that he knew Christ three times before the cock crowed. The sinfulness of all was a theme on which the Puritans constantly harped.

In winter, the meetinghouse was scarcely warmer than the snowy fields outside. There may have been a fireplace, but the heat did not reach those sitting more than ten feet from it. The congregation bundled in fur envelopes—not sleeping bags; there was a fine for nodding off. People rested their feet on brass or iron foot warmers holding coals brought from home. If foot warmers were prohibited as a fire hazard, worshipers might bring a well-trained dog to lie on their feet.

Women sat on the left side of the meetinghouse with their daughters. Men sat on the right, but boys, apt to be mischievous, were placed around the pulpit where a warden could lash out at the fidgety ones with a switch. He probably had his work cut out often, for the service went on and on, sermons running at least an hour and a half

and sometimes three hours. And, lest anyone wonder how long the sermon was lasting, an hourglass sat conspicuously on the preacher's pulpit; when the sand ran down, it was turned by the warden.

The Puritans allowed no instrumental music in the meetinghouses but they sang psalms from the Bay Psalm Book, published in Massachusetts. It was composed with accuracy of translation in mind, not poetry. Psalms exquisitely beautiful in the King James version of the Bible (which the Puritans would not use) were awkward and strained. For example, in the Puritan translation, the magnificent Psalm 100 is barely comprehensible.

> The rivers on of Babylon, there when we did sit downe;
> Yes even then we mourned, when we remembered Sion.
> Our harp we did hang it amid upon the willow tree,
> Because there they thus away led in captivitie,
> Required of us a song, thus asks mirth; us waste who laid
> Sing us among a Sion's song unto us then they said.

Puritan singing appalled outsiders; it was a "horrid medley of confused and disorderly noises."

Services ended about noon. Families returned home for a meal that had been prepared before sundown the previous day. Like Jews on the Sabbath, the Puritans took the Lord's Day seriously: no cooking, no work, and certainly no play. Even conversation was spare. It was no more proper to talk about workaday tasks than to perform them. Pious families discussed the morning's sermon or other religious subjects. In the afternoon, they returned to the meetinghouse to hear secular announcements and another sermon.

Neither Maine nor New Hampshire made much money for their proprietors and Massachusetts Bay disputed their rights to the land. In 1680, to end the squabble, the Crown took control of New Hampshire, making it a **royal colony.** In the meantime, Massachusetts gained Maine by subterfuge. In 1677, a Boston merchant, John Usher, purchased the white elephant from Gorges's heirs for £1,250. Usher immediately deeded the land to Massachusetts Bay. The "Maine District" remained a part of Massachusetts for almost fifty years after the American Revolution.

The Puritans knew that the bottomlands of the Connecticut River valley were fertile. Moreover, Connecticut was a rich source of beaver that the Mohawks, an Iroquois tribe, were trapping, selling the pelts to the Dutch in New Netherlands. In 1636, with both farming and the fur trade in mind, Rev. Thomas Hooker, an ultra-strict Puritan, led a contingent of his followers to the river, where they founded Hartford.

Hartford was forty miles from Long Island Sound, in the middle of the woods. It was also in the heart of the hunting grounds of the Pequot Indians, a fierce tribe then suffering from Mohawk incursions. Now pressed from the East too, the Pequot tried to form an anti-Mohawk alliance with Massachusetts. But when the Puritans dithered, they concluded they had to neutralize the whites, whom they considered weaker than the Mohawks. In May 1637, the Pequot attacked Wethersfield, not far from Hartford.

After Roger Williams, at Winthrop's request, convinced the Narraganset Indians to remain neutral, Massachusetts Bay, Connecticut, a few men from Plymouth, and several Indian tribes sent an army into Connecticut. By night, they surrounded a town the Pequot thought was secretly located and set it afire. As the Pequot fled, the invaders shot and killed more than 400 of them, women and children as well as warriors. After a few more battles, an attack by the Mohawk, and more than a little treachery, the Pequot were annihilated except for the purposes of founding gambling casinos.

During the Pequot War, two Massachusetts ministers founded New Haven on Long Island Sound on land claimed by New Netherlands. New Haven is best known for having more rigorous blue laws than even Massachusetts. It remained small and, in 1662, was absorbed into Connecticut.

PROPRIETARY COLONIES

Plymouth, Massachusetts Bay, Rhode Island, and Connecticut were *corporate* colonies. Their charters from the king were their constitutions. While acknowledging the king's sovereignty they were, in practice, self-governing commonwealths. Officials elected by heads of household, who (except in Rhode Island) were members of the established church (what eventually came to be known as the Congregationalist Church), governed the colonies.

Virginia was a **corporate colony** until 1624 when James I revoked its charter and took direct control of it. As a *royal* colony, Virginia was governed by the king through an appointed governor. Royal colonies had elected assemblies with considerable say in how money was spent. But the royal governor could veto any law assemblies enacted and he controlled the patronage, or who was appointed to offices that paid salaries. By the time of the American Revolution in 1776, nine of the thirteen colonies were royal colonies.

A **proprietary colony,** such as Maryland and early New Hampshire, had yet another kind of government. The king gave all the powers he exercised in royal colonies to highly placed people who, for one reason or another, he wished to benefit. Proprietary colonies were governed much as royal colonies were governed except that lords proprietors, rather than the king, appointed the governor.

MAKING MONEY

Lord Baltimore hoped that Maryland would be a Catholic colony. But he, like Mason and Gorges, hoped to profit from his colony too. One of his (and other lords proprietors') methods of making money was feudal, hearkening back to the Middle Ages. Settlers were given land by headright, so many acres (50 to 100) for each member of the colonist's

Double Dutch

The Dutch of New Netherlands coined the word *Yankee*. "Jan Kies" (John Cheese) was their collective term for New Englanders, just as American soldiers in Vietnam called the enemy "Charlie."

The English retaliated with a host of insulting uses of Dutch. A one-sided deal was a "Dutch bargain," a potluck dinner a "Dutch lunch." Liquor was "Dutch courage," a frog was a "Dutch nightingale," and a prostitute was a "Dutch widow."

household—himself, his wife and children, and other dependents, including servants.

They were then obligated to pay the proprietor (or king) an annual quitrent. This was not rent as we understand it. The settlers owned the land; they were not tenants. Nor was a quitrent quite a tax. The quitrent principle dated from the era when the feudal system was breaking up in England (around 1300) and landowners commuted, or changed, their tenants' obligation to labor for them so many days each year into an annual cash payment in perpetuity. People owning land in "free and common socage" were "quit" of their old obligations to serve their lord as a soldier, to shear sheep, to repair the castle moat, or whatever. But there was an annual payment in recognition of what they had been granted.

Colonial quitrents were small: the idea was to attract people to America, not to discourage them with extortionate demands. Thus, for each acre freeholders in Maryland owned, they paid an annual quitrent of two pence worth of tobacco. The quitrent for a hundred acres in New York was a bushel of wheat each year. In Georgia, the quitrent was two shillings per fifty acres.

It wasn't much, but for the proprietor of a vast domain, thousands of pittances added up to a handsome income while the quitrents the lords proprietors owed the king were purely symbolic: two Indian arrowheads a year for Maryland, two beaver pelts a year for Pennsylvania.

NEW NETHERLAND BECOMES NEW YORK

In 1646, the Dutch West India Company named Peter Stuyvesant governor of New Netherlands. He was dictatorial, ill-tempered, bigoted, and cantankerous. ("His head is troubled," people said, not to his face, "he has a screw loose.")

Linguistic Legacies

The Dutch, who were numerous in New Jersey, Pennsylvania, and Delaware, as well as in New York, contributed a great many words to American English: baas, a common Dutch word for "master," became "boss"; koeckjes became cookies, koolsla Cole Slaw, and Sinter Klaas, Dutch for St. Nicholas became the American Santa Claus, replacing the English Father Christmas. Some other words from the Dutch are blunderbuss, scow, sleigh, stoop, bedspread, and poppycock.

A Bizarre Constitution

The Carolina proprietors had bizarre plans for their colony. The scheme was outlined in The Fundamental Constitutions of Carolina, the brainchild of Anthony Ashley Cooper (later the Earl of Shaftesbury). Its 120 painfully detailed articles were written by his secretary, John Locke, who must have found them absurd for he is known to history as a philosopher of political liberty.

The Fundamental Constitutions divided Carolina into square counties, in each of which the proprietors (the "seigneurs") owned 96,000 acres. Other contrived ranks of nobility called "caciques" (an Indian title) and "landgraves" (European) had smaller but still ample tracts. Humble "leetmen" (a medieval term) and even humbler African slaves, over whom their owners had "absolute power and authority" would contribute the labor.

Was it all a promotional device designed to attract buyers of land with the promise of puffed-up titles? Maybe, but in 1671, Sir John Yeamans claimed the right to be governor because he was a landgrave and the appointed governor a mere cacique. In any case, with land so abundant, the constitution was unworkable and repeatedly revised. It did not much affect the actual development of the Carolinas.

But Stuyvesant was an effective governor. When he took over, New Netherlands' future was doubtful. Stuyvesant brought prosperity, maintained good relations with both Algonkian and Iroquois Indians, promoted immigration so that population increased from 700 to 6,000, and added New Sweden to the colony.

Most New Netherlanders were Dutch, but the colony's population was far more diverse than the population of the English colonies. There were Swedes and Finns on the Delaware River, a large English population everywhere, a substantial black population, most of them slaves but many free, and even a Jewish community. (The Jews were not to Stuyvesant's liking; he wanted to expel them but was overruled by his bosses in the West India Company.)

Stuyvesant had two problems he could not overcome: his personal unpopularity and England's displeasure with the Dutch wedge between New England colonies and the tobacco colonies. After seventeen years as governor, Stuyvesant had offended just about everyone in New Amsterdam, including his council. In 1664, four warships sailing for the Duke of York (the brother of Charles I) threatened to bombard New Amsterdam if it did not accept English rule. However, the commander, James Nicholls, offered generous terms if the Dutch did not resist: the Dutch language and the Dutch Reformed Church would have official status, and Dutch inheritance laws, which differed significantly from England's, would be enforced.

Stuyvesant wanted to fight. In a rage, he ripped to pieces the letter from Nicholls. But New Netherlands' number two man, Nicholas De Sille, pieced the document together and the council unanimously overruled the sputtering governor. Without a shot, New Netherlands became New York, and New Amsterdam the city of New York.

A SUCCESSFUL TRANSITION

New York was the Duke of York's proprietary colony until, in 1685, he was crowned King James II, whence it became a royal colony. James II, unpopular at home, largely because he was a Roman Catholic, was fairly well liked in New York because of his liberal policies. Few Dutch departed. De Sille stayed as, indeed, did Stuyvesant, who had many properties in New York, and Dutch immigrants continued to come to the colony.

But James was not universally popular. In 1689, after he was dethroned back home, a German merchant, Jacob Leisler, led a somewhat ragtag group to seize control of New York City. He proclaimed his loyalty to England's new rulers, William (a Dutchman) and Mary (the daughter of James II). But when their troops arrived to restore order, Leisler's men fired on them. They were arrested and eight were sentenced to hang. Leisler and one other were hanged; the others were pardoned. William and Mary restored the policies of tolerance of James II.

THE CAROLINA GRANT

In 1663 (a year before the takeover of New York), Charles II granted the land lying between 36 and 31 degrees north latitude (the northern boundary of the state of North Carolina and the southern boundary of South Carolina) to eight nobles and gentlemen, including Virginia's governor, Sir William Berkeley. There were already a few colonists living on Albemarle Sound within the new colony of Carolina (named for the king—Carolus is Latin for Charles). They had been sent there by Berkeley a decade earlier to defend Virginia's southernmost plantations from the Tuscarora Indians. Even after the eight proprietors took over, however, population grew slowly. Most settlers were rather poor, small-scale farmers who dribbled down from Virginia.

Carolina's first significant settlement was farther south, Charleston (more flattery of the king), founded in 1669. Many of the first white settlers were planters from the West Indian island of Barbados, where land had become exorbitantly expensive. Barbados was England's most lucrative colony. It grew sugar, for which all Europe had developed a craving. The cane was planted and harvested by African slaves worked far harder and treated far worse than blacks in Virginia, Maryland, and New York. The Barbadians brought both their slaves and their harsh slavery laws to southern Carolina.

At first, the economy of Charleston and its hinterlands was diversified. The whites bought hides and furs from the Muskohegan tribes that reached as far into the interior as present day Alabama. Timber and other naval stores were harvested from Carolina's pine forests. Some tobacco was grown and, on the sandy "sea islands" that rimmed the coastline, cotton. All except the fur trade depended on slave labor and the African population increased faster than the white

MAP 3:2 The Middle Colonies

All of the Middle Colonies except Pennsylvania were carved out of the Dutch New Netherlands, which surrendered to an English fleet in 1664. All, including Pennsylvania, were originally proprietary colonies. Pennsylvania remained a Penn family property until the American War for Independence. New York, New Jersey, and Delaware all became royal colonies.

TWO CAROLINAS

Three hundred miles of sandy beaches, islands, piney woods, swamps, and meandering waterways separated the settlements of northern and southern Carolina. Overland connections barely existed; communication was by sea. The two regions differed economically and socially. The northerners grew tobacco, mostly on farms rather than on large plantations. Few whites owned slaves, none in large numbers. Charleston, the colonial capital, virtually ignored the northern settlements.

In contrast, the rice planters of southern Carolina prospered; the biggest landowners became fabulously rich. Unlike Virginia tobacco planters, however, Carolina rice growers did not live on their lands. The low country that produced their wealth was—thanks to mosquito-borne diseases like malaria and yellow fever and waterborne sickness, particularly dysentery—"in the spring a paradise, in the summer a hell, and in the autumn a hospital." Carolina's elite built town houses in Charleston, which was open to sea breezes, and left the sickness and death of the pestilential rice plantations to white overseers poor enough to risk their lives and to slaves, who had no choice in the matter. If the rice grandees visited their plantations at all (and many did not for years at a time), it was for a month or two in winter and spring. Thus, unlike in Virginia, where planters lived among their servants and slaves, southern Carolina's elite was urban, interested in the land only in that it enriched them.

For administrative purposes, the increasingly unpopular proprietors divided the colony into North and South Carolina with separate assemblies. It was not enough. The proprietors' ineffective defense against Indian attacks and a raid by the Spanish and French caused an ongoing, sometimes violent, unrest among the whites of Albemarle Sound. In 1729, the Crown revoked the proprietors' charter and established North and South Carolina as separate royal colonies.

population. By 1700, half of Carolina's 5,000 people were African or African Americans, a far greater proportion than in any other English colony.

Indeed, African slaves introduced the crop that made South Carolina rich. They had grown rice in Africa and discovered that the marshy lowlands along the Ashley and Cooper Rivers made ideal rice fields. As an export, rice was less lucrative than sugar but more profitable than tobacco. The slaves found themselves raising their food not on a small scale but rice by the hundreds of tons on large plantations.

NEW JERSEY AND THE QUAKERS

New Jersey began as two colonies and ended up as one. In 1665, the Duke of York gave Lord John Berkeley and Sir George Carteret the part of his Dutch conquest west of the Hudson River. The two proprietors divided their grant roughly north to south, Carteret taking East New Jersey facing New York harbor and the Atlantic, Berkeley the western half facing the Delaware River. In 1674, West New Jersey was sold to two members of a fringe religious sect, the Society of Friends, or "Quakers," as

---

Thou, Thy, and Thee

Like French, Spanish, Italian, and German, the English language once had two forms of the pronoun to address another person. Thou (like *tu* in French) was used when speaking to family members, intimate friends, children, social inferiors, and God in prayer—it survives in the Christian Lord's Prayer: "hallowed be thy name." You (like *vous* in French) was for formal conversation, with casual acquaintances or strangers, and when addressing social superiors.

Thou, thy, and thee were beginning to be abandoned in the late 1600s in favor of using you in all cases, as we do today. However, the rules were well-known. When Quakers expressed their belief in the spiritual equality of all by addressing strangers and even nobles and the king himself as thou, thy, and thee. It was taken as profoundly ill-mannered, an insult. Not, however, by Charles II when his favorite Quaker, William Penn, called him thee. The king thought it was great fun.

Colonial Williamsburg Foundation

Charleston, South Carolina was the only true city in the colonies south of Philadelphia. Built between the Ashley and Cooper Rivers, it had a superb harbor from which to export rice, cotton, furs and hides, and, later indigo. More African slaves were imported into Charleston than into any other port.

members were called because they trembled with emotion at their religious services.

The Quakers were ridiculed, harassed, and sometimes brutally persecuted in old England and in Massachusetts. Massachusetts hanged several when, after they were banished to Rhode Island, they returned and resumed preaching their belief that God communicated directly with all men and women. Their doctrine was more obnoxious to the Puritans than Anne Hutchinson's. She had said that God inspired some people; the Quakers said God inspired everyone.

The Friends worried authorities in old England because they were pacifists. Friends were forbidden to take up arms, even in self-defense. Armies of the era were not made up of draftees, but pacifism was still bothersome because war was a routine part of effecting national policy. Then, the Quakers said that because of every person's divine "inner light," there was no need for priests, ministers, or bishops. They challenged the Church of England more radically than Puritans did.

When haled into court, Quakers refused to take oaths—to swear on the Bible. Some refused to remove their hats in the presence of social superiors, a pointed insult to magistrates because most Quakers were of the lowest ranks of English society.

Finally, the doctrine of the equality of all before God meant that women participated in Quaker services and preached in the streets. It was an affront to one of society's most basic rules, that women were subordinate to men and played no role in public life.

Charles II, seated, is receiving William Penn. Royal etiquette was that when the king was seated, no one else sat until he invited them to, at dinner, for instance. Protocol also had it that no one wore a hat in the king's presence—ever. Penn's Quaker religion taught that a man took off his hat for no other man precisely because doing so was an act of deference and all were equal before God. The custom amused the good-natured Charles II. He not only tolerated Penn's impropriety, he joked about it with his courtiers.

MAP 3:3 The Southern Colonies

The Carolina colony was chartered in 1663, a year before the English seized New York from the Dutch, but developed slowly. The population, mostly around Charleston in the south, was tiny when the Quakers' "great migration" to New Jersey and Pennsylvania began 20 years later. Northern Carolina remained thinly populated with tobacco growers but, by the early 1700s, the Charleston area—South Carolina—had become a valuable producer of rice. It was also vulnerable to Spanish raids, thus the founding in 1732 of Georgia. It was intended as a defensive buffer between South Carolina and Spanish Florida.

The proprietors of West New Jersey hoped that their co-religionists would flee persecution at home, go to their colony for religious freedom, and, of course, purchase land from them. They did. Beginning in 1675, Quakers by the thousand crossed the ocean, mostly, at first, to West New Jersey. It was a "great migration" almost as carefully orchestrated as the Puritan migration a generation earlier, and it involved even more people. In 1682, 2,000 Quakers came to America in twenty-three ships. Between 1682 and 1685, ninety ships brought more Quakers than remained in England. By 1750, the Society of Friends was the third largest religious denomination in English America. By 1683, however, most headed not for New Jersey, but for a new colony on the western bank of the Delaware.

PENNSYLVANIA: "THE HOLY EXPERIMENT"

Charles II had a lot of courtiers and creditors clamoring for favors. Proprietary colonies were a cheap way to oblige them. They cost the king nothing.

The most unusual of the king's beneficiaries, and the most successful proprietor he created, was **William Penn,** the wealthiest and most influential Quaker in England, and the most visionary. That so highly placed a gentleman should worship with cobblers and housemaids amused the good-natured king. When Penn, hat on head, was ushered into his presence, Charles removed his own headgear, remarking that it was customary, when the king was present, for only one man to wear a hat.

Charles owed Penn £16,000 for services Penn's dead father, an admiral in the navy, had rendered. In 1681, to cancel the debt, he carved what are now the states of Pennsylvania and Delaware out of the Duke of York's property and chartered the land to Penn as Pennsylvania—"Penn's Woods." The king picked the name, not Penn, in honor of Penn's father. For Charles II, it was a bargain: he disposed of a £16,000 debt with distant woodland when other proprietorships were changing hands for £1,000. The next year, Penn purchased what is now Delaware from the Duke of York, annexing it to Pennsylvania as the "three lower counties." (Delaware was detached from Pennsylvania in 1701 and became a royal colony. New Jersey, where William Penn also was a proprietor, became a royal colony the same year.)

Penn envisioned his colony not only as a refuge for Quakers but as a "Holy Experiment" governed on Quaker principles. All religious faiths were tolerated. Penn paid the Indians higher prices for land than the governments of other colonies and insisted that the natives be treated justly. Early Pennsylvania suffered no Indian wars. And Penn sold land at bargain prices, a shilling to three shillings an acre at a time when a carpenter made three shillings a day in wages.

Eccentrics Welcome

William Penn's toleration extended to eccentrics. In 1694, a German, Johannes Kelpius and about forty followers who called themselves "The Woman in the Wilderness," built a 40' by 40' "monastery" outside Philadelphia. They had individual cells but gathered in a common room to eat, pray, study, and perform chemistry experiments. Kelpius kept a telescope, attended around the clock, on the roof. Suffering no interference, The Woman in the Wilderness survived for fifty years. Its third leader, affectionately known as Der alte Matthai (Old Matthew), wandered benignly around Philadelphia in a snowy white gown, carrying an alpenstock.

Philadelphia (like Charleston) was a planned city. The streets of the "greene countrie towne" were laid out on a grid-iron, making possible a tidiness that even the well-ordered Puritans had been unable to command of Boston. Philadelphia became the largest and most prosperous city in English North America, partly because of Quaker liberality. By the mid-1700s, it was "the second city of the British empire," smaller only than London in the English-speaking world.

GEORGIA: A PHILANTHROPIC EXPERIMENT

Georgia was the last of the "thirteen colonies." It was chartered in 1732, with Savannah established the next year, as a military buffer state protecting valuable South Carolina from the Spanish in Florida. Spanish forces had seriously threatened Charleston during a war between 1702 and 1713. A tough, battle-hardened soldier, James Oglethorpe, was put in command of the colony.

Command is the proper word. Georgia was neither a corporate, proprietary, nor royal colony. Trustees who met in England governed it. Most of them sympathized with Oglethorpe's vision of Georgia as a social experiment as well as a fortress. Oglethorpe was troubled by the misery of England's urban poor, the alcoholism widespread among them, and laws that imprisoned people for debt, creating more poverty as well as convicts guilty of, at worst, poor financial judgment. He thought of Georgia as a place in which jailed debtors might have a fresh start. He persuaded the trustees to ban alcohol from the colony and also slavery. Oglethorpe recognized that, in South Carolina, slavery had made it possible for a small elite of great planters to lord it over everyone else. He meant Georgia to be a colony of small, self-sustaining farmers (the maximum land grant was 50 acres), living close together so that they could be mobilized quickly against the Spanish.

Georgia was a success as a buffer state. In 1742, a Spanish flotilla of 36 ships brought 2,000 soldiers from Cuba to capture Savannah. With just 900 men, Oglethorpe sent them packing. Oglethorpe then retaliated, destroying a fortified Spanish town north of St. Augustine.

As a philanthropic enterprise, Georgia failed. The trustees sent about 1,800 debtors and paupers, and about 1,000 people came on their own. Many of them were South Carolinians who brought their slaves in defiance of Georgia law. Oglethorpe, although as tyrannical a personality as Peter Stuyvesant, could not stop them. Nor could he keep Georgians away from their rum. He returned to England disgusted. In 1752 the trustees surrendered control of the colony to the king, a year earlier than the charter required.

FURTHER READING

General Charles M. Andrews, *The Colonial Period of American History*, 1934–1938; Daniel Boorstin, *The Americans: The Colonial Experience*, 1958; Alan Taylor, *American Colonies*, 2001; Jack P. Greene, *Pursuits of Happiness: The Social Development of Early Modern British Colonies and the Formation of American Culture*, 1988; Jack P. Greene and J. R. Pole, eds., *Colonial British America, 1607–1789*, 1984; John J. McCusker and Russell Menard, *The Economy of British North America*, 1985; Stanley Katz, *Colonial America: Essays in Political and Social Development*, 1992; John E. Pomfret with Floyd Shumway, *Founding the American Colonies*, 1970; Alison Games, *Migration and the Origins of the English Atlantic World*, 1999; David Hackett Fisher, *Albion's Seed: Four British Folkways in America*, 1989.

New England Governor William Bradford, *History of Plimmoth Plantation*, (numerous editions); George Langdon, *Pilgrim Colony: A History of New Plymouth, 1620–1691*, 1966; John Demos, *A Little Commonwealth: Family Life in Plymouth Colony*, 1970; David Cressy, *Coming Over: Migration and Communication Between England and New England in the Seventeenth Century*, 1987; Harry Stout, *The New England Soul: Preaching and Culture in Colonial New England*, 1986; Charles Hambrick-Stowe, *The Practice of Piety*, 1982; David Hall, *Worlds of Wonder, Days of Judgement: Popular Religious Belief in Early New England*, 1989; Andrew Delbanco, *The Puritan Ordeal*, 1989; Emery Battis, *Saints and Sectarians: Anne Hutchinson and the Antinomian Controversy in Massachusetts*, 1962; Sydney V. James, *Colonial Rhode Island: A History*, 1975.

The Middle Colonies Edwin B. Bronner, *William Penn's "Holy Experiment,"* 1962; Gary Nash, *Quakers and Politics: Pennsylvania, 1681–1726*, 1971; James T. Lemon, *The Best Poor Man's Country: A Geographical Study of Early Southeastern Pennsylvania*, 1972; Richard and Mary Dunn, *The World of William Penn*, 1986; Michael Kammen, *Colonial New York*, 1975; Robert C. Ritchie, *The Duke's Province*, 1977; Joyce D. Goodfriend, *Before the Melting Pot: Society and Culture in Colonial New York City, 1664–1730*, 1992; Russell Shorto, *The Island at the Center of the World: The Epic Story of Dutch Manhattan* (2004); Edwin G. Burrows and Mike Wallace, *Gotham: A History of New York City to 1898*, 1999; J. E. Pomfret, *The Province of East and West New Jersey*, 1956; Brendan McConville, *These Daring Disturbers of the Public Peace: The Struggle for Property and Power in Early New Jersey*, 1999.

The Carolinas and Georgia William S. Powell, *Colonial North Carolina*, 1973; Eugene Sirmans, *Colonial South Carolina*, 1966; Robert M. Weir, *Colonial South Carolina: A History*, 1983; Robert Orwell, *Masters, Slaves, and Subjects: The Culture of Power in the South Carolina Low Country*, 1998; Phinizy Spalding, *Oglethorpe in America*, 1977.

KEY TERMS

The following terms are covered in this chapter and can also be found in the list of Key Terms at the back of the book.

Anne Hutchinson	John Winthrop	proprietary colony	royal colony
blue laws	Pilgrims	Puritans	William Penn
corporate colony	Plymouth Company	Roger Williams	

 ## ONLINE SOURCES GUIDE

Use this listing to find online documents, images, interactive maps, simulations, and other resources related to this chapter:

American History Resource Center
http://history.wadsworth.com

Selected Documents

Ann Bradstreet, Verses upon the Burning of Our House
Ann Bradstreet, A Dialogue between Old England and New
William Bradford, Of Plimouth Plantation (1620)
The Mayflower Compact
John Winthrop's Shipboard Sermon, A Model of Christian Charity
William Penn, Some Account of the Province of Pennsylvania (1681)
Edward Randolph's Letters describing colonial avoidance of trade regulations
Robert Beverly's Report on decline of Native American populations in Virginia (1705)

Selected Images
John Winthrop, Governor of Massachusetts Bay Colony
Engraving of the defeat of Pequot, 1637
William Penn
Puritans entering a meetinghouse
Hingham, Massachusetts meetinghouse

Simulations
Colonial Expansion (Choose an identity as an Aztec, Jamestown settler, or a Puritan in New England and make choices based on the circumstances and opportunities afforded.)

Interactive Timeline (with online readings)
English America: The Thirteen Colonies 1620–1732

Additional resources, exercises, and Internet links related to this chapter are available on *THE AMERICAN PAST* web site: http://history.wadsworth.com/americanpast8e

Discovery

What are the differences and similarities in North American colonial development?

In thinking about this question, begin by breaking it down into the components shown below. A discussion of the significance of each component should appear in your answer.

Geography: For this exercise, review Maps 3.1, 3.2, and 3.3 and study this image, "New England framed home." Look at the three maps of the colonies. What geographical features are common in all of these European colonies? What does this suggest is important to the early colonies? On what were these colonies going to depend?

Look at the image of the New England home. What is the traditional view of frontier homes and how does it differ from the photograph of the New England home? Why was the New England home constructed in this fashion? How does it follow from the geography of the region? What influences from England might be seen here? How would this type of home differ from what might be used in the other colonies?

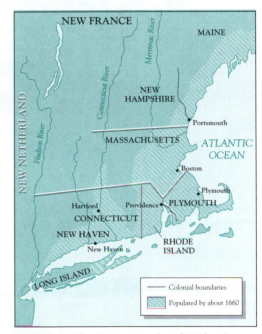

MAP 3:1 The New England Colonies

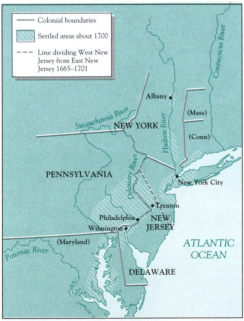

MAP 3:2 The Middle Colonies

MAP 3:3 The Southern Colonies

Photograph by Wilfred French,
Courtesy of the Society for the Preservation of New England Antiquities

New England framed home

Government and Law: For this exercise, read the following document excerpt, "Mayflower Compact." What were the various stated motives for the founding of colonies in America?

Mayflower Compact

Having undertaken for the Glory of God, and Advancement of the Christian Faith, and the Honour of our King and Country, a voyage to plant the first colony in the northern parts of Virginia; do by these presents, solemnly and mutually in the Presence of God and one of another, covenant and combine ourselves together into a civil Body Politick, for our better Ordering and Preservation, and Furtherance of the Ends aforesaid; And by Virtue hereof to enact, constitute, and frame, such just and equal Laws, Ordinances, Acts, Constitutions and Offices, from time to time, as shall be thought most meet and convenient for the General good of the Colony; unto which we promise all due submission and obedience.

To read extended versions of the documents, visit the companion Web site
http://history.wadsworth.com/americanpast8e; click on "Discovery Sources."

CHAPTER 4

English Intentions, American Facts of Life

Colonial Society in the 1600s

Reproduced from the Collections of the Library of Congress

And those that came were resolved to be Englishmen,
Gone to the world's end but English every one,
And they ate the white corn kernels, parched in the sun
And they knew it not but they'd not be English again

Stephen Vincent Benét

In 1660, King Charles II was an exile. He had fled England when a Parliamentary army defeated his father in battle, then beheaded him. The "Commonwealth of England" was governed for a decade by a military dictator, a Puritan, Oliver Cromwell.

Cromwell died in 1658 and England's experiment with republican government fizzled. People generally were weary of Cromwell's Massachusetts-like blue laws: no theater, no games on Sunday, and so on. Powerful nobles, men never comfortable without a king, invited Charles II to return.

Charles executed those who had signed his father's death warrant and he scrapped the puritanical laws. However, the king endorsed many other laws enacted during the Commonwealth. Among these was a series of **Navigation Acts** that set down the rules governing colonial trade. Charles II was not the wisest of kings, but he understood, as he said in 1668, "the thing that is nearest the heart of the nation is trade." The Navigation Acts of the 1660s defined England's and, later, Great Britain's colonial policy for a century.

English and British

Even today the terms *English* and *British* are often confused. English refers to a language, of course, and to a nationality. Henry VII, John Cabot's patron, was King of England, so the colonies founded on Cabot's discoveries were English colonies. In 1603, the King of Scotland became James I of England; Scotland and England never again had different monarchs. However, the two countries retained their own parliaments, laws, and possessions. (There was an unsuccessful Scottish attempt at colonization in Central America, but the colonies that existed belonged to England.)

That is, until 1707. In that year, England and Scotland were united under one parliament as the United Kingdom of Great Britain. Scots remained Scots and English remained English, but both were also now British, and the American colonies became British colonies.

Boundary Dispute

One of several border disputes resulting from the Crown's carelessness in making gifts of American land pitted Maryland against Pennsylvania. In the Maryland charter of 1632, the colony's northern line was set vaguely at "under the Fortieth Degree of North Latitude." William Penn's charter, granted fifty years later, set Pennsylvania's southern line at 40 degrees north latitude.

So what was the problem?

The problem was that William Penn, misinformed that the 40th parallel was forty miles farther south than it actually is, located his capital, Philadelphia, just below 40 degrees. The city was thriving when surveyors discovered Penn's mistake so he was not about to abandon his "greene countrie towne" to the Calverts of Maryland.

Luckily for Penn, there was that vague "under the Fortieth Degree" in Maryland's charter. And, when the issue overheated, the Penn family was in better odor at court than the Catholic Calverts were. Pennsylvania kept Philadelphia. Exactly where the Pennsylvania–Maryland line ran, however, was disputed until 1763 when two surveyors employed by both colonies, Charles Mason and Jeremiah Dixon, marked it at 39°, 43', 18", the "Mason-Dixon Line."

TRADE

Overseas trade was central to a theory of national greatness now known as **mercantilism.** It was first described systematically in the 1630s by Thomas Mun, a shareholder in the greatest trading venture of all, the East India Company. Mun's book, *England's Treasure by Foreign Trade,* was published during the reign of Charles II, in 1664.

MERCANTILISM

The object of mercantilism was to strengthen England by increasing the nation's store of coin: gold and silver—the gold and silver of all the realm's subjects, not just what was in the royal treasury. The key to accumulating coin, Mun said, was a favorable balance of trade; that is, for the English "to sell more to strangers yearly"—to foreigners—"than wee consume of theirs in value." Thus the word *mercantilism,* for merchants trading abroad (*mercator* is Latin for merchant) were the country's moneymakers and merchants were mercantilism's chief proponents.

So, the argument ran, when a merchant dispatched a ship from Bristol to west Africa with a cargo of woolen cloth, traded the cloth for slaves, transported the slaves to Spanish Cuba where they were exchanged for sugar which was sold in Italy or Denmark for gold, the profit on each transaction increased "England's treasure" at the expense of every other party involved. The African slave traders, the Cuban sugar planters, and the Danes and Italians were merely consuming; English merchants brought gold home.

The merchants' success depended on the government—the Crown—acting aggressively to nurture, protect, encourage, and favor them with subsidies, special privileges, and naval protection. To a mercantilist, there was no better reason for the Crown to go to war than to protect or to expand foreign trade, and no issue more important when writing peace treaties than winning control of overseas ports or concessions for England's merchants.

Manufacturing was important to mercantilists. Manufacturing added cash to raw materials at no cash expense. Even in the Middle Ages, long before Thomas Mun put pen to paper, England's kings concluded that it was economic lunacy to export raw wool to the low countries (present-day Belgium and Holland) and then buy it back in the form of cloth. The cloth, having been spun into yarn, woven, and dyed in the low countries, commanded a considerably higher price than the sacks of English wool that went into it. The difference in value was the gold and silver drained out of England.

So the Crown prohibited the export of raw wool. With subsidies and other favors, kings and parliaments encouraged the

Colonial Society and Economy 1600–1700

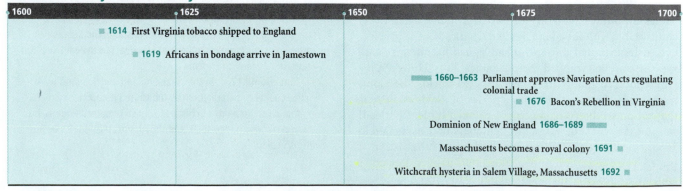

| 1600 | 1625 | 1650 | 1675 | 1700 |

- 1614 First Virginia tobacco shipped to England
- 1619 Africans in bondage arrive in Jamestown
- 1660–1663 Parliament approves Navigation Acts regulating colonial trade
- 1676 Bacon's Rebellion in Virginia
- Dominion of New England 1686–1689
- Massachusetts becomes a royal colony 1691
- Witchcraft hysteria in Salem Village, Massachusetts 1692

An English merchant's warehouse and wharf. His "counting room" (office) was inside, and was possibly his family's residence too. Vessels were unloaded and loaded on wharfs stretching for miles on the Thames—London's river—and in Plymouth, Bristol, and other ports.

West Indies. England (Great Britain) purchased furs both for luxurious adornment and for the manufacture of felt for hats. The finest furs came from Muscovy, as Russia was known.

As a maritime nation, Britain consumed vast quantities of timber just to build ships. A full-size warship consumed 2,000 oak trees, some of them one and a half feet in diameter. But the country's forests had been harvested for centuries; they had disappeared in much of the country. "Good old English oak" was not plentiful enough to meet the planking needs of the nation's many shipyards. Virtually all the long straight-grained trees from which masts were made had to be purchased in Scandinavia. Teak became invaluable to ship-builders because of its resistance to rot, and luxurious woods like mahogany and black, iron-hard ebony were tropical. Naval stores—tar, pitch, and turpentine manufactured from pine—and fiber for the manufacture of rope were also essential to shipbuilding.

spinners, weavers, and dyers whose skills and labor added to the value of English cloth sold abroad in competition with the cloth of the low countries. In treaties with other states—forced on them by the mouths of cannon, if necessary—the Crown secured markets for the nation's cloth makers. Seventeenth-century mercantilists urged the Crown to promote other kinds of manufacturing—making of iron products, for example—with similar inducements.

THE COLONIAL CONNECTION

In the best of all possible mercantilist worlds, England would be self-sufficient. Its people would produce everything they consumed and buy nothing abroad. Gold and silver earned from exports would roll in; none would depart.

In the real world, self-sufficiency was a fantasy. An island nation in a northerly latitude, England imported any number of tropical products. Cotton came from Egypt and the Middle East; silk from Italy and east Asia; spices (of course, always spices) came from the Indies, and by the end of the seventeenth century, tea had made its appearance and soon became the "national beverage."

The English produced little wine but they drank a good deal of it. It was imported from France, Portugal, and the German Rhineland. Sugar was still a luxury but getting cheaper; those who could afford it bought lots of it, increasingly from the

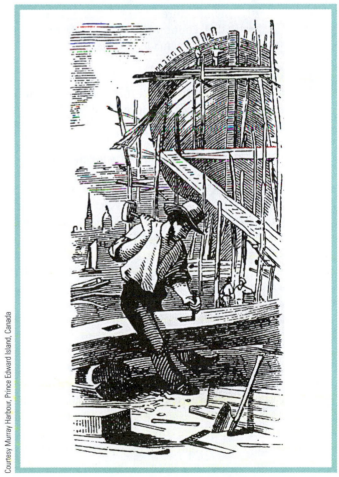

Shipbuilders lined every navigable river in England. They needed prodigious quantities of lumber, particularly well-seasoned ("winter-cut"), flawless oak for the ribs of vessels. Scholars estimate that the largest naval vessels consumed parts of 2,000 oak trees! North America—one sprawling forest—was a major source of supply. New England's pineries also provided long, straight-grained trees for masts.

This is where colonies entered the mercantilist equation. Colonies reduced England's dependence on foreigners for both essential imports and luxuries. By seizing islands in the West Indies like Barbados (in 1627) and Jamaica (1655), English sailors created dependable sources of sugar both to sate its own people's sweet tooth and to sell to other countries. A shaky English enclave in Central America (present-day Belize) shipped mahogany and logwood (source of a precious dye) back home. The North American colonies were almost entirely forested with both hardwoods like oak and maple and, in New England, with towering, straight-grained pines. America's woods teemed with beaver, mink, otter, and other furred animals, and with deer, the hides of which made a leather more versatile than leather from cattle and sheep. And, of course, there was tobacco, which had almost as many markets as sugar did.

Money spent in the colonies was a subtraction from the national store of gold just as money spent in Scandinavia or Portugal was. But few imports from the colonies were paid for with coin. Mercantilists, the Crown, defined colonies as producers of (cheap) raw materials and colonials as consumers of (costly) manufactures. The balance of trade was favorable to the mother country—exceedingly favorable—so long as the mother country made the rules.

THE NAVIGATION ACTS

The Navigation Acts of 1660–1663 (others were added later) minced no words in defining the purpose of the American colonies as the enrichment of the mother country. The welfare of the colonies was not ignored. However, when the economic interests of colonials clashed with the economic interests of the English, the latter were the people who counted. Colonies were tributaries of the empire; they were not partners with the mother country.

So the Navigation Acts stipulated that all colonial trade be carried in vessels built and owned by English or colonial merchants. These ships were to be manned by crews in which at least three seamen in four were English or colonials. Not even lowly seamen's wages were to be paid to foreigners who might take their meager earnings home with them.

Next, the Navigation Acts required that European goods intended for sale in the colonies be carried first to certain English ports called *entrepôts* (places, or clearinghouses, from which goods are distributed). There they were monitored, taxed, and only then shipped to America. The purpose of this law was to ensure a precise record of colonial trade, to collect taxes on, for example, French, Spanish, and Portuguese wines which were coveted in the colonies, and to see to it that English merchants and even port laborers benefited from transactions that involved no English products.

The Navigation Acts designated some colonial exports—the most valuable—as **enumerated articles.** These could be shipped only to English ports, even if they were destined for sale elsewhere. Once again, the object was to ensure that part of the profit in the colonies' sales in Europe or Africa went into English purses. Enumerated articles bound for France or Poland or Italy were taxed. These duties were an important

source of government revenue. Charles II collected £100,000 a year just from the tax on tobacco.

The enumerated articles included most colonial products that readily sold on the world market: sugar and molasses made from sugar, furs and hides, naval stores, rice, cotton, and tobacco. Foodstuffs ("bulk goods")—grain, livestock, salted fish, lumber not suited to shipbuilding—were less profitable and not enumerated. Rum, because it was so cheap, was overlooked. Colonials could ship these products directly to foreign ports and they did. The North American colonies fed the sugar islands of the West Indies—French, Spanish, Dutch, Danish, as well as English—and New England annually shipped thousands of tons of salted cod to Portugal, Spain, and Italy.

MERCANTILISM IN THE SOUTH

The Navigation Acts applied uniformly to every colony. However, the colonies' widely varying climates and landforms meant that they had sharply differing economies. These and differing social structures meant that England's commercial code affected colonials in sharply differing ways.

Well before 1700, the North American colonies were defined geographically: the New England colonies, the southern colonies, and "the middle colonies." New England was New Hampshire, Massachusetts (including Maine), Rhode Island, and Connecticut. The southern colonies were Maryland, Virginia, North Carolina, South Carolina, and, after 1732, Georgia. In between were what had been New Netherlands, the middle colonies: New York, New Jersey, Pennsylvania, and Delaware.

English merchants prized the southern colonies. Like the sugar islands of the West Indies, they grew two profitable enumerated articles—tobacco and rice. Like the West Indies, the southern colonies were home to a large, bonded labor force, mostly white servants in the 1600s, black slaves after 1700. Their masters had to clothe and shoe their laborers with English manufactures and provide them with tools manufactured in the mother country. By 1700, the planter elite of Maryland, Virginia, and South Carolina were rich enough to covet and consume every luxury that any merchant ever thought to load on a sailing ship.

TOBACCO'S LUSTER LOST

The American colonies had a monopoly on tobacco production in the empire. English farmers were forbidden to grow it. By the 1660s, however, Maryland's and Virginia's (and, on a

The Tobacco God

When Edward Seymour was asked to support the creation of a college in Virginia because the ministers trained there would save souls, he replied, "Souls! Damn your souls! Make tobacco!"

much smaller scale, North Carolina's) advantage was not enough to ensure prosperity. In just a decade, the wholesale price of tobacco (the price at which the planters sold) collapsed from two pence and a halfpenny a pound to a halfpenny. So much leaf was being grown (elsewhere in the world too) that the world's smokers, chewers, and snorters no longer demanded it at any price. It was cheap.

Complaining about the forces of a world marketplace was like complaining about the weather. Tobacco planters could do nothing about them. They could, however, blame hard times on the Navigation Acts. The Dutch reached markets the English did not, planters argued, but the Navigation Acts forbade selling an enumerated article to the Dutch. Planters complained: "If the Hollanders must not trade to Virginia, how shall the planters dispose of their tobacco? . . . The tobacco will not vend in England, the Hollanders will not fetch it from England. What must become thereof?"

One thing that "became thereof" was evasion of the Navigation Acts. Smuggling (illegal trade) was common and by no means unrespectable. Dutch tobacco buyers illegally tying up at wharves on the Chesapeake rarely had to listen to lectures about the sanctity of English trade law. If they paid a farthing more per pound than the going English rate, they did not sail off in ballast. Widespread evasion of the Navigation Acts was not difficult because of the topography of the Chesapeake region.

THE TIDEWATER

The Chesapeake is the estuary (where fresh river water mixes with salt sea water) of not one but many streams. Among countless briny creeks are several sizeable rivers: the Choptank, Nanticoke, and Wicomico in Maryland, the Potomac (bigger than the Seine), Rappahannock, York, and James (larger than the Thames) in Virginia.

They are broad and slow-moving rivers for miles from the open bay; ocean tides reach far inland. The vessels of the seventeenth and eighteenth centuries could sail as far as salt water reached. Ships at anchor might careen in sticky black mud at low tide. But twice each day, salt water returned to float them and their cargos back to sea.

The most desirable farm land was on the "necks" between the navigable rivers. There, in the words of a Virginia planter, Robert Beverley, ships could tie up "before the gentleman's door where they find the best reception or where 'tis most suitable to their Business." By 1700, most land with river frontage, called the "Tidewater," had been consolidated into large tobacco plantations worked by white servants and black slaves, but owned by just a few hundred great planter families, the Tidewater aristocrats. Not only did they sell their tobacco and receive English goods they had ordered on their own wharves, they hosted the small scale tobacco growers whose farms were inland.

Those were exhilarating days when the tobacco factors (agents) arrived. Indians and landless, poor whites hired

A tobacco "factor" (buyer) and a planter (Peter Jefferson, father of Thomas Jefferson) negotiating the sale of the year's crop at the planter's wharf. Tobacco was packed in hogsheads, huge barrels, as most goods transported by ship were. No matter how heavy, barrels could be rolled; good ones were watertight, and, properly stacked in the hold on their sides, they did not shift in rough seas.

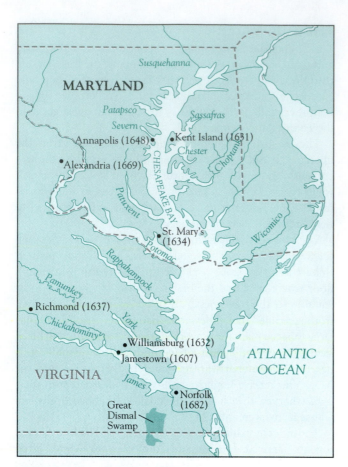

MAP 4:1 The Chesapeake Estuary
Seagoing ships could sail miles up many of the broad rivers of the Virginia and Maryland Tidewater, and transact their business on the premises of hundreds of plantations. The few towns of the region were centers of government. They were nearly deserted when the assemblies and courts were not in session; they were not commercial centers.

themselves out to roll hogsheads (large barrels) of tobacco to the dock alongside servants and slaves. Middling landowners and their wives, called the "yeomanry," danced, drank, raced on foot and horseback, shot targets, and bought what they thought they could afford from the visiting merchants. Ships were variety shops. There would be spades, shovels, axes, and saws; household items such as kettles, pots, pans, sieves, funnels, pewter tankards, and tableware; oddments such as buttons, needles, thread, pins, and ribbons. There were textiles for both the planter families' fine clothing and rough wraps for poor farmers, servants, and slaves; shoes and boots; bricks, nails, and paint; goods to trade with the Indians (all of this plus trinkets, mirrors, and the like); and firearms, shot, and gunpowder. For the wealthy few there were luxuries: silver candlesticks, chests and other fine furniture, wine, brandy, spices, books, even violins and harpsichords with which to grace a parlor and cheer an evening. Everyone discussed the news of battles and kings that the ships brought. Some received letters from old country family, friends, and business agents. The sailors

enlivened the carnival with their giddiness at being ashore after a couple of months at sea, spending their wages, as tradition required, on games and rum and the favors of women of three races. For the women of the yeomanry, whose only chance to socialize the rest of the year might be an hour after church on Sunday, the arrival of a tobacco ship was the high point of the year.

THE FIRST FAMILIES OF VIRGINIA

The excitement of the tobacco factor's annual visit briefly masked a potential conflict within tobacco colony society and a potential for resentment of the mother country. Because ships had easy access to plantations throughout the Chesapeake, no cities developed in Virginia and Maryland, no urban ports. The colonial capitals, Jamestown (Williamsburg after 1699) and St. Mary's (Annapolis after 1695) were ghost towns when the assembly was not meeting and the courts were not in session, which was most of the year.

The fact that there were no cities meant there were no urban merchants (who doubled as bankers), nor a class of artisans who elsewhere (in old England, in New England, in the middle colonies) had interests different than those of farmers, and who were often at odds with them. As the only wealthy people in the tobacco colonies, the great planters of the Tidewater had no opposition with which to contend for political power.

Servants, slaves, and the poor were numerous—six Virginians in seven were "Poor, Indebted, Discontented" according to the royal governor—and therefore worrisome. But they did not vote. Yeoman farmers, owners of small tracts of land, did vote, but dependably for Tidewater aristocrats whom they admired and whose circles they aspired to join.

The "first families of Virginia" were conscious of themselves as an elite with common social and political interests. With each passing year, they grew more tightly-knit by intermarrying, thus creating a social class of cousins. In 1724, all twelve members of Virginia's Royal Council and half of the members of the House of Burgesses were related to one another by blood or marriage.

The first families did not trace their ancestry to the founding of Jamestown (as prominent New Englanders liked to trace their American origins to the *Mayflower*). Probably, little pioneer blood flowed in their veins. The "starving times" of 1607–1610 and two devastating Indian massacres had snuffed out many a bloodline in the making. High mortality from disease interrupted other lines of descent. Well into the 1600s, life expectancy in Virginia was ten years shorter than it was in old England, twenty years shorter than in New England. Virginia's population remained an immigrant population for decades.

The founders of the "first families" (and Virginians of lower station) came to America beginning in the late 1640s. **Sir William Berkeley,** royal governor from 1646, called them "distressed cavaliers." That is, they were royalists (known as **cavaliers**) who had supported Charles I in the Civil War that ended with the King's execution. Under Oliver Cromwell they fell on hard times.

Finding the Way

to measure height of
thereby determine
ude.

Cross Staff

Sailors in the African or Asian trade found their way by the ancient expedient of keeping the coastline in sight. They sailed like pilots of small airplanes fly, by following landmarks. It was in this way that the Vikings made it to Newfoundland in 1000. After a short dash across the open ocean from Greenland to Baffin Island (a passage possibly discovered by accident), land was rarely out of sight. Their first voyage to Iceland more than a century earlier was a much bolder enterprise than crossing from Greenland to North America. Deepwater seamen—transatlantic sailors beginning with Columbus and Cabot—depended on the compass and the cross-staff, back-staff, or astrolabe.

The Chinese discovered that magnetized iron pointed north. Italians adapted the knowledge into a navigational instrument. By the seventeenth century, the ship's compass was a magnetic needle delicately balanced on a brass bowl with a flat top marked with 16 directions (north, east, south, and west, of course; NE, SE, etc.; and NNE, ENE, ESE, SSE). The compass was within sight of the helmsman and mounted on pivots so that it remained level when the vessel pitched and rolled.

The cross-staff, back-staff, and astrolabe enabled navigators to measure the angle between the horizon and the sun by day and, by night, the North Star (the Southern Cross below the Equator). With this information, navigators could determine their latitude; that is, the distance of their position from the equator. With one of these instruments, sailors knew on which east–west line their ship was sailing.

So a captain headed for Cape Cod, which he knew was located at about 42 degrees north latitude, and sailed southerly out of England until his astrolabe told him he was at 42 degrees. Then, using the compass, checking the astrolabe for corrections several times daily, he sailed due west.

What sailors could not determine with any accuracy was longitude—their position on the imaginary arcs that run north–south from pole to pole. On an east to west voyage

such as across the Atlantic, navigators could only determine by reckoning how far they had sailed from their port of departure and how far they were from their destination.

There were rude instruments for determining a ship's speed, which is what longitude is on an east–west voyage. The log line was a rope knotted every 48 feet with a wooden float tied to the end. It was thrown overboard and, measuring minutes with a sandglass, the captain counted the number of knots that passed over the stern in a given period of time. Because the log was not blown as the ship was, the speed of the wind could be roughly estimated. However, the logline did not take account of ocean currents that could radically increase or decrease a ship's progress: the log was in the grip of the current, just as the ship was.

Not until the mid-eighteenth century was the problem of determining longitude systematically attacked. In 1752, a German astronomer, Tobias Mayer, devised a set of tables and a mathematical formula for determining longitude from the position of the moon. His method worked, but was impractical. A skilled mathematician needed four hours to complete the calculation. Few ships' captains were so skilled. None had four hours to spare even two or three days a week. In 1767, the Royal Observatory at Greenwich, England (which, much later, was universally accepted as 0 degrees longitude) issued the Mariner's Almanac, a volume of tables that abbreviated the calculations but diluted their accuracy.

Not until the invention of the "chronometer," a highly accurate clock undisturbed by the ocean's rough handling of it, was longitude mastered. Set at the beginning of a voyage at Greenwich time, the chronometer told a navigator, wherever in the world he was, what the time was at 0 degrees longitude. He compared that with the time aboard ship (determined from the position of the sun), and thus, with simple arithmetic done in a few minutes, he established his ship's longitude.

Many of those who emigrated to Virginia were far from destitute. They were the offspring of established merchant and artisan families, of the landowning yeomanry and gentry, and some, like Berkeley himself, were from noble families. Out of favor in Cromwell's England, they had good reason to remove to the end of the world and—they brought money with which to acquire and expand Tidewater lands, and to buy servants and slaves to work their fields. Many were educated; Berkeley had a university degree. They were genteel, on the well-mannered side; and they often had "connections" back home.

In recruiting such settlers, Governor Berkeley was doing something new in the colonies: seeking people to buy large parcels of land (Berkeley had plenty to sell) rather than people to labor. (There were also plenty of poor people who came as servants during the mid-1600s.) Berkeley favored the distressed cavaliers and organized them into a clique that maintained him in power. Berkeley himself became quite rich in land and servants, and not just in Virginia: he was one of the lords proprietors of North Carolina. If the governor slipped into corruption (by our definition of the word), he was also constructive. Under his sometimes-dictatorial supervision, Virginia's population increased fivefold, from 8,000 to 40,000.

CONFLICT IN THE PIEDMONT

After 1670, Berkeley and his Tidewater cronies confronted a crisis that undid the once untouchable governor, rattled the planter elite, and when the crisis passed, left the great planters chronically in debt to English merchants, generation after generation.

In one way, the collapse of tobacco prices during the 1660s benefited the richest Tidewater planters. They increased their acreage by buying cheaply the small, marginal farms that were hit hardest by the tobacco depression. With Berkeley a leading participant, they compensated for their own loss of income from tobacco by investing in the fur and hide trade with the Indians to the west.

The trouble was that farmers bought out by Tidewater planters were moving west, along with recent immigrants to Virginia. Together they pushed into Indian lands in the "Piedmont," the foothills of the Appalachians where land was cheap. They were joined on the frontier by desperate hardscrabble dirt farmers, many of them freed servants. They were a rude and boisterous lot who dealt roughly with the Indians and suffered when the Indians retaliated. The settlers of the Piedmont demanded that Berkeley order a massive attack on the tribes and drive them away from white settlement. The Indians, notably the Susquehannock, who sold hides and furs to the Tidewater planters, complained about white incursions into their hunting grounds.

Berkeley devised a compromise. He began to build a line of nine defensive stockades on the headwaters of the main rivers. Each was to be manned by 50 soldiers, with a cavalry of 125 to patrol between the forts. Before the defensive line was completed, however, it was obvious it was not going to work. Indian marauders had no trouble slipping between the forts, raiding isolated white settlements, and disappearing. Moreover, like American frontiersmen for two centuries to come, Virginia's backcountry settlers did not think in terms of holding a line against the Indians. Ever increasing in numbers, they meant to clear the land they wanted of the natives.

BACON'S REBELLION

When the death toll of backcountry whites climbed to 300, with dozens of women and children kidnapped, the Piedmont settlers rebelled. Nathaniel Bacon, a recent immigrant and distressed cavalier of some means, set himself up as the commander of a force of 500 that decimated the Oconeechee tribe. The Oconeechee had not attacked any whites; indeed, the tribe had expressed interest in an alliance with the Virginians against the Susquehannock! No matter—they were Indians. Bacon crushed them and turned his army toward Jamestown.

Angry words in the streets led the governor to arrest Bacon as a rebel, but he soon released him when Bacon's frightening followers made it clear they were quite capable of laying the little town to waste. Bacon was shaken, and departed; but after an uneasy spell of stalemate, he returned to Jamestown with a larger force, blustered that he would hang the governor, and declared that he was in charge "by the consent of the people." Berkeley fled across the Chesapeake and sent a ship to England with the alarming story.

For several months, Nathaniel Bacon governed Virginia. Then, in October 1676, he fell ill and died at only 29. He must have been a charismatic figure. With Bacon gone, the rebels scattered into the forests. Berkeley returned with a squadron of three warships and 1,100 troops. Their commander signed treaties with the Indians, tacitly admitting that frontier whites were the cause of the violence. In the meantime, Berkeley rounded up and hanged several dozen of Bacon's men.

But the governor was finished. Charles II was disgusted by Berkeley's blunders and ruthlessness. He remarked that "the old fool has hanged more men in that naked country than I have done for the murder of my father." He fired Berkeley and recalled him to England where he died within a few months.

Ill feeling between Tidewater and Piedmont did not die. The Tidewater aristocracy continued to dominate Virginia's economy, government, and culture, and the people of the backcountry continued to resent them.

BIG SPENDERS

After 1700, the great planters of Virginia and Maryland cultivated a gracious style of life modeled after the life of the English country gentry. They copied as best they were able the manners, fashions, and quirks of English squires and their ladies. When tobacco was returning a decent price (never again was it the bonanza crop it had been), they built fine houses in the style of English manors and filled them with good English-made furniture. They stocked their cellars with port and Madeira, hock from the Rhineland, and claret from France, which they generously poured for one another at dinners, parties, balls, and simple visits that marked the origins of the famous "southern hospitality."

Some Tidewater families educated their sons at Oxford, Cambridge, or the Inns of Court—the law schools of England.

BACON'S REBELLION.

Nathaniel Bacon confronting Governor Berkeley. The artist's sympathies are obvious: Bacon is a dashing cavalier, as are his backup men. Berkeley and his cohorts are cringing, terrified. To this artist, Bacon was battling a tyrant. A Tidewater planter's pictorial interpretation of Bacon's Rebellion would more likely depict Bacon and his followers as a mob of frontier hooligans.

If they feared the effects of English miasmas on innocent American bodies (smallpox, a deadly scourge in Europe, did not spread so easily in rural America), they schooled their heirs at the College of William and Mary, founded at Williamsburg in 1693.

The grandeur of the great planters' social and cultural life must not be overstated. William Byrd of Westover (one of the richest of the Tidewater elite—he owned 179,000 acres when he died in 1744) was very well-educated and cultured; he preferred the high life in London to Virginia. When his first wife, Lucy Park, died, Byrd sailed to England to find the daughter of a wealthy nobleman to succeed her. When Byrd found just the lady and proposed, the bride he chose had an annual income equal to Byrd's entire fortune. Quite naturally, her father rejected Byrd as too poor for her. William Byrd looks like a duke in a portrait he commissioned in London. The fact was, even the grandest of tobacco planters was a poor relation among the English upper classes.

Like many poor relations with pretensions, Tidewater planters were constantly in debt. When profits from tobacco drooped, Virginians and Marylanders could not or would not break the habits of consumption they had cultivated. They continued their annual orders of luxuries from England. To pay the bill, they mortgaged future crops—at a discount, of course—to the merchants who took their tobacco and who were to deliver their goods. It was not unusual that, by the time the tobacco went into the ground in spring, the imports it was to pay for had already been purchased and, in the case of wine, consumed.

Planter debt gratified mercantilists. It meant yet more money in the form of interest and discounts flowing from colony to mother country. In time, chronic indebtedness would make anti-British rebels of practically the entire Tidewater aristocracy.

SOUTH CAROLINA

The social structure of South Carolina was similar to that of Virginia and Maryland: a small, wealthy, intermarried elite living on the labor of white servants and black slaves governed a struggling class of small farmers gone west into the foothills. The rhythms of life in South Carolina were, however, quite different from those in the Chesapeake. The cash crops were rice, some cotton, and by the mid-1700s, indigo, a plant that yielded a blue pigment for dying cloth.

Indigo was developed as a crop by Eliza Lucas Pinckney of Barbados, on her father's South Carolina plantation.

Rice and indigo nicely complemented one another. They required intensive labor at different seasons, so South Carolina's slaves produced wealth for their masters twelve months a year. However, because the marshy rice lands were breeding grounds for mosquitoes and mosquito-borne diseases—malaria and the dreaded yellow fever—the slaves and white overseers were left to be bitten, sicken, and die while South Carolina's planters lived in airy Charleston.

By congregating in a genuine city, South Carolina's elite was even more conscious of its privileged position, and more united in its determination to preserve it. No colony (or state) was dominated by so small a ruling aristocracy as ran South Carolina for more than 200 years.

NEW ENGLAND

The European populations of Virginia, Maryland, and New England were almost entirely English. (There was a sprinkling of Huguenots—French Protestants—in South Carolina.) However, whereas most of the distressed cavaliers of the Chesapeake came from the southern counties of the old country, New England Puritans were overwhelmingly from the East. The sharp distinction between the flat New England accent and the "southern drawl," already noticeable in the 1700s, reflect the distinct regional origins of southerners and New Englanders.

However, the culture and social structure peculiar to colonial New England was largely the product of the northern colonies' religious heritage—Puritanism—and New England's climate and the land itself.

GEOGRAPHY AND SOCIETY

The preeminent geographic facts of life in New England were the long, cold winters (which meant a short growing season) and the rocky character of the soil.

Winter and summer, temperatures in New England were 10 to 30 degrees cooler than they were in Virginia. The lethal diseases (tropical in origin) that plagued life in the South were less threatening in temperate New England; and some were unknown there. Consequently, New Englanders lived longer than southerners. Twice as many children in Massachusetts survived infancy than survived in Virginia. One result of this godsend was larger families and a more rapid natural increase in population. Indeed, colonial New England was the world's

A New England stone fence on a property line in New England. During the seventeenth century, farmers piled the stones they did not use in construction in piles "out of the way." They affirmed property lines by "walking" them in a group each year. In the eighteenth and nineteenth centuries, the indestructible stones were put to use as the picturesque fences we know today.

How Do You Deal with a Ten-Ton Boulder?

Clearing New England's soil of rocks was not simply a matter of hauling 50- and 100-pound stones to the edge of the woods. Granite boulders could weigh tons. Farmers let the largest outcroppings go, to become highlights of suburban landscaping today. Other big ones, definitely in the way, had to be broken up. Sledgehammers were useless. There was no dynamite and gunpowder was too expensive. The solution was water. Cracks in boulders were filled with water in winter. Falling temperatures froze the water into ice, which is greater in volume than water, and split the rocks or, at least, widened the crack for another go the next year.

Health Food

The staples of the New England diet were corn boiled into mush or baked into a crumbly bread; wheat bread (whole grain, of course); apples—raw, dried, baked in pies, or in the form of vinegar and cider; maple syrup or molasses for a sweetener; and large quantities of meat and fish.

In the late twentieth century, when health food devotees discovered that colonial New Englanders had a life expectancy exceeding that of any other people of their era, they fastened on the whole grains, apples and vinegar, and unrefined sweeteners as the secret (while overlooking New England's large meat consumption). One of the countless "miracle" diets of the era was based on Puritan grub.

first society in which it was commonplace for people to have personally known their grandparents.

In its soil, New England was less fortunate. Geologically, the entire region is a glacial moraine. It was there that the continental glaciers of the last ice age halted their advance. When they receded (melted) they left behind the rocks and gravel they had scooped from the earth on their journey from the Arctic.

Before New England's farmers could plow effectively, they had to clear rocks by the thousands from their fields, breaking up the large boulders, and hauling off what were not needed for construction to wasteland or, in time, to stack them in the stone fences that are so picturesque to those of us who did not have to build them. This back-wrenching toil went on for generations, for each winter's freeze heaved more rocks to the surface.

The intensive labor required to clear the land reinforced the Puritans' commitment to a society of small, family farms. The demanding New England countryside produced a variety of foods so the population of the closely regulated townships was fairly dense. But there were no grand plantations in New England. A household might well take in a servant or two—usually the adolescent children of relatives or neighbors; and there were African slaves, most of them domestic servants, in every sizeable New England town. But the small size of farms meant that families grew enough food to feed themselves and, at most, a small surplus to sell in the towns. Quite unlike Marylanders and Virginians, no New Englanders grew rich farming.

THE NEED FOR COIN

The crops New Englanders produced in no plenitude were much the same as those that the mother country grew—grain, squash, beans, orchard nuts, apples, livestock. So English mercantilists looked at New England with less interest than they looked at the South.

Indeed, the mother country's merchants, shipbuilders, and fishermen found competitors in New England. Boston was sending ships down the ways before 1640. The shipwright's craft flourished in every town with a harbor. Whaling, a

calling New Englanders would come to dominate, began as early as 1649. Nantucket and New Bedford, Massachusetts became synonymous with whalers. Fishermen sailed out of Portsmouth, Marblehead, New London, and dozens of other ports to harvest more than their share of the codfish of the North Atlantic. It was a short trip from New England to the Grand Banks of Newfoundland, the world's richest fishery, compared to the transatlantic voyage European fishermen had to make. New Englanders undersold European fishermen in European markets.

As for commerce, by 1700 the label "Yankee trader" conjured up the image of a shrewd businessman not quite to be trusted. Newport, Rhode Island, was a center of the African slave trade, another profitable business the English would have preferred to reserve for themselves.

New Englanders had no choice but to compete with the mother country. It took money—gold and silver—to purchase English manufactures. With no cash crop like tobacco or rice, whaling, fishing, and trade were the obvious solutions to the colonies' balance of payments problem.

YANKEE TRADERS

Where did New England merchants sail? By the time of the American Revolution, just about everywhere in the world, even China. The term *Yankee trader* was universally known to signify a shrewd deal-maker, even one who was not above chicanery.

During the 1600s and early 1700s, however, the New Englanders were Atlantic traders. There were several triangular routes, voyages of three legs, which their ships regularly plied—at least in part. They carried rum distilled in New England to west Africa, traded it for captives, and transported them to the West Indies (usually to Barbados or Jamaica, but illegally to Cuba and French Guadeloupe and Martinique) where they were exchanged for sugar, or molasses—a saleable commodity back home and the raw material from which rum was made.

Or a New Englander carried provisions from the middle colonies—wheat and livestock, plentiful in New York and Pennsylvania—to the West Indies where just about all

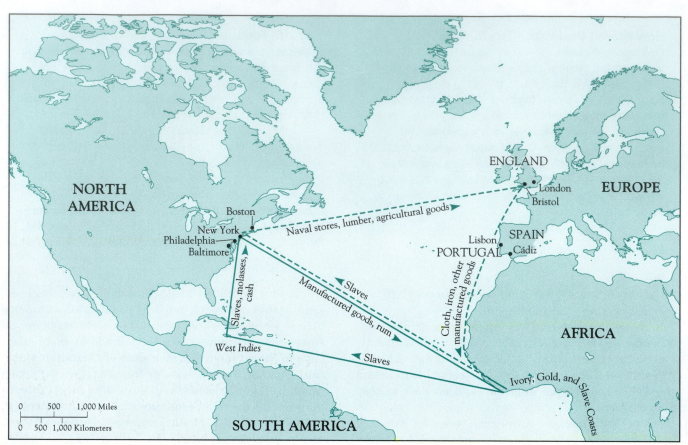

MAP 4:2 Two Triangular Trade Routes
Not every British and colonial ship plied one of those "triangles" regularly. Seafaring merchants were opportunists, taking on profitable cargos (and destinations) that presented themselves. But much of the colonial trade flowed in these three-legged patterns.

foodstuffs except garden produce had to be imported. West Indian sugar and molasses were carried to England; and English manufactures—from cloth and tools to luxuries—were transported back home.

Other merchants carried Maryland and Virginia tobacco to England; manufactures to the West Indies; and West Indian slaves, mostly of African birth, to South Carolina, Virginia, and Maryland. Before 1700, very few enslaved blacks came directly from Africa to the North American colonies. Even after 1700, most slaves sold in North America spent sometime in Barbados or Jamaica where they were "seasoned," that is, restored to something resembling health and fitness after their harrowing voyage across the Atlantic.

Most New England merchant vessels never crossed the Atlantic. They were "coasters," smaller sloops and schooners that transported whatever wanted moving from one colonial port to another: Portsmouth, Boston, Newport, New Haven, New York, Philadelphia, Charleston, and dozens of small towns with an anchorage. Long distance overland travel was difficult for a man or woman on horseback until nearly the end of the colonial era. Shipping freight overland was unheard of—everything moved on water.

In a word, New England merchants were themselves mercantilists. They competed with the English, carrying the same goods on the same routes. Unsurprisingly, British mercantilists looked on New England with, at best, indifference. The northernmost colonies produced nothing profitable; New England merchants competed with the traders of the mother country.

AN INDEPENDENT SPIRIT

Indeed, the charters of Plymouth, Massachusetts, Rhode Island, and Connecticut gave those colonies such extensive powers of self-government that they functioned much like independent commonwealths. New Englanders (most of them) drank toasts to the king. A few of the grandchildren of the Puritans still entertained the fiction that they were members of the Church of England. But these were little more than pieties during a century when two English kings were dethroned, one of them decapitated, and when it often took two months for a message from the mother country to reach her daughters.

During the decade Oliver Cromwell ruled England, the New England colonies ignored almost every directive he issued. In 1652, Massachusetts minted its own coin, the "Pine Tree Shilling," thereby assuming a right reserved to sovereigns since antiquity. Nor did Massachusetts retreat when Charles II became king in 1660. Indeed, the colony continued to strike the shilling after Charles II was crowned. Charles was forced to go to court, suing to have the Massachusetts charter revoked. In 1684, he won his case.

THE DOMINION OF NEW ENGLAND

The next year, the new king, James II, combined all the New England colonies into a single Dominion of New England. (New York and New Jersey were later added.) He abolished local assemblies and endowed his governor, Sir Edmund Andros, with a viceroy's powers. Andros had some success in New York but he never had a prayer in New England. James II, unpopular at home because he was Roman Catholic, was forced in 1688 to flee from England, replaced on the throne by joint monarchs, William and Mary. Mary was James II's Protestant daughter; her husband, William, the military leader of the Dutch.

The news of the overthrow of James II inspired popular uprisings in several colonies. In Maryland, John Coode seized power from the Catholic proprietors whom Coode assumed had fled with James II. In New York, a German named Jacob Leisler gained control of the city, claiming that, in the name of the new sovereigns, William and Mary, he was ridding New York of "Popish Doggs & Divells." In New England, the merchant elite, never truly subservient to Andros, simply resumed acting as it always had—independently. Prudently, Andros put to sea.

However, the Calverts of Maryland had played safe; they never committed to James II. When the dust settled, they regained their proprietary rights. In New York, Leisler, giddy with power, ordered a volley fired at newly arrived troops who really did act for William and Mary. He and an aide were sentenced to be "hanged by the Neck and being Alive their bodies be Cutt Downe to the Earth that their Bowells be taken out." On second thought, the judge decided that hanging would be enough.

As for the Dominion of New England, William and Mary knew better than to revive it. Colonial opposition had been too emphatic for that. They restored the charters of Connecticut and Rhode Island (where there had been little tumult) but, with a court's decision on their side, the king and queen had no intention of allowing Massachusetts to return to its independent ways. In 1691, they combined

Plymouth and Massachusetts into one royal colony. After 1691, the governor of the Bay Colony was no longer elected. He was appointed by the Crown, as were the governors of New Hampshire, Virginia, New York, and the Carolinas.

This was no easy pill for latter-day Puritans to swallow. Their forebears had been divinely mandated to govern Massachusetts as a godly commonwealth. That God should allow the Crown to take their "city on a hill" from them was a profound punishment calling for anguished prayer and soul-searching.

WITCHCRAFT

Puritan soul-searching when the entire community suffered God's anger focused on vile sins that the community was not punishing. Some believed they had identified that sin when two pubescent girls in Salem Village, a kind of suburb of the town of Salem, were seized in fits of screaming and crawling about making odd throaty sounds. Their physician found no earthly affliction and reckoned that the girls were being tortured by Satan's servants: witches. The girls confirmed his diagnosis.

Few laughed at the suggestion of witchcraft, and no one with any sense laughed in public. Most Europeans and Americans believed that individuals could acquire supernatural powers (like the torture of little girls) by promising to serve Satan, a bargain almost always sealed by having sexual intercourse with him. (Or, for men, with satanic spirits called succubi.) It was a serious business. Witchcraft was a capital crime; the Bible said, "Thou shalt not suffer a witch to live." Since the Reformation, tens of thousands of Europeans had been executed for witchcraft. In the 1640s in East Anglia, the heartland of the Massachusetts emigration, as many as 200 witches were executed. Several people had been hanged as witches in the colonies; one in Boston in 1691.

Just what set off the girls who started the witchcraft hysteria in Salem in 1692 cannot be known for certain. It may have been the spooky tales told to them by a West Indian

Courtesy Peabody Essex Museum, Salem, Massachusetts

A veiled woman (or girl) accuses a young woman of witchcraft. This victim of the Salem hysteria has better prospects than most of those who were fingered. She lives in a substantial house and has a male defender. Most of the women hanged at Salem were poor and friendless, easy targets.

slave, Tituba, in the home of the Reverend Samuel Parish. In any case, finding themselves the center of attention, the girls began to accuse other villagers of bewitching them. Their targets could not have been better chosen for vulnerability by a committee of sociologists. Most were women, as were almost all the accusers. Some of the victims were eccentrics (conformist New England still looked askance at eccentricity); others unpopular in the village for good reason and bad; several were loners without friends to defend them. Only a few of the accused women had husbands or adult sons— freeholder voters— to speak up on their behalf. Tituba was a slave, easy pickings (although, in the end, she was not hanged). Another Salem witch was an impoverished hag who may have been senile; yet another was deaf and probably never fully understood the charges against her. An 88-year-old male witch was notorious as a crank and, in his younger years, an unabashed open adulterer.

Accusers and accusations multiplied. Of some 130 people who were fingered as witches, 114 were charged. Of those who were found guilty, 19 were hanged. Although some of Massachusetts's most distinguished men were caught up in the hysteria, including Judge Samuel Sewall and the eminent

minister, Cotton Mather, the authorities called a halt to the frenzy when people of their own eminence (notably the wife of the governor) were named as witches. Of the 19 souls executed, only one was a male of respectable social station.

THE MIDDLE COLONIES

William Penn did not believe in witchcraft. When, during the Salem hysteria, he was asked if there might not be witches in Pennsylvania too, he replied that settlers were free to fly about on broomsticks in his colony. The liberality of the middle colonies—religious tolerance first and foremost— was rooted in Quaker principles in Pennsylvania, New Jersey, and Delaware. In New York it was the consequence of a population too diverse for regimentation.

Liberality and an abundance of good, cheap land made the middle colonies the preferred destination of immigrants who were able to pay the transatlantic fare, and even of the poor, who had to sign on as servants. Just two years after Penn selected the site of Philadelphia, it was a city of 300 houses and 2,500 people. When Pennsylvania was twenty years old, its population was the third largest in the colonies. Philadelphia was never the "greene countrie towne" Penn had envisioned, every house having "room enough for House, Garden and small Orchard." Laid out on a tidy gridiron (Philadelphia and Charleston were America's first "planned cities"), it was quite compact. New York City, contained behind a wall (present-day Wall Street) out of fear of Indians, was even more densely populated.

BALANCED ECONOMIES

The growing season in the middle colonies was one to two months longer than it was in New England. The soils in the alluvial valleys of the Hudson, Delaware, Schuylkill, and Susquehanna Rivers were rich and deep (and without glacial rocks). Outside Philadelphia the soil was mildly alkaline, enriched by eroded limestone; it was perfect for growing wheat. Almost from the start, middle colony farmers produced a surplus they could sell. Because individual landholdings were much larger than the New England colonies apportioned to families, all but the poorest middle colony farmers could pasture more animals than they needed for their own meat—something else to sell. Most farmers, on however small a scale, were commercial, not subsistence farmers. Pennsylvania's surpluses were so great it was called the "breadbasket of the colonies."

There were great estates along New York's Hudson River. With, eventually, more than a million acres and tens of thousands of tenants, the famous Renssaelerwyck put the largest Tidewater plantations to shame. But there were few such agribusinesses in New Jersey and Pennsylvania. It was the proprietors' policy in the Quaker colonies to sell lands in family-size parcels. Those farmers who made some money took in servants to improve their productivity or purchased slaves. Indeed, New York, New Jersey, and Delaware had large African and African-American populations. But families owning dozens of slaves, common in the South, were rare. The common pattern was for a well-off but still working farm family to own two, four, maybe six slaves, often a family—the adult men working the fields, the women and girls helping to run the home.

Middle colony farmers did not themselves export their grain, cattle, hogs, and horses, as Tidewater planters exported their tobacco. They sold to "middlemen," merchants in New York and Philadelphia who had markets overseas, largely in the sugar islands of the West Indies. The wealthiest merchants—intermarried Dutch and English families in New York, Quakers in Philadelphia—dominated the colonial assemblies and sat in the governors' councils. Farmers were not without political power; they voted. But the merchant aristocracy of the cities, allied with the governors, ensured that farmers were underrepresented in the assemblies. Until the 1750s, between 70 and 80 percent of Pennsylvania's assemblymen were Quakers, most from Philadelphia.

DIVERSE POPULATIONS

New Jersey and Pennsylvania (including Delaware until 1701) officially tolerated all religious denominations. In New York, the Church of England and the Dutch Reformed Church were established; members had privileges not shared by others. However, other laws proscribing other forms of worship were ignored except, for example, when anti-Catholic feelings boiled over (and Catholics were few). Indeed, a Roman Catholic, Thomas Dongan, was briefly governor of the colony. A Jewish synagogue founded under Dutch rule continued to function unmolested under the English. A visiting Virginian marveled that New Yorkers "seem not concerned what religion their neighbor is, or whether hee hath any or none."

The populations of New England and the South (always excepting black slaves) were ethnically homogenous. Almost all white people were of English ancestry. This was not so in the middle colonies; their populations were diverse from the beginning. The Dutch were a large minority in New York. Outside of Manhattan, they clustered in Dutch Villages, preserving their language and customs. Even in the city, most Dutch married among themselves. However, the upper classes freely intermarried with upper-class English and often became members of the Church of England.

The city of New York was, even in colonial times, an ethnic jumble of whites and blacks (many of them free), people of mixed European and African blood, and pockets of just about every Western European people. Isaac Jogues, a French priest passing through the city, heard eighteen languages spoken on New York's streets.

There were numerous Dutch, Swedes, and Finns in New Jersey, Delaware, and Pennsylvania before the English colonies were chartered. William Penn advertised for immigrants in the German and Swiss states along the war-torn Rhine River. The first to respond belonged to persecuted religious sects known as "Anabaptists," a name they did not like, or "Mennonites," which they accepted. Like the Quakers, they were pacifists. They wanted to farm and developed the rich rolling land west of Philadelphia into model farms. Some of their descendants, still observing some seventeenth-century customs, are the "Pennsylvania Dutch." Other Germans (Lutherans and Catholics) founded Germantown, now a neighborhood of modern Philadelphia.

FURTHER READING

General D. W. Meinig, Atlantic America 1492–1800, vol. I of *The Shaping of America: A Geographical Perspective on 500 Years of History,* 1986; Daniel Boorstin, *The Americans: The Colonial Experience,* 1958; Jack P. Greene and J. R. Pole, eds., *Colonial British America,* 1984; Alan Taylor, *American Colonies,* 2001; Jack P. Greene, *Pursuits of Happiness: The Social Development of Early Modern British Colonies and the Formation of American Culture,* 1988; John J. McCusker and Russell Menard, *The Economy of British North America,* 1985; David Hackett Fisher, *Albion's Seed: Four British Folkways in America,* 1989.

Trade Ralph Davis, *The Rise of the Atlantic Economies*, 1973; Kenneth R. Andrews, *Trade, Plunder, and Settlement: Maritime Enterprise and the Genesis of the British Empire, 1480–1630*, 1984.

The Southern Colonies David L. Ammerman, ed., *The Chesapeake in the Seventeenth Century*, 1979; Gloria Main, *The Tobacco Colony: Life in Early Maryland, 1650–1719*, 1982; William S. Powell, *Colonial North Carolina*, 1973; Robert M. Weir, *Colonial South Carolina: A History*, 1983; Robert Orwell, *Masters, Slaves, and Subjects: The Culture of Power in the South Carolina Low Country*, 1998; Wilcomb E. Washburn, *The Governor and the Rebel*, 1957.

The Middle Colonies Gary Nash, *Quakers and Politics: Pennsylvania, 1681–1726*, 1971; James T. Lemon, *The Best Poor Man's Country: A Geographical Study of Early Southeastern Pennsylvania*, 1972; Richard and Mary Dunn, *The World of William Penn*, 1986; Michael Kammen, *Colonial New York*, 1975; Robert C. Ritchie, *The Duke's Province*, 1977; Joyce D. Goodfriend, *Before the Melting Pot: Society and Culture in Colonial New York City, 1664–1730*, 1992; Russell Shorto, *The Island at the Center of the World: The Epic Story of Dutch Manhattan*, 2004; Edwin G. Burrows and Mike Wallace, *Gotham: A History of New York City to 1898*, 1999; J. E. Pomfret, *The Province of*

East and West New Jersey, 1956; Brendan McConville, *These Daring Disturbers of the Public Peace: The Struggle For Property and Power in Early New Jersey*, 1999.

New England Bernard Bailyn, *The New England Merchants in the Seventeenth Century*, 1955; Stephen Foster, *The Long Argument: English Puritanism and New England Culture, 1570–1700*, 1991; Philip J. Greven Jr., *Four Generations: Population, Land, and Family in Colonial Andover, Massachusetts*, 1970; Howard S. Russell, *A Long, Deep Furrow: Three Centuries of Farming in New England*, 1976.

Witchcraft Marion G. Starkey, *The Devil in Massachusetts*, 1969; Paul Boyer and Stephen Nissenbaum, *Salem Possessed*, 1974; John Demos, *Entertaining Satan: Witchcraft and the Culture of Early New England*, 1982; Carol Karlsen, *The Devil in the Shape of a Woman*, 1987; Frances Hill, *The Salem Witch Trials*, 2000; Mary Beth Norton, *In the Devil's Snare: The Salem Witchcraft Crisis of 1692*, 2002.

Navigation Dana Sobel, *Longitude: The True Story of a Lone Genius Who Solved the Greatest Scientific Problem of His Time*, 1995.

KEY TERMS

The following terms are covered in this chapter and can also be found in the list of Key Terms at the back of the book.

cavaliers	**mercantilism**	**Sir William Berkeley**	**Tidewater**
enumerated articles	**Navigation Acts**		

ONLINE SOURCES GUIDE

Use this listing to find online documents, images, interactive maps, simulations, and other resources related to this chapter:

American History Resource Center
http://history.wadsworth.com

Selected Documents
Nathaniel Bacon's Declaration of the People
John Eliot's Brief Narrative, Progress of the Gospel among the Indians in New England
Jeremiah Dummer, A Defence of the New England Charters
John Wise's Argument for Local Government Authority

Selected Images
Depiction of Salem witch trials
Tobacco worker
Iroquois "savage" by a French artist

Simulations
Colonial Expansion (Choose an identity as an Aztec, Jamestown settler, or a Puritan in New England and make choices based on the circumstances and opportunities afforded.)

Document Exercises
1676 Bacon's Declaration

Interactive Timeline (with online readings)
English Legacies, American Facts of Life: Colonial Society in the 1600s

Additional resources, exercises, and Internet links related to this chapter are available on *THE AMERICAN PAST* **web site:** http://history.wadsworth.com/americanpast8e

Discovery

What difficulties did England encounter while governing its overseas empire? How did it respond to these problems?

In thinking about this question, begin by breaking it down into the components shown below. A discussion of the significance of each component should appear in your answer.

Economics and Technology: For this exercise, please read the following document excerpts, "Edward Randolph, 'Letters and Official Papers'" and "Jeremiah Dummer, 'A Defence of New England Charters.'" What problems did Randolph say that the colonists were causing the empire? How does this contrast with Dummer's view? Why did the English feel that it was important to control trade within its colonies? What had been the previous position of the English government? How do you think the change in regulations might have spurred colonial anger?

Edward Randolph, "Letters and Official Papers"

At last in the year 1681 His Matie confirmed me in that Office by a Commission under the Great Seal, which they did also invalidate by a Law made to that purpose, Directing the Officer of the Customs not to Act but by a Warrant from their Governor, and with the Assistance of a civill Officer, and by that shift, they kept up their illegall Trade untill the time that Mr Dudley was President, and Sr Ed-mond Andros afterwards made Governor of that Colony, Then severall Vessells from Scotland, Cadiz and Malaga & others from New-England, were Seized and Condemned in the Courts of Boston for trading irregularly, of which some were of considerable Value. This highly exasperated the Traders and Masters of Ships against me, for they taking advantage of the late tumult in Boston, I was seized upon and hurried to the common Goale by a Company of Ship Carpenters, Ship Chandlers and others whose Livelyhood depended upon the Sea, being thereto Impowered by those in the present Governmt whence I hardly escaped with my life, tho' soon after they set at liberty eight persons committed for murder and Piracy.

Jeremiah Dummer, "A Defence of New England Charters"

Invited and encourag'd by these Advantages, a considerable Number of Persons dissenting from the Discipline of the Establish'd Church, tho' agreeing with it in Doctrine, remov'd into those Remote Regions, upon no other View than to enjoy the Liberty of their Consciences without Hazard to themselves, or Offence to others. Thus the Colonies went on increasing and flourishing, in spite of all Difficulties, till the Year 1684, when the City of London lost its Charter, and most of the other Corporations in England, influenced by fear of Flattery, complimented King CHARLES with a Surrender of theirs. In this general Ruin of Charters at Home, it could not be expected that those in America should escape. It was then that a Quo Warranto was issu'd against the Governor and Company of the Massachusetts-Bay and soon after a judgment was given against them in Westminster Hall. At the same Time Sir Edmund Andross, then the King's Governour of New-England, did by Order from Court repair to Hartford, the Capital of Connecticut, with arm'd Attendants, and forcibly seiz'd their Charter for the King. Rhode-Island, finding there was no Remedy to be had, made a Vertue of Necessity and peaceably resign'd theirs. But as soon as the News arriv'd of the happy Revolution in England, these two last mention'd Governments re-assum'd their Charters, and put themselves under the old Form of Administration in which they have continu'd ever since. The Government of the Massachusetts, cautious of offending their Superiours at Home, and considering there was a Judgement against them in the Court of Chancery, tho' most unfairly and illegally obtain'd, did not think it adviseable to make this Step; but sent Agents to Court to supplicate, in a humble Manner the Restoration of their Charter. To what Mismanagement or other Cause it was owing, that they did not obtain it, and that this Loyal Corporation was the only one either in Old or New-England, that did not recover its lost Liberty under our late Glorious Deliverer King WILLIAM, 'tis now too late, and therefore to no Purpose, to enquire. A new Charter was order'd which the Province now has, and is not much more than the Shadow of the old One. For by these new Letters Patents, the Appointment of a Governour, Lieutenant-Governour, Secretary, and all the Officers of the Admiralty is vetted in the Crown. The Power of the Militia is wholly in the Hands of His Majesty's Governour, as Captain-General. All Judges, Justices, and Sheriffs, to whom the Execution of the Law is intrusted, are nominated by the Governour, with the Advice of His Majesty's Council. The Governour has a Negative upon the Choice of Councellors, which is both peremptory and unlimited: He is neither oblig'd to render a Reason, nor restrained to any Number. All Laws enacted by the General Assembly are to be sent Home for the Royal Approbation or Disallowance. There is, besides, one very comprehensive Article inserted in this Charter, that no Laws, Ordinances, Elections, or Acts of Government whatsoever, shall be of any Validity, without the Consent of the King's Governour signify'd in Writing.

To read extended versions of the documents, visit the companion Web site http://history.wadsworth.com/americanpast8e; click on "Discovery Sources."

CHAPTER 5

Other Americans

Colonial Indians and Africans

Roberta Wilson

Why will you take by force what you may obtain by love? Why will you destroy us who supply you with food? What can you get by war?

Chief Powhatan

Is it not enough that we are torn from our country and friends to toil for your luxury and lust of gain? Must every tender feeling be likewise sacrificed to your avarice?

Olaudah Equiano

Swedes, Finns, Dutch, Huguenots—all left marks on America that are visible today. As did two European ethnic groups that came to the colonies in great numbers after 1700: Germans and Scotch-Irish, and the French and Spanish on whom the expanding United States impressed its institutions. In time, however, their descendants were assimilated into a culture that was English in its essentials. The principles of American law were English. So were American political ideals and practices and, of course, the language of the country.

But Americans have never been exclusively European. There were Africans in Virginia in 1619 and on Manhattan Island in 1624. And then there were those people who had not come to the colonies from somewhere else, those for whom North America was the "Old World," the entire world before they knew that white and black people existed.

EASTERN WOODLANDS INDIANS

From the Atlantic to the Mississippi River, North America was forest. Seamen approaching the continent smelled the fragrance of pine days before they saw the land. There were gaps in the endless woods, natural openings, and prairies, some of them sizeable. Indians had cleared other large tracts of trees to create farmland or to improve hunting by encouraging the growth of the sun-loving grasses, berries, and shrubs on which moose, elk, deer, bear, and bison fed. There were park-like landscapes in New England that were man-made—oaks and maples towering over brushless ground providing clear bow and arrow shots at animals. Much of Virginia's Shenandoah Valley was a checkerboard of open land and groves. But, mostly, the eastern half of what is now the United States was forest.

Bow and Arrow

The bow and arrow is a sophisticated tool; it is astonishing that it was developed independently by so many of the world's peoples. The bows of most Eastern Woodlands Indians were made from a single piece of wood like the famous English longbow, but it was shorter: 5 feet was typical. Different tribes preferred different woods: hickory, ash, or elm. A few tribes made composite bows, laminating or binding animal sinews to willow for increased pull and resilience. Lethality at short range was important; accuracy at long distances was not. The Indians hunted and battled in forests; if a target was visible, it was rarely farther than 30 yards away.

And so, while climate varied radically between Maine and Spanish Florida, the economy of the "Eastern Woodlands Indians" (as anthropologists would later call them) was much the same for all.

HUNTERS

All eastern Indians hunted and fished. Men and adolescent boys using bows and stone-tipped arrows harvested meat for sustenance and furs and hides for clothing. They ranged as far from their villages as it took to feed their village for a few days, but not so far that they were unable to carry their kill home before it spoiled.

The extent of a tribe's hunting grounds was also limited by the proximity of neighbors. There were no "borders" between tribal territories in the European sense of the word. "They range rather than inhabite," a Virginian wrote. A Dutchman in New York elaborated: "wind, stream, bush, field, sea, beach, and riverside are open and free to everyone of every nation with which the Indians are not embroiled in open conflict." There was no concept of individuals or tribes owning land.

The Indians were, however, territorial, particularly because conflict between tribes was chronic. Hunting parties ran hunters from other tribes out of the neighborhood if they had the muscle. Hunting parties confident enough to intrude into other tribes' territories did so. The Wampanoag and Massachusetts Indians had been contesting hunting grounds with the Narragansett of Rhode Island long before the Puritans brought the concept of "this land is mine" to New England. And the Narragansett skirmished with the Pequot of Connecticut to their west who, in turn, contended with Mohican, Mohegan, and Mohawk to the west of their territory.

Most tribes fished using hooks, traps, and weirs (fixed nets) in creeks, rivers, and lakes. No eastern Indians were deep-sea sailors, but they harvested the rock-rimmed coves of New England and the tangle of saltwater inlets that run from New Jersey to Georgia. Indians on the Delaware and Chesapeake Bays netted crabs and gathered clams and oysters. In New England, even lobsters could be had in shallow waters.

FARMERS

Men cleared fields for farming by slash-and-burn, a technique well-suited to a world in which land was plentiful and labor scarce. They girdled the trees; that is, they stripped the trunk of bark and hacked a gash several inches into the exposed wood. This prevented the circulation of sap; the trees died. When the leaves fell, admitting sunlight, the underbrush was burned.

That was it so far as the men were concerned. Indian women were the farmers. (And the gatherers; seasonally they collected fruits, berries, nuts, and roots.) In the ghost forests slash-and-burn created—the lifeless tree trunks stood for years—the women planted maize ("Indian corn"), squash of uncountable varieties, climbing beans, melons, cabbages, gourds for vessels, and, almost universally, tobacco. Maize, beans, and squash were the staples. The **Iroquois** called them the "three sisters" because they were planted together in mounds. The corn stalks served as poles for the climbing beans; the large leaves of the squash plants acted as mulch, stifling weeds and preserving moisture.

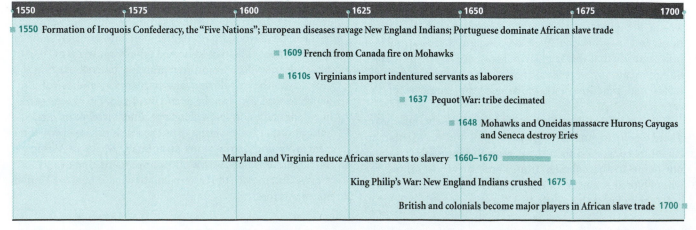

Indians and Africans in Early Colonial History 1550–1700

| 1550 | 1575 | 1600 | 1625 | 1650 | 1675 | 1700 |

1550 Formation of Iroquois Confederacy, the "Five Nations"; European diseases ravage New England Indians; Portuguese dominate African slave trade

1609 French from Canada fire on Mohawks

1610s Virginians import indentured servants as laborers

1637 Pequot War: tribe decimated

1648 Mohawks and Oneidas massacre Hurons; Cayugas and Seneca destroy Eries

Maryland and Virginia reduce African servants to slavery **1660–1670**

King Philip's War: New England Indians crushed **1675**

British and colonials become major players in African slave trade **1700**

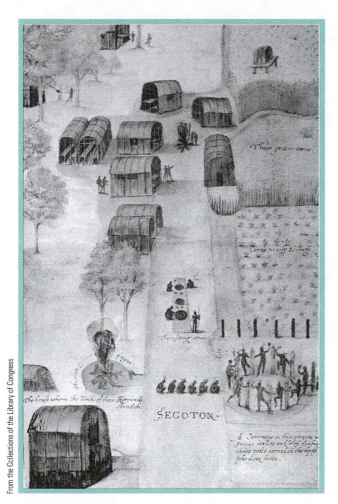

From the Collections of the Library of Congress

This watercolor of the village of Secotan in North Carolina was painted by John White in 1585. It shows an orderly society and the fact that the inhabitants planted at least two crops of corn each year in order to extend their food supply. If hostile tribes visited often, villages were surrounded with palisades: upright logs planted in the ground to form a wall.

growers. Many other tribes, however, neglected agriculture, loading their women with other chores. (A squaw's work—*squaw* was the colonists' rendition of the **Algonkian** word for woman—was literally never done.) The corn ran out so regularly in Virginia that Powhatan women regarded digging for tuckahoe (an edible root) as an annual chore. (They hated it—the work was cold and wet.)

John Smith observed that the Powhatan gorged and fattened up in the fall and were scrawny by spring. (As were those among Smith's Jamestowners who were still alive.) Analyses of bones in the graveyards of pre-colonial New England show a high incidence of malnutrition and anemia. Indians living along the St. Lawrence River were familiar with scurvy, a vitamin C deficiency. When the first French explorers there sickened with the disease, Indians showed them a cure—a spruce tea. Fear of famine explains why, unlike in Mesoamerica, Eastern Woodlands communities were small. The Powhatan gathered in camps of a thousand in the late summer, but broke up into small, scattered villages as winter descended.

Colonists often described the Indians as nomads. They were not; no eastern peoples were full-time wanderers. Seminomadic (a term seventeenth-century English did not have) is more accurate. The woodlands tribes relocated their villages every several years when the men had over-hunted the range, the women had exhausted the soil, or when everyone was sick and tired of the lice and filth that had accumulated.

LANGUAGE

Languages were more numerous in North America than in Europe. In the Eastern Woodlands, however, every tribe's language fell into one of four "linguistic families." That is, within each family, the languages had evolved from a single root language just as Spanish, French, and Italian evolved from the Latin. Siouan and **Muskogean**-speaking peoples were found mostly in the southern interior. However, just about every tribe with which the early English colonists interacted spoke an Algonkian or Iroquoian language.

The first Native American words the settlers of Virginia and New England heard spoken were Algonkian: Powhatan in Virginia, Wampanoag in Massachusetts. Other Algonkian-speaking tribes were the Mohegan, Massachusetts,

Maize and beans, kept dry, lasted a year. With meat supply often problematical, avoiding springtime hunger depended on a village's store of corn. The Mohawk of New York maintained vast fields and corn reserves; they were large-scale

Sustained Yield

Not long after the founding of Massachusetts Bay, a Narragansett sachem, Miantomi, lamented: "Our fathers had plenty of deer and skins, our plains were full of deer, as also our woods, and of turkeys. . . . But these English have gotten our land, they with scythes cut down the grass, and with axes fell the trees, . . . and their hogs spoil our clam beds, and we shall all be starved."

Miantomi was one of the first Indians who understood that it was the different use to which the colonists put land that destroyed the Indian way of life. It was not, as some have said, that Indians lovingly preserved nature: the Miami of the Ohio Valley thought nothing of starting uncontrollable forest fires just to drive a few hundred bison to a killing field. Still, some Indians were explicitly conscious of

the need to maintain, by human restraint, the game that provided their food. The Choctaw of Mississippi monitored the number of deer they killed each year. When the herd was reduced to the minimum size necessary to sustain its numbers, they forbade further hunting. Better a season of scarcity than unsolvable starvation two years on.

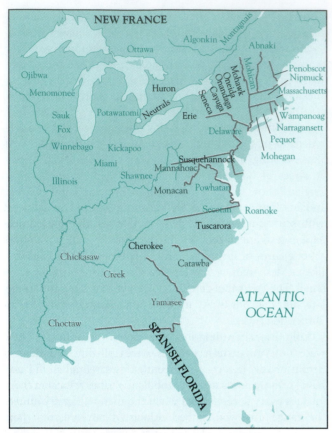

NEW FRANCE

MAP 5:1 Eastern Woodlands Indians During the Colonial Era

Every eastern tribe, often every band within a tribe, was effectively independent. The numerous Creek towns periodically formed confederations but they were unstable and did not last long. In 1607, most Chesapeake Indian villages acknowledged Powhatan as "Paramount Chief," but that coalition too was shaky with outlying villages ever restive. Only the Five Nations—the Iroquois Confederacy—of New York, founded about 1550, preserved political unity.

Narragansett, Abnaki, and Pequot in New England; the Mahican and Lenni-Lenape (Delaware) in the middle colonies; and south of the Great Lakes, the Miami, Shawnee, Potowatomi, Illinois, Kickapoo, Fox, Sauk, and Chippewa (Ojibwa). Quite a few Algonkian words and place names are now fixtures of American English: hickory, hominy,

moccasin, succotash, tomahawk, totem, and wigwam; Massachusetts, Connecticut, and Chesapeake.

By no means could all Algonkian speakers understand one another, anymore than a Sicilian can understand a Parisian. The greater the distance between two tribes, the further back in time their common ancestors, the greater the differences between their languages. Neighboring Algonkian tribes like the Wampanoag and Massachusetts conversed easily, but in one corner of North Carolina, several small tribes that had resided within ten miles of one another for a century could trade (or squabble) only by means of sign language.

One of the largest southern tribes, the Cherokee, spoke an Iroquoian language, as did the Tuscarora of North Carolina. Most Iroquoian speakers lived farther north: the Susquehannock in Virginia; the Erie south of Lake Erie; and the Seneca, Cayuga, Onandaga, Oneida, and Mohawk tribes of New York.

WARFARE

Two tribes having a mutually beneficial trade (or a frightening common enemy) might be allies for decades. Wariness of outsiders, however, is the essence of tribal culture. Whereas most eastern peoples' name for themselves translates as something like "the human beings," they called other tribes "the things" or worse: "bloodsuckers" or "man-eaters."

Warfare was chronic in the world of the Indians because males aspired, above all else, to bravery. An individual's reputation for courage was the key to his status in the tribe. Consequently, when a gang of young men on a hunt happened on young men from another tribe, reckless belligerence was common. A New Englander who lived among Indians wrote that they battled as if "for a pastime."

Oral tradition told of massacres of whole villages, but wholesale bloodshed on the European model was not typical of Indian warfare. Neither their military technology nor the object of wars nor the Indians' manner of battle was adapted to mass slaughter. Their weapons were made of wood and stone, which meant fighting at close quarters. Palisaded villages—surrounded by a wall of upright logs—were usually secure against such "low-tech" assaults. And bravery meant fighting boldly, not necessarily killing enemies and certainly not splitting a baby's head open with a tomahawk. The object of planned assaults was stealing corn or meat or seizing women and children to adopt.

What's in a Name?
The name many Indian tribes gave themselves translates as "the people" or "the human beings." Tribes usually referred to other Indians in unflattering terms. "The other things" was mild. More common were insults like "Mohawk," which is Narragansett for "blood sucker"; "Sioux" is Chippewa for "snake." Curiously, the colonists adopted the insulting name as often as the name by which peoples called themselves.

Sometimes the colonists gave tribes an entirely irrelevant European name that stuck. They called the Lenni-Lenape "Delawares" because their heartland bordered the river the English called the Delaware. The tribe, soon pushed to the Ohio River valley, adopted it. A Canadian Iroquois band that refused to ally with either the French or the English became known as "Neutrals" and they adopted the name.

Finally, Indian warriors did not, like Europeans, fight as a trained, coordinated, disciplined unit. They ambushed enemies, and battled one on one in chaotic mêlées. When things got too hot, they fled. Roger Williams said, "the Indians' Warres are far less bloudy and devouring than the cruell warres of Europe." When, in 1637, soldiers from Massachusetts and Connecticut shot down Pequot Indians who were attempting to flee their burning village, the New Englanders' Narragansett allies, incredulous and perhaps disgusted (the battle was won; it was over!) shouted at them to stop.

THE IROQUOIS CONFEDERACY

The most powerful eastern Indians were the five "Iroquois Nations" (known as the Iroquois Confederacy) that occupied most of what is now upstate New York. Until about 1550, the Seneca, Cayuga, Onandaga, Oneida, and Mohawk fought as fiercely among themselves as other tribes. They were notorious for torturing the prisoners they took.

Torture, like farming, was woman's work. Captives were forced to "run the gauntlet"—to race between two lines of shrieking women swinging clubs and thrusting with spears. From among the survivors, the women selected those they would adopt into their clans (subdivisions of the tribe that shared the same longhouse). The leftovers were tied to trees and slowly roasted by small fires built at their feet, skinned, dismembered finger by finger and limb by limb, and blinded with firebrands—not necessarily in that order. When a victim passed out, torture was suspended until he regained consciousness. The fun was in the captive's agony, not his death.

About 1550, a visionary known to history as **Hiawatha** set out to end this cycle among the five tribes. He traveled tirelessly from one nation to another preaching the advantages of cooperation. Astonishingly, Hiawatha succeeded. All five tribes retained their independence—their sovereignty in Europeans' terms. Each tribe governed itself and was free to make war on tribes outside the confederation without consulting the others.

However, the leaders of the **Five Nations** vowed not to make war on one another. Inevitable disputes—if, for example, a Seneca killed a Cayuga—were resolved without further bloodshed at an annual meeting of delegates from all five tribes at the chief town of the Onandaga, the central-most of the Nations. It worked. Hiawatha's confederation kept the peace among the New York Iroquois for more than two centuries.

EMPOWERED WOMEN

A tribe's delegates at the annual meetings were men who were selected by women. Indeed, among the Iroquois, women, not men, owned property. Descent was matrilineal, traced from mother to daughter, not from father to son as among Europeans. Women governed the clans, for they were the only permanent clan members. When a couple married, the groom left his mother's longhouse and moved to his wife's house. He became a member of her clan, socializing, hunting, wandering, and warring alongside his wife's unmarried brothers and her sisters' and cousins' husbands. If his wife tired of him, divorce was easy—he moved out of his ex-wife's longhouse and returned to his mother's house. The children stayed.

Iroquois social stability depended on matrilineal clans. The Iroquois had a lackadaisical attitude about who had sexual relations with whom. The paternity of a child, therefore, could not be reliably known. So, father–son relationships counted for little—clan membership counted for a lot.

Iroquois women also held extensive political power within tribes because Iroquois men were endlessly on the move. With their own towns secure from attack thanks to the confederation, the young men could range aggressively far into the hunting grounds of other tribes, usually itching for a fight.

A momentous fight occurred in 1609. About 200 Mohawk on Lake Champlain stumbled on a party of Montaignais and Huron from the north, accompanied by a few oddly dressed white men. They were French from newly founded Quebec; the governor of the colony (and namesake of the lake), Samuel de Champlain, was one of them. When the Mohawk

Roberta Wilson

The Iroquois longhouse (this one is Mohawk) was a unique Indian residence that reflected the clan structure of Iroquois tribes. Many families of the same clan—all related to one another through women: mothers, daughters, and sisters—lived in "apartments" separated by partitions (not very private) on both sides of an aisle. Such intimate living arrangements reinforced the solidarity of the women of the clan. Husbands were from other clans, to avoid inbreeding, and lived with their wives unless there was a divorce, which was common and usually initiated by the wife. If there was a divorce, the man returned to his mother's longhouse and to membership in her clan.

advanced, Champlain and two others opened fire with arquebuses (matchlock muskets). Loaded with shrapnel, each shot felled several Mohawk. Bewildered and terrified (it was their introduction to firearms), the survivors fled. They would have their revenge on more than one occasion, including the Huron massacre of 1648.

A WORLD TURNED UPSIDE DOWN

Battling with strangers was nothing new to the Indians, but the diseases the white people brought with them were. As early as 1550, European fishermen holed up for the winter on

New England shores, trading and carousing with the coastal tribes. (It was in such a camp that Samoset of Plymouth learned to speak English.) The fishermen infected the natives with highly contagious Old World diseases to which they had little resistance: diphtheria, cholera, and typhus at first—later measles, smallpox, and others. (Africans would introduce plasmodium malaria and yellow fever.) Infected coastland Indians, in turn, spread the new sicknesses to inland tribes that had never seen a white man. The Indian population of Massachusetts may have been 80,000 in 1550. There were no more than 40,000 when the Pilgrims arrived at Plymouth.

SEPARATE SPHERES

Except in the devastation both suffered from Old World disease, the experience of the Indians who were confronted by the English was quite unlike that of Native Americans who lived in lands the Spanish conquered. First of all, there were not so many of them; about 150,000 Indians lived in the parts of North America the English penetrated during the 1600s. More Aztecs lived on the shores of Lake Texcoco. Nevertheless, the English had a more difficult time dominating the Indians than the Spanish did. This was, in part, because English colonization was not primarily military as Spanish colonization was. The English were uninterested in conquering the Indians and living among them as rulers. They meant to clear the land they wanted of Indians, and live apart from them.

The sexual ratio among the English made segregation by race plausible. The Spanish conquerors of Santo Domingo, Cuba, Mexico, and Peru were soldiers—all males; decades passed before more than a handful of Spanish women came to America. But, except for Virginia and Maryland, families and English women looking for husbands settled the English colonies. Men did not look to the tribes for wives and mistresses to the extent the conquistadors did. They married "their own kind." One scholar has identified only three Indian–white marriages in Virginia during the colony's first century, including John Rolfe and Pocahontas!

There was plenty of nonmarital miscegenation, of course: English–Indian, English–African, and African–Indian. But because it was not difficult for an Englishman to find a white wife, it was easy to look down on interracial couplings, to associate it with low-life whites, and to consign "half-breed" offspring to the Indians and blacks. English culture was not intrinsically more racist than Spanish culture. But colonial Americans were, from early on, able to make more of race than the Spanish were, and they did.

THE INDIANS AND CHRISTIANITY

Like the Spanish (and French in Canada), the first colonists meant to convert the Indians to true religion—Protestant Christianity in their case. Looking into the Bible to explain who the natives were, the Puritans concluded that they were descendants of the "ten lost tribes of Israel" whom they would win "to the knowledge and obedience of the true God and Saviour of Mankind." The great seal of Massachusetts depicted an Indian pleading "Come over and help us."

However, creating a replica of England—where there were no Indians—was much more important to Puritans than Indian souls. A few ministers, most famously John Eliot, "the Apostle to the Indians," devoted their lives to saving Indians. But John Cotton, the most prestigious preacher in Massachusetts, better represented the colonial mind when he called the Indians "children of Satan who should be blasted in all their green groves and arbours."

Few Indians converted to Puritan Protestantism. In 1675, after a half century of English presence, there were only thirteen villages of "praying Indians" in all of New England. By way of contrast, Spanish priests commonly converted just about all the Indians in a region to Roman Catholicism within decades. Why such a difference?

It was a central tenet of Roman Catholicism that every human being, saint and sinner alike, should belong to the Church. ("Catholic" means "universal.") The Puritans believed that only a minority of their own people was saved. It was not easy to convince Indians to embrace the belief that just about all of them were damned to hell's fire.

Over a millennium, Catholic missionaries had preached to peoples of a hundred diverse cultures. Accepting baptism was what mattered; Catholic missionaries took little interest in changing cultural practices so long as they did not clash head-on with Church teachings. Indeed—anything to baptize—they tailored their message and even their own behavior to the cultures of the peoples among whom they worked. They emphasized similarities between the beliefs of Aztec, Chinese, Iroquois, and whomever, on the one hand, and Roman Catholic teachings on the other in order to make Catholicism more congenial. The Roman Church was comfortably "multi-cultural."

English colonists, by way of contrast, were intensely nationalistic. Their religion—Puritan or Anglican—was inextricably tangled with English ways of eating, dressing, working, looking at the world. Even John Eliot insisted that

---

Legal Loopholes

Like the Spanish, New Englanders contrived legalistic justifications for taking Indian land. The Puritans looked to the Bible. In 1630, John Cotton found in the book three ways by which "God makes room for a people."

First, if they won control of land in a just war, which God blessed. ("Thou didst drive out the heathen before them," Psalms 44:2)

Second, strangers could purchase land or accept land as a gift "as Abraham did obtaine the field of Machpelah" or as the Pharoah gave the land of Goshen "unto the sons of Jacob."

Third, and here was major-league legal loophole-making: "when Hee makes a Countrey though not altogether void of inhabitants, yet voyd in that place where they [the newcomers] reside . . . there is liberty for the sonne of Adam or Noah to come and inhabite, though they neither buy it, nor aske their leaves."

Pennsylvania's Friendly Reputation

Early Pennsylvania was famous for its peaceful relations with the Indians, a reputation in which the Quakers took sometimes unhumble pride. There was no armed conflict with Indians in Pennsylvania until the mid-1700s when the non-Quaker, quick-to-fight Scotch–Irish pushed into Indian lands.

The Quakers' pacifism and their belief in the equality of all people before God had much to do with this extraordinary history. Addressing the Delaware Indians from whom he bought the site of Philadelphia, William Penn said that he wished to enjoy his colony "with your Love and Consent, that we may always live together as Neighbors and Friends."

There are always debunkers: some historians have argued that the Quakers were lucky. Before they arrived in New Jersey and Pennsylvania, European disease had reduced the once numerous Lenni-Lenape (Delaware) of the country to a tiny remnant. Both banks of the Delaware River had been virtually depopulated. The Susquehannock, whose hunting grounds extended into southern Pennsylvania, had been triply savaged by disease, the Iroquois Confederacy, and Virginians. The Quakers found it easier to be friendly than colonists elsewhere did.

Christian Indian men farm and women weave, that they live not in wigwams but in English houses, that they barber their hair just as the Puritans did, even that they stop using bear grease to ward off mosquitoes. Small wonder his successes were so modest.

Finally, Catholicism had long been the religion of people, who, like the Indians, could not read or write. Catholic worship was ritualistic, ceremonial, and mysterious. Protestants, especially Puritans, were a "people of the Book," the Bible. Religious services consisted of long sermons by learned preachers who minutely dissected biblical passages, which were well known to English listeners because the pious among them read the good book daily. A religion that began and ended with a book was, if not incomprehensible to Indians, without much appeal. The only interest North Carolina tribe Indians took in the Bible, an appalled settler reported, was in rubbing its soft vellum binding on their bellies.

LAND HUNGER

The goal of English colonization—to replicate as closely as possible the way of life the settlers knew back home—had no place in it for Indians. So, the colonists sought to acquire land by purchase or force, pushing the dispossessed Indian survivors beyond the pale of white settlement. The English (and Dutch) concept of private property—this belongs to me exclusively and no one else may so much as walk across it without my permission—required that Indians move on. In any case, intensive agriculture made the Indian way of life unfeasible; they had little choice but to find new homes. "Our fathers had plenty of deer and skins, our plains as also our woods, and of turkeys," a Narragansett sachem said, "but these English . . . with their scythes cut down the grass, and with axes fell the trees; their cows and horses eat the grass, and their hogs spoil our clam beds, and we shall all be starved."

Conscientious colonials devised moral and legal justifications for taking Indian land. The Pilgrims approved their occupation of Plymouth on their legal principle of *vacuum domicilium*—no one was living there when they arrived. Roger Williams purchased Providence, Rhode Island from the Narragansett and because he was a trader. Useful to the Indians, he remained personally hospitable. William Penn and the Quakers conscientiously paid fair prices for the land they settled and Pennsylvania had more amicable relations with the Indians than any other colony.

The Dutch paid for Manhattan Island three times over because the sellers, three different tribes, viewed the transaction differently from the buyers. They thought that, in return for goods, they were accepting the Hollanders' presence on the island. The Dutch, of course, thought they were purchasing exclusive rights to it. The Indians had the better claim to be bewildered. Jasper Danckhaerts wrote of a transaction in New York in 1679: "The Indians hate the precipitancy of comprehension and judgement [of the whites], the excited chatterings, . . . the haste and rashness to do something, whereby a mess is often made of one's good intentions."

Many colonials lacked good intentions. When conflict erupted, they shot, took, and shrugged. Possession by right of conquest had a long pedigree and compelling recommendations to the party with the military edge.

TRADE

Eastern Woodlands Indians were not flabbergasted by the appearance of whites as the Arawak and Mexicans had been. European fishermen had camped on Atlantic beaches for decades before the founding of Jamestown and Plymouth. Gossip among tribes had informed peoples of the interior existence of whites before they confronted an Englishman face to face.

The earliest English settlements posed little military threat, however, and the English offered highly desirable goods in trade. There were the famous baubles, of course: glass beads, ribbons, trinkets, and mirrors. The Indians accorded them the high status and price of any novelty. It was with $24 worth of such gewgaws that Peter Minuit "purchased" Manhattan Island in 1626. A European product brimming with tragedy, but coveted nonetheless, was liquor, usually rum (cheap brandy in New France). Some Eastern tribes made a weak beer from corn but nothing so potent as distilled spirits. From the first, the Indians took with tragic zest to "firewater." It devastated many tribes both physically and morally.

Scalping

In the 1870s, a crusader for Indian causes, Susette LaFlesche, persuaded audiences all over the United States that scalping—a gory practice that was universally appalling—had been taught to the Indians by the English and French. Her evidence was the fact that colonial assemblies paid Indian allies a bounty for each enemy scalp they delivered. LaFlesche's contention was revived in the 1980s and 1990s when it was fashionable to look on Indian–white relationships as all virtuous on one side (the Indians) and all evil on the other (the whites).

It was all nonsense. Seventeenth-century Europeans had a large repertory of gory practices, but there is no record of scalping among Europeans, not even a word for the practice in the English, French, and Dutch languages, until 1535 when Jacques Cartier observed Indians along the St. Lawrence River taking their dead enemies' hair as trophies.

Important to a people who smelted no metals were European commodities that improved their standard of living: brass and iron vessels; tools (spades, hatchets); woven blankets (which were warmer than hides) and other textiles; and firearms, which allowed the Indians to hunt more efficiently and get a military leg up on old tribal enemies.

In return, the Indians provided foodstuffs to the earliest settlers. When the English became agriculturally self-sufficient, they supplied furs and hides in exchange for goods that had become necessities in a native economy that was no longer self-sufficient.

A HURON—TYPE.

Culver Pictures

A Huron warrior. The Huron befriended the French, a decision that doomed them. Their numbers were reduced by disease, particularly smallpox. The tragedy caused some to abandon the Christianity to which the French had converted them. Then, in 1648, a massive attack by Mohawk and Oneida Indians wiped out nearly all the Catholic Huron who were still alive. Although they were longtime enemies of the Mohawk and Oneida, the Huron were Iroquois too. The dress and hairstyle of the warriors who slaughtered were much the same as this man's.

FURS AND A NEW KIND OF WAR

Furs and hides played a far greater part in the decline of the Eastern Woodlands peoples than liquor or the superiority of English weapons. The English (and Dutch and French) appetite for animal skins resulted in the destruction of the ecology of which the Eastern Indians had comfortably been a part. Before the whites arrived, the Woodlands tribes killed only the moose, deer, beaver, and other animals that they needed for food and clothing. Why kill more? Because the Indians were few, their needs had a minimal impact on the animal population. Indeed, their harvests of game probably had a healthy effect on wildlife by preventing overpopulation and disease.

Europeans could not get too many skins and pelts. The upper classes back home coveted the lush furs of the beaver, otter, marten, and weasel. Inferior furs were chopped and pressed to make felt for hats and dozens of other saleable goods. Leather made from deerskins was superior, for many purposes, to leather made from cattle and hogs. In order to buy more of the goods the Europeans offered, the eastern tribes soon virtually exterminated the deer and beaver in hunting grounds that had been adequate for their needs for centuries. This forced the tribes that supplied the Europeans to expand their operations aggressively into the hunting grounds of other peoples. Indian warfare, once highly formalized and not very bloody by European standards, became savage with extermination of rivals for the fur trade—the major object.

Thus, the Dutch in Fort Orange (Albany, New York) first bought furs from the Mahican, an Algonkian tribe. When the Mahican hunting grounds were trapped out, the Dutch turned to the neighboring Mohawk. Powerful and aggressive, the Mohawk (and their allies in the Iroquois Confederacy) began to range farther in all directions than they had reason to do, before furs became European trade goods. In 1637, they helped New Englanders in the Pequot War. Between 1643 and 1646, they cooperated with the Dutch in devastating the Mahican and other Algonkian tribes. In March 1648, a thousand Mohawk and Seneca warriors—a number unprecedented in Indian warfare—marched to north of the Great Lakes and swooped down on several Huron villages. They killed (according to estimates to be entertained with caution) 10,000 men, women, and children. The next year, to the west, Cayuga and Seneca virtually destroyed the Erie as a functioning tribe and then drove other tribes out of ancestral homes in the Ohio River Valley.

So valuable to the English were the Iroquois as suppliers of furs and hides that several colonial assemblies encouraged them to destroy their competitors by paying bounties for scalps, more for a man's than for a woman's, but more for a woman's than for a live captive.

KING PHILIP'S WAR

After a few early skirmishes with the Massachusetts tribe, the Puritans maintained uneasy but peaceful relations with the Massachusetts and Chief Massasoit's Wampanoag Indians for forty years. Thanks largely to Roger Williams, the powerful Narragansett were not aggressive. Indeed, they too cooperated in the war against the Pequot in 1637.

The long peace came to an end in 1675 when Plymouth hanged three Wampanoag for murdering Sassamon, a "praying Indian." Massasoit had disapproved of English ways but tolerated them. The new Wampanoag chief, **Metacomet** (whom New Englanders called "King Philip") hated the intruders, in part because of a personal insult, largely because he understood that the colonists were not just another tribe but, with their numbers, were destroying the Indian way of life. Secretly, he persuaded two other chiefs, Pomham of the Nipmuck and Canonchet of the Narragansett tribes (old enemies of the Wampanoag) to join him in a coordinated attack on outlying colonial towns. It was the first pan-Indian (that is, inter-tribal) attempt to preserve traditional culture and was, briefly, very successful.

Through most of 1675, the alliance was unstoppable. Fifty-two of ninety New England towns were attacked, wiping twelve of them off the map. About 500 soldiers were killed and as many as 1,000 "civilians" (one of thirty-five New Englanders). It was devastating. But it was also too late. King Philip's warriors ran short of provisions and their leaders began to quarrel among themselves. Most of the "praying Indians" allied themselves with the colonists; the Mahican and the remnants of the Pequot tribe declared neutrality, and the ever-expansive Mohawk attacked Philip's followers from the rear. In an attack on the Narragansett, the New Englanders killed 2,000 to 3,000. (The total death toll among the natives is unknown.) King Philip was killed, his head mounted on a stake in Boston in best seventeenth-century fashion. Canonchet's head was impaled in Hartford, Connecticut.

MIXED FEELINGS

The aftermath of King Philip's War dramatized the difference between white and Indian conceptions of race. The Indians were quintessentially tribal: they thought in terms of "us versus them"—members of the tribe were in an entirely different category of people than all those who were not part of the tribe. However, there was not a scintilla of racism in their minds. Captives adopted into the tribe—white as well as Indians born into another tribe—were fully accepted as "brothers" and "sisters." Indeed, tribes that lost population because of disease or war raided other tribes and white settlements specifically to replenish their numbers.

Among the colonists, however, what was at first a disdain for Indian culture—the English compared them to the long-despised Irish—became racist. The Indians were "savage" not simply because their customs were not English, but because they were intrinsically inferior. Indians—all Indians—were enemies. After King Philip's War, Massachusetts banished most of the "praying Indians" (who had supported the whites against King Philip!) to an island—interned them. In the end, only four of thirteen Christian Indian villages were rebuilt.

Not every colonial shared these feelings. Benjamin Franklin, the Pennsylvanian who sanctified hard work and the squirreling away of money, betrayed a wistfulness when he wrote of the Indians: "Having few artificial wants, they have abundance of leisure for improvement by conversation. Our laborious manner of life, compared with theirs, they esteem slavish and base." Whites captured and adopted by Indians commonly refused to return to white society while, as another Pennsylvanian wrote, "we have no examples of one of these Aborigines having free choice becoming European."

That was overstating it. Many Indians chose European ways only to discover that their race excluded them. Generally, however, the natives despised the culture of the whites. In 1744, Virginia invited the Iroquois to send six boys to the College of William and Mary. The confederacy replied that it had had bad luck with Indian lads educated at New England colleges. "When they came back to us, they were bad runners, ignorant of every means of living in the woods, unable to bear either cold or hunger, knew neither how to build a cabin, take a deer, or kill an enemy; they were totally good for nothing."

However, the Iroquois understood that the Virginians meant well: "If the gentlemen of Virginia will send us a dozen of their sons, we will take great care of their education, instruct them in all we know, and make men of them."

AMERICANS FROM AFRICA

To farmers in the colonies, the Indians were impediments. They were in the way like the massive oaks and maples of the forests. They had to be cleared, like the trees, preferably by peaceful purchase, but by force if necessary.

Colonists, particularly farmers, looked on America's third great people as desirable, indeed essential in the southern colonies where large plantations with a large labor force were the way to wealth. These were Africans, most of them from west Africa. They were brought to America against their will but neither that fact, nor their race, set them apart from many whites—at first. Indeed, the first African Americans arrived quite by accident. In time, however, the African presence solved the greatest problem of making a living by farming in North America. Land to cultivate was limitless; backs to bend over it were few.

SLAVERY AND THE ENGLISH

Enslaved Africans and their children had been the backbone of the labor force in the West Indies, on the Spanish mainland, and in Portuguese Brazil long before Jamestown was founded. So, the English, particularly those in the tobacco

A Servant's Contract

A contract of 1659 between "Richard Smyth of Virginia, planter, and Margaret Williams of Bristol, spinster" (an unmarried woman), was a typical indenture:

Witnesseth that the said Margaret doth hereby covenant, promise, and grant to and with the said Richard, his executors and assigns [the master could sell her services to another], from the day of the date hereof, until her first and next arrival at Virginia, and after, for and during the term of four years, to serve in such service and employment as the said Richard or his assigns shall there employ her, according to the custom of the country in the like kind. In consideration whereof the said master doth hereby covenant and grant to and with the said servant to pay for her passing [her transportation to Virginia], and to find and allow her meat, drink, apparel, and lodging, with other necessaries during the said term; and at the end of the said term to pay unto her one axe, one hoe, double apparel, fifty acres of land, one year's provision, according to the custom of the country.

colonies who needed cheap, dependable labor, had an example to which to look.

The colonists did not, however, turn to Africa or to slavery to bring their crops in—not right away. The English lacked a tradition of owning human beings as property. Slavery, even serfdom, had vanished from England centuries earlier. As for Africa, the English, unlike the Spanish and Portuguese, had little experience of trade or war with its darker-skinned peoples. By the latter 1500s, some English seafarers, notably John Hawkins and Francis Drake, were buying and selling black slaves in the Caribbean, but mostly they had seized them from the Spanish. As late as 1618, when an African merchant on the Senegal River offered slaves to Richard Jobson in payment for English trade goods, Jobson replied indignantly that "we were a people who did not deal in any such commodities, neither did wee buy or sell one another, or any that had our owne shapes." The African was astonished, telling Jobson that other white men who came to his country wanted nothing but slaves. The English captain answered that "they were another kinde of people different from us."

Had this goodly man's principles prevailed, North America would have been spared a great historical wrong, the enslavement of Africans and their descendants on the basis of their race. However, just months after the curious incident on the Senegal—and a year before the *Mayflower* anchored at Plymouth, Massachusetts—the history of African Americans began at Jamestown, with their enslavement for life in the near future.

NEW USES FOR AN OLD INSTITUTION

During the 1600s, the colonists solved the labor shortage by adopting and adapting an English institution that was well established—indentured servitude. An indenture was a contract. For example, a man who wanted his son to learn a trade signed an indenture with a master of the craft: a blacksmith, a baker, a cooper who made barrels, all kinds of skilled work. In return for the boy's labor and obedience for a period of years—commonly seven (age 14 to 21)—a master agreed to shelter, clothe, and feed him and to teach the boy the "mysteries" of his craft. It was an effective means of transmitting skills from generation to generation.

The English also used servitude (bondage for a period of years) to provide for orphans. Children whose parents died or abandoned them were farmed out as menial servants to families that agreed to bear the expense of raising them in return for their labor. There was no education involved in such arrangements; the parish, required by the Crown to care for the helpless, spared itself the expense of supporting orphans. The families that took them in got the labor of workers who could not quit, at no cost beyond the price of meals, clothing, and a corner for sleeping.

Apprentices and servants were not slaves; they were not property. They had rights as people their masters were obligated to respect. Their term of servitude was written down in black and white: the day came when the apprentice and maidservant walked off as a free man and free woman. Servants were not free. Under the Elizabethan Statute of Artificers of 1562, masters held the same broad authority over them that parents exercised over their natural children: servants were bound to obey their master; they could not do as they pleased; they could not marry without his consent. The master had a parent's right to administer corporal punishment, which could be nasty. The maltreated servant is a

Seven Years

The earliest servants in Virginia were bound for seven years, the traditional term of an apprenticeship.

Why seven? Two reasons:

Custom divided a person's minority, which ended at age 21, into three equal parts: seven years of infancy; seven years of childhood; and seven years of semi-

adulthood (not then called adolescence). The years from 14 to 21 were commonly (although not always) the years of apprenticeship for boys, and when girls were taught domestic arts.

Seven years as a term of servitude had a biblical justification. In Genesis 29, Jacob labored seven years for Laban in order to win the hand of Laban's daughter, Rachel.

The seven years "seemed unto him but a few days, for the love he had for her," which was surely not the way indentured servants in the colonies looked upon their servitude. They would have found much more relevant the fact that Laban tricked Jacob, marrying him to Laban's elder daughter, Leah, at the end of his term, then forcing Jacob to labor another seven years to get Rachel.

stock character in literature and folklore: Cinderella comes to mind. (There were kindly masters too, of course; the human species includes all kinds.)

The institution was perfect for colonists who needed laborers. It was difficult, even impossible, to hire unskilled workers for wages. So, colonists recruited impoverished adults or adolescents—not the elderly or children, of course—to sign indentures to work for them for an agreed upon number of years (the term varied), in return for their passage across the ocean; and, when they were freed they were to receive two changes of clothing (one for church), perhaps some tools or some money, and sometimes a patch of land. In Virginia's early decades, there was a bonus for the planter who brought servants over: 50 acres per head.

Established planters and farmers did not make a perilous crossing to Europe to recruit servants personally. Owners of ships recruited people to sign indentures, transported them to America, and sold their contracts. In the Netherlands and the Rhineland of Germany, the recruiters, undoubtedly fast-talking sales types, were called "spirits" or "soul-sellers." Servants who did not know to whom they would be bound were called redemptioners. Some languished for months in what amounted to prisons in New York and Boston until a buyer could be found.

SERVANTS

The system worked quite well. There were plenty of poor men and women willing to sell three or four years of their lives in order to escape hopelessness in the old country and the chance that, when their service was completed, they might make a decent, independent life for themselves.

Then there were involuntary servants and redemptioners. Jobbers kidnapped boys off the streets of English seaports and men foolish enough to get drunk on the waterfront when a half-filled servant ship was anchored in the harbor. Judges punished minor crimes (and, often enough, major ones) by sentencing convicts to "transportation" to the colonies and indentured servitude. Some historians estimate that half the European emigrants to the American colonies came as **indentured servants.**

Well into the 1700s, servants brought in the bulk of tobacco in Virginia and Maryland. Many farmers in the middle colonies were able to raise enough grain and livestock for export—and payment in cash!—by taking in servants at a cost of £6 to £30 each, depending on how many years the servant was obligated to work. If a servant did not die—and that was not a remote possibility, especially during the 1600s—the cost of the indenture was a fraction of the cost of a free man's or woman's wages. And servants could not quit if a better job showed up. If he ran away and was caught, the courts almost always added time to his term of servitude.

Most indentured servants during the 1600s were British: English, Scots, Welsh, and Irish. After 1700, German servants were numerous, especially in the middle colonies. The institution did not die out until the era of the American Revolution.

The "N" Word
The document describing the arrival of the first Africans in Jamestown referred to them as "negars." There was nothing derogatory in the word; it was the writer's attempt to spell the Spanish word for black and a black person, negro; a Jamestowner would associate Africans forced to labor with Spain's islands in the West Indies. Colonists got the spelling correct in writing, "negro," usually not capitalized. But pronunciation remained "naygur" and eventually "nigger." At first, the word was not in itself meant offensively, although general white contempt for African Americans coincided with their reduction to the status of slaves in the later 1600s. The clear distinction between the words Negro and nigger developed during the 1700s.

The first African Americans were servants, not slaves. In 1619, a Dutch vessel sailed into the Chesapeake and sold about twenty black Africans, whom they had probably captured from a slave ship bound for the Spanish West Indies, to the Jamestowners. The Virginians continued to buy any "negars" who were brought to colony, but blacks did not become an important part of the labor force for more than fifty years. In 1660, African Americans were just 4 percent of the population in Virginia and Maryland. New Netherlands, still Dutch in 1660, had a higher proportion of Africans in its population, 15 percent.

Until about 1670, black Virginians and Marylanders had a legal status similar to that of white servants. If they survived, they were freed after a term of service comparable to what whites served. One African who arrived in Jamestown in 1619 took the name Anthony Johnson and became a prosperous planter with several white servants bound to him. By 1650, there was a free black population in the Chesapeake colonies. Africans newly arrived in New Netherlands were defined as slaves—property. They were not a submissive lot, however. After a few years, a group of blacks successfully pressured the West India Company—which was the government—to grant them "half freedom": married males could acquire property of their own and buy their families from their white owners.

THE EMERGENCE OF SLAVERY

By 1670, however, the status of black servants was radically redefined in Virginia and Maryland. The assemblies in both colonies enacted laws providing that blacks who were not already free—and those yet to arrive—would serve their masters as servants (the term was still used) *durante vita,* throughout life. Blacks became property instead of persons under contract. The point was underlined when laws were passed defining a child's status as following the status of the mother. A slave woman's children were her master's property too, just as his cow's calf and his mare's foal were. In the law, African-American slaves were chattels.

Why the fatal change? In part, Virginia and Maryland and, eventually, all the colonies, took their cue from South Carolina. Many of that colony's first white settlers were from the British West Indian island of Barbados where slavery on the Spanish model was well established.

But there was more to it than imitation. The Chesapeake's rich tobacco planters, who made the colony's laws, could reclassify blacks to their own benefit. It was obviously in their interest that their field hands labor for them for life rather than for a few years. Enslaving white servants was out of the question; their rights as persons was sacrosanct. African servants, however, had no claim on the "rights of Englishmen." English law and tradition did not protect them.

An increase in the supply of captive Africans encouraged tobacco planters to make the most of them as laborers. The English were latecomers in the business of buying slaves in Africa but, by 1660, English merchants were making up for lost time. In 1663, the Crown created the Royal African Company to ensure that the big profits to be made selling slaves in the colonies went into English rather than foreign purses—mercantilism again!

White servants were the "better buy" until about the end of the century. Slaves had to be purchased in Africa; white servants were free in Europe—they were recruited. Transportation costs from Africa were considerably more than the costs of the much shorter voyage from Europe. The asking price of a lifetime worker was higher than the price of a white servant who would be free in a few years. As a rule, a slave cost three times as much as a servant of the same age and sex.

The high mortality rate in the tobacco colonies also favored the purchase of white servants. So long as every newcomer, black and white, stood a dismayingly good chance of contracting a fatal disease within a year—smallpox, influenza, dysentery, typhoid fever, typhus, malaria, and yellow fever—it made better sense financially to buy cheaper white servants than expensive black slaves. Life expectancy for male immigrants to Maryland (including the well-to-do) was 43. Governor Berkeley of Virginia estimated that four out of five servants (black and white) died within a year or two of

arriving. When *durante vita* meant a year or two, it did not mean very much.

During the late 1600s, however, the mortality rate on the Chesapeake steadily improved and planters noticed that Africans were more likely to survive attacks of yellow fever and malaria than whites were. (Yellow fever and the most dangerous form of malaria, plasmodium, were emigrants from Africa; blacks were, in fact, more likely to have inherited immunities to them than whites were.) With everyone living longer and blacks more resistant to two of the worst diseases of the country, planters now had an incentive to save money on the annual cost of a laborer rather than on the initial outlay—the purchase price. It made sense to buy workers who served longer and whose offspring increased their owners' wealth.

THE SERVANT PROBLEM

Yet another inducement to prefer black slaves was the nuisance involved in managing white servants. Planters' letters were filled with complaints about their servants' insolence, negligence, and laziness; about stolen food and drink, rowdy all-night parties, and pregnancies, which exempted women from work for as long as a year. White servants who knew the ropes took their masters to court charging mistreatment or some other breach of contract; black slaves, being property, had no right to sue. Servant plaintiffs did not often win their

A SLAVE-SHED.

North Wind Picture Archives

These wretched captives were fated to be slaves somewhere in the Americas, if they survived the Middle Passage. Seized by people of another tribe, they would soon be marched to the coast where European or possibly American slave traders waited to purchase them.

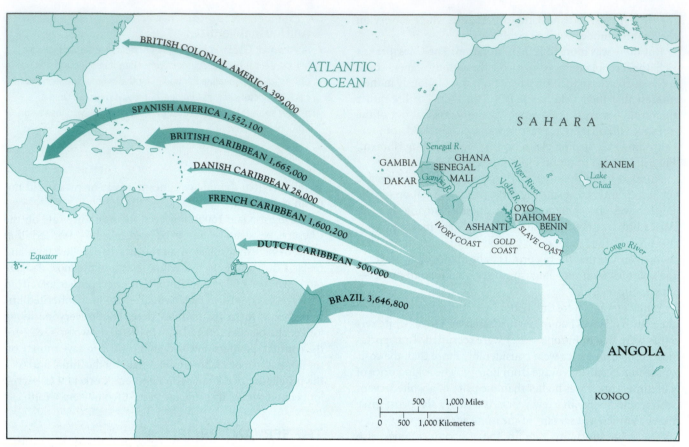

MAP 5:2 **The Atlantic Slave Trade**

Slavery looms large in American history, but the Thirteen Colonies and the United States were minor players in the Atlantic slave trade as a whole. Even the tiny Dutch sugar islands of the West Indies imported more captive Africans than colonial Americans did. Slaves who produced sugar were worked so hard they did not reproduce naturally. Sugar planters constantly imported new workers to replace those who died. On the mainland, African Americans had children at a normal rate almost from the start.

cases, but it happened now and then; at best, being hauled to court was a bother for a busy planter.

Then there were runaways. Even in the oldest tobacco-growing areas, the country was mostly woods. Plantations were mere gaps in the forest. In Virginia and Maryland, roads were only tracks, some of them so narrow two horsemen could not pass without jostling one another.

It was not easy for white servants to make successful escapes, but it was far from impossible. They could hide in the forests. If they made it to a city like Philadelphia, they could lose themselves in the crowds of strangers. Immigrants known to no one streamed through colonial ports. The few law enforcement officers could not practically ask every white stranger to prove he was not a runaway.

A runaway black, by reason of race, stood out in the city throngs. Unknown blacks were so few that it was worth a constable's time to ask them to show their papers. Black seamen and free blacks knew to treasure and protect the proof of their status. Any black woman or man without documents was assumed to be a runaway and jailed until his or her master— masters advertised runaways and could be contacted—

showed up and paid the costs of keeping the runaway plus a fee. Such fees were an important part of sheriffs' and city constables' income. And so the badge of race contributed to the turn toward African slavery.

In 1670, there were 20,000 blacks in Virginia, a large majority of them slaves. After 1700, the colony's slave population grew rapidly until, by the time of the Revolution, it approached 300,000. By 1720, 67 percent of South Carolina's population was black, and nearly all were slaves. A British officer observed, "They sell the servants here as they do their horses, and advertise them as they do their beef and oatmeal." New Jersey and New York had large slave populations. Virtually every prosperous Dutch farmer in New York owned a few slaves. The institution was legal in all thirteen colonies.

THE AFRICAN SLAVE TRADE

The buying and selling of slaves was an ancient institution in west Africa. Since the Middle Ages, Muslim Arabs and Berbers of present-day Morocco and Algeria had crossed the

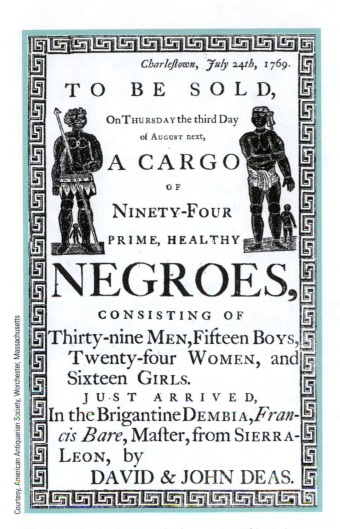

A typical advertisement of a slave auction. This one in Charleston in 1769 was unusual in that the people to be sold had been brought directly from Africa. Most African slaves in the colonies made a stop in the West Indies where they were "seasoned." Their origin in Sierra Leone may mean they were purchased at the slave station on Sherbro Island.

Sahara in caravans to Timbouctou where they purchased black Africans, gold, and ivory. Some caravans paused for a rest in towns near Cape Branco (Mauritania) where, in the 1440s, the Portuguese founded Arguin, the first European slave trading station in Africa. The Portuguese bought from the caravaners but recognized that they could bypass these middlemen by setting up farther south. The Portuguese soon had stations at regular intervals around the Gulf of Guinea, then in Angola, and eventually in east Africa. By 1600, when the Dutch, French, and others began to horn in on the Portuguese monopoly of the slave trade, as many as 200,000 west Africans had already been torn from their homeland. About 50,000 were taken to Europe, 25,000 to Portugal's island colonies in the Atlantic, and the rest to Brazil and Spanish colonies in the New World.

Dutch and French slave traders sometimes built their own coastal forts, and sometimes seized slave stations from the overextended Portuguese. Then came the English and, soon enough, Swedes, Danes, German Brandenburgers, and American colonials, notably from Newport, Rhode Island, a city that was built on the African slave trade.

A COLLABORATIVE ENTERPRISE

Some whites ventured up the rivers of west Africa and seized or "panyared" villagers themselves. An English trader explained: "In the night we broke into the villages and, rushing into the huts of the inhabitants, seized men, women, and children promiscuously." But such expeditions were rare; they were dangerous. Europeans died in great numbers from tropical diseases; and native African slave dealers, who had the power in the interior and did not take kindly to whites competing at their end of the business.

So, the slave trade was a collaboration between African suppliers and white buyers with, in the 1700s, people of mixed white and black blood (lançados in Portuguese, tapoeijers in Dutch, mulattos to the English) acting as brokers. The African slave trade was never race versus race; it was a multiracial business.

Tribal kings and lesser chiefs sold their criminals, both garden variety troublemakers and ugly types, and prisoners they had taken in war to the Europeans. As the European demand for slaves grew and profits soared, aggressive peoples like the Mandingos, Wolofs, Yoruba, and, later, the Ashanti launched raids far inland solely for the purpose of capturing merchandise. The economy of the great Ashanti Confederation rested on the commerce in slaves. By 1750, King Tegbesu of Dahomey annually pocketed £250,000 selling slaves destined for the Americas.

Captives were marched to the coast in coffles (tied or chained together neck to neck) along the great rivers of west Africa—the Senegal, Gambia, Volta, Niger, and Congo—as well as along numerous smaller streams. They were sold on the coast where they were held, sometimes in dungeons, until a ship arrived. Lançados sometimes grouped captives on beaches and hailed passing vessels. The big slave trading companies had permanent forts; freelance slave traders literally cruised the shoreline looking for slaves for sale. Even at the major port of Elmina, slaves were ferried in canoes from shore to ship.

Unknown numbers died between capture and the day they were put aboard a ship. Slaves in coffles who faltered, delaying the march, were routinely killed. The ocean crossing, called the "Middle Passage," was deadlier. Rather than providing the most healthful conditions possible for their human cargos to keep mortality low, the Atlantic slave traders crammed as many as they could in the hold "like herrings in a barrel."

A DEADLY BUSINESS

Not even the business of warfare was so drenched in death as the African slave trade was. It is the ultimate testimony to human greed and desperation that so many people were

Slave Stations

"Slave stations" or "factories" were houses of business and forts. The first one, Arguin, an octagonal structure the Portuguese built on Cape Blanco in the 1440s, was constructed of stone brought from Portugal as ballast. Elmina on the Gold Coast (Ghana), built by the Portuguese but seized by the Dutch in 1637, was, according to a French visitor, "justly famous for beauty and strength." The walls of other stations were pounded earth, built by slaves. Indeed, some slave stations, including Elmina between 1480 and 1520, imported slaves from other ports on the Gulf of Guinea.

Stations on the mainland, at the mouths of river, were walled to protect the European merchants from attacks by Africans either to free captives or to seize them for sale elsewhere. The slavery business was as competitive as it was ugly. Stations were also tempting targets because they were warehouses for gold and ivory as well as for slaves.

The forts' cannons, however, were trained on the sea, not the land. Europeans of other nations in ships were a greater threat than the Africans, the most powerful of whom were trading partners—the Mandingos at Goreé, the Yoruba at Whydah, and the Wolofs at Fort James. Some slave stations changed owners several times. Arguin was Spanish between 1580 and 1638 when the French seized it. Brandenburgers (Prussian Germans) took it over at the end of the century. The Dutch bought Arguin in 1721, only to lose it to the French. Cabo Corso, built by Swedes in 1655, fell to the Dutch, the Danes, and the English in just ten years.

The most desirable location for a slave station was an island off the coast. Island forts were easier to defend and healthier places than stations on the mainland. The Portuguese, the first Europeans in the slave trade, had and held São Tomé and Principe, strategically located midway between the Slave Coast and Angola, the two most important sources of enslaved Africans.

Visitors described São Tomé and Principe as stunningly "beautiful." Life at Goreé, the preferred market for slave traders out of Newport, Rhode Island, was said to be "pleasant." It is difficult to understand how anyone came up with those words. The forts were places of horror, routine brutality, filth, disease, and death. Courtyards were filled with slaves tied to posts and penned in stockades while their captors waited for buyers. In the stone forts, they were packed into pitch-black dungeons. They died wholesale, and so did the European merchants and soldiers posted to the forts: their mortality rate was 80 percent.

Because of the Europeans' vulnerability to tropical diseases, most "middle managers" at the forts—those who negotiated directly with suppliers—were people of mixed blood, mostly Portuguese-African *lançados*. The Portuguese presence in west Africa was two centuries old by 1700; the *lançado* population was large. Not quite accepted by either Portuguese or Africans, they carved a niche for themselves as go-betweens. On the Guinea Coast, *lançados* dominated the slave trade for almost a century.

Each station had its church, Roman Catholic in the Portuguese and French forts, Protestant in the others. Besides religion, the only relief for Europeans from the ugly business—and the consciousness that the chances of seeing Europe again were one in five—was alcohol. The slave trading companies were generous. The ships sent to carry slaves to the Americas carried immense quantities of wine and liquors, most commonly cheap rum, distilled from sugar cane raised in the West Indies by African slaves.

---

engaged in it for so long. The number of captives who died in the coffles cannot be estimated. Four of five Europeans posted to coastal slave stations were buried there. If only one in twenty slaves crossing the Atlantic died aboard ship, the voyage was so extraordinary a success its operators and owners celebrated with a party. If one slave in five on the Middle Passage died, unusually high but far from unknown, there was still a profit. A slave for whom a *lançado* charged £5–£10 sold in the New World for £25 and more. Only as the eighteenth century progressed did mortality on the Middle Passage decline. Then, ships' captains reported (proudly, it sometimes seems) that, proportionally, more slaves survived than crewmen. One seaman in five sailing the Middle Passage failed to complete the voyage. (One in 100 sailors on North Atlantic crossings died.)

The reason Africans died was not because the slave ships were sailed by sadists (although some of them were). Transporting slaves was a business and it was calculated early on in the trade that it was more profitable to pack captives in and absorb large losses caused by the greater filth and disease than it was to provide the captives with enough individual room so that they could live with minimum decency. Indeed, the mortality rate on the European servant ships, which were also packed solid, was as high as on the Middle Passage. In 1720, the *Honour* left England for Annapolis, Maryland with sixty-one convicts; twenty survived. In 1731, the *Love and Unity* sailed from Rotterdam to Philadelphia with 150 Dutch and German redemptioners; it arrived with thirty-four. In 1751, the *Good Intent* had a terrible time with weather and was 24 weeks at sea: there was no one left to sell as a servant.

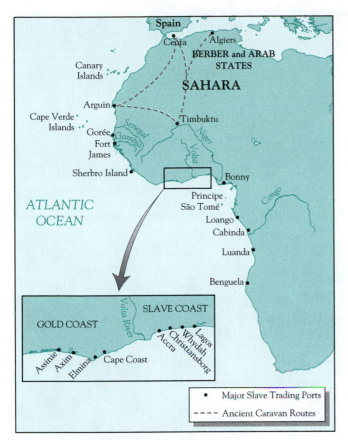

MAP 5:3 West African Slave Stations
This map shows only the most important and longest lasting slave stations from which virtually all the Africans taken to North America were sold and shipped. There were many others. At one time, on a 12-mile stretch of the Guinea Coast (the mainland opposite Sherbro Island) there were five forts representing five European nations. On the Gold Coast, "free lancers" held captives on beaches and hailed passing ships. An Englishwoman, Betsy Heard, married to an African, ruthlessly ran a major operation for several years.

A description of a 15-week crossing of a redemptioner's ship in 1750 could as well describe many—much longer!—voyages of the Middle Passage: "The ship is full of pitiful signs of distress—smells, fumes, horrors, vomiting, various kinds of sea sickness, fever, dysentery, headaches, heat, constipation, boils, scurvy, cancer, mouth-rot, and similar afflictions."

WEST AFRICAN ROOTS

Only a small proportion of the Africans enslaved and torn from their homelands were destined for Britain's North American colonies. Excluding the black Africans enslaved by north Africans and sold in the Muslim countries, probably 10 million people were forcefully taken from Africa by sea. By far the largest part of those that survived became Brazilians, 3.6 million. About 1.6 million ended up in the Spanish-American empire, approximately the same number in the French Caribbean (especially San Domingo, Haiti) and in Britain's West Indian islands. The North American colonies

were, by comparison, a minor market. Between 1619 and 1808, when the United States outlawed the African slave trade, about 400,000 blacks were shipped to North America.

Almost all of them were purchased on the coast of the Gulf of Guinea in regions then called the Slave Coast, the Gold Coast, and the Ivory Coast, now the nations of Gambia, Senegal, Guinea, Liberia, Sierra Leone, Ivory Coast, Ghana, Togo, Benin, and Nigeria. Toward the end of the colonial period and after the United States gained its independence, increasing numbers of Angolans (from what is now the Congo as well as Angola), many of them warriors captured in the region's unending tribal wars, were imported. (The Portuguese and French enslaved east Africans too, but few of them ended up in North America.) So, most African Americans of today who are not recent immigrants have west African roots.

Linguistically, however, most slave ships were Babels. European captains deliberately purchased slaves from as many language groups as were available so that few could understand one another. The idea was to minimize the threat of mutiny. There were plenty of uprisings when Africans found themselves faced with a situation they could not comprehend: what west African from the interior could have imagined the ocean, let alone wooden prisons that floated on it? Most successful mutinies occurred within sight of the African coast. Slave uprisings on the high seas sometimes succeeded in capturing the ship, but if all the seamen were killed, the rebels discovered they did not know how to sail the ships and died of hunger or thirst. Slave traders returned to port with tales of finding ships adrift, their deck littered with corpses.

Relatively few Africans destined to be sold in North America were transported directly from Africa. A glance at a map reveals why—every week at sea increased the death toll. Because most slave traders rode the same favorable westerly winds Columbus followed from the Canary Islands, their first landfall was in the West Indies. Even when the cargo was destined for Virginia or South Carolina, prudent slaver captains paused at a West Indian island to replenish water and stores and to put the slaves ashore for what was called "seasoning."

Seasoning meant little more than recovering from the ordeal of the crossing: rest, fresh air, and at least a few weeks of food that was better than slops. With a healthier cargo to sell, slavers then proceeded to Savannah, Charleston, the Chesapeake, or a northern port.

Many American slave traders never laid eyes on Africa. They carried grain and livestock to the West Indies and traded their cargos for slaves recently brought across the Atlantic. In the eighteenth century, some troublesome—that is, rebellious—colonial slaves were sold to the West Indies. It was a dreaded punishment; slaves knew from those who had been on the sugar islands that, as bad as their lot in Virginia or Maryland, it was preferable to the slave's life in the West Indies. Sugar was so profitable that planters routinely worked their slaves to death.

View of Mulberry, House and Street, by Thomas Coram, oil on paper, Gibbes Museum of Art/Carolina Art Association

Slave cabins at Mulberry Plantation, South Carolina. They are far more substantial than most slave housing in the early 1700s; it was more commonly primitive and squalid. Mulberry was a frontier plantation. The handsome "big house" was designed as a fortress in which slaves could shelter with the planter's family (and be prevented from running away) in the event of an Indian attack.

FURTHER READING

General Alvin M. Josephy, *The Indian Heritage of America*, 1968; Harold E. Driver, *Indians of North America*, 1970; Wilcomb E. Washburn, *The Indian in America*, 1975; Robert F. Spencer and Jesse Jennings, et al., *The Native Americans: Ethnology and Background of the North American Indians*, 1977; and *The Cambridge History of the Natives of the World*, vol. 3, North America, 1993.

People of the Eastern Woodlands James Axtell, *The European and the Indian: Essays in the Ethnohistory of Colonial North America*, 1981; *The Invasion Within: The Contest of Cultures in Colonial America*, 1985; and *Beyond 1492: Encounters in Colonial America*, 1988; Colin G. Calloway, *War, Migration, and the Survival of Indians*, 1990; *Dawnland Encounters: Indians and Europeans in Northern New England*, 1991; *New Worlds for All: Indians, Europeans, and the Remaking of Early America*, 1997; and *The World Turned Upside Down: Indian Voices from Early America*, 1994 (a collection of Indian speeches and writings); William Cronon, *Changes in the Land: Indians, Colonists, and the Ecology of New England*, 1983; Neal Salisbury, *Manitou and Providence: Indians, Europeans, and the Making of New England*, 1982; Richard White, *The Middle Ground: Indians, Empires, and Republics in the*

Great Lakes Region 1650–1815, 1991; Karen O. Ordahl, *Indians and English: Facing Off in Early America*, 2000; Peter C. Mancall and James H. Morrell, eds., *American Encounters: Natives and Newcomers from European Contact to Indian Removal*, 2000; Russell Bourne, *Gods of War, Gods of Peace: How the Meeting of Native and Colonial Religions Shaped Early America*, 2002; Laura M. Stevens, *The Poor Indians: British Missionaries, Native Americans, and Colonial Sensibilities*, 2005; Francis Jennings, *The Ambiguous Iroquois Empire: The Covenant Chain Confederation of Indian Tribes with English Colonies*, 1984; Daniel K. Richter, *The Ordeal of the Longhouse: The People of the Iroquois League in the Era of European Civilization*, 1992.

The First African Americans, Servants, and Slavery David B. Davis, *The Problem of Slavery in Western Culture*, 1966; Kenneth Stampp, *The Peculiar Institution*, 1956; Ira Berlin, *Many Thousands Gone: The First Two Centuries of Slavery in North America*, 1998; David W. Galenson, *White Servitude in Colonial America*, 1981; Edmund S. Morgan, *American Slavery, American Freedom*, 1975; Philip D. Curtin, *The Atlantic Slave Trade*, 1969; Hugh Thomas, *The Slave Trade: The Story of the Atlantic Slave Trade, 1440–1870*, 1997.

KEY TERMS

The following terms are covered in this chapter and can also be found in the list of Key Terms at the back of the book.

Algonkian	**Five Nations**	**indentured servants**	**Metacomet**
durante vita	**Hiawatha**	**Iroquois**	**Muskogean**

 ## ONLINE SOURCES GUIDE

Use this listing to find online documents, images, interactive maps, simulations, and other resources related to this chapter:

American History Resource Center
http://history.wadsworth.com

Selected Documents
John Eliot's A Brief Narrative of the Progress of the Gospel amongst the Indians in New England
Robert Beverly's Report on the Decline of Native American Populations in Virginia
Reverend Solomon Stoddard's Plan for Hunting Native Americans With Dogs

Selected Images
Engraving of 1690 battle between Champlain and Iroquois
Pocahontas
Massacesoit/Wampanoag/pilgrims meeting
Iroquois savage by a French artist
Algonkian constructing family lodge

Simulations
Colonial Expansion (Choose an identity as an Aztec, Jamestown settler, or a Puritan in New England and make choices based on the circumstances and opportunities afforded.)

Interactive Timeline (with online readings)
Other Americans: The Indians, French, and Africans of Colonial North America

Additional resources, exercises, and Internet links related to this chapter are available on *THE AMERICAN PAST* web site: http://history.wadsworth.com/americanpast8e

Discovery

How did non-colonists fare within the English colonies?

In thinking about this question, begin by breaking it down into the components shown below. A discussion of the significance of each component should appear in your answer.

Economics and Technology: For this exercise, please study these two images, "Wretched Captives," and "A typical advertisement," and review the map shown here. What was the English reasoning or justification for importing large numbers of slaves? How was this related to the economic factors that were discussed in the Discovery section of the previous chapter? Note the two images. What is the difference, do you think, between the capture of slaves among Africans and the use of slaves among English colonists? How is the portrayal of Africans in both images used to help de-humanize them? Why would this be important among the English?

A SLAVE-SHED.

North Wind Picture Archives

Wretched Captives

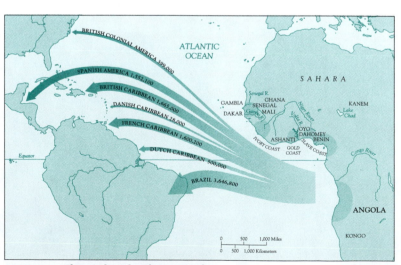

Courtesy, American Antiquarian Society, Worchester, Massachusetts

Typical advertisement

MAP 5:2 The Atlantic Slave Trade

Culture and Society: For this exercise, please reflect on the chapter section "Mixed Feelings" and read the following document excerpt, "Richard Hutchinson, 'The Death of King Philip.'" How did the portrayal of Native Americans by the colonists contribute to a feeling of cultural superiority? How did the idea that Native Americans were still "savages" help determine colonial policies toward Native Americans? How would this help to justify their actions? Do you think some cultures are more "developed" than others? Is there a linear development?

Richard Hutchinson, "The Death of King Philip," excerpt from *The Warr in New England Visibly Ended*, 1677

While we were thus beset with Difficulties in this Attempt, the Providence of God wonderfully appeared, for by Chance the Indian guide and the Plimouth Man, being together, the Guide espied an Indian and bids the Plimouth-man shoot, whose Gun went not off, only flashed in the Pan; with that the Indian looked about, and was going to shoot, but the Plimouth-man prevented him, and shot the Enemy through the Body, dead, with a Brace of Bullets; and approaching the Place where he lay, upon Search, it appeared to be King Philip, to their no small Amazement and great Joy. This seasonable Prey was soon divided, they cut off his Head and Hands, and conveyed them to Rhode-Island, and quartered his Body, and hung it upon four Trees. One Indian more of King Philip's Company they then killed, and some of the Rest they wounded but the Swamp being so thick and miry, they made their Escape.

To read extended versions of the documents, visit the companion Web site http://history.wadsworth.com/americanpast8e; click on "Discovery Sources."

CHAPTER 6

Competition for a Continent

French America and British America 1608–1763

North Wind Picture Archives

This country has twice the population of New France, but the people there are astonishingly cowardly, completely undisciplined, and without any experience in war. . . . It is not at all like that in Canada. The Canadians are brave, much inured to war, and untiring in travel. Two thousand of them will at all times and in all places thrash the people of New England.

French Officer, Troupes de la Marine

A perfidious enemy, who have dared to exasperate you by their cruelties, but not to oppose you on equal ground, are now constrained to face you. . . . A few regular troops from old France, . . . those numerous companies of Canadians, insolent, mutinous, unsteady, and ill-disciplined. . . . As for those savage tribes of Indians, whose horrid yells in the forest have struck many a bold heart with affright, terrible as they are with a tomahawk and scalping-knife to a flying and prostrate foe, you have experienced how little their ferocity is to be dreaded by resolute men upon fair and open ground. . . .

General James Wolfe, to his troops before Quebec

In 1603, a celebrated French soldier, **Samuel de Champlain,** sailed to North America to look for the Northwest Passage and a site for a French colony. Champlain explored the St. Lawrence River to above the location of present-day Montreal. In 1605, he left a few men on the western shore of Nova Scotia (which the French called Acadia) to lay the foundations of Port Royal. (A handful of Frenchmen had been living with Indians at Tadoussac on the St. Lawrence as early as 1600.) But New France, as the French named Canada (an Indian word) had its real beginnings in 1608, just months after Jamestown was founded. In that year, Champlain built Quebec (an Algonkian word meaning "the narrows") on a cliff on the great river's north bank. It was after wintering at Quebec that Champlain opened fire on the Mohawks on Lake Champlain.

NEW FRANCE AND LOUISIANA

French designs on North America were the same as those of the English and the Dutch. They hoped to find the all-water route to the Indies that just had to exist. Like the first settlers of Jamestown, they dreamed of gold. French investors in the Company of the Indies, like shareholders in the London and Plymouth Companies, hoped to profit by exploiting the resources of the New World—whatever they might prove to be.

TOO FEW PEOPLE

There the similarities between New France and British America ended. English men and women crossed the Atlantic in droves; French men and women did not. During Quebec's first thirty years, only 300 French (not counting soldiers) settled along the St. Lawrence and stayed. Between 1630 and 1640, 30,000 Puritans emigrated to just one of the half dozen English colonies, Massachusetts.

It was not that French peasants led enviable lives at home. It was the climate and soil of New France, which held few charms for a peasant who owned even a tiny patch of "sweet France." Canada's growing season was even shorter than New England's, winter was colder, the soil rockier. Two-thirds of the emigrants to New France gave up and returned home to feed the anti-Canadian prejudice with tales of woe and weather. Strikingly—for four Europeans in five were rural people—a high proportion of those who stayed in Canada came from cities and towns.

France could have populated Canada with religious dissenters as the English had populated New England. France had its own Puritans, Calvinist Protestants called Huguenots who were more numerous (and more troublesome to the king) than the Puritans in England. Where they were in the majority, zealous Huguenots harassed Catholics, destroyed churches, and defied the monarchy. In most of France, however, the Huguenots were the victims of persecution and many wanted to go abroad. All the failed French colonies of the 1500s were Huguenot colonies; Port Royal in Acadia was mostly Huguenot. But the kings of France forbade any but Catholics in New France. After 1685, when the Huguenots lost the limited toleration they had enjoyed, tens of thousands left the country—moving to Holland, England, and the English colonies. Many were quite rich and well educated; many more were solidly middle class, energetic and industrious. New France would likely have prospered had the Huguenots settled there.

Louis XIV, king for seventy years, tried to induce French Catholics to go to Canada. Indentured servants' terms were legally limited to three years; when freed, servants were given generous land grants. Louis even tried force. Entire villages in impoverished Brittany were shipped to Quebec. Soldiers posted in Canada were ordered to remain when they were discharged. Orphan girls and the daughters of peasants who got in trouble with the tax collector were shipped to Canada to be the wives of men already there. Although the king

No Protestants in the English colonies were fractionally as devoted and industrious in converting and educating Indians as the Jesuit priests of New France. Hated by Protestants for their effectiveness and smeared as unscrupulous, they were, indeed, zealots. When the Iroquois tortured and killed six Jesuits during the 1640s, the order in France was swamped by dozens of young priests begging to go to New France. Well-educated themselves, they founded schools for Indian boys and men wherever they went. Ursuline nuns founded schools for Indian girls.

disapproved, so were prostitutes, rounded up in Paris and seaports.

Nothing worked. New France would not grow. By 1713, after a century of settlement, the French population in all of North America was 25,000, about the same number as lived in the single English colony of Pennsylvania, which was only thirty years old.

INDIAN FRIENDS

The French had their Indian troubles too. After thirty years of defeat by Huron armed with French muskets, the Iroquois Confederacy had its revenge, killing thousands of Huron and their French priests. In 1683, the Iroquois soundly defeated the French in battle, coming within an ace of overrunning Quebec. French fur trappers so feared the Iroquois they made detours of hundreds of miles to avoid them. As late as 1684, the Algonquin, first friends and next-door neighbors of the

Savages

The Spanish, Portuguese, English, Dutch, Swedes, Danes—every European people that established colonies in the Americas called the native inhabitants Indians—except the French. They had the word, the Indies were *les Indes*. But in New France, natives, both friends and enemies, were *les sauvages,* the savages. In French, the word is not complimentary, but neither is it intrinsically derogatory as it has become in English.

Indian Slaves

The French, too, had slaves. Africans were imported, usually from San Domingo (Haiti) into Louisiana. In Canada, Indians were held as slaves even though the Catholic Church and King Louis XIV had forbidden the enslavement of Indians. Curiously, Indian slavery was forced on the French by Indians. Taking captives was a central feature of intertribal warfare. The Indian allies of the French presented them with enemies they had captured as slaves; to have insulted their allies' generosity by letting the captives go was not the French way. So they put them to work.

The Indians gave the French white colonial captives too. They were not enslaved but held as hostages, exchanged for French the Americans had captured, or ransomed.

French for seventy-five years, erupted in anger and killed thirty whites.

In general, however, the French had far better relations with Indians than the English did. Their numbers were too few to threaten the Indians with inundation as the English colonials did. Canada's farmland was a narrow belt along the St. Lawrence; farms did not expand endlessly into Indian hunting grounds as those in England's colonies did. The fur trade, which Indians saw as a blessing, providing them with European goods, was virtually the whole of New France's economy.

Whereas the English colonials remained apart from Indians, the French encouraged intermarriage and amalgamation. "Our sons shall wed your daughters," Champlain said, "and we shall be but one people." In general, the French won friendship, respect, and loyalty from the tribes with which they dealt; Indians who aligned with the English colonists did so because they had been defeated or because it was expedient to do so. Suspicion characterized English–Indian relations.

New England ministers who devoted their lives to Indians can be counted on the fingers of one hand. (There were fewer in the southern colonies.) The French flooded New France with nuns and priests whose assignment was to baptize *les sauvages.* Ursuline sisters operated schools for Indian girls, whom they converted to Roman Catholicism and then sent back to their villages where, as wives, they were themselves effective missionaries.

Most priests in New France were **Jesuits,** members of the Society of Jesus. Jesuits were the Church's militant elite: very well educated, disciplined, dedicated to spreading their religion, and ready, even eager to die for it. They learned the language of every tribe they targeted for conversion and lived among them. Unlike New England's ministers, they took no interest in changing anything in Indian culture except their religion. They saw nothing ungodly in wearing breechcloths, tattooing faces, or sitting on the ground. They were indulgent of Indian practices that they believed were immoral; better a baptized sinner who could repent than a sinner outside the Church doomed to hell. They were superbly successful missionaries wherever they went. When hostilities with the Iroquois nations ended late in the 1600s, the Jesuits made more converts among them in a decade than English Protestants had made in a half century.

INTREPID EXPLORERS

Good relations with Indians made it possible for the French to become the most adventurous and accomplished explorers in North America since Coronado. Trappers, traders, and priests

Colonial Wars 1688–1763

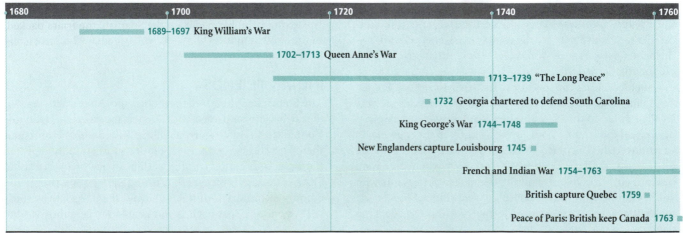

1680	1700	1720	1740	1760

1689–1697 King William's War

1702–1713 Queen Anne's War

1713–1739 "The Long Peace"

1732 Georgia chartered to defend South Carolina

King George's War 1744–1748

New Englanders capture Louisbourg 1745

French and Indian War 1754–1763

British capture Quebec 1759

Peace of Paris: British keep Canada 1763

Brown Brothers

In 1673, a French Jesuit stationed in what is now Michigan, Father Jacques Marquette, joined forces with Louis Joliet, an experienced woodsman, and several Indians to voyage by canoe down the Mississippi to the mouth of the Arkansas River. It was the greatest expedition of discovery for 150 years. They covered 2,500 miles in four months. Marquette was taken seriously ill on the return trip but Joliet brought him back at the risk of his own life. Marquette died a short time later at age 38.

plunged far into the forests around the Great Lakes while the much more numerous English huddled close to the ocean, still fearful of Indian attack. Unlike the English, the *coureurs de bois* (not quite translatable as "runners of the woods"), young men building up a nest egg before marrying—usually to an Indian woman—adopted the Indians' ways of surviving in the wilderness. When a governor of Virginia reached the crest of the Appalachians, he celebrated by covering a table with pressed linen and setting it with china, silver, and crystal. Frenchmen already exploring the Missouri River, 700 miles farther west, hunkered in the dirt, roasted a slab of venison, and ate it with their hands.

French explorers charted what is now the central third of the United States, from the Appalachian ridges to the Rockies. In 1673—a decade before William Penn set foot in Pennsylvania—Louis Joliet, a trapper and scholar, and **Jacques Marquette,** a Jesuit priest, crossed Wisconsin to the Mississippi River and, with Indian companions, paddled two canoes to the mouth of the Arkansas River. They turned back only because Indians there told them of white people farther south whom Marquette and Joliet correctly reckoned to be Spaniards, enemies who would imprison them. They

covered 2,500 miles in 4 months, informing Quebec that rumored Mississippi existed and that it flowed into the Gulf of Mexico.

In 1682—a half century before the founding of Georgia—Robert Cavelier, the Sieur de La Salle, reached the mouth of the great river. In 1699, Pierre le Moyne, the Sieur d'Iberville, founded New Orleans on the delta. To put Spanish Florida on notice that France was on the Gulf to stay (in its second American province, Louisiana), the French established forts at Biloxi and then at Mobile, which had the best harbor on the Gulf.

French America (New France and Louisiana) was a flimsy empire: a string of isolated log forts and trading posts at long intervals on the Great Lakes and Mississippi River. It was similar in structure to Portugal's commercial empire of the 1500s. Kaskaskia and Cahokia in the Illinois country and St. Louis where the Missouri River meets the Mississippi were dots on a map, manned by a few traders and soldiers. Portugal's dots were connected by the seas, France's by lakes, rivers, creeks, portages (a place where the canoes had to be carried, ported, from one waterway to another).

IMPERIAL STANDOFF

The Dutch, English, and French had picked apart the Portuguese empire from slave station to trading post until only remnants remained. New France was overextended, as Portugal had been, but it remained intact during the 1600s thanks to Indian allies, professional military garrisons in Quebec and Montreal, and the English colonists' preoccupation with their own development. The colonists and the Canadians skirmished, but mostly through Indian proxies: the Iroquois destroyed a small French town not far from Montreal; the Abenaki who were French allies, attacked Pemaquid, now Bristol, and other towns on the coast of Maine.

Louisiana's security was, on the face of it, more precarious. Spain, also a long-standing enemy of France, had pushed from Mexico to what is now the Texas-Louisiana border, within striking distance of New Orleans. Pensacola, in Florida, threatened the French from the east. But the Spanish were also overextended. When, in 1693, mission Indians in Texas were hit by an outbreak of smallpox and (quite correctly) blamed it on the Spanish, the friars packed up and left rather than be killed in an uprising, as priests in New Mexico had been. Spain's hold on northern Florida was firmer but there, too, disease had reduced their once numerous Timecuan allies to a fraction of their original numbers.

Moreover, Spanish Florida faced another enemy to the north, South Carolina. In 1688, South Carolinians destroyed the Spanish missions in Guale, in present-day Georgia. The same year, the undeclared little wars in North America were absorbed into a big war formally declared in Europe (with, ironically, England and Spain on the same side). With one brief interruption, the colonies—some of them, some of the time—battled the French for 24 years.

European Wars, American Wars

This table provides the European names and the American names of the four major wars—worldwide wars, actually—between 1689 and 1763. Note that in several cases, the dates of hostilities differ slightly. By the 1700s, European nations declared wars. Americans were colonials; the mother country handled the declarations. They, like the Indian allies and enemies, went to war when they attacked or were attacked.

Europe's Wars		The Colonies' Wars	
Dates	Name	Dates	Name
1688–1697	War of the League of Augsburg	1689–1697	King William's War
1701–1713	War of the Spanish Succession	1702–1713	Queen Anne's War
	[The "Long Peace," 1713–1740]		
1740–1748	War of the Austrian Succession	1744–1748	King George's War
1756–1763	Seven Years War	1754–1763	French and Indian War

A CENTURY OF WAR

In 1688, an alliance led by William III of England went to war with France in the War of the League of Augsburg. The colonials called their theater of the war "King William's War." Few Americans cared who ruled the Netherlands—the issue between Louis XIV and the League. But the New England colonies had their own reasons for a conflict with France: French ships out of Port Royal harassed New England fishermen and merchant ships, and the French in Quebec armed Indians on the New England frontier.

Between 1688 and 1763, Europeans fought four major wars, France and Great Britain always on opposite sides. The colonials gave their own name to each of them—the British monarch's name—reflecting their lack of interest in the issues at stake in Europe. Indeed, because Indians were major belligerents in the fighting in North America, often outnumbering European soldiers and colonial militiamen in battles, it is more accurate in the context of American history to look at a longer period, from 1689 to 1815—a century with interruptions—of the same war. The British resolved their imperial competition with France for control of North America in 1763. Americans destroyed the military might of the Eastern Woodlands Indians only in 1815.

Learning from the Colonials

If colonials borrowed military techniques from the Indians, Indians learned from Europeans too. Most important, of course, were firearms. Both the French and the English supplied their Indian allies with muskets. Not only did the Indians soon become experts with the (not very accurate) weapons, they learned gunsmithing, how to repair the easily broken muskets. While Indians had palisaded their villages with logs before the arrival of Europeans, they learned the superiority of earthworks and even stone fortifications. There were skilled stonemasons among the tribes of New England and New York.

EUROPEAN WAR-MAKING

European warfare was becoming less brutal in the late 1600s, a trend that would continue for a century. The soldiers in the Thirty Years War (1618–1648) and Oliver Cromwell's ravage of Ireland a few years earlier had been so vicious toward non-combatants—pillaging, raping, and murdering wholesale—that even monarchs recoiled in disgust.

An innovation in weaponry also served to encourage more "civilized" warfare. Muskets were now the foot soldier's standard armament. To make the most of musket fire, armies formed lines and fired volleys in battle rather than, as in the past, advancing in "a brute mass." Keeping infantrymen in a disciplined formation meant long, exhaustive training: drill, drill, drill. Where kings and queens had hired mercenaries when they needed them, and then dismissed them, creating and maintaining a professional army was extremely expensive. The rulers who footed the bills made it clear to their officers that they were not to waste the lives of soldiers in whom they had invested so much money. Generals were to do battle only when by maneuvering into a superior position, the odds of victory were stacked in their favor. Generals who faced defeat were to retreat and "live to fight another day" or, if they were trapped, surrender and save the army.

The maxims of war, wrote the novelist, Daniel Defoe, were "never fight without a manifest advantage, and always encamp so as not to be forced to it." He added sarcastically that armies "spend a whole campaign in dodging, or, as it is genteelly called, observing one another, and then march off into winter quarters."

To be effective, discipline had to be constant. Soldiers could no longer be told to "live off the land" as in Germany during the Thirty Years War. It was when they foraged for food and loot that conscienceless mercenaries laid waste to churches, cottages, and fields and terrorized the people unlucky enough to be in their paths. (Three to four million of Germany's twenty million people disappeared during that war.) Keeping troops under control, therefore, meant supplying them with food and drink, a new and expensive military specialization, and punishing them harshly when they looted.

THE "AMERICAN STYLE" OF WAR

None of this affected North Americans any more than the question of who would rule the Netherlands or be king of Spain. Very few professional British soldiers were stationed in the colonies; the professionals in New France stayed close to Quebec and Montreal. Colonials had long since adopted Indian ways of war that the earliest settlers had despised. Europeans called it the "American style"—ambush and surprise raids. Colonials "crept on their bellies," which was the antithesis of the disciplined European march. Like the Indians, colonials were "bellicose individuals" in battle, doing what they chose to do, not what an officer ordered.

And they were savage. Although officers trained in Europe sometimes tried to observe "rules" requiring the decent treatment of prisoners, they frequently could not control Indians they thought they commanded. Colonial assemblies showed little sympathy for the new European niceties. During Queen Anne's War, Massachusetts paid £40 for the scalp of an enemy. During King George's War, the bounty was raised to £105 for the scalp of an Indian male older than 12, and £50 each for the scalps of women and children.

TWO INCONCLUSIVE CONFLICTS

Little was accomplished in King William's War and Queen Anne's War but killing and destruction. In 1689, Abenaki Indians attacked several Massachusetts towns on the Maine Coast. In 1690, Indians with a few French officers attacked Schenectady in New York and Casco in Maine. When a hundred Casco villagers tried to surrender, the Indians slaughtered them. In 1693, a French and Indian force devastated the Mohawk and Onandaga, demoralizing the Iroquois Confederacy.

New Englanders, led by Massachusetts, organized two amphibious forces, one to attack Quebec, the other Port Royal. The Quebec expedition was incompetently commanded and got nowhere. The New Englanders occupied Port Royal in 1689 and the French regained it two years later. In Europe, there was more maneuvering than battling. In 1697, the Peace of Ryswick ended the fighting on the basis of *status quo ante bellum*—the situation as it was before the war.

This assured there would be another war, which erupted in 1701, Queen Anne's War or, in Europe, the War of the Spanish Succession. Spain was now an ally of France rather than an enemy. This meant that South Carolina and Spanish Florida, where King William's War had been ignored, were engaged. Their war was an exercise in incompetence. In 1702, about 500 Carolinians and 300 Indians on 14 ships besieged St. Augustine. It was a ramshackle town; many people lived in huts made of sticks and reeds. But the attackers could not take it and when two Spanish warships arrived from Cuba, they fled. A French and Spanish attack on Charleston was likewise a fiasco.

DEERFIELD AND PORT ROYAL

In New England, the French and their Indian allies renewed what the French called *petite guerre* ("little war"), surprise raids on outlying colonial towns. The most dramatic was

North Wind Picture Archives

BURNING OF DEERFIELD, MASSACHUSETTS.

Deerfield, Massachusetts was no mere cluster of frontier cabins when Indians and French soldiers burned it to the ground in 1704. It was a substantial, comfortable town founded 35 years earlier. The utter destruction of so apparently secure a place set all New England on edge.

the assault on Deerfield, Massachusetts in February 1704. Deerfield was a substantial village of more than forty structures and about 270 people. All the previous year, it had been well prepared for an assault. But winter in New England, the ground deep in snow, meant security, or so everyone assumed. At four in the morning, after a long march on snowshoes (an Indian invention), Abenaki Indians and a few French officers attacked. Within two hours, before the sun rose, they killed 44, including 9 women and 25 children, and took 109 captives. Only 133 Deerfielders managed to escape. Only 59 of the 109 captives ever returned. One who stayed in Canada was Eunice Williams, daughter of the village minister, who became a Catholic and married an Indian—the cruelest cut of all.

In 1707, Massachusetts again sent a force against Port Royal. Two assaults failed, with the New Englanders suffering terrible casualties. When British warships arrived with a large force of professional soldiers, Port Royal surrendered. In the Treaty of Utrecht in 1713, Britain took Acadia from France, giving the new colony the name of Nova Scotia. But when the French built a new fortress, Louisbourg, on Cape Breton Island, the threat to New England shipping was revived.

The Treaty of Utrecht had significant consequences in Europe. French defeats at the hands of two great generals, the

British Duke of Marlborough and Prince Eugene of Savoy, ended a generation of fear that France would dominate all of western Europe. The "balance of power" in Europe—two blocs of nations of equal military strength—ushered in a "long peace" of almost thirty years. For Americans, the long peace was a time of astonishing growth and profound social and cultural developments that created a mature and confident society where there had been precariously established outposts of England.

SOCIAL DEVELOPMENTS

Between 1700 and 1776, the population of the colonies increased tenfold, from about 250,000 people to 2.5 million. With its rich and ever expanding agricultural hinterland, Philadelphia bypassed the older cities of Boston, New York, and Charleston to become North America's metropolis; indeed, Philadelphia was the second largest city in the British Empire, smaller only than London.

Except for African-American slaves and free blacks, who formed a caste submerged by prejudice and force, colonial Americans enjoyed more personal freedom than any people in the world. Nowhere did so great a proportion of the population have a voice in government as in the colonies. The "standard of living" (not an eighteenth century term) was unparalleled anywhere. There were fewer fabulously rich and fewer utterly destitute people in the colonies than in any other country.

NATURAL INCREASE

Large families and longer life expectancy accounted for some of this astonishing growth. In New England, those who survived childhood enjoyed a life expectancy nearly as high as it is today. New Englanders were the first people in history to know their grandparents as a matter of routine—their grandfathers, anyway.

Unlike today, when women outlive men by a half dozen years, men often survived longer in the eighteenth century. The reason for this was childbirth. The lives of many young women were snuffed out by puerperal fever, an infection due to poor sanitation. However, a New England male of 20 was more likely to die at 70 years of age than 60; a man of the middle colonies at older than 60. Life expectancy was shorter in the South, 45 in Virginia and Maryland, 42 in the Carolinas and Georgia. (Life expectancy for a white man of 20 in the British West Indies was 40; West Indian slaves died in such chilling numbers, there was virtually no natural increase of the black population during the 1700s.)

Families were large, some very large. Benjamin Franklin, born in 1706, was the tenth child in his family. Patrick Henry, born in 1736, a future leader of the American Revolution, was one of nineteen children. John Marshall, born in 1755 and a future Chief Justice of the Supreme Court, had fourteen brothers and sisters. In 1766, Jacob Van der Bilt left a widow and eleven children. His son, Jacob, was survived by seven children. One of them, Cornelius (the father of the railroad magnate, Cornelius Vanderbilt) left nine heirs.

From the Collections of the Library of Congress

One of several German language newspapers published in colonial Philadelphia. Benjamin Franklin and others worried that the city might become more German than English. In 1776, The Declaration of Independence was published in German before it was published in English. It was seriously proposed (although not seriously received by many people) that German be made the official language of the infant United States.

Epidemics of contagious diseases such as diphtheria, yellow fever, typhus, and smallpox periodically ravaged colonial cities. In Boston in 1721, 6,000 people were afflicted with smallpox; more than 800 of them, almost ten percent of the population, died. Farm families, with a narrow circle of personal contacts, were not so vulnerable.

GERMAN AND IRISH IMMIGRANTS

The population explosion was fed by immigrants, as many as 800,000 between 1700 and 1776. Cheap land was the attraction; sales records show it changing hands for 3 pence to £1 per acre. English men and women continued to arrive, but they were outnumbered by Germans and **Scotch-Irish,** Protestants from northern Ireland whose forebears, a century and more earlier, had come from the lowlands of Scotland.

Most of the Germans and Scotch-Irish stepped ashore in Philadelphia. (In just one week in August 1773, 3,500 immigrants arrived in the city.) Pennsylvania already had a German community, the Quaker-like Mennonites for whom William Penn had provided a refuge from persecution. Most of them were farmers in what are now Lancaster and York counties west of Philadelphia, the ancestors of the "Pennsylvania

Women Voters

Only Virginia specifically barred women heads of household from voting. Elsewhere it was a nonissue: women and men alike assumed that government was a man's affair. Here and there, eccentric or very bold women showed up at the polls and (perhaps amidst masculine laughter) were allowed to vote. In New York in 1737, "two old Widdows" cast ballots. A few Massachusetts townships seem to have allowed propertied widows to vote.

James Logan, the Penn family's agent in Philadelphia, wrote in consternation: "I must own, from my experience in the land office, that the settlement of five families from Ireland gives me more trouble than fifty of any other people." But Logan and others used their toughness against the Indians. The Scotch-Irish wanted land. To get it after 1700, they had to move deep into the backcountry of Pennsylvania, Virginia, and the Carolinas. There, inevitably, they fought the Indians on whose hunting grounds they had encroached. For a century, the Scotch-Irish would be the vanguard of westward expansion and the fiercest of Indian fighters. Benjamin Franklin, who generally espoused an aggressive Indian policy, had nothing ill to say of them.

Dutch." The eighteenth-century German immigrants, mostly Lutherans but some of them Catholics, also came to farm but others were artisans and laborers who settled in Philadelphia and nearby Germantown (now a part of Philadelphia).

Germans were so numerous (a third of Pennsylvania's population in 1776) that they aroused anxieties among other Philadelphians, including the city's most famous citizen, Benjamin Franklin. Calling them "the most stupid of their nation," he feared they would "never adopt our Language or Customs" and will "Germanize us instead of us Anglifying them."

The Scotch-Irish immigrants were even more numerous. Between 1717 and 1776, as many as 250,000 (a third of Ireland's Protestants) came to America. They were more widely disliked than the Germans because they dispersed, populating the frontiers everywhere except in New England, where they were bluntly told they were not welcome. In Worcester, a mob burned a Scotch-Irish Presbyterian church that was under construction.

The Scotch-Irish were disliked because they were a rough, contentious, combative, and clannish people. Their ancestors had fought with the English who had persecuted them because of their Presbyterian faith. Pushed into Ireland they lived in an unending state of hostility with the Catholic Irish whose lands had been taken from them and given to the Presbyterians. They huddled "together like brutes without regard to age or sex or sense of decency," said one colonial who did not admire them. "Ignorant, mean, worthless, beggarly," an Anglican minister called them. Another said that "they delight in their present low, lazy, sluttish, heathenish, hellish life, and seem not desirous of changing it."

FAMILY AND PROPERTY

The family had a standing in colonial law and custom that, today, can be difficult to comprehend. Families, not individuals, were the political unit. Only male heads of households owning property voted, no matter there were two or three adult sons at home. (Unmarried women who inherited property could be heads of household but they could not vote.) How much property was required for a man to participate in elections varied from colony to colony, but it was generally not much: a farm that produced an income of 40 shillings in Massachusetts and Connecticut; a "competent estate" in Rhode Island; 50 acres in six colonies; 25 improved acres in Virginia. In Great Britain only one adult male in three could vote; almost three in four qualified in the colonies. Actual participation was less: one fourth of male Bostonians actually cast votes, about 40 percent of eligible Pennsylvanians and New Yorkers. Farmers living far from county seats had other things to do on election day, and, before the 1760s, candidates for public office rarely differed on "issues." Why bother?

Property laws were written by propertied men and designed to preserve the social integrity and privileges of the propertied families. Virginia, Maryland, and South Carolina enacted laws of primogeniture and entail. If a head of household died intestate (without leaving a will), all his land passed to his eldest son (primogeniture means "first-born"). Wealthy planters almost always did this anyway because at least the core of their landed estates was entailed: by law, it

Dutch Women's Rights

Married women in New Netherlands had significantly different property rights than married women in the English colonies. They owned family property jointly with their husbands, not in coverture. When one spouse died, the survivor inherited the whole. If the survivor was a woman and she remarried, her property from her previous marriage remained hers independently of

her second husband. He had no say in how she used it. When she died, the property from her first marriage was divided equally among the sons and daughters from her first marriage.

The English guaranteed these property laws when New Netherlands surrendered in 1664. Only during the 1700s did they fall into disuse. Even then, ethnically Dutch women in New York clung to another Dutch

practice at odds with English custom. As late as the nineteenth century, they continued to use their maiden names throughout life, not their husbands' surnames. Thus, Annetje Krygier, married to Jans van Arsdale, remained Annetje Krygier until she died. In sharp contrast, many English church registries did not list a woman's surname even in the record of her marriage: coverture with a vengeance.

had to be passed on intact to a single heir. In Virginia in 1760, 80 percent of the cultivated land was entailed. (A daughter inherited estates only if there were no sons.)

The purpose of the laws was to preserve the riches and social privileges of the wealthy—in effect to protect social station against human nature. That is, if an estate of a thousand acres and 30 slaves, enough to support a household in grand style, was divided among four or five children, the result would be four or five households of middling means. If these properties were subdivided among the next generation, the result, from grandparents to grandchildren, would be a gaggle of struggling subsistence farmers where once there had been a grandee.

SOCIAL MOBILITY

Propertied men were not insensitive to the fate of their younger sons. They could and did bequeath them money (personal as opposed to real property) or acquired land for them that was not entailed. As in Great Britain, second sons were educated in a profession: the ministry, medicine, the law, or (less likely in the colonies) the military. A profession maintained their social status as gentlemen, and the possibility of making an advantageous marriage.

George Washington, for example, was a second son. His older brother, Lawrence, inherited the extensive family lands. He helped George train as a surveyor (which meant land speculator in the colonies) in the hope he would himself "found a family"; that is, acquire property. Washington was also an officer in the Virginia militia and he kept an eye toward that other avenue to acquiring property: marrying an

heiress or a wealthy widow. George found one in Martha Custis. So did William Carter in 1771 when, to the merriment of the Virginia Gazette, he married the Widow Ellison, "aged eighty-five; a sprightly old tit, with three thousand pounds fortune."

Wealthy men attended to their daughters' futures by providing dowries (money and slaves, rarely land) handsome enough to attract wealthy husbands. Women who came into property, as daughters without brothers or as widows, were surrounded by suitors not many days after the funeral. (Washington and Martha Custis married shortly after her first husband died.) The woman who wanted to control her property, which only an unmarried woman could do, had to have a strong will to resist the pressure on her to marry.

WOMAN'S PLACE

A propertied woman who married did not, as is often said, lose her property to her husband. It remained her property; she could bequeath it to anyone she liked. However, her husband had the use of it. He could not sell it, but he managed it and the income it provided was his. The legal principle of **coverture** held that "husband and wife are one and that one the husband." In the law, a married woman's person was submerged into the person of her husband.

The law provided a married woman with some protection. When her husband died, the widow was entitled to one-third of the income of the estate that passed to her elder son. This entitlement was called a dower (a reference to the dowry she had brought to the marriage) and the widow was known as a dowager.

If colonial women's status was inferior to that of men, they enjoyed more favorable situations than women in Europe. In most colonies, husbands were forbidden to beat their wives, in some even to strike them. At least one Massachusetts man was fined because, in public, he referred to his wife as "my servant." Europeans unfailingly commented on the deference colonial men paid women, and the protections women were provided by custom. In the former Puritan colonies, a woman could sue for divorce on the grounds of adultery, bigamy, desertion, impotence, incest, or absence for a period of seven years.

THE LOWER ORDERS

Property laws meant little to people on the bottom. The larger northern cities—Boston, New York, Philadelphia—all had their "lower orders": ex-servants, slaves and poor free blacks, sailors on leave, and roustabouts. They found enough work to keep them alive, but too little to feel a sense of belonging to the community or to have much respect for conventional morals.

Even small seaports had a disreputable quarter where drunkenness and brawling were endemic and the makings of a mob were ever present. The patterns of underclass crime were much as they are today. In New York, men committed 95 percent of violent crimes and 74 percent of thefts. Rape must have been common but was rarely prosecuted because

Coverture in the Graveyard

The submersion of a married woman's person into the person of her husband continued after death in the Upper Burial Ground, a cemetery in Germantown, Pennsylvania. Until about 1800, almost no married women buried there are registered in cemetery records by their own names. Instead, their burials are recorded as "Johannes Koch's wife," and so on. A few unmarried women were buried under their own names but widows were not. Their burials were entered as "Widow Hoess" or "Alois Miller's widow." Children—there are plenty of them—are identified as their father's, not their mother's. A poignant series of burials in 1769 reminds us of how different life was 250 years ago:

Oct 26 Johannes Kehrbach's child
Nov 1 Johannes Kehrbach's child
Nov 4 Johannes Kehrbach's third child

(Yet another was buried May 31, 1773.)

convictions were difficult. The victim was unlikely to be a "woman of virtue" and her personal morality was of compelling pertinence to judges and juries. Statutory rape cases were virtually unknown. The traditional English age of consent was ten! Colonial assemblies upped this, but only to twelve or fourteen.

With witchcraft prosecutions disreputable after the Salem hysteria, the only major crime associated with women was infanticide. With high infant mortality a fact of life, like rape, it was a difficult crime to prove in court. In New York between 1730 and 1780, twenty women were charged with killing their newborns but only one was convicted. Illegitimate births were common. A third of all colonial births—not just among the lower classes!—occurred outside marriage or in noticeably less than nine months after the wedding.

SLAVE REBELLIONS

The lowliest of the lowly were the slaves. Except in New York, they were not numerous north of the Mason-Dixon line, the boundary between Pennsylvania and Maryland that was surveyed in 1769. Slaves were only 8 percent of the population in Pennsylvania, 3 percent in Massachusetts.

In the southern colonies, slavery grew in importance during the eighteenth century. The number of blacks in Virginia, most of whom were slaves, rose from about 4,000 in 1700 to 42,000 in 1743, and to more than 200,000 at the time of the American Revolution. In a few Virginia counties and over much of South Carolina, blacks outnumbered whites.

Slaves rebelled now and then. In 1712, slaves in New York City staged an uprising and, in 1741, a series of arsons in the city was blamed on a cabal of slaves and poor whites. Probably there was no organized conspiracy. Nevertheless, eighteen blacks and four whites were hanged; thirteen African Americans were burned alive (the punishment for arson); seventy were sold to the West Indies.

In 1730, about 300 Christian slaves in Virginia fled into the Great Dismal Swamp, an uncharted tangle of marshes and dense woods on the Virginia–North Carolina border. Hired Indians tracked them and most were captured. (Virginia hanged twenty-nine of the leaders.) But the Great Dismal remained a refuge for a community of runaway blacks, tribeless Indians, and alienated poor whites for decades, their numbers possibly as many as a thousand.

In 1739, about twenty slaves from the **Stono** plantation near Charleston seized guns, killed several planter families and almost captured the lieutenant governor. About 150 other slaves joined them. "With Colours displayed, and two Drums beating," they began to march toward Florida where, they had learned through an astonishingly efficient slave grapevine, the governor of the Spanish colony would grant them freedom. Judging from their names, some of the rebels were Catholics, probably converted in the Congo before they were enslaved, and favorably disposed toward the Spanish for religious reasons.

Most of the Stono rebels were captured within a week but some managed to reach St. Augustine. They settled to the north of the town in the fortified African-American village of Santa Teresa de Mose. They swore to "shed their last drop of blood in defense of the Great Crown of Spain, and to be the most cruel enemies of the English." The attraction Santa Teresa held out to slaves in South Carolina was great enough that, in 1640, Georgia's Governor Oglethorpe attacked the village.

POLITICS: IMPERIAL AND COLONIAL

For a quarter of a century, from 1713 to 1739, France and Britain were at peace and the colonies prospered. Tobacco was no longer a bonanza crop, but it was profitable. The export of rice, indigo, naval stores, and hides and furs continued to be lucrative, although these items were harder to get. The middle colonies, especially Pennsylvania, fed the West Indies where sugar cultivation was so intensive slaves had no time to grow much of their own food. Colonials even began to export ginseng root to China. The colonial merchant marine grew in size so there was almost as much tonnage registered in American as in British ports. In the troubled times to come, Americans would look back on the "long peace" of 1713–1739 as a golden age.

SALUTARY NEGLECT

They identified the good times with the policies of the British prime minister, Robert Walpole. Avuncular and easygoing, fancying his daily outsized bottle of port, Walpole believed that the best way to govern was to govern as little as possible. So far as the colonies were concerned, things were going well if they were bustling, prosperous, and content. Their exports and imports were enriching British merchants. Why in the world do anything to disturb them? Walpole's policy—"leave

Piracy's Golden Age

There have been pirates as long as ships have carried cargoes worth stealing. From about 1660 to 1725, the crime was a major problem in American waters.

Pirates are seafaring armed robbers, usually murderers, accomplices at least. They were not rapists only because they preyed on merchant ships, which rarely had women aboard.

Pirates in the West Indies were called buccaneers because the first of them were riffraff from the mountains of Hispaniola who cooked their meat by slow-smoking it (*boucaner* in French). The commercial wars of the 1600s attracted them to maritime robbery when, to save money on naval expenditures, France, Holland, Spain, and England commissioned privateers, well-armed privately owned ships who, for a percentage of the take, were licensed to attack the enemy's merchantmen. Privateering was lucrative so, when peace treaties were signed, some privateers found it difficult to give up the trade. They went on to steal from ships without regard to the flag their victims flew. In 1701, the British hanged Captain William Kidd, a New Yorker, for piracy. Just a few years earlier, they had issued him the privateer's Letters of Marque and Reprisal.

What kind of men became pirates? In the early 1720s, 98 percent of those who were captured said they started life

From the Collections of the Library of Congress

as "honest seamen" on the merchantmen on which they came to prey. A large number said that liquor led them to opt for their life of crime. Indeed, life on a pirate vessel can seem, in the records, to have been one long drunken revel so that, on a given day, most of the crew was incapacitated.

There was more to it than drink. An honest seaman's life was dull and laborious. Pay was poor; punishments were brutal. Piracy offered excitement, eternally an attraction to young men agitated by raging hormones. Pirates might risk their lives during robberies, and the gallows was their fate if they were caught. But each job filled their purses and, whether or not they were drunk nonstop between hits, they did not work very much. A merchant sloop of 100 tons was sailed by a crew of about a dozen; the same vessel under the black flag of piracy carried eighty men. If they captured slaves, they did the work while the pirates looked for buyers. Captain Kidd told of stealing "twelve slaves of whom we intended to make good use of to do the drudgery of our ship."

Pirate crews were large because numbers were the key to their success. They were robbers; they did not want to destroy the ships they attacked. (Their cannon were for defense.) They wanted victims' vessels undamaged so they

well enough alone," "let sleeping dogs lie"—was known as **salutary neglect.** Inaction was the best action, even if it meant overlooking colonial violations of the Navigation Acts, which were common.

Alas for history's Walpoles, there are always people who demand government action on behalf of their interests or whims. In 1732, London hatmakers complained that the growth of that industry in the northern colonies was hurting their sales in North America. The prime minister quieted them by forbidding colonials to sell hats outside the boundaries of their own colony; it was also an offense to train African Americans in the craft. London's hatters were mollified. American hatmakers ignored the laws. Colonial officials rarely enforced it. Walpole dined with his friends.

The Molasses Act of 1733 was a response to complaints by sugar planters in the British West Indies that Americans were buying molasses from French islands, where it was cheaper. Mercantilism, they argued, entitled them to a monopoly of the molasses market in New England (where most of it was distilled into rum, the common man's liquor, and valuable in the African slave trade.)

In the Molasses Act, Walpole levied a 6 pence per gallon duty on French molasses, placating British sugar planters, and then made little effort to collect it, satisfying colonials who were buying molasses from the French. Fraudulent invoices stating that French molasses came from British Jamaica or Barbados did not fool customs collectors, but they could be bribed.

could take everything worth taking—often enough, the captured ship. The captain of a merchantman with twelve seamen (who were not fighting men) was foolish to resist eighty vicious pirates armed with cutlasses, knives, and pistols. Few did. Merchants knew that those who gave up without a fight were usually spared the hideous cruelties of which the pirates were capable. The principle was the same as the advice given today to people confronted on a dark street by a thug with a knife: give him the wallet.

A pirate vessel had to be fast. Pirates had to catch their victims in order to intimidate them with their numbers and ferocity. A few famous pirates like Bartholomew "Black Bart" Roberts and Edward "Blackbeard" Teach had large 40-gun ships; most pirates sailed sloops, large enough to accommodate a hundred drunken cutthroats, but speedy.

Treasure—"pieces of eight!"—was, of course, the most desirable booty. When pirates tortured captives who had given up without resisting, it was usually to learn where any money aboard had been hidden. Mostly, however, pirates took the food and drink they wanted for their own use and had to be satisfied with whatever cargo was aboard, even low-cost bulk items—hogsheads of molasses or tobacco.

Selling such contraband was a problem. Pirates could not anchor in a port and advertise for buyers. There were a few wide-open pirate towns in the Bahamas and Belize where merchants of dubious integrity would come for the bargains available. The governor of Jamaica encouraged pirates to come to Port Royal; armed pirate ships in the harbor discouraged attacks by the Spanish and French. Blackbeard was scouting Ocracoke Inlet in North Carolina for the site of a new pirate entrepôt when he was killed in 1718. But none of the sanctuaries lasted for long. The wildest of them, Port Royal, was destroyed by an earthquake in 1692, much to the satisfaction of moralists.

Curiously, pirate vessels were more democratic than New England town meetings. Where to hunt prey, from Newfoundland to the West Indies, was determined by majority vote, as was the decision whether or not to attack a vessel. The captain (who was elected and could be voted out) claimed a far smaller share of booty than the masters of merchantmen or whalers (or privateers) received. His allowance of food and drink was the same as that of the crewmen. Only when "fighting, chasing, or being chased" did he have the absolute authority of a naval commander.

During piracy's "golden age," most pirates were British or colonials, blacks and whites. At his last stand, Blackbeard had 13 whites and 6 blacks with him. In 1722, Black Bart's huge force of 268 included 77 blacks. Unlike their white shipmates, blacks had a chance to escape hanging; they had to argue they were slaves—contraband, not crewmen—and not be contradicted by witnesses who had seen them resisting capture.

The golden age came abruptly to an end during the Long Peace when the colonial powers directed their warships against the pirates. In 1720, between 1,500 and 2,000 pirates in about twenty-five ships worked the Caribbean and the North American coast. By 1723, their numbers were down to 1,000, by 1726 to 200. In 1718, there were fifty attacks on merchant vessels in American waters but just six in 1726. Relentless pursuit and prompt hanging were effective; so were announcements of pardons. Many pirates had, they claimed, been forced into the life when, honest seamen, they were captured by pirates. The large number of men who immediately applied for pardons implies they were telling the truth.

Another law ignored in the interests of prosperity and calm was passed in 1750 at the behest of English ironmakers, who wanted a monopoly of the colonial market. The act forbade colonists to engage in most forms of iron manufacture. Not only did colonial forges continue to operate with impunity, several colonial governments actually subsidized the iron industry within their borders. Salutary neglect was a wonderful way to run an empire—as long as times were good.

ASSEMBLIES AND GOVERNORS

One consequence of Walpole's easygoing colonial policy was the steady erosion of the mother country's political control of her American daughters. Piecemeal during the eighteenth century, colonial assemblies increased their power at the expense of royal governors (proprietors' governors in Maryland and Pennsylvania).

The key to this shift in the balance of government was the British political principle that the people, through their elected representatives, must consent to all tax laws. In Great Britain, Parliament held the power of the purse; all money bills had to be approved by the House of Commons. In the colonies, the elected assemblies—whether called the House of Burgesses or the House of Delegates—made this important prerogative their own.

Colonial governors were authorized to veto any bill of which they disapproved, including budget bills. But political realities required them to be cautious. When the governor's

Collection of The New-York Historical Society

And the Governor Wore Organdy

Of the few nobles who accepted appointments as royal governors, by far the worst was Edward Hyde, Viscount Cornbury, who was governor of New York and New Jersey between 1701 and 1709. He was a disaster. He aggravated political division dating to Leisler's Rebellion in 1688 and harassed the Dutch Reformed Church which had supported royal government. Within a few years, Lord Cornbury knew he had made a mess of things. He lamented that "a Porter in the streets of London is a happier man than a Governor in America." He begged Queen Anne to relieve him. When she finally did, he was thrown into New York's debtors' prison from which he was released only when he inherited his father's title, Earl of Clarendon, and, undoubtedly more important to him at the moment, his father's money.

It was whispered (and said aloud after Cornbury went home) that he dressed in women's clothing, openly sashaying on the ramparts surrounding the governor's palace; that he invited the men at a banquet to fondle his wife's ears, which he believed beyond compare. (Lady Cornbury was herself accused of stealing jewelry—earrings?—from homes she visited.)

The evidence the governor was a cross-dresser is not reliable. The allegations, although numerous, were made by his bitterest political enemies or were hearsay, remarks in letters of what the writer had been told but had not himself seen. There is a portrait said to be of Cornbury in a gown worthy of a queen. (One of his alleged explanations of his peculiarity was that he represented Queen Anne and therefore should appear to be her.) Critics of the tale have no conclusive evidence to discredit it, but they establish a reasonable doubt, which is all that is asked of defense attorneys.

---

dispute with the assembly got nasty, the assembly could deny the governor the funds he needed for day-to-day expenses, even the money to maintain his personal household; that is, "starve him into compliance" as a hungry royal governor of New York phrased it.

The power of the purse was a formidable weapon. Few who served as governors in America were excessively wealthy before they took their jobs. Englishmen and Scots rich enough to maintain themselves opulently in London or Edinburgh did not choose to rough it in Portsmouth, Williamsburg, or Charleston. Most royal and proprietary governors were men on the make. They sought positions overseas because—another blessing of salutary neglect—Walpole winked at personal profiteering by royal officials. To make money in the colonies, however, governors had to get along with powerful colonials, the men who sat in their councils or were elected to seats in the assemblies.

Of course, it was possible to get along too well with influential Americans, to yield too much to them. That would excite the displeasure of Crown or proprietor. But during the era of salutary neglect, it came easily for governors to be cooperative: so long as trade was bustling and the quitrents flowed back to Great Britain, a governor was doing the important part of his job.

CULTURE AND RELIGION

Colonial culture was British culture. Educated Americans imported their books and periodicals from England along with fine fabrics for their clothing and candelabra for the dining rooms. Colonial ladies and gentlemen—particularly in the South—patterned their manners and avocations on those of the English country gentry. Young George Washington's mania for fox hunting—riding to the hounds, an exhilarating but dangerous and peculiarly English sport—was so avid that a number of observers mentioned it, but Washington never lacked for company. Although New Englanders sent their brighter sons to Harvard or Yale Colleges, and Virginia had the College of William and Mary, some planters shipped their sons to Britain to be educated, particularly at the law schools in London. Few were such fanatic Anglophiles as William Byrd II of Virginia or Pennsylvania's Benjamin Franklin—both preferred lively London society to home—but if colonial Anglophobes existed, they were few and quiet.

THE DECLINE OF THE CHURCHES

Religion and church were less important to the eighteenth-century colonial elite than it had been to their grandparents. Most of New England's wealthy merchants still rented pews

THE HANCOCK MANSION.

The splendid home of wealthy merchant, John Hancock, in Boston. His luxurious life bore little resemblance to the Spartan lives of his Puritan forebears. Nor did his "liberal" religious views have much in common with the Calvinism of seventeenth century Boston. In 1776, Hancock would win immortality for putting his name on the Declaration of Independence in an outsized signature.

in the Congregational Churches, as the Puritan meeting-houses of their grandparents were now called. But the old teachings lost their hold on them. Indeed, many prominent Bostonians whose ancestors had crossed the ocean on the *Mayflower* or *Arabella* crossed the street to join the Church of England.

To hard-shelled latter-day Puritans, the Congregationalism of Boston and Harvard College had itself gone flabby. Strict Calvinists who believed Harvard was teaching loose doctrine and morals founded Yale College in New Haven, Connecticut in 1701. Only twenty years later, Yale was rocked; its rector, Timothy Cutler, and almost the entire faculty—all ministers—resigned, announcing that they were sailing to England to be ordained as Anglican priests.

As the established church in the mother country, New York, and the southern colonies—and, in Massachusetts, the church of the royal governor—the Anglican Church was the socially prestigious church; membership in it was almost a prerequisite to political preferment. It was not a demanding church, as much a social as a religious institution. Its ministers baptized babies, wed men and women, buried the dead, and kept their sermons short and undisturbing. The "low church" movement that began in the 1660s rejected the rituals and superstitions of the almost Catholic "high church" and the enthusiastic and disruptive fanaticism of Puritans and Quakers.

Like refined and worldly descendants of Puritans in Massachusetts, Pennsylvania Quakers who had prospered and lost their parents' zeal became Anglicans. In Philadelphia,

indeed, Benjamin Franklin could win universal respect as the city's first citizen while affiliated with no church at all.

THE ENLIGHTENMENT

Traditional religion lost its hold on upper- and middle-class colonials, primarily because of the prosperity and comfort more and more of them enjoyed. When worldly life is good, people of every era and faith have tended to relegate religious beliefs and practices to the periphery of their lives—a few hours on Sunday and baptisms and weddings. Moreover, educated Europeans and colonials of the era were profoundly drawn to the spirit of the **Enlightenment,** a revolutionary way of looking at the world that took shape during the latter 1600s.

Two of the key figures of the English Enlightenment were Isaac Newton and John Locke. In *Principia Mathematica* (1687) and *Opticks* (1704), Newton demonstrated that forces as mysterious as those that determined the paths of the planets and even the nature of light and color could be rationally explained through observation and mathematical calculation. The order, symmetry, and "laws" of the physical world were knowable. John Locke's "Essay Concerning Human Understanding" (1690) argued that all human knowledge was learned through experience. God did not implant ideas in the human mind; when a human being was born, his mind was a blank slate. Everything men and women learned they learned from others.

Pioneers of modern science such as William Harvey, who discovered how the human circulatory system worked,

© Bettmann/Corbis

George Whitefield usually preached to crowds of thousands, but a dozen insistent colonials hungry for the salvation he promised was enough to get him started. Whitefield preached outside more than in churches, not only because of the size of the crowds he attracted but because disapproving Old Light ministers locked their doors against him.

showed that yet another mystery was no mystery at all. Indeed, Benjamin Franklin won his reputation as the greatest of American colonials by explaining electricity. He and thirty other colonists were members of London's Royal Society, which was dedicated to the advancement of science.

The Enlightenment turned few people into atheists, but it reduced the role of God in nature and human affairs to that of the Creator. Even men and women who continued to attend religious services became deists. Yes, of course, there was a God, but, like a clockmaker, after he created the universe and set it in motion, he just let it run according to laws that his human creatures could discover and understand. People of the Enlightenment scorned and even ridiculed traditional ministers who preached that an Indian attack, a yellow fever epidemic, or a hurricane were expressions of God's anger.

THE GREAT AWAKENING

Church attendance by uneducated colonials of humbler people also declined in the early eighteenth century, in part because of the "liberalization" of the three major American denominations: Congregationalism in New England; the Quakers in Pennsylvania, New Jersey, and Delaware; and the Anglican Church in the South and in New York. Deism and

genteel religion had little appeal to people who looked to religion for emotional fulfillment.

Then, as if they had been combusted in a fire of God's making (which some of them believed to be so), passionate preachers calling for a revival of true faith seemed to be everywhere in the colonies within just a few years. The first signs of the **Great Awakening** were in New Jersey and Pennsylvania during the 1620s among Presbyterians and the Calvinistic Dutch Reformed Church. In 1734, Jonathan Edwards, the Congregationalist minister in Northampton, Massachusetts, began to preach sermons emphasizing the sinfulness of humanity, the torment all deserved to suffer in hell, and that salvation could be had only through divine grace, which God visited on men and women in the form of an intensely emotional conversion experience. Edwards did not honey his message. "The God who holds you over the pit of hell," he said in his most famous sermon, "much as one holds a spider or some loathsome insect over the fire, abhors you, and is dreadfully provoked."

In 1736, an already famous English preacher, George Whitefield, arrived in Georgia and—he could not be exhausted—made the first of five preaching tours the length of colonial America, often addressing thousands in open-air meetings, speaking 60 hours a week. During one 78-day period, he delivered more than a hundred lengthy sermons.

When he spoke in Philadelphia, Benjamin Franklin was so awed by the power of Whitefield's voice—he called it "an excellent piece of music"—that he methodically backed away from the preacher to measure at what distance he could still understand his words. Franklin then hurried home to calculate how many people could, in theory, hear Whitefield at one time.

Some of the revivalists were sincere believers of high integrity. Jonathan Edwards took care not to inspire false conversions with theatrical arm-waving and flouncing about. It was said that during his sermons he stared at the bellpull at the entrance to his church and carefully modulated his voice. Other preachers, including Whitefield, were more demonstrative. A few, like James Davenport, ranted and raved, whooped and hollered, danced and pranced about the platform, tore their clothes from their bodies, rolled their eyes like lunatics, and fell to the floor. "Strike them, Lord, strike them!" Davenport cried when the local sheriff, convinced he was insane, tried to restrain him. Davenport has a better claim to being the father of the American revival, as it evolved, than Jonathan Edwards.

"NEW LIGHTS," "OLD LIGHTS," AND THE IDEA OF EQUALITY

The Great Awakening divided most Protestant denominations into "Old Lights" (conservative defenders of the established churches) and "New Lights" (the Great Awakening rebels). New Lights said that Old Light ministers were dull because they were not truly saved; they had not been blessed with God's grace. Most New Lights were contemptuous of learning. God did not speak through ministers with college degrees; he spoke to those whom he struck with lightning although they had not spent a day at school in their lives.

Old Lights responded that New Light preachers deceived their listeners and even themselves. Charles Chauncy, an Old Light Boston Congregationalist wrote that a revivalist in the city "mistakes the working of his own passions for divine communications, and fancies himself immediately inspired by the SPIRIT OF GOD, when all the while, he is under no other influence than that of an over-heated imagination."

Congregationalists and Presbyterians split into two mutually hostile factions. The Anglican Church eventually calved the Methodist Church. Before the Great Awakening, the three largest religious groups in the colonies were the Anglicans, Congregationalists, and Quakers. By the end of the century, the three largest were the Baptists, Methodists, and Presbyterians.

In disdaining educated ministers in favor of preachers personally inspired by God (shades of Anne Hutchinson!), and in saying that salvation was available to everyone, the New Lights planted the seeds of a belief in the equality of all men and women, eventually a central principle of American culture. What has been called the "feminization of American Protestantism" began with the Great Awakening. Before the eighteenth century, women were submissive and secondary to men in churches. By 1800, 75 percent of Protestant church members in the United States were women.

MAP 6:1 French and British Empires in North America Until 1763

France claimed much more American acreage than Britain did. However, beyond narrow agricultural strips on the St. Lawrence River and Gulf Coast—the cities of Montreal and Quebec and the towns of New Orleans, Biloxi, and Mobile—French America was largely wilderness, the Indians' country.

The Great Awakening also spawned a multiplication of American colleges. Old Lights, alarmed at New Light rejection of learning, founded Brown in Rhode Island, King's College (Columbia) in New York, and Queen's College (Rutgers) in New Jersey. New Light Presbyterians, not as scornful of education as Baptists and Methodists, founded the College of New Jersey in 1747; it was later renamed Princeton.

BRITAIN'S GLORIOUS TRIUMPH

The "long peace" ended in 1739 when Parliament declared war on Spain. Supposedly, all London was enraged when a merchant, Robert Jenkins, with one of his ears in a box he carried everywhere, told everyone who asked that it had been cut off by a Spanish customs agent.

In fact, conflicts with Spain had been piling up, not the least of them the ongoing quasi-war between Spanish Florida and British South Carolina and newly founded Georgia.

KING GEORGE'S WAR

Now feeble Spain was virtually a dependency of France so, in 1740, France joined the war. The next year, the War of Jenkins Ear merged into the War of the Austrian Succession when Prussia (subsequently a French ally) attacked Austria (backed by Great Britain after 1743). The Americans—who knew anything of Austrian affairs?—called the conflict King George's War.

Georgia and South Carolina exchanged attacks with Florida; both parties had Indian allies. *Petite guerre* flickered again on New England and New York frontiers. The great event in the North, however, was in 1745 when a force of 4,000 militia, mostly from Massachusetts, besieged and captured the French fortress at Louisbourg on Cape Breton Island. Never had colonial soldiers won such a victory. Louisbourg was a state-of-the-art fortress; the French boasted that it was impregnable, "the Gibraltar of North America," and British generals agreed. New Englanders had a right to exult.

But the joy was short lived. Three years later, in the Treaty of Aix-la-Chapelle, the British returned Louisbourg to France in return for French concessions in Europe, where they and the Prussians had won most of the battles.

Parliament reimbursed Massachusetts for the cost of the Louisbourg campaign, but there was no way to restore the 500 lives lost on Cape Breton Island, nor the fact that, at Louisbourg, French ships that harassed New Englanders once again had a sanctuary.

Peace lasted only eight years. The war between France and Britain that erupted in 1756—called the Seven Years War in Europe—differed significantly from the three Anglo–French conflicts that preceded it. First, it was a worldwide war; the British and French faced off on the high seas, in the West Indies, and in India as well as in Europe and North America. Second, the war began in North America. It was not a European war into which the colonies were drawn; it was an American war that, within a few years, sucked in all the European powers. Finally, although it could hardly be known at the time, it was to be a decisive war with an overwhelming

victor and a dispossessed loser, a conclusion unknown in European war for centuries.

A YOUNG VIRGINIAN MAKES HIS MARK

On the face of it, the British position in North America was far superior to that of France and Spain. The population of the British colonies was 1.2 million. There were only about 50,000 whites in French America, fewer than 20,000 Spanish north of Mexico. For the first time, Britain sent a large force of professional soldiers to America. They soon outnumbered French troops stationed there.

However, the French had the goodwill of most of the Indian tribes west of the Appalachians between the Ohio River and the Great Lakes, where the war began. Virginia claimed this territory; wealthy Virginians, among them a 22-year-old planter named George Washington, were already speculating in land there. They had secured large tracts of land that they intended to subdivide into farms to sell to settlers. Their "property," however, was worthless so long as Indians controlled the Ohio River valley.

With even the heart of New France still thinly populated, the French did not think of populating the Ohio country. But they coveted it for its furs and the numerous Indians that were a lucrative market for French goods. French interests and Indian interests were identical: keep the British colonials out. Without their Indian allies, the French would have been helpless. Indians outnumbered French soldiers in every battle except Louisbourg and Quebec. Americans called the conflict the French and Indian War.

In 1753, the French began to lay out a string of forts in western Pennsylvania. Governor Robert Dinwiddie of Virginia sent young George Washington west to inform the French that they were trespassing. Washington was received cordially but, of course, his message was ignored. Although he had no military experience, the next year Washington was sent back with a small armed force to build a Virginian fort where the Allegheny and Monongahela Rivers joined to form the Ohio (the site of Pittsburgh today). He never got that far. Run off by Indians and French, he holed up in appropriately named Fort Necessity; it was a palisade, hurriedly slapped together. He was "soundly defeated" (Washington's words) in a skirmish he prudently kept almost bloodless, then was sent home. The French built Fort Duquesne at the conjunction of the three rivers.

American Soldiers: An Opinion Poll

George Washington claimed that his Virginians fought much better at Braddock's defeat than the British regulars. If so, according to the British commanders of the French and Indian War, it was an astonishing aberration. A sampling of their opinions of the Americans they commanded:

General Braddock: "slothful and languid"
General Abercromby: "vagabonds"
Lord Loudoun: "the lowest dregs"
General Wolfe: "contemptible cowards"
General Forbes: "the scum of the worst of people . . . a bad collection of Broken Innkeepers, Horse Jockeys, and Indian traders"

Germ Warfare

Tradition has it that Braddock and, later, Jeffery Amherst, employed a primitive form of germ warfare against the Indians, seeing to it that blankets that had covered smallpox victims fell into natives' hands. Only one such incident, however, is documented. In June 1763, when the war with the French was effectively over, Amherst (who despised Indians) approved giving two such blankets and a handkerchief to Indians at truce talks. Using disease systematically as a weapon was not British policy.

BRADDOCK'S DEFEAT

Washington's humiliation prompted the British to send 1,400 regulars, commanded by General Edward Braddock, to Virginia. Washington, now officially a soldier, was named Braddock's American aide in charge of about 450 Virginia volunteers. Braddock had the men to take Fort Duquesne—a cakewalk. Only 72 French soldiers, 150 Canadians, and 600 Indians defended it, and the Indians argued that Braddock's army was too strong. They were persuaded to stay, however, and Braddock played into French and Indian hands. He was a brave soldier, even reckless, but he was arrogantly inflexible. According to Washington's post mortem, Braddock refused to hear Washington's explanation of how Indians battled, of the necessity of quietly scouting ahead of the army. Braddock marched his army in a column as if in open country rather than on the narrow trail they hacked out of the wilderness as they went.

Had the French and the Indians remained in Fort Duquesne, they would have been overwhelmed. Instead, they sallied out and hit the British and Virginians in the forest, completely surprising them. Washington later claimed that his Virginians, familiar with fighting Indians, did well. But the British column was hemmed in; forming the conventional battle line was out of the question. The soldiers piled up into one another creating an unmissable target. Braddock and 976 others were killed or wounded. Only 39 French and Indians were lost.

PITT, AMHERST, AND WOLFE

In London, the news of Braddock's defeat was just one item on a depressingly long list. The overall commander of British troops in the colonies, John Campbell, Lord Loudoun (whose personal baggage when he arrived in New York filled an entire ship) was clearly ineffective. General James Abercomby was utterly incompetent; with 12,000 troops at his disposal he was badly defeated by 3,000 French and Indians under Louis de Montcalm near New York's Lake George. There were also defeats in Europe and India. The war seemed to be ending as King William's, Queen Anne's, and King George's wars had ended, with a negotiated peace and New France and the Indians hemming in the British colonies.

Then, a remarkable man, energetic and imaginative, took charge of the war in Parliament. **William Pitt** insisted that, above all else, France must not be ascendant in North America. He convinced Parliament to send only a token army to Europe; instead, with borrowed money, Parliament paid huge subsidies to Prussia, now Britain's ally, to tie down the French army, preventing France from matching the massive force (more than 20,000 soldiers) Pitt sent to North America. Pitt also recruited Americans into the regular army, and curried the vanity of the commanders of colonial volunteers by recognizing the ranks colonial assemblies had bestowed on them.

Pitt had an eye for generals. He put the able **Jeffery Amherst** in overall command with instructions to strike at the heart of New France, Louisbourg, and Quebec. Amherst commanded the Louisbourg campaign. The assault that toppled the fortress was led by **General James Wolfe,** a high-strung, possibly disturbed young man (fellow officers thought he was unbalanced). Wolfe got lucky; he tried to call off the attack but could not get his orders to the front lines and the French panicked. Amherst was impressed. He put Wolfe in charge of an advance on Quebec via the St. Lawrence River while Amherst, returning to New York, would lead a second army to the French capital overland.

THE FALL OF QUEBEC . . . AND THE FRENCH EMPIRE

Amherst was delayed. Wolfe found himself alone below Quebec's cliffs. Several frontal attacks were easily repulsed. Wolfe then tried to draw the French commander, Montcalm, out of the city by destroying a thousand French farms. Montcalm did not budge. It was September 1759; the leaves were turning and the Canadian winter was weeks away. Montcalm reasoned that Wolfe would have to retire to winter quarters in Louisbourg. Why waste his soldiers?

Wolfe too felt the temperatures dropping and gambled. Under cover of night on September 12, he led 4,000 troops up Quebec's cliffs on a steep, narrow trail that had been left virtually unguarded. When the sun rose the next day, Montcalm was stunned to see a British army in battle formation on open ground called the Plains of Abraham. Montcalm's situation was far from desperate. His troops outnumbered Wolfe's. Wolfe's line of supply was inadequate and vulnerable. He had managed to haul only a few cannon up the cliffs while Montcalm's artillery was abundant. He could have bombarded Wolfe's exposed army or, simply, sat tight.

But Montcalm inexplicably—military historians have puzzled over his decision—took his army out of the fortified city to battle Wolfe on equal terms. At 130 yards, the French fired a volley; the British did not respond. At 100 yards and again at 70 yards, they volleyed again; British soldiers crumpled to the ground but the line remained intact. Only when the French closed to 40 yards did the British open fire, mowing the French soldiers down. The battle lasted fifteen minutes. Both

Cajuns

In 1755, when French Acadians in Nova Scotia refused to take an oath of allegiance to King George (they feared they would be forced to fight the French), the British panicked. They forced 6,000 people on ships and deported them to other British colonies where they were simply dumped. Some, in time, found their way back to Nova Scotia. Others settled in French Louisiana where they became known as "Cajuns," a corruption of Acadians. Henry Wadsworth Longfellow, who also immortalized Hiawatha and Paul Revere, wrote a poignant narrative poem, "Evangeline," about the tragic attempt of an Acadian woman to find the lover from whom she was separated.

Cajuns spoke a French dialect (as well as English) until quite recently. They are still a self-conscious ethnic group in Louisiana.

The New-York Historical Society

General James Wolfe died defeating the French outside their fortress at Quebec. A difficult man in life—some thought him mad—the dead Wolfe was immortalized as a national hero. The pensive Indian is an Iroquois, the Native American ally indispensable to British success.

Montcalm and Wolfe were killed. The French army was demoralized. The British occupied Quebec.

Fighting continued elsewhere, and bickering over the terms of the peace dragged on for three years. So far as Americans were concerned, the war was over. In the Peace of Paris of 1763, the map of North America was redrawn from scratch. Great Britain took Florida from Spain and Canada from France. To compensate Spain for the loss of Florida, France was forced to hand over Louisiana, the central third of what is now the United States, to her ally. The sprawling French American empire in the western hemisphere was reduced to its possessions in the West Indies and two tiny, rocky islands in the North Atlantic where French fishermen could shelter but which were militarily useless.

FURTHER READING

General Daniel Boorstin, *The Americans: The Colonial Experience,* 1958; Richard Hofstadter, *America at 1750,* 1971.

New France Bruce G. Trigger, *Natives and Newcomers: Canada's "Heroic Age" Reconsidered,* 1985; William J. Eccles, *The French in North America, 1500–1783,* 1998; Allen Greer, ed., *The Jesuit Relations: Natives and Missionaries in Seventeenth Century North America,* 2000; James Pritchard, *In Search of Empire: The French in the Americas, 1670–1730,* 2004.

Wars Douglas E. Leach, *Arms for Empire: A Military History of the British Colonies in North America,* 1973; Francis Jennings, *The Ambiguous Iroquois Empire: The Covenant Chain Confederation of Indian Tribes with English Colonies,* 1984, and *Empire of Fortune,* 1990; John E. Ferling, *A Wilderness of Miseries: War and Warriors in Early America,* 1980, and *Struggle for a Continent: The Wars of Early America,* 1993; James Merrell, *Beyond the Covenant Chain:* *The Iroquois and Their Neighbors,* 1987; Colin G. Calloway, *War, Migration, and the Survival of Indian Peoples,* 1990.

Colonial Society Bernard Bailyn, *Voyagers to the West: A Passage in the Peopling of America on the Eve of the Revolution,* 1986; Bailyn and Philip D. Morgan, eds., *Strangers Within the Realm: Cultural Margins of the First British Empire,* 1991; T. J. Davis, *A Rumor of Revolt: The "Great Negro Plot" in Colonial New York,* 1985; James G. Leyburn, *The Scotch-Irish: A Social History,* 1962; David Hackett Fisher, *Albion's Seed: Four British Folkways in America,* 1989; David Cordingly, *Under the Black Flag: The Romance and Reality of Life Among the Pirates,* 1995.

Political Developments Bernard Bailyn, *The Origins of American Politics,* 1968; Stephen Webb, *The Governors-General,* 1979; James Henretta, *Salutary Neglect,* 1972.

Religion and Culture Louis B. Wright, *Cultural Life of the American Colonies,* 1957; Jack P. Greene, *Pursuits of Happiness: The Social Development of Early Modern British Colonies and the Frontier of American Culture,* 1988; Alan Heimert and Perry Miller, eds., *The Great Awakening,* 1967; Perry Miller, *Jonathan Edwards,* 1958; Edwin S. Gaustad, *The Great Awakening in New England,* 1957; Henry F. May, *The Enlightenment in America,* 1976; Ned Landsman, *From Colonials to Provincials: Thought and Culture in America 1680–1760,* 1994.

The French and Indian War Howard H. Peckham, *The Colonial Wars, 1689–1762,* 1964; Fred Anderson, *A People's Army: Massachusetts Soldiers and Society in the Seven Years War,* 1984, and *Crucible of War: The Seven Years War and the Fate of Empire in British North America,* 2001; Francis Jennings, *Empire of Fortune: Crowns, Colonies, and Tribes in the Seven Years War,* 1988; Ian K. Steele, *Warpaths: Invasions of North America,* 1994.

KEY TERMS

The following terms are covered in this chapter and can also be found in the list of Key Terms at the back of the book.

coverture	Huguenots	Louisbourg	Scotch-Irish
Enlightenment	Jacques Marquette	*petite guerre*	Stono
General James Wolfe	Jeffery Amherst	salutary neglect	the "American Style"
Great Awakening	Jesuits	Samuel de Champlain	William Pitt

 ## ONLINE SOURCES GUIDE

Use this listing to find online documents, images, interactive maps, simulations, and other resources related to this chapter:

American History Resource Center
http://history.wadsworth.com

Selected Documents
Letter from Father Marquette to Father Dablon (1672)
Excerpts from Jonathan Mayhew's Two Discourses delivered October 25, 1759
Thomas Paine's "Common Sense"
John Dickinson's "Letters from a Farmer in Pennsylvania"
The Liberty Song (1768)

Selected Images
The Battle of Quebec, 1759
Benjamin Franklin and grandsons in Paris

Document Exercises
1754 The Albany Plan of Union

Interactive Timeline (with online readings)
A Maturing Society: Society, Culture, War in the 1700s

Additional resources, exercises, and Internet links related to this chapter are available on *THE AMERICAN PAST* web site: http://history.wadsworth.com/americanpast8e

Discovery

What social changes occurred in the first half of the 1700s that would help spur the later revolutionary movement?

In thinking about this question, begin by breaking it down into the components shown below. A discussion of the significance of each component should appear in your answer.

Religion and Philosophy: For this exercise, please read the following document excerpts: "Jonathan Edwards, 'Sinners in the Hands of an Angry God,'" and "Jonathan Edwards, 'The Great Awakening in New Hampshire ca. 1735.'" Compare and contrast these two religious accounts. How do they differ in their views of sin, salvation, and redemption? What changed in the colonies in the mid-1700s that sparked such a revivalist movement? How does this reflect the decline of Puritanism? What effect might this religious revivalism have on local politics?

Jonathan Edwards, "Sinners in the Hands of an Angry God"

. . . That world of misery, that lake of burning brimstone, is extended abroad under you. There is the dreadful pit of the glowing flames of the wrath of God; there is hell's wide gaping mouth open; and you have nothing to stand upon, nor any thing to take hold of: there is nothing between you and hell but the air; it is only the power and mere pleasure of God that holds you up.

You probably are not sensible of this; you find you are kept out of hell, but do not see the hand of God in it; but look at other things, as the good state of your bodily constitution, your care of your own life, and the means you use for your own preservation. But indeed these things are nothing; if God should withdraw his hand, they would avail no more to keep you from falling, than the thin air to hold up a person that is suspended in it.

Your wickedness makes you as it were heavy as lead, and to tend downwards with great weight and pressure towards hell; and if God should let you go, you would immediately sink and swiftly descend and plunge into the bottomless gulf, and your healthy constitution, and your own care and prudence, and best contrivance, and all your righteousness, would have no more influence to uphold you and keep you out of hell, than a spider's web would have to stop a fallen rock. Were it not for the sovereign pleasure of God, the earth would not bear you one moment; for you are a burden to it; the creation groans with you; the creature is made subject to the bondage of your corruption, not willingly; the sun does not willingly shine upon you to give you light to serve sin and Satan; the earth does not willingly yield her increase to satisfy your lusts; nor is it willingly a stage for your wickedness to be acted upon; the air does not willingly serve you for breath to maintain the flame of life in your vitals, while you spend your life in the Service of God's enemies. God's creatures are good, and were made for men to serve God with, and do not willingly subserve to any other purpose, and groan when they are abused to purposes so directly contrary to their nature and end. And the world would spew you out, were it not for the sovereign hand of him who hath subjected it in hope. There are black clouds of God's wrath now hanging directly over your heads, full of the dreadful storm, and big with thunder; and were it not for the restraining hand of God, it would immediately burst forth upon you. The sovereign pleasure of God, for the present, stays his rough wind; otherwise it would come with fury, and your destruction would come like a whirlwind, and you would be like the chaff of the summer threshing floor. . . .

Jonathan Edwards, "The Great Awakening in New Hampshire ca. 1735"

Particularly, I was surprized with the relation of a young woman, who had been one of the greatest company-keepers in the whole town. When she came to me, I had never heard that she was become in any wise serious, but by the conversation I then had with her, it appeared to me, that what she gave an account of, was a glorious work of God's infinite power and sovereign grace; and that God had given her a *new* heart, truly broken and sanctified. I could not then doubt of it, and have seen much in my acquaintance with her since to confirm it.

Though the work was *glorious*, yet I was filled with concern about the *effect* it might have upon others. I was ready to conclude, (though too rashly) that some would be hardened by it, in carelessness and looseness of life; and would take occasion from it to open their mouths in *reproaches* of religion. But the *event* was the *reverse*, to a wonderful degree. God made it, I suppose, the *greatest occasion of awakening* to others, of any thing that ever came to pass in the town. I have had abundant opportunity to know the effect it had, by my private conversation with many. The news of it seemed to be almost like a *flash of lightning*, upon the hearts of young people, all over the town, and upon many others. Those persons amongst us, who used to be farthest from seriousness, and that I most feared would make an ill improvement of it, seemed greatly to be *awakened* with it. Many went to talk with her, concerning what she had met with; and what appeared in her seemed to be to the satisfaction of all that did so.

Presently upon this, a great and earnest concern about the great things of religion, and the eternal world, became *universal* in all parts of the town, and among persons of all degrees, and all ages. The noise amongst the dry *bones* waxed louder and louder; all other talk but about spiritual and eternal things, was soon thrown by; all the conversation, in all companies and upon all occasions, was upon these things only, unless so much as was necessary for people carrying on their ordinary secular business. Other discourse than of the things of religion, would scarcely be tolerated in any company. The minds of people were wonderfully taken off from the *world*, it was treated amongst us as a thing of very little consequence. They seemed to follow their worldly business, more as a part of their duty, than from any disposition they had to it; the *temptation* now seemed to lie on that hand, to *neglect* worldly affairs too much, and to spend too much time in the immediate exercise of religion. This was exceedingly misrepresented by reports that were spread in distant parts of the land, as though the people here had wholly thrown by all worldly business, and betook themselves entirely to reading and praying, and such like religious exercises.

To read extended versions of the documents, visit the companion Web site http://history.wadsworth.com/americanpast8e; click on "Discovery Sources."

CHAPTER 7

Family Quarrels

Dissension in the Colonies 1763–1770

Harcourt Picture Collection

Magnanimity in politics is not seldom the truest wisdom; and a great Empire and little minds go ill together.

Edmund Burke

In 1763, church bells pealed in the colonies, possibly every bell from Maine to Savannah. Americans were exultant: it was good to be British, to be a part of the people who had humbled Europe's richest and most powerful nation.

By 1775, only twelve years later, a good many of the same Americans were taking up arms and learning to be soldiers, prepared to fight the British army that had taken Quebec. In 1776, the colonies' political leaders proclaimed the independence of the "United States of North America."

One of those men, Oliver Wolcott of Connecticut, wondered what had gone wrong. "So strong had been the Attachment" of Americans to Great Britain, he wrote, that "the Abilities of a Child might have governed this Country."

Wolcott blamed the breakup on British folly, incompetence, and tyranny. He had a point about folly and incompetence. Blunder after stupidity upon miscalculation tells the story of Parliament's and the king's colonial policy between 1763 and 1776. But it would be a mistake, given the education in tyranny that the twentieth century has provided us, to entertain Wolcott's claim that **King George III** and Parliament were tyrants. He was far from alone in using the word; by 1776, "Tyranny!" had become a catchphrase; no

patriotic speech or pamphlet was complete without it. But it was nonsense. Excepting the slaves, colonial Americans enjoyed more political and personal freedom than any people on the continent of Europe, or in Africa, Asia, or South America.

What turned men like Oliver Wolcott into rebels was Great Britain's mismanagement of a badly needed reform of the administration of the empire combined with the failure or refusal of colonial politicians to accept any departure from Robert Walpole's policy of "salutary neglect"; and, in the end, the colonials' refusal to shoulder the responsibilities along with the privileges of being British. The sequence of events that led from 1763 to the War for Independence is not a story of American righteousness versus British villainy; it is merely history.

IMPERIAL PROBLEMS

Wolfe's capture of Quebec put Canada in British hands. Even before negotiators gathered in Paris to write a treaty, however, there was a debate as to whether the British should keep Canada as the reward of victory, or the French West Indian

White Gold, Black Death

Sugar was the most profitable crop grown in the British Empire; by the mid-eighteenth century, it had long since displaced tobacco. Per capita consumption of sugar in Britain doubled every several decades as the population became addicted to sweet coffee, tea, chocolate, candies, and cakes. Even the poorest Londoners smeared molasses on their bread.

There was little art in cultivating and processing it. Cuttings were planted in holes dug with hoes; there was no plowing, and little need for livestock except to pull wagons. The cane is ready for harvest in fifteen months. The stalks are cut and crushed to extract juice, which is boiled, skimmed, and cooled. The crystals are separated from the molasses (most of which was distilled into rum).

Sugar cane needs fertile soil, hot weather, and lots of rain, which the West Indies provided, as well as hordes of laborers, which Africa provided: an astonishing 150 slaves for each 100 acres of cane, three or four times as many slaves as were needed to grow tobacco, which was considered a labor-intensive crop.

And the work was heavier than tobacco-growing and the West Indies unhealthier than the mainland. The West Indies—French, Dutch, Spanish, and Danish—devoured African lives. Sugar planters found it cheaper to work their slaves to death and import new ones than to nurture their health. Between 1700 and 1775, 1.2 million Africans were brought to just the British West Indies. Women were worked as hard as men: their fertility was low and miscarriages high. Infanticide was common in the West Indies; women smothered their infants rather than raise them to the life of misery they knew.

islands of Martinique and Guadeloupe. The British had captured them too, but France's price for ending the costly war in 1763 was the return of one or the other, Canada or the islands.

CANADA OR SUGAR?

The Duke of Bedford and others argued that Britain should give Canada back. Endless forest was not so grand a trophy. What use was Siberia to Russia? The Indians of Canada—former French allies—were numerous, powerful, and hostile. Were not the Indians of the Ohio Valley, also pro-French, enough of a problem? The 50,000 *habitants,* the French Canadians—all Roman Catholics!—would be nothing but trouble. The British had deported a few thousand Acadians out of fear of a rebellion. The Catholic Irish had regularly risen against British authority for two centuries and they showed no sign of calming down. What sense did it make to take another alien people into the empire?

Martinique and Guadeloupe, by way of contrast, were tiny. Small military garrisons could manage them. The handful of French planters that lived on the islands cared less about the design of the flag flying over the harbor forts than the fact that the soldiers there were primed to keep the masses of their slaves in check. The West Indian market, moreover, was very attractive to British merchants. Before the war, two-thirds of France's exports had gone to the West Indies: luxuries for the planters, cheap clothing and shoes for the slaves, and, every year, more slaves from Africa.

There was yet another argument in favor of keeping the sugar islands and giving Canada back. By 1763, the thirteen Atlantic colonies constituted a substantial country. Was it not possible, even likely, that the Americans had been loyal to

Sugar, grown in the West Indies, was the most profitable colonial crop in the eighteenth century. The British West Indies imported far more Africans than the mainland colonies so their owners bought more cheap clothing from British merchants. The sugar slave's life was more wretched than that of a North American slave. In addition to field work, slaves crushed the cane to extract liquid, then, in "boiler houses" like this one—nightmarish factories—they boiled the juice to produce molasses and sugar crystals.

Great Britain only because they feared the French and their Indian allies at their back door? Remove the French from Canada, thus choking off the Indians' supply of arms, and the Americans would no longer need British military protection. They might as well unite, in the words of a Swedish observer, Peter Kalm, and "shake off the yoke of the English monarchy." Others echoed Kalm. At least sixty-five pamphlets published in London argued the Canada-versus-West Indies question.

In the end, Great Britain kept Canada and handed Martinique and Guadeloupe back to France. There was a £140 million national debt to pay and British taxpayers were already pressed to the limit. If Canada (and Louisiana) remained French, another expensive North American war was as inevitable as tomorrow. Influential colonials like former Governor William Shirley of Massachusetts and Benjamin Franklin, who was living in London as Pennsylvania's agent, warbled lyrically of the potential of the Canadian landmass.

British sugar planters in the West Indies also favored keeping Canada and they had pull; Jamaica's sugar crop alone was worth five times the value of the exports of all the mainland colonies combined. They feared that raising the Union Jack over Martinique and Guadeloupe would glut the sugar market in the empire, driving down the price of their "white gold." Even the French negotiators preferred losing Canada and getting their sugar islands back. And, in the end, George III and Parliament were confident of American loyalty no matter the circumstances.

Americans were overjoyed. The Peace of Paris of 1763 not only removed the French menace from the frontiers of the northern colonies, but Britain took Florida from Spain. South Carolina was no longer threatened from the south; Georgia need no longer be considered a military colony but could be developed as a producer of rice and cotton. Spain took Louisiana over from France, but Louisiana was far away.

SOLVING THE FRENCH AND INDIAN PROBLEM

In the Peace of Paris, "His Britannick Majesty" agreed "to grant the liberty of the Catholick religion to the inhabitants of Canada." It was a necessary concession, but nonetheless significant. Parliament saddled Britain's Roman Catholic community, small as it was, with disabilities. Even smaller numbers of Catholics in several of the thirteen colonies were generally unmolested but unpopular. And there was a big difference between tolerating a genteel Catholic minority in Maryland and the odd Roman church in Philadelphia and New York, and coming to terms with sprawling Canada where almost everyone—Indians included—was Catholic.

Still, as in Ireland, the British held the power in Canada and the *habitants* had no tradition of representative government or making demands on authorities; New France had been governed by the military. To French Canadians, taking orders from officers in red uniforms was not much different in day-to-day terms than taking orders from French officers in blue and buff. By dealing diplomatically with the leadership of the Canadian Church, the British generals in Canada were able to govern the new province without significant resistance.

The Indians of the Ohio Valley presented a far more difficult problem. Unlike the French army, the warriors of the Ohio had not been decisively defeated in battle. The Treaty of Paris might proclaim them subjects of King George. In reality, they were securely in possession of the forests west of the Appalachians and comfortable in a culture that was nearly intact, even stronger because of all they had borrowed from the French.

So diplomatic with the *habitants*, the army blundered in dealing with the Indians. General Jeffery Amherst looked on them as "wretched people" whose proper condition was subjection. He informed the western tribes that they would not receive the regular "gifts" of blankets, iron and brass tools and vessels, firearms, and liquor that they were accustomed to getting from the French.

Neolin, a religious leader of the Delaware, a tribe that had been driven west by colonial expansion, preached that "if you suffer the English among you, you are dead men." An Ottawa chieftain, **Pontiac,** ("I am a Frenchman and will die a Frenchman.") attacked the British fort at Detroit. Eighteen tribes on a thousand-mile front soon joined him. Detroit and Fort Pitt (formerly Fort Duquesne) held out, but ten other western forts were overrun; 2,000 colonials were killed in Virginia and Pennsylvania, more than were lost in any

Quarrels with the Mother Country 1760–1770

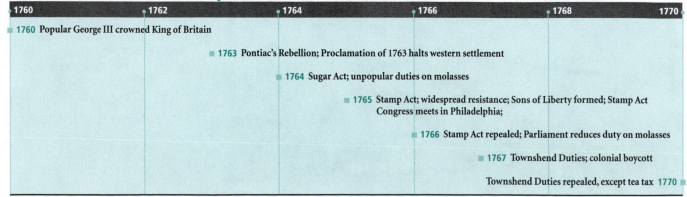

1760	1762	1764	1766	1768	1770

1760 Popular George III crowned King of Britain

1763 Pontiac's Rebellion; Proclamation of 1763 halts western settlement

1764 Sugar Act; unpopular duties on molasses

1765 Stamp Act; widespread resistance; Sons of Liberty formed; Stamp Act Congress meets in Philadelphia;

1766 Stamp Act repealed; Parliament reduces duty on molasses

1767 Townshend Duties; colonial boycott

Townshend Duties repealed, except tea tax 1770

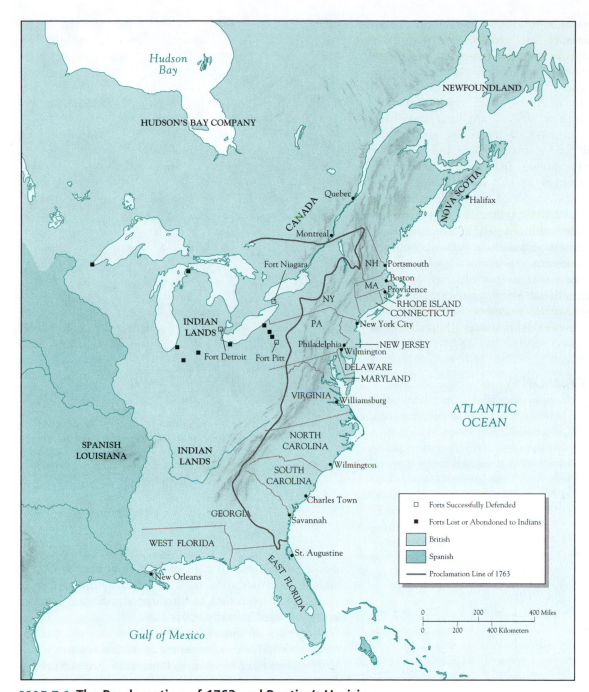

MAP 7:1 The Proclamation of 1763 and Pontiac's Uprising
Pontiac's well-coordinated warriors either captured or forced the abandonment of all the forts the British had inherited from France except Fort Niagara, Fort Detroit, and Fort Pitt (Pittsburgh). The multitribal assault was devastating. For a brief moment, as in King Philip's War eighty-eight years earlier, the Indians seemed to have halted the white incursions into their lands. Like Metacomet before him, however, Pontiac was defeated.

battle of the French and Indian War. Amherst spoke of germ warfare ("Try to inoculate the Indians by means of Blankets, as well as to try Every other Method than can serve to Extirpate this Execrable Race."), although it is not clear that his instructions were carried out. Militarily, however, the British forces quickly regrouped and defeated Pontiac at Bushy Run near Pittsburgh. Even then, they had only stunned the Indians, not "extirpated" them.

THE PROCLAMATION OF 1763

Amherst resumed the gift giving. In October 1763, in order to let tempers cool, the Crown drew an imaginary line on the Appalachian divide, the crest between the sources of the rivers that emptied into the Atlantic and those that flowed into the Ohio–Mississippi River system. The king proclaimed, "We do strictly forbid, on pain of our displeasure, all our loving subjects from making any purchases or settlements whatever" west of the line. Frontiersmen already living west of the mountains were ordered to return east of the mountains. Impatient emigrants were urged to go to northern New England, Upper Canada (Ontario), Georgia, and Florida. Land sales west of the Appalachians were frozen.

The Proclamation Line was, as one land speculator, George Washington, called it, "a temporary expedient to quiet the minds of the Indians." No one considered the Proclamation Line permanent. Indeed, royal superintendents of Indian affairs began to purchase land west of the line from Indians even before news of the Proclamation had reached the remote tribes. In the south, the Line of 1763 was redrawn—farther west—within a few months. Regularly over the next decade, trans-Appalachian lands were opened to speculation and settlement.

Nevertheless, by interfering temporarily, even on paper, with the colonial lust for land, British policy touched a tender nerve. Americans would remember the **Proclamation of 1763** as an early example of King George III's campaign to throttle their "liberties."

MONEY, MONEY, MONEY

Rattled by Pontiac's rebellion, General Amherst asked for a permanent American garrison of 5,000 to 6,000 troops. Parliament sent him 10,000. Although—several years later—Americans would say that the redcoats were sent to police them, Parliament had more innocent motives for its generosity with the army; there were thousands of French and Indian War veterans in Britain, and the British had never liked standing armies at home in peacetime. American duty was popular with the redcoats; there would be no fighting with the French gone, and the locals were, after all, British too, friendly—not a subject population to be kept down like the Irish. In the Quartering Act of 1765, Parliament put the financial responsibility of providing food, drink, and shelter for the quasi-pensioners, about £200,000 a year, on the colonies to which the troops were posted.

The cost of supporting 10,000 soldiers was the least of Parliament's financial woes. William Pitt's war had been very expensive, and he had financed it by borrowing. In 1763, the

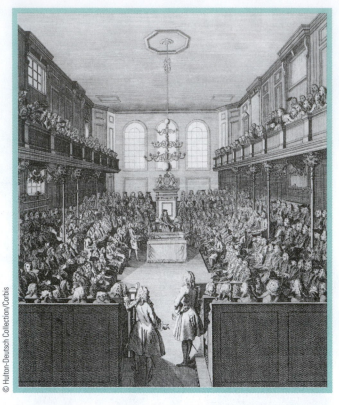

Parliament consisted of two houses: the House of Lords in which most seats were held by some 200 peers or nobles; and the House of Commons, pictured here, to which 588 members were elected. The electorate was so small, however, that most members of the Commons were of the same social class as the Lords.

national debt of £140 million was twice what it had been before the war. The running costs of governing the empire were up. Not only were there the new acquisitions, annual administrative expenses in the thirteen mainland colonies had quintupled from £70,000 to £350,000.

Parliament cut some expenditures; the Royal Navy's budget was slashed from £7 million in 1762 (the last year of actual fighting) to £2.8 million in 1766, and to just £1.5 million in 1769. Parliament might also have economized by cleaning up waste and corruption at home, of which there was plenty: bribes and kickbacks in awarding padded government contracts; parasitical aristocrats drawing big salaries for jobs with few or no duties; others drawing pensions for rendering no particular services.

PARLIAMENT AND KING

But to attack waste, corruption, and patronage would have struck at the essence of eighteenth-century government. The men who sat in Parliament were members of the same, small social class of landowners tightly connected by intermarriage. The heads of just 200 titled families, dukes, marquesses, earls, and viscounts sat in the House of Lords. Most members of the House of Commons, who were chosen by a very small electorate (300,000 men, 3 percent of the population), were

---

£/s/d

The British monetary unit is the pound sterling, designated by a stylized capital L with one or two slashes: £. ("L" is the first letter of the Latin word for pound.) Since 1970, British money has been decimalized: there are 100 New Pence (p) to the pound. Before 1970, the pound was divided into twenty shillings, designated "s". The shilling was divided into 20 pence ("d" for the Latin word for penny, *denarius*).

So, amounts of money were expressed in pounds, shillings, and pence, £/s/d. (The smallest British coin was a farthing: one-fourth of a penny. A guinea, only briefly a coin but often used in stating prices until 1970, was 21 shillings, £1/1s.)

however, he was immensely popular in the colonies. Taverns and towns were named in his honor. Statues of him were erected, including a grand one of George seated on a horse, in the center of New York.

In fact, George III was more decent and appealing a person than any British monarch for a century before him (or any since). He was sociable and unaffected; he rarely wore a wig, even on state occasions. His "common touch" was entirely authentic. Interested in agriculture, he could converse comfortably for hours with a rude farmer, even pitch in to fork hay or try his hand guiding a plow. He was a faithful, loving husband and a doting father. (He had fifteen children.) As a king he was conscientious, hardworking, and well meaning, sincerely devoted to the welfare of the English people. (He never even visited Scotland or Ireland.) He respected the British constitution. Hardly a tyrant, he accepted the supremacy of Parliament and the limits on his powers; he approved of them.

Alas—it ran in the family—he was not very bright and he shared the tunnel vision of the English upper class. His habit of ending many of his sentences ". . . what, what, what?" was comical. His failure to see the American colonials as anything but ignorant, rustic yokels who should do as their betters told them to do would prove disastrous. He was not alone in that prejudice.

GEORGE GRENVILLE

The unenviable job of solving Britain's financial crisis fell to **George Grenville,** who, in 1763, was named First Lord of the Treasury (secretary of the treasury, we would say) over the objections of King George, who disliked him intensely. Grenville's family was plenty old and distinguished but, like few of his colleagues, he was highly talented; he was a financial expert who thought in terms broader than double-entry bookkeeping.

He also understood that the empire had become too large and scattered to be managed by "salutary neglect." There were twenty colonies just in the western hemisphere. If each one of them, from populous Massachusetts and Virginia to the ménage of pirates called British Honduras was allowed to go its own way as in the past, the result would be chaos, one local headache after another. Indeed, William Pitt (Grenville's brother-in-law) had made it clear during the French and Indian War that salutary neglect was a thing of the past. It had been all very well to wink at colonials playing loose with the Navigation Acts because British merchants were doing £2 million in trade with Americans each year, but the huge national debt demanded order and revenue.

Grenville could not reduce the debt by raising taxes at home. Landowners were already paying 20 percent of their income in taxes. When Parliament jiggered a minor tax on apple cider, the daily beverage in southwestern England, there were riots. However, while Britishers were taxed twenty-six shillings a year per capita, a British subject living in Massachusetts paid taxes of one shilling a year, the average Virginian a mere five pence. (One shilling equaled twelve pence.) And these were the people who had gained the most

George III was popular in the colonies during the 1760s. Genuinely an Englishman, he had been raised English—unlike his German great grandfather, George I (who did not speak English) and his grandfather, George II, who had no interest in governing. His mother told him, "George, be a king." He tried.

younger sons or cousins of peers, or gentlemen who had married women of the nobility. Lords and commoners alike had yet other relations and friends looking to live off a piece of the patronage at Parliament's disposal.

Although some members of Parliament called themselves "Whigs" or "Tories," there were, in fact, no organized political parties. Parliament was a patchwork of factions some of which were held together by a principle, some by blood and marriage, some just to have a bloc of votes to trade for patronage.

The monarchy had long since lost the power to issue proclamations without Parliament's approval. But George III, crowned in 1760 at the age of 22, was an active and powerful politician not only because of royal prerogatives that survived and the deference of Tories, but because he was intensely interested in politics. He used the considerable royal patronage at his disposal to form his own Parliamentary faction known as **"the king's friends."**

By 1776, rebellious Americans would denounce George III as a tyrant and "the royal brute," blaming him for dozens of oppressions, some of them imaginary. During the 1760s,

George Grenville was an aristocrat who climbed to the top of the slippery pole of British politics. He hoped to reorganize the disorderly British Empire under firm Parliamentary control. His plans were dashed when Americans resisted his Sugar Act of 1764 and Stamp Act of 1765.

from the French and Indian War. Grenville concluded that the colonials had to shoulder a heavier financial burden.

There was no faulting Grenville's reasoning. Indeed, none of the Americans who protested British tax policies after 1763 denied that the colonies had a moral obligation to contribute financially to the empire. (Plenty of them ignored the issue, however.) Unfortunately, if the thirteen colonial assemblies had been willing to vote Grenville the money he said the Exchequer must have, they never got the chance to do so. Grenville did not request grants from each colony as his predecessors, including Pitt, had done. He bundled his money problem together with his intention to bring order and Parliamentary authority to imperial administration. Grenville told Americans how much they would pay and how they would pay it.

THE SUGAR ACT

The **Sugar Act** of 1764 replaced the ineffective Molasses Act of 1733. The old 6d per gallon tax on molasses imported from non-British (mostly French) islands was so high that few merchants paid it. They presented customs collectors with transparently false documents certifying that their cargos of molasses came from British Barbados or Jamaica along with a

bribe of a penny or two per gallon. If they were arrested as smugglers, they could count on juries of their neighbors to acquit them regardless of the evidence (and join them afterwards for a tot of rum, which was made from molasses).

The Sugar Act struck at lax law enforcement and promised to generate income for Great Britain. (So widespread was smuggling that Grenville thought the Act would generate between £40,000 and £100,000 a year.) It enlarged the colonial customs service and provided that accused smugglers be tried in vice-admiralty courts in which judges, not juries, decided guilt. To encourage American importers to obey the law, Grenville reduced the duty on molasses to 3d a gallon. (The Sugar Act also levied duties on some wines, coffee, silks, and other luxury items. They were minimal; Grenville wanted revenue, not to deny colonials their pleasures.)

In New England, where molasses was a major import, protest was loud and fierce. The Boston town meeting declared that citizens would import no British goods of any kind until Parliament repealed the tax. New York followed suit. Even "the young Gentlemen of Yale College" announced that they would not "make use of any foreign spirituous liquors" until Grenville backed down. This sacrifice, heroic for students, was eased by the availability of oceans of domestic beer and cider.

Grenville was unimpressed. He assumed that the Americans simply did not want to pay any taxes they could avoid. It was not an unreasonable conclusion, as a glance at the editorial columns of newspapers today will attest. Sippers of rum and Madeira wine wanted their beverages priced as cheaply as motorists want their gasoline.

THE RIGHTS OF BRITISH SUBJECTS

And yet, there was a principle at stake in the protest too. Most politically conscious colonials were heirs of Britain's "country party," Whigs, as opposed to the "court party," Tories. British Whigs believed that Parliament was the foundation of British liberties and that Parliament, not the king, must be the supreme authority of government.

Whiggery dominated British politics between 1688 and the accession of George III. Parliament had beheaded one king (Charles I), deposed another (James II), and created two kings who had no claim on the throne through inheritance (William III and George I: thirty-nine other people had better claims to the throne than he did). The Tories had opposed George I, favoring the Stuart "pretenders" who were descendants of James II. By the 1760s, however, they had accepted George III (great grandson of George I), who preferred them to Whigs because they believed the king should have increased political powers.

The most important of the "rights of British subjects" to which the Whigs clung was the principle that British subjects, through Parliament, must consent to the taxes they paid. Colonial Whigs conceded that Parliament had enacted the Sugar Act; however, Parliament represented the British people, not them. The thirteen colonial assemblies represented them; the assemblies were their parliaments and only their assemblies could tax them. On this foundation was

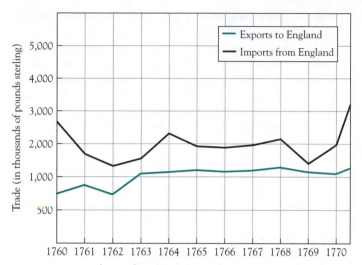

CHART 7:1 Value of Colonial Trade with Great Britain (in British Pounds)

The boycott of British imports called by the Sugar Act protesters had some effect, but not much. Only with the more broadly supported boycott following the Townshend Acts of 1767 was there a decline in imports that greatly affected British merchants.

built a decade of debate about the nature of representation in the British empire.

Daniel Dulany of Maryland responded to the Sugar Act by comparing it to the Molasses Act that it replaced. As a tax designed to reduce the importation of French molasses into the empire, Dulany said, the Molasses Act had been a regulation of trade. It was, therefore, legitimate; Parliament had the right to regulate trade for the entire empire. (John Dickinson of Delaware and Pennsylvania later refined the argument.) The Sugar Act of 1764, on the other hand, was not designed to keep foreign molasses out of the colonies; its purpose was to raise money. So far as Grenville was concerned, the more foreign molasses the colonies imported, the better. The official name of the Sugar Act was the American Revenue Act.

It was Grenville's goal, revenue, that raised the constitutional question of the right of British subjects to consent to taxes levied on them. The Sugar Act was a tax levied by a body that did not represent colonials; they had not consented to it.

TRIAL BY JURY

The Sugar Act raised another "rights" issue: the right of a British subject accused of a crime to be tried before a jury of his peers. This ancient right (its origins went back to the Magna Carta of 1215), colonials believed, set the British people apart from (made them the superiors of) the French, Spanish, Poles, Chinese, Hottentots, and Shawnee of the world. By denying accused smugglers a jury trial, George Grenville and Parliament were tampering with the essence of British liberty.

It is impossible to say what would have happened if Grenville's program had ended with the Sugar Act. Some

Americans were noisy; some of the language was inflammatory. But there was no violence. The Sugar Act protest began with a debate on a high level and ended with a perfectly legal boycott of imports from Great Britain designed to bring pressure on Parliament. To the extent that colonial opposition to the tax on molasses was a garden-variety dislike of taxes (no matter who levied them), the protest might well have petered out as Grenville expected it to do. The 1764 duties affected only bibbers and people in the molasses business, none of them gravely. In fact, the boycott made hardly a blip in colonial imports and when, in 1766, the tax on molasses was reduced to a penny a gallon (the level of the traditional bribes) the protests evaporated, although "the principle of the thing" remained intact.

But Grenville did not stop with the Sugar Act. In 1765, he proposed a tax on Americans that could not be ducked by smuggling or protested with a boycott.

THE STAMP ACT CRISIS

The English had been paying a stamp tax since 1694. In order to be binding, some legal documents had to be inscribed or printed on paper that was embossed with a government stamp. Purchase of the essential paper constituted payment of a tax. The tax could not be evaded short of committing a far more serious crime, forgery. Registrars did not accept a sale of real estate that was not recorded on stamped paper. Contracts written on ordinary foolscap could be thrown out of court.

THE STAMP ACT OF 1765

Grenville's **Stamp Act of 1765,** which applied to the colonies, went further than the English law. In addition to legal documents such as wills, bills of sale, licenses, deeds, insurance policies, and contracts, it required that newspapers, pamphlets, handbills, even playing cards be printed on the embossed government paper. The tax varied from a halfpenny on a handbill announcing a sale of taffeta to £10 for a tavern

---

Stamps

What we call a postage stamp was unknown in the eighteenth century. The adhesive-backed proof that postage has been paid on a letter was introduced only in 1834 (the perforations between stamps in 1854). When it appeared, the speakers of no European language except English chose the word stamp as the name of the ingenious device. To them, and to colonial Britons and Americans, a stamp was an image impressed—stamped—into paper, not something stuck on it. Eighteenth-century stamping was what we call embossing.

Thus, the stamp that caused all the excitement in 1765 was an embossment, pressed into the paper to be used for licenses, newspapers, and so on. Very few colonials ever saw Stamp Act stamps (except of course, those who burned the stamped paper). Only a few sheets of stamped paper were sold in Georgia—none in any other colony.

keeper's license to sell liquor. The sum was significant in both cases; Grenville expected to make a great deal of money from the Act. Enforcement of the Stamp Act was entrusted to vice-admiralty courts.

Grenville tried to curry American favor by offering generously paid collectorships to prominent colonials—patronage worked in Parliament—and by providing that all money raised by the Stamp Act would be used solely in "defending, protecting, and securing the colonies." Not a farthing would go to Great Britain, not even to retire the national debt.

A few prominent Americans were dazzled by the job offer, much to their later regret. In London, Benjamin Franklin tried to get a collectorship for a crony back in Pennsylvania. Richard Henry Lee of Virginia who, eleven years later, would propose the resolution declaring American independence, applied for a job as a stamp tax collector in 1765.

But the proviso that all Stamp Act revenues would be spent in the colonies did not pacify those who had protested against the Sugar Act on the principle of "no taxation without representation." It raised their opposition to a higher level because the Stamp Act was not only designed to raise money, as the Sugar Act was, it was a direct tax on transactions entirely within a colony, which the Sugar Act—an import duty—was not. The fact that all revenues from the Stamp Act would be spent within the colonies only made the point clearer. Only a colonial assembly, in which the people of the colony were represented, could enact such a direct tax. (Massachusetts had experimented with a stamp tax in 1755.) Parliament had no more right to enact such a tax on Georgians and Marylanders than the New York colonial assembly had.

These points were alluded to during Parliament's debate of Grenville's proposal but they made no impression. The Stamp Act sailed through Parliament on a vote of 204 to 49.

A STUPID LAW

Parliament's nonchalance in passing the Stamp Act was remarkable because, constitutional niceties aside, it was a sloppily written, politically stupid law. Courts could invalidate deeds not printed on stamped paper but a will hastily written by a dying man was to be invalid? Were constables to interrupt every card game they noticed to examine the playing cards for stamps? Were authorities to devote their time to tracking down the source of an unstamped handbill blowing down the street?

The burden of the taxes that could be easily enforced fell heavily on just those people who were in the best positions to stir up a fuss. Newspaper editors, with their influence on public opinion, were hit hard by the Stamp Act. Advertisements, a newspaper's bread and butter, were taxed two shillings; every page of every edition had to be printed on stamped paper. Printers, who made a living by putting out broadsides—posters used for announcing goods for sale and public meetings—including protest meetings!) saw their business taxed at every turn of the press.

Lawyers, already the single largest professional group in colonial public office, and persuaders by profession, had to pay a tax on every document with which they dealt. Keepers of taverns, to be saddled with expensive licenses by the law, were influential figures in every town and neighborhood. Their inns and ordinaries were the gathering places where—over rum, brandy, coffee, and tea—locals gathered to read newspapers and discuss affairs, such as taxes.

What was worse, these groups were concentrated in cities where they could easily meet with one another, cooperate, organize, and have an impact out of proportion to their numbers. It was one thing to upset such people one group at a time—as the Sugar Act had riled shippers and distillers—but the Stamp Act hit all of these key elements of the population at once, and the protestors won the support of large numbers of working people and even the tumultuous underclass of the cities.

RIOT

Parliament approved the Stamp Act in February 1765; it was to go into effect in November. As soon as the news of the tax reached the colonies, they erupted in anger. Local organizations called Sons of Liberty (a phrase used to describe Americans by one of their parliamentary friends, Isaac Barré) condemned the law and called for another boycott of British imports.

Some of the Sons of Liberty turned to violence. When the stamped paper was delivered to warehouses in port cities, mobs broke in and made bonfires of it. Men appointed stamp masters were shunned or hanged in effigy if they were

How Many Lawyers Does It Take To . . . ?

Colonials went to court often enough in property disputes and to collect debts. But professional lawyers were few until the middle of the eighteenth century. There were only three lawyers in New York in 1692, seven in 1700. Boston as late as 1720, had only three.

In part, this was because there were no law schools in the colonies. The first college to offer lectures in law was William and Mary in 1779 (although the lecturer, George Wythe had privately trained a number of lawyers, Thomas Jefferson among them). The first permanent school of law was founded in 1812 at the University of Maryland.

Also, in part, lawyers had a bad reputation for getting in the way of justice with their hair-splitting and for being chiefly concerned with diverting as much of the money in their clients' purses to their own as their ingenuity allowed. Massachusetts enacted a law forbidding the practice of law in 1641, Virginia in 1658.

By the end of the colonial period, this prejudice was beyond memory. Of the fifty-six signers of the Declaration of Independence in 1776, twenty-four were lawyers. Of the fifty-five delegates to the Constitutional Convention of 1787, thirty-one were lawyers.

Metropolitan Museum of Art

A New Hampshire man who applied to be a seller of Stamp Act paper is tortured in effigy, probably just outside his home. He was a lucky one. Mobs like this—riffraff, but substantial workingmen too—beat and tortured other men who had taken the job.

lucky; others were roughed up. A few were stripped, daubed with hot tar, rolled in chicken feathers, and were carried about town, straddling a fence rail.

One official in Maryland fled for his life to New York. That was a mistake, because the New York Sons of Liberty were the most volatile of all. They located the Marylander and forced him to write a letter of resignation. Led by Isaac Sears, the captain of a merchant vessel, the New Yorkers frightened their own lieutenant governor so that he went into hiding. When they could not find him, they burned his carriages. In Boston, the crowd looted and burned the homes of several British officials.

Rowdies are seldom popular, but the Stamp Act rioters were. When one governor was asked why he did not call out the militia to restore order, he pointed out that it would mean arming the very people who were wreaking havoc in the streets. Isaac Barré had warned Parliament of resistance. But everyone was caught short by what seemed to be half the colonial population on a rampage.

THE STAMP ACT CONGRESS

Among those taken aback were wealthy colonials who opposed the Stamp Act but shuddered when they heard the sounds of a mob. A mob was a beast that, in a twinkling,

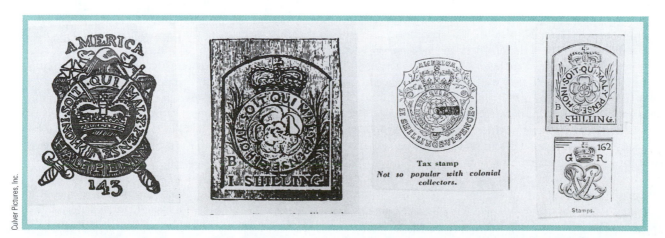

Culver Pictures, Inc.

Tax stamp
Not so popular with colonial collectors.

These stamps, what we call embossments—images pressed into paper—were the cause of the Stamp Act uproar of 1765. Few colonials ever saw them. A few were sold in Georgia, none anywhere else. The stamped paper was burned by rioters or returned to Britain and scrapped.

School for Politicians

Far more Americans than Britons were eligible to vote for their representatives. Only about one in four adult British males could vote for members of the House of Commons and, possibly as few as one in six. (Historians differ on this.) In sharp contrast, three of four adult white male colonials could vote and some of the disenfranchised were sons of farmers who hoped to have their own farms and, therefore, the franchise.

Because voters were so numerous in the colonies, men who stood for office (they did not *run* for office in the eighteenth century) had to be far more adept at popular politicking than members of the House of Commons, many of whom had to win the approval of only a handful of voters. This is a part of the reason for the often remarked fact that the two generations of American political leaders who led the protests of British policies in the 1760s and 1770s, launched the War for Independence, wrote the Constitution in 1787 and won popular support for it, and created a functioning republican government were so very remarkable. They were trained in the demanding school of colonial politics.

Elections in about half the colonies were by voice vote (notably the most populous colony, Virginia), by paper ballot in the others. Nowhere, however, were members of the assemblies elected by secret ballot. European political philosophers disliked secret elections, fearing they encouraged bribery and ballot box stuffing. In colonial elections, the contending candidates and a voter's neighbors knew how he voted.

Electioneering and elections were face-to-face and personal. Districts were small—they had to be. Every eligible voter had to be able to get to the polls and back home in a day when the fastest means of transportation was a walking horse. In Virginia, candidates for a seat in the House of Burgesses knew the names of most of the men who stepped forward—out of doors, weather permitting—to announce his choice. Every voter certainly knew a great deal about the candidates because they were almost inevitably among the largest landowners in the county. Small farmers had no time to spare for sessions of the legislature in Williamsburg and they were deferential to their social superiors.

Their social superiors did not degrade themselves, like candidates today, by toadying to voters. They stood at the polling table and, when a voter announced their names, stepped forward and thanked him. Candidates did, however, "entertain" voters, setting out food and drink at the polling place.

In the northern cities, personal acquaintance of candidates and voters was less likely than in rural areas, but candidates—equally dignified on election day and also, for the most part, upper crust merchants and lawyers—were well-known to voters. An ambitious politician in Boston and other New England towns made his reputation and won his following with his eloquence or by the positions he took at town meetings, which men sufficiently interested to cast a vote on election day were apt to attend regularly. Voter participation, however, was probably no greater than it is today, particularly in the countryside. Recent immigrants had rarely been eligible voters in Great Britain, Ireland, or Germany; hard-working farmers were likely to consider a day in the fields better spent than a day at the county seat.

As in Great Britain, there was nothing resembling a political party in any of the colonies. From Maryland south, in fact, there were no factions as there were in Parliament. Candidates for seats in the southern assemblies stood for election as individuals and won or lost largely on the personal respect they commanded. In several northern colonies, there were differences in the politics of candidates roughly analogous to the Tory–Whig division in Parliament. The governor of Pennsylvania, appointed by the Penn family, the proprietors of the colony but no longer Quakers, used their patronage to build a "court party" supporting them. The Whiggish opposition was largely made up of Quakers dedicated to keeping the governor's power in check, and reducing it when there was an opportunity to do so. The "Quaker party" was almost always in the majority.

There were similar rivalries in New York and Massachusetts assemblies between the royal governors' supporters and those ever on guard against an increase in executive power, a frame of mind that played a large role in the resistance to "tyranny" in the dozen years leading up to the Revolution.

Assembly debates, usually closely covered in newspapers with some speeches printed word for word, were usually decorous and dignified. Most members were of the colonial elite, personally and socially acquainted with their opponents as well as their allies, and often related, at least by marriage. But there were exceptions, more numerous as the break with Great Britain neared. In a speech attacking the Stamp Act in Virginia's House of Burgesses in 1765, a newly elected Burgess, Patrick Henry, concluded a speech by saying, "Caesar had his Brutus, Charles the First his Cromwell, and George III . . . may profit by their example." He was shouted down with cries of "Treason!" Not incidentally, Henry was no rich planter but a self-taught trial lawyer born the son of tavern keepers, people socially far below the gentility. Even Thomas Jefferson, a rebel like Henry but a wealthy planter, despised him for his vulgar manners.

shifted its depredations from one target to another when the exhilaration of hell-raising obscured the initial excuse for it. The urban colonial elite—merchants, lawyers—were men with something to lose. They wanted the Stamp Act repealed, but not by mob violence. John Dickinson, a cautious, conservative Quaker grandee, hoped to bring pressure on Parliament through the influential British merchants who dominated the colonial trade.

In October 1765, Dickinson and thirty-six other delegates from nine colonies, most of them conservative men, assembled in New York City as what they called the Stamp Act Congress. They adopted fourteen resolutions and a "Declaration of Rights and Grievances" addressed to the king. It condemned the Sugar Act, Stamp Act, and other parliamentary policies on the grounds that they violated the British constitution. The delegates to the Congress carefully and prominently made it clear they acknowledged "all due subordination" to the Crown.

What did "all due subordination" mean—loyalty to the king? Unquestionably: just about everyone in 1765 agreed on the importance of the monarch as the symbol that unified a people. Lése-majesté, "injuring the king," was the gravest of political crimes. It was punished by hanging followed by disembowelment and quartering—harnessing four horses to each of the traitor's limbs and cracking the whip. But the Stamp Act protesters insisted that colonials were not subordinate to Parliament because it did not represent them.

WHAT IS REPRESENTATION? THE COLONIAL CASE

Colonials did not elect members of the House of Commons—it was that simple. Their own assemblies, which they did elect, represented them. They alone were empowered to tax them.

The colonial case is easy to understand today because our concept of representation reflects it. In order to be represented in government, a citizen must be entitled to vote for a city council member, county supervisor, state legislator, representative, or senator. Senators from Kentucky do not represent Iowans, who have no voice in electing them. Every significant liberalization of voting requirements in United States history—extension of the suffrage to men who did not own property, to African-American men, and to women—was based on the principle that a person must have the right to vote in order to be represented.

James Otis of Massachusetts spoke for this way of thinking at the Stamp Act Congress when he proposed that Parliament put an end to the problem by allowing colonials to elect members of Parliament. (Benjamin Franklin also toyed with this idea.) But most of Otis's colleagues ignored his proposal. They did not want to send representatives to Parliament. They wanted Parliament to recognize the authority of their own assemblies.

Parliament rejected the idea of Americans electing members of the House of Commons not because they feared American political power, but because, by British lights, colonials were already constitutionally represented.

VIRTUAL REPRESENTATION: THE BRITISH CASE

By eighteenth-century standards, Parliament was quite correct. The British concept of representation differed (and differs) from our own. For example, it was not (and is not) required that a member of the House of Commons reside in the electoral district that sends him or her to the House of Commons. Although it is unlikely to happen today, a member of Parliament may never set foot in the district that elected him. Actual residence is not required, and was not in the eighteenth century because, it was assumed, each member of the House of Commons virtually represented all Britons. Edmund Burke, a steady friend of Americans, made the point to citizens of Bristol who elected him when he said: "You choose a member . . . but when you have chosen him, he is not a member of Bristol, but he is a member of Parliament."

Only 3 percent of the British population voted. But the members of Parliament they elected represented everyone. Indeed, in the 1760s, a dozen or so members of the House of Commons were elected from districts where, because of shifts of population, voters numbered only a dozen or so. Several of these "rotten boroughs" (they had their critics) had a single voter; one had been under water for two centuries. Several cities did not elect members of Parliament because they did not exist when seats in the House of Commons were handed out. But, according to the principle of **virtual representation,** Parliament represented them.

In fact, colonials practiced virtual representation. George Washington and other Virginians were elected to the colonial House of Burgesses from counties in which they did not reside. They were candidates for seats in more than one county in an election so that they were covered in the event they were defeated in one of them. Few objected to the practice. It was assumed that those who were elected would act with the interests of all Virginians in mind.

The colonists also practiced virtual representation in their restriction of the suffrage to free, white, adult male heads of household who owned property. The number of actual voters in colonial elections amounted to a small proportion of the inhabitants of the colony. Nevertheless, the colonists considered propertyless white men, all women and children, and even, in a strange way, African-American slaves, to be virtually represented in their elected assemblies. The assumption was that assemblymen acted on behalf of all, not just on behalf of those who voted for them.

This was precisely the position Parliament took when the colonials complained that they were not represented in Parliament: the colonists were virtually represented.

ACT TWO

The Stamp Act crisis was not resolved by adding up debaters' points. The violence of the colonial protesters alarmed Parliament as much as it alarmed the men of the Stamp Act Congress. Nor could Parliament ignore the fact that twenty-seven respectable, well-to-do, and conservative colonial

Courtesy Peabody Essex Museum, Salem, Massachusetts

■ *A "souvenir teapot" celebrating the repeal of the Stamp Act. It was made in Great Britain for the colonial market. The potteries of Staffordshire were multi-product, mass-production operations, manufacturing everything from everyday tableware to items like this teapot, exploiting a topical "specialty market" much like people today who silk-screen the latest slogan on t-shirts. After the Revolution, the potteries shipped statuettes of George Washington to the United States.*

stated that Parliament "had, hath, and of right ought to have, full power and authority to make laws and statutes of sufficient force and validity to bind the colonies and people of America, subjects of the Crown of Great Britain, in all cases whatsoever."

Not only did the Declaratory Act deny American claims for the authority of their own assemblies, the wording of the bill was lifted from a 1719 law that made Ireland completely subject to Great Britain. That should have given colonial protesters pause, for the status of the despised Irish was precisely what they were determined to avoid. But few noticed. Their friend, Lord Chatham, was installed as prime minister and he ignored the Declaratory Act with the slickness of Robert Walpole. Chatham also reduced the Sugar Act duty on molasses from 3d to a penny per gallon (the level of the bribes importers had been paying customs agents for decades).

political leaders were sufficiently concerned about the Stamp Act to travel to New York and write a remonstrance of their grievances. Never before had such a statement issued from the colonies.

REPEAL BUT NOT VICTORY

Members of Parliament who had voted against the Stamp Act praised the Congress. William Pitt, now in the House of Lords as the Earl of Chatham, rejoiced "that America has resisted. Three millions of people so dead to all the feelings of liberty," he said, "so voluntarily to submit to be slaves, would have been fit instruments to make slaves of the rest." Edmund Burke, a conservative traditionalist, viewed the colonists as defenders of British tradition, Grenville's backers as dangerous innovators. The radical John Wilkes egged on the colonials as his natural allies in his agitations on behalf of a free press. Charles Fox, a future cabinet minister, part cynical opportunist and part man of high principle, praised the Americans, as did Isaac Barré, a former soldier who had fought with Wolfe at Quebec.

The majority found no merit in the colonial argument that Parliament could not constitutionally tax them but, in 1766, they repealed the Stamp Act. George III was not unhappy to see Grenville fall on his face (the king soon dismissed him); "the king's friends" voted for repeal. When the news reached the colonies, the celebrations were so giddy that few paid attention to the fact that Parliament had not yielded on principle. On the same day the Stamp Act was repealed, Parliament enacted the **Declaratory Act,** which

A LIST of the Names of *those* who AUDACIOUSLY continue to counteract the UNITED SENTIMENTS of the BODY of Merchants thro'out NORTH-AMERICA ; by importing British Goods contrary to the Agreement.

John Bernard,
(In King-Street, almost opposite Vernon'sHead.
James McMasters,
(On Treat's Wharf.
Patrick McMasters,
(Opposite the Sign of the Lamb.
John Mein,
(Opposite the White-Horse, and in King-Street.
Nathaniel Rogers,
(Opposite Mr. Henderson Inches Store lower End King-Street.
William Jackson,
At the Brazen Head, Cornhill, near the Town-House.
Theophilus Lillie,
(Near Mr. Pemberton's Meeting-House, North-End.
John Taylor,
(Nearly opposite the Heart and Crown in Cornhill.
Ame & Elizabeth Cummings,
(Opposite the Old Brick Meeting House, all of Boston.
Israel Williams, Esq; & Son,
(Traders in the Town of Hatfield.
And, *Henry Barnes,*
(Trader in the Town of Marlboro'.

The following Names should have been inferted in the Lift of Juftices.

County of Middlefex.	County of Lincoln.
Samuel Hendley	
John Borland	John Kingfbury
Henry Barnes	
Richard Cary	County of Berkfhire.
County of Briftol.	Mark Hopkins
George Brightman	Elijah Dwight
County of Worcefter.	Ifrael Stoddard
Daniel Blifs	

Rare Books Division, The New York Public Library, Astor, Lenox and Tilden Foundations

■ *By 1770, when protesters called for a boycott of these merchants who were selling goods imported from Britain, the furor over the Townshend Acts was already abating.*

Then, in one of those accidents of history that have grave consequences, Chatham was taken seriously ill and ceased to play an active part in government. The man who stepped into the vacuum his absence created was as bad a stroke of luck for the colonials as Grenville had been.

"CHAMPAGNE CHARLEY" AND THE TOWNSHEND DUTIES

Charles Townshend lacked Grenville's breadth of vision, but he was clever and no more wicked a fellow than Grenville. Indeed, Townshend was rather on the convivial and jolly side. He was nicknamed "Champagne Charley" because he frequently arrived at the House of Commons unsteady on his feet and even giggling. (In fairness to Townshend, Parliament convened in the evening; on a given night, any number of members were at less than their best.)

Townshend was Chancellor of the Exchequer, and he hoped to be prime minister. To earn that prize, he intended to cut taxes at home and make up for the shortfall in revenue by taxing the colonies. Townshend examined the distinctions Americans drew between external taxes regulating trade and internal taxes for the purpose of raising money. He thought the distinction nonsense but (so he thought) he accommodated colonial sensibilities by designing a series of duties that were clearly external. The **Townshend Duties** taxed paper, paint, lead, glass, and tea—all goods that the colonies imported. He had no trouble persuading Parliament to enact the duties in 1767.

Townshend thought he had solved the problem. Instead, his design for collecting revenues from the colonies was seriously flawed. If none of the goods Townshend taxed were produced in more than dribbles in the colonies, all except tea could be; paint, glass, and papermaking technologies were not secrets. Moreover, they could, in the short run, be done without; Townshend invited a boycott, and he got one. British–American trade fell off by 25 percent and then by 50 percent. Townshend had told Parliament that his duties would bring in £40,000 annually. The actual take in 1768 was £13,000 and, in 1769, less than £3,000. That was not enough to operate a few frontier forts.

There was little violence. The boycott was organized and controlled by conservative merchants still nervous about the Stamp Act riots. They argued that, when the British merchants who sold the colonies felt the pinch of the boycott, they would collectively pressure Parliament for repeal. The boycott, although never close to total, was effective enough. In 1770, Parliament repealed the Townshend Duties except for a 3d per pound duty on tea. The tea tax was a mini-Declaratory Act, Parliament's restatement of its right to tax the colonies.

FURTHER READING

General J. R. Alden, *A History of the American Revolution*, 1969; Bernard Bailyn, *The Ideological Origins of the American Revolution*, 1967, and *British Politics and the American Revolution*, 1965; Jack P. Greene, *The Reinterpretation of the American Revolution*, 1968; Merrill Jensen, *The Founding of a Nation*, 1968; Robert Middlekauff, *The Glorious Cause: The American Revolution, 1763–1789*, 1982; Don Higginbotham, *The War of American Independence, 1763–1789*, 1971; Alfred T. Young, *The American Revolution: A Radical Interpretation*, 1976; Pauline Maier, *From Resistance to Revolution, 1765–1776*, 1972; Edward A. Countryman, *The American Revolution*, 1987.

Problems of 1763 Howard H. Peckham, *Pontiac and the Indian Uprising*, 1947; Wilbur R. Jacobs, *Wilderness Politics and Indian Gifts*, 1966; Gregory E. Dowd, *A Spirited Resistance: The North American Indian Struggle for Unity, 1745–1815*, 1992; Evans Dowd, *War Under Heaven: Pontiac, the Indian Nations, and the British Empire*, 2002; Philip Lawson, *The Imperial Challenge: Quebec and Britain in the Age of the American Revolution*, 1989.

Taxing the Colonies John L. Bullion, *A Great and Necessary Measure: George Grenville and the Genesis of the Stamp Act, 1763–1765*, 1982; Edmund S. Morgan and Helen M. Morgan, *The Stamp Act Crisis*, third edition, 1995; Peter D. Thomas, *British Politics and the Stamp Act Crisis* 1975, and *The Townshend Duties Crisis: The Second Phase of the American Revolution, 1767–1773*, 1987; Philip Reid, *Constitutional History of the American Revolution: The Authority of Rights*, 1987; John W. Tyler, *Smugglers and Patriots: Boston Merchants and the Advent of the American Revolution*, 1986; Jay Fliegelman, *Prodigals and Pilgrims: The American Revolution Against Patriarchal Authority, 1750–1800*, 1982.

KEY TERMS

The following terms are covered in this chapter and can also be found in the list of Key Terms at the back of the book.

Declaratory Act	Pontiac	Sugar Act	vice-admiralty courts
George Grenville	Proclamation of 1763	"the king's friends"	virtual representation
King George III	Stamp Act of 1765	Townshend Duties	

ONLINE SOURCES GUIDE

Use this listing to find online documents, images, interactive maps, simulations, and other resources related to this chapter:

American History Resource Center
http://history.wadsworth.com

Selected Documents
The Stamp Act (1765)
Imperial Official William Knox's Essay on American Taxation

Selected Images
George Grenville
Engraving of John Wilkes

Cartoon opposing stamp tax
Opponents of crown tar and feather Boston tax collector

Interactive Timeline (with online readings)
Years of Tumult: The Quarrel with Great Britain 1763–1770

Additional resources, exercises, and Internet links related to this chapter are available on *THE AMERICAN PAST* web site: http://history.wadsworth.com/americanpast8e

Discovery

What political and economic divisions had developed between the English government and its North American colonies?

In thinking about this question, begin by breaking it down into the components shown below. A discussion of the significance of each component should appear in your answer.

Economics and Technology: For this exercise, please read the following document excerpt: "Stamp Act." What does the Stamp Act say? How does the Stamp Act differ from previous British taxes? Why had taxes become such a contentious issue between the colonies and Britain? Was this a concept worth dying for?

Stamp Act

Whereas, by an act made in the last session of Parliament, several duties were granted, continued, and appropriated towards defraying the expenses of defending, protecting, and securing the *British* colonies and plantations in *America;* and *whereas* it is first necessary that provision be made for raising a further revenue within your Majesty's dominions in *America,* towards defraying the said expenses; we, your Majesty's most dutiful and loyal subjects, the Commons of *Great Britain,* in Parliament assembled, have therefore resolved to give and grant unto your Majesty the several rights and duties hereinafter mentioned; and do most humbly beseech your Majesty that it may be enacted. And be it enacted by the King's most excellent Majesty, by and with the advice and consent of the lords spiritual and temporal, and commons, in this present Parliament assembled, and by the authority of the same, that from and after the first day of *November,* one thousand seven hundred and sixty-five, there shall be raised, levied, collected, and paid unto his Majesty, his heirs and successors, throughout the colonies and plantations in *America,* which now are, or hereafter may be, under the dominion of his Majesty, his heirs and successors . . .

Economics and Technology: For this exercise, please study Chart 7.1 and image, "A List of the Names" below. How are the Townsend duties a reaction to American anger over earlier economic measures such as the Stamp Act? In what ways do they directly respond to American criticisms? Look at the boycott list. Compare that to the chart. How effective were these types of boycotts from the Sugar Act through the Townsend Acts? Why were they not more effective? Why did they collectively stir American anger?

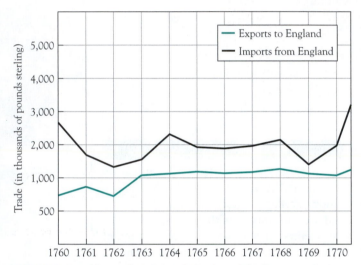

CHART 7:1 Value of Colonial Trade with Great Britain (in British Pounds)

A LIST of the Names of *thofe* who AUDACIOUSLY continue to counteract the UNITED SENTIMENTS of the BODY of Merchants thro'out NORTH-AMERICA; by importing Britifh Goods contrary to the Agreement.

John Bernard,
(In King-Street, almoft oppofite Vernon'sHead.

James McMafters,
(On Treat's Wharf.

Patrick McMafters,
(Oppofite the Sign of the Lamb.

John Mein,
(Oppofite the White-Horfe, and in King-Street.

Nathaniel Rogers,
(Oppofite Mr. Henderfon Inches Store lower End King-Street.

William Jackfon,
At the BrazenHead, Cornhill, near theTown-Houfe.

Theophilus Lillie,
(Near Mr. Pemberton'sMeeting-Houfe,North-End.

John Taylor,
(Nearly oppofite the Heart andCrown inCornhill.

Ame & Elizabeth Cummings,
(Oppofite the Old Brick Meeting Houfe, all of Bofton.

Ifrael Williams, Efq; & Son,
(Traders in the Town of. Hatfield.

And, *Henry Barnes,*
(Trader in the Town of. Marlboro'.

The following Names fhould have been i ferted in the Lift of Juftices.

County of Middlefex.	County of Lincoln.
Samuel Hendley	
John Borland	John Kingfbury
Henry Barnes	
Richard Cary	County of Berkfhire.
County of Briftol.	Mark Hopkins
George Brightman	Elijah Dwight
County of Worcefter.	Ifrael Stoddard
Daniel Blifs	

A List of the Names

To read extended versions of the documents, visit the companion Web site http://history.wadsworth.com/americanpast8e; click on "Discovery Sources."

CHAPTER 8

From Riot to Rebellion

The Road to Independence 1770–1776

Reproduced from the Collections of the Library of Congress

He has dissolved Representative Houses . . . He has obstructed the Administration of Justice . . . He has kept among us, in times of peace, Standing Armies . . . He has plundered our seas, ravaged our Coasts, burnt our towns, and destroyed the lives of our people.

The Declaration of Independence

I can have no other Object but to protect the true Interests of all My Subjects. No People ever enjoyed more Happiness, or lived under a milder Government, than those now revolted Provinces. . . . My Desire is to restore to them the Blessings of Law and Liberty . . . which they have fatally and desperately exchanged for the Calamities of War, and the arbitrary Tyranny of their Chiefs.

George III

The repeal of the Townshend Duties did not touch the issue of Parliament's right to tax the colonies. Nevertheless, almost everyone who had been involved in the debate was relieved to see an end to confrontation and boycott. For three years after 1770, Parliament avoided provocations. In America, anti-British protests were few and muted.

In fact, tensions may have been easing before mid-1770 when news of the repeal reached the colonies. A door-to-door survey of New Yorkers revealed that a majority was willing to buy all the Townshend items except tea, which could be had more cheaply from Dutch smugglers. Imports into New England, the most obstreperous colonies, began a steady rise from £330,000 at the peak of the boycott to £1.2 million,

more than ever before. As perhaps most people always do, Americans seem to have wanted calm, a resumption of daily life unaggravated by the folderol of politics.

STORMS WITHIN THE LULL

Still, several incidents between 1770 and 1773 indicated that not all was well in British North America. On the streets of Boston, a bloody brawl between workingmen and some British soldiers dramatized a simmering hostility toward the redcoats stationed in the city. In North Carolina, frontier settlers took up arms against the elite of the eastern counties

Reproduced from the Collections of the Library of Congress

This engraving of the Boston Massacre, by silversmith Paul Revere, was meant to be propaganda, not an accurate portrayal of the incident. The redcoats were actually backed against a wall and were in some danger; the mob was large, not just the few victims of the British volley shown here. Revere himself, giving testimony in court, drew a map of the incident that depicted it accurately.

who governed the colony. And in Rhode Island, farmers protected smugglers who burned a British patrol boat.

THE BOSTON MASSACRE

On March 5, 1770, the weather in Boston was frigid. The streets were icy; heaps of gritty snow blocked the gutters. No doubt aggravated by the severity of the winter, which brought unemployment as well as discomfort, some men and boys exchanged words with British soldiers who were patrolling the streets. A handful of hecklers became a crowd cursing and throwing snowballs at the redcoats. A few dared the soldiers to use their muskets.

When the mob pressed close on King Street, backing the redcoats against a wall, they fired. Five Bostonians, one a boy, another an African American named Crispus Attucks, fell dead. Boston, a city of 15,000, was shocked. A few men who had been active in the Stamp Act protest tried to revive anti-British feelings. A silversmith, **Paul Revere,** engraved a picture of the "Boston Massacre" that misrepresented what happened (as Revere admitted in court). His print depicted soldiers aggressively attacking innocent people. **Samuel Adams,** an Anglophobic former brewer, circulated the prints and tried to rouse tempers. Joseph Warren, a physician, embroidered passionately on the theme. "Take heed, ye orphan babes," he told a public meeting, "lest, whilst your streaming eyes are fixed upon the ghastly corpse, your feet slide on the stones bespattered with your father's brains."

But their agitation got nowhere. Most Bostonians seemed to blame the incident on the mob. John Adams, cousin of Samuel and a friend of Warren, represented the soldiers in court. Adams was nobody's stooge, least of all a stooge of the British. He was strong-headed to the point of self-righteousness and a critic of British policies. Indeed, in arguing the redcoats' case, Adams criticized the policy of stationing professional soldiers in cities like Boston. "Soldiers quartered in a populous town will always occasion two mobs where they prevent one," he said. "They are wretched conservators of the peace."

Nevertheless, Adams blamed an unsavory mob, not the accused redcoats, for the incident. The jury agreed, acquitting all of the defendants but two and sentencing them only to branding on the thumb, a slap on the wrist by eighteenth-century standards.

A DANGEROUS RELATIONSHIP

The significance of the Boston Massacre, and the Battle of Golden Hill in New York in January (another brawl with soldiers) was that the vast majority of colonials let them pass. Still, they dramatized a sore spot in colonial city life:

The Road to Independence 1770–1776

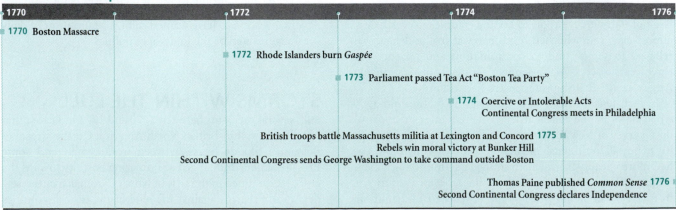

| 1770 | 1772 | 1774 | 1776 |

■ **1770** Boston Massacre

■ **1772** Rhode Islanders burn *Gaspée*

■ **1773** Parliament passed Tea Act "Boston Tea Party"

■ **1774** Coercive or Intolerable Acts
Continental Congress meets in Philadelphia

British troops battle Massachusetts militia at Lexington and Concord **1775** ■
Rebels win moral victory at Bunker Hill
Second Continental Congress sends George Washington to take command outside Boston

Thomas Paine published *Common Sense* **1776** ■
Second Continental Congress declares Independence

Blue Anchor Inn ~Philadelphia ~ 1776

An upscale colonial tavern, the Blue Anchor in Philadelphia. The diners are well-mannered gentlemen, more likely travelers than locals. Upper-class men dined out when they were in all-male circumstances such as during the Continental Congresses in Philadelphia. Couples living at home rarely did; they entertained one another at their homes. Workingmen's taverns and ordinaries were not so genteel as the Blue Anchor. They were more apt to be "holes in the wall."

Americans did not much like having soldiers in their midst. Property owners resented paying for their keep. Working people disliked rubbing shoulders with men who commanded little respect. Others were hostile to the redcoats for the time-honored reason that they were outsiders.

Eighteenth-century soldiers were tough and lusty young men isolated from society. Some had been pressed into service from Britain's poorest class; a few were convicted criminals (although rarely for serious crimes) who were in the army because it was offered to them as an alternative to prison. The majority, workingmen who had voluntarily enlisted, was stereotyped as "scum" along with the others.

So long as the soldiers were posted at frontier forts or lived in isolated bases such as Castle Island in Boston Harbor, there was little conflict. However, after the Stamp Act riots, the Crown stationed large detachments of redcoats within cities and towns. Some 4,000 soldiers were camped on Boston Common at the time of the massacre. Others, under the terms of the Quartering Act of 1765, were billeted in vacant buildings.

This brought the tightly knit redcoats into intimate daily contact with working-class colonials. Some found girlfriends, stirring up resentment on that primeval count. Others coarsely accosted young women. Off-duty redcoats competed with local men and boys for casual work. There had been a fistfight over jobs at a Boston rope maker's a few days before the Massacre. Redcoats also passed idle hours in taverns where colonials gathered.

Inns and taverns were not just places where travelers supped and bedded down. They were a focal point of urban social life, neighborhood social centers like contemporary English pubs. Workingmen popped in throughout the day for a cup of tea or coffee or a shot of rum, a mug of mulled cider, a pipe of tobacco, and a chat about work and politics. With plenty of time on their hands, unemployed men and seamen between voyages fairly lived in the "ordinaries," as bars were called, if only to warm themselves before the fire. The intrusion into this world of uniformed foreigners— some redcoats were colonials, but not many—laughing loudly and carrying on by themselves, caused resentments even when, as between 1770 and 1773, political relations with the mother country were good.

STREET PEOPLE

The redcoats had more to do with the anti-British feelings of lower-class colonials than Parliamentary taxation did. Poor people did not worry the fine points of the British constitution, and they were central to the protest that boiled over into riot in 1765 and rebellion after 1773. Workingmen, the

Redcoats

© Historical Picture Archive/Corbis

British officers rarely spoke well of their troops. They are "men fit to kill and be killed," one said, and that was mild. The word "scum" recurs so often in officers' written remarks that it must have been a conversational staple. Americans considered the redcoats as the off-scourings of British streets and jails, the lowest of the low.

Actually, most enlistees had respectable enough, if humble origins. They were laborers from English, Scottish, and Irish farms, villages, and towns; fewer from cities. Men enlisted for the sometimes generous bounties towns offered to fill the quotas the army assigned them; because the army offered a security that casual labor did not; or simply because their lives were stultifying and a recruiter could make the soldier's life look exciting. There were criminals in the army, young men convicted of petty crimes given a choice between enlistment and jail, but it was not an army of criminals.

There were draftees too, men pressed into service in the language of the day. Regiments unable to fill their ranks sent out press gangs to force unemployed young men living off the poor laws (on welfare, we would say), and many of them were unsavory types. But such men were not numerous in the army that fought in America. Enlistments during the war were high. Before the war, the British army

unemployed, boisterous street boys and apprentices, and the disreputable fringe elements of colonial society did the dirty work in the Stamp Act crisis. They were the ones who taunted the soldiers and were killed in the Boston Massacre.

The colonial "street people" were themselves social outcasts by virtue of their poverty, their occupation or lack of one, and their race. Seamen, suspect because they came and went and belonged to no community but their own, were prominent in colonial crowds. Crispus Attucks was an out-of-work seaman. Free blacks congregated in cities and urban slaves mixed with them. John Adams described the mob on King Street as "Negroes and mulattoes, Irish teagues and outlandish jack-tars." And yet, the revolution he was to join with enthusiasm owed much to the boldness of this motley bunch.

The role of alcohol in the agitation should be noted. Soldiers were a bibulous lot. It was standard military practice to pass around strong drink before battle, and the royal governor of New York dissolved the colonial assembly in 1766 when its members refused to provide the redcoats with their

signed up, on average, 2,000 each year. There were 15,000 enlistees in 1778, and about 9,000 in 1779. Two-thirds of them were Scots.

Moreover, because pressed soldiers were the most likely to desert, the army preferred to send them to posts where desertion was next to impossible, like Gibraltar; or where it was difficult, such as in the West Indies where the greater brutality of pressed and convict redcoats found its outlet against slaves, about whom no one much cared.

A large number of enlistees found the life congenial. Of 485 men in the 29th Regiment of Foot when it was sent to fight the Americans, 273 had more than six years of service. Pay was low, just 8d a day, but when the men were not in action, they were given two twenty-day leaves of absence a year. They ate better than they had as laborers; a week's rations included 7 pounds of bread, 7 pounds of beef (or 4 pounds of pork), 3 pints of peas, plus some butter and oatmeal. There was a daily rum ration; it varied although some rations would be enough to knock most people today unconscious. When in camp, the army enforced surprisingly high sanitary standards, but not so in Boston in 1775–1776. The trapped men were "dirty as hogs" and suffered from "camp fever" which might have been typhus (contracted from flea bites) or typhoid (from contaminated drinking water).

The red uniforms were, when fairly new, the best clothing most soldiers had ever worn. The famous tall bearskin hats served no function except, perhaps, to make the men look taller to their enemies. (The average redcoat was 5 feet 7 inches tall.)

Training (drilling) was rigorous, for it was the essence of eighteenth century armies. The workday for trainees was nine hours. Experienced redcoats had more time off, thus the competition with Bostonians for jobs that contributed to the tensions that led to the Boston Massacre. The men were kept in good condition for marching by running, carrying musket and a full pack. Redcoats marched at 75 steps a minute—pretty brisk—and were expected to handle 120 steps a minute in a pinch.

The infantryman's weapon was the "Brown Bess," a .78 caliber flintlock musket little modified since its introduction in 1703. It was about 5 feet long with a 17-inch bayonet inserted into a socket for hand-to-hand fighting. The soldier removed a paper-wrapped cartridge of gunpowder from a pouch, bit off the end, poured a few grains in the pan where the hammer would throw a spark, pour the rest down the muzzle, then add the wadded paper and a ball, and ram the charge and bullet home with a ramrod. A well-trained soldier could load and fire five times a minute. The musket was accurate at 60 yards; farther than that a hit was luck. Nobody aimed more than approximately, anyway, for they fired in volleys. In heavy rain, Bess was useless.

Generally, the redcoats were well disciplined. The casualties Major Pitcairn's column sustained on the retreat from Concord were not high because, as myth has it, they marched in tight "European" formation while the minutemen, intelligently, sniped at them from cover. Casualties would have been greater if the soldiers had panicked and run. On either side of the road, the column was protected by flanking parties that picked their way through fields and woods. Americans who were killed or captured during Pitcairn's retreat had inevitably been surprised when a detachment of redcoats attacked them from behind.

Until the last two years of fighting, the redcoats were much better trained than Washington's Continentals. Man for man, they were far better soldiers than state militiamen, especially with bayonets. A European stereotype of American soldiers—"they're afraid of cold steel"—which lasted through the Civil War into World War I, had its origins in the War for Independence.

Officers did lose control of their men when a battle had been particularly savage and a unit had suffered heavy casualties. Then, enraged soldiers, having seen friends killed, lost control of themselves and murdered prisoners. On a few occasions, officers encouraged looting and even atrocities in violation of the "rules of war," and at the risk of losing discipline.

---

accustomed ration of five pints of beer or four ounces of rum a day.

Colonials were hard drinking too, and people on the bottom, with more to forget, were the thirstiest of them. Many signal episodes on the road to independence seem to have been carried out by men in their cups. "The minds of the freeholders were inflamed," wrote an observer of the Stamp Act protest in South Carolina, "by many a hearty damn . . . over bottles, bowls, and glasses." The crowd that precipitated the Boston Massacre had come out of the taverns. The Sons of

Liberty, who ignited the last phase of the revolutionary movement with the Boston Tea Party of 1773, assembled over a barrel of rum.

Upper-crust protest leaders had mixed feelings about this kind of support. They were more than willing to exploit angry, inebriated crowds by stirring up resentment of the British, then winking at the mobs' mockeries of the law. John Adams, so scornful of the Massacre mob in 1770, called the men at the Boston Tea Party of 1773 "so bold, so daring, so intrepid." But many thoughtful upper-class colonials, and not just those who remained loyal to Great Britain, worried about "the rabble." They knew that mobs do not always fade graciously away after having played their historic role.

THE REGULATORS

Tensions between the people living on the colonies' western frontiers and residents of the longest settled regions dated to Bacon's Rebellion in 1676. They were exacerbated in the 1700s by the huge influx of Scotch-Irish who, by the 1760s, were the most conspicuous element in the western reaches. They faced the same problem Bacon's followers had: ongoing conflict with Indians, which they believed colonial governments did too little to assist. The strong ethnic consciousness of the Scotch-Irish, their own clannishness coupled with the disdain of the easterners, who were largely English in ancestry, aggravated the conflict.

In 1763, after the Pennsylvania assembly ignored the requests of Scotch-Irish settlers in Paxton on the Susquehanna River to protect them from the raiding Susquehannock, the settlers themselves launched a devastating attack on the tribe. The assembly ordered the leaders of the assault arrested. Instead, the "Paxton Boys," fully armed, marched on Philadelphia. Much of the city was near panic when Benjamin Franklin

(an advocate of an aggressive Indian policy) persuaded the Irishmen to leave, promising to use his influence to cancel the arrest warrants and increase western representation in the assembly—which he did.

In the backcountry of South Carolina between 1767 and 1769, frontiersmen did rebel against the colonial assembly, which was dominated by Charleston planters; just as Philadelphia merchants, who had refused to set up county governments in the West, dominated Pennsylvania. They created their own counties to which they paid taxes that were supposed to go to Charleston. The rebels called themselves Regulators because they said they would regulate their own affairs.

In North Carolina, a similar dispute led to actual battle. A band of westerners rode east to demonstrate their resentment of the colony's penny-pinching policies and there was no Ben Franklin to mediate. In May 1771, they were met and defeated by a smaller but better-trained militia at the Battle of Alamance. Only nine men were killed. (Six Regulators were later hanged.) But the clash did not sweeten the bitterness in the backcountry. When the War for Independence began, backcountry Carolinians were more likely than any other lower-class white colonials to align with the British.

■ *Rhode Islanders burning the grounded British customs schooner, Gaspée, in Narragansett Bay in 1772. It was a gravely serious incident, legally a rebellion and, therefore, punishable by death, because the Gaspée was a royal vessel. That an intensive investigation could not turn up one person to provide testimony identifying the perpetrators is as good an example of the power of community solidarity as can be found.*

THE *GASPÉE*

In June 1772, the **Gaspée,** a British schooner patrolling Narragansett Bay spotted a vessel suspected of smuggling and chased it toward Providence. About seven miles from the city, the *Gaspée* ran aground. That night, men from eight boats boarded the schooner, roughly set the crew ashore, and burned it to the waterline.

Because the *Gaspée* was a royal vessel, this was an act of rebellion. The authorities had good reason to believe that the ringleader of the gang was a merchant named John Brown, who had had several run-ins with customs collectors. However, neither a £500 reward nor the fact that Rhode Island's elected governor took part in the investigation persuaded anyone to provide evidence against him. The Commission of Inquiry disbanded only in June 1773. By then, the three-year lull in British–colonial relations was drawing to a close.

THE MARCH TOWARD WAR

In the spring of 1773, Parliament again enacted a law that angered Americans. This time, however, instead of spontaneous protests under the control of no one in particular, resistance to British policy was organized by a number of able, deliberate men.

They may be described as professional agitators. Some were orators ("rabble rousers" to the British), others propagandists of the pen. Several were able organizers willing to devote their time to the humdrum tasks of shaping anger into rebellion. There can be no revolutions without such revolutionaries, only tumult. Men like James Otis and Samuel Adams of Massachusetts and **Patrick Henry** of Virginia made the difference between spontaneous incidents like the burning of the *Gaspée* and calculated provocations like the Boston Tea Party.

THE TROUBLEMAKERS

James Otis was a Boston attorney, once an effective prosecutor before the unpopular vice-admiralty courts. Like some celebrated criminal attorneys today, he was a showman, excitable and a practitioner of "anything-to-win-a-case" argumentation. His rhetoric was often ugly. He described one group of courtroom adversaries as a "dirty, drinking, drabbing, contaminated knot of thieves," and, what's more, "Turks, Jews, and other infidels, with a few renegade Christians and Catholics." This sort of thing always has its enthusiasts. Otis could fire up the passions of a jury or a town meeting as few of his contemporaries could.

In 1761, Otis led Boston's fight against "writs of assistance." These were broad search warrants empowering customs agents to enter warehouses and homes to search for any evidence of smuggling; they did not have to specify the evidence for which they were looking. Arguing against the writs, Otis made them an issue of the sacred, basic rights of British subjects, apparently coining the phrase soon to be the slogan of a revolution: "taxation without representation is tyranny." John Adams would later say of Otis that "then and there the child Independence was born."

Reproduced from the Collections of the Library of Congress

Samuel Adams was unique among American protest leaders. His origins were respectable, but modest: he had been a brewer. He was no orator; he was visibly nervous whenever he had to speak before a crowd. Just why he was so hostile to the British so early on—he was just about the first prominent colonial to speak of independence—cannot be explained. But his unique high standing among both wealthy merchants and Boston's "street people" made him the key figure in Massachusetts's rebellion.

For inflammatory rhetoric, Patrick Henry of Virginia was Otis's equal. Not well read, no deep thinker, Henry was a sharp-tongued Scotch-Irish shopkeeper who became one of the colony's most effective trial lawyers and a member of the House of Burgesses, a station to which few of his class rose. He first won notice when he denounced the king—in vivid, quotable language—for reversing a law passed by the Burgesses, something monarchs had been doing since 1624. During the Stamp Act excitement, Henry made his "Caesar had his Brutus" speech. He was one of the first colonials to call for the establishment of an army to fight the British and, in May 1775, won fame from New Hampshire to Georgia by concluding a speech with the words "Give me liberty or give me death."

Less excitable than Otis and Henry, and no orator (he was nervous at a podium, trembling and stumbling over his words), Samuel Adams of Massachusetts was the most substantial revolutionary of the three. A brewer (and a tax collector between 1756 and 1764), Adams thereafter devoted himself to moral censorship and anti-British agitation. Personal morality and civic virtue were fundamental to his dislike of British rule. He was obsessed by the concept of republican virtue that the educated people of the era attributed to the ancient Greeks and Romans. Adams said that Boston should reconstitute itself as a "Christian Sparta." Humorless, bored by socializing, he believed that political power was legitimate only when in the hands of men who lived austerely and were ever vigilant to preserve liberty.

Adams was in the midst of every major protest in Boston: against the Sugar Act, the Stamp Act, and the Townshend Duties; and he was the primary agitator in attempting—unsuccessfully—to exploit the Boston Massacre. He was indispensable to the move toward independence, a sober organizer amongst oratorical prima donnas like Otis and James Warren. He was the man who handled the tasks that transform protest into politics. He also served as a go-between for the Boston elite (men like the rich merchant, John Hancock) and the Sons of Liberty; men of Adams's own artisan class, and through them, the crowd.

FATAL TURN: THE TEA ACT

Samuel Adams may have been thinking about independence from Great Britain by the mid-1760s. If so, he shared his thoughts with few others. He knew that to espouse radical causes alone was to alienate people who looked to him as a leader. His cousin John Adams to the contrary, "the child Independence" was born not when James Otis challenged the writs of assistance, nor when Patrick Henry threatened George III with executioners. The baby was delivered on May 10, 1773, when Parliament's Tea Act became law. After the Tea Act, the colonial quarrel with "Mother Britain" did not, as before, burn itself out and die. It intensified by progressive steps to an explosion.

Ironically, the Tea Act was not, like the Stamp Act and the Townshend Duties, motivated by the desire to raise money in the colonies. Parliament's leaders had not given up on that project, but they were understandably gun shy about new taxes. Their purpose in enacting the Tea Act was unrelated to North American policy; they wanted to save the **East India Company,** a huge corporation invaluable to the Crown because, in return for a monopoly of trade with India, the company governed much of the subcontinent, even maintaining its own army. The East India Company was empire on the cheap. In 1773, however, it was also on the verge of bankruptcy. In just a few months, East India shares plummeted in value from £280 to £160.

The Company had an asset: 17 million pounds of tea stored in warehouses. The directors proposed to a friendly Parliament (many members owned shares in the tottering corporation) that the company be given a monopoly on tea sales in the colonies rather than, as it was then doing, auctioning it to merchants involved in the colonial trade. Because of what was left of the Townshend boycott, they were not buying much anyway. The directors pointed out that because they would be dumping the warehoused tea to raise whatever cash could be had, their price would be substantially lower than the price of smuggled Dutch tea that inveterate American sippers were buying. To sweeten the cup, the company asked Parliament to repeal the Townshend tax on tea that had been left in place.

The Morning After

The men of Boston who dumped the tea into Boston harbor had been drinking, but not all suffered hangovers. One participant remembered what he did the morning after the Boston Tea Party:

The next morning, . . . it was discovered that very considerable quantities of it were floating upon the surface of the water, and to prevent the possibility of any of its being saved for use, a number of small boats were manned by sailors and citizens, who rowed them into those parts of the harbor wherever the tea was visible, and by beating it with oars and paddles so thoroughly drenched it as to render its entire destruction inevitable.

Parliament met the East India Company nine-tenths of the way. The prime minister, Frederick, Lord North, supported by George III, saw a chance to succeed where Grenville and Townshend had failed. Even with the tax, East India Company tea would be a bargain. It would cost Americans money to uphold the cause of no taxation without representation. Like many others in Great Britain, Lord North and the king believed that the colonial protest was about greed, not principle.

TEA PARTIES

They were wrong. When a dozen East India Company ships carrying 1,700 chests of tea sailed into American ports, they were greeted by the rowdiest defiance of British authority since 1765. Tea Act tea may have been cheap, but buying it would set the precedent of Parliament granting monopolies on goods colonials had to import.

The tea was landed in Charleston; it was hastily locked up in a warehouse where an angry crowd could not get to it. The governors of New York and Pennsylvania ordered the tea ships to return to England for fear of riots. In Annapolis, Maryland, a tea ship was burned. But it was a milder action in Boston that triggered the crisis.

The American-born governor of Massachusetts, Thomas Hutchinson, would not permit the tea ships to depart Boston. Instead, while sparks flew at public meetings, he hatched a plan to get the cargo under his control—royal control—rather than the Company's. He would seize the tea for failure to pay port taxes. Any violence against it then would be an act of rebellion.

It was a clever idea, but Samuel Adams was cleverer and quicker. On December 16, 1773, the day before Hutchinson would gain custody of the tea, Adams presided over a protest meeting attended by a third of the population of Boston. Some sixty Sons of Liberty slipped out of the meetinghouse, had a few drinks, dressed up as Mohawk Indians, and boarded the East India Company ships. To the cheers of a crowd, they dumped 342 chests of tea worth £10,000 into Boston Harbor.

The Indian costumes were a touch of political genius. They disguised the perpetrators, but also lent the air of a prank to

Americans throwing the Cargoes of the Tea Ships into the River, at Boston

© Corbis

■ *The Boston Tea Party: an early woodcut, hurriedly prepared to be printed and circulated as propaganda, like Paul Revere's more famous engraving of the Boston Massacre. The destruction of the tea was well-organized and flawlessly executed by the Sons of Liberty, led by Samuel Adams.*

an act of gross vandalism: thus the Boston "Tea Party." Adams and his collaborators, such as John Hancock, knew that Britain could not let the incident pass and they guessed that Parliament would overreact. Parliament did, grotesquely and foolishly. Instead of flushing out the individuals involved in the party and trying them as vandals (the dumped tea had not been under government control), Lord North decided to punish the people of the city of Boston and the colony of Massachusetts, making an example of them. It was a terrible mistake, and yet, even **General Thomas Gage,** who knew America well and happened to be in London when news of the Tea Party arrived, approved of the plan.

THE INTOLERABLE ACTS

A few parliamentary leaders like reliable Lord Chatham warned that the Coercive Acts of 1774—Americans called them the Intolerable Acts—were ill advised, but Lord North easily pushed them through Parliament. First, the port of Boston was closed to all trade until such time as the city (not the culprits) paid for the spoiled tea. Second, the new governor (General Gage) was empowered to transfer out of the colony the trials of soldiers or other British officials accused of killing protesters. (It was not unreasonable for colonials to interpret this as an invitation to the redcoats to shoot on the slightest of pretexts.) Third, the Massachusetts colonial

Salt in the Wound: The Quebec Act

The Quebec Act of 1774 was not one of the Coercive Acts. It was not intended to punish the colonials or force them into better behavior. It had been in the works long before the Boston Tea Party. But it, too, agitated New Englanders by bestowing official status on the Catholic religion in the province of Quebec. (The 1763 Treaty required only

toleration.) British and colonial anti-Catholicism was not so rabid as it had been, but it was not dead. In the Gordon Riots in London in 1780, mobs burned the churches and homes of Catholics for three days.

Colonials having no particular hostility toward Roman Catholics were angered by another provision of the Quebec Act: the extension of the province of Quebec into the Ohio Valley. Had not the French and Indian

War been fought to expel the French (and Canadians) from these lands? Speculators with claims to Ohio Valley land and farmers eyeing the possibility of moving there were alarmed.

Finally, the Quebec Act did not provide for an elective assembly in Quebec, which was particularly disturbing because of Parliament's attacks on elected bodies in Massachusetts.

The Way We Were

Before 1776, few colonials thought in terms of independence. The goal of the quarrel with Great Britain was to go backward, to things as they were before 1763. Benjamin Franklin's advice was to "repeal the laws, renounce the right, recall the troops, refund the money, and return to the old method of requisition."

government was overhauled with elected bodies losing powers to the king's appointed officials. Fourth, a new Quartering Act further aggravated civilian–soldier relations. It authorized the army to house redcoats in occupied private homes, a gratuitous provocation.

Lord North hoped that by coming down hard on Massachusetts, he would not only intimidate protest leaders in other colonies, but also isolate the Bay Colony, which had never been popular elsewhere in North America. Instead, the Coercive Acts proved to be intolerable everywhere. Several cities shipped food to paralyzed Boston. More ominous than charity, when Massachusetts called for a "continental congress" to meet in centrally located Philadelphia to discuss a united response to the Intolerable Acts, every colony except Georgia sent delegates.

REBELLION

The Tea Act marks the beginning of a progressive march toward rebellion; the Intolerable Acts mark the beginning of a coordinated colonial resistance. Before 1774, only the informal Committees of Correspondence, groups exchanging news and views among the colonies via the mail, connected one colony's protestors to protesters elsewhere. Now, while the delegates to the Continental Congress who trickled into Philadelphia during the summer came as New Hampshiremen and New Yorkers and Carolinians, they acted in concert "continentally" with something like formal authority.

THE FIRST CONTINENTAL CONGRESS

The fifty-six delegates to the First Continental Congress began their discussions on September 5. One of them, hometowner Benjamin Franklin, was already famous in Europe for his experiments with electricity. Samuel Adams and Patrick Henry were known throughout the colonies thanks to newspapers. The others, however, were men of only local renown. Because every one of the colonies had closer relations with Great Britain than with the other American provinces, few of the delegates had met their colleagues from other colonies.

They differed in temperament, in their sentiments toward Great Britain, and in their opinions as to what should be done, could be done, and what ought not be done. But they got along remarkably well. The heritage they were soon to rebel against gave them much in common. They were all gentlemen in the English mold: merchants, planters, and professionals—particularly lawyers. They prized education and civility. They knew how to keep debates decorous and impersonal. In the evening, they recessed to a round of festive dinners and parties

with Philadelphia high society. George Washington of Virginia rarely dined in his own chambers. John Adams gushed in letters to his wife, Abigail, about the lavishness of the meals he was served. Only Samuel Adams, nurturing his ideals of Roman republican frugality, shunned the social whirl, and won the reputation of being a stick-in-the-mud.

None of the delegates had an "ideology"; few had even an agenda. They were troubled and angry, even those who, in the end, would later remain loyal to Great Britain. But they were uncertain, even vacillating. The Congress was on the verge of adopting a series of conciliatory resolutions moved by Joseph Galloway of Pennsylvania when Paul Revere of Boston arrived in Philadelphia after a frantic ride with a set of defiant declarations called the **Suffolk Resolves.** (Boston was in Suffolk County.) The tenor of the Suffolk Resolves was utterly at odds with Galloway's resolutions, but the Congress adopted them.

Still, there was no king baiting in the style of Patrick Henry. Indeed, the delegates toasted themselves tipsy every evening raising glasses to King George. They agreed that Parliament had the right to regulate trade within the empire (without exploring the question of how that could be done without duties).

George III, unfortunately, was not in a conciliatory mood. His gravest shortcomings, his disdain for colonials and the simplicity of his mind, came to the fore. "Blows must decide whether they are to be subject to the country or independent," he told Lord North at a time when no colonial leader of consequence had publicly mentioned force as a means of resistance or independence as an conceivable alternative to colonial status. The king's intransigence left the delegates the options of submission or responding in kind to the king's threats. One of the Congress's last actions before adjourning was to call on Americans to organize and train militias.

MILITIAS

Little encouragement was needed in the Massachusetts countryside where, with tempers aflame, men had oiled their guns and begun to assemble regularly at musters. Long before the Intolerable Acts, every township was required by law to have a training band. All men were obligated to serve except clergymen, college students and professors, the mentally incompetent, and, since 1691, Quakers. In 1774, militiamen ranged in age from sixteen to fifty, with men over fifty and up to seventy on an emergency "alarm list." Since 1711, thirty men from each town were to be ready to march with "a minute's warning"—the so-called "minutemen."

Other colonies had similar arrangements. When there was no war, no one had paid them much attention and, as a consequence, professional soldiers did not hold colonial militias in much esteem. During the French and Indian War, General John Forbes had said "there is no faith or trust to be put in them." George Washington, himself soon to be commanding thousands of militia, would use almost identical words to describe them.

One problem was the fact that many militiamen owned no muskets. A New Hampshire militia captain said that half of

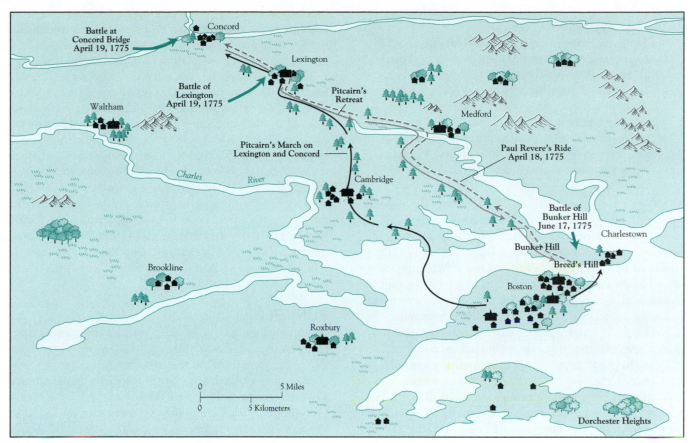

Map 8:1 The First Battles, April–June 1775
The British march to Lexington and Concord, and their retreat to Boston, was through farmland marked by stone fences and extensive woodlots, which enabled "minutemen" to inflict numerous casualties on the retreating column from cover. The militia surrounded Boston, which presented the British in Boston with no supply problems—British ships controlled the harbor. However, their occupation of high ground north of the city was threatening if the Americans brought in artillery. In June, in what was misleadingly called the Battle of Bunker Hill, the British actually assaulted and captured Breed's Hill, but at terrible cost.

his soldiers were unarmed. When Thomas Jefferson was governor of Virginia, he fretted over the militia's shortage of firearms but (astonishingly) consoled himself that there would be so many deserters that the shortfall would be eliminated. The image of early Americans as armed to the teeth is a myth. One study of western New England, where Indians still threatened, revealed that just 14 percent of men had guns and half of those were broken. That figure is much too low, but many of the militia at the first battle of the Revolution, at Concord, were unarmed.

Militiamen were poorly trained, if trained at all. In most colonies, musters were held only four times a year. (Professional soldiers drilled daily for months.) Many of the men looked on the musters mainly as social occasions, which appears to have been the case. Officers were elected on the basis of their popularity. If any of them had any knowledge of drill, on which armies were based, they lacked the authority to force their soldiers to it. A British drill officer punished soldiers who did not take drill seriously with a flogging; that did not happen at American militia musters.

Like the redcoats, militiamen who did own firearms had smoothbore muskets, "Brown Besses" as likely as not.

Colonials were much more likely to be marksmen than the redcoats were because they used their muskets primarily for hunting. In Pennsylvania, many people had adopted the *Jaeger*, a rifle introduced there by German immigrants. Americans extended the length of the rifle's barrel for even greater accuracy at long distances. A British officer observed, "provided an American rifleman were to get a perfect aim at 300 yards at me, standing still, he most undoubtedly would hit me unless it was a very windy day."

LEXINGTON AND CONCORD

There were no riflemen in Massachusetts, however, so when General Gage decided to seize rebel supplies said to be stored at Concord, twenty-one miles from Boston, he did not worry about the minutemen or any other militia. Early on the morning of April 19, 1775, with no warning, 800 to 900 redcoats were awakened, given a single day's rations, handed thirty-six rounds of powder and ball each, and marched toward Concord. They carried no knapsacks; it was to be a one-day operation. Howe advised the commander of the column, Major John Pitcairn, that Samuel Adams and John Hancock were believed to be in Concord; Pitcairn was to arrest them.

The British Were Not Coming

Paul Revere (and William Dawes and Samuel Prescott) did not rouse every Middlesex village and town by shouting, as legend has it, "the British are coming!" In April 1775, Revere and other Americans thought themselves to be quite as British as soldiers from Yorkshire and Ayrshire. They may have shouted that "the redcoats" were on the march, possibly "the lobsters," two derogatory American terms for British soldiers. Most likely they shouted, "the Regulars are coming." Massachusetts militiamen thought of themselves as soldiers too; the redcoats were members of the regular army.

The nighttime march was meant to be a surprise; the troops were ordered to be as quiet as possible. But the Sons of Liberty had been watching. Paul Revere and two others galloped off ahead of them in different directions to arouse the militias. Revere was the most effective. He not only awakened every house he passed by shouting, "The regulars are coming!" but at the homes of known Sons of Liberty, made sure that riders were dispatched along roads he would not be covering.

When Major Pitcairn arrived at Lexington, a few miles shy of Concord, he found seventy armed but uneasy village militiamen drawn up in a semblance of battle formation. (But no minutemen; Lexington had ignored the requirement to maintain such an elite unit.) Pitcairn detached several companies from the column and quickly formed a professional battle line of tough, grim men.

Twice Pitcairn ordered the colonials to disperse. Some witnesses said that (sensibly) they were beginning to do so when a shot rang out. No one knew who fired it, a colonial hothead determined to force the issue or a British soldier mishandling his musket. It did not matter. Although not ordered to respond, the redcoats volleyed, clearing Lexington Green in minutes.

Pitcairn marched on to Concord, where a much larger force of Americans mobilized by Revere met them at a bridge inside the town. Surprised by the size of the resistance and worried by the Americans' superior position, Pitcairn ordered a retreat to Boston. All the way back, militiamen sniped at the British soldiers from behind trees and stone fences, inflicting serious casualties. By the time the redcoats reached the city, 73 were dead and 174 were wounded. The casualties owed nothing to American marksmanship; the militiamen had fired, according to one calculation, 75,000 rounds. Elated nevertheless, the militia, joined by thousands more from all over Massachusetts and Rhode Island, set up camps surrounding Boston. Within two weeks, they numbered 16,000.

BUNKER HILL

In London, Edmund Burke pleaded with Parliament to evacuate Boston and allow tempers to cool. As usual, the most thoughtful politician of the age was heard for his eloquence, then ignored. Lord North dispatched an additional 1,000 troops to Boston and three more generals: Henry Clinton, John "Gentleman Johnny" Burgoyne, and William Howe. Curiously, all three, as well as Gage, were personally sympathetic to Americans.

The British were surrounded but that meant little. They could be supplied by sea. However, the city was at risk of bombardment from high ground north and south of the city—

John Carter Brown Library

One of numerous depictions of the "battle" at Lexington, each one of which portrays the incident in a different light. This one conveys an image of, on the left, disciplined "minutemen" in a battle line driving off redcoated jackals who have burned the village. In fact, the Massachusetts militiamen collected on Lexington Green understood they could not stand up to the British regulars and were probably dispersing when they were fired on.

Breed's Hill and Bunker Hill to the north across the Charles River, Dorchester Heights to the south overlooking Boston Harbor. (Unknown to the British at the time, the Americans had only about a half dozen cannon.) General Clinton asked Gage to order him to occupy Dorchester Heights. Howe asked to be sent to seize Breed's Hill. Then, the day before Howe was to move, 1,600 Americans dug in on Breed's Hill.

Howe sent 2,000 crack troops up the slopes. Puzzlingly, no one returned their fire. Then, when the Americans could "see the whites of their eyes" (in other words, when they could aim rather than volley), they let loose. The redcoats staggered and retreated. They regrouped and again advanced, and again they were thrown back. Now, however, Howe correctly calculated that the Americans were short of powder and shot. Reinforcing his badly mauled line with fresh men, Howe took Breed's Hill with bayonets.

The British had won, or had they? Hearing that 200 men had been killed and 1,000 wounded, General Clinton remarked that too many such victories would destroy the army's capacity to fight. Several units were destroyed. The Royal Welsh Fusiliers, three officers commanding thirty-five men, were reduced to one corporal and eleven privates. The King's Own Grenadiers, with forty-three officers and men before Lexington, listed twelve men "effective" after Bunker Hill. Half the officers who had marched to Concord were dead or seriously wounded; ninety-two officers had been lost.

Clinton was right. The misnamed Battle of Bunker Hill was a moral victory for the Americans—an American triumph. General Gage remarked of the Americans, "in all their wars against the French they never showed so much conduct, attention and perseverance as they do now." He was shaken. He refused to allow Clinton to move on Dorchester Heights even though it was not occupied.

TICONDEROGA

The rebels' morale had another boost in the spring of 1775. Soon after Lexington and Concord, the Massachusetts Committee of Safety instructed **Benedict Arnold,** scion of a wealthy Connecticut family and a proven soldier, to raise an army and attack Fort Ticonderoga on Lake Champlain. Before he started, Arnold learned that backwoodsmen from what is now Vermont, a kind of guerrilla group calling themselves the **Green Mountain Boys,** were preparing to march on the same fort, led by an eccentric land speculator named Ethan Allen.

Arnold caught up with the Green Mountain Boys, but he was unable to get the headstrong Allen to recognize his authority. Quarreling all the way to the fort, the two shut up just long enough to capture Ticonderoga on May 10. When the British commander, who had heard nothing of Lexington and Concord, asked in whose name he was being asked to surrender, Allen allegedly replied, "in the name of the great Jehovah and the Continental Congress." Striking and memorable as the words are, Allen was unlikely to have spoken them just so, since he was a militant atheist.

The Arnold-Allen group captured several other British forts. They were not big battles, they were hardly battles at all.

The British garrisons, languishing in the forests, were caught entirely by surprise. But along with Bunker Hill, these actions established that a war had begun, forcing Americans to take sides. Nowhere was the psychological impact greater than in Philadelphia, where another congress was already in session.

THE SECOND CONTINENTAL CONGRESS

The delegates to the Second Continental Congress were less conservative than those of the first. Joseph Galloway was not present; Thomas Jefferson, a 32-year-old Virginian who had written several scorching anti-British polemics, was.

The situation had changed since the First Continental Congress. Armed rebellion, barely imagined a year earlier, was a reality. Without bloodshed, royal authority was disintegrating everywhere as governors fled to the safety of British warships and self-appointed committees of rebels took over the functions of government. The Congress was in danger of being left behind by events. To assert its authority, the delegates sent George Washington of Virginia (a delegate who showed up wearing his military uniform) to take command of the troops around Boston in the Congress's name.

Delegates discussed independence, but not officially. In its "Declaration of the Cause and Necessity of Taking up Arms" in July 1775, Congress insisted that the rebels sought only their rights as British subjects. But the inconsistency of shooting at George III's soldiers while swearing loyalty to the king was preying on many minds. With Lord North refusing to propose any kind of compromise, Congress held back only because of a thread of sentiment—the sense that monarchy was essential to good government.

CUTTING THE TIE

The man who snipped this thread of sentiment was not an American, but an Englishman. Thomas Paine was 38 years of age in 1775, and only recently arrived in the colonies, sponsored by Benjamin Franklin. Perhaps because both men were of the artisan class, (Thomas Paine was a corset maker) Franklin saw beyond Paine's history of failures in business, his "loathesome" personal appearance, and a vanity that many others could not suffer.

COMMON SENSE

Paine's egotism and contentiousness were hard to take. But his talents as a propagandist were formidable. In January 1776, he published a pamphlet that ranks with Luther's *95 Theses* and the *Communist Manifesto* as works of few words that shaped the course of history. In **Common Sense,** Paine argued that it was foolish for Americans to risk everything for the purpose of British approval. He shredded Americans' attachment to King George III, whom he called a "Royal Brute." Indeed, Paine attacked the idea of hereditary monarchy. Kingship was "an office any child or idiot may fill, . . . to be a king requires only the animal figure of a man."

With a genius and a gift for the right words that would produce many stirring calls on behalf of democracy and liberty over the next twenty years, Paine made converts by the

Culver Pictures, Inc.

John Trumbull's classic painting of the signing of the Declaration of Independence depicts an assembly that never existed. By the time the document was ready for signing, most of the delegates had left for home. They signed without ceremony, singly or in twos and threes, later on in the summer or fall of 1776. However, Trumbull went to great lengths to find likenesses of every signer.

thousands. Within a year, a population of 2.5 million bought 150,000 copies of *Common Sense;* within a decade, half a million copies. Every American who could read must have at least skimmed it; many others must have heard it read aloud. Paine boasted that it was "the greatest sale that any performance ever had since the use of letters."

Paine's depiction of the king seemed to come to life with every dispatch from London. George III refused even to listen to American suggestions for peace, and he backed Lord North's proposal to hire German mercenaries to crush the rebels. As the spring of 1776 wore on, colony after colony formally nullified the king's authority within its boundaries.

Some instructed their delegates in Philadelphia to vote for independence.

INDEPENDENCE

On June 7, Richard Henry Lee of Virginia introduced the resolution that "these United Colonies are, and of right ought to be, free and independent states." For three weeks the delegates debated the issue. New England and the southern colonies were solidly for independence. The middle colonies were divided. New York never did vote for independence, but Pennsylvania, the large, prosperous, strategically located "keystone" of the colonies, gave in when the pacifistic John Dickinson, a

The Funny "S"

In documents of the revolutionary era, including the Declaration of Independence, the letter *s* is often written *f*. This not a lower case *f*. Note that the character has only half a crossbar, and sometimes not that.

The letter *f* is an *s*, pronounced just as the familiar *s* character is. The unfamiliar *f*

originated in German handwriting and was adopted by printers in the German printed alphabet. It made its way to England because the moveable type used by the earliest English printers was imported from Germany.

The use of *f* was governed by strict rules. It was a lowercase letter, never a capital at

the beginning of a proper noun or sentence; the familiar *S* served that purpose. The *f* appeared only at the beginning or in the middle of a word in lower case, never at the end. Thus, *business* was *bufinefs* and *sassiness* was *faffinefs*. Printers abandoned this form of the letter during the early nineteenth century.

Yelping and Driving

Samuel Johnson, recognized during his lifetime as the greatest figure of English letters, did not like Americans. Among their unpleasant traits, Dr. Johnson said, was that they were shameless hypocrites. "Why is it," he wrote in 1775, "that we hear the loudest yelps for liberty among the drivers of negroes?" His point, of course, was not lost on Americans (Thomas Jefferson among them) who subscribed to the phrase "all men are created equal" yet held one American in five in slavery.

King George's Spectacles

John Hancock, as president of the Second Continental Congress, was the first to sign the Declaration of Independence. He inscribed his name in an elegant hand, outsized so that, Hancock said, King George could read his name without his glasses. In fact, Hancock often signed his name flamboyantly, as on the Olive Branch Petition, an earlier, conciliatory message to King George. And he was risking nothing in making his name clear to the king. He already had a price on his head because of his role in organizing the Boston Tea Party. Many of the other signers were, in fact, bolder, for they had previously been unknown to the king.

Quaker, and the cautious financier, Robert Morris, agreed to absent themselves so that the deadlock in the delegation could be broken in favor of the resolution. (Both men later supported the patriot cause.)

Delaware, also divided, swung to the side of independence when Caesar Rodney galloped full tilt from Dover to Philadelphia, casting the majority vote in his delegation. On July 2, the maneuvers concluded, Congress broke America's legal ties with England. "The second day of July 1776," an excited John Adams wrote to Abigail, "will be the most memorable epoch in the history of America." He was two days off. The "Glorious Fourth" became the national holiday when, on that day, the congress gathered to adopt its official statement to Americans and to the world of why it chose to dissolve the political bands that tied America to Great Britain.

THE DECLARATION OF INDEPENDENCE

Officially, the Declaration of Independence was the work of a committee consisting of Thomas Jefferson, Roger Sherman of Connecticut, John Adams, Benjamin Franklin, and Robert Livingston of New York. In fact, appreciating better than we do that a committee cannot write coherently, the work of composition was assigned to Jefferson because of his "peculiar felicity of style." The lanky Virginian, sometimes as careless of his personal appearance as Tom Paine, holed up in his rooms and emerged with a masterpiece.

Franklin and Adams changed a few words, and the Congress made some alterations, the most important of which was to eliminate Jefferson's sly, backhanded attack on

Common Knowledge

Jefferson did not try to be original when he wrote the Declaration of Independence. His purpose was to call on ideas that were in the air, familiar to all, so as to sell the American cause. His famous restatement of the natural rights of man, for example, was taken from a speech that Samuel Adams made in Boston in November 1772: "Among the natural rights of the colonists are these: first, a right to life; secondly, a right to liberty; thirdly, to property; together with the right to support and defend them in the best manner they can." This statement itself was an elaboration of philosopher John Locke's writings, with which every educated Briton and colonial was familiar.

the institution of slavery. King George, Jefferson wrote, "has waged cruel war against human nature itself, violating its most sacred right of life and liberty in the persons of a distant people who never offended him, captivating them into slavery in another hemisphere." Whatever and whomever were to be blamed for slavery, George III was not one of the culprits. Jefferson knew it, as did fellow southerners in the Congress, especially South Carolinians who, wedded to the institution, insisted the section be deleted.

George III was blamed for practically everything that was wrong in the colonies in part to personalize the struggle that had already begun. The king had done nothing without a majority of Parliament supporting him, but to demonize Parliament, when the rebels insisted on the supreme authority of their elected assemblies, would have been awkward at best.

UNIVERSAL HUMAN RIGHTS

The Declaration is not remembered for its catalog of George III's high crimes and misdemeanors. It is one of history's great political documents because, in his introductory sentences, Jefferson penned a stirring statement of universal human rights. Jefferson did not write solely of the rights of American colonials. He put their case for independence in terms of the rights of all human beings: "We hold these truths to be self-evident, that all men are created equal, that they are endowed by their Creator with certain unalienable Rights, that among these are Life, Liberty and the pursuit of Happiness." And he tersely codified the principles that government drew its authority only from the consent of the people governed. When the people withdrew that consent and were faced with coercion, they had the right to rebel.

Wording from the Declaration of Independence would, over two centuries, be borrowed by many peoples asserting their right to freedom, from the republics of Central and South America early in the 1800s to the Vietnamese on September 2, 1945. In the United States, groups making demands on society—from African Americans to feminists and labor unions to organizations lobbying against smoking tobacco in bar rooms—have based their demands on their inalienable rights. In the summer of 1776, however, Americans were not thinking of the Declaration's future. The job was to confirm it on the battlefield.

FURTHER READING

General Bernard Bailyn, *The Ideological Origins of the American Revolution*, 1967; Don Higginbotham, *The War of American Independence, 1763–1789*, 1971; Alfred T. Young, *The American Revolution: A Radical Interpretation*, 1976; Pauline Maier, *From Resistance to Revolution, 1765–1776*, 1972; Robert Middlekauff, *The Glorious Cause: The American Revolution 1763–1789*, 1982; Stephen Conway, *The War of American Independence 1775–1783*, 1995; John Ferling, *A Leap in the Dark: The Struggle to Create the American Republic*, 2003.

Landmarks Hiller B. Zobel, *The Boston Massacre*, 1970; Marjoleine Kars, *Breaking Loose Together: The Regulator Rebellion in Pre-Revolutionary North Carolina*, 2002; Benjamin W. Labaree, *The Boston Tea Party*, 1964; Philip Lawson, *The Imperial Challenge: Quebec and Britain in the Age of the American Revolution*, 1989; David Hackett Fischer, *Paul Revere's Ride*, 1994.

Redcoats and Militiamen John Shy, *Toward Lexington: The Role of the British Army on the Coming of the Revolution*, 1965; John E. Ferling, *A Wilderness of Miseries: War and Warriors in Early America*, 1980; Sylvia R. Frey, *The British Soldier in America: A Social History of Military Life in the Revolutionary Period*, 1984; Robert A. Gross, *The Minutemen and Their World*, 1976; Charles Royster, *A Revolutionary People at War: The Continental Army and American Character 1775–1783*, 1980.

The First Battles Robert L. O'Connell, *Of Arms and Men: A History of War, Weapons, and Aggression*, 1989; Peter D. Thomas, *Tea Party to Independence: The Third Phase of the American Revolution, 1773–1776*, 1991; Mark V. Kwasny, *Washington's Partisan War, 1775–1783*, 1996; David McCullough, *1776*, 2005.

Declaring Independence Carl Becker, *The Declaration of Independence*, 1922; Garry Wills, *Inventing America: Jefferson's Declaration of Independence*, 1978; Pauline Maier, *American Scripture: The Making of the Declaration of Independence*, 1997.

Biographies Bernard Bailyn, *The Ordeal of Thomas Hutchinson*, 1974; Richard R. Beeman, *Patrick Henry: A Biography*, 1974; Eric Foner, *Tom Paine and Revolutionary America*, 1976; Noel B. Gerson, *The Grand Incendiary: A Biography of Samuel Adams*, 1973; Ira D. Gruber, *The Howe Brothers and the American Revolution*, 1972; Pauline Maier, *The Old Revolutionaries: Political Lives in the Age of Samuel Adams*, 1980; John K. Alexander, *Samuel Adams: America's Revolutionary Politician*, 2002; Willard Sterne Randall, *Benedict Arnold: Patriot and Traitor*, 1990; Richard Brookhiser, *Founding Father: Rediscovering George Washington*, 1996.

KEY TERMS

The following terms are covered in this chapter and can also be found in the list of Key Terms at the back of the book.

Benedict Arnold	*Gaspée*	**Patrick Henry**	**Regulators**
Common Sense	**General Thomas Gage**	**Paul Revere**	**Samuel Adams**
East India Company	**Green Mountain Boys**	**Quebec Act**	**Suffolk Resolves**

ONLINE SOURCES GUIDE

Use this listing to find online documents, images, interactive maps, simulations, and other resources related to this chapter:

John Hancock
Samuel Adams
Thomas Paine

American History Resource Center
http://history.wadsworth.com

Selected Documents
The Coercive Acts (1774)
Thomas Paine's Common Sense *(1776)*
Thomas Paine's The Crisis

Selected Images
John Dickinson, author
The Boston Tea Party

Simulations
The American Revolution

Interactive Timeline (with online readings)
From Riot to Rebellion: The Road to Independence 1770–1776

Additional resources, exercises, and Internet links related to this chapter are available on *THE AMERICAN PAST* web site: http://history.wadsworth.com/americanpast8e

Discovery

How are words and images used to justify actions in time of war, especially in the case of the American Revolution?

In thinking about this question, begin by breaking it down into the components shown below. A discussion of the significance of each component should appear in your answer.

Government and Law: For this exercise, please read the following document excerpt: "Declaration of Independence." What was the reasoning for moving toward independence? How did the colonists move from disagreeing over taxes to complete separation? Did the colonists fully embrace all of the principles implied in the Declaration of Independence? Do you see any hypocrisy among these individuals? How long would it take to fulfill all of the principles stated? How could they reconcile not fulfilling them?

Declaration of Independence

We hold these Truths to be self-evident, that all Men are created equal, that they are endowed by their Creator with certain unalienable Rights, that among these are Life, Liberty and the Pursuit of Happiness— That to secure these Rights, Governments are instituted among Men, deriving their just Powers from the Consent of the Governed, that whenever any Form of Government becomes destructive of these Ends, it is the Right of the People to alter or to abolish it, and to institute new Government, laying its Foundation on such Principles, and organizing its Powers in such Form, as to them shall seem most likely to effect their Safety and Happiness. Prudence, indeed, will dictate that Governments long established should not be changed for light and transient Causes; and accordingly all Experience hath shewn, that Mankind are more disposed to suffer, while Evils are sufferable, than to right themselves by abolishing the Forms to which they are accustomed. But when a long Train of Abuses and Usurpations, pursuing invariably the same Object, evinces a Design to reduce them under absolute Despotism, it is their Right, it is their Duty, to throw off such Government, and to provide new Guards for their future Security. Such has been the patient Sufferance of these Colonies; and such is now the Necessity which constrains them to alter their former Systems of Government. The History of the present King of Great-Britain is a History of repeated Injuries and Usurpations, all having in direct Object the Establishment of an absolute Tyranny over these States.

Culture and Society: For this exercise, please study these three images: "The Boston Massacre," "The Boston Tea Party," and "The 'Battle' at Lexington." Look closely at all of these pictures. How are the British depicted? How are the Americans depicted? What values do you think the images are attempting to portray? How accurately do you think these images portray the actual incidents? For what purpose might they have been created originally?

The Boston Massacre

Americans throwing the Cargoes of the Tea Ships into the River, at Boston

The Boston Tea Party

The 'Battle' at Lexington

To read extended versions of the documents, visit the companion Web site http://history.wadsworth.com/americanpast8e; click on "Discovery Sources."

CHAPTER 9

The War for Independence

Winning the Revolution 1776–1781

North Wind Picture Archives

The history of our Revolution will be one continual lie from one end to the other. The essence of the whole will be that Dr. Franklin's electrical rod smote the earth and out sprang George Washington. That Franklin electrified him with his rod—and thenceforward these two constructed all the policy, negotiations, legislatures, and war.

John Adams

The signers of the Declaration of Independence pledged their lives, their fortunes, and their sacred honor to the cause of independence. This was no empty vow. Had George III won the quick victory he expected, the delegates to the **Second Continental Congress** would have been punished, at least some severely. There might well have been hangings. The noose had been the fate of Irish rebels and would be again. The Americans called themselves patriots. To the king they were traitors.

AN IMBALANCE OF POWER

To European onlookers—notably the French—patriot chances of winning the war were not bright: 1775 was a year of victories, but the battles were small and decided nothing. The first months of 1776 brought mixed news. The Americans around Boston, now commanded by George Washington of Virginia, forced the British to evacuate the city. But an offensive in Canada was a disaster.

THE ARMIES

After Bunker Hill, Lord North's military advisor, Lord George Germain, dispatched 32,000 soldiers in 400 ships to join the redcoats already in America. It was the largest military operation in British history. Fewer than half were British regulars. Germain had contracted with several petty German princes, who rented out well-trained soldiers, for the services of 18,000 men (eventually 30,000); the fee was £7 a head, double if the man was killed. The mercenaries came from six different principalities, but Americans lumped them together as "Hessians." (Two of the suppliers were the states of Hesse-Cassell and Hesse-Hanau.) During much of the war, Britain never had fewer than 50,000 troops ready for battle; in 1781, there were 92,000 redcoats and Hessians in Canada, the thirteen colonies, Florida, and the West Indies.

In 1775 and 1776, the Americans could field only hastily mobilized militias. Washington thought no better of them as soldiers than British officers did. He wrote of the "unaccountable kind of stupidity" of the troops around Boston he was sent to command, calling the army "a mixed multitude of people . . . under very little discipline, order, or government." They came and went; from day to day, Washington did not know how many men he commanded.

A few militias were excellent fighting forces, including the "Rhode Island Army of Observation" brought to Boston by General Nathanael Greene, who would prove to be one of the best American battle commanders. Later in the war, South Carolina's militia stood almost alone against a crack British army, avoiding a pitched battle, but harassing the redcoats to distraction. Even the militias least reliable in battle freed other men to fight by policing areas the British did not occupy, which was almost all of the countryside.

The Continental Army created by the Congress was, by 1778, well trained and effective. But "continentals" usually enlisted for a year at a time. Washington never personally had more than 18,500 continentals and, on several occasions, his army dwindled to 5,000.

The British navy was without an equal in the world. The patriot navy was a cipher at the start and never more than a joke. Washington had to pay personally for the first American warship, the *Hannah,* a schooner with only four guns. (Some merchant vessels were better armed.) The Continental Congress eventually appropriated funds to build thirteen frigates, one for each state, but the eleven that were completed fared poorly: one was destroyed in battle, seven were captured, two were scuttled to keep them out of British hands, and one was accidentally set afire by its own crew.

LOYALISTS: WHITE, BLACK, AND RED

By no means were Americans united behind the cause of independence. John Adams estimated that a third of the white population was loyal to the king. That may have been overstating it. Nevertheless, when the British evacuated Boston, 1,000 Americans went with them. When Howe established his headquarters in New York, the redcoats were received more as liberators than the British army and one American in thirty left the country to live in England, the West Indies,

Fears of a Loyalist

The Reverend Mather Byles was an oddity, a Massachusetts Congregationalist minister who opposed the Revolution. Almost all of them were militant patriots. In a sermon of 1776, Byles explained his fear that the Revolution would liberate an undesirable trend toward democracy. "Which is better," he asked, "to be ruled by one tyrant three thousand miles away, or by three thousand tyrants not a mile away?" The question has not yet been definitively answered.

and Canada. As late as 1812, 80 percent of the population of Upper Canada (Ontario) was American-born.

Most northern Anglicans were loyalists. So were merchants with close commercial ties to Britain and, in the South, farmers from the backcountry Regulator counties. Imperial officials supported the Crown, of course, as did a few rich South Carolina and Georgia planters.

The British won support among southern slaves by promising freedom in return for military service. Some 50,000 African Americans ran away from their masters during the war. Both George Washington and Thomas Jefferson lost slaves to the British. When the war ended, Britain evacuated about 20,000 black loyalists to Nova Scotia, England, Jamaica, and Sierra Leone in West Africa.

Alexander Hamilton, Washington's aide-de-camp, urged southern patriots to free slaves who agreed to take up arms on the American side. "I have no doubt," he wrote, "that the Negroes will make excellent soldiers." His proposal got nowhere. Indeed, when Washington first arrived outside Boston and discovered that many Massachusetts militiamen were black, he discharged them. He had to countermand his order; free blacks in the North were pro-independence, they wanted to fight, and they brought pressure on the army to sign them up. About 5,000 African Americans, almost all northerners, fought on the patriot side.

The War for Independence 1776–1783

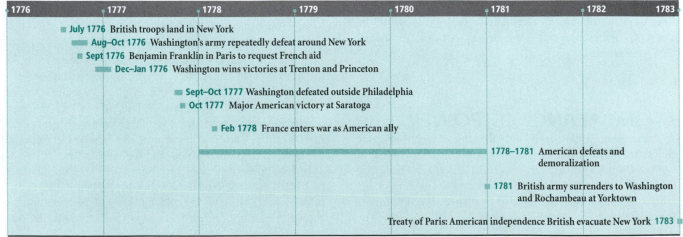

| 1776 | 1777 | 1778 | 1779 | 1780 | 1781 | 1782 | 1783 |

■ July 1776 British troops land in New York
■■ Aug–Oct 1776 Washington's army repeatedly defeat around New York
■ Sept 1776 Benjamin Franklin in Paris to request French aid
■■ Dec–Jan 1776 Washington wins victories at Trenton and Princeton

■ Sept–Oct 1777 Washington defeated outside Philadelphia
■ Oct 1777 Major American victory at Saratoga

■ Feb 1778 France enters war as American ally

1778–1781 American defeats and demoralization

■ 1781 British army surrenders to Washington and Rochambeau at Yorktown

Treaty of Paris: American independence British evacuate New York 1783 ■

After the French and Indian War, New Yorkers erected a much admired equestrian statue of George III in the king's honor. It represented no small expenditure for a provincial city. In the excitement following the Declaration of Independence, New York patriots pulled the statue down. The bronze was melted and used in making munitions for Washington's army.

Indians lined up on both sides. The Revolution split the 200-year-old Iroquois Confederacy in two. At first, the Six Nations (the Tuscarora had joined the original five) tried to be neutral. However, a well-educated Mohawk, Thayendanega, who took the name **Joseph Brant** when he converted to Anglicanism, convinced most Mohawk, Seneca, and Cayuga warriors to side with the British. In 1777, the Oneida and Tuscarora aligned with the patriots. Actually, the war shattered individual tribes as well as the Confederacy: some Iroquois from every tribe fought on both sides.

The Revolution was, in part, a continuation of the 150-year war of whites against Indians. George Washington's single biggest operation before Yorktown was not against the British but a 1779 assault on the Mohawks.

PATRIOT CHANCES

For all the discouraging signs, the patriot cause was far from hopeless. The Americans were fighting a defensive war in their homeland, a kind of conflict that always bestows advantages on rebels. The patriots did not have to destroy the British armies. Rebels on their own ground need only hold on and hold out until weariness, demoralization, dissent, and a painful defeat here and there take their toll on the enemy.

An army attempting to suppress a rebellion, by way of contrast, must wipe out the enemy military and then occupy and pacify the entire country. The Americans' friend in Parliament, Edmund Burke, pointed out the immensity of this challenge as early as 1775. "The use of force alone is but temporary," he said. "It may subdue for a moment; but it does not remove the necessity of subduing again; and a nation is not governed which is perpetually to be conquered."

The British were never able to crush the patriot military; they came close only once. Redcoats occupied most port cities for much of the war; as late as 1780, they captured Charleston.

Vision of the Future

Circumstances, John Adams believed, made him a politician and a revolutionary. But he envisioned another kind of future for his country: "I must study politics and war, that my sons may have liberty to study mathematics and philosophy, geography, natural history and naval architecture, navigation, commerce, and agriculture, in order to give their children a right to study painting, poetry, music, architecture, statuary, tapestry and porcelain."

Joseph Brant, painted by Gilbert Stuart several years after the War for Independence. Brant, a Mohawk, was as devoted to the British as Pontiac had been to the French. He committed his tribe to the loyalist cause but was defeated by Americans at Fort Stanwix in 1777 shortly before the decisive battle at Saratoga. The Mohawk were destroyed as a military force two years later.

But only one American in twenty lived in the seaports. From first to last, the countryside remained largely under patriot control, providing a vast sanctuary for American armies. The huge British garrisons in the cities had to be provisioned from abroad. Grain for horses had to be carried by ship from England and Ireland; at one point, it was thought hay would have to be brought across the ocean.

The patriots had British friends to speak on their behalf. Politicians like Burke, Charles Fox, John Wilkes, and the Marquis of Rockingham sniped at Lord North's ministry throughout the war. They believed that the Americans were more right than wrong. Privately, Lord North had grave doubts about the British cause.

The patriots also had reason to hope for foreign help. Since 1763, the major powers of Europe had been uneasy with Great Britain's preeminence. From Spanish Louisiana, Governor Bernardo de Gálvez surreptitiously provided arms. France, so recently humiliated by the British, was even more helpful. In May 1776, the French government began to funnel money and arms to the rebels through a not-so-secret agent, Pierre de Beaumarchais, who also provided money to the Americans from his own purse. During the first two years of the war, 80 percent of patriot gunpowder came from France.

BOSTON WON, NEW YORK LOST

In September 1776, the Congress sent Benjamin Franklin, 70 years old but just slightly creaky, to Paris to lobby for a French alliance. Franklin was a social sensation. The French

Benjamin Franklin, assigned to win an alliance with France, loved living in Paris. The French aristocracy adored him, titillated by his American simplicity, which Franklin encouraged. John Adams, also in Paris, thought Franklin spent much time partying (and lecherously courting a scandalous widow), but the old reprobate got the job done.

aristocracy was in the throes of a "noble savage" craze, enamored of primitives like their own peasants and the rustic Americans—who were thought to lead happy, wholesome lives because of their simplicity and closeness to nature. Well aware of this nonsense, Franklin (who liked the high life) appeared at court and balls wearing homespun clothing, no wig on his bald head, and the rimless bifocal spectacles he had invented. French high society loved it, but the foreign minister, Charles, Count Vergennes, was cautious. By the fall of 1776, the Continental Army had suffered an almost fatal defeat. Vergennes insisted that the Americans must win a major battle before he committed France to more than financial assistance.

STALEMATE AT BOSTON

General William Howe, who succeeded Gage as British commander in Boston, was also cautious. Given Washington's assessment of the American army outside Boston—untrained, undisciplined men coming and going; only nine rounds of gunpowder per soldier; and just six artillery pieces—Howe may have missed an opportunity to trounce the patriots in the summer of 1776.

But he had good reasons not to attack. Howe's redcoats were outnumbered—the terrible casualties they had sustained at Bunker Hill haunted him—and anti-British Boston was not the best of bases. Howe wanted to evacuate the city and establish his headquarters in friendlier New York. He asked London for permission to leave and his request was approved, but the exchange of messages took too long for Howe to organize the massive operation before winter.

Personally, Howe did not much care, Bostonians said; he was having too good a time with his beautiful mistress:

> Sir William Howe, he, snug as a flea,
> Lay all this time a-snoring;
> Nor dreamed of harm, as he lay warm
> In bed with Mrs. Loring

George Washington had no mistress in his quarters across the river in Cambridge; he faithfully wrote weekly to his wife about, among other things, the intense dislike he had taken to New Englanders. He made an exception of Nathanael Greene of Rhode Island and Henry Knox of Massachusetts who, like Greene, had taught himself the arts of generalship

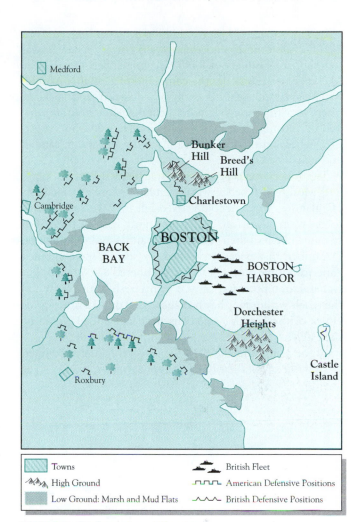

Towns **British Fleet**
High Ground **American Defensive Positions**
Low Ground: Marsh and Mud Flats **British Defensive Positions**

MAP 9:1 Stalemate at Boston, June 1775–March 1776

After the shock of the Battle of Bunker Hill, both the British within Boston and the Americans surrounding the city dug in and sat. General Howe wanted to evacuate Boston in 1775 but permission arrived too late in the year. In March 1776, George Washington seized Dorchester Heights and installed artillery capable of razing Boston and at least damaging the British fleet. Howe hurriedly evacuated the city.

out of books. Greene talked Washington out of a winter assault on Boston across frozen Back Bay. The ice was thin, he pointed out, and the bay was well covered by British artillery. Knox talked Washington into authorizing him to take a party 300 miles to Fort Ticonderoga, where Americans had captured dozens of cannon and mortars, and bring them to Boston.

QUEBEC AND DORCHESTER HEIGHTS

Knox's feat was next to miraculous. Just to cross snowbound Massachusetts was a chore. With eighty yoke of oxen (which had to be fed), Knox hauled fifty-eight mortars and cannon (three of the mortars weighed a ton each; one cannon weighed 5,000 pounds) to Boston by the end of February. The scale of his success was dramatized by another American winter campaign that ended in disaster.

Mrs. Loring

General Sir William Howe consorted openly in both Boston and New York with his American mistress, Elizabeth Loring. She was not a courtesan but the wife of a loyalist, Joshua Loring, who did not mind being cuckolded. Actually, Loring was less cuckold than pimp. Howe rewarded his good sportsmanship by showering Loring with lucrative contracts supplying the British army. Such arrangements were not unknown among British aristocrats; what is curious is the fact that the adulterous woman was the object of nastier gossip than her profiteering husband.

In September 1775, General Philip Schuyler had led 2,000 New Yorkers from Ticonderoga toward Canada. There he was to join forces with about 1,100 New Englanders crossing the Maine wilderness under the command of **Benedict Arnold.** Arnold's expedition was sadly ill-equipped and luckless. There were not enough tents to shelter the men from snowfall and they lost most of their provisions. The 600 who made it to Quebec were reduced to eating flour and water, candles and soap.

The Americans captured poorly defended Fort St. John's and Montreal. Quebec was defended by only 1,150 Scots Highlanders when Arnold arrived but they were soon reinforced from downriver. Unlike the French in 1759, the British remained behind their fortifications and Arnold's assault on December 30 was easily crushed. By spring, the combined American force outside Quebec numbered 8,000 troops but General John Burgoyne arrived with a fresh British army and the rebels withdrew. They had succeeded only in making enemies of the French Canadians they had hoped would be their allies.

In the meantime, the British in Boston had a bad winter. Weather crippled their line of supply. At least seventy ships from Britain were blown south and spent the winter in the West Indies. Soldiers pulled down a hundred buildings, including Old North Church, for firewood. Disease was rife.

Dorchester Heights, about a mile and a half from the British front lines, remained a no man's land until March. Neither Howe nor Washington sent troops there because the high ground was accessible only by a narrow spit of land, and therefore was easy for the enemy to cut off. The arrival of Knox's artillery, however, made the risk well worth taking for Washington. On the night of March 5, 1776, as unnoticed as Wolfe's ascent to the Plains of Abraham, the Americans moved the cannon and mortars to the high ground. Morning revealed to Howe that Washington was capable of razing Boston and a British barrage revealed that their artillery could not be sufficiently elevated to reach Washington's guns. American soldiers gathered 700 cannonballs that had landed harmlessly on the hillside.

Worse than the threat to the city, Dorchester Heights overlooked much of Boston Harbor where Howe's lifeline, the British fleet, was anchored. Howe sent a message that, if the Americans did not interfere with his evacuation, he would not destroy Boston. Washington was faced with a dilemma.

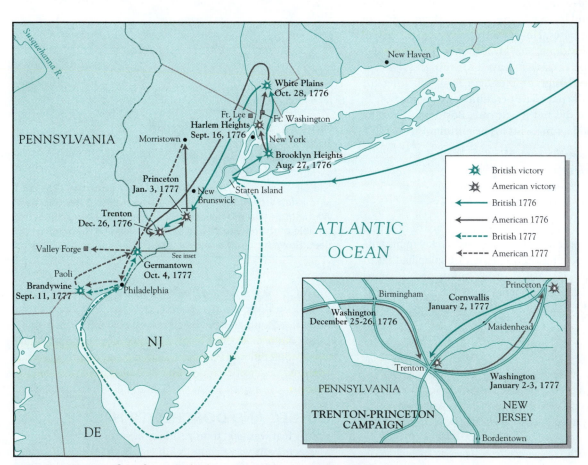

MAP 9:2 Years of Defeat and Discouragement, 1776–1777
The year 1776 was a bad one for the patriot military. General Washington was chased out of Long Island, Brooklyn, and Manhattan Island, and fled across New Jersey. He avoided disintegration only when he captured Trenton and Princeton at the end of the year. The next year was no better for Washington. He was repeatedly driven back from Philadelphia.

Military Music

Drum, fife, and trumpet were an essential part of armies. Boys 12 and 13 years old beat snare drums to set the cadence for soldiers on the march. If his men stepped off 96 paces of 30 inches each in a minute, a commander knew that the army was covering 3 miles in 50 minutes, allowing 10 minutes per hour for a breather and a drink.

Fifers tootled both to entertain the men and to communicate orders: the "Pioneers' March" was the signal for road-clearing crews to get started ahead of the infantry. "Roast Beef" meant it was time to eat. Fife and drum were also vital in battle. The men could hear them above the roar of firearms when they might not hear an officer's shouts.

Cavalry also used music for communication, using kettle drums instead of snare drums, so as not to be confused with infantry; and valveless trumpets (bugles) instead of fifes because, requiring only one hand to play, they could be played on horseback.

Knox's cannon might have been capable of wasting the British army and navy. But Boston was patriot country. If it were burned to the ground, Americans in other cities might blame Congress and the Continental army. Washington did not respond when, beginning March 10, the British evacuation began. About 120 ships took 9,000 troops, 1,200 soldiers' wives and children, 1,100 loyalists, Howe, and Mrs. Loring to Halifax, Nova Scotia.

HUMILIATION IN NEW YORK

Halifax was for regrouping and reinforcement by both redcoats and Hessians. Howe intended to establish his headquarters in New York, then a city of 20,000, larger than Boston and centrally located. Washington got there first, occupying Manhattan Island and the western end of Long Island, present-day Brooklyn. (In 1776, Brooklyn was a village.) He had between 8,000 and 10,000 troops in the vicinity or on the way.

On June 29, the first British ships arrived in New York Harbor—100 of them by sunset, including one monster carrying sixty guns and two with fifty. And more arrived daily from Halifax, the West Indies, and England until 400 ships were anchored in the harbor. About 32,000 soldiers, half British, half Hessians, mustered on Staten Island. Surveying the situation, one of Washington's aides wrote in his journal, "It is a mere point of honor that keeps us here."

Late in August, Howe invaded Long Island. Because Washington's right flank had been left unguarded, the British and Hessians almost surrounded his army. It could have been the end of the war, but most of the Americans slipped away to Brooklyn Heights, high ground on the East River across from Manhattan. In a brilliantly executed overnight maneuver, Massachusetts fishermen managed to ferry about 5,000 of the army to Manhattan. Howe was right behind them, capturing 3,000 at Fort Washington and forcing General Greene to abandon Fort Lee, across the Hudson River in New Jersey. Once again Washington and his bedraggled troops escaped within hours of capture north to White Plains, where the Americans were again defeated, then across the Hudson into New Jersey. When Washington was able to count heads in New Brunswick, he had only 3,500 soldiers under his personal command and half of them were marking time until their enlistments expired a few weeks later.

Howe and his generals enjoyed the New York campaign. It was all chase and reminded them of a fox hunt. When British buglers sounded the foxhunters' tally-ho, Washington, always super-sensitive about his dignity, was infuriated. The remnants of the Continental Army that fled across yet another river, the Delaware, into Pennsylvania, were demoralized and ready to desert en masse. In Philadelphia, a day's march to the south, the Continental Congress panicked and fled to Baltimore. It was mid-December 1776, less than six months after the Declaration of Independence had been approved.

SAVING THE REBELLION

"These are the times that try men's souls," Thomas Paine wrote. "The summer soldier and the sunshine patriot will, in this crisis, shrink from the service of his country." Thousands of captured patriot soldiers took an oath of allegiance to the Crown. The Revolution was close to being snuffed out.

Howe considered finishing Washington off, but decided to soldier by the book, which said that an army went into winter quarters in December. Howe and the army settled into New York where the population was friendly, including a huge contingent of prostitutes whom both Americans and British described as a terrifying lot: "bitch foxly jades, hogs, strums." Howe placed small advance garrisons in Princeton and Trenton to keep an eye on what was left of Washington's army.

Washington was no more an innovator than Howe was. Had his army not been near disintegration, he too would have followed the book into winter quarters. Instead, on Christmas night, the fishermen rowed Durham boats, lumbering 40-foot-long vessels used to transport pig iron from Pennsylvania to New Jersey, forty men in each. At 8:00 A.M. (two hours behind schedule), the Americans surprised the 1,500 Hessians in Trenton and, in a 15-minute battle, killed and wounded over 100 and made prisoners of 900. The Americans suffered only five casualties.

Withdrawing across the Delaware, the Americans returned to New Jersey, eluded a large army under General Charles Cornwallis, and attacked the British garrison at Princeton, taking 300 more prisoners. Howe withdrew his forward line to New Brunswick and Washington made his winter quarters in Morristown, New Jersey.

The Continental Insurance Companies

Burgoyne's march from Montreal to Saratoga was frustrated at every turn. When he surrendered to General Horatio Gates in October 1777, the news was enough to bring France into the war as an American ally.

Trenton and Princeton were small battles. Given the size of his army in New York, Howe's losses were minor. But Washington had boosted patriot morale when it was at its lowest point. His sallies across the Delaware saved the rebellion. Reading of Washington's campaign, King Frederick the Great of Prussia described it as brilliant.

BRITISH STRATEGY

The plan to win the war in 1777 was for Howe to move north up the Hudson River, joining forces with Iroquois warriors led east on the Mohawk River by Joseph Brant and Barry St. Leger, and a large British army coming south out of Montreal. Their pincers movement would isolate New England from the rest of the colonies. With the Royal Navy blockading New England's ports, the British army could easily subdue Massachusetts, Connecticut, and Rhode Island. If the loss of New England was not enough to persuade Washington to ask for terms, the British would then move against his army.

Germain was persuaded to approve the plan by General John Burgoyne, who had returned to England from Boston and was betting his career on the campaign. A playwright and bon vivant popular in London society, Burgoyne would command the 8,000 strong army and more than 100 cannon in Montreal. But Howe, in New York, sabotaged it. Perhaps because he saw that Burgoyne would get most of the credit

for the victory, or perhaps because he was persuaded by Joseph Galloway (Pennsylvania's most prominent loyalist) that Philadelphia was ripe for plucking, Howe moved south instead of north, leaving only 3,000 troops under General Henry Clinton to hold New York.

War Crimes

Soldiers and Indians on both sides were guilty of atrocities. Colonel Henry Hamilton, the British commander of Fort Detroit, was called the "hair-buyer" because he paid Indians for patriot scalps, including those from the heads of women and children. In 1776, Cherokees devastated the Virginia and Carolina frontiers, massacring everyone in their path. In July 1778, loyalists and Indians scourged Pennsylvania's Wyoming Valley and, in November, a similar force swept through Cherry Valley in New York. About 200 patriots were murdered in Pennsylvania; 40 in Cherry Valley.

At King's Mountain in 1780, American troops fired on redcoats who had surrendered. Virginia and North Carolina militia burned 1,000 Cherokee villages and destroyed 50,000 bushels of corn, not bothering to count the fatalities. In March 1782, Pennsylvania militia murdered 96 Delaware Indians who had tried to stay out of the conflict.

THE WATERSHED CAMPAIGN OF 1777

Howe moved to Pennsylvania by sea. Washington followed overland and, on September 11, was defeated at Brandywine Creek, southwest of Philadelphia. On September 26, after another victory at Paoli, Howe occupied Philadelphia. On October 4, Washington attacked at the suburb of Germantown. Although he came close to victory, in the end he was repulsed. His army had to fall back to winter quarters at Valley Forge, which was not even a town but rolling farmland. Howe was again ensconced in a comfortable and friendly city.

Alas for glory, Howe's success was badly tarnished by events in the forests of New York. In June, Burgoyne had left Montreal, heading south with 4,000 redcoats; 3,200 Hessians; several hundred Canadians, loyalists, and Indians; and 138 cannon. The 3,500 Americans at Fort Ticonderoga fled without a fight. (No one, it seems, ever held Fort Ticonderoga.) But Burgoyne's progress was slow; for three weeks, the column advanced no more than a mile a day. In part, the problem was too much unessential baggage on a road that was little more than an Indian trail. Burgoyne's personal effects—a living and dining suite, linens, china, and crystal fit for London—filled thirty carts; and 2,000 camp followers slowed the march down. But mostly, Burgoyne was delayed because his axe men had to clear the road of trees that the Americans had felled across it.

Then there was bad news from west, east, and south. St. Leger and Brant's army of Mohawk disintegrated after a series of battles with Nicholas Herkimer and Benedict Arnold around Fort Stanwix, not halfway across New York. Militia wiped out Hessians Burgoyne sent east on a routine mission of seizing supplies in Bennington, Vermont. By this time, Burgoyne knew that Howe was en route to Philadelphia.

Occupation of New England was out of the question. The best Burgoyne could hope for was to save his army by retreating to Canada. Instead, he dug in near Saratoga and hoped for help from General Clinton in New York. American General Horatio Gates jumped on Burgoyne's blunder and surrounded his army. On October 17, he accepted the surrender of 5,700 soldiers. The **Battle of Saratoga** was the most important event of the year, perhaps of the war. All New England remained under patriot control.

THE TIDE TURNS

Saratoga was precisely the news for which Franklin and his colleagues were waiting in Paris. The victory allayed Vergennes's doubts about the patriots' chances. The rout of an army of 8,000 crack redcoats and German mercenaries was no skirmish. When Lord North heard of the defeat, he wrote to Franklin that King George would end the war on the terms demanded by Americans up to July 1776. The Intolerable Acts and other obnoxious laws enacted between 1763 and 1775 would be repealed. Great Britain would concede the colonies control of their internal affairs in return for swearing loyalty to the king. In effect, Lord North proposed to organize the empire as a commonwealth of autonomous dominions, the

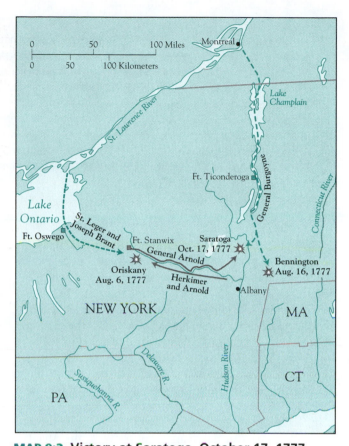

MAP 9:3 Victory at Saratoga, October 17, 1777
While Washington's army sat outside Philadelphia defeated and demoralized, the British and Hessians suffered a series of defeats in New York at Fort Stanwix, Bennington, and most important, at Saratoga, where a British army surrendered. Saratoga heartened the French to join the Americans as allies.

status Britain was to accord Canada, Australia, and New Zealand in the nineteenth century.

But victory is a tonic, and American blood was up. By the end of 1777, American animosity toward the mother country had intensified. Patriot propagandists made hay of the murder and scalping of Jane McCrea (a loyalist, ironically) by Indians under Burgoyne's command, who went unpunished. In New Jersey, British troops had brutally bullied farmers, raping women and girls. The old rallying cry, the "rights of British subjects," had lost its magic. The French offered a military alliance that was more attractive than returning, however triumphantly, to the British Empire.

FOREIGN FRIENDS

In December 1777, Vergennes formally recognized the United States. In February 1778, he signed a treaty of alliance, to go into effect if France and Britain went to war (which they did in June). The agreement provided for close commercial ties between France and the United States and stated that France would assert no claims to Canada after the war. France's reward at the peace table would be in the West Indies.

The war could not have been won without the French alliance. Not only did "America's oldest friend" pour money and men into the conflict, France provided a fleet, which the Americans lacked and could not hope to create. Individual patriot seamen like John Paul Jones ("I have not yet begun to fight") and John Barry won naval victories. But the superiority of the Royal Navy enabled the British to hold Philadelphia and New York for most of the war, and to capture Charleston, Savannah, and Newport near the end. Without the French navy, the entire American coastline might have been blockaded.

In fact, patriot merchantmen had little difficulty moving goods in and out of the many small ports on the Atlantic. Until 1781, when the British occupied the island, Dutch St. Eustatius, in the West Indies was, along with French Martinique, the major destination of American merchants. Holland was neutral, but well disposed to the Americans. Ships of all nations brought cargos destined for America to St. Eustatius, where American sloops and schooner ships collected them for delivery to the continent. When the British fleet finally seized St. Eustatius with a surprise attack, they found fifty American merchant ships in the harbor, and 2,000 American seamen in the port.

Spain had no love for anti-colonial rebels but, in her own interests, sent Bernardo de Gálvez into British Florida, where he soon occupied every fort. Vergennes averted a war brewing between Prussia and Austria that would have tied down French troops in Europe, a traditional British objective. He persuaded both countries, as well as Russia, to declare their neutrality. Vergennes denied Britain the allies she needed.

MERCENARIES FOR LIBERTY

Peace in Europe meant that many military professionals were unhappily unemployed. Aristocratic officers, hungry for commissions with salaries attached, flocked to the United States. There was plenty of deadwood in the bunch, but others were able soldiers and some were motivated by more than money.

Commodore John Barry was an Irishman; John Paul Jones a Scot. Marie Joseph, the Marquis de Lafayette, was a 19-year-old noble (the British called him "the boy") who proved to be an excellent field commander. He took no money; on the contrary, he spent generously from his fortune on the American cause. Also an idealist was Casimir Pulaski, a Pole who had fought Russia for his country's independence. Recruited in Paris by Benjamin Franklin, Pulaski was a romantic figure, a cavalry commander in gaudy uniform and waxed mustache. He was killed leading a charge at the Battle of Savannah late in the war. Johann Kalb, a Bavarian who affected the title Baron de Kalb, also lost his life during the war, at the Battle of Camden.

Jean Baptiste, the Comte de Rochambeau, arrived in Newport, Rhode Island in 1780 and played a key role in the decisive American victory at Yorktown, Virginia the next year. More valuable than combat officers (American officers were not short on boldness and bravery) were specialists like Thaddeus Kosciusko, a Polish engineer expert in building fortifications—a military field in which few Americans were trained. Friedrich Wilhelm von Steuben, a Prussian who also styled himself Baron, was an expert in drill. He supervised the training at Valley Forge in the winter of 1777–1778 that transformed Washington's continentals into a disciplined army. By 1781, fully one patriot officer in five was a foreigner.

THE WAR DRAGS ON

Steuben arrived in the nick of time. Washington lost 2,500 men to disease and exposure during the winter at Valley Forge and, by the spring of 1778, it was obvious that the war

North Wind Picture Archives

Washington and "the boy," the French general Lafayette, at Valley Forge during the dismal winter (for the patriots) of 1777–1778. Lafayette was twenty-five years younger than Washington, but they became close friends and remained so until Washington's death. Lafayette regarded Washington as the giant of the age.

would go on for years. The Americans did not dare to force the issue in an all-or-nothing battle. Their strategy was to hold on, fighting only under auspicious conditions. Lord Germain and General Clinton (who took over from Howe in May 1778) could hope only to throttle the American economy with a naval blockade and concentrate land operations in the South.

Beginning with the occupation of Savannah, Georgia, in December 1778, the redcoats won a series of victories in the South, but they could not break the stalemate. For each British victory, the Americans won another; or, in losing ground, they cost the British so heavily that the redcoats had to return to the coast, within reach of supply ships.

Washington effectively knocked the Mohawk out of the war in 1779, reducing the tribe to famine by destroying thousands of acres of corn. But the war was wearing heavily on the American side. Prices of necessities soared. Imports were available only at exorbitant costs. When the Continental Congress failed to pay and provision troops in 1780 and 1781, mutinies erupted on the Connecticut, Pennsylvania, and New Jersey lines. In September 1780, Washington

learned that Benedict Arnold, commanding the important fortress at West Point in New York, sold it and his services to the British for £20,000.

The campaign of 1781 opened with American spirits lower than they had been since before Trenton. Washington was idle outside New York. The most active British army, led by Lord Charles Cornwallis, lost a battle at Cowpens, South Carolina, but then repeatedly pummeled Nathanael Greene the breadth of North Carolina. Cornwallis then joined with other commanders (including Benedict Arnold) to amass 7,500 men in Virginia.

WASHINGTON SEIZES AN OPPORTUNITY

Cornwallis had his problems, however. Anywhere away from navigable waters was dangerous ground. On August 1, 1781, he set up what he regarded as a routine encampment at Yorktown, Virginia, on the same neck of land as the first permanent English settlement in America. Cornwallis requested supplies and instructions from General Clinton in New York. In mid-August, with Clinton dawdling, Washington learned

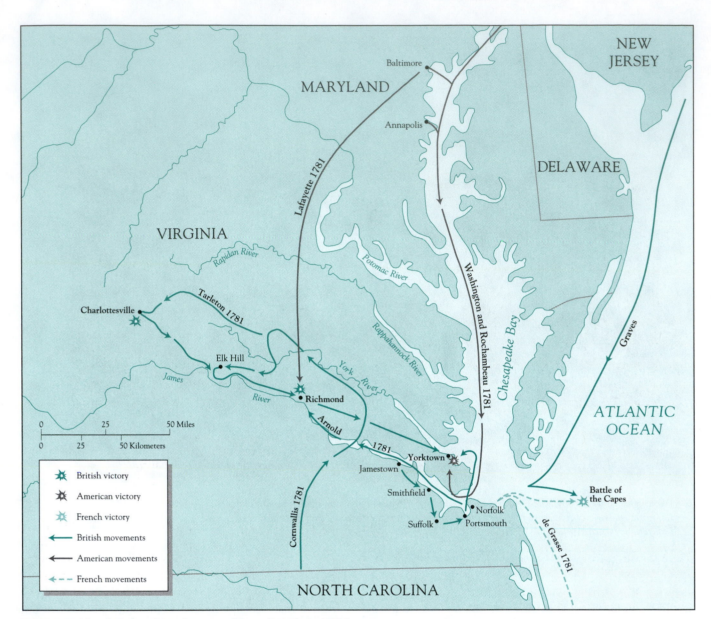

MAP 9:4　**The Battle of Yorktown, May–October 1781**
After wandering around South Carolina, harassed by American militia under Francis Marion, General Cornwallis moved into Virginia, setting up headquarters at Yorktown. There, he assumed, he could be resupplied or evacuated by sea. The coordinated arrival of a large American army and the French fleet resulted in the British defeat that ended the war.

that a French admiral, Count François de Grasse, was sailing from the West Indies to the Chesapeake Bay with 3,000 French troops aboard twenty-five warships.

Yorktown was George Washington's backyard. He knew the terrain intimately; he knew that if de Grasse could cut Cornwallis off by sea, the British were trapped. Even then, however, because he had nearly completed plans to attack New York, Washington had to be persuaded—pressured, even—by Rochambeau to rush to Virginia. Maneuvering around New York so that a confused Clinton would sit tight, Washington raced the best of his army, from Rhode Island, New Jersey, and New York, across New Jersey. In September, his troops joined with French troops under Lafayette,

Rochambeau, Steuben, and those de Grasse had landed. The combined army of 17,000 outnumbered Cornwallis's 8,000, almost the first time in the war that the patriots enjoyed numerical superiority. A majority of the "American army" was French.

YORKTOWN

Cornwallis did not panic. His men were well dug in, and he expected to move them out by sea. But between September 5 and 10, de Grasse sent the British evacuation fleet sailing off empty to New York. Further defense was futile. On October 17, Cornwallis asked for terms, and on October 19, he surrendered.

There are dozens of artists' depictions of the British surrender of Yorktown, each with its unique point of focus. This one makes a point more important than the contest of ceremonial one-upmanship between Cornwallis and Washington: emphasis on the critical part played by sea power—de Grasse's French fleet's control of the Chesapeake, which prevented a British evacuation.

Lord Cornwallis was no America basher. He had been only one of four lords in Parliament to oppose the Declaratory Act. But he found his defeat at Yorktown humiliating. Claiming sickness, he sent an aide to the field to surrender his sword. The aide tried to hand it to Rochambeau, but the French general gestured him to Washington. Rather than accept the symbol of capitulation from an inferior officer, Washington delegated the honors to General Benjamin Lincoln, whom the British had similarly humiliated at Charleston. During the ceremonies, the British army band played the hymn, "The World Turn'd Upside Down."

THE TREATY OF PARIS

The British could have fought on. They still had 44,000 troops in North America, far more than the patriots and French. But eighteenth-century wars were fought with limited objectives, balancing the values of the goals with the costs of reaching them. Rulers did not burrow into bunkers and tell their subjects to fight nobly on until the last of them was dead. In February 1782, the House of Commons voted to end the war. Lord North resigned and was succeeded by the Marquis of Rockingham, the Whig who had arranged the repeal of the Stamp Act in 1766.

It took two years to put the Treaty of Paris together. In part, the delay was due to growing suspicions between the Americans and the French. And with good reason: the American legation in Paris came to terms with the British without the French at the table. The treaty, signed in September 1783, recognized the independence of the United States with the Mississippi River the western boundary. Americans were to have fishing rights off British Newfoundland and Nova Scotia (which New Englander John Adams made his personal project), and the Continental Congress promised not to molest loyalists and to urge the states to compensate them for property that had already been seized.

Between Yorktown and the Treaty

Between 1781 and 1783, when the Treaty of Paris was signed, British troops remained in New York City so Congress could not disband the Continental Army. It set up quarters in Newburgh, New York, and Congress was negligent in providing for the soldiers. Washington, who sorely wanted to get back to his Virginia plantation, remained with the troops. He nagged Congress to vote them pensions and bounties and, by his own example, discouraged a full-blown mutiny.

British soldiers left New York City once the treaty was signed. For decades, New Yorkers celebrated Evacuation Day, November 25, with more gusto than they observed July 4. Independence Day was comparatively decorous; Evacuation Day was party time.

Ignoring the Revolution

John Adams said that one American in three was a patriot, one in three a loyalist, and one in three was not particularly interested in the war. Whether or not he had his fractions right, Adams was being honest, with himself as well as with others. He was admitting that a good many Americans simply did not care about a cause that he considered sacred.

Americans who tried to ignore the war were found in every part of the country. They were most likely to be harassed for their indifference—and they were bullied, as loyalists were—if they lived in a vociferously patriot area. New Jersey's Francis Hopkinson, a poet-politician, categorized Americans as "birds" (patriots), "beasts" (loyalists), and "bats," who claimed to be birds around birds and beasts around beasts. There was no minding one's own business in Hopkinson's War for Independence; one was either with him and the patriots, or against them.

It was easier to sit out the war west of the Appalachians. There were battles on the frontier but they were mostly with Indians, episodes in a conflict that began long before 1775 and would continue when the Revolutionary War was over. In fact, the most famous frontiersman and Indian fighter of the era, Daniel Boone, avoided involvement in the war even though he was a major in the Virginia militia. He continued to hunt, build roads, and dream of getting rich speculating in land. His reputation suffered because he sat the war out. He was accused of collaborating with the Shawnee, who were British allies, of being, in other words, a loyalist or one of Hopkinson's "bats."

Boone was born in Pennsylvania in 1734 and emigrated with much of his family to western North Carolina. In 1755, he was a teamster on the disastrous Braddock march to Fort Duquesne. (Given his lowly job, he did not make the acquaintance of Braddock's aide, George Washington.) Boone hated farming. He took a variety of jobs, including driving a team, to avoid it; he most enjoyed hunting deer and selling the venison. Boone spent much of the 1760s and 1770s in the forests of what is now Kentucky and saw the land there (as George Washington saw the land north of the Ohio River) as a commodity on which a man could get rich. In one way, Kentucky was a better bet for a land speculator than Ohio because the Indian population was

sparse. Both the Cherokee from the south and the Shawnee from the north hunted in Kentucky and traded with one another—Boone had run-ins with both tribes—but neither people lived there in great numbers.

In 1775, when the fighting began back East, Boone was supervising thirty axe men building the "Wilderness Road" through the Cumberland Gap into Kentucky where he intended to connect it to the ancient "Warrior's Path," a north–south route. Just when news of the Declaration of Independence and the all-out war with the British reached him is not clear but he did sign on as a scout for the Virginia militia. Almost immediately he was captured by the Shawnee and taken by them to be questioned by British officers north of the Ohio River. Boone was gone for a year and said little about his captivity when he returned. When accused of being a Tory, he denied it, but refused to elaborate. Had he been "back East," he might not have gotten off with mere suspicion.

Boone returned to developing his townsite at Boonesboro and several other frontier settlements where he claimed land. His fame as a woodsman—Boone engineered a spectacular and well-publicized rescue of his daughter, who had been kidnapped by Indians—made him Kentucky's most effective promoter, but his land speculations all failed. In part, Boone's undoing was having a sense of personal honor in a business in which ethics were an unacceptable burden. He sold thousands of acres cheaply to compensate associates for losses for which he felt responsible. He spent thousands on lawyers but had no stomach for going to court himself; land speculation was a profession which was half litigation, and Boone lost almost all of his courtroom contests.

In 1799, Boone moved to Missouri and never returned to Kentucky. He was broke and bitter. When, in 1815, a Kentucky creditor showed up to ask for his money, Boone's son told him, "You have come a great distance to suck a bull and, I reckon, you will have to go home dry."

Boone was nationally famous most of his life. After he died, he was installed in the American pantheon as the first and even the greatest of frontiersmen. But, if he was no Tory during the Revolution, he was no patriot either. He was not particularly interested.

THE FATHER OF HIS COUNTRY

American independence made a celebrity of George Washington in Europe as well as in the infant United States. Adulation was heaped on the "father of his country" from every European capital, London included. It was an astonishing rise in fame for a man who had been a rich Virginia planter in 1775 when the Continental Congress singled him

out to command an army that did not then exist, but who otherwise was of no notable accomplishment.

Even Washington's military record (in the French and Indian War) was spotty. He had played no part in the heady political debates of the previous decade. John Adams was too catty when he said that Washington was "too illiterate, unlearned, unread for his station and reputation." Washington

General George Washington, painted by John Trumbull a few months after the decisive **Battle of Yorktown.** *The portrait captures Washington's heroic image in Europe as well as in the effectively independent United States. Washington was quartered with his army north of New York City, which was still occupied by the British.*

as when he commented on the alliance with France that "men are very apt to run into extremes; hatred to England may carry some into excessive Confidence in France."

But it was true that he was no intellectual, as many men of the Revolutionary era were. He had no formal education. He sat silently during debates and was, according to Thomas Jefferson, a dull conversationalist, "not above mediocrity, possessing neither copiousness of ideas, nor fluency of words."

His record as a commander and strategist during the War for Independence was mixed. He had to be talked out of an assault on Boston in 1775 that would have been a disaster, and nagged into trapping Cornwallis at Yorktown. (He wanted to assault New York.) Any number of his subordinate generals were better in the thick of a fight, which Washington recognized—without rancor or envy—as clearly as he recognized that he had nothing to contribute to political debate.

So, why was he great? Because he alone kept an army in the field—and therefore kept the rebellion alive—in the face of battlefield defeats, superior British forces, inadequate provisions, epidemic disease among his men, poor shelter and a sometimes shameful lack of support from the Continental Congress, including even obstruction and schemes to dump him. If it sometimes seemed he was always in retreat, it was his retreats (brilliantly executed in New York in 1776) that kept the Revolution alive. Washington understood this. "We should on all occasions avoid a general action," he wrote to the Congress, "when the fate of America may be at stake on the issue." He would not fight a battle that, if lost, meant the end of the war.

In order to understand Washington's greatness, it is necessary to fall back on the intangibles that transfixed his contemporaries. Radicals like Samuel Adams, conservatives like Alexander Hamilton, intellectuals like Thomas Jefferson, warriors like Israel Putnam, and cultivated European aristocrats like Lafayette and Rochambeau all deferred to the Virginian. Washington's deportment, integrity, personal dignity, and disdain for petty squabbles set him a head taller than the best of his contemporaries. He held the Revolution together with that not quite definable quality known as "character." If the very idea rings a little sappy in our time, the dishonor is not to Washington or to the era of the Revolution.

was, in fact, well read; he had a large personal library and subscribed to as many as ten newspapers. He wrote (on concrete subjects) with admirable clarity and he was often shrewd

George Washington

George Washington was a fourth-generation Virginian. His great-grandfather, John Washington, emigrated in 1657, one of the "distressed cavaliers" recruited by Governor Berkeley. George's father, Augustine Washington, was a prosperous planter; in addition to seven children, he left his wife, leaving 10,000 acres of mostly prime tidewater land and forty-nine slaves to work it. When George's elder brother, Lawrence,

died without children in 1752, the estate, including Mount Vernon, was his. By 1775, he held title to 60,000 acres, mostly in the Ohio Country.

Washington was tall—6 feet 2 inches to 6 feet 4 inches—"straight as an Indian," trim, and athletic. His face was scarred from smallpox and, famously, he had few teeth and wore dentures more for the sake of appearance than chewing; they were painful.

Washington was a superb horseman. When people complimented Thomas Jefferson for his skills with a horse, he said that Washington was far better. Washington was a fanatic fox hunter, spending sometimes seven hours in the saddle chasing his hounds. Less often mentioned of Washington's equestrian feats, his personal servant, a slave named Billy Lee, was always on his own horse right behind the general.

FURTHER READING

General Robert Middlekauff, *The Glorious Cause: The American Revolution 1763–1789*, 1982; Stephen Conway, *The War of American Independence 1775–1783*, 1995; John Ferling, *A Leap in the Dark: The Struggle to Create the American Republic*, 2003; Alfred T. Young, *The American Revolution: A Radical Interpretation*, 1976; John Shy, *A People Numerous and Armed*, 1976.

Loyalists Robert M. Calhoon, *The Loyalists in Revolutionary America*, 1973; Paul H. Smith, *Loyalists and Redcoats: A Study in British Revolutionary Policy*, 1964; Judith Van Buskirk, *Generous Enemies: Patriots and Loyalists in Revolutionary New York*, 2002; Mary Beth Norton, *The British-Americans: The Loyalist Exiles in England, 1774–1789*, 1972.

Military History Don Higginbotham, *The War of American Independence: Military Attitudes, Policies, and Practice*, 1971; Philip Lawson, *The Imperial Challenge: Quebec and Britain in the Age of the American Revolution*, 1989; Sylvia R. Frey, *The British Soldier in America: A Social History of Military Life in the Revolutionary Period*, 1984; Charles Royster, *A Revolutionary People at War: The Continental Army and American Character 1775–1783*, 1980; Robert L. O'Connell, *Of Arms and Men: A History of War, Weapons, and Aggression*, 1989; Mark Kwasny, *Washington's Partisan War, 1775–1783*, 1996; Peter D. Thomas, *Tea Party to Independence: The Third Phase of the American Revolution, 1773–1776*, 1991; Mark V. Kwasny, *Washington's Partisan War, 1775–1783*, 1996; David McCullough, *1776*, 2005; Walter Edgar, *Partisans and Redcoats: The Southern Conflict that Turned the Tide of the American Revolution*, 2001.

Special Topics Mary Beth Norton, *Liberty's Daughters*, 1980; Barbara W. Tuchman, *The First Salute: A View of the American Revolution*, 1988; Barbara Graymont, *The Iroquois in the American Revolution*, 1972; Colin G. Calloway, *The American Revolution in Indian Country*, 1995; Sylvia R. Frey, *Water from the Rock: Black Resistance in a Revolutionary America*, 1991; Richard B. Morris, *The Peacemakers*, 1965.

Biographies Ira D. Gruber, *The Howe Brothers and the American Revolution*, 1972; Pauline Maier, *The Old Revolutionaries: Political Lives in the Age of Samuel Adams*, 1980; Willard Sterne Randall, *Benedict Arnold: Patriot and Traitor*, 1990; Joseph J. Ellis, *Founding Brothers: The Revolutionary Generation*, 2000; Richard Brookhiser, *Founding Father: Rediscovering George Washington*, 1996.

KEY TERMS

The following terms are covered in this chapter and can also be found in the list of Key Terms at the back of the book.

Battle of Saratoga   **Benedict Arnold**

Battle of Yorktown

Joseph Brant   **Second Continental Congress**

ONLINE SOURCES GUIDE

Use this listing to find online documents, images, interactive maps, simulations, and other resources related to this chapter:

American History Resource Center
http://history.wadsworth.com

Selected Documents
A Continental Army Soldier's Account of His Experiences in 1780
Thomas Paine's The Crisis

Selected Images
Landing of U.S. Marines at New Providence Island Bahamas, 1776
Burning of New York City, September 1776
General William Howe

Continental army recruiting poster
Nancy Hart defends her home against British soldiers
British surrender at Yorktown, 1781

Simulations
The American Revolution (Choose an identity as a patriot, a loyalist, or a woman and make choices based on the circumstances and opportunities afforded.)

Interactive Timeline (with online readings)
The War for Independence: Winning the Revolution 1776–1781

Additional resources, exercises, and Internet links related to this chapter are available on *THE AMERICAN PAST* web site: http://history.wadsworth.com/americanpast8e

Discovery

How can individuals, both commonplace and famous, affect the outcomes of wars?

In thinking about this question, begin by breaking it down into the components shown below. A discussion of the significance of each component should appear in your answer.

Warfare: For this exercise, please read the following document: "Letter from Esther Reed to General Washington." How do modern Americans who remain on the home front sacrifice during a time of war? Do they at all? What role did women such as Esther Reed attempt to play during the war? How does this compare to the roles of women such as Deborah Sampson and Molly Hays, whose stories are related in the sidebar, "Women Warriors"?

Letter from Esther Reed to General Washington

Philadelphia, July 4th, 1780.
Sir,
The subscription set on foot by the ladies of this City for the use of the soldiery, is so far completed as to induce me to transmit to your Excellency an account of the money I have received, and which, although it has answered our expectations, it does not equal our wishes, but I am persuaded will be received as a proof of our zeal for the great cause of America and our esteem and gratitude for those who so bravely defend it.

The amount of the subscription is 200,580 dollars, and £625 6s. 8d. in specie, which makes in the whole in paper money 300,634 dollars.

The ladies are anxious for the soldiers to receive the benefit of it, and wait your directions how it can best be disposed of. We expect some considerable additions from the country and have also wrote to the other States in hopes the ladies there will adopt similar plans, to render it more general and beneficial.

With the utmost pleasure I offer any farther attention and care in my power to complete the execution of the design, and shall be happy to accomplish it agreeable to the intention of the donors and your wishes on the subject.

The ladies of my family join me in their respectful compliments and sincerest prayer for your health, safety, and success.

I have the honour to be, With the highest respect, Your obedient humble servants,
E. Reed.

Government and Law: For this exercise, please study the two images of Washington and "the boy," Lafayette and the portrait of General George Washington. Notice the similarities in the portrayals of Washington. Which characteristics most stand out? How do these relate to him as a war-time commander? What values or qualities is each artist attempting to emphasize or portray? How accurate do you believe these images to be? How do these compare to modern political leaders and our portrayals of them?

Washington and Lafayette

General George Washington

To read extended versions of the documents, visit the companion Web site
http://history.wadsworth.com/americanpast8e; click on "Discovery Sources."

CHAPTER 10

Inventing a Country

American Constitutions 1781–1789

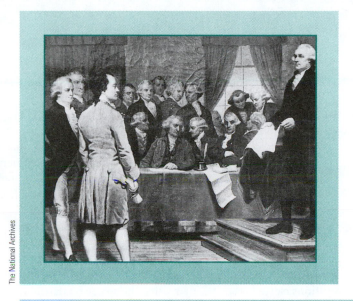

The National Archives

Without some alteration in our political creed, the superstructure we have been seven years raising at the expense of so much blood and treasure must fall. We are fast verging to anarchy and confusion.

George Washington

There was nothing novel in fighting for independence. Beginning in ancient Mesopotamia, the cradle of civilization, the history of empires has been a history of subordinate peoples rising up to free themselves from the rule of others. The Revolution was, however, singular in the fact that the patriots had to invent themselves as Americans. They were not already "a people" as, for example, the Dutch were when they won their independence from Spain. Nor had the colonials been conquered by a foreign power like the Irish. Most colonials were British by descent and, until 1775, they defined themselves as, first, British and, secondly, as New Hampshiremen or Virginians or Georgians.

The Articles of Confederation, which the patriots wrote early in the war, created the "United States," but the first American Constitution—for that is what the Articles were—did not create a nation or a nationality. Each of the thirteen states that joined together to fight the British remained explicitly, indeed, emphatically, independent of one another.

STATE CONSTITUTIONS

Connecticut and Rhode Island, as corporate colonies, had been largely self-governing since their inception. They converted their colonial charters into state constitutions by jiggling the wording, deleting references to the king, and the like. The constitutions the other eleven states wrote from scratch were more telling; to varying degrees, they institutionalized the patriots' intense hostility to things British.

The fact that the state constitutions were written and sought to cover every contingency state governments would face was itself a break with British practice. The British constitution was largely unwritten; it included a few basic documents but mostly it consisted of customs and traditions. The unwritten character of the British constitution had been a big part of the problem that led to the rebellion: just what was the extent of the king and Parliament's authority over the colonies? The patriots believed that king and Parliament had violated the unwritten British constitution in trying to tax the colonies. But they could win the point only by taking

And They're Off . . .

Reaction against things British found form in more than written constitutions. When the United States adopted the dollar as its monetary unit, it was in part a patriotic statement. British and colonial currency were based on the pound sterling (£). *Dolar* was one name given to a Spanish silver coin

that, as the *Thaler,* dated back to medieval Germany. Adopting the dollar was something of a declaration of financial independence. It was also, however, commonsensical: there were far more Spanish dollars circulating in the infant United States than there were British pounds.

It was also during the Confederation period that Americans began to run their horse races counterclockwise around the track rather than clockwise as they were run in Britain and had been run in the colonies. No one has identified the element of common sense in that innovation.

up arms. Written constitutions can be violated too, of course. However, as Thomas Jefferson wrote, "They furnish a text to which those who are watchful may again rally and recall the people." Americans wanted their constitutions in black and white.

LIMITING POWER, STRIKING DOWN PRIVILEGE

In Great Britain, Parliament was the government. There was no appealing Parliament's actions, as the Americans discovered. Parliament was supreme. The Americans' state constitutions, however, were written not by their parliaments, the thirteen state assemblies, but by conventions elected specifically for the purpose of constitution-making. A convention superior to a state assembly was "the only proper body" to write a constitution; the assembly's function was "to make Laws agreeable to that Constitution." The point was that sovereignty (ultimate government power) rested with the people (as the word was then defined). Constitution-making called for a special expression of the people's will.

The patriots had resented royal officials as arbitrary because they were unbeholden to them. They guarded against creating a homegrown elite entrenched in public office by requiring that nearly all state officials stand for election every year. Even

then, executive officers had little power. State governors were empowered to administer laws and dress up and act dignified on ceremonial occasions. Pennsylvania's 1776 constitution abolished the office of governor. (Nor did the Articles of Confederation provide for a chief executive.)

Another anti-British resentment was reflected in the disestablishment of the Church of England in every colony where it had been the official church, funded by taxes everyone paid no matter what church they chose to attend. The Church of England lost its privileges with independence. The Protestant Episcopal Church (the name of the church Anglicans formed) was just another private denomination legally on a par with the Quakers, Presbyterians, Baptists, and, for that matter, the sparse scattering of Catholic parishes and Jewish synagogues. It too depended on its members' contributions to pay ministers and patch leaky roofs.

In New Hampshire, Connecticut, and Massachusetts, the Congregationalist church had been established and so it was to remain for forty years after independence. (The Constitution of 1787 forbade the federal government to establish a religion, but not the states.) Five other state constitutions expressed a "preference" for Protestant Christianity. Roman Catholics were not permitted to vote in North Carolina until 1835. Jews could vote in Pennsylvania, Rhode Island, and New York.

An Infant Government 1777–1791

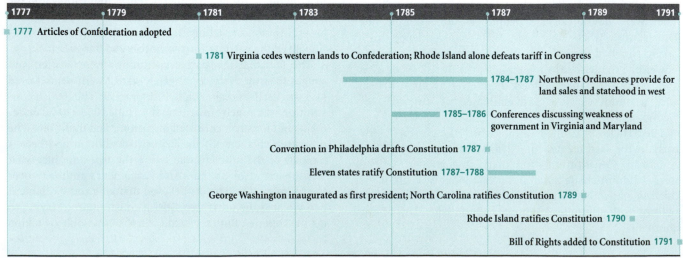

1777	1779	1781	1783	1785	1787	1789	1791

■ **1777 Articles of Confederation adopted**

■ **1781 Virginia cedes western lands to Confederation; Rhode Island alone defeats tariff in Congress**

1784–1787 Northwest Ordinances provide for land sales and statehood in west

1785–1786 Conferences discussing weakness of government in Virginia and Maryland

Convention in Philadelphia drafts Constitution 1787 ■

Eleven states ratify Constitution 1787–1788

George Washington inaugurated as first president; North Carolina ratifies Constitution 1789 ■

Rhode Island ratifies Constitution 1790 ■

Bill of Rights added to Constitution 1791 ■

North Wind Picture Archives

In 1776, New Jersey gave the vote to "all free inhabitants" who met the state's residency and property requirements, thus enfranchising some free blacks and a few women, mostly widows. For twenty years, some qualified African Americans and women voted. Protest was minimal. Indeed, a 1790 law referred to voters as "he or she." Then, in Elizabeth, New Jersey in 1797, seventy-five Federalist Party women showed up at the polls en masse. The Federalists lost but narrowly, and the victorious Jefferson Republicans noticed. Firmly in control of the state in 1807, they disenfranchised women and blacks and eliminated the property requirement for white males.

DEMOCRATIC DRIFT

Every state extended the franchise to more people than had enjoyed the right to vote under colonial law. However, every state except Georgia, Pennsylvania, and Vermont (a state in fact although not in name until 1791) required that voters own property—not very much in most states; only the very poor had no say in government. Women who met the property test could vote in New Jersey. New Jersey, Massachusetts, and New Hampshire made no distinctions between free blacks and whites at the polls. Five other states (including North Carolina) allowed property-owning blacks to vote for several years, but then canceled the African-American franchise on racial grounds.

Eight states specified rights that were guaranteed to every citizen, beginning with Virginia's constitution in 1776. After the vice-admiralty courts, the quartering acts, and the arbitrary actions of the British army, Americans heady with independence were determined that there be no vagueness in the matter of the government's power over individuals. The rights later listed in the first ten amendments to the United States Constitution—the Bill of Rights—were found in one or another of the state constitutions written during the Revolution.

LIBERTY'S LIMITS: WOMEN

In 1777, when the air was thick with talk of liberties, Abigail Adams wrote a letter to her husband, John, who was engaged in writing the Articles of Confederation, to ask "in the new code of laws" to "remember the ladies and be more generous and more favorable to them than your ancestors. Do not put such unlimited power into the hands of husbands. Remember, all men would be tyrants if they could."

She was too insightful a woman to hope for much. (Abigail and John discussed public affairs constantly and Abigail's correspondence with her friend, Mercy Otis Warren, was heavy with politics.) Still, she was not alone in hoping that the expansion of liberties and rights would extend beyond men. A woman describing herself as a "matrimonial republican" wrote to a newspaper: "Marriage ought never to be considered a contract between a superior and an inferior, but a reciprocal union of interest, an implied partnership of interests, where all differences are accommodated by conference."

Liberty and Indians

Most northern Indians sat out the Revolutionary War or sided with the British. The loyalist tribes were crushed, morally as well as militarily, by the American victory. About half of the once feared Mohawk tribe followed Joseph Brant to Canada. In the Northwest Territory, tensions were building but there were no significant conflicts during the 1780s. Kentucky, south of the Ohio River, was another story. Southern tribes killed about 1,500 settlers who were flooding like a tide through the Cumberland Gap from Virginia.

Back in Williamsburg, Governor Patrick Henry made a novel proposal to put an end to the bloody chronic hostilities: amalgamation of red and white. The state would pay £10 to every free white person who married an Indian plus £5 for every child born of such unions. The state assembly was uninterested. Some years later, Supreme Court Chief Justice John Marshall commented that Henry's idea "would have been advantageous to this country. . . . Our prejudices, however, opposed themselves to our interests, and operated too powerfully for them."

She was describing a "companionate marriage" of equals, something only couples considered highly eccentric would practice—fifty years in the future! The term "companionate marriage" would not be coined for a century. But devoted and doting a husband as John Adams was—in his eyes *because* he was a loving husband—neither he nor any other political mover and shaker of the era thought twice about altering a married woman's subordination to her husband. The idea of an equality of the sexes was beyond the comprehension of the era. When the first feminist manifesto, *Vindication of the Rights of Women,* was published in 1792 by an English woman, Mary Wollstencroft, it was not even thought worth the time to ridicule it, or even read it, by prominent men on both sides of the Atlantic.

MANUMISSION IN THE SOUTH

If a revision of the status of women was not on the table, African-American slavery was. None of the southern states came close to abolishing slavery, but they enacted laws indicating hopes that the institution's days were numbered. Even South Carolina, where proslavery feelings were strongest, was among the eleven states that forbade the further importation of slaves from abroad.

Petition for Freedom

On November 12, 1779, nineteen of New Hampshire's African Americans petitioned the state assembly to free slaves on the basis of the ideals of liberty the patriots were touting. The petition concluded:

> Your humble slaves most devoutly pray for the sake of injured liberty, for the sake of justice, humanity and the rights of mankind, for the honor of religion and by all that is dear, that your honors would graciously interpose in our behalf, and enact such laws and regulations, as you in your wisdom think proper, whereby we may regain our liberty and be ranked in the class of free agents, and that the name of slave may not more be heard in a land gloriously contending for the sweets of freedom.

New Hampshire adopted a gradual emancipation law.

In part, the increasing revulsion among southern whites was moral and religious. All but a few southern Quakers succumbed to antislavery pressure from their northern brethren and freed their slaves. John Payne (the father of future first lady Dolley Madison) emancipated his slaves in 1783 and moved to Philadelphia. The denominations vitalized by the Great Awakening in the South—Methodists, Baptists, and Presbyterians—were antislavery in their early days. In 1781, the Methodist church forbade its ministers to own slaves.

Confederation-era antislavery was also political and philosophical. "All men are created equal," Jefferson had written in the Declaration of Independence. "Oh the shocking, the intolerable inconsistence" of owning slaves, a pamphleteer, Samuel Hopkins wrote. Wealthy tobacco planters, who still dominated the states of the upper South, were particularly troubled to own slaves while uttering (in the sardonic words of England's Samuel Johnson) "the loudest yelps for liberty." Their state assemblies made it easier for individuals to manumit (free) their slaves, and they did, with the rate of **manumission** increasing during the 1790s.

Between 1776 and 1810, Marylanders freed a fifth of the slaves in the state. Delaware's slave owners were even more rigorous. In 1790, 70 percent of the state's black population was enslaved. By 1810, almost 80 percent of African Americans in Delaware were free. Many slave owners, no doubt, were encouraged to free their slaves because Delaware forbade the sale of slaves out of state.

Because some southerners who freed their slaves were rich and well known, their acts of emancipation may have inspired others to do the same. Motivated by a religious conversion, Robert Carter of Nomini Hall, the head of one of Virginia's proudest families, freed 500 slaves. When Richard Randolph (the Randolphs were also of the cream of Virginia society) died at age 26 in 1796, his will emancipated his 200 slaves. He gave some of them 400 acres, "Israel Hill," on which to get a start as freemen. Randolph was explicit, not to say impassioned, in explaining his action. He freed his slaves "to make retribution, as far as I am able, to an unfortunate race of bondmen, over whom my ancestors have usurped and exercised the most lawless and monstrous tyranny, and in whom my countrymen (by iniquitous laws, in contradiction of their own declaration of rights, and in violation of every sacred law of nature . . .) have vested me with absolute property. . . ."

Slaves in Pennsylvania

No northerners owned slaves by the hundred, as some southerners did; few owned as many as a dozen. Most commonly, farmers (and city people) owned only two or three slaves. The absence of an influential social class with a great deal of money invested in slaves was a major reason why abolition was easy in the northern states.

Simon Vanarsdalen of Bucks County, Pennsylvania, a prosperous farmer but by no means wealthy or a landed grandee, owned a large number of slaves by northern standards. Just how many is unknown but, when he died in 1770, he bequeathed "Black Eve," "Black Cuff," "Black Henry," and "my negro wench called Poll or Mary" to his children with instructions that they inherit "the remainder of my negroes" after the death of my wife.

Ten years later, any of them who were at least 28 years of age were freed by Pennsylvania's emancipation law.

ABOLITION IN THE NORTH

The northern states set in motion mechanisms by which slavery would gradually disappear and in two instances abolished slavery outright.

Quasi-independent Vermont (which became a state in 1791) forbade slavery as early as 1777. Pennsylvania, where antislavery Quakers were still a potent political force, was the first state to adopt a program of gradual **abolition.** In 1780 the assembly provided that all persons born in the state were free—no exceptions. Slaves born in Pennsylvania before 1780 became free at age 28. Buying slaves was forbidden; owners of slaves were forbidden to take them out of the state to sell them. Slaves brought into Pennsylvania were legally free after residing in the state for six months. With Quakers like the tireless tailor, Isaac Hopper, helping African Americans in the courts, Pennsylvania's combination of laws was highly effective. Slave owners found the legal restrictions on the use of their property (and social pressures) so burdensome that most of them freed their slaves before the law did. By 1800, there were only 1,700 slaves in Pennsylvania.

Most northern states patterned their own gradual abolition laws on Pennsylvania's. Even Rhode Island, where several hundred influential merchants were engaged in the African slave trade, adopted an emancipation program.

In Massachusetts, slavery was abolished at one blow in 1783. **Elizabeth Freeman,** a slave, sued her master for her freedom on the basis of a paraphrase of the Declaration of Independence in the recently adopted state constitution: "All men are born free and equal." The judges agreed with her, ruling slavery unconstitutional in the state. By 1800, there were only 1,300 slaves in the five New England states.

AMERICA UNDER THE ARTICLES OF CONFEDERATION

The collective affairs of the thirteen states were governed by the Articles of Confederation, which reflected the same ideals and sentiments as the state constitutions. Drafted during the heady years 1776 and 1777, the Articles created no president, indeed, no executive power independent of the Congress. Congress alone was the government. Members were elected annually and could serve only three years out of every six. That is, a man elected to Congress three years in a row was ineligible to serve again until he sat out for three years. Americans would have no permanently seated office holders.

DIVIDED AUTHORITY

The United States of America was explicitly not a nation. It was, a bit vaguely, "a firm league of friendship." Georgia, North Carolina, and the rest retained their "sovereignty, freedom, and independence." Each state, no matter how large or small its population (there were twelve Virginians for every Delawarean) was the equal in Congress of every other. Delegates voted not as individuals, but as members of their state's delegation. If two of three of a state's delegates voted "nay," that state cast a single negative vote in Congress. No provision of the Articles asserted the sovereignty of the states (and the weakness of the Confederation) than the fact that a taxation bill required the approval of all thirteen states!

Congress was not powerless. The Articles authorized it to maintain an army and navy, to declare war and make peace, and to maintain diplomatic relations with foreign countries and the Indian tribes, which were defined as nations. Congress was entrusted with the maintenance of the post office inherited (in pretty good shape) from the colonial era and it was empowered to establish a system of uniform weights and measures. Congress could mint coins, issue paper money, and borrow money.

However, the Articles also permitted the individual states to issue money and to ignore the Confederation's standards of measurement. Indeed, states could individually negotiate commercial treaties with other countries. A state could even, "with the consent of Congress," declare war (as a state!) on a foreign nation. Under the Articles, it would have been impeccably constitutional if New Jersey went to war with Holland while neighboring Pennsylvania agreed by treaty to sell gunpowder to the Dutch. (It never happened.)

The weakness and confusion of the ties binding the states under the Articles were not the fruit of incompetence or inexperience. The weakness of the Confederation Congress and the right of individual states to shrug off most of its actions were consciously written into the Articles because of the revolutionary generation's aversion to powerful centralized government. The Articles may have been a mistake. John Jay of New York said so not long after the peace treaty with Great Britain: "I am uneasy and apprehensive, more so than during the war. . . . We are going and doing wrong . . . I look forward to evils and calamities." With each new year, increasing

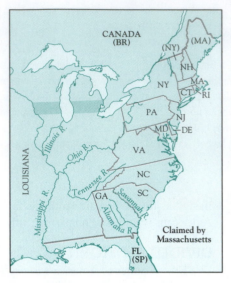

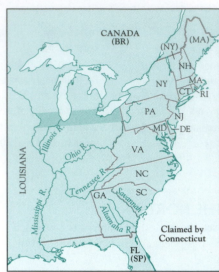

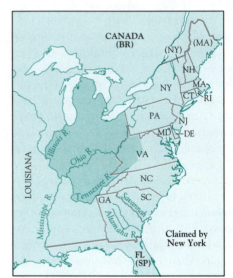

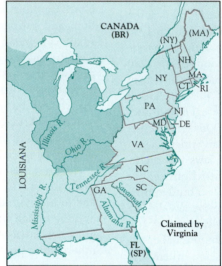

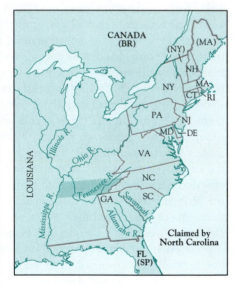

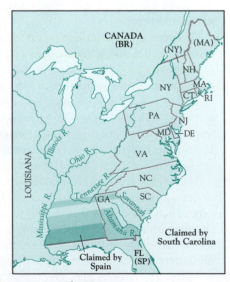

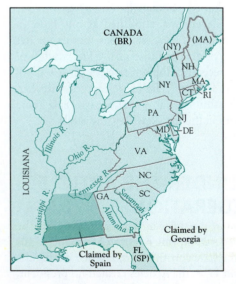

MAP 10:1 The Western Lands Mess

This series of maps shows better than any written account can, just what a mess of conflicts the states' claims to western lands created. Thus, the charters of the Massachusetts and Connecticut colonies set their western boundaries at the Pacific Ocean. Both states conceded that subsequent royal grants to New York and Pennsylvania took some of their lands from them (and, of course, that the

numbers of Americans (but probably not a majority) came to agree with him. But there was nothing accidental in the design of the government.

THE WESTERN LANDS

The Confederation had its achievements. It was under the Articles that the war with Great Britain was prosecuted. The Confederation Congress created a bureaucracy in Philadelphia (the capital) that administered the government's day-to-day business as well as could be done. States did contribute to the Confederation treasury. And Congress solved a conflict of interests big enough to have torn apart a far more powerful government.

The issue was the land between the Appalachians and the Mississippi River. Who owned it? The Treaty of Paris said that the United States did. Seven old colonial charters said that seven of the thirteen states did, and their claims overlapped. The charters had been drafted between 1606 and 1732 by British officials who had little knowledge of North American geography and less regard for what their predecessors in boundary drawing had already given away.

So, Virginia's colonial charter (the oldest) gave the state boundaries that flared north at the crest of the Appalachians, encompassing the northern half of the region. New York claimed the same territory and even farther south than Virginia. Connecticut conceded that New York's and Pennsylvania's charters, both drafted later than Connecticut's, had removed the lands of the states of New York and Pennsylvania from Connecticut's colonial land grant; but claimed that a "western reserve" in what is now northern Ohio, Indiana, and Illinois was still in Connecticut's jurisdiction. Massachusetts, North Carolina, South Carolina, and Georgia also had claims on the West based on their colonial charters.

The snarl was complicated further by the fears in the six states with no western claims: New Hampshire, Rhode Island, New Jersey, Pennsylvania, Delaware, and Maryland. Reasonably enough, citizens of those states worried that the landed states would finance their governments indefinitely by selling their western lands, thus reducing taxes of next to nothing, and attracting people of the unlanded states to emigrate. On these grounds, Maryland refused to sign the Articles of Confederation until 1781.

There was an obvious solution to the problem, suggested by John Dickinson as early as 1776. However, because it called on human beings to give up wealth for the sake of an abstract ideal, it was not a solution that promised to be easy. Dickinson proposed that the states with claims to western lands cede them to the Confederation so that all states shared in the benefits of owning them.

Remarkably, thanks to Virginia, the state with the best western claims and the first to give them up, Dickinson's call was heeded. Virginia's leaders had good reasons to make a sacrifice in order to keep the Confederation together. It was the largest and richest state with a third of the country's population and a third of its commerce. Its first citizen, George Washington, was also the first citizen of the United States; other Virginians played prominent roles in the Confederation government. Moreover, it was commonly believed that free republican institutions could not survive in empire-size states. For the sake of hard-won freedoms, Virginia's leaders preferred to see new sovereign states be carved out of the West to endless bickering in a fight to retain a "Great Virginia."

THE NORTHWEST ORDINANCES

In January 1781 (before the battle of Yorktown!), Virginia ceded the northern part of its claims to the Confederation. Within a few years, all the states with western claims except Georgia followed suit. In 1792, Virginia added its southern claims to what was by then a national domain. (Georgia held out long after it had become ridiculous to do so, until 1802.)

This remarkable act—European nations went to war over far lesser tracts of real estate—was followed by a series of congressional acts that were equally novel, the **Northwest Ordinances** of 1784, 1785, and 1787. They created procedures by which five states—equal in all ways to the thirteen states—would, once they were settled, be carved from the "Northwest Territory" north of the Ohio River and east of the Mississippi. (The states of the "Old Northwest" are Ohio, Indiana, Michigan, Illinois, and Wisconsin.) The Ordinance of 1785 provided for the survey of the territory and the orderly sale of surveyed lands, the income from which went to the Confederation.

In the Northwest Ordinances, the United States asserted that it would have no subordinate colonies, as the thirteen colonies had been subordinate to Great Britain. When the population of a "territory" in the Northwest equaled the population of the smallest existing state (Delaware in 1787), and fulfilled other reasonable requirements, that territory would be admitted to the Confederation as a state. In the end, the Confederation added no states; but the principles

MAP 10:1 *Continued*

treaty with Great Britain set the western boundary of the United States at the Mississippi River). However, both Massachusetts and Connecticut claimed that their northern and southern borders still extended west of New York and Pennsylvania. Connecticut called the upper third of what are now the states of Ohio, Indiana, and Illinois its "Western Reserve." Legally, they had a case.

But the case was not unassailable. Virginia's grant of land from the king in 1606 predated every other colony's documentary claim. Virginians (with pretty good arguments going for them) rejected the contentions of other states that the Crown had modified Virginia's boundaries.

It would have been impossible for the most learned and most just of judges to untangle the conflicts by adjudication. The dispute—and the prize was a rich one—could be resolved in one of only two ways: power (war) or what astonishingly was actually done—all states with western claims giving them up to the Confederation.

Laying Out the Land

People flying across the United States for the first time are struck by the fact that, once west of the Appalachians, the country has been graphed. Even when the terrain is uncooperative, town and county lines and farm and ranches are rectangular, usually squares, neatly aligned north and south and east and west. This impressing of geometry on nature is a legacy of the Northwest Ordinances.

Using lines of latitude as boundaries was already old hat in North America. Most east to west colonial borders (the Massachusetts-Connecticut line, for example) were straight lines because Crown officials in London who drafted colonial charters knew next to nothing about American geography; they could not name rivers, ridge lines, or other natural features as boundaries as they did in Ireland during the same years.

The streets of Charleston, Philadelphia, and Savannah intersected at right angles not because of geographical ignorance but for the sake of tidiness. Property parcels in those cities were, of course, rectangular. The streets of much older Boston meandered, European-style, but the Massachusetts Bay colony, followed by Connecticut and New Hampshire, later laid out new townships using straight lines. The New England Puritans controlled the expansion of settlement as best they could. New lands were

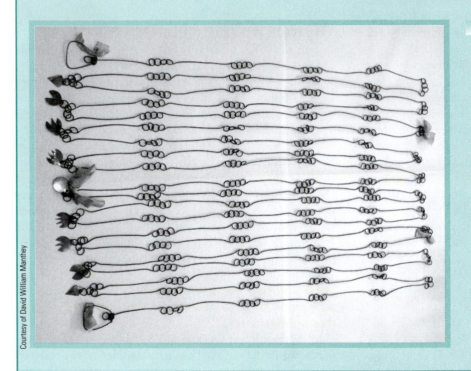

Courtesy of David William Manthey

Gunter's Chain, the unique tool of the eighteenth century surveyor. A "chain" was 22 yards (66 feet); 80 chains was a mile. Twenty-five "links" was a "perch," the surveyor's term for a rod or pole (16 1/2 feet), then a common measure of land. Note that every tenth link is marked—like a tape measure today. On some Gunter's Chains, every twenty-fifth link was marked.

laid down in the Northwest Ordinances were adopted by the constitutional government established in 1787.

Thomas Jefferson was one of the architects of the Northwest Ordinances. He claimed that he was the author of yet another of its remarkable provisions. The Ordinance of 1787 forbade slavery in the Northwest Territory. The West would be reserved for the independent family farmers whom Jefferson idealized. They would be protected from economic competition with men owning vast tracts of land worked by slaves.

THE RECTANGULAR SURVEY

Another novelty of the ordinances was its orderly system of surveying and then selling the western lands. During the colonial period, and after independence in territory not regulated by the Northwest Ordinance, property lines were described by **metes and bounds.** That is, a would-be buyer located the land he wanted at the land office (which incorporated the description in a deed) by referring to adjacent properties that were already deeded and by natural features such as creeks, outcroppings of rock, and even temporary markers, as in this legal description of a 140-acre parcel in Kentucky: "Beginning at the mouth of a branch at an ash stump thence up the creek south 20 poles to 2 beach, thence east 41 poles to a small walnut in Arnett's line, thence north 50 east 80 poles to a linn hickory dogwood in said line, thence north 38 poles to an ash, thence west 296 poles with Potts's line till it intersects with Tolly's line, thence south 30 west 80 poles to a whiteoak and sugar, thence east 223 poles to beginning." (*Branch* was another word for creek. *Pole* was a synonym for a *rod*, a

developed not by individuals but by already organized communities to which the colonial government granted whole townships contiguous to already established towns. That often meant geometric boundaries and, sometimes, rectangular townships. (Some townships in New Hampshire, oddly, were parallelograms.)

The Northwest Ordinance of 1785 raised this orderliness a notch in virtually ignoring natural features in surveying the Northwest Territory previous to offering land there for sale. It called for crisscrossing the Territory north to south and east to west with straight lines forming squares. The survey of the "first seven ranges" in eastern Ohio began in 1785. (A range was a north–south stack of 36-square-mile townships.)

The survey was put under the supervision of Thomas Hutchins, who was instructed to begin at the high water mark of the Ohio river opposite the border between Pennsylvania and Virginia (now West Virginia). Arriving at what was then wilderness in August 1785, Hutchins used a navigational instrument, either a Davis quadrant or a sextant (invented in Philadelphia in 1731) to identify the starting point as north latitude 40 degrees, 38 minutes, 27 seconds (40°, 38', 27"). (Hutchins's calculation later proved to be slightly off, but not enough that, had he been captaining a ship at sea, he would have missed even a tiny islet.)

Hutchins marked the spot and, a month later, returned with eight of the thirteen surveyors Congress had authorized for the job. (Each state was supposed to send a surveyor.) He hired about thirty men to fell trees so as to clear sight lines and to handle the heavy and cumbersome "Gunter's Chains" that, along with compasses and "Theodolites," were the surveyor's peculiar tools.

A Theodolite was a telescope with a plumb line for positioning it (the first placement being at Hutchins's

marker) and cross hairs for precise sighting. A Gunter's Chain consisted of 100 links just under eight inches in length so that it was 22 yards (66 feet) long. Today, the "chain" seems like an awkward, even absurd standard of measure. In fact, it was ingeniously handy for quantifying land. Twenty-two yards was equal to 4 *rods* (surveyors called them "perches") of 16.5 feet. The rod has just about vanished as a measure today but it was an everyday term in the eighteenth century; and 25 links was a much more convenient measure for calculation than 16.5 feet.

Eighty chains (320 perches) equaled a mile on the button. A square mile—called a "section" by the Northwest Ordinances—equaled 640 acres; an acre equaled 40 square perches. The dimensions of the Gunter's Chain made excellent sense.

Hutchins's crew did not make much progress in 1785. They had run one line for only four miles when they disbanded out of fear that unwelcoming local Indians, who knew very well what the survey meant, were about to attack them. Hutchins returned in August 1786 with twelve surveyors (Delaware never did send one) and a larger crew of armed axe men and chainmen. They surveyed four of the seven ranges when, again, Indians scared them off. They finished the job in 1787 at a cost to the government of $14,876.43.

The "first seven ranges"—minimum parcel, a section at a minimum cost of $1 per acre—went on sale immediately in New York, which had replaced Philadelphia as the capital. Speculators hoping to make a fortune in real estate (a perennial American dream) purchased 108,431 acres for a total of $176,000; the more desirable land sold for more than $1 per acre. The first recorded buyer of a piece of the great National Domain was one John Martin who paid the minimum for 640 acres: Section 20 of Township 7, in Range 4, about ten miles due west of Wheeling, West Virginia.

---

measure (16.5 feet) now obsolete but an everyday term in the eighteenth century.)

A problem with settlers of new land identifying their properties by metes and bounds was that they selected only prime land and excluded steep hillsides, rocky ground, marshes, and other wasteland from their purchase. Once they were established, settlers did not waste the wasteland. They quarried rock and gravel from it, cut timber and firewood, and grazed livestock on it. But no one had paid for it and no one paid taxes on it.

To avoid this in the Northwest Territory, Congress designed the **rectangular survey.** Before land was available for purchase, surveyors crisscrossed it with lines creating townships 6 miles square that were subdivided (also in squares) into 36 "sections" of one square mile (640 acres). Buyers located

the land they wanted, but they had to purchase the entire section, good farmland and wasteland alike. The government was not left owning irregular pockets of unsellable land.

A section, the smallest tract that could be purchased under the Northwest Ordinance at a minimum of a dollar an acre, was far more land than a family needed or could make use of and, in most cases, $640 was more than pioneering farmers, poor almost by definition, could afford to spend. Congress was selling to developers, speculators who could afford to buy in sections and subdivide them into farm-size parcels for sale at a profit. Congress did not want to involve the government in the massive job of retailing; nor did land speculators, who knew how to lobby congressmen. Congress did, however, attend to the educational needs of the communities that would emerge in the Northwest Territory. Section 16 of each

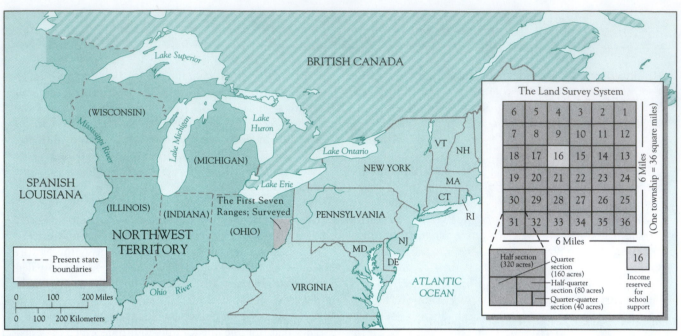

MAP 10:2 The Northwest Territory and the Rectangular Survey
The ingenious "rectangular survey" system. An American innovation, it provided for orderly disposition of the "national domain," government land, to settlers. Land distribution in the colonies (and in Kentucky during the 1780s) was often chaotic and resulted in endless legal conflicts over property lines. The rectangular survey was later applied to the Louisiana Purchase and the Mexican Acquisition that rounded out the United States as we know it.

township was withheld from sale, reserved to provide money (from leases) to fund schools.

DIFFICULTIES AND FAILURES

Despite the Confederation's achievements, each year that passed convinced more and more prominent people—particularly those like Hamilton and George Washington, who thought of themselves as Americans and not as New Yorkers or Virginians—that the Confederation government was too weak, and that a disaster was lurking in the near future.

MONEY PROBLEMS

Finance was a tenacious problem. Even during the war, delegates in Congress bickered and connived, denying or delaying the funds needed to fight. Congress dithered for hours as to whether a man who claimed a mere $222.60 for ferrying troops should be paid. The difficulty was that all thirteen states had to approve financial measures. In 1781, Rhode Island alone, representing 2 percent of the country's population, refused to approve a tariff of 5 percent on imports. On another occasion, New York killed a tax bill the other twelve states approved.

Because Congress could not levy taxes, it resorted to a dangerous alternative to pay its bills, printing increasingly larger amounts of paper money popularly called "continentals." From $6 million in paper money in 1775, Congress printed $63 million in 1778 and $90 million in 1779. No one accepted the bills at face value when they were still crisp from the printer. By 1783, it required $167 paper dollars to purchase what one

silver Spanish dollar bought. "Not worth a continental" was a catchphrase that long survived the Articles of Confederation.

Seven states also printed paper money. The assembly of Rhode Island, controlled by farmers in debt, churned it out in bulk; Rhode Island's was worthless outside the state and tales were told of creditors fleeing Rhode Island to prevent those who owed them paying them in the state's legal tender. Merchants needed a sound paper currency valid in every state and accepted abroad. Such a currency, they said, needed a strong central government backing it.

DIPLOMATIC VULNERABILITY

Squabbles among the states made it difficult for American diplomats to negotiate with other nations and invited foreign meddling. In 1784, a Spanish diplomat, **Diego de Gardoqui,** played on the commercial interests of the northern states in the hopes of splitting the United States in two. He offered to open Spanish ports to American ships (which meant northern ships) if Congress gave up Americans' treaty rights to export goods via the Mississippi River.

New Englanders and New Yorkers cared little about trade on the Mississippi. Their delegations tried to ram de Gardoqui's treaty through Congress. Had they succeeded, the southern states would have been under great pressure to go their own way. The Mississippi and Ohio River system was vital to the tens of thousands of southerners who had moved to what are now Kentucky and Tennessee but were still claimed by Virginia, the Carolinas, and Georgia.

Britain schemed to detach Vermont from the United States. Claimed by both New York and New Hampshire, the

Confederation era money ("not worth a continental"). The "dollar" was borrowed from Spain. However, the Spanish divided their dollar into eighths. The division into sixths illustrated here was a British practice (recall the famous sixpence coin). Decimalization—100 cents to the dollar—was adopted in 1791.

isolated Green Mountain country functioned as an independent commonwealth during the 1780s, dominated by Ethan and Levi Allen, two eccentric and scheming Revolutionary War veterans. The Allens tried to make a treaty with the British that would have tied Vermont more closely to Canada than to the Confederation. Congress was powerless to stop them, even militarily; the Continental Army had shrunk to 700 men. Only because the British failed to act decisively did the project fall through.

WOUNDED PRIDE

Britain refused to turn over a string of Great Lakes forts that were American under the terms of the Treaty of Paris. Nor did the British send a minister (ambassador) to America. A British diplomat joked that it was too expensive to outfit thirteen men with homes and the other accoutrements of office in the thirteen sovereign states. In London, the American minister to Great Britain, John Adams, was mocked when he acted with the dignity of a national legate.

There were insults elsewhere. A world-traveling American sea captain said that the United States was regarded "in the same light, by foreign nations, as a well-behaved negro is in a gentleman's family"; that is, as an inferior scarcely to be noticed. Even the venal Barbary States of northern Africa made light of Americans. These little principalities lived by piracy, collecting tribute from nations trading in the Mediterranean. When Americans lost the protection the British annually purchased for vessels flying the Union Jack, they were sunk or captured. The bey (governor) of Algiers sold American crews into slavery when Congress was unable either to ransom them (ransom was another Barbary specialty) or to launch a punitive expedition. It was a sorry state of affairs for the young men of the Revolution who had crowed of national greatness.

CALLS FOR CHANGE

A trivial conflict in domestic waters triggered the movement to overhaul the government. In March 1785, a small group of Marylanders and Virginians gathered at Mount Vernon, George Washington's home on the Potomac, to discuss the conflicting claims of Maryland's and Virginia's fishermen in the Chesapeake Bay. They were unable to come up with a boundary acceptable to the two states' fisheries. They did, however, conclude that the problem was only one in a morass of disputes between states and between states and the Confederation. They invited all thirteen states to send delegates to a meeting the next year in Annapolis, Maryland, to discuss what might be done.

Only five states responded; decisive action was out of the question. Only Washington's former aide-de-camp, 30-year-old Alexander Hamilton of New York, was undiscouraged. He persuaded the other men who had wasted their time traveling to Annapolis to try again in more centrally located Philadelphia. They should prepare, Hamilton told them, to discuss all the "defects in the System of the Federal Government."

Hamilton and a few others, notably James Madison of Virginia, who was scarcely older than Hamilton, had more than jawing in mind. They intended a bloodless coup d'état, peacefully replacing the Articles of Confederation with a completely new frame of government. Rumors of their intentions spread quickly and met less than resounding approval. Virginia Governor Patrick Henry, Madison's

The Oyster War

Usually, when a waterway is a boundary, the line is drawn at the *thalweg,* the deepest part of the creek, river, or bay. However, the boundary between Maryland and Virginia in the Chesapeake Bay was the high tide line on the Virginia side. This peculiar specification gave Marylanders the right to harvest oysters on Virginia shores. Virginia oystermen were not delighted. Periodically, they engaged in shooting wars with Marylanders. An "oyster war" was one of the disputes that first brought together the men who would eventually write the Constitution. Over the years, at least fifty oystermen were killed in the wars; the last known fatality was in 1959. Even today, Chesapeake oystermen are forbidden to have firearms on their boats.

© Bettmann/Corbis

▪ *Shays' Rebellion began as riotous behavior, bullying and beating up Massachusetts state officials, for example. But it evolved quickly into a worrisome, if short-lived, armed insurrection.*

rival in state politics, said that he "smelled a rat" and refused to endorse the proposal. Rhode Island officially declared that the state would not participate. Hamilton's Philadelphia convention would likely have fizzled like the Annapolis meeting had it not been for a wave of protests in western Massachusetts that turned into armed rebellion.

SHAYS' REBELLION

Farmers in western Massachusetts resented the fact that the state's tax laws favored trade at the expense of agriculture. In 1786, hundreds of them held meetings at which they demanded that their property taxes be reduced. To make up for the loss of revenue, they called for the abolition of "aristocratic" public offices in the state government in Boston.

In several towns, angry crowds surrounded courthouses, harassed lawyers and judges, whom they considered parasites, and forcibly prevented the collection of debts. In September, a Revolutionary War veteran, Daniel Shays, led 2,000 armed men against the state arsenal in Springfield.

Shays and his followers did not regard themselves as revolutionaries. They believed they were carrying on the spirit and struggle of the War for Independence against a privileged elite. Then minister in France, Thomas Jefferson agreed with them. "A little rebellion now and then is a good thing," he wrote to a friend. "The tree of liberty must be refreshed from time to time with the blood of patriots and tyrants." (So long as he was not on the scene, Jefferson was titillated by social disorder.)

Shays' Rebellion collapsed in December. But the men who were preparing to gather in Philadelphia the next summer, and some who were just considering it, determined not to face another such crisis. To them, it was not Jefferson's pine tree of liberty that needed attention; it was the ailing oak of social stability and order. Washington, Hamilton, and conservatives like them believed that disorders like the uprising in Massachusetts were the inevitable consequence of weak government.

The "Founding Fathers" in Philadelphia. This is an imagined reconstruction painted after the Convention. The delegates admitted no nondelegates to the meeting room. George Washington is presiding. Seated second from left is an idealized Benjamin Franklin. The oldest delegate at 81, Franklin was not so lively as he is shown to be here. He died within three years.

THE CONSTITUTION

The American Constitution has been hailed with a reverence that can be described as religious. Jefferson called the men who wrote it "demigods." In fact, the Constitution has been a remarkably successful frame of government, and the generation of political leaders who wrote and debated it was richer in talent than any generation of American politicians since. But the Founding Fathers were not demigods. They were well-to-do, privileged, conservative men of their time who found a good deal about their time alarming.

THE CONSTITUTIONAL CONVENTION

The convention began on May 25, 1787. The fifty-five delegates almost immediately agreed that the Articles of Confederation could not, realistically, be revised. Ironically, it was much easier to effect a coup d'état, to create a government from scratch, than it was to amend the articles. Amendment required that all thirteen states concur. Rhode Island had already made it quite clear that it opposed any changes. This did not bother the men at Philadelphia; they were quite willing to have a new union of twelve states in place of the confederation of thirteen.

The Constitutional Convention met in secret from beginning to end. For four months the delegates bolted the doors and sealed the windows of the Pennsylvania State House (Independence Hall)—which was a demigod-like sacrifice in the hot and humid Philadelphia summer. Every delegate swore not to discuss the proceedings with outsiders. George Washington, who presided, was furious when one delegate could not account for a single page of notes he had taken.

There was nothing sinister about the secrecy. The goal of the convention—a new frame of government—was common knowledge. The delegates sequestered themselves because they wanted to proceed with caution. As James Wilson of Pennsylvania said, "America now presents the first instance of a people assembled to weigh deliberately and calmly, and to decide leisurely and peaceably, upon the form of government by which they will bind themselves, and their posterity." No small business that: never before had a nation been invented. There was an immediate, practical reason for secrecy too: the delegates were politicians. Successful politicians calculate every word they utter in public so as to please or, at least, so as not to displease the people who elect them to office. The delegates to the convention, to their credit, wanted to voice their honest opinions rather than, as

A History Book that Made History

Thomas Jefferson called the men who wrote the Constitution "demigods." His piety was insincere. With the notable exception of James Madison, the men who gathered in Philadelphia in 1787 and remained active in politics became Jefferson's enemies.

However, nineteenth-century Americans looked back on the "Founding Fathers" as beings more than human in their wisdom and visionary foresight. The Constitution was a sacred thing, miraculous even. It "was intended to endure for ages to come," said John Marshall, the great Chief Justice of the Supreme Court. The Constitution, said Henry Clay, "was not made merely for the generation that then existed but for posterity—unlimited, undefined, and endless, perpetual posterity." British Prime Minister William Gladstone called the Constitution "the most wonderful work ever struck off at a given time by the brain and purpose of man."

It was, therefore, a blasphemy when, in 1913, Columbia University Professor Charles A. Beard published *An Economic Interpretation of the Constitution.* The men who wrote the Constitution and jiggered through its ratification were not visionaries, Beard said. They were (too simply, but only a little) money men or the friends of money men; speculators in government "paper"— state and federal bonds, promissory notes given to veterans of the Revolution—who feared that unless they established a centralized government friendly to their financial interests, they would never be able to redeem the instruments they had bought up, often at a steep discount. Nor was the Constitution acclaimed by "We the People," Beard said. The common people did not want the new government, but many of them could not vote because, in some states, many did not own enough property to qualify as voters or because, in other states, pro-Constitution Federalists ignored the anti-Constitution popular vote and ratified it anyway. In brief, the Constitution was written not with "endless, perpetual posterity" in mind but because it served the immediate financial interests of a few.

For half a century, Beard's interpretation was gospel in university-level history courses. Since the 1950s, however, "revisionist" historians have discredited one and a half of three of Beard's major arguments.

1. While speculators favored the Constitution and profited from its adoption, they did not dominate the Constitutional Convention or the state ratification conventions. Beard was half wrong.

2. By eighteenth-century standards, the ratification elections were very democratic. Because property ownership was so widespread, only the very poorest of men could not participate in them. Beard was mistaken.

3. Two of the thirteen states (North Carolina and Rhode Island) refused to ratify the Constitution. (They surrendered to the inevitable only after the new government was a going concern.) In three of the four largest states (Massachusetts, Virginia, New York), the Constitution was ratified only because delegates elected to vote against it voted for it. There were also manipulative shenanigans in the convention in the other large state, Pennsylvania. Beard was quite right to say that "We the People" did not clearly "ordain and establish" the "most wonderful work."

politicians must do most days of their lives, truckle to popular prejudice.

Moreover, the delegates knew that there would be opposition to the constitution they wrote. Wilson said that "the people" were assembled in Independence Hall. The Constitution begins with the words "We the People of the United States." In fact, most of the Founding Fathers represented just one of several American political tendencies, and they knew it. They wanted their program complete before they had to debate its merits.

THE DELEGATES

They finished in September 1787, whence most of the delegates scattered north and south to lobby for their states' approval. (A few did not sign the document.) They were a formidable lot, all of them influential at home by virtue of their wealth, education, and political prominence. Of the fifty-five, only two, Roger Sherman of Connecticut, who had been a cobbler as a young man, and Alexander Hamilton, the bastard son of a ne'er-do-well merchant in the West Indies, could be said to have been weaned on anything less glittering than a silver spoon.

Lifetimes devoted to justifying independence and creating state governments made many of the delegates keen students of political philosophy. During the years just preceding the convention, James Madison augmented his library with 200 books on the subject. Just as important was the delegates' practical experience: seven had been state governors; thirty-nine had sat in the Continental Congress.

The Founding Fathers were young. Only nine signers of the Declaration of Independence were among them (and three of them were nonsigners of the Constitution). Only Benjamin Franklin at 81 was antique. The other delegates averaged 40 years of age; ten delegates were less than 35 years of age; one was 26. Such men had been barely old enough in 1776 to play minor roles in the war. They had been children during the Stamp Act crisis. They were heirs of the Revolution, not makers of it.

The youth of the Founding Fathers is of some importance in understanding the nature of the Constitution they wrote. Most of the delegates had never thought of themselves as colonials. By 1787, most wanted to think of themselves not as New Hampshiremen or South Carolinians, but as Americans. Unlike their more provincial forebears, they had moved freely and often from one state to another. In the Continental Army (a third of the delegates had been soldiers, mostly junior officers) and in the Confederation Congress, they met and formed relationships with men from other states. They thought in terms of a continent rather than of coastal enclaves looking back to a mother country for an identity.

A CONSERVATIVE MOVEMENT

Youth does not, as we are often told to think, equate with radicalism. The men who drew up the Constitution were conservatives in the classic (not the contemporary) meaning of the word. They did not believe with Jefferson (then in France) that human nature was essentially good and eternally malleable, that people and society were perfectible if

Alexander Hamilton was one of the youngest Founding Fathers. He thought the Constitution allowed the states too much power and the president too little. But he accepted it in the spirit of give-and-take compromise that Benjamin Franklin eloquently asked of the delegates. And, for Hamilton, the imperfect Constitution was an infinite improvement on the Articles of Confederation, which he despised.

left free. Most of the Founding Fathers feared the darker side of human nature. They believed that, without strong institutional restraints, selfish individuals were quick to trample on the rights of others. To such conservatives, democracy and liberty did not go hand in hand. On the contrary, if "the people" were unchecked, they would destroy liberty, and a good deal more. Rufus King of New York defined democracy as "madness." John Adams who, like Jefferson, was serving in Europe, called rule by the masses of people "the most ignoble, unjust, and detestable form of government."

The most pessimistic of the lot was Alexander Hamilton. Sent by friends who recognized his genius to King's College in New York (now Columbia University), Hamilton never returned to the West Indies. He quit college to serve Washington as an aide during the war, impressing the General with his intelligence and, no doubt, with his conservatism, for Washington too viewed democracy with distaste. Hamilton may never have actually said that "the people" were "a great beast," but the alleged quotation nicely sums up his feelings on the subject.

Had Hamilton been English, he would have defended those institutions that British conservatives believed helped to control the passions of the masses: the monarchy, the aristocracy, the established church, and the centuries-old accretion of law and custom that is the British constitution. In fact, Hamilton admired British culture and government. Like Edmund Burke, he thought of the American Revolution as a conservative movement. In rebelling, the Americans had defended tradition against a reckless, innovative Parliament.

In the Constitution, Hamilton wanted to recapture some lost traditions. He suggested that the president and the senators be elected for life, thus creating a kind of monarch and aristocracy. He was unable to sway his fellow delegates. Many of them shared Hamilton's sentiments, but they understood better than he ever would that Americans would never tolerate institutions that even hinted of aristocracy. What the majority of delegates did approve, and Hamilton accepted as preferable to "anarchy and convulsion," was a system of government that was in part democratic (by eighteenth-century standards) but in which democracy was limited. The government they created was, in John Adams's word, "mixed," a balance of the "democratical" principle (power in the hands of the many); the "aristocratical" (power in the hands of a few); and the "monocratical" (power in the hands of one).

CHECKS, LIMITS, BALANCES

The House of Representatives was democratical. Representatives were elected frequently (every two years) by a broad electorate—most free, white, adult males. The Senate and the Supreme Court reflected Adams's aristocratical principle. Senators were elected infrequently (every six years) and by state legislatures, not by popular vote. They were thus somewhat insulated from the fickleness of the democratical crowd.

The Supreme Court was almost totally insulated from popular opinion. Justices were appointed by the president, but, once confirmed by the Senate, they were immune to his or the Senate's or the people's influences. Justices served for life. They could be removed from the bench only by a difficult impeachment process.

The monocratical principle was established in the presidency and was, therefore, the most dramatic break with the Confederation government. The president alone represented the whole nation, but he owed his power neither directly to the people nor to Congress. An electoral college that played no other role than selecting the president put him into office.

An intricate web of checks and balances tied together the three branches of government. Only Congress could enact a law, and both democratic House and aristocratic Senate had to agree to every syllable. The president could veto an act of Congress if he judged it adverse to the national interest. However, Congress could override his veto by a two-thirds majority of both houses.

Judging specific cases according to these laws was the job of the judiciary, with the Supreme Court the final court of appeal. In time (this was not written into the Constitution), the Supreme Court established a quasi-legislative role of its own in the principle of judicial review; that is, in judging according to the law, the Supreme Court also interpreted the law. Implicit in this process was the power to declare a law unconstitutional and, therefore, void.

Finally, the Constitution could be amended, although the process for doing so was deliberately made quite difficult. An amendment may be proposed in one of two ways: two-thirds of the states' legislatures can petition Congress to summon a national constitutional convention. Or, and this is the only method by which the Constitution has in fact been amended, Congress can submit proposals to the states. If three-fourths of the states ratify a proposed amendment, it becomes part of the Constitution.

THE FEDERAL RELATIONSHIP

Another web of checks and balances defined the relationship between the central government and the states. Under the Articles, the United States was a confederation of independent states that retained virtually all the powers possessed by sovereign nations. Under the Constitution, the balance shifted, with preponderant and decisive powers going to the federal government. The states were not reduced to administrative districts, as Hamilton would have liked. Nationalistic sentiments may have been high in 1787, but local interests and jealousies were a long way from dead. If the Constitution were to win popular support, the states had to be accommodated.

Small states like Delaware, New Jersey, and Connecticut were particularly sensitive in this matter. If they were not to be bullied or even absorbed by larger, wealthier neighbors, delegates from the small states insisted, they must be accorded fundamental protections. These they received in the decision that states rather than population would be represented in the Senate. That is, each state elected two senators, no matter what its population. Virginia, the largest, was ten times as populous as Delaware, but had the same number of senators. Without this "great compromise," which was accomplished only after intense debate in July 1787, the Constitution would not have been completed.

THE CONSTITUTION AND SLAVERY

The question of slavery necessitated another compromise. Virtually none of the delegates from the northern states were sympathetic to the institution. Some, including Benjamin Franklin, Alexander Hamilton, John Jay, and Gouverneur Morris were active abolitionists. Jay purchased several slaves in order to free them. Some of the Virginians like Washington and Madison regarded slavery as a curse—a dozen years later, Washington freed all his slaves in his will—but with the African-American population of the South so large, they feared that emancipation would mean social disorder far worse than Shays' Rebellion. Only the South Carolinians and Georgians can be described as proslavery as a group.

Even their sensibilities had been jarred by a decade talking about liberty. Tellingly, the word *slave* does not appear in the Constitution. But slavery, unnamed, does. In Article I, Section 9, which guaranteed the importation of Africans for twenty years, slaves are referred to obliquely as "such Persons as any of the States now existing find proper to admit." Elsewhere, slaves are identified as "all other persons."

This was the term employed in the **three-fifths compromise** by which a serious North–South conflict was averted. The northern delegates wanted to count slaves for purposes of apportioning taxation among the state on the grounds that their labor produced wealth, but not when apportioning seats in the House of Representatives; slaves, after all, did not vote and their interests were not, like the interests of women, represented by fathers, husbands, and sons. Southern delegates, with nothing resembling a comparable argument, wanted to count slaves when apportioning Representatives but not when apportioning taxes.

For the northern delegates, it was a matter of forgetting the new Constitution or making a deal. The compromise that was worked out was so contrived as to be grotesque. Each slave (and indentured servant) in a state was counted as three-fifths of a person in apportioning that state's tax burden and its representation in the House. Politically, this gave southern white voters considerably more power than northern voters. In 1800, the three-fifths compromise would determine the winner of a presidential election.

RATIFICATION

The Constitution was to go into service when conventions in nine states ratified it. Three did so immediately, Delaware and Connecticut almost unanimously, thanks to the "great compromise" that gave them equality with the large states in the Senate. Pennsylvania's ratification also came quickly, but in a manner that dramatized the widespread opposition to the new government and the determination of the supporters of the Constitution, who called themselves "Federalists," to have their way.

FEDERALIST SHENANIGANS

"Federalist" was something of a misnomer, since Federalists proposed to replace a genuinely federated government with a more centralized one. In Pennsylvania, the Federalists secured ratification only by physically forcing two anti-Federalist members of the state convention to remain in their seats when they tried to leave the hall. This irregular maneuver—not that the anti-Federalist strategy of paralyzing the convention was admirable—was necessary to guarantee a quorum so that the Federalist majority could legally register a pro-Constitution vote.

In Massachusetts, Antifederalists claimed that scheduling the election of delegates to the ratification convention in midwinter prevented many snowbound Antifederalist farmers from getting to the polls. Even then, ratification was approved in Massachusetts by the narrow margin of 187 to 168 only because several delegates pledged to vote against the Constitution actually voted for it.

In June 1788, Edmund Randolph of Virginia, an announced Antifederalist, changed his vote and took a coterie of followers with him; the Federalist victory in Virginia was by a vote of only 89 to 79. A switch of six votes would have reversed the verdict in the largest state, and that, in turn, would have kept New York in the Antifederalist camp.

In New York, a large Antifederalist majority was elected to the ratifying convention. After voting to reject the Constitution, the convention reversed its decision when news of Virginia's approval reached the state. Still, the vote was closer than it was in Massachusetts and Virginia, a razor-thin 30 to 27.

There is good reason to believe that if an open, democratic, countrywide referendum had been held in 1787, the Constitution would have been rejected.

THE ANTIFEDERALISTS

North Carolina was decisively Antifederalist. Only in November 1789, eight months after the new government began to function, did the state reluctantly ratify and join the Union. Rhode Island held out longer, until May 1790. Rhode Island became the thirteenth state only when Congress threatened to pass a tariff that would have shut its produce out of the United States.

Today, when the Constitution has worked successfully for 200 years, it can appear that the anti-Federalists of 1787 were cranks. In fact, their reasons for favoring the Articles of Confederation were firmly within the tradition of the Revolution.

Among the Antifederalists were fiery old patriots who feared that centralized power was an invitation to tyranny.

Unpredictable Critic

Mercy Otis Warren, sister of hell-raiser James Otis and wife of another prominent patriot was of a type familiar today. In the vanguard of many radical causes, her blood was the bluest Massachusetts produced and she knew it. She condescended even to those just a notch below her in social status like John and Abigail Adams. Her condescensions were subtle because her pen was among the deftest of her era— she was often as eloquent as Jefferson. Warren wrote several plays reviling loyalists and also a history of the Revolution.

Mercy Otis Warren was not happy with America under the Articles of Confederation. She called the country a "restless, vigorous youth, prematurely emancipated from the authority of a parent, but without the experience necessary to direct him to act with dignity or discretion."

That sounds like a Federalist in the making, but Warren was no Federalist. She regarded the Constitution as a plot, sinister in ways she (untypically) never quite defined in writing. Mercy Warren fit into not a "type" of the 1780s. There was no other informed American so critical of both the Articles of Confederation and the Constitution.

Samuel Adams, still padding about Boston shaking his head at moral decadence, opposed the Constitution until Massachusetts Federalists, needing the old lion's support, agreed to press for a national bill of rights. In Virginia, Patrick Henry battled James Madison around the state. Some of Henry's arguments against the Constitution were rather bizarre. At one point he concluded that the Constitution was an invitation to the pope to set up court in the United States. Henry had his eccentricities.

But he and other Antifederalists also argued that free republican institutions could survive only in small countries such as Switzerland, the city states of ancient Greece, and, of course, an independent and sovereign Virginia. When the Roman republic became an empire, they pointed out, Rome became despotic. The same thing would happen, Antifederalists warned, to a large, centrally governed United States.

Answering such arguments was the Federalists' most difficult task. Madison, Hamilton, and John Jay of New York took it upon themselves to do so in eighty-five essays later collected under the name the Federalist Papers—which is still a basic textbook of political philosophy. They argued that a powerful United States would guarantee liberty. These ingenious essays, however, were probably less important to the Federalist victory than their agreement, quite reluctant in Hamilton's case, to add a bill of rights to the Constitution.

THE BILL OF RIGHTS

The Constitutional Convention paid little attention to the rights of citizens. The Founding Fathers were by no means hostile to individual rights, but their preoccupation was strengthening government. And they assumed that the rights of individuals were protected in the state constitutions.

Because the Constitution created a national government superior to the states, however, Antifederalists like Samuel Adams and Edmund Randolph agreed to scrap their opposition to ratification only when the rights that had been adopted by the states since 1776 were guaranteed on the federal level. The Bill of Rights, the first ten amendments to the Constitution, was ratified in 1791, but tacitly agreed upon during the ratification process. The First Amendment guaranteed freedom of religion, speech, the press, and peaceable assembly. The Second Amendment guaranteed the right to bear arms. The Third and Fourth Amendments guaranteed security against the quartering of troops in private homes (which was still a sore point with older Americans) and against unreasonable search and seizure.

The famous Fifth Amendment is a guarantee against being tried twice for the same crime and, in effect, against torture. It is the basis of a citizen's right to refuse to testify in a trial in which he or she is a defendant. (British practice did not allow a defendant to testify.) The Sixth Amendment also pertains to criminal trials. It guarantees the right to a speedy trial and the right to face accusers: no secret witnesses. The Seventh and Eighth Amendments likewise protect the rights of a person who is accused of committing a crime.

The Ninth and Tenth Amendments are catchalls. They state that the omission of a right from the Constitution does not mean that the right does not exist, and that any powers not explicitly granted to the federal government are reserved to the states.

FURTHER READING

General Gordon S. Wood, *The Creation of the American Republic, 1776–1787,* 1969, and *The Radicalism of the American Revolution,* 1991.

The Confederation Period Jackson T. Main, *The Sovereign States, 1775–1783,* 1973; Kenneth Silverman, *A Cultural History of the American Revolution,* 1976; Richard B. Morris, *The Forging of the Union, 1781–1789,* 1987; Willi P. Adams, *The First American Constitution,* 1988; Larry E. Tise, *The American Counterrevolution: A Retreat from Liberty, 1783–1800,* 1998; David Szarmary, *Shays' Rebellion,* 1980; Leonard L. Richards, *Shays' Rebellion: The American Revolution's Final Battle,* 2002; Richard H. Kohn, *Eagle and Sword: The Federalists and the Creation of the Military Establishment in America, 1783–1802,* 1975; Andro Linklater, *Measuring America: How the United States was Shaped by the Greatest Land Sale in History,* 2002.

The West Gregory E. Dowd, *A Spirited Resistance: The North American Indian Struggle for Unity, 1745–1815,* 1992; R. Douglas Hurt, *The Ohio Frontier: Crucible of the Old Northwest, 1720–1830,* 1996; Peter S. Onus, *Statehood and Union: A History of the Northwest Ordinance,* 1987.

The Constitution Richard Beeman, Stephen Botein, and Edward C. Carter, *Beyond Confederation: Origins of the Constitution and American National Identity,* 1987; Herbert J. Storing, *What the Anti-Federalists Were For,* 1981; Richard B. Bernstein, *Are We to be a Nation?: The Making of the Constitution,* 1987; Morton White, *Philosophy, the Federalist, and the Constitution,* 1987; Gary Nash, *Race and Revolution,* 1990; Thornton Anderson, *Creating the Constitution,* 1993; Jack N. Rakove, *Original Meanings: Politics and Ideas in the Making of the Constitution,* 1996; Akhil Reed Amar, *The Bill of Rights: Creation and Reconstruction,* 1998; Saul Cornell, *The Other Founders: Anti-Federalism and the Dissenting Tradition in America, 1788–1828,* 1999; Michael Kammen, *A Machine that Would Go by Itself: The Constitution in American Culture,* 1986; Robert A. Rutland, *The Ordeal of the Constitution: The Anti-Federalists and the Ratification Struggle of 1787–1788,* 1966; Garry Wills, *Explaining America, The Federalist,* 1981.

Biographies Lance Banning, *The Sacred Fire of Liberty: James Madison and the Founding of the Federal Republic,* 1995; Stuart Leibiger, *Founding Friendship: George Washington, James Madison, and the Creation of the American Republic,* 1999; Richard Brookhiser, *Founding Father: Rediscovering George Washington,* 1996; Joseph J. Ellis, *Founding Brothers: The Revolutionary Generation,* 2000, and *His Excellency, George Washington,* 2004; Ron Chernow, *Alexander Hamilton,* 2004; Walter Stahr, *John Jay: Founding Father,* 2005.

KEY TERMS

The following terms are covered in this chapter and can also be found in the list of Key Terms at the back of the book.

abolition	**manumission**	**rectangular survey**	**three-fifths compromise**
Diego de Gardoqui	**metes and bounds**	**Shays' Rebellion**	
Elizabeth Freeman	**Northwest Ordinances**		

ONLINE SOURCES GUIDE

Use this listing to find online documents, images, interactive maps, simulations, and other resources related to this chapter:

American History Resource Center
http://history.wadsworth.com

Selected Documents
James Madison, The Federalist Papers, No. 10
The Virginia Statute for Religious Freedom
The Articles of Confederation
The Constitution of the United States
The Bill of Rights and Amendments to the Constitution

Selected Images
1787 Constitutional Convention in Philadelphia
James Madison
Alexander Hamilton
Boston's Faneuil Hall, 1789

Interactive Timeline (with online readings)
Inventing a Country: American Constitutions 1781–1789

Document Exercises
1781 Articles of Confederation/U.S. Constitution
1785 Thomas Jefferson on Slavery
1787 Federalist No. 10 by James Madison
1789 James Madison's Speech on Amendments

Discovery

Winning the American Revolution and solidifying its accomplishments were two different things. In what ways did America change following the Revolution? What impact did this have on America's future?

In thinking about this question, begin by breaking it down into the components shown below. A discussion of the significance of each component should appear in your answer.

Geography: For this exercise, please study the series of maps in Map 10:1, The Western Lands Mess. What problems are apparent in the new territories? How did claims to those lands impede the start of an American government? On what basis were those claims made? What areas might cause the most problems for the new government?

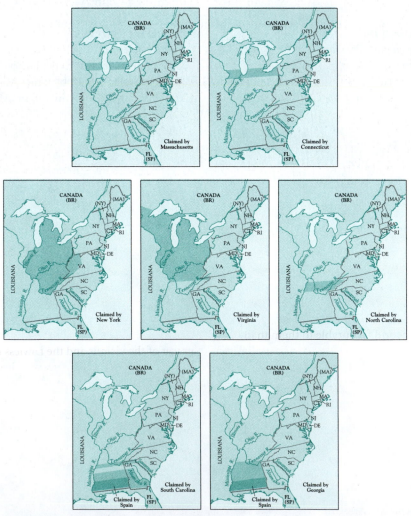

MAP 10:1 The Western Lands Mess

Culture and Society: For this exercise, please study this image, "New Jersey Gives the Vote to all 'Free Inhabitants,'" and read the following letter: "Abigail Adams to John Adams." Which groups were not included in the new-found ideas of independence and freedom? Why were they excluded? How did they attempt to have their voices heard? What reasons were used to exclude these groups?

North Wind Picture Archives

New Jersey Gives the Vote to All

Abigail Adams to John Adams, Braintree, 31 March 1776

I long to hear that you have declared an independancy-and by the way in the new Code of Laws which I suppose it will be necessary for you to make I desire you would Remember the Ladies, and be more generous and favourable to them than your ancestors. Do not put such umlimited power into the hands of the Husbands. Remember all Men would be tyrants if they could. If perticuliar care and attention is not paid to the Laidies we are determined to foment a Rebelion, and will not hold ourselves bound by any Laws in which we have no voice, or Representation.

That your Sex are Naturally Tyrannical is a Truth so thoroughly established as to admit of no dispute, but such of you as wish to be happy willingly give up the harsh title of Master for the more tender and endearing one of Friend. Why then, not put it out of the power of the vicious and the Lawless to use us with cruelty and indignity with impunity. Men of Sense in all Ages abhor those customs which treat us only as the vassals of your Sex. Regard us then as Beings placed by providence under your protection and in immitation of the Supreem Being make use of that power only for our happiness.

To read extended versions of the documents, visit the companion Web site http://history.wadsworth.com/americanpast8e; click on "Discovery Sources."

CHAPTER 11

We the People

Putting the Constitution to Work 1789–1800

Reproduced from the Collections of the Library of Congress

The father of his country.
  Francis Bailey

First in war, first in peace, first in the hearts of his countrymen.
  Henry Lee

America has furnished to the world the character of Washington. And if our American institutions had done nothing else, that alone would have entitled them to the respect of mankind.

  Daniel Webster

Neither before nor after the Constitution was ratified did anyone in the United States wonder in writing who would bear the burden of being the first president. George Washington towered so far above every other American that, to no one's surprise, all sixty-nine members of the electoral college chose him to fill an office that was, at the time, unique in the world. After a slow, triumphal procession from Virginia to New York City (then the capital), Washington took the presidential oath on April 30, 1789.

The Constitution directed that each elector vote for two candidates with the second place finisher becoming vice president. (This system caused a problem in 1796 and a crisis in 1800; it was abandoned before the 1804 election.)

John Adams believed that his services to the country entitled him to that honor and thirty-four electors, not quite half of them but enough to elect Adams, agreed.

THE FIRST PRESIDENCY

Washington was more than first in the hearts of his countrymen. He was possessed of qualities perhaps indispensable to overseeing the launch of a government designed from scratch. He was committed to the republican ideal. His sense of duty was the very core of his personality. He was aware that events had made him one of his civilization's most respected

Washington was hurrahed and feted all the way from Mount Vernon to his inauguration in New York City, then the nation's capital. He crossed the Hudson in a splendidly decorated barge and took the presidential oath on a balcony, cheered by thousands in the street below.

figures, which increased his obligation to act wisely and prudently. He knew that, as first president, he would set a precedent with every deed, from signing an act of Congress into law to the manner in which he greeted a guest for dinner.

SETTING PRECEDENTS

It is fortunate that Washington was a dedicated republican and it was by no means a given that he should have been. The advisor he trusted most, Alexander Hamilton, was not. Nor were many members of the Order of Cincinnatus, a society of Revolutionary War officers. Before the Constitution fixed presidential terms at four years, they had wanted to make him a president for life, an elected monarch. Washington politely but decisively quashed the suggestion. When the new government was mustering itself in New York in 1789, it was proposed that Washington be addressed as "Your Elective Majesty." He toyed with "His High Mightiness" but (thankfully) settled for "Mr. President."

Washington was not "one of the boys." He was fussy about the trappings of his office. He insisted his servants dress in livery (clothing identifying them as servants) and powdered wigs. He was driven about New York in a splendid carriage drawn by matched cream-colored horses. When he toured

the country—Washington visited every state while he was president—he stopped his utilitarian overland coach before entering towns and mounted a fine, large charger on which he sat "straight as an Indian." He consciously affected the appearance and manners of a European prince. On a bet that he would not dare do it, Gouverneur Morris chummily slapped Washington on the back at a public function. The president stared him down with such iciness that Morris retreated stammering from the room. Morris said it was the costliest bet he ever won.

In being as much monument as man, Washington won an even greater respect than his generalship of the Revolution had earned him. No Europeans feared the United States, but neither did they mistake George Washington for a head-scratching bumpkin.

THE CABINET

Washington was accustomed to wielding authority. Rarer qualities among men raised high by history were his awareness of his personal limitations and his receptivity to advice, even when it contradicted his own impulses. He did not resent brighter people (as, for instance, George III did). Washington sought out intelligent and learned people and listened to them, and he had those who disagreed hash out their arguments in his presence.

Political considerations entered into his appointments of the men who headed the five executive departments under him who were soon collectively known as the president's "cabinet." (The word does not appear in the Constitution.) He chose Edmund Randolph to be attorney general because Randolph had been a prominent member of the Anti-Federalists, and Washington wanted to win their support for the government. He named Samuel Osgood to be postmaster general so that Massachusetts, the only state to rival Virginia in importance, would have two cabinet members, as his own state of Virginia did.

But the other three men in the first cabinet Washington chose mainly because he admired them and respected their advice. Secretary of war, Henry Knox (Massachusetts), had been one of Washington's favorite generals and had remained a friend. Secretary of state, Thomas Jefferson (Virginia) was the author of the Declaration of Independence, but, more important, he had lived six years in France, America's ally—for four years as minister—and he was popular there. Moreover, Jefferson was widely considered a friend of democratic government, which neither Washington, Adams, or other cabinet members were, and he had contacts throughout the country with those who agreed with him. Washington wanted to please them, too.

The most important cabinet post, because of the complex and serious financial problems the government faced, was secretary of the treasury. Washington's pick to fill this vital position was as foreordained as the electoral college's choice of the first president. Alexander Hamilton of New York had been Washington's aide-de-camp during the war; he was one of the

The Cincinnati

Lucius Quinctius Cincinnatus was a Roman farmer who was twice made dictator for six months when enemies threatened the republic. Both times Cincinnatus was quickly victorious. Instead of exploiting the months of his dictatorship to enrich himself, however, he resigned immediately and went back to his plow. Educated Americans who were steeped in ancient history likened George Washington, also a selfless patriot, to Cincinnatus.

In 1784, Continental Army officers organized the Society of the Cincinnati (the plural of Cincinnatus). The club was controversial from the start. The Cincinnati met in secret and membership was hereditary: only the first-born sons of charter members were eligible to join. The Cincinnati had adopted the aristocratic principle of primogeniture that Revolutionary-era state governments had abolished in property law. Thomas Jefferson, called the society "a nascent nobility."

Some of the Cincinatti discussed—no one knows how many or how seriously—the desirability of making George Washington a dictator. Rumors of a military coup in the making flew and Washington quashed the idea as soon as he heard of it. The original Cincinnati grew long in the teeth without biting. Chastened by their unpopularity, they abandoned primogeniture, opening membership to all male descendants of Revolutionary officers. The Society evolved into an organization "devoted to the principles of

Military men wear medals. The old soldiers in the Order of the Cincinnatus wore this one to identify themselves. The inscription reads: "All sacrificed to serve the republic."

the Revolution, the preservation of history and the diffusion of historical knowledge," as which it exists today.

most energetic proponents of the Constitution (he wrote fifty-one of the long and closely argued Federalist Papers), and his expertise in financial matters was universally recognized and almost universally admired. Like Washington, he was strongly nationalistic and highly conservative. Did Washington know, when he brought Hamilton and Jefferson together, that he would hear both sides of every basic political question argued as articulately as they possibly could be? If not, he was soon to learn it.

THE NATIONAL DEBT

To pay the government's running expenses, Hamilton asked Congress to enact a 5 percent tariff on imports. The duty was low, not enough to impede sales of foreign goods in the

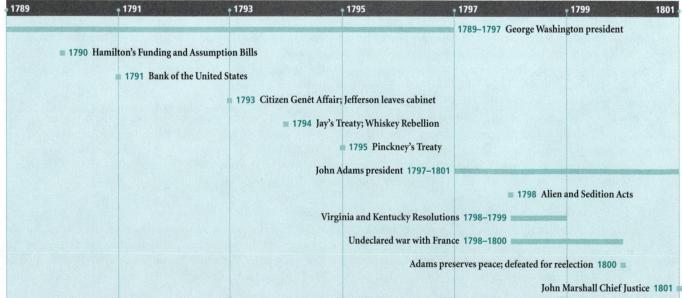

The Federalist Presidents 1789–1801

1789	1791	1793	1795	1797	1799	1801

1789–1797 George Washington president

1790 Hamilton's Funding and Assumption Bills

1791 Bank of the United States

1793 Citizen Genêt Affair; Jefferson leaves cabinet

1794 Jay's Treaty; Whiskey Rebellion

1795 Pinckney's Treaty

John Adams president 1797–1801

1798 Alien and Sedition Acts

Virginia and Kentucky Resolutions 1798–1799

Undeclared war with France 1798–1800

Adams preserves peace; defeated for reelection 1800

John Marshall Chief Justice 1801

The first cabinet, left to right: the president, Secretary of War Henry Knox (depicted at less than his usual 300 pounds), Attorney General Edmund Randolph, Secretary of State Thomas Jefferson, and Jefferson's rival, Secretary of the Treasury Alexander Hamilton.

United States (mostly French and British manufactures), and the 5 percent figure enabled Hamilton to make a larger statement, which he was always keen to do. Rhode Island, standing alone, had crippled the Confederation government by vetoing a 5 percent duty.

Revenue from the tariff was not enough to sustain the government in a crisis such as war, but it was also a lesser demand on the treasury. The government, like all governments, would need to borrow money now and then—often! For that, the government had to have sound credit. Foreign governments, banks at home and abroad, and even individuals who could afford to buy government bonds of a few hundred dollars, had to be assured that the United States was a good risk, that their loans would be repaid.

In 1789, the United States was a terrible financial risk. The Confederation Congress had been badly delinquent in repaying the money it had borrowed. The United States owed $12 million to foreigners and $44 million to Americans. The creditors were wary. Would the new government repudiate the old government's obligations? It happened often enough,

kings refusing to honor the debts of the kings they had ousted. In January 1790, Hamilton reassured the lenders by asking Congress to fund the entire Confederation debt at face value. That is, by retiring Confederation bonds by issuing new federal bonds, dollar for dollar, in their place (restructuring the debt, we might say) the government would assert, with no immediate expenditure, its financial reliability.

No one in Congress objected to **funding** the debt owed abroad. The United States was cash poor. Any big future loans would have to be floated in Europe. The Dutch and the French governments (and Dutch bankers) must have confidence in the new government. However, Hamilton's proposal to pay American creditors at the face value of the Confederation paper they held met stiff resistance.

THE FIRST DEBATE

The issue was speculation. Most of the domestic debt dated to the war years when, moved by patriotism (to feed and clothe the soldiers) as well by the chance to earn some interest, thousands of Americans bought government bonds.

Continental Army soldiers had been given promissory notes when there was no cold cash with which to pay them. As the years passed and the Confederation failed to redeem these obligations, lenders and veterans lost hope. They sold their holdings at big discounts to speculators willing to take a chance that, eventually, they would collect on the paper. For modestly fixed people, getting 20 or 30 cents on the dollar from someone willing to pay was better than getting nothing from the government ever. By 1790, most Confederation obligations were in the strongboxes of financial adventurers.

Not all of them had been so adventurous. As James Madison explained in the House of Representatives in opposition to the funding bill, some speculators, learning in advance that Hamilton would propose payment of the debt at face value, had scoured rural villages, buying up, dirt cheap, all the old bonds and notes they could find. In our parlance, they had traded on "insider information."

Congress should not reward profiteers, Madison said. He proposed to fund debts at face value (plus 4 percent annual interest) only when the people who presented them had themselves loaned the money to the government. Speculators who had bought Confederation debts from the original lenders would get half face value.

Morally, Madison's argument was appealing. It rewarded those who had stepped forward during the times that tried men's souls. Hamilton replied that morality was beside the point. At issue was the government's credit. By rewarding people who had money—capitalists—including speculators, his funding bill would encourage them to be lenders in the future. Hamilton believed that the support of the monied classes was the key to the success of the new government.

Hamilton's realism was compelling. It did not hurt that several dozen members of Congress stood to profit personally from his funding bill. The House of Representatives chose his proposal over Madison's three to one.

ASSUMPTION

Hamilton's second proposal concerning government debt had tougher sledding. He wanted the federal government to assume responsibility for the debts the states had contracted during and since the war, a total of $25 million. In addition to yet further demonstrating the federal government's solid credit, Hamilton believed that the British government's eternal indebtedness—and its constant repayment of its debts!—explained the extraordinary economic growth of Great Britain during the eighteenth century. A national debt, Hamilton said, to the bewilderment of Thomas Jefferson and his supporters, is a national blessing. That is, the treasury's ongoing repayment of government loans plus interest would finance economic development.

Finally, by taking over the debts that states had not paid, Hamilton the nationalist would reduce the prestige and power of the recently sovereign states relative to the prestige and power of the federal government—the government that paid the bills.

The trouble was that the southern states, notably Virginia, had generally been more responsible in paying back lenders than the New England states, notably Massachusetts, had been. James Madison pointed out that Virginians, who had dutifully been paying state taxes to retire Virginia's debt, would, if the federal government assumed all state debts, have to pay federal taxes to pay back the money Massachusetts had borrowed and failed to repay. His arithmetic showed that whereas **assumption** would relieve Virginia of $3 million in debt, Virginians would pay $5 million in taxes to repay the federal debt.

It was not a good deal and, although the numbers were smaller, other southern states were looking at the same kind of trade-off. For the northern states on the other hand, assumption was a bargain. In the House of Representatives, pretty much along sectional lines, assumption was defeated 31–29.

HORSE TRADE: ASSUMPTION FOR THE CAPITAL

Hamilton did not take the defeat very well. He was not going to accept losing by the closest vote possible. Fortuitously, he had a horse to trade, his considerable influence in the northern states as to where the permanent capital of the United States would be located.

New York, Hamilton's hometown, was the capital in 1790 but everyone except New Yorkers agreed that it was not going to stay there. New York was too far north, just 300 miles from Boston (and a quick hop by sea) but 800 miles from Charleston, 900 from Savannah. Moreover, far from the metropolis of today, New York was still something of a backwater. As president, Washington had a fine home, but John Adams had to go out of town to find a house to rent. Secretary of State Jefferson roomed at a tavern; Speaker of the House James Madison lived at a boarding house.

Philadelphia had the best claim to be the permanent capital. It was a hundred miles to the south of New York, an easy trip from Virginia, the most populous state; it was much larger than New York, with many more amenities, and it was the city where independence was declared and the Constitution written. However, no fewer than fifteen other places were seriously bidding to be selected—Trenton in New Jersey, Baltimore and Frederick in Maryland, and two sites where there was no city, where a capital would be built from scratch, one on the Susquehannah River, one on the Potomac. Another twenty-five towns offered their names because lightning can strike anywhere.

Hamilton quietly proposed to Madison that if the enactment of assumption were arranged, Hamilton would deliver enough northern congressmen to locate the permanent capital in the South, on the Potomac. Madison was interested but was already deferring to Jefferson, his inferior in many ways. At an historic dinner, the deal was made. Madison sat out a second vote on assumption and it was enacted. Hamilton convinced enough northern congressmen to approve a site on the Potomac (the future Washington, D.C.) as the permanent capital, with Philadelphia the capital in the interim. Pennsylvanians were as jubilant as Virginians; they were sure that the Potomac capital would never be built and the government would stay in Philadelphia.

A NATIONAL BANK

Hamilton had been an ardent patriot during the Revolution. He was also, however, a lifelong Anglophile. He admired

The Granger Collection, New York

Hamilton's darling, which President Washington approved only reluctantly, the First Bank of the United States in Philadelphia. Imposing in size, its classical design, borrowed from ancient Greece, was novel and deliberate. Size conveyed power and reliability. The classical façade hearkened to the republics of antiquity, with which Americans liked to identify.

British institutions such as the national debt and the Bank of England, a powerful central bank chartered by Parliament to handle the government's revenues, issue paper money, and, so far as it was able, to maintain order on the financial side of the national economy.

Hamilton's Bank of the United States (BUS), to which Congress voted a twenty-year charter in 1791, was patterned on the Bank of England. While it would be the repository of all the government's money, it was a private institution. The president named five of its directors; twenty were elected by shareholders, men of Hamilton's monied classes again. With the vast wealth at its disposal, the BUS would wield great power over other banks and the country's money supply.

Hamilton pushed the bank through Congress, but Jefferson urged Washington to veto the bill. He argued that Congress had exceeded the powers given it by the Constitution. Nothing in the document gave the government the authority to create such an institution.

Washington had presided at the Constitutional convention where, indeed, nothing had been said about national banks. He was impressed by Jefferson's reasoning. But Hamilton won the day. The point was, he argued in his report to the president, nothing in the Constitution prohibited Congress from chartering a national bank. The BUS was justified under Article I, Section 8, which authorized Congress "to make all laws which shall be necessary and proper for carrying into execution," among other things, the regulation of commerce, and to "provide for . . . the general welfare," which, to Hamilton, the bank would do by using its powers to maintain a dependable currency beneficial to all. Washington was uneasy about it, but he signed the bill.

In the bank debate, Jefferson and Hamilton formulated fundamentally different theories of the Constitution.

Hamilton's **broad construction** permitted Congress to legislate on any matter that was not specifically prohibited by the Constitution. Jefferson's **strict construction** held that if the Constitution did not spell out and properly punctuate a governmental power in black and white, it denied that power to Congress and the president.

HAMILTON REBUFFED

The BUS was Hamilton's last hurrah. Congress rejected the fourth pillar of his financial edifice, the protective tariff he called for in his "Report on Manufactures" in December 1791. In that report, Hamilton argued that the United States had a solid agricultural and commercial base. (There were as many American as British ships engaged in overseas trade.)

However, the country still imported almost all its manufactured goods from Great Britain. Hamilton wanted to encourage American investors to put money into manufacturing by protecting them against established British manufacturers who could easily undersell American competitors who were just starting out. The idea was to lay an import duty on, for example, cloth and shoes from Britain that increased the retail price enough that American textile mills and shoe manufacturers could compete.

Consumers—which meant mostly farmers and southern planters in the 1790s—opposed protective tariffs. They were not interested in paying higher prices for goods in order to subsidize the enrichment of American manufacturers. Southern planters led the opposition. They bought shoes and cloth for their numerous slaves not a pair and a yard at a time, but in large quantities. It was a "business expense." Raising the retail price of textiles by 40 or 50 percent to benefit would-be mill owners in New England was unacceptable.

Family farmers in the middle colonies, who grew grain and raised livestock for export without slaves, were concerned that Britain and France would retaliate against high import duties by excluding their products from lucrative markets such as the West Indies. Even some New England merchants, staunch Hamiltonians in other matters, disliked the protective tariff. Their business was transporting goods; the more cargos that needed moving about the better. Already, British mercantilist laws restricted their activities within the British empire. They could not afford to have their own government shutting down yet more trade.

Hamilton's plan to promote manufacturing in the United States may have been his most far-seeing program. And, because the big loser if America manufactured its own goods was Great Britain, it gave the lie to his enemies' accusation, beginning to be heard in 1792, that Hamilton was a stooge for the British. But there was too much opposition. Import duties remained low; they provided revenue but no protection for "infant industries."

TROUBLES ABROAD

By 1792, Hamilton and Jefferson's differences on policy had grown into an ugly personal hostility. Even in their separate letters to Washington urging him to agree to a second term, they sniped at one another. Jefferson wanted to resign from the cabinet. In part, he vacillated his entire life between intense political ambition and a longing to retire to his beloved home, Monticello, in the Virginia foothills. In part, he wanted out because he had lost every contest with Hamilton for Washington's endorsement.

Washington was aware of the fact that his ambitions for the United States did not accord with Jefferson's. However, his appreciation of Jefferson's abilities was genuine; in 1792, when Washington was unanimously reelected, he persuaded Jefferson to remain at his post. In 1793, foreign policy problems further divided and embittered Jefferson and Hamilton so that, on the last day of the year, Jefferson resigned and went home.

THE FRENCH REVOLUTION

In 1789, the year of Washington's first inauguration, France exploded in revolution. Just about every American rejoiced. Had not the Declaration of Independence spoken of the inalienable rights of all people? Was not the beloved Lafayette one of the leaders of the movement to expand the liberties of the French people on the American model? Lafayette sent Washington the key to the Bastille, a royal prison that, in the first act of the Revolution, a Parisian mob had stormed. Curiously, for Washington did not much like mobs, he prized the gift, displaying it prominently in his home. It became fashionable among Americans to festoon their hats with cockades of red, white, and blue ribbon—the badge of the French revolutionaries.

But the French Revolution was not a flattering imitation of the American Revolution. It moved rapidly beyond a demand for liberty to the ideals of equality and fraternity. Conservatives like Washington and Hamilton balked at talk of wiping out social distinctions. As for fraternity, it soon came to mean more than national brotherhood. The idea of the nation as a morally bound community became a rationale for ensuring that no one disagree with, or merely displease, the brotherhood's guardians.

Moderates like Lafayette, who had envisioned a liberal, democratic constitutional monarchy, were undercut at one end by the nobility's resistance to any change and King Louis XVI's clumsy scheming with foreign powers to restore him to power; and, on the other end, by radicals who proclaimed a republic, executed nobles simply because they were nobles, and, in January, 1793, beheaded the king. During the "Reign of Terror," radicals known as Jacobins guillotined or drowned thousands of nobles, political rivals, and even ordinary people who ran afoul of a low-level Jacobin bully. The virtual dictator of France during the Terror, Maximilien Robespierre, tried to purify the country by wiping out religion—in France, Roman Catholicism. He converted Paris's cathedral of Notre Dame into a "Temple of Reason" where paunchy politicians and actresses performed contrived rituals that struck some as blasphemous, others as ridiculous.

Despite the bloodshed and horrors, many Americans remained avid pro-French "francomen." William Cobbett, an Englishman then living in the United States, observed with

MORT DE LOUIS XVI, LE 21 JANVIER 1793

Place de la Concorde : on voit à gauche le socle de la statue de Louis XV déboulonnée

(Extrait des *Révolutions de Paris*)

Americans greeted the first stages of the French Revolution with joy: the French, like themselves, were establishing a constitutional government of the people. When the Revolution turned violent with mass murders of first nobles and then revolutionaries who disagreed with those in power, conservatives like President Washington and most ordinary people, grew disillusioned. A hard core, notably Thomas Jefferson, overlooked the atrocities, but support for the French "Reign of Terror" was not popular.

distaste that crowds of city people guillotined dummies of Louis XVI "twenty or thirty times every day during one whole winter and part of the summer."

CITIZEN GENÊT

Well before the Reign of Terror, conservatives like Washington, Hamilton, and John Adams were dismayed by the direction the French had taken. Worse, France's declaration of war on Great Britain early in 1793 presented them with a touchy diplomatic problem. The United States had an anti-British mutual assistance treaty with France that the French government called on Washington to honor by going to war with Britain. The thought of the still shaky young nation challenging the powerful Royal Navy caused shudders in Washington's cabinet.

Luckily, there was a loophole in the treaty, explained, as usual, by that peerless discoverer of loopholes, Hamilton. The 1778 treaty obligated the United States to join France in a war against Great Britain only when Britain was the aggressor, which was not the case in 1793. Moreover, Hamilton argued, the treaty had been contracted with the French monarchy which—to put it delicately—no longer existed: Louis XVI was

guillotined ten days before France declared war. Washington announced that the United States would be neutral, "impartial toward the belligerent powers." Then, in April 1793, a new French minister, **Citizen Genêt,** arrived in Charleston.

Genêt was young (30), brilliant (he spoke seven languages), and as subtle as fireworks. Within days of stepping ashore, he began commissioning Americans as French privateers, sending them to sea to seize British ships. The raiders soon brought eighty British "prizes" into American ports where Genêt presided over trials and awarded a share of the loot to the captors. This was all standard procedure, except: during a war between France and Britain with the United States a proclaimed neutral, Genêt was commissioning privateers, an act of war, and presiding over a French court on American soil. Indeed, Genêt sometimes acted as if he were the governor of a French colony.

By the time the minister called on the president, Washington was livid. He received the minister coldly, commanding him to cease commissioning privateers and bringing captured British vessels into American ports. Genêt bowed, retired, and shortly thereafter commissioned a captured

British vessel, the *Little Sarah,* as a privateer. Washington ordered him to return to France.

This was not good news. Back in France, Genêt's party had been ousted from power; the Reign of Terror was in full swing. Going home meant a rendezvous with Madame la Guillotine. Suddenly abject, Genêt asked Washington for political asylum, and the president granted it. Genêt married into the wealthy Clinton family of New York and lived a long, quiet life as a gentleman farmer.

BRITISH THREATS TO NEUTRALITY

Now it was Britain's turn to sabotage Washington's determination to stay out of the war. The British proclaimed they would fight the war at sea under the Rule of 1756. This policy stated that ships of neutral countries could not trade in ports from which they had been excluded before the war.

The proclamation was aimed at American merchants who were carrying grain and livestock to the French West Indies—Martinique, Guadeloupe, and Haiti, which had been closed to Americans before 1793. The profits were astronomical. Merchants who had recently been struggling suddenly found themselves rich. They did not want to give up the new business.

The British did not want war with the United States, but they were concerned about the explosive growth of the American merchant marine that the French trade stimulated. Would they defeat the French only to discover that

upstart Yankees had filched their overseas trade? The Rule of 1756 was aimed more at retarding the growth of American commerce than economic warfare against the French. In any case, the rule was rigorously prosecuted. In 1793 and 1794, British warships and privateers seized 600 American vessels, half of them in West Indian waters.

The merchants of Philadelphia, New York, and Boston protested, but few demanded war. Their dislike of "French atheism" outweighed their financial losses. Common seamen were more bellicose not only because they were interned for months when the ships they were sailing were seized, but because of British impressment.

Great Britain authorized naval commanders to replace sailors who died or deserted by pressing (forcing) substitutes into service. If a ship was in port, navy press-gangs roamed the streets drafting likely young men. At sea, shorthanded warships ordered merchant vessels flying the Union Jack to heave to—the proverbial shot across the bow—whence press-gangs boarded them and took their pick of the crew. Impressment was unpopular among British seamen. It was even more aggravating to Americans when the British impressed sailors from American vessels. The British claimed they impressed only British-born seamen. But there were plenty of them on American ships and some were naturalized American citizens.

Pro-French Americans set up a clamor: protest meetings, torchlight parades, and vituperative attacks on presidential

Turning Forests into Farms

How They Lived

Before the rectangular survey opened the Northwest Territory to settlement, the northern frontier was in western Pennsylvania, where the Whiskey Rebellion erupted in 1794. There were few Indian problems in the region. The tribes had been pushed or had retreated to the west. Otherwise, the experience of pioneering in Pennsylvania's hardwood and conifer forests was much the same as it was in Kentucky and would be in Ohio.

Settlers tried to arrive in April. Winter's snow had melted, but the trees were just beginning to leaf. The pioneers' first job was to kill them and to build a cabin so as to be sheltered by mid-May when a crop of corn, beans, and squash was planted. Pines, spruce, and firs—softwoods with long, straight trunks—were felled for the logs with which cabins and barns were built. Oaks and maples were girdled to kill them. Crops were planted among the dead trunks. Only later were they chopped down. Frontier "fields" were far from pretty, but the soil was rich. Even in the first year, a farmer harvested 40 to 50 bushels of corn, wheat, or rye per acre.

Building a log cabin required just one tool, an axe, and little skill—only the muscle power to move the logs into position. If a man owned an adze, he hewed (squared) the logs on two sides for a tighter fit when they were stacked, but that could also be done with an axe. The ends of each log were notched so that, by locking them perpendicularly, it was possible to construct walls without uprights. The only task of cabin building requiring more than a single man's and woman's labor was raising the roof beam. For this, neighbors were summoned and entertained as thanks for their help. Even the author of an article in the *Columbian* magazine in 1786, who described the pioneers as the dregs of society, admired the fact that roofs were raised "without any other pay than the pleasures which usually attend a country frolic."

Log cabins were tight, strong buildings. The walls, chinked with moss and mud, provided better insulation from cold and heat than sawn clapboards did. The logs were plenty of protection from arrowhead, musket ball, and even fire. To burn a log cabin, it was necessary to ignite the shingled or thatched roof.

A yoke of oxen (a pair), maybe a few horses, perhaps a milk cow, were hobbled as often as they were fenced. Their forelegs were bound loosely enough that they could walk, but too tightly for running away. Hogs were for meat. They were cheap and, more than a match for any predator, they ran loose. They were hunted rather than rounded up for slaughter in October. Salt was a necessity; the pork was heavily salted to preserve it and packed in barrels. Deer were abundant; with fresh venison to supplement the salt pork, meat shortages were less of a problem than keeping deer and domestic animals out of the fields and garden.

For this, pioneers built zigzag fences. Logs split into rails—again, only an axe and wooden wedges were needed—were stacked alternately, at angles a little more than 90 degrees zigzag. No postholes needed digging. They were not very good fences—deer could leap them and the largest hogs could push them over. But they were a first line of defense.

According to the *Columbian,* "the first settler in the woods" rarely stayed more than a year or two. He was "generally a man who has outlived his credit of fortune in the cultivated parts of the State." Not a very good citizen, he was an anarchic, irreligious, and hard-drinking individual who "cannot bear to surrender up a single natural right for all the benefits of government." Soon restless, he sold out to a newcomer who improved the farm, felling and burning the dead hardwoods and adding to the cabin. The people of the second wave of settlement, often enough, were in the business of turning a profit by improving the land and selling it. Only the "the third and last species of settler," a solid citizen whose habits were a relief to the author, was "commonly a man of property and good character" who helped create a community.

policy in newspapers, although not yet on the president himself. Jefferson, living in retirement in Virginia, was himself silent. In confidential letters, however, he egged on political allies like James Madison and newspaper editors like the intemperate Philip Freneau. The nation's honor was being insulted, they said.

JAY'S TREATY

By April 1794, war fever was so heated that, in a last-ditch effort to cool it down, Washington rushed Chief Justice John Jay across the Atlantic to appeal to the British for a settlement. Just sending Jay to beg (as the Anglophobes saw it) further agitated the fury. When the news trickled back that Jay was gaily hobnobbing in London society and had kissed the queen's hand, the anti-administration press had a field day. Many opposition newspapers reprinted an anonymous ditty:

May it please your highness, I John Jay
Have traveled all this mighty way,
To enquire if you, good Lord will please
To suffer me while on my knees,
To show all others, I surpass,
In love, by kissing of your___.

The British wanted peace too. They agreed to compensate Americans whose ships had been seized in the West Indies, and opened some trade in India to Americans from which they had previously been excluded. Finally, the British agreed to evacuate a number of western forts that they should have turned over to the United States in 1783. This was not as meaningless as it might sound; the United States had not seen to it, as promised in the Treaty of 1783, that money owed to British subjects be repaid.

But nothing was said of impressment, the point of conflict most charged with emotion, nor about British aid to Indians who were warring against settlers in the Northwest Territory, nor about slaves who had escaped to Canada, matters that had aroused anti-British feelings in the West and South.

Jay was less than delighted with his work. Washington was unhappy with the treaty; he had hoped to placate westerners and farmers. Washington kept the terms of Jay's Treaty secret for weeks; he was tempted simply to bury it. In the end, he concluded that war was the only alternative to ratifying it.

As expected, the publication of the treaty's terms caused an uproar. To westerners and southerners and Anglophobes hot to fight Great Britain, the only beneficiaries of Jay's Treaty were the same wealthy northeastern merchants who were reaping the rewards of Hamilton's financial program. But many northeasterners were dissatisfied too. Jay was so violently attacked— "Damn John Jay! Damn everyone that won't put lights in his windows and sit up all night damning John Jay!" Jefferson's political allies chanted—that he resigned from the Supreme Court and retired to private life. For the first time, newspapers calling themselves "Republican" opposed to the "Federalist" administration attacked Washington personally.

In fact, the two political parties had been taking shape since Hamilton and Jefferson clashed in 1790 and 1791. Social conservatives, dedicated to clear-cut social inequalities as essential to stability, and horrified by the French Revolution (men like Washington, Adams, and Hamilton), and those with mercantile and financial interests were Federalists. The party was strongest in the northeastern states but many wealthy southerners, particularly in South Carolina, were Federalists. Most southern planters, however, especially in Virginia, still rankling from the costs of assumption—small farmers, generally, and westerners almost unanimously—and people who wanted a more democratic government and were excited by the radical political experiments in France, were Republicans. They would soon call themselves Jefferson Republicans when Thomas Jefferson agreed to accept open leadership of the party in 1796.

PINCKNEY'S TREATY

Indirectly, although few Republicans admitted it, Jay's Treaty led to major benefits for westerners. Spain was negotiating a peace treaty with France. However, Spanish diplomats feared that when Spain abandoned the anti-French alliance, the British would retaliate, in league with the Americans with whom—thanks to Jay's Treaty—they were reconciled, to seize Spanish Louisiana. The colony was poorly defended; it would fall easily to a combined attack of Americans by

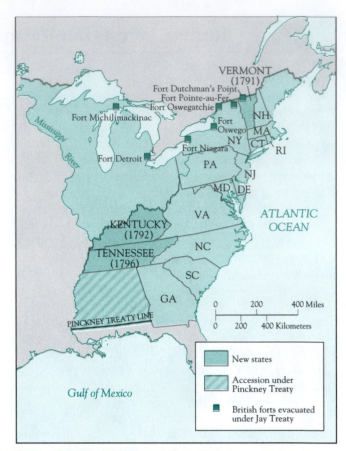

MAP 11:1 The Federalist Treaties

Britain's agreement to turn over seven frontier forts to the United States was not perceived as a diplomatic victory because the British had violated the Treaty of Paris in continuing to occupy them. In giving up, in Pinckney's Treaty, claims to what are now the states of Mississippi and Alabama (except the Gulf Coast), Spain eliminated a dispute with the United States that would likely have led to war.

land and the British by sea. Spanish anxieties were by no means far-fetched. Some Kentuckians had—unauthorized— begun to prepare an attack on New Orleans on their own.

In order to head off loss of Louisiana, Spanish diplomats reversed a decade of trying to close the Mississippi to American trade. Out of the blue, they offered the American minister in Spain, Thomas Pinckney (who had recently been threatened with expulsion), to open the Mississippi River to American navigation and to grant Americans the "right of deposit" in New Orleans. That is, Americans were given the privilege of storing and selling their exports (mostly foodstuffs and timber from the Northwest) in the Spanish city.

The **Treaty of San Lorenzo (Pinckney's Treaty)** was a major triumph for the Washington administration. If the United States had been the weaker party in the Jay Treaty sentiment, Spain played that role in Pinckney's. And the 100,000 Americans living in Kentucky, Tennessee, and the Northwest Territory—most of them Jefferson Republicans— had a reason to calm down.

THE TUMULTUOUS NORTHWEST

Washington had already appealed to the westerners for support by crushing the military power of the Indians in the Northwest Territory. It had not been easy. The tribes living in Ohio and Indiana—Shawnee, Miami, Potawatomi, Ojibwa, even Iroquois, refugees after their defeat during the Revolution—were numerous, well organized, well armed by the British in Canada, and determined to hold the line against white expansion into their lands.

THE DARK AND BLOODY GROUND

The Northwest Ordinance of 1787 had stated that "the utmost good faith shall always be observed towards the Indians; their lands and property shall never be taken from them without their Consent; and in their property, rights and liberty they shall never be invaded or disturbed." The frontiersmen who were moving into the Territory (and Kentucky and Tennessee) were not the sort to take note of such sentiments if they ever read them. They were tough, rugged people; if appalled Easterners who observed them are to be believed, they were "depraved" and violent: "Like dogs and bears, they use their teeth and feet, with the most savage ferocity, upon one another."

And they used their rifles on Indians who stood in their way. War, in the form of skirmishes, was constant. Both Indians and whites were responsible for massacres of entire camps and towns. Privately, Washington blamed the whites. Nothing but "a Chinese Wall or a line of troops" could stop their illegal "encroachment," he said. However, when the Indians threatened large-scale war, he did not hesitate to send armies west to fight them.

Most Americans' image of wars with Indians is set on the Great Plains in the late nineteenth century: the Seventh cavalry versus the mounted Sioux, Cheyenne, and Commanche in eagle feather war bonnets. In fact, the Indian wars on the

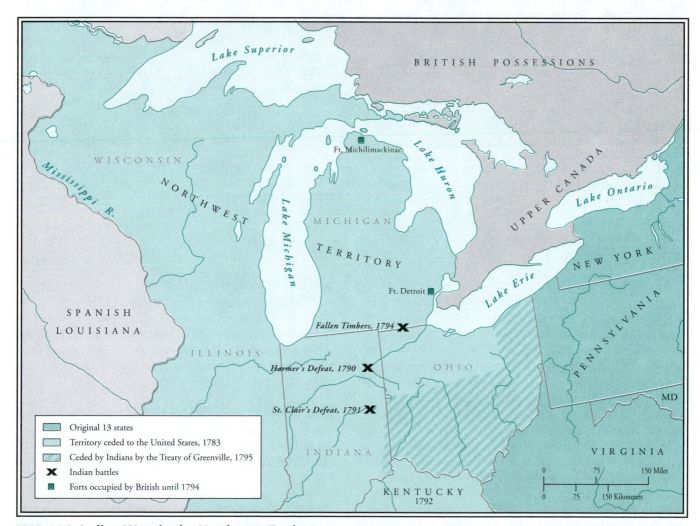

MAP 11:2 Indian Wars in the Northwest Territory

After victories over American militia in 1790 and 1791, the Indians of the Northwest Territory met their match in an army led by "Mad Anthony" Wayne in the Battle of Fallen Timbers. In the Treaty of Greenville signed after Fallen Timbers, the defeated Indians gave up their claims to most of Ohio. However, Wayne did not destroy their ability to resist. The Northwest Indians would make one last stand twenty years on.

Brown Brothers

The Whiskey Rebellion began with assaults on federal tax collectors like this man, stripped, tarred, and feathered. Washington tried to calm the settlers by promising a reduction in the tax on whiskey. They resisted, forcing the president to mobilize an army to suppress them. Washington, perhaps just to insult the rebels, called them mental defectives. Hamilton regarded them as what we would call "low-life," but, then, his definitions of low-life sometimes included a large proportion of the population.

Great Plains involved far fewer soldiers and Indians than the wars in the Northwest Territory during the 1790s, and they were far less bloody. George Armstrong Custer's column at the endlessly celebrated battle of the Little Big Horn in 1876 numbered 265 men. In Ohio in 1794, General Anthony Wayne commanded an army ten times that number. Deaths in Kentucky were so numerous that both Indians and whites called Kentucky "the dark and bloody ground."

In 1790, Washington sent General Josiah Harmer to subdue the Miami and Shawnee who, under the command of Little Turtle, had been harassing white settlements. Poorly supplied, wracked by dysentery and malaria, and handicapped by unfamiliarity with the country, Harmer and his men were decimated near the site of present-day Fort Wayne, Indiana. The next year, a better-prepared expedition under Arthur St. Clair met the same fate: 600 soldiers were killed.

Washington blamed both defeats on the fact that the soldiers were militiamen, for whom he never had a good word. In 1794, he gave General **"Mad Anthony" Wayne** command of troops

from the regular army. Wayne defeated Indians from several tribes at the Battle of Fallen Timbers. (The trees on the battlefield, near present-day Toledo, Ohio, had been leveled by a tornado.) In the Treaty of Greenville that followed, the battered tribes ceded the southern half of Ohio and a sliver of Indiana to the United States. The line was drawn—until the southern half of Ohio was populated.

THE WHISKEY REBELLION

The men and women of the frontier were heavy drinkers. They launched their days with an "eye-opener" or "flemcutter": homemade whiskey. A jug sat on shop counters like a dish of mints today; general stores doubled as saloons. Westerners swigged whiskey with their meals and like water when they worked. Preachers refreshed themselves with "the creature" during their sermons. Virginian William Henry Harrison said that he "saw more drunk men in forty-eight hours succeeding my arrival in Cincinnati than I had in my previous life."

Disease explains some of the drinking. Frontier settlers suffered chronically from the alternating chills and fevers of malaria. (They called it the "ague".) The medicine for which they reached was alcohol. Isolation also contributed. Travelers in the Ohio valley invariably described conversations with men, and especially women, who commented mournfully on the lack of company. Whiskey was a companion.

Finally, whiskey was cheap. The corn and rye from which it was made were easy to grow. The technology was simple: ferment the mash of grain and water; boil it in an enclosed "kettle"; condense the steam—alcohol vaporizes at a lower temperature than water. Fuel was free, the wood from endless land clearing that had to be burned anyway. Many family farmers kept a small still percolating day and night. And whiskey was a cash crop. Before Pinckney's Treaty opened the Mississippi to American trade, the westerners' only market was back East, by land over the Appalachians. The cost of transporting a low-value bulk commodity like grain was prohibitive. A pack horse could carry about 200 pounds: four bushels of corn. Four bushels of corn, in the food-rich United States, sold for pennies. However, a horse could carry the equivalent of 24 bushels of grain when it was converted into liquor. A gallon of whiskey sold for 25 cents, which provided just enough profit to make the trek over the mountains plausible.

In 1791, to augment federal revenues, Hamilton slapped an excise tax of 7 cents per gallon on distilled liquor. It was enough to wipe the out the western distillers' profits. Like Daniel Shays's followers in Massachusetts a few years earlier, but far more violent, farmers in western Pennsylvania kidnapped a federal marshal and terrorized tax collectors. When one tax collector summoned 12 soldiers to protect his house, 500 rebels attacked and burned the man's barn, stables, and crops, roughed up federal tax collectors, and rioted. Other mobs destroyed the stills of neighbors who had paid the tax.

Washington first tried to negotiate a peaceful end to the crisis. Even Hamilton expressed his willingness to make "any reasonable alterations" in the tax to make it more palatable. But the Whiskey Rebels had been carried away by the excitement and pro-French rhetoric, calling for the erection of guillotines. Washington set out at the head of 15,000 troops to suppress the rebellion. Just the news an army was on the way was enough to scatter the mobs. Washington left the column to return to Philadelphia but Hamilton, who had yen for military glory he was never able to satisfy, pushed on. He was denied a battle but managed to arrest a few rebels who were convicted of treason and sentenced to death. Washington pardoned them, calling them mental defectives.

In one sense, the suppression of the **Whiskey Rebellion** was a farce. An army as large as the one that defeated the British—and much larger than Wayne's army at Fallen Timbers—was mobilized to crush a rebellion it could not find. But the political significance of the episode was profound. The Federalist Hamilton was delighted to assert the national government's power to enforce order entirely within one state with troops raised in other states. The resentment of the western Pennsylvanians, however, ensured that when they got the chance, they would vote for the emerging Jefferson Republican party against the Federalists.

THE PRESIDENCY OF JOHN ADAMS

They got their chance in 1796 when Washington resisted every plea to once again stand for reelection. In retiring (quite happily) after two terms, he not only set a precedent that would not be broken for 144 years, he astonished both Americans and Europeans: he was indeed a Cincinattus voluntarily walking away from power to be a farmer. Even George III said that Washington's retirement made him "the most distinguished of any man living . . . the greatest character of the age." (A few years later, when Napoleon clung to power at the cost of thousands of lives, he remarked, perhaps scornfully, of those who urged him to retire, "They wanted me to be another Washington.")

THE ELECTION OF 1796: SURPRISING RESULTS

Because Washington made his retirement official only with his Farewell Address of September 1796, the presidential campaign was the shortest in history. (Twenty-first century Americans may look back at it wistfully.) Privately, however, the politicians had been at their machinations for months. With Vice President John Adams slated to stand for the Federalists, James Madison pressured Thomas Jefferson to be a candidate. Only Jefferson, he said, had a chance to defeat a Federalist, a party in the sinister hands of the despised Alexander Hamilton, and his pro-British foreign policy; his dedication to aristocracy and even monarchy at the expense of the people's liberties; his circle of banker and speculator friends; and his determination to make the federal government ever more powerful at the expense of the states. Indeed, Madison and Jefferson accused Hamilton of corruption.

Jefferson had not abandoned politics when he retired to his plantation in 1793. Hours each day he read and responded to dozens of letters from politicians from every state who agreed with him. But he had a mind-boggling variety of interests besides politics and a powerful aversion to confrontation and even face-to-face disagreement and criticism. The quiet life at Monticello suited him; between 1793 and 1797, the farthest he ever traveled from his home was seven miles. He may have succumbed to Madison's nagging more for personal than political reasons. He confided to his daughter that his isolation sometimes depressed him, making him "unfit for society, and uneasy when necessarily engaged in it."

The Republicans nominated Jefferson and Aaron Burr of New York, Hamilton's chief rival in state politics. As required in the Constitution, they were not officially identified as presidential and vice presidential candidates, but the head of the Jefferson Republican party was, of course, Jefferson.

The Federalists named Thomas Pinckney of South Carolina to run with John Adams. Quietly, but not quite secretly,

The Vice Presidency: Not a Crime
The vice president's only constitutional functions are to preside over the Senate, casting the deciding vote when there is a tie, and to step in if the president dies, resigns, or is removed from office. Thomas Jefferson is the only ambitious politician who has been happy in the post.

John Adams called the vice presidency "the most insignificant office that ever the invention of man contrived." John Nance Garner, vice president between 1933 and 1941, said the job wasn't "worth a pitcher of warm spit." Finley Peter Dunne, who wrote a popular newspaper column in Irish-American dialect at the turn of the

twentieth century, summed it up: "Th' prisidincy is th' highest office in th' gift iv th' people. Th' vice-presidincy is th' next highest an' the lowest. It isn't a crime exactly. Ye can't be sint to jail f-r it, but it's a kind iv a disgrace."

Alexander Hamilton began to scheme to put Pinckney rather than Adams into the presidency. Pinckney was pliable; Hamilton believed that he would be easily persuaded to carry out Hamilton's wishes. Adams was self-centered and suspicious of everyone, especially men like Hamilton who had instructions, often not tactfully conveyed, for everyone. Hamilton tried to ensure that Pinckney would win more electoral votes than Adams by urging South Carolina's eight electors to vote for Pinckney but to "throw away" their second vote on someone other than Adams.

All eight South Carolinians did so. But Hamilton's scheme blew up in his face because New England Federalists learned of the conspiracy and twenty-two of them voted for Adams but not for Pinckney. Worse, the candidate on whom South Carolina's electors "threw away" their second vote was Thomas Jefferson. Adams won, but barely. Needing 70 electoral votes to have a majority, Adams won 71. And Pinckney was not second; thanks to South Carolina's votes, Thomas Jefferson won 68 votes to Pinckney's 59. The president and vice president represented the two opposing parties. The Founding Fathers could not have anticipated such an outcome because they did not anticipate political parties.

JOHN ADAMS, "HIS ROTUNDITY"

After 200 years, it is easy to admire John Adams. When he was dispassionate, he was a moderate man who acted according to admirable principles. He could be humorous. When scandalmongers said absurdly that Adams sent Charles Cotesworth Pinckney to London to procure four loose women for his and Adams's use, he responded, "I do declare upon my honor, General Pinckney has cheated me out of my two." His relationship with his wife, Abigail, was unique in their era. He discussed public issues with her in detail, sought her advice, and often took it. "The President would not dare to make a nomination without her approbation," an opponent said.

Benjamin Franklin said that Adams was "always honest and often great." He then added, however, that Adams was "sometimes mad." Neurotically insecure, Adams was vain and often peevish. A raging temper, quick to erupt, incinerated his judgment. All work and duty, he was socially inept. A friend commented, "He cannot dance, drink, game, flatter, promise, dress, swear with the gentlemen . . . or flirt with the ladies."

Adams was laughably pompous. When wits sniggered at his short, dumpy physique, a sharp contrast to Washington's height and military bearing (they called him "His Rotundity"),

Adams isolated himself. He spent less time in the capital that any other president; for four years, he was one day in four at his home in Quincy, Massachusetts. Washington was absent from his post less than one day in eight.

His presidency might have gone better had it not been for James Madison's political partisanship and astuteness. Adams and Jefferson had once been close personal friends. Just before they were inaugurated, Adams told Jefferson that he hoped they could be reconciled and put the interests of good government above their political differences. Jefferson wrote a reply in which he went even farther in pledging Adams his cooperation and support. However, he showed it to Madison, who was horrified. If—when—Jefferson and Adams differed publicly, Madison pointed out, Adams would publish Jefferson's letter and Jefferson would be the one discredited. Jefferson did not send the letter.

Far more damaging, Adams retained Washington's cabinet intact. Two of his advisors were incompetent. Hamilton had urged Washington not to appoint them, which proved ironical, for they and another member of Adams's cabinet served as Hamilton's spies and saboteurs. They reported cabinet proceedings to Hamilton and obstructed Adams when Hamilton told them to do so. Adams's Federalist Party was split in two factions from day one.

WAR SCARE WITH FRANCE

Like Washington, Adams faced the threat of war, this time with France. Angered by Jay's Treaty, the French government ordered its navy and privateers to treat American ships as fair game. By the time Adams was inaugurated in March 1797, they had seized 300 American vessels. Moreover, the French defined American sailors captured off British ships (many of whom had been pressed involuntarily into service) as pirates who could legally be hanged. The American minister in Paris, Charles Cotesworth Pinckney, was threatened with arrest. The French minister in the United States, Pierre Adet, railed against Adams almost as intemperately as Genêt had assailed Washington.

Hamilton's "High Federalists," who had shrugged off British seizures of American ships, demanded war with France. Determined to keep the peace, Adams dispatched John Marshall and Elbridge Gerry to join Pinckney in Paris to negotiate an end to the "quasi-war."

They were shunned for weeks, unable to get near the French foreign minister—the charming, devious, and corrupt

North Wind Picture Archives

President John Adams was able and principled but "sometimes mad." His mind was the equal of the mind of any of his contemporaries. His personal integrity was equal to Washington's and far superior to Jefferson's and Hamilton's. He was, unfortunately, as vain and pompous as human beings come, and he lacked tact and social graces.

Charles Maurice de Talleyrand. Then, Talleyrand sent word through three henchmen—identified in code as "X," "Y," and "Z" (hence, **the X, Y, Z Affair**)—that he would speak with the Americans if they agreed in advance to a loan to France of $12 million and a personal gift to Talleyrand of $250,000.

Bribes were routine in diplomacy, but the sum Talleyrand demanded was excessive and the tempers of the Americans were worn thin from waiting and humiliation. "Not a sixpence," Pinckney snapped. (In the United States, Pinckney's reply was dressed up (and converted into American currency) as "millions for defense but not one cent for tribute."

The High Federalists were delighted. Hamilton pressured Adams to mobilize an army of 10,000 men. The aged Washington agreed to be its commander on the condition that Hamilton be second in command. Adams resisted. It offended his principles and his vanity that Washington should, in effect, issue an order to the sitting president. It would demoralize the army to jump Hamilton's rank over a large

number of Revolutionary War officers senior to him. And, after Hamilton's scheme to deny him the presidency in 1796, Adams was as suspicious of his ambitions and motives as Jefferson was. He feared a military coup.

Adams was more comfortable with the navy. Sea power posed no threat to civil government; a people cannot be subdued by ships. Moreover, while it was difficult to say where France and America might battle on land, an undeclared war already raged on the seas. Adams authorized the construction of forty frigates and lesser warships, a huge jump from the three vessels he inherited from Washington's administration.

THE ALIEN AND SEDITION ACTS

The Jefferson Republicans, still pro-France despite its corrupt and semi-dictatorial government, loudly opposed all preparations for war. Again, Jefferson was personally silent, speaking through cat's-paws, several of them, like journalist James Callendar, rather sleazy characters. In 1798, the Federalists responded to the criticism with a series of laws called the Alien and Sedition Acts.

The first Alien Act extended the period of residence required for American citizenship from five to fourteen years. A second authorized the president to deport any foreigner whom he deemed "dangerous to the peace and safety of the United States." The two laws were blatantly partisan, tacit admission that most immigrants became Republicans. Leaving no doubt of their political purpose, the Alien Acts would expire shortly after Adams's term ended in 1801.

The Alien Acts had few consequences. The Sedition Act did. It provided stiff fines and prison sentences for persons who published statements that held the United States government in "contempt or disrepute." Twenty-five cases were brought to trial; ten people were convicted. Most were journalists but when Adams visited Newark, New Jersey and was saluted with a volley of gunfire, one said, "There goes the president and they are shooting at his ass." Another responded, "I don't care if they fire through his ass," and the court ruled that the words were seditious.

THE VIRGINIA AND KENTUCKY RESOLUTIONS

Jefferson and Madison believed the Alien Acts violated the Bill of Rights and were therefore unconstitutional. But who was to declare that an act of Congress signed by the president was invalid? The Constitution did not say. The answer Jefferson and Madison gave was to haunt American history for half a century and contribute to the tragedy of the Civil War.

The Virginia Resolutions, written by Madison and adopted by the Virginia legislature, and the Kentucky Resolutions, which Jefferson wrote, proclaimed that the federal government was a compact of sovereign states. Congress, therefore, was the creation of the states. If Congress enacted a law that a state deemed unconstitutional, that state had the right to forbid its enforcement within the state.

It is difficult to understand how Madison, the most nationalistic of Americans in 1787 and a nationalist again when he was president, could espouse such a doctrine.

A Death in the Family

George Washington, 67 years of age, took to his bed in December 1799 with a sore throat and fever. Modern physicians have diagnosed a bacterial infection, strep throat. Bacteria were unknown in 1799, but Washington's doctors could only have hastened his death. The gargles (tea and vinegar) and syrups (molasses, vinegar, and butter) to ease the pain in his throat did not hurt; and the emetics (tartar and calomel) might have helped reduce his fever. But the bloodlettings—applying leeches to Washington—a therapy doctors seem to have prescribed whenever they were confused, surely weakened the old man. The doctors took 82 ounces, five pints, of blood in about a week! Blood donors today rest briefly after being relieved of a single pint.

He hinted at his uneasiness when, after reading Jefferson's first draft of the Kentucky Resolutions, he persuaded him to delete the word nullify to describe a state's right to ignore a federal law; it was too strong a word. Perhaps the explanation is Madison's boundless admiration of and devotion to Jefferson. When they disagreed, Madison sometimes could sway Jefferson. But he never differed openly with him.

There was logic in the Virginia and Kentucky Resolutions, but their implications were ominous. Had the principle on which they were based been established, the United States would have reverted halfway to the state supremacy of the Articles of Confederation. As it was, they were nothing more than abstractions, statements. No other state legislature adopted them. The death of George Washington in December 1799 briefly calmed political tempers and, as the election of 1800 drew nearer, it became obvious to the Jefferson Republicans that the unpopularity of the Alien and Sedition Acts was winning voters to their party.

FURTHER READING

General Gordon S. Wood, *The Radicalism of the American Revolution*, 1991; Stanley Elkins and Eric McKitrick, *The Age of Federalism: The Early American Republic, 1788–1800*, 1993; Jack Larkin, *The Reshaping of Everyday Life 1790–1840*, 1988; Cynthis A. Kierner, *Scandal at Bizarre: Rumor and Reputation in Jefferson's America*, 2004; Joseph J. Ellis, *Founding Brothers: The Revolutionary Generation*, 2000; Joyce Appleby, *Inheriting the Revolution: The First Generation of Americans*, 2000, and *Capitalism and the New Social Order: The Republican Vision of the 1790s*, 1984.

The Washington Administration Joseph J. Ellis, *His Excellency, George Washington*, 2004; Garry Wills, *Cincinattus: George Washington and the Enlightenment*, 1984; Richard Brookhiser, *Founding Father: Rediscovering George Washington*, 1996; Joseph J. Ellis, *American Sphinx: The Character of Thomas Jefferson*, 1996; Stephen F. Knott, *Alexander Hamilton and the Persistence of Myth*, 2002; Ron Chernow, *Alexander Hamilton*, 2004.

Foreign Policy Jerald Combs, *The Jay Treaty*, 1970; Walter Stahr, *John Jay, Founding Father*, 2003; Daniel G. Lang, *Foreign Policy in the Early Republic: The Law of Nations and the Balance of Power*, 1985; Albert Bowman, *The Struggle for Neutrality: Franco-American Diplomacy During the Federalist Era*, 1974.

The West Gregory Evans Dowd, *A Spirited Resistance: The North American Indian Struggle for Unity, 1745–1815*, 1992; Robert V. Hine and John Mack Faragher, *The American West: A New Interpretive History*, 2000; Reginald Horsman, *Expansion and American Indian Policy, 1783–1812*, 1992; Stephen Aron, *How the West Was Lost: The Transformation of Kentucky from Daniel Boone to Henry Clay*, 1996; Thomas G. Slaughter, *The Whiskey Rebellion: Frontier Epilogue to the American Revolution*, 1986.

Party Politics Richard Buel, Jr., *Securing the Revolution: Ideology in American Politics, 1789–1815*, 1972; John Hoadley, *Origins of American Political Parties, 1789–1803*, 1986; Lance Bannon, *The Jeffersonian Persuasion: Evolution of a Party Ideology*, 1980; Garry Wills, *A Necessary Evil: A History of American Distrust of Government*, 1999; James Roger Sharp, *American Politics in the Early Republic: The New Nation in Crisis*, 1995; Joanne B. Freeman, *Affairs of Honor: National Politics in the New Republic*, 2001.

John Adams David McCullough, *John Adams*, 2001; Lynne Withey, *Dearest Friend: A Life of Abigail Adams*, 1981.

KEY TERMS

The following terms are covered in this chapter and can also be found in the list of Key Terms at the back of the book.

assumption	funding	the X, Y, Z Affair	Whiskey Rebellion
broad construction	"Mad Anthony" Wayne	Treaty of San Lorenzo	
Citizen Genêt	strict construction	(Pinckney's Treaty)	

ONLINE SOURCES GUIDE

Use this listing to find online documents, images, interactive maps, simulations, and other resources related to this chapter:

American History Resource Center
http://history.wadsworth.com

Selected Documents
The Treaty of Greenville (1795)
George Washington, Sixth Annual Address to Congress (1794)
The Alien and Sedition Acts (1798)
Washington's Farewell Address

Selected Images
Abigail Adams
John Jay
James Madison
Alexander Hamilton
Sequoya
Pittsburgh in 1790
Diagram of slave ship
Boston's Faneuil Hall, 1789

Interactive Timeline (with online readings)
We The People: Putting the Constitution to Work
1789–1800

Document Exercises
1798 Mr. Gordon's Speech on the Alien Bill

Discovery

In what ways did Washington establish precedents for the first American government that would be observed by future administrations?

In thinking about this question, begin by breaking it down into the components shown below. A discussion of the significance of each component should appear in your answer.

Government and Law: For this exercise, please study this image, "The Whiskey Rebellion," and read the following document excerpts: "Washington's Warning to the Insurgents," and "Tully on the Insurrection in the Western Country." What are the reasons given for sending the military to suppress the Whiskey Rebellion? Why is this considered of such national importance? How does this differ from earlier fears about the power of national government? How does this show an evolution of the Americans toward the importance and power of a national government, especially in light of the failures of the Articles of Confederation?

Brown Brothers

The Whiskey Rebellion

Washington's Warning to the Insurgents

And whereas, by a law of the United States, entitled 'An act to provide for calling forth the militia to execute the laws of the Union, suppress insurrections, and repel invasions,' it is enacted, 'that, whenever the laws of the United States shall be opposed, or the execution of them obstructed in any State by combinations too powerful to be suppressed by the ordinary course of judicial proceedings, or by the powers vested in the marshals by that act, the same being notified by an associate justice or the district judge, it shall be lawful for the President of the United States to call forth the militia of such State to suppress such combinations, and to cause the laws to be duly executed; and, if the militia of a State, when such combinations may happen, shall refuse or be insufficient to suppress the same, it shall be lawful for the President, if the legislature of the United States shall not be in session, to call forth and employ such numbers of the militia of any other State, or States, most convenient thereto, as may be necessary, and the use of the militia so to be called forth may be continued, if necessary, until the expiration of thirty days after the commencement of the ensuing session; provided always, that, whenever it may be necessary in the judgment of the President to use the military force hereby directed to be called forth, the President shall forthwith and previous thereto, by proclamation, command such insurgents to disperse and retire peaceably to their respective abodes within a limited time . . .'

Tully on the Insurrection in the Western County

Let us see then what is this question. It is plainly this – Shall the majority govern or be governed? Shall the nation rule or be ruled? Shall the general will prevail, or the will of a faction? Shall there be government, or no government? It is impossible to deny that this is the true, and the whole question. No art, no sophistry can involve it in the least obscurity.

The Constitution you have ordained for yourselves and your posterity contains this express clause: 'The Congress shall have power to lay and collect taxes, duties, imposts, and excises, to pay the debts, and provide for the common defence and general welfare of the United States.' You have, then, by a solemn and deliberate act, the most important and sacred that a nation can perform, pronounced and decreed, that your representatives in Congress shall have power to lay excises. You have done nothing since to reverse or impair that decree.

Your representatives in Congress, pursuant to the commission derived from you, and with a full knowledge of the public exigencies, have laid an excise. At three succeeding sessions they have revised that act, and have as often, with a degree of unanimity not common, and after the best opportunities of knowing your sense, renewed their sanction to it, you have acquiesced in it, it has gone into general operation: and you have actually paid more than a million of dollars on account of it.

But the four western counties of Pennsylvania, undertake to rejudge and reverse your decrees. You have

said, 'The Congress shall have power to lay excises.' They say, 'The Congress shall not have this power.' Or, what is equivalent – they shall not exercise it: for a power that may not be exercised is a nullity. Your representatives have said, and four times repeated it, 'An excise on distilled spirits shall be collected.' They say it shall not be collected. We will punish, expel, and banish the officers who shall attempt the collection. We will do the same by every other person who shall dare to comply with your decree expressed in the constitutional charter; and with that of your representatives expressed in the laws. The sovereignty shall not reside with you, but with us. If you presume to dispute the point by force, we are ready to measure swords with you, and if unequal ourselves to the contest, we call in the aid of a foreign nation. We will league ourselves with a foreign power.

Politics and Foreign Relations: For this exercise, please study this image, "Mort de Louis XVI" and read the following document excerpt: "George Washington on Foreign Affairs." What reasons did Washington give for avoiding alliances with foreign powers? Did he appear to favor one foreign power over another? How might images such as the illustration of Louis XVI's execution be inflammatory to European governments of the time? Why were Americans initially pleased by what was occurring there? Why might the American government want to remain neutral despite the feelings of many American citizens?

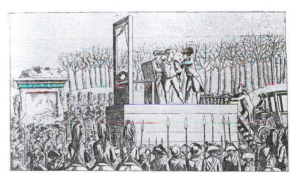

MORT DE LOUIS XVI, LE 21 JANVIER 1793
Place de la Concorde : on voit à gauche le socle de la statue de Louis XV déboulonnée
(Extrait des *Révolutions de Paris*)

Mort de Louis XVI

George Washington on Foreign Affairs

. . . After deliberate examination, with the aid of the best lights I could obtain, I was well satisfied that our country, under all the circumstances of the case, had a right to take, and was bound in duty and interest to take, a neutral position. Having taken it, I determined, as far as should depend upon me, to maintain it, with moderation, perseverance, and firmness. . . .

The duty of holding a neutral conduct may be inferred, without any thing more, from the obligation which justice and humanity impose on every nation, in cases in which it

is free to act, to maintain inviolate the relations of peace and amity towards other nations.

The inducements of interest for observing that conduct will best be referred to your own reflections and experience. With me, a predominant motive has been to endeavour to gain time to our country to settle and mature its yet recent institutions, and to progress without interruption to that degree of strength and consistency, which is necessary to give it, humanly speaking, the command of its own fortunes. . . .

To read extended versions of the documents, visit the companion Web site http://history.wadsworth.com/americanpast8e; click on "Discovery Sources."

CHAPTER 12

Jeffersonian America

Expansion and Frustration 1800–1815

Smithsonian Institution, Bureau of American Ethnology

The immortality of Thomas Jefferson does not lie in any one of his achievements, or in the series of his achievements, but in his attitude toward mankind.

Woodrow Wilson

In 1800, Thomas Jefferson was again to challenge John Adams for the presidency. At the beginning of the year, the political leanings of the states were much as they had been in 1796; the vote in the electoral would again be close. The Federalists were dominant in New England states (although the Jefferson Republicans had grown to be a genuine opposition party in Massachusetts). Except for Charleston and a few pockets in Virginia, the southern states were Republican. The middle states were divided but only New York was hotly contested.

Popular opinion had been wrenched in both directions during Adams's presidency. The Federalist Alien and Sedition Acts were unpopular, but a decade of Republican endorsement of the French Revolution came back to haunt Jefferson and his party when news of the X, Y, Z Affair fired a wave of anti-French war fever. Had Adams nourished that fever, as the Hamilton Federalists were doing, he might well have been reelected. Instead, Adams risked another French insult by sending a new set of negotiators to France in a last ditch effort to keep the peace. On the eve of the election, they secured a settlement. The "quasi-war" was over, but Adams's peace may have sent Republican voters angry with their pro-French leaders back to the party.

THE ELECTION OF 1800

Still, what "the people" wanted did not determine the election winner in 1800. Only five of sixteen states chose electors by popular vote. The bizarre election of 1800—there has never been another like it—was thrown into disarray by the Republican leadership to coordinate their electors and, in the end, after months of scheming, the losers in the electoral college, the Federalists, named the new president.

A COMPLICATED COUNT

In 1796, Adams defeated Jefferson in the electoral college 71 votes to 68. In 1800, Jefferson won by a slightly larger margin, 73 to 65. New York was a key to the swing, and poor Adams knew he had lost New York's votes long before the electors were chosen. In a nasty fight for control of the state in the spring, the Jefferson Republicans, led by Aaron Burr, defeated Hamilton's Federalists. State officials (thanks in part

The African-American Vote

Yet another twist in the bizarre vote count of 1800 was little noted at the time: Jefferson won the election because of the three-fifths compromise, the constitutional provision that slaves (who, obviously, did not vote) count as three-fifths of a person in assigning electoral votes to each state.

Jefferson won 53 of the slave states' 67 electoral votes. If slaves had not been "represented" in the electoral college, Adams would have been reelected president. Historians have calculated that Jefferson owed 14 of his electoral votes (almost 20 percent of them) to the three-fifths compromise.

Monticello: Jefferson's home in Charlottesville, Virginia, the center of one of several plantations he owned. Here, for most of his life, he studied and carried on a correspondence that required many hours daily. He took little interest in agriculture but regularly observed a small, slave-operated shop in which nails were manufactured. Monticello was the love of his life but his debts were so great that his daughter had to sell it.

to Hamilton) chose New York's electors; now they were Jeffersonians. New York's switch from 1796 subtracted 12 electoral votes from Adams's column and added them to Jefferson's.

Even then, Adams would have won the election had his vice presidential candidate, Charles Cotesworth Pinckney, had better control of South Carolina politics. Pinckney, urging loyalty to the Federalist ticket, insisted that South Carolina's eight electors vote for him and Adams. Had they done so, Adams would have been elected president and Pinckney vice president. But the electors wanted to vote for Pinckney and Jefferson, as they had done in 1796. (That formula would have elected Jefferson with Pinckney his vice president.) Pinckney would have none of it and South Carolina's votes went to Jefferson and Burr.

A FAILURE TO COMMUNICATE

That was not the end of it. No Republican elector "threw away" one of his votes on someone who was not a candidate so that Jefferson, the party's choice for president, would have one vote more than the vice presidential candidate, Aaron Burr. (The losing Federalists did not make the same mistake; one Rhode Island elector voted for Adams and John Jay.)

So Jefferson and Burr both had 73 electoral votes. The Constitution provided that, in such a case, the House of Representatives chose the president voting not as individuals but as states, Articles of Confederation style. Republicans had a majority in half of the sixteen state delegations in the House, one short of the majority needed to elect Jefferson. The Federalists controlled six delegations. Two state delegations were evenly split between Republicans and Federalists.

Most of the Federalists preferred Burr, not because he was brilliant, which he was, but because he was an opportunist, a man who would deal. Jefferson the Federalists regarded as immoral, an atheist, a dangerous democratic demagogue, and a French revolutionary who would have blood run in the streets to have his way. (It had been a dirty campaign.)

For thirty-five ballots, the tally was the same: Jefferson eight, Burr six, abstaining two. Burr was in seclusion; he refused to plot with the Federalists but he was willing to have the election stolen for him. He issued only a weak, ambivalent statement saying that Jefferson should be selected. Some Hamiltonian Federalists, through intermediaries, tried—

delicately—to win concessions from Jefferson. He was not antagonistic, but he refused to commit himself to win an office that was rightfully his.

PRESIDENT JEFFERSON

In the end, Jefferson's nemesis, Alexander Hamilton, urged House Federalists to elect Jefferson. Hamilton only disliked Jefferson; he detested Burr. Burr, he said, would surround himself with rogues; "his private character is not defended by his most partial friends." It was not saying much, but Jefferson had "pretensions to character." After the thirty-fifth ballot on a Saturday, Delaware's sole Representative, Federalist James A. Bayard, announced that on Monday he would change his vote from Burr to Jefferson, giving Jefferson a majority. The game was over; several other Federalists faced up to the facts and Jefferson was named president ten states to four with two states abstaining.

So that the fiasco would not be repeated, the **Twelfth Amendment** to the Constitution, ratified in 1804, provided that electors would vote separately for president and vice president, the system in place today.

THE SAGE OF MONTICELLO

Jefferson said that once a man "cast a longing eye" on public office, "a rottenness begins in his conduct." He said quite frequently that he preferred the quiet life of scholar and tinkerer at Monticello to the confrontations of politics and the disquiet of public office. He was dissembling about politics. On the most peaceful days at Monticello, he devoted hours to writing letters to his political supporters. He was an inveterate schemer and manipulator.

As for disliking government service, he was undoubtedly sincere, for his public career had not been distinguished. The vice presidency was a job that made no demands. As secretary of state, Jefferson had been eclipsed, even humiliated, by Hamilton. His four years as minister to France were more holiday than work. His stint as governor of Virginia during the Revolution was a disaster. He was accused of cowardice in the state assembly for fleeing his post when the British invaded the state.

This was unfair. A British detachment had been specifically assigned to capture Jefferson as a trophy and it came close to succeeding. Was he to deliver himself to the redcoats? It was true enough, however, that Jefferson was not personally brave. His enemy Hamilton liked to crack that he was "womanish." (Jefferson was not immune to such jibes nor was he above the gospel of manliness. A superb horseman, he delighted in Hamilton's "timidity" in the saddle.)

But Jefferson's lack of achievement in public office was part of Woodrow Wilson's point when he said that he has been remembered because he put into admirable words a vision of human nature and human liberties that have become our civilization's ideals.

JACK-OF-ALL-TRADES

Jefferson was a scholar with interests ranging from philosophy through linguistics to natural science. His library numbered 6,000 books; it became the core of the Library of Congress, which continued to use Jefferson's classification system until, eighty-two years later, it devised its own. He was a musician; he played the violin, quite well according to those who heard him. He was an architect. He designed and built and redesigned and rebuilt Monticello several times. He

Wine Snob

Jefferson was a moderate drinker. He did not touch spirits, but he liked his wine at dinner, rarely more than two glasses. He subjected many a guest to perhaps lengthier disquisitions on the nuances of the wine they were sipping than they appreciated. As early as 1773, Jefferson gave Filippo Mazzei of Florence 200 acres adjoining his plantation so that he could plant a vineyard from Italian cuttings. Unfortunately, just as it was beginning to produce, Mazzei enlisted to fight the British and never returned.

designed the buildings of the University of Virginia, which he founded. He was an inventor, with the dumbwaiter and the swivel chair among his credits.

He wrote better than any other president has. His English was precise in vocabulary and mellifluous in its rhythms. He authored only one short book, *Notes on Virginia,* but it is superb. Mostly, he wrote letters, a lot of them; 18,000 survive. When it is remembered that most were responses to letters he received—his topic was assigned to him, in other words; he wrote back "off the top of his head" with no rewrites—his perceptiveness and the quality of his language are astonishing.

As a thinker Jefferson was neither original nor profound. His mind was compartmentalized, unlike Hamilton's or Adams's or Madison's. One historian has called him a "fragmentarian," which is a good reason to take care when using the term "Jeffersonian" to describe anything more systematic than a point of view. Inevitably, he was inconsistent and self-contradictory. In the abstract, he praised farming above all other ways of life but the nitty-gritty of agriculture bored him. He called cities "pestilential to the morals, the health, and the liberties of man," and was particularly harsh on New York and Philadelphia. But he lived ecstatically in Paris at a time when the misery of the Parisian poor—a

The Jefferson Republicans Triumphant 1801–1815

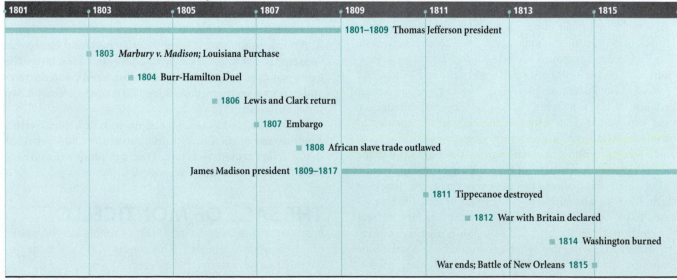

1801	1803	1805	1807	1809	1811	1813	1815

1801–1809 Thomas Jefferson president

1803 *Marbury v. Madison*; Louisiana Purchase

1804 Burr-Hamilton Duel

1806 Lewis and Clark return

1807 Embargo

1808 African slave trade outlawed

James Madison president 1809–1817

1811 Tippecanoe destroyed

1812 War with Britain declared

1814 Washington burned

War ends; Battle of New Orleans 1815

Shop 'Till You Drop

Jefferson is the patron saint of economical government, an honor he deserves. He insisted that Gallatin count pennies when he drafted federal budgets. Personally, however, Jefferson was a spendthrift. He spent as much as $2,800 a year on wine, and up to $50 a day on groceries when a turkey cost 50 cents. Twice when he had a new architectural idea, he had much of

Monticello torn down and rebuilt. In Paris during the 1780s, he lived as extravagantly as the French nobles with whom he hobnobbed; when he visited John and Abigail Adams (they were then personal friends) the frenzy of his shopping spree appalled the thrifty New Englanders.

Already rich in land and slaves, he inherited more acreage and slaves from his wife when she died in 1782—and also a

huge debt her father had bequeathed her. Jefferson was never again out of debt and he never made a serious attempt at belt tightening to reduce it. He sold slaves, land, and even his beloved library when creditors threatened to take legal action. Even then, when he died in 1826, he saddled his daughter with so much debt that she had to sell Monticello, national shrine that it was.

large majority of the population—made New York and Philadelphia look like heavenly cities.

He denounced slavery eloquently in his younger years and, his entire life, when pressed, he said the institution was a curse on everyone involved in it. But he owned hundreds of slaves each of the last fifty years of his life and allowed only two to go free (both, probably, his own children). When he needed money, he raised it by selling slaves, 160 on a single occasion. And, when northerners began to criticize southerners for clinging to slavery, he was all but explicit in saying that if the institution was seriously threatened, Virginia would be justified in leaving the Union.

Jefferson could be juvenile, as when he said that every generation should write its own constitution and that, given a choice between government without newspapers and newspapers without government, he would opt for the latter. It takes an exhausting search, but he even wrote a few sentences that, on a freshman's term paper, would be circled in red ink: "The President is fortunate to get off as the bubble is bursting, leaving others to hold the bag."

CONTINUITIES

Jefferson was a hypnotic conversationalist but he hated to give speeches. He mumbled his inaugural address, which—tacitly acknowledging that, days earlier, Federalists had ensured his election—was conciliatory and non-partisan. "Every difference of opinion is not a difference in principle," he said, "We have called by different names brethren of the same principle. We are all republicans, we are all federalists."

Jefferson did quietly shelve some of his pre-presidential positions and he left some Federalist programs in place. Nothing more was heard of the right of states to nullify federal laws within their borders. He allowed Hamilton's financial edifice to stand; like Washington and Adams, he deposited federal revenues in the Bank of the United States that he had called unconstitutional and a servant of speculators. He appointed as secretary of the treasury a Swiss-born Pennsylvanian, Albert Gallatin, who was a responsible money manager.

DEPARTURES

However, Jefferson rejected the Hamiltonian shibboleth that national debt was a blessing. Gallatin devised a schedule for eliminating the government's debt by 1817. Jefferson slashed

expenditures high under Washington and Adams. The army's appropriations budget was reduced from $4 million to $2 million, the navy's from $3.5 million to $1 million. Jefferson pardoned everyone convicted under the Sedition Act, all of them his supporters, of course. He restored the five-year residency for citizenship and replaced many Federalists drawing government salaries with Republicans. He did not have much patronage to hand out. The federal government employed 3,000 but most were postal employees and customs collectors who were paid little for doing hard work. Jefferson had only about 300 more or less desirable jobs at his disposal.

Jefferson brought a new style to the presidency. He disliked the pomp and protocol of the Federalist administrations. Instead of bowing, he shook hands. He abolished presidential levees (regularly scheduled, highly formal receptions) and, much to the annoyance of high-ranking officials and diplomats, he paid scant attention to the rules assigning a rank of precedence—a chair at the dinner table, a position in a procession—to every senator, representative, judge, cabinet member, and minister from abroad. Even at state dinners, guests had to scramble for the places they believed appropriate to their dignity. At the small dinner parties he preferred, Jefferson served his guests himself.

Jefferson's "republican simplicity" was made easier by the move of the capital, the summer before his inauguration, from sophisticated Philadelphia to Washington. Washington was not really a city in 1801. It was a hodgepodge of partly constructed public buildings and ramshackle boarding houses isolated from one another by dense woods and swamps in which strangers regularly got lost. There were few private homes. For decades to come, there would be no houses suitable for congressmen's families. Wives and children stayed home. Capital social life was masculine and on the raw side: smoky card games, heavy drinking, even brawls.

These departures hardly constituted the "Revolution of 1800" that Jefferson called his election. The only fundamental innovation in government during Jefferson's presidency was effected by his cousin but also his personal enemy, the Federalist Chief Justice of the Supreme Court, John Marshall.

MARBURY V. MADISON

During John Adams's last weeks as president, he appointed forty-two Federalists to various federal courts. Federal judges served for life, so Adams was securing long-term employment for loyal supporters and ensuring Federalist principles in the judiciary for years.

However, the document that entitled one William Marbury to a judgeship was, somehow, not gotten to him before March 4, when Jefferson was sworn in. The Judiciary Act of 1789 required the secretary of state to deliver such commissions once they were signed. However, Jefferson's secretary of state, James Madison, refused to do so. Marbury sued for a *writ of mandamus,* a court order that means "we compel" a government official to perform a duty.

In 1803, the case reached the Supreme Court. As he would for three decades, Chief Justice Marshall dominated the other justices. The force of his personality was such, his willingness to do the lion's share of the Court's work was so eager, and his legal arguments were so acute, that Marshall almost always had his way.

In the case of *Marbury* v. *Madison,* Marshall scolded Madison for his unseemly behavior. However, instead of commanding him to deliver Marbury's commission (which might well have precipitated a grave constitutional crisis), Marshall ruled that Madison need not do so because the section of the Judiciary Act Marbury cited was unconstitutional (for reasons unrelated to his dispute with Madison). Congress did not have the power, under the Constitution, to enact the law it had.

JUDICIAL REVIEW

Marbury v. *Madison* may not have been unassailable constitutional law. It was, however, a political masterstroke with profound implications. By sacrificing the paycheck of one Federalist politico and negating part of one Federalist law, Marshall asserted the Supreme Court's power to decide whether or not acts of Congress signed by the president were constitutional, voiding those the Court decided were not. The Supreme Court, Marshall said, not only judged cases according to the law; it judged the validity the law itself.

Nothing in the Constitution vested the Court with this substantial power; short of Constitutional amendment, it trumped both the executive and legislative branches of the government. Implicitly, *Marbury* v. *Madison* condemned the contention in the Kentucky and Virginia Resolutions that state legislatures had the power to find federal laws unconstitutional. (Marshall could not have known that Jefferson and Madison had written the resolutions, but he knew that Jefferson Republicans had.) Marshall had no intention of wielding the power of **judicial review** recklessly. His Court never again judged an act of Congress unconstitutional. But he put a mighty power on the books.

Unable to fight Marshall on high ground, Jefferson launched a campaign of machination and low blows against the Federalist judiciary. He tried to get rid of some Federalist judges by abolishing their jobs. Then the Republicans impeached and removed from office a Federalist judge in New Hampshire, John Pickering. Pickering was easy pickings; he was given to drunken tirades in court and was probably insane.

But Jefferson went too far when his supporters inched closer to Marshall by impeaching Supreme Court Justice Samuel Chase. Chase was an inferior jurist. He was grossly prejudiced, overtly partisan, and sometimes asinine. But the Senate, despite a Republican majority, refused to find him guilty of the "high crimes and misdemeanors" that the Constitution defines as grounds for impeachment. Like other presidents unhappy with the Supreme Court, Jefferson had no choice but to wait until seats fell vacant in order to change its complexion. He was to appoint three Justices, but they too were captivated by Marshall's mind and will.

THE LOUISIANA PURCHASE

If John Marshall tweaked the Constitution, Jefferson gave it a shake in the most significant achievement of his presidency, the purchase of Louisiana for $15 million. The Louisiana of 1803 was not the present-day state of the name. As a French (later Spanish) colony, Louisiana included the better part of the thirteen states that lie between the Mississippi River and the Rocky Mountains, 828,000 square miles. The United States paid less than three cents an acre for Louisiana; it was the greatest real estate bargain of all time.

SUGAR AND FOODSTUFFS

The purchase was possible because the Emperor of the French, Napoleon Bonaparte, was forced by events to abandon his plan to revive France's continental American empire. France still retained two small sugar-producing islands in the West Indies—Martinique and Guadeloupe—and, nominally, large and lucrative San Domingo, where a large slave population produced coffee as well as sugar.

But they produced little food. To feed the slaves, the islands imported foodstuffs, mostly from Louisiana, Spanish since 1763. In 1801, Napoleon forced Spain, a client state, to return Louisiana to France. The transfer was supposed to be secret but was common knowledge. There were only about 50,000 people of European descent in the province but, with enough French immigrants, it would be an agricultural cornucopia.

On Napoleon's instructions, the Spanish revoked the right of deposit in New Orleans that Pinckney's Treaty had gained for the United States. This was bad news for the 400,000 Americans living in the Mississippi Valley. Annually, they had been shipping 20,000 tons of provisions to New Orleans as well as lumber in the form of the rafts that carried the grain and livestock. To westerners, in James Madison's words, the Mississippi was "the Hudson, the Delaware, the Potomac, and all the navigable rivers of the Atlantic formed into one stream." Jefferson added, "There is on the globe one single spot, the possessor of which is our natural and habitual enemy. It is New Orleans."

War with France, so recently averted, seemed inevitable. Congress voted to call up 80,000 state militiamen. But an overland attack on New Orleans would have to be backed up by a naval blockade, which Jefferson's evisceration of the

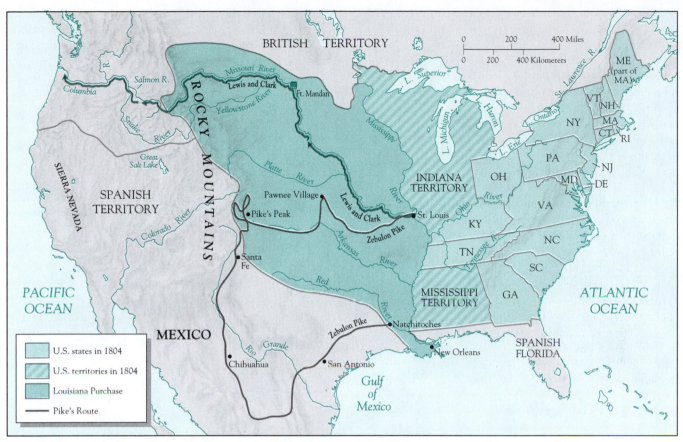

MAP 12:1 Louisiana and the Expeditions of Discovery, 1804–1807

The Louisiana Purchase doubled the area of the United States. Except for the banks of the Mississippi and Missouri Rivers, little was known about the country and its native peoples until the federally sponsored explorations of the Lewis and Clark expedition through the northern parts of Louisiana and of a semiofficial Zebulon Pike party in the south.

navy made impossible. Moreover, while Jefferson was never a pacifist, he always preferred diplomatic resolutions of conflicts to war.

AN OFFER NOT TO BE REFUSED

He instructed his minister to France, Robert Livingston, to offer Napoleon $2 million (voted him by Congress) for a tract of undeveloped land on the lower Mississippi where the Americans could build their own entrepôt for western exports. In January 1803, uneasy because there had been no message from Livingston, Jefferson sent James Monroe to Paris to offer up to $10 million (a sum that had appeared in no congressional appropriation) for New Orleans and West Florida (the gulf coast of Mississippi and Alabama).

When Monroe arrived, he was stunned to learn that, just a few days earlier, the French foreign minister (Talleyrand again) had offered to sell Livingston the whole of Louisiana for $15 million. This remarkable turnabout had nothing to do with American wants and needs. Louisiana had become worthless to Napoleon. Black rebels in Haiti had, with the help of tropical disease, utterly destroyed one of Napoleon's best armies. Some 30,000 experienced French troops had been lost. Haiti was in the hands of its former slaves. "Damn

sugar," Napoleon exploded on hearing of the debacle, "Damn coffee. Damn colonies! Damn niggers!"

He might have added Great Britain to the list for Napoleon was planning to go to war with the old enemy and he knew that as soon as he did, the Royal Navy would seize New Orleans and occupy Louisiana. So, he decided to trade the province for money.

CONSTITUTIONAL NICETIES

Livingston and Monroe signed off on the Louisiana Purchase and Jefferson sealed it despite the fact that Congress had authorized spending $2 million, not $15 million. Much more embarrassing—for Jefferson's party controlled Congress—the Constitution said nothing about such acquisitions nor did it provide for conferring citizenship on the French and Spanish residents of Louisiana as the agreement with Napoleon required. According to the "strict construction" of the Constitution that Jefferson had propounded, the Louisiana Purchase was unconstitutional.

Jefferson, sheepishly, wrote, "What is practicable must often control what is pure theory." Confidentially, he instructed Republicans in Congress that "the less we say about constitutional difficulties respecting Louisiana the better."

York was one of the most valuable members of the Lewis and Clark expedition, strong, rarely ill, resourceful in the wilderness, decisive in crises. He was William Clark's slave and, despite his services, Clark had to be pressured to reward him with his freedom by friends distressed by Clark's reluctance to do so.

The Louisiana Purchase was too amazing a stroke of good fortune to be rejected. Jefferson said (without much thought) that it would provide farms for Americans for a thousand years. Even Republicans far more zealous in their Jefferson principles than the president, notably John Randolph of Roanoke, held their tongues. Federalists gleefully made hay of Jefferson's "hypocrisy" but they did not oppose a nationalistic stroke bolder than anything Hamilton had dared.

THE MAGNIFICENT JOURNEY

Geographically, Louisiana was a mystery. Only a few trappers and traders had wandered far from the Mississippi and Missouri River. Congress appropriated a modest $2,500 to finance an expedition of exploration to gather scientific information and to search for a feasible overland route to the Pacific.

Jefferson assigned the mission to a Virginia neighbor, Meriwether Lewis, to head the expedition. Lewis persuaded William Clark, his friend and former commanding officer, to be a co-commander (although, officially, Lewis was the chief). Jefferson, who was himself no traveler, attended to the

most picayune details of preparation, listing in his own hand the provisions the explorers would need.

The journey of Lewis and Clark exceeded anything ventured by conquistadors or voyageurs. A party of forty men (and, for most of the way, a girl and her baby) and a Newfoundland dog rowed, poled, and pulled their skiffs up

African American Explorer

In the informality wilderness enforces, William Clark's slave, York, participated in the great expedition as an equal. Meriwether Lewis recorded that when Indians first saw York, they thought he was a white man wearing paint and tried to remove it. Lewis noted that "instead of inspiring any prejudice, his color served to procure him additional advantages from the Indians," a decorous way of saying that a number of Indian ladies wanted to have a black child. Clark freed York after the expedition, but rather gracelessly. Despite York's invaluable services, Clark had to be pressured by Lewis and others to do the right thing.

From the Collections of The New Jersey Historical Society, Newark, New Jersey

Pike's Expedition

Shortly before Lewis and Clark arrived back in St. Louis in 1806, **Zebulon Pike**, an army officer with seventeen men, left the city to explore the southern part of the Louisiana Purchase. At the Rockies ("Pike's Peak") he headed south to Santa Fe and deep into Mexico, returning to Louisiana the next year. His exploits were not so celebrated as those of the Lewis and Clark Expedition, in part because Jefferson suspected him of scouting for Aaron Burr. Unknowingly, he may have been doing just that. He was sent west not by the president but on the orders of Louisiana governor Wilkinson, whose actual relationship with Burr is unknown.

Young Aaron Burr painted by Gilbert Stuart. He was handsome, charming, intelligent, and persuasive. But unlike his political enemy, Hamilton, and his sometimes political ally, Jefferson, he was guided by no principles and he had no goals but his own advancement. Even his friends conceded his amorality. The nature of his later adventures, obscure at the time, remain mysterious. Burr put little in writing; his "papers" are scant.

the Missouri to the spectacular falls now the site of Great Falls, Montana. Learning from the Mandan, Shoshone, and Nez Percé Indians that a portage of sixteen miles would bring them to a river flowing westerly, they deduced that it was a tributary of the Columbia River. (The mouth of the Columbia had been discovered only in 1792.) They reached the Pacific on November 15, 1805. There they lived four and a half months—it rained every day but twelve—and returned to St. Louis in September 1806.

Lewis and Clark were among the last Americans to contact Indians untouched by white civilization. Their experience is instructive. Although they had a few uneasy moments with the Sioux and Shoshone on the journey west, the explorers were involved in nothing resembling conflict with the many tribes with whom they dealt. (There was a skirmish with Blackfoot Indians on the return trip.) The native peoples of the interior were not only friendly, they were hospitable and generous once they learned that Lewis and Clark were not members of enemy tribes. When Lewis needed to prove this, he exposed his arm, which was not sunburned brown, to show that his skin was white. York, Clark's slave, was a source of endless fascination because of his color. Indians rubbed him raw, thinking he had painted himself black.

The touchiest moment on the westbound trip was with the Shoshone, who, at first, were not friendly. In the single most astonishing moment of the journey, Sacajawea, a Shoshone teenager carrying her infant son, recognized her brother among the Shoshone warriors. Sacajawea had been kidnapped by another tribe as a girl and been purchased as a wife by a Frenchman whom Lewis and Clark hired as a guide.

The tribes of the Pacific coast were familiar with whites—American and British seamen, whalers, and fur traders who camped among them. One woman had the name "Jonathan Bowman" tattooed on her leg. The coastal Indians had adopted into their language the words "misquito," "powder," "shot," "nife," "file," "damned rascal," and "son of a bitch."

THE BURR-HAMILTON DUEL

Louisiana also attracted the attention of Vice President Aaron Burr. His political fortunes tumbled downhill immediately after the election of 1800. Jefferson snubbed him, believing (incorrectly) that Burr had tried to betray him when the deadlocked electoral college sent the election to the House of Representatives. And the energetic Burr found the emptiness of the vice presidency stultifying.

When men like Burr are bored, they scheme. When Burr schemed, he schemed big. Apparently—Burr's plots were so secretive (he put almost nothing on paper) that little of them can be confirmed—Burr discussed detaching New York and New England from the United States with a few embittered Federalists called the "Essex Junto." The plan—if it got far enough to be called a plan—depended on Burr winning the governorship of New York. He was defeated, in part because of campaign propaganda authored by Alexander Hamilton. The men exchanged insults. Burr challenged Hamilton to a duel.

Hamilton disapproved of dueling; his son had been killed in one shortly before Burr's challenge. But the era's code of masculine honor left him no way out. On July 11, 1804, Burr and Hamilton, with their seconds and surgeons, and two .54 caliber dueling pistols, rowed across the Hudson to Weehawken, high on the New Jersey Palisades. They fired at one another from 20 paces. Hamilton's bullet went astray; his seconds said he deliberately shot high, as reluctant duelists often did. Burr aimed; his bullet pierced Hamilton's liver and lodged in his spine. He died the next day.

The first secretary of the treasury was never beloved, but the death of so eminent a man in a duel was shocking. Burr was indicted for murder in New York and New Jersey. He fled to the South while friends ironed out his legal difficulties. Not yet fifty years of age and full of energy, his political career was finished. What next?

THE BURR CONSPIRACY

Burr went west. He linked up with one Harman Blennerhasset, an Irish exile who lived opulently, on wealth never explained, on an island in the Ohio River. Blennerhasset financed the construction of thirteen flatboats, including a barge for Burr outfitted with glass windows, a fireplace, a promenade deck, and a wine cellar. With sixty men, the flotilla meandered slowly down the Ohio and the Mississippi.

Burr met secretly with Andrew Jackson, a prominent politician and soldier in Tennessee, and, in New Orleans, with the head of the French Ursuline Convent, Louisiana's most powerful woman. He had a number of discussions with James Wilkinson, the territorial governor of Louisiana and a character so chicaning and devious that, next to him, Burr was a choirboy.

What did they plan to do? Later, Burr was accused by some of planning to invade Spanish Mexico, by others of detaching the Louisiana Territory from the United States. Jefferson was of a mind to believe the worst. Wilkinson, possibly in a panic

as to what he had said in the secret talks, accused Burr of treason. Burr was arrested and tried in Richmond before Chief Justice John Marshall.

Marshall was apt to snipe at anything dear to Jefferson, even if it was to the benefit of the likes of Aaron Burr. But he was justified in his insistence that treason be defined as requiring an overt act. No matter: the prosecution's case was sloppy; few accusations were corroborated; and the unsavory Wilkinson was a weak reed on which to support so serious an allegation. Burr was acquitted. He lived abroad for a few years, then returned to New York where he prospered as a lawyer.

FOREIGN WOES

Like Washington and Adams, Jefferson was frustrated by foreign affairs. Unlike his predecessors, Jefferson contributed to his discomfiture by reducing the navy Adams had created to a few ships. The American merchant fleet was rivaled in size only by Great Britain's. A country with such vital interests in international trade needed to be able to protect its ships. Jefferson's agrarianism could be extreme and tunnel-visioned and, in his second term, he paid for it.

The Rhode Island Historical Society

Stephen Decatur led several punitive expeditions against the Barbary States. In this painting his fleet is bombarding Tripoli in present-day Libya. Decatur's assaults were popular and effective in the United States—but only for a time. The Barbary States remained a threat to commerce in the Mediterranean until France began to seize control of north Africa.

THE BARBARY PIRATES

One trouble spot was the Mediterranean, where the Barbary ("Berber") states of Morocco, Algiers, Tunis, and Tripoli seized the vessels of nations that did not pay tribute to the beys and pashas who ruled them. They held captured crews for ransom and, if they were not ransomed, enslaved them. France, Britain, Spain, Holland, and Venice found the expense of such "protection money" less than the cost of posting warships permanently off north African shores. During the 1790s, the United States paid too, possibly as much as $2 million over a decade.

The indignity of paying tribute, even when dressed up as gifts, rankled on Jefferson. He ignored the demand of the pasha of Tripoli for the 1801 installment. Tripolitan pirates promptly seized the crew of several American ships and demanded ransom. Instead, Jefferson dispatched warships commanded by Stephen Decatur and William Eaton. When the frigate *Philadelphia* ran aground in Tripoli, 309 officers and men were captured. After four years of intermittent bombardment, a daring amphibious raid by marines led by Decatur ("to the shores of Tripoli," as in the Marine Corps hymn), and Eaton's capture of the port in 1805, a settlement was negotiated. All the Americans were freed in return for a payment of $60,000. Barbary piracy continued for another decade when Decatur returned to the Mediterranean and France began to establish imperial control over north Africa.

CAUGHT IN THE MIDDLE AGAIN

A more serious problem was the Anglo-French war that began shortly after the purchase of Louisiana. Jefferson declared neutrality and, as during the 1790s, American shipowners reaped bonanza profits trading with both sides. Particularly lucrative was the re-export trade: West Indian sugar and molasses brought to the United States, then shipped to Europe under the neutral American flag. In two years, the re-export business quadrupled in value from $13 million to $60 million.

Then, in 1805, the war reached an impasse. The Royal Navy was supreme at sea; Napoleon, after three major victories in rapid succession, was unchallengeable on the European continent. Both sides dug in for a protracted economic war, each aiming to ruin the other by crippling its trade. The British issued the Orders in Council, which forbade neutrals (meaning the United States) to trade in Europe unless their ships first

A British press gang forces a crewman from an American merchantman into service in the Royal Navy. The British insisted that they pressed only British subjects, but many men born under the British flag considered themselves Americans, and mistakes were made. If a pressed seaman survived and later proved he was American-born, he was released but not compensated.

called at a British port to purchase a license. New England merchants, who inclined to be pro-British anyway, did not find the Orders intolerable; Britain was on the way. However, Napoleon retaliated with the Berlin and Milan decrees of 1806 and 1807. They enacted what Napoleon called the Continental System: the French would seize neutral vessels that observed the Orders in Council.

American merchants were caught in the middle. Within a year the British seized 1,000 American ships and the French about 500. Even then, the wartime trade was profitable. A Massachusetts senator calculated that if a merchant sent three ships out and two were dead losses, the profits from the third made up for his losses. Statistics bear him out. In 1807, at the height of the seizures, Massachusetts merchants earned $15 million in freight charges.

IMPRESSMENT AGAIN

There was more at stake than confiscated ships. The Royal Navy, bigger than ever, had an enormous manpower shortage. Commanders with crews decimated by disease, desertion, and battle turned again to impressing replacements from American as well as British vessels. The British insisted that they pressed only British subjects. There were plenty of them on American vessels; a seaman of an American ship was paid as much as three times as much as British merchant sailors were. Probably 10,000 of the 42,000 men sailing American ships had been born in Britain or in British colonies.

Many of them were naturalized American citizens, a transfer of allegiance the British did not recognize. And there were plenty of "mistakes," American-born sailors impressed into the Royal Navy. Between 1803 and 1812, about 6,000 United States citizens were forced into service by British press gangs. (If naval commanders at sea were not inclined to observe the rules strictly, British courts were; some 4,000 pressed Americans were released when they reached a British port.)

The **impressment** crisis came to a head in June 1807. When HMS *Leopard,* with fifty guns, was resupplying in the Chesapeake Bay, four sailors deserted. Safely on American soil, they taunted their officers and told them they had signed up in the American navy, aboard a frigate, the *Chesapeake.* The *Leopard* sailed off and waited for the *Chesapeake.* When the American ship refused to allow the British to board, the *Leopard* fired three broadsides, killing eighteen sailors. A press gang boarded and seized the four deserters.

Three of the four were blacks, two of them American born. Newspapers and politicians made little of their race (which would have diluted the impact of their propaganda) but much of Britain's arrogant insult of the nation's honor. They had a point; the *Chesapeake* was not a merchantman making a dollar for a Boston merchant, but a flagship of the American navy. The patriotic uproar was deafening. Jefferson, who had hoped to resolve the impressment crisis by negotiation, had to act. Still, he meant to avoid war with Great Britain. He chose what he called "peaceable coercion," the Embargo Act of 1807.

THE EMBARGO

The Embargo Act forbade American ships in port to set sail for foreign ports. (Ships bound for another American port— the coastal trade—were not affected.) Foreign vessels in American ports had to depart in ballast (carrying boulders or other worthless bulk in their hulls; no cargos). All imports and exports were prohibited. Jefferson was applying the same economic pressure on Great Britain that had been so successful in his youth in winning the repeal of the Townshend Acts. He believed that the American trade was so vital to Great Britain that the Embargo would win a satisfactory settlement of the conflict without going to war.

Unfortunately, he overrated the importance of the American trade. The British had other sources of the foodstuffs the Americans produced, not as profitable or convenient, but adequate. Moreover, the interdiction of trade was riddled with holes. American merchant vessels left port with cargos bound for other American ports and sailed to the West Indies or Great Britain. Smugglers taking exports across the border into Canada were so numerous and brazen that customs officials could only watch.

Worse, the Embargo hurt Americans more than it hurt the British. Exports, $108 million in 1807, collapsed to $22 million in 1808. Seaports from Baltimore north to Portland, Maine had ships rotting at anchor and tens of thousands of seamen and shore laborers out of work. Small businesses dependent on their wages closed their doors. The Federalist party, badly maimed when Jefferson was reelected in 1804, began to make a comeback in New England and New York. Farmers in Pennsylvania and the western states remained good Republicans but they complained vociferously when their crops, raised for export, could not be sold.

Although Jefferson continued to believe it would work, Congress did not. In the final days of Jefferson's administration, Congress repealed the Embargo Act as of March 15, 1809, placating the president by replacing it with the Non-Intercourse Act, which reopened trade with all nations except Britain and France. Non-Intercourse provided that the president could reopen trade with either of the warring nations when it agreed to respect American shipping.

Not happily, Jefferson signed the repeal of the Embargo and the Non-Intercourse Acts just three days before he was to turn the presidency over to his handpicked successor, James Madison.

JEMMY APPLEJOHN AND THE WAR OF 1812

James Madison was a profound political philosopher whose writings are still studied. But Madison was even less suited to be a head of a government than Jefferson was. His only

The Two-Term Tradition

When Washington rejected a third term as president, he made no point of principle about it. He was old and tired, he said. When Jefferson said he would retire after two terms, he understood that his choice was historically significant. "A few more precedents," he wrote, "will oppose the obstacle of habit to anyone after a while who shall endeavor to extend his term. Perhaps it may beget a disposition to establish it by an amendment to the Constitution."

Madison, Monroe, and Andrew Jackson all retired after two terms. So did Ulysses S. Grant, although he later tried to run again. Theodore Roosevelt retired after nearly eight years in office although, having been elected only once, he could have run again without violating the tradition. Like Grant, Roosevelt tried to get the White House back four years after leaving it. Woodrow Wilson and Calvin Coolidge would both have liked to have had a third term, but dared not say it, so powerful had the tradition become. Only in 1940, with Europe at war, did Franklin D. Roosevelt seek and win a third term (and four years later, a fourth).

Republican hatred for FDR was so intense that, in 1947, two years after Roosevelt died, they had a kick at him by proposing the Twenty-Second Amendment to the Constitution. Ratified, it forbids a president more than two terms. Ironically, the two presidents since who could probably have won a third term, had it been constitutional, were Republicans, Dwight D. Eisenhower and Ronald Reagan.

The Emperor of America

Madison was content to be addressed as "Mr. President" but, in a communiqué, the Bey of Algiers called him:

His Majesty, the Emperor of America, its adjacent and dependent provinces and coasts and wherever his government may extend, our noble friend, the support of the Kings of the nation of Jesus, the most glorious amongst the princes, elected among many lords and nobles, the happy, the great, the amiable, James Madison, Emperor of America.

executive experience was as Jefferson's secretary of state and he lacked his idol's prestige. Jefferson's enemies vilified him; Madison's enemies (the same crowd) ridiculed him. They mocked his short stature—his famous wife, Dolley, towered over him—his pinched face, deeply furrowed even at age fifty. The writer Washington Irving quipped that "Little Jemmy" looked like a "withered applejohn," a dried apple. Madison was "too timid," Federalist Fisher Ames said. He was "wholly unfit for the Storms of War," according to a young Jefferson Republican, Henry Clay.

NON-INTERCOURSE AND MACON'S BILL NO. 2

The embargo expired on March 15, 1809, when the Non-Intercourse Act was to go into effect. Before that date, David Erskine, the British minister in Washington, signed a treaty agreeing to the terms under which Madison was empowered to resume trade with Great Britain. In April, Madison did so and hundreds of American ships left port with cargos destined for Great Britain. Many had loaded up with British manufactures and were headed back when the British foreign minister repudiated Erskine's treaty. A humiliated and angry Madison reinstated Non-Intercourse while customs officials tried to clean up the mess—which goods coming into port were legal, which not?

In May 1810, Congress replaced Non-Intercourse with Macon's Bill No. 2. It opened commerce with both Britain and France with the proviso that if either of the two ceased to molest American shipping, the United States would cut off trade with the other. Macon's Bill No. 2 invited mischief. It pledged the United States to become, in effect, the ally in an economic war with whichever of the two belligerents acted first.

Napoleon acted, or seemed to do so. In fact, his revocation of parts of the Continental System concerning American shipping was transparently designed to embroil the Americans and British in a shooting war. It did, despite the fact that Britain revoked the Orders in Council in order to re-open trade with the United States. Once again, and not for the last time, the weeks it took for communications to cross the Atlantic played a major role in events. The British met American demands on June 16, 1812. Two days later, pressured by anti-British "War Hawks" in Congress, Madison asked Congress for a formal declaration of war.

OPPOSITION TO THE WAR

Madison asked for war in the interests of American commerce and the thousands of American seamen who were being impressed into the Royal Navy. However, New England's mercantile interests opposed going to war and they remained hostile to the war effort throughout the conflict. In the House of Representatives, New England, New York, and New Jersey voted 34 to 14 against the declaration of war. Not a single Federalist voted for war. Connecticut's governor refused to allow militia to leave the state. In 1814 and 1815, Federalists from Massachusetts, Connecticut, and Rhode Island met in Hartford to discuss their grievances with "Mr. Madison's War."

A few delegates at the Hartford Convention spoke openly in favor of seceding from the union. Although Republicans called the convention itself treasonous, moderate Federalists unsympathetic to the "young hotheads" controlled the meeting. The Convention's resolutions called only for such reforms as reducing the political power of the southern states (which New Englanders blamed for the war), and abolishing the three-fifths compromise, for example.

A few southern congressmen denounced the war, notably John Randolph of Roanoke and his followers, the *Tertium Quids* (Latin for the "third somethings"; they were not Federalists, they said, not Republicans, but something else). The Quids had broken with Jefferson and Madison in 1806. They considered themselves the true Jeffersonians. Jefferson and Madison had betrayed the party's pure principles, which Randolph listed as love of peace, hatred of offensive war, jealousy of the state governments toward the general government; a dread of standing armies; a loathing of public debt, taxes, and excises; tenderness for the liberty of the citizen; and Argus-eyed jealousy of the patronage of the President. In 1812, Randolph accused Madison of embracing Hamiltonian militarism. Not one to mince words, he said that the president's army was an assembly of "mercenaries picked up from brothels and tippling houses."

THE WAR HAWKS

Who wanted war? Most Republicans representing agricultural regions voted for it. The Pennsylvania, southern, and western delegations in the House voted 65 to 15 to go to war. They were led by a young and exuberant circle of congressmen—many just elected for the first time—known as **"War Hawks."** They brimmed with the cocky belligerence of youth and they were super-nationalists. They had been educated by Jefferson and his followers to regard Great Britain as the national enemy. They dreamed of completing the Revolution by conquering Canada and annexing it to the United States.

The notion of conquering Canada was not far-fetched. Many Americans had settled in Upper Canada, present-day Ontario. Some openly called for making the region an American state. Militarily, the prospects looked good. Locked in mortal battle with Napoleon, Great Britain had reduced the professional army in Canada to a few thousand soldiers. Canadian militias had no better reputations than those of their American counterparts.

Frontier Society   *How They Lived*

Europeans touring newly settled parts of the United States, such as the Northwest Territory, complained about the food, invariably greasy fried salt pork and cornmeal mush or fire-roasted corn bread. They were shocked by the heavy drinking. But most of all they shuddered at the isolation in which the people lived. Frances Trollope, an English woman who wrote a celebrated book, *The Domestic Manners of the Americans,* met a tough pioneering woman just a few miles outside of bustling Cincinnati. The woman showed off her farm, boasting that it produced everything her household consumed except tea, sugar, and whiskey. When Mrs. Trollope rose to depart, her hostess sighed and said, "'Tis strange for us to see company; I expect the sun may rise and set a hundred times before I shall see another human that does not belong to the family."

Frontier life was lonely, but it was not without social occasions. In northern Ohio during the 1820s, which William Cooper Howells, a printer, saw develop from wild forest into a populous industrial center, he looked back on the parties of his youth with fond nostalgia. Ohio pioneers, Howells wrote, combined amusement with work. The raising of a cabin or barn was done collectively by neighbors. The host had cut all the logs he needed. They were brought to the building site by means of a community "logroll." The men who were best with an ax notched the logs at each end; others raised them into place. "The men understood handling timber," Howells wrote, "and accidents seldom happened, unless the logs were icy or wet or the whisky had gone around too often." Howells himself, still quite a young man in Ohio's early years, took pride in taking on the job of "cornerman." While others built the walls, he "dressed up" the corners with an axe. "It was a post of honor." The job was less laborious than that of raising the walls, but it took a head that "was steady when high up from the ground."

When a gathering of men for such a purpose took place there was commonly some sort of mutual job laid out for

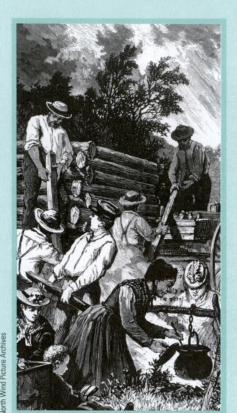

North Wind Picture Archives

women, such as quilting, sewing, or spinning up a lot of thread for some poor neighbor. This would bring together a mixed party, and it was usually arranged that after supper there should be a dance or at least plays which would occupy a good part of the night and wind up with the young fellows seeing the girls home in the short hours or, if they went home early, sitting with them by the fire in that kind of interesting chat known as sparking.

In addition to logrolling and barn raisings, the tedious task of processing flax (for linen and oil) was done in combination with a community party. Other tasks—splitting logs into rails for fences, for example—were spiced up by holding a competition. Abraham Lincoln first ran for political office on his reputation as a virtuoso rail-splitter. But by far the most enjoyable kind of work party, remembered wistfully in practically every reminiscence, was the husking bee. Not only was the job of husking Indian corn less laborious than other jobs, the bees took place in the autumn, when the harvest was done and the weather cool.

The ears of corn were divided into two piles. Two captains chose up sides, selecting their teams alternately from among the young men, boys, young women, and girls. The two teams fell to husking, standing with the heap in front of them, and throwing the husked corn to a clear space, and the husks (for animal fodder) behind them. There was no pause except to take a pull at the jug of inspiration that was passed along the line.

When one team had finished husking, they let out a great shout (which was the signal to lay a community dinner on the table), briefly exchanged taunts for the excuses of the losers, and then finished the husking. Another "rule of the game" that increased interest was the provision that a boy who husked a red ear could claim a kiss from one of the girls. But Howells concluded: "I never knew it necessary to produce a red ear to secure a kiss when there was a disposition to give or take one."

Canada's only formidable defenders had been the Indian tribes of the Northwest Territory. They bitterly resented the Treaty of Greenville; they were numerous and well armed by the British, and they had been revitalized by a religious revival and the emergence of the greatest of Native American leaders. Had Indian power been intact in 1812, the War Hawks might have been less cocky. But it was not. In November 1811, it had been shattered.

THE PROPHET AND THE PANTHER

Canada's defense depended on the Delaware, Pottawottamie, Miami, Shawnee, and some refugee Iroquois living south of the Great Lakes. Demoralized after their defeat at Fallen Timbers in 1794, the Indians of present-day Indiana and Illinois were revitalized, about ten years later, by a reformed Shawnee drunk turned visionary, **Tenskwatawa.** Americans called him "The Prophet."

Tenskwatawa preached pan-tribalism. That is, Indians must give up their ancient tribal hostilities and recognize

Smithsonian Institution, Bureau of American Ethnology

Tecumseh, a Shawnee, was born about 1768. No other Indian leader quite measures up to him. He understood the culture of the white settlers. He was, in fact, well educated, perhaps better educated than the British officers in Canada with whom he dealt. He was devoted to preserving Indian cultures but did not share the mysticism of his brother, a religious teacher. Had he been at Tippecanoe, in 1811, it is unlikely the Indians would have suffered their crushing defeat there. In 1813, Tecumseh was killed in battle.

that all Indians together had a common enemy in the relentlessly advancing whites. In order to stop the whites, The Prophet said, Indians must cease imitating them and adopting white ways. They must move out of American-style houses, discard clothing made of purchased cloth, and stop using the white man's tools. The Prophet even preached that Indians must extinguish all their fires, for they had been ignited using the whites' flint and steel, and start new ones using Indian methods. Most important of all, they must give up the white man's alcohol, which was, obvious to all, the major element in the moral decay of the Indians.

White settlers in the Northwest Territory paid little attention to the Indian religious revival until 1808, when Tenskwatawa's followers expelled Christian Indians from tribal lands and founded a town, Tippecanoe or Prophetstown, which was soon quite large. There, The Prophet's brother, Tecumseh ("Panther Lying in Wait"), by force of his intelligence and charismatic personality, made himself the chief of a confederation of virtually all the tribes of the Northwest Territory.

Tenskwatawa was a mystic, sometimes cockeyed, and, as he was soon to prove, no warrior. Tecumseh had both feet on the ground; his reputation for bravery in battle dated back to the Indian victory over St. Clair in 1792, when he was a teenager. Most important, Tecumseh understood and appreciated the Americans' culture and strengths far better than his brother did. For ten years, he had lived among whites, developing a strong personal friendship with a prominent Ohioan, James Galloway. Galloway owned 300 books with which Tecumseh educated himself. In 1808, he proposed marriage to Galloway's daughter, Rebecca. She consented on the condition that Tecumseh abandon Indian ways—which he had never rejected— so that they would live like Americans.

Tecumseh was torn. In the end, more sensible than most people in love, he concluded that he could not reject his culture. He left Rebecca and Ohio to join his brother at Tippecanoe. The rational Tecumseh modified some of the Prophet's commandments. He exempted the white man's firearms from the Prophet's list of taboos and he ended the persecution of Christian Indians. He embarked on long journeys to convert more tribes to the Prophet's revitalization movement or, at least, to Tecumseh's alliance. His effectiveness— even the nobility of his character—was universally recognized. The British knew that he and his confederation were Canada's chief defense against the Americans. His enemy, William Henry Harrison, the territorial governor of Indiana, called him "one of those uncommon geniuses who spring up occasionally to produce revolutions and overturn the established order of things."

TIPPECANOE

In 1811, Tecumseh embarked on the most important of his journeys. He went deep into the South to enlist the powerful Cherokee, Creek, Choctaw, and Chickasaw in his confederacy. Had he succeeded and launched a coordinated attack on the frontier from Lake Michigan to the Gulf of Mexico, the white westerners would have suffered a devastating defeat.

It was not to be. Allowing blood relationship to rule his better judgment, Tecumseh put The Prophet in control of Tippecanoe during his absence. He told Tenskwatawa emphatically that he must keep the peace with the whites at any cost until he returned. The mystical Prophet, who believed in his visions, was not the man to whom to entrust so difficult and delicate a task.

In November 1811, Governor Harrison arrived at Tippecanoe, camping about a mile away from the town with 1,000 soldiers. He had come to fight but was surprised and alarmed to discover that he was badly outnumbered by well-armed Indian warriors, possibly as many as 3,000. He was leaning toward withdrawing to fight another day on better terms when The Prophet ordered an attack on the American camp. The Indians came within an ace of overrunning Harrison's army but his line held and the Americans counterattacked, winning the day. Tippecanoe's inhabitants scattered, most fleeing to Canada. Harrison leveled the town. He was a hero to the War Hawks who were elected to Congress the month of the great victory. They took their seats in Congress unrestrained by fear of Tecumseh's Confederacy.

BATTLING BUNGLERS

The American assault on Canada was a fiasco. New York militia refused to cross the Niagara River. They delayed their mass desertion only long enough to watch a duel between two American officers (which Canadians across the river also enjoyed). Surprised at American ineffectiveness, the British, Canadians, and Indians counterattacked and captured Detroit. An Indian force destroyed the stockade at Chicago, then called Fort Dearborn.

A Canadian-Indian offensive (in five of the seven land battles of the war, Indians outnumbered white soldiers on the British side) was stymied when, in September 1813, Captain **Oliver Hazard Perry** secured control of Lake Erie for the Americans. Receiving his famous message, "We have met the enemy and they are ours," William Henry Harrison then led 4,500 men toward York (now Toronto), the capital of Upper Canada.

There, the British and Canadians proved as inept as the Americans. According to Tecumseh, who was with them, they were cowards. He told the British commander, "We must compare our father's conduct to a fat dog that carries its tail upon its back, but when afrightened drops it between its legs and runs off." Harrison defeated the combined British, Canadian, and Indian force at the Battle of the Thames, and burned the public buildings in the city. Tecumseh was killed.

In the meantime, the British invaded New York via Burgoyne's route and were stopped at Lake Champlain, again by the navy commanded by Captain Thomas Macdonough. Ironically, whereas Americans won few victories on land, American naval forces on both the lakes and the ocean won most of their encounters.

The British revenged the burning of York in August 1814 when they launched a daring amphibious raid on Washington, D.C. The troops burned the Capitol and the White House. British officers claimed that they ate a dinner, still warm, that had been set for James and Dolley Madison. In fact, the president narrowly escaped capture when he drove out to rally the American army, and it fled without fighting, abandoning him.

THE BATTLE OF NEW ORLEANS

Napoleon's abdication in the spring of 1814 freed British troops for American service. Anglo-American peace talks in Ghent (Belgium) dragged on inconclusively, while 8,000 excellent and experienced troops under General Sir Edward Pakenham sailed to the Gulf of Mexico with orders to seize New Orleans. The city was undefended. It augured to be an American disaster. Instead, Packenham was humiliated and the Tennessean who hurriedly organized the defense of New Orleans eclipsed William Henry Harrison overnight. Indeed. Andrew Jackson became the most celebrated American general since George Washington.

Jackson was a self-taught lawyer, a slave owner, a land speculator, an Indian fighter, and a notorious duelist. At New Orleans, he cobbled together a defense force of 2,000 Kentucky and Tennessee volunteers (whom he had trouble getting to the city), New Orleans merchants, two battalions of free blacks, some Choctaw Indians, and artillerymen in the employ of a pirate-businessman, Jean Lafitte. Jackson threw up earthworks five miles south of New Orleans—the Mississippi River on his right, an impenetrable swamp on his left. He created a wide-open battlefield with his own army well protected.

"The Star-Spangled Banner"

On the evening of September 13, 1814, a lawyer named Francis Scott Key was detained on a British ship where he was arranging for the release of a prisoner. That night, the British shelled Fort McHenry, the chief defense for the city of Baltimore. The fort held out and the sight of the American flag waving atop its ramparts the next morning inspired Key to write a verse, "The Star Spangled Banner," while he was rowed to shore.

Key did the nation no favor by choosing as the music for his verse an English song, "To Anacreon in Heaven." Perhaps because "Anacreon" was a drinking song, sung by people who, at the moment, did not care what they sounded like, "The Star Spangled Banner" resists attractive vocalization by all but the most gifted professionally trained singers. This unfortunate reality has not discouraged the assignment of important renditions of the song to teenage rock and roll guitarists, actresses from television comedies, and mayors' nephews.

"The Star-Spangled Banner" has not been the national anthem for very long. Although unofficially sung as one since Key published it in 1814, it was not officially adopted by Congress until 1931 after a century worth of evidence that the tune, at least, was not a good choice.

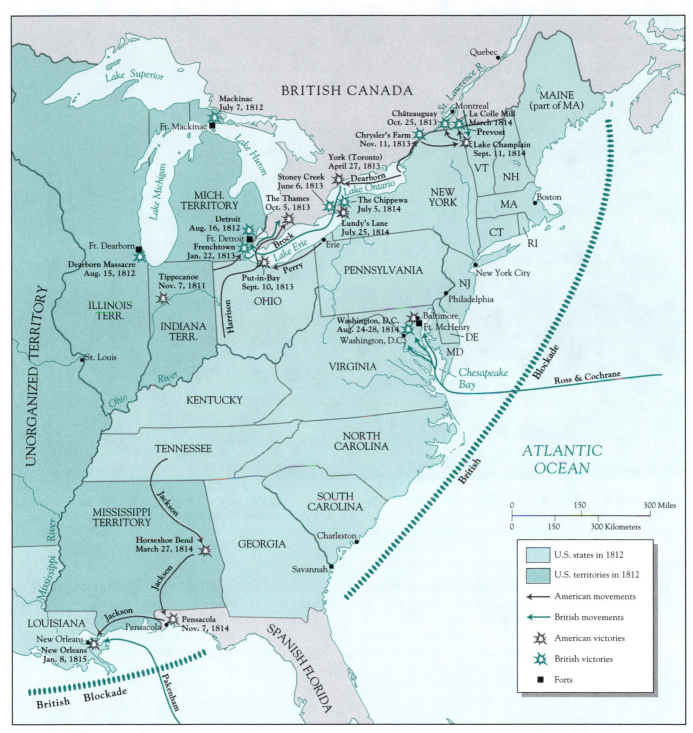

MAP 12:2 The War of 1812

Until the final battle of New Orleans, the War of 1812 was fought at sea and on the Canadian-American border. The capitals of both belligerents—York (now Toronto) in April 1813 and Washington in August 1814—were burned by the enemy.

Packenham should have paid closer attention to the setup Jackson had prepared. But, like so many British generals, he disdained American soldiers too reflexively to bother noticing. He sent his army through the morning fog in a straightforward frontal assault. Lafitte's cannoneers raked the British with grapeshot. When the redcoats were 200 yards from Jackson's earthworks, the riflemen opened up with "a leaden torrent no man on earth could face." More than 2,000 British soldiers fell dead—one in four on the expedition! They never got close to the American lines. In the mist and gunpowder smoke, few ever saw the fortifications. Only seven Americans were killed, four of them when they mindlessly pursued the fleeing British. After the battle, Jackson hanged as many American soldiers for desertion as were killed during it.

The Granger Collection, New York

The Battle of New Orleans. Like many patriotic paintings, this splendid one was more concerned with arousing national pride (and celebrating Andrew Jackson) than in accuracy. The British troops never got closer than a hundred yards of the American position. General Jackson did not direct the battle from a vantage in which he could be easily killed by the enemy.

Ironically, the **Treaty of Ghent,** which restored British-American relations to what they had been before the war, had already been signed. Nevertheless, the news of Jackson's astonishing victory had an electrifying effect on the country. So glorious a conclusion to an unnecessary and mostly calamitous war seemed to many a divine reaffirmation of the nation's destiny. When, within three years, Jackson crushed the

Creek in the southeast and Stephen Decatur returned to the Barbary Coast to sting the Algerians, Americans could imagine they had won respect in a world where armed might was the measure of greatness. According to another of those measures, a nation's sway over vast territory, the United States had already captured European attention.

FURTHER READING

General Marshall Smelser, *The Democratic Republic, 1801–1815,* 1992; Joanne B. Freeman, *Affairs of Honor: National Politics in the New Republic,* 2001; Robert Tucker and David Hendrickson, *Empire of Liberty: The Statecraft of Thomas Jefferson,* 1990; Peter Onuf, *Jefferson's Empire: The Language of American Nationhood,* 2001; R. Kent Newmeyer, *The Supreme Court under Marshall and Taney,* 1986.

Thomas Jefferson John Ferling, *Adams vs. Jefferson: The Tumultuous Election of 1800,* 2004; Joseph J. Ellis, *American Sphinx: The Character of Thomas Jefferson,* 1996; Andrew Burstein, *Jefferson's*

Secrets: Death and Desire at Monticello, 2005; Roger Kennedy, *Burr, Hamilton, and Jefferson: A Study in Character,* 2000; Christopher Hitchins, *Thomas Jefferson: Author of America,* 2005; Annette Gordon-Reid, *Thomas Jefferson and Sally Hemmings: An American Controversy,* 1997.

Louisiana and Exploration Alexander Deconde, *This Affair of Louisiana,* 1976; Roger G. Kennedy, *Mr. Jefferson's Lost Cause: Land, Farmers, Slavery, and the Louisiana Purchase,* 2003; Stephen Ambrose, *Undaunted Courage: Meriwether Lewis, Thomas Jefferson, and the Opening of the American West,* 1996; James Ronda, *Lewis* *and Clark Among the Indians*, 1984, and *Finding the West: Explorations with Lewis and Clark*, 2001; Carolyn Gilman, *Lewis and Clark: Across the Great Divide*, 2003.

Madison and His Presidency Jack M. Rakove, *James Madison and the Creation of the American Republic*, 1990; Drew McCoy, *The Last of the Fathers: James Madison and the Republican Legacy*, 1989; Robert A. Rutland, *The Presidency of James Madison*, 1990; Lawrence Kaplan, *"Entangling Alliances With None": American Foreign Policy in the Age of Jefferson*, 1987.

War With the Indians and Great Britain Gregory E. Dowd, *A Spirited Resistance: The North American Indian Struggle for Unity, 1745–1815*, 1992; R. David Edmunds, *The Shawnee Prophet*, 1983, and *Tecumseh and the Quest for Indian Leadership*, 1984;

John Sugden, *Tecumseh: A Life*, 1998; Jeffrey Bolster, *Black Jacks: African American Seamen in the Age of Sail*, 1997; Donald R. Hickey, *The War of 1812: A Forgotten Conflict*, 1989; J. C. A. Stagg, *Mr. Madison's War: Politics, Diplomacy, and Warfare in the Early American Republic*, 1983; Steven Watts, *The Republic Reborn: War and the Making of Liberal America 1790–1820*, 1987; Richard Buel Jr., *America on the Brink: How the Political Struggle Over the War of 1812 Almost Destroyed the Young Republic*, 2005; Robert V. Remini, *The Battle of New Orleans*, 1999.

Individuals Leonard Baker, *John Marshall: A Life in Law*, 1974; Nathan Schachner, *Aaron Burr*, 1984; Ron Chernow, *Alexander Hamilton*, 2004; Stephen K. Knott, *Alexander Hamilton and the Persistence of Myth*, 2002; Thomas J. Fleming, *Duels: Alexander Hamilton, Aaron Burr, and the Future of America*, 1999.

KEY TERMS

The following terms are covered in this chapter and can also be found in the list of Key Terms at the back of the book.

Barbary Pirates	**Oliver Hazard Perry**	**Treaty of Ghent**	**"War Hawks"**
impressment	**Tenskwatawa**	**Twelfth Amendment**	**Zebulon Pike**
judicial review	**The Burr Conspiracy**		

ONLINE SOURCES GUIDE

Use this listing to find online documents, images, interactive maps, simulations, and other resources related to this chapter:

American History Resource Center
http://history.wadsworth.com

Selected Documents
Thomas Jefferson: Constitutionality of the Louisiana Purchase (1803)
Marbury v. Madison (1801)
The Treaty of Ghent
The Star Spangled Banner

Selected Images
New Jersey woman voting in 1807
1805 portrait of Thomas Jefferson
John Marshall, Chief Justice of the Supreme Court

Battle between U.S.S. *Constitution* and H.M.S. *Guerriere*, August 1812
Oliver Hazard Perry at Battle of Put-In-Bay, September 1813
Tecumseh's Death at Battle of Thames

Interactive Timeline (with online readings)
Jeffersonian America: Expansion and Frustration 1800–1815

Document Exercises
1803 Gallatin Budget

Discovery

In what ways did the theme of expansionism characterize Jeffersonian America, and how did it shape the future of America?

In thinking about this question, begin by breaking it down into the components shown below. A discussion of the significance of each component should appear in your answer.

Social and Political: For this exercise, read the document excerpts "Thomas Jefferson, Constitutionality of the Louisiana Purchase (1803)" and "*Life of Ma-Ka-Tai-Me-She-Kia-Kiak or Black Hawk* dictated by Himself." Who were the inhabitants of the Louisiana Purchase? Who does Paine indicate lives there? What is his solution for handling those people? How does he feel they will acclimate themselves to being American? What potential problems exist when bringing those people into the United States? Why does Black Hawk oppose the treaty of annexation? How does what Black Hawk experienced foreshadow the fate of the Native Americans as a group? Does he seem to be resisting the government as a whole?

Thomas Jefferson, Constitutionality of the Louisiana Purchase (1803)

Thomas Paine to John C. Breckinridge

I know little and can learn but little of the extent and present population of Louisiana. After the cession be completed and the territory annexed to the United States it will, I suppose, be formed into states, one, at least, to begin with. The people, as I have said, are new to us and we to them and a great deal will depend on a right beginning. As they have been transferred backward and forward several times from one European Government to another it is natural to conclude they have no fixed prejudices with respect to foreign attachments, and this puts them in a fit disposition for their new condition. The established religion is roman; but in what state it is as to exterior ceremonies (such as processions and celebrations), I know not. Had the cession to France continued with her, religion I suppose would have been put on the same footing as it is in that country, and there no ceremonial of religion can appear on the streets or highways; and the same regulation is particularly necessary now or there will soon be quarrels and tumults between the old settlers and the new. The Yankees will not move out of the road for a little wooden Jesus stuck on a stick and carried in procession nor kneel in the dirt to a wooden Virgin Mary. As we do not govern the territory as provinces but incorporated as states, religion there must be on the same footing it is here, and Catholics have the same rights as Catholics have with us and no others. As to political condition the Idea proper to be held out is, that we have neither conquered them, nor bought them, but formed a Union with them and they become in consequence of that union a part of the national sovereignty.

The present Inhabitants and their descendants will be a majority for some time, but new emigrations from the old states and from Europe, and intermarriages, will soon change the first face of things, and it is necessary to have this in mind when the first measures shall be taken. Everything done as an expedient grows worse every day, for in proportion as the mind grows up to the full standard of sight it disclaims the expedient. America had nearly been ruined by expedients in the first stages of the revolution, and perhaps would have been so, had not *Common Sense* broken the charm and the Declaration of Independence sent it into banishment.

Life of Ma-Ka-Tai-Me-She-Kia-Kiak or Black Hawk dictated by Himself

. . . Some moons after this young chief descended the Mississippi, one of our people killed an American—and was confined in the prison at St. Louis, for the offence. We held a council at our village to see what could be done for him—which determined that Quash-qua-me, Pa-she-pa-ho, Ou-che-qua-ka, and Ha-she-quar-hi-qua, should go down to St. Louis, see our American father, and do all they could to have our friend released; by paying for the person killed—thus covering the blood, and satisfying the relations of the man murdered! This being the only means with us of saving a person who had killed another—and we then thought it was the same way with the whites!

The party started with the good wishes of the whole nation—hoping they would accomplish the object of their mission. The relatives of the prisoner blacked their faces, and fasted—hoping the Great Spirit would take pity on them, and return the husband and father to his wife and children.

Quash-qua-me and party remained a long time absent. They at length returned, and encamped a short distance below the village—but did not come up that day—nor did any person approach their camp! They appeared to be dressed in fine coats, and had medals! From these circumstances, we were in hopes that they had brought good news. Early the next morning, the Council Lodge was crowded—Quash-qua-me and party came up, and gave us the following account of their mission:

"On their arrival at St. Louis, they met their American father and explained to him their business, and urged the release of their friend. The American chief told him wanted land—and they had agreed to give him some on the west side of the Mississippi, and some on the Illinois side opposite Jeffreon. When the business was all arranged, they expected to have their friend released to come home with them. But about the time they were ready to start, their friend was let out of prison, who ran a short distance, and was shot dead! This is all they could recollect of what was said and done. They had been drunk the greater part of the time they were in St. Louis."

This is all myself or nation knew of the treaty of 1804. It has been explained to me since. I find, by that treaty, all our country, east of the Mississippi, and south of the Jeffreon, was ceded to the United States for one thousand dollars a year! I will leave it to the people of the United States to say, whether our nation was properly represented in this treaty? Or whether we received fair compensation for the extent of country ceded by those four individuals? I could say much about this treaty, but I will not at this time. It has been the origin of all our difficulties.

Government and Law: For this exercise, read the document excerpts "The Treaty of Greenville" and "James Madison to the Senate and House of Representatives." What does Madison consider to be one of the causes for declaring war against Great Britain? What does this suggest about American views of Native Americans and their actions? How might Americans have been at fault? Did the Americans live up to their treaty with the Native Americans?

Treaty of Greenville (1795)

. . . In consideration of the peace now established, and of the cessions and relinquishments of lands made in the preceding article by the said tribes of Indians, and to manifest the liberality of the United States, as the great means of rendering this peace strong and perpetual, the United States relinquish their claims to all other Indian lands northward of the river Ohio, eastward of the Mississippi, and westward and southward of the Great Lakes and the waters, uniting them, according to the boundary line agreed on by the United States and the King of Great Britain, in the treaty of peace made between them in the year 1783. . . .

James Madison to the Senate and House of Representatives, June 1, 1812

. . . In reviewing the conduct of Great Britain toward the United States our attention is necessarily drawn to the warfare just renewed by the savages on one of our extensive frontiers—a warfare which is known to spare neither age nor sex and to be distinguished by features peculiarly shocking to humanity. It is difficult to account for the activity and combinations which have for some time been developing themselves among tribes in constant intercourse with British traders and garrisons without connecting their hostility with that influence and without recollecting the authenticated examples of such interpositions heretofore furnished by the officers and agents of that Government. . . .

To read extended versions of the documents, visit the companion Web site http://history.wadsworth.com/americanpast8e; click on "Discovery Sources."

CHAPTER 13

Beyond the Appalachians

The West in the Early Nineteenth Century

Reproduced from the Collections of the Library of Congress

When I reflect that all this grand portion of our Union, instead of being in a state of nature, is now more or less covered with villages, farms and towns, . . . that hundreds of steamboats are gliding to and fro over the whole length of the majestic river, . . . When I remember that these extraordinary changes have all taken place in the short period of twenty years, I pause, wonder, and although I know it all to be fact, can scarcely believe its reality.

John J. Audubon

The Appalachians are not high as mountains go. Nevertheless, they were an impediment to the development of the lands west of them because they consist of a series of almost uninterrupted ridges extending from Alabama to Maine. Livestock and wagons could cross the range through only a few passes—along the Mohawk River in New York, for example, and through the famous Cumberland Gap from Virginia to Kentucky. And the Cumberland Gap climbed to 1,600 feet above sea level. The Whiskey Rebellion dramatized the difficulties of east–west transportation—whiskey was the only thing trans-Appalachian Pennsylvanians produced that had enough cash value per pound to make it worth hauling over the ridge. The only states beyond the Appalachians in 1800 were Vermont, Kentucky, and Tennessee.

THE FIRST AMERICAN WEST

After 1800, the population growth and economic development of "the West" were explosive. By 1830, a quarter of the American people lived west of the Appalachians. A majority of them had been born "back East." They (or their parents, if they had come as children) had cut their ties to home and family, packed up the little they could cart, and struck off westward despite the possibility of conflict with Indians when they got there—because, beyond the Appalachians, land was so cheap. In a country still mostly agricultural, land was synonymous with independence and opportunity.

The West, which was to loom large in American imaginations for a century, was as much an idea as a place, for its location constantly shifted. Well before 1830, Americans had redefined the word *frontier*, almost forgetting its traditional meaning. In Europe, a frontier was a boundary between principalities. To Americans it was the vague belt of territory where their civilization edged on wilderness and the domain of "wild Indians" began. No one spoke of the Canadian or Florida frontiers: those were borders or lines. It was the Kentucky frontier and the Indiana frontier.

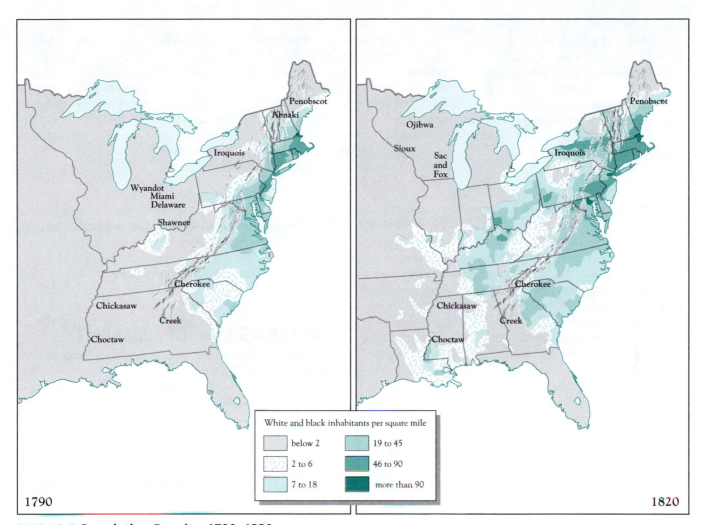

MAP 13:1 Population Density, 1790–1820

These two maps reveal two historically significant developments. First: a dramatic increase in population and population density in the Northeastern states but comparatively less growth in the southern states. Second: a tremendous expansion of settled land west of the Appalachians, including, in New York, western Pennsylvania, Ohio, and Kentucky, pockets of dense population.

European frontiers were relocated in fits and starts, back and forth, as a consequence of wars or princely marriages. The American frontier was constantly moving, often enough after wars with the Indians, but always in the same direction.

POPULATION EXPLOSION

Between 1800 and 1820, the white and black population of Mississippi grew from 8,000 to 75,000. Alabama, with about 1,000 whites and blacks in 1800, was home to 128,000 in 1820.

The states north of the Ohio River grew even more dramatically. In 1800, there were 45,000 white people in Ohio and a few African Americans, all of them free because the Northwest Ordinance prohibited slavery. Ten years later, the state's population was 230,000. By 1820, trans-Appalachian Ohio was the fifth largest state in the Union. By 1840, with 1.5 million people, it was fourth; only New York, Pennsylvania, and Virginia had more people. Ohio, little more than a generation old and still near wilderness in the center, was more populous than Finland, Norway, or Denmark.

Between 1800 and 1840, the mostly white population of Indiana grew from a few hundred to 685,856; Illinois from next to nil to 476,183. In 1800, Michigan consisted of one wretched fort inherited from the French and British—Fort Detroit. In the 1830s, New Englanders flocked like passenger pigeons to Michigan's "oak openings," fertile flats amidst the forests. By that time, the Mississippi River itself had ceased to be a frontier. Missouri, on the west bank, had been a state for ten years.

PEOPLE ON THE MOVE

The abundance of cheap land does not by itself explain the extraordinary river of people that flowed west. Russia had much more barely populated land in Siberia but, even after the Czar freed the serfs, few peasants headed to the "East" to settle. They had to be dragooned into moving to the country.

The Kentucky Long Rifle

The gun that won the trans-Appalachian West was the Kentucky long rifle. It had a 44-inch barrel and enough maple stock to make it the height of an average man. However, it weighed only eight pounds, a considerable recommendation to those who had to carry one.

The long rifle was a muzzle loader. With the butt on the ground, a charge of coarse black powder (measured by dead reckoning) was poured down the muzzle into the breech, classically from a "powder horn," an ox horn sealed against moisture. Then a ball—wrapped in greased linen or a leather patch to seal the explosion—was rammed

home, then a wad of paper to keep the ball in place.

In even the most practiced hands, the long rifle failed to fire one time in four. The phrase "flash in the pan" derives from the all too common, aggravating phenomenon of a charge that flashed when the trigger was pulled but failed to send the ball on its way.

But Americans were not peasants, conservative and fearful of the new. Always excluding slaves, Americans exploited their freedom to live where they chose and they were inherently restless, as nervous and agitated as the "painters" (panthers) they chased out when they pushed ever deeper into the woods. To Europeans, and sometimes to themselves, Americans were incapable of putting down roots.

The young couple saying their marriage vows and promptly clambering aboard a wagon to head west was as familiar a scene in New England as stone fences. During the first decades of the century, white Virginians, many with their slaves in tow, headed across the mountains as rapidly as a high birth rate could replace them. In central and western Pennsylvania, where a major wagon road ran west, the regional economy was closely tied to emigration. Inns and the stables of horse and oxen traders (teams needed to be replaced frequently) dotted the highway. Pennsylvania's Conestoga Valley gave its name to a type of wagon manufactured there, a high-slung, heavy-wheeled vehicle that could roll where there was no road. (And it gave the name to a cheap cigar, the "stogie," that so many Conestoga wagon drivers clenched between their teeth it might as well have been required by law.)

"In the United States," marveled Alexis de Tocqueville, the most observant of foreign tourists, "a man builds a house in which to spend his old age, and he sells it before the roof is on." An Englishman looking over lands near the Ohio river reported that if, to be polite, he admired the improvements a recent settler had made on his land, the man was likely to propose selling him everything on the spot so that he could start improving again farther west. A joke of the era had it that, in the spring, American chickens crossed their legs so they could be tied up for the next push west.

PATTERNS OF SETTLEMENT

Some of these eternal pilgrims were simply antisocial, the "eye-gougers" and "frontier scum" of legend and reality. Others were as respectable as the King James Bible and wanted as much company as they could persuade to join them on the frontier. They meant to recreate the way of life they had known back East, but better, because out west they would hold title to much more land than they could afford, or even find for sale, east of the mountains.

Yet other pioneers were developers—a profession still with us and sometimes still honored—dreamers, schemers, and promoters of new Edens, Romes, and Lexingtons. Poor and struggling men like Abraham Lincoln's father, Thomas, who made a career of clearing a few acres of forest and building a cabin to sell to a newcomer, were small-time developers. More important to western development were men with some capital (or credit) who purchased large tracts of land—a section or two or more—trumpeted its glorious fertility and future, and sold, at a profit, farm-sized parcels: "quarter sections" (160 acres) or "quarter quarter-sections" (40 acres),

Tying the West to the East 1800–1830

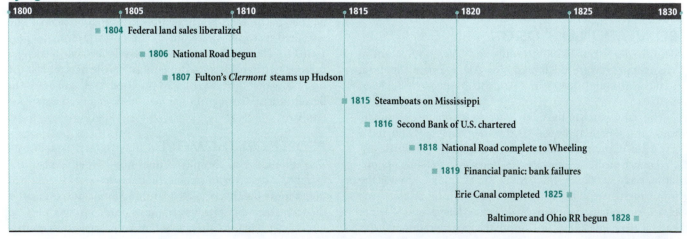

| 1800 | 1805 | 1810 | 1815 | 1820 | 1825 | 1830 |

- 1804 Federal land sales liberalized
- 1806 National Road begun
- 1807 Fulton's *Clermont* steams up Hudson
- 1815 Steamboats on Mississippi
- 1816 Second Bank of U.S. chartered
- 1818 National Road complete to Wheeling
- 1819 Financial panic: bank failures
- Erie Canal completed 1825
- Baltimore and Ohio RR begun 1828

The Conestoga wagon was big and rugged. An early standard was 19 feet long at the top of the bucket, 14 feet at the bed. The bucket was 4 feet deep. Such a wagon could carry six tons. (Some claimed ten.) Like a boat, the Conestoga wagon was tightly caulked. If it was emptied, it could be floated across a river.

The front wheels were usually four feet in diameter providing almost two feet of clearance. The rear wheels were six feet across so that, when the wagon needed a push, the spokes provided handholds with good leverage. The famous canvas bonnet was stretched on iron hoops and kept possessions and sleeping emigrants dry when it rained.

Conestogas crossing the Appalachians were drawn by one or two yokes (pairs) of oxen. They were kept moving by goading and constantly repeated voice commands. (Oxen have short memories.) You could hear an ox team coming. And there were barking dogs too, trained to run alongside, preventing other dogs from harassing the oxen. Later in the century, when Conestoga wagons were adapted for transcontinental treks, teams of six horses or mules—which were faster than oxen—were driven from a seat on the wagon.

which was about right for a family in the well-watered trans-Appalachian West.

Some boosters laid out what they called cities divided into town lots suitable to a blacksmith or printer. They named streets before a tree in imagined intersections had been felled. Some town fathers were merchants or even manufacturers who intended to stay in the settlements they named for themselves often enough, and prosper as the country grew. Others were professional boomers who moved on as soon as they made their bundle (or lost it); they were quite as rootless as the hunters and trappers that farmers displaced.

WESTERN CITIES

The army was the cutting edge on some frontiers. Soldiers posted in the West to keep an eye on Indians had to be fed, clothed, and entertained. Shopkeepers and saloonkeepers clustered around military installations. The security the fort provided encouraged trappers, hunters, and others who tramped the woods to congregate within or near them during times of Indian trouble. And many Indians hooked by American goods—alcohol all too often—left their tribes to make a sort of life on the fringes of the army towns. Tribal Indians arrived periodically to trade. The wants of this diverse assortment of westerners stimulated the growth of a mercantile economy before there was much tillage in the neighborhood. Farmers followed urbanization. Vincennes, Detroit, and other towns developed in this manner.

Cities came first along major rivers too. Only after a fairly advanced (if not refined) urban life had evolved did the hinterland fill in with farmers to provision places like

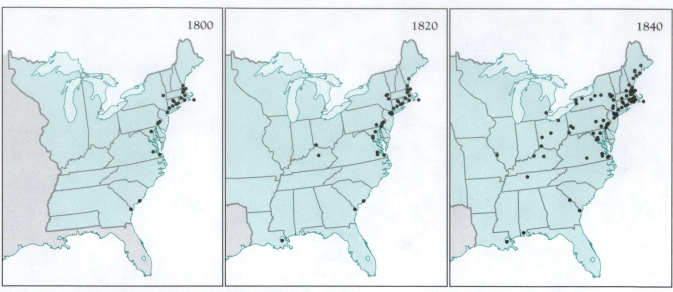

MAP 13:2   **Cities of At Least 5,000 Inhabitants, 1800–1840**

Eastern cities in number and size between 1800 and 1840. Most striking in these maps, however, was the multiplication of cities in the West where there had been none in 1800 and only three in 1820.

SOUTH WATER STREET.   CHICAGO. 1834.

Chicago Historical Society

In 1834, Chicago was a decidedly unimpressive cluster of rude one- and two-room buildings on a muddy flat barely higher than Lake Michigan. The town grew slowly until it became the northern terminus of the Illinois Central Railroad and, later, the western terminus of several eastern trunk lines. Chicago's population exploded when the transcontinental railroads were built, bringing the "Windy City" the produce of the last American West.

Cincinnati, Louisville, and Nashville, built on sites at which river travelers could conveniently beach canoes and tie up rafts and keelboats. Such towns became rest stops and jumping-off points for emigrants bound farther west. When the cotton lands of the lower Mississippi boomed, sending out calls for provisions for the slaves who raised the lucrative crop, the river ports became entrepôts of grain and livestock. Cincinnati, "the Queen City of the West," was famous for its slaughterhouses and packing plants when, not many miles away, the great hardwood forests blocked the sun from the earth and lonely men and women battled malaria.

Most astonishing is how quickly western cities became manufacturing centers. In 1815, when there were no more than fifteen steam engines in all of France (a nation of 20 million people), half-wild Kentucky boasted six steam mills turning out cloth and paper. Before the War of 1812, St. Louis had a steam mill six stories high. Like medieval burghers determined to outdo the cathedral spires of the rival cities, Cincinnatians built a mill nine stories high.

By 1828, Cincinnati boasted nine factories building steam engines, nine cotton mills, twelve newspapers, forty schools, two colleges and a medical school. A metropolis it was, but unmistakably western too: only one street was paved and unslaughtered pigs were everywhere.

SPECULATION AND FEDERAL LAND POLICY

Such rapid development encouraged heated financial speculation. Many went to Illinois or Michigan or Alabama neither to farm, run a shop, nor pack pork. They were speculators with dreams of growing rich by the timeless, risky game of buying land cheap and selling it dear. Some were sharpers by any era's standards, out to line their pockets without concern for law, ethics, or common decency.

Speculation in western lands made the price at which the federal government disposed of the public domain—and the terms of purchase—a matter of considerable interest to both speculators and to those who wanted to settle and farm. Originally (in the Northwest Territory), the federal government sold land for a minimum of $1 per acre (the price could be bid higher at auctions) in minimum parcels of a section, 640 acres. Actual settlers neither needed so much land nor, in most cases, could afford to spend $640. But the federal government was not so much encouraging speculators as sparing itself the prodigious administrative costs of selling farm-sized parcels.

A Federalist revision of the law in 1796 favored large-scale speculators—Hamilton's capitalist elite. It increased the minimum price per acre to $2 payable within one year, difficult terms for an entry-level speculator operating on a shoestring and illusions. Moreover, under the 1796 law, only half the land available for purchase could be bought in sections; the other half was sold in 8 section units: 5,120 acres! There were few takers. In four years, the government disposed of fewer than 50,000 acres.

In 1800, half-section parcels were available for the first time. The minimum price remained $2 an acre but the purchaser could extend payments over four years and there was an 8 percent discount for those who paid cash, which few speculators did.

LIBERAL LAND POLICY BACKFIRES

In 1804, the Jefferson Republicans were in power. They reduced the smallest parcel available to 160 acres and the per acre minimum price to $1.64. So as to encourage cash-poor settlers to buy, the land office required a small down payment. Unfortunately, the Land Act of 1804 encouraged the most reckless kind of speculation. For very little cash outlay—and that could be borrowed from newly chartered state banks that churned out paper money—speculators could get title to numerous 160-acre parcels which, they expected, they would sell at a profit before too many bank loans and installment payments at the land office came due. Many a man got rich quick by shuffling land and loans. Each fabulous success story told at a tavern or plantation house encouraged others to have a go in the gold mine. After the War of 1812, land values soared as speculators grasping wads of bank notes bid prices up at auctions and bought properties from one another. Paper-rich speculators bid some prime cotton acreage in Alabama and Mississippi up to $100 an acre.

It was all, in the language of the era, a "bubble." Land values bore no relationship to the wealth that the land, actually in use, could produce. They were inflated with air: borrowed bank notes ostensibly redeemable in gold and silver but, in fact, just paper, and the illusion that no matter how apparently absurd the price one paid for land, someone willing to pay more was coming to town. In 1815, the government sold a million acres; in 1819, more than 5 million.

It was not just the price of land that rose. With so much paper money circulating, the prices of all commodities rose. Cotton, tobacco, and grain prices climbed. Back East, groceries, rents, and wages rose.

THE PANIC OF 1819

The bubble had to burst and it did, in 1819. Speculators found no buyers for parcels of their landed empires and defaulted at both the land office and the bank. Acreage the government thought it had sold reverted to the public domain. Wildcat banks, no coin in their vaults and no loans being paid, closed their doors by the dozens weekly, rendering the notes they had issued worthless. The price of cotton collapsed, causing planters to default on their loans. Nationwide, about half a million wage workers lost their jobs, and many their homes.

What caused the Panic of 1819? At bottom, like all booms that bust, its cause was the human capacity for greed and even more marvelous capacity for self-deception. Crazed speculations, whether in land, diamonds, dot-com stocks, or even in tulip bulbs (as happened in seventeenth-century Holland), are based on the "greater fool" principle. People pay absurd prices for a commodity in the belief that a "greater fool" willing to pay even more for it is just around the corner. When the supply of greater fools runs dry, or the money that has fueled the speculation loses value, the bubble bursts and fortunes disappear.

The Panic of 1819 had specific causes too. Those who suffered from it, needing a scapegoat, focused on those causes rather than on human frailty. British buyers looked elsewhere for cotton when the price of American cotton rose too high. The wildcat banks were poorly capitalized and irresponsible. They printed and loaned out far more paper money than, given their tiny gold and silver reserves, they could redeem if more than a few people with a wad of banknotes demanded coin. State legislatures chartered the wildcat banks without regard for their flimsy foundations. The Second Bank of the United States, chartered in 1816 to monitor and restrain state banks, failed to do so. In 1817, after encouraging the purchase of federal land with borrowed paper money, the Bank abruptly ordered that the land office accept only specie—gold and silver coin. People and interests picked the scapegoat that most persuasively absolved them of their contributions to the disaster.

McCULLOCH V. MARYLAND

The Panic itself cleaned out the worst of the state banks. In 1820, Congress abolished credit purchases of federal land and tried to dispose of the properties that had reverted to the government by reducing the minimum tract for sale to 80 acres and the minimum price per acre to $1.25. Defenders of the Second Bank of the United States blamed not the principle of a national bank but the incompetence of the board of directors appointed in 1816. Die-hard Jeffersonians blamed the BUS. The legislatures of six states where the Bank had branches levied heavy taxes on its transactions.

The BUS cashier in Maryland refused to pay the tax on the grounds that, although it was a private institution, it was also public, chartered by the federal government and therefore not subject to state regulation of any kind. In 1819, Republican presidents had appointed five of the seven justices. However, the aging old Federalist John Marshall had converted most of them to a Hamiltonian view of the Constitution. In *McCulloch* v. *Maryland* (1819), the Court ruled unanimously that the state of Maryland violated the Constitution when it taxed the BUS. "The power to tax involves the power to destroy," Marshall wrote. If Maryland were permitted to tax the BUS, what was to stop the state from taxing other federal agencies such as the customs houses or the post office?

Marshall asserted the superiority of the federal government over the states in McCulloch. He also made Hamilton's "broad

---

Western Eloquence

Simeon Cragin, a land speculator, made the following statement before a land auction in Missouri.

> I own fourteen claims, and if any man jump one of them, I will shoot him down at once, sir. I am a gentleman, sir, and a scholar. I was educated at Bangor, have been in the United States Army, and served my country faithfully. I am the discoverer of the Wopsey, can ride a grizzly bear, or whip any human that ever crossed the Mississippi, and if you dare to jump one of my claims, die you must.

Frontier Violence

The Mississippi valley frontier's reputation for violence may have been overstated. John J. Audubon, who wandered the region for twenty-five years collecting and painting specimens of birds and animals, thought so. In twenty-five years, he said, he was personally threatened only once, in 1812, when an Indian warned him that frontier thugs planned to rob and kill him at the cabin where he was lodging. Fortuitously, two more travelers arrived before bedtime and nothing happened.

"Indeed," Audubon wrote, in an overstatement of his own, "so little risk do travelers run in the United States that no one born there dreams of any [violence] to be encountered on the road."

---

construction" of the Constitution the law of the land by declaring (almost in Hamilton's own words) that Congress had acted constitutionally in creating the Bank. "Let the end be legitimate, let it be within the scope of the constitution, and all means which are appropriate, which are plainly adapted to that end, which are not prohibited, but consist with the letter and spirit of the constitution" are constitutional.

PROGRAMS

The word squatter did not have a disagreeable ring in the trans-Appalachian West. To western farmers, squatters were settlers who, out of orneriness, innocence, or ignorance of the law, developed farms on the public domain before the government offered it for sale. They cleared and sometimes plowed fields and built cabins and barns. Such improved land was particularly attractive to speculators because the squatter's labor had substantially increased the property's value. When the Land Office held its auction, many squatters saw their claims "jumped." They were outbid for their homes by speculators waving wads of bank notes.

Some squatters responded with vigilante action. Banded together in "land clubs," they threatened physical reprisals against anyone who bid on a member's land. Not infrequently, they made good on their threats. But speculators determined to get improved squatter land could and did hire thugs, never hard to find on the frontier, who were more than a match for farmers. And the law was on the speculators' side; the squatters had no legal claim to the land they had improved.

"OLD BULLION" BENTON

Squatters and their sympathizers turned to their representatives in Congress. Their hero after 1820, when the new state of Missouri named him senator, was **Thomas Hart Benton,** known as "Old Bullion" because, after the debacle of 1819, he despised all kinds of paper money. To Benton, gold—bullion—was the only real money. Born in North Carolina, he meant to make a political career in Tennessee but, after a gunfight with Andrew Jackson, the most powerful man in the state, Benton had to go west again—to Missouri.

Although he was well-read in the classics and liked to speckle his oratory with allusions to Greece and Rome,

Benton knew how to turn on the boisterous bluff that appealed to rough-hewn westerners. "I never quarrel, sir," he told an opponent in a debate. "But sometimes I fight, sir; and when I fight, sir, a funeral follows, sir."

Benton was a populist. He trumpeted the interests of the common people against the rich, bankers, paper money, land speculators, anyone and anything else he defined as inimical to the common man. Throughout his long career—thirty years in the Senate—he fought and dickered for an ever more liberal land policy, favoring settlers over speculators. His pet project was "squatters' rights," or **preemption.** Preemption provided that people who settled on and improved land before the government offered it for sale be permitted to purchase the land at the government minimum. They were not required to bid against others at auction.

Another Benton program was **graduation:** land that was unsold after government auction would be offered at half the minimum price and, after a passage of time, at a quarter. The price of the land would be graduated downward so as to increase the number of people able to afford it. Eventually, Benton hoped, long unsold land would be given away to people willing to settle it.

Benton's sentiments were more Jeffersonian than anything Jefferson ever proposed. Land was for use; it was not a commodity the value of which was to be manipulated by speculators for their own enrichment. He favored those who tilled the soil, "the bone and sinew of the republic" in Jefferson's phrase, over financial interests associated with the Federalists and, later in Benton's career, with the Whig party.

SECTIONAL TENSIONS

Southerners and northeasterners inclined to oppose policies that disposed of public land cheaply. People living on Virginia's James neck or on the oldest streets of Plymouth had no interest in acquiring land in Missouri and Michigan. But they had a significant stake in the price at which the federal government disposed of the public domain. Western land sales provided much of the government's revenues. If the land was sold off as cheaply as Benton wanted to sell it, the tariff—duties on imports, the other major source of federal income—might have to be increased. Southern planters, whose slaves were clothed and shod in cheap imports from Britain, opposed tariffs that raised the prices they had to pay for such goods. Finance the federal government, they said, with revenues from land slaves.

Manufacturers, a rising political force in the Northeast after the War of 1812, agreed that the price of western land should be kept high—but for an entirely different reason. They feared that dirt-cheap land would lure to the West the hard-pressed New England farm families among whom mill owners found their workforce. The smaller the labor pool, the fewer people willing to work in factories, the higher the wages manufacturers had to pay.

If the Northeast and South found a common cause in maintaining the price of western land, the two sections were at odds on the tariff. Northeastern manufacturers wanted import duties as high as Congress could be persuaded to

North Wind Picture Archives

Henry Clay was keenly intelligent, a dazzling orator, famously handsome, graciously mannered, witty, and sociable. He charmed women and won the friendship and loyalty of men. He was equally comfortable sipping claret with an elegant lady and playing faro with the boys until the whiskey was gone. Although he was a poor shot, Clay fought several duels, almost a prerequisite of success in western politics.

raise them. Their mills were "infant industries." They needed protection—a "protective tariff"—if they were to survive. They could not compete with older, more efficient British factories in an open market. They would be undersold and go out of business. By raising the prices of British goods by adding import duties to them, American mills could charge enough for their products to prosper.

On one issue or another, each of the three "sections" (Northeast, South, and West) had interests that pitted it against the other sections on clear-cut geographical lines. The man who made it his business to reconcile these clashing sectional interests was Henry Clay of Kentucky.

THE NATIONAL ROAD

Henry Clay was born in Virginia in 1777. Trained as a lawyer, he moved to Lexington, Kentucky at the age of 21 and prospered as a planter, land speculator, and in state politics. He was elected to Congress in 1810. No sooner did he arrive in Washington than the House elected him Speaker. A freshman Representative could win so coveted a post over veteran

American Roads

A functional north–south highway had been put together piecemeal in the Northeast over a two-hundred-year period. The Old Post Road connecting Boston and New York was open to travel by horse-drawn stagecoaches all year (although it was a depressingly uncomfortable trip). New York (Newark, New Jersey, actually) was connected to Philadelphia by a reliable graveled highway with ferry service across the Delaware River. Another road connected Philadelphia to Baltimore and Washington.

These highways were maintained by county and state governments with some federal help. The Old Post Road was originally developed for riders carrying mail.

Turnpikes were built by investors whose profits (they hoped) would come from collecting tolls. The word turnpike referred to the fact that, at the regularly spaced toll stations, the roadway was blocked by a long pole resembling a pike. When a user paid the toll, the pike was turned so that he could pass.

The most successful toll road, the Lancaster Pike (present-day highway U.S. 30) connected the rich farm town of Lancaster, Pennsylvania to Philadelphia, 60 miles away. By 1820, there were 4,000 miles of turnpike in the United States, some surfaced with macadam. A cheaper surfacing common in northern New England and in the western states was made by laying heavy planks or logs across the roadbed. Log-paved roads were called corduroy roads for the obvious reason. The ride was not comfortable, but as long as the logs lasted, they kept horses and wagons out of the mud.

---

congressmen with connections because almost half the members of the House in 1811 were first-timers like Clay. This was the War Hawk Congress and Clay was one of the war party's most eloquent spokesmen.

Clay remained a strident nationalist after the war. A few years when the entire country seemed united by patriotic fervor (the "Era of Good Feelings"; see Chapter 14) enabled him to earn a national reputation as a promoter of federally financed **internal improvements,** what we would call "public works." In the early decades of the nineteenth century, internal improvements meant improving harbors, dredging rivers, and, most of all, building long-haul highways. In order to justify the use of federal money, improvements had to benefit the people of more than one state.

The greatest federal project underway during Clay's first years in Washington was the **National Road.** Begun in 1806, completed in 1818, it connected Cumberland, Maryland at the head of navigation on the Potomac River with Wheeling on the Ohio River. It was expensive; only the federal government could have built it. Including the cost of quite beautiful stone bridges, it cost $13,000 per mile of 60-foot-wide roadway, the center 20 feet surfaced with macadam, finely crushed rock compacted to form a foundation that raised the road above ground level so that it drained. (The chief curse of dirt roads was the mud holes churned up by narrow wagon wheels.)

The National Road was a godsend to farmers and merchants who lived within reach of the Ohio River, including, of course, Kentuckians. By boat, wagon, and boat again, crops could be gotten to the Atlantic, and manufactures could be brought back. The National Road eliminated the problem that had led to the Whiskey Rebellion—western farmers unable to sell their grain in any other shape than distilled spirits. Until the opening of the Erie Canal in 1825, the National Road was also the preferred route of emigrants moving west.

Henry Clay became the National Road's adoptive father. He took the lead in persuading Congress to finance its extension through Ohio and Indiana to Vandalia, Illinois. By veering northwesterly, the highway brought the benefits of through transportation to farmers who lived far from the Ohio River. And, not incidentally, for Clay was politically ambitious, it won him a sometimes adoring following outside of Kentucky.

THE AMERICAN SYSTEM

Clay was disturbed when, after 1820, the Northeast, South, and West began to take sharply conflicting positions along geographical lines—as sections—on land policy, the tariff, continued federal financing of internal improvements, and, of course, slavery. Clay was a Jefferson Republican but only because, when he entered politics, it was the only political party that existed outside of New England. In his heart, Clay was a Federalist. Like Alexander Hamilton, he was a nationalist; he envisioned the United States as a great, single, unified nation and deplored those who trumpeted the prerogatives, even the sovereignty of the states. Like Hamilton, he saw mutually advantageous national economic development as the key to overcoming the threat of sectionalism.

Unlike Hamilton, who represented one extreme on the political spectrum of the 1790s, Clay stuck to the middle of the road; he was comfortable with democracy (although he was no populist like Benton), and he was always open to a compromise. Indeed, he was always ready to seize the initiative in engineering compromises.

His **American System** proposed to reconcile the conflicting economic interests of the Northeast, South, and West with a program of Hamiltonian comprehensiveness. To westerners, the American System offered a program of federally financed internal improvements the western states could not themselves afford, and parts of the liberal land policy for which Benton called. Clay was willing to lower the minimum price at which the federal government sold lands and he accepted the principle of graduation.

To manufacturers, Clay argued, immigrants would more than make up for any population loss due to the emigration of northerners to the West. And the ever more populous, mostly agricultural West would provide a huge market for their products. By supporting federal road construction, they would improve their access to the West. The clincher in winning support in the Northeast was the American System's high protective tariff. Clay advocated import duties so substantial they would not only ensure the survival of northeastern mills in the face of foreign competition, they would effectively subsidize greater profits and, therefore, further industrial development.

Again reflecting his debt to Hamilton, Clay defended the Second Bank of the United States as the indispensable moderator of the finance essential to his vision of a nationally integrated economy. He attributed the Bank's contributions to the Panic of 1819 to the incompetence of the directors who were installed when the Bank was chartered in 1816. He had a point about that, and the management problem was remedied in 1822 when a talented and conservative Philadelphian, Nicholas Biddle, emerged as the Bank's uncontested boss.

The American System won widespread, although not universal, support in the North and West. Politically, its weakness

MAP 13:3 Rivers, Roads, and Canals 1820–1860

During the first half of the nineteenth century, the United States boasted two of the world's longest continuous highways, the routes followed today by U.S. 1/I-95 and U.S. 40/I-70 (the National Road). American canals, now almost all gone, were far more extensive than the long-distance highway network.

was that Clay offered the South nothing that it did not already have. A tariff-subsidized textile industry in the Northeast would grow, Clay argued, buying ever more cotton, the South's most lucrative crop. In time, when American mills were as efficient as British mills, their products would be as cheap as British goods were.

In effect, Clay was asking cotton planters to subsidize Northeastern industry in the short run by paying higher prices jacked up by the tariff, for cloth, shoes, and other manufactures. In return there would be a domestic market for cotton in the future when American manufactures would drop in price. The trouble was, southern cotton planters did not need a domestic market. The mills of Manchester, Leeds, and Bradford in England—and mills in France, too—gobbled up all the fiber the South could grow. All the American System offered the South was a wonderful future in which they had trouble believing, and higher prices today.

Moreover, southerners had historically been more suspicious of nationalism than northerners and westerners. And during the 1820s, slavery was emerging as an issue that isolated the South as a section. Except for Louisiana sugar growers, who wanted tariff protection from the West Indies, few southerners signed up for the American System.

THE TRANSPORTATION REVOLUTION

Clay had to be content with levering bits and pieces of the American System through Congress, but not his comprehensive scheme. The American economy developed—explosively!—and was integrated nationally not by "government planning," but by technological innovation exploited for gain by entrepreneurs operating in a wide-open market economy. There was one significant exception, a publicly funded internal improvement bigger and more daring than the National Road. But it was not the federal government that financed it; it was the state of New York.

THE ERIE CANAL

In 1817, the New York state legislature funded the construction of a canal connecting the Hudson River (thereby New York City) with Lake Erie (thereby the entire Great Lakes basin above Niagara Falls). It was a monumental undertaking. At the time, the longest canal in the United States ran less than 30 miles; the route of the Erie Canal was 364 miles long. And yet, the big ditch, 4 feet deep and 40 feet wide, was completed in eight years. It was expensive, $7 million or

The Erie Canal. Long stretches were idyllic, as this artist has depicted it at a set of two locks. Other canal towns were rough-and-tumble places, as "wild" as the cow towns and mining camps of a later era.

Digging the Erie Canal

By 1790, there were about thirty canal companies in the United States. Most ran for only a few miles, around river rapids and waterfalls so that cargos did not have to be portaged. George Washington was interested, intellectually and financially, in a canal that circumvented the falls of the Potomac.

Any number of visionaries who crossed New York State via the Mohawk River and then overland to the Great Lakes observed that on that route alone was a canal through the Appalachians imaginable. At only a few places, most dauntingly the Niagara Escarpment (over which Niagara Falls drops), were there significant obstacles to be overcome.

To most practical-minded men, the idea was fantastic. It was more than 300 miles from Albany, on the Hudson River, to Lake Erie. A few men, however, were not dissuaded. Led by **DeWitt Clinton,** a rising politician, they had the route surveyed and commissioned reports from engineers on how to overcome the obstacles. Clinton petitioned Thomas Jefferson for federal aid but he called the project "little short of madness." (He meant the immense cost of the project, not its feasibility.) President Madison also turned Clinton down in 1816.

The next year, however, Clinton, just elected governor of New York, persuaded the state legislature to fund what his critics called "Clinton's Folly." The digging began almost immediately at several points along the route (so as to create jobs—and thus win popular support—across the state). It was pick and shovel work, digging a ditch 4 feet deep and 40 feet wide. Oxen, mules, and horses hauled the excavated earth and rock away, but the digging was done by hand. Laborers, drawn at first from the local population, including farmers during their idle winter months, were paid $1 a day if they provided their own meals, $13 a month with meals and a daily half pint of whiskey provided.

Local labor pools were not up to the task. On long stretches of the route, through forests and where it was rocky, there were no farms or towns and, therefore, no local workers. However, Clinton was popular among New York's growing Irish population because he had sponsored the law that ended restrictions on Catholics' right to vote. Immigrants barely getting by in New York City and impoverished Irish in the old country who heard of the "big ditch" flocked upstate. They were soon the bulk of the 3,000-4,000 strong workforce.

The durable stereotype of the Irish as drunken brawlers got a boost during the digging of the Erie Canal. All young men, almost all without wives and children to support, they supported grog shops and brothels instead.

The building of the Erie Canal was the greatest construction project of its time, its progress followed in European as well as American newspapers. It was not all plain digging and shoveling. In several locations, the banks of the canal were so porous they sucked the ditch dry. Workers "puddled" the clay, turning it again and again, kneading it until it became impermeable. One hill was traversed by digging through it; the canal lay 30 feet below the surface. One valley was crossed without locks by heaping up a 70-foot embankment. The Genesee River, that flooded destructively almost annually, was crossed by an aqueduct 800 feet long. Another aqueduct ran 3,000 feet and reached as high as 30 feet above the ground. On heavily populated sections, bridges crossing the canal were built every quarter mile.

The most dramatic spot on the canal was where the cliff of the Niagara Escarpment rose 60 feet. The canal negotiated it with five pairs of locks, one after another. (The locks at Lockport, an appropriately named new town, were built in pairs so eastbound and westbound traffic could move along simultaneously.) The Erie Canal opened in November 1825.

---

almost $20,000 per mile. But the Erie was so successful that the state paid the interest on its bonds in one year and retired the bonds in twelve.

The canal made New York City "the great depot and warehouse of the western world." It funneled the agricultural produce, lumber, and minerals of the northern two-thirds of the old Northwest Territory through New York. The manufactures the people of Ohio, Indiana, Illinois, Michigan, and, later, Wisconsin bought were handled by New York merchants. The Erie Canal displaced the National Road as the emigrants' preferred way west. Travel on the Erie was much quicker than overland travel: six to eight days from Albany to Buffalo (a city the canal created) without an hour of physical exertion. In 1845, about 100,000 people moved west via the canal. Mostly, the Erie Canal moved freight cheaply. It cost $10 (eventually $8) to ship a ton the entire

length, about a tenth of what it cost to move a ton the same distance overland.

Canal boats were flat-bottomed. They could be no longer than 78 feet to fit into the eighty-four locks that raised and lowered them; most boats were shorter. The maximum beam (width) of a canal boat was 14 to 15 feet so that there was plenty of clearance between boats being towed in opposite directions. The number of boats in service at any one time varied from 3,400 to 5,000.

THE "CANAL EXPERIENCE"

The "navigators," as canal boat workers good-humoredly called themselves, worked two six-hour shifts each day, two crews alternating. (Canal boats moved around the clock.) The mules that towed the boats, two or three of them per boat, had it a little easier than their tenders; they worked five-hour shifts. An expert crew could unharness one mule, get her to her stall in the boat, and harness her relief in fifteen minutes. But the job was usually done at a more leisurely pace. It was when the tow mules were changed that canalers took a breather and had a bite to eat. The boats moved at two miles per hour westbound and three eastbound (there was a current in the canal!)

Accommodations on passenger boats ranged from painfully Spartan to nearly luxurious. (Going first class cost five cents a mile.) Aft—in the rear of the boat—was the passenger cabin, about ten feet by twelve. Travelers sat and ate there during the day and slept there at night, two to a drop-down bunk three feet wide. Their luggage was stowed in a hold below the cabin.

The stable for the mules was fore (in the front), their hay and grain in a center compartment. In good weather, passengers got off and walked along the towpath for exercise, or they could sit on the roof. That, however, was not relaxing in populated areas where the canal ran under numerous bridges that the boats barely cleared. Anyone on the roof had to lie flat or be knocked in the head. One verse in the canalers' anthem, "Fifteen Years on the Erie Canal," had it:

> Low bridge, everybody down,
> Low bridge, for we're coming to a town

Ladies and gentlemen could not have been enthusiastic about hurriedly jumping up from a chair and flopping down flat. Then again, many may have found behavior out of character to be great fun.

The navigators, many of them Irishmen who had dug the big ditch, were a rough lot, both boat-owning entrepreneurs and "hoggies," the boys who walked with the mules. A canal song less genteel than "Fifteen Years" poked fun at those menial workers:

> Hoggie on the towpath,
> Five cents a day,
> Picking up horseballs
> To eat along the way.

Towns at toll booths and locks were notorious for their whorehouses and drunken fistfights. In 1835, the Bethel Society—evangelical Protestants trying and generally failing to improve navigator morals—counted 1,500 grog shops along the Erie (an average of four per mile but they were, of course, in clusters).

By the 1840s, 30,000 people made their living on the canal: lock tenders, toll house workers, and repairmen (all state employees); and the navigators, saloonkeepers, and others catering to the needs of workers and travelers.

ANOTHER BOOM AND BUST

When the Erie Canal was begun, there were about 100 miles of canal in the United States. When it was finished, those who had ridiculed "Clinton's Folly" went berserk in their rush to duplicate the bonanza the Erie created for New York.

The most ambitious of the competitors was **the Mainline Canal** in Pennsylvania. Smarting under their loss of commercial preeminence to New York, Philadelphia merchants pressured the state legislature into pumping millions into a waterway across Pennsylvania. The Mainline was shorter than the Erie. However, while the New York canal rose to 650 feet above sea level at its highest point, and required 84 locks to cross the state, the Mainline Canal climbed to 2,200 feet and needed 174 locks.

And not only locks were needed. At the Allegheny ridge, the highest in the Pennsylvania Appalachians, boats had to be hauled out of the water and winched up and over the mountain on fantastic inclined planes. It was a horrendous bottleneck. Miraculously, the Mainline Canal was completed and more or less functioned; Pennsylvania operated 608 miles of canal at the peak of the canal craze. But it was not the gold mine the Erie was. There were too many bottlenecks crowded with swearing boatmen in the mountains—where no boatman belonged.

All in all, some 4,000 miles of canal were dug in imitation of the Erie. Another 7,000 miles were on the drawing boards when the bubble burst. Although many canals were invaluable to local use, only a few made enough money to cover the investment in them. So many states saddled themselves with debt to fund poorly conceived projects that many politicians, including westerners, swore never again to finance any kind of state-owned internal improvements. As late as 1848, the constitution of the new state of Wisconsin forbade the expenditure of tax money on public works. The bitter reaction to the canal bust ensured that railroads (which helped end the canal age) would not be built and owned by government but by private entrepreneurs.

EARLY RAILROADS

Canals were destined to be superceded by a machine that proved workable in England in 1825, the year the Erie was completed. The steam locomotive that could pull dozens of heavily laden cars on iron tracks had several advantages over canals. Canals were plausible only when the terrain was not theatrical—in reasonably flat country—and where the water supply was plentiful and constant. Canals shut down during

It cost more to ship by railroad than by canal, but canals could not be dug over mountains. This locomotive was one of the first to cross the Appalachians. The celebrants posing on the "cowcatcher" are probably company officials and their wives. Unless the engine had been scoured for the occasion, they were dirty when they climbed down.

the winter when they froze over. Railroads could be built almost anywhere; trains were several times faster than canal boats and, except during catastrophic blizzards, they operated every day and night of the year. Even eight-foot snowdrifts could be cleared from the tracks in a few hours.

The New York and Erie Railroad

In order to offset the economic advantages that the Erie Canal had brought to the northern counties of New York State, the southern counties proposed to build a railroad between the Hudson River and Lake Erie. Chartered on April 24, 1832, the New York and Erie Railroad (commonly called the Erie) ran 446 miles between Piermont on the Hudson (26 miles from New York City) and Dunkirk on Lake Erie.

In 1851, trains carried President Millard Fillmore and his cabinet on what was then the longest continuous railroad in the world. Secretary of State Daniel Webster had, it was reported, "on a flat car, at his own request, a big easy rocking-chair provided for him to sit on. He chose this manner of riding so that he could get a better view and enjoy the fine country through which the railroad passed."

The first two American railroads were built in 1827. Both were just a few miles long; they replaced long used wagon roads. One connected the granite quarries of Quincy, Massachusetts with the Neponset River. The other carried coal from Carbondale, Pennsylvania to the Lehigh River. Quarrying and mining companies built them for their exclusive use.

Elsewhere, entrepreneurs built railroads that would haul any kind of freight any customer would pay to have moved, including the transport of travelers. Most were quite short, connecting cities with their hinterlands or other cities nearby. In 1833, with 136 miles of track, the Charleston and Hamburg was the longest railroad in the world.

Shipping by rail was more expensive than shipping by canal. Start-up costs were formidable. Right-of-way had to be secured by hook or crook. Construction was usually cheaper per mile than digging a canal but still costly. And unlike canals (and turnpikes), that collected tolls from users who owned their boats, mules, wagons, and teams, railroad companies had to buy locomotives and rolling stock. Investors were reluctant to risk their money anywhere but in areas where plenty of customers already lived.

The railroad's full potential lay in using it—like the National Road and the Erie Canal—over long distances,

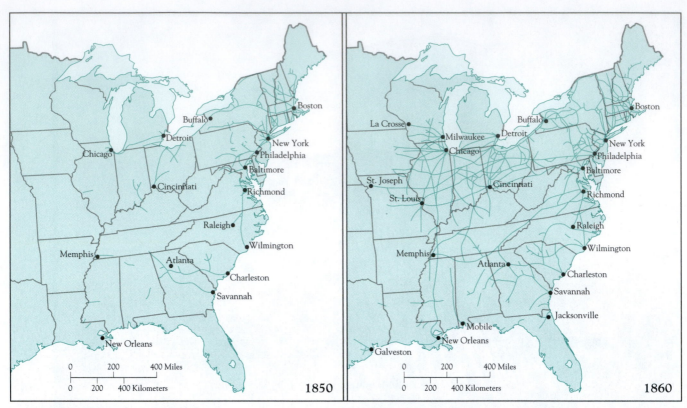

MAP 13:4 Railroads, 1850–1860
In 1850, American railroads were short and fragmented, serving only small, local regions. By 1860, there were several routes running continuously from the Northeast to the West for a thousand miles. The process of binding the country together in a national economy was well underway.

connecting distant regions. The first entrepreneurs to recognize this were Baltimoreans hoping to put their city back into competition with New York City for the trade of the West. In 1828, work began on America's first trunk line, the Baltimore and Ohio.

The B&O was plagued by financial difficulties; on several occasions, construction was suspended for years while the company hunted for more capital. Finally, in 1853, the line was completed to Wheeling on the Ohio River. In the meantime, another trunk line, the Erie Railroad, was completed. It extended 441 miles across New York State and was the longest railroad company in the world. Indeed, the United States was the world's premier railroad country. When American railroad mileage reached 6,000 (in 1848), there were fewer than 3,000 miles of track in the rest of the world.

"OLD MAN RIVER"

With its two great tributaries, the Ohio and Missouri Rivers, and dozens of smaller but navigable feeders, the Mississippi River drains the central third of the North American continent. Westerners who lived in the Mississippi Valley shipped their corn and livestock to New Orleans on log rafts that, broken up and sawed into lumber, supplemented income. A youthful Abraham Lincoln once shipped aboard a Mississippi raft.

The catch was moving goods upstream. Despite the width of the river, sailing ships were of little use. The Mississippi

current was more powerful than the strongest winds. Channels deep enough to float ocean-going vessels were too narrow for tacking; worse, they were constantly shifting as the river created sandbars and washed others away.

Some cargo was moved upstream in 50-foot-long "keelboats" by a procedure so laborious that one can feel faint reading about it. When the river bottom was deep enough to allow movement close to the banks, ropes were secured to trees upstream and the crew heaved the keelboat forward. Away from the riverbanks, the work was even harder. Bracing a long, sturdy pole in the muddy bottom, lines of crewmen walked bow to stern, poling the boat slowly forward, then returned to the bow, and on and on. A keelboat could move fifteen miles a day. Hauling a cargo from New Orleans to Louisville took between three and four months.

Because crews had to be large, shipping by keelboat was very expensive. It was feasible to ship only the costliest cargos upriver: cloth, leather products, iron and steel tools, and furniture. It cost far less to move a ton of freight from Europe to New Orleans than from New Orleans to St. Louis.

QUEENS OF THE MISSISSIPPI

The marvel that solved the problem of upstream transportation on the shallow Mississippi was the flat-bottomed steamboat. A Connecticut Yankee named John Fitch, then living in Philadelphia, ran a practical 45-foot steamboat down and up

© Bettmann/Corbis

The flat bottoms and shallow drafts of Mississippi steamboats allowed them to tie up at river banks in order to take aboard cotton directly from a plantation, as shown here. They also stopped when they needed cordwood. Locals, often slaves working on their own time, set up piles of wood, like roadside fruit stands today, to attract the boats.

the Delaware River in 1787. (Several delegates to the Constitutional Convention witnessed the spectacle.) But Fitch never exploited his invention. The steamboat had to be reinvented in 1807 by Robert Fulton, this time in New York. Fulton's *Clermont* wheezed, chugged, and clanked up the Hudson River to Albany at five miles per hour. The *Clermont* was three times as long as John Fitch's boat, but the dimension that thoughtful people noticed was that it drew only seven feet of water. The boat was able to clear shallows and underwater obstacles such as snags (fallen trees) that would ground or sink a sailing ship.

Steamboats more than paid their way on eastern rivers. But it was on the Mississippi, Missouri, and Ohio that they were indispensable. Fulton understood this; just a few years after his success with the *Clermont* he went west and built the first Mississippi paddle wheeler. It was not powerful enough to buck the river's currents, however. A competitor's boat was; in 1815, it made the first steam-powered upstream voyage from New Orleans to Louisville. By 1817, there were 17 steamboats on the Mississippi. By 1830, there were 187 with new ones being constructed more quickly than the old ones blew up.

Boiler explosions were no small problem. In order to minimize the weight of the boats, boilers were constructed more flimsily than good sense prescribed. Nonetheless, after the *Tecumseh* set a record of eight days and two hours from New Orleans to Louisville in 1827, riverboat captains found it difficult to resist the challenge of a race. Speed sold tickets and attracted shippers. So, despite the opulence of some steamboats, traveling on one was a bit of a gamble. At the peak of the steamboat age, 500 people died in accidents each year. In the explosion of the *Moselle* in 1838, 150 people were lost.

Steamboats drew very little water. Sandbars piled up to just feet below the surface and they shifted location constantly. The Missouri River was shallower than the Mississippi. If the competition to design boats with ever shallower drafts was less dramatic than the competition to set speed records, it was also less dangerous, and much more important. The champion was the **Orphan Boy,** launched in 1841. Loaded with 40 tons of freight plus passengers, it skimmed atop water only two feet deep. Dozens of paddle wheelers carried even heavier cargos drawing three or four feet. The steamboats' shallow drafts not only solved the problems of shifting sandbars and snags, it enabled the boats to tie up at river banks anywhere to take on the cordwood the boats burned in prodigious quantities.

FURTHER READING

General D. W. Meinig, *The Shaping of America: A Geographical Perspective on 500 Years of History*, vol. 2: *Continental America, 1800–1867*, 1993; Charles G. Sellers, *The Market Revolution: Jacksonian America, 1815–1846*, 1991; Jack Larkin, *The Reshaping of Everyday Life, 1790–1940*, 1988; Daniel Feller, *The Jacksonian Promise: America, 1815–1840*, 1993; Henry L. Watson, *Liberty and Power*, 1990; Jean Mathews, *Toward a New Society: American Thought and Culture, 1800–1830*, 1990.

Land Policy and Internal Improvements Malcolm J. Rohrbaugh, *The Trans-Appalachian Frontier: People, Societies, Institutions*, 1978; Daniel Feller, *The Public Lands in Jacksonian Politics*, 1984; Stephen Aron, *How the West Was Lost: The Transformation of Kentucky from Daniel Boone to Henry Clay*, 1996; Joan E. Cashin, *A Family Venture: Men and Women on the Southern Frontier*, 1991; John Mack Faragher, *Sugar Creek: Life on the Illinois Prairie*, 1986; John L. Larson, *Internal Improvement: National Public Works and the Promise of National Government in the Early United States*, 2001; Philip D. Jordan, *The National Road*, 1948.

Canals and Railroads Ronald E. Shaw, *Erie Water West: A History of the Erie Canal, 1792–1854*, 1966; Carol Sheriff, *The Artificial River: The Erie Canal and the Paradox of Progress, 1817–1863*, 1996; Dan Murphy, *The Erie Canal: The Ditch that Opened a Nation*, 2001; Peter L. Bernstein, *The Wedding of the Waters: The Erie Canal and the Making of a Great Nation*, 2005; Ronald E. Shaw, *Canals for a Nation: The Canal Era in the United States, 1790–1860*, 1990; Albert Fishlow, *American Railroads and the Transition of the Ante-Bellum Economy*, 1965; James A. Ward, *Railroads and the Character of America, 1820–1887*, 1986; George R. Taylor, *The Transportation Revolution, 1815–1860*, 1951; David F. Hawke, *Nuts and Bolts of the Past: A History of American Technology, 1776–1860*, 1988; David Nye, *Consuming Power: A Social History of American Energies*, 1998.

Biography William Chambers, *Old Bullion Benton: Senator from the New West*, 1970; Robert V. Remini, *Henry Clay: Statesman for the Union*, 1991; Merrill D. Peterson, *The Great Triumvirate: Webster, Clay, and Calhoun*, 1987.

KEY TERMS

The following terms are covered in this chapter and can also be found in the list of Key Terms at the back of the book.

American System	internal improvements	preemption	Thomas Hart Benton
DeWitt Clinton	National Road	the Mainline Canal	
graduation	*Orphan Boy*		

ONLINE SOURCES GUIDE

Use this listing to find online documents, images, interactive maps, simulations, and other resources related to this chapter:

American History Resource Center
http://history.wadsworth.com

Selected Images
The Mohawk and Hudson Railroad's DeWitt Clinton
Erie Canal, Lockport, NY

Interactive Timeline (with online readings)
Beyond the Appalachians: The West in the Early Nineteenth Century

Discovery

How did the economic changes of the early nineteenth century contribute to the rising sectional tensions that would plague the United States later?

In thinking about this question, begin by breaking it down into the components shown below. A discussion of the significance of each component should appear in your answer.

Geography: For this exercise, study Maps 13:1 and 13:2. Compare the growth of the population in cities in early nineteenth-century America. What patterns are immediately clear? Where is the population concentrated and why? How would this create differing views of the role of government in society and the economy? How would this contribute to differing economic development in different sections of the country?

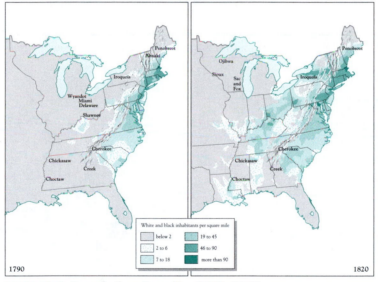

White and black inhabitants per square mile

below 2   19 to 45

2 to 6   46 to 90

7 to 18   more than 90

1790   1820

MAP 13:1 Population Density, 1790–1820

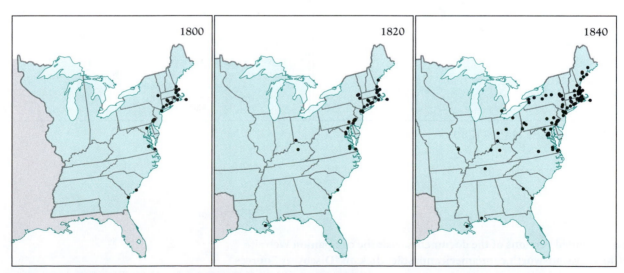

1800   1820   1840

MAP 13:2 Cities of At Least 5,000 Inhabitants, 1800–1840

Economics and Technology: For this exercise, study "The Erie Canal" image and Map 13:4. How did the Erie Canal transform New York and the rest of the United States? What impact did it have on development in rural areas? What other kinds of transportation experienced a boom in the mid-nineteenth century? Look at the map of railroads in the United States. What areas experienced the most growth in those twenty years? Do you see differences in the regions? What might explain those differences?

The Erie Canal

Courtesy of The New-York Historical Society, New York City

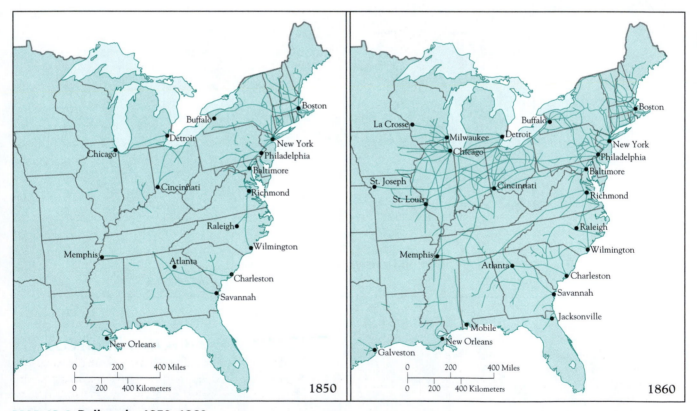

1850

1860

MAP 13:4 Railroads, 1850–1860

To read extended versions of the documents, visit the companion Web site http://history.wadsworth.com/americanpast8e; click on "Discovery Sources."

CHAPTER 14.

Nation Awakening

Political and Economic Development 1815–1824

© Bettmann/Corbis

Our country! In her intercourse with foreign nations, may she always be in the right; but our country, right or wrong.

Stephen Decatur

I can never join with my voice in the toast which I see in the papers attributed to one of our gallant naval heroes. I cannot ask of heaven success, even for my country, in a cause where she should be in the wrong. Let justice be done though the heavens fall. My toast would be, may our country be always successful, but whether successful or otherwise, always right.

John Quincy Adams

Henry Clay's vision of an integrated national economy did not spring full-blown from his personal ruminations. The American System was the product of a brief era when a nationalistic spirit transcended sectional loyalties. Sectionalism was there, but it was muted during what a New England editor called the "Era of Good Feelings."

The upsurge of nationalism began in 1815 with Andrew Jackson's victory at New Orleans and Stephen Decatur's punishment of the insolent Algerians. It was shaken in 1820 when northern and southern congressmen exchanged unbrotherly remarks in a debate as to whether Missouri should be admitted to the Union with a state constitution that legalized slavery. It ended in 1824 when another indecisive presidential election was resolved by seating a candidate who finished second in both popular votes and electoral votes.

THE ERA OF GOOD FEELINGS

In the decade after the divisive War of 1812, Americans everywhere embraced an image of themselves as a new chosen people, unique on the face of the earth, unsullied by the corruptions of Europe, nurtured by their closeness to nature, and committed in the marrow of their bones to liberty, democracy, and progress.

It was during this period that the Fourth of July became a day of raucous popular celebration. Formerly observed with religious services and decorous promenades of the social elite in city squares, the Glorious Fourth burst into prominence as a day when everyone paid homage to independence with games, feasting, excessive drink, and boisterous gaiety.

Historical Society of Pennsylvania

The Fourth of July, 1818. Twenty years earlier, it was a holiday to which only the genteel paid much attention, promenading in their best clothing. After the war of 1812, Independence Day became pretty raucous, lubricated by free-flowing liquor.

PATRIOTIC CULTURE

Patriotism permeated popular art. Woodcarvers and decorators trimmed canal boats, sailing ships, stagecoaches, and private homes with screaming eagles clutching braces of arrows; the idealized, vigilant female figure that represented liberty; and the flag, the only national ensign that had progress sewn into it. Between 1816 and 1820, six new stars were added to Old Glory as six new states entered the Union.

The needlepoint samplers that girls made to display their mastery of womanly skills depicted patriotic as often as religious themes: the Stars and Stripes, or the brave sayings of national heroes like Nathan Hale's "I regret that I have but one life to give for my country" and Decatur's "Our country right or wrong." Newspapers published exuberant verses touting the glories of the United States. Songwriters churned out lyrics that celebrated American grandeur.

Nationalism and Industry 1790–1830

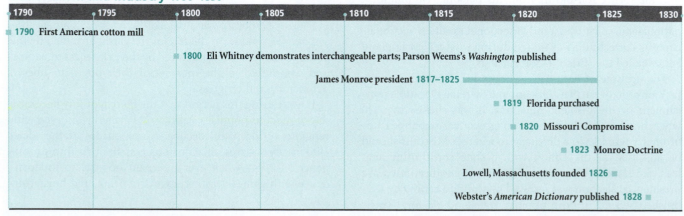

1790	1795	1800	1805	1810	1815	1820	1825	1830

1790 First American cotton mill

1800 Eli Whitney demonstrates interchangeable parts; Parson Weems's *Washington* published

James Monroe president 1817–1825

1819 Florida purchased

1820 Missouri Compromise

1823 Monroe Doctrine

Lowell, Massachusetts founded 1826

Webster's *American Dictionary* published 1828

Noah Webster

Not all of Noah Webster's spelling reforms caught on, although some may be found in student essays to this day: *karacter*, *wimmen*, *definit*, *fether*, *tung*, *bred* (bread). In fact, after a trip to England in 1828 where he was wowed by British sophistication, Webster recanted his spellings of *flavour*, *kerb*, *gaol*, and other words, but it was too late. He was brilliant; he taught himself twenty languages. He was also humorless, without social graces, and unbearably pious. He prepared an edition of the Bible in which he left out words "offensive to delicacy," including *breast*.

> *Many words are offensive, especially for females, as to create a reluctance in young persons to attend Bible classes and schools, in which they are required to read passages which cannot be repeated without a blush; and containing words which on other occasions a child ought not to utter without rebuke.*

It is at least as likely that the Sundays when the offensive texts were studied were the most popular.

noble was the father of his country that he could not fib; so far did he tower above other nations' heroes that even in physical strength he was a superman: "It is hardly an exaggeration to say that he was as pious as Numa; just as Aristides; temperate as Epictetes; patriotic as Regulus; impartial as Severus," Weems wrote, challenging readers' recollection of ancient history even in an era when the subject was taught in every school.

Another influential author of the era was Noah Webster, whose *American Spelling Book*, first published in 1783, sold more than sixty million copies in perhaps 300 editions. From the "blue-backed speller," schoolchildren learned that the American tongue was superior to British English because Webster had stripped it of Old World affectations. Many of the differences in spelling between American English and British English today (*labor*, *theater*, *curb*, and *jail* as opposed to *labour*, *theatre*, *kerb*, and *gaol*) owe to Webster's tinkering.

Noah Webster was also the father of that great event of the American elementary school, the spelling bee, for he was a stickler for uniform spelling and uniform pronunciation. It saddened him that even so great a figure as William Clark, in his journal of the great expedition across the continent, spelled mosquito nineteen different ways. Webster's *American Dictionary of the English Language*, published in 1828, distinguished American English from British English by including hundreds of words adopted from Indian languages.

In 1817, Attorney General **William Wirt** published a biography of Patrick Henry in which he implied that Virginians led the movement for independence and fought the war more-or-less single-handedly. Virginians loved it. Piqued patriots from other states responded with inevitably overblown celebrations of their homegrown demigods: Massachusetts's Paul Revere, Rhode Island's Nathaniel Greene, South Carolina's Francis Marion, and so on.

Less controversial because of its singular subject was Mason Locke Weems's *The Life and Memorable Actions of George Washington*. Although originally published in 1800, Weems's unblushing exercise in hero worship peaked in popularity during the 1810s and 1820s, running through fifty-nine editions. It was Weems who invented the story of the boy Washington chopping down the cherry tree and of an older Washington throwing a silver dollar across the Rappahannock River. So

NATIONALISM IN THE COURTROOM

On the Supreme Court, Chief Justice John Marshall had never ceased, through the Jeffersonian heyday, to write nationalism into constitutional law. He continued to buttress the primacy of the federal government over the states in a series of decisions that still rank among the most important in Supreme Court history. Despite Jefferson's hatred for him, and his own reputation for physical laziness and squalid personal habits, Marshall dominated his fellow Supreme Court justices until near the end of his thirty-five years as head of the Court.

He converted many of Jefferson's, Madison's, and Monroe's Republican appointees to his nationalism. In chambers by

The Sanctity of Contracts

Scarcely less important to John Marshall than the federal government's superiority to the states was his devotion to the sanctity of contracts. This was itself often a "Federalist" versus "Republican" issue because the offending party, in several of Marshall's decisions, was a state legislature dominated by Jeffersonians.

Fletcher v. Peck (1810) required Marshall to have a strong stomach. In 1794, an utterly corrupt Georgia legislature—just about every member was bribed—sold 35 million acres in what is now Alabama

and Mississippi to several speculators for 1.5 cents an acre. Two years later, an entirely new legislature rescinded the sale and voided the deeds of everyone who had already purchased some of the land from companies. (Most buyers were parties to the fraud.) One buyer, Robert Fletcher, sued to have the recision invalidated as a violation of the Constitution's "contract clause" (Article 1, Section 10). Repellent as he found the corruption, Marshall held that the original sale was nonetheless a legal contract and could not be rescinded.

In *Dartmouth College v. Woodward* (1819), Marshall ruled that a royal charter of 1769 granting self-governance to Dartmouth College, a private corporation in the law, was a contract. It could not, therefore, be invalidated by the New Hampshire state legislature, no matter how much invalidation might be in the public interest.

In *Ogden v. Saunders* (1827), Marshall found himself in dissent in a contract case. All those years of Republican presidents appointing justices had caught up with him. In a 4–3 decision, the Court ruled that contract rights were not absolute.

day, in the evening at his boardinghouse where several justices had rooms, over law books and over tumblers brimming with whiskey, Marshall whittled away at the powers of the states. He was rarely in dissent in important cases and wrote almost all the Court's decisions that had far-reaching consequences, assigning colleagues to less important cases.

In *Fletcher v. Peck* (1810), the Marshall court declared a state law unconstitutional, establishing the power of the Supreme Court over legislation concerned exclusively with a state's domestic affairs. In *Martin* v. *Hunter's Lessee* (1816), Marshall established the Court's authority to reverse the decision of a state court. In *McCulloch v. Maryland* (1819), Marshall told the state of Maryland (and other states) that it could not tax even a quasi-federal agency (the Bank of the United States), and made broad construction of federal powers the law of the land. *Gibbons* v. *Ogden* (1824) denied the states any voice in regulating interstate commerce. Aaron Ogden held a monopoly on steamboat navigation on the Hudson River granted by the New York state legislature. Thomas Gibbons had a federal license to run steamboats between New York and New Jersey. Marshall ruled that Gibbons's federal license nullified Ogden's state-granted monopoly.

John Marshall was Chief Justice during the administrations of six presidents, three of whom served two full terms. In 1833, Joseph Story, the only Supreme Court justice of the era in Marshall's league (and to whose disagreements Marshall listened respectfully), published *Commentaries on the Constitution of the United States*. Essentially, this classic textbook was a commentary on fundamental law as John Marshall had defined it.

SUCCESSFUL DIPLOMACY

The gentleman who presided over the "Era of Good Feelings" was, like three of the four presidents who preceded him, a Virginian: James Monroe of Westmoreland County. His is a blurred figure in the history books; a personality, like his face, with no hard edges.

Monroe's achievements can be listed. He was one of Jefferson's most loyal followers (although, in 1808, he tried to

---

The Year Without a Summer

For those who lived through it, especially easterners, 1816 was less memorable for James Monroe's election than for the fact that there was no summer. On June 6, one to two feet of snow fell over much of the Northeast. Temperatures were twenty or thirty degrees cooler than usual and almost every day was cloudy. It snowed again in both July and August.

Only in the twentieth century was the summerless year explained. Mount Tamboura in Java had erupted, filling the atmosphere with a cloud of dust dense enough to filter the sun over much of the world. Europe had less of a summer than Americans did.

---

defeat James Madison, Jefferson's pick, for the party's presidential nomination). He was an able diplomat, a good administrator, and incorruptible. "Turn his soul wrong side outwards," Jefferson said, "and there is not a speck on it." It can be noted that his wife was thought one of the country's most beautiful women. Portraits of James show that, in his dotage, he dressed eccentrically in the old-fashioned knee breeches of the Revolutionary era; his contemporaries had long since been pulling on the utilitarian trousers of the nineteenth century each morning.

But a two-dimensional oil painting James Monroe remains. Perhaps it is because he was not a man of the mind as Jefferson and Madison were. Perhaps it is because his presidency was an effortless success. Presidents tried by crisis are memorable. Monroe was confronted with only a few "problems," and they were promptly resolved. Happy presidencies, like Leo Tolstoy's happy families, are all the same and therefore not so interesting. In his second inaugural address in 1821, Monroe could intone the bromide that United States "will soon attain the highest degree of perfection of which human institutions are capable." What else is there to say?

THE POLITICS OF CALM

The founding fathers expected that the United States would be governed without contention between political parties. Something similar came to pass during Monroe's presidency. The Federalist party, hostile to the War of 1812, collapsed when the war was concluded with Jackson's symbolic but glorious victory at New Orleans. Instantly, Federalist opposition to the war seemed more like disloyalty than good sense, even in New England.

The number of Federalist congressmen declined from 68 during the war to 42 in 1817 and 25 in 1821 (compared with 158 Jefferson Republicans). By 1821, there were only four Federalists in a Senate of 48 members. Old John Adams, in retirement in Quincy, took little interest in the evaporation of the party he had helped to found. His son, John Quincy Adams, joined the party of Thomas Jefferson and Monroe named him secretary of state.

Until 1824, Republican congressmen and senators, meeting in a **caucus,** chose their presidential candidate and, in effect, the next president. Monroe, the choice of the caucus in 1816, handily defeated Federalist Rufus King. King won the electoral votes of only Delaware, Connecticut, and Massachusetts. The next year, when President Monroe visited Boston, where Jefferson had been loathed and Madison despised, the city cheered, praised, honored, and dined him.

In 1820, Monroe was unopposed. (One member of the electoral college cast his vote for John Quincy Adams so that no president but Washington would have the distinction of being his country's unanimous choice.) With only one political party, the United States had, in effect, no parties at all.

Unsurprisingly, voters and even politicians were indifferent to presidential politics. In 1816, William Crawford of Georgia would probably have won the Republican nomination over Monroe if he had thought the prize worth a fight.

He did not; so his supporters did not bother to attend the caucus.

Nor was there much popular interest in the elections. In 1816, only six of nineteen states chose presidential electors by popular vote alone; in 1820, only seven of twenty-four states did. In most of the other states, legislatures named the electors and they treated the task as they would have treated a motion to grant a pension to a retiring doorkeeper. In 1820, in Richmond, Virginia, a city of 12,000, only seventeen men bothered to vote.

There is nothing intrinsically wrong in a subdued president and popular indifference to politics, particularly according to the Jeffersonian faith. Jefferson said that the government that governed least governed best. If Monroe was neither mover nor shaker, history's movers and shakers have often done a good deal of mischief along with any legacies for which they can be honored. Monroe left little legacy; he did no mischief. He was competent, conscientious, and content to allow perhaps the greatest of all Secretaries of State, John Quincy Adams, peacefully and without bluster, to effect several diplomatic coups.

CANADA AND FLORIDA

The noteworthy achievements of the Monroe administration were diplomatic. And foreign affairs were so adroitly managed by Secretary of State Quincy Adams as to look effortless. In the Rush-Bagot Agreement of 1817, Adams arranged with Great Britain virtually to demilitarize the Great Lakes. It saved both countries money and freed lakefront towns from the fear of naval bombardment. The treaty also set the Canadian-American border west of the Great Lakes at 49 degrees north latitude, where it remains today. Britain conceded Americans' rights equal to those of British subjects in the "Oregon Country"—present-day Oregon, Washington, and British Columbia. That was a major victory for Quincy Adams; if the British claim to Oregon was just a claim and the British presence in Oregon minimal, the United States claim was flimsier and had no presence there worth noticing.

America's southern neighbor, the once-mighty Spanish Empire, collapsed during the Monroe administration. By 1819, armies led by José de San Martín and Bernardo O'Higgins had ended Spanish rule in southern South America. Simon Bolivar was near victory in the northwest of the continent. Mexican independence, proclaimed in 1810 by a village priest, Miguel Hidalgo y Castillo, had been virtually assured in 1819 by an army commanded by Augustin de Iturbide. (Mexican independence officially dates from 1821.) Only Cuba, Puerto Rico, and San Domingo remained under Spanish control.

Florida was nominally Spanish but troubled and unstable, almost anarchic. Four-fifths of the peninsula was unexplored. The interior was not a Spanish domain; it was firmly in the hands of Indians, including the aggressive Seminole, a branch of the Creek nation that had adopted numerous blacks who had escaped both Spanish masters and Georgia planters. Except for small and sleepy Spanish communities in Pensacola and St. Augustine, and a string of missions among the Indians, virtually all Florida's white (and slave) population lived on Key West, an island almost as close to Cuba as to the Florida mainland. Many of the whites on Key West were French, British, and American.

In 1818, Andrew Jackson demonstrated how weak Spain's hold on Florida was. Pursuing Creek warriors, his army pushed brazenly across the border. In the tiny town of Suwanee, he arrested two British subjects whom he accused of arming the Creek and encouraging them to attack Americans. (One of them may have been innocent.) Jackson hanged both for treason to the United States. It was extraordinary high-handedness; they were British subjects and Jackson was on foreign soil! Jackson then captured Pensacola, deposing the Spanish governor.

When the Spanish minister protested, a deadpan Quincy Adams responded by offering to buy Florida for $5 million. Spain had good reason to take the money. Some of Jackson's troops (although not the general) were still in Pensacola. Clearly, the town would fall to a small invasion force. Georgia and Alabama planters had puttered about over the border looking for cotton lands. American seizure of the province looked to be inevitable—Quincy Adams said as much (diplomatically) to the Spanish minister. With Spanish hopes of holding on to Mexico still alive, there were no troops available to defend Florida.

In the **Adams-Oñis Treaty** of 1819, Spain ceded Florida to the United States. A meaningless face-saving provision of the treaty drew the border between Louisiana and Spanish Texas where Spain had claimed it to be.

CONCERNS—RUSSIAN AMERICA AND THE CONCERT OF EUROPE

John Quincy Adams was a tireless worker. His every initiative was successful. He left the nation no mischievous legacies. And he thought ahead—for posterity (the Canadian border and American rights in Oregon); and about what might cause problems two or three or ten years down the road.

During Monroe's second term, Adams had two concerns. Russia, Austria, and France were dedicated, in the so-called

Russian California

By 1821, when the Czar hinted that Russia was in California to stay, the Russia America Company's Indian hunters had just about wiped out the sea otters that were the reason Fort Ross was established. For two decades, the tiny colony supplied Russian settlements in Alaska with grain and meat, but never adequately. In 1839, the Company contracted with the British Hudson's Bay Company to feed Alaska and decided to abandon Fort Ross. Mexico would not pay for the stockade, village, herds, a few cannon, and Russian claims because, to the Mexicans, the Russians were trespassing on Mexican territory. The Russia America company sold out to Johann Augustus Sutter, a Swiss adventurer who held a vast Mexican land grant and was soon to become internationally famous as the man who owned the land where the great gold rush started.

"Concert of Europe," to cooperate in restoring the world to what it had been before the French Revolution. All three powers were making noise about sending armies to the western hemisphere to restore Spain's empire. Such an intervention was not imminent, but Quincy Adams was not one to ignore possibilities.

Also bothersome was Russian activity on the Pacific coast of North America, in the Oregon Country and farther south, in the Mexican province of Alta California (Upper California, now the state of California). Russian claims to Alaska dated to 1741; the first permanent Russian settlement in Alaska was founded in 1784. A few years later, the Czar turned over administration of his distant property to the Russia America Company. The Company aggressively expanded settlement and extended its fur trapping operations to the south. Furs were its sole source of income.

Russian trappers and Alaskan Indian hunters harvested furs on the coasts and up the rivers of the Oregon Country. But then they moved on. In 1812, however, about twenty-five Russians and eighty Alaskans built a substantial redwood stockade, complete with blockhouses and cannon, and a village at **Fort Ross,** less than eighty miles from Spain's port of Yerba Buena (San Francisco), even closer to the mission town of Sonoma. The territory was universally recognized as Spanish (Mexican after 1821). But neither collapsing Spain nor unstable Mexico could do more than protest.

By 1821, the sea otters, whose lush furs had drawn the Russians to Fort Ross, were hunted out. However, the Russia America Company showed no signs of departing. The Company had established a number of farms and ranches in the vicinity of Fort Ross to raise grain, cattle, and sheep to feed its still lucrative settlements in Alaska.

Fort Ross was on Mexican land, not American. It was 1,700 miles and three mountain ranges away from St. Louis, the westernmost American city. The rare American ship that sailed California waters looked on Fort Ross as a godsend, an anchorage, and a speck of civilization on a wild coast. Then the Czar proclaimed that all foreign ships were banned within 100 miles of Russian America. How he was going to enforce such a policy was moot; it was a challenge.

THE MONROE DOCTRINE

President Monroe's annual message to Congress in December 1823 included a long section based on Quincy Adams's diplomatic concerns, probably written by him. Monroe began with a specific reference to "the respective rights and interests" of Russia and the United States on the Pacific coast. He informed Congress that he had asked Russia to join in "amicable negotiations" to resolve the conflict.

From an incidental, localized, and even trivial diplomatic matter, Monroe moved abruptly (thus dramatically) to the hemispheric subject of the "American continents!" North and South America, he declared, were "henceforth not to be considered as subjects for future colonization by any European powers." The United States never had and never would interfere in the European nations' affairs "relating to themselves." The "system" of the Americas had become "essentially different" from the "system" of the European powers, with the independence of the republics of Central and South America. Monroe was talking about colonies.

With existing colonies in the Americas, the United States had no quarrel. (Seven European nations had them.) However, Monroe said, "We should consider any attempt on their part to extend their system to any portion of this hemisphere as dangerous to our peace and safety." Monroe made it clear that the United States would regard any attempt to reestablish Spain's authority in her lost colonies as "manifestation of an unfriendly disposition toward the United States." In less diplomatic words, European military intervention in the western hemisphere meant war with the United States.

John Quincy Adams did not originate the **Monroe Doctrine** (a name given to it seventy years later). The British foreign minister, George Canning, had quietly proposed to him that Great Britain and the United States jointly proclaim the Americas closed to further colonization. (The Spanish Empire had been closed to British trade; Great Britain was the chief economic beneficiary of Latin American independence.) Adams decided that the United States would act alone without even informing Canning in advance. In a joint proclamation, the United States would look like "a cock-boat in the wake of the British man-of-war." By defining the

Female CEOs

A few women headed manufacturing companies. Rebecca Lukens owned and managed the Lukens Steel Company for twenty-five years. Her father had turned the company over to her husband, Charles Lukens. When he died in 1825, Rebecca was 30 years old with three young children. Nevertheless, she took over management of the factory and won the respect of other ironmasters.

Some goods resisted machine manufacture and continued to be produced by the "putting-out" system. Abby Condon of Penobscot, Maine became a cottage industry jobber during the Civil War when she won a government contract to provide mittens, at 25 cents a pair, for the Union army. She recruited knitters all over northern New England, collected the mittens, and delivered them to the army. When the war ended, the wholesale price of mittens collapsed to six cents a pair. Had Mrs. Condon's mittens been made by expensive machines in a factory, she would have been bankrupt. Thanks to the no overhead putting-out system, she stayed in business with as many as 250 knitters in her network. In 1882, when a knitting machine was finally perfected, Mrs. Condon purchased four and built a factory to house them. When she died in 1906, she owned 150 knitting machines. Her business consumed six tons of woolen yarn a year and produced 96,000 pairs of mittens.

Monroe Doctrine in terms of separate American and European destinies, he was able to assert the pride and confidence of the United States. All the while he knew that, if push came to shove, the Royal Navy would be there to help.

INDUSTRIALIZATION

Hamilton envisioned the United States as a major manufacturing nation. Although he fastidiously avoided profiting from speculation in the public paper to which his policies gave value, he was a major investor in the development of mills in Paterson, New Jersey, across the river from New York. Only after his death, however, did his dream (and Jefferson's nightmare) of an industrial United States become a reality. To some extent in the West, but mostly in New England and the Middle Atlantic states, manufacturing came to rival or exceed agriculture and even trade in economic importance. With the multiplication and growth of factories, the population of the Northeast shifted from farms and villages to towns and cities dedicated to manufacturing.

THE INDUSTRIAL REVOLUTION

Machine technology, the **factory system** as the chief means of producing goods, and urbanization—the "Industrial Revolution"—were not revolutionary in the sense that the nature of people's lives changed overnight. But the gradual, piecemeal consequences of machines that made goods quickly and cheaply changed the terms of human existence far more profoundly than any battle or beheading of a king ever did.

Thus, in the United States today, less than 8 percent of the population lives on farms; virtually no household in the country produces more than a tiny fraction of the food it consumes and the goods it uses. Most people buy commodities they need (or fancy) with money they have been paid for performing highly specialized jobs. Even the typical farm family raises one or two crops for market and purchases the same industrially produced and packaged milk, meat, vegetables, clothing, and other goods and luxuries that a family living in a fourth floor apartment buy.

Before the industrial revolution, in colonial and early national America, this situation was reversed. Roughly 90 percent of the population lived on farms. Households produced a sizable proportion of the food they consumed and many of the goods they needed. Purchases were few: shoes; some clothing; tools such as axes and guns; pottery and tin or pewter ware; specialized services such as milling flour, shoeing horses, and so on.

Many necessities ordinary people improvised from available materials. The preindustrial farmer or shopkeeper had to be handy. A man with a door to hang often made the hinges. A woman who kept a tidy house made the broom with which she swept it. In all but the half dozen largest cities, townspeople who were not rich or destitute maintained gardens, often a milk cow (even in the middle of big cities like Philadelphia and Boston), and sometimes a brood

A commercially printed fabric of the 1810s. It may have been used as a wall covering (wallpaper) but more likely it was made into drapes. Even the most patriotic families must have tired of it quickly.

sow. The Industrial Revolution changed all that, if not overnight, then within the experience of a generation.

IT STARTED WITH CLOTH

The first industrial machines manufactured cloth, unsurprisingly. Cloth is a nigh universal necessity but making it by hand is a complex multi-step process, each step tedious and time-consuming. First the fiber—some from animals (wool and silk); some from plants (hemp and flax, the fiber from which linen is made); and the king of them all, cotton—must be cleaned and carded, combed out and unsnarled.

Then it is spun, twisted uniformly to form a continuous yarn of uniform thickness. Different cultures devised different but similar devices to spin yarn quickly and uniformly; almost all involved a wheel of some kind. The European and American "spinning wheel," resembling a rickety wagon wheel, is the central fixture in our image of a preindustrial home. To spin yarn properly required long practice as well as a knack for the job; not everyone who tried to learn the skill succeeded. Once mastered, spinning was monotonous. In western culture, it was woman's work, performed when more pressing duties were done. (The legal term for an unmarried older woman was spinster, reflecting the fact that such women lived with a relative and, not having the duties of the mistress of the house, used their time to spin yarn.)

After spinning came knitting or crocheting, also women's work, or weaving, sometimes done by men.

Because the process from the harvest of fiber to the production of a bolt of cloth was so time consuming, handmade textiles not made at home for the use of the household were expensive, even the cloth that was made into everyday clothing. The poor did, literally, dress in rags. Some scavenged cast-off rags because they too, however dirty and torn, had cash value.

COTTAGE INDUSTRY

Well-to-do people did not pick and shear, wash, card, spin, and weave cloth. From time immemorial, some people have made cloth to sell to them. In the United States, owners of slaves had to buy cheap textiles with which to clothe their slaves. Before the industrial revolution, cloth for these markets was made by "cottage industry," by what was sometimes called "the putting-out system."

A dealer in textiles (or "factor") contracted with farm wives and their daughters to receive fiber he "put out" into their homes, spinning it into yarn in their spare time or, often enough for daughters, full-time. Pay was "by the piece," an agreed price for each yard of yarn spun. The factor then put the yarn out into a cottage specializing in weaving.

This system of production did not disturb traditional ways of life. Households involved in cottage industry were able to participate in the money economy to the extent of their earnings. However, women and girls who spun for money remained, essentially, farmwives, spinsters, and farmers' daughters not yet of marrying age. Their values and the rhythm of their lives were the same as those of their neighbors who were not involved in "putting out." Because the weaver's loom was more expensive than the spinning wheel, cottagers who weaved were more likely to do it full-time, and not farm. But they too worked in their homes, in villages among other weavers.

MACHINES AND POWER

In England in the mid-1700s, manufacturing underwent a fundamental change. Inventors devised machines powered by water mills that spun cotton into yarn and—soon enough—powered looms that wove cloth a hundred and

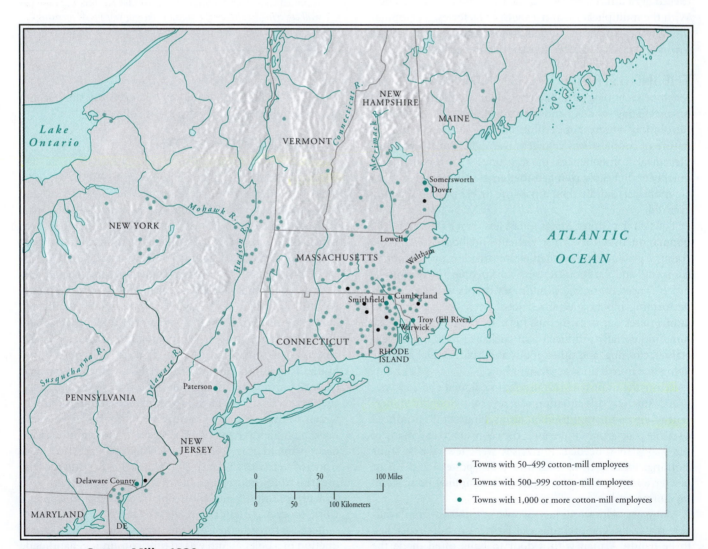

MAP 14:1 Cotton Mills, 1820

The mill towns appear to be scattered randomly; they were not. They were built at the "fall line" on rivers, where uplands dropped sharply to the coastal plan and streams tumbled on rapids or over waterfalls. Lowell, Massachusetts was built at the 32-foot falls of the Merrimack River. Up the Merrimack, at Manchester, New Hampshire, a "hideous rapids" dropped 85 feet. Paterson, New Jersey was built where the Passaic River, searching for the Hudson River, found a shortcut by creating a dramatic falls. Note how few mills there were on the mostly slow-flowing Connecticut River.

more times faster than hand spinners and hand weavers. What was more, the machines ran constantly until they broke down; hand workers had to rest. Setting aside the start-up costs of the machinery, the cost of machine-made cloth was a tiny fraction of the cost of homespun.

With a virtual monopoly of the new technology, Britain prospered as the world's supplier of cheap fabric. Women from Canada to Calcutta were delighted to be relieved of the tedium of spinning and weaving. British cloth was so cheap that all but the destitute could afford it (and its quality was better than that of most handmade cloth). The instantaneous success of spinning machines and power looms, and the riches they earned their owners, soon set inventors to work on machines with which to industrialize other kinds of manufacturing.

A single water mill could power dozens of machines. Industrial production of cloth, therefore, was centralized in factories. Instead of working in scattered cottages, as hand spinners and weavers did, the raw materials brought to them, workers in the new factory system came to the mill. The relentless, uninterrupted pace of the machines meant that, unlike workers in the putting-out system, they worked "full-time" and did nothing else. Full-time in the late eighteenth and early nineteenth centuries was as long as there was light by which to see, daybreak to sundown, sixteen hours a day during the summer.

Thus came the industrial revolution. Machines revolutionized the way cloth was made, the speed with which it was made, and the quantities in which it was made. The factory system revolutionized the way people involved in manufacturing lived. No longer did they spin or weave at home on farms during spare moments, or in cottages in villages. They became town and city dwellers, clustered around the mills that themselves clustered around the rapidly flowing waterways that powered the machines. Virtually all of their waking hours (Sundays excepted) were spent in factories tending machines. They paid their rent and bought their food and other necessities with the wages they were paid. They produced nothing for themselves, as farmers did. They were wage earners and consumers in a market economy.

The Granger Collection, New York

The first spinning mill in America, built in 1790 by Samuel Slater and Moses Brown in Pawtucket, Rhode Island. Note the dam across the river. The reservoir it created provided a steady supply of water that was diverted into a mill race that flowed in a torrent from right to left behind the mill, turning the waterwheel that powered the spinning machines. The first factories were small and designed with some attention to aesthetics—as evidenced by the cupola.

TECHNOLOGICAL PIRACY

The British tried to protect their technological monopoly as magicians guard their bags of tricks. It was illegal to export textile machinery or the plans for them. Additionally, engineers familiar with the new machines and even mechanics who repaired them were forbidden to leave the country.

One particularly knowledgeable engineer was Samuel Slater. He had been an apprentice to Sir Richard Arkwright, one of the founding fathers of the industrial revolution. Arkwright had invented both carding and spinning machines and he was a pioneer in the development of the factory system. Slater, learning that American investors were offering rewards to anyone who could build a spinning mill in the United States, memorized intricate drawings and long lists of specifications. He slipped away from his home and, in disguise, shipped off to the United States. There he struck a bargain with a Rhode Island merchant, Moses Brown, who had experimented unsuccessfully with spinning machines.

Brown put up the money; Slater contributed the know-how. In 1790, they opened a small water-powered cotton mill in Pawtucket, Rhode Island. The little factory housed only seventy-two spindles, a pipsqueak operation by British standards. Still, their six dozen spindles were the equivalent of seventy-two spinning wheels in seventy-two cottages.

Operating expenses were low. One supervisor (Slater, at first) and nine children between the ages of seven and twelve

American Ingenuity

The American fascination with gadgets is as old as the republic. European tourists observed—some with a chuckle, some aghast—that Americans dove into tinkering without planning. As an archetypical American engineer was supposed to have said, "Now, boys, we have got her done. Let's start her up and see why she doesn't work."

Between 1790 and 1800, Americans took out 306 patents. Between 1850 and 1860, the Patent Office registered more than 28,000. A year earlier, in 1849, an Illinois lawyer named Abraham Lincoln patented a device to float steamboats over shoals. Lincoln never learned if his invention worked because he never started it up.

ran the mill. Their wages ranged between 33 and 60 cents a week. Within a few years, Slater was rich and Brown richer than he had been. Slater lived to be one of New England's leading industrialists, owning mills in three states.

There were other such acts of technological piracy. In 1793, two brothers from Yorkshire, John and Arthur Schofield, emigrated illegally to Byfield, Massachusetts where they established the first American woolens mill. Francis Cabot Lowell of Massachusetts smuggled plans for a power loom out of England. Throughout the nineteenth century, Englishmen would bring valuable technological information to America in their sea trunks or heads.

Once aroused, Americans proved more than able to advance the industrial revolution on their own. Alexander Hamilton had observed "a peculiar aptitude for mechanical improvements" in the American people. In the 1820s, a foreign observer marveled that "everything new is quickly introduced here. There is no clinging to old ways; the moment an American hears the word 'invention' he pricks up his ears."

INVENTORS GALORE

Oliver Evans of Philadelphia earned nationwide fame when he contrived a continuous-operation flour mill. One man was needed to dump grain into one end of an ingenious complex of machinery. Without further human attention, the grain was cleaned, ground, weighed, and packed in barrels. Only at the end of the line was a second man required to pound a lid on the keg. Evans saved millers half their payroll.

In 1800, Eli Whitney devised a rotary cutting tool that quickly and cheaply milled small cast iron parts. Whitney's invention augured to make highly skilled gunsmiths obsolete. For, in making new guns and watches, and in repairing broken ones, they had to construct each of dozens of moving parts from scratch. Every musket and rifle was "custom made," their locks (the devices that fired the guns) were individually fashioned by hand; no two guns were the same. When one part was broken, the gunsmith had to dismantle the lock and make a replacement that fit perfectly. Whitney's milling device made it plausible to mass-produce parts of gunlocks that were interchangeable.

He appeared before a congressional committee with ten functional muskets he had constructed. He took them apart, shuffled all the components into a pile, and, picking parts out at random, reassembled ten muskets. His dramatic little show won him a government contract to make 10,000 of the weapons.

Many cultures produce inventors; the United States was peculiar in that the nation raised the inventor to the status of a hero, almost the equivalent of a conquering general. Even bastions of tradition embraced practical science. In 1814, Harvard College instituted a course called "Elements of Technology." In 1825, Rensselaer Polytechnic Institute, a college devoted entirely to the new learning, was founded at Troy, New York. Others followed in quick succession, for Americans found nothing bizarre in teaching engineering side by side with Greek and Latin. Indeed, they were increasingly more likely to be suspicious of the classics than of engineering.

A COUNTRY MADE FOR INDUSTRY

A cultural predilection to technology was only one American advantage in making the most of the Industrial Revolution. The United States was also blessed with the other prerequisites of an industrial society: "raw materials," the natural resources machines turned into saleable goods; capital, surplus money to finance the building of factories; and access to plenty of labor, people to operate the machines.

The Granger Collection, New York

The Second Bank of the United States in Philadelphia, chartered by Congress in 1816. After several years of incompetent management (the BUS contributed to the Panic of 1819), it became a valuable source of capital for manufacturers.

Roads

One dictionary defines *road* as "an open way, generally public, for the passage of vehicles, persons, and animals."

With a few exceptions, the roads of the colonies and early nation were not good. Most were dirt tracks that became impassable quagmires after the spring thaw and even after a heavy summer rain. Maintenance was poor. Responsibility for repairs was usually put on those who lived along the highway. Connecticut, for example, required "every teeme and person fitt for labour" living along a road to devote two days a year to maintenance.

People with access to water that would float a boat preferred to travel, as well as move their goods, by water. From Portsmouth to Savannah, rivers and sheltered coastal inlets were filled with small vessels sailing or being rowed to and fro. On horseback, it took George Washington four days to get from Mount Vernon to Williamsburg, so bad was overland travel in Virginia. By boat, the trip took less than two days. Providence was connected to Hartford and New Haven by the Pequot Trail, but anyone living near Long Island Sound traveled by water. Philadelphia was only a hundred miles from New York, and there was a highway connecting the two cities as early as 1700. Nonetheless, travelers who had the means rounded New Jersey by schooner or sloop.

Early American highways followed routes blazed by Indians. The Boston Post Road (present-day U.S. Route 1) followed the Pequot Trail. The road British General Braddock built to battle the French and Indians followed Nemacolin's Path. Daniel Boone renamed the Shawnees'

The Granger Collection, New York

and Cherokees' Warriors Path through Kentucky the Wilderness Road.

There was no money to be made in road building so only government, with interests other than profit, could undertake big projects. Until the adoption of the Constitution, the federal governments helped to finance post roads (roads over which letters were carried) but they needed to accommodate only horses.

The great breakthrough in road surfacing was the work of a Scotsman, John McAdam, who discovered that it was not necessary to construct a roadbed of large stone blocks, as the Romans had done, in order to have a roadway that remained passable come high water. His road base (named macadam after him), raised a foot or two above the terrain for drainage, was constructed of small, uniformly sized stones, broken by hand; or, if a natural gravel deposit was available, mined. The traffic would continually compact the roadbed.

A cheaper surface in forested areas was made by laying 8-foot logs of 6 to 8 inches in diameter across the roadway. Eight feet of good old dirt road ran alongside so that vehicles could pass, although not always cordially. Known as corduroy roads, for obvious reasons, they were built in newly developed areas until late in the nineteenth century. Corduroy roads could be dangerous if teamsters were careless entering or leaving them. But they were cheap and easy to repair by replacing rotted logs with newly cut ones.

RESOURCES AND CAPITAL

For a people still providentially minded, it was as if the Creator had shaped the northeastern states with water-powered machinery in mind. From New England to New Jersey, the country was traversed with fast-running streams that, dammed and channeled, provided power for factories. When steam power proved superior to water power in some ways, there were plenty of forests and abundant deposits of coal to stoke boilers. America's forests and vast agricultural base produced the raw materials industrialization required, from lumber to leather to hemp for rope. During the years the tex-

tile industry was growing in New England, cotton cultivation expanded across the lower South to provide enough fiber for the mills of both America and Great Britain.

Money to buy machinery and build factories was provided, at first, by northeastern merchants. Ironically, the Embargo and Non-Intercourse Acts, and the disruption of overseas trade during the War of 1812—all of which northeastern merchants had opposed—persuaded many of them to divert their capital from shipping to mills, much to their advantage in the long run. In 1800, before the long war between France and Britain, there were seven spinning mills in New England with a total of 290 spindles. After fifteen years of restrictions on trade and maritime war, there were 130,000 spindles in 213 factories in Massachusetts, Connecticut, and Rhode Island alone. Aware of a good thing once it enriched them beyond an overseas merchant's dreams, investors never looked back. The American merchant fleet, once equal in ships to Great Britain's, steadily declined. Industry steadily expanded. By 1840, there were two million spindles in the United States.

The Second Bank of the United States, after weathering harsh political criticism after the Panic of 1819, was another fount of capital. Conservatively managed after 1822, it supported state banks that observed BUS standards for the ratio between the amount of money they printed and their gold and silver reserves by lending approved banks money that, in turn, the state banks loaned to manufacturers. Banks were, like creeks and rivers, a source of energy.

INDUSTRY AND POLITICS

As manufacturing became central to the economy of the New England states, New England's politics changed character. Overseas merchants had generally opposed high tariffs on imported goods. Their business was moving goods—the more goods to be shipped the better—and if manufactures came from Great Britain, better they cost as little as possible in the United States so that more people could afford them. Alexander Hamilton failed to get the high protective tariff he wanted in part because many of New England's congressmen, faithful Federalists on other issues, voted with Jeffersonian farmers and southern planters (consumers of British manufactures) to defeat him.

As late as 1816, some New England congressmen were voting against high protective tariffs. One was Daniel Webster, a 34-year-old lawyer and representative from New Hampshire who numbered Portsmouth merchants among his clients. Webster moved to Massachusetts and soon numbered textile manufacturers among his most lucrative clients. In 1823, when Webster returned to Congress as a Massachusetts resident, he dedicated his eloquence to calling for the high protective tariffs he had denounced four years earlier.

Manufacturers dictated the Northeast's political interests. Politically, mill owners were not competitors but united in their demands, and they were efficient. John Randolph of Virginia, who despised their program, explained why: "Do but ring the firebell, and you can assemble all the manufacturing interests of Philadelphia in fifteen minutes. Nay, for that matter, they are always assembled."

THE FIRST FACTORY WORKERS

Slater and Brown hired children to tend the first American spinning machine. Young children continued to fill factory jobs involving no great strength and little danger. In cotton mills, for example, "bobbin boys" carried boxes of wooden bobbins (spools) wound with newly spun yarn from spinning rooms to weavers and boxes of bobbins they'd unwound back to the spinners. As spinning machines were enlarged, children were too short to reach far enough to perform some of the tasks tending the machines required.

And the machines could be dangerous. The bobbins spun at hundreds of revolutions a minute; the power from the water mill was transferred to the machinery by a dizzying network of broad leather belts on pulleys turning almost as fast. An operator had to take care lest hair, clothing, or a hand be caught in the works. Such an accident could mean scalping, loss of a limb, or death. Children at their freshest are not attentive; and they tire quickly from monotonous routine.

Some factory owners, notably at Fall River, Massachusetts, hired entire families to work their mills. Their reasoning was rooted in the way of life they knew: families ran farms—adult males shouldering the heavy work; women the jobs requiring skill but less physical strength; children saving adults time by fetching water and firewood, feeding chickens, and the like. Why not hire families to divide up millwork similarly? The "Fall River system" was a failure. The pace of factory work was entirely different from the rhythms of life on a farm. The head of the family's authority over his wife and children inevitably clashed with the mill owner's authority over all of them. First in Rhode Island, then elsewhere, including Fall River, mill owners put the man of the house on a small farm and put his wife and children to work in the mills.

THE LOWELL GIRLS

A more successful system, because it found a niche within the traditional social structure beneficial both to mill owners and to ever-struggling New England farmers was the "Lowell System." Francis Cabot Lowell built several large mills at Waltham, Massachusetts in 1813, and, in 1826, in a town he founded and named after himself. Lowell staffed his mills by dispatching recruiters to roam rural New England. They persuaded farmers to send their teenage daughters to work in Lowell's mills. For seventy hours a week tending machines, the girls and young women earned $3, paying half of that for room and board at Lowell's strictly-supervised lodging houses. The rest of their pay the girls could send home or save so as to have a dowry.

The long workweek put off no one. It was a normal enough regimen for a farm girl. The money was attractive. Farming the stony New England soil never made anyone rich. Yankee farmers had large families; they liked the prospect of subtracting one diner from the table. Lowell did not offer lifelong careers. The idea that anyone should toil in a mill through life appalled him as it appalled tradition-minded farmers. The "Lowell Girls" would work two, three, four years, accumulate an attractive dowry—which, in theory, got them better husbands—quit their jobs, and live as God intended, as farmwives.

The trick was to persuade straitlaced, religious New Englanders to allow daughters of 17 to leave home. Lowell worked it by providing a strictly regulated life for his employees during off-hours as well as when they were working. The girls lived in company-run dormitories, attended church services, and were kept busy (as if seventy hours at work each week were not enough) with a variety of educational and cultural programs.

University of Massachusetts, Lowell

New England mill girls in smocks to protect their clothing from dirt, lint, and tears. They were likely to work only a few years, then marry. Their wages were invaluable to their families; New England farms produced little income. They also earned dowries that their families (particularly if there were several sisters) could not afford. Factory work was hard and the hours long, but many of the girls found the social experience of so many companions exhilarating.

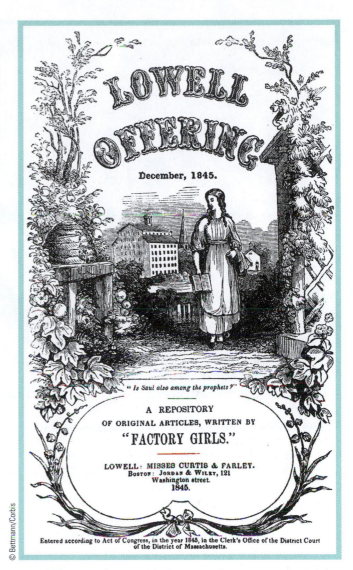

© Bettmann/Corbis

The paternalistic supervision of the "factory girls" at Francis Cabot Lowell's mills was comprehensive. Attendance at church was mandatory; employees presented slips signed by ministers to their supervisors each Monday morning. "Dating" was closely monitored; the Lowell girls were less likely to get pregnant than girls on New England farms. In a literary magazine the employees themselves produced, they published their own poetry, stories, and essays.

Most of the first American industrial workers were women; the rest were children. In 1820, about half the factory hands in Massachusetts mills were under 16 years of age. A society of farmers, in which everyone down to six years of age had assigned chores, did not find this inhumane. And the pace of the early factory, although more demanding than work on a farm, was far more leisurely than work on a twenty-first century assembly line. Operatives minding textile machines shut them down when they thought it necessary to do so. In some mills, girls were permitted to entertain visitors while they watched their spindles. English tourists commented that American factories were idyllic compared with England's "dark, satanic mills." Nevertheless, life at Lowell was not idyllic. In 1834 and 1836, angry Lowell Girls shut down the mills until their demands for better compensation were met.

THE SOUTH AT THE CROSSROADS

While westerners tamed forests and northeasterners built mills, towns, and cities, southerners reaffirmed an agrarian society largely based on slavery. There were those who would have had it otherwise. In 1816, when Daniel Webster was still speaking for the shipping interests of old New England, John C. Calhoun of South Carolina promoted the construction of cotton mills in the state.

But Calhoun's flirtation with industrialization, like his War Hawk super nationalism in 1812, was not to last. His

Culver Pictures, Inc.

A lithograph celebrates the economic revolution the cotton gin worked in the lower South. The satisfaction of the planter in top hat as he shows seed-free cotton to a visitor makes sense—cotton was making him rich. It is more difficult to accept the delight his slaves find picking and hauling the cotton and cranking the gin from sunup to sundown.

vocation would be defending the plantation South and slavery. Ironically, this clever political theorist (and less able politician) was chained to such anachronistic institutions because of a machine—its technology brilliantly simple, its consequences profound.

SLAVERY IN DECLINE

When John C. Calhoun was born in 1782, African-American slavery appeared to be dying out. The northern states abolished the institution when Calhoun was a child. In the tobacco South, as the world price of the crop dropped and dropped, planters found the costs of their numerous slaves too great for the profits from their fields. Even South Carolina's rice and indigo lost some of their luster when British subsidies ended following independence.

Southerners, as well as northerners, were shaped by the ideals of the Declaration of Independence. Many patriot planters, some famous, like George Washington, freed their slaves. As late as 1808, few southerners objected when Congress outlawed the further importation of Africans from abroad; 1808 was the first year the Constitution permitted Congress to end the African slave trade. At the peace talks in Ghent in 1815, American and British commissioners discussed Anglo-American cooperation to suppress slave traders on the African coast.

By 1815, however, the likelihood that the states of the deep South would abolish slavery had vaporized. The reason was an "absurdly simple contrivance" invented by Eli Whitney.

THE COTTON GIN

In 1793, seven years before his demonstration to Congress of **interchangeable parts,** Eli Whitney was living on a plantation near Savannah. There he saw his first cotton plants and learned that they flourished all over the upland South, where there was plenty of rain and 210 frost-free days spring to fall. Cotton fiber sold on the world market for 30 to 40 cents a pound—a fabulous price. The trouble was that separating the fiber from the plant's oily, sticky green seeds by hand was so time consuming that cost of labor ate up most of the wholesale price. Only the nimblest could process much more than a pound of the fluff a day, not enough to pay anyone to do it; not enough even to assign a slave, who represented an investment of hundreds of dollars, to the job.

After only a few days of thinking about the problem, Whitney put together a small machine—he called it an "engine," thus the name cotton "gin"—that worked miraculously well. Whitney dumped cotton bolls into a box with slots in the bottom, too narrow for the seeds to pass through them. A drum studded with wire hooks revolved so that the hooks snagged the fibers, pulling them through the slots,

Slave-trader, Sold to Tennessee,

Arise! Arise! and weep no more dry up your tears, we shall part no more. Come rose we go to Tennessee. that happy shore. to old virginia never — never — return.

the Company going to Tennessee from Staunton. Augusta County, the law of virginia Suffered them to go on. I was Astonished at this boldness, the carrier Stopped a moment. then Ordered the march, I Saw the play it is Commonly in this State. with the negro's. in droves Sold,

The cotton boom created a seller's market in slaves in the lower South. Virginia, Maryland, and even Kentucky slave owners, growing low-profit crops, often on exhausted soil, frequently had more slaves than they needed. Several visitors to Jefferson's Monticello commented on the leisurely life his slaves led. In the cotton belt, by way of contrast, planters typically had more land than they had slaves to work it. They paid twice the prices at which slaves were sold in the Upper South. Consequently, there was a busy trade in sending slaves "down the river" to be sold. This watercolor depicts a group of slaves being marched to new homes and a harder life. Such scenes were common on major roads to the deep south like the Natchez Trace across Tennessee.

leaving the seeds behind. (The seeds were not wasted; they were fed to hogs or pressed to make oil.) Another drum, revolving in the opposite direction, brushed the fiber from the wire hooks.

It was a magnificent device. A single slave cranking a small gin could clean 10 pounds of cotton a day ($3 to $4 at 1790 prices). A larger machine turned by a horse on a windlass could clean 50 pounds a day ($15 to $20!). When steam-powered gins were developed, the capacity for producing cotton was limited not by processing capacity but by the number of acres that a planter could acquire and cultivate.

Whitney himself made little money from his invention. It was so splendidly simple a device that it was easy for others to make gins that, with trivial modifications, were not covered by Whitney's patents.

THE REVIVAL OF SLAVERY

Technology had come to the South, but industry had not. Eli Whitney's machine revived the one-crop economy that planters of Washington's generation had considered the South's curse. (During the last ten years of his life, Washington refused to grow any tobacco at Mount Vernon

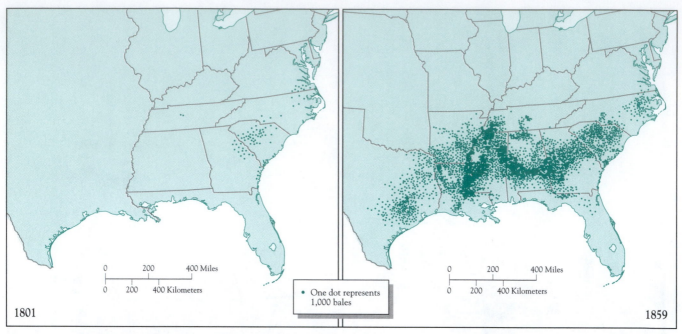

1801

1859

One dot represents 1,000 bales

MAP 14:2 The Spread of Cotton Cultivation
Short-staple, green-seed cotton grew "like a weed" on the uplands of the lower south. It was not a valuable crop until Eli Whitney's cotton gin made it possible to extract the oily seeds without fouling the precious fiber. Then, commercial cotton cultivation spread "like a weed."

because dependence on tobacco alone put a planter at the mercy of a single market price over which he had no influence.)

Cotton, like tobacco, was well adapted to gang cultivation. The crop required plenty of unskilled labor: plowing, planting, chopping (or weeding, an endless process in the hot, fertile South), ditch digging and maintenance, picking, ginning, pressing, baling, and getting it to buyers.

The fertile upland black belt that extends from South Carolina and Georgia through eastern Texas was natural cotton country. Southerners streamed into the "Old Southwest"—Alabama, Mississippi, and northern Louisiana—and eventually into Arkansas across the Mississippi River. In 1800, excluding Indians, there were about 1,000 people in what is now Alabama. In 1810, there were 9,000; in 1820, 128,000! The growth of Mississippi was less dramatic but not lethargic: in 1800, 8,000; in 1810, 31,000; in 1820, 75,000.

Nor was this an emigration of only buckskin-clad frontiersmen with no more baggage than a long rifle and a frying pan. Wealthy planters from the old states sold their land and made the trek, bringing their bondsmen and women with them. In 1800, there were 4,000 blacks in Alabama and Mississippi. In 1810, there were 17,000, virtually all of them slaves. In 1820, the African-American population was 75,000. Almost half the people of Mississippi were slaves.

The demand for "prime field hands"—young, healthy men—to toil in the cotton fields caused the price of slaves to soar. The average purchase price of a slave doubled between 1795 and 1804. In Louisiana, by 1810 slaves cost twice what they cost in Virginia. Blacks who were becoming financial

burdens in Maryland and Virginia became valuable commodities in the cotton South. The most humane masters found it difficult to resist the temptation of the high prices offered for their slaves. Although it was illegal to do so, some slave owners in Delaware and New Jersey smuggled their slaves out of state and shipped them to the cotton states.

THE MISSOURI CRISIS

Because New York's and New Jersey's abolition laws freed slaves only when they reached a certain age, and did not free some older slaves, there were perfectly legal slave owners in both states in 1819.

However, there was a clear-cut line between states where slavery was forbidden and states where the institution was protected. In the East, the dividing line began with the semicircular Pennsylvania-Delaware border and extended west along the Mason-Dixon Line (the Maryland-Pennsylvania border) that was already the symbol of the North-South split. West of Pennsylvania, the dividing line was the Ohio River. The states of the Northwest Territory were free by an act of Congress. Kentucky, south of the Ohio and settled largely by Virginians, was a slave state.

In 1819, at the mid-point in President Monroe's "Era of Good Feelings," extremely bad feelings erupted in Congress. The cause was the relationship of the location of the mouth of the Ohio River and the situation of Missouri Territory, which, in that year, applied for statehood with a constitution protecting the institution of slavery. All but a slender strip of Missouri lay north of the point where the Ohio emptied into the Mississippi.

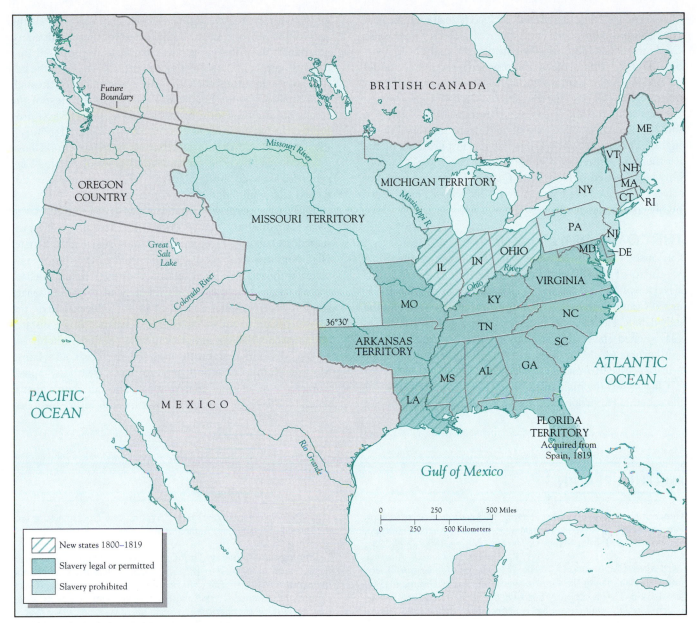

MAP 14:3 The United States in 1820

After an ugly debate in Congress, Missouri was admitted as a slave state in 1820. Note that virtually all of Missouri lies north of the mouth of the Ohio River that had become the unofficial dividing line between slave states and free states. For that reason, many northern congressmen wanted to forbid slavery in Missouri. Southerners erupted in anger.

Henry Clay jerry-built a compromise: Missouri was admitted with slavery but, north of its southern boundary at 36° 30′ north latitude, all future states would be free states. Maine was immediately admitted as a free state to "balance" free states and slave states at twelve of each. Before 1820, Maine was a "district" of Massachusetts, a status its inhabitants resented.

Missouri had been settled largely by southerners but mostly by family farmers. Southern planters who owned large numbers of slaves headed south, to cotton country. It was no secret that there were several hundred slaves in Missouri Territory, but they were so few—fewer than there were in New Jersey—that antislavery northerners had not much thought about the issue before 1819. Those who did assumed that Missouri would provide for the emancipation of the few slaves living there by compensating slave owners for their losses.

Missourians had little stake in protecting slavery, but they were nevertheless southern farmers who assumed blacks should be slaves, and for whom economic improvement meant becoming a slave owner. Missouri's white population was inflexible on the question.

Missourians and other southerners became antagonistic when Congressman James Tallmadge of New York proposed that Missouri be admitted as a state only after its proposed constitution was amended to forbid the further importation of slaves and to free all slaves within the state when they reached

25 years of age. Most of Tallmadge's speech dealt with the negative economic and social consequences of slavery, but he also condemned it as an immoral institution. Once the breach was opened, dozens of northern congressmen leapt into it. One described slavery as "a sin which sits heavily on the soul of every one of us."

On reading the highly charged rhetoric, Thomas Jefferson said that he was startled as if he had heard "a firebell in the night." That is, he was terrified of the implications of the northerners' criticism because attacks on morality could only be answered in kind. John Quincy Adams, no friend of slavery, expressed his concern about his fellow northerners' highly charged language.

THE COMPROMISE

Curiously, President Monroe was not unduly disturbed. A Virginian of the Revolutionary generation, he still hoped slavery would, in time, die out peacefully in the South. He urged Congress to devise a compromise that would end the ugly debate. Henry Clay put the package together that did so. Clay owned slaves but also hoped that, in time, rational southerners would do away with the offensive and certainly unprogressive institution.

Clay earned the nickname, "The Great Compromiser," for his scheme. He proposed that Missouri be admitted to the Union with its proslavery constitution. That was, after all, the wish of the Missourians, and it placated southern politicians. To mollify the antislavery northerners, Clay proposed that the southern boundary of Missouri, 36° 30'—close to the latitude of the mouth of the Ohio River—be extended through the remainder of the Louisiana Purchase to the crest of the Rocky Mountains. North of the line slavery was forever prohibited. In territories south of 36° 30' (Arkansas Territory), the voters would decide whether or not they would have slavery when the time for statehood arrived. Finally, Clay proposed that the "Maine District" of Massachusetts be detached and admitted to the Union as a free state.

There were twenty-two states in 1819, eleven free, eleven slave. By admitting Maine along with Missouri, Clay preserved the balance of free states and slave states in the Senate. His intentions were good; Clay, like many other politicians, believed that the sectional bitterness of the Missouri debate was a passing phenomenon. However, by horse trading Senate seats in order to quiet a clash of moral values in 1820, the Missouri Compromise legitimized a balance of slave states and free states that could not be maintained indefinitely.

The Missouri Compromise ended the crisis and James Monroe enjoyed a second peaceful term. Tempers cooled. Congressmen who had glared at one another shook hands, voted for Clay's Compromise, and turned to other business.

FURTHER READING

General D. W. Meinig, *The Shaping of America: A Geographical Perspective on 500 Years of History*, vol. 2: *Continental America, 1800–1867*, 1993; John Mayfield, *The New Nation, 1800–1845*, 1981; Charles G. Sellers, *The Market Revolution: Jacksonian America, 1815–1846*, 1991; Robert H. Wiebe, *The Opening of American Society: From the Adoption of the Constitution to the Eve of Disunion*, 1984; Jack Larkin, *The Reshaping of Everyday Life, 1790–1940*, 1988; Daniel Feller, *The Jacksonian Promise: America, 1815–1840*, 1993; Henry L. Watson, *Liberty and Power*, 1990; Jean Mathews, *Toward a New Society: American Thought and Culture, 1800–1830*, 1990.

Nationalism Jill Lepore, *A is for America; Letters and Other Characters in the Early United States*, 2002; Richard J. Moss, *Noah Webster*, 1984; E. Jennifer Monaghan, *A Common Heritage: Noah Webster's Blue Back Speller*, 1983; David Mickelthwait, *Noah Webster and the American Dictionary*, 2000; R. Kent Neumeyer, *The Supreme Court under Marshall and Taney*, 1968; Morton J. Horwitz, *The Transformation of American Law, 1780–1860*, 1977.

James Monroe William P. Cresson, *James Monroe*, 1971; Harry Ammon James, *James Monroe: The Quest for National Identity*, 1971; Noble E. Cunningham, *The Presidency of James Monroe*, 1996.

Diplomacy Ernest R. May, *The Making of the Monroe Doctrine*, 1976; Donald J. Weber, *The Spanish Frontier in North America*, 1992; James E, Lewis, *The American Union and the Problem of Neighborhood: The United States and the Collapse of the Spanish Empire, 1783–1829*, 1998; William E. Week, *John Quincy Adams and American Global Empire*, 1992; Greg Russell, *John Quincy Adams and the Public*

Virtues of Diplomacy, 1995; Gary V. Wood, *John Quincy Adams and the Spirit of Constitutional Government*, 2004.

Technology and Industry Thomas C. Cochran, *Frontiers of Change: Early Industrialists in America*, 1981; David J. Jeremy, *Transatlantic Industrial Revolution: The Diffusion of Textile Technologies between Britain and America*, 1981; David F. Hawke, *Nuts and Bolts of the Past: A History of American Technology, 1776–1860*, 1988; Walter Licht, *Industrial America: The Nineteenth Century*, 1995; Arand R. Mayr and Robert C. Post, eds., *Yankee Enterprise: The Rise of the American System of Manufactures*, 1981; Carroll Pursell, *The Machine in America: A Social History of Technology*, 1995; David Nye, *Consuming Power: A Social History of American Energies*, 1998.

Factory Workers Cynthia Shelton, *The Mills of Manayunk: Industrialization and Social Conflict in the Philadelphia Region, 1787–1837*, 1986; Bruce Laurie, *The Working People of Philadelphia, 1800–1850*, 1980, and *Artisans and Workers: Labor in Nineteenth Century America*, 1989; Jeanne Boydston, *Home and Work: Housework, Wages, and the Ideology of Labor in the Early Republic*, 1990; Thomas Dublin, *Women at Work: The Transformation of Work and Community in Lowell, Massachusetts, 1810–1860*, 1979, and *Transforming Women's Work: New England Lives in the Industrial Revolution*, 1994.

The Missouri Compromise Glover Moore, *The Missouri Controversy*, 1953; Donald L. Robinson, *Slavery in the Structure of American Politics, 1765–1820*, 1979; Don E. Fehrenbacher, *The Slaveholding Republic: An Account of the United States Government's Relationship to Slavery*, 2001.

KEY TERMS

The following terms are covered in this chapter and can also be found in the list of Key Terms at the back of the book.

Adams-Oñis Treaty	**factory system**	**interchangeable parts**	**Monroe Doctrine**
caucus	**Fort Ross**	**Missouri Compromise**	**William Wirt**

 ## ONLINE SOURCES GUIDE

Use this listing to find online documents, images, interactive maps, simulations, and other resources related to this chapter:

American History Resource Center
http://history.wadsworth.com

Selected Images
John Quincy Adams, Sixth President of the United States

Interactive Timeline (with online readings)
Nation Awakening: Political and Economic Development 1815–1824

Discovery

How did changes in transportation and markets reinforce the existing social fabric and regional differences?

In thinking about this question, begin by breaking it down into the components shown below. A discussion of the significance of each component should appear in your answer.

Economics and Technology: For this exercise, read the document excerpts "*The Harbinger*, Female Workers of Lowell (1836)" and "Morality of Manufactures" and study Map 14:1. Look at the map concerning the location of cotton mills. How would this have helped spur the growth of industry in the North? Who would work in these mills? What effect might it have on the towns or communities? Consider the two documents concerning the positives and negatives of manufacturing. What arguments are made concerning the negatives? What arguments are made concerning the positives? Who do you think has the better argument? Do we see these kinds of issues today?

The Harbinger, Female Workers of Lowell (1836)

. . . In Lowell live between seven and eight thousand young women, who are generally daughters of farmers of the different states of New England. Some of them are members of families that were rich in the generation before. . . .

The operatives work thirteen hours a day in the summer time, and from daylight to dark in the winter. At half past four in the morning the factory bell rings, and at five the girls must be in the mills. A clerk, placed as a watch, observes those who are a few minutes behind the time, and effectual means are taken to stimulate to punctuality. This is the morning commencement of the industrial discipline (should we not rather say industrial tyranny?) which is established in these associations of this moral and Christian community.

At seven the girls are allowed thirty minutes for breakfast, and at noon thirty minutes more for dinner, except during the first quarter of the year, when the time is extended to forty-five minutes. But within this time they must hurry to their boardinghouses and return to the factory, and that through the hot sun or the rain or the cold. A meal eaten under such circumstances must be quite unfavorable to digestion and health, as any medical man will inform us. After seven o'clock in the evening the factory bell sounds the close of the day's work.

Thus thirteen hours per day of close attention and monotonous labor are extracted from the young women in these manufactories. . . . So fatigued—we should say, exhausted and worn out, but we wish to speak of the system in the simplest language—are numbers of girls that they go to bed soon after their evening meal, and endeavor by a comparatively long sleep to resuscitate their weakened frames for the toil of the coming day.

Morality of Manufactures, 1823

. . . Before I commenced the erection of these works, said Mr. S. and established in this place the branch of cotton manufacture, the process of which you have been just examining, the man who built, and now owns that neat little tenement, had no place to shelter himself and his numerous family, but the wretched hovel which you may observe at a few rods distance from his present abode. At that time, continued my informant, his only occupation was that of fishing or rambling in the mountains in pursuit of such game as chance might throw in his way. Of the little he obtained by this occasional and precarious mode of subsistence, a large proportion was expended in the purchase of rum; in the use of which he indulged to such an extent as to brutalize his faculties, and render him a pest to society, as well as a curse to his family; which he kept in a state of the most deplorable and squalid poverty. Of his children three of four were daughters, of various ages, from seven or eight to fourteen years; these, said Mr. S. on commencing my establishment, I took into the factory; where, from that period to the present time, they have always had constant and regular employment. The proceeds of their first week's labor, amounting to six or seven dollars, when paid and taken home to their parents, was an amount which, it is probable, they never before at any one time possessed. The almost immediate effect on the mind of the father appears to have been a conviction that his children, instead of being a burden which he despaired of supporting, and, therefore, never before made an effort to accomplish, would, on the contrary, by the steady employment now provided for them, be able, by their industry, not only to sustain themselves, but also contribute to the maintenance and support of the other members of the family. From that moment, it would appear, as if he had determined to reform his vicious habits, and to emerge from that state of degradation and wretchedness into which he had plunged himself and family. He has done so, said Mr. S. and, instead of being a pest,

he has become a useful member of society; instead of being a curse to his family, and occupying with them that wretched hovel yonder, fit only for swine to wallow in, he has, by his own exertions, aided the industry and good conduct of his children, lately purchased the soil, and erected the comfortable cottage, which said Mr. S. smiling, appears so powerfully to attract your notice. . . .

Economics and Technology: For this exercise, study Map 14:2 and read the document excerpt "Cotton Boom in Alabama and Mississippi, ca. 1820s." Look at the map concerning cotton production. What explains such growth in production? Read the excerpt from the "Cotton Boom." Who is doing the work? How long does the work take during the course of a day? Does the author consider the work from a social perspective at all? What kinds of economic comparisons is he making?

MAP 14:1 Cotton Mills, 1820

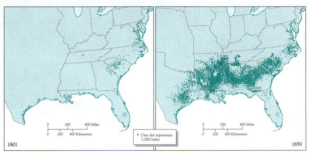

MAP 14:2 The Spread of Cotton Cultivation

Cotton Boom in Alabama and Mississippi, ca. 1820s

. . . Under this stimulating process prices rose like smoke. Lots in obscure villages were held at city prices; lands, bought at the minimum cost of government, were sold at from thirty to forty dollars per acre, and considered dirt cheap at that. . . . Society was wholly unorganized: there was no restraining public opinion: the law was well-nigh powerless—and religion scarcely was heard of except as furnishing the oaths and *technics* of profanity . . .

Larceny grew not only respectable, but genteel, and ruffled it in all the pomp of purple and fine linen. Swindling was raised to the dignity of the fine arts. Felony came forth from its covert, put on more seemly habiliments, and took its seat with unabashed front in the upper places of the synagogue . . .

"Commerce was king"—and Rags, Tag, and Bobtail his cabinet council. Rags was treasurer. Banks, chartered on a specie basis, did a very flourishing business on the promissory notes of the individual stockholders ingeniously substituted in lieu of cash. They issued ten for

one, the *one* being fictitious. They generously loaned all the directors could not use themselves, and were not choice whether Bardolph was the endorser for Falstaff, or Falstaff borrowed on his own proper credit, or the funds advanced him by Shallow. The stampede towards the golden temple became general: the delusion prevailed far and wide that this thing was not a burlesque on commerce and finance . . .

Paper fortunes still multiplied—houses and lands changed hands—real estate see-sawed up as morals went down on the other end of the plank—men of straw, corpulent with bank bills, strutted past them on 'Change. They began, too, to think there might be something in this new thing. Peeping cautiously, like hedge-hogs out of their holes, they saw the stream of wealth and adventurers passing by—then, looking carefully around, they inched themselves half way out—then, sallying forth and snatching up a morsel, ran back, until, at last, grown more bold, *they* ran out too with their horded store, in full chase with the other unclean beasts of adventure . . .

To read extended versions of the documents, visit the companion Web site http://history.wadsworth.com/americanpast8e; click on "Discovery Sources."

CHAPTER 15

The People's Hero

Andrew Jackson and a New Era 1824–1830

Thomas Sully, General Andrew Jackson, 1845, 97 × 61¼, oil on canvas. In the Collections of the Corcoran Gallery of Art, Washington, D.C. Gift of William Wilson Corcoran

Thou great democratic God!, . . . who didst pick up Andrew Jackson from the pebbles; who didst hurl him upon a warhorse; who didst thunder him higher than a throne! Thou who, in all Thy mighty, earthly marchings, ever cullest Thy selected champions from the kingly commons.

Herman Melville

Except an enormous fabric of executive power, the President has built up nothing. . . . He goes for destruction, universal destruction.

Henry Clay

The one-party system of the Monroe years had its virtues. At the top, at least, administration was efficient. In Congress debate was candid and eloquent, almost always on a higher plane than has been in eras of intense partisanship. At its best, loyalty to party is less edifying than loyalty to home, country, or principle. More often, it is tawdry, rewarding hacks simply because they echo the party line. The Era of Good Feelings was spared the worst American politics can produce, but it was not spared men of ambition. And a single party in good order could not accommodate every politician who aspired to the job at the top.

In 1824, as James Monroe prepared to pack up and retire to Virginia—where both Jefferson and Madison still lived— the Jefferson Republican party, albeit civilly, divided not into two but into half a dozen coteries gathered around Monroe's would-be successors. New York Governor DeWitt Clinton,

now a national figure because of the Erie Canal's success, sent out (in today's political jargon) "feelers." But he was not a national figure and soon gave up the project. John C. Calhoun of South Carolina, Monroe's secretary of war, withdrew his candidacy early. The president favored another southerner and cabinet member, Secretary of the Treasury William Crawford. Calhoun was just 42, fifteen years younger than anyone who had been elected to the presidency. He could wait; he announced he would stand for vice president. That left four strong contenders.

THE SKEWED ELECTION OF 1824

During the quarter century in which the Jefferson Republicans dominated national politics, three traditions had grown up around the presidency: **King Caucus,** the **Virginia Dynasty,**

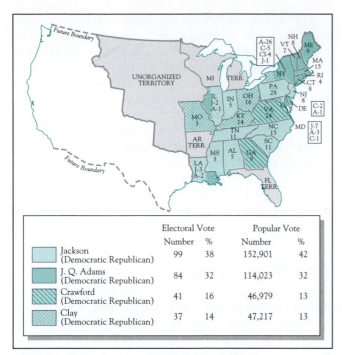

MAP 15:1 **Presidential Election of 1824**
Andrew Jackson won more electoral votes in the southern states than William Crawford did. He carried Indiana, "Clay Country," and Pennsylvania, the second biggest state, in Quincy Adams's Northeast. He was the only truly national candidate.

and succession to the White House by the secretary of state, who was appointed by his predecessor. In 1824, two of these institutions were toppled and the third was discredited.

CAUCUS, DYNASTY, AND SUCCESSION

"King Caucus" was the name given (by those who did not much like it) to the procedure by which the Jeffersonians had nominated their presidential candidates. Republican members of Congress met in caucus, haggled (never very much), and named their choice. Until 1824, unsuccessful candidates gracefully accepted King Caucus's decision. Indeed, after losing to Madison in the caucus of 1808, Monroe joined Madison's cabinet. **William F. Crawford,** who half-heartedly opposed Monroe in 1816, joined his cabinet.

Madison and Monroe both stepped from the office of secretary of state into the White House. An orderly means of succession seemed to be established—presidents, like Roman emperors, "adopting" their heirs.

Caucus

Caucus is an American word. It was not found in British newspapers until the end of the nineteenth century. However, it appears unself-consciously in John Adams's diary as early as 1763; others remembered the word in common usage in New England decades earlier. The word is of Algonquian origin. Captain John Smith mentions *ca-cawaassaugh* meaning "one who advises."

Already, Americans spoke of a "Virginia Dynasty." All three of the Jefferson Republican presidents—Jefferson, Madison, and Monroe—were Virginians. Until 1824, it was all quite tidy and, to Virginians, quite proper.

In 1824, however, the secretary of state was John Quincy Adams, so much a Massachusetts man that southern Jeffersonians regarded him as a Federalist in disguise. They were suspicious of Adams's strident nationalism and disliked his belief that the national government should use its powers to shape both economy and society.

Most southerners—including the president—wanted William Crawford nominated. Crawford was a Georgian; but he had been born in Nelson County, Virginia, which was enough to qualify him for the dynastic succession. He was a party-line Jeffersonian suspicious of centralized power and an exponent of Jefferson's "strict construction" theory of the Constitution, battered as it was by 1824. The caucus nominated him—too easily: The only congressmen to attend it were southern Crawford supporters. Those who opposed his nomination, including Speaker of the House Henry Clay, refused to lend legitimacy to Crawford's nomination by staying away. Crawford's rivals were all nominated by state legislatures. King Caucus was dead.

CANDIDATE STEW

The Massachusetts legislature nominated John Quincy Adams. His supporters, mostly in the Northeast, could point to his eight productive years as secretary of state as preparation for the presidency. Principally, however, Adams's strengths were his New England heritage and Northeastern points of view. Quincy Adams advocated a high tariff to protect industry, and he supported active and massive federal financial investment in internal improvements.

Henry Clay's political views were indistinguishable from Quincy Adams's. Had the election of 1824 been a contest between competing ideologies, even competing parties, either Clay or Adams would have been pressured to step aside in favor of the other. But it was neither; it was a competition among prominent, ambitious individuals to whom the programs they espoused were second in importance to their desire to be president. There was a personal angle to the fact that Clay and Quincy Adams divided the vote of those who shared their views. When the two men were commissioners in Ghent, negotiating the treaty to end the War of 1812, Clay had lived the high life in off-hours, drinking, gambling, and womanizing. Quincy Adams, personally fastidious, thought Clay dissolute. Clay thought Quincy Adams prissy and humorless.

Clay knew that Quincy Adams would win in New England. He hoped that his yeoman work in Congress for internal improvements would sweep the western states and his sponsorship of the Missouri Compromise would win votes in the upper South. Had there not been another westerner in the race, Clay might well have won.

But another westerner there was, and a formidable westerner at that. Clay was well known; Andrew Jackson was celebrated, the hero of New Orleans and the conqueror of

Losers Who Won

John Quincy Adams is the only president who won fewer electoral votes than another candidate, but he was not the only president to win with fewer popular votes than opponents. In 1876 Republican Rutherford B. Hayes won fewer votes than Democrat Samuel J. Tilden, but Hayes was inaugurated. In 1888 Republican Benjamin Harrison lost the popular vote to Democrat Grover Cleveland but won handily in the electoral college. In 2000 the Democratic candidate, Albert Gore, had a substantial popular majority but lost in the electoral college to Republican George W. Bush.

the Creek nation. So magical was his name, his admirers did not care that where Jackson stood on the political issues of the day was something of a mystery. As an admirer put it, "He has slain the Indians and flogged the British, and therefore is the wisest and greatest man in the nation."

So Jackson was not merely a second western candidate; he was a national hero. Clay won only four electoral votes outside of the West. Crawford won just five outside the South. Adams won seven electoral votes outside the Northeast. Only Jackson carried states in all three sections; he was the only national candidate.

WHO WON?

Jackson won more popular and electoral votes than any of his opponents, but his 99 electoral votes were 32 short of a majority. As in the election of 1800, the job of naming the president fell to the House of Representatives with members voting by states. The terms of the Twelfth Amendment provided that the House choose from among the top three finishers in the electoral college. This eliminated Clay from contention; he had finished fourth. Crawford was out of the running less because he finished third than because he had suffered a stroke that left him bedridden and unable to speak.

So it was between Jackson and the electoral college runner-up, John Quincy Adams. Jackson's supporters believed they had it in the bag. Not only had Jackson been the choice of more voters and electors than Adams, he had won three western states, five southern states, and, in the Northeast, Pennsylvania, the second largest state in the Union. The House of Representatives was morally bound to formalize the election of the man who was the people's choice.

It was a good argument—the democratic argument—but it did not carry the day. Instead, largely because of the political principles and personal ambitions of Henry Clay, the Speaker of the House, and, some say, the impulse of an elderly New York congressman, Stephen Van Rensselaer, the prize went to the second-place finisher in the election, John Quincy Adams.

NEW YORK ELECTS QUINCY ADAMS

The state delegations in the House were divided down the middle between Jackson and Quincy Adams. New York was the swing state. New York had given 26 of its 36 electoral votes to Adams, and only one to Jackson. However, its congressmen were split between the two candidates. Some representatives were persuaded by the Jacksonians' appeal to democracy. Others had ties to the Albany Regency, a party faction that leaned toward Jackson. New York would probably have voted for Jackson, and given him the presidency, had it not been for the influence Henry Clay wielded as Speaker of the House. Clay disliked Jackson, a feeling that would soon graduate to detestation. The importance to congressmen of retaining the Speaker's favor prevented a Jackson stampede among the New Yorkers.

The deadlock in the New York delegation was broken by Stephen Van Rensselaer. He later explained that, just before the roll call, he bowed his head to pray for divine guidance and saw on the floor a piece of paper on which was written "Adams." Taking it as a sign, he voted for Quincy Adams, giving him New York's vote and the presidency. Jackson's backers were enraged. Divine guidance had not elected

Quincy Adams and Andrew Jackson 1824–1838

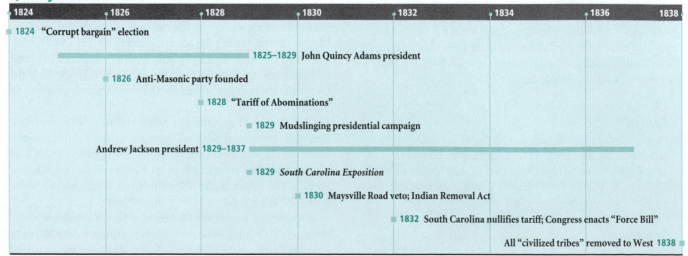

1824	1826	1828	1830	1832	1834	1836	1838

- 1824 "Corrupt bargain" election
- 1825–1829 John Quincy Adams president
- 1826 Anti-Masonic party founded
- 1828 "Tariff of Abominations"
- 1829 Mudslinging presidential campaign
- Andrew Jackson president 1829–1837
- 1829 *South Carolina Exposition*
- 1830 Maysville Road veto; Indian Removal Act
- 1832 South Carolina nullifies tariff; Congress enacts "Force Bill"
- All "civilized tribes" removed to West 1838

Quincy Adams, they said, Henry Clay had. When the new president named Clay secretary of state, Jackson's backers claimed that the two men had negotiated a **"corrupt bargain"**: the presidency for Quincy Adams in return for the position of heir apparent for Clay.

Clay could not very well deny presidential ambitions. Unable in 1824 to foresee the emergence of a new two-party system, he recognized that his prospects were dim as Jackson's

ally. The general was surrounded by heirs apparent: Vice President Calhoun, Richard M. Johnson of Tennessee, and others. Adams had no coterie of politicians around him. He had lived abroad most of his life and had stood aloof from politics as secretary of state. Clay could reasonably see himself as Adams's successor. Moreover, if Clay and Adams were not personally fond of one another, their positions on the issues of the day were identical. No one knew much of anything about Jackson's politics—except that he hated banks. The Bank of the United States was the cornerstone of Clay's American System.

"CORRUPT BARGAIN!"

It is difficult to believe, however, that there was a bargain. Quincy Adams and Clay did not, as the Jacksonians claimed, sit down at a table—or have agents meet—and work out a trade-off. Clay was not above such an arrangement. How else did a "Great Compromiser" operate but by political horse-trading? But John Quincy Adams would have bristled at any such proposition. He valued his principled New England integrity to the extent that it incapacitated him for public life in the age of democratic politics and partisan solidarity. In 1809 he had resigned as senator from Massachusetts, the only elective office he ever held, when the Massachusetts legislature criticized him for supporting the embargo. He was no doubt thanking Clay for his support when he named him secretary of state, but there was no deal.

There was, however, a duel. John Randolph (a Crawford supporter, not a Jacksonian) believed there had been a bargain between "the puritan" (Quincy Adams) and "the blackleg" (Clay), a literary allusion to the Henry Fielding novel *Tom Jones*. "Blackleg" was a nasty insult, particularly when applied to Clay, who whiled away many a night playing cards. (A blackleg was a gambler who cheated.) Clay challenged Randolph to a duel. Fortunately, neither man really hated the other. After a few shots that drew no blood, they embraced and went home, everyone's honor intact.

PLAIN SEWING DONE HERE

SYMPTOMS OF A LOCKED JAW

An overly optimistic pro-Clay cartoon. It shows Henry Clay sewing closed the mouth of Andrew Jackson to stop his false accusations of the "corrupt bargain" between Clay and President John Quincy Adams. In fact, Jackson did not speak publicly about the alleged bargain; he left that to his henchmen. And Clay's lengthy rebuttal of the charge, published in 1827, did not silence anyone. The corrupt bargain issue contributed to Quincy Adams's defeat in 1828 and shadowed Clay for the rest of his life.

THE AGE OF THE COMMON MAN

Like his father, John Quincy Adams brought impressive credentials to the presidency. Of his contemporaries, only Henry Clay—surely not General Jackson—was as qualified

John Randolph of Roanoke

John Randolph had the sharpest tongue in Congress. Representatives hesitated to debate him not only because his arguments were powerful, but because he insulted his opponents' intelligence in refuting them. Randolph was what today would be called "emotionally disturbed." Apparently he had episodes of insanity.

Randolph owned 300 slaves but consistently maintained that he hated slavery. He was—most of the time— the kindest of masters. Even a Federalist abolitionist from Massachusetts who visited Randolph's plantation, Josiah Quincy, said that the slaves there loved him. However, neighbors, also slave owners, said that when Randolph was out of his mind, he was cruel and brutal.

Randolph wrote three wills. In two of them he freed all his slaves and provided money so that they could establish themselves. In a third will, he ordered his slaves sold at auction, the proceeds divided among his heirs. The court ruled that Randolph had not been "of sound mind" when he wrote the third will and freed the slaves.

as he, and Clay's credentials were of an entirely different kind. Although Jackson could claim to have been slashed in the face by a British officer at the age of 14, John Quincy Adams at 14 was already in government service as secretary to an American minister abroad (his father). He had himself been minister in several European countries, senator from Massachusetts, and a secretary of state whose successes in that office are unrivaled.

ANOTHER UNHAPPY ADAMS

Also like his father, Quincy Adams's qualifications to be president ended with his curriculum vitae. Temperamentally, he was out of tune with his times; he was incapable of providing what more and more people were demanding of their leaders. In an age of vivid political personalities—Benton, Clay, Jackson, Calhoun—Quincy Adams excited no one. Among a people that prized equality and easy informality, Adams was standoffish, stuffy, and self-conscious of his abilities, learning, ancestry, and achievements. In an era when government was becoming more democratic at every level, Adams spoke contemptuously of being "palsied by the will of our constituents."

Worst of all, political horse-trading, if far from new, was becoming open, frank, fast, and furious. Quincy Adams tried to stand above partisan politics. He allowed open enemies he could have fired to remain in office. To remove them and fill their posts with his supporters, Adams felt, would be to stoop to the shabby politics of which he was accused in the corrupt bargain controversy.

Adams was also thin-skinned and short-tempered. He took criticism and sometimes mere suggestions as affronts to his office and his person. He cut himself off not only from a majority of voters but also from allies who had honest, often minor disagreements with him. By the end of his term, he had a smaller political base in Washington than any previous president, including his unhappy father.

A DEMOCRATIC UPHEAVAL

Quincy Adams's concept of himself as a member of a "natural aristocracy" of wealth, talent, education, culture, and manners was the viewpoint of a dying generation of American politicians. During the 1820s, and obvious to those who would see even before 1824, politics was ceasing to be primarily the concern of the leisured, educated classes. Politics (and highly partisan newspapers) preoccupied the white male population. The great French commentator on American attitudes and folkways, Alexis de Tocqueville, wrote that "almost the only pleasure which an American knows is to take part in government." A less sympathetic visitor to the United States, Mrs. Frances Trollope, was appalled

Few presidents have come to the White House with qualifications like John Quincy Adams's. He was American minister in the Netherlands, Prussia, Russia, and Great Britain; a senator; and secretary of state for eight years. He was also proud to the point of arrogance, not a recommendation in an increasingly democratic era.

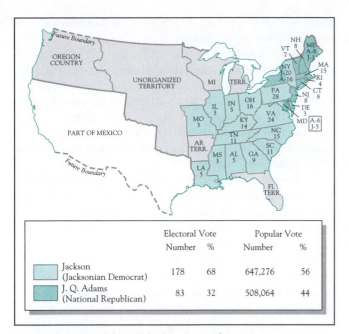

MAP 15:2 Presidential Election of 1828
Jackson swept the electoral college in 1828. He won Clay's Kentucky and even one vote in Adams's New England.

that American men would rather talk politics than mend their fences and tend their crops.

In part, this great democratic upheaval was the fruit of half a century of Jeffersonian rhetoric that flirted with democracy. The Jeffersonians never ceased saying that the people should rule. Like a slogan in a television commercial endlessly repeated, the idea caught on. The democratic upheaval of the 1820s and 1830s was also the consequence of the extraordinary growth and energy of the young republic. An increasingly prosperous people needed to struggle less to survive and had more time to think about public affairs. With issues like the tariff, land policy, and internal improvements bearing heavily on individual fortunes, ordinary men had good reason to take an interest in politics.

Finally, the wave of democratic spirit that swept Andrew Jackson on its crest had a peculiarly western source. To attract population, the young western states extended the right

Interviewing the President

John Quincy Adams was excessively stiff and formal when acting in an official capacity. He was, however, infinitely more accessible than modern presidents surrounded by bodyguards ready to incapacitate anyone who acts slightly out of the ordinary. If Quincy Adams had a yen for fresh air, he put on his hat and walked out the door. In hot weather, he rose early, walked to the Potomac, shed his clothes, and had a swim. A woman journalist, failing for weeks to make an appointment with the president, followed him one morning. Once he was in the water, she sat on his clothes and refused to budge until Adams, treading water, answered her questions—in good humor.

to vote to all free, adult white males. All six states admitted to the Union between 1816 and 1821—Indiana, Mississippi, Illinois, Alabama, Missouri, and, back East, Maine, required no property ownership for voting. Western states enacted other laws designed to appeal to people of modest station. Kentucky abolished imprisonment for debt in 1821. No longer could a man or woman be jailed for financial misfortune (or calculated dereliction).

Democratization spread south and east. Fearful of losing population to the West, most eastern states responded to liberal western laws by adopting universal white manhood suffrage. In 1824 about half the states still had some property qualifications for voting. By 1830 only North Carolina, Virginia, Rhode Island, and Louisiana did, and Rhode Island's conservatism in the matter was misleading. Still governed under the state's colonial charter, which could not be easily amended, Rhode Island was rocked by a brief violent uprising in 1842, Dorr's Rebellion, which resulted in an extension of the vote to all adult white males.

In 1800 only two of sixteen states named presidential electors by popular vote. In 1824 eighteen of twenty-four states did. By 1832 only planter-dominated South Carolina still named electors in the legislature.

Given the right to vote, free adult white males did. In 1824, the first presidential election in which there was widespread popular participation, about one-quarter of the country's eligible voters cast ballots. In 1828 one-half of the eligible voters voted; in 1840 more than three-quarters. If such a proportion of eligible voters voted today, it would be accounted a political revolution.

THE "WORKIES"

Newly enfranchised voters built parties around social issues. During the 1820s, "workingmen's parties" sprang up in eastern cities. Casually called the "Workies" and supported largely by mechanics, as skilled artisans were known, they pushed in city and state elections for a variety of reforms to protect their particular interests: abolition of imprisonment for debt, which hit independent artisans hard; mechanics' lien laws, which prevented creditors from seizing their tools; laws giving employees, rather than creditors, first crack at a bankrupt employer's assets; and free public education for all children. To the workingmen of the Northeast, education was the equivalent of the westerner's free land, the key to moving up in the world.

The Workies had their victories, especially in New York. But the party's support dwindled when middle-class visionaries joined the parties and tried to commit them to far-reaching reforms. Scotland-born Frances "Fanny" Wright, a feminist before feminism's time, advocated equal rights for women and "free love"—the freedom of all, unmarried and married, to enjoy sexually the person they loved—from Workie platforms.

Fanny's embrace of the Workies was the kiss of death. Mechanics had no more interest in modifying the legal status of women than mainstream politicians did; they were quite as committed to traditional sexual morality as their ministers

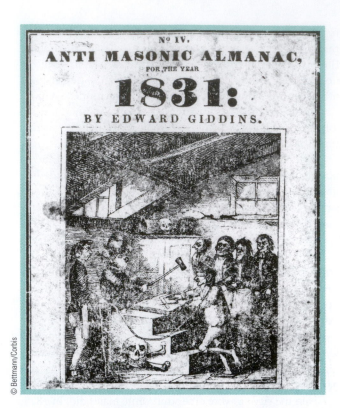

© Bettmann/Corbis

Founded in 1826, the Anti-Masonic Party had astonishing success in the Northeast for a few years. It elected fifty-three members of the House of Representatives in 1832. In part, it reflected the cult of the common man; its supporters regarded the secret organization as a conspiracy that discriminated against non-Masons in business and government. As shown in this illustration, however, Anti-Masonic propaganda focused on what supporters believed were the Masons' lurid, even obscene secret rituals.

were. No doubt as likely to dally as people of the middle and upper classes, mechanics were conscious of the fact that their social status was superior to that of the urban underclass in part because of the promiscuity of the lower orders. Once most of the Workies' bread-and-butter reforms were enacted, they left the party and drifted into the Jacksonian camp.

THE ANTI-MASONIC PARTY

The **Anti-Masonic party** was a curious expression of the democratic upheaval of the 1820s and 1830s. It was founded in upstate New York when a bricklayer named William Morgan

Party Conventions

One legacy of the Anti-Masonic party remains alive, if not in good health: nominating presidential candidates at party conventions. In 1831 the Anti-Masonic party, meeting in Baltimore, was the first party to do so. The idea caught on immediately. In 1832 the Democratic-Republican party (the Democrats) met in convention to nominate their hero, Andrew Jackson. A few years later, the Whig party, founded in 1834, was organized nationally at a nominating convention.

published an exposé of the Society of Freemasons and, shortly thereafter, was murdered.

Founded in London in 1717 by intellectuals who believed in God but not necessarily in Christian forms of worship, the Masonic Order devised its own secret rituals drawn in part from what was then known about ancient Egypt in the time of the building of the pyramids—thus the stonemason regalia (and the pyramid topped by an all-seeing eye still on the back of the dollar bill). Benjamin Franklin and George Washington were both Masons.

By the 1820s the order was quite large; membership was restricted mainly to middle- and upper-class businessmen and professionals. In small towns, invitations to join were usually snapped up; being a Mason was a sign that a man had "arrived." The increasingly elaborate hocus-pocus of lodge meetings and handshakes and passwords by which Masons could identify one another were considered sacred secrets. Much of Morgan's book dealt with Masonic rituals and regalia. He quoted the initiation ceremony during which a new member swore "to keep all Masonic secrets under the penalty of having his throat cut, his tongue torn out, and his body buried in the ocean." When Morgan disappeared and a corpse apparently mutilated according to regulations was dragged out of the Niagara River, outrage swept the state.

Politicians made much of the fact that Morgan was a workingman. The order, they said, was a conspiracy aimed at keeping Masons on top and the common man down. The handshakes and passwords, they pointed out, quoting from Morgan's book, were to identify brother Masons so as to do business with them rather than with "any other person in the same circumstances."

The Anti-Masonic party was a rebellion against the establishment. Every governor of New York between 1804 and 1828 had been a Mason. No more, the Anti-Masons said. Preferential treatment had no place in a free economy. Secret societies had no place in a free society. Indeed, if a man was required to keep secrets from his own wife, he was violating the sanctity of marriage as surely as if he practiced free love.

A brace of political leaders who would later play important roles in national politics were Anti-Masons during the 1820s and 1830s: Thaddeus Stevens, Thurlow Weed, William H. Seward, and a future president, Millard Fillmore. In 1832 the party's presidential candidate, William Wirt, won 33,000 votes and carried the state of Vermont; the party elected fifty-three candidates to Congress.

The Anti-Masons had difficulty with the fact that the universal hero George Washington had been a Mason. They had none with the fact that Andrew Jackson was quite active in the order. They were staunch anti-Jacksonians. When, in 1834, the anti-Jackson Whig party was organized, most Anti-Masons supported it.

THE REVOLUTION OF 1828

Thomas Jefferson had called his election the "Revolution of 1800." There was a greater break with what had gone before in 1828 than there had been in 1800. Andrew Jackson's

The "coffin handbill," a widely distributed anti-Jackson advertisement describing in detail the men Jackson had "murdered." Most of Jackson's "victims" were militiamen under his command executed for desertion or mutiny. These were legitimate capital crimes, although Jackson was, in fact, much more liberal in his use of the firing squad than other generals.

Dueling the American Way

A duel is a prearranged combat in cold blood between two gentlemen in front of witnesses governed by strict rules. The issue was the honor of a man who believed he had been insulted, or the honor of a woman under his protection. It was not necessary that duelists fight to the death. Merely observing the intricate code that governed challenges and acceptance confirmed one's honor. Many American duels—fought with a pair of identical pistols made specifically for dueling—ended when each party discharged his weapon in the general direction of the other. The point was the display of bravery. That was why only gentlemen dueled; the vulgar multitude brawled.

Although Edward Doty and Edward Leicester fought something like a duel in Virginia in 1621, the custom was almost unknown in colonial America; scholars have found records of but a dozen before 1776. Then, during the Revolutionary War, French officers introduced the *Code Duello,* the rules of duel etiquette, to their American friends. American officers took so zealously to the institution that even before the war was over, a Frenchman wrote, "The rage for dueling here has reached an incredible and scandalous point." A decade later, when some aristocrats fled the French Revolution to Louisiana, they made New Orleans the dueling capital of America. On one Sunday in 1839, ten duels were fought in the Crescent City. A woman wrote that the young men of her acquaintance kept score of their duels as young ladies kept count of marriage proposals.

Dueling spread rapidly as sudden wealth created men in a hurry to prove their gentility. Timothy Flint wrote of Mississippi, "Many people without education and character, who were not gentlemen in the circles where they used to move, get accommodated here from the tailor with something of the externals of a gentleman, and at once set up in this newly assumed character. The shortest road to settle their pretensions is to fight a duel."

Button Gwinnet, a signer of the Declaration of Independence from Georgia, was killed in a duel in 1777. James Madison fought a duel in 1797. Maryland-born Commodore Stephen Decatur fought a duel in 1801 and was killed in another in 1820. Of the four presidential candidates in 1824, three were duelists. In 1806 William Crawford killed one opponent in a Georgia election in a duel and wounded another. Henry Clay had several duels. Andrew Jackson's enemies tried (without success) to blacken his character because he had killed men in duels. Only John Quincy Adams and, by 1824, almost all New Englanders disdained dueling as they disdained everything they associated with the South. As early as 1802, two New England Federalists in Congress, Josiah Quincy and Timothy Pickering, let it be known they would neither challenge anyone to a duel nor accept challenges. They paid a price: their Republican opponents did not restrain their language in debates. But that was better than a ball of lead in the intestines. (Curiously, Quincy was, for many years, warm personal friends with John Randolph of Roanoke, who was not only a duelist, but the antithesis of a New England Federalist.)

In 1828 Andrew Jackson's enemies said that he had been involved in a hundred duels. That figure is unlikely—not even Old Hickory was tough and lucky enough to beat those odds. But he fought several, and the written terms of one of them have survived. In 1806 Jackson faced Charles Dickinson, a Nashville lawyer: "It is agreed that the distance shall be 24 feet, the parties to stand facing each other, with their pistols drawn perpendicularly. When they are ready, the single word 'fire' is to be given, at which they are to fire as soon as they please. Should either fire before

---

overwhelming victory in the election of 1828 ended an era of transfers of the presidency from incumbent to secretary of state (all of them decorous transfers until 1824). Jackson's election was an unambivalent repudiation of the sitting administration. And Jackson was the first chief executive to come from a western state. (He was the first president not from Virginia or Massachusetts.) Finally, the 1828 election campaign, because it took place in a democratic society, was noisier and harder fought than any that had gone before, and at least as "dirty" as the Federalist versus Republican campaign of 1800.

SLINGING MUD

Jackson followed precedent by taking no part in the campaign of 1828. He sat in his plantation home, the Hermitage in Tennessee, while his supporters, calling themselves **Democratic-Republicans,** fired insulting salvos at President Adams. They depicted Quincy Adams as a usurper (the "corrupt bargain"), an elitist, a man with effete European tastes who squandered money filling the White House with elegant furniture and its cellar with European wines. The Jacksonians made a great fuss over Adams's purchase of a billiard table; billiards, because of the high cost of the table, was an aristocrat's game. (Adams had bought a billiard table, but paid for it out of his own pocket, not from the White House budget.)

Alarmed by the effectiveness of the attacks, Adams supporters replied that Jackson was a savage and a murderer. Calling themselves National-Republicans, they reminded voters that Jackson had, in violation of Spanish sovereignty, executed two British subjects in Spanish Florida in 1818.

the word is given, we [the seconds of both parties] pledge ourselves to shoot him down instantly. The person to give the word to be determined by lot, as also the choice of position." Dickinson fired first, wounding Jackson. "Back to the mark, sir," Jackson said when Dickinson staggered in fear of what was to come. Then, according to Jackson's enemies, Jackson's pistol misfired, and in violation of the Code Duello, he pulled the hammer back and fired again. This breach of honor haunted Jackson for the rest of his life because Dickinson died.

Thomas Hart Benton fought a grotesque duel with a man named Charles Lucas. They fired at one another at a distance of ten feet! Or rather, Benton fired at a distance of ten feet and put a ball in Lucas's heart. To Benton's credit, he was ashamed of the affair. He burned all the documents pertaining to the duel and never spoke of it. Another episode that mocked the duelists' pretensions to gentlemanly honor involved Col. William Cumming and a prominent Jeffersonian congressman, George McDuffie of South Carolina. President Monroe and John C. Calhoun tried to stop it. Calhoun concluded that Cumming was insane, and subsequent events indicated he probably was. Cumming wounded McDuffie. When told McDuffie had repeated his insult to Cumming's honor, Cumming demanded a rematch. Cumming's shot missed; he then stooped in a crouch. McDuffie, disgusted, walked away. Cumming had the brass to demand they meet again. At the third duel, Cumming's ball broke McDuffie's arm.

The most famous American duel is, of course, the Burr–Hamilton duel of 1804. Friends of the dead Hamilton later said that he opposed dueling on principle. Maybe—the duel with Burr was the first as well as the last he fought; but Hamilton had been involved in at least ten "affairs of honor," exchanges of letters about an alleged insult. None resulted in duels because Hamilton understood human nature and was a master of the ritual. His many affairs of honor were resolved by carefully worded explanations or apologies, sometimes mutual apologies, that satisfied the honor of both parties—that is, until 1804.

By the 1820s, dueling was a crime almost everywhere in the United States, even in most southern states. South Carolina imposed a fine of $2,000 and a year in prison for seconds as well as duelists. Alabama's anti-dueling law indicates that the institution had lost its gentlemanly luster by the time it was enacted in 1837; among prohibited weapons were those instruments "known as Bowie knives or Arkansas Tooth-picks." (Fannie Kemble told of a duel in Georgia in which one of the terms was that the winner could cut the loser's head off and impale it on a stake on the property line the two honorable gentlemen were disputing.)

Authorities could and did prevent duels if they got wind of them before they occurred. Cumming and McDuffie had to cross from South Carolina to North Carolina to fight their second duel. But it was next to impossible to prosecute duelists after the fact where dueling was socially acceptable, as in the South, even if one of the men was killed. How could a jury be convinced that a man had committed murder, as some states defined a killing in a duel, when the dead man had a loaded pistol in his hand, or one he had just fired at the alleged murderer? The survivor was not going to testify. Nor were the only eyewitnesses, the seconds; they were accessories to the crime, whatever it was. People who knew all about the affair in advance could provide only hearsay evidence. Even the highest-profile American duel, the Burr–Hamilton affair, was not prosecuted in either New Jersey or New York.

(Neither they nor Jackson knew that, in the Monroe cabinet's discussion of the matter, Quincy Adams had defended Jackson.) They printed broadsides that listed the men whom Jackson had killed in duels and the soldiers whom he had executed.

The assault that enraged Jackson was the accusation that he and his beloved wife, Rachel, had lived in sin. "Ought a convicted adultress and her paramour husband," wrote a Cincinnati editor, "be placed in the highest offices in this free and Christian land?" The circumstances surrounding the Jacksons' first years together were and are murky. On the record, however, was the fact that Rachel Jackson's divorce from her first husband was not legally final when she and Andrew wed, so some years later they had to go through a mortifying second ceremony. Laxity in observing marriage customs was not unusual on the frontier. When Daniel Boone was absent from home for two years and returned to find he had a son a few months old who had been fathered by Boone's brother, he shrugged. But whatever Rachel Jackson's moral code might have been when she was a young woman, in 1828 she was a dowdy, prim, and pious old lady, and the story, printed in every anti-Jackson newspaper in the country, tortured her. When she died shortly after the election, Jackson blamed Adams and his supporters for his deeply felt loss.

In the meantime, the Jacksonians had responded in kind. They dug up a preposterous tale that, when he was minister to Russia, Adams had procured the sexual favors of a young American girl for the dissolute czar. Then there were whispers of bizarre perversions in the Adams White House.

© Bettmann/Corbis

Inauguration Day, March 1829. Washington never saw such a display of raucous celebration (President Jackson's enemies said "mob rule") when thousands of Jackson's supporters flocked to the capital to honor their hero. Although he did not say so, Jackson was himself alarmed. He fled the reception at the White House through a window.

Negative campaigning had come to American politics with a vengeance.

THE SYMBOL OF HIS AGE

Mudslinging did not determine the outcome of the election of 1828. John Quincy Adams's failure to capture the popular imagination, the shadow of the corrupt bargain, and a sectional alliance led by Jackson, Vice President Calhoun, and Martin Van Buren of New York turned that trick. Jackson swept to victory with 56 percent of a total vote three times as large as the vote in 1824 and a 178 to 83 victory in the electoral college.

On Inauguration Day in March 1829, it became obvious that Andrew Jackson had captured the imagination of the common man. About 10,000 people crowded into Washington, shocking genteel society with their drinking, coarse shouting, and boisterous invasion of the White House. Invited by the new president, the mob muddied the carpets, broke crystal stemware, and stood on expensive upholstered sofas and chairs to catch a glimpse of their gaunt, white-haired hero.

The adoring mob was so unruly that Jackson's friends feared he might be injured. They spirited the president away through a window; he spent his first night as president in a hotel. Back at the executive mansion, servants lured the mob outside by setting up bowls of lemonade, whiskey punch, and tables heaped with food on the lawn.

The man whom these people idolized was by no definition a "common man." Jackson's talents were exceptional, his will almost inhuman. Nor was he the vicious desperado whom the Adams forces depicted. Jackson was "erect and dignified in his carriage," in the words of Fanny Kemble, an Englishwoman who met him. He was a gentleman whose manners were courtly.

Jackson thought well enough of himself, but he also believed that his success—he was the first log cabin–born president—was due to the openness of American society. All people were not equally talented, but American society provided everyone the opportunity to exploit his abilities and enjoy the fruits of his labor unimpeded by artificial social and economic obstacles. The government's task was to preserve this opportunity by striking down obstacles to it, such as laws that benefited some and therefore handicapped others.

Jackson's concept of government was therefore essentially negative, quite the opposite of Quincy Adams's and Clay's, which held that government was an active force for progress. Jackson believed that government should, as far as possible, leave people, society, and the economy alone so that natural

Andrew Jackson. Artist Thomas Sully's portrait captures Jackson's majestic side; he looks more like a British nobleman here than an Indian fighter or, certainly, the hero of the common man. There was such a side to Jackson. Visitors expecting to find a rough-hewn, tobacco-spitting frontiersman were surprised by Jackson's gracious manners.

social and economic forces and human initiative could operate freely.

ATTITUDES OF THE HERO AND HIS PEOPLE: WOMEN AND CHILDREN

Jackson's concept of equal, unimpeded opportunity extended only to white males; but in this, too, as in his attitudes toward women, children, blacks, and Indians, he embodied the prejudices of his era.

Jackson believed that women lived—and should live—in a "sphere" quite apart from the competitive world of men. It was men's destiny to struggle in an often brutal world; women's role was to guard home and hearth from worldly nastiness. In religious and moral sensibility, they were superior to men. Indeed, so that men could find moral and spiritual refreshment at home, they had to shelter women from a

public life that would harden or corrupt them. Jackson and most Americans (women certainly included) agreed with the clergymen, increasingly dependent on female congregants, who preached the "Gospel of Pure Womanhood." Woman's "chastity is her tower of strength," one wrote, "her modesty and gentleness are her charm, and her ability to meet the high claims of her family and dependents the noblest power she can exhibit to the world." The Rev. Edward Kirk of Albany, New York, preached that "the hopes of human society are to be found in the character, in the views, and in the conduct of mothers."

The reward due women for accepting a private and submissive role in society was the right to be treated with deference. Jackson was famous for his chivalry. Rough as the old soldier's life had been, he was prim and prudish in mixed company. Even in the absence of women, he habitually referred to them as "the fair." Adding the word "sex" would have offended his sense of delicacy.

Toward children, foreign visitors were appalled to discover, the old soldier was a pussycat. The man who aroused armies to bloodlust and slaughtered enemies without wincing, the president who periodically exploded in rages that left him and everyone else trembling, beamed happily as young children destroyed rooms in the White House before his eyes. The British minister wrote that he could not hear the president's conversation because the two men were surrounded by caterwauling children. Jackson smiled absentmindedly and nodded all the while. At the table, the president fed children first, saying that they had the best appetites and the least patience.

Indulgence of children was not universal in the United States. Strict Calvinists in New England and elsewhere still raised their children with the "Good Book" and the strap. But many Europeans commented in horror that American children had the manners of "wild Indians." Some foreigners also noticed that American children were more self-reliant than European children because of the freedom that was allowed them. It was this quality—"standing on your own two feet"—that Jackson and his countrymen valued in their heirs.

RACE

Toward Indians and blacks, Jackson also reflected the prejudices of his age. Blacks were doomed to be subject to whites by the Bible and nature. Blacks were slaves; they were intended to be slaves. American blacks were fortunate to be the slaves of enlightened, Christian masters. Jackson never troubled himself with the implications of owning slaves while believing in equal rights because, to him, the values of the Declaration of Independence were never intended to apply to African Americans. After fifty years of the Declaration and human bondage coexisting, all but a small minority of Americans felt the same.

As a westerner, Jackson had thought a great deal about Indians. He spent many years at war with them. He was the conqueror of the Creeks, the most numerous and most aggressive of the southeastern tribes.

Although he was ruthless in the Indian wars, Jackson was not the simple "Indian hater" his enemies portrayed. He found much to admire in Native Americans (as he did not in African Americans). He admired their closeness to nature, a view promoted during the 1820s by the popular novelist and Jackson supporter, James Fenimore Cooper, and their courage in resisting their conquerors. There was a tinge of regret, a sense of tragedy, in Jackson's statement to Congress that the white and red races simply could not live side by side. Left in that situation, the Indians would simply die out. He adopted and raised a Creek orphan he found in the ashes of a town his soldiers had burned.

GOVERNMENT BY PARTY

Attitudes are not policies, but President Jackson lost no time in establishing the latter. As the first president to represent a political party without apologies, he made it clear that he would replace federal officeholders who had opposed his election with his own supporters.

There were about 20,000 federal jobs in 1829; Jackson eventually dismissed about one-fifth of the employees he inherited from the Adams administration. Even recognizing that some federal officeholders had supported Jackson, that was far from a clean sweep. John Quincy Adams, who never dismissed anyone, privately admitted that many of the people Jackson fired were incompetent.

As for those who were able and lost their jobs, Jackson said that every government job should be designed so that any intelligent, freeborn American citizen could perform it adequately. If that were so, it was perfectly legitimate to say, as New York Jacksonian William Marcy said, "To the victor belongs the spoils."

Attacks on the "**spoils system**" were noisy but short-lived. When the anti-Jackson forces won power in 1840, they carved up the spoils of office far more lustily than Jackson's lieutenants had done. The "patronage," a politer term for the spoils, became an established feature of American party politics.

ISSUES OF JACKSON'S FIRST TERM

When he became president, Jackson did not have particularly strong opinions on the questions of the tariff or internal improvements. In his first address to Congress, he called for a protective tariff, but he later drifted (again without passion) to the southern position of a low tariff solely for the purpose of earning revenue.

CONSTITUTIONAL INCONSISTENCIES

As a pioneer in Nashville, Jackson was aware of the need for good roads and rivers free of snags. He had lobbied for federally financed internal improvements that would benefit Tennessee. By 1829, however, he had developed constitutional scruples about the federal government financing internal improvements that directly benefited the citizens of only one

state, or so he said. In 1830 he vetoed a bill to pay for the construction of a road between Maysville and Lexington, Kentucky, a distance of about twenty miles. He told Congress that it was the responsibility of the state of Kentucky to pay for an internal improvement that lay entirely within the state. If the Constitution was amended to authorize projects like the Maysville Road, he would approve them.

Jackson's rationale was not new. James Madison had vetoed similar projects; Madison refused to fund the Erie Canal because it lay entirely within New York. In the Maysville Road veto, Jackson seems to have been more interested in taking a slap at Henry Clay (whose hometown was Lexington) and in pleasing southern planters, who opposed all large federal expenditures, than in constitutional niceties. Later in his presidency, Jackson approved without comment internal improvement bills supported by members of his party.

On the central constitutional issue of the era—the clash of the power of the states and the power of the federal government, a matter of debate from the day the Constitution was ratified—Jackson was also inconsistent. He deferred to the state of Georgia when it violated federal treaties with Indians even after the Supreme Court ruled that the treaties were binding. But when South Carolina attempted to defy an act of Congress that he had signed, he moved quickly and decisively to crush the challenge, coming close to dusting off his old uniform, polishing his sword, and personally leading an army south.

INDIAN REMOVAL

The destruction of Tecumseh's tribal alliance in the War of 1812 and Jackson's defeat of the Creeks destroyed the last major Indian military powers east of the Mississippi. The federal government tried to avoid constant skirmishing between white pioneers and surviving tribes by negotiating treaties, at the rate of almost one a year, by which one tribe after another ceded its lands and moved into the Louisiana Purchase to find new homelands.

A few tribes resisted. In the Southeast, the Seminoles of Florida harassed outlying American settlements; they never were truly defeated, just worn down. In 1831 Black Hawk, a chief of the Sauk and Fox of Illinois and Wisconsin, led a last-ditch attempt to drive frontier farmers back. His warriors were cornered, and hundreds of Sauks and Foxes were slaughtered. The remnant of the tribes was "removed" to beyond the Mississippi.

Some prominent Americans—Thomas Jefferson, for example—continued to hope that if the Indians stayed in one place and, as individuals, began to farm as whites did, they would be amalgamated peacefully into American society. Most, however, including presidents Monroe, Quincy Adams, and Jackson, believed the Indians' tenacity in clinging to their traditional cultures made it impossible for whites and Indians to live side by side. The only alternative to wars, in which the Indians would be exterminated, was the **removal** of the tribes to an "Indian Territory" far to the west (in what is now Oklahoma) that the federal government would guarantee to them, prohibiting white incursions.

Courtesy of the Edward E. Ayer Collection, Newberry Library, Chicago

Sequoyah with the syllabary he created so that the Cherokee language could be written and printed in phonetic characters. Sequoyah understood that the letters in books represented the sounds of spoken English, but he could not read. In effect, he invented a means of writing and reading Cherokee from scratch, knowing only the principle of written language.

Four large tribes of the Southeast—the Cherokee, Creeks, Choctaws, and Chickasaws—resisted removal by consciously and deliberately undercutting the Americans' rationale for the policy: the incompatibility of Indian and white cultures. Beginning in the 1790s in the case of the Cherokee, the tribe closest to large white populations, they gave up wandering and hunting and began to farm commercially as whites did, even growing cotton with slave labor. Whites called them **"the civilized tribes."**

But being civilized was not enough to save their homes. The Creeks were too weak after their defeat in war to resist removal. The Choctaw and Chickasaws were defrauded. Federal agents bribed renegade chiefs to sign removal treaties that were then enforced on the entire people. Between 1830 and 1833, the Choctaws were forced to march west under army supervision. The Cherokee, the most "civilized," fought removal with remarkable solidarity, appealing to the law. Their rebuff revealed that, in their greed for land, Americans did not really believe that cultural differences alone justified Indian removal; so did the Indians' race.

SEQUOYAH AND THE CHEROKEE

The Cherokee had traded with Americans as soon as there was an established colony in Charleston, South Carolina. Until the late 1700s, they were the largest tribe in the South and dominated about 70,000 square miles, mostly in northern Georgia and Alabama. By 1800 their numbers had been reduced to about 16,000 and their range to 20,000 square miles. However, they had almost entirely ended intertribal conflicts, and their leaders had concluded that to prevent being overrun by the whites, they must make peace with them and become more like them.

So the Cherokee allied with Jackson in his war against the Creeks. They intermarried with whites and blacks, farmed intensively, and founded permanent towns indistinguishable in appearance and function from towns in South Carolina and Georgia. Many were Christians. They funded schools and built mills. They had a more efficient police force than neighboring whites did. They elected their leaders according to a constitution based on the American Constitution. They sent their brightest young men to the United States to be educated. And a remarkable uneducated individual, Sequoyah, also known as George Guess, devised a means by which the Cherokee could read, write, and publish in their own Iroquoian language.

Sequoyah was a silversmith who did not speak or read English. However, he grasped the principle of written language when it was explained to him that the individual characters on the pages of books represented sounds. Had Sequoyah been literate, he would have done what other Indians had done: adapted the letters of the Latin alphabet to his tribe's language. Instead, beginning in 1809, Sequoyah

---

Writing Down Words

To us, just learning the basics of reading pictographic languages, like Chinese, seems so difficult it is a wonder that hundreds of millions of people can do so. Most Chinese symbols represent things, qualities (like color), actions, and abstract ideas. A person must memorize several thousand to read anything more advanced than an advertisement for toothpaste.

Alphabetical systems, such as our own, represent sounds with letters or combinations of letters. English uses twenty-six letters, of course. The sounds of Russian require several more, whereas almost perfectly phonetic Italian uses fewer. Hawaiian is written with just thirteen Latin letters.

A syllabary is well suited to spoken languages having relatively few syllables (sounds combining a consonant sound and a vowel sound). Sequoyah's Cherokee syllabary had only eighty-six characters—readily learned. An English syllabary wouldn't work well: it would have about 500 characters. However, had Hawaii produced a syllabary for its language before American missionaries wrote it using their alphabet, it could have been written with just forty characters.

started from scratch and created not an alphabet but a syllabary: eighty-six symbols that represented the eighty-six syllables that Sequoyah counted in Cherokee speech. It was the same method of writing that had been developed in Minoan Crete two thousand years earlier, and in several other cultures. The Cherokee nation immediately adopted Sequoyah's syllabary, teaching it in schools and publishing books in it. A newspaper, the *Cherokee Phoenix,* was published in both English and Cherokee.

THE CHEROKEE GO TO COURT

By the late 1820s, life in the Cherokee nation was scarcely distinguishable from life in neighboring Georgia. But white Georgians wanted Cherokee land. In 1828 the state legislature asserted its authority over Cherokee territory. The Cherokee asked the Supreme Court to invalidate Georgia's claims on the grounds that the Cherokee people comprised an independent nation. The Court rejected the Indians' argument. Writing for the majority in *Cherokee Nation v. Georgia* (1831), John Marshall denied Cherokee independence, but he left the tribe a significant opening. The Cherokee nation was, Marshall wrote, a "domestic, dependent nation" within the United States, like the "ward" of a guardian.

In the meantime, the state of Georgia arrested Samuel Worcester, a Congregationalist minister, for violating a Georgia law requiring "white persons" to apply for a license before they entered Indian lands. Financed by the Cherokee, Worcester sued for his release on the grounds that Georgia was violating Cherokee treaties with the United States and congressional acts regulating Indian affairs. In other words, a state was defying federal power, an issue on which Marshall had made his nationalism quite clear. Indeed, treaties between the United States and a "domestic dependent nation" were contracts, another of Marshall's interests. The Cherokee brief was brilliantly composed.

With only one dissenting vote, the Court ruled that the Cherokee nation was a "distinct community, occupying its own territory, with boundaries accurately described . . . which the citizens of Georgia have no right to enter." The law under which Worcester had been arrested was invalid.

THE TRAIL OF TEARS

Marshall's decision in *Worcester* was unambiguous, and the Cherokee celebrated. But Georgia gambled or, perhaps, secured confidential assurances from Jackson through intermediaries. The president was, after all, an Indian fighter, and Georgia had voted for him in 1828. The state defied the Supreme Court and held onto its prisoner. State commissioners engineered purchases of lands from Cherokees who could be bought and began preparations to remove by force Indians who resisted.

President Jackson may not actually have said, "John Marshall has made his decision, let him enforce it," as he was quoted. But he did nothing to stop Georgia's takeover of the Cherokee nation. By 1838 the dispossession of the Cherokee was complete. On what the Indians called the "Trail of Tears," they were marched 1,200 miles to Indian Territory, accompanied by federal troops. An officer sent to supervise one of the marches, General John E. Wool, was disgusted by his assignment: "The whole scene since I have been in this country has been nothing but a heartrending one." The Indians were forced from their homes under the gaze of "vultures ready to pounce on their prey and strip them of everything they have."

Two thousand died in camps waiting for the migration to begin, another 2,000 on the trail. About 15,000 Cherokees made it to Oklahoma, along with smaller numbers of Choctaws, Chickasaws, and Creeks.

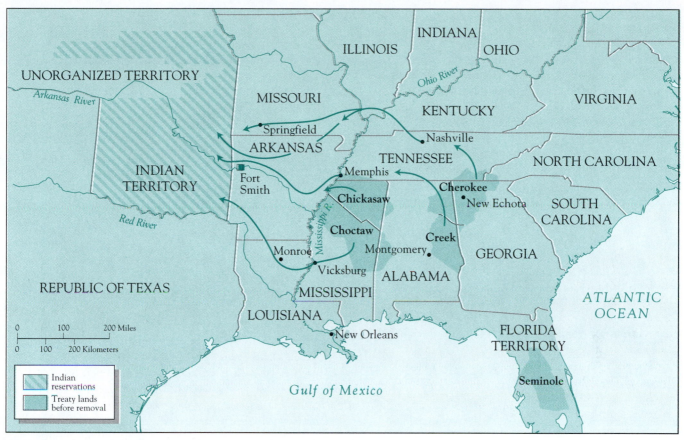

MAP 15:3 Removal of the Southeastern Tribes, 1820–1840

Removal of the southeastern tribes, 1820–1840. Removing the "civilized tribes" from their southeastern homeland was a cynical land grab. The southeastern nations had proved that they could function and prosper side by side with whites—the pious rationale for removal was that Indians never could—by incorporating much of the mainstream culture into their own. They had firm treaties with the U.S. government confirming their rights to their lands. The Cherokee won two rulings in the Supreme Court in their favor. Still they were forced to leave.

THE SOUTH AND THE TARIFF

South Carolina had less luck defying the federal government than Georgia did. The issue that brought the state (and Vice President Calhoun) into conflict with Jackson was the tariff. In 1828, before Jackson's election, Congress enacted an extremely high protective tariff. Southern planters hated what they called the "Tariff of Abominations." Cotton growers believed that their crop was paying the country's bills and underwriting industrial development in the North.

They had a point. Cotton accounted for fully half of American income from abroad. Some of this wealth was effectively diverted into the hands of northern manufacturers by the tariff, which, by raising the price of imported products, permitted American mill owners to charge more for the goods they produced. As long as a majority of congressmen favored high tariffs, however, what could be done?

As a young man, Vice President Calhoun had favored protective tariffs. He had hoped to see South Carolina develop mills to spin and weave its cotton—factories in the fields. Those hopes came to nothing. The cotton industry and most other manufacturing were centered in New England and the middle states. South Carolina's economy was almost exclusively agricultural; the state grew and exported cotton and imported its manufactures. The price of cotton depended on a world market under no one's control. The price of manufactures was artificially propped up by a tariff enacted, in effect, by northern congressmen with a few southern allies. (Kentucky hemp growers and Louisiana sugar growers favored high tariffs to protect their crops from foreign competitors.)

When the Tariff of Abominations was enacted, the heavily industrialized northeastern states had eighty-seven representatives in Congress. The cotton states of the South had thirty-one; even adding Virginia's votes, the core of the anti-tariff faction in the House numbered just fifty-three.

NULLIFICATION

Compromise was impossible, Calhoun concluded. Northern and southern positions were irreconcilable. The only political solution was "surrender, on one side or the other."

This famous painting depicting the Cherokee on their "Trail of Tears" from Georgia to Oklahoma only hints at the horrors of the trek. The procession looks almost triumphant. Cherokee migrants and sympathetic army officers who accompanied them—and the number of deaths on the journey, a quarter of those who started—described a horror.

In 1829, Calhoun secretly wrote *The South Carolina Exposition and Protest*. It was an ingenious but mischievous interpretation of the relationship of the states to the federal union that provided South Carolina and other southern states a rationale for defying the federal tariff. The *Exposition* took up where Madison's and Jefferson's Virginia and Kentucky Resolutions left off. Calhoun stated that the United States had been created not by the people of America (John Marshall's premise) but by the people acting through the states of which they were citizens. This was not splitting hairs. Calhoun was saying that the states were sovereign, not the federal government. The United States was a voluntary compact of the states.

If, therefore, the U.S. Congress enacted and the president signed a law that was intolerable to a sovereign state, that state had the right to nullify the law (to prevent its enforcement) within its borders. Such a nullification could be overridden only by three-quarters of the other states. (Calhoun was here referring to the Constitution's amendment procedure, which requires the ratification of an amendment by three-fourths of the states.) In such an event, Calhoun concluded, the nullifying state could choose between "surrender" to the other states or leaving the Union via secession.

SOUTH CAROLINA ACTS, THE PRESIDENT RESPONDS

Calhoun and his supporters were content to leave the *South Carolina Exposition* in the abstract in the hope that the big Jacksonian majority elected to Congress in 1830 would repeal the Tariff of Abominations and enact a low tariff. However, in 1832, while slightly lowering rates, Congress adopted a tariff that was still protective, and Jackson signed it. South Carolinians blew up, electing a convention that declared the Tariff of 1832 "null and void" within the borders of the state. State officials were ordered not to collect tariff payments, and federal officials in the state were warned that collection of the duties was "inconsistent with the longer continuance of South Carolina in the Union."

Jackson exploded in one of his rages. South Carolinians would rather rule in hell, he said, than be subordinate in heaven. They could write a dozen expositions, but if "a single drop of blood shall be shed there" in interfering with the collection of the tariff, "I will hang the first man I can lay my hand on engaged in such treasonable conduct, upon the first tree I can find."

Congress supported him with a "Force Bill." It authorized the army to collect duties in South Carolina. The bloodshed for which Jackson was waiting seemed inevitable. It was avoided because the nullifiers were disheartened by the refusal of any other state to nullify the 1832 tariff and because Henry Clay, after meeting with Calhoun, put together a tariff with duties just low enough that he and the nullifiers could claim victory but not so low as to arouse fury in the industrial states. In 1833 the state rescinded its nullification of the tariff. However, it pointedly did not repudiate the principle of nullification.

Jackson let it ride. It was just paper, like *Worcester* v. *Georgia.* He had had his way—and he had identified a new enemy, his own vice president.

FURTHER READING

Biographies Donald B. Cole, *Martin Van Buren and the American Political System,* 1984; John Nive, *Martin Van Buren: The Romantic Age of American Politics,* 1983; Merrill D. Peterson, *The Great Triumvirate: Webster, Clay, and Calhoun,* 1987; Robert V. Remini, *Henry Clay: Statesman for the Union,* 1991.

Indian Removal John Ehle, *Trail of Tears,* 1988; Michael D. Green, *The Politics of Indian Removal: Creek Government and Society in Crisis,* 1982; William G. McLaughlin, *Cherokee Renascence in the New Republic,* 1986; Ronald Satz, *American Indian Policy in the Jacksonian Era,* 1974; Anthony Wallace, *The Long Bitter Trail: Andrew Jackson and the Indians,* 1993.

Jackson: Life, Character, Values Joanne B. Freeman, *Affairs of Honor: National Politics in the New Republic,* 2001; Robert V. Remini, *Andrew Jackson and the Course of American Freedom,* 1981, *Andrew Jackson and the Course of American Democracy,* 1984, and *Andrew Jackson and His Indian Wars,* 2001; M. P. Rogin, *Fathers and Children: Andrew Jackson and the Destruction of American Indians,* 1975; Bertram Wyatt-Brown, *Honor and Violence in the Old South,* 1986.

Nullification Richard E. Ellis, *The Union at Risk: Jacksonian Democracy, States' Rights, and the Nullification Crisis,* 1987; William W. Freehling, *Prelude to Civil War: The Nullification Controversy in South Carolina, 1816–1836,* 1966; John Niven, *John C. Calhoun and the Price of Union,* 1988.

Politics and Parties Daniel Feller, *The Public Lands in American Politics,* 1984; Lawrence F. Kohl, *The Politics of Individualism: Parties and the American Character in the Jacksonian Era,* 1989; Richard McCormick, *The Party Period and Public Policy: American Politics from the Age of Jackson to the Progressive Era,* 1986, and *The Second American Party System: Party Formation in the Jacksonian Era,* 1966; Harry L. Watson, *Liberty and Power: The Politics of Jacksonian America,* 1990.

KEY TERMS

The following terms are covered in this chapter and can also be found in the list of Key Terms at the back of the book.

Anti-Masonic party	**King Caucus**	**"the civilized tribes"**	**William F. Crawford**
"corrupt bargain"	**removal**	**Virginia Dynasty**	*Worcester* v. *Georgia*
Democratic-Republicans	**"spoils system"**		

ONLINE SOURCES GUIDE

Use this listing to find online documents, images, interactive maps, simulations, and other resources related to this chapter:

American History Resource Center
http://history.wadsworth.com/rc/us

Selected Documents
Andrew Jackson's first annual message (1829)
Andrew Jackson's letter to Captain James Gadsden (1829)
"Memorial of the Cherokee Nation" (1830)

Selected Images
Henry Clay
John Quincy Adams
Andrew Jackson
John C. Calhoun

Interactive Time Line (with online readings)
Hero of the People: Andrew Jackson and a New Era
1824–1830

Discovery

How did Jackson enhance the use of presidential power while in office?

In thinking about this question, begin by breaking it down into the components shown below. A discussion of the significance of each component should appear in your answer.

Government and Law: For this exercise, please look at the "Inauguration Day" image and read the excerpts "Jackson Announces His Policy of Rotation in Office" and "Margaret Bayard Smith Describes the Inaugural Celebration." What did Jackson's election and inauguration symbolize to many Americans? Why was this the case? How was Jackson's inauguration symbolic of the political changes of this period? Note the illustration and account of Jackson's inauguration. Is Smith's account of the inaugural celebration positive or negative? How does she explain the behavior of the crowd? How does Jackson's policy of rotation in office represent the political changes of the period? Do you think the inaugural crowd would be pleased with this policy?

© Bettmann/Corbis

Inauguration Day

Jackson Announces his Policy of Rotation in Office, 1829

FIRST ANNUAL MESSAGE.
Fellow-Citizens of the Senate and House of Representatives: . . .

There are, perhaps, few men who can for any great length of time enjoy office and power without being more or less under the influence of feelings unfavorable to the faithful discharge of their public duties. Their integrity may be proof against improper considerations immediately addressed to themselves, but they are apt to acquire a habit of looking with indifference upon the public interests and of tolerating conduct from which an unpracticed man would revolt. Office is considered as a species of property, and government rather as a means of promoting individual interests than as an instrument created solely for the service of the people. Corruption in some and in others a perversion of correct feelings and principles divert government from its legitimate ends and make it an engine for the support of the few at the expense of the many. The duties of all public officers are, or at least admit of being made, so plain and simple that men of intelligence may readily qualify themselves for their performance; and I can not but believe that more is lost by the long continuance of men in office than is generally to be gained by their experience.

I submit, therefore, to your consideration whether the efficiency of the Government would not be promoted and official industry and integrity better secured by a general extension of the law which limits appointments to four years.

In a country where offices are created solely for the benefit of the people no one man has any more intrinsic right to official station than another. Offices were not established to give support to particular men at the public expense. No individual wrong is, therefore, done by removal, since neither appointment to nor continuance in office is a matter of right. The incumbent became an officer with a view to public benefits, and when these require his removal they are not to be sacrificed to private interests. It is the people, and they alone, who have a right to complain when a bad officer is substituted for a good one. He who is removed has the same means of obtaining a living that are enjoyed by the millions who never held office. The proposed limitation would destroy the idea of property now so generally connected with official station, and although individual distress may be sometimes produced, it would, by promoting that rotation which constitutes a leading principle in the republican creed, give healthful action to the system. . . .

Andrew Jackson.

Margaret Bayard Smith Describes the Inaugural Celebration, 1829

[Washington] March 11th, Sunday [1829]

[To Mrs. Kirkpatrick]

. . . We stood on the South steps of the terrace; when the appointed hour came saw the General and his company advancing up the Avenue, slow, very slow so impeded was his march by the crowds thronging around him. Even from a distance, he could be discerned from those who accompanied him, for he was only uncovered, (the Servant in presence of his Sovereign, the People). The south side of the Capitol was literally alive with the multitude, who stood ready to receive the hero and the multitude who attended him. "There, there, that is he," exclaimed different voices. "Which?" asked others. "He with the white head," was the reply. "Ah," exclaimed others, "there is the old man and his gray hair, there is the old veteran, there is Jackson." At last he enters the gate at the foot of the hill and turns to the road that leads round to the front of the Capitol. In a moment every one who until then had stood like statues gazing on the scene below them, rushed onward, to right, to left, to be ready to receive him in the front. Our party, of course, were more deliberate, we waited until the multitude had rushed past us and then left the terrace and walked round to the furthest side of the square, where there were no carriages to impede us, and entered it by the gate fronting the Capitol. . . . At the moment the General entered the Portico and advanced to the table, the shout that rent the air, still resounds in my ears. When the speech over, and the President made his parting bow, the barrier that had separated the people from him was broken down and they rushed up the steps all eager to shake hands with him. It was with difficulty he made his way through the Capitol and down the hill to the gateway that opens on the avenue. Here for a moment he was stopped. The living mass was impenetrable. After a while a passage was opened, and he mounted his horse which had been provided for his return (for he had walked to the Capitol) then such a cortege as followed him! Country men, farmers, gentlemen, mounted and dismounted, boys, women and children, black and white. Carriages, wagons and carts all pursuing him to the President's house. . . . [W]e set off to the President's House, but on a nearer approach found an entrance impossible, the yard and avenue was compact with living matter. The day was delightful, the scene animating, so we walked backward and forward at every turn meeting some new acquaintance and stopping to talk and shake hands. . . . We continued promenading here, until near three, returned home unable to stand and threw ourselves on the sopha. Some one came and informed us the crowd before the President's house, was so far lesson'd, that they thought we might enter. This time we effected our purpose. But what a scene did we witness! The *Majesty of the People* had disappeared, and a rabble, a mob, of boys, negros, women, children, scrambling fighting, romping. What a pity what a pity! No arrangements had been made no police officers placed on duty and the whole house had been inundated by the rabble mob. We came too late. The President, after having been *literally* nearly pressed to death and almost suffocated and torn to pieces by the people in their eagerness to shake hands with Old Hickory, had retreated through the back way or south front and had escaped to his lodgings at Gadsby's. Cut glass and china to the amount of several thousand dollars had been broken in the struggle to get the refreshments, punch and other articles had been carried out in tubs and buckets, but had it been in hogsheads it would have been insufficient, ice-creams, and cake and lemonade, for 20,000 people, for it is said that number were there, tho' I think the number exaggerated. Ladies fainted, men were seen with bloody noses and such a scene of confusion took place as is impossible to describe,—those who got in could not get out by the door again, but had to scramble out of windows. At one time, the President who had retreated and retreated until he was pressed against the wall, could only be secured by a number of gentleman forming around him and making a kind of barrier of their own bodies, and the pressure was so great that Col. Bomford who was one said that at one time he was afraid they should have been pushed down, or on the President. It was then the windows were thrown open, and the torrent found an outlet, which otherwise might have proved fatal.

To read extended versions of the documents, visit the companion Web site http://history.wadsworth.com/americanpast8e; click on "Discovery Sources."

16 In the Shadow of Old Hickory

Personalities and Politics 1830–1842

Reproduced from the Collections of the Library of Congress

He prefers the specious to the solid, and the plausible to the true. . . . I don't like Henry Clay. He is a bad man, an impostor, a creator of wicked schemes. I wouldn't speak to him, but by God, I love him.

John C. Calhoun

[Calhoun is] a smart fellow, one of the first among second-rate men, but of lax political principles and a disordinate ambition not over-delicate in the means of satisfying itself.

Albert Gallatin

Such is human nature in the gigantic intellect, the envious temper, the ravenous ambition, and the rotten heart of Daniel Webster.

John Quincy Adams

Thank God. I—I also—am an American.
Daniel Webster

To the people of the country who idolized him, Andrew Jackson was "Old Hickory," a tough, timeless frontiersman as straight as a long rifle. In person, however, he was a frail, 62-year-old wisp of a man who often looked to be a day away from death. Over six feet in height, Jackson weighed only 145 pounds. His posture was, indeed, soldierly, but he was frequently ill. He suffered from chronic lead poisoning (he carried two bullets in his body), headaches, diarrhea, kidney disease, and edema, a painful swelling of the legs. Coughing

fits beleaguered him. When he was sworn in as president in 1829, many who knew him wondered if he would live to finish his term.

VAN BUREN VERSUS CALHOUN

Vice president John C. Calhoun had a more than academic interest in Jackson's health. When Jackson accepted Calhoun as his vice president in 1828, he was not merely pocketing

16, 22, 24

High Praise

The testimony to Calhoun's integrity was almost unanimous. It was complimented even by two of the nation's leading abolitionists, men sworn to destroy the institution Calhoun swore to preserve: slavery. William Lloyd Garrison called him "a man who means what he says and never blusters. He is no demagogue." Wendell Phillips spoke of "the pure, manly and uncompromising advocate of slavery; the Hector of a Troy fated to fall."

South Carolina's electoral votes. He was naming his heir apparent as the next presidential candidate of what the Jacksonians now called the Democratic-Republican Party and, possibly—for Jackson was not oblivious to his age and health—president within four years.

JOHN C. CALHOUN

Like Jackson, Calhoun was Scotch-Irish, the descendant of those eighteenth-century emigrants dependably described as hot-tempered and pugnacious. Calhoun was, in fact, again like Jackson, passionate and willful. Portrait painters captured a burning in his eyes just short of rage but never the slightest hint of a smile. Photographers, coming along late in his life, confirmed the painters' impressions. "There is no recreation in him," a woman friend said, "I never heard him utter a jest." Did he ever enjoy a moment's peace of mind? Harriet Martineau, a perceptive Englishwoman who wrote a

book about the United States called him "the cast-iron man, who looks as if he had never been born, and never could be extinguished."

As a young man, Calhoun had been a nationalist who urged South Carolinians to build spinning mills amidst their cotton fields. In 1815, as earnestly as Henry Clay, he wanted to "bind the nation together with a perfect system of roads and canals." In 1816, he introduced the bill that chartered the Second Bank of the United States, arguing the desirability of a powerful national regulator of the nation's money supply. John Quincy Adams said that Calhoun was "above all sectional and factious prejudices," that he had a "fair and candid mind."

Fair Calhoun remained until the very end of his life. He was certainly more candid in his views than his illustrious contemporaries. But several slips into prevarication when he was Jackson's vice president cost him dearly.

By 1828, when South Carolina had not industrialized and its planters and politicians embraced agrarian opposition to protective tariffs and large federal expenditures, Calhoun was no longer a nationalist. He opposed the tariffs of 1828 and 1832 as well as costly internal improvements. He wrote *The South Carolina Exposition and Protest* justifying state nullification of federal laws but, knowing the doctrine would not sit well in the Northeast and still ambitious to be president, he kept his authorship secret.

So fundamental a difference with Jackson was quite enough in itself to kill Calhoun's expectations to be anointed the president's successor. However, it was on a question of

The New York Historical Society

President Jackson never asked Peggy O'Neill to cavort for the members of his cabinet, as in this lampoon of the affair, but he defended her chastity at length and told them that their wives should receive her. Secretary of State Martin Van Buren, the beneficiary of the hubbub, is at the right studying Mrs. Eaton through a lorgnette, hand-held eyeglasses associated with pretentious women and effeminate men.

personal morals and etiquette and Jackson's discovery of an opinion Calhoun had expressed a decade earlier that made enemies of the president and vice president.

PEGGY O'NEILL TIMBERLAKE EATON

Peggy O'Neill was the once fetching daughter of a Washington hotel keeper with whom a number of congressmen boarded, including Jackson when he was a senator between 1823 and 1825. She married a seaman named Timberlake who was, as seamen are apt to be, rarely at home. In her husband's absence, or so much of Washington society whispered, she found solace in the arms of Tennessee congressman John Eaton, whom Jackson named secretary of war.

Such conjunctions were not unusual in the capital. It was no longer the all-male city it had been when Jefferson was president but quarters suitable to congressmen's families were still scarce. Some bachelors like Eaton and even lonely husbands found lady friends; as long as they were discreet, little was made of it. Henry Clay was reputed to be a roué. Richard M. Johnson, who would be vice president between 1837 and 1841, was known to cohabit with a black woman who was also his slave.

But Johnson did not bring his common law wife to social functions. Peggy (O'Neill) Eaton became an affair of state when her husband died at sea and she married Eaton. He and Peggy assumed that, as man and wife, they would join Washington society together.

This was asking too much of respectable women, including Floride Calhoun, the vice president's sternly moralistic wife. She became the ringleader of the wives of cabinet members who snubbed Mrs. Eaton. Jackson was furious. When his niece and official hostess refused to receive Peggy, Jackson told her to move out of the White House. Jackson found Peggy Eaton charming and blameless. At a cabinet meeting summoned to discuss the matter, he pronounced

A Foolish Lady

There was nothing amusing about Peggy Eaton's final years. As a well-off widow of 59, she married a 19-year-old dancing teacher, Antonio Buchignani. Momentarily, she was sensible enough to protect her wealth with a prenuptial agreement. But she reverted to the foolery of love almost immediately and gave her husband a $14,000 house. He stole and pawned her silver. When he threatened to leave her, she turned over almost everything she owned to him. Buchignani then ran off with Peggy's granddaughter.

her "as chaste as a virgin." Advisors who wished to remain in his favor assured him, as Amos Kendall, a Kentucky editor did, that her only fault was being "too forward in her manners." (Another Jacksonian, Louis McLane, wisecracked that Eaton had "married his mistress—& the mistress of 11 dozen others," but not within Jackson's hearing.)

Jackson's endorsement meant nothing to the ladies of Washington society. And if women were excluded from public life, the rules of morality and society were squarely within their sphere and, within that sphere, prudent husbands did as they were told. Few ladies called on Peggy Eaton and she continued to stand conspicuously alone at balls and dinners. Only Secretary of State Martin Van Buren who, as a widower, had no spouse to oblige, dared to be seen admiring her gowns and bringing her refreshments.

THE RISE OF THE SLY FOX

Charm and chitchat came easily to Van Buren. His worst enemies conceded his grace and wit. His portraits, in contrast to Calhoun's, show a twinkle in his eye and a good-natured, easy-going smile.

Democrats versus Whigs 1828–1845

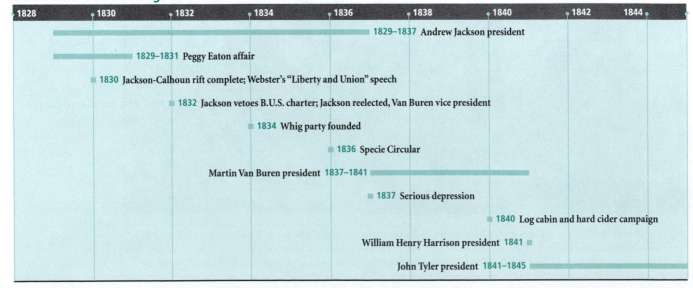

| 1828 | 1830 | 1832 | 1834 | 1836 | 1838 | 1840 | 1842 | 1844 |

1829–1837 Andrew Jackson president

1829–1831 Peggy Eaton affair

1830 Jackson-Calhoun rift complete; Webster's "Liberty and Union" speech

1832 Jackson vetoes B.U.S. charter; Jackson reelected, Van Buren vice president

1834 Whig party founded

1836 Specie Circular

Martin Van Buren president 1837–1841

1837 Serious depression

1840 Log cabin and hard cider campaign

William Henry Harrison president 1841

John Tyler president 1841–1845

But Martin Van Buren was much more than a jolly Dutchman. He was a devilishly clever politician, almost always several moves ahead of his rivals, particularly when they were impassioned true believers like Calhoun. Van Buren's wiles earned him the nickname "the Sly Fox of Kinderhook" (his hometown in New York).

He was the most successful political organizer of his time. He owed his high position in Jackson's cabinet to delivering a majority of New York's electoral votes to the Democratic-Republican ticket in 1828. (New York had voted for John Quincy Adams in 1824.) He understood that a political party had first and foremost to be a vote-gathering machine; it had to win elections. Therefore, a party must reward the activists who corralled the voters by appointing them to government jobs.

Van Buren was ambitious for himself. His sensitivity to the feelings of Peggy Eaton may have been quite sincere, but his courtesy to her also won Jackson's friendship where, previously, they had been political allies. Then, with the Eaton mess paralyzing the administration—it took more of Jackson's time during his first two years as president than any other matter—Van Buren suggested to the perplexed president a way out.

Van Buren proposed that he would resign as secretary of state, and Eaton would resign as secretary of war. The other members of the cabinet, whose wives were causing the president so much anxiety, would have no choice but to follow their example. Jackson would be rid of the lot, but no particular wing of the Democratic-Republican Party could claim to have been wronged. Jackson appreciated both the strategy and Van Buren's willingness to sacrifice his prestigious office. He appointed a new cabinet and rewarded Van Buren by naming him minister to England, then, as now, the plum of the diplomatic service.

CALHOUN SEALS HIS DOOM

The Sly Fox of Kinderhook was lucky, too. While he calculated each turning with an eye on a distant destination, Calhoun bumped into posts like a blind cart horse. While the Eaton business was still rankling Jackson, the president discovered in some old cabinet reports that, ten years earlier, Secretary of War Calhoun wanted to punish Jackson for his unauthorized invasion of Florida and John Quincy Adams had defended Jackson. Confronted with the evidence, Calhoun tried to explain his way out of the fix in a long and convoluted monologue. The president cut him off by writing, "Understanding you now, no further communication with you on this subject is necessary." To Jackson's credit, he tried to reconcile personally with Quincy Adams, but Adams, to his discredit, publicly snubbed the president.

There was not much further communication between Jackson and Calhoun on any subject. In April 1830, they attended a formal dinner during which twenty of Calhoun's cronies offered toasts to states' rights and even nullification. When it was the president's turn to lift a glass, he rose, stared at Calhoun, and toasted, "Our Union: It must be preserved." Calhoun got in the last word of the evening. He replied, "The

Courtesy Chicago Historical Society

■ *Martin Van Buren was a dapper dresser, a good-humored bon vivant, shrewd, and preternaturally shrewd. He was also unfailingly lucky until, when he was president, the country was rattled by a serious depression that no political career could have survived.*

Union, next to our liberty, the most dear." But Jackson took satisfaction in the fact that, as he told the story, Calhoun trembled as he said it.

The old duelist delighted in such confrontations. Van Buren took pleasure in his enduring good luck, for he was in England during the nastiest squabbling between Jackson and Calhoun, when even the slyest of foxes might have stumbled across a hound.

And Calhoun blundered again, ensuring that Van Buren would succeed Jackson. Seeking personal revenge, Calhoun cast the deciding vote in the Senate's refusal to confirm Van Buren's diplomatic appointment. This brought the New Yorker back to the United States, but hardly in disgrace. Jackson was yet more deeply obligated to him. Van Buren was named vice-presidential candidate in the election of 1832, as he probably would not have been had Calhoun left him in London.

THE WAR WITH THE BANK

Jackson's health did not improve. He suffered two serious hemorrhages of the lungs as president. But he was still alive in 1832 and, apparently, never thought of retiring after one term. The presidential contest of 1832, unlike the personalities and smears campaign of 1828, centered on a serious issue, the future of the Bank of the United States. It need not have been an issue; the Bank's charter had four years to run. Jackson's dislike of the Bank was on record but he had, like his predecessors, deposited the government's revenues with it. It was Henry Clay, in a political miscalculation that was to lead to much financial mischief, who made the Bank the issue of the year.

THE POWERS OF THE BANK

Every cent the government collected in excise taxes, tariffs, and from land sales went into the BUS. It was a huge, fabulously rich institution. Its twenty-nine branches controlled about a third of all bank deposits in the United States, and did some $70 million in transactions each year.

With such resources, the Bank held immense power over the nation's money supply and, therefore, the economy. In an impolitic but revealing moment, **Nicholas Biddle** told congressmen that the BUS was capable of destroying any other bank in the country.

What he meant was that the BUS was likely to have in its possession more paper money issued by a state chartered bank than the bank had specie (gold and silver) in its vaults. If the BUS presented this paper for redemption in specie, the issuing bank would be bankrupt and the investment and deposits in it wiped out.

On a day he was more tactful, Biddle said that the BUS exercised "a mild and gentle but efficient control" over the economy. Because the state banks were aware of the sword the BUS held over them, they maintained larger reserves of gold and silver than they might otherwise have done. Rather than ruining banks, the BUS ensured that they operated more responsibly.

A PRIVATE INSTITUTION

Biddle was as proud of the public service he rendered as of the Bank's annual profits. Nevertheless, the fact remained that the Bank was powerful because of its control of the money supply—a matter of profound public interest—but was itself a private institution. BUS policies were made not by elected officials, or by bureaucrats responsible to elected officials, but by a board of directors responsible to shareholders.

This was enough in itself to earn the animosity of a president who abhorred special interests. Biddle therefore attempted to make a friend of the president by generous loans to key Jackson supporters, and he presented the president with a plan to retire the national debt—a goal dear to Jackson's heart—with the final installments coinciding with the anniversary of the Battle of New Orleans. It was to no avail. Jackson told Biddle that it was not a matter of disliking the BUS more than he disliked other banks; Jackson did not trust any of them. Like old Bullion Benton, he was a hard-money man. Faced with a stone wall in the White House, Biddle turned to Congress for friendship.

THE ENEMIES OF THE BANK

Biddle needed powerful friends because the BUS had plenty of enemies. Except for their fear or resentment of the Bank, however, they had little in common.

First was the growing financial community of New York City—the bankers and brokers who would soon be known collectively as "Wall Street." Grown wealthy from the Erie

A satirical six-cent bill supposedly printed by one of Jackson's irresponsible "pet banks," the Humbug Glory. It is covered with Democratic Party symbols: Jackson on the penny, a leaf from a hickory tree, and, curiously, a donkey, which became a symbol of the Democratic Party only a generation later.

Canal and New York's role as the nation's leading port, they were keen to challenge Philadelphia's last financial powerhouse, the BUS.

Second, the freewheeling bankers of the West disliked Biddle's restraints, "mild and gentle" as they were. Just as during the 1810s, they were caught up in the financial opportunities of land speculation and the rapid growth of western cities. Curiously, some of the most avid allies of the president who hated all banks were bankers and, generally speaking, not the most virtuous of their profession.

A third group anxious to see the BUS declawed was the old-fashioned fraternity of hard-money men like Jackson and Thomas Hart Benton. They disapproved of the very idea of an institution that issued paper money in quantities greater than it had gold and silver on hand. Thirty years earlier, the decidedly un-Jacksonian John Adams had condemned the principle of modern banking. Indeed, the hard-money position was, in part, generational, but not entirely. Mechanics, especially in the East, many of them former "Workies" but now Democratic-Republicans known as "Locofocos" (after a brand of smoker's matches with which they had illuminated a darkened auditorium), were hard-money men. They had too often been paid in bank notes that, when they presented them to landlords and shopkeepers, were discounted because the banks that had issued them were shaky. They wanted to be paid in coin.

THE BANK WAR

In 1832, the BUS had four years before its charter expired or Congress renewed it. Biddle was confident; he had plenty of time to prepare for the day of reckoning by making loans to well-established congressmen and senators, retaining them as legal counselors, or providing jobs to their political cronies. In another one of his tactless moments, he said that he could "remove all the Constitutional Scruples in the District of Columbia" by handing out "a dozen cashierships, and 100 clerkships to worthy friends [of congressmen] who have no character and no money."

Henry Clay, now a National-Republican senator from Kentucky, had different ideas. He wanted to run for president against Jackson, but knew he could not defeat the "Old Hero" in a contest of personalities. He needed an issue. He persuaded a reluctant Biddle to apply for a new charter immediately. National-Republicans and pro-Bank Democrats—a majority in both houses (Clay had counted heads)—would vote for it. It was unlikely that Jackson would grit his teeth and sign the bill but, if he did, all well and good for Biddle. If, as was more likely, Jackson vetoed the charter, Clay would have the issue on which to wage his anti-Jackson presidential campaign. Clay believed that, because the bank had proved its value to the economy, he would defeat Jackson by promising to rescue it. He argued to Biddle that a Jackson veto in 1836, when the charter expired, could not be so readily reversed (which was not necessarily so).

Clay was not the last presidential nominee to believe that, presented with a clear, concrete issue, voters would choose their president rationally rather than emotionally. And so, his well-laid plans proceeded smoothly, except for the outcome. Congress rechartered the Bank. Jackson vetoed the bill. Clay ran for president on the issue. Clay went down to defeat—resoundingly. Jackson won 55 percent of the popular vote and 219 electoral votes. Clay won only 49 electoral votes. (Anti-Masonic candidate William Wirt won 7 electoral votes, and South Carolina gave its 11 votes to an ally of Calhoun, John Floyd.)

FINANCIAL CHAOS

It was Jackson's turn not to wait until 1836. "The Bank is trying to destroy me," he had said, "but I will destroy the Bank." He already hated Henry Clay. Now he personified the BUS—the "Monster Bank!"—and he hated it. In September 1833, six months after his second inauguration, Jackson ceased depositing federal revenues in the Bank. Instead, he scattered the government's accounts among state-chartered institutions, which his beaten enemies called his **pet banks.**

The BUS, on federal instructions, continued to pay the government's bills. Within just three months, federal deposits in the BUS sank from $10 million to $4 million. Biddle had no choice but to reduce the scope of the Bank's operations. He also chose, at least in part to retaliate against Jackson, to call in debts owed the Bank by other financial institutions. The result was a wave of bank failures that wiped out the savings of tens of thousands of people, just what Jackson had feared BUS power might mean.

Under pressure from the business community, Biddle relented. He let state banks' debts ride and actually reversed direction, increasing the money supply by making loans to state banks. The result was a speculative mania such as, before 1832, the BUS had prevented. Many of the eighty-nine pet banks to which Jackson had entrusted federal money proved to be among the least responsible in feeding the speculation.

In 1836, Henry Clay made his contribution to what would be the most serious American depression since Jefferson's embargo. He convinced Congress to pass a distribution bill that apportioned $37 million among the states to spend on internal improvements. The politicians reacted as politicians presented with a windfall usually do: they spent recklessly on the least worthy of projects. Values in land, both in the undeveloped West and in eastern cities, soared. Federal land sales rose to $25 million in 1836. Seeking to get a share of the freely circulating cash, new banks were chartered at a dizzying rate. There had been 330 state banks in 1830; there were almost 800 in 1836.

There was no powerful Bank of the United States to cool things down. Its charter expired on schedule and Biddle

Reproduced from the Collections of the Library of Congress

An aged Jackson, after leaving the presidency. He was 70 when he retired to the Hermitage, his plantation near Nashville, in 1837. He lived there quietly until 1845 while both Democrats and Whigs politicked in his shadow.

transformed what was left of it into a Pennsylvania chartered state bank. Jackson tried to end the speculative frenzy in the only way within his powers. In July 1836, he issued the **Specie Circular** requiring that all payments on purchases of federal lands be in gold and silver coin; paper money was no longer acceptable.

The Specie Circular stopped the runaway speculation, but as a stone wall stops a runaway horse. Land sales collapsed. Neither land speculators nor ordinary people developing farms could make their installment payments. Banks that had fueled the speculation with paper money that the government would not accept and, soon enough, few others would accept at face value, collapsed. The financial disaster spread to the East when gold and silver flowed westward and eastern bank notes lost value. Unable to pay their workers in anything resembling money, employers laid them off.

THE GIANT OF HIS AGE

In tandem with Clay and Biddle's political gamble in 1832, Jackson's financial policy, founded on ignorance, prejudice, and pigheadedness, ended in disaster. If he had been president during the depression of 1837, it would have blasted even his popularity. Instead, it ended the career of his successor,

Martin Van Buren. By the time the economy hit bottom, Jackson had retired to Tennessee.

The man whom many thought would die before he finished a term as president, had cut and chopped his way through eight pivotal years in the history of the nation. Though aching and coughing and refusing to mellow (Jackson said his biggest regret was not shooting Henry Clay and hanging John C. Calhoun), Jackson would live for nine more years, observing from his mansion (the Hermitage) an era that unfolded in his shadow. He was never a wise man. His intelligence was limited; his education spotty; his prejudices often ugly. He was easily ruled by his passions and confused them with the interests of the country. His vision of America was pocked with more flaws than that of many of his contemporaries—including his enemies, such as the not unflawed Henry Clay.

But for all that, Andrew Jackson was his times made flesh. He was the personification of a democratic upheaval that changed the character of American politics. He presided over a time of ferment in nearly every facet of American life. He set new patterns of presidential behavior by aggressively taking the initiative in making policy. Jackson also impressed his personality on a political party. Even the Whig party that was formed in 1834 to oppose Jackson was held together by little more than its supporters' antipathy to "the Gin'ral" and his memory.

THE SECOND AMERICAN PARTY SYSTEM

In 1828, John Quincy Adams and Andrew Jackson ran for president under the half-fiction that they were both Jefferson Republicans. In fact, Adams's National-Republicans and Jackson's Democratic-Republicans were not organized political parties. They were names adopted by loose coalitions of the supporters of regional leaders, notably Clay with Quincy Adams and Van Buren and Calhoun with Jackson.

During Jackson's presidency, Van Buren, Amos Kendall, and others put together a true political party with a nationwide organization. The senators who clung to the name National-Republican were still a loose alliance bound together only by the fact that they opposed Jackson's policies.

By 1834, the Jacksonians called themselves the Democratic Party. In that year, the National-Republicans, former Anti-Masons, and Democrats who had soured on Jackson organized the Whig party to mount an organized presidential campaign in 1836, and the **Second American Party System** was born.

John C. Calhoun was a Democrat in everything but the disappointment of his presidential ambitions at the hands of Jackson and Van Buren.

THE WHIGS

The name Whig was borrowed from Great Britain. Historically, the British Whigs had fought to reduce the power of the monarchy and ensure that Parliament governed the country.

The Whigs took their name from the British party that had originated as the defenders of the powers and prerogatives of Parliament as opposed to the authority of the monarchy. The American Whigs deftly depicted Jackson as a would-be king. One of the few principles that held the Whigs together was their insistence that Congress, not the president, was the center of governmental power.

The American Whigs related to them because, they said, Jackson, "King Andrew I," with his frequent vetoes of congressional acts—12 in eight years—was usurping representative government.

Beyond their opposition to Jackson, the Whigs were a diverse group. In the Northeast, the Whig party included most people of education, means, and social status. Four out of five merchants were Whigs. To some extent, the northeastern Whigs were heirs of the Federalist tradition, which had survived in the Jefferson Republican party in the views and policies of men like John Quincy Adams. The Whigs were not antidemocratic; but they did not worship "the common man" as the Democrats said they did. The Whigs understood that "the people" could become a mob and create a tyrant as, indeed, in their hysterical moments, they saw Andrew Jackson. The great French commentator on Jacksonian America, Alexis de Tocqueville, observed that "all the enlightened classes" opposed Jacksonian democracy.

In both the West and the Northeast, supporters of Clay's American System were Whigs. They believed that government had an active role to play in promoting national progress. Davy Crockett, remembered now as a frontiersman and martyr for Texas, was known in the 1830s as a best-selling humorist and a Whig congressman from Tennessee who excoriated Jackson and Van Buren.

A Whig editor in New York nicely summed up the philosophical difference between Whigs and Democrats.

> *The government is not merely a machine for making wars and punishing felons, but is bound to do all that is within its power to promote the welfare of the people. Its legitimate scope is not merely negative, representative, defensive, but also affirmative, creative, constructive, beneficent.*

Evangelical moralists and reformers were Whigs. They wanted to enlist the affirmative, creative, constructive, and beneficent powers of government in the causes of strict observance of the Sabbath, temperance in the use of alcohol,

---

An Unlikely Democrat

James Fenimore Cooper, the author of *The Leatherstocking Tales,* including *The Last of the Mohicans,* was a very rich, cultivated, and cosmopolitan New York aristocrat. His forebears had been Federalists. He had scant sympathy for "the people." He was involved in a long lawsuit with his neighbors near Cooperstown, New York, when he forbade them to swim and picnic, as they had been doing for decades, in a lake on his property. The dispute inspired him to write a book critical of the pushy demands of the lower orders. He should have been a Whig.

But he was not. He was an active Democrat. Why? Because Cooper deplored "Wall Street Whiggery, . . . a race of cheating, lying, money-getting blockheads" even more than he deplored dirty farmers cooling off in his lake. They would speculate in anything, he wrote, "in the general delusion of growing rich by pushing a fancied value to a point still higher." In those sentiments, he was a true-blue Jacksonian.

Alma Mater

Students today would find little that was familiar if they were transported to a college of the Jacksonian era. Studies more closely resembled those of a midieval university than college curricula in the twenty-first century.

Almost all colleges were private institutions. As late as 1860, only 17 of America's 246 colleges and universities were state-funded. With a few exceptions, the others were funded and closely administered by Protestant denominations to train ministers and to maintain or win other young men to their creeds. This was particularly true of the colleges founded during the Jacksonian years when dozens of new colleges were founded by evangelical Protestants committed to reforming society as well as to saving souls.

All but a handful of colleges were male institutions. Women's social role was domestic. Women were seen as the guardians of morality, but that task called for sequestration from the amoral, even sordid worlds of commerce and politics. Women had no need of the higher learning nor, certainly, did they belong in the professions, least of all the ministry.

There were dissenters. In 1833, Ohio's Oberlin College, a hotbed of evangelical reform, began to admit women as students and, year by year, a few other colleges and universities followed suit. In 1837, two all woman colleges were founded, Georgia Female College in Macon (now Wesleyan College) and Mount Holyoke in South Hadley, Massachusetts. However, women's colleges became numerous only in the final decades of the century.

Higher education was not career-oriented. Students were not taught the specifics involved in the occupation or profession to which they aspired. The young man who wanted to be an engineer, an architect, or a businessman apprenticed himself to someone in those callings; he learned "on the job." Although some universities had established medical and law schools, apprenticeship was also the most common means of preparing for those professions, too.

The heart of college curricula remained what it had been for centuries. The sequence of courses was strictly prescribed. Everyone studied the liberal arts and sciences (*liberal* meaning knowledge "suitable to a free man"). Colleges taught Latin, Greek, sometimes Hebrew; literature; natural science; mathematics; and political and moral philosophy in conformity with the doctrines of the church that supported the institution. Rhetoric, both theory and a great deal of public speaking, was an important, even central subject.

The colleges were small. Except at the very oldest institutions such as Harvard and Yale—and some public institutions like the University of Virginia—the typical student body rarely numbered more than a few dozen, the typical faculty perhaps three or four professors and an equal number of tutors (assistant professors). In so small a community, faculty and students all knew one another by sight and name. But there was none of the chumminess and unbecoming forced intimacy so common today. Professors erected a high wall of formality between themselves and those they taught, both because of their belief in hierarchy and out of the fear that friendliness would lead to a breakdown in discipline. The stiff-necked behavior of instructors often also owed to the fact that many of them were little older and sometimes even younger than their students. Joseph Caldwell became *president* of the University of North Carolina when he was 24 years old.

Ostensibly, student behavior was regulated by a long list of detailed rules. Students were expected to toe the line

---

helping the physically and mentally handicapped, and a welter of other social reforms. Northern and western Whigs thought of their party as "the party of hope," the Democrats as "the party of fear"—fear of progress.

Southern Whigs had less interest in social reform. Wealthy planters who were nationalistic or disturbed by the growing power of the Democratic masses of white southerners were Whigs. Most Louisiana sugar planters and Kentucky hemp growers were Whigs because they needed tariff protection for their crops; southern Democrats, including cotton planters, were fanatically opposed to protection, as the nullification crisis demonstrated.

Most Anti-Masons became Whigs, some of them, no doubt, simply because Jackson was an active Mason. Many New Englanders of modest means were Whig because of their traditional suspicion of things southern; the Democrats were the majority party in most of the southern states.

Antislavery people everywhere, including blacks in the few states where they were able to vote, were Whigs.

In 1834, the new party won 98 seats in the House of Representatives and almost half the Senate, 25 seats to the Democrats' 27. For twenty years, while unlucky in presidential elections, the Whigs fought the Democrats as equals in House, Senate, and in the states.

THE GODLIKE DANIEL

Next to Henry Clay, the best-known Whig was Daniel Webster of Massachusetts. At the peak of his powers in the 1830s, he was idolized in New England, the "Godlike Daniel." The adoration owed to Webster's personal presence and his peerless oratorical powers. With a great face that glowered darkly when he spoke, his eyes burned like "anthracite furnaces." A look from him, it was said, was enough to win most debates. Webster was described as "a steam engine in

not only in class but also in their private lives. Attendance at religious services was mandatory at church institutions. Strict curfews determined when students living in dormitories extinguished their lamps. Even impoliteness was to be punished by a fine or suspension.

The lists of institutional rules had more to do with reassuring parents and donors than with reality. College students were at least as rambunctious as students today. They defied their professors by day—the distinguished political philosopher Francis Lieber had to tackle students he intended to discipline—and they taunted them by night. A favorite prank was stealing into the college chapel and ringing the college bell until dawn or until some enraged professor emerged in his nightshirt. Students threw snowballs and rocks through tutors' windows. They led the president's horse to the roof of three- and four-story buildings. Students at Dickinson College in Pennsylvania sent a note to authorities at Staunton, Virginia, where Dickinson's president was visiting, informing them that an escaped lunatic was headed that way, would claim to be a college president, and should be returned under guard.

There were rebellions as violent, if on a smaller scale, than the student uprisings of the 1960s. Professors were assaulted—stoned, horsewhipped, and fired on with shotguns. At the University of Virginia in 1840, Professor Nathaniel Davis was murdered. Writing to his own son at college in 1843, Princeton professor Samuel Miller warned against sympathizing with potential rebels. Miller lived in fear of student uprisings, perhaps because one rebellion at Princeton was so serious that the faculty had to call in clubwielding townspeople to put it down.

The Vietnam war and the anger of African-American students underlay the student protests of the 1960s. What caused student rebelliousness in the Jackson era?

One explanation is that college rules were written at a time when most students were 14 to 18 years old—high school age by present-day standards. By the 1820s, students were often in their mid-twenties and, in a tougher world, much more mature and self-sustaining than people in their twenties today. They were simply not inclined to conform to behavior appropriate to adolescents. In a society that took pride in individual freedom, they were quite capable of reacting violently.

Moreover, many college students lived not in dormitories but in private lodgings in town. They fraternized largely with other students and developed a defiant camaraderie directed against outsiders. Enjoying broad freedoms in their off-campus lives, they were unlikely to conform to strict rules of behavior when they were at the college.

Finally, while the rules were strict, enforcement was erratic. "There were too many colleges," historian Joseph F. Kett wrote, "and they needed students more than students needed them." Faculty members, ever nervous for their jobs, overlooked minor offenses until they led to greater ones, at which point, suddenly, they drew the line. Inconsistency, as ever, led to contempt for authority.

Colleges might suspend the entire student body for "great rebellion." However, financial pressures usually resulted in everyone's readmission for the price of a written apology. Samuel Miller described student rebels as "unworthy, profligate, degraded, and miserable villains," but if they had the tuition, there was a place for them, if not at their alma mater, then at another college up the road.

---

trousers" and "a small cathedral in himself." An admirer said he was "a living lie because no man on earth could be so great as he looked."

Webster was not a fraction as great as he looked. He was an able enough administrator and an effective diplomat. But Webster's character was less than shining. Of humble origin, he took too zestfully to the high life that his success as a lawyer opened up to him. He dressed grandly, savored good food, and basked in the company of the wealthy. He was also an alcoholic and he invested his money as foolishly as he spent it. He should have been quite rich; he never was. He was constantly in debt and effectively sold himself to industrialists and bankers who regularly bailed him out of his financial difficulties by sending him gifts of money, no visible strings attached. During Jackson's war on the BUS, Webster not too subtly threatened to end his services as legal counsel to the Bank unless Nicholas Biddle paid him off. Biddle did.

Webster came to expect money in the mail after every speech on behalf of the tariff or even the ideal of the Union. All of this was more or less common knowledge. So, while he remained popular in New England until the end of his career, his not-so-secret vices provided an easy target for the Democrats.

UNION AND LIBERTY

And yet, it was this flawed man who gave glorious voice to the ideal that was to sustain the indisputably great Abraham Lincoln during the Civil War. In 1830, when Calhoun and Jackson were toasting the relative values of union versus liberty, Webster rose in the Senate to tell the nation that "Liberty and Union, now and for ever," were "one and inseparable."

He was replying to Robert Hayne of South Carolina, himself a fine orator who, when Calhoun was vice president, spoke Calhoun's lines on the floor of the Senate. Hayne identified the

Daniel Webster has the floor in the celebrated Webster-Hayne debate of January 1830. Senator Robert Hayne of South Carolina is seated dead center. In an artistic masterstroke, the painter shows John C. Calhoun in shadows at the left. As vice president, Calhoun could not speak, but he was the coauthor of Hayne's defense of the South, sectionalism, and nullification. The debate was Daniel Webster's finest hour. Parts of his speech exalting the Union as the fount of American liberty were memorized by northern schoolchildren for generations.

doctrine of nullification with American liberty. In a brilliantly crafted speech that kept every senator in his seat for two days, Webster, a superb lawyer, dissected Calhoun's doctrine legally, constitutionally, and historically.

In a ringing rhetorical climax, he declared that it was not state sovereignty, but the Constitution that was the well-spring of American liberty, and the indissoluble union that was liberty's protector. "It is, Sir, the people's Constitution, the people's government, made for the people, made by the people, and answerable to the people."

The liberty and union speech transformed a political abstraction, the Union, into an object for which people were willing to die.

1836: WHIGS VERSUS A DEMOCRAT

In 1836, for all their talk about the Union and the American nation, the Whigs could not agree on a presidential candidate. Henry Clay was still the party's most distinguished member. But the Whigs wanted to win; Clay had been trounced in 1832 on an issue of his own choosing. The Democratic candidate, vice president Van Buren, was not the national figure Jackson was. Therefore, the Whigs decided to run different candidates against him in states where each was popular. If they denied Van Buren a majority in the electoral college, as in 1824, the election would be decided in the House of Representatives where the Whigs and anti-Van Buren Democrats like Calhoun

were likely to control a majority of state delegations. There they would unite behind whichever of their three candidates qualified for the run-off.

Webster was the candidate in lower New England and New York (although Van Buren was bound to carry his home state). Hugh Lawson White of Tennessee was the candidate in the southern states. In the Northwest and upper New England, the Whigs' man was William Henry Harrison, the hero of the Battle of Tippecanoe. The Whig strategy got a boost when South Carolina, overwhelmingly Democratic, refused to give its votes to Calhoun's enemy, Van Buren, and nominated a Calhoun henchman, Willie P. Magnum.

The popular vote was close. Van Buren won just 26,000 votes more than the three Whigs. And, as they expected to do, the Whigs increased their representation in the House; they would have elected their man there. But Van Buren won a comfortable 170 to 124 majority in the electoral college. Daniel Webster failed to win in neighboring Connecticut and Rhode Island. Harrison lost in Michigan and Illinois. In the South, White carried only Tennessee and Georgia. Martin Van Buren was president.

DEPRESSION

Election to the presidency was just about the last good thing that happened to Martin Van Buren. When his administration was just a few months old, the country reaped the

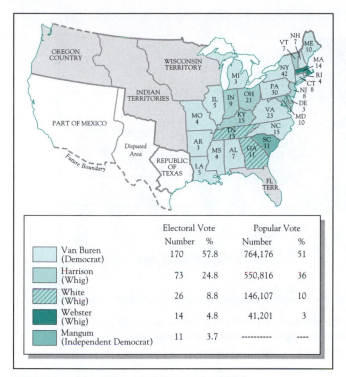

MAP 16:1 Van Buren's Victory in 1836
The Democrats and Whigs were both national parties. Both carried states in North, South, and West; a Whig carried Jackson's Tennessee. But the tactic of sending the election to the House of Representatives by running three sectional candidates failed. Van Buren outpolled each of the favorite sons in some states in their own sections for an easy victory in the electoral college.

	Electoral Vote		Popular Vote	
	Number	%	Number	%
Van Buren (Democrat)	170	57.8	764,176	51
Harrison (Whig)	73	24.8	550,816	36
White (Whig)	26	8.8	146,107	10
Webster (Whig)	14	4.8	41,201	3
Mangum (Independent Democrat)	11	3.7	----------	----

Pop Art

In 1834, with the hero of the common man in the White House, Nathaniel Currier of New York democratized art in America. He began to sell prints depicting natural wonders, marvels of technology such as locomotives, battles such as New Orleans, portraits of prominent people, and scenes of everyday life, both sentimental and comical.

Currier and Ives (the partner arrived in 1852) sold their prints for as little as 25 cents for a small black and white to $4 for a hand-colored engraving 28 by 40 inches. They were affordable but just expensive enough to be acceptable as a wall-hanging in a self-conscious, middle-class household.

More than 7,000 different Currier and Ives prints were produced by a process that can only be called industrial. Some artists specialized in backgrounds, others in machinery, others in faces, yet others in crowd scenes. By the late nineteenth century, it was a rare American who could not have identified "Currier & Ives" to an enquirer.

government intervention in the economy—it is difficult for any administration to survive a serious depression. The president, who reaps the credit for blessings that are none of his doing, gets the blame when things go badly. By early 1840, the Whigs were sure that hard times would put their candidate into the White House.

"TIPPECANOE AND TYLER TOO"

But who was to be the sure-thing candidate? Clay believed that he *deserved* the nomination. For twenty-five years, he had promoted a coherent national economic policy that, for the most part, the Whigs had adopted. For half that time he led the fierce fight against the Jacksonians.

But Clay's distinguished career was also his weakness. In standing in the vanguard for so long, in brokering so many deals, Clay inevitably made enemies. His fellow Whig, Edmund Quincy, wrote (in dreadfully purple prose) of "the ineffable meanness of the lion turned spaniel in his fawnings on the masters whose hands he was licking for the sake of the dirty puddings they might have to toss him."

Victory-hungry young Whigs like Thurlow Weed of New York argued against nominating Clay because of the baggage he carried. Better, Weed said, to choose a candidate who had little or no political record, but who, like Jackson, could be peddled as a symbol. The first and foremost object of a political party, Weed said, echoing Martin Van Buren, was to win elections. Only then could it pursue its goals.

Weed's candidate was William Henry Harrison. He had done better than Webster and White in 1836. He was the scion of a distinguished Virginia family; his father signed the Declaration of Independence. He was associated with no controversial political position. Best of all, like Jackson, he was both a westerner and a military hero, the victor of Tippecanoe. When the Whigs nominated him, his handlers admonished one another, "let him say not one single word

whirlwind of Jackson's Specie Circular. Drained of their gold and silver, several big New York banks announced in May that they would no longer redeem their notes in specie. Speculators and honest workingmen alike found themselves holding paper money that even the institutions that issued it would not accept.

In 1838, the country sank into depression. In 1841 alone, 28,000 businesses declared bankruptcy. Factories closed. Several cities were unsettled by riots of unemployed workers. Eight western state governments defaulted on their debts.

Van Buren tried to meet the fiscal part of the crisis. A good Jacksonian, he attempted to divorce the government from the banks, which, with some justice, he blamed for the disaster. He established the **subtreasury system,** by which, in effect, the government kept its funds in its own vaults. The Clay and Webster Whigs replied that what was needed was an infusion of money into the economy, not burying it out of reach. But they could not carry the issue.

Van Buren also maintained the Democratic faith by refusing to take any measures to alleviate popular suffering. The founding fathers, he said (in fact he was voicing Jackson's sentiments), had "wisely judged that the less government interfered with private pursuits the better for the general prosperity."

Whatever the virtues of Van Buren's position—whatever the convictions of most Americans on the question of

A TIPPECANOE PROCESSION.

■ *In 1840, the Whigs built mock-up log cabins for rallies in support of William Henry Harrison's candidacy. Among other gimmicks new to election campaigns and routine thereafter were great balls covered with slogans and rolled from town to town on an axle. The phrase "keep the ball rolling," still common parlance, dates from the landmark campaign.*

about his principles or his creed, let him say nothing, promise nothing. Let no [one] extract from him a single word about what he thinks. . . . Let use of pen and ink be wholly forbidden as if he were a mad poet in Bedlam."

To appeal to southerners, John Tyler of Virginia was nominated vice president: thus the slogan "**Tippecanoe and Tyler Too!**"

POLITICS AS MARKETING

The Whigs intended to campaign simply by talking about Harrison's military record. Then a Democratic newspaper editor made a slip that opened up a whole new world in American politics. Implying that Harrison was incompetent, the journalist sneered that the old man would be happy with an annual pension of $2,000, a jug of hard cider, and a bench on which to sit and doze at the door of his log cabin.

Such snobbery was ill suited to a party that had come to power as the champion of the common man. The Whigs, who suffered Democratic taunts that they were elitists, charged into the breach. They hauled out miniature log cabins at city rallies and country bonfires. They bought and tapped thousands of barrels of hard cider. They sang raucous songs like:

> *Farewell, dear Van,*
> *You're not our man,*
> *To guide our ship,*
> *We'll try old Tip.*

Stealing another leaf from the Jacksonian book, the Whigs depicted Van Buren as an effeminate fop who sipped

champagne, ate fancy French food, perfumed his whiskers, and flounced about in silks and satins. Before he departed for Texas, death, and immortality at the Alamo, the colorful Whig politician Davy Crockett said that Van Buren was "laced up in corsets such as women in a town wear, and if possible tighter than the best of them. It would be difficult to say from his personal appearance whether he was man or woman, but for his large red and gray whiskers."

It was all nonsense. Harrison lived in no log cabin but in a mansion. He was no simple country bumpkin but rather the opposite, a pedant given to tedious academic discourse on subjects of little interest to emotionally healthy people. Van Buren, while indeed a dandy, was of modest origins (his father had kept a tavern). He was earthy and he espoused to much more democratic ideals than did old Tippecanoe.

But nonsense worked, as it often does. Although Van Buren won 47 percent of the popular vote, he was trounced in the electoral college 60 to 234. Jacksonian chickens had come home to roost. Rarely again would a presidential election be contested without great fussing about symbols, images, and irrelevancies.

With their successful appeal to the prejudices of the common man, the Whigs of 1840 demonstrated that the democratic upheaval of the Age of Jackson was complete. Never again in the egalitarian United States would there be political profit in appealing to the superior sensibilities of the better sort. Perhaps what is most noteworthy about the election of 1840 is that a political candidate was marketed as a commodity—Harrison was "packaged"—long before the techniques of modern advertising were formulated.

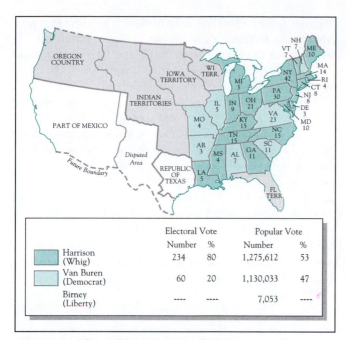

MAP 16:2 The Whig Victory of 1840
The Whigs ran a nonissue, all hoopla campaign in 1840, stealing the Democrats' pose as the party of the common man. Whig strategists persuaded candidate William Henry Harrison to say nothing of substance. But Van Buren would have been defeated whatever the Whigs did. No president during a serious depression has ever won reelection.

FATE'S CRUEL JOKE

Wherever William Henry Harrison stood on specific issues, he was fully in accord with one fundamental Whig principle—that Congress should make the laws and the president execute them. He was quite willing to defer to the party professionals, particularly Clay, whom he admired, in making policy. With Whig majorities in both houses of Congress, the Great Compromiser had every reason to believe that, if not president in name, he would direct the nation's affairs. Old Tip dutifully named four of Clay's lieutenants to the cabinet.

Harrison would have done well to defer to Daniel Webster in his field of expertise—oratory. Webster wrote an inaugural address for Harrison, but the president politely turned it down, having prepared his own. It is the longest, dullest inaugural address in the archives, a turgid treatise on Roman history and its relevance to the United States of America circa March 1841. Harrison delivered it out of doors on a frigid, windy day. He caught a cold that turned into pneumonia. For weeks he suffered, half the time in bed, half the time receiving Whig office seekers as greedy for jobs as the Democrats of 1828. Then he ceased to rise and dress. On April 4, 1841, exactly one month after lecturing the country on republican virtue, he passed away.

JOHN TYLER

At first the Whigs did not miss a stride. Clay lectured "Tyler Too" that he was an "acting president." He would preside over the formalities of government while a committee of Whigs chaired by Henry Clay made policy decisions. John Quincy Adams, now a Whig congressman from Massachusetts, concurred. Tyler would have none of it. He was a man of little imagination and provincial views but he was nobody's stooge. Tyler insisted that the Constitution authorized him to exercise the same presidential powers that he would exercise if he had been elected.

Tyler tried to get along with Clay. He went along with the abolition of the subtreasury system, and, although a low-tariff man, he agreed to an increase of rates in 1842 as long as the rise was tied to ending federal finance of internal improvements. Tyler also supported Clay's attempt to woo western voters from the Democrats with his Preemption Act of 1841. This law provided that a family who squatted on up to 160 acres of public land could purchase it at the minimum price of $1.25 per acre without having to bid against others.

A PRESIDENT WITHOUT A PARTY

But Tyler was not a real Whig. He had split with Jackson over King Andrew's arrogant use of presidential power. His views on other issues were closer to those of John C. Calhoun than to the nationalism and activism of the Whigs. Most notably, Tyler wanted no new BUS. He warned Clay not to try to force one on him.

Clay tried anyway, and Tyler vetoed one bank bill after another. Furious, the Whigs expelled the president from the party, and Tyler's entire cabinet, inherited from Harrison, resigned (except Secretary of State Webster, who wanted to complete some touchy negotiations with Great Britain). Clay left the Senate in order to devote full time to winning the presidential election of 1844.

Tyler's new cabinet was made up of nominal southern Whigs who shared Tyler's views. The president's plan was to piece together a new party of states rights Whigs like himself and maverick Democrats like John C. Calhoun. Toward this end, he named Calhoun secretary of state.

BRITISH-AMERICAN FRICTION

The major accomplishments of the Tyler administration were in the area of foreign affairs: resolving a series of potentially dangerous disputes with Great Britain, and paving the way for the annexation of the Republic of Texas.

Daniel Webster engineered the first. One problem was a boundary dispute between Maine and New Brunswick. According to the Treaty of 1783, the line ran between the watersheds of the Atlantic and the St. Lawrence River. Both sides had agreed to the boundary as it had been drawn on a map in red ink by Benjamin Franklin.

The map had disappeared, however, and in 1838 Canadian lumberjacks began cutting timber in the Aroostook Valley, which the United States claimed. A brief "war" between the Maine and New Brunswick militias ended with no deaths, and Van Buren managed to cool things down. But he could not resolve the boundary dispute.

The Canadian-American line west of Lake Superior was also in question, and there were two more points of friction because of unofficial American assistance to Canadian rebels and the illegal slave trade in which some Americans were involved. The slavery issue waxed hot late in 1841 when blacks on the American brig *Creole* mutinied, killed the crew, and sailed to Nassau in the British Bahamas. The British hanged the leaders of the mutiny but freed the other slaves, enraging sensitive southerners.

THE WEBSTER-ASHBURTON TREATY

Neither Britain nor the United States wanted war, but the Canadians' determination to build a road through the disputed Aroostook country stalled a settlement. Fortuitously, Daniel Webster found a kindred spirit in the high-living British negotiator, Lord Ashburton.

Over lots of brandy, they worked out a compromise. Webster made a big concession to the British, too big so far as Maine's loggers were concerned. Never above chicanery,

Webster forged Franklin's map to show a red line that gave Maine less territory than he "won" from Ashburton. He warned that the United States had better take what it could get. (The real Franklin map surfaced some years later, and showed that the United States was shorted.)

Ashburton was generous, too. He ceded a strip of territory in northern New York and Vermont to which the United States had no claim, and also about 6,500 square miles at the tip of Lake Superior. Wilderness at the time, it was later known as the Mesabi Range—one of the world's richest iron ore deposits.

When the Senate ratified the Webster-Ashburton Treaty in 1842, every outstanding issue between the United States and Britain was settled, except the two nations' joint occupation of the Oregon Country on the Pacific coast. Webster had good reason to be pleased with himself, and he joined his fellow Whigs in leaving John Tyler's cabinet.

FURTHER READING

The Jackson Presidency Robert V. Remini, *Andrew Jackson and the Course of American Freedom*, 1981, *Andrew Jackson and the Course of American Democracy*, 1984, and *The Revolutionary Age of Andrew Jackson*, 1985; Edward Pessen, *Jacksonian America: Society, Personality, and Politics*, 1978; Andrew Burstein, *The Passions of Andrew Jackson*, 2005; John F. Marszallek, *The Petticoat Affairs: Manners, Mutiny, and Sex in Andrew Jackson's White House*, 1997; Anthony Wallace, *The Long Bitter Trail: Andrew Jackson and the Indians*, 1993; John Ehle, *Trail of Tears*, 1988.

Party Politics Richard McCormick, *The Party Period and Public Policy: American Politics from the Age of Jackson to the Progressive Era*, 1986, and *The Second American Party System: Party Formation in the Jacksonian Era*, 1966; Harry L. Watson, *Liberty and Power: The Politics of Jacksonian America*, 1990; Lawrence F. Kohl, *The Politics of*

Individualism: Parties and the American Character in the Jacksonian Era, 1989.

Democrats D. B. Cole, *Martin Van Buren and the American Political System*, 1984; John Niven, *Martin Van Buren: The Romantic Age of American Politics*, 1983; M. L. Wilson, *The Presidency of Martin Van Buren*, 1984; John Niven, *John C. Calhoun and the Price of Union*, 1988.

Whigs D. W. Howe, *The Political Culture of the American Whigs*, 1979; Merrill D. Peterson, *The Great Triumvirate: Webster, Clay, and Calhoun*, 1987; Robert V. Remini, *Henry Clay: Statesman for the Union*, 1991; Sydney Nathan, *Daniel Webster and Jacksonian Democracy*, 1973; M. G. Baxter, *One and Inseparable: Daniel Webster and the Union*, 1984; Mark Derr, *The Frontiersman: The Real Life and the Many Legends of Davy Crockett*, 1993.

KEY TERMS

The following terms are covered in this chapter and can also be found in the list of Key Terms at the back of the book.

Daniel Webster	pet banks	Specie Circular	"Tippecanoe and Tyler too!"
Nicholas Biddle	Second American Party System	subtreasury system	
Peggy (O'Neill) Eaton			

🌐 ONLINE SOURCES GUIDE

Use this listing to find online documents, images, interactive maps, simulations, and other resources related to this chapter:

American History Resource Center
http://history.wadsworth.com

Selected Documents
Memorial of the Cherokee Nation (1830)
Black Hawk, "Life of Black Hawk" (1833)
The Harbinger, *Female Workers of Lowell (1836)*

Selected Images
The Brooklyn Ferry 1839
1830's three-dollar bill
Andrew Jackson
Andrew Jackson's first inaugural reception
Nicholas Biddle, President of the Second Bank of the
   United States
Daniel Webster
Martin Van Buren

1840 election prediction
Whigs during Log Cabin campaign, 1840.

Interactive Timeline (with online readings)
In the Shadow of Old Hickory: Personalities and Politics,
1830–1842

Document Exercises
1839 Slave Trade Book

Discovery

What was the role of personalities in American politics in the Jacksonian Era?

In thinking about this question, begin by breaking it down into the components shown below. A discussion of the significance of each component should appear in your answer.

Government and Law: For this exercise, study the images "Daniel Webster has the floor" and "King Andrew." How did the political parties use imagery to support their candidates or denigrate their opposition? How is Daniel Webster portrayed in this painting? How is John C. Calhoun portrayed? To which party do you think the artist belonged? How is Jackson portrayed in the "King Andrew" cartoon? What are the Whigs saying about him? What are they saying about his politics?

King Andrew

Courtesy Boston Art Commission

Daniel Webster has the floor

Government and Law: For this exercise, read the excerpts "Of the Ability of the State to Provide Ample Funds for Internal Improvements, 1819" and "Maysville Road Veto Message" and look at the "King Andrew" cartoon again. Consider these two views of federal obligations for economic improvements in the states. What justification does Murphey offer for federal assistance in internal improvements in North Carolina? Does he have a positive or negative view of the national government? What justification does Jackson provide for vetoing the internal improvements? Does he follow a strict or loose interpretation of the Constitution? How did vetoes such as this one contribute to the portrayal in the political cartoon? Is this a fair portrayal?

Archibald Murphey, Of the Ability of the State to Provide Ample Funds for Internal Improvements, 1819

For more than two thirds of the imported merchandize sold in North Carolina, are purchased in New-York, Philadelphia, Baltimore, Richmond, Petersburg, Norfolk and Charleston; and the duties upon this merchadize are paid at the Custom Houses of New-York, Pennsylvania, Maryland, Virginia and South Carolina. There can be little doubt, that the revenue derived by the General Government from North-Carolina, since the adoption of the Federal Constitution has exceeded twenty millions of dollars. This fact reminds us more sensibly than any other, of the humiliating condition of the State. Whilst we have thus liberally contributed to the support and the aggrandizement of the Union, how have we been viewed by the General Government, or by our Sister States? Have we not been uniformly treated with cold neglect by the one, and open contempt by the others? There is no citizen of the State, whose sensibility is not depraved, who has noticed the passing events of the times, and not suffered a severe mortification from the reflection that such has been our treatment. We have been considered the outcasts of the Union, whose virtue and intelligence gave no claim to the high honors of the Government, and whose integrity was unworthy of a share in its administration. We have planted a colony that has outstripped us in public distinction; we have ceded this colony, with its extensive territory, (now forming a distinguished State,) to the General Government; we have been an obedient and patriotic people; and what have we got in return? We have been honoured by the appointment of one of our citizens to a Foreign Embassy; of another to the Bench of the Supreme Court of the United States; and of a third, as Comptroller of the Treasury. We have had two miserable Light Houses erected, one at Cape Hatteras, the other at Bald Head, near Smithville. Out of the many millions which we have paid, not two hundred thousand have been expended for this State. What had been the cause of this neglect? It is to be found in the supineness and apathy of the State; in its want of pride and character. We are never thought of, until the election of a President of the United States is coming on; and then we are complimented for our good sense, our stern Republicanism, and devotion to the good cause; we have tacked to the Virginia Ticket, and we vote accordingly. When this Farce is over, we are laughed at for a few weeks, and no more remembered until the next election come[s] on, and then the same Farce is acted over again. . . .

Andrew Jackson, Maysville Road Veto Message, 1830

The constitutional power of the Federal Government to construct or promote works of internal improvement presents itself in two points of view—the first as bearing upon the sovereignty of the States within whose limits their execution is contemplated, if jurisdiction of the territory which they may occupy be claimed as necessary to their preservation and use; the second as asserting the simple right to appropriate money from the National Treasury in aid of such works when undertaken by State authority, surrendering the claim of jurisdiction. In the first view the question of power is an open one, and can be decided without the embarrassments attending the other, arising from the practice of the Government. Although frequently and strenuously attempted, the power to this extent has never been exercised by the Government in a single instance. It does not, in my opinion, possess it; and no bill, therefore, which admits it can receive my official sanction.

But in the other view of the power the question is differently situated. The ground taken at an early period of the Government was "that whenever money has been raised by the general authority and is to be applied to a particular measure, a question arises whether the particular measure be within the enumerated authorities vested in Congress. If it be, the money requisite for it may be applied to it; if not, no such application can be made." The document in which this principle was first advanced is of deservedly high authority, and should be held in grateful remembrance for its immediate agency in rescuing the country from much existing abuse and for its conservative effect upon some of the most valuable principles of the Constitution. The symmetry and purity of the Government would doubtless have been better preserved if this restriction of the power of appropriation could have been maintained without weakening its ability to fulfill the general objects of its institution, an effect so likely to attend its admission, notwithstanding its apparent fitness, that every subsequent Administration of the Government, embracing a period of thirty out of forty-two years of its existence, has adopted a more enlarged construction of the power . . .

To read extended versions of the documents, visit the companion Web site http://history.wadsworth.com/americanpast8e; click on "Discovery Sources."

CHAPTER 17

Religion and Reform

Evangelicals and Enthusiasts 1800–1850

© Bettmann/Corbis

God has found it necessary to take advantage of the excitability there is in mankind, to produce powerful excitements among them, before he can lead them to obey. Men are so spiritually sluggish, there are so many things to lead their minds off from religion, and to oppose the influence of the Gospel, that it is necessary to raise an excitement among them, till the tide rises so high as to sweep away the opposing obstacles.

Charles G. Finney

Religious insanity is very common in the United States.
Alexis de Tocqueville

During Andrew Jackson's lifetime, from the Revolution to the 1840s, America's religious profile itself underwent a revolution. The United States was still "a Protestant country" in 1840. But an old man or woman in that year who could recall the kinds of churches people attended in 1776 would remember attachments and practices as alien in 1840 as the custom of toasting the health of His Majesty, King George III.

AGE OF REASON, AGE OF REACTION

Before independence, the four largest American denominations were the Congregationalists (as latter-day Puritans were called), the Church of England, the Presbyterians, and the Quakers. There were about 470 Congregationalist meeting-houses during the revolutionary era, 300 Anglican churches, 250 Quaker meetings, and about 250 Presbyterian churches.

Other churches were prominent regionally: the Dutch Reformed church in New York and German pietists (Mennonites, Amish, Moravians) in eastern Pennsylvania. There were tiny Catholic communities in Maryland, Philadelphia, and New York; German Lutherans in Philadelphia; and synagogues in Newport, New York, Philadelphia, Charleston, and Savannah. Baptists were fairly numerous. But, by far, most American churchgoers were Congregationalists, Anglicans, Quakers, or Presbyterians.

DEISTS

Any Americans who were atheists kept their convictions to themselves. Known atheists were permitted to vote in only a few states. In the revolutionary era, however, many educated people, including some of the most prominent "founding fathers," were deists. Deists were children of "the age of reason," the Enlightenment. They believed in a supreme being but not in a God constantly at work in the world, like the Puritan God. Nor did they accept the Bible as literal truth or believe in denominational creeds. To deists, Jesus was a great moral teacher, but he was not divine.

Franklin and Jefferson were deists. Washington almost certainly was. He belonged to the Anglican church in Virginia but he attended services only when ceremonial duties or good manners required. Other deists were church members for family, social, or political reasons.

Deists were not hostile to churches—for others. Conservatives among them believed that traditional faiths imbued the uneducated and superstitious with morality and ethics; churches were pillars of social stability. They opposed officially established churches. Thomas Jefferson regarded his bill disestablishing the Anglican church in Virginia as one of his greatest achievements. Deists advocated religious freedom and granting civil rights without any religious test. At New York's constitutional convention, Gouverneur Morris successfully defeated John Jay's motion to deny the vote to Catholics. (Jay was not a deist.) Morris thought Catholic doctrines outlandish, but curiously, when he lived in France he was offended by the disrespectful manners of Catholic aristocrats when they were in church.

RATIONALISM VERSUS CALVINISM

Anglicanism declined sharply after independence, in part because of the rationalism of the times, in part because most Anglican ministers had been loyalists. In New England, rationalism reduced the numbers of Congregationalists church by church. That is, each Congregationalist meeting was self-governing, independent of any other authority. When a majority of church members redefined their beliefs, the congregation ceased to be Congregationalist.

The attrition began in 1785. A Boston church eliminated all references to the Trinity from its prayers because, its members had concluded, the doctrine was idolatrous. Other New England congregations, mostly in towns and cities and mostly middle- and upper-class in membership, followed suit. Some took the name Unitarian, others Universalist because they rejected the central Calvinist doctrine of predestination. God did not elect a few "saints" to be saved, they said, consigning the rest of humanity to damnation. Universalists and Unitarians believed that grace was available to all; it was universal. God was not the wrathful Jehovah of the Puritans; he was merciful and loving.

When **William Ellery Channing,** one of Congregationalism's most prominent ministers, declared himself a Unitarian in 1819, dozens of New England churches followed him. Channing preached that God had "a father's concern for his creatures, a father's desire for their improvement, a father's equity in proportioning his commands to their powers, a father's joy in their progress, a father's readiness to receive the penitent, and a father's justice for the incorrigible."

Unitarians and Universalists said they sought to be godly by following the precepts of Jesus without (Thomas Jefferson's words) "hocus-pocus phantasms." Universalists were generally a notch or two lower on the social scale than Unitarians. New England's educated elite, including presidents John and John Quincy Adams, was Unitarian. By 1805, so was Harvard's president. A few years later, a newcomer to Boston observed that "all the literary men of Massachusetts were Unitarians; all the trustees and professors of Harvard College were Unitarians; all the elite of wealth and fashion crowded Unitarian churches." Even Thomas Jefferson, who spurned organized religion, thought that Unitarianism was "the pure and uncompounded" religion of "the early ages of Christianity."

RELIGIOUS FERMENT

Presbyterians, like Congregationalists, were strict Calvinists and lost members because of it. In describing his childhood, John Fitch (the inventor of the steamboat) spoke for many when he bitterly recalled his father as "a bigot and one of the most strenuous of the sect of Presbyterians [who] thought that the extent of his duty toward me was to learn me to read the Bible, that I might find the way to Heaven."

A Presbyterian minister who rejected predestination founded the Disciples of Christ. The Disciples democratized heaven. Salvation was available to all but not without effort. People had to pray for God's grace, which would be visited upon them in an emotional conversion experience. No intermediaries were needed. Christians who were "saved" had a personal one-on-one relationship with God.

The Disciples, most Baptists, and Methodists were called "evangelical" because they aggressively preached their gospel—they evangelized. They believed they had a duty to urge others to seek salvation. The evangelical denominations soon outstripped the traditional churches in membership (and many Congregationalists and Presbyterians eased slowly away from strict Calvinism). Along with Jacksonian democracy, evangelicalism was the most dynamic force molding America during the 1820s, 1830s, and 1840s; for the evangelicals believed they had an obligation to save society as well as souls from sin.

CANE RIDGE

In August 1801, somewhere between 10,000 and 30,000 trans-Appalachian pioneers gathered at Cane Ridge, Kentucky, near a log Presbyterian church. Even at 10,000 the "camp meeting" was larger than any American city away from salt water. The labor-hardened pioneers, many of them Scotch-Irish, were at Cane Ridge to listen to ministers of various denominations and no denomination at all. Some of the preachers had roofed platforms built in advance; others climbed atop stumps. Their messages were the same: all were sinners damned to burn in hell unless they repented and prayed for God's grace.

Conversions were numerous and passionate. A Methodist preacher wrote that "at one time I saw at least *five hundred* swept down in a moment as if a barrage of a thousand guns had been opened upon them." Sinners fell to their hands and knees, weeping uncontrollably. Others scampered about on all fours, barking like dogs. The most celebrated manifestation of God's presence was the "jerks": people afflicted with them lurched about, their limbs snapping uncontrollably. At Cane Ridge a rumor spread that a man who cursed God had been seized by the jerks and had broken his neck.

There were plenty of scoffers there. Such a mass of humanity in the middle of the endless woods was itself exhilarating; who could miss such an occasion? Young men, in particular, came for the company, the showmanship, and to exploit the occasion with thievery, heckling, drinking, and

the sexual opportunities religious excitement dependably provided. A joke had it that more souls were begotten at camp meetings than were saved. Opportunists had plenty of opportunities for thirty years. Camp meeting revivals became regular events in the western states, although never again on the scale of Cane Ridge.

GROWING CHURCHES

The Disciples of Christ was founded in 1804 by the Presbyterian minister at Cane Ridge, Barton W. Stone. "Calvinism is among the heaviest clogs on Christianity," Stone wrote; "it is a dark mountain between heaven and earth." In 1832 Stone's church merged with another Presbyterian offshoot, the Campbellites, to become a major denomination. Doctrines were of little importance to the Disciples; what counted was every Christian's personal relationship with God.

The Baptists, an old church—some dated American Baptist origins to Roger Williams—embraced evangelicalism and grew exponentially in the early 1800s, especially in the South. Like the Disciples, the Baptists had little time for detailed creeds. Religion was individual and personal; all souls had access to God. God meant all men and women to interpret the Bible for themselves.

The Methodist church was the fastest-growing denomination of the early 1800s. Methodism originated within the Church of England, which, its founders said, was too formal and cold. Indeed, along with conventional Anglican ministers, Methodist preachers were suspect during the Revolution because the founder of the movement, John Wesley, condemned the War for Independence. In 1784, however, Francis Asbury declared the independence of the Methodist Episcopal Church of America, and the new denomination grew exponentially. In 1770 no more than 1,000 Americans called themselves Methodists. In 1820 Methodists numbered 250,000, and many more were "adherents" who attended Methodist

Religion and Reform 1800–1850

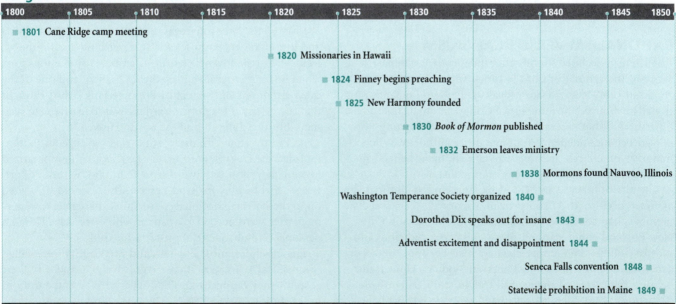

1800	1805	1810	1815	1820	1825	1830	1835	1840	1845	1850

1801 Cane Ridge camp meeting

1820 Missionaries in Hawaii

1824 Finney begins preaching

1825 New Harmony founded

1830 *Book of Mormon* published

1832 Emerson leaves ministry

1838 Mormons found Nauvoo, Illinois

Washington Temperance Society organized 1840

Dorothea Dix speaks out for insane 1843

Adventist excitement and disappointment 1844

Seneca Falls convention 1848

Statewide prohibition in Maine 1849

▨ *A camp meeting. The preacher has most of the crowd writhing hysterically. To the right, a few well-dressed visitors are unmoved, perhaps amused; they are there for the show. Skeptical spectators were fixtures at revivals. They were quite welcome; often enough to keep the preachers' hopes high, scoffers were carried away by the electric atmosphere and converted.*

services but did not join the church. By 1850 one in three church members in the United States was a Methodist.

Early Methodism had its contradictions. It appealed to simple, uneducated people but founded colleges. Its preachers called for free, voluntary, individual conversion but saddled members with strict rules of behavior; Wesley and Asbury condemned enthusiasm, "a religious madness arising from some falsely imagined influence or inspiration of God," but Methodists sponsored the often crazy camp meetings and were notorious for "sudden Agonies, Roarings and Screamings, Tremblings, Droppings-down, Ravings and Madnesses."

The Methodists' emotionalism helps explain why rural areas that had been nominally Anglican, notably the Delmarva Peninsula, became almost entirely Methodist. African Americans—slave and free—flocked to the Methodist church as they had resisted formal, liturgical Anglicanism. In 1816 Richard Allen, a black Philadelphian disgusted by discrimination in St. George's, the oldest Methodist church, founded the African Methodist Episcopal Church. By the end of the nineteenth century there were more black American Methodists than there were Methodists in all England.

The Methodists pioneered the "circuit rider" as a means of ministering to westerners too thinly dispersed to support a full-time minister. Intensely devoted, poorly paid, unmarried, itinerant preachers rode an unending circuit of ten or twenty little settlements. They forded swollen creeks in all weather, carrying little on their horses but a Bible. They preached, performed marriages and baptisms, took their rest and meals in the cabins of the faithful, and rode on. For three decades, the most famous of them, Finis Ewing and Peter Cartwright, were rarely off their horses for more than three days at a time.

THE SECOND GREAT AWAKENING

Middle- and upper-class townspeople, particularly in the Northeast, were uneasy with the excesses of camp meeting revivalism. In the early 1820s, a popular novelist (and Methodist), Catherine Arnold Williams, described one in Rhode Island she attended:

> There was a preacher on the stump speaking loudly and vehemently; a black man also on the stand, and nobody attending to either; the noise could not have been exceeded by the confusion of Babel. . . . One woman flew past, throwing her arms abroad, and shouting "there are grapes here and they are good, heavenly times! Heavenly times!"

But many such people responded to a more restrained evangelicalism that they called "the Second Great Awakening." The most famous of the urban preachers was Charles Grandison Finney, who, as a worldly young law student in 1821, woke up one morning having been summoned by God to save souls. Finney devised the "anxious bench" directly in front of his pulpit; it was for those who sensed they were about to be saved. "Do it!" he told them, "Get saved!"

Finney's converts were usually more restrained than camp meeting people. There was plenty of weeping at the huge Brooklyn Tabernacle where he preached for many years, but little crawling about and barking. In 1835 Finney became a professor of theology at Oberlin College in Ohio. There, like the Disciples, and unlike southern Baptists, Finney promoted a variety of social and political reforms to "perfect" society. The greatest of the evangelical reforms was the abolition of slavery. At first, all the evangelical churches were antislavery. During the 1780s, Methodist ministers were commanded to free their slaves. The Baptist and Presbyterian churches in the slave states of Kentucky and Tennessee called for the abolition of slavery there. Most northern evangelicals remained antislavery. But by the 1830s, southern evangelicals had made their peace with the institution.

REFORMERS

For evangelicals, the war against sin was fought not only within souls but in society. They believed it was their sacred obligation to battle against social evils as well as individual sinfulness. "Christianity is practical in its very nature and essence," wrote William Goodell in 1837. "It is a life, springing out of a soul imbued with its spirit. . . . Do you love God whom you have not seen? Then magnify that love."

For the first time, women were at the forefront of a great social and political movement. Even before the evangelical churches took shape, women outnumbered men as church members. The disparity increased with the Second Great Awakening. Any number of students of the history of religious enthusiasm have seen the phenomenon as an agency of female emancipation. In 1839 the American Female Moral Reform Society was organized. Less than a decade later, American feminism was born.

GALLAUDET, HOWE, AND DIX

Some evangelical reformers were specialists. Thomas Gallaudet was troubled by society's indifference to the deaf. Traditionally, Americans regarded deafness, blindness, and other disabilities as punishments for sin, as trials designed by God, or simply as unhappy circumstances visited on some by the roll of life's dice. In any case, nothing could be done about them. Care of the disabled was a family responsibility. Individuals who strived to overcome handicaps were edifying, but the problem was personal, not social.

Gallaudet believed that the Christian was his brother's keeper; the unique social isolation of the deaf was, for him, everyone's concern. In 1815 he went to England to study new techniques for teaching lip-reading and sign language to the deaf. He was disgusted to discover that the system was a trade secret, guarded by those who knew and profited from knowing it. With a Frenchman who shared his ideals, Gallaudet returned to the United States and, in 1817, founded the American Asylum, a free school for the deaf in Hartford, Connecticut. Gallaudet taught his techniques to every interested party and encouraged others to establish similar institutions in other cities.

Samuel Gridley Howe organized the Perkins Institute for the Blind in Boston. He also publicized his techniques and toured the country with a young girl named Laura Bridgman who was both deaf and blind. Howe had established communication with her, laying to rest the widespread assumption that such seriously handicapped people were hopeless. The most overwhelming impediments to human fulfillment, Howe said, could be overcome if men and women did their moral duty.

The insane aroused less sympathy than did the physically handicapped. Traditionally, the retarded and harmless idiots were cared for by their families and otherwise ignored (or mocked). Dangerous lunatics were locked up. The line between violent insanity and criminality was blurred. Many a lunatic was hanged; others were recognized as lacking moral responsibility but, nonetheless, were confined in prisons or asylums where treatment consisted of restraint.

In 1841 Dorothea Dix, a Massachusetts teacher, discovered in the Cambridge House of Correction that the insane were locked in an unheated room, even in winter. At 39, Dix had lived a genteel, sheltered personal life. She was pious and shy. Her discovery of evils in the treatment of the insane galvanized her, and she became one of the most effective reformers of the century.

In 1843 she scolded the Massachusetts state legislature because of the "state of insane persons confined within this Commonwealth in *cages, closets, cellars, stalls, pens! Chained, naked, beaten with rods, and lashed* into obedience." Dix's revelations did not square with New Englanders' image of themselves as the nation's most enlightened people. ("O New England," Noah Webster wrote, "how superior are thy inhabitants in morals, literature, civility, and industry!"). The Massachusetts legislature promptly passed a bill to enlarge the state asylum and improve conditions elsewhere. Dix then carried her message throughout the nation and the world. She persuaded Congress to establish St. Elizabeth's Hospital for the Insane and fifteen states to build humane asylums.

CRIME AND PUNISHMENT

The penitentiary also attracted the notice of reformers. Large prisons for convicts serving long terms were new to the United States. Until the late eighteenth century, long prison terms were rare. The most serious crimes were punished by hanging; there were as many as sixteen capital offenses in some states. Other felonies merited a flogging or physical mutilation. Thomas Jefferson advocated the castration of rapists and homosexuals, and boring half-inch holes through

A pillory (top) and whipping post at New Castle, Delaware. Corporal punishment of criminals, including executions, was public in most states during the antebellum period. It was believed that witnessing punishment deterred crime despite centuries of evidence that people turned out to watch whippings and hangings because they enjoyed them. Delaware did not abandon flogging (for wife beaters) until the 1950s, but whippings there had long ceased to be public.

Do-Gooders

Few reformers of any age have been easygoing people. Most have been so consumed by their cause that they are soon tiresome to those who do not agree with them with the same intensity. Orestes Brownson was friendly with most of the New England utopians and reformers of the era; he ran through more causes than any of them. Somehow he retained (or gained) the detachment to write, "Matters have come to such a pass that a peaceable man can hardly venture to eat and drink, to go to bed or to get up, to correct his children or to kiss his wife, without obtaining the permission and the direction of some moral society." Brownson turned out to have been, like de Tocqueville, a prophet too.

System, obvious almost immediately, were twofold: Individual cells were extremely expensive, and total isolation resulted in many mental breakdowns.

The Auburn System, named after the town in which New York's state prison was located, addressed the problem of isolation by marching prisoners each day to large workrooms and a common dining hall. Conversation was forbidden, both to prevent education in crime and to keep order. The Auburn System was adopted by other states, including Pennsylvania.

DEMON RUM

Undesirable behavior among the masses also inspired reforms. For example, Americans drank heavily. Per capita consumption peaked in the 1820s at more than 7½ gallons of alcohol a year for each American man, woman, and child. In part, this incredible bibulousness owed to the fact that grain was abundant and cheap. American farms produced much more than was needed as food or could find markets abroad. English-style ales, cider, and rum were the everyday beverages of the East. In the West, the daily tonic was whiskey. Wine and brandy—most of it imported—were fixtures of middle- and upper-class life.

Except among the dregs of society, drunkenness was considered sinful or at least disagreeable. Before 1800, Dr. Benjamin Rush of Philadelphia systematically described the physically destructive effects of excessive drinking. With the blossoming of the evangelical spirit, anti-alcohol reformers added two more arrows to the quiver. First, they published statistics showing that a substantial number of crimes were committed by people who were drunk. Second, they drew a connection between poverty and drinking. Some said that the miseries of poverty led to drunkenness. Others, steeped in the evangelical sense of individual responsibility, believed that drunkenness caused poverty.

In either case, alcohol was an evil to be destroyed. By 1835 there were 5,000 temperance societies in the United States with a membership of more than a million. In 1840 six reformed alcoholics founded a national organization, the Washington Temperance Society. Two years later a more militant association, the Sons of Temperance, began to promote sobriety as a

the noses of lesbians. In Massachusetts in 1805, counterfeiters, arsonists, wife beaters, and thieves were whipped, their ears cropped, or their cheeks branded with a hot iron.

During the 1790s, influenced by an Italian criminologist, Cesare Beccaria, most states reduced the number of capital offenses, abolished mutilation, and restricted the use of whipping. They turned to prisons as the proper response to serious crime. The purposes of prisons were punishment and the protection of society; conditions of confinement were universally execrable. Connecticut housed its state prison in an abandoned mine shaft.

Reformers pointed out that the security of society was not improved if prison transformed every convict into a resentful, hardened criminal. In confining burglars with rapists, prisons became schools of crime. The evangelical alternative was the correctional institution, the prison as a place for moral and social rehabilitation. Theories as to how best to accomplish this worthy goal differed. The **Pennsylvania System** kept convicts in solitary confinement. The idea was that inmates would meditate on their crimes (like a sinner contemplating his sins on the "anxious seat") and leave prison determined not to offend again. The flaws of the Pennsylvania

European Observers

Literary Europeans thought of the United States as a cultural backwater. White Americans were of little more interest than the Indians whom they dispossessed and the Africans they enslaved. Sidney Smith, a British wit, wrote in 1820, "In the four quarters of the globe, who reads an American book? or goes to an American play? or looks at an American picture or statue? What does the world yet owe to American physicians or surgeons? What new substances have their chemists discovered? or what old ones have they analyzed? What new constellations have been discovered by the telescopes of Americans? What have they done in the mathematics?" Few of Smith's readers would have felt he had overdone it, including Americans who imported Smith's *Edinburgh Review*.

The next year, two New Yorkers won some literary respect in Europe. Washington Irving published two stories, "Rip Van Winkle" and "The Legend of Sleepy Hollow," that won acclaim in Great Britain. James Fenimore Cooper was lionized for his *Leatherstocking Tales,* novels about the clash of civilization and nature on the American frontier. Notably, both lived in Europe for long periods—Cooper for seven years, Irving for seventeen.

Still, it was American popular culture rather than high culture that came to interest Europeans, particularly the novelty of Jacksonian democracy and American religious enthusiasm. Before 1828, the year of Jackson's election, only some forty books about America were published in Europe. In the decade that followed, hundreds were written in at least a dozen languages. Popular British authors such as Frederick Marryat, Anthony Trollope, Harriett Martineau, and Charles Dickens crossed the Atlantic specifically to describe the scenery, explain the political institutions, and wonder about the manners, morals, and quirks of Americans. The greatest of the books was *Democracy in America,* published in 1835 and 1840 by a French aristocrat, Alexis de Tocqueville.

Tocqueville found much to admire in Americans. Because he was a traditionalist, he was surprised to discover that democratic government worked. However, because Tocqueville believed that stability and continuity in human relationships were essential to a healthy society, he was troubled that Americans were always on the move, loved the new and disdained the old indiscriminately, and were consumed by a relentless pursuit of money. Much of *Democracy* could have been written last month. Tocqueville also observed that Americans were chauvinistic: "A stranger who injures American vanity, no matter how justly, must make up his mind to be a martyr."

Frances Trollope, whose *Domestic Manners of the Americans* (1832) was much more popular than the "American book" of her famous writer son Anthony, came to the United States not to write but to go into business in Cincinatti. She did not like Americans a bit. "I do not like their principles. I do not like their manners. I do not like their opinions." With the eye of an eagle and a wit as sharp as talons, Mrs. Trollope swooped through American parlors, kitchens, cabins, steamboats, theaters, churches, and houses of business, finding something

basic religious duty. One of the Sons' most effective lecturers was John B. Gough, an ex-drunk who rallied audiences with the lurid language of the camp meeting revivalist: "Crawl from the slimy ooze, ye drowned drunkards, and with suffocation's blue and livid lips speak out against the drink."

PROHIBITION

Temperance reformers quarreled and parted ways as promiscuously as drunks. One cleavage ran between advocates of moderation in the use of alcohol and complete abstainers.

The Pledge

In 1840 an Irish priest, Theobald Mathew of the Teetotal Abstinence Society, toured the United States and administered "The Pledge" to more than half a million Irish Catholics. The pledge was never to touch another drop of liquor. It is not known how many pledgers kept their promises. It is, however, safe to say that Father Mathew's campaign did not perceptibly alter the stereotype of Irish Americans as habitually drunk.

The former argued that drunkenness was the evil, not alcohol itself. They saw no evil in the occasional sip of wine or restorative dram. The abstainers, observing that alcohol was addictive, concluded that it was inherently dangerous and sinful. Moderation was asking for trouble. It was necessary to swear off drink "T-totally."

Then the teetotalers divided between "**moral suasionists**," who said abstinence was an individual responsibility, and "legal suasionists," who called for the prohibition of the manufacture and sale of liquor. People must be *prevented* from sinning. In 1838 Massachusetts experimented with a law designed to cut down alcohol consumption among the poor. The Fifteen Gallon Law prohibited the sale of whiskey or rum in quantities smaller than fifteen gallons. However, the temper of the Age of Jackson ran against any law that privileged the rich, who could afford to buy spirits in bulk. The Fifteen Gallon Law was repealed within two years.

In 1845 New York adopted a good Jeffersonian law, which authorized local governments to forbid the sale of alcohol within their jurisdictions. Within a few years, five-sixths of the state was "dry." In 1846 the state of Maine, led by Neal Dow, a

wrong with everything. Like Tocqueville's generalizations, some of her anecdotes are eerily contemporary. She cited an English resident of the United States who told her "that in following, in meeting, or in overtaking, in the street, on the road, or in the field, at the theater, the coffee house, or at home, he had never overheard Americans conversing without the word *dollar* being pronounced between them."

Mrs. Trollope observed that Americans rushed through hastily prepared meals. They jogged rather than walked. (Frederick Marryat wrote that a New York businessman "always walks as if he had a good dinner before him and a bailiff after him.") Americans fidgeted when detained by some obligation lest they miss something happening in another part of town. When they did sit down they whittled, so incapable were they of stillness. At least two foreign tourists remembered as a symbol of their American experience the spectacle of a team of horses pulling a house on rollers from one site to another. Nothing in the United States was rooted—neither homes nor customs nor social relationships nor religious beliefs that had served humanity for centuries.

Charles Dickens came to the United States to persuade American publishers, who pirated his books, to pay him royalties. He failed, as Mrs. Trollope failed in business, and this no doubt colored his negative reflections in *American Notes* (1842). Fanny Kemble, an actress, came to America in 1832 and was a great success. However, she was swept off her feet and off the stage by Pierce Butler. She knew he was rich before they married in 1834 but, curiously, not that his family owned 700 slaves, making the Butlers one of the nation's largest slave-owning families. Fanny Kemble's first book about America, published in 1835, contradicted Mrs. Trollope in finding Americans courteous, but agreed with her in other particulars—for example, the difficulty of finding solitude among a people who "take pleasure in droves, and travel by swarms," and the headaches of managing servants in a society in which all were equal. It was "a task quite enough to make a Quaker kick his grandmother."

Those were white servants working for wages, of course. The slaves who served Fanny Kemble at her husband's Georgia plantation she found ignorant and dirty but hardly impudent. When she first arrived, she was mystified that the slaves kissed her dress, hugged her, and showered her with endearments. She later learned that she and the children she was expected to bear represented a better future for them than they had anticipated. Before marrying her, Pierce Butler had been considering selling the plantation and slaves, which would have meant the breakup of their families. With Fanny in residence, there was hope.

But Fanny did not remain for long. She left the plantation after less than a year, disgusted by the injustice and cruelties of slavery. She became an abolitionist, divorced her husband, and wrote an account of her life in Georgia that, unlike much antislavery propaganda, was firsthand, forthright, and unexaggerated. Published during the Civil War, Kemble's journal was instrumental in dulling what sympathy for the South there was in Great Britain.

Portland businessman, adopted the first statewide prohibition law. By 1860 thirteen states had followed suit. But alcohol was too important a part of the culture to be abolished by ordinance. Prohibition laws were flagrantly violated, and by 1868 they were repealed in every state except Maine.

Temperance and prohibition were largely evangelical Protestant movements directed at native-born, old-stock Americans. In the 1840s, however, the crusade against alcohol took on a new urgency because of the huge influx of immigrants who had (as far as reformers were concerned) an inordinate devotion to beer and whiskey.

Germans in America

Germans were so numerous in independent Texas in 1843 that the Texas Congress published the Lone Star Republic's laws in the German language as well as in English. By 1860 there were 100,000 Germans in New York City. They supported twenty churches, fifty schools, five printers, and a theater.

THE STRESSES OF IMMIGRATION

About 8,400 Europeans came to the United States in 1820, hardly enough to excite notice. More than 23,000 arrived in 1830, however, and 84,000 in 1840. Then came the deluge: In 1850, 370,000 people stepped from crowded immigrant ships onto the wharves of the eastern seaports. Not only were the numbers unprecedented, a large majority of the immigrants were adherents of religious faiths of little note in the United States before 1840.

Immigration of Germans, negligible since independence, exploded. In 1820, 968 Germans entered the United States; 1850 saw the arrival of 79,000. Religiously, they were evenly divided between Lutherans and Roman Catholics. Even more numerous (and annoying to old-stock Americans) were the Irish. About 3,600 Irishmen and women came to the United States in 1820, half of them Protestant. Some 164,000 arrived in 1850, the vast majority Roman Catholic. Between 1830 and 1860, when the general population slightly more than doubled, the Roman Catholic population of the United States increased tenfold, from 300,000 to more than 3 million.

Pennsylvania militia attempting to subdue anti-Catholic rioters in Philadelphia in 1844. There were other outbreaks of anti-Catholic, anti-Irish violence during the period; a convent in Charlestown, Massachusetts, was burned by a mob. Philadelphia established a professional police force in 1845 as a consequence of the riot. Several of the first professional police forces in cities were inspired not by conventional crime but by social disorder.

THE "WHORE OF BABYLON"

The inundation was difficult for many Protestants to swallow. They did not look upon Roman Catholicism as just another Christian denomination; the Church of Rome was the Bible's Whore of Babylon, a fount of evil. The pope, the spiritual leader of the world's Catholics, was also the political head of a reactionary and repressive principality: the Papal States of Central Italy. His political principles—monarchy, submission

Anti-Catholic? Anti-Irish?

The 1844 riot in Philadelphia is sometimes described as an anti-Catholic riot, sometimes as anti-Irish. It was both and, yet, not quite either. The targets of the Protestant mob were Irish Catholics; but most of the Protestant aggressors were Irish too—Orangemen who had been battling their Catholic fellow countrymen in the old country for two centuries.

So it was an anti-Catholic riot. But while the Protestant mob burned two Irish Catholic churches to the ground, they ignored two German Catholic churches on streets they controlled for several days.

to authority, and religious conformity—were the antitheses of American ideals. Irish immigrants were particularly devoted to their faith, looking for guidance to the numerous priests who accompanied them.

Some Protestants feared that they were shock troops of political reaction. Many Whigs—and northern evangelicals were Whigs in their politics—found it enough to worry about that the Irish flocked to the Democratic party. Moreover, most of the newcomers were destitute. Landless in overpopulated Ireland, they died by the hundreds of thousands when, beginning in 1845, the crop on which the Irish survived, the potato, was destroyed almost annually by a blight. Those who could fled to Great Britain and, if they could scrape together fares as low as $12, to the United States in sailing ships as crowded as slave ships had been with a comparable mortality rate. Once in the United States, the Irish accepted work at almost any rate of pay. In addition to distaste for their Catholic religion, Protestant workingmen regarded the Irish as a threat to their high standard of living.

The painter and inventor of the telegraph, Samuel F. B. Morse, lobbied to forbid the immigration of Catholics. Street wars between Protestant and Irish Catholic workingmen erupted in northeastern cities. An anti-Catholic book,

The Tactless Archbishop

Anti-Catholicism was not without provocation. John Joseph Hughes, the Catholic bishop of New York after 1842, wrote, "Protestantism is effete, powerless, dying out . . . and conscious that its last moment is come when it is fairly set, face to face, with Catholic truth."

The Awful Disclosures of Maria Monk, sold 300,000 copies even after a committee of distinguished Boston clergymen visited the Canadian convent where, allegedly, Maria Monk and other nuns were kept as sex slaves for priests, and declared the book nonsense. In 1834, aroused by sermons on the theme, a mob burned an Ursuline convent in Charlestown, Massachusetts. In Philadelphia in 1844, twenty people were killed and over a hundred injured in a riot pitting Protestants against Catholics.

Anti-Catholicism took political shape in the Order of the Star-Spangled Banner, a secret organization dedicated to shutting off further immigration. The order's members were called "Know-Nothings" because, when asked about the organization, they replied, "I know nothing." After 1850 the order came above ground as the American party. Capitalizing on the disintegration of the Whigs, the anti-Catholic, anti-immigrant party swept to power in several states, including Massachusetts. At its peak, the American party elected seventy-five congressmen.

The majority of Protestants disapproved of political action (and certainly of mob action) against Catholics. Many, however, supported attempts by evangelical missionary societies to convert Catholics. The American Tract Society and the American Bible Society distributed literature among the Catholic population. By 1836, the Tract Society estimated that it had sold or given away more than 3 million publications explaining Protestant beliefs.

BLUE OWYHEE

It took the rise of evangelicalism to make Americans missionaries. Converting the Indians to Christianity had never attracted more than a handful of ministers of the traditional churches. That changed in the early nineteenth century; but, oddly enough, rather than ride a horse to the West, the earliest zealous missionaries sailed halfway around the world to Pacific islands known only since the War for Independence: Owyhee or, as it would soon be spelled, Hawaii.

Hawaii was familiar to whalers from New Bedford and Nantucket. The islands' location in the central Pacific—quite by themselves—made Hawaii an essential landfall for ships that often needed three years in the Pacific to fill their holds with valuable whale oil. They refit their vessels in Lahaina and Honolulu, rested, recovered from scurvy, and took on provisions. The diseases they brought devastated the Polynesian population. Between 1778 and 1804, the Hawaiian population was halved, from about 300,000 to 150,000. The goods the whalers brought to pay for provisions transformed the simple economy of the islands and corrupted Hawaiian culture as thoroughly as the white advance across the continent changed Indian life.

In 1819 a young Hawaiian Christian came to New England with whalers and told the students of Andover Theological Seminary of the harm done to his homeland by American whalers. The next year several young ministers and their wives, sisters, and mothers shipped out to the islands. Their letters home, widely published in newspapers, encouraged others to follow—dozens, even a hundred in a year.

Like John Eliot two centuries earlier, many of the missionaries insisted Hawaiians embrace proper New England clothing and manners as well as the gospel. The best-known example of the missionaries' inability to distinguish religion from culture was the insistence of some that, in Hawaii's warm, humid climate, girls and women cover up their breasts and legs in full-length calico and even flannel "Mother Hubbard" dresses.

But too much has been made of that. For the most part, the American mission to Hawaii was a great success. Native Hawaiian culture had been shattered by contact with the basest exemplars of American and European society. (Even other seamen, not a respectable lot, looked down on whalers.) The missionaries, a majority of them women, found a religious void in which to work. By 1830, missionary schools enrolled 52,000 Hawaiians (40 percent of the population), teaching evangelical religion in the Hawaiian language, which the Americans put into writing.

FEMALE ACTIVISTS

New England women were the backbone of the missionary movement, particularly "spinsters" (unmarried women): Many ministers who went to Hawaii took sisters as well as their wives. Women were the workhorses of many other evangelical projects, and Dorothea Dix was not unique in being the most prominent person in her chosen field. Women led the movement to expand public education and edited temperance newspapers. Anna Ella Carroll authored *The Great American Battle,* in which she warned that Catholicism would "swallow up America."

The prominence of women in New England evangelicalism owes in part to the fact that the section had a surplus of them. The West attracted so many young males that, however great the pressure on young women to marry, there were not enough potential husbands to go around. In Catholic countries, single women became nuns. In New England, they devoted their energies to church work; in the age of evangelicalism, that included reform movements. Many women found active public life rewarding. However, because there were strict limitations on what women were permitted to do, many female temperance advocates and, especially, abolitionists remained aware of the inferiority of their status.

SENECA FALLS

In the summer of 1848, a small group of activist women (and a few men) called for a convention to be held at Seneca Falls,

New York, to consider the "Declaration of Sentiments and Resolutions" they had drafted. The declaration was a deadly serious parody of the Declaration of Independence:

> When in the course of human events it becomes necessary for one portion of the family of man to assume among the people of the earth a position different from that which they have hitherto occupied, but one to which the laws of nature and nature's God entitle them, a decent respect to the opinions of mankind requires that they should declare the causes that impel them to such a course. . . .

The injustices suffered by women included the denial of the right to vote even when it was extended to "the most ignorant and degraded men"; the forfeiture by a married woman of control over her own property; a husband's considerable authority over his wife, which "made her, morally, an irresponsible being"; and the exclusion of women from the professions and other gainful employment. Most of the organizers of the Seneca Falls convention were Quakers, members of a sect that, traditionally, practiced near-equality for women. But women of several evangelical denominations attended the meeting.

The Declaration was signed by sixty-eight women and thirty-two men, but the convention was discussed avidly in newspapers. Lucretia Coffin Mott and **Elizabeth Cady Stanton,** two of the organizers, continued to play an important part in this first feminist movement for a generation. Among the attendees was Amelia Jenks Bloomer, a temperance reformer who was soon famous as the advocate of a new style of dress that bore her name.

Evangelical reformers were generally (but not unanimously) sympathetic to the cause of women's rights. However, they urged feminists like Mott, Stanton, and Susan B. Anthony, a schoolteacher who soon became Stanton's lifelong collaborator, to defer their campaign until the most important evangelical reform had succeeded. This was the abolition of slavery, a cause entering its final phase when the Seneca Falls convention was called.

"I do not see how anyone can pretend that there is the same urgency," the African-American abolitionist Frederick Douglass said, "in giving the ballot to the woman as freedom to the Negro." Stanton, Mott, and Anthony, who were abolitionists before they were feminists, agreed.

HOME-GROWN RELIGION; UTOPIAN REFORM

The evangelical denominations—and evangelicals within the old churches—were the mainstream of American religious life and social reform in the early nineteenth century. It was also an era, however, when at least two uniquely American religions were born. And when people at least as unhappy with American society as the evangelicals were gave up on changing it, they tried to live good lives by withdrawing into utopian communities.

Courtesy American Antiquarian Society

William Miller's predictions of the end of the world in 1843 or 1844, based on years of studying prophecies, were illustrated in this Adventist chart tracing the rise and fall of earthly kingdoms from Babylon through the "Mahometans." Like many Protestant denominations of the era, the Millerites focused on the popes of Rome as the most wicked of earthly rulers.

THE BURNED-OVER DISTRICT

In 1831, after a decade of poring over Biblical prophecies and compiling endless columns of mathematical calculations, William Miller announced that the Second Coming of Christ—the end of the world, when sinners would be hurled into the fiery pit—was not, after all, in the unimaginable

Jehovah's Witnesses

The Jehovah's Witnesses were a later offshoot of the Millerites. Like the Adventists, they looked forward to the end of the world. The founder of the denomination, Charles Taze Russell, was a denomination-hopper—in turn a Presbyterian, Congregationalist, and Adventist. He and his successors, claiming papal-like authority to explain what the scriptures meant, dated the end of the world as coming in 1878, then in 1881, 1914, 1925, and most recently, 1975. Then 144,000 select would live in heaven; faithful witnesses would live in an earthly paradise; and everyone else would be destroyed.

future. It would occur between March 21, 1843, and March 21, 1844. Miller convinced thousands of the validity of his prophecy when, at the beginning of the fateful year, an omen appeared in the sky. (It was Halley's Comet.) Millerites in upstate New York sold their possessions, contributing the proceeds to the sect. On the last day of Miller's year, numerous people climbed hills in "ascension robes" sold to them by Joshua Himes, an associate of Miller, so as to be the first in heaven before the damnations began. When the sun set without incident—it was called the "Great Disappointment"— Miller went back to his computations, found an error, and rescheduled the Second Coming for October 22.

Fewer people got their hopes up this time. After the "Second Disappointment," the remnants of the sect were bewildered and aimless until 17-year-old Mary Harmon (later Mary Harmon White) experienced a series of visions in which Christ told her he had not returned to earth on schedule because Christians still worshipped on Sundays rather than on the sabbath (Saturday) as the Bible instructed. Mother White's Seventh Day Adventists adopted the more serviceable doctrine that the world would end *soon*.

The Millerites were concentrated in a part of western New York State that was called the "burned-over district" because religious revivals of every stripe had repeatedly swept over it, scorching the psyches of its inhabitants. Belief in magic was widespread. Prophets with novel messages popped up regularly. Lucina Umphreville proclaimed that God forbade carnal intercourse; another woman said that God told her she and her minister could lie together without sinning if they did it without lust.

Charles Grandison Finney was from the **burned-over district.** So were the Fox sisters, Margaret and Kate, who announced in 1848 that they could communicate with the dead. For a fee, they would—as "mediums"—relay questions to deceased parents and spouses or, for that matter, George Washington. The answers were conveyed in a darkened room by mysterious raps: one for yes, two for no. In 1850 the sisters took their seances to New York City, where they were flooded by anxious customers. Other "Spiritualists" emerged all over the country. The seance mania soon cooled off, but Spiritualism survived as yet another American sect.

The Fox sisters were frauds. Late in life, one of them confessed that they had created the "raps" by popping trick joints in their legs. But Mother White seems to have believed sincerely in her revelations, which continued throughout her life. The most successful of the burned-over district prophets, Joseph Smith, had little sincerity and a little fraud in him.

THE MORMONS

Joseph Smith was a daydreaming, part-time treasure hunter who, on a countryside ramble when he was 20, met an angel, Moroni. Moroni showed him gold plates bearing mysterious inscriptions that, with the help of miraculous stones, Smith was able to read. In 1830, with his family and some neighbors already convinced, Smith published his translation of the

"Reformed Egyptian" as the *Book of Mormon,* a "Bible of the New World." It told of the Nephites, descendants of lost tribes of Israel who had come to America, whom Christ visited, and their enemies, the Lamanites—the Indians.

The book lacked the poetry and substance of the Bible. Few pored over it as millions have studied the Bible. Mark Twain called the *Book of Mormon* "chloroform in print," saying that the phrase "and it came to pass" appeared 2,000 times. Smith himself lost interest in his book within a few years.

But it was an astonishing success. Smith's Church of Jesus Christ of the Latter Day Saints had 50 members when the *Book of Mormon* was published, 1,000 members the next year, and thousands more each succeeding year. To people told from childhood that the United States was a new Eden, it was not preposterous that Christ should have visited America. The Puritans had believed that the Indians were descendants of the lost tribes of Israel. Poor people unsettled by the frenzied pace of the Age of Jackson flocked to the church. Josiah Quincy pitied the Mormons, as they were called, as "feeble or confused souls who are looking for guidance." The Quaker poet John Greenleaf Whittier was kinder. He wrote that the Mormons "speak a language of hope and promise to weak, heavy hearts, tossed and troubled, who have wandered from sect to sect, seeking in vain for the primal manifestation of divine power."

The Mormons believed that God spoke directly to Joseph Smith, and they could not get enough of what he had to say. Between 1830 and 1834, Smith had more than 100 revelations. At first his religion was Protestant Christianity with the Native American gimmick. However, Smith's revelations increasingly took the Mormons beyond Christian doctrinal boundaries. "Proxy baptism," for example—Mormons saving ancestors who died before Smith's latter-day revelations by being baptized in their place—was an entirely original concept. "Plural marriage" (polygamy), a revelation Smith shared with only a few close associates and the women he secretly wed, was far from original, but it was a practice that Christians had rejected as sinful since ancient times.

And yet Smith was so magnetic a personality he was "one in 100 million," and the comforts of belonging to the tight-knit Mormon community so reassuring, that the Latter Day Saints grew constantly despite their unpopularity with "gentiles," as they called outsiders.

If Smith was at first surprised by the immense power he held over his followers, he was soon comfortable exercising it. Moving to Kirtland, Ohio, he founded a bank with freely given money. It failed in the Panic of 1837; some suspected him of stealing from it. Then Smith was accused of adultery, which was a crime as well as a sin. He moved to western Missouri, where many Mormons had already settled. There the hostility was not just verbal. Hard-bitten gentiles burned Mormon houses and businesses and killed several people. The Mormons retaliated, forming a paramilitary force, and responded in kind. There were plenty of thugs among them willing to do whatever Joseph Smith commanded. But they were outgunned, and the state put a price on Smith's head. He had to flee; most of the church members followed him.

Joseph Smith reviews the Mormons' "Legion" at Nauvoo, Illinois. The crack, spit-and-polish character of the soldiers depicted here is overdrawn. Nonetheless, the Nauvoo Legion was the largest and best-armed militia in Illinois, probably in the United States, and its unquestioning allegiance to Smith alarmed non-Mormons in western Illinois.

DEATH IN NAUVOO

Smith settled the Mormons in **Nauvoo,** Illinois, on the banks of the Mississippi. By 1844 it was the largest city in the state. Because Smith could deliver the votes of the entire city as a bloc, both Democrats and Whigs vied for his favor. He was given permission to organize the Nauvoo Legion. Officially a unit of the state militia, it was in fact Smith's private army. The legion was half the size of the U.S. army.

Again, however, Smith's sexual appetites came close to destroying his authority. He continued to contract secret plural marriages with women whom he found attractive; it was easy enough to send their husbands out of town on a church errand. At least one dutiful Mormon married his teenage daughter to the "Prophet, Seer, and Revelator." Smith's wife, who did not buy Smith's plural marriage revelation, chased two wives he was keeping in their home (which was also a hotel) down the street with a broom. When an unwilling bride and her husband exposed Smith, an angry Mormon crowd gathered outside his home. Smith denied he had committed adultery and denounced polygamy as a sin. Considerable numbers of Mormons who knew he was lying left Nauvoo.

But most remained, and the Mormons prospered. Their collective wealth (only a few were individually rich), their undisguised dislike of outsiders, and fear of the Nauvoo Legion begat envy and resentment locally. Smith let his power over Mormons obliterate his judgment when dealing with non-Mormons. In sermons reported in newspapers, he said such things as "I will consecrate the riches of the gentiles unto my people which are the House of Israel." Then, in 1844, he declared that he was a candidate for the presidency of the United States, which destroyed his ability to play off the Whigs and the Democrats for his support. When he ordered a mob to destroy the office and press of a critical newspaper, he was arrested and jailed in nearby Carthage. With the collusion of state militia who were guarding him, a mob murdered him.

UTAH: THE MORMON ZION

Without Smith, internal dissension would likely have split the Mormons into a number of tiny sects. (One scholar has counted 200 splinter groups in Mormon history.) But a leader as singular as the First Prophet but in an entirely different way immediately stepped forward. Brigham Young was short, stout, and homely, whereas Smith was tall and handsome. Young sincerely believed in Mormon doctrines, whereas Smith several times hinted the whole business was a scam. Most important, whereas Smith's brain swirled constantly with nebulae, Brigham Young was hard-headed and practical; he had "both feet on the ground." As head of the church for fourteen years, Smith had at least 135 divine revelations. In thirty-three years as president, Brigham Young had one, and it had nothing to do with religion. It concerned the logistics of removing the Mormons from the hostile United States to the Great Salt Lake Basin, then nominally in Mexican territory.

Young chose the desolate alkaline desert precisely because it was so forbidding a land: "No other well-informed people can covet its possession." There, thanks to Mormon industriousness, Young supervised the building of a city of broad avenues and blooming gardens supported by irrigation ditches bringing water from the Wasatch Mountains. Within a few years more than 10,000 people lived in what is now northern Utah. A well-organized network of missionaries, especially in Britain and Scandinavia, provided a constant influx of immigrants into what the Mormons called Desert.

The Latter-Day Saints did not, however, escape from the United States. Even while Salt Lake City was being surveyed, American victory in the Mexican War brought the Mormon Zion into the United States. But Young handled threats from the federal government, including military intervention, with a shrewdness of which Joseph Smith would not have been capable. When Abraham Lincoln was asked why he did not assert more federal authority in Utah, he recalled how, when settlers clearing land ran across a log that was too hard to split, too wet to burn, and too heavy to move, they just plowed around it.

UTOPIAN COMMUNITIES

The Adventists and the Mormons were not evangelicals. They had no interest in reforming society. The Adventists looked forward to the end of the world because it meant the destruction of all sinners—just about everyone but themselves. For fifty years after the publication of the *Book of Mormon*, the Latter Day Saints looked on Americans as their mortal enemies; non-Mormons were irredeemable. The utopians gave up on reforming society from within. They withdrew so that they, at least, could live as God or their philosophical leaders believed people should live.

Jacksonian America was famous for its many utopian communities. Poets Samuel Taylor Coleridge and Johann

Wolfgang von Goethe both came close to emigrating so as to live in one. Robert Owen, a rich Scottish manufacturer famous for generosity with his employees, founded New Harmony in Indiana in 1825. Owen believed that private property was the root of social ills, a view all the utopians shared. If property were held in common, life need not consist of drudgery, a struggle to survive, but could be morally and intellectually fulfilling for all. Socializing property in Great Britain or the United States was, of course, a fool's errand. Owen's plan was to build New Harmony as a shining example of what socialism could do, believing that ultimately society would get the point.

Unfortunately, New Harmony attracted too many people interested passionately in philosophical discussions but not much in doing their share of the labor. In between the uplifting conversations, they disappeared. Believing deeply in the goodness of human nature, Owen was incapable of throwing freeloaders out. In 1827, somewhat poorer, he returned to Scotland.

Another star-crossed utopia was Fruitlands, Massachusetts, the brainstorm of Bronson Alcott, described by everyone who knew him as lovable. (He is best known today as the father of the author Louisa May Alcott.) He was a magnificent eccentric. Like many intellectuals, he did not cope well with workaday life. He could button his shirt, but that was about it. He inaugurated Fruitlands by planting several apple trees within two feet of the community house front door, dropped his shovel, and returned to his meditations and endless conversations.

There was no Robert Owen to subsidize Alcott's crackpot heaven. One Fruitlander refused to weed the garden because weeds had as much right to grow as vegetables did. Samuel Larned lived for one year on nothing but crackers (so he said) and the next year on nothing but apples. Another utopian showed his superiority to social conventions by greeting people with "Good morning, God damn you!" Everyone at Fruitlands agreed that cows were loathsome in all ways; Alcott forbade the use of their manure as fertilizer. A hired girl was expelled when she slipped off to a neighboring farm to eat some beef. Fruitlands survived for several years only because Mrs. Alcott, who did not take her husband seriously, did most of the work.

THE SHAKERS

The most successful utopians were a religious group, the Shakers. Founded in England by Mother Ann Lee, the Shakers, like Owen, thought that private property corrupted people.

◼ *The library at the Oneida Community. Oneida's founder, John Humphrey Noyes, believed that owning property in common and dividing labor equitably among all would create plenty of time for study and other fulfilling and ennobling activities. Other utopian communities were inundated by parasites and collapsed. Oneida did not tolerate freeloaders (long on sitting in the library but hard to locate when labor called), and it thrived.*

Mother Lee also believed that sexual intercourse was the sin of Adam and Eve. The Shakers were celibate. Believing (like the Millerites) that the end of the world was near, there was no need to perpetuate the human race by the disgusting means required. Men and women lived separately in, by the 1830s, about twenty tidy, comfortable, and prosperous Shaker communities from Maine to Kentucky. Both sexes came together for meals, conversation, and religious services.

The Shakers were not harassed. Sexual abstinence might be peculiar, but it offended no one. Unlike the Mormons, the Shakers were hospitable to outsiders. They were famous for their fine craftsmanship: Shaker-design furniture, still an American standard; wooden clothespins and an apple parer that the Shakers invented; and flat brooms, which they may have invented. Indeed, the Shakers performed a valuable social service: They took in and raised orphans, giving them the option, once they reached adulthood, to remain as a Shaker or return to "the world."

SEXUAL LIBERATORS

Charles Fourier, a Frenchman, devised a complicated scheme for communities he called "phalansteries." He took a view of sex rather different than Mother Lee's. He outlawed marriage; he believed that sexual exclusivism, more than private property, was what corrupted people. Phalanstery sex life was not to be promiscuous. Fourier drew up all sorts of regulations to match people of disparate ages and personality types. Fourier approved of homosexuality and even sadomasochistic practices, which he called "amorous manias." (Interestingly, Fourier's most careful biographer believes he died a virgin.) There were a number of short-lived phalansteries in the United States. The most famous, because it attracted some of New England's literary elite, was Brook Farm in Massachusetts. (The Brook Farmers dispensed with Fourier's kinkiness.)

John Humphrey Noyes disapproved of both private property and marriage. Wedlock, he said, was itself a form of private property. Under American law and customs, husbands effectively "owned" their wives. Hence both were miserable. Noyes's alternative was "complex marriage." In his utopia at Oneida, New York, every man was married to every woman and vice versa. Couples who chose to have sexual relations for pleasure (the initiative was the woman's) could do so, but not for the purpose of procreation. Noyes was an exponent of what would be called eugenics in the twentieth century. While Oneida was setting an example for the world, the community would improve the quality of the human race by allowing only those superior in health, constitution, and intellect to reproduce. After long and ardent study, Noyes concluded that he was an ideal male breeder.

© Bettmann/Corbis

Oneida's sexual practices enraged neighbors, who brought them to the attention of the authorities. Noyes fled to Canada to escape arrest. The community lived on but ceased to preach Noyes's sexual doctrines. Economically, Oneida was as successful as the Shakers. The community prospered from the manufacture of silverware, silks, and a superior animal trap for fur-bearing animals that was designed there. Oneida abandoned complex marriage in 1879 and, in 1881, communal ownership of property. The community was reorganized as a commercial corporation.

FURTHER READING

Adventists and Mormons Leonard J. Arrington, *Brigham Young: American Moses*, 1984; Frederic J. Baumgartner, *Longing for the End: A History of Millennialism in Western Civilization*, 1999; Paul Boyer, *When Time Shall Be No More: Prophecy Belief in Modern American Culture*, 1992; Fawn M. Brodie, *No Man Knows My History: The Life of Joseph Smith, the Mormon Prophet*, 1945, 1971; Richard L. Bushman, *Joseph Smith and the Beginnings of Mormonism*, 1984; John Shipps, *Mormonism: The Story of a New Religious Tradition*, 1985.

Evangelicals at Work Ruth Bordin, *Women and Temperance*, 1981; F. L. Byme, *Prophet of Prohibition: Neal Dow and His Crusade*, 1961; Thomas J. Curran, *Xenophobia and Immigration, 1820–1930*, 1975; David Gallagher, *Voice for the Mad: The Life of Dorothea Dix*, 1995; Patricia Grimshaw, *Paths of Duty: American Missionary Wives in Nineteenth Century Hawaii*, 1989; Gerald M. Grob, *The Mad among Us: A History of the Care of America's Mentally Ill*, 1994; Earl F. Kaestle, *Pillars of the Republic: Common Schools and American Society*, 1960; Dale T. Knobel, *Paddy and the Republic: Ethnicity and Nationality in Ante-Bellum America*, 1980, and *America for the Americans: The Nativist Movement in the United States*, 1996; M. E. Lender and J. K. Martin, *Drinking in America: A History*, 1982; Michael Meranze, *Laboratories of Virtue: Punishment, Revolution, and Christianity in Philadelphia, 1760–1835*, 1996; W. G. Rorabaugh, *The Alcoholic Republic: An American Tradition*, 1979; David J. Rothman, *The Discovery of the Asylum*, 1970; Ian R. Tyrrel, *Sobering Up: From Temperance to Prohibition*, 1979; Mary Zwiep, *Pilgrim Path: The First Company of Women Missionaries to Hawaii*, 1991.

Reform: General Robert H. Abzug, *Cosmos Crumbling: American Reform and the Religious Imagination*, 1994; Stuart M. Blumin, *The Emergence of the Middle Class*, 1989; Richard J. Cawardine, *Evangelicals and Politics in Ante-Bellum America*, 1993; Lori D. Ginzberg, *Women and the Work of Benevolence: Morality, Politics, and Class in the Nineteenth Century United States*, 1990; Steven Mintz, *Moralists and Modernizers: America's Pre-Civil War Reformers*, 1995; R. G. Walters, *American Reformers: 1815–1860*, 1978.

Religious Upheaval S. E. Ahlstrom, *A Religious History of the American People*, 1972; Jon Butler, *Awash in a Sea of Faith: Christianizing the American People*, 1990; Frederick Dreyer, *The Genesis of Methodism*, 1999; Charles Hambrick-Stowe, *Charles Grandison Finney and the Spirit of American Evangelism*, 1996; Nathan D. Hatch, *The Democratization of American Christianity*, 1989; David Hempton, *The Religion of the People: Methodism and Popular Religion, 1750–1900*, 1996; Christine L. Heyrman, *Southern Cross: The Beginnings of the Bible Belt*, 1997; Paul Johnson, *A Shopkeeper's Millenium: Society and Revivals in Rochester, New York, 1815–1837*, 1978; Martin E. Marty, *Righteous Empire: The Protestant Experience in America*, 1970, and *Pilgrims in Their Own Land: 500 Years of Religion in America*, 1984.

The Woman's Movement Lois Banner, *Elizabeth Cady Stanton*, 1980; Carl M. Degler, *At Odds: Women and the Family in America from the Revolution to the Present*, 1980; Eleanor Flexner, *Century of Struggle: The Women's Rights Movement in the United States*, 1975; Gerda Lerner, *The Woman in American History*, 1970; Alma Lutz, *Susan B. Anthony*, 1979; William L. O'Neill, *Everyone Was Brave: The Rise and Fall of Feminism in America*, 1970; Mary P. Ryan, *Womanhood in America*, 1975.

Utopian Communities Spencer Klaw, *Robert O. Thomas, The Man Who Would Be Perfect*, 1977; Stephen J. Stein, *The Shaker Experience in America*, 1992.

KEY TERMS

The following terms are covered in this chapter and can also be found in the list of Key Terms at the back of the book.

burned-over district	**"Great Disappointment"**	**"moral suasionists"**	**Pennsylvania System**
Elizabeth Cady Stanton	**Millerites**	**Nauvoo**	**William Ellery Channing**

ONLINE SOURCES GUIDE

Use this listing to find online documents, images, interactive maps, simulations, and other resources related to this chapter:

American History Resource Center
http://history.wadsworth.com/rc/us

Selected Documents
The Married Women's Property Act (1848)
The Seneca Falls Declaration (1848)
Elizabeth Cady Stanton, Declaration of Sentiments (1848)

Selected Images

Joseph Smith, founder of the Church of Jesus Christ of Latter Day Saints

Corporal punishment administered in New Castle, Delaware

Tree of Temperance

Lydia Maria Child, antislavery advocate and champion of women's rights

Lucretia Coffin Mott

Interactive Time Line (with online readings)

Enthusiasm: Evangelicals, Utopians, Reformers

Document Exercises

1842 American Transcendentalism

Discovery

What social and religious changes resulted from the economic changes of the early nineteenth century?

In thinking about this question, begin by breaking it down into the components shown below. A discussion of the significance of each component should appear in your answer.

Religion and Philosophy: For this exercise, read these two accounts of religious revivals: "William Sprague Describes Revivals, 1833" and "Tocqueville Witnesses American Religious Enthusiasm." Do they differ in their analysis of the revivals and those participating in them? What does Sprague believe causes these revivals? What does Tocqueville believe? Does revivalism exist today? If so, where do we see it? How has it impacted the modern generations? With which author do you agree?

William Sprague Describes Revivals, 1833

. . . Now if such be the nature of religion, you will readily perceive in what consists a *revival* of religion. It is a revival of scriptural knowledge; of vital piety; of practical obedience. The term *revival of religion* has sometimes been objected to, on the ground that a revival of any thing supposes its previous existence; whereas in the renovation of sinners, there is a principle implanted which is entirely new. But though the fact implied in this objection is admitted, the objection itself has no force; because the term is intended to be applied in a general sense, to denote the improved religious state of a congregation, or of some other community. And it is moreover applicable, in a strict sense, to the condition of Christians, who, at such a season, are in a greater or less degree revived; and whose increased zeal is usually rendered instrumental of the conversion of sinners. Wherever then you see religion rising up from a state of comparative depression to a tone of increased vigor and strength; wherever you see professing Christians becoming more faithful to their obligations, and behold the strength of the church increased by fresh accessions of piety from the world; *there* is a state of things which you need not hesitate to denominate a revival of religion.

Such a state of things may be advantageously represented under several distinct particulars.

1. The first step usually is an *increase of zeal and devotedness on the part of God's people.* They wake up to a sense of neglected obligations; and resolve to return to the faithful discharge of duty. They betake themselves with increased earnestness to the throne of grace; confessing their delinquencies with deep humility, and supplicating the aids of God's Spirit to enable them to execute their pious resolutions, and to discharge faithfully the various duties which devolve upon them. There too they importunately ask for the descent of the Holy Ghost on those around them; on the church with which they are connected; on their friends who are living at a distance from God; on all who are out of the ark of safety. . . .

2. Another prominent feature in the state of things which I am describing, is *the alarm and conviction of those who have hitherto been careless.* Sometimes the change in this respect is very gradual; and for a considerable time nothing more can be said than that there is a more listening ear, and a more serious aspect, than usual, under the preaching of the word; and this increased attention is gradually matured into deep solemnity and pungent conviction. In other cases, the reigning lethargy is suddenly broken up, as if there had come a thunderbolt from eternity; and multitudes are heard simultaneously inquiring what they shall do to be saved. . . .

3. It also belongs essentially to a revival of religion, that there are those, from time to time, *who are indulging a hope that they are reconciled to God, and are born of the Spirit.* In some cases the change of feeling is exceedingly gradual, insomuch that the individual, though he is sensible of having experienced a change within a given period, is yet utterly unable to refer it to any particular time. Sometimes the soul suddenly emerges from darkness into light, and perceives a mighty change in its exercises, almost in the twinkling of an eye. Sometimes there is a state of mind which is only peaceful; sometimes it mounts up to joy and ecstacy. In some cases there is from the beginning much self-distrust; in others much—too much confidence. But with a great variety of experience, there are many who are brought, or who believe themselves brought, into the kingdom of Christ. They give reason to hope they have taken the new song upon their lips. . . .

Tocqueville Witnesses American Religious Enthusiasm, 1831–1832

Causes of Fanatical Enthusiasm in Some Americans

Although the desire of acquiring the good things of this world is the prevailing passion of the American people, certain momentary outbreaks occur, when their souls seem suddenly to burst the bonds of matter by which they are restrained, and to soar impetuously toward Heaven.

In all the States of the Union, but especially in the half-peopled country of the far West, wandering preachers may be met with who hawk about the word of God from place to place. Whole families—old men, women, and children, cross rough passes and untrodden wilds, coming from a great distance to join a camp-meeting, where they totally forget for several days and nights, in listening to these discourses, the cares of business and even the most urgent wants of the body.

Here and there, in the midst of American society, you meet with men, full of a fanatical and almost wild enthusiasm, which hardly exists in Europe. From time to time, strange sects arise, which endeavour to strike out extraordinary paths to eternal happiness. Religious insanity is very common in the United States.

Culture and Society: For this exercise, read the excerpts "Elizabeth Cady Stanton, Declaration of Sentiments (1848)" and "Observations on the Real Rights of Women. 1818." On what is the Declaration of Sentiments patterned? Why did the writers make that choice? What other groups at that time could have made and did make similar arguments? Compare the declaration with the other document. What does the author of "Observations" believe is a woman's role? How would she view the Declaration of Sentiments? Does the author of "Observations" believe that women are not capable of the same things that men can do? Does the women's rights movement still have this split today? If so, how so?

Elizabeth Cady Stanton, Declaration of Sentiments (1848)

When, in the course of human events, it becomes necessary for one portion of the family of man to assume among the people of the earth a position different from that which they have hitherto occupied, but one to which the laws of nature and of nature's God entitle them, a decent respect to the opinions of mankind requires that they should declare the causes that impel them to such a course.

We hold these truths to be self-evident: that all men and women are created equal; that they are endowed by their Creator with certain inalienable rights; that among these are life, liberty, and the pursuit of happiness; that to secure these rights governments are instituted, deriving their just powers from the consent of the governed. Whenever any form of government becomes destructive of these ends, it is the right of those who suffer from it to refuse allegiance to it, and to insist upon the institution of a new government, laying its foundation on such principles, and organizing its powers in such form, as to them shall seem most likely to effect their safety and happiness. Prudence, indeed, will dictate that governments long established should not be changed for light and transient causes; and accordingly all experience has shown that mankind are more disposed to suffer, while evils are sufferable, than to right themselves by abolishing the forms to which they are accustomed. But when a long train of abuses and usurpations, pursuing invariably the same object, evinces a design to reduce them under absolute despotism, it is their duty to throw off such government, and to provide new guards for their future security. Such has been the patient sufferance of the women under this government, and such is now the necessity which constrains them to demand the equal station to which they are entitled. . . .

Observations on the Real Rights of Women, 1818

It must be the appropriate duty and privilege of females to convince by reason and persuasion. It must be their peculiar province to sooth the turbulent passions of men, when almost sinking in the sea of care, without even an anchor of hope to support them. Under such circumstances women should display their talents by taking the helm, and steer them safe to the haven of rest and peace, and that should be their own happy mansion, where they may always retire and find safe asylum from the rigid cares of business. It is women's peculiar right to keep calm and serene under every circumstance in life, as it is undoubtedly her appropriate duty, to sooth and alleviate the anxious cares of man, and her friendly and sympathetic breast should be found the best solace for him, as she has an equal right to partake with him the cares, as well as the pleasures of life.

It was evidently the design of heaven by the mode of our first formation, that they should walk side by side as mutual supports in all times of trial. There can be no doubt, that, in most cases, their judgement may be equal with the other sex; perhaps even on the subject of law, politics, or religion, they may form good judgement, but it would be improper, and physically very incorrect, for the female character to claim the statesman's birth or ascend the rostrum to gain the loud applause of men, although their powers of industry may be equal to the task. . . .

To read extended versions of the documents, visit the companion Web site http://history.wadsworth.com/americanpast8e; click on "Discovery Sources."

CHAPTER 18

A Different Country

The South and Slavery

Reproduced from the Collections of the Library of Congress

There must doubtless be an unhappy influence on the manners of our people produced by the existence of slavery among us. The whole commerce between master and slave is a perpetual exercise of the most boisterous passions, the most unremitting despotism on the one part, and degrading submissions on the other. Our children see this and learn to imitate it. . . . The parent storms, the child looks on, catches the lineaments of wrath, puts on the same airs in the circle of smaller slaves, gives loose to the worst of passions and thus nursed, educated, and daily exercised in tyranny, cannot but be stamped by it with odious peculiarities.

Thomas Jefferson

Doodling at his desk one day, Thomas Jefferson drew up a list of character traits in which, he suggested, northerners and southerners differed. Northerners were cool and sober, he wrote; southerners were fiery and "voluptuary." Northerners were hard-working, self-interested, and devious; southerners were lazy, generous, and candid. Northerners were "jealous of their own liberties, and just to those of others"; southerners were "zealous for their own liberties, but trampling on those of others."

He had a point. Jefferson usually did. And it could not have been easy for a man who called Virginia "my country" to tote up the unattractive characteristics he found in his own people. Still, to fixate on differences between northerners and southerners would be to obscure the reality that they shared a common language and the same religious, cultural, and political heritage. By 1826, the year Jefferson died, they also shared fifty years of history as citizens of a country in which laws were made by elected representatives. Until about 1826, a large majority of Americans regarded the institution of slavery as, at best, an undesirable burden that history had saddled upon them. Most southerners and northerners believed that the United States would be a better place if slavery could be abolished without causing a social upheaval.

SOUTHERN ANTISLAVERY

In the northern states, the institution was dead by 1826. The only slaves north of the Pennsylvania–Maryland border were a few thousand in New York and New Jersey who had been in

The Strange Case of the State of Delaware

Originally, Delaware was part of Pennsylvania; antislavery Quakers were numerous in the northern part of the state. Southern Delaware was settled by Marylanders; white people there were generally proslavery. Nevertheless, fewer people in Delaware had an economic stake in slavery than New Jerseyans and New Yorkers and their states abolished the institution. Nor did the southern whites' fear that they would be overrun by freed blacks make sense in Delaware. In 1830 slaves were only 3 percent of the state's population. Free blacks numbered about 15 percent of Delaware's people and while they were notorious for helping runaway slaves from Maryland and Virginia escape to the North, they were a peaceable community.

So why did Delaware not rid itself of the institution? The legislature enacted several laws expressing distaste for slavery. It was illegal to import more slaves into the state and to sell Delaware slaves out of state. Several bills to abolish slavery failed in the legislature by narrow margins.

In the end, fear of black rebellion, irrational as it was in Delaware, and the reasonable anxiety that a free Delaware would be a magnet for runaways from Virginia and Maryland kept the state a slave state. After Nat Turner's rebellion in 1831, Delaware enacted a series of laws that restricted the free movement of *all blacks,* not just slaves.

bondage before the dates the legislature set after which every person born or entering the states was free by law.

QUESTION OF NUMBERS

None of the states south of Delaware, Maryland, and Kentucky adopted similar laws. Except in Delaware, slaves were so numerous in the states south of the Mason–Dixon line that lawmakers feared that if they were freed from their masters' restraints, the destitute masses would create a social upheaval with horrors that would dwarf the horrors of the French Revolution. White southerners could point to a terrifying precedent in the recent past. In 1791, 100,000 blacks in Haiti had rebelled and slaughtered every white person who was unable to flee to the few safe havens on the island. Refugees who came to the United States made San Domingo (as Haiti was then called) synonomous with uncontrolled blacks.

It had been easy, southerners said, for the northern states to abolish slavery. In the North, blacks were numerically insignif-icant. In 1830 there were 125,000 African Americans among a total northeastern population of 5.54 million: 2 percent. There were 42,000 blacks among the 1.6 million people of the old Northwest, about the same percentage. So tiny a minority was no threat to social stability. Blacks could be ignored, disdained, or pushed aside among themselves to rot or die (as, indeed, most African Americans in the North were).

But blacks were a substantial portion of the population of the South, 2.16 million in 1830 alongside 3.54 million whites: 38 percent. Blacks were in the majority in many areas—overwhelmingly in coastal South Carolina and Georgia and along the Mississippi River.

It was not just the specter of Saint-Domingue, as often as that unhappy island was mentioned. Planters and farmers in Virginia and Maryland could imagine bringing in their crops with hired workers or free tenants. But the cotton, rice, and sugar growers of the lower South could not. They wanted more slaves. Indeed, the owners of Maryland's and Virginia's worn-out and often unprofitable tobacco plantations found

The South Closes Ranks 1800–1857

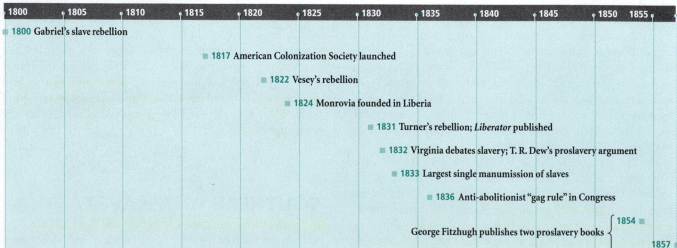

1800 Gabriel's slave rebellion

1817 American Colonization Society launched

1822 Vesey's rebellion

1824 Monrovia founded in Liberia

1831 Turner's rebellion; *Liberator* published

1832 Virginia debates slavery; T. R. Dew's proslavery argument

1833 Largest single manumission of slaves

1836 Anti-abolitionist "gag rule" in Congress

George Fitzhugh publishes two proslavery books { 1854
1857

A Lesson for Many Ages

John Randolph despised everything about slavery. He never bought or sold a slave. He voted to abolish the slave trade in the District of Columbia, calling it "infamous." He never passed up an opening for an antislavery witticism. In the early 1830s, when the Greeks were fighting for independence from the Turkish empire, all things Greek were the rage among trendy Americans. After listening to a southern lady gushing about "the noble Greeks" and their fight for freedom, Randolph pointed with his riding crop to some slave children playing nearby. "Madam," he said, "the Greeks are at your door."

that there was still money in being slave owners: by sending their slaves to the cotton kingdom to be sold.

Finally, slave owners of the upper South who had no stomach for selling their slaves "down the river" were not about to allow their state legislatures to free their slaves without compensating them for the money invested in them. Whenever an antislavery legislator calculated the costs of compensated emancipation in a southern state, the total was so great as to kill the proposition.

RELIGION, MANUMISSION, AND RACE

Some white southerners were vocally antislavery well into the 1820s. Individual slave owners with troubled consciences continued to free their own slaves in large numbers, as many southerners of the Revolutionary generation had done. Others continued to search for a formula by which they could do away with slavery without plunging their state into social, economic, and financial turmoil.

Southern Quakers, numerous in Delaware and North Carolina, had freed their slaves well before 1800. The first wave of Methodist preachers to scour the South made many converts and, with mixed success, prevailed on Methodist slave owners to set their people free. The large free black communities in Kentucky and on the Delmarva Peninsula owed largely to Methodist abolitionism.

Individual manumissions of large numbers of slaves at a stroke were less common after 1800 than earlier, probably because masters without antislavery scruples could sell slaves in the cotton states of the deep South. Still, there were manumissions. A former governor of Virginia, James Wood, took his slaves to Ohio, freed them, and set them up with farms. He returned home and became president of the Virginia Abolition Society. His antislavery sentiments did not damage him politically; he remained a member of the Council of State.

One of the largest single manumissions of slaves in American history—about 300 people—occurred in 1833 when John Randolph of Roanoke, Virginia died. As he usually did during life, Randolph had a pointed remark to make in his will: "I give and bequeath my slaves their freedom, heartily regretting that I have ever been the owner of them." Randolph also provided money so they could get started in a free state.

Randolph had asserted on several occasions that blacks were not inherently inferior to whites. When they appeared to be, he said, it was because they had been warped by slavery. By the 1820s, James Madison had concluded that blacks were the intellectual equals of whites. In that conviction, Madison and Randolph were rare exceptions among white southerners (or among white northerners, for that matter). Most whites were sincerely convinced that African Americans lacked the intelligence, industriousness, and moral fiber it

■ *Monrovia was built on an uninhabited stretch of coast beginning in 1822. This engraving shows the city in about 1847, when Liberia declared its independence from the American Colonization Society.*

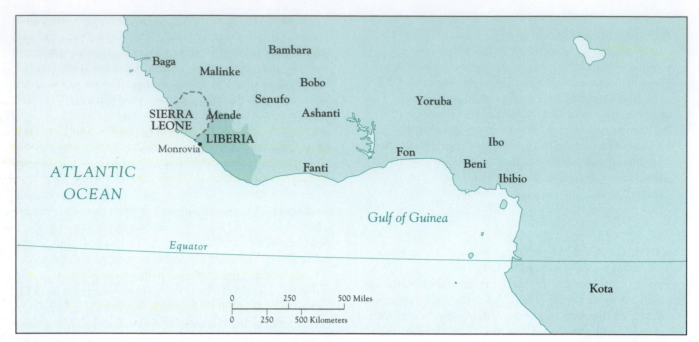

MAP 18:1 Liberia

As early as 1787, British abolitionists settled freed West Indian slaves at what became Freetown in Sierra Leone. An African-American sea captain, Paul Cuffee, scouted the coast to the south for a site to which free American blacks might move. In 1822 Monrovia (named for President James Monroe) was founded by the American Colonization Society. In 1847 Liberia, its native tribes dominated by Americans, declared its independence.

took to get by in America's competitive society. Being slaves protected them from society as well as society from them.

THE COLONIZATION MOVEMENT

The **American Colonization Society** was founded by antislavery southerners in 1817 to answer those who said that freeing slaves in the southern states would create catastrophic social problems. With the active support of distinguished men such as Madison, Monroe, John Marshall, and Henry Clay, the society's purpose was to raise money to assist free blacks in "returning" to west Africa, where the Society would aid them in creating a viable economy and government. The original goal of the colonization movement (similar societies were founded in several southern states) was to encourage both manumission and, in time, legal abolition.

In 1821 the society financed the emigration of a few former slaves to Sierra Leone, a British colony on what was then called the Guinea Coast. Sierra Leone was a British colony established as a refuge for slaves freed in the British West Indies. The next year, the society, with some government funds, purchased a stretch of coastline south of Sierra Leone and established Liberia. In 1824 construction of its capital, named Monrovia after President Monroe, was begun.

LIBERIA

Altogether, about 11,000 African Americans went to Liberia. The country functioned rather like an American territory except that the Colonization Society, not the government, appointed the governor of the colony. In 1847 the Liberians, dominated by former Americans, declared the nation's independence. When, later in the nineteenth century, European powers carved up Africa among them, Liberia and Ethiopia were the only two independent nations on the continent.

Despite Liberia's success, the experience of the American Colonization Society showed that sending free blacks to Africa was unrealistic. The slave population of the United States was 1.5 million in 1820 and 2 million in 1830—more than could survive on a swampy strip of African seacoast. Moreover, while white southerners were glad to see free blacks emigrate, few of them manumitted their slaves so they could go. Most of the Liberians were African Americans who were already free.

And few American blacks were interested in going to Africa. The 10,000–11,000 who went represented only about 7 percent of the South's free black population. There were 37,000 free blacks in Virginia alone in 1820. It is remarkable that as many

Discoverer of Liberia

During the 1810s Paul Cuffee, an African-American master mariner, called at Freetown in Sierra Leone, west Africa, after the British had established a colony for free blacks there. Cuffee scouted the coast south of Freetown, hoping to locate a site where free American blacks might go. It is not clear if Cuffee picked the future location of Monrovia in Liberia, but he was the first American to think of the region as a homeland for African Americans who wanted out of the United States.

people went to Liberia as did. Unenviable as were the conditions with which free blacks lived, unless they or their parents had been born in Africa, they were, simply, not Africans. Most black Americans were generations removed from their African roots; they felt little attraction to a land that was as unknown (and forbidding) to them as it was to white Americans.

Within a few years, few white southerners thought of Liberia and colonization in antislavery terms. When the Mississippi Colonization Society was founded in 1829, its pronounced purpose was to rid the state of free blacks. Its officers disassociated themselves from the old goal of encouraging planters to free their slaves. Except for one last debate, by 1830 the southern antislavery movement was dead.

THE LAST DEBATE

In December 1831, Governor John Floyd of Virginia asked the legislature to consider a plan for the gradual abolition of slavery in the state. Unlike in the northern states, slave owners would be compensated with money for their lost property, just as the state compensated the owners of real estate seized to build a fort or a road. For three weeks in January 1832, the legislature discussed the proposal, for the most part moderately and intelligently.

Even the staunchest proslavery legislators were defensive. Typically they introduced their speeches by regretting the fact that blacks were ever brought to Virginia, and by saying that the state would be a better place if it had been developed by free white labor. However, the past was unchangeable. In 1832 African Americans constituted almost half of Virginia's population; so large a population of free blacks was out of the question. Virginia already had a law requiring slave owners who manumitted their slaves to find homes for them in other states. The colonization movement was obviously a failure. However tragic it was for the Old Dominion, Virginia must continue to be a slave state.

The belief that a biracial society would not work carried the day, but just barely. The legislature rejected Floyd's scheme by 73 to 58. A switch of 8 votes would have altered the course of American history because the other states of the upper South—Delaware, Maryland, and Kentucky—would likely have followed Virginia's lead. Had those states phased slavery

out, the institution would not have split the Union down the middle. It would have been the peculiar institution of a few states in the deep South no more able to threaten the Union than the six states of New England. As it was, once Virginia's debate was concluded, no significant body of southern whites ever again considered the possibility of ridding themselves of their "burden."

THREATS TO THE SOUTHERN ORDER

Both Floyd's proposal and the Virginia legislature's rejection of it were profoundly influenced by two events that electrified the South in 1831: the emergence in the North of a new kind of antislavery agitator, and a bloody rebellion of slaves in southern Virginia—the third large conspiracy of slaves in thirty years, and the first in which white people were murdered.

EARLY ABOLITIONISTS

Since the War for Independence, the debate over slavery had revolved around questions of political principle, economic wisdom, and social consequences. In the middle colonies, however, the Quakers, who emphasized the equality of all men and women before God, early on saw slavery as a religious question. French-born Anthony Benezet of Philadelphia began to condemn slavery as immoral around 1750 where he was a teacher of black children. About the same time, another Quaker, John Woolman of New Jersey, took it upon himself to tell members of his meeting who owned slaves that the practice was sinful. Woolman began to travel to Quaker meetings throughout the middle colonies and upper South carrying a "minute" (a statement that he was a Quaker in good standing). At meetings, where everyone who felt moved to speak spoke, Woolman repeated and developed his message. Individually, he admonished Quakers who owned slaves to free them, and many did. By 1800 few Quakers in good standing still owned slaves.

Woolman had concerned himself almost exclusively with other Quakers. However, the Quaker vote was vital to the abolition of slavery in Pennsylvania, and by 1800, Quakers began to assist slaves seeking freedom in the courts and to help runaways put distance between themselves and their masters. Quakers joined antislavery evangelicals in active, public condemnations of the institution. In 1821 a New Jersey–born Quaker, Benjamin Lundy, began publishing *The Genius of Emancipation,* one of the first newspapers dedicated to abolition. A good Quaker, Lundy meant to persuade white southerners of the sinfulness of slavery, not to antagonize them. He espoused gradual emancipation so as to avoid sudden social dislocations, and he advocated colonizing African Americans in Liberia, Haiti, Canada, and Texas—then a part of Mexico.

Most Unitarians and Universalists, like the Quakers, were moderate and conciliatory in their antislavery sentiments. William Ellery Channing told southerners, "We consider

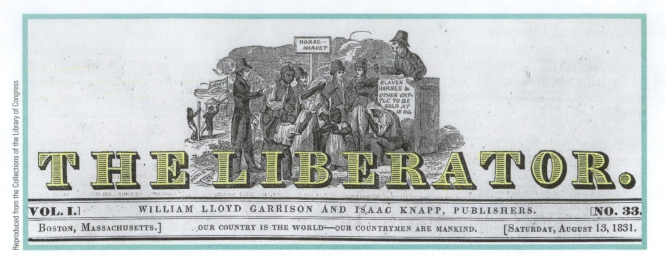

■ *The masthead of William Lloyd Garrison's* The Liberator *when it first appeared in 1831. It was a weekly and the most uncompromising of the many abolitionist newspapers. Garrison's writings were often intemperate, for which he made no apologies: slavery was sinful; God had not admonished Christians to be well-mannered in confronting sin. Many abolitionists disapproved of Garrison's rhetoric, but* The Liberator *had many readers, perhaps in part because Garrison published sensational accounts of cruelty to slaves that others considered indelicate.*

slavery your calamity and not your curse." Antislavery evangelicals, by way of contrast, considered slavery the South's sin and slave owners sinners. There was to be no mollycoddling of sinners; if they did not repent and cease to be slave owners, they were the enemy.

DAVID WALKER AND WILLIAM LLOYD GARRISON

In 1829 a black cloth dealer in Boston, David Walker, published a pamphlet called *The Appeal.* Walker reviewed familiar arguments about the immorality and injustice of slavery, reported instances of extreme cruelty toward slaves, and attacked, point by point, justifications for continuing to preserve slavery written by well-known men, including Thomas Jefferson. Walker added a declaration that shocked Quakers and Unitarians as well as slave owners: Unless whites abolished slavery, Walker said, black people had a moral right, indeed a duty, to rise up and destroy slavery violently. Walker was an evangelical; he backed up almost every point he made, including his call for violence, with quotations from the Bible.

When an African-American minister in Savannah received fifty copies of *The Appeal* in the mail, the Georgia legislature offered $1,000 to anyone who would bring Walker to the state to face trial. Walker's career as an abolitionist was short. In 1830 he was found dead in his shop. There was no hard evidence, but some Bostonians believed he was murdered.

William Lloyd Garrison was another Boston evangelical who had worked with Benjamin Lundy in publishing *The Genius of Emancipation.* There was scarcely an evangelical reform that Garrison did not support. Because he was also a pacifist, however, he disapproved of David Walker's call to arms.

But Garrison had no objection to Walker's use of intemperate language. A spare, intense young white man of 24,

Garrison believed slavery to be the most abominable of sins. His rhetoric was incendiary and personal, aimed at the sinners. "I am aware," Garrison wrote in the first issue of his abolitionist newspaper, *The Liberator,* which appeared in 1831, "that many object to the severity of my language; but is there not cause for severity? I will be as harsh as truth, and as uncompromising as justice. On this subject I do not wish to think, or speak, or write, with moderation. No! No! Tell a man whose house is on fire to give a moderate alarm; tell him to moderately rescue his wife from the hands of the ravisher; tell the mother to gradually extricate her babe from the fire into which it has fallen; but urge me not to use moderation in a cause like the present."

> ## Southern Anxieties
>
> Both antislavery and proslavery southerners feared slave rebellion. The difference between them was the tone in which they expressed it.
>
> Thomas Ritchie, an antislavery Virginian:
>
> > To attempt to excite discontent and revolt, or publish writings having this tendency, obstinately and perversely, among us, is outrageous—it ought not to be passed over with indifference. Our own safety—the good and happiness of our slaves—requires it.
>
> Edward D. Holland, a proslavery South Carolinian:
>
> > Let it never be forgotten that our NEGROES are truly the Jacobins of the country; that they are the anarchists and the domestic enemy, the common enemy of civilized society, and the barbarians who would, IF THEY COULD, become the DESTROYERS of our race.

The Granger Collection, New York

Gabriel's and Vesey's rebellions were exposed before they began. Nat Turner's was not because he informed only a few trusted friends of his plans. Turner may have been familiar with the fact that Vesey's plot was revealed to whites by one of the many slaves who knew of his plans. It had been only nine years since Vesey and thirty-four others had been hanged. The slave grapevine could and did convey news hundreds of miles in a week or two. White efforts to keep newspapers from slaves were never entirely successful.

Garrison described the slave owner's life as "one of unbridled lust, of filthy amalgamation, of swaggering braggadocio, of haughty domination, of cowardly ruffianism, of boundless dissipation, of matchless insolence, of infinite self-conceit, of unequaled oppression, of more than savage cruelty."

Garrison was not popular in the North. Even in Boston, a center of evangelicalism and antislavery sentiment, he was hooted and pelted with stones when he spoke in public. On one occasion, a mob threw a noose around his neck and dragged him through the streets. He may well have been hanged had not a group of abolitionist women momentarily stunned the mob with their boldness and rescued him. (Garrison was also a supporter of women's rights.)

In the South, Garrison was a monster—not merely because he was against slavery, at least not at first. Garrison and other evangelical abolitionists were accused of inciting slave rebellion, which in 1831 was no abstraction.

REBELLIONS

In 1800, less than a decade after the massacres of whites in Haiti (and just two years after a second, lesser wave of killings), Richmond narrowly averted a slave rebellion led by a blacksmith slave, Gabriel Prosser, who was probably inspired by the uprising in Haiti. Gabriel, white Virginians observed when the scare was over, was literate, as were many of his friends and cronies, both black and white, who were, like him, skilled tradesmen. They had regularly discussed politics in their off hours.

Just how long Gabriel and his associates had been planning a rebellion is unclear, but it was set for August 30, 1800. With a core of about 150, Gabriel expected hundreds of slaves who had heard of the plan to join his army. The rebels' instructions were to kill only those who resisted them, and to

spare Quakers and Methodists, who were known to oppose slavery. The objective was to capture Virginia's governor (James Monroe) and several key points in the city, then to negotiate a settlement. Gabriel was not apocalyptic; he was realistic about what a few hundred rebels could do. Nor did he share the Haitians' blanket hatred of whites. He expected poor whites to join his struggle against the slave-owning aristocracy that dominated Virginia.

But the uprising never happened. Torrential rains on August 30 prevented the rebels from assembling. A few slaves acting suspiciously were arrested and questioned, and Gabriel's plot was exposed. Twenty-seven of the leaders were hanged; others were sold outside the state.

In 1822 a free black carpenter and Methodist preacher in Charleston, South Carolina, **Denmark Vesey,** devised a plan for a slave uprising with a Haitian connection. Vesey's idea was for slaves to sack the city for arms and provisions, seize ships in the harbor, and sail to Haiti. Vesey talked the plot up among slaves in Charleston, including house servants who, their owners were later shocked to learn, were not so devoted to their masters and mistresses that they did not listen to Vesey and expose him. Vesey's chief collaborator, known only as Gullah Jack, was an Angola-born plantation slave who had met Vesey at the African Methodist church. He recruited rebels on plantations outside Charleston. Many were also Africans. South Carolina had imported 40,000 African slaves in 1807, the last year it was legal to purchase slaves from abroad; and illegal slave traders had continued to call at the port.

The rising was scheduled for June 16. Two days earlier, an informer revealed the plan. Vesey, Gullah Jack, and thirty-three others were hanged. No one knew (or knows) how many slaves were involved, but white South Carolinians remained, understandably, uneasy.

African Slave Traders: Defying the Law

As of January 1, 1808, it was illegal to import slaves from abroad. It was the first day that the Constitution permitted Congress to forbid the "African slave trade."

The Constitution's attention to the foreign slave trade, protecting it for twenty years, then authorizing its termination, sheds light on the founding fathers' hope that slavery's days were numbered, and the fact that Georgia and South Carolina disagreed with that consensus. Most Americans saw the abolition of the foreign slave trade as a first step toward abolishing the institution of slavery. James Madison wrote, "Happy would it be for the unfortunate Africans if an equal prospect lay before them of being redeemed from the oppression of their European brethren."

But South Carolina's and Georgia's delegates to the Constitutional convention balked. Their states were importing a good many slaves from Africa and the West Indies. They made it clear that without temporary protection of the trade, they would not ratify the Constitution. So the Constitution prohibited Congress from forbidding the "Importation of such Persons as any of the States now existing shall think proper to admit" until 1808. This provision was specifically exempted from the amendment process. It could not be changed; each state's right to two senators is the only other part of the Constitution future generations were forbidden to amend.

Attitudes toward the African slave trade were unchanged in 1807. Congress voted to abolish the African slave trade right on schedule. However, during the last year the trade was legal, South Carolina imported more slaves than the state had in any previous year.

Enforcing the ban was difficult. Major African suppliers of slaves like the Ashanti king were mystified by news of the American action. Other purveyors of slaves were angry, saying that the termination of the business was an insult to Islam. (There were more slaves in Africa in 1807 than in all of the Americas.) The British, who also abolished the African slave trade, bore the major burden of patrolling the west African coast for violators. By the 1840s, more than thirty naval ships were assigned to African waters. Sailors boarded vessels violating the ban and returned captives to Africa. The U.S. navy assigned a squadron of eight ships to Caribbean waters to search suspicious vessels. Between May 1818 and November 1821, American sailors freed 573 Africans.

From an American perspective, the term *African* slave trade is misleading. In colonial times, few slave traders carried captives directly from Africa to North America. It was the terrible nature of the business. So many captives died on the middle passage that profits depended on making the voyage as short as possible. The quickest Atlantic crossing was to Brazil, a partial explanation of the fact that 40 percent of Africans sent as slaves to the Western Hemisphere went to Brazil. Few slave traders sailed in one stage from Africa to North America because that meant adding weeks to their voyage (and deaths to their balance sheets) when they could avoid both problems by calling in the West Indies and selling their captives there. Most American slave buyers purchased their slaves in the West Indies after they had been "seasoned," a euphemistic way of saying that they had recovered from the horrors of the middle passage. Almost all Africa-born slaves in the United States spent some time in the West Indies.

This remained the case after 1808 because of the added risks of transporting Africans illegally. There were still plenty of slaves for sale in Africa. King Gezo of Dahomey (whose bodyguard was a platoon of tall, fierce women) sold 9,000 slaves annually between 1809 and 1850. The major middlemen at Sangha were an American, Paul Faber, and his African wife, Mary, who kept meticulous books, as if they were grocers. Most of those slaves went to Brazil and Cuba, where slave traders headed for Charleston, Savannah, or New Orleans bought their cargos. They preferred small, fast vessels to outrun naval ships on the lookout for them.

By 1839 many southerners and some northerners were sympathetic to the illegal slave trade. There were plenty of willing buyers. The boom in cotton had sent the price of America-born slaves soaring; newly imported Africans were cheaper than native slaves. Northern shipyards continued to build vessels designed for the slave trade. Of 170 slave trade expeditions identified by the British between 1859 and 1862, 74 had been outfitted in New York. The schooner *Wanderer*, ostensibly a yacht, was built for John Johnston of New Orleans in 1856. The tip-off of its real purpose was its oversized water tanks. Still, the *Wanderer* was not seized until it had successfully landed 325 slaves at Jekyll Island, South Carolina, in December 1858.

The penalties for being convicted of slave trading were harsh. The British equated slave traders with pirates; they hanged them. There was a price to pay if captured by Americans too. By the 1850s, however, it was difficult to get a conviction from a southern jury. In 1859 a U.S. warship brought the *Emily*, obviously a slaver, into port; the case was dismissed. In 1860 the owner of the *Wanderer* was acquitted in Savannah and permitted to buy his ship back for a quarter of its value. In the law, crewmen on a slaver could be prosecuted, but they rarely suffered more than a slap on the wrist. With little deterrence, seamen found it difficult to ignore the fact that wages on a slave ship running illegally from Cuba were as high as $10 a day, an astronomical sum.

WANTED: Nat Turner

"Five feet 6 or 8 inches high, weighs between 150 and 160 pounds, rather bright complexion, but not a mulatto. Broad shoulders, large flat nose, large eyes. Broad flat feet, rather knock-kneed, walks brisk and active. Hair on the top of the head very thin, no beard, except on the upper lip and at the top of the chin. A scar on one of his temples, also one at the back of his neck. A large knot on one of the bones of his right arm, near his wrist, produced [by] a blow."

NAT TURNER

Gabriel and Vesey were rational rebels. Neither fantasized that slaves could destroy their enemies; neither was blood-thirsty. Their objectives were limited and realistic. Nat Turner, whose rebellion in August 1831 was not discovered before it began, was an altogether different sort. An ordinary field hand in southern Virginia who had been taught to read by his first owner (his owner in 1831 was illiterate), he was a pious Baptist who pored endlessly over the Bible. Hardly realistic, he was mentally disturbed, perhaps even psychotic. Turner had visions and heard voices. He took a solar eclipse in February 1831 as God's go-ahead to slaves to rise up and kill all whites. Unlike Gabriel and Vesey, Turner had no goal other than an apocalypse. That he had any followers at all indicates how desperate some of the slaves of Southampton County found their lives.

Turner was shrewd enough to divulge his plans to very few trusted friends. (He may have known that Vesey's rebellion was squelched because of an informer.) On the night of August 21, 1831, armed with little more than farm tools, Turner's band swept quickly across the county, killing sixty whites and recruiting supporters from among their slaves. The murders were over in a couple of days, although it was six weeks before the last of seventy rebels were rounded up. Turner and thirty-nine others were hanged. Others, who were acquitted of shedding blood, were sold out of the state. Rumor had it that in the panic of the first days, whites had murdered many other blacks and never reported the killings.

Turner's rebellion terrified slave owners, especially those who lived in parts of Louisiana, Mississippi, and South Carolina where blacks overwhelmingly outnumbered whites by as many as twenty to one. Mary Boykin Chesnut, the wife of a planter, was not musing over a demographic curiosity when she described her home, Mulberry, as "half a dozen whites and sixty or seventy Negroes, miles away from the rest of the world."

White belief in black inferiority meant that some southerners were unwilling to admit that blacks, left to their own devices, were capable of mounting a rebellion like Turner's. It was no coincidence, they said, that the massacre in Southampton County followed the fiery first issue of *The Liberator* by eight months. They took note of the fact that Turner knew how to read, and blamed white abolitionists like Garrison for the tragedy.

THE SOUTH CLOSES RANKS

Once Virginians decided that the Old Dominion would remain a slave state, the South stood almost alone in the western world. The northern states had abolished the institution. The Spanish-speaking republics of the Americas had done so. Great Britain had recently emancipated slaves in its colonies. In the entire Christian world, slavery survived only in the Spanish colonies of Cuba and Puerto Rico, the tiny French islands of Martinique and Guadeloupe, in a few small Portuguese enclaves, and in Brazil.

After 1832, southerners began to recognize that their slavery was a peculiar institution, almost unique to the American South. They moved on three fronts to protect it. They attempted to insulate the South from outside ideas that threatened slavery and suppressed criticism of the institution at home. Slave owners ceased to chastize their forebears for clinging to slavery and to regret it to outsiders as a historical tragedy or a necessary evil; they devised the argument that slavery was a positive good that benefited both slave owner and slave—indeed, southern society. Finally, they reformed the states' slave codes—the laws that governed the peculiar institution—both improving the material conditions under which slaves lived and instituting stricter controls over the black population.

SUPPRESSING DISCUSSION

Most southern states forbade the circulation of abolitionist literature. The post office authorized southern postmasters to examine the mail and destroy material that was locally objectionable. Innumerable copies of *The Liberator* and other antislavery newspapers were burned.

Georgia's legislature offered a reward of $5,000 to any person who would bring William Lloyd Garrison into the state to stand trial for inciting rebellion. That fact that a state legislature was willing to encourage an abduction (Garrison had no intention of taking a vacation in Georgia) indicates the depths of hatred for abolitionists in the South. Only in border states like Maryland and Kentucky could abolitionists like John Gregg Fee and Cassius Marcellus Clay continue to speak without fear of anything worse than heckling and harassment. Elsewhere in the South, the expression of antislavery opinions was no longer acceptable.

In the House of Representatives, beginning in 1836, southern congressmen, with the support of some northern Democrats, annually adopted a procedural rule that petitions to the House calling for the abolition of slavery in the District of Columbia be tabled without discussion. That is, the petitions were simply set aside. There were a lot of them. By March 1838, tabled petitions filled a room twenty feet by thirty feet. Former President John Quincy Adams, now a member of Congress, argued that the "gag rule" violated the right to free speech. Adams considered zealots like Garrison irresponsible, but he insisted that abolitionists had a constitutional right to be heard. In 1838 Congressman Robert Rhett of South Carolina replied that the Constitution should be amended to limit First Amendment freedom of speech when the subject was slavery.

A "POSITIVE GOOD"

Shortly after Virginia's debate on the future of slavery, a professor of economics at the College of William and Mary, Thomas Roderick Dew, published a systematic defense of slavery. He said that as a means of organizing and controlling labor, the slavery system was superior to the free wage worker system of the North and Europe. By 1837 southern preachers and politicians were parroting and embroidering on Dew's theories. In the Senate, John C. Calhoun declared that compared with other systems by which racial and class relationships were governed, "the relation now existing in the slaveholding states is, instead of an evil, a good—a positive good"—better for everyone concerned, slaves included, than other economic systems.

In *A Sociology for the South,* published in 1854, **George Fitzhugh** of Virginia amassed statistics and other evidence with which he argued that the southern slave lived a better life than did the northern wage worker or the European peasant.

In every society, Fitzhugh wrote, someone had to perform the drudgery. In the South, menial work was done by slaves who were cared for from cradle to grave. Not only did the slave owner feed, clothe, and house his workers, but he also supported slave children, the injured and the disabled, and the elderly—all of whom were nonproductive. Fitzhugh pointed out that by comparison, the northern wage worker was paid only as long as there was work to be done and the worker was fit to do it. The wage worker who was injured was cut loose to fend for himself. His children, the elderly, and the incompetent were no responsibility of capitalist employers and the "free labor" system in which they took pride.

Consequently, Fitzhugh said, the North was plagued by social problems unknown in the South. The North teemed with obnoxious, nattering reformers. The lower classes were irreligious and, in their misery, drunken and tumultuous. The free working class was tempted by socialist, communist, and other doctrines that threatened the social order. By comparison, Fitzhugh claimed, southern slaves were contented, indeed happy. "A merrier being does not exist on the face of the globe," Fitzhugh wrote, "than the Negro slave of the United States."

Even John Randolph, who hated slavery, told of touring Ireland attended by his valet slave. Both men were shocked by the squalor in which the Irish lived. His slave told him that he "was never so proud of being a *Virginia slave*. He looked with horror upon the mud hovels and miserable food of the *white slaves.*"

THE BIBLE, THE ANCIENTS, AND CULTURE

The **"positive good"** proslavery argument was new. Before Nat Turner and *The Liberator,* only the odd eccentric South Carolinian had suggested that slavery was a positively desirable institution. The new southern ideology incorporated religious, historical, cultural, and social arguments alongside the economic justifications for the peculiar institution.

The Bible sanctioned slavery. The ancient Hebrews—the patriarchs Abraham, Isaac, and Jacob—owned slaves with God's blessing. When a slave approached Christ saying he wished to follow him as a disciple, Christ said that he should return to his master, serve him, and, as a slave, practice Christ's teachings.

Dew and others pointed out that the great civilizations of antiquity, Greece and Rome, were slaveholding societies. Hardly a barbaric institution, slavery had made possible the high cultures that were still closely studied in American colleges and universities for their art, literature, and wisdom. Slavery made possible a leisured, gracious, and cultured upper class that preserved the highest refinements of human achievement. Southern planters pointed out that more southerners than northerners were college educated. Even as late as 1860, there were more than 6,000 college students in Georgia, Alabama, and Mississippi and fewer than 4,000 in the more populous and intellectually pretentious New England states.

As an aristocracy, southern planters were closer to the tradition of the gentlemanly founding fathers than were the vulgar, money-grubbing capitalists of the North. Because gentlemen dominated politics in the South, the southern states were better governed than the northern states were. In the North, demagogues won elections to high position by playing to the whims and passions of the dregs of society. Some planters liked to think of themselves as descendants of the cavaliers of seventeenth-century England. The South's favorite novels were Sir Walter Scott's tales of knighthood and chivalry.

Currier and Ives published prints with which people who could not afford paintings decorated the walls of their homes. Subject matter was diverse, ranging from natural wonders (Niagara Falls) to sailing ships to homey, and humorous scenes. The prints always aimed to please, never to provoke; Currier and Ives were in business. This depiction of a cotton plantation at picking time is idyllic. Everyone seems to be enjoying a pleasant summer day. In fact, cotton-picking time meant frantic, hard work and long hours for every hand available, often including otherwise privileged "house slaves" and children left to themselves the rest of the year.

RACE: THE TRUMP CARD

But did all these "proofs" justify denying personal freedom to human beings? Yes, Fitzhugh said in a second book, *Cannibals All!*, published in 1857. The Negro race was incapable of civilization's higher callings. In return for enjoying the fruits of their labor, the owners of slaves did blacks a favor by providing for their necessities and protecting them against competition (and inevitable conflict) with poor whites (of whose virtues Fitzhugh and other upper-class southerners had no exalted opinions).

Here and there, a few southerners argued that African Americans were not quite human. Dr. Josiah Nott, a well-known medical researcher, collected skulls from all over the world. He measured brain cavities by drilling holes in them, filling them with buckshot, and then measuring the shot. He concluded that blacks had significantly smaller brains than whites.

Few southerners bought Nott's theories. Different species do not produce fertile offspring, and the number of mulattos in the southern "black" population was pretty convincing evidence that blacks and whites were both *Homo sapiens*. White southerners, almost all religious, preferred to add to their quivers the argument that by bringing blacks from

Africa and exposing them to Christianity, whites had done them the greatest service of all.

MANAGEMENT

Positive-good southerners equated happiness with the material conditions of slave life—housing, clothing, diet—and compared them favorably with the conditions under which the poorest wage workers of the North lived. By the 1850s, when Fitzhugh wrote, most southern state legislatures had, in fact, defined minimum living standards as part of their slave codes. Magazines like the *Southern Agriculturalist* featured exchanges among slave owners about how well they treated their people and what kinds of improvements were desirable.

The most obvious reason for keeping slaves adequately housed, clothed, and fed was practical: a healthy slave worked more efficiently and was less likely to rebel or run away. Also underlying the trend toward improvement in the conditions of slave life after the 1830s was the South's determination to give the lie to the abolitionists' depiction of slavery as a life of unrelenting misery. Planters who provided decent accommodations for their slaves took pleasure in showing "the quarters," as slaves' cabins were called, to

The "quarters" of a plantation on the South Carolina coast. The cabins are ruder than slave housing on some other plantations, much more solid and better roofed than slave housing on others. Grouping the cabins together served several purposes. It made the master's accounting for the whereabouts of his slaves easier and provided the slaves with a kind of village social life so that they were less likely to wander looking for company.

northern and foreign visitors. They reassured themselves that they were just the beneficent patriarchs that the positive-good writers described.

CONTROL

Visitors were less likely to be apprised of new measures of slave control that were introduced after the Turner conspiracy. By 1840 the states of the deep South had adopted laws that made it extremely difficult for a slave owner to manumit his slaves. Even Virginia, where manumission had been honored as the act of a gentleman, required newly freed blacks to leave the state. (The law was difficult to enforce and widely evaded.) It was a crime in some southern states to teach a slave to read; Gabriel, Vesey, and Turner had all been literate and, in fact, voracious readers.

County governments were required to maintain slave patrols. Some counties required all fit white males to take turns on the patrols; most hired "paddyrollers," as slaves called the patrollers. These mounted posses of armed whites policed the roads and plantations, particularly at night. They had the legal right to break into slave cabins or demand at gunpoint that any black (or white) account for himself or herself. Usually rough, hard-bitten men who were so poor that they would take the unsavory job, the **paddyrollers** were brutal even with unoffending slaves who were carrying the written

passes they were required to have when off their master's property. Blacks hated and feared them. Their mere presence and arrogance cast a cloud of repression over the country.

Free blacks—there were about 250,000 in the South by 1860, one to every fifteen slaves—carefully protected the documentary evidence of their status. Kidnappings of free blacks, and sale of them as slaves elsewhere in the South, were far from unknown.

The mere existence of a free African-American population among slaves was a bothersome problem for slave owners. It was as important to the institution that blacks be convinced that God and nature intended them to be slaves as it was to persuade other whites that slavery was a positive good. If slaves saw free blacks prospering, the argument disintegrated. Slave owners also believed that free blacks were likely to stir up discontent among slaves, and they were probably right. These factors produced the laws requiring masters who freed their slaves to take them out of state and pressure (and sometimes laws) forcing free blacks to move to towns and cities. In fact, free blacks who had no land to farm needed no persuasion to congregate in towns. Only there could they find work and a social life; and living in numbers among other free African Americans provided some security. A free black family living in a remote rural area was vulnerable to abuse, and worse, abduction and enslavement.

Muslim Slaves

The west African peoples who supplied British and American slavers with their captives raided Islamic tribes in the interior. One scholar estimates that 30,000 Muslims were sold in North America. A few distinguished themselves by virtue of their literacy and abilities. About 1730, Job Ben Salomon Jallo of Senegal took two slaves to sell in the Mandingo country along the Gambia River. He was himself enslaved and sold to an English captain who took him to Annapolis, Maryland. He astonished his owner when he asked to write a letter to his father to arrange his ransom. He was freed, and he returned to the Gambia via England where he became an agent of the Royal African Company, buying slaves in his homeland for export to the Americas.

Omar ibn Said, a slave in South Carolina, impressed his owner because he was literate in Arabic. He was not freed, but he was exempted from labor. Salil Bilali (called "Tom") supervised 450 slaves on St. Simon's Island, Georgia. The *Southern Agriculturalist* singled it out as a model plantation. Ibrahim Abd ar-Rahman was a plantation manager in Natchez, Mississippi. He became a national figure when he met a white man whom, incredibly, he had met in Africa. With his help, Ibrahim spoke with both Henry Clay and John Quincy Adams, who assisted him in raising the money to buy his freedom and the freedom of his American wife and several of his grandchildren. He went to Liberia in 1829.

RELIGION: A THREAT TO CONTROL

Probably fewer than half of southern slaves were Christians at the time of the Revolution. Neither masters, slaves, nor ministers took much interest in converting them. The rise of the Methodists, the reinvigoration of the Baptists, the purchase of Louisiana (where most slaves were Roman Catholics), and the end of the legal importation of slaves from Africa after 1807 changed that. Within a few decades after 1800, almost all slaves embraced one or another form of Christianity, usually evangelical varieties. Indeed, religious observance—almost always highly personal and emotional—became an important part of slave culture.

All southern states had laws, inherited from colonial times, specifying that conversion to Christianity did not affect a slave's status. Nevertheless, religious zeal in the quarters presented a problem of control. Denmark Vesey had been a Methodist minister; Nat Turner had been led to rebellion by Bible reading; David Walker's *Appeal* was laced with biblical quotations.

Some masters took their slaves to their own churches where the minister was expected, now and then, to deliver a sermon based on biblical stories such as that of Hagar: "The angel of the Lord said unto her, return to thy mistress, and submit thyself under her hands." Other masters permitted blacks to have preachers of their own. These often literate and more often eloquent men were instructed—explicitly or tacitly—to steer clear of lessons that might cast doubt on the rightness of slavery. Most toed the line; it was an African-American minister in Savannah who informed the authorities that Walker's *Appeal* had been sent to the state. Others conveyed their antislavery message by placing heavy emphasis on the ancient Israelites' bondage in Babylon and Egypt and their ultimate deliverance.

FURTHER READING

General David Brion Davis, *The Problem of Slavery in the Age of Revolution, 1770–1823*, 1975; Don E. Fehrenbacher, *The Slave-Holding Republic: An Account of the United States Government's Relations to Slavery*, 2001; Daniel Feller, *The Jacksonian Promise: America 1815–1840*, 1995; D. W. Meinig, *The Shaping of America: A Geographical Perspective on 500 Years of American History*, vol. 2, *Continental America, 1800–1867*, 1993; Peter J. Parish, *Slavery: History and Historians*, 1989.

Rebellions and Reactions James T. Baker, *Nat Turner: Cry Freedom in America*, 1998; Thomas Bender, *The Anti-Slavery Debate*, 1992; Douglas R. Egerton, *Gabriel's Rebellion: The Virginia Slave Conspiracies of 1800 and 1802*, 1993, and *He Shall Go Free: The Lives of Denmark Vesey*, 1999; Allison G. Freehling, *Drift toward Dissolution: The Virginia Slavery Debate of 1831–1832*, 1982; Scot French, *The Rebellious Slave: Nat Turner in American Memory*, 2004; Robert J. Loewenburg, *Freedom's Despots: The Critique of Abolitionism*, 1986; Henry Mayer, *All on Fire: William Lloyd Garrison and the Abolition of Slavery*, 1998; David Robertson, *Denmark Vesey*, 1999;

James Sidbury, *Plowshares into Swords: Race, Rebellion, and Identity in Gabriel's Virginia, 1730–1810*, 1997.

Slave Owners Edward A. Ayers, *Vengeance and Justice: Crime and Punishment in the Nineteenth-Century American South*, 1984; Dickson D. Bruce, *Violence and Culture in the Antebellum South*, 1979; Victoria E. Bynum, *Unruly Women: The Politics of Social and Sexual Control in the Old South*, 1992; Bruce Collins, *White Society in the Antebellum South*, 1985; William J. Cooper, *The South and the Politics of Slavery, 1828–1856*, 1978; Barbara J. Fields, *Slavery and Freedom on the Middle Ground: Maryland during the Nineteenth Century*, 1985; Elizabeth Fox-Genovese, *Within the Plantation Household: Black and White Women of the Old South*, 1988; Eugene D. Genovese, *The World the Slaveholders Made*, 1988; James Oates, *The Ruling Race: A History of American Slaveholders*, 1982; Brenda Stevenson, *Life in Black and White: Family and Community in the Old South*, 1996; Bertram Wyatt-Brown, *Honor and Violence in the Old South*, 1986, and *Southern Honor: Ethics and Behavior in the Old South*, 1988.

The South and Colonization Bertram Wyatt Brown, *The Shaping of Southern Culture: Honor, Grace, and War, 1760s–1890s,* 2001; Eric Burin, *Slavery and the Peculiar Solution: A History of the American Colonization Society,* 2005; Clement Eaton, *A History of* *the Old South,* 1975; I. A. Newby, *The American South,* 1979; James Oates, *Slavery and Freedom: An Interpretation of the Old South,* 1990; Gavin Wright, *The Political Economy of the Cotton South,* 1998.

KEY TERMS

The following terms are covered in this chapter and can also be found in the list of Key Terms at the back of the book.

American Colonization Society	**"gag rule"**	**paddyrollers**	**"positive good"**
Denmark Vesey	**George Fitzhugh**		

ONLINE SOURCES GUIDE

Use this listing to find online documents, images, interactive maps, simulations, and other resources related to this chapter:

Interactive Time Line (with online readings)
A Different Country: The South

American History Resource Center
http://history.wadsworth.com/rc/us

Selected Images
Slave quarters near Charleston, South Carolina
William Lloyd Garrison
Southern yeoman farmer's home

Discovery

How did southerners justify and perpetuate slavery?

In thinking about this question, begin by breaking it down into the components shown below. A discussion of the significance of each component should appear in your answer.

Culture and Society: Read "J. H. Hammond, Slavery in the Light of Political Science (1845)" and "A Fugitive Slave Writes to His Former Master, 1844." By what authority does the author of the first excerpt justify slavery in southern society? Based on that belief, in what ways might southerners feel that they are helping slaves? What justifications does the author provide in the document? How might his arguments cause southerners to entrench themselves in their support of slavery? In what ways might this argument be dangerous? The author of the second excerpt also implies a belief in Christianity. In light of this, how can you reconcile the two positions?

J. H. Hammond, Slavery in the Light of Political Science (1845)

. . . It is impossible, therefore, to suppose that slavery is contrary to the will of God. It is equally absurd to say that American slavery differs in form or principle from that of the chosen people. *We accept the Bible terms as the definition of our slavery, and its precepts as the guide of our conduct. We desire nothing more. Even the right to buffet,"* which is esteemed so shocking, finds its express license in the gospel." 1 Peter ii. 20. Nay, what is more, God directs the Hebrews to "bore holes in the ears of their brothers" to *mark* them, when under certain circumstances they become *perpetual slaves.* Exodus xxi. 6.

   I think, then, I may safely conclude, and I firmly believe, that American slavery is not only not a sin, but especially common led by God through Moses, and approved by Christ through his apostles. And here I might close its defense; for what God ordains, and Christ sanctifies should surely command the respect and toleration of man. But I fear there has grown up in our time, a transcendental religion, which is throwing even transcendental philosophy into the shade a religion too pure and elevated for the Bible; which seeks to erect among men a higher standard of morals than the Almighty has revealed, or our Saviour preached and which is probably destined to do more to impede the extension of God's kingdom on earth than all the infidels who have ever lived. Error is error. It is as dangerous to deviate to the right hand as to the left. And

when men, professing to be holy men, and who are by numbers so regarded, declare those things to be sinful which our Creator has expressly authorized and instituted, they do more to destroy his authority among mankind than the most wicked can effect, by proclaiming that to be innocent which lie has forbidden. To this self-righteous and self-exalted class belong all the abolitionists whose writings I have read. With them it is no end of the argument to prove your propositions by the text of the Bible, interpreted according to its plain and palpable meaning, and as understood by all mankind for three thousand years before their time. They are more, ingenious at construing and interpolating to accommodate it to their newfangled and ethereal code of morals, than ever were Voltaire and Hums in picking it to pieces, to free the world from what they considered a delusion. When the abolitionists proclaim "manstealing" to be a sin, and show me that it is so written down by God, I admit them to be right and shudder at the idea of such a crime. But when I show them that to hold "bondmen forever" is ordained, by God *they deny the Bible, and set up in its place a law of their own making.* I must then cease to reason with them on this branch of the question. Our religion differs as widely as our manners. The great Judge in our day of final account must decide between us. . . .

A Fugitive Slave Writes to His Former Master, 1844

From Henry Bibb to William Gatewood, Detroit, March 23, 1844 in *Narrative of the Life and Adventures of Henry Bibb, an American slave, written by himself.*

March 23, 1844 Detroit

Dear Sir:—I am happy to inform you that you are not mistaken in the man whom you sold as property, and received pay for as such. But I thank God that I am not property now, but am regarded as a man like yourself, and although I live far north, I am enjoying a comfortable living by my own industry. If you should ever chance to be traveling this way, and will call on me, I will use you better than you did me while you held me as a slave. Think not that I have any malice against you, for the cruel treatment which you inflicted on me while I was in your power. As it was the custom of your country, to treat your fellow men as you did me and my little family, I can freely forgive you.

I wish to be remembered in love to my aged mother, and friends; please tell her that if we should never meet again in this life, my prayer shall be to God that we may meet in Heaven, where parting shall be no more.

You wish to be remembered to King and Jack. I am pleased, sir, to inform you that they are both here, well, and doing well. They are both living in Canada West. They are now the owners of better farms than the men are who once owned them.

You may perhaps think hard of us for running away from slavery, but as to myself, I have but one apology to make for it, which is this: I have only to regret that I did not start at an earlier period. I might have been free long before I was. I think it is very probable that I should have been a toiling slave on your property today, if you had treated me differently.

To be compelled to stand by and see you whip and slash my wife without mercy, when I could afford her no protection, not even by offering myself to suffer the lash in her place, was more than I felt it to be the duty of a slave husband to endure, while the way was open to Canada. My infant child was also frequently flogged by Mrs. Gatewood, for crying, until its skin was bruised literally purple. This kind of treatment was what drove me from home and family, to seek a better home for them. But I am willing to forget the past. I should be pleased to hear from you again, on the reception of this and should also be very happy to correspond with you often, if it should be agreeable to yourself. I subscribe myself a friend to the oppressed, and Liberty forever.

To read extended versions of the documents, visit the companion Web site http://history.wadsworth.com/americanpast8e; click on "Discovery Sources."

CHAPTER 19

The Peculiar Institution

Slavery as It Was Perceived; Slavery as It Was

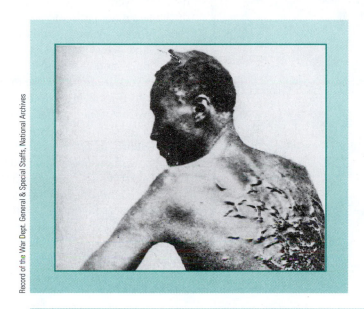

Record of the War Dept. General & Special Staffs, National Archives

Oppression has, at one stroke, deprived the descendants of the Africans of almost all the privileges of humanity. The Negro of the United States has lost all remembrance of his country; the language which his forefathers spoke is never heard around him; he abjured their religion and forgot their customs when he ceased to belong to Africa, without acquiring any European privileges. But he remains halfway between the two communities; sold by the one, repulsed by the other; finding not a spot in the universe to call by the name of country, except the faint image of a home which the shelter of his master's roof affords.

Alexis de Tocqueville

The Thirteenth Amendment, added to the Constitution in 1865, is just two sentences long. But it changed the United States more radically than any of the other twenty-six. It states that "neither slavery nor involuntary servitude . . . shall exist within the United States." The Thirteenth Amendment destroyed a two-century-old institution that mocked the ideals of individual freedom and equality before the law that since independence, Americans had proclaimed, made the United States unique among the nations of the world.

In fact, in 1865 the United States was almost unique in the Western world in permitting some human beings to own others, as they might own furniture or horses and a wagon—as personal property. Aside from Islamic countries and parts of sub-Saharan Africa and Asia—places Americans dismissed as "oriental" or savage—the institution of slavery survived only in Brazil, Cuba, Puerto Rico, and in the southeastern United States. Even in Russia, a country synonymous in the West with backwardness, the czar had freed the serfs, and they had not been *property*. Southerners called slavery "our **peculiar institution**," and not apologetically.

"DE OLD PLANTATION"

Apologists for slavery and abolitionists, all in the North after the watershed 1830s, purveyed to the world two images of African-American slavery that did not merely differ, but were irreconcilable. "Positive-good" southerners depicted a benign, paternalistic institution beneficial to slave as well as slave owner; abolitionists portrayed a relationship between masters and slaves that dehumanized the latter and made evil whip-wielding brutes of their owners.

The Granger Collection, New York

Publicity for a minstrel show. The stereotypical characters are exuberant, simple, idle, and ecstatically happy. So popular were the minstrels during the 1850s that there were 100 different touring troupes during the decade.

entertainment that evolved during the 1830s and, by the 1850s, had been experienced by a majority of Americans: the minstrel show.

THE MINSTRELS

By the 1830s, light musical entertainment alternated on the stages of American theaters with dramatic plays and comedies. They were "variety shows," precursors of the vaudeville of the late nineteenth and early twentieth centuries. Musicians, singers, dancers, comics, jugglers, sleight of hand artists, and actors doing skits or declaiming poetry took turns doing short routines. By the 1850s, the growing railroad network made it possible for traveling troupes of performers to turn a profit doing "one-night stands" in very small towns, sleeping in cheap hotels and rushing to catch a morning train that took them the next night to their next booking thirty or fifty miles down the line. Admission was cheap; it was "low-brow" entertainment calculated to appeal to the largest possible audience. The comedy was broad and physical, and the songs and skits were sentimental.

In Louisville, Kentucky in 1830, a traveling performer, Thomas D. "Daddy" Rice, saw an African American in rags dancing on the street for the pennies of passers-by. Rice copied the man's dance on stage, and blackening his face (probably with soot from an oil lamp or burned cork), he called his act "Jumpin' Jim Crow." He was a sensational success and, as always in show business, soon had imitators.

A songwriter, Daniel D. Emmett, and an impresario, Edwin P. Christy, broadened "blackface" entertainment beyond Jumpin' Jim Crow. As the centerpiece of their variety shows, they created what became the standardized **minstrel show.** The minstrels (a medieval word meaning, originally, traveling musicians) sat in a line of chairs across the stage. In the center was the master of ceremonies, "Mr. Interlocutor," a white man who spoke in a stilted, often "British" accent. Most of the rest of the cast were white too, but in blackface. (There were some successful African-American minstrels who also "blacked up"!) Most were the usual singers and dancers and so on, who did their routines when called upon by Mr. Interlocutor.

What made the minstrels distinctive were the two "end men" at either side of the cast: "Brother Tambo" (he played a tambourine) and "Brother Bones," whose instrument was "the bones," two hog's ribs which, in fact, slaves used for rhythm in their music. Brother Tambo was a dim-witted

Most American whites subscribed to neither image. A majority of northerners were indifferent to slavery as it affected slaves. Abolitionists were a minority, and the militant ones were not popular. A majority of southern whites knew the workings of the institution too well to think of the slaves' lives as easygoing and their masters as preoccupied dawn to dusk with the well-being of "their people."

In the contest for the minds of ordinary northerners, curiously, the abolitionists' chief rivals were not positive-good southerners like Thomas Roderick Dew and George Fitzhugh, whose books few people read, but a popular stage

Slavery Real and Imagined 1840–1860

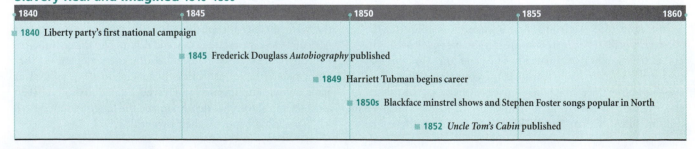

1840	1845	1850	1855	1860

■ **1840** Liberty party's first national campaign

■ **1845** Frederick Douglass *Autobiography* published

■ **1849** Harriett Tubman begins career

■ **1850s** Blackface minstrel shows and Stephen Foster songs popular in North

■ **1852** *Uncle Tom's Cabin* published

plantation slave sometimes called "Jim Crow." The other was a black city slicker, dandy, and confidence man sometimes called Zip Coon. Between songs and dances, they insulted one another and Mr. Interlocutor with broad comedy.

The makeup and dialect were grotesque stereotypes, but the minstrel show was not vicious. The end men were good-natured, even lovable. The city slicker's schemes to bilk Mr. Tambo were usually foiled by his own bumbling, sometimes by Mr. Tambo's previously disguised native shrewdness. If the blackface characters were not threatening, however, they were lazy and childlike. They affirmed white convictions about African Americans. Minstrel show slaves enjoyed life on "the old plantation," the setting of the shows. They knew no better; they were incapable of knowing better; there was no injustice in the fact that African Americans were slaves.

Neither Emmett nor Christy was interested in making proslavery propaganda. Both were northerners; in fact, Emmett's father was a prominent abolitionist. They and their many imitators were interested in making money in show business, which minstrel shows did. Christy's Minstrels packed a large New York theater for 2,500 performances. But the minstrels helped calm anxieties about slavery among ordinary white people that the abolitionists struggled to arouse.

STEPHEN FOSTER

Stephen Collins Foster, who eclipsed Daniel Emmett as a writer of "Ethiopian songs" for minstrel shows, was the first great American composer of popular music and, possibly, still the greatest of all. His first hit, a nonsense song, "Oh! Susannah," published in 1848, became the anthem of the "forty-niners," the men who rushed to California the next year to mine for gold. (Originally it was a song sung by a black man to his black lover, written for the minstrel shows.)

Although Foster was written off in the late twentieth century as a racist, few of his lyrics were condescending to African Americans. He publicly regretted writing one early song that he later found patronizing, and he deleted a dubious verse from "Oh! Susannah." Foster's intention was to humanize the characters of his songs and to dignify relations among African Americans and between whites and blacks, including master and slave.

"Massa's in de Cold, Cold Ground" and "Old Black Joe" (1860), which was not written in dialect, have been attacked because they depict slaves devoted to "Ol' Massa," but there is no hint of an apology for slavery in them; the songs gush with sentimentality, but the warmth of a human relationship was Foster's theme. "Nelly Was a Lady" (1849) told of the love between slave husband and slave wife, an emotion tacitly denied by apologists for slavery. (This was a theme Hollywood filmmakers still suppressed a century later.)

Indeed, Foster may have been an abolitionist. If so, he was not an activist because a successful writer for minstrel shows could not afford to be. However, his best friend was one of Pittsburgh's most prominent antislavery advocates. In "Old Folks at Home" (1851), in which a slave far from "de old plantation" longs for familiar surroundings, there is an implication that the singer is a runaway. "Ring, Ring de Banjo," written the same year, is explicitly about a slave fleeing his master.

When Foster realized that his songs were being used to justify the magnolia blossom and simple-minded "darky" version of slavery, he instructed singers not to mock black people or their sentiments. He stopped writing in dialect and told Edwin P. Christy that he detested the "trashy and really offensive words" of other writers' minstrel show songs. He refused to call his verses "Ethiopian songs," insisting they be called "plantation songs" and, later, "American melodies."

For all his efforts, Foster, who died before he was forty, was remembered as an apologist for slavery, one of the creators of the sympathetic image of slavery that culminated in popular culture in Margaret Mitchell's novel of 1936, *Gone with the Wind,* and Hollywood's classic film based on the book.

THE ABOLITIONISTS

Abolitionists saw a different slavery. To zealous black and white lecturers, journalists, and preachers who crisscrossed the northern states, the slave's world was a hell of blacksnake whips; brutal slave catchers and bloodhounds; children torn from their mothers' breasts to be sold; and squalor, disease, and near starvation at the hands of callous, arrogant masters.

William Lloyd Garrison was the nation's best-known abolitionist because his fierce language infuriated southerners. Proslavery propagandists dependably named him when they claimed that abolitionists were tearing the country apart. Their relentless attacks on Garrison may, more than any other factor, account for the wide circulation of his *Liberator,* because many other prominent abolitionists disapproved of the extremities of his rhetoric. One who did not was Wendell Phillips, who, like Garrison, said "my curse be on the Constitution" because it sanctioned slavery. A well-to-do Boston

Garrison on the Constitution

William Lloyd Garrison broke few if any laws unrelated to slavery. But his view of the Constitution was less than patriotic. He called it "a covenant with death and an agreement with hell" because, however evasively, it sanctioned slavery.

"A sacred compact, forsooth! We pronounce it the most heaven-daring arrangement ever made for the continuance and protection of a system of the most atrocious villainy ever exhibited on earth." Garrison once burned a copy of the Constitution during an antislavery speech.

It was because of Garrison's insistence on distancing himself from anything that smacked of evil that many earnest and active abolitionists who wanted to convert others, including southerners, to antislavery distanced themselves from him.

Anti-Slavery Almanac.

Old Sturbridge Village, photo by Henry E. Peach

25

1840.

"OUR PECULIAR DOMESTIC INSTITUTIONS."

There was nothing romantic about the South the abolitionists depicted: Slavery produced a society of torturers, brawlers, murderers, lynch mobs, drunken gamblers, duelists, and men who whipped children. It was hardly more realistic than the South of the minstrels. There was no possibility of discussion between subscribers to the two visions.

lawyer, Phillips refused to allow his family to use sugar or wear cotton clothing because they were produced by slaves.

WELD AND HIS CONVERTS

Like Garrison, Theodore Dwight Weld was an evangelical. Unlike Garrison, he tried not to antagonize southerners, emphasizing Christian love rather than righteousness. Weld was probably the best abolitionist orator, "as eloquent as an angel and as powerful as thunder." But because his pamphlets and speeches were not sensational, many people who knew quite well who Garrison was never heard of Weld.

Weld made many important converts to the antislavery cause. He convinced two wealthy New York merchants, Arthur and Lewis Tappan, to devote large chunks of their fortunes to the American Anti-Slavery Society, Kenyon and Oberlin (abolitionist colleges in Ohio), and the **underground railroad,** an informal series of networks that aided runaway slaves in escaping.

James G. Birney, an Alabama planter, freed his slaves at Weld's behest and founded an abolitionist newspaper. Birney advocated working within the political system (which Garrison spurned), and in 1840 and 1844, he was the Liberty party's presidential candidate. (The party was a bust; Birney drew only 2 to 3 percent of the popular vote.) Moderate as he was, Birney was driven out of Alabama and then Kentucky. Just a generation earlier, an abolitionist could sit on the state council of Virginia. By 1840 abolitionists living in slave states feared for their lives.

Not even **Sarah and Angelina Grimké,** daughters of a high-ranking South Carolina family, were immune from mob violence. When Angelina spoke against slavery, the hall in which she spoke was burned to the ground. The Grimkés moved north, where in 1838 Angelina married Theodore Dwight Weld.

BLACK ABOLITIONISTS

The abolitionist movement might have foundered without Garrison, Weld, and the Tappans, but its most dependable supporters were the free blacks of the North. Although generally poor, African Americans contributed a disproportionate part of the money that funded antislavery newspapers and sent antislavery lecturers on their tours.

Several prominent abolitionists were black. Sojourner Truth was the name adopted by Isabella Van Wagenen, a physical giant of a woman born a slave in New York in 1797. Freed in 1827, she worked as a domestic servant, was briefly a Millerite, then burst on the abolitionist scene as one of the movement's most popular orators. Sojourner Truth was illiterate to the end—she died in 1893 at 96—but she transfixed audiences by accompanying her speeches with songs she had herself composed.

The most distinguished black abolitionist was Frederick Douglass. Born a slave in Maryland, he escaped to Massachusetts, educated himself as well as Harvard educated most of its graduates, and in 1845 wrote his autobiography, an indictment of slavery more meaningful than any of

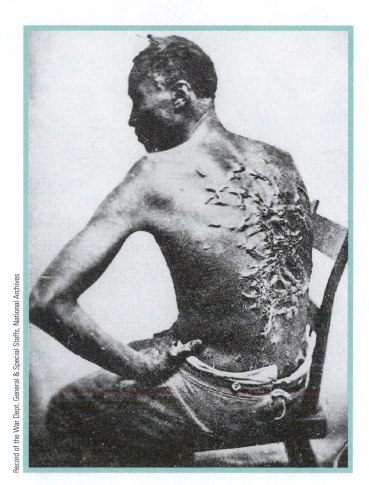

The abolitionists did not have to resort to imagined cruelties to indict slave owners. Slaves who had been viciously whipped like this man sometimes accompanied abolitionist lecturers on their speaking tours.

Garrison's because Douglass knew slavery firsthand. When his book made him famous, his former master set out to re-enslave him, and Douglass fled to England. There he furthered his education and earned enough money from writing and lecturing to pay his master off.

MRS. STOWE AND UNCLE TOM

The most telling antislavery argument was that slavery reduced human beings to the status of livestock. So philosophic a point, however, did not lend itself to an appeal to the emotions. Consequently, both black and white abolitionists focused on the deprivations and cruelties suffered by slaves. Some antislavery lecturers traveled with runaway slaves whose backs had been disfigured by brutal whippings.

The single most effective abolitionist propaganda was *Uncle Tom's Cabin, or Life among the Lowly,* written by Harriet Beecher Stowe, the member of a distinguished family, and published in 1852. Not only did Stowe's book sell an astonishing 300,000 copies within a year of publication (the equivalent of more than 3 million sales today), but it was adapted into plays performed by professional and amateur troupes in small towns and cities alike. So influential was

Mrs. Stowe's tale of Uncle Tom, a submissive and loyal old slave, that when Abraham Lincoln met her during the Civil War, he remarked, "So you are the little woman who wrote the book that made this great war."

The underlying theme of **Uncle Tom's Cabin** was that no matter how well-intentioned an individual slave owner, he cannot help but do wrong by living with an inherently evil institution. Uncle Tom's first owner is the epitome of the kind, paternalistic planter beloved of positive-good theorists and minstrels. He genuinely loves Uncle Tom. Nevertheless, when financial troubles require him to raise money, he sells Tom. Heartbroken, he promises that, as soon as he is able, he will find Tom and buy him back. The point was that the noblest of white men sells the best of black men when the law allows such a transaction.

It was not this insight, however, that made *Uncle Tom's Cabin* so popular. The book owed its success to the lurid cruelties that Tom witnesses and suffers. Mrs. Stowe herself thought that this was the book's contribution. When southerners complained that she had distorted the realities of slave life, she responded in 1853 with *A Key to Uncle Tom's Cabin,* which set out the documentary basis of her allegations in quotations from southern newspapers.

WHAT SLAVERY WAS LIKE

Which vision of slavery was true—Mrs. Stowe's or George Fitzhugh's? Both and neither. Proslavery and antislavery partisans dealt with the peculiar institution as though it were monolithic, the same in Virginia and Texas, on cotton plantation and New Orleans riverfront, on sprawling plantation and cramped frontier homestead, for field hand and "big house" butler. In the law—the classification of human beings as property—it was one thing. The experience of slavery, however, was as diverse as the South.

STRUCTURE OF THE INSTITUTION: WHITE PERSPECTIVE

The census of 1860, the last taken when slavery was legal, reveals that nearly 4 million people lived in bondage, equally divided between males and females. All but a handful lived in the fifteen states south of the Mason–Dixon Line and the Ohio River. West of the Mississippi River, Missouri, Arkansas, Louisiana, and Texas were slave states. Some Indians in Indian Territory owned black slaves.

One white southern family in four owned slaves. Even when those whose living depended directly on the existence of the institution—overseers, slave traders, patrollers—are added in, however, a minority of white southerners had a material stake in slavery.

The great planter class (the only slave owners in the world of the minstrel shows) was quite small. In 1860 only 2,200 people, less than 1 percent of the southern population, owned 100 or more slaves. Only 254 owned 200 slaves or more. Nathaniel Heyward of South Carolina was at the top of the pyramid, owning 2,000 slaves on seventeen plantations.

Fugitive Slaves

The underground railroad was an informal network of "lines" with "stations" and "conductors" who helped African Americans escape from slavery. Stationmasters concealed runaways in their homes from their masters, law officers, and professional slave catchers; they fed the fugitives and sent them on their way to the next station.

Actually, the underground railroad existed before the railroad did. During the 1790s Isaac Harper, a Quaker who assisted slaves in winning their freedom in Philadelphia courts, decided that, to win in one case, he had to break the law. He concealed a slave who was being pursued by his legal owner from Maryland, then took him by night to a farmer outside the city who gave him a job.

This was a violation of the **Fugitive Slave Act** of 1793, which enabled masters to repossess slaves who had escaped to states where slavery had been abolished. Harris and other Quakers, who were law-abiding in other matters, believed they had a moral duty to help African Americans escape from slavery, law or no law. "We might as well look for a needle in a haystack as for a nigger among Quakers," a frustrated slave owner complained. Another said, "There is no use in trying to capture a runaway slave in Philadelphia."

In 1820 the Pennsylvania assembly came close to nullifying the federal fugitive law. Only a constable with a warrant could legally take custody of an alleged runaway. Anyone else who did so (the owner or a hired slave catcher) could be fined $2,000 and imprisoned for up to twenty-one years. In court, an owner's claim that he owned a certain person was not admitted into evidence. He had to bring someone else to court to swear he owned the slave in order to prove his claim. This was so expensive a procedure that many owners of runaway slaves just gave up.

Others, however, did not. So to give runaways a reasonable chance to stay free, antislavery Pennsylvanians established a network of houses across the state and in New Jersey—about twenty miles apart—at which runaways were welcome to hide and rest during the day while, at night, they made their way to the next station and north to New York or New England. Similar "lines" were developed in Ohio and Indiana for slaves who managed to get across the Ohio River, the boundary between slave states and free states.

There was an underground railroad in Kentucky, Virginia, and Maryland, too. Some slaves helped others get to a free state. A few southern whites helped too, although usually, Quaker stationmaster Levi Coffin said, in the South "it was done for money."

A white man got Jarm Logue started on his escape by selling him food and a revolver and giving him some interesting advice. As long as he was in a slave state, the man told Logue, "If you go dodging and shying through the country, you will be suspected." Logue, he said, should move about boldly and confidently, as if he were a free black. He should stop only at the "big houses" to ask for food, as a man who was free would do. Alfred T. Jones also traveled through Kentucky openly. He used a pass from his owner that he had forged. Looking back on his escape years later, Jones remembered, "I could hardly put two syllables together, but in fact, one half the white men there were not much better." His phony pass got him to Ohio, where he made contact with the underground railroad.

Southern congressmen tried repeatedly to strengthen federal laws providing for the return of slaves who escaped to free states. By the 1840s, between 1,000 and 1,500 were making it to the North each year. The Fugitive Slave Act of 1850 bypassed antislavery state judges in the North by

---

A more typical slave owner was Jacob Eaton of North Carolina. On his 160-acre farm he worked side by side with the slave family he owned. Eaton's yeoman class—small independent farmers who owned up to nine slaves—was the backbone of both the South and the slavery system. About 74 percent of slave owners fell into the yeoman category. Another 16 percent of slave owners owned between ten and twenty people. Just 10 percent of slave owners owned more than twenty slaves.

STRUCTURE OF THE INSTITUTION: BLACK PERSPECTIVE

If the big plantation was rare from a white perspective, life in the shadow of the big house was more common in African-American lives. By 1860 more than half the South's slaves

lived on what we would think of as a plantation rather than a farm. Half a million, one in eight, belonged to members of the great planter class.

There were black slave owners. The census of 1830 revealed 3,775 free African Americans in possession of 12,760 slaves. A few, most of them in Louisiana, were "great planters," although not, one may be sure, invited to balls and dinners. Andrew Durnford of New Orleans owned seventy-seven slaves. When questioned, Durnford said that owning slaves was self-interest. It was the only way to wealth in the South. Although he contributed to the American Colonization Society, Durnford freed only four slaves during his lifetime, just one in his will.

More typical of black slave owners was Dilsey Pope, a free black woman in Georgia, who owned her husband. Most southern states had laws requiring slave owners who freed

creating special federal commissioners to assist and rule on the claims of slave owners and professional slave catchers. Anyone who helped a fugitive slave "directly or indirectly" was fined and jailed. The commissioners were empowered to "compel" bystanders to assist them in capturing a fugitive. The law jeopardized the freedom even of African Americans who had lived in a free state for years. One of the first persons arrested under the 1850 act—and returned to slavery!—was a man who had lived free in Indiana for nineteen years.

The underground railroad did not shut down after 1850; it lengthened its "track." It was now necessary to spirit runaway slaves out of the United States into Canada. During the first three months the law was in effect, 3,000 African Americans crossed the border. Between 1848 and 1853, the black population of Upper Canada (Ontario) increased from 20,000 to 35,000.

Eighty percent of the blacks in Canada were from Virginia, Maryland, and Kentucky. Walking to a station in a free state from the deep South was not a realistic possibility, although at least one slave from Georgia, Charles Ball, actually did this. Ball planned carefully and saved money to buy food. He "followed the North Star" by night, although on several cloudy nights Ball discovered he had walked in circles. Once the presence of slave catchers so frightened him that he hid in the woods for eleven days. It took him nine months to reach the Pennsylvania line.

Other slaves from the deep South escaped by going to seaports like Mobile and Savannah, where they located a sailor from a vessel bound for the North who, for a price, would hide them aboard. But not many: some southern ports did not allow free black seamen ashore in order to prevent such arrangements. Suspect ships were thoroughly searched before they cast off. The penalties in southern states for helping a slave to escape were severe: ten years in prison in Louisiana, hanging in North Carolina. No one was hanged for the offense, but Florida branded SS for "slave stealer" on a convicted white sailor's cheek.

Men outnumbered women and children on the underground railroad, and for good reason. The risk of capture (and severe punishment) was high. Josiah Henson had to threaten his wife that he would go without her to persuade her (at the last minute) to accompany him. "We should die in the wilderness," she told him, "we should be hunted down with bloodhounds, we should be brought back and whipped to death." In truth, the Hensons had a harrowing journey. In 1830, when they made their flight, central Ohio was still virtual wilderness. Only friendly Indians saved them from starvation. Sandusky, on Lake Erie, was crawling with professional slave catchers, who collected fees of more than $100 for each slave they caught that far north.

The Hensons got lucky. The captain of a boat headed for Buffalo, on the Canadian border, agreed to take the family along even though this meant, after leaving port by day, returning to shore after dark to escape the notice of the slave catchers. In Buffalo, the captain paid the Hensons' fare on a ferry that crossed the Niagara River to Ontario. In words that may be disturbing today but were not to Josiah Henson when he was boarding a ferryboat to Canada in 1830, the captain told him, "Clap your wings and crow like a rooster; you're a free nigger as sure as the devil."

How many slaves escaped to freedom on the underground railroad or by their own devices? No one really knows; estimates range between 70,000 and 100,000. Between one-fourth and one-third went all the way to Canada even before 1850, although, after emancipation in 1865, many returned to the United States.

their slaves to send them to a free state. Free black women and men who bought their spouses out of slavery were able to keep their families together only by owning them as slaves. It may be that this was the case in many, even most, instances of blacks owning slaves. Dilsey Pope's story was unusual— bizarre actually—in that she and her husband had a vicious quarrel and Mrs. Pope sold him to a white neighbor. When the couple reconciled, as couples do, the new owner refused to sell Mr. Pope back to his wife. The marriage had no standing in Georgia law because one party to it was a slave. The Popes were without legal recourse.

FIRST LIGHT TO SUNDOWN

A few blacks enjoyed the advantages of living as domestic servants: better food, clothing, and beds. Cooks, maids, butlers, valets, and footmen made life more pleasant for the great planters who could afford them, but they did not make money for their masters. "House slaves" were few. The vast majority of slaves were field hands who raised a cash crop by means of heavy labor from first light to sundown almost year-round. For a slave owner to justify investing capital in a labor force rather than hiring free laborers, it was necessary to keep the property hopping.

Cotton was by far the most important southern product (and also the most important American product). During the 1850s, an average annual crop of 4 million bales brought more than $190 million into the American economy from abroad. Cotton represented two-thirds of the nation's total exports and (in 1850) employed fully 1.8 million slaves out of 3.2 million. In 1860 the twelve richest counties in the United States were cotton counties. Other cash crops

Washington the Slave Owner

George Washington owned 300 slaves. His record as a master was mixed. On the one hand, according to a visitor from Poland, the slaves' houses at Washington's River Farm were "more miserable than the most miserable cottages of our peasants." (Washington himself was embarrassed by living conditions at River Farm, one of his plantations.) And he had several of a slave's teeth pulled to make dentures for himself.

On the other hand, Washington respected his slaves' family and marriage relationships. He temporarily separated husbands and wives, and some of his slaves were married to the slaves of other planters or to free blacks. Washington meticulously recorded who was tied to whom, and he refused to sell slaves "because they could not be disposed of in families . . . and to disperse the families I have an aversion."

Washington's plantations were within four miles of one another, so "nightwalking" (conjugal visits) was an annoyance about which he complained but knew better than to try to prohibit. Washington provided that his slaves be freed only after his wife's death because they had intermarried with Martha Washington's "dower Negroes" and it "would excite the most painful sensations" if they were to be separated.

dependent on slave labor were tobacco (350,000 slaves), sugar (150,000), rice (125,000), and hemp (60,000), from which rope and sacking for cotton bales were made.

Southern farmers and planters strived to be self-sufficient. Therefore, slaves raised corn, vegetables, and hogs for food, and hay for fodder, as well as the cash crop. There was plenty of work to be done on a farm or plantation year-round. Thomas Jefferson heated Monticello with ten cords of wood

a month in winter—a lot of bucking logs. The calendar of a cotton plantation was packed with jobs, major and odd, except for a short period around Christmas, to which the slaves looked forward as "laying-by time."

Because slaves were expensive—by the 1850s a prime field hand (a healthy male in his twenties or early thirties) cost $2,000—planters preferred to hire free blacks or Irish immigrants for unhealthful and dangerous jobs. Few risked their

© UPI-Bettmann/Corbis

The daily life a majority of slaves experienced: plowing for, planting, chopping, and (shown here) picking cotton. "Chopping cotton" (hoeing the weeds) was hard work, but picking was frantic. The cotton had to be out of the fields and under cover before autumn rains. On all but the largest plantations, every slave was sent to the fields, including house servants and children able to walk.

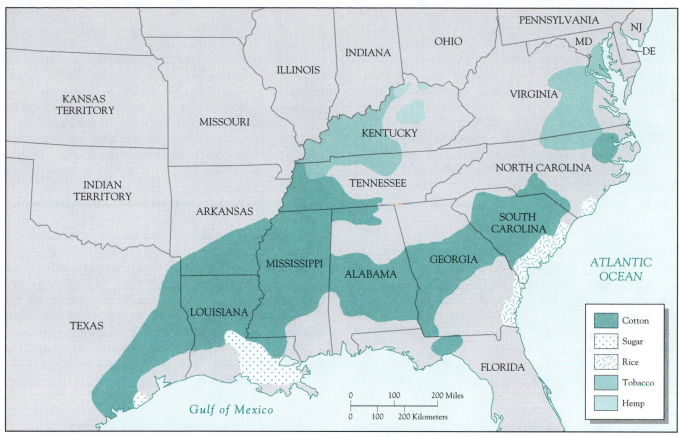

MAP 19:1 Major Southern Crops, 1860

Cotton was king. Almost two-thirds of African-American slaves raised cotton or at least lived on cotton plantations. Growing and processing sugarcane in Louisiana and rice, mostly in South Carolina, was even harder or, at least, more unhealthful than growing cotton. Tobacco was still the chief cash crop in the upper South, and hemp (for making rope and sacking) was a slave-grown crop in Kentucky. Slaves everywhere raised much of the corn that they ate.

costly human property on draining swamps or working at the bottom of chutes down which 600-pound bales of cotton came hurtling at high speeds. It was a lot cheaper to give the widow of a dead employee a $5 gold piece.

THE RHYTHMS OF LABOR

By the 1850s, a slave produced from $80 to $120 in wealth each year and cost between $30 and $50 to feed, clothe, and shelter. The margin of profit was not large enough to allow

King Cotton

Southern politicians repeatedly lectured northerners that the South supported the national economy. That is, the money that cotton brought in from abroad provided most of the surplus capital that paid for the industrialization of the nation.

They were right. Cotton did industrialize the United States before the Civil War. However, the antislavery movement had another way of looking at these economics. Who, they asked, raised, picked, and ginned the precious cotton? Slaves did.

the small-scale slave owner to live without working in the fields along with his slaves.

Planters who owned ten to twenty slaves were freed of menial tasks. However, because few slaves worked any harder than they were forced to do (their share of the fruits of their labor was fixed), they had to be supervised constantly: bribed, cajoled, threatened, or whipped. If a man owned more than twenty slaves, he could afford to hire an overseer or put a **slave driver** (himself a slave) in charge. On large plantations, masters had little contact with their field hands, which was itself a balm for the conscience.

Slaves on large plantations worked according to the task system or the gang system. Under the task system, a specific job was assigned to each slave each day. When it was done, the slave's time was his or her own. For some planters this was the most efficient form of organization because, when provided with an incentive, however meager, the slaves worked harder. Other planters complained that the task system resulted in slipshod work as the slaves rushed to get to their own chores or recreation.

Under the gang system, slaves worked from sunrise to sundown in groups under a white overseer or black driver.

The Health of Slaves

In an age when nothing was known of scientific nutrition, the slaves' diet was comparable to that of poor southern whites and free blacks, and likely better on plantations where slaves were permitted to keep gardens. The life expectancy of slaves was about the same as that of free blacks and poor whites in the South. Statistical surveys done about 1860 showed southern slaves averaging three inches more in height than the west Africans from whom they were descended. They were two inches taller than Trinidadians, who had been free since 1830, and an inch taller than British marines.

Who knows how frequently they felt the sting of the black-snake? The lash was always in evidence, however, in black hand as well as white. Frederick Douglass remarked that "everybody in the South wants the privilege of whipping someone else."

SLAVE TRADERS

Slaves were defined in law as chattel property: personal possessions legally much the same as cattle, hogs, a necklace, or a share of stock. They could be bought, sold, bartered, willed, or given away. The commerce in slaves was brisk and profitable.

Even defenders of slavery admitted that the slave trade was ugly. The slave auction was a livestock auction often accompanied by coarse sexual joking. Prospective buyers crowded around the auction block, determining the age of the slaves for sale by examining their teeth, as they would vet a horse. Slaves were made to run to test their wind. Buyers wiped their bodies with rags to determine if the auctioneer had dyed gray hair black or rubbed oil into aged dry skin. If adolescent girls were for sale, sexual innuendos often floated around the crowd. Foreigners, northerners, and many southerners were simultaneously disgusted and fascinated by slave auctions, much as American tourists in Mexico today react to bullfights.

Masters aspiring to be patriarchs disapproved of the slave trade, describing traders as base, crude, unworthy men. Nevertheless, as Harriet Beecher Stowe and others pointed out, without the slave trade there could be no slavery. If some humans were to be property, owners had to be free to buy and sell them. Where there is trade, there must be brokers.

The general flow of the commerce was "down the river"—the Mississippi—from the declining tobacco states to the cotton states of the deep South. Professional slave traders

Missouri Historical Society

■ *A slave auction in St. Louis. There is much more decorum in this depiction than there is in the accounts of northerners and foreigners who witnessed auctions. If some buyers were, no doubt, as well dressed as the gentlemen here, not everyone in attendance was.*

purchased blacks in Virginia, Maryland, and Kentucky and marched them, like their African ancestors, in coffles to Memphis or New Orleans, where as many as 200 companies were in the business.

LIFE IN THE QUARTERS

The slave codes of most southern states provided that slaves had no civil rights. They could not own property under the law; therefore, they could not legally buy or sell anything. They could not make contracts. They could not marry legally. (How, if they could, was a planter to sell a woman without her husband?) They could not testify in court against any white person (nor could free blacks in southern states). They could not leave the plantation without written permission.

It was a crime for a slave to strike a white person under any circumstances, even to defend his life. Slaves could not carry firearms. They could not congregate in more than small groups except at religious services under white supervision. They could not be abroad at night. And in most southern states, it was a crime for a white or another black to teach a slave to read.

The slaves' legal rights were the right to life and, under most slave codes, the right to a minimum standard of food, clothing, and shelter.

HUMANS WITHOUT HUMAN RIGHTS

The actual experience of slave life often deviated from the letter of the slave codes. For example, a master could not legally kill his slave, but it was not accounted murder when a slave died during "moderate" or "reasonable" correction, words highly debatable in court. Whipping was the most common form of corporal punishment, and fifty lashes—quite enough to kill a man—was not an uncommon punishment. In the end, the slaves' only guarantees against brutality at the hands of their masters were the gospel of paternalism, social expectations of the master by his peers, religious scruples, and the slaves' cash value.

There are few better guarantees of a man's good behavior than his knowledge that bad behavior will cost him money. But that applies to men who are thinking. Slave owners (and surely their overseers) flew into uncontrolled rages and accidentally killed slaves. Because their property rights in their slaves almost always took precedence in court over the slaves' human rights, owners were rarely punished for such crimes. After an incident of hideous torture in Virginia in 1858, with a slave dying after twenty-four hours of beating and burning, the court punished the sadistic master by imprisoning him. But he did not forfeit ownership of the blacks he owned.

A DIVERSE INSTITUTION

Even if the laws protecting slaves were defective, many slave owners were moved by their religion, their sense of decency, and by their aspiration to be seen as benevolent patriarchs to care generously for their slaves, even in violation of the slave codes.

A family that owned only one or two slaves occasionally developed a relationship much like partnership with them. White owners and black slaves ate the same food, slept in the same cabin, and worked together intimately. However, the slave on a large plantation was likelier to be better off because of the poverty of the struggling small farmer.

After about 1840, large-scale slave owners generally provided adequate rations of corn meal, salt pork, and molasses. It was common to allow slaves to keep their own vegetable plots of several acres and even chickens. Some masters did not keep their own gardens and coops, but purchased vegetables and eggs from their slaves. They concluded, sensibly, that if both master and slave were in the vegetables and chicken businesses, no one could tell from where the slaves' dinners came. For the same reason, few slave owners allowed slaves to raise hogs for their own use. Pork was one of the staples; the planter needed to control its production and distribution.

Some slaves were permitted to buy and sell beyond the boundaries of the plantation and to keep the money they earned. Along the Mississippi, task system slaves working on their own time cut firewood for steamboats. Some sold chickens and eggs in towns, and here and there a slave had a shotgun for hunting. One remarkable slave entrepreneur was Simon Gray, a skilled flatboatman whose owner paid him $8 a month to haul lumber to New Orleans. Gray commanded crews of up to twenty men, including free whites, and kept detailed accounts. He eventually bought his freedom.

A few masters permitted their slaves to save money to purchase their freedom, their spouses', or their children's, but the deal depended on the owner's personal decency. No contract with a slave was enforceable in most southern states. (Kentucky was an exception.)

A well-known example of wide-open violation of a slave code was the model plantation of Joseph Davis, brother of Jefferson Davis, the future president of the Confederate States of America. Ignoring a Mississippi state law forbidding the education of blacks, Joseph Davis maintained a formal school and teacher for the children of the quarters.

It is important to recall, however, that for every master like Joseph Davis, there were a dozen who kept their slaves just sound enough to work and a dozen more who, out of stupidity, ignorance, or malevolence, treated them worse than they treated their mules. The editor of a southern magazine made no comment when a subscriber wrote, "Africans are nothing but brutes, and they will love you better for whipping, whether they deserve it or not."

PROTEST

Whether their master was kindly or cruel, their material circumstances adequate or execrable, the majority of slaves hated their lot in life. While some were sincerely attached to their masters, and while rebellion by more than one slave at a time was rare after Nat Turner, blacks resisted slavery in various ways. When freedom became a realistic possibility during the Civil War, slaves deserted their homes by the thousands to flee to Union lines. A South Carolina planter

Why Br'er Possum Loves Peace

Violent resistance by slaves was unusual because it was suicidal. Elders in the quarters counseled young hotheads to keep their wits and act docile; and unless pushed beyond the breaking point, they did. An Uncle Remus fable shared with whites only after emancipation explains.

Mr. Dog attacks Br'er Coon and Br'er Possum. Br'er Coon fights back and drives Mr. Dog away, but at the price of serious injury. Br'er Possum plays possum, plays dead.

Br'er Coon represents blacks who want to fight back. He berates Br'er Possum for cowardice. "I ain't runnin' wid cowards deze days," sez Br'er Coon.

Br'er Possum replies that just because he did not fight Mr. Dog does not mean that he is a coward: "I wan't no mo' skeer'd dan you is right now . . . but I'm de most ticklish chap w'at you ever laid eyes on, en no sooner did Mr. Dog put his nose down yer 'mong my ribs dan I got ter laffin. . . . I don't mine fightin,' Br'er Coon, no mo' dan you duz . . . but I declar' ter grashus ef I kin stan' ticklin."

Note that it is *Mr.* Dog, not Br'er; the tale is about the races. *Mr.* means a white man; *Br'er,* "Brother," means a fellow black.

wrote candidly after the war, "I believed these people were content, happy, and attached to their masters." That, he concluded sadly, had been "a delusion."

MALINGERING AND THIEVING

He might have been spared his disappointment had he given deeper consideration to white people's stereotypes of slaves. It was commonly held that blacks were inherently lazy and irresponsible. In fact, most free blacks worked quite hard, and the same slaves whose laziness was an aggravation in the cotton fields toiled in their own gardens from dawn to dusk on Sundays, and often by moonlight during the week. The only incentive for a slave to work hard for the master was negative—the threat of punishment. That was often insufficient to cause men and women to ignore the blazing southern sun. When the overseer or driver was over the hill, it was nap time.

Theft was so common on plantations that whites concluded that blacks were congenital thieves. Again, the only incentive not to steal a chicken, a suckling pig, or a berry pie was fear of punishment. If a slave was not caught, he had no reason to believe he had done wrong. One chicken thief who was caught in the act of eating his prize explained this point to his master: If the chicken was master's property and he was master's property, then master had not lost anything because the chicken was in his belly instead of scratching around the yard. It is not known if his meditation saved the philosopher from a whipping.

Daniel Webster's Slave

Daniel Webster, representing a state that abolished slavery before he was born, bought a slave, Paul Jennings, to be his butler in Washington. When he was criticized, Webster freed Jennings, but then again, he did not. Jennings had to sign a contract to work off the price Webster had paid for him.

As far as Jennings was concerned, he was still a slave. In 1848 he joined other slaves to charter a sloop in which they planned to escape north. Jennings changed his mind at the last minute and dropped out of the expedition, to his good fortune. The sloop was becalmed in the Chesapeake, and the passengers were arrested and punished.

RUNNING AWAY

The clearest evidence of slave discontent was the prevalence of runaways. Only blacks who lived in states that bordered the free states—Delaware, Maryland, Kentucky, and Missouri—had a reasonable chance of escaping to permanent freedom. Some "rode" the underground railroad, rushing at night from hiding places in one abolitionist's home, often a black abolitionist's, to another.

Harriet Tubman, who escaped from her master in 1849, returned to the South nineteen times to lead other blacks to freedom. The "Black Moses" was a hands-on and very brave and shrewd abolitionist. Tubman went south only in winter, when the nights were longer and few people were outdoors. She herself never went on a plantation; she selected a rendezvous several miles away and sent others to tell the slaves where she was.

Departure was almost always on Saturday night. The runaways, whom Tubman called her "cargo," would be missed Monday morning, but their master would not be alarmed until Monday evening. It was common for slaves, tired or disgusted, to disappear for a few days; the vacation was worth a whipping to many. So Tubman had a two-day head start. She moved only by night, depending on African-American families known to her, free and slave, for food and shelter. (Collaborators also helped by tearing down notices of the runaways.) If Tubman had to enter a town for some reason, she approached from the north and left in a southerly direction. She was in appearance and manners "a very respectable Negro, not at all a poor fugitive."

In a dangerous business (if caught she faced serious penalties) Tubman was no sunshine and sugar social worker. She refused to accept "cargo" she judged weak: "If he was weak enough to give out, he'd be weak enough to betray us all." She told her runaways she would shoot anyone who gave up and probably would have done so. On one occasion, to get a complainer moving, she frightened him so with her threats he moved.

LET MY PEOPLE GO

The culture of the quarters will never be fully understood because the slaves left few written records. However, some reliable conjectures can be ventured based on what is known of African-American religion and folklore.

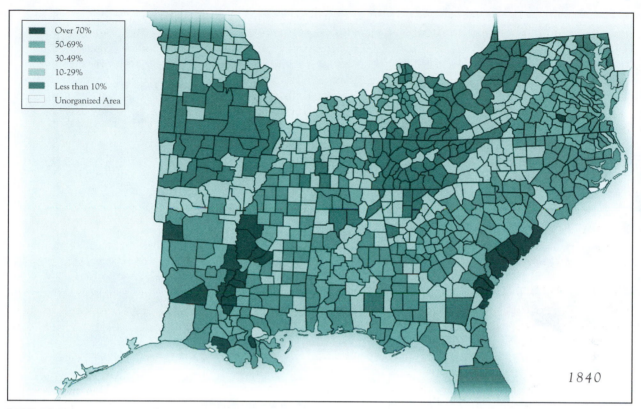

MAP 19:2

Slaves were most numerous in the cotton belt, especially along the Mississippi River and in the South Carolina, where, in many counties, they out numbered whites. The oldest parts of Virginia were also heavily black in population. Slaves were fewest in the Appalachian mountains and foothills, and in Missouri.

By the 1850s most slaves had embraced an evangelical brand of Protestant Christianity, most commonly Baptist or Methodist in temper. Their religious services centered on animated sermons by unlettered but charismatic preachers, along with exuberant rhythmic singing of hymns borrowed from the white churches and also what became known as Negro spirituals.

In both sermons and spirituals, the slaves explicitly identified with the ancient Hebrews. While in bondage in Babylon and Egypt, the Hebrews had been, nevertheless, in their simplicity and misery, God's chosen people. The protest—for God delivered the Hebrews from their captivity—was too obvious to be lost on whites. But so long as they were convinced—and the slaves obliged them—that blacks associated freedom with the afterlife, "crossing over Jordan," slave religion was not stifled.

"BRED EN BAWN IN A BRIER PATCH"

Another thinly masked form of protest were the folktales for which black storytellers became famous, particularly the Br'er Rabbit stories that were collected after the Civil War as *Uncle Remus: His Songs and Sayings*. In these yarns, elements of which have been traced back to west African folklore, the rabbit, the weakest of animals and unable to defend himself by force, survives and flourishes through wit and complex deceit.

In the most famous of the Uncle Remus stories, "How Mr. Rabbit Was Too Sharp for Mr. Fox," Br'er Fox has the rabbit in his hands and is debating with himself whether to barbecue him, hang him, drown him, or skin him. Br'er Rabbit assures the fox that he will be delighted with any of these fates just so long as the fox does not fling him into a nearby brier patch, which he fears more than anything. Of course, that is exactly what Br'er Fox does, whence Br'er Rabbit is home free. "Bred en bawn in a brier patch, Br'er Fox," Br'er Rabbit shouts back tauntingly, "bred en bawn in a brier patch." The slaves, unable to taunt their masters so bluntly, satisfied themselves with quiet trickery and coded tales about it.

Freedom Song

When Israel was in Egypt land
Let my people go
Oppressed so hard they could not stand
Let my people go
Go down, Moses,
Way down in Egypt land
Tell old Pharaoh
To let my people go

Sophia Smith Collection, Smith College, Northhampton, Mass.

Harriett Tubman (on the left) with a "cargo" she has led from slavery in Maryland to relative safety in Pennsylvania. To be assured of their freedom after 1850, these fugitives had to make their way to Canada via the underground railroad. Tubman made nineteen trips into the South at great risk to herself. Legally she was still a slave, and the penalties for helping slaves escape were harsh.

It is worth noting that in the Uncle Remus stories, Br'er Rabbit now and then outsmarts himself and suffers for it. As in all social commentary of substance, the slaves were as sensitive to their own foibles as to those of their masters.

THE SLAVE COMMUNITY

Like Br'er Rabbit, slaves presented a different face to whites than to their own people. Individuals played on white beliefs in their inferiority by pretending to be lazy, dimwitted, comical "Sambo," devoted to "Ol' Marse" and patently incapable of taking care of himself. Observant whites noticed that Sambo was quick-witted enough when they surprised him while he was talking to other slaves, or that he literally slaved in his garden and slept only when in the fields of cotton.

Recent historical research indicates that the slave family was more vital than the family among poor whites and African Americans today. Both parents were present in two-thirds of slave families, the same proportion as among European peasants at that time. Perhaps the most striking demonstration of the resilience of African Americans during slavery times is the fact that in 1865, when slavery was abolished, there were ten times as many blacks in the United States as had been imported from Africa and the West Indies between 1619 and 1807. The American slave population was the only slave population in the Western Hemisphere to increase as a result of natural reproduction.

FURTHER READING

General Daniel Feller, *The Jacksonian Promise: America 1815–1840*, 1995; Don E. Fehrenbacher, *The Slave-Holding Republic: An Account of the United States Government's Relations to Slavery*, 2001; D. W. Meinig, *The Shaping of America: A Geographical Perspective on 500 Years of American History*, vol. 2, *Continental America, 1800–1867*, 1993; Peter J. Parish, *Slavery: History and Historians*, 1989; Gavin Wright, *The Political Economy of the Cotton South*, 1998.

Abolitionists Ronald Abzug, *Passionate Liberator: Theodore Dwight Weld and the Dilemma of Reform*, 1980; Thomas Bender, *The Anti-Slavery Debate*, 1992; Anna Bontemps, *Free at Last: The Life of Frederick Douglass*, 1971; M. L. Dillon, *The Abolitionists: The Growth of a Dissenting Minority*, 1974; Julie Ray Jeffery, *The Great Silent Army of Abolitionism: Ordinary Women in the Antislavery Movement*, 1998; Aileen S. Kraditor, *Means and Ends in American Abolitionism: Garrison and His Critics on Strategy and Tactics, 1834–50*, 1967; Gerda Lerner, *The Grimké Sisters from South Carolina: Rebels against Slavery*, 1967; Robert J. Loewenburg, *Freedom's Despots: The Critique of Abolitionism*, 1986; Waldo C. Martin, *The Mind of Frederick Douglass*, 1984; Henry Mayer, *All on*

Fire: William Lloyd Garrison and the Abolition of Slavery, 1998; William S. McFeely, *Frederick Douglass,* 1990; Nell Irvin Painter, *Sojourner Truth: A Life, a Symbol,* 1996; Benjamin Quarles, *Black Abolitionists,* 1969; J. B. Stewart, *Holy Warriors: The Abolitionists and American Slavery,* 1976; Shirley Yee, *Black Women Abolitionists: A Study in Activism, 1828–1860,* 1992.

Fugitives Fergus M. Bordewich, *Bound for Canaan: The Underground Railroad and the War for the Soul of America,* 2005; Kate Clifford Larson, *Bound for the Promised Land: Harriett Tubman, Picture of an American Hero,* 2003; Albert J. Van Frank, *The Trials of Anthony Burns: Freedom and Slavery in Emerson's Boston,* 1996.

Slave Culture Mia Bay, *The White Image in the Black Mind: African-American Ideas about White People, 1838–1925,* 2000; Ira Berlkin, *Many Thousands Gone: The First Two Centuries of Slavery in North America,* 1998; John Blassingame, *The Slave Community,*

1972, and *Slave Testimony,* 1977; A. Roger Ekirch, *At Day's Close: Night in Times Past,* 2005; Elizabeth Fox-Genovese, *Within the Plantation Household: Black and White Women of the Old South,* 1988; George M. Frederickson, *The Black Image in the White Mind,* 1971; Eugene Genovese, *Roll Jordan Roll,* 1975; Herbert G. Gutman, *The Black Family in Slavery and Freedom, 1750–1925,* 1976; Vincent Harding, *There Is a River: The Black Struggle for Freedom in America,* 1981; Walter Johnson, *Soul by Soul: Life Inside the Ante-Bellum Slave Market,* 1974; Lawrence W. Levine, *Black Culture and Black Consciousness: Afro-American Folk Thought from Slavery to Freedom,* 1977; Albert J. Raboteau, *Slave Religion: The "Invisible Institution" in the Ante-Bellum South,* 1978; Brenda Stevenson, *Life in Black and White: Family and Community in the Slave South,* 1996; Sterling Stuckey, *Slave Culture: Nationalist Theory and the Foundation of Black America,* 1987; Deborah Gray White, *Ar'n't I a Woman?: Female Slaves in the Plantation South,* 1985.

KEY TERMS

The following terms are covered in this chapter and can also be found in the list of Key Terms at the back of the book.

Fugitive Slave Act	**"peculiar institution"**	**slave driver**	***Uncle Tom's Cabin***
minstrel show	**Sarah and Angelina Grimké**	**Stephen Collins Foster**	**underground railroad**

ONLINE SOURCES GUIDE

Use this listing to find online documents, images, interactive maps, simulations, and other resources related to this chapter:

American History Resource Center
http://history.wadsworth.com/rc/us

Selected Documents
Interviews with former slaves (conducted in the 1930s)

Selected Images
Harriett Beecher Stowe
Scene from *Uncle Tom's Cabin*

William Lloyd Garrison, founder of American antislavery movement
Frederick Douglass
Runaway slave poster

Interactive Time Line (with online readings)
The Peculiar Institution: Slavery as It Was Perceived and as It Was

Discovery

In what ways did Americans oppose slavery prior to the Civil War?

In thinking about this question, begin by breaking it down into the components shown below. A discussion of the significance of each component should appear in your answer.

Culture and Society: For this exercise, read the document excerpt "Peter Osborne Speaks to a Crowd," and study these images. Look at the abolitionist depiction of slave society. In what kinds of activities are the southerners engaging? What does this suggest that the artist thinks about southern society? How are the slaves being used in this image? Compare this with the photograph of the slave's back after repeated whippings. How inflammatory do you think both of these images would be in creating support for the abolitionist movement? What is Osborne's argument concerning Independence Day? How does this compare with the "Declaration of Sentiments" in Chapter 17? To what does Osborne compare the abolitionist movement?

Record of the War Dept. General & Special Staffs, National Archives

Former Slave

Old Sturbridge Village, photo by Henry E. Peach

Abolitionist View of Slave Society

Peter Osborne Speaks to a Crowd Celebrating American Independence, 5 July 1832

Delivered to the people of color in the African Church in the city of New-Haven, Connecticut.

Fellow Citizens—On account of the misfortune of our color, our fourth of July comes on the fifth; but I hope and trust that when the Declaration of Independence is fully executed which declares that all men, without respect to person, were born free and equal, we may then have our fourth of July on the fourth. It is thought by many that this is as impossible to take place, as it is for the leopard to change his spots; but I anticipate that the time is approaching very fast. The signs in the north, the signs in the south, in the east and west, are all favorable to our cause. Why, then, should we forbear contending for the civil rights of free countrymen: What man of rational feeling would slumber in content under the yoke of slavery and oppression, in his own country? Not the most degraded barbarian in the interior of Africa.

If we desire to see our brethren relieved from the tyrannical yoke of slavery and oppression in the south, if we would enjoy the civil rights of free countrymen, it is high time for us to be up and doing. It has been said that we have already done well, but we can do better. What more can we do? Why, we must unite with our brethren in the north, in the south, and in the east and west, and then with the Declaration of Independence in one hand, and the Holy Bible in the other, I think we might courageously give battle to the most powerful enemy to this cause. The Declaration of Independence has declared to man, without speaking of color, that all men are born free and equal. Has it not declared this freedom and equality to us too?

What man would content himself, and say nothing of the rights of man, with two millions of his brethren in bondage? Let us contend for the prize. Let us all unite, and with one accord declare that we will not leave our own country to emigrate to Liberia, nor elsewhere, to be civilized nor christianized. Let us make it known to America that we are not barbarians; that we are not inhuman beings; that this is our native country; that our forefathers have planted trees in America for us, and we intend to stay and eat the fruit. Our forefathers fought, bled and died to achieve the independence of the United States. Why should we forbear contending for the prize? It becomes every colored citizen in the United States to step forward boldly and gallantly defend his rights. What has there been done within a few years, since the union of the colored people? Are not the times more favourable to us now, than they were ten years ago? Are we not gaining ground? Yes—and had we begun this work forty years ago, I do not hesitate to say that there would not have been, at this day, a slave in the United States. Take courage, then, ye African-Americans! Don't give up the conflict, for the glorious prize can be won.

Culture and Society: For this exercise, read the document excerpt from *Uncle Tom's Cabin*. How did the images portrayed in *Uncle Tom's Cabin* inflame both the North and the South? How would this passage in particular upset both northerners and southerners? Do you think it gives an accurate depiction of slavery?

Excerpt from Harriet Beecher Stowe, *Uncle Tom's Cabin*, 1852

. . . Legree now turned to Tom's trunk, which, previous to this, he had been ransacking, and, taking from it a pair of old pantaloons and a dilapidated coat, which Tom had been wont to put on about his stable-work, he said, liberating Tom's hands from the handcuffs, and pointing to a recess in among the boxes,—

"You go there, and put these on."

Tom obeyed, and in a few moments returned.

"Take off your boots," said Mr. Legree.

Tom did so.

"There," said the former, throwing him a pair of course, stout shoes, such as were common among the slaves, "put these on."

In Tom's hurried exchange, he had not forgotten to transfer his cherished Bible to his pocket. It was well he did so; for Mr. Legree, having refitted Tom's handcuffs, proceeded deliberately to investigate the contents of his pockets. He drew out a silk handkerchief, and put it into his own pocket. Several little trifles, which Tom had treasured, chiefly because they had amused Eva, he looked upon with a contemptuous grunt, and tossed them over his shoulder into the river.

Tom's Methodist hymn-book, which in his hurry, he had forgotten, he now held up and turned over.

"Humph! pious, to be sure. So, what's yer name,—you belong to the church, eh?"

"Yes, Mas'r," said Tom, firmly.

"Well, I'll soon have that out of you. I have none o' yer bawling, praying, singing niggers on my place; so remember. Now, mind yourself," he said, with a stamp and a fierce glance of his gray eye, directed at Tom, "I'm your church now! You understand,—you've got to be as I say."

To read extended versions of the documents, visit the companion Web site http://history.wadsworth.com/americanpast8e; click on "Discovery Sources."

CHAPTER 20

From Sea to Shining Sea

American Expansion 1820–1848

Reproduced from the Collections of the Library of Congress

Our manifest destiny is to overspread the continent allotted by Providence for the free development of our yearly multiplying millions.

John Louis O'Sullivan

Poor Mexico, so far from God, so close to the United States.
Porfirio Díaz

Thomas Jefferson's generation believed that the Louisiana Purchase had established the western boundary of the United States for all time. The Rocky Mountains were as formidable a natural boundary as any in the world with (so most people believed) uninhabitable desert between the mountains and California. In the north, the War of 1812 dashed the hopes of the mentally balanced that Canada would one day be American; but in 1817 the British and Americans agreed not to keep warships on the Great Lakes, a first step toward a completely demilitarized border. As long as Florida remained Spanish and a safe sanctuary for hostile Indians, there was a problem to the south. But the Adams–Oñis Treaty of 1819 added Florida to the Union. On every side, Americans were secure.

But they were not necessarily satisfied. The Adams treaty established the Sabine River as the boundary between the United States and Spanish Mexico; but it was a dubious line because the lands across the narrow river were fertile, well-watered, and sparsely populated. By 1821 Mexico had won independence from Spain. The Sabine was now the boundary between the United States of America and the weak new Los Estados Unidos de Mexico. Americans began to cross the Sabine by the thousands.

THE MEXICAN BORDERLANDS

New Spain was the jewel of the Spanish Empire for three centuries. An elite of Spanish-born *gachupines* and Mexican-born but white *criollos* monopolized the best lands, living fat off the labor of the Indians. But they were few. Mexico was home to the greatest of indigenous New World civilizations, an amalgam of Spanish and Indian cultures. Most Mexicans were *mestizos,* a mix of European and Native American blood—a new people.

MEXICO LOOKS NORTH

Just as the American population emigrated to the west, the population of Mexico emigrated north, but more slowly. Spanish and Mexican pioneers and friars planted outposts deep in what is now the American Southwest. The rivers of Texas, especially the Rio Bravo of the north (the Rio Grande), were dotted with presidios (military bases) and missions more numerous than the old French trading posts along the Mississippi. The northernmost was at Santa Fe, about seventy-five miles south of the restive Indian pueblo at Taos.

Beginning in 1769, a Franciscan priest, **Junípero Serra,** established a string of missions in California, the northernmost at Sonoma above San Francisco Bay. His plan, completed after his death, made it possible for a foot traveler along the *camino real* ("royal highway," which is now California Highway 1 and U.S. Route 101) to find shelter every night in a hospitable compound. As in New Mexico, a gracious but simple way of life evolved among the small numbers of *californios* who settled there.

THE SANTA FE TRADE

The Spanish had banned Americans from California and New Mexico, including traders. Violators were arrested and deported. In 1821 independent Mexico opened trade with the United States, and William Becknell, an alert entrepreneur in Independence, Missouri, immediately set off cross-country in a wagon packed with American manufactures: cloth, shoes, tools, and some luxury items. Feeling his way by compass and by dead reckoning across what is now Kansas, he blazed an 800-mile-long trail to Santa Fe. The 7,000 inhabitants of the town were so remote from the Mexican heartland that they paid Becknell handsomely for his goods with furs and gold.

Annually for fourteen years, a convoy of wagons rolled down the **Santa Fe Trail.** A few Missourians, such as Kentucky-born horse handler Christopher "Kit" Carson, settled in New Mexico, happily adapting to the gracious Spanish–Indian culture. Nevertheless, the presence of even a few *sassones* (Saxons) in New Mexico forged a link between the country and the United States that was—no matter what flag flew—more substantial than the link between Santa Fe and Mexico City.

THE GREAT AMERICAN DESERT

Americans believed that the American territory the Santa Fe traders crossed was worthless except as a highway. At about 100° west longitude (central Kansas), the land gradually rises from an elevation of 2,000 feet to, at the base of the Rockies, 5,000 to 7,000 feet. These high plains lie in the rain shadow of the Rockies. Before the winds from the West reach the plains, the moisture in them is scooped out by the great mountains. Save for cottonwoods along the rivers, few trees grew on the plains. The vastness of the landscape unnerved Americans, who were accustomed to dense forests. When they gazed over the windblown buffalo grass, they thought not of farmland but of the ocean. Indeed, the Santa Fe traders called their

Culver Pictures

The "Great American Desert" was no desert. It was almost treeless plains, but it was peerless grazing land. Once settlers broke the tough sod and dug wells to compensate for the sparse summer rainfall, the eastern half of the plains produced grain in abundance.

wagons "prairie schooners." Less imaginative military map-makers labeled the country "the Great American Desert."

It was a mistake to believe that only land that grew trees naturally would support crops. However, it was true enough that the tough sod of the plains was more than a fire-tempered wood or even a cast iron plowshare could turn over. And there was not enough rainfall to nourish grain. Travelers in the region observed that the grass that fattened 10 million bison would fatten cattle too. But it was difficult to imagine how such hypothetical steers might be transported to eastern markets. All agreed that the Indians of the plains were welcome to what they had.

THE TEXANS

The Great Plains extended into Texas, a district of the Mexican state of Coahuila. There cattle could be grazed within driving distance of the Gulf of Mexico and shipped by boat to New Orleans. In 1819 a Connecticut Yankee named Moses Austin was attracted by the possibilities of grazing and the suitability of eastern Texas to cotton cultivation. He proposed to the Mexicans that, in return for land grants, Americans would settle there and provide a counterforce to the Comanche, raiders feared throughout northern Mexico.

Moses Austin died, but in 1821 his son Stephen concluded the negotiations. He was licensed to bring 300 American families to Texas, each to receive 177 acres of farmland and 13,000 acres of grassland. The settlers would abide by Mexican law, adopt the Spanish language, and observe the Roman Catholic religion.

Many of the early settlers were baptized Catholic, including Stephen Austin, and he banned Protestant clergymen from the province. But he did not force American immigrants to become Catholic, and most did not. When, in 1826, a ragtag force from Louisiana seized Nacogdoches, just inside Texas, Austin drove them out. He was a good Mexican citizen.

Nevertheless, with land costing a tenth of the price of similar land in Louisiana (and land grants much larger), Texas was soon overwhelmingly "anglo" in population. By 1834, 15,000 of the 20,000 whites in Texas were from the United States. Texas was more American than Mexican in culture.

Santa Anna's Legacy

Santa Anna's first presidency was ruined by Texans. However, he bore little animosity toward Americans. Between 1841 and 1844, exiled from Mexico, he lived in New York, where he unwittingly helped to inflict an addiction on Americans. Santa Anna chewed chicle, sap from the sapodilla tree. When he hurried back to Mexico in 1844, he left some behind. It fell into the hands of Thomas Adams, who marketed it as an alternative to chewing tobacco, a ubiquitous habit thought filthy in polite society. Adams made a decent living from "chewing gum." Fifty years later, it made William Wrigley rich when he hit on the idea of sweetening and flavoring the chicle, calling it "Juicy Fruit."

The Texans never did bridle the Comanche (they remained free agents until the Civil War), but they prospered and paid their taxes. There was no conflict with Mexican authorities until Mexico abolished slavery in 1829. Slavery had become as vital to the economy of Texas as it was in neighboring Louisiana. There were about 2,000 slaves in the total non-Indian population of about 22,000.

For several years the Texans ignored the prohibition of slavery. Then, in 1833, General Antonio Lopez de Santa Anna seized power. He was a far less accommodating president than his predecessors had been. Santa Anna wanted to put an end to the squabbling that had plagued Mexican politics since independence by promoting a sense of Mexican nationality. He centralized the government and canceled American trading privileges in Santa Fe. Texans feared for the considerable autonomy they had enjoyed and their lucrative economic connections with the United States, to say nothing of their slaves.

A small number of Anglo and Hispanic Texans rebelled, seizing the only military garrison in Texas at San Antonio. At first, like the Americans of 1775, the rebels claimed that they were fighting only for the rights they had traditionally exercised. However, they had far less in common with their mother country than the rebels of 1775 had with Great Britain. Some spoke of independence from the start.

Expansion 1815–1850

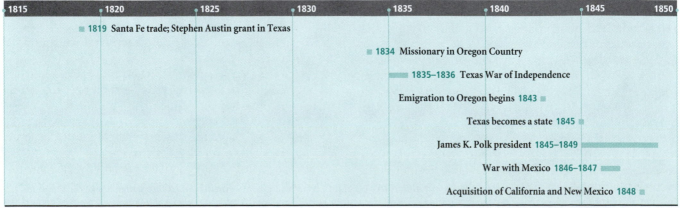

| 1815 | 1820 | 1825 | 1830 | 1835 | 1840 | 1845 | 1850 |

1819 Santa Fe trade; Stephen Austin grant in Texas

1834 Missionary in Oregon Country

1835–1836 Texas War of Independence

Emigration to Oregon begins 1843

Texas becomes a state 1845

James K. Polk president 1845–1849

War with Mexico 1846–1847

Acquisition of California and New Mexico 1848

MAP 20:1 **The United States in the Mexican Borderlands, 1819–1848**
The Santa Fe Trail, a commercial incursion into the Spanish borderlands, and American settlement of eastern Texas were both welcomed by the infant republic of Mexico. It was the Americanization of East Texas that led to conflict and Texas independence.

THE ALAMO AND SAN JACINTO

Like George III, Santa Anna had no intention of negotiating with rebels. He welcomed the uprising in Texas as an opportunity to rally the Mexican people around a national cause. In 1836 he led an army of 6,000 to San Antonio, knowing he could easily overcome the 200 Texans and a few newly arrived Americans who were holed up in an old mission compound called the **Alamo** ("cottonwood tree").

Among the defenders were men well-known in the United States. The garrison commander was William Travis, a prominent Texan who had taken over for James Bowie, inventor of the famous double-edged knife, who was unable to rise from a sickbed. More famous in the United States was

the anti-Jackson Whig politician from Tennessee, David "Davy" Crockett.

Santa Anna could have passed the Alamo by, leaving a small detachment to contain the small garrison. The real threat to Mexico lay farther east, where Sam Houston, an old crony of Andrew Jackson, was frantically trying to raise an army. Houston had big problems. By no means did every Texan support the rebellion. Others were reluctant to confront professional soldiers. By moving quickly, Santa Anna might easily have snuffed out the insurrection.

Instead, he sat in San Antonio for ten days, daily more infuriated that the defenders of the Alamo, whose cause was hopeless, would not surrender. When he finally attacked at

© Bettmann/Corbis

A fanciful depiction of the final moments at the Alamo. Commander Travis is at the left. The heroic figure in fringed buckskin and coonskin cap is Davy Crockett, who, if he ever wore a coon tail on his hat, did not at the Alamo. Some accounts of the battle have Crockett fighting to the end, as in this picture; others say he was shot from a distance by a sniper; yet others have him surrendering only to be executed.

tremendous cost to his army, he ordered all prisoners executed. (The few women in the Alamo were spared.) Two weeks later, at Goliad, Santa Anna massacred 365 Texans who also had surrendered. The atrocities rallied Texans, including many of Mexican culture, to the fight against Santa Anna.

On the banks of the Rio San Jacinto on April 21, Sam Houston's army routed the Mexicans and captured Santa Anna. To secure his release, Santa Anna agreed to the independence of Texas with a southern boundary at the Rio Grande rather than at the Rio Nueces, which had been the boundary of the district of Texas. As soon as he was free, Santa Anna repudiated the agreement and refused to recognize the Republic of Texas. But the demoralized Mexican army was in no condition to mount another campaign, and most Texans discreetly remained north of the Nueces.

THE LONE STAR REPUBLIC

In October 1836, Sam Houston was inaugurated president of a republic patterned on the United States. Texas legalized slavery and dispatched a minister to Washington. Houston hoped that his old friend Andrew Jackson would annex Texas to the United States. In his nationalistic heart, Jackson liked the idea of sewing the "Lone Star" of the Texas republic on the American flag. However, Congress was embroiled in a nasty debate in which the question of slavery was being bandied about. Jackson did not want to complicate matters by proposing the admission of a new slave state. He recognized Texan independence to spare his successor that decision, but only on his last day in office.

President Van Buren opposed the annexation of Texas. He was spared a debate on the question when depression distracted Congress. The Texans, disappointed and worried about a Mexican invasion to reassert Mexican authority, looked to Europe for an ally. They sent out feelers to the empire-minded King Leopold I of Belgium, offering him land in return for a loan and a military presence. The United States warned Leopold off.

The Texans turned to the British, who were unlikely to be intimidated by the United States, and they were happy to oblige—up to a point. That is, the British coveted Texas cotton, and the idea of an independent Texas under British protection as a barrier to further American expansion in the Southwest was appealing. The hang-up was Texan slavery. Parliament had recently abolished slavery in the empire; public opinion was hostile to the institution. No British government could get away with establishing a protectorate over a slaveholding state. So the Texas–British connection remained almost entirely commercial.

THE OREGON COUNTRY

The American government was uneasy about British influence in Texas. There was also a point of conflict between the two nations on the Pacific coast of North America in what was known as the Oregon Country. This land of mild climate, prosperous Indians, sheltered harbors, spruce and fir forests, and rich valley farmlands was not the property of any single nation.

A DISTANT LAND

Spain's (and therefore Mexico's) claim to Oregon was never more than nominal. Spanish and Mexican influence ended just north of San Francisco, and it was shaky there. So after 1819, when the northern boundary of Mexico was set at 42° north latitude (the present California–Oregon line), the claim was itself overreaching.

The Russians had founded a string of fur-trapping stations on the Pacific coast to within 100 miles of San Francisco Bay.

Trappers and Indians

To survive, the mountain men needed the friendship of at least one Indian tribe, a good reason in itself to take an Indian wife. With tribal enmities strong, however, identification with one people meant that others were enemies. In confrontations, the trappers' rifles gave them no edge. The large-bore Hawkens they favored for their stopping power were accurate to a hundred yards, twenty or thirty yards more than an Indian archer's arrow. However, it took half a minute to reload a Hawken. A good bowman could shoot ten arrows in that time.

The Indians most respected were the Blackfeet. So great was the fear of them that when, by 1840, overtrapping had destroyed the beaver population all over the West, the animals remained numerous in Blackfoot country.

However, by the 1820s, Russian and Alaskan Indian trappers had looted the Pacific coves of the sea otters whose furs had brought them there. In 1825, when the British Hudson's Bay Company agreed to provide food to Russia's Alaskan settlements, Fort Ross in California became useless. Russia withdrew its claims to 54° 40' north latitude, the present southern boundary of the state of Alaska.

Thus between 42° and 54° 40' lay the Oregon Country. Both British and American fur trappers wandered it, but they were few. To avoid a conflict, and to warn other nations off, Britain and the United States easily agreed to a **joint occupation.** Neither country gave up its claims to Oregon, but neither needed to devote unavailable resources to defend them. Citizens of both countries had equal rights there.

THE MOUNTAIN MEN

The trappers in the Oregon Country were after beaver. Beaver pelts had been a staple of North American trade since the seventeenth century. By the 1800s, the Rocky Mountains and the Oregon Country were the only regions where the animals had not been trapped to near-extinction.

American and Canadian veterans of the War of 1812, the kind of men whose ties to home had been cut by their military experience, disappeared into the Rockies for eleven months each year. These "mountain men" probably never numbered more than 500 in a given season. About half took Indian

Harvesting the Beaver

Trapping beaver was not a Sierra Club wilderness adventure. It was hard work—and cold work, because the best pelts were taken when beavers were wearing their winter coats. The entrance to a beaver burrow was several feet below the surface of a river or pond. A trap weighing five pounds was anchored near the entryway and baited with the beaver's marking scent. The beaver died by drowning.

After cleaning, the pelt of an adult animal weighed up to two pounds. At the annual rendezvous trappers were paid $3 per pound (more if they took their pay in merchandise); so to earn enough income for a year, a mountain man had to harvest hundreds of animals each year. To move their cargo, they needed pack horses, which were expensive.

Jedediah Smith bought broken-down nags by the dozen in California for $10 each and sold them for $50 to $150 in the mountains to horseless trappers who had no choice but to pay. Individuals were often horseless: Indians stole them and the trappers grossly abused them, loading horses undernourished on iffy mountain pasture with 200 pounds of furs or supplies. They died off as quickly as the beavers.

Zorro and the Californios   *How They Lived*

Alta California—Upper California—was thinly populated when the United States seized it, but it was not empty. Indians were numerous in California's mild climate. Several thousand Mexicans had followed the mission fathers in the late eighteenth and early nineteenth centuries. Some of these *californios,* as they called themselves, clustered around small market towns and *presidios,* military installations: San Diego, Los Angeles, Monterey, Yerba Buena (San Francisco), and Sonoma. Others were ranchers living on vast government land grants. A few Americans had taken out Mexican grants.

The *californios* were rich in acres but not money or luxuries. The only commodities California produced for the international market were hides and tallow, the fat of cattle and sheep cooked down for use in soap and candle manufacture. Even the richest *californios* lived in adobe homes of one or two stories. Furniture, iron products, and most other manufactures were made by Indian craftsmen. Diet was ample (plenty of beef), but *californio* cuisine was inelegant.

The *californios* at the top of the social pyramid were proud of their independence and self-sufficiency. They were *hidalgos,* they believed, rightful rulers but also the protectors and benefactors of the poor Mexicans and Indians.

The *californio* community was divided down the middle by the American invasion. Some, feeling little commitment to distant Mexico, quickly made peace with the gringos and salvaged at least some of their property and social position. Others resisted and won a few small battles before being overcome.

It was not the American army that turned the *californio* world upside down, but the gold rush of 1849 and 1850. Spanish-speaking ranchers were literally overrun by the tens of thousands of gold seekers. Among those who were ruined was Salomon María Simeón Pico, the son of a soldier who had been granted eleven Spanish leagues (48,829 acres) between the Tuolumne and Stanislaus Rivers. According to legend, Pico not only lost his herds and land, but his wife was raped and died soon thereafter.

It is impossible to separate legend from fact in Pico's subsequent career. It is probable that he became a masked highwayman on the *camino real* between Santa María and Santa Barbara, and he may have cut an ear off each of his mostly gringo victims. (Pico, the story goes, strung his trophies and carried them on his saddle horn like a lariat.) It is less likely that he gave his loot to impoverished *californio* families, but he was a popular hero even during his lifetime. Pico moved about California with impunity for eight years, no doubt aided by the fact that his two brothers were the mayors of San Luis Obispo and San Jose.

Pico's most famous scrape with the law came in November 1851 when he shot the hat off the head of Los Angeles Judge Benjamin Hayes. Although himself wounded, Pico escaped to Baja California, where in 1854 he was arrested by Mexican police and summarily executed.

In the 1920s, as "Zorro" (the Fox, a name Pico never used), he became a popular fictional hero in the United States. In 1919 Johnston McCulley collected the Pico legends, deftly adapted them for an American readership, and published them as *The Curse of Capistrano.* In McCulley's books, Pico was Don Diego Vega and he lived not in California's American era but earlier, when California was firmly Mexican. His enemies were not gringos but corrupt Mexican authorities.

Don Diego was a gracious *hidalgo* by day who, by night, donned a mask not for the purpose of robbery but to fight for justice and something like what would be called "the American Way." So admirable a fellow could not be amputating ears. McCulley's Zorro left his trademark by cutting a "Z" on his victims' cheeks. Even that was too nasty for television. In the 1950s, when Zorro came into American living rooms on the small screen, he contented himself to cut "Z" into the bark of trees, on the sides of buildings, or, bloodlessly, on the clothing of his adversaries. Rather more remarkable, the television Zorro devoted a good deal of his time to protecting decent gringos from venal Mexicans.

---

wives. All but those soon dead learned Indian ways to survive in the most rugged of wilderness.

Late each summer, the trappers brought their furs to prearranged locations on the Platte, Sweetwater, and Big Horn rivers for the "rendezvous," the first of which was held in 1825. For a few weeks, buyers from the British Hudson's Bay Company and John Jacob Astor's American Fur Trading Company, mountain men, and Indians of many tribes traded, drank, enjoyed a riotous orgy, and now and then bit off the ear of an old pal. Of more lasting significance was the knowledge of western geography the mountain men

imparted to company agents and, through them, to the folks back home. Most important was the intelligence that although it would be a long, hard trip, it was possible to cross overland to the Pacific with wagons.

Some mountain men were legends during their lifetimes. Jedediah Smith opened South Pass in Wyoming, the route that would be followed by most overland emigrants. Smith was almost as famous because, unlike other trappers, he was pious and abstemious; he neither drank alcohol nor slept with Indian women. Jim Beckwourth, the son of a slave woman and her white owner, discovered the lowest (and therefore

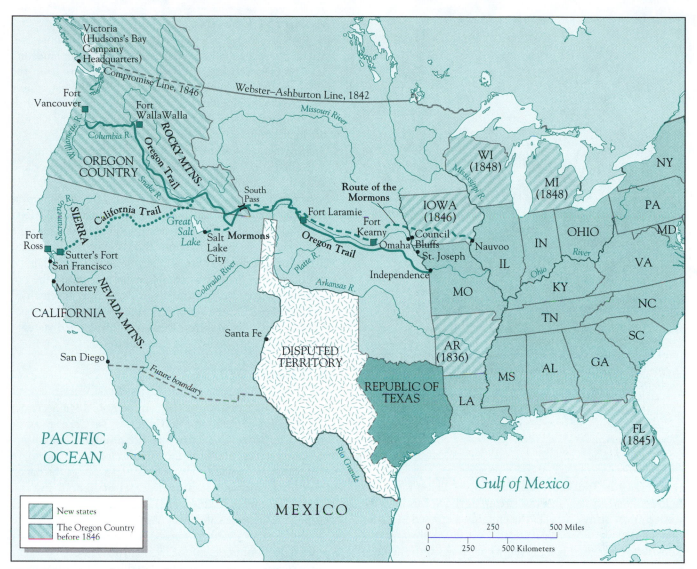

MAP 20:2 Americans in the West, 1819–1848
Britain and the United States divided the Oregon Country in 1846 along the 49th parallel. Present-day California and northern Utah were still Mexican territories when Americans began to settle there in numbers.

the least snowy) pass through the Sierra Nevada. His cronies valued him for his toughness and bravery, but even in a world in which the tall tale was king, it was said that one was wise not to believe a word Beckwourth said. There was little race consciousness in the mountains. Polette Labrass was an African American who traveled with Jedediah Smith. Many of the French Canadian trappers were *metís,* or "half-breeds."

Jim Bridger, perhaps the greatest mountain man of them all, was a walking, talking atlas; he explored almost every nook of the Rockies. He was the first non-Indian to lay eyes on the Great Salt Lake.

THE OREGON TRAIL

Among the first to make the six-month journey for the purpose of settling in Oregon were missionaries. In 1834 the Methodists sent Jason Lee, a longtime circuit rider, to preach

the gospel to the Indians. In 1835 four Nez Percés visited the American Board of Foreign Missions and, so the board reported, persuaded them that the gospel their tribe wanted to hear was Presbyterian. In 1836 **Marcus and Narcissa Whitman** carried it to them on foot. (The Whitmans converted a Scot, a French Canadian, and a Hawaiian, but no Indians; in 1847 Indians blamed a measles epidemic on the Whitmans and murdered them.) The Catholic University at St. Louis sent Father Pierre-Jean de Smet to the Oregon Country.

The long trek usually began at Independence, a city that had specialized in outfitting overland travelers since the Santa Fe Trail was opened. The first great "Oregon or Bust" wagon trains were organized there in 1843, a thousand emigrants in all. They swore to strict rules of behavior and cooperation for the duration of the crossing, and hired mountain men as guides.

A mountain man drawn by the famous illustrator of the West, Frederic Remington. Remington never knew the real thing; he was born in 1861. But his research was solid. This crusty character, the runtiness of the ponies, and the excessive load on the trapper's pack animal capture written descriptions of antebellum mountain men.

The Oregon Trail crossed Kansas to the Platte River and followed that broad, shallow stream to Fort Laramie, the westernmost army outpost. The emigrants crossed the Continental Divide at South Pass and struggled through the Rockies to near the Snake River, which flows into the great Columbia and the Pacific. A wagon train covered up to twenty miles a day or as few as none at all, depending on the terrain and the weather. At night, exhausted by the tremendous labor of moving a hundred wagons and several hundred head of cattle, horses, and mules, the migrants drew their prairie schooners into a hollow square or circle.

The Indians of the plains and mountains did not threaten large, well-organized expeditions. Although they were hardly delighted to see hordes of white strangers crossing their ancestral hunting lands (3,000 in 1845 alone), these whites were, at least, passing through. Although the tribes of the plains skirmished constantly with one another, not many had firearms during the 1840s. The Oregon-bound travelers worried less about Indian attacks than about theft. Indians made a game of stealing horses that strayed too far from the caravans. They also traded with the whites and picked up the discarded items that soon littered the trail. Long before the annual river of wagons wore ruts into the sod and rock—which can be seen here and there today—the Oregon Trail was marked with broken furniture, empty barrels, incapacitated wagons, the skeletons of cattle and horses, and simple grave markers. Death from accident or disease, particularly cholera, was common. But it was impossible to lose the way.

MANIFEST DESTINY

By 1845 the American population of the Columbia and Willamette valleys had grown to 7,000. The British Hudson's Bay Company prudently moved its headquarters from the mouth of the Columbia to Vancouver Island. What is now the state of Washington was a buffer zone between British and American population centers. Still, occasional clashes threatened joint occupation.

The Americans wanted to annex the Oregon Country to the United States. In July 1843 a group met at Champoeg and established a provisional territorial government under the American flag. A few politicians back east supported them, as much to taunt the British as for any realistic hope of affecting policy. The idea of territorial expansion was taking on a positive dignity—even, to some, the guise of a sacred duty. Increasingly, some Democratic party propagandists claimed that the United States had an obligation to increase the domain in which democracy and liberty held sway. It remained for a New York journalist, John O'Sullivan, to coin a phrase. It was, he said, the "**Manifest Destiny**" of the United States—clearly God's will—to expand from sea to sea.

THE TEXAS DEBATE

Some southerners added slavery to the list of American institutions to be carried across the continent. In 1843 Secretary of State John C. Calhoun told Congress that Texas must be annexed lest growing British influence result in the abolition of slavery there. He won the support of some northern Democrats such as Lewis Cass of Michigan, James Buchanan of Pennsylvania, and Stephen Douglas of Illinois. But not enough of them: In 1844 the Senate rejected Calhoun's proposal by a 2 to 1 vote. Every Whig but one voted nay.

Most northern Whigs opposed the addition of new slave states to the Union except for Florida (which became a state the next year). Aside from Indian Territory, slavery was made illegal in all the western lands by the Missouri Compromise of 1820. Moreover, the Whigs argued that annexing Texas would lead to a war with Mexico in which the Mexicans, not the Americans, would be in the right.

Both of the likely presidential nominees of 1844 were unhappy to see Texas annexation shaping up as the principal issue of the campaign. Henry Clay knew that his Whig party, already strained by slavery issues, might split in two over

Dark Horse

The term *dark horse*, which Americans applied to surprise presidential candidates, came from a novel, *The Young Duke*, published in 1832 by future British prime minister Benjamin Disraeli: "A dark horse which never had been thought of, and which the careless St. James had never even observed in the list, rushed past the grandstand in sweeping triumph." The phrase had entered racetrack lingo when the Democrats nominated James K. Polk to run for president in 1844. Other dark horse presidential candidates were James A. Garfield (1880), William Jennings Bryan (1896), and Wendell Willkie (1940).

#1940 Association of American Railroads

Where the overland trail reached the Snake River, it forked. The Oregon Trail continued along the Snake to the northwest; the California Trail branched southwest into what is now Nevada. This extraordinary photograph, with two wagon trains side by side, indicates how crowded the trail could be.

Texas. Martin Van Buren, who commanded a majority of delegates to the Democratic nominating convention, had the same problem. The Democrats were torn between proslavery and antislavery factions. If the two candidates took opposite stands on the question, both of their parties would be disarrayed as voters voted on Texas rather than on party lines. Neither of the partisan old rogues wanted that. They met quietly and agreed that both would oppose annexation and compete on more comfortable issues.

Their unusual bargain presented lame-duck President Tyler with an opportunity. He would be a third candidate favoring annexation. Tyler had no party behind him, so his announcement did not disturb Clay and Van Buren. Then occurred one of those unlikely events that unexpectedly change the course of history. Manifest Destiny Democrats revived a neglected party rule that a presidential nominee must win the support of two-thirds of the delegates to the convention, not just a simple majority. Having declared against annexation, Van Buren was stymied. Pro-Texas Democrats numbered far more than a third of the delegates.

After eight ballots, the convention turned to a **dark horse candidate**—that is, a man who was not a contender for the nomination. He was James Knox Polk of Tennessee, a protégé of Jackson not yet 50 years old. (Supporters called him "Young Hickory.") Polk was a Van Buren man, but personally he favored annexation of Texas. He was a perfect compromise candidate.

THE ELECTION OF 1844

"Who is Polk?" the Whigs asked scornfully when they heard the news. The sarcasm was misplaced. Polk had not been seeking the nomination, but he was well known among politicians. He had been governor of Tennessee and had served in Congress for fourteen years, several of them as Speaker. His career and personality were tiny set beside those of Henry Clay. A frail, small man with a look of melancholy about him, Polk was priggish, sniffily disapproving of alcohol, dancing, and playing cards. But he was not obscure, and he was widely recognized as a competent legislator.

Denver Public Library, Western History Collection

A family bound overland poses. They are sunburned, dirty, and weary but still look plenty tough and determined.

At first, Henry Clay was pleased to have Polk as his opponent. After three attempts, he would be president at last! The partyless Tyler and the colorless Polk would divide the pro-Texas vote. The anti-Texas vote, including the antislavery Democrats who would have voted for Van Buren, were his.

Then another piece of sky fell. Tyler withdrew, and every wind brought Clay news that Manifest Destiny was carrying the day. He began to waffle on expansion; never was it more apparent that Clay's ambition to be president consumed him. His equivocation cost him the election by alienating anti-annexation Whigs in New York State, which, as was so often true in the nineteenth century, was the key to the election. Polk carried New York by a scant 5,000 votes. Counties that had voted Whig for ten years gave 16,000 votes to James G. Birney, the candidate of the abolitionist Liberty party, which was, of course, anti-Texas.

Encouraged by the election and egged on by Secretary of State Calhoun, Tyler moved on the Texas question. He could not muster the two-thirds vote in the Senate that ratification of a treaty requires, but he had a simple majority of both houses of Congress behind him. Three days before Polk's inauguration, Congress approved a joint resolution with the Texas Congress, making the Lone Star Republic the twenty-eighth state.

A VERY SUCCESSFUL PRESIDENCY

Polk might have looked mousy; as president he was anything but. He proved to be a master politician, a shrewd diplomat, and, in terms of accomplishing what he set out to do, one of the most successful of presidents. When he took his oath of office, Polk announced he would serve only one term. His goals were to secure Texas to the Union, acquire New Mexico and California from Mexico, and annex the Oregon Country.

Texas statehood was already in the bag. The hardworking president (he was a micromanager: "I prefer to supervise the whole operations of the government myself, rather than entrust the public business to subordinates") immediately turned to Oregon. He embraced a chauvinistic slogan of the day: "**Fifty-Four Forty or Fight!**" (seizing all of Oregon up to the boundary of Russian America at 54° 40' north latitude). He alarmed the British by threatening a war neither nation wanted and which the United States—planning on war with Mexico—could scarcely afford. Polk then presented it as a concession to Britain that he would settle for an extension of the Webster–Ashburton line, 49° north latitude, as the northern boundary of American Oregon. The Oregon Country would be cut in half, with Britain retaining all of Vancouver Island. Great Britain accepted. Except for a minor adjustment of the line in the Strait of Juan de Fuca in 1872, the American–Canadian boundary was final in 1846.

Polk was candid about his designs on California and New Mexico. The United States had no legal claim in either Mexican province. Nor could Polk claim, as he could about Texas and Oregon, that California and New Mexico were peopled largely by Americans. Unassimilated gringos were few in New Mexico, and there were only about 700 Americans in California compared with 6,000 *californios*. In 1842 an American naval officer, Thomas ap Catesby Jones, somehow got it into his head that the United States was at war with Mexico and seized Monterey, the provincial capital of California. When he learned that he was mistaken, he had to run down the flag and sail off, rather the fool. But Jones was

From the Collections of the Library of Congress

A splendid pictorial representation of Americans' thoughts about western expansion. Led by a classical (giant) depiction of civilization, who is helpfully stringing telegraph wire, prospectors, farmers, the overland emigrants and the overland stage, the railroad, and, in the distance, a pony express rider drive the bison, Indians, and a wild beast into oblivion.

merely a few years ahead of his time. When Mexico turned down Polk's offer to buy California and New Mexico for $30 million, he set out to take them by force.

WAR WITH MEXICO

The luckless Santa Anna was back in power in Mexico City. This time, however, he moved cautiously, ordering Mexican troops not to provoke the Americans. It was no use: Polk was determined to have war. He drew up an address to Congress for a declaration of war because the Mexican government owed $3 million to American banks, pretty weak stuff. Polk ordered General Zachary Taylor of Louisiana to take 1,500 men from the Nueces River in Texas to the Rio Grande. In April 1846, sixteen American soldiers were killed in a skirmish with a Mexican patrol.

Affecting moral outrage, Polk rewrote his speech, declaring that because of Mexican aggression, a state of war between the two nations already existed. Constitutionally, this was nonsense; Congress alone has the power to declare war. But patriotic danders were up; both houses of Congress rubber-stamped Polk's action. The Mexican army was larger than the American army, but most Mexican troops were ill-equipped, demoralized by endless civil war, and commanded by officers who owed their commissions to social status rather than merit. In less than two years, the Americans conquered much of the country.

In the summer of 1846, Stephen W. Kearny occupied Santa Fe without resistance. He then marched his troops to California, where he found that the Americans and a few *californio* allies already had won a nearly bloodless revolution and established the Bear Flag Republic. Kearny had only to raise the American flag and defeat a few scattered Mexican garrisons.

Gringos

The origin of the word *gringo*, once a pejorative Mexican term for Americans, now inoffensive, is obscure. One theory is that it originated during the American occupation of Mexico City when a song popular with American troops began, "Green grows the grass. . . ." To Mexicans this was gobbledygook, but they caught the first two syllables and used them to refer to the *norteamericanos*. Another theory is that the word was a corruption of *griego*, "Greek," which Mexicans applied to foreigners in the same sense that Americans said, "It's Greek to me."

In September, Taylor advanced into northern Mexico, defeating Mexican armies at Matamoros and Nuevo León (also known as Monterrey). Although "Old Rough and Ready," as his men called him, showed shrewd tactical judgment, the Nuevo León garrison escaped. Polk, who disliked Taylor, used this mistake as an excuse to divert some of Taylor's troops to a command under General Winfield Scott. Nevertheless, in February 1847 Taylor became a national hero when, with his shrunken army, he was attacked at Buena Vista by Santa Anna himself. Old Rough and Ready won a total victory.

The next month, March 1847, Scott landed at Vera Cruz and fought his way toward Mexico City along the ancient route of Cortés. He won a victory at Cerro Gordo and an even bigger one at Chapultepec, where he captured 3,000 men and

MAP 20:3 **The Mexican War, 1846–1847**
Mexico lost a third of its territory in the war with the United States, somewhat more if disputed territory is included.

General John E. Wool and his staff in Saltillo, shortly before or after the battle of Buena Vista in 1846. This is believed to be the earliest surviving photograph of American soldiers.

eight generals. On September 14, 1847, Scott donned one of the gaudy uniforms he loved (his men called him "Old Fuss and Feathers") and occupied Mexico City, "the Halls of Montezuma."

By the Treaty of Guadalupe Hidalgo, signed in February 1848, Mexico ceded the Rio Grande boundary, California, and New Mexico, which included the present states of Arizona and Nevada (and the Mormon Zion in Utah). The United States paid Mexico $15 million and assumed responsibility for about $3 million that the Mexican government owed Americans. Mexico was dismembered like a carcass of beef. One-third of its territory was detached largely because the United States was strong enough to take it. Although the ineptitude of the Mexican military played a part in the national disaster, the partition of the country could not but leave a bitterness in the historical memory of the Mexican people.

THE OPPOSITION

The Mexican War was popular in the United States. The army could accept only a fraction of the young men who volunteered to fight. Most battles were American victories, and only 1,700 soldiers died in battle (11,000 soldiers succumbed to disease). About 50,000 Mexicans lost their lives.

Nevertheless, the war had its critics. Many Whigs, including a young congressman from Illinois named Abraham Lincoln, voted against the declaration. In the Senate, Thomas Corwin of Ohio warned his pro-war colleagues, "If I were a Mexican, I would tell you, 'Have you not room in your own country to bury your dead men? If you come into mine, we will greet you with bloody hands, and welcome you to

hospitable graves.'" (As president two decades later, Lincoln named Corwin minister to Mexico, knowing that his sympathies would be remembered.)

In New England, politicians and clergymen condemned the war from platform and pulpit. Ralph Waldo Emerson and much of the Massachusetts cultural establishment opposed it. Henry David Thoreau went to jail rather than pay a tax he said would help pay for adding new slave states to the Union.

Not even the army was unanimously keen on the fight. Years later in his autobiography, Ulysses S. Grant, a captain in 1846, remembered, "I was bitterly opposed to the measure, and to this day regard the war . . . as one of the most unjust ever waged by a stronger against a weaker nation. . . . Even if the annexation itself could be justified, the manner in which the . . . war was forced upon Mexico cannot."

The vote in the Senate ratifying the Treaty of Guadalupe Hidalgo was only 38 to 14. Had four senators changed their votes, the treaty would not have been approved.

EXPANSION RUN AMOK

Cynical as the Mexican acquisition was, it was moderate compared to the suggestions of some expansionists. Some southerners wanted Polk to seize even more of Mexico, and he was leaning in that direction when the Treaty of Guadalupe Hidalgo arrived in Washington. When a rebellion broke out in the Yucatán Peninsula in 1848, Polk asked Congress to authorize the army, which was still in Mexico, to take over the tropical province. Curiously, some antislavery northerners were sympathetic. Because slavery was illegal in Mexico, they believed that new American states carved from the country would come into the Union as free states. Thus did slavery obsess and warp the minds of so many Americans

The president also had designs on Cuba, where 350,000 slaves had long excited the imagination of proslavery southerners. Polk wanted to present the Spanish government there with a choice between selling the rich sugar island or running the risk of a rebellion fomented by the United States, followed by American military intervention.

Even more bizarre was J. D. B. De Bow, an influential southern publisher. He wrote that it was the American destiny to absorb not only all Mexico, but also the West Indies, Canada, and Hawaii. And that was for appetizers. De Bow continued,

> The gates of the Chinese empire must be thrown
> down by the men from the Sacramento and the
> Oregon, and the haughty Japanese tramplers
> upon the cross be enlightened in the doctrines
> of republicanism and the ballot box. The eagle
> of the republic shall poise itself over the field of
> Waterloo, after tracing its flight among the gorges
> of the Himalaya or the Ural Mountains, and a
> successor of Washington ascend the chair of
> universal empire.

FURTHER READING

General Paul H. Bergeron, *The Presidency of James K. Polk,* 1987; John Mack Faragher and Robert V. Hine, *The American West: A New Interpretive History,* 2000; Don E. Fehrenbacher, *The Slaveholding Republic: An Account of the United States Government's Relationship to Slavery,* 2001; Reginald Horsman, *Race and Manifest Destiny: The Origins of American Racial Anglo-Saxonism,* 1981; Patricia Limerick, *Legacy of Conquest: The Unbroken Past of the American West,* 1987; D. M. Pletcher, *The Diplomacy of Annexation: Texas, Oregon, and the Mexican War,* 1973; Richard D. White, *"It's Your Misfortune and None of My Own": A History of the American West,* 1992.

Mountain Men and Oregon Jennifer S. Brown, *Strangers in Blood: Fur Trade Company Families in Indian Country,* 1980; Malcolm Clark, Jr., *The Eden-Seekers: The Settlement of Oregon, 1812–1862,* 1981; John Mack Faragher, *Women and Men on the Oregon Trail,* 1979; David A. Johnson, *Founding the Far West: California, Oregon, and Nevada, 1840–1890,* 1992; Theodore J. Karamanski, *Fur Trade and Exploration: Opening the Far Northwest, 1821–1852,* 1983; Laura Parker, *Jim Bridger, Mountain Man,* 1981; Glenda Riley, *The Female Frontier,* 1988; John D. Unruh, *The Plains Across: The Overland Emigrants and the Trans-Mississippi West, 1840–1860,* 1979; D. J. Wishart, *The Fur Trade of the American West, 1807–1840,* 1979.

The Southwest David J. Beber, *The Mexican Frontier: The American Southwest under Mexico,* 1982; William Y. Chalfant, *Dangerous Passage: The Santa Fe Trail and the Mexican War,* 1994; Mark Derr, *The Frontiersman: The Real Life and Many Legends of Davy Crockett,* 1993; Cheryl J. Foote, *Women of the New Mexico Frontier, 1846–1912,* 2005; Gregory M. Franzwa, *The Santa Fe Trail Revisited,* 1989; Paul D. Lack, *The Texas Revolutionary Experience: A Political and Social History, 1835–1836,* 1992; Timothy Matovina, *Tejano Religion and Ethnicity: San Antonio, 1821–1860,* 1995; Michael A. Morrison, *Slavery and the American Southwest: The Eclipse of Manifest Destiny,* 1997; Donald J. Weber, *The Spanish Frontier in North America,* 1992.

The War with Mexico K. Jack Bauer, *The Mexican–American War, 1846–1848,* 1974; John S. D. Eisenhower, *So Far from God: The U.S. War with Mexico, 1846–1849,* 1989; Iris Engstrand et al., *Culture y Cultura: Consequences of the U.S.–Mexican War, 1846–1848,* 1998; Paul Foos, *A Short, Offhand, Killing Affair: Soldiers and Social Conflict during the Mexican–American War,* 2002; Robert W. Johansen, *To the Halls of Montezuma: The Mexican War in the American Imagination,* 1985; James McCaffrey, *Army of Manifest Destiny: The American Soldier in the Mexican War,* 1992.

KEY TERMS

The following terms are covered in this chapter and can also be found in the list of Key Terms at the back of the book.

Alamo	**"Fifty-Four Forty or Fight!"**	**Junípero Serra**	**Marcus and Narcissa Whitman**
dark horse candidate	**joint occupation**	**"Manifest Destiny"**	**Santa Fe Trail**

 ## ONLINE SOURCES GUIDE

Use this listing to find online documents, images, interactive maps, simulations, and other resources related to this chapter:

American History Resource Center
http://history.wadsworth.com/rc/us

Selected Documents
John Fremont, "The Exploring Expedition to the Rocky Mountains, Oregon, and California"

Selected Images
Stephen F. Austin
Alamo
Sam Houston
American troops under Zachary Taylor storming Monterey, September 1846

Interactive Time Line (with online readings)
From Sea to Shining Sea: American Expansion, 1820–1848

Discovery

What role did Manifest Destiny play in the development of the American character?

In thinking about this question, begin by breaking it down into the components shown below. A discussion of the significance of each component should appear in your answer.

Geography: For this exercise, study Map 20:2 and the painting on Westward Movement. Look at the map of overland trails. Which parts of this journey do you believe would be most difficult? What kinds of problems and dangers might these groups encounter? How does the painting of America's Westward Movement help explain why emigrants were willing to risk everything to move west? What did they hope to achieve?

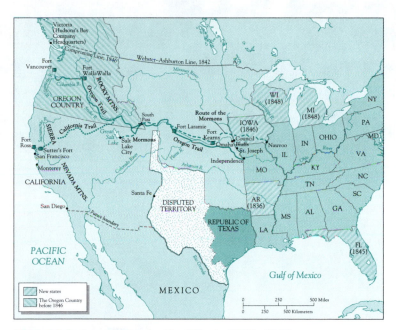

MAP 20:2 **Americans in the West, 1819–1848**

Westward Movement

Culture and Society: For this exercise, study the three images. What is the common theme of all three images? What did it require to be an American who moved west? What difficulties had to be overcome? Why would people be willing to face these trials? Was the risk worth the reward? What kinds of people paved the way for American expansion? Do you believe these individuals were thinking of "Manifest Destiny" as they moved west? How is this same drive seen in Americans today?

Culver Pictures

Great American Desert

From Harper's Magazine

Mountain Man

#1940, Association of American Railroads

Fork of the California and Oregon Trails

To read extended versions of the documents, visit the companion Web site http://history.wadsworth.com/americanpast8e; click on "Discovery Sources."

CHAPTER 21

Apples of Discord

The Poisoned Fruits of Victory 1844–1854

North Wind Picture Archives

KANSAS A FREE STATE.
Squatter Sovereignty
VINDICATED!
NO WHITE
SLAVERY!

The United States will conquer Mexico, but it will be as the man who swallows the arsenic which brings him down in turn.

Ralph Waldo Emerson

Even before Mexico officially transferred the title to New Mexico and California to the United States, the fruits of the American victory in the war looked like the apples of discord of the Greek myths. The new territories Polk had boasted he would win set northerner against southerner as viciously as the Greek goddesses scrambled after the prized apple tossed among them. The apple in the myth was golden. It would be gold that ushered in the sectional conflict of the 1850s that led to the terrible American Civil War.

THE SECTIONAL SPLIT TAKES SHAPE

Slavery had been the subject of acrimonious conflict before the Mexican War. Since the 1830s, abolitionists and slavery's defenders had hurled anathemas at one another. But before the Mexican War, the slavery debate had been a debate between zealots. Mainstream politicians, northern and southern, stayed out of it, including slave owners like Henry Clay, who regretted slavery, and Andrew Jackson, who did not.

John Quincy Adams was antislavery from his boyhood to his death on the floor of Congress in 1848. He fought for the right of abolitionists to be heard in Congress, but he repeatedly condemned extremists like William Lloyd Garrison as irresponsible mischief-makers. Daniel Webster said that the abolitionists had contributed "nothing good or valuable" to the country.

Thomas Hart Benton was disgusted by both abolitionists and his fellow southerners who were obsessed with defending slavery. It was like, he said, the biblical visitation of plagues on Pharaoh's Egypt: "You could not look on the table but there were frogs. You could not sit down at the banquet table but there were frogs, you could not go to the bridal couch and lift the sheets but there were frogs! We can see nothing, touch nothing, have no measures proposed, without having this pestilence thrust before us."

CONGRESS AND SLAVERY: A DEAD LETTER

Benton, Clay, Quincy Adams, Webster and many others were impatient with the proslavery versus abolitionist debate because they were practical politicians. The name-calling could only embitter people against one another. There was nothing the federal government could do about slavery where it existed. The Constitution defined slavery as a "domestic institution"; that is, it was for the individual states to decide whether they would permit the ownership of slaves, as indeed the states had done.

Slavery could be abolished nationally by constitutional amendment, but no one entertained such an amendment as within the realm of reality. Three-fourths of the states must ratify an amendment. Half the states had clearly chosen to protect slavery within their borders. When William Lloyd Garrison called on the free states to leave the Union, it was because, constitutionally, slavery could not be abolished.

The Constitution did empower Congress "to exercise exclusive legislation in all cases whatsoever" over the District of Columbia. So abolitionist congressmen could and did call for the abolition of slavery in Washington or, at least, a ban on the buying and selling of slaves in the capital. Some moderate southerners were open to putting an end to the slave trade in the capital for cosmetic reasons. Slave auctions were ugly affairs. Why, the argument went, put them on view in a city that almost all foreigners visited? Washington's slave owners would hardly be inconvenienced; if they chose to buy or sell a slave, they need only cross the Potomac to Alexandria in Virginia.

Did Congress have the power to abolish the interstate slave trade? Not really: the "interstate commerce clause" was not then interpreted as applying to, for example, a slave trader purchasing a slave in Maryland, taking him to Mississippi, and selling him there. The purchase, the transport, and the sale were looked upon as three different transactions, not part of a "stream of commerce."

Congress had the power to enact laws concerning slaves who ran away from their masters and crossed state lines. The Fugitive Slave Act of 1793 provided that such runaways be returned to their owners. The law was evaded or obstructed in many free states, and by the late 1840s, the states of the upper South had a serious runaway problem: between 1,000 and 1,500 slaves, mostly from Maryland, Virginia, and

The Berrien Proviso

Another rider of the era, proposed in February 1847 by Senator John M. Berrien, was less successful than David Wilmot's. The Berrien Proviso stated that "the true intent of Congress in making this appropriation [for the army is] that the war with Mexico ought not to be prosecuted by this Government with any view to the dismemberment of that republic." Even in the northern states, Berrien's anti-expansionism was unacceptable.

Kentucky, were getting away each year. While abolitionist congressmen talked of ending slavery in Washington, proslavery southerners demanded a fugitive slave law that could not be obstructed. Southern hotheads proposed reopening the African slave trade, which Congress had the authority to do, but that was absurd; it would bring the United States into head-on conflict with Great Britain and the royal navy.

Congress also had the power to protect or prohibit slavery in the western territories. Politically, however, that too was a dead letter in 1848. The Missouri Compromise of 1820 had permitted slavery in the West only south of 36° 30' latitude. The only territory below that line that was not already a slave state was Indian Territory (Oklahoma). Some Indians living there owned slaves and were proslavery. But it was *Indian* territory; in that status, Oklahoma could not be a state.

Before the acquisition of land from Mexico, slavery was—at the federal level—a dead letter.

THE WILMOT PROVISO AND FREE SOIL PARTY

Southern proslavery extremists were so keen on the war with Mexico because by adding new territories to the United States, new slave states could be added to the Union. In 1846, hoping to foil this design, Congressman David Wilmot of Pennsylvania attached a **rider** to several bills appropriating money to fight the war. The **Wilmot Proviso** declared that "neither slavery nor involuntary servitude shall ever exist" in

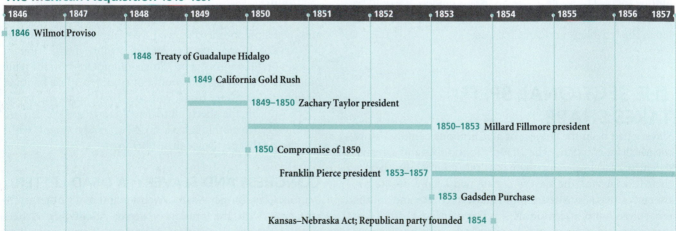

The Mexican Acquisition 1846–1857

1846	1847	1848	1849	1850	1851	1852	1853	1854	1855	1856	1857

1846 Wilmot Proviso

1848 Treaty of Guadalupe Hidalgo

1849 California Gold Rush

1849–1850 Zachary Taylor president

1850–1853 Millard Fillmore president

1850 Compromise of 1850

Franklin Pierce president **1853–1857**

1853 Gadsden Purchase

Kansas–Nebraska Act; Republican party founded **1854**

any lands taken from Mexico. The House of Representatives attached the Wilmot Proviso to fifty bills between 1846 and 1850. Every northern Whig and all but four northern Democrats voted for it in 1846. Every northern state legislature except New Jersey's officially endorsed it. It was not that so many northerners were abolitionists. Only a minority of northerners cared about slavery in the southern states. However, like Thomas Jefferson in drafting the Northwest Ordinance, the majority of northerners (and some southerners) believed that the West should be reserved for family farmers. Slavocrats, the planter aristocracy, had to be kept out lest they dominate the West as they dominated the South.

The Wilmot Proviso never became law. John C. Calhoun led the fight against it in the Senate. As usual, he was logical (although not necessarily constitutionally correct). The Constitution, Calhoun said, guaranteed to the citizens of all states who emigrated to the territories the same rights they enjoyed at home. The citizens of some states could own slaves. Therefore, they had the right to take their slaves with them if they went west into the former Mexican lands.

Slave state senators were equal in number to free state senators. With the help of a few northern Democrats, the Senate deleted the Wilmot Proviso from every bill to which the House attached it.

When President Polk endorsed Calhoun's reasoning, a large number of northern Democrats bolted the party and organized the Free Soil party. Some were abolitionists, but by no means all. As a party, the Free Soilers allowed that the people of the South had the constitutional right to preserve slavery at home. Most Free Soilers cared little about the injustice and suffering of African Americans. Some were vociferous racists who wanted to exclude blacks as well as slaves from the West. As late as 1857, Oregon prohibited the emigration of free blacks into the state.

However, they insisted, the Mexican Acquisition must be dedicated to "Free Soil! Free Speech! Free Men!"—the party's slogan.

THE ELECTION OF 1848

Polk, as he promised, did not stand for reelection in 1848. In fact, he had so worn himself out working that he died four months after leaving the White House, only 54 years of age. The Democrats nominated one of his northern supporters, the competent but gloriously dull Lewis Cass of Michigan. The Whigs, having lost once again with Clay in 1844,

returned to the winning formula of 1840—a popular general whose views were unknown. They nominated the hero of the close-run battle of Buena Vista, Zachary Taylor of Louisiana. Taylor owned a great many slaves but (as far as anyone knew) was no proslavery fanatic. (He wasn't.) Whig strategists gambled that he would carry southern states that would otherwise be lost to the Democrats because northern Whigs had supported the Wilmot Proviso.

Taylor was a remarkable presidential candidate. "He really is a most simple-minded old man," said Whig educator Horace Mann. "Few men have ever had more contempt for learning," wrote General Winfield Scott. "He doesn't know himself from a side of sole leather in the way of statesmanship," wrote Horace Greeley. A coarse, cranky, and blunt-spoken old geezer of 64, Taylor admitted he had never bothered to vote in his life. When the letter from the Whig party announcing his nomination arrived, he refused to pay the postage due on it. When someone else did, he responded diffidently, "I will not say I will not serve if the good people were imprudent enough to elect me."

The Free Soil party named a more distinguished and able candidate than either major party, former president Martin Van Buren. Along in years, he had announced his opposition to slavery in the territories. Van Buren did not have a chance, but his name on the ballot determined the election. He won more votes in New York than Lewis Cass, throwing the state's thirty-six electoral votes to Taylor. With New York State, as in 1844, went the election.

THE CRISIS OF 1850

Congressional Whigs hoped that Taylor's victory would cool the southern passions aroused by the Wilmot Proviso and the Free Soilers, allowing the party to divert interest from the slavery issue back to government promotion of orderly national economic development. As they had hoped with William Henry Harrison in 1841, they hoped that Old Rough and Ready—would be happy to be a figurehead president, as they had hoped Harison would be, allowing Congress's top Whigs to make policy. Taylor might have enjoyed such a presidency, but he was destined to have no peace; and when he was criticized, he reacted angrily. Events in distant California, unfolding even as he was nominated and elected, caused a crisis that almost destroyed the Union in 1850.

Junk Mail

Had the leaders of the Whig party been up to date in 1848, they might have spared themselves the embarrassment of having Zachary Taylor refuse to pay the postage due on the letter notifying him of his presidential nomination. In the previous year, 1847, the U.S. Post Office had begun to issue adhesive-backed paper stamps that permitted the sender to pay the postage. Apparently the idea had not yet caught on.

No Name City

In the national capital in 1850, California meant sectional crisis. However, when the first California legislature met, the delegates were more interested in making some citizens feel comfortable in the new state. The first law enacted by the legislature reduced the statute of limitations so that Californians with perhaps murky pasts back east could not easily be extradited. The second enactment made it easier for an individual to change his name.

California State Library

Placer miners at Spanish Flat, California. They are using a long tom, shoveling gravel into a box through which a constant stream of water is being sluiced. With luck, there will be several ounces of gold dust in the bottom of the long tom when the sun goes down. Note the rocks at the feet of the miner on the right. They were picked out of the gravel by hand.

GOLD!

On the evening of January 24, 1848, a carpenter from New Jersey, James Marshall, took a walk along the American River where it tumbles through the foothills of the Sierra Nevada. Marshall worked for John Augustus Sutter, a Swiss adventurer

The Gold Rush That Wasn't

In 1844, four years before Marshall's discovery, Pablo Gutiérrez discovered gold in the bed of the Bear River. He immediately secured a land grant of 22,000 acres that included what he hoped would be a rich mine. When he went to Sacramento to buy mining equipment, Sutter was preoccupied with a social tumult near Monterey. He persuaded Gutiérrez to go there to learn what was happening, and Gutiérrez was killed by the rebels. The gold fever of 1844 died with him. His Bear River grant was sold to William Johnson, who knew nothing of Gutiérrez's discovery. No matter: The Bear was overrun in 1849 and 1850 by miners who ignored Mexican land grants, and the deposit was rediscovered.

who had turned a Mexican land grant into a feudal domain. Sutter's castle was an adobe fort on the Sacramento River, defended by cannons he had purchased from the Russians when they abandoned Fort Ross.

Marshall was building a sawmill for Sutter. He was inspecting the tail race, the ditch that returned rushing water to the river after it powered the mill. He picked up a curious metallic stone. "Boys," he told his workmen, "I think I have found a gold mine."

He had, and that was that for the sawmill. Sutter's employees dropped their hammers and set to shoveling gravel from the river, separating the sand and silt from what proved to be plenty of gold dust and nuggets. Briefly, Marshall's discovery was the end of San Francisco. A town of 500, it was depopulated when "everyone," including the recently arrived American military garrison, headed for the hills.

The next year—1849—80,000 people descended on California. Some came overland; some sailed by clipper ship around Cape Horn; yet others took a steamship to Panama, hiked across the isthmus, and got to the diggings on another ship, when they could hail one. Mexicans came from Sonora. Chileans found berths on the clippers when they put into port for provisions. By the end of the year, the population of California was about 100,000, more than lived in the states of Delaware or Florida. By the end of the year, the Forty-Niners produced $10 million in gold. They said, plausibly enough, that their numbers and their value to the nation merited immediate statehood. When Congress convened in December 1849, California's provisional constitution was already on the table.

By an overwhelming majority, California's citizens prohibited slavery in the golden state.

POLITICAL TRAUMA

It all happened so fast. It was a small wonder much of Congress was hysterical. The first vague news of the California discovery reached Washington in December 1848, a month after Zachary Taylor's election. The astonishing gold rush began immediately. It was still under way in October when California's constitution was delivered to Congress. In December the president urged immediate acceptance.

The southern senators and congressmen were in a panic. They had thought of the war as a seizure of lands in which slavery would be established. They assumed that California, the best of the Mexican acquisition, would be populated slowly— it was a long way from the United States—and in part by southerners and their slaves. When, some years down the line, it was time to create a state on the Pacific coast, at least part of California would apply for admission as a slave state.

Now, even before Congress had created a territorial government in California, proslavery southerners saw their entirely reasonable expectations pulverized. The worst of it was that California statehood would mean the South's end of equality with the free states in the Senate, with two more embryonic free states about to hatch in Oregon and Minnesota.

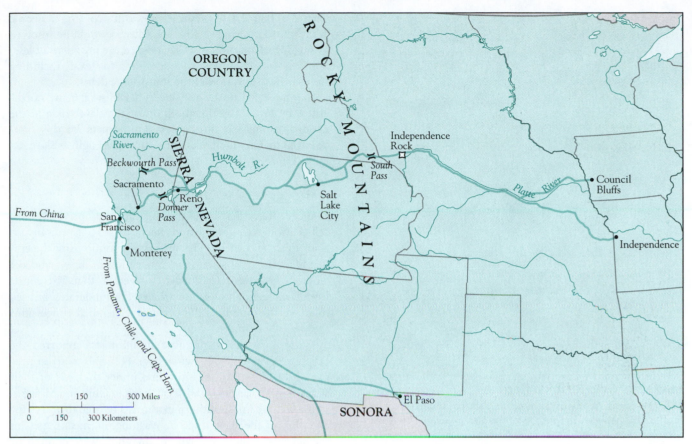

MAP 21:1 The Gold Rush
The overland route of the Forty-Niners was long known by mountain men and, most of the way, for several years, to emigrants to Oregon. It became a virtual highway only with the Gold Rush.

Even with the three-fifths compromise inflating the number of slave state congressmen, the South was easily outvoted by free state representatives on sectional issues. Thus the repeated approval of the Wilmot Proviso in the House. Southerners looked to senators, half of them from slave states, plus a handful of pro-South northern Democrats, to protect the South's sectional interests, which by 1850 pretty much boiled down to protecting slavery.

A large majority of southern senators and congressmen immediately declared they would vote against California statehood, no matter the 100,000 population, no matter the $10 million annual gold production. The North's toleration of abolitionists and the "slave stealers" of the underground railroad made it impossible for the South to trust the goodwill of the North. The South had to have the Senate as a check on northern fanatics.

HENRY CLAY'S LAST STAND

The announcement infuriated President Taylor. He said that he would himself take up arms to defend his right to his 100-odd slaves. But Taylor was a nationalist. National pride, prosperity, and security demanded that California be admitted immediately as a state. His dander up, he further angered his fellow southerners when he recommended that a boundary dispute between Texas and New Mexico Territory be resolved in favor of New Mexico. Taylor's decision had nothing to do with the fact that Texas was a slave state. Like just about every other army officer who served in Texas during the Mexican War, he despised Texas (and Texans). Moreover, Texas was already the largest state in area, and the state's claim to part of New Mexico Territory was weak.

Tempers were boiling. The election of a Speaker of the House, usually a formality, required sixty-three ballots. In the Senate, Henry Clay, frail and weary at 72, and beyond all hope of being president, tried to cap his career as the Great Compromiser by proposing a permanent solution to the question of slavery in the Mexican Acquisition as, thirty years earlier, his Missouri Compromise had settled the same question on the Louisiana Purchase.

Clay's **Omnibus Bill** was a compromise in the old tradition: it required both sides to make significant concessions in the interests of the common good, the Union. California would be admitted as a free state. The rest of the Mexican Acquisition would be organized as territories with no reference to the status of slavery there. Clay meant to hold out to proslavery southerners the possibility of future slave states in

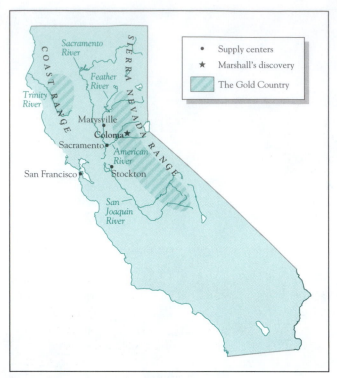

MAP 21:2 Gold Rush California
The gold camps (many of them actually sizable towns) were located on the western foothills of the Sierra Nevada. They were supplied through San Francisco and river towns like Marysville, Sacramento, and Stockton.

what are now Utah, Nevada, New Mexico, and Arizona. Texas's border dispute with New Mexico would be resolved as Taylor had announced (Clay needed the president's blessing) but with face-saving concessions to Texas, including Congress's assumption of the state's large debts.

Clay appealed to the antislavery feelings of many northerners by proposing the abolition of the slave trade in the national capital. To compensate southerners for this symbolic rebuff, Clay included a new, stronger Fugitive Slave Act in the Omnibus Bill.

IMPASSE

Two decades earlier, the Omnibus Bill would probably have sailed through Congress amid cheers, tossed hats, and invitations to share a bottle. The spread of abolitionism, the epidemic of runaway slaves, the annexation of Texas, and the fabulous growth of California changed all that. Extremists from both sections, and more than a few moderates, refused to accept the Omnibus Bill because it included concessions they refused to make.

Many northerners, not just abolitionists, abhorred the Fugitive Slave Act. By allowing federal officials to arrest people who had committed no crime under the laws of their states, it made slavery quasi-legal there, in Ohio and Maine as well as in Alabama. Southern extremists refused to accept the abolition of the slave trade in Washington, meaningless as the act was except as a symbol. Symbols were enough by 1850; slavery was nothing to be apologized for, to be hidden;

The great debate of 1850. Henry Clay is making his eloquent plea for compromise in the cause of the Union. John C. Calhoun, accurately depicted as near death, is the third senator from the right. Daniel Webster, seated at the left, head in hand, would soon speak magnificently in support of Clay and to his disgrace in Massachusetts.

The Granger Collection, New York

How They Mined the Gold

The Sonorans who rushed north to California on hearing of John Marshall's discovery knew how to mine. Mexicans had been mining metals before Cortés. Cornishmen from southwestern England were miners too. But very few of the thousands of American men who rushed overland or by ship to California were familiar with even the rudiments of mining. Fortunately, their ignorance did not much matter. Forty-Niner mining was **placer mining:** the gold was pure gold—in nuggets or dust (tiny flakes, actually)—and had only to be washed out of the sand and gravel of creek and river beds.

The labor was hard, but the technology was simple. To determine if there was gold in a creek, a miner "panned" it. That is, he scooped up a pound or two of silt, sand, and pebbles in a sturdy, shallow pan; removed the stones by hand; and then agitated the finer contents, constantly replenishing the water in the pan so that the lighter mud and sand washed over the sides while the heavier gold dust remained.

When miners discovered enough "color" to warrant mining the placer, they staked a claim and built a "rocker" or a "long tom," two easily constructed devices that performed the washing process on a larger scale. The rocker was a watertight wooden box, three to five feet long and a foot or so across. It was mounted on a base like that of a rocking chair so that it could be tipped from side to side. In the bottom of the box were wooden riffles or a sheet of corrugated metal, and sometimes a fine wire mesh. These simulated the crevices in a creek bed, where the gold naturally collected. Into the rocker, by means of a sluice, also easily built of two planks, ran a stream of water. While one partner shoveled gravel and sand into the box, another rocked it and agitated the contents with a spade or a pitchfork. The lighter worthless mineral washed out (stones, again, were manually discarded), and the gold remained at the bottom to be retrieved at the end of the day, weighed, divided, and cached.

The long tom took more time to build, but it was more productive. In effect, the water-bearing sluice was extended into a long, high-sided, watertight box with riffles in the bottom. With a long tom, all the miners in a partnership could shovel gravel rather than spending effort in rocking.

The placer mines were known as the "poor man's diggings" because placer mining required little money, just a grubstake. In fact, the man with capital had no advantage over a man with a few months' supply of food and a place to get out of the rain. The placer miner needed only a few tools and materials. Because just about everyone in California hoped to strike it rich, few were willing to work for set wages, no matter how high they were—and miners with a good claim offered plenty. The lucky discoverer of a valuable gold deposit had to take on partners if he wanted to work it efficiently.

As long as the "poor man's diggings" held out, life in the mining camps was democratic and egalitarian. No one was allowed to stake a claim larger than he and his partners could mine within a season or two. Law and order in the earliest mining camps was maintained by the informal common consent of the men who lived in them. Except for small military units that were plagued with desertion, there was no formal legal authority in California until late 1850, and no significant government presence in many of the gold fields for several years thereafter.

Not all the fruits of democracy were edifying. A man with the majority of a camp behind him could "get away with murder." Miner democracy did not extend to other than native-born Americans and immigrants from western Europe. Despite the fact that the Forty-Niners learned what they knew of mining from the Sonorans, they expelled them from all but the southernmost gold fields within a year. Chileans, being Spanish speakers, came up against the same prejudice.

Treated worst of all were the Chinese. Because their culture was so alien and because they worked in large groups, thus spending less to live, the Chinese frightened the Forty-Niners. They feared that the "Celestials," as they called the Chinese, would drag down the standard of living for all. In fact, Chinese miners did not compete with American miners. They worked placer deposits that had been abandoned by whites and the few African-American miners as too thin to be worth the work. Other Chinese who came to the "Golden Mountain" to mine drifted into California's towns and cities in the face of Forty-Niner hostility and settled for other jobs.

---

it was a positive good, a point of pride. President Taylor's animosity to Texas had become so heated that his friends in Congress resented compensating the Lone Star state in any way.

In a word, the *spirit* of compromise was dead. New York's William H. Seward called the very idea of compromise "radically wrong and essentially vicious." **Fire-eaters**—militantly proslavery young southern congressmen as intem-

perate in their speech as William Lloyd Garrison—swore to yield nothing. John C. Calhoun, once master of cold logic, was reduced to the sophistry of a cynical county seat lawyer. Obsessed with restoring the veto of bills before Congress, the slave states had lost in the Senate when California became a state. Calhoun proposed that the Constitution be amended to provide for two presidents, one from the North, one from the South, each with the power to veto acts of Congress. The old man was so pathetic he could ignore the unanimous historical evidence of the unworkability of such a scheme. He passed his last days, dying painfully of throat cancer, surrounded by a gaggle of romantic young disciples with, among them, half the brain he had once had in his head.

Henry Clay plugged away, mustering his eloquence one last time. "I have heard something said about allegiance to the South," he told the Senate, "I know no South, no North, no East, no West, to which I owe any allegiance. The Union, sir, is my country."

Because his terminal disease left him almost voiceless, Calhoun's answer had to be read for him. Where Clay appealed to ideals long obsolete, Calhoun was realistic about the circumstances of 1850: "The cry of 'Union, Union, the glorious Union!' can no more prevent disunion than the cry of 'Health, health, glorious health!' . . . can save a patient lying dangerously ill."

Daniel Webster, the last of the Senate's aged triumvirate, had his last word too. It ranked with his greatest orations, and it destroyed him politically. Webster supported the Omnibus Bill. To save the Union, he said, he would vote even for the fugitive slave law in Clay's proposal. Webster was vilified in New England. Nothing better illustrates what the infection of extremism does to people than the fact that New Englanders who had winked for decades at Webster's personal corruption now consigned him to hell for advocating compromise in a crisis that was tearing the Union apart. "The word 'honor' in the mouth of Mr. Webster," wrote Ralph Waldo Emerson, "is like the word 'love' in the mouth of a whore."

Millard Fillmore, Whig president following the sudden death of Zachary Taylor in 1850. Fillmore has been, quite unfairly, an object of redicule. He was a moderate, responsible president whose support of the Compromise of 1850 helped to avert a secession crisis in that year.

THE COMPROMISE

The Omnibus Bill was voted down, and no matter. President Taylor would have vetoed it on the Texas compensation issue. It was the most innocuous part of the Omnibus Bill, a few dollars. But Taylor was a crusty and stubborn man, the officers who served under him during the war could have told the Whigs. By gagging on paying the Texas debt when the Union was near splitting, Taylor demonstrated that he was no politician.

Clay left Washington, without hope, probably disgusted, almost certainly depressed. He was 73; he had seen five far lesser men than he in the presidency; his dreams of an American nation were dashed. In his absence, fate intervened to make a semblance of his Omnibus Bill imaginable, and a resourceful young senator half his age devised a formula to make it a reality.

DEATH OF A SOLDIER

Exit Zachary Taylor: on July 4, 1850, the president attended a ceremony on the Capitol mall, where for two hours he sat hatless in the blazing sun listening to long-winded orators. Back at the White House, he wolfed down cherries and cucumbers and several quarts of iced milk and water. A few hours later the old man took to bed with stomach cramps.

Instead of leaving him alone, his doctors bled him and administered one powerful medicine after another—ipecac to make him vomit, quinine for his fever, calomel as a laxative, and opium for the pain to which they had contributed. Old Rough and Ready was murder on Mexicans and Texans, but he could not handle the pharmacopoeia of the nineteenth century. He died on July 9.

He was succeeded by Vice President Millard Fillmore. Fillmore is often ridiculed as the least memorable of American presidents. A New Yorker born in poverty, he educated himself to be a lawyer. As a young man, he flirted with third-party politics, winning his first election as an Anti-Mason. Like most other Anti-Masons, he became a Whig when the short-lived excitement evaporated, and he served quite ably in Congress as a Clay–Webster man. He was neither proslavery nor antislavery, which, along with his New York connections, made him a wiser choice for vice president in 1848 than John Tyler had been in 1840. Suddenly president in July 1850, he did not declare publicly in favor of the compromise Taylor had condemned, but it was reasonably assumed that, as a good Whig without Taylor's crotchets, he favored it.

THE "LITTLE GIANT"

It was not a Whig, however, who picked up the shreds of the Omnibus Bill and pasted them back together. It was a Democrat from Illinois, just three years in the senate and not yet 40 years of age: **Stephen A. Douglas** of Illinois. Barely five feet in height and already portly, Douglas did not cut much of a figure. But he was known in Illinois as the "Little Giant" because of his oratorical powers and his political finesse as the state's Democratic party tactician. Douglas wanted to be president, but at his age, he knew better than to be in a hurry. He had devoted his three years in the senate to ingratiating himself with both northern and southern Democrats, and with Whigs too. He was on the verge of being considered a "national figure" when the sectional crisis catapulted him into the first rank of national figures.

Buttonholing individual senators and representatives by the dozen, Douglas tirelessly explained his plan for shimming Clay's collection of compromises through Congress. Rather than introduce them in a single bill, Douglas proposed to carve the Omnibus Bill into five separate bills. He maneuvered these individually through Congress by patching together different majorities—more buttonholing, more persuasion, more just wearing his colleagues down—for each one.

Douglas's strategy was ingenious and complex. He could count on northern senators and representatives of both parties to vote for California statehood and the abolition of the slave trade in the District of Columbia. Both sailed through the House. In the Senate, he won the votes of enough southern Whigs from the border states (southern Whigs did not make a religion of slavery) to slip the bills through with slim majorities.

Douglas started with a solid southern Democratic bloc for the Fugitive Slave Act. Northern Whigs were opposed to it, but, arguing for the necessity of preserving the Democratic party in both sections, Douglas added enough northern Democratic senators and representatives to make a majority.

Douglas's manipulations were brilliant, but the "Compromise of 1850" was no compromise at all. In a compromise, contending parties each give up some of their wants to win others and to restore cooperation where there has been a deadlock. That did not happen in 1850. A large majority of northern and southern congressmen yielded nothing. Only 4 of 60 senators voted for all of Douglas's bills! Only 11 voted for five of six. (Even Douglas was absent for the vote on the Fugitive Slave Act.) Only 28 of 240 Representatives voted for all six bills. Clay's Omnibus Bill was a compromise. Douglas's "compromise" was sleight of hand. It did not restore a spirit of intersectional cooperation to Congress (or to the nation). Sectional animosities in Congress were as bitter after Douglas's trick as before.

CHANGING OF THE GUARD

The Congress of 1849–1851 saw the nation's second generation of political leaders—the men of the age of Andrew Jackson—pass the torch to a third generation. Andrew Jackson was already gone, dead in 1845. Calhoun died in March 1850, croaking to his young disciples, "the South, the poor South." Henry Clay and Daniel Webster passed on two years later. Thomas Hart Benton survived until 1858, but in the new

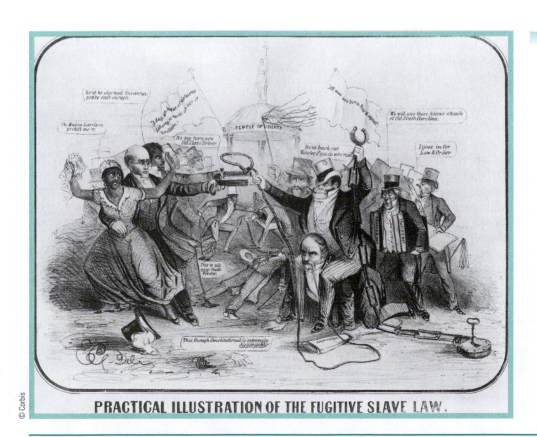

An antislavery cartoon attacking the Fugitive Slave Act of 1850. Abolitionist William Lloyd Garrison is protecting the runaway slave woman at left (with a gun, curiously— Garrison was a pacifist). Daniel Webster, who voted for the law, is the mount for a stereotypical Irishman (most Irish voters were Democrats friendly to slavery) bearing chains for the woman and a noose for Garrison.

PRACTICAL ILLUSTRATION OF THE FUGITIVE SLAVE LAW.

atmosphere of bitter sectional hostility, there was no place for him. Because he prized the Union more than he prized slavery, he lost his Senate seat in 1850, was defeated in a race for the House in 1856, and lost when he ran for governor of Missouri.

The Whig party, the refuge of moderates, dwindled after 1850. Some younger southern Whigs outdid the Calhounites in their obsession with defending slavery. Robert Toombs of Georgia supported the Compromise of 1850; within a few years he was himself a fire-eater, as proslavery extremist politicians were called. Only in the border states did a few old Henry Clay Whigs continue to win elections because they were respected as individuals.

In the North, the Whigs were weakened by tensions between **"cotton Whigs" and "conscience Whigs."** Cotton Whigs tried to downplay the slavery issue because they knew it would split the party in sectional lines and because of the importance of southern cotton to the northern textile industry. Conscience Whigs were abolitionists, and like the southern Democratic fire-eaters, they were young members of a new generation. Among the ablest was William H. Seward of New York, a former Anti-Mason. Thaddeus Stevens of Pennsylvania was a staunch believer in racial equality whom southerners hated above all other abolitionists. Charles Sumner of Massachusetts, who succeeded Webster as New England's most prominent senator, was as obnoxious personally as any southern fire-eater.

With the Free Soilers gone from the Democratic party to form their own, most northern Democrats were friendly to the South and slavery, but to different degrees. A few northern Democrats preached positive-good propaganda with the best of them. Others, notably Stephen A. Douglas, did not look on slavery as a desirable institution, but their sensibilities were not outraged by its existence in the South. For the sake of Democratic party unity, they were willing to make concessions to southern Democrats.

FRANKLIN PIERCE

The election of Franklin Pierce as president in 1852, and the events of his administration, finished off the Whig party. Pierce was a longtime Democratic regular from New Hampshire who had been popular in Congress during the 1830s and 1840s. Handsome, charming, and sociable (too sociable, maybe—one colleague called him the "hero of many a well-fought bottle"), he quit politics to fight in the Mexican War and then returned to New Hampshire to practice law.

At the Democratic convention in 1852, Pierce was New Hampshire's **favorite son** candidate, selected after forty-eight ballots when no other candidate could win two-thirds of the delegates. Pierce was acceptable, even desirable, to southern Democrats because of his record of vilifying abolitionists and praising slavery. He won just over 50 percent of the popular vote, but he won in all but a few states, winning 254 electoral votes to Whig candidate General Winfield Scott's 42.

Rarely have American voters made so bad a mistake. If Pierce calmed southern apprehensions because he was pro-southern, Scott was himself a southerner, a Virginian. Scott, for all his personal pomposity, was able, temperate, and decisive—just what the country needed after the trauma of 1850. Pierce was at best a dubious leader. As a fellow New Hampshire man commented, "Up here, where everybody knows Frank Pierce, he's a pretty considerable fellow. But come to spread him out over the whole country, I'm afraid he'll be dreadful thin in some places."

Pierce's wife, to whom he was devoted, hated politics and Washington, D.C. She was an emotionally fragile woman who was completely shattered when, just before Pierce's inauguration, their young son was killed in a railroad accident.

Anthony Burns

Anthony Burns, a slave, fled Virginia for Boston in 1854. He was arrested under the Fugitive Slave Act of 1850, and a furious mob of abolitionists almost freed him. Federal troops had to be brought in to guard Burns, and he was returned to his owner in Virginia, who sold him for $900. But Burns was intelligent and self-educated; he could write; and he was determined to be free. Thanks to the publicity given his case, Bostonians raised the money to buy his freedom and sent him to Oberlin College.

Southern fire-eaters had rejoiced when Burns was re-enslaved. Southerners with cooler heads pointed out that it had cost $100,000 to return one man to slavery. "A few more such victories and the South is undone," wrote the *Richmond Enquirer*.

© Corbis

Preoccupied with his wife's distress, Pierce leaned heavily on his personal friend, whom he named secretary of war, Jefferson Davis of Mississippi. Indeed, Davis was—without sinister motives or hidden goals—the dominating personality of the Pierce administration.

THE KANSAS–NEBRASKA ACT

A RAILROAD TO CALIFORNIA

Jefferson Davis was certainly proslavery—his brother was one of Mississippi's biggest slave owners—but he was not a fire-eater. He had presidential ambitions of his own and wanted to persuade northern Democrats that he was a nationally minded man. He looked like an aristocrat but was, in fact, of modest background; he was born in a log cabin in Kentucky. He was one of the Mexican War's genuine battlefield heroes, having distinguished himself for bravery in several battles.

With the support of the distracted Pierce, Davis tried to revive the expansionism of the 1840s with unsuccessful attempts to annex Hawaii and Cuba. (Cuba, with its many slaves, figured prominently in southern imaginations.) He tacitly supported American filibusters—freelance adventurers, mostly southerners, who led private armies into unstable Central America in the hopes of creating personal empires.

Filibusters

The word *filibuster* is a corruption of the Dutch *vrijbuiter*, meaning "freebooter." The filibusters of the 1850s were mostly southern veterans of the Mexican War who saw greater opportunities as warriors in Central America and the Caribbean than back home on a farm. The first filibuster was a Cuban rebel, Narciso Lopez; most of his soldiers, however, were American. In 1850, with financial support from southerners, he tried to overthrow the Spanish regime in Cuba. The plan was to annex Cuba, where slavery was still legal, to the United States. The Spanish executed fifty of Lopez's Americans. Chastened, the federal government arrested Mississippi governor John A. Quitman before he could lead a filibustering expedition to resume the fight.

Secretary of War Jefferson Davis supported the most famous of the filibusters, William Walker. An extraordinary adventurer, probably more interested in personal glory than in adding slave states to the Union, Walker invaded Baja California in 1853 but was driven out within weeks. Reorganizing his little army, he went to Nicaragua, which was then in an almost anarchic state. With the support of Nicaraguan rebels as well as his American mercenaries, Walker proclaimed himself president of the country. As a roving warlord, Walker actually ran Nicaragua for two years. When things turned sour, an American warship rescued him. He tried again, this time in Honduras. Walker was executed by a firing squad there in 1860.

Slavery in the State of Maine

The Missouri Compromise provided that slavery was "forever forbidden" in the *territories* of the Louisiana Purchase north of 36° 30'. But did that mean that the *states* that emerged in those lands were forbidden to legalize slavery? Legally, no. Before he signed the Missouri act, President Monroe consulted with his advisers. All, including John Quincy Adams, said that once a territory had become a state, its domestic institutions were its own business. In other words, had the state of Maine voted to legalize slavery as late as 1864, it was constitutionally free to do so just as Maryland and Delaware were constitutionally free to abolish slavery in those states.

In practice, prohibiting slavery in the territories meant that states that developed there would be free states. There would be no slave owners at the state's constitutional convention.

But Davis's most important project was the construction of a transcontinental railroad that tied California to the old states. That the railroad would eventually be built, everyone knew. Davis wanted its eastern terminus in the South, knowing that the California trade would enrich the city that was the eastern gateway of the line. From an engineering perspective, the best route was through Texas and along the southern boundary of the country. There were no mountains of any consequence on the route except in the southern New Mexico Territory, just above the Gila River (present-day Arizona). There, to keep the projected railroad on the flat, it would be necessary to build in Mexico, which was unacceptable.

To remedy the problem, Davis sent James Gadsden, a railroad man, to Mexico City. For $10 million he purchased a 30,000-square-mile triangle of arid but level land. Davis, it appeared, had plucked a plum for the South that would also be a great national enterprise—big enough, perhaps, to make its chief proponent president.

DOUGLAS'S SCHEME

Senator Stephen A. Douglas wanted the transcontinental railroad for Chicago in his home state. However, the central route had drawbacks the southern route did not. It crossed several major mountain ranges, and beyond Missouri, it ran through unorganized territory, those parts of the Louisiana Purchase that had been left to the Indians. The only federal presence was a series of forts protecting the overland trail. There was no territorial government. Southern politicians could kill the central route and win the transcontinental for the South simply by refusing to organize territorial governments west of Missouri.

Douglas hatched a scheme to seduce the southerners by playing on the issue that obsessed them: slavery. In May 1854 Douglas introduced a bill to organize Kansas and Nebraska territories. The bill explicitly repealed the section of the Missouri Compromise that prohibited slavery there. Instead, Douglas said, the people of Kansas and Nebraska territories would decide for themselves whether they would allow or

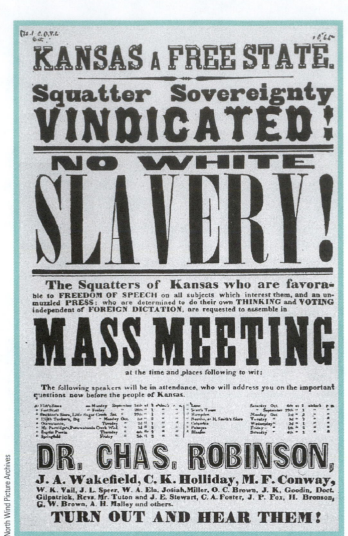

KANSAS A FREE STATE.

Squatter Sovereignty

VINDICATED!

NO WHITE

SLAVERY!

The Squatters of Kansas who are favorable to FREEDOM OF SPEECH on all subjects which interest them, and an unmuzzled PRESS; who are determined to do their own THINKING and VOTING independent of FOREIGN DICTATION, are requested to assemble in

MASS MEETING

at the time and places following to wit:

The following speakers will be in attendance, who will address you on the important questions now before the people of Kansas.

DR. CHAS. ROBINSON,

J. A. Wakefield, C. K. Holliday, M. F. Conway,
W. K. Vail, J. L. Speer, W. A. Ela, Josiah Miller, O. C. Brown, J. K. Goodin, Doct. Gilpatrick, Revs. Mr. Tuton and J. E. Stewart, C. A. Foster, J. P. Fox, H. Bronson, G. W. Brown, A. H. Malley and others.

TURN OUT AND HEAR THEM!

North Wind Picture Archives

A poster announcing an anti-Kansas–Nebraska rally. There were thousands of such meetings all over the North within weeks of Congress's enactment of the law. Rarely has there been so spontaneous a widespread protest.

prohibit the institution. "Popular sovereignty," Douglas said, was the democratic solution to the problem of slavery in the territories.

Southern congressmen jumped for the bait like trout after a bad winter. No one had illusions about slavery in Nebraska Territory, through which the central route would run. It bordered on the free state of Iowa and would inevitably be populated by antislavery northerners. Kansas, however, abutted on Missouri, where slavery was unimportant economically but an emotionally passionate issue, even with poor whites who owned no slaves.

Douglas's popularity soared in the South, and he laid plans to exploit it when he ran for president in 1856. As in 1850, he presented himself as a broker between the sections. To southerners, he was the man who opened Kansas to slavery. To northerners, he was the man who got the transcontinental railroad.

In fact, while most northern Democrats supported him, Douglas was vilified by antislavery northerners (Free Soilers and Whigs) as a "**doughface,**" a Democrat who kneaded his face into one shape in the North, another in the South—in effect a northern man with southern principles. The epithet was also applied to Pierce and to the Democratic presidential nominee in 1856, who was not Douglas, but James Buchanan of Pennsylvania.

THE REPUBLICAN PARTY

When southern Whigs voted for the Kansas–Nebraska Act, the Whigs of the North bade them farewell. Many northern Whigs were abolitionists. Those who were not, like Abraham Lincoln of Illinois, regarded the Missouri Compromise as sacred, the one inviolable hedge against the expansion of slavery. Whigs like Lincoln were willing to tolerate slavery in the South, even protect it for the sake of national unity, but they were unwilling to accept its expansion.

With the old party dead, the northern Whigs joined with the Free Soilers, former Democrats, to form the Republican party. So spontaneous was the eruption of anti-Kansas–Nebraska sentiment that the birthplace of the Republican party is disputed. (Ripon, Wisconsin has the best claim.) The fact is, the Republican party combusted and coalesced all over the North spontaneously. Rather more striking, the Republican demand that the Kansas–Nebraska Act be repealed was so popular that the infant party captured the House of Representatives in the midterm election of 1854, months after Kansas–Nebraska became law.

At first the Republicans were a single-issue party: no further expansion of slavery. However, its Whig leaders knew that the Free Soilers, with the same single-issue platform, had never won more than 10 percent of the vote nationally. So the Republicans worked out a comprehensive program. They stole Douglas's thunder on the railroad issue by insisting that the transcontinental be built on the central route. They appealed to Democratic farmers by advocating a Homestead Act giving western lands free to families who would actually settle and farm it.

From the Whigs, the Republicans inherited the demand for a high protective tariff, thus winning some manufacturing interests to their side. And appealing to industrial capitalists was the Republican demand for a liberal immigration policy, which would attract cheap European labor to the United States. Also from the Whigs, Republicans inherited a disdain for Democrats as the country's vulgar, self-serving, and ignorant. Poet Walt Whitman put it in a diatribe not to be topped. The Democrats of Washington were:

> the meanest kind of bawling and blowing officeholders, office-seekers, pimps, malignants, conspirators, murderers, fancy-men, custom-house clerks, contractors, kept-editors, spaniels well-train'd to carry and fetch, jobbers, infidels, disunionists, terrorists, mail-riflers, slave-catchers, pushers of slavery, creatures of the President, creatures of would-be

Presidents, spies, bribers, compromisers, lobbyers, sponges, ruin'd sports, expell'd gamblers, policy-backers, monte-dealers, duellists, carriers of conceal'd weapons, deaf men, pimpled men, scarr'd inside with vile disease, gaudy outside with gold chains made from the people's money and harlot's money twisted together, crawling serpentine men, the lousy combinings and born freedom-settlers of the earth.

The Republicans (the exact opposite of the Democrats on every count, of course) were not a national party, as the Whigs had been. Their program appealed only to northerners. They did not even put up candidates for office in most slave states. Their hopes of national victory lay in a sweep of the free states, which indeed would be quite enough to control the House and win the presidency. In that hope, government by a party frankly representing only one section of the country lay a new threat to national unity.

FURTHER READING

General William W. Freehling, *The Road to Disunion*, 1990; Kenneth S. Greenber, *Masters and Statesmen: The Political Culture of American Slavery*, 1985; Michael F. Holt, *The Political Crisis of the 1850s*, 1978; Bruce Levine, *Half Slave and Half Free: The Roots of the Civil War*, 1992; James M. McPherson, *Battle Cry of Freedom: The Civil War Era*, 1988; Leonard Richards, *The Slave Power: The Free North and Southern Domination, 1780–1860*, 2000; Richard A. Sewell, *A House Divided: Sectionalism and Civil War, 1848–1860*, 1988.

The Crisis of 1850 K. J. Bauer, *Zachary Taylor: Soldier, Planter, Statesman of the Old Southwest*, 1985; Holman Hamilton, *Prologue to Conflict: The Crisis and Compromise of 1850*, 1964; John Mayfield, *Rehearsal for Republicanism: Free Soil and the Politics of Anti-Slavery*, 1980; Merrill Peterson, *The Great Triumvirate: Webster, Clay, and Calhoun*, 1987; Robert Remini, *Henry Clay: Statesman for the Union*, 1991.

Kansas and Dred Scott Nichole Etcheson, *Bleeding Kansas: Contested Liberty in the Civil War Era*, 2004; Don E. Fehrenbacher, *The Dred Scott Case: Its Significance in American Law and Politics*, 1981; Kenneth M. Stampp, *America in 1857: A Nation on the Brink*, 1990; Gerald W. Wolff, *The Kansas–Nebraska Bill: Party, Section, and the Coming of the Civil War*, 1977; David Zarefsky, *Lincoln, Douglas, and Slavery: In the Crucible of Debate*, 1990.

The Republican Party Eric Foner, *Free Soil, Free Labor, Free Men: The Ideology of the Republican Party before the Civil War*, 2nd ed., 1995; William E. Gienapp, *The Origins of the Republican Party, 1852–1856*, 1987; Michael F. Holt, *The Rise and Fall of the American Whig Party*, 1999; Richard H. Sewell, *Ballots for Freedom: Antislavery Politics in the United States, 1837–1860*, 1976; Kenneth Winkle, *The Young Eagle: The Rise of Abraham Lincoln*, 2003.

KEY TERMS

The following terms are covered in this chapter and can also be found in the list of Key Terms at the back of the book.

"cotton Whigs" and "conscience Whigs"

"doughface"

favorite son

fire-eaters

Omnibus Bill

placer mining

rider

Stephen A. Douglas

Wilmot Proviso

ONLINE SOURCES GUIDE

Use this listing to find online documents, images, interactive maps, simulations, and other resources related to this chapter:

American History Resource Center
http://history.wadsworth.com/rc/us

Selected Documents
Walt Whitman preface to Leaves of Grass *(1855)*
Excerpts from Narrative of the Life of Frederick Douglass
John L. O'Sullivan, "Annexation" (1845)

Selected Images
Return of Thomas Sims and Anthony Burns

Interactive Time Line (with online readings)
Apples of Discord: The Poisoned Fruits of Victory, 1844–1854

Discovery

How did expansion and the fight over slavery affect American society in the 1850s?

In thinking about this question, begin by breaking it down into the components shown below. A discussion of the significance of each component should appear in your answer.

Government and Law: For this exercise, read the document excerpts "The New York *Herald* Supports the Compromise of 1850" and "Calhoun's Speech on the Compromise of 1850." What justification does the New York *Herald* give for supporting the Compromise of 1850? What fears does the newspaper express? What kinds of people does it claim are undermining the compromise efforts? Why does Calhoun oppose the compromise? What are his fears? What does he believe will be happening soon? Who does he believe has to compromise more in order for the union to remain as one? Why?

The New York *Herald* Supports the Compromise of 1850

From The New York *Herald*, September 8, 1850

. . .—leaving, only the Fugitive Slave bill, and the bill for the abolition of slave traffic in the District of Columbia, to be disposed of, the former having been passed by the Senate, and the later being now under consideration in that body. . . . The whole of this disagreeable subject will, therefore, be shortly wound up, and a quietus put to the ultras and fanatics of different sections of the Union, who have exerted themselves to the utmost to keep alive the slavery agitation, and maintain an estrangement of feeling between the Northern and the Southern States. The subject, therefore, which has caused so much disquietude and uneasiness to the friends of the Union everywhere, as well as to the admirers of our political institutions at home and abroad, is set at rest in a manner satisfactory to all, and no impediment now exists in the way of this republic pursuing the even tenor of its way, and arriving at that extraordinary and unlimited commercial and political greatness which destiny long since shadowed forth for it. . . .

Now that the danger which immediately threatened the perpetuity of the Union has been safely passed, and the public mind can reflect calmly on the escape which the country has had, the statement who nobly and patriotically threw aside all predilections and feelings, and stood together shoulder to shoulder, in restoring harmony in our public councils, as well as throughout the country, must not be overlooked. To the efforts of Messrs. Clay, Webster, Cass, Foote and Dickinson, supported by Mr. Hilliard and others in the House, in the country indebted for the adjustment of a question which, at one time, wore a dreadful and ominous aspect. . . . At this important juncture, those statemen stepped into the breach, and by their moral firmness and patriotism hushed the storm and calmed the waves of disunion. . . .

Calhoun's Speech on the Compromise of 1850

Having now, Senators, explained what it is that endangers the Union, and traced it to its cause, and explained its nature and character, the question again recurs, How can the Union be saved? To this I answer, there is but one way by which it can be, and that is, by adopting such measures as will satisfy the States belonging to the southern section that they can remain in the Union consistently with their honor and their safety. There is, again, only one way by which that can be effected, and that is, by removing the causes by which this belief has been produced. . . .

The North has only to will it to accomplish it—to do justice by conceding to the South an equal right in the acquired territory, and to do her duty by causing the stipulations relative to fugitive slaves to be faithfully fulfilled—to cease the agitation of the slave question, and to provide for the insertion of a provision in the Constitution, by an amendment, which will restore to the South in substance the power she possessed of protecting herself, before the equilibrium between the sections was destroyed by the action of this Government. There will be no difficulty in devising such a provision—one that will protect the South, and which at the same time will improve and strengthen the Government, instead of impairing and weakening it.

But will the North agree to do this? It is for her to answer this question. But, I will say, she cannot refuse, if she has half the love of the Union which she professes to have, or without justly exposing herself to the charge that her love of power and aggrandizement is far greater than her love of the Union. At all events, the responsibility of saving the Union rests on the North, and not the South. The South cannot save it by any act of hers, and the North may save it without any sacrifice whatever, unless to do justice, and to perform her duties under the Constitution, should be regarded by her as a sacrifice.

To read extended versions of the documents, visit the companion Web site http://history.wadsworth.com/americanpast8e; click on "Discovery Sources."

CHAPTER 22

The Collapse of the Union

From Debate to Violence 1854–1861

Reproduced from the Collections of the Library of Congress

Shall I tell you what this collision means? They who think it is accidental, unnecessary, the work of interested or fanatical agitators, and therefore ephemeral, mistake the case altogether. It is an irrepressible conflict between opposing and enduring forces.

William H. Seward

"A house divided against itself cannot stand." I believe this government cannot endure permanently half-slave and half-free. I do not expect the Union to be dissolved—I do not expect the house to fall—but I do expect it will cease to be divided.

Abraham Lincoln

By devising the Kansas–Nebraska Act, Stephen A. Douglas believed he had become the Democratic party's sure-thing presidential nominee in 1856. He thought he had added the gratitude of southerners to the northern Democrats who were beholden to him for resolving the crisis of 1850.

In fact, Douglas had become Pandora, the woman of Greek mythology who opened a box from which all the evils people plague one another with escaped into the world. In the story, seeing what she had done, Pandora closed the lid of the box before hope was lost. Douglas had his hopes after 1854. But they were dashed by events directly traceable to Kansas-Nebraska, and unlike before 1854, they were often violent.

BLEEDING KANSAS

The southern congressmen who voted to create Kansas territory assumed that it would be populated gradually by proslavery Missourians from next door and then—thanks to **popular sovereignty**—apply for admission to the Union as a slave state. The northern Democrats who had voted for Kansas–Nebraska would, of course, vote for Kansas statehood.

They (and Douglas) were utterly unprepared for the explosion of anti-Kansas–Nebraska feeling in the North. Of forty-four northern Democrats who voted in favor of the bill, thirty-seven were defeated in the 1854 election—by the Republican party that had been organized only months

Border Ruffians

Missouri's western tier of counties was known as a violent region before and after the issue of slavery aroused tempers there. During the 1840s, western Missourians drove Mormon settlers out with the connivance of the state government. After the Kansas–Nebraska Act, proslavery western Missourians were denounced as **border ruffians** for their raids in eastern Kansas. A disproportionate number of dubious characters of the Civil War era had roots there. Western Missouri was prime recruiting ground for Quantrill's Raiders, notorious Confederate irregulars responsible for terrorist attacks on civilians. William Quantrill's right-hand man, Bloody Bill Anderson, scalped the northerners he killed. Future outlaws Jesse and Frank James and the Younger brothers came from western Missouri, as did the "bandit queen," Myra Belle Shirley, or Belle Starr.

earlier. Indeed, the Republicans won a majority in the House of Representatives and won control of all but two northern state legislatures, giving them fifteen Senate seats. If the Republicans got control of both houses, Kansas–Nebraska would be repealed.

FREE SOILERS AND BORDER RUFFIANS

Equally dismaying was the wildfire speed with which abolitionists mobilized to make Kansas a free state under the rules of popular sovereignty. Organizations such as Eli Thayer's New England Emigrant Aid Company urged northern farmers thinking of going west to go to Kansas. They sweetened the pot by financing the costs of emigration and helping free-state voters to set up a farm or business when they got there. Within two years, Thayer's group sent 2,000 people to Kansas. Undoubtedly, their effective propaganda—abolitionists praised the soil and climate of Kansas as if they pocketed a percentage of every land sale in the territory—encouraged many other northerners to go on their own.

Proslavery southerners could not match such a campaign. No part of the South was so densely populated as New England was; there was not the same economic incentive to go west. Southerners who were thinking of emigration were more interested in the cotton lands of Arkansas and Texas than in the prairies and plains of Kansas. Not even western Missourians, for whom moving to Kansas meant a short ride, went in any great numbers. Except for bustling Independence, western Missouri was itself thinly populated

The Granger Collection, New York

Border ruffians on a raid of free-state settlers in Kansas. It is, obviously, a hostile northern depiction. The men who lived in the far west of Missouri were mostly poor and many of them were tough characters, but not all of those who harassed free staters in Kansas were frontier scum of this caliber.

frontier. The western counties wanted more settlers; they had no surplus to send west in the interest of a cause.

The ink with which President Pierce signed the Kansas–Nebraska Act was scarcely dry, and it was already a toss-up whether slave-state voters or free-state voters would write the Kansas state constitution.

If few western Missourians moved to Kansas, some of the rougher sort—and western Missouri was tough country—were willing to vote fraudulently in Kansas elections and even to terrorize the free staters who had settled there. About 5,000 Missourians voted in the election of a territorial legislature in March 1855. In one district in which there were eleven cabins, 1,828 proslavery votes were recorded. Free-state Kansans were intimidated by armed riders, told to get out, and roughed up. Cabins and barns were burned by "border ruffians," as free staters called the Missourians.

That thousands of young Missourians should have participated in so ugly a campaign indicates that the conflict had more to do with racism and adolescent hormonal upheaval than promoting slavery. Most western Missourians were struggling farmers; only a few owned slaves, and none owned very many. Most border ruffians were teenagers and young men who owned nothing; but, like young men since time began, they found bullying and generally raising hell an inviting prospect.

LAWRENCE AND "BULLY" BROOKS

It is impossible to say how many of the innumerable beatings, robberies, and arsons, along with the murders of six free staters in 1855 and early 1856, could be attributed to the slavery controversy, and how many would have occurred had slavery not been an issue. American frontiers were unstable as a rule. But the sustained violence of the summer of 1856—"**Bleeding Kansas**," northern newspapers called the territory—was clearly a miniature civil war fought over slavery. Nor were the free staters all passive victims. They formed paramilitary cavalries, called **jayhawkers,** that were as nasty as the border ruffians, beating and robbing proslavery Kansans and raiding Missouri.

On May 21, 1856, a large gang of border ruffians and proslavery Kansans rode into the antislavery town of Lawrence, Kansas. They shot it up and set several buildings afire. Only one person was killed (a Missourian crushed by a falling wall); but in other incidents, probably the work of the same gang, several free-state settlers were murdered.

In Washington at about the same time, Massachusetts Senator Charles Sumner delivered a speech he called the "Crime against Kansas." Like Garrison, Sumner was a pacifist; also like Garrison, he was given to vituperative language that pacifists ought to avoid. During his review of the proslavery violence in Kansas, Sumner threw in a gratuitous personal insult of an elderly senator from South Carolina, Andrew Butler, who was sitting nearby. Butler suffered from a physical defect that caused him to salivate when he spoke. Sumner coarsely alluded to his slobbering as emblematic of the bestiality of slave owners.

Two days later, Butler's nephew, a congressman named Preston Brooks, entered the Senate chamber, approached Sumner from behind, and beat him senseless with a heavy cane—more a club than a walking stick. Brooks explained his action by citing the Code Duello, which held that a gentleman avenged another gentleman's personal insult by challenging him to a duel. But a gentleman horsewhipped or caned a social inferior who insulted him or a member of his family.

In fact, Brooks mocked the code of honor. He did not humiliate Sumner with a few sharp raps, which was what the Code Duello prescribed; he bludgeoned him until Sumner was near death. Rather than disown Brooks as a bounder, southerners feted him at banquets, making him gifts, amidst appreciative laughter, of gold-headed canes to replace the one he had broken. When Brooks resigned his seat in the House, his district reelected him resoundingly. Sumner, who had himself overstepped the bounds of Senate etiquette, albeit with words, became a martyr in the North. His injuries were so severe that he was unable to return to work for several years, but Massachusetts reelected him so that his empty desk would stand as a rebuke to southern barbarism.

POTTAWATOMIE BROWN

Back in Kansas, a man named John Brown snapped. Brown was a zealous abolitionist who had helped the underground railroad in Ohio and then joined five of his sons who had

The Breakup of the Union 1856–1861

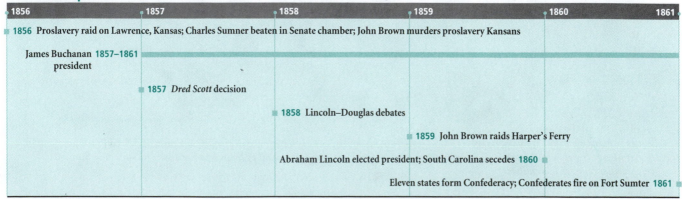

| 1856 | 1857 | 1858 | 1859 | 1860 | 1861 |

1856 Proslavery raid on Lawrence, Kansas; Charles Sumner beaten in Senate chamber; John Brown murders proslavery Kansans

James Buchanan 1857–1861 president

1857 *Dred Scott* decision

1858 Lincoln–Douglas debates

1859 John Brown raids Harper's Ferry

Abraham Lincoln elected president; South Carolina secedes 1860

Eleven states form Confederacy; Confederates fire on Fort Sumter 1861

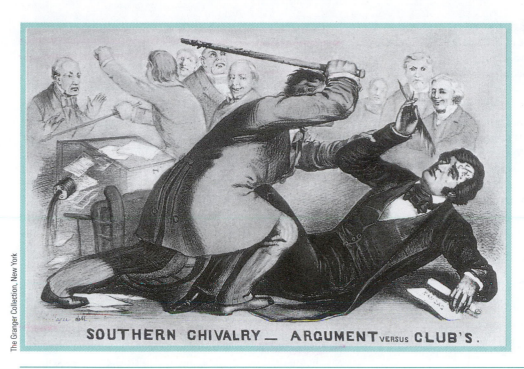

SOUTHERN CHIVALRY — ARGUMENT versus CLUB'S.

Preston Brooks's clubbing of Charles Sumner readily lent itself to the antislavery movement's portrayal of proslavery southerners as barbarians and Sumner as a man of the pen. Note the senators in the background—southerners, obviously—ignoring or laughing at Brooks's brutality.

JOHN BROWN

moved to Kansas to vote free state. So far as is known, Brown had never committed an act of violence (except on his children, whom he beat with a severity unusual even for the time.) However, on the night of May 24, with four of his sons and two other men, he descended on the cabins of five proslavery Kansans on Pottawatomie Creek, called them outside, and hacked them to death, apparently with farm tools.

Southern politicians, who had joked about the border ruffians as if they were pranksters, howled in humanitarian anguish. Northern abolitionists, who had wrung their hands over the clubbing of Senator Sumner, were silent about what was a cold-blooded ritual murder. (It was not a retaliation for Lawrence. None of Brown's victims had been involved in the raid.) That such a man should be excused and subsequently canonized by educated New Englanders who were inclined to parade their gentility and moral rectitude indicates the extremity of the hatred between antislavery northerners and proslavery southerners. Extremists on both sides no longer played by the rules of politics or common decency. They endorsed as justified anything done in the name of "the South, the poor South" or for the holy cause of striking the chains from the bondmen.

FUGITIVE SLAVES

By 1856 it was not only Kansas, so recently the land of opportunity for slavery but now all too likely the site of an impending defeat, that was driving proslavery southerners to distraction. The Fugitive Slave Act of 1850, the great concession to the South in the Compromise of 1850, was not quite a dead letter. But it had not solved the problem of runaway slaves as it was intended to do.

Before 1850, between 1,000 and 1,500 slaves each year had escaped to northern states. Once in Indiana, Ohio, or Pennsylvania, many were helped by the underground railroad to escape farther north, where with additional aid from antislavery blacks and whites, they found work and disappeared into the population. Even when a slave owner or a professional slave catcher (bounty hunters, in effect) located and arrested runaways, antislavery state and county judges often found technicalities that prevented the return of the fugitives to the South.

The Fugitive Slave Act of 1850 bypassed northern law officers and courts by creating federal commissioners empowered to arrest, judge, and return runaways. The law levied harsh punishments on any person helping a runaway slave "directly or indirectly." The commissioners could "compel" a bystander to assist in restraining a fugitive slave who was resisting, and could punish anyone who refused to help. The law put in jeopardy the freedom of African Americans who had lived as free men and women in the North for years. One of the first people returned to slavery by commissioners had lived in the North for nineteen years.

At first, the Fugitive Slave Act lived up to southern expectations. During the first three months the law was in effect, hundreds of fugitives were returned to their masters. Where slave catchers had been successful only within a few dozen miles of a slave state, they now operated as far north as Wisconsin and Boston. Within three months, 3,000 African Americans who had lived securely in the North fled to Canada to escape the reach of American law.

Antislavery northerners reacted with the same fury with which they responded to the Kansas–Nebraska Act. If a man or woman could be snatched from the streets and returned to slavery without recourse to the courts, slavery was de facto as legal in Wisconsin and New Hampshire as it was in Alabama—no matter that the people of the state had abolished the institution.

By 1856 the underground railroad had adjusted to the new circumstances and extended its "tracks" so that runaways could get all the way to Canada. Arrests and returns declined. In a few cases mobs used force to free fugitive slaves whom commissioners had taken into custody. Northerners saw the federal law as the arrogance of the slave power. Southerners saw northern resistance to the law as acts of war against their institutions.

A HARDENING OF LINES

In normal times, politicians who argue emotionally with one another in the halls of Congress often socialize outside the Capitol. Calhoun, Webster, and Clay made small talk at receptions. Even Andrew Jackson and Nicholas Biddle managed civil conversation when they met socially. By 1856 this was no longer so. Some congressmen, both northerners and southerners, carried firearms on the floor. They withdrew into their own tribes for social occasions. Against this backdrop the presidential election of 1856 was held.

THE ELECTION OF 1856

The Democrats had no choice but to nominate a doughface; a southerner could not win. But not any northerner would do. Southerners insisted on a northern Democrat who was emphatic in his sympathies for the South and slavery. Had Kansas not become a battleground in 1855, the Democrats would surely have picked Stephen A. Douglas. But the Little Giant, a hero in the South when he opened the territories to slavery in 1854, lost his southern following when the opening created by the Kansas–Nebraska Act proved to be little more than hypothetical.

Even Douglas retreated from his position in 1854. Alarmed by the hostility to Kansas–Nebraska in Illinois, Douglas now assured his constituents and northerners generally that they need not worry about Kansas becoming a slave state. Kansas would be a free state, Douglas said, because of the unsuitability of Kansas to plantation agriculture. With the success of the emigrant aid societies in sending thousands of antislavery northerners to the territory, Douglas's reasoning rang unpleasantly true in proslavery ears.

The Democrats nominated James Buchanan of Pennsylvania, a man of pedestrian talents and effeminate manner. (Andrew Jackson called him "Miss Nancy"—a sissy, even a homosexual, in nineteenth-century parlance.) Buchanan had been a party yes-man who was lucky. He had been out of the country serving as minister to Great Britain between 1853 and 1856; he had said little about Bleeding Kansas. He was, however, congenial to southern extremists

because, along with several other diplomats, he signed the Ostend Manifesto—a call for the United States to purchase Cuba, which, since California statehood, many southerners envisioned as a slave state.

The Republicans nominated John C. Frémont, nationally celebrated as "the Pathfinder," the dashing leader of two western expeditions that helped map the way to Oregon and California. In fact, Frémont was no giant of character or intellect. His greatest recommendation was his wife, Jessie Benton, the beautiful, willful, and intelligent daughter of Old Bullion Benton. In 1856, however, Frémont was a natural choice for the Republicans: he was a military hero like the only two successful Whig candidates for president, and he was a Free Soiler. (He was also an abolitionist, but that was not common knowledge.)

Frémont's name was not listed on the ballot in a single southern state. Nonetheless, he won a third of the popular vote and the electoral votes of New England and New York. Buchanan won every slave state, where his only opposition was the anti-immigrant, anti-Catholic American or "Know-Nothing" party. He also won the electoral votes of New Jersey, Pennsylvania, Indiana, and Illinois. The Know-Nothing candidate was former president Millard Fillmore, who sidestepped the Kansas question for good reason: many northern Know-Nothings were antislavery; Fillmore's southern supporters, of course, were not. Fillmore won 44 percent of the popular vote in the slave states, where there were few Catholics to worry about; there were still a great many southern Whigs who could not bring themselves to vote for a Democrat.

DRED SCOTT

Buchanan's presidency began with a bang. In his inaugural address he hinted that the issue of slavery in the territories would shortly be settled for all time. Two days later, on March 6, 1857, Americans learned what he meant when the Supreme Court handed down a decision in the case of *Dred Scott v. Sandford.*

Dred Scott was a slave in Missouri. For much of his life he was the valet of an army officer. In 1834 Scott accompanied his master to Illinois, where slavery was prohibited under the Northwest Ordinance. Briefly, then, he lived in a part of the Louisiana Purchase where slavery was illegal under the Missouri Compromise.

In 1844 Scott's owner died, bequeathing him to his widow, who disliked slavery. Rather than simply manumit him, she was persuaded by abolitionists to cooperate in creating a test case. Scott sued his owner (eventually a man named Sandford) for his freedom on the grounds that for four years he was held as a slave in territory where Congress had prohibited slavery.

Missouri courts had released slaves with cases identical to Scott's, but that was before sectional animosity had become so bitter. Judges too had changed. Scott lost his case on the grounds that whatever his legal status may have been when he was in Illinois twenty years earlier, he became a slave again

Dred Scott, his wife, and (above them) their daughters. This sympathetic presentation of the beleaguered family indicates how anger in the North toward "the slavocrat conspiracy" had spread far beyond the abolitionists. Frank Leslie's was no antislavery propaganda sheet but a general periodical that usually avoided strong political stands in order to appeal to the broadest possible readership.

legally when he returned to Missouri. By 1856 the *Dred Scott* case was before the Supreme Court.

CHIEF JUSTICE TANEY'S FINAL SOLUTION

Every justice commented individually on the case, which was unusual. However, Chief Justice Roger B. Taney, a slave owner and an old Jackson henchman from Maryland, spoke for the majority when he declared that because Scott was black, he could not be a citizen of Missouri, which restricted citizenship to white people. Therefore, Scott could not sue in Missouri courts.

The Court could have left the decision at that. Several justices did; the legal reasoning was plausible, and such a decision would have raised few hackles (not even Scott's; he had been assured he would be freed when the case was concluded).

Unfortunately, Taney, like so many Supreme Court justices in recent decades, wanted to make his mark on history. He did. With the highly irregular input of president-elect Buchanan, Taney believed he had discovered the ultimate constitutional solution to the question that was tearing the country apart—the status of slavery in the territories. In fact, the doctrine Taney propounded had been anticipated in detail by John C. Calhoun.

Taney declared that the Missouri Compromise (and, by extension, the Northwest Ordinance) had been unconstitutional in prohibiting slavery in the territories because the Constitution forbade Congress to discriminate against the citizens of any state. A state legislature could outlaw slavery because the states were sovereign. But neither Congress nor a territorial legislature (a creature of Congress) could do so because that would deny the right of the citizens of states where slavery was legal to take their property into the territories. The Constitution forbade such discrimination.

THE REPUBLICAN PANIC

The Republicans were floored. The essence of their program was to win a majority in Congress so as to restore a Missouri Compromise–like prohibition of slavery in the western territories. In telling them they could not do so, Taney had hit at their reason for existing. Just as proslavery southerners had seen the Fugitive Slave Act effectively nullified by the underground railroad, antislavery northerners saw their political intentions frustrated by extrapolitical forces.

To Republicans, the history of the question of slavery in the territories was a step-by-step whittling away of the will of the majority to prevent the expansion of slavery. That is, between 1820 and 1854, under the Missouri Compromise, slavery was illegal in all territories north of 36°30'. The Kansas–Nebraska Act of 1854 legalized slavery in a territory where it had been forbidden if a majority of citizens in that territory voted to do so. Now the *Dred Scott* decision of 1857 prevented a majority of a territory's population from keeping slavery out because *Dred Scott* v. *Sandford* killed the principle of popular sovereignty too.

Republicans spoke of the "slave power"—a "**slavocracy**" government by a small coterie of slave owners determined to force their abominable institution on everyone, a conspiracy that now included the Supreme Court. The fire was fanned in October 1857 when President Buchanan endorsed the **Lecompton Constitution,** a constitution for Kansas that made it a slave state. The Lecompton Constitution was at best dubious. It had been drafted by one of two rival territorial legislatures: proslavery Kansans met at Lecompton, free staters at Topeka. Nevertheless, Congress might have accepted it—Democrats had a majority in both houses—but for the fact that Stephen A. Douglas and other northern Democrats, hard-pressed in the North because they appeared to be proslavery, insisted that the Lecompton document be ratified in a referendum in which all Kansans voted.

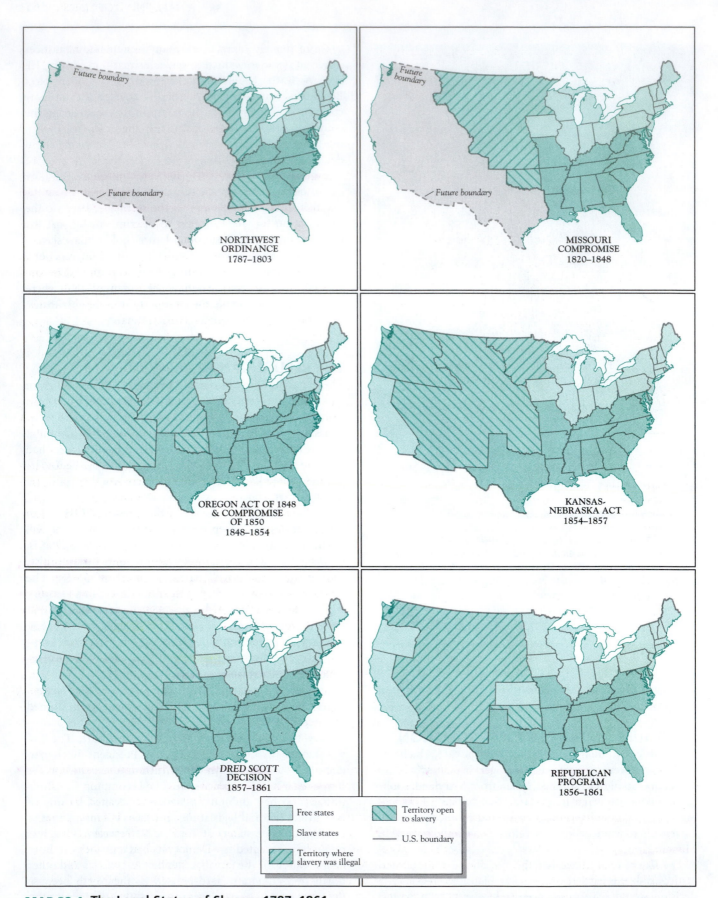

MAP 22:1 The Legal Status of Slavery 1787–1861

This series of maps explains why ever-increasing numbers of northerners who were not abolitionists were frustrated during the 1850s. While a majority of Americans clearly wanted no slavery in the territories, every change in the status of the institution since 1820 increased the area of the territories in which slavery was legal.

Map labels:

NORTHWEST ORDINANCE 1787–1803

MISSOURI COMPROMISE 1820–1848

OREGON ACT OF 1848 & COMPROMISE OF 1850 1848–1854

KANSAS-NEBRASKA ACT 1854–1857

DRED SCOTT DECISION 1857–1861

REPUBLICAN PROGRAM 1856–1861

Legend:
- Free states
- Slave states
- Territory where slavery was illegal
- Territory open to slavery
- U.S. boundary

CHIEF JUSTICE ROGER B. TANEY

Roger B. Taney, Chief Justice of the Supreme Court, is remembered only for writing the destructive majority opinion in the Dred Scott *Case, which injected the Court into the center of the divisive political issue of slavery's status in the territories. Taney's pro-slavery "solution" to the problem was gratuitous; Scott v. Sandford could have been decided with a simple, impeccably judicial ruling. Of an old Maryland planter family, Taney's avid proslavery sentiments were his great weakness as a jurist. Constitutional historians consider his career as a whole exemplary. Taney was a Unionist; he administered the inaugural oath to Lincoln and remained on the Court until his death in 1864.*

LINCOLN AND DOUGLAS: TWO NORTHERN ANSWERS

In 1858 Douglas, so recently a shoo-in to be president, now feared that he might lose his Senate seat. The Republicans painted him as a proslavery doughface. If few of Illinois's Democrats were antislavery, many of them opposed the expansion of slavery into the territories. Having presented himself as a friend of the South in 1854, in 1858, to be re-elected to the Senate, Douglas had to argue that popular sovereignty would ensure that the territories would be free of slave owners.

His task was complicated by the *Dred Scott* decision because it denied territorial legislatures, as well as Congress, the power to keep slavery out. In a way, the *Scott* decision worked to the benefit of the Republican candidate for Douglas's seat, a former Whig congressman and successful lawyer from Springfield, Abraham Lincoln.

Douglas and Lincoln were not competing for a majority of the popular vote; in 1858 Senators were elected by state legislatures. But both campaigned hard on behalf of the candidates for seats in the legislature who would vote for them. Knowing he was in a very close race, Douglas agreed to a series of debates with Lincoln at towns around the state.

How, Lincoln asked Douglas at most of the debates, could slavery be kept out of the territories after the *Dred Scott* decision? Douglas had an answer, which he spelled out at a debate in Freeport in August. A territorial legislature, Douglas said, could ensure that no slave owners brought their slaves to that territory simply by failing to enact a slave code: the laws in every southern state that protected a master's property rights in his slaves. No slave owner would be so foolish as to take his valuable human property to a place where there were no laws to ensure his power over his slaves. (In California, in fact, slave owners watched their slaves simply walk away from them because there were no laws protecting slavery.) The Supreme Court might be able to overturn a territorial law, Douglas pointed out, but the Court could not force a territorial legislature to enact a law it did not choose to enact.

The **Freeport Doctrine** was ingenious; Douglas was a superb lawyer. And he defeated Lincoln in the election, although narrowly. But events proved that Lincoln was correct that southern extremists would be stopped by nothing. When presented with the logic of the Freeport Doctrine, southerners demanded that Congress enact a *national* slave code that would affirmatively protect slavery in the territories.

Race

Few whites, including abolitionists, believed in racial equality. Thus it was in the political interest of northern Democrats to accuse the Republicans of advocating "race mixture." "I am opposed to Negro equality," Stephen A. Douglas said in a debate with Abraham Lincoln in Chicago. "I am in favor of preserving, not only the purity of the blood, but the purity of the government from any mixture or amalgamation with inferior races."

This kind of attack put Republicans on the defensive. They had to assure voters that their party's opposition to slavery did not mean they believed in the equality of the races or even equal civil rights for African Americans. Lincoln replied to Douglas, "I protest, now and forever, against that counterfeit logic which presumes that because I do not want a Negro woman for a slave, I necessarily want her for a wife. . . . As God made us separate, we can leave one another alone, and do one another much good thereby."

Lincoln shrewdly took the debate back to the territorial question by saying, "Why, Judge, if we do not let them get together in the Territories, they won't mix there." Implicitly, Lincoln was approving of laws (such as Oregon's) that forbade free blacks as well as slaves in the state.

John Brown as Martyr

John Brown was content to be doomed. He believed that his death would serve the antislavery cause. Shortly before his execution, he wrote to his wife, "I have been whipped but am sure I can recover all the lost capital occasioned by that disaster by only hanging a few minutes by the neck." He was right. Within two years of his execution, he was considered a martyr to the cause of antislavery.

John Brown's Mountains

The Appalachians, where John Brown said his slave rebellion would be based, contained many corners that were nearly impenetrable. During the Civil War, Confederate draft dodgers and deserters roamed the mountains with little fear of being caught. Folklorists have suggested that some Appalachian hollows were so isolated that Elizabethan patterns of speech and seventeenth-century ballads survived there almost unchanged into the twentieth century, while they had long since disappeared elsewhere in the English-speaking world. "Moonshiners" are still associated with Appalachian "hillbillies" because it was easier to conceal an illegal still deep in the mountains than anywhere else in the United States.

John Brown was not crackbrained when he argued that a guerrilla band could function in the mountains.

JOHN BROWN RETURNS

John Brown went into hiding after the Pottawatomie murders, but not for long. Although he was wanted for murder in Kansas, he discovered that he could move around openly in northern New York and New England. Prominent New England abolitionists and their wives were titillated rather than appalled by the Kansas murders. They invited him to dinners where he showed off the Bowie knife and revolver he tucked into his boots and excited his hosts with repartee such as "Talk! talk! talk! That will never free the slaves. What is needed is action—action" and "Caution, caution! Sir, I am eternally tired of hearing that word caution. It is nothing but the word of cowardice."

This kind of bravado is often effective among cautious, self-protective people who like to talk about sacred causes. Brown persuaded six well-to-do abolitionists to give him

A curiously neutral nineteenth-century drawing of John Brown and his followers in the final minutes in the roundhouse at Harper's Ferry. Southerners depicted Brown as a devil, northern abolitionists as a godly crusader. The man in Brown's arms is his son, who was already dying when marines stormed the ill-chosen fortress. Brown himself was seriously wounded when he was captured. He lay on a stretcher at his trial.

money to launch a slave rebellion in the South. He divulged few details of his plans; the "Secret Six" who financed him did not want to know too much. He did tell Frederick Douglass what he planned to do: with a small, disciplined cadre of whites and blacks, he would seize the federal arsenal in Harpers Ferry, Virginia (now West Virginia), capture guns and ammunition, arouse slaves in the area to join him, and escape into the Appalachians, which rose steeply around Harpers Ferry. From the mountains, Brown's guerrilla army would swoop down on plantations, free a few slaves at a time, and enlarge the corps. Before long, Brown predicted, slave rebellions would erupt all over the South, decisively destroying the peculiar institution.

Douglass was no pacifist, as many abolitionists were; he was not opposed to employing force to destroy slavery. But he wanted no part of Brown's scheme. It was doomed to failure, Douglass said; Harpers Ferry was "a perfect steel trap." He told Brown to call his project off.

Critics of **John Brown's Raid** after the fact, including many historians, have echoed Douglass. They said that it proved that the old man was out of his mind. Brown was certainly no rock of emotional stability. But he was not insane; there was nothing crazy about the idea of a small guerrilla force operating from a remote and shifting base, avoiding battles in which conventional military forces have the overwhelming advantage, and winning the support of ordinary people, in Brown's instance the slaves. Such tactics often succeeded in producing a revolution in the twentieth century. The odds were never with Brown, but they were not prohibitive.

THE RAID AND THE REACTION

Better evidence of problems in Brown's mental processes was the fact that he abandoned his plan almost as soon as he got started. On October 16, 1859, his phalanx of nineteen, including several African Americans, easily captured the arsenal. Then Brown either lost his nerve or deluded himself into believing that the slaves in the area were going to join him. Instead of making for the hills just outside the doors of

The Irish Famine and the Know-Nothings

Anti-Catholicism was a powerful force in America from the start. To the Puritans of New England, the Roman Church was not just another Christian denomination, but the "Whore of Babylon," the devil's church. Even Anglicans in the other colonies, similar as their ceremonies were to Catholic ceremonies, were fiercely anti-Catholic, perhaps because the most important difference between the Church of England and the Church of Rome was the fact that the former did not acknowledge the pope. As long as the northern colonies were threatened by the Catholic French in Canada and the Catholic Spanish in Florida, the question of security reinforced Americans' anti-Catholic bias.

The foreign threats were gone after 1819, and there were too few Catholics in the United States to occasion any worry: just 120 churches, many of which were missions among the Indians. One of the signers of the Declaration of Independence, Charles Carroll of Maryland, was a Catholic. His brother, John Carroll, was the first Catholic bishop in the country, and he endorsed both the separation of church and state and religious toleration.

Beginning about 1820, however, increasing numbers of Irish Catholics emigrated to the United States. Ireland was frighteningly overpopulated. With about 1.5 million people in 1750, thanks largely to the introduction and universal cultivation of the potato, the Irish population doubled and doubled again until, in 1840, it reached 9 million (far more than live in Ireland today). Already, among the English, the Irish had a reputation for senseless combativeness. In England, an observer said, murder was "a private act perpetrated by some ruffian for the sake of gain." In Ireland, murder was committed by a crowd of barbarians "who have no other reason for fighting than because half of the number are called O'Sullivan and the other O' something else." Irish tumultuousness on the Erie Canal fixed the stereotype in American minds.

In 1845 disaster hit a country already half-starving. A blight destroyed the potato crop in most of Ireland, and the blight returned almost annually into the 1850s. Perhaps a million people died of starvation or of diseases that a healthy population would have overcome. Several million emigrated to Britain, Canada, and especially to the United States. Many more died trying to get to America. The mortality rate on Irish immigrant ships exceeded the death rate among Africans in the Middle Passage of the eighteenth century. In America, the Irish clustered in disease- and crime-ridden slum neighborhoods. Their willingness to

take jobs at any rate of pay frightened American working people. Curiously, more Irish were literate than were Americans. But their inclination to fights and drunkenness and their intense devotion to Roman Catholicism and their priests worried Protestant Americans.

Middle- and upper-class Americans did not compete with the Irish for jobs. However, many people feared that the masses of Irish were, with their first loyalty to the Church of Rome, subverting American principles. Pope Pius IX, elected in 1846, was an unbending enemy of religious toleration, democracy, republican government, and individual rights and civil liberties. He took little direct interest in the United States; but his demons were European liberals who patterned their demands on American achievements.

This was the context in which prominent Americans like inventor and painter Samuel F. B. Morse became full-time crusaders against further Irish immigration and proponents of laws designed to inhibit Catholic worship and political participation. In 1849 a secret anti-Catholic, anti-Irish organization, the Order of the Star Spangled Banner, was organized to enact anti-immigrant and anti-Catholic laws. Members were called "Know-Nothings" because, when asked about the order, they said, "I know nothing." When the Know-Nothings came into the open as the American party, their success was astonishing. They won the mayoralty of New York City, the governorship and all but one seat in the Massachusetts assembly, and 40 percent of the vote in large parts of the South in the presidential election of 1856. The Know-Nothings circulated an old (and discredited) anti-Catholic tract, *The Awful Disclosures of Maria Monk*, which depicted nuns as the sexual slaves of Catholic priests. A convent in Charleston, Massachusetts, was burned to the ground.

The increasing bitterness of the fight over slavery killed off the Know-Nothing movement as rapidly as it had appeared. Until the *Dred Scott* decision, the party had dodged the slavery issue; southern Know-Nothings were inclined to be proslavery, although not extremists. Northern Know-Nothings were also moderates on the issue, usually not abolitionists but opposed to slavery in the territories. After *Dred Scott,* the territorial question became so consuming that the anti-Catholic passions evaporated. Most northern Know-Nothings became Republicans and voted for Abraham Lincoln in 1860 despite his disapproval of anti-Catholicism. Other ex-Know-Nothings voted for John Bell.

the arsenal, he holed up in the roundhouse, where he was promptly surrounded by U.S. marines under the command of Colonel Robert E. Lee. In two days Lee's professionals killed ten of Brown's followers and captured the others, including Brown. He was immediately tried for treason against the state of Virginia, found guilty, and hanged in December.

Most northerners were shocked by the raid and grimly approved of the speedy trial and execution of the old man. "It was not a slave insurrection," Abraham Lincoln said. "It was an attempt by white men to set up a revolt among slaves. . . . It was so absurd that the slaves saw plainly enough it could not succeed." But for southerners, if their fears of slave rebellion were rarely dwelled upon publicly, they were always in mind. They saw Brown's raid as an attempt by abolitionists to instigate an uprising that would leave them, their wives, and their children dead in their beds. Virginia governor Henry A. Wise, who interviewed Brown and was impressed by him, dismissed the suggestion that he was a lone lunatic. Brown was "fanatic, vain, and garrulous," Wise said, but also "cool, collected, and indomitable, . . . firm, truthful, and intelligent." By implication, Brown was like other northern abolitionists—a deadly serious and capable enemy.

Southern hysteria was confirmed by the fact that a few abolitionists openly praised Brown as a hero and a martyr. Ralph Waldo Emerson said that Brown's death made the gallows as holy as the Christian cross. Brown was hanged in December 1859. The following year, 1860, was an election year. Could the South trust a Republican president to protect southern whites against other John Browns? An increasing number of southerners thought not.

THE ELECTION OF 1860

Southern fire-eaters declared that if the Republicans won the presidency, the southern states would secede from the Union. Then, having threatened northern voters, the extremists not only failed to work against a Republican victory, but they guaranteed it. They split the Democratic party that had served their interests so well.

THE DEMOCRATS SPLIT

In 1860 the Democratic party was almost the last national institution in the United States. The Methodists had split into northern and southern churches in 1844, the Baptists in 1845, and the Presbyterians after 1850. Fraternal lodges broke in two. The Whig party, the country's nationalist party, was a fading memory. The Republican party was exclusively a northern institution. Only within the Democratic party did men from both sections still come together to try to settle sectional differences.

In April 1860, with the gun smoke of Brown's Raid still in the air, the Democratic convention met in Charleston. The majority of the delegates, including many southerners, supported the nomination of Stephen A. Douglas. The candidate had to be a northerner like Buchanan and Pierce. Douglas was the one Democrat open to southern needs who

could win in the North too. But the delegations of eight southern states dominated by extremists announced that they would support Douglas only if he repudiated the Freeport Doctrine and supported their demand for a federal slave code.

Douglas's supporters pointed out that if he did so, he would drive northern Democrats into the Republican party. The Democrats had to be satisfied with the one candidate who could keep the Republicans out of the White House. Unmoved, the eight hard-line delegations walked out of the convention. The Douglas forces recessed without nominating their leader, hoping to talk sense into the minority.

The Democrats reassembled in Baltimore in June. Again the southern extremists refused to budge. Disgusted by what they considered political suicide, the regular Democrats nominated Douglas for president and a southern moderate, Herschel V. Johnson of Georgia, as his running mate. The southern Democrats nominated John C. Breckinridge of Kentucky; to give the ticket a semblance of national support, they chose an Oregon doughface, Joseph Lane, as their vice presidential candidate.

REPUBLICAN OPPORTUNITY

The Republicans met in Chicago. They were optimistic but cautious. With the Democrats split, victory was likely. But if they ran too extreme an antislavery candidate—as they believed Frémont had been in 1856—many northern voters would back Douglas. Even worse would be winning on too radical a platform: southerners would make good on their threat to secede, which no one but a few abolitionists like William Lloyd Garrison wanted.

So the convention backed off from the sometimes radical rhetoric of previous years and rejected party stalwarts William H. Seward of New York and Salmon P. Chase of Ohio. Seward had spoken of "a higher law than the Constitution" in condemning slavery and, worse, of an "irrepressible conflict" between North and South. Chase had been a militant abolitionist for more than a decade.

Instead, the Republicans picked the comparatively obscure Abraham Lincoln, who was not, however, unknown thanks to nationwide newspaper coverage of his debates with Douglas. Lincoln was rock solid on the fundamental Republican principle: slavery must be banned from the territories. But he was not an abolitionist. He had steered clear of the Know-Nothings and maintained a good relationship with German voters; and he was moderate, humane, and ingratiating in manner. In a speech introducing himself to eastern Republicans in New York City in February 1860, he struck a note of humility, prudence, and caution. Not only was slavery protected by the Constitution in those states where it existed, Lincoln said, but northerners ought to sympathize with slave owners rather than vilify them. Lincoln himself was born in Kentucky, a slave state. He knew that a quirk of fate would have made him a slave owner. By choosing him, the Republicans accommodated southern sensibilities as far as they could without giving up their basic principles.

The Republican platform was comprehensive: a high protective tariff, a liberal immigration policy, the construction of a transcontinental railway, and a homestead act (free farms in the West for actual settlers). The platform was designed to win the votes of rather disparate economic groups often at odds with one another: eastern industrial capitalists, workers, and midwestern farmers. Moreover, by avoiding a single-issue campaign, the Republicans hoped to signal to the South that they were not, as a party, antislavery fanatics. They even named a vice presidential candidate who had been a Democrat as late as 1857, Hannibal Hamlin of Maine.

THE OLD MAN'S PARTY

A fourth party entered the race, drawing its strength in the states of the upper South: Maryland, Virginia, Kentucky, and Tennessee. Henry Clay's brand of Whiggery—sectional compromise and a deep attachment to the Union—was strong in the border states. The platform of the Constitutional Union party consisted, in effect, of stalling: it was a mistake, its leaders said, to force any kind of sectional confrontation while tempers were up; put off the problem of slavery in the territories to a later day when tempers had cooled.

For president the Constitutional Unionists nominated John Bell of Tennessee, a protégé of Clay. For vice president they chose the distinguished Whig orator Edward Everett of Massachusetts. Republicans and Democrats alike dismissed them as "the old man's party."

REPUBLICAN VICTORY

Abraham Lincoln won 40 percent of the popular vote, but he carried every free state except New Jersey, which he split with Douglas. He won a clear majority in the electoral college. Breckinridge won only 18 percent of the national vote, but he was the overwhelming choice of the South; he won a plurality in eleven of the fifteen slave states. Between the two, appealing to sectional feelings, Lincoln and Breckinridge won a decisive majority of voters.

Douglas, one of the two candidates appealing to nationalist sentiments, won a mere twelve electoral votes (Missouri and New Jersey), but he ran second to Lincoln in most northern states and to Breckinridge in some states in the South. John Bell carried three border states and was strong almost everywhere. Even if the Douglas and the Bell votes had been combined, however, Lincoln would have been elected. Nevertheless, inasmuch as many Lincoln and some Breckinridge supporters had no desire for a civil war, it seems clear that most Americans wanted some kind of settlement.

SOUTH CAROLINA LEADS THE WAY

If so, they did not get their wish. Having announced that Lincoln's election meant secession, the fire-eaters of South Carolina (where there was no popular vote for presidential electors) called a convention that, on December 20, 1860, unanimously declared that "the union now subsisting between South Carolina and the other States, under the name of the 'United States of America,' is hereby dissolved."

During January 1861 six states of the deep South followed suit, declaring that a Republican administration threatened their "domestic institutions." Then came a glimmer of hope. The secession movement stalled when none of the other slave states approved secession ordinances. While they rejected secession, however, conventions in the border states declared their opposition to any attempt by the federal government to use force against the states that had seceded. By rebuffing the big talkers on both sides, the leaders of the border states hoped to force a compromise.

The outgoing president, James Buchanan, was not the man to engineer such a compromise. No one had much respect for Old Buck, including his own southern adviser, who now betrayed him. His secretary of war, John Floyd of Virginia, transferred tons of war matériel to states that either had left the Union or were on the verge of leaving. Floyd's act skirted close to treason, but Buchanan did nothing.

Other Buchanan allies resigned their offices and left Washington, hardly pausing to remember the president who had worked on their behalf. The first bachelor ever to occupy the White House was quite alone, and he knew it. After a hand-wringing message sent to Congress in which he declared that while secession was illegal, he as president was powerless to do anything about it, Buchanan sat back to wait for the day he could go home to Pennsylvania.

THE CONFEDERACY

As Buchanan slumped, Senator John J. Crittenden stood up. Like many Kentuckians, Crittenden had made a career of mediating between the North and the deep South. Now he proposed that rather than break up the Union, divide the territories. Extend the Missouri Compromise line to the California border; guarantee slavery to the south of it, and forbid slavery to the north.

THE COMPROMISERS FAIL

Because of the *Dred Scott* decision, Crittenden's plan could not be put into effect by congressional action; the territories could be divided only by constitutional amendment. Crittenden hoped that the specter of civil war, now chillingly real with militias drilling in both the North and South, would prompt both northern and southern state legislatures to act in haste.

With some encouragement and a bit more time, they might have done so. There was a flurry of enthusiasm for Crittenden's compromise on both sides of the Mason–Dixon line. But before the southern extremists were forced to take a stand, President-elect Lincoln quashed the plan. His reasons were political but nonetheless compelling. His Republican party was a diverse alliance of people who disagreed with one another on many issues. The one adhesive that bound them together was the principle that slavery must not expand into the territories. If Lincoln gave in on this point, he would take office with half his party opposing him.

Lincoln also discouraged a second attempt at compromise, a peace conference held in Washington in February 1861.

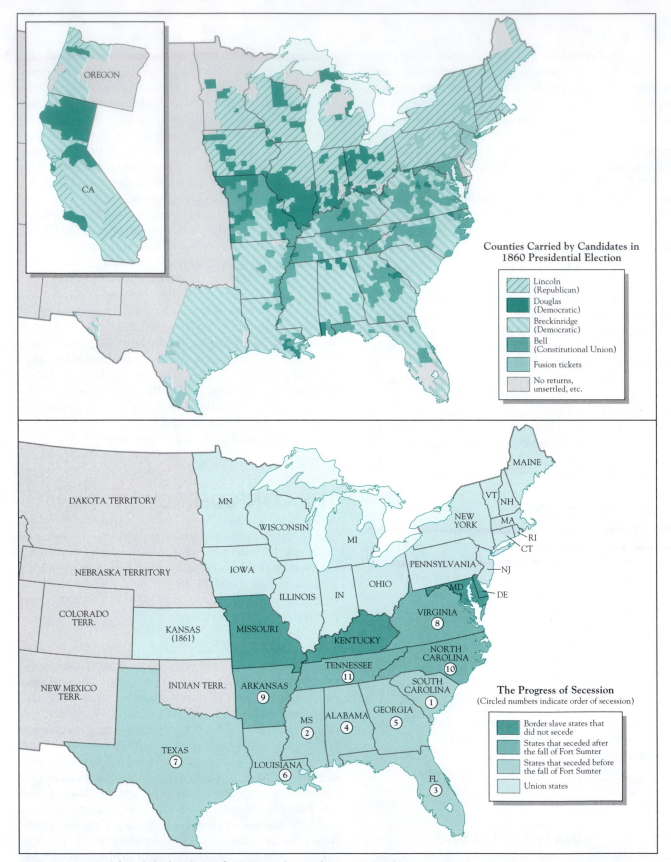

Counties Carried by Candidates in 1860 Presidential Election

- Lincoln (Republican)
- Douglas (Democratic)
- Breckinridge (Democratic)
- Bell (Constitutional Union)
- Fusion tickets
- No returns, unsettled, etc.

The Progress of Secession
(Circled numbers indicate order of secession)

- Border slave states that did not secede
- States that seceded after the fall of Fort Sumter
- States that seceded before the fall of Fort Sumter
- Union states

MAP 22:2 Presidential Election of 1860 and Southern Secession

Note, in the upper map, Lincoln's sweep in the North and Breckinridge's in the South. Bell won majorities in the border states—slave states in the upper South where only a minority shared the militant proslavery views of other southerners. Few counties gave Douglas a majority, but he finished second almost everywhere in both the North and the South.

The lower map indicates the order in which the eleven Confederate states seceded from the Union. Virginia, North Carolina, Kentucky, and Tennessee resisted secession until Lincoln's call for troops after the fall of Fort Sumter. Four slave states did not secede.

It was a distinguished assembly, chaired by former president John Tyler. Tyler had been a southern extremist, and a few months later, he would support the secession of Virginia. But he worked hard for a settlement in February, proposing a series of constitutional amendments along the same lines as Crittenden's.

Once again, Lincoln drew the line on allowing slavery in the southern territories. Instead, he endorsed an amendment (immediately passed by both houses of Congress) that would forever guarantee slavery in the states where it already existed. As he well knew, this was a largely symbolic gesture. But the question was moot by February 1861; heady with the excitement of creating a new nation, the secessionists had lost interest in preserving the Union.

THE CONFEDERATE STATES OF AMERICA

According to secessionist theory, the seven states that left the Union were now independent republics. However, no southern leader intended his state to go it alone. Although they were disappointed that eight of the fifteen slave states refused to join them, they met in Montgomery, Alabama, shortly before Lincoln's inauguration, and established the Confederate States of America.

The government of the Confederacy differed little from the one that the secessionists had repudiated. All United States laws were to remain in effect until amended or repealed, and they adopted the Constitution of 1787, plus amendments, almost word for word. The changes they made reflected the South's obsession with slavery and with Calhoun's political theories, and resulted in several curious contradictions.

Thus the Confederates defined the states as sovereign and independent but called their new government permanent. Even more oddly, the Confederates declared that individual states might not interfere with slavery, a restriction on states' rights that no prominent Republican had ever suggested.

The Confederates also modified the presidency. The chief executive was to be elected for a term of six years rather than four, but he was not permitted to run for a second term. Although this seemed to weaken the office, the Confederates allowed the president to veto parts of congressional bills rather than, as in the Union, requiring the president to accept all or nothing.

JEFF DAVIS

As their first president, the Confederates selected Jefferson Davis. On the face of it, he was a good choice. His bearing was regal, and he was the model slave owner, the sort that southerners liked to pretend was typical of the institution. Davis also seemed to be a wise choice because he was not closely associated with the secessionist movement. Indeed, Davis asked his fellow Mississippians to delay secession until Lincoln had a chance to prove himself. When his state overruled him, Davis delivered a moderate, eloquent, and affectionate farewell speech in the Senate. By choosing such a man, rather than a fire-eater, the Confederates demonstrated their willingness to work with southerners who opposed

Jefferson Davis, first and only president of the Confederacy. Davis was zealously proslavery and supported every measure to expand it to the territories. But he hoped to save the Union; he tried to delay Mississippi's secession, arguing that the state should wait until Lincoln was inaugurated and had the opportunity to make concessions to the South.

secession; there were plenty of them. With the respected Davis, the Confederacy could also appeal to the eight slave states that remained within the Union.

In other ways, the choice of Jefferson Davis was ill-advised. It was not so much the coldness of his personality; George Washington had been icy. Davis's weakness was that despite his bearing, he lacked self-confidence and was, consequently, easily irritated and inflexible. He proved incapable of cooperating with critics, even those who differed with him on minor points. He seemed to need yes-men in order to function, and, as a result, he denied his administration the services of some of the South's ablest statesmen.

Worse, Davis was a dabbler. Instead of delegating authority and presiding over the government, he repeatedly interfered in the pettiest details of administration—peering over his subordinates' shoulders, arousing personal resentments among even those who were devoted to him. He had been a good senator and secretary of war, but he was not up to being the "Father of His Country."

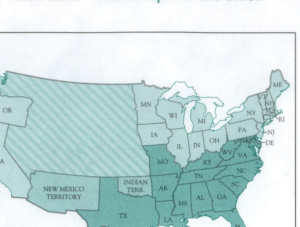

MAP 22:3 Crittenden's Compromise Plan of 1861
Crittenden's compromise recognized the justice of northern anger over the Kansas–Nebraska Act and the *Dred Scott* decision as his idol, Henry Clay, would have done. He tried to restore and extend the Missouri Compromise line; but by 1861 the Republicans would not tolerate even the legal possibility that New Mexico might be a slave state, and southern Democrats wanted nothing less than Chief Justice Taney's guarantee of slavery in the territories. (See Map 22:1 on p. 362.) They wanted secession and, if necessary, war.

Map legend:
- Free states
- Slave states
- Territory where slavery was illegal
- Territory open to slavery

ABE LINCOLN

By comparison, Abraham Lincoln knew the value of unity and competent help. Rather than shun his rivals within the Republican party, he named them to his cabinet. Seward became secretary of state; Salmon P. Chase was Lincoln's secretary of the treasury. After a brief misadventure with an incompetent secretary of war, Simon Cameron, Lincoln appointed a Democrat, Edwin Stanton, to that post because his talents were obvious. Lincoln wanted able aides, not pals or toadies. Within their departments, Lincoln's cabinet officers were free to do anything that did not conflict with general policy. As a result, a cantankerous and headstrong group of men never challenged Lincoln's control of basic policy.

Lincoln differed from Davis in other ways. Far from regal, he was an awkward, plain, even ugly man. Tall and gangling, with oversized hands and feet, he impressed those who met him for the first time as a frontier oaf. His enemies called him "the baboon." Some of his supporters snickered at his clumsiness and were appalled by his fondness for dirty jokes.

But both friends and enemies soon discovered that the president was no yokel. Lincoln had honed a sharp native

First Blood
The first blood of the Civil War was not shed at Fort Sumter. No one was killed there. The first deaths of the Civil War occurred in Baltimore a week after the fall of Sumter. A mob attacked soldiers from Massachusetts on the way to Washington as they marched from one railroad terminal to another. The soldiers fired back. Twelve members of the mob and four soldiers were killed.

intelligence on a stone of lifelong study, and he proved to be one of the three or four most eloquent chief executives. And yet behind his brilliance was a humility born of modest background that can be found in no other American president.

Lincoln needed all his native resources. On March 4, 1861, when he was sworn in before a glum Washington crowd, the Union was in tatters. During the previous two months, the Stars and Stripes had been hauled down from every flagstaff in the South except for one at Fort Pickens in Pensacola, Florida, and another at Fort Sumter, a rocky island in the harbor of Charleston, South Carolina.

A WAR OF NERVES

Neither of the forts threatened the security of the Confederacy. They were old installations designed for defense and were manned by token garrisons. But symbols take on profound importance in uneasy times, and the southern fire-eaters, itching for a fight, ranted about the insulting "occupation" of "their country" by a "foreign power."

Davis was willing to live with the Union forts for the time being. He understood that the Confederacy could not survive as long as it consisted of just seven states. His hope was to delay a confrontation with the North until he could make a foreign alliance or induce the eight slave states that remained in the Union to join the Confederacy. He feared that if he fired the first shot, the states of the upper South might support the Union.

The fire-eaters disagreed. They believed that a battle, no matter who started it, would bring the other slave states to their side. Nevertheless, when the commander at Fort Sumter announced that he would soon have to surrender the fort for lack of provisions, Davis had his way.

Within limits, Lincoln also favored delaying confrontation. He believed that the longer the states of the upper South did not secede, the less likely they were to go. Moreover, the leaders of Virginia, Kentucky, Tennessee, and Arkansas formally warned him against using force against the Confederacy. If the Union fired the first shot, they would secede.

Finally, Lincoln did not have the people of the North solidly behind him. Northern Democrats might not support an act of aggression, and Winfield Scott, Lincoln's chief military adviser, told him that the army was not up to a war of conquest. Some abolitionists who were also pacifists, such as Horace Greeley and William Lloyd Garrison, urged the president to "let the wayward sisters depart in peace."

Reproduced from the Collections of the Library of Congress

Fort Sumter the day after it was surrendered to the Confederacy. The commander of the fort was expected to make only a symbolic resistance; Sumter was at the mercy of the batteries in Charleston, but the fort took a terrific shelling as this photograph shows.

Lincoln had no intention of doing that. He was determined to save the Union by peaceful means if possible, by force if necessary. He reasoned that if the Confederates fired the first shot, the border states might secede anyway, but at least the act of rebellion would unite northerners. If he delayed a confrontation indefinitely, he still might lose the border states and have a divided, uncertain North.

This was the reasoning behind Lincoln's decision to resupply Fort Sumter. He announced that he would not use force against the state of South Carolina. There would be no arms in the relief ship, only food, medicine, and other nonmilitary supplies. He repeated his wish that the crisis be resolved peacefully. But he insisted on his presidential obligation to maintain the government's authority in Charleston Harbor.

Lee's Loyalty

Robert E. Lee was perhaps the most respected soldier in the army. When he was asked if he would support the Union or the South in the event of a civil war, Lee replied, in effect, that he would support neither. He would support his native state, Virginia: "If Virginia stands by the old Union, so will I. But if she secedes (though I do not believe in secession as a constitutional right, nor that there is sufficient cause for revolution) then I will follow my native state with my sword and, if need be, with my life."

It is impossible to consider Lee's choice dishonorable and remain an admirer of Thomas Jefferson (and many other Virginians and Massachusetts men of Jefferson's generation): Jefferson made it clear on numerous occasions that Virginia, not the United States, was his homeland.

And so the war came. When the relief ship approached the sandbar that guarded Charleston Harbor, the Confederacy attacked. On the morning of April 12, 1861, artillery under the command of General P. G. T. Beauregard opened fire. The next day, Sumter surrendered. Davis was reluctant to the end. In a sense, he lost control of South Carolina.

THE BORDER STATES TAKE SIDES

The Battle of Fort Sumter served both Confederate and Union purposes. Although Lincoln was able to call for and get 75,000 volunteers, his call for troops pushed four more states into the Confederacy: Virginia, North Carolina, Tennessee, and Arkansas. In deference to Virginia's importance, the capital of the new nation was moved from Montgomery to Richmond.

Secessionist feeling was strong in the slave states of Maryland, Kentucky, and Missouri. Lincoln was able to prevent them from seceding by a combination of shrewd political maneuvers and the tactful deployment of troops. Delaware, the fifteenth slave state, never seriously considered secession.

Then, in the contest for the border states, the North won a bonus. The mountainous western part of Virginia was peopled by farmers who owned few slaves and who traditionally resented the planter aristocracy that dominated Virginia politics. The westerners had no interest in fighting and dying to protect the human property of the rich flatlanders. In effect, the fifty western counties of Virginia seceded from the Old Dominion. By an irregular constitutional process, the Republicans provided the means for West Virginia to become a Union state in June 1863.

For the border states, the Civil War was literally a war between brothers. Henry Clay's grandsons fought on both sides. Several of President Lincoln's brothers-in-law fought for the South, and Jefferson Davis had cousins in the Union army. The most poignant case was that of Senator Crittenden of Kentucky, who had tried to head off war with a compromise. One of his sons became a general in the Union army and another a general in the Confederate army.

FURTHER READING

General William W. Freehling, *The Road to Disunion,* 1990; Michael F. Holt, *The Political Crisis of the 1850s,* 1978; Bruce Levine, *Half Slave and Half Free: The Roots of the Civil War,* 1992; James M. McPherson, *Battle Cry of Freedom: The Civil War Era,* 1988; David Potter, *The Impending Crisis, 1848–1861,* 1974; Leonard Richards, *The Slave Power: The Free North and Southern Domination, 1780–1860,* 2000; Richard A. Sewell, *A House Divided: Sectionalism and Civil War, 1848–1860,* 1988; Kenneth M. Stampp, *The Imperfect Union: Essays on the Background of the Civil War,* 1980.

Brown's Raid Paul Finkelman, *His Soul Goes Marching On: Responses to John Brown's Harpers Ferry Raid,* 1995; Truman Nelson, *The Old Man John Brown at Harpers Ferry,* 1973; Franny Nudelman, *John Brown's Body,* 2004; Stephen Oates, *To Purge This Land with Blood: A Biography of John Brown,* 1984; Merrill D. Peterson, *John Brown: The Legend Revisited,* 2005; David S. Reynolds, *John Brown, Abolitionist: The Man Who Killed Slavery, Sparked the Civil War, and Seeded Civil Rights,* 2005; John Stauffer, *The Black Hearts of Men,* 2002.

Kansas and *Dred Scott* David Donald, *Abraham Lincoln,* 1995; Nichole Etcheson, *Bleeding Kansas: Contested Liberty in the Civil War Era,* 2004; Don E. Fehrenbacher, *The Dred Scott Case: Its Significance in American Law and Politics,* 1981; James A. Rawley, *Race and Politics: "Bleeding Kansas" and the Coming of the Civil War,* 1969; Kennneth M. Stampp, *America in 1857: A Nation on the Brink,* 1990; Kenneth Winkle, *The Young Eagle: The Rise of Abraham Lincoln,* 2003; Gerald W. Wolff, *The Kansas–Nebraska Bill: Party, Section, and the Coming of the Civil War,* 1977; David Zarefsky, *Lincoln, Douglas, and Slavery: In the Crucible of Debate,* 1990.

Politics Tyler Anbinder, *Nativism and Politics: The Know-Nothing Party in the Northern United States,* 1992; Eric Foner, *Politics and Ideology in the Age of the Civil War,* 1980, and *Free Soil, Free Labor, Free Men: The Ideology of the Republican Party Before the Civil War,* 2nd ed., 1995; Robert E. May, *The Southern Dream of a Caribbean Empire, 1854–1861,* 1973; Kerby A. Miller, *Emigrants and Exiles: Ireland and the Irish Exodus to North America,* 1985; Richard H. Sewell, *Ballots for Freedom: Antislavery Politics in the United States, 1837–1860,* 1976; Kenneth A. Stampp, *America in 1857: A Nation on the Brink,* 1990; Kenneth Winkle, *The Young Eagle: The Rise of Abraham Lincoln,* 2003.

Secession W. L. Barney, *The Road to Secession,* 1972; Stephen A. Channing, *Crisis of Fear: Secession in South Carolina,* 1970; Daniel W. Crofts, *Reluctant Confederates: Upper South Unionists in the Secession Crisis,* 1989; Charles B. Dew, *Apostles of Disunion: Southern Secession Commissioners and the Causes of the Civil War,* 2001; Maury Klein, *Days of Defiance: Sumter, Secession, and the Coming of the Civil War,* 1997; R. A. Wooster, *The Secession Conventions of the South,* 1962.

KEY TERMS

The following terms are covered in this chapter and can also be found in the list of Key Terms at the back of the book.

"Bleeding Kansas"	**jayhawkers**	**Lecompton Constitution**	**popular sovereignty**
border ruffians	**John Brown's Raid**	**Ostend Manifesto**	**"slavocracy"**
Freeport Doctrine	**"Know-Nothing" party**		

ONLINE SOURCES GUIDE

Use this listing to find online documents, images, interactive maps, simulations, and other resources related to this chapter:

American History Resource Center
http://history.wadsworth.com/rc/us

Selected Documents
The First Lincoln and Douglas Debate (1858)

Selected Images
Know-Nothings' portrayal of an ideal American
Announcement of antislavery meeting in Kansas Territory
Harper's Ferry, Virginia
John Brown

Interactive Time Line (with online readings)
The Collapse of the Union: The Road to Secession, 1854–1861

Discovery

How did the United States find itself on the brink of the Civil War prior to the presidential election of 1860?

In thinking about this question, begin by breaking it down into the components shown below. A discussion of the significance of each component should appear in your answer.

Government and Law: For this exercise, read the document excerpts "John Brown Addresses the Court, 1859" and "Correspondence of Lydia Maria Child." What was John Brown accused of doing? Why would this be particularly frightening for southerners? Why would responses such as Child's increase tensions with southerners? If you were a southerner at the time and you read Child's letter, what would be your position regarding abolitionists and northerners in general?

John Brown Addresses the Court, 1859

From "Speech and Sentence of Brown," *The Life, Trial and Execution of Capt. John Brown: Being a Full Account of the Attempted Insurrection at Harper's Ferry, Va.*

I have, may it please the Court, a few words to say. In the first place, I deny everything but what I have all along admitted, of a design on my part to free slaves. I intended certainly to have made a clean thing of that matter, as I did last winter when I went into Missouri, and there took slaves without the snapping of a gun on either side, moving them through the country, and finally leaving them in Canada. I designed to have done the same thing again on a larger scale. That was all I intended to do. I never did intend murder or treason, or the destruction of property, or to excite or incite the slaves to rebellion, or to make insurrection. I have another objection, and that is that it is unjust that I should suffer such a penalty. Had I interfered in the manner which I admit, and which I admit has been fairly proved—for I admire the truthfulness and candor of the greater portion of the witnesses who have testified in this case—had I so interfered in behalf of the rich, the powerful, the intelligent, the so-called great, or in behalf of any of their friends, either father, mother, brother, sister, wife, or children, or any of that class, and suffered and sacrificed what I have in this interference, it would have been all right, and every man in this Court would have deemed it an act worthy of reward rather than punishment. This Court acknowledges, too, as I suppose, the validity of the law of God. I see a book kissed, which I suppose to be the Bible, or at least the New Testament, which teaches me that all things whatsoever I would that men should do to me, I should do even so to them. It teaches me further to remember them that are in bonds as bound with them. I endeavored to act up to that instruction. I say I am yet too young to understand that God is any respecter of persons. I believe that to have interfered as I have done, as I have always freely admitted I have done in behalf of His despised poor, is no wrong, but right. Now, if it is deemed necessary that I should forfeit my life for the furtherance of the ends of justice, and mingle my blood further with the blood of my children and with the blood of millions in this slave country whose rights are disregarded by wicked, cruel, and unjust enactments, I say let it be done. Let me say one word further. I feel entirely satisfied with the treatment I have received on my trial. Considering all the circumstances, it has been more generous than I expected. But I feel no consciousness of guilt. I have stated from the first what was my intention, and what was not. I never had any design against the liberty of any person, nor any disposition to commit treason or excite slaves to rebel or make any general insurrection. I never encouraged any man to do so, but always discouraged any idea of that kind. Let me say also in regard to the statements made by some of those who were connected with me, I fear it has been stated by some of them that I have induced them to join me, but the contrary is true. I do not say this to injure them, but as regretting their weakness. Not but joined me of his own accord, and the greater part at their own expense. A number of them I never saw, and never had a word of conversation with till the day they came to me, and that was for the purpose I have stated. Now, I am done. . . .

Correspondence from Lydia Maria Child to Governor Henry Wise, Virginia

. . . If Captain Brown intended, as you say, to commit treason, robbery, and murder, I think I have shown that he could find amply authority for such proceedings in the public declarations of Governor Wise. And if, as he himself declares, he merely intended to free the oppressed, where could he read a more forcible lesson than is furnished by the state seal of Virginia? I looked at it thoughtfully before I opened your letter; and though it had always appeared to me very suggestive, it never seemed to me so much so as it now did in connection with Captain John Brown. A liberty-loving hero stands with his foot upon a prostrated despot; under his strong arms, manacles and chains lie broken; and the motto is, "Sic Semper Tyrannis;" "Thus be it ever done to tyrants." And this is the blazon of a State whose most profitable business is the internal slave-trade!—in whose highways coffles of human chattels, chained and mana-cled, are frequently seen! And the seal of the coffles are both looked upon by other chattels, constantly exposed to the same fate! What if some Vezey, or Nat Turner, should be growing up among those apparently quiet spectators? It is in no spirit of taunt or of exultation that I ask this question. I never think of it but with anxiety, sadness, and sympathy. I know that a slave-holding community necessarily lives in the midst of gunpowder; and, in this age, sparks of free thought are flying in every direction. You cannot quench the fires of free thought and human sympathy by any process of cunning or force; but there is a method by which you can effectually wet the gunpowder. England has already tried it, with safety and success. Would that you could be persuaded to set aside the prejudices of education, and candidly examine the actual working of that experiment! Virginia is so richly endowed by nature that free institutions alone are wanting to render her the most prosperous and powerful of the States.

In your letter you suggest that such a scheme as Captain Brown's is the natural result of the opinions with which I sympathize. Even if I thought this to be a correct statement, though I should deeply regret it, I could not draw the conclusion that humanity ought to be stifled, and truth struck dumb, for fear that long-successful despotism might be endangered by their utterance. But the fact is, you mistake the source of that strange outbreak. No abolition arguments or denunciations, however earnestly, loudly, or harshly proclaimed, would have produced that result. It was the legitimate consequence of the continual and constantly-increasing aggressions of the slave power. The slave States, in their desperate efforts to sustain a bad and dangerous institution, have encroached more and more upon the liberties of the free States. Our inherent love of law and order, and our superstitious attachment to the Union, you have mistaken for cowardice; and rarely have you let slip any opportunity to add insult to aggression.

To read extended versions of the documents, visit the companion Web site http://history.wadsworth.com/americanpast8e; click on "Discovery Sources."

CHAPTER 23

Tidy Plans, Ugly Realities

The Civil War through 1862

The Cooper Union Museum, New York

> *Our new Government is founded upon . . . the great truth that the Negro is not the equal to the white man; that slavery, subordination to the superior race, is his natural and moral condition. This, our new Government, is the first, in the history of the world, based upon this great physical, philosophical, and moral truth.*
>
> *Alexander H. Stephens*

> *The first blast of civil war is the death warrant of your institution.*
>
> *Benjamin Wade*

The bombardment of Fort Sumter answered the big question: there would be a war. When Lincoln called for volunteers to suppress the rebellion, and Davis summoned the manhood of the South to defend its honor and independence, both were flooded with recruits. By the summer of 1861 the Union had 186,000 soldiers in uniform, the Confederacy 112,000.

But what kind of war would it be? What would battle be like? Nowhere had such large armies clashed since the Napoleonic Wars in Europe half a century earlier. During the Mexican War, the United States had fielded no more than 10,000 men at a time. Now, just fifteen years later, two American forces faced the challenge of feeding, clothing, sheltering, transporting, training, and controlling a mass of humanity ten and twenty times that size.

THE ART AND SCIENCE OF WAR

The American Civil War took up where Napoleon and Wellington left off. American officers were trained—indirectly—in a theory of battle devised by a Swiss officer who had served both the French and the Russians, **Antoine-Henri Jomini.** A textbook derived from Jomini's *Art of War* was read at West Point, where most of the major commanders of the Civil War learned their craft.

POSITION, MANEUVER, AND CONCENTRATION

Jomini emphasized position and maneuver as the keys to winning battle. The goal of the commanding general was to occupy high ground, ascertain the weakest point in the enemy's lines, and concentrate his power there. The general

Photo by Timothy O'Sullivan, Chicago Historical Society

■ *Wagons of a Union supply unit in Virginia. The North's massive resources and efficiency in supplying troops were immense advantages over the Confederacy.*

who prepared more thoroughly, better exploited the terrain, and moved his troops more skillfully than his opponent would break through the opposing line and force the enemy from the field.

The strategic object was to capture and occupy politically or economically important enemy cities, particularly the enemy's capital. The idea was that after losing what we call a national infrastructure, the enemy would have nothing for which to fight. Napoleon defeated his enemies in Europe (except Russia) when he occupied their major cities.

Jomini reduced battle situations to twelve models. Therefore, officers well-versed in his theories (and with a brain in their heads) should know, in general, what their adversaries had in mind at all times. So long as both sides observed the rules, there would be no long casualty lists. The general who was outfoxed knew that his duty was to disengage so that his men could fight another day under more favorable circumstances. Retreat, far from shameful, was among the most important of military maneuvers because it preserved an army as a functioning machine.

Military Stalemate 1861–1863

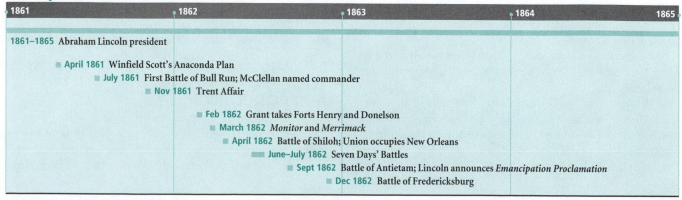

1861	1862	1863	1864	1865

1861–1865 Abraham Lincoln president

■ **April 1861** Winfield Scott's Anaconda Plan
■ **July 1861** First Battle of Bull Run; McClellan named commander
■ **Nov 1861** Trent Affair
■ **Feb 1862** Grant takes Forts Henry and Donelson
■ **March 1862** *Monitor* and *Merrimack*
■ **April 1862** Battle of Shiloh; Union occupies New Orleans
■ **June–July 1862** Seven Days' Battles
■ **Sept 1862** Battle of Antietam; Lincoln announces *Emancipation Proclamation*
■ **Dec 1862** Battle of Fredericksburg

The Organizational Chart

The smallest unit in the armies was the company of 100 men, commanded by a captain and two lieutenants. Ten infantry companies made up a regiment under a colonel. However, regiments were often undermanned because of casualties and disease. Four or more regiments made a brigade under a brigadier general. Three brigades were a division. Two to four divisions were a corps. At one time or another during the war, the Union army had twenty-five corps, but by 1865 many had been liquidated because of losses, the men in them assigned to others.

THE ARMIES

Civil War armies were made up of cavalry, artillery, and infantry, with support units such as the Corps of Engineers (which constructed fortifications) and the Quartermaster Corps (entrusted with supply).

The cavalry's principal role was reconnaissance. Horse soldiers were an army's eyes (although there was some experimentation with anchored balloons in the Civil War). Battle plans were based on the information the cavalry brought back from sometimes spectacular rides that circled the enemy force. Because of their mobility and speed, cavalry units were also used for raids: plunging deep into hostile territory, burning and destroying what they found, sometimes seizing useful booty, and hightailing it out before they were confronted by big guns and masses of infantry.

In a pitched battle, cavalry dismounted to reinforce weak points in the enemy lines; if enemy troops retreated, the horse soldiers pursued, harassed, and scattered them. But cavalrymen were lightly armed by definition; for all the dash and flash, cavalry played a minor role in pitched battle. Early in the war, the generals learned that against infantrymen armed with accurate rifled muskets, the gallant old cavalry charge was suicidal.

The artillery was slow to move and, with its toil, noise, and grime, unglamorous. But as Napoleon had shown, big guns were critical to both attack and defense. On several occasions the Confederates had too few horses to move their cannons into a useful position. At least once, at Missionary Ridge outside Chattanooga, Union forces had the same problem.

Before an attacking army moved, its artillery slugged away at enemy positions with exploding shells, "softening them up."

When in a defensive position, artillery greeted attacking infantry and cavalry with grapeshot or canister. Canister was a tin cylindrical projectile filled with small lead or iron balls in sawdust. The canister disintegrated immediately upon firing and was devastating at 100 to 200 yards. Grapeshot consisted of somewhat larger balls in canvas bags. It was used on a charging army at longer ranges. Examinations of dead soldiers after some Civil War battles revealed that an attacking army suffered more from artillery than from small arms. (In other battles, however, five soldiers were killed by minié balls fired by muskets for every one killed by grapeshot and canister.) Soldiers wryly joked that they fired a man's weight in lead and iron for each enemy they killed. A Union expert found their calculation to be conservative; he said that 240 pounds of gunpowder and 900 pounds of lead were expended for every Confederate soldier felled.

As always, the infantry was the backbone of the army. The cavalry might worry the enemy, and the artillery weaken him, but it was the foot soldiers, squander ammunition as they might, who slogged it out face-to-face, took the casualties, and won and lost the battles.

THE INFANTRY IN BATTLE

The basic infantry unit was the brigade of 2,000 to 4,000 men, depending on what battle and disease had done to it. Under the command of a brigadier general, the soldiers formed double lines in defense or advanced over a front of about a thousand yards. During the first campaigns of the Civil War, captains in the front lines tried to march the men in step, as had been the practice in the Napoleonic Era. But with the greater firepower of the 1860s, formality was sensibly abandoned. It was enough that the men continued to trot or walk into grapeshot, **minié balls** (conical bullets), noise like a thunderstorm in hell, and a haze of black, sulfurous smoke. Junior officers led the charge, so the ranks of lieutenant and captain suffered high casualties. More senior officers walked behind the lines to discourage stragglers. They carried revolvers and were authorized to shoot men who panicked and broke ranks, and they did.

If the advancing army was not forced to turn back, the final phase of battle was hand-to-hand combat. The attackers clambered over the enemy's fortifications of earth and lumber. Attackers and defenders swung their muskets at one another like the baseball bats they played with in camp until the defenders broke and ran or the attackers were killed or

Bibles, Whiskey, and ID

As the war ground on, veteran soldiers tended to grow quiet and reflective before a battle. Many read their Bibles. The American Bible Society printed 370,000 more Bibles in 1861 than in 1860. Five million in various formats, most pocket sized, were given to soldiers by the end of the war. When, in the war's final months, the Confederacy could devote no resources to printing Bibles, Union armies sent them between the lines under a flag of truce.

Some soldiers took a few quick pulls of whiskey before battle. Friends made promises to look for one another at the end of the day and, if one of them was dead, to send his personal belongings to his family. During the brutal battles before Richmond, soldiers wrote their names and addresses on pieces of paper pinned to their clothing on the assumption that there would be no friends alive to identify them.

captured. The men had bayonets, but neither side succeeded in training the soldiers to use them well.

There was plenty of shooting but not much aiming. Except for special units of sharpshooters, few foot soldiers were marksmen. There was little sense in taking on the big and expensive job of training large numbers of men in the skill of hitting small targets at great distances. With a few important exceptions (Antietam, Gettysburg), Civil War battles were not fought in open country. The men confronted one another in dense woods on terrain broken by hills, creeks, stone fences, and ditches. In several battles, attackers had to clamber up Appalachian cliffs on all fours. Often opposing soldiers could not see one another until they were on the verge of touching.

Even in open country, hundreds of cannons and tens of thousands of muskets filled the air with a dense, acrid smog that, on a windless day, shrouded the battlefield. (Smokeless powder was still in the future.) Even if a soldier could shoot well, there was little he could aim at to prove it.

BILLY YANK AND JOHNNY REB

As always, the men who fought the Civil War were young, most between the ages of 17 and 25 with drummer boys of but 12. They came from every state and social class, although when both sides adopted draft laws (the Confederacy in April 1862, the Union in March 1863), the burden fell more heavily on poorer farmers and working people than on the middle and upper classes.

This was because the draft laws included exemptions favoring the well-to-do. The Confederates exempted men who owned twenty or more slaves. This was sorely resented by "**Johnny Reb,**" the common soldiers, few of whom owned one. Both the Confederate and Union draft laws allowed a man who was called to service to pay for a substitute at a price that was beyond the means of the ordinary fellow who did not want to go. In the North, a draftee could hire another to take his place or pay the government $300 for an exemption.

In July 1863 working-class resentment of the draft law led to a weeklong riot in New York City. Mobs of mostly Irish workingmen sacked draft offices, attacked rich men, and harassed and lynched blacks, whom they considered the cause of the war and a threat to their jobs. Some 60,000 people were involved; at least 400 were killed, and some $5 million in property was destroyed.

In the South, resistance to conscription took the form of thousands of draft dodgers and deserters heading west or into the Appalachians and the Ozarks, where some organized outlaw gangs, raided farms, and occasionally skirmished with Confederate troops. Most southern opposition to the war centered in the poorer mountain counties of western Virginia, North Carolina, and eastern Tennessee.

Both Union and Confederate armies were plagued by a high desertion rate: about 10 percent through most of the war. "**Bounty jumpers**" were professional deserters. Because some units paid cash bounties to men who signed up, a few made a lucrative but risky business of enlisting, skipping out at the first opportunity, and looking for another unit offering bounties. In March 1865 Union military police arrested John O'Connor, who was surely the champion. He confessed to enlisting, collecting a bounty, and deserting thirty-two times.

The penalty for desertion was death, but remarkably few deserters were actually shot, fewer than 200. Instead, deserters were branded with a "D" on buttock, wrist, or cheek, put back in the army in none too desirable a situation, and watched.

Shirking was not typical of either army. During the war 1.5 million young men served in the Union army, and more than 1 million, from a much smaller population, with the Confederates. Whatever their resentments, ordinary people thought they had something at stake in the conflict. Despite their exemption, southern slave owners served in proportion to their numbers.

IT'S A WOMAN'S WAR TOO

A few women, although on no payroll, worked as spies during the war. The most famous Confederate agent was Rose O'Neal Greenhow, a Washington widow with entrée into Washington society. During 1861 she forwarded information learned from Union officers to Richmond, but she was caught before the end of the year and deported through southern lines. There may have been dozens of less respectable pro-Confederate women in Washington, their names unknown, who wheedled information from officers with whom they slept. There were plenty of Confederate sympathizers of both sexes in the city.

Wilhelmina Yank and Joanna Reb

Women, posing as men, fought in the Civil War. Official records list 127 female soldiers who were discovered (six because they became pregnant). One historian suggests the number was closer to 400. Among them were Jennie Hodges, who fought for an Illinois regiment as Albert Cashier; her sex was not discovered until "Albert" died in 1911. Sarah Lemma Edmonds was Franklin Thompson in the Second Michigan. Passing as Lyons Wakeman in the 153rd Regiment of the New York State volunteers, Sarah Rosetta Wakeman rose to the rank of major.

DESPERATE HAND TO HAND COMBAT BETWEEN UNION CAVALRY, COMMANDED BY GEN. AVERILL, AND STUART'S REBEL TROOP, AT KELLEY'S FORD, ON THE RAPPAHANNOCK, VA., MARCH 17.
FROM A SKETCH BY AN OFFICER.

A clash of Union and Confederate cavalry. Skirmishes of this kind were what lent an aura or romance to the cavalry, but they were rare in the Civil War. The cavalry's chief task was reconnaissance; its secondary task was raiding behind enemy lines. Battles like this one occurred when raiders were caught by opposing cavalry as when Union General Philip Sheridan caught Confederate General Jubal Early in the Shenandoah Valley in 1864.

Harriet Tubman continued to penetrate Virginia in her role of harmless "mammy," reporting back to the Union army the disposition of rebel troops and locations of fortifications. Mary Elizabeth Bowser, a domestic slave in Jefferson Davis's household in Virginia, could read and passed whatever information she could to Union forces. Slaves were sources of information for the Union armies everywhere, although they were often unreliable. An abolitionist Union officer was not surprised by slave spying: "After all, they had been spies all their lives."

Nurses were the most numerous and prominent female soldiers in the cause. Shortly after Fort Sumter, Elizabeth Blackwell, the first American woman medical doctor, organized what became the United States Sanitary Commission, which put 3,000 nurses in army hospitals. At first the army did not want them. Closeness to the front lines and the gore and male nakedness of the hospitals did not accord with the ideals of the gospel of true womanhood. But spokeswomen like Clara Barton (later founder of the American Red Cross) and Dorothea Dix, both women of impeccable propriety, wore the generals down. The fiercest opponents of female nurses were forced to admit that they were infinitely superior to the disabled men who had previously assisted in army hospitals.

A shortage of male workers, due to the size of the armies and full employment in industry, opened jobs in the federal bureaucracy for women at the lowest levels. After the war, the taboo broken, the number of female civil servants steadily increased until they were a majority of federal employees in Washington. In the South more than the North, because there the manpower shortage was far more serious, women took heavy and dirty factory jobs. And dangerous ones: about 100 southern women were killed in explosions in munitions plants.

THE SOBERING CAMPAIGN OF 1861

Army life also meant drilling day in and day out. But those who rallied to the colors in the spring of 1861 thought of the war as a great adventure, a vacation from the plow and hog trough that would be over too soon. They trimmed themselves in gaudy uniforms. Some, influenced by pictures of Turkish soldiers in the recently concluded Crimean War, called themselves "Zouaves" and donned fezzes and baggy

Manassas or Bull Run?

Early in the war, the Confederacy named battles after the nearest town. So they called the first battle, on July 21, 1861, Manassas. The Union army named some battles after the nearest waterway; thus Manassas was the Battle of Bull Run. The Union's Antietam (a creek) was the South's Sharpsburg (a town in Maryland).

The Confederacy named armies after the states they were initially assigned to defend, or part of a state in the case of Robert E. Lee's Army of Northern Virginia. The Union named its armies after rivers: the Army of the Potomac, the Army of the Ohio. There was a Confederate Army of Tennessee and a Union Army of the Tennessee, the river of that name.

The Union rout at Manassas/ Bull Run. It was total at the end of the day, but the Confederate army had itself come so close to disintegration that a follow-up march on Washington was out of the question.

pantaloons. Other units adopted names that would have been more appropriate to a boys' club. One Confederate regiment was called "The Lincoln Killers."

ON TO RICHMOND

Abraham Lincoln shared the illusion that the war would be short and painless. He waved off General Winfield Scott's warning that it would take three years and 300,000 men to crush the rebellion. Lincoln asked the first volunteers, mostly state militiamen, to enlist for only ninety days. That would be enough. Southerners too spoke of "our battle summer." The soldiers and civilians on the two sides disagreed only as to who would be celebrating when the leaves fell in the autumn of 1861.

These pleasant illusions were blown away on a fine July day about twenty miles outside Washington. Believing that his volunteers could take Richmond before their enlistments expired, Lincoln sent General Irvin McDowell marching directly toward the Confederate capital with 30,000 troops but not a single reliable map of the country. Laughing and joking as they went, sometimes shooting at targets, the boys from Ohio and Massachusetts were accompanied by a parade of carriages filled with congressmen, socialites, newspaper reporters, and curiosity seekers. The crowd carried picnic lunches and discussed where in Richmond they would enjoy a late supper.

They were met by a Confederate force of 22,000 under the command of General Beauregard, recently arrived from Fort Sumter. The rebels had hastily dug in on high ground behind a creek called Bull Run, near a railroad crossing named Manassas Junction. McDowell attacked immediately, guessing the Confederate left flank to be the weakest point in the line. He was right about that. Although his troops were shocked by the ferocity of the musket fire that greeted them, they almost cracked the southern line.

Had it cracked, the war might have been over in the upper South. To the rear of Beauregard's line, the road to Richmond was wide open. At the critical moment, however, 9,000 Virginians commanded by Joseph E. Johnston arrived on the field after a frantic train ride from the Shenandoah Valley. A brigade under the command of Thomas J. Jackson, a 37-year-old mathematics instructor at Virginia Military Academy, shored up the sagging Confederate left. The Union soldiers fell back and then broke in a panic, fleeing for Washington along with the spectators.

CELEBRATIONS AND RECRIMINATIONS

The South had a victory and a hero. At the peak of the battle, a South Carolinian rallied his men by shouting, "There stands Jackson like a stone wall." The name stuck, for it seemed appropriate to more than Thomas J. Jackson's performance on the battlefield. He was introspective and humorless; his dullness as a lecturer was legendary among his students at Virginia Military Institute, where he taught mathematics before the war. Jackson was a stern Scotch–Irish Presbyterian who took long, cold showers to kill his sexual impulses. Southern civilians canonized him, but his troops never loved him, as they do some generals.

But they were awed by Jackson because he came to life when the bullets whistled. He never yielded a line to the enemy, and he was a genius at maneuvering troops. For two years Jackson would do what the South needed done, inserting his men in critical positions and standing like a stone wall.

By way of contrast, General Beauregard's reputation collapsed after Bull Run because he failed to follow up his victory by marching on Washington. He was replaced as Confederate commander in Virginia by Joseph E. Johnston, who had brought the troops and Stonewall Jackson from the Shenandoah Valley.

Johnston was the superior field commander, but Beauregard was not to blame for the South's failure to capture Washington. As Johnston himself put it, "The Confederate army was more disorganized by victory than that of the United States by defeat"; and a disorganized army is no army

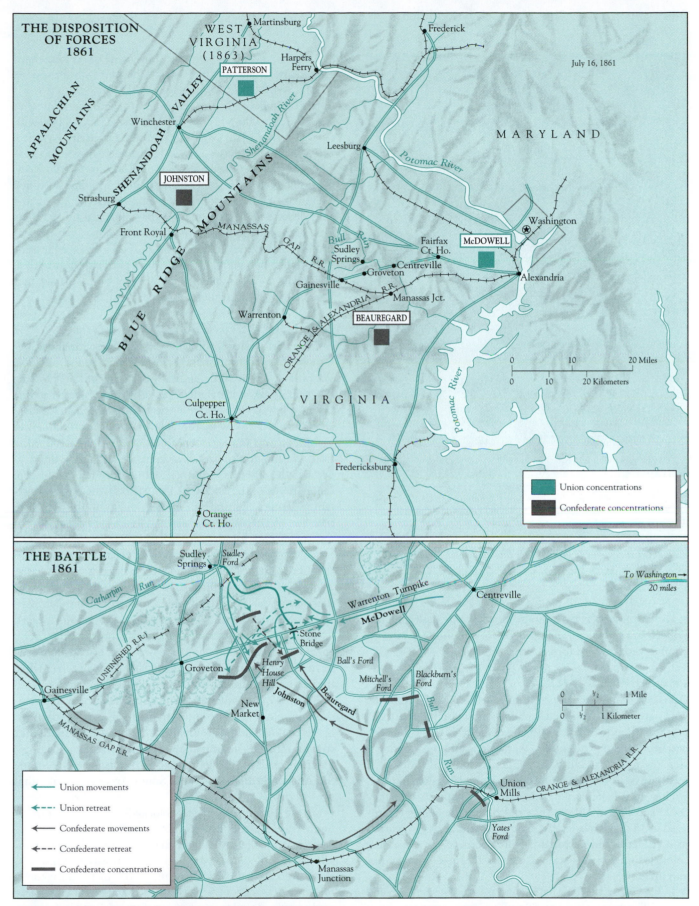

MAP 23:1 The Battle of Bull Run, July 21, 1861

McDowell's army advanced from Washington along the highway that led to Winchester in the Shenandoah Valley. The battle lines stretched along Bull Run, a creek, straddling the Warrenton turnpike. Confederate generals Johnston and Jackson rushed reinforcements to the scene on the Manassas Gap railroad.

Thomas J. "Stonewall" Jackson was the hero of the Confederacy's first summer. He was polite at the many celebrations at which he was feted but probably did not enjoy himself much. Jackson was the most strictly self-disciplined of Presbyterians. He once said he did not drink whiskey because he liked it too much.

at all. All the better generals at Bull Run, plus desk men like Robert E. Lee, who was President Davis's military adviser, emphasized the need for intensive training.

THE SUMMER LULL

Davis, who had been a pretty good officer in the Mexican War, agreed. He cautioned Richmond society that there was more fighting to come. But few seemed to listen. Casualties had been minor. The soldiers were cocky and overconfident after their victory. Southern politicians spoke as though the war were over. Volunteer officers nagged their tailors to finish sewing gold braid onto their dress uniforms so that they could show them off once or twice before the Union capitulated. And they bickered. At an endless round of gala parties in Richmond, old personal jealousies erupted as blustering colonels and generals blamed one another for blunders real and imaginary.

In the North, the defeat at Manassas taught a sorely needed lesson. The spectacle of McDowell's troops throwing down their guns and trotting wild-eyed into Washington, where they slept in doorways and on the sidewalks, alarmed Lincoln and brought him around to Winfield Scott's way of thinking.

The war would be no summer's diversion but a long, hard fight. Now when Lincoln asked Congress for troops, he wanted 300,000 men for three years.

Lincoln relieved Irvin McDowell from command of what was now called the Army of the Potomac, replacing him with George B. McClellan. After distinguishing himself in Mexico, McClellan was stationed at West Point, where he was an innovator with an eye for self-promotion. He introduced a bayonet drill he called the "McClellan Bayonet Drill" and modified a Hungarian saddle for the cavalry, which he called the "McClellan Saddle." (It remained the standard until 1920.) As president of the Illinois Central Railroad (for which Lincoln had been a lawyer), McClellan was a superb organizer and administrator. In November 1861, when Winfield Scott retired, McClellan took overall command of the Union armies that were being drilled throughout the Midwest.

NORTHERN STRATEGY

A three-part strategy Winfield Scott had recommended became, with modifications, Union policy. First and obvious, Washington had to be defended by the Army of the Potomac; if Washington was lost, Lincoln could not very well have continued the war. However, the Army of the Potomac was also an offensive army with the goal of capturing Richmond. Richmond was important not only because, just 100 miles from Washington, it was the Confederate capital, but also because the city was a railroad hub and a major industrial center, home of the Tredregar Iron Works, which was to sustain Virginia's fighting machine throughout the war. The rebellion might have continued had Richmond fallen early in the war, but not for long.

Second—and Lincoln the westerner needed no tutoring on this—because the Ohio–Mississippi waterway was vital to the economic life of the Midwestern states, Union armies would strike down the valley. Their object was to gain complete control of the Mississippi as soon as possible to permit western farmers to resume the export of foodstuffs, by which they lived, and to split the Confederacy in two. The trans-Mississippi front (Arkansas and Texas) could be left to small forces while the Union concentrated its power in the East.

Third, the Union would use its overwhelming naval superiority to blockade the South, strangling its export economy. If the Confederates were unable to sell cotton abroad, they could not buy the manufactures, particularly the munitions, that were essential in a lengthy war. Scott called the blockade the **Anaconda Plan,** after the South American snake that slowly crushes its prey.

On the face of it, an effective blockade was out of the question. The Confederate Atlantic and Gulf coastlines were labyrinths of inlets, sheltered channels, coves, bays, bayous, salt marshes, and lonely broad beaches. It was impossible to prevent every vessel from reaching shore or from making a break for the high seas. Nevertheless, a national commerce could not be rowed through the surf or unloaded in swamps. The commanders of the Union navy felt confident that with time and more ships, they could bottle up the Confederate ports.

The Granger Collection, New York

Facing Battle

The battle experience was much the same whether a soldier wore blue or gray—except that northern troops were better supplied with shelter, clothing, shoes, medicine, food, and arms and ammunition. It is difficult to say how much this meant to the outcome of the war. Cold, wet, tired, and ill soldiers are surely less effective than well-equipped ones. Confederate troops without shoes—not uncommon— were generally excused from charging enemy lines. Nevertheless, "Johnny Reb," the Confederate foot soldier, won the respect of both his officers and his enemies as a fighting man. As early as the second Battle of Bull Run in 1862, the commander of a unit called Toombs's Georgians told of leading so many barefoot men that they "left bloody footprints among the thorns and briars."

Johnny Reb and his Union counterpart, Billy Yank, knew when they were going to fight. In only a few large battles was an army caught by surprise. Preparations for massive attack were so extensive that getting caught napping, as Grant's men were at Shiloh, was rare. In fact, the men who would be defending a position were generally prepared for battle with extra rations and ammunition earlier than the attackers, who were provisioned only when they were about to move.

Two or three days' rations were distributed before a battle. Historian Bell I. Wiley suggested that in the Confederate ranks:

> This judicious measure generally fell short of its object because of Johnny Reb's own characteristics: He was always hungry, he had a definite prejudice against baggage, and he was the soul of improvidence. Sometimes, the whole of the extra rations would be consumed as soon as it was cooked, and rarely did any part of it last for the full period intended.

Such recklessness could have serious consequences because battle was heavy labor. Reports of units incapacitated by hunger after a day's fighting were common. The men did learn early on to attend carefully to their canteens. Waiting, marching, and running in the heat, cold, rain, and the grime and dust of battle meant constant thirst.

As short a time as possible before a battle, each infantryman was given forty to sixty rounds of ammunition for the cartridge box he wore on a strap slung over a shoulder. (Soldiers rarely carried ammunition when no battle was anticipated because the powder so quickly became damp and useless.) The Springfield repeating rifles took a round that looked like a modern cartridge. The muzzle-loading musket—which was used by all the Confederates and most Yankees—took a round that consisted of a ball and a charge of powder wrapped together in a piece of paper that was twisted closed at the powder end. To load the musket, a soldier bit off the twist so that the powder was exposed, pushed the cartridge into the muzzle of his gun, inserted the paper he held in his teeth to keep the ball from rolling out, and rammed a rod (attached to his gun) into the barrel to the breech. Each time he fired, he had to fall to one knee in order to reload. That moment, and when men were retreating, was more dangerous than when troops were advancing.

On the eve or morning of a battle, the commanding general addressed his troops either personally or in written orations read by line officers. Confederate General Albert Sidney Johnston took the high road in his speech before Shiloh:

> The eyes and the hope of eight millions of people rest upon you. You are expected to show yourselves worthy of your race and lineage; worthy of the women of the South, whose noble devotion in this war has never been exceeded in any time. With such incentives to brave deeds and with the trust that God is with us, your general will lead you confidently to the combat, assured of success.

Others, like, General T. C. Hindman in December 1862, were demagogues:

> Remember that the enemy you engage has no feeling of mercy. His ranks are made up of Pin Indians, free Negroes, Southern Tories, Kansas jayhawkers, and hired Dutch cutthroats. These bloody ruffians have invaded your country, stolen and destroyed your property, murdered your neighbors, outraged your women, driven your children from their homes, and defiled the graves of your kindred.

DIXIE'S CHALLENGE

Southern strategy had a simpler design but a flimsier foundation. To win its independence, the Confederacy needed to conquer nothing. The South had only to turn back Union advances until Britain or France, where there was self-serving sympathy for the southern cause, came to the rescue—or until the people of the North grew weary of fighting and forced Lincoln to negotiate. In the broadest sense, the story of the Civil War tells how southern hopes were dashed and how, although long frustrated and delayed, the Union strategy succeeded.

Indians in Gray and Blue

Most Native Americans sat out the war, no doubt heartened that the whites were fighting among themselves for a change. Most Cherokee, Creeks, Choctaws, and Chickasaws were pro-Confederate because, in Indian Territory, some of them owned slaves. John Ross, a Cherokee chieftain, called the southern rebellion "a great and glorious cause." About 5,500 Native Americans fought on the Confederate side, about 4,000 for the North. An Iroquois officer served on General Grant's staff.

The Confederacy's hope of foreign intervention died first. In the case of France, it may have been doomed from the beginning by the erratic personality of the French emperor, Napoleon III. On one day a scheming power politician who recognized that an independent Confederacy might be molded into a French dependency, Napoleon III was on the next day a flighty romantic.

At first, while leading the Confederates on, he delayed when the more prudent British dithered. (Napoleon did not want to intervene in the war without British approval.) Then, when he was approached by Mexican aristocrats who, in order to defeat a mestizo and Indian revolution, offered to make an emperor of Napoleon's nephew, Maximilian of Austria, Napoleon III saw a far greater opportunity in the Civil War than an independent South. While the United States at peace would have resisted French interference in Mexico—it was not so long since some American expansionists spoke of annexing the whole country—the United States tearing itself apart was helpless to act. Anyway, what self-respecting emperor wanted a dependency of quarrelsome, headstrong cotton planters when he could tread in the footsteps of Cortés? Not Napoleon III. By the end of 1862 he was avoiding Confederate diplomats in Paris.

The pro-Confederate sentiments of the British government were solidly founded. Southern cotton fed the massive British textile industry, and British industrialists generally supported Henry Lord Palmerston's Liberal government. Moreover, many English aristocrats looked upon the southern planters as rough-cut kinsmen, flattering in their Anglophilia and imitation of the British upper classes. And then, far-seeing British politicians saw an opportunity to shatter the growing power of the United States, which, they understood, was destined to eclipse Great Britain's.

The trouble was slavery. British public opinion was staunchly antislavery. British hostility toward slavery had prevented an alliance with Texas. Lord Palmerston was not willing to risk the wrath of antislavery voters unless the Confederates demonstrated that they had a real chance of winning. Britain would not help the South fight an open-ended war of defense.

A combination of Confederate blunders in export policy, bad luck, Union diplomatic skill, and a Union victory that put an end to the Confederacy's brightest hour dashed the dream of redrawing the map of North America.

DIPLOMACY

The blunder was Jefferson Davis's calculation that he could blackmail Britain into coming to the aid of the South. In the excited solidarity of the Confederacy's first days, he prevailed on cotton shippers to keep the crop of 1860 at home, storing it in warehouses. The idea was to put the pinch on British mill owners so that they would set up a cry for a war to liberate the coveted fiber.

"Cotton diplomacy" did not work. English mill owners had seen the war coming and stockpiled huge reserves. When these supplies ran out in 1862 the price of cotton tripled, inducing farmers in Egypt and the Middle East to expand their cotton cultivation. Within a year, they were filling much of the gap created by the American war. To make matters worse, Union troops captured enough southern cotton in 1861 and 1862 to keep the mills of New England humming and even to sell some to Britain.

As the war dragged on, **cotton diplomacy** was completely scuttled by two successive poor grain harvests in western Europe. Fearing food shortages, monarchist Britain discovered that Union wheat was more royal than King Cotton. Blessed with bumper crops in those years, northern farmers shipped unprecedented tonnages of grain to Europe at both financial and diplomatic profit.

In November 1861 a zealous Union naval officer almost ruined the northern effort to keep Britain neutral. The captain of the U.S.S. *San Jacinto* boarded a British steamer, the *Trent,* and seized two Confederate diplomats who were aboard, James M. Mason and John Slidell. Northern public opinion was delighted, but Lincoln took a dimmer view. The British minister in Washington came close to threatening war. For the president, Mason and Slidell were two hot potatoes, and he took advantage of the first lull in the public celebrations to hasten them aboard a British warship. "One war at a time," he remarked to his cabinet.

No harm was done. In France, Slidell was frustrated by Napoleon III's Mexican ambitions. In England, Mason proved no match for the Union minister, Charles Francis Adams, in the delicate game of diplomacy. Mason managed to see two commerce raiders, the *Florida* and the *Alabama,* constructed for the Confederacy and put to sea. But Adams cajoled and threatened the British government into preventing a sister ship and several Confederate rams from leaving port. He moved with great skill and energy through the salons of London—it ran in the family—and kept Great Britain out of the war until the North turned the tide in its direction, when the possibility of British intervention quietly died.

1862 AND STALEMATE

As hopes of bringing England in dimmed, the South looked increasingly to northern sympathizers and defeatists to aid their cause. Some northerners frankly favored the South. Former President Franklin Pierce openly hoped for a Confederate victory. Pro-southern sentiment was strongest in the Union slave states of Maryland, Kentucky, and Missouri, but it was also significant in the lower counties of Ohio, Indiana, and Illinois, a region with a strong southern heritage. However, these "**copperheads**," as northerners who sympathized with the South were called (after the poisonous snake that strikes without warning), were never able to mount a decisive threat to the Union war effort. Except in Maryland, they were a minority, and Lincoln played freely with their civil liberties in order to silence them.

LINCOLN AND THE COPPERHEADS

One of the president's most controversial moves against opponents of the war was his suspension of the ancient legal right of *habeas corpus,* a protection against arbitrary arrest that is basic to English and American law. At one time or another, 13,000 people were jailed, almost always briefly, because of alleged antiwar activity. Lincoln also used his control of the post office to harass and even suppress anti-administration newspapers.

The noisiest copperhead was Clement L. Vallandigham, a popular Democratic congressman from Ohio. His attacks on the war effort were so unsettling that, after General Ambrose Burnside jailed him, Lincoln feared he would be honored as a martyr. The president solved the problem by handing Vallandigham over to the Confederates as if he were a southern agent. Identifying Vallandigham with treason was unfair but politically shrewd; in 1863 he was forced to run for governor of Ohio from exile in Canada. At home, or even in prison, he might have won. But *in absentia* he was defeated, and when he returned to the United States the next year, he was harmless enough that Lincoln could ignore him.

More worrisome than the copperheads was defeatism, the belief that the war was not worth the expense in blood and money. Each time Union armies lost a battle, more northerners wondered if it would not be wiser to let the southern states go. Or, they asked, was it really impossible to negotiate? Was Lincoln's Republican administration, rather than the southern states, the obstacle to a compromise peace?

It was in fact impossible for Lincoln to secure reunion on any other basis than military victory. Even at the bitter end of the war, when the Confederacy was not only defeated but devastated, Jefferson Davis insisted on southern independence as a condition of peace. As long as the South was winning battles, negotiation was out of the question.

And the South won most of the battles in 1861 and 1862. The show belonged to Stonewall Jackson and General Robert E. Lee, who succeeded Joseph Johnston as commander of the Army of Northern Virginia when, at the Battle of the Seven Pines on May 31, 1862, Johnston was seriously wounded. Time after time, Lee and Jackson halted or drubbed the Army of the Potomac. Nevertheless, even in his most triumphant hour in the summer of 1862, Lee's military genius was limited by his supreme virtue, his devotion to Virginia.

Lee's cause was not so much the Confederacy as the dignity of "Old Virginny." He did not like slavery, the obsession of the southern hotheads. He may never have owned a slave himself, and he had freed his wife's slaves in 1857 when he was executor of her father's will. He looked on cotton planters from the deep South as grasping parvenus. He had opposed Virginia's secession until it was a fact. Consequently, Lee never fully appreciated the fact that while he was defending the Old Dominion with such mastery, the southern cause was slowly throttled at sea, in the dozens of coastal enclaves Union troops occupied, and in the Mississippi Valley.

THE CAMPAIGN IN THE WEST

Lincoln, although no military man (and the author, himself, of several Civil War blunders), understood the importance of the West. "We must have Kentucky," he told his cabinet. Without Kentucky—the southern bank of the Ohio River— he feared the war would be lost. Even before the army recovered from the defeat at Manassas, Lincoln approved moving a large force into the state under the command of Generals Henry Halleck and Ulysses S. Grant. In early 1862 Grant thrust into Tennessee, quickly capturing two important forts, Henry and Donelson. They guarded the mouths of the Tennessee and Cumberland Rivers, two waterways of infinitely greater value than muddy Bull Run. Moving on, however, General Grant stumbled into the battle that taught both sides that they were not playing chess.

Moving up (south on) the Tennessee River unopposed, Grant intended to attack Corinth, Mississippi. He knew that Confederate General Albert Sidney Johnston planned to defend the town, but he had no idea that Johnston was also prepared to attack. On April 6, 1862, while camped at Shiloh, Tennessee, Grant's soldiers were caught in their bedrolls by 40,000 rebels. Many were killed before they awoke. The others held on, but just barely. Only that night, when Union reinforcements arrived under General Don Carlos Buell, did the Confederates withdraw.

Albert Sydney Johnston, regarded by some military historians as one of the Confederacy's best field commanders, was killed at Shiloh. Other southern losses numbered 11,000 of 40,000 troops engaged. The Union lost 13,000 of 60,000 men. Bodies were stacked like cordwood while massive graves were dug. Acres of ground were reddened with blood, and the stench of death sickened the survivors at their grisly job of cleaning up. Compared with the minor casualties at Bull Run, Shiloh was a horror.

Grant was disgraced. He was accused of being drunk on the night before the attack. Soldiers of the two armies ceased to fraternize between battles, as they had in the woods of Tennessee, where Confederate and Union guards conversed

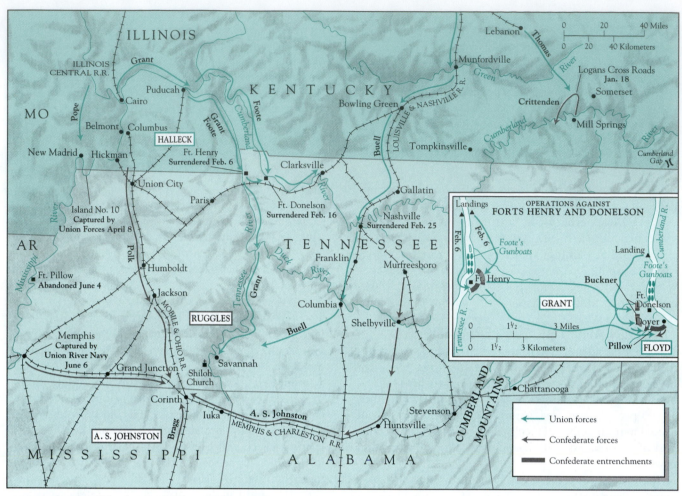

MAP 23:2 The War in the West, 1862
The importance of the Tennessee and Cumberland Rivers for communication and transportation can be clearly seen in this map. Thus the importance of the surrender of Forts Henry and Donelson to General Grant in February 1862. Grant's advance through Tennessee was without incident. Then came bloody Shiloh on the Mississippi border.

in the night and traded tobacco for coffee. Bull Run showed that there would be a long war; Shiloh showed that it would be a national tragedy. Not even the success of naval officer David G. Farragut a short time after Shiloh, which put the Union in control of New Orleans, could cure the sense of melancholy that followed on the terrible battle.

THE WAR AT SEA

Confederate seamen on the commerce raiders *Florida, Alabama,* and *Shenandoah* saw quite a bit of the world. These fast, heavily armed ships destroyed or captured more than 250 northern vessels ($15 million in ships and cargo) in every corner of the seas. Sailors on the commerce raiders experienced naval warfare at its most exhilarating.

For the Union sailors assigned to the blockade, by way of contrast, days were long and boring, spent slowly patrolling the waters outside southern ports in scorching sun and winter winds. In 1861 and 1862, blockade duty was also frustrating. Most blockade runners, Confederate and foreign, outran the navy's ships in and out of southern ports. Steamers

specially built for the purpose were low-slung so as not to be seen until within a few miles, and they were narrow in the beam. Blockade runners did not cross the ocean. European shippers brought the goods the Confederates wanted—everything from munitions to cloth—to Bermuda or one of the West Indies. There the merchandise was picked up and paid for with cotton or bills of exchange issued as loans by English banks willing to gamble on a Confederate victory. Blockade running was ferrying, with quick turnarounds.

The Confederates threatened to break the Union blockade of the Chesapeake Bay in March 1862. An old warship, the **Merrimack,** had been armored with iron plates so that she had the shape of a tent. Cannonballs fired at the ship ricocheted harmlessly off the slanting superstructure. The *Merrimack* was not heavily armed; it was primarily a ram, with a heavy iron blade prow that could slice through a wooden hull. Within a few hours of her debut, the *Merrimack* sank several Union warships.

Left unopposed for a few weeks, this single ship might have opened the Chesapeake to a flourishing trade. But the

■ *Confederate commerce raiders under construction in Liverpool. Three put out to sea, the most famous being the* Alabama, *which savaged Union shipping. American minister Charles Francis Adams persuaded the British not to release raiders to the Confederacy after it became likely the Union would win the war. Adams was the son of John Quincy Adams and the grandson of John Adams: diplomacy ran in the family.*

Merrimack did not have even a few days. Fortuitously, the Union navy also had an experimental ironclad vessel ready to go. The even odder-looking *Monitor* resembled a cake tin on a platter skimming the waves. The cake tin was a turret containing a big gun; it was not necessary to turn the vessel to fire, only the turret. Its round shape deflected projectiles as the *Merrimack's* sloping walls did. Its decks, barely above the level of the water, provided no target at all.

For five hours on March 9, 1862, the two ships had at one another, then disengaged. The battle was technically a draw, but effectively a Union victory. The *Merrimack* had to retreat for repairs. In May the Confederates destroyed the vessel so that it would not fall into Union hands. And once again, the material disparity between the two nations told in the long run. The South never built another *Merrimack*. The *Monitor* was a prototype for a flotilla of others like it.

MCCLELLAN AND THE "SLOWS"

In creating the Army of the Potomac, George McClellan made a valuable contribution to the Union cause. Not only were his men better trained than most southern troops, but they usually were better armed. While the Confederates had to import or capture most of their arms, McClellan (and his successors) had a limitless supply of munitions and constantly improved firearms. The Springfield repeating rifle, introduced late in the war, allowed Union soldiers to fire six times as fast as musket-armed Confederates.

McClellan was probably the best desk general either army produced. He knew how to create an edge in numbers, training, and equipment—and his soldiers were devoted to him. McClellan thought of himself as a battlefield commander too, a Napoleon; he posed, strutted, and issued bombastic proclamations to his troops. But a fighting general he was not. Confronted with an enemy army, he lost confidence: he ceased to advance and told Lincoln he needed more troops even when his army outnumbered Lee's by two to one. It was partly a matter of personality but not entirely. McClellan was a Democrat and (with little justification) developed a contemptuous dislike of Lincoln. He had his own war plan. He did not want to crush the South. He believed that merely by creating a terrifying military machine, he could persuade the Confederates to give in and negotiate a peace:

The Granger Collection, New York

The Union had no better organizer and executive than General George McClellan. But he was no field commander. He dallied, even avoided battle, because of either an aversion to exposing his men to high casualties, hopes for negotiation with the Confederacy, or both.

To Lincoln, who did not much like McClellan either, it was simpler. Lincoln said that McClellan was ill: he had a bad case of "the slows."

THE PENINSULA CAMPAIGN

When McClellan finally moved in April 1862, he did not drive directly toward Richmond as McDowell had. Instead, he moved his army by sea to the peninsula between the York and James Rivers. In a month he had 110,000 troops poised to take Richmond from the south, bypassing the city's fortifications.

The plan was ingenious; it should have worked. The Confederate Army of Northern Virginia was outnumbered and caught by surprise. Having outmaneuvered General Johnston, however, McClellan did not, as Jomini prescribed, hurl his overwhelming force at the enemy's weakness. He established what looked like a permanent defensive camp on the peninsula and sat, fiddled, and fretted. He overestimated the size of the Confederate force facing him and demanded reinforcements from Lincoln.

Lincoln refused to send them for good reason: Lee had accurately sized up the situation, including McClellan's insecurity, and fooled Lincoln into thinking that Washington itself was in danger. He gambled that McClellan would not move from the South and sent Stonewall Jackson on a diversionary mission toward Washington. (Jackson did not have the numbers to bring off an actual assault on the capital.) The ruse was successful. Lincoln called off the transfer of troops to the peninsula, whence Jackson rapidly returned to reinforce the Confederates facing McClellan. By the time McClellan angrily gave in to the president's impatient demand for aggressive action, Lee and Jackson had 85,000 men dug in where, a week earlier, they would have had to fight in open country.

Seven days of nearly constant battle followed between June 26 and July 2, 1862. Again overly cautious and outsmarted on the field, McClellan was fought to a standstill. Even then he held a favorable position. His supply lines were intact; Richmond was cut off from the Chesapeake and the sea; its only supply lines lay to the west. And Confederate morale was badly shaken by the 25 percent casualties the men had suffered. If McClellan had advanced only a few more miles—far from an impossible task—Richmond could have been bombarded, forcing Lee to attack.

It was Lincoln's turn to blunder. Still failing to appreciate that Stonewall Jackson's advance on Washington had been a feint, he called off the Peninsula Campaign, ordered the Army of the Potomac back to Washington, and replaced McClellan with General John Pope, who proposed to take the "safe" Manassas route to Richmond.

Pope was a good brigadier, even a good division commander. He had won several impressive victories in the West and was a favorite with the abolitionists in Congress because of his opposition to slavery. But he lacked imagination, and (like McClellan) he was no match on the battlefield for the wily Lee and Jackson. At the end of August, Lee met him on the same ground as the first Battle of Manassas and beat him back more easily than Beauregard had repulsed McDowell the previous year.

ANTIETAM

Lincoln had no choice but to recall McClellan, which confirmed the general's conviction that he should not be subject to Lincoln's orders. The Richmond–Washington battlefront bogged down into a stalemate that dimly prefigured the trench warfare of World War I fifty years in the future. The situation was favorable to the Confederacy, but Jefferson Davis, like Lincoln, was vexed by pressures to "do something." Dissatisfied with Lee's brilliance in repelling Union advances, the critics wanted the war carried into the North. The chances of British intervention were rapidly fading. Only a major victory on Union soil could bring Britain into the war, just as the American victory in Saratoga in 1777 had brought France into the War for Independence.

Unfortunately, while Lee worked defensive miracles with inferior numbers, his army of 40,000 was not up to an

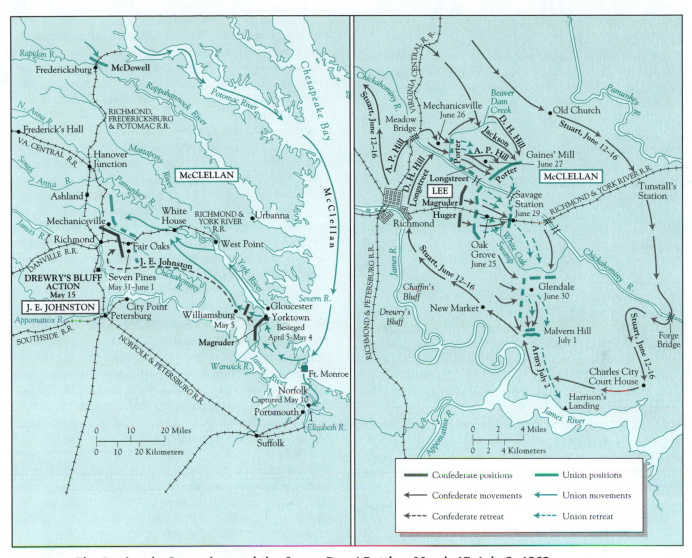

MAP 23:3 The Peninsula Campaign and the Seven Days' Battles, March 17–July 2, 1862
The Peninsula Campaign was brilliant in conception. By approaching Richmond from the southeast, virtually all the fortifications built to defend the city to the north were rendered irrelevant. But McClellan dawdled. Although his numerical advantage was overwhelming, he wanted more troops before he moved. Brilliant improvised maneuvers by Johnston, Jackson, and Lee fought McClellan to a standstill practically within sight of the Confederate capital.

advance when the enemy was 70,000 strong. Moreover, Lee suffered a stroke of appalling bad luck when his written battle plans, wrapped around a pack of cigars, fell into Union hands. McClellan caught Lee when he was unprepared to fight, at Sharpsburg in Maryland, near Antietam Creek.

The fighting was as vicious and gory as at Shiloh. Antietam was the worst single day of the entire war. Lee lost a quarter of his men. His army was in such disarray that it was in no condition to retreat in order back into Virginia. His supply lines were cut. Stoically, Lee waited for a counterattack that would destroy his army. To his amazement, McClellan did not move. He was down with "the slows" again. On the second night after the battle, hardly believing his luck, Lee was able to slip back to the sanctuary of Virginia.

Prisoners and Race

During the first years of the war, Union and Confederate armies routinely exchanged prisoners taken in battle. The exchanges ended in 1864 for two reasons. First, Grant opposed them because his war of attrition was designed to reduce the Confederate armies to ineffectiveness. He did not want to return captured rebels so they could fight again: "We would have to fight on until the whole South is exterminated." Second, the Confederates refused to exchange captured African-American soldiers (and they treated them viciously, in several cases, murdering soldiers who had surrendered). In this, at least, Lincoln insisted that black soldiers be treated according to the same rules that white soldiers were.

EMANCIPATION: A POLITICAL MASTER STROKE

During the first year of the war, Lincoln insisted that his aim was not the destruction of slavery but the preservation of the Union. He constantly reassured uneasy political leaders from the loyal slave states, especially in Maryland, where pro-Confederates were numerous. When General Frémont freed captured slaves as contraband, Lincoln countermanded his order and wrote to Frémont's wife, Jessie, "The General should never have dragged the Negro into the war. It is a war for a great national object and the Negro has nothing to do with it."

His actions aroused increasing opposition in Congress. Republicans who had not been abolitionists began to side with abolitionists, who argued that, in a war brought on by slave owners, destroying the institution should be a war aim alongside the restoration of the Union. Lincoln looked at the issue from a different perspective: what policies were most likely to bring victory. In August 1862, just before Antietam, abolitionist newspaper editor Horace Greeley publicly demanded that Lincoln move against slavery. The president replied, "If I could save the Union without freeing any slave, I would do it; and if I could save it by freeing all the slaves, I would do it; and if I could do it by freeing some and leaving others alone, I would also do it."

In fact, Lincoln had already decided to free some of the slaves. In the summer of 1862 he read to his cabinet a proclamation that, as of a date to be decided, all slaves held in territory still under the control of rebels were henceforth free. His purpose was to convince Confederate leaders that the only realistic way to preserve slavery was to come to terms before the cutoff date.

Secretary of State William Seward, who had been thought too keenly antislavery to be a Republican presidential candidate, was now the voice of caution. He persuaded Lincoln to keep the *Emancipation Proclamation* secret until the North won a major battlefield victory. Otherwise, Seward argued—and it was a good point—Lincoln's proclamation would look like an act of desperation. The major victory was Antietam. On September 22, 1862, five days after the battle, Lincoln issued his proclamation, to go into effect January 1, 1863.

A few abolitionists pointed out that Lincoln's proclamation did not free a single person. It did not apply to the loyal slave states or to those parts of the Confederacy occupied by Union troops in September: most of Tennessee and several southern seaports. This was true enough but meaningless. The Emancipation Proclamation was a master stroke. It reassured Unionist slave owners by allowing them to keep their slaves. But it permitted northern generals to make use of African Americans who, once Union armies were nearby, fled to them by the thousands—which Lincoln had previously forbidden. Many young black men wanted to join the Union army, but as long as they were legally slaves, they could not be enlisted. Now, however, they could be hired to dig fortifications and perform other labor.

Lincoln came around only slowly to enlisting African-American troops, even though free blacks in the North had already begun to train in militias. After the Emancipation Proclamation, however, and the unending demands from Lincoln's generals for more soldiers, he relented. Fully 150,000 blacks served in Union blue. One Billy Yank in eight was black.

African-American units were usually assigned the dirtiest duty and, when sent into combat, the most dangerous tasks. Many white officers looked upon them as cannon fodder. Other officers, however, were moved by their soldiers' bravery. Black soldiers were paid only half a white soldier's wages, about $7 a month, and, when captured, they were treated brutally by Confederates. And yet, because they were fighting for freedom rather than for an abstraction, black soldiers were said to bicker and gripe far less than whites did, and their desertion rate was a fraction of the desertion rate among whites.

FIGHTING TO MAKE MEN FREE

The Emancipation Proclamation served Lincoln as a trial balloon. Without committing himself either way, he was able to test northern opinion on the subject of abolition. When Union soldiers adopted Julia Ward Howe's abolitionist "Battle Hymn of the Republic" as their anthem ("let us fight to make men free") Lincoln learned that by striking at slavery, he had improved morale. He had also ensured British neutrality.

Finally, Lincoln mollified—for a time—his chief critics within the Republican party. Called the Radicals because they wanted an all-out conquest of the South and a radical remaking of its social institutions, this group controlled the Joint Committee on the Conduct of the War. The Radical leaders, Thaddeus Stevens in the House and Charles Sumner in the Senate, were not satisfied with the Emancipation Proclamation. They wanted a constitutional amendment that would abolish slavery in the Union as well as in the Confederacy. But Lincoln's action subdued their criticisms. Lincoln also played for Radical support by once again dismissing the Democrat McClellan and appointing another antislavery general, Ambrose E. Burnside, as commander of Union forces in the East.

STALEMATE RENEWED

Burnside did not want the job. An excellent corps commander, he believed the complexities and responsibilities of directing an entire army were beyond him. Indeed, he made a blunder that astonished even the Confederates. On December 13, 1862, Burnside ordered a frontal assault on an impregnable southern position on high ground near Fredericksburg, Virginia. The slaughter of Union soldiers shocked even veterans of Antietam. Union General Darius Crouch exclaimed, "Oh, great God! See how our men, our poor fellows are falling!" Robert E. Lee remarked to an aide that "it is well that war is so terrible or we would grow too fond of it." Burnside retreated, in tears and broken. And the Union and

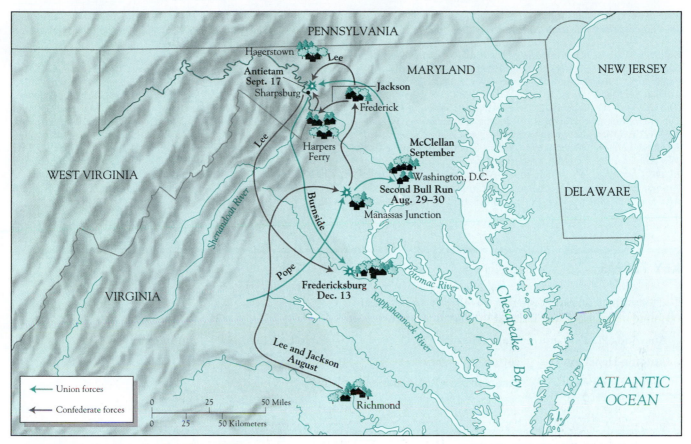

MAP 23:4 Stalemate in the East, 1862
Lee and Jackson displayed their mastery of tactics at the Second Battle of Bull Run in August 1862; but in September their army was almost destroyed at Antietam on the Maryland side of the Potomac, in part because Lee's plans fell by a fluke into McClellan's hands. Lee's reputation was restored when Union troops made an ill-advised attempt to cross the Rappahannock at Fredericksburg at the end of 1862.

Confederate armies settled down to winter quarters on either side of the Rappahannock River.

The war also bogged down in the West. After Shiloh, a Confederate force under General Braxton Bragg moved across eastern Tennessee into Kentucky in an attempt to capture that state. At Perryville on October 8, he fought to a draw against General Don Carlos Buell, decided his supply lines were overextended, and moved back into Tennessee. On the last day of 1862, Bragg fought another standoff with the Union army at Murfreesboro. Both sides went into winter quarters—neither beaten, neither within sight of victory.

FURTHER READING

General Gabor Borit, *Why the Civil War Came*, 1996; David J. Eicher, *The Longest Night: A Military History of the Civil War*, 2001; Edward Hagerman, *The American Civil War and the Origins of Modern Warfare*, 1988; Herman Hattaway and Archer Jones, *How the North Won: A Military History of the Civil War*, 1980; D. W. Meinig, *The Shaping of America: A Geographic Perspective on 500 Years of History*, vol. 2, *Continental America, 1800–1867*, 1993; Ivan Musicant, *Divided Waters: The Naval History of the Civil War*, 1995; Geoffrey C. Ward, *The Civil War*, 1999.

Commanders Gabor Borit, *Lincoln's Generals*, 1994; Joseph G. Glathaar, *Partners in Command: The Relationships between Leaders in the Civil War*, 1993; Joseph L. Harsh, *Confederate Tide Rising: Robert E. Lee and the Making of Southern Strategy, 1861–1862*, 1998; William S. McFeeley, *Grant*, 1981; Alan Nolan, *Lee Considered: General Robert E. Lee and Civil War History*, 1991; Stephen B. Oates, *With Malice toward None*, 1979; Charles B. Royster, *The Destructive War: William Tecumseh Sherman, Stonewall Jackson, and the Americans*, 1991; Brooks D. Simpson, *Ulysses S. Grant*, 2000.

The Confederacy David F. Berenger et al., *Why the South Lost the Civil War*, 1986; William Blair, *Virginia's Private War: Feeding Body and Soul in the Confederacy, 1861–1865*, 1998; Drew Gilpin Faust, *The Creation of Confederate Nationalism*, 1988, and *Mothers of Invention: Women of the Slaveholding South in the American Civil*

War, 1996; Gary W. Gallagher, *The Confederate War*, 1997; Emory M. Thomas, *The Confederate Nation, 1861–1865*, 1979.

Soldiers William Blair, *Virginia's Private War: Feeding Body and Soul in the Confederacy, 1861–1865*, 1998; Dudley T. Comish, *The Sable Arm*, 1966; Lauren M. Cook, *They Fought Like Demons: Women Soldiers in the American Civil War*, 2002; Robert Durden, *The Gray and the Black*, 1972; James W. Geary, *We Need Men: The Union Draft in the Civil War*, 1991; Joseph Glathaar, *Forged in Battle: The Civil War Alliance of Black Soldiers and White Officers*, 1990; Elizabeth Leonard, *All the Daring of the Soldier: Women in the Civil War Armies*, 1999; Gerald E. Linderman, *The Experience of Combat in the Civil War*, 1987; Richard M. McMurry, *Two Great Rebel Armies*, 1989; James M. McPherson, *For Cause and Comrades: Why Men Fought in the Civil War*, 1997; Reid Mitchell, *The Vacant Chair:*

The Northern Soldier Leaves Home, 1993; J. Tracy Power, *Lee's Miserables: Life in the Army of Northern Virginia from the Wilderness to Appomattox*, 1998.

The Union Jean Baker, *Affairs of Party: The Political Culture of the Northern Democrats in the Mid-Nineteenth Century*, 1983; Lawanda Cox, *Lincoln and Black Freedom*, 1981; Eric Foner, *Politics and Ideology in the Age of the Civil War*, 1980; J. Matthew Gallman, *The North Fights the War: The Home Front*, 1994; Elizabeth D. Leonard, *Yankee Women: Gender Battles in the Civil War*, 1994; Philip S. Palaudan, *"A People's Contest": The Union and the Civil War, 1861–1865*, 1988, and *The Presidency of Abraham Lincoln*, 1994; James A. Rawley, *The Politics of Union*, 1974; Joel Silber, *A Respectable Minority: The Democratic Party in the Civil War Era*, 1977.

KEY TERMS

The following terms are covered in this chapter and can also be found in the list of Key Terms at the back of the book.

Anaconda Plan	**"copperheads"**	**"Johnny Reb"**	**minié balls**
Antoine-Henri Jomini	**cotton diplomacy**	***Merrimack***	
"bounty jumpers"	**Emancipation Proclamation**		

 ## ONLINE SOURCES GUIDE

Use this listing to find online documents, images, interactive maps, simulations, and other resources related to this chapter:

American History Resource Center
http://history.wadsworth.com/rc/us

Selected Documents
Southern Confederacy: Our Cause before the World
Excerpt from Mary Boykin Chestnut's Wartime Diary from the Southern Home Front

Selected Images
Abraham Lincoln
Jefferson Davis
Northern view of Jefferson Davis
General Robert E. Lee
Recruiting station, New York City

Interactive Time Line (with online readings)
Tidy Plans, Ugly Realities: The Civil War through 1862

Discovery

How was the fervor in going to war tempered by the realities of conflict?

In thinking about this question, begin by breaking it down into the components shown below. A discussion of the significance of each component should appear in your answer.

Warfare: For this exercise, read the document excerpts from the Emancipation Proclamation and "The Capture of Fort Pillow, 1864." How many slaves were actually freed by the Proclamation? Is it a political document? How so? What happened at Fort Pillow? Were African Americans the only ones who suffered? Who does the author believe bears the brunt of the responsibility?

By the President of the United States of America: A Proclamation (1863)

Abraham Lincoln

Whereas on the 22nd day of September, A.D. 1862, a proclamation was issued by the President of the United States, containing, among other things, the following, to wit:

"That on the 1st day of January, A.D. 1863, all persons held as slaves within any State or designated part of a State the people whereof shall then be in rebellion against the United States shall be then, thenceforward, and forever free; and the executive government of the United States, including the military and naval authority thereof, will recognize and maintain the freedom of such persons and will do no act or acts to repress such persons, or any of them, in any efforts they may make for their actual freedom.

"That the executive will on the 1st day of January aforesaid, by proclamation, designate the States and parts of States, if any, in which the people thereof, respectively, shall then be in rebellion against the United States; and the fact that any State or the people thereof shall on that day be in good faith represented in the Congress of the United States by members chosen thereto at elections wherein a majority of the qualified voters of such States shall have participated shall, in the absence of strong countervailing testimony, be deemed conclusive evidence that such State and the people thereof are not then in rebellion against the United States."

Now, therefore, I, Abraham Lincoln, President of the United States, by virtue of the power in me vested as Commander-In-Chief of the Army and Navy of the United States in time of actual armed rebellion against the authority and government of the United States, and as a fit and necessary war measure for supressing said rebellion, do, on this 1st day of January, A.D. 1863, and in accordance with my purpose so to do, publicly proclaimed for the full period of one hundred days from the first day above mentioned, order and designate as the States and parts of States wherein the people thereof, respectively, are this day in rebellion against the United States the following, to wit:

Arkansas, Texas, Louisiana (except the parishes of St. Bernard, Palquemines, Jefferson, St. John, St. Charles, St. James, Ascension, Assumption, Terrebone, Lafourche, St. Mary, St. Martin, and Orleans, including the city of New Orleans), Mississippi, Alabama, Florida, Georgia, South Carolina, North Carolina, and Virginia (except the forty-eight counties designated as West Virginia, and also the counties of Berkeley, Accomac, Morthhampton, Elizabeth City, York, Princess Anne, and Norfolk, including the cities of Norfolk and Portsmouth), and which excepted parts are for the present left precisely as if this proclamation were not issued.

And by virtue of the power and for the purpose aforesaid, I do order and declare that all persons held as slaves within said designated States and parts of States are, and henceforward shall be, free; and that the Executive Government of the United States, including the military and naval authorities thereof, will recognize and maintain the freedom of said persons.

And I hereby enjoin upon the people so declared to be free to abstain from all violence, unless in necessary self-defence; and I recommend to them that, in all case when allowed, they labor faithfully for reasonable wages.

And I further declare and make known that such persons of suitable condition will be received into the armed service of the United States to garrison forts, positions, stations, and other places, and to man vessels of all sorts in said service.

And upon this act, sincerely believed to be an act of justice, warranted by the Constitution upon military necessity, I invoke the considerate judgment of mankind and the gracious favor of Almighty God.

The Capture of Fort Pillow, 1864

. . . After the rebels were in undisputed possession of the fort and the survivors had surrendered, they commenced the indiscriminate butchery of all the Federal soldiers. The colored soldiers threw down their guns and raised their arms in token of surrender, but not the least attention was paid to it. They continued to shoot down all they found. A number of them finding no quarter was given, ran over the bluff to the river, and tried to conceal themselves under the bank and in the bushes, were pursued by the rebel savages, and implored to spare their lives. Their appeals were made in vain, and they were all shot down in cold blood, and in full sight of the gunboat. I passed up the bank of the river and counted fifty dead strewed along. One had crawled into a hollow log and was killed in it; another had got over the bank into the river, and got to a board that ran out into the water. He lay on it on his face, with his feet in the water. He laid there when exposed stark and stiff. Several had tried to hide in crevices made by the falling bank, and could not be seen without difficulty, but they were singled out and killed. From the best information I could get the white soldiers were, to a very considerable extent, treated in the same way. One of the 13th Tennessee on board—D.W. Harrison—informs me that after the surrender he was below the bluff, and one of the rebels presented a pistol to shoot him. He told him he had surrendered and requested him not to fire. He spared him, and directed him to go up the bluff to the fort. Harrison asked him to go before him, or he would be shot by others, but he told him to go along. He started, and had not proceeded far before he met a rebel who presented his pistol. Harrison begged him not to fire but paying no attention to his request, he fired and shot him through the shoulder, and another shot him in the leg. He [sic] full, and while he lay unable to move, another came along and was about to fire again, when Harrison told him he was badly wounded twice, and implored not to fire. He asked Harrison if he had any money. He said he had a little money and a watch. The rebel took from him his watch and ninety dollars in money, and left him. Harrison is probably fatally wounded. Several such cases have been related to me, and I think, to a great extent, the whites and negroes were indiscriminately murdered. The rebel Tennesseans have about the same bitterness against Tennesseans in the Federal army, as against the negroes. I was told by a rebel officer that Gen. Forrest shot one of his men and cut another with his saber for shooting down prisoners. It may be so, but he is responsible for the conduct of his men, and Gen. Chalmeres stated publicly while on the Platte Valley, that though he did not encourage or countenance his men in shooting down negro captives, yet that it was right and justifiable.

To read extended versions of the documents, visit the companion Web site
http://history.wadsworth.com/americanpast8e; click on "Discovery Sources."

CHAPTER 24

Driving Old Dixie Down

General Grant's War of Attrition 1863–1865

National Park Service, Harpers Ferry Center

The rebels now have in their ranks their last man. The little boys and old men are guarding prisoners and railroad bridges, and forming a good part of their forces, manning forts and positions, and any man lost by them cannot be replaced. They have robbed the cradle and the grave.

Ulysses S. Grant

By the spring of 1863, the Confederacy was suffering severe shortages and an inflation of the currency just short of runaway. In the Union, the problem was frustration. Lincoln had men, matériel, and money, but he could not find a general who would both fight and win. In the East, Robert E. Lee had defeated or confounded four commanders. In the West, the situation was a little more encouraging. Southern Louisiana and western Tennessee were occupied but not secure; even Kentucky was vulnerable to Confederate cavalry raids.

THE CAMPAIGNS OF 1863

The third summer of the war began with more bad news for the Union. By the end of the year, however, the tide had unmistakably turned against the South. Lee's second invasion of the Union ended in a Confederate disaster worse than Antietam. In the West, Union armies broke the stalemate, and Lincoln found a general in whom he could be confident. Oddly enough, he was a man who had flirted with demotion and even discharge after the disaster at Shiloh.

CHANCELLORSVILLE

After Burnside's debacle at Fredericksburg, his most outspoken critic was General Joseph Hooker, called "Fighting Joe" because of his aggressiveness. Hooker had a history of indiscretion. He had resigned from the army in 1853 when Winfield Scott chastised him for badmouthing fellow officers.

Hookers

It is a common misconception that use of the term *hookers* to refer to prostitutes was a kind of tribute to General "Fighting Joe" Hooker, who was not interested in keeping whores away from the Army of the Potomac. Not true: *hooker* in its colloquial sense was included in the second edition of John R. Bartlett's *Dictionary of Americanisms,* published in 1859. Apparently the term originated in North Carolina and refers to the obvious— the custom of an aggressive prostitute to hook her arm around the arm of a potential client.

Reproduced from the Collections of the Library of Congress

■ *Robert E. Lee took great pride in his family heritage. He was an aristocrat, always soberly dignified, "the marble man." He owned no slaves, opposed secession, and looked down upon newly rich cotton planters from the deep South. Lee did not so much join the Confederacy as he defended Virginia.*

After Fredericksburg, Hooker openly criticized Lincoln for timidity. What the country needed for the duration of the war was a dictator, he said. In one of the most unusual commissions ever given a military officer, Lincoln wrote Hooker that only victorious generals could set up dictatorships. If Hooker would win the victory that the North badly needed, Lincoln would run the risk that Hooker was a Napoleon.

Hooker distinguished himself in battle before and after Chancellorsville: in the Seven Days' Battles, Lookout Mountain, and Chattanooga. He was with William Tecumseh Sherman all the way from Atlanta to the sea. In May 1863 he put together the Army of the Potomac's best battle plan since the Peninsula Campaign. He crossed the Rappahannock River with more than twice as many soldiers as Lee's 60,000. Once again Lee gambled. He threw away the book and divided his army, left his fortifications, and hit Hooker from two directions near the town of Chancellorsville.

Lee was losing his bet. His men were on the brink of running. Then Hooker did something entirely out of character. At the moment Fighting Joe should have attacked, he ordered a withdrawal. His field commanders were incredulous. One told the courier who delivered the order, "You are a damned liar. Nobody but a crazy man would give such an order when we have victory in sight!" General Henry Slocum galloped personally to Hooker's headquarters to confirm a message he could not believe.

Once again, Lee was the victor, if through little of his own doing. The Army of the Potomac suffered 11,000 casualties. Hooker, humiliated, was soon relieved of command. However, the Battle of Chancellorsville also exposed a weakness in the South's fighting capacity that could only grow more serious. Lee's losses were larger than Hooker's, with a population base less than half that of the Union's. If the war continued indefinitely as it had been going, even with Lee winning most of the battles, the Confederacy would run out of soldiers.

The casualty at Chancellorsville Lee noticed most was his "strong right arm," Stonewall Jackson. His death too was a fluke. Returning from a reconnaissance mission, Jackson was shot by his own troops and died. Lee said he could never replace Jackson and never placed the same kind of confidence in any other general.

THE FORTRESS OF VICKSBURG

In the West, the Union's object was still winning control of the Mississippi River. By holding fast to a 150-mile stretch of

The North's War of Attrition 1863–1865

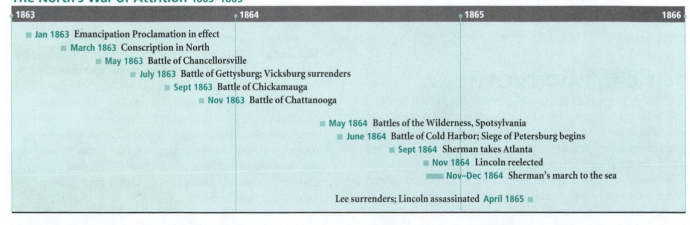

1863	1864	1865	1866

■ Jan 1863 Emancipation Proclamation in effect
■ March 1863 Conscription in North
■ May 1863 Battle of Chancellorsville
■ July 1863 Battle of Gettysburg; Vicksburg surrenders
■ Sept 1863 Battle of Chickamauga
■ Nov 1863 Battle of Chattanooga

■ May 1864 Battles of the Wilderness, Spotsylvania
■ June 1864 Battle of Cold Harbor; Siege of Petersburg begins
■ Sept 1864 Sherman takes Atlanta
■ Nov 1864 Lincoln reelected
■■ Nov–Dec 1864 Sherman's march to the sea

Lee surrenders; Lincoln assassinated April 1865 ■

As a soldier, Grant took little interest in his appearance. Only his epaulets indicated his rank. But his subordinates soon learned that he sized up battle situations calmly and almost always accurately. He had his share of luck, but he was, in the end, the best general of the war.

laced by creeks and bayous—a tangle of woods, earth, brush, and water. When Union forces approached, struggling through the morass, the Confederate garrison sallied out and repelled every assault. Vicksburg was as near and as far from the Union's western armies as Richmond was from the Army of the Potomac.

U. S. GRANT

Then, within a few weeks, an unlikely candidate for the laurels of the war hero broke the western stalemate. He was young General Ulysses S. Grant, just 41 years old but with, it seemed, a century's worth of failures behind him. A West Point graduate, Grant was cited for bravery in the Mexican War but then shunted off to duty at a lonely desert fort and then to a cold, wet, and lonelier outpost on the northern California coast. (McClellan, by way of contrast, was stationed at West Point.) Grant took to the whiskey bottle in California, and after a dressing down by his superior, he resigned from the army. In business and trying to farm back in Illinois, he failed. When the Civil War began, he was a clerk in a relative's store—a charity job.

The Civil War was a godsend for men like Grant. Critically short of officers, the army did not quibble that Joe Hooker had been disruptive and Grant a drunk. Grant was given the command that won the first notable Union victory of the war, the capture of Forts Henry and Donelson. Then, however, came the disaster at Shiloh and revived suspicion of Grant's friendship with the bottle.

He looked like a drunk. Everyone who met Grant commented on his unimpressive presence. He was dumpy; his beard was carelessly trimmed; his uniform was perpetually rumpled and soiled. From a few yards away he could be mistaken for an aging sergeant in danger of demotion to corporal. Up close Grant struck some as listless, even stupid. But he was neither; and although he, like most officers, enjoyed his whiskey in the evening, he was not a sot.

Grant understood battle and, soon enough, showed that he understood war. He was capable of boldness equal to Stonewall Jackson's and Joe Hooker's, and he had Lee's confidence with large commands. His written instructions to his subordinates would have allayed the worries of those who doubted him, had they seen them. Dashed off on his knee, they were clear, precise, even literary on occasion; Grant emphasized his points with metaphors.

THE SIEGE

At Vicksburg, Grant scored a feat of old-fashioned military derring-do and then sat down to a model exercise in siege

the river between Vicksburg, Mississippi, and Port Hudson, Louisiana, the rebels were able to shuttle goods and men from one end of the Confederacy to the other. The farmers of the Midwest were unable to export their crops down the Mississippi and had to depend on railroads, which did the job but were more expensive than river transport and cut into farmer income.

The key to the impasse was Vicksburg. The city sat on high cliffs at a sweeping bend in the Mississippi. A Confederate force commanded by a renegade Pennsylvania Quaker, John C. Pemberton, manned heavy artillery on the top of the bluffs. Vessels passing below ran the risk of being blown out of the water. Infantry could not approach the city from the north because Vicksburg was ringed with rugged woodland

Loaded Guns

Some 24,000 of 37,000 muskets and rifles that were collected from the battlefield at Gettysburg were still loaded; they were never fired. About 6,000 of them had between three and ten charges in them. The soldiers were so excited that they continued to reload without discharging their weapons.

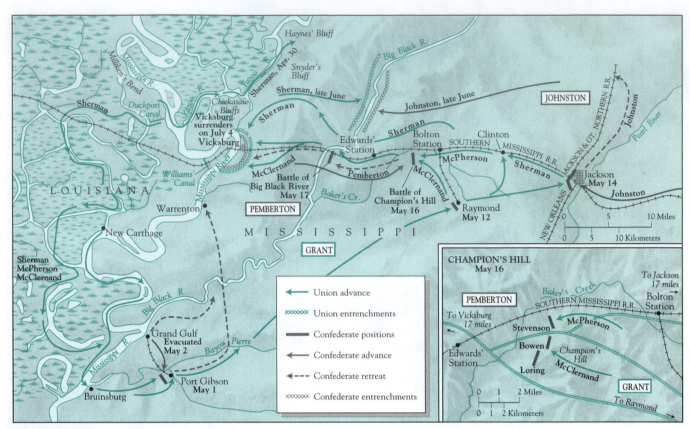

MAP 24:1 Grant's Vicksburg Campaign
The campaign that made Ulysses S. Grant's reputation: it was a combination of daring, risky maneuvers that bewildered the Confederates and a classic siege, isolating fortress Vicksburg, bombarding the city into rubble, and starving its defenders and civilian population.

warfare, not maneuvering with an army but strangling the base that sustained the enemy. First, unknown to Pemberton, Grant transferred most of his army to the west bank of the Mississippi, marched the men swiftly to a few miles below Vicksburg, and then recrossed the river, ferried by gunboats that raced by night under the Confederate guns.

Having bypassed the rugged country where Pemberton had been unbeatable, Grant abandoned his supply lines, a risky maneuver in hostile territory that confused the Confederates for that reason. What did Grant know that they did not? Was there another Union army moving in from elsewhere? There was not. Grant charged to the east and frightened a small Confederate force under Joseph Johnston to withdraw from the area. Grant feigned a full assault on Jackson, the capital of Mississippi, and when its defenders were holed up in the town, he reversed direction, turning back west to Vicksburg.

The Draft Riot

The first two weeks of July 1863 were the happiest in the North since the war began. Instead of constant defeats merely punctuated by occasional victories, the Union won two great victories on the same day: Vicksburg and Gettysburg. The high spirits were suffocated on July 13 when massive riots against the new draft law erupted in New York City. For three days, thousands of workingmen, a majority of them Irish, attacked draft offices, any obviously rich men they ran across (wealthy men could buy their way out of the draft), and African Americans. The mob even burned an orphanage for black children.

What caused the explosion? Why were Irish Americans generally (not just in July 1863) so hostile to blacks? It was not a matter of a lack of patriotism. There were thirty-eight "Irish regiments," all volunteers in the Union army. The Irish did not bring negrophobia with them from Ireland. When Frederick Douglass toured Ireland, he was astonished at the absence of color prejudice. The earliest Irish Catholic immigrants in New York shared neighborhoods with blacks, and if those districts were not known for the gentility of the citizens, no observers mentioned racial hostility.

Possibly, Democratic party politics imbued the Irish with antiblack attitudes. Most of the Irish were Democrats, and the New York party defended the South and slavery. The riots of July 1863 also owed in part to the fact that several "Irish regiments" sustained terrible casualties at the battles of Fredericksburg and Gettysburg. The mobs attacked African Americans because they blamed the war and the deaths on slaves.

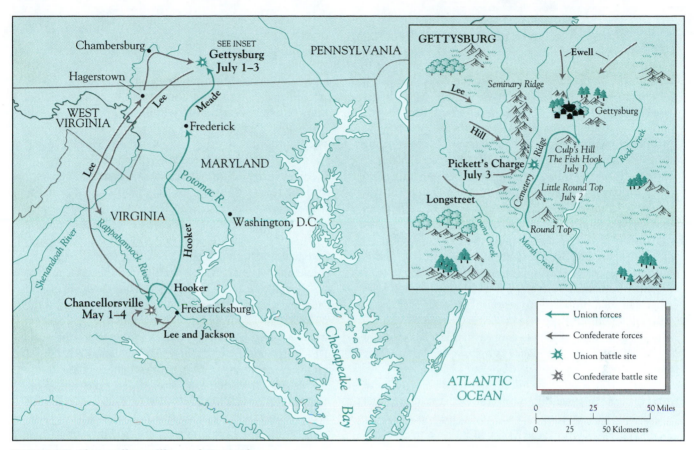

MAP 24:2 Chancellorsville and Gettysburg
Had General Joseph Hooker been aggressive at Chancellorsville as he had been earlier in the war and afterward, he would likely have been the hero of the war. But he withdrew when victory was within his grasp. His defeat made Lee's immediate offensive into Pennsylvania possible, but at Gettysburg the Confederacy's offensive capability was destroyed.

The befuddled Pemberton was trounced in a series of brief battles outside the city. In a little more than two weeks, Grant had fooled half a dozen good generals and won half a dozen confrontations; he had 8,000 Confederate prisoners. On May 19, with Pemberton penned up in Vicksburg, Grant sat his tired army down to bombard the city. Nothing was settled. Vicksburg was a natural fortress and still commanded the river below. But Union forces had broken through where they had been helpless for a year. Richmond was alarmed.

THE GETTYSBURG CAMPAIGN

Some of Lee's advisers urged him to dispatch part of the Army of Northern Virginia to hit Grant from the rear and lift the siege. But Lee thought he could raise the siege without dividing his army by invading Pennsylvania, thus threatening Washington from the north where that city's fortifications were vulnerable. Lincoln, he calculated, would be forced to call Grant's troops east to save the capital if, indeed, Lee had not already taken it.

It was quite a good plan. Had Lee succeeded, his reputation as a strategist would have equaled his reputation as a battlefield tactician. But he failed because, ironically, in the most famous battle of the Civil War, Lee made the most serious tactical mistake of his career.

At first, all went well. Lee's thrust into Pennsylvania (no plans wrapped around lost cigars this time) surprised the Army of the Potomac, now commanded by General George Meade. Meade was mystified; Lee's whereabouts were unknown. A colorless but methodical general, Meade drifted northwest able only to hope he would find Lee on ground favorable to his army. Forward units of both armies bumped into each other near Gettysburg, Pennsylvania, on July 1, 1863. The Confederates were looking for shoes. The Union forces were looking for the Confederates.

Both armies descended on rolling farmland south of Gettysburg. The Confederates occupied the battlefield from the north, the Yankees from the south. Both established strong positions on parallel ridges about half a mile apart, the rebels on Seminary Ridge, the Union troops on Cemetery Ridge.

Deciding to move before Meade's entrenchments were complete, Lee attacked with his left and almost won the battle on the first day. His men pushed Meade's line back until it was curled into the shape of a fishhook. Then, however, the Union line held, and Lee could not flank it without exposing the rest of his army to a counterattack that would split the Confederate army in two.

On July 2 Lee attacked on his right, at the other end of the Union line, at the eye of the fishhook. Once again, the rebels

Marching through Georgia

Late in the summer of 1864, General William Tecumseh Sherman, with a battle-tempered army of 60,000, occupied Atlanta, Georgia, the most important Confederate city aside from Richmond. But Atlanta was an insecure prize. The civilian population was fiercely hostile. A strong Confederate army under General John Bell Hood of Texas, its exact whereabouts unknown to Sherman, menaced both the city and Sherman's supply line, 100 miles of easily raided railroad to Chattanooga, Tennessee. Sherman had good reason to be apprehensive about defending an unfriendly city deep in unfriendly country.

He proposed to General Grant that he evacuate Atlanta, burning everything that might be of use to Hood's army: "Let us . . . make it a desolation," he urged on August 10. Sherman then proposed to "astonish" the Confederates by marching without supply lines across Georgia, "smashing things generally" and making a rendezvous with a naval squadron at Savannah. His men would "eat out" the country.

Sherman had more in mind than the vulnerability of his position. He meant to punish the civilians of the heart of the South for causing and sustaining the war, to lay the countryside waste as cavalry general Philip Sheridan had done in the Shenandoah Valley. Both Grant and Lincoln were reluctant. If Sherman's army was forced to surrender while marching across Georgia—a real possibility—the Confederate will to fight on would be reinvigorated. In the end, Grant swayed the president on the basis of his confidence in Sherman's assessment of his situation.

On November 11 Sherman's men evacuated Atlanta. To move quickly lest they be caught by the Confederates, the men marched in four parallel columns, cutting a swath thirty to sixty miles wide through the rich Georgia countryside. Each column usually stretched out for five miles when, after fifteen miles of marching, it paused for the night's rest. They were not opposed. Hood decided, with good reason, to recapture Tennessee rather than pursue Sherman. (He was defeated there.)

Sherman charged his men to "discriminate" against the rich in seizing the food, mules, horses, oxen, and hogs they needed to keep moving. He told his officers to leave enough at every farm for the people who lived there to survive. "Soldiers must not enter the dwellings of the inhabitants, or trespass." Officers were to punish soldiers guilty of unprovoked abuse of civilians.

Whether Sherman meant to enforce these regulations strictly or was just covering himself in the inevitable event of violations, his troops' adherence to the rules was spotty, and Sherman shrugged off accusations of their bad behavior with the observation that his men had suffered brutality at the hands of the rebels. In fact, crime against persons was not wholesale. Only six rapes were documented, a remarkably low figure with 60,000 men on a rampage. Georgians in Sherman's path knew that women were safe. Frequently, when Sherman's army approached, the men of the plantations and farms hid, leaving their wives and daughters to plead for mercy or glower with hatred at the Yankees. One Confederate soldier wrote that "the Federal army generally behaved very well. . . . I don't think there was ever an army in the world that would have behaved better, on a similar expedition. . . . Our army certainly wouldn't."

This was a rare southern voice. Almost every other witness of the march, Union as well as Confederate, trembled in describing the damage Sherman's army did. The typical farm or village was not hit just once but several times, first by foraging parties ("pioneers") seizing food and livestock, and then by the column itself, the first comers looting, the rear guard burning or shooting the animals that were still alive. An estimated 15,000 horses, 20,000 cattle, and 100,000 hogs were seized, eaten, or destroyed. Half a million bushels of corn disappeared, along with 100,000 bushels of freshly harvested sweet potatoes.

For a century, Sherman's march across Georgia was burned into the southern psyche. Even at the time, many northerners protested. For the most part, however, Sherman's vengeance filled a deeply felt need in the hearts of northerners. They believed the war should have been ended before Sherman's men left Atlanta. General Lee, in Virginia, was obviously finished by November 1864. By preparing for another campaign in the spring, he seemed to be ready to add tens of thousands more to the appalling casualty lists for the sake of no plausible object. The Confederacy was dead. Sherman's terrible rampage was emotional compensation for frustration in the Union.

---

came within a few yards and a few hundred men of breaking through. But when the sun set on the second day, Union troops under Joshua Lawrence Chamberlain of Maine had survived horrendous casualties to hold a bulbous knoll called Little Round Top. It was a valuable position—indeed, a decisive one. The troops that occupied Little Round Top—Chamberlain was flooded with reinforcements overnight—could enfilade the open fields between the two armies. That is, they could shoot into an advancing army from the side, vastly increasing the odds of finding targets.

That night, Lee's imagination failed him. Badly outnumbered now, he guessed correctly that Little Round Top had been reinforced. He rejected another assault on the fishhook in favor of a massive do-or-die frontal attack on the Union center. General James Longstreet argued long, loudly, intemperately (almost insubordinately), and late into the night against Lee's plan. He compared it to Burnside's charge at a powerful Confederate position at Fredericksburg. Longstreet pointed out that with two days in which to dig in on Cemetery Ridge—by 1863 the first thing both armies did on a battlefield was dig deep trenches—the Union troops would be invulnerable. Longstreet urged Lee to sit tight, improve the Confederate entrenchments, and force Meade to attack. In the war to that date, the advantage had always rested with the defensive army.

PICKETT'S CHARGE

Stonewall Jackson might have persuaded Lee to change his plan. James Longstreet could not. But his assessment of the situation was dead right. General Meade had bet on an assault on his center, and he concentrated his forces there. On the afternoon of July 3, he had the satisfaction of seeing his decision pay off. Between one and two o'clock, howling the eerie rebel yell, 15,000 men in gray began to trot across the no-man's-land. This was **Pickett's Charge,** somewhat of a misnomer because the angry Longstreet was in command of it. The attack was a nightmare. The men were slaughtered first by artillery and then by minié balls. The most destructive fire came from Little Round Top.

About a hundred Virginians and North Carolinians actually reached the Union lines. There was a split second of glory, but there were too few rebel soldiers. They were surrounded by a thousand Union soldiers and killed or captured.

Pickett's Charge lasted less than an hour. When the survivors dragged themselves back to Seminary Ridge, 10,000 men were dead, wounded, or missing. Five of twenty regimental commanders were wounded; the other fifteen were dead. So were two brigadier generals. Robert E. Lee rode among the survivors, restraining his tears, apologizing over and over.

On July 4, with 28,000 fewer soldiers than he had led into Pennsylvania, Lee waited for the Union counterattack. It never came. Meade was still ruminating over Pickett's Charge. He would not expose his men to the experience of crossing an open field into the mouths of cannon. By nightfall, a drizzle became a downpour, making the Potomac impassable and setting up Lee's army for a plucking. Defeated and huddled together, the Confederates were in a worse position than they had been after Antietam. But the rain discouraged Meade too. He did not attack. "We had them within our grasp," Lincoln fumed in a rare display of temper; "We

had only to stretch forth our hands and they were ours. And nothing I could say or do could make the Army move."

HIGH TIDE

For all Lincoln's disappointment, Gettysburg was an important victory. It ravaged southern morale: sensible Confederates understood that their armies would never again be capable of an offensive campaign. Lincoln was still without the decisive, relentless general who would exploit the Union's advantages. Meade had done well, but Lincoln would not forgive him for allowing Lee to escape. Then came news from the West. The victory at Gettysburg had not yet been digested in Washington when a spate of telegrams informed the president that the siege of Vicksburg had also ended on July 4, 1863.

Literally starving, after having stripped the streets of pets and the cellars of rats, the army and people of Vicksburg had surrendered. Five days later, Port Hudson, Louisiana, the last Confederate stronghold on the Mississippi, gave up without a fight. Union General Nathaniel Banks took 30,000 prisoners. Within a week, the Confederacy lost several times more men than the rebels had put into the field at the first Battle of Bull Run.

THE TENNESSEE CAMPAIGN

Worse followed bad. In September, a theretofore cautious Union general, William S. Rosecrans, attacked the last large Confederate army in the West. Rosecrans pushed Braxton Bragg out of Tennessee and into northern Georgia. Union troops occupied Chattanooga, a railroad center on the Tennessee River.

Like Grant at Shiloh, however, Rosecrans was surprised by a counterattack. On September 19, reinforced by grim Confederate veterans of Gettysburg, Bragg hit him at Chickamauga Creek. It was one of the few battles of the war in which the Confederates had the larger army, 70,000 to Rosecrans's 56,000, and numbers told. The rebels smashed through the Union right, scattering the defenders. It would have been a total rout but for the stand on the Union left flank led by a Virginian who had remained loyal to the Union, George H. Thomas, the **"Rock of Chickamauga."** Thanks to Thomas, the Union troops were able to retire in good order to the fortifications of Chattanooga.

Wisely, Bragg decided to besiege rather than attack the city. Unlike Grant at Vicksburg, however, Bragg had enemies to his rear. On learning that the Union army was bottled up, Grant himself marched his men to Chattanooga and, by rail, brought an additional 23,000 troops from the East, also Gettysburg veterans. Late in November, his men (departing from Grant's orders, actually) drove Bragg's Confederates from strongholds on Missionary Ridge and Lookout Mountain and back into Georgia.

The long campaign for Tennessee was over. It took two years longer than Lincoln had scheduled, but at last the Confederacy was severed in two. After Vicksburg and Chattanooga, there was no doubt about the man who was to lead the Union army in the end game. Early in 1864, Lincoln promoted U. S. Grant to the rank of lieutenant general and gave him command of all Union forces. Grant turned his western command over to his strong right arm, William Tecumseh Sherman.

TOTAL WAR

Grant had shown that he could be a daring tactician of the old school. At Vicksburg, with dash and flash, he outsmarted and outmaneuvered the enemy. Now he informed Lincoln that his primary object was not the capture of Confederate flags, commanders, cities, and even territory, but the total destruction of the enemy's ability to fight. Richmond mattered to Grant not because Jefferson Davis was there, but because it was an industrial center.

The Union's numerical and matériel superiority was overwhelming. Grant intended to put it to work. He would force the Confederates to fight constant battles on all fronts simultaneously. Unlike in the past, when Union forces "acted independently and without concert, like a balky team, no two ever pulling together," Grant intended to coordinate every army offensive. Unlike McClellan, Grant was willing to sustain high casualties on the cold-blooded but rational grounds that the North could bear the losses and the South could not. Grant discontinued prisoner exchanges to cut off that Confederate source of manpower. He supported the naval blockade with more enthusiasm than his predecessors at the head of the army. He appreciated that, by 1864, the blockade was strangling the southern economy.

Grant's kind of warfare was not chivalrous. It involved wreaking devastation not only on soldiers but on a society. It was left to Grant's favorite commander, William Tecumseh Sherman, to give it a name. "War is hell," Sherman said. He was a no-nonsense man, even unpleasant in his refusal to dress up dirty work with fuss, feathers, and pretty words.

Sherman's assignment was to move from his base in Chattanooga toward Atlanta, the railroad center of the lower South that was defended by the Army of Tennessee under Joseph E. Johnston. Grant, with General Meade as his field commander, would personally direct the assault on Richmond.

GRANT BEFORE RICHMOND

The war of attrition—grinding down the Confederacy—began in May 1864. With 100,000 men, Grant marched into **The Wilderness,** dense scrub forest near Chancellorsville. There he discovered that Lee was several cuts above the

A Union supply depot in Virginia. Grant's army before Richmond was abundantly supplied. The troops at Petersburg were treated to a grand dinner on Thanksgiving of 1864. The Confederates facing them had corn meal mush. By the end of winter, thousands of the rebel soldiers were shoeless. If the outcome of the war is to be attributed to a single factor, that factor is the Union abundance of matériel.

Confederate commanders he had faced in the West. Badly outnumbered, Lee took advantage of the thick woods and neutralized Grant's greater numbers, surprising Grant by attacking. Although the Union suffered 18,000 casualties to Lee's 12,000, replacements were rushed to Grant from Washington. Lee counted his dead, sent his wounded men home, and unhappily counted the declining numbers of soldiers who were fit.

Now it was Lee's turn to discover that he too was up against a new kind of adversary. Instead of withdrawing so that his men could lick their wounds and regroup, Grant shifted his army to the south and, two days later, attacked again at Spotsylvania Courthouse. He thought Lee would have no time to construct fortifications. Overnight, however, Lee's men somehow dug protective trenches. For five days, spearheaded in places by African-American troops, the Army of the Potomac attacked. Grant lost 12,000 men, almost twice Lee's casualties. Northern congressmen and editors, including a few Republicans, howled that Grant was a butcher. Lincoln was alarmed. But Grant was unmoved. He sent a curt message to the president that he intended "to fight it out on this line if it takes all summer."

Again, Grant swung to the south and Lee's men miraculously dug in again. Lee rallied his shrinking army and somehow managed to scratch together enough munitions and

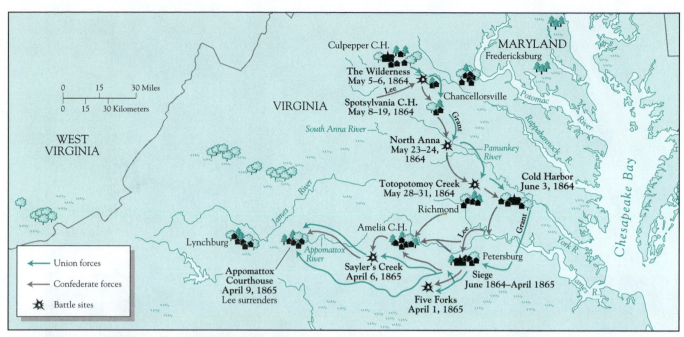

MAP 24:3 Grant before Richmond, 1864–1865
Grant was a kind of general Lee had not seen in Virginia. When his assaults were rebuffed, he moved south and attacked again. The casualties at each battle were horrendous. Grant was determined to reduce Lee's army by attrition. Lee was fighting a war of attrition too. He hoped that by inflicting even greater casualties on the North, he would persuade northern voters to defeat Lincoln in the fall of 1864 and negotiate a peace.

provisions to keep his men in the field. In June, at Cold Harbor, ten miles from Richmond, the two armies fought another gory battle. Before they charged, Union troops wrote their names on scraps of paper and pinned the tags to their uniforms. They expected to die. Even Grant was rattled by the casualty list. He later wrote that the attack at Cold Harbor was his worst mistake in the war.

PETERSBURG AND THE SHENANDOAH

At the time, he just swung south again to Petersburg, a railroad center that was the key to Richmond's survival. Grant might have broken into the town but for the failure of

General Benjamin Butler, a political general in charge of 30,000 reinforcements, to join him in time. After four days, the summer only begun, Grant stopped and ordered a siege.

The Army of the Potomac had lost 65,000 men in a month and a half, more men than Lee had in his army. (Lee lost almost 40,000.) One Maine regiment of 850 soldiers (already shorthanded) reported 218 fit for duty. Democratic party newspapers made the most of the gore; and, looking forward to the November election, the Democrats called the war a "failure." The siege of Petersburg would last nine months, seven months longer than Vicksburg, through the worst winter of the war.

The Battle of the Crater
Early in the siege of Petersburg occurred one of the war's most bizarre battles. It was Ambrose Burnside's idea, and it had merit. Pennsylvania coal miners dug a tunnel under a salient in the Confederate lines and planted four tons of gunpowder beneath a critical point in the fortifications. The plan was to detonate the charge and send an assault force led by a battle-tested unit of African-American troops.

At the last moment, the blacks were replaced by a green white unit, with the African Americans demoted to a support role. Some said the reason for the change was the Union officers' fears they would be accused of using black troops as cannon fodder. (The charge had been levied before.)

In any case, the assault was a disaster for both white and black soldiers. The explosion blasted a crater 170 feet long, 60 feet wide, and 30 feet deep, larger than expected. Confederate troops a hundred yards on either side of the hole were killed or fled. The gap in the lines was wide

enough for a brigade to march through in half an hour.

Incomprehensibly, the general in command waited more than an hour before ordering the troops to advance. (Critics said he was drunk.) And he sent them not around the crater but into it! The Confederates had regrouped and slaughtered the Union soldiers in the trap they had themselves created. Black soldiers who tried to surrender were murdered.

Wounded soldiers outside a makeshift hospital. Army surgeons were dedicated and inexhaustible. They learned a great deal during the war. After a battle, however, their daylong and nightlong work was mainly amputating shattered limbs. They could do little about infection.

In July Lee tried a trick that, with Stonewall Jackson in charge, had worked perfectly in 1862. He sent General Jubal Early on a cavalry raid toward Washington. The hope was that, just as Lincoln had called off the Peninsula Campaign because he feared the capital was in jeopardy, he would panic again and weaken Grant's forces. Early's raid was sensational. His men actually rode to within sight of the Capitol dome. But it was the Confederacy's last hurrah. Grant knew it was only a raid, and this time Lincoln had full confidence in his general. (In fact, Lincoln nearly got himself shot by a sniper when he rode out to see Early's men and did not take cover until forced by soldiers to do so.) Grant's army stayed at Petersburg. He countered Early by sending Union cavalry under General Philip Sheridan to intercept Early, preventing him from rejoining Lee.

Sheridan chased Early into the Shenandoah Valley, the fertile country to the west of Richmond that had been an untouched Confederate sanctuary and Richmond's breadbasket for three years. Sheridan defeated Early three times. More important, he laid waste to the land that had fed the Army of Northern Virginia, burning houses, barns, and crops, and slaughtering what livestock his men did not eat. He reported that when he was done, a crow flying over the Shenandoah Valley would have to carry its own provisions.

SHERMAN IN GEORGIA

General Sherman would be equally destructive in scouring Georgia. He moved into the state at the same time Grant attacked at The Wilderness. At first he was foiled by a brilliant harassing action commanded by Joseph E. Johnston. But an impatient Jefferson Davis, unaware that Johnston's army was not up to a major battle with Sherman, replaced him with a courageous but reckless Texan, John B. Hood, whom Sherman promptly defeated. On September 2, 1864, with Grant beginning his third month outside Petersburg, Union troops occupied Atlanta. The loss of the city was a devastating blow to the economy of the lower South and to Confederate morale.

Just as important, the capture of Atlanta took the sting out of Democratic opposition to continuing the war. At the end of

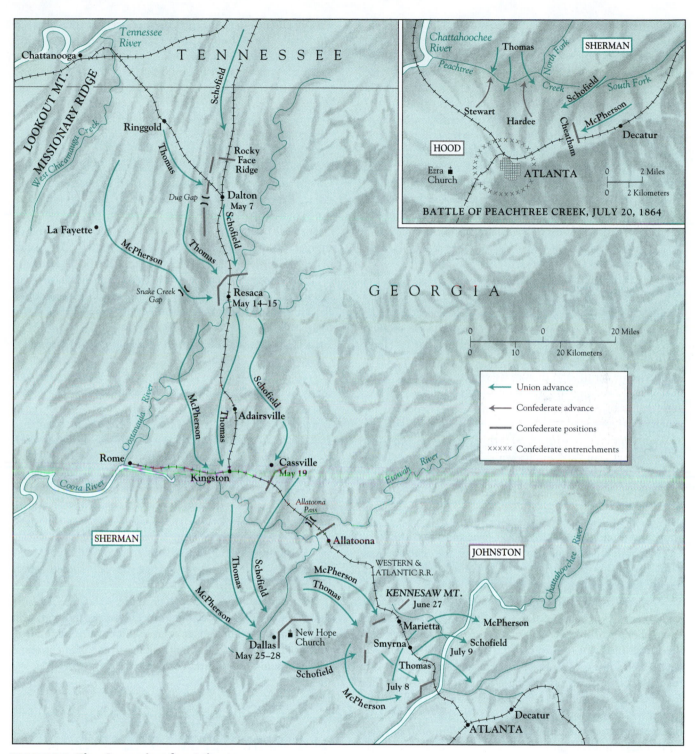

MAP 24:4 The Campaign for Atlanta
Sherman's advance from Chattanooga to Atlanta was timed to coincide with Grant's assault on Richmond; the Confederates would be unable to shift troops from front to front. President Lincoln owed his reelection in November 1864 to Sherman's capture of Atlanta rather than to Grant, whose bloody attacks were repeatedly stopped.

August, the Democrats nominated former general McClellan to oppose Lincoln in the presidential election. Although McClellan knew not to promise southern independence, he effectively said he would call for a truce and negotiate with the Confederates. Lee and Davis were heartened; if the Confederate army could hold out until November, McClellan might very likely win the election. Lincoln prepared himself for defeat at the polls. In effect, Lee fought a war of attrition in the early fall of 1865—not against Grant's army (that was out of the question), but aimed at northern morale.

In Atlanta, Sherman hatched a dangerous plan. He told Grant and Lincoln that he wanted to abandon the city, which he could defend only at great cost; abandon his supply lines; and march "to the sea," to Savannah. He would scourge the countryside, "making Georgia howl." Grant and Lincoln both opposed the plan. They could smell victory; the situation called for caution, not Sherman's potentially disastrous gamble. They pointed out that Hood's Army of Tennessee, 40,000 strong, would have an edge on an army without supply lines. Sherman responded that he had 60,000 men. If Hood pursued him (which he doubted he would), George Thomas in Tennessee, who commanded another 60,000 troops, would rush by railroad to attack Hood from the rear. Grant was persuaded, more by his loyalty to Sherman than by confidence in Sherman's scenario. Once again, Lincoln backed Grant despite his personal reservations.

Sherman ordered the civilians of Atlanta to evacuate the city and put everything of military value to the torch. (By accident, much of the residential city was also destroyed.) His army set out in four columns to the southeast, moving at top speed to avoid a battle. There was no battle. Hood too was aware of Thomas's presence and chose to attack in Tennessee rather than to pursue Sherman. Thomas defeated him twice, reducing the Army of Tennessee to a shell like Lee's Army of Northern Virginia—not important but not much of a threat.

Sherman's men destroyed everything of use to the Confederacy in a swath sixty miles wide. They not only tore up the Atlanta–Savannah railroad, but they burned the ties and twisted the iron rails around telegraph poles. "**Sherman bow ties**," the soldiers called them. Sherman's purpose in laying Georgia waste was to punish the people of Georgia. Those who caused and supported the war (and profited from it, as Georgia had) would suffer for the suffering they had abetted. This was total war. Not only was the Confederate army the enemy; so were the people of the Confederacy.

Sherman reached Savannah on December 10; the city surrendered two weeks later. Except for Richmond and Charleston (where it all began), every major southern city was occupied by Union troops. Sherman removed Charleston from the list. Rested and resupplied from the sea, his army turned north, scorching the earth in South Carolina too, until he was told to ease up. Sherman's goal was to join forces with Grant and finish off Lee. In the West, Hood's maimed army, again under Johnston's command, did not dare attack Thomas again.

THE SUDDEN END

The final battle was never fought. In February 1865, Jefferson Davis sent Confederate Vice President Alexander H. Stephens and two others to meet with Lincoln and Secretary of State Seward on a ship off Hampton Roads, Virginia. Another Confederate diplomat met with newspaper editor Horace Greeley in Canada. Incredibly, their instructions were to insist on Confederate independence as a condition of peace. Davis was out of touch; there was nothing left.

Lee and Davis tried to solve their critical manpower problem by proposing to the Confederate Congress that they recruit slaves. Although it was unsaid, it was assumed that after the war, slave volunteers would be freed. Lee, at least, and probably Davis too, understood that even if Confederate independence was, by a miracle, won, slavery was doomed anyway. Hundreds of thousands of slaves had fled their masters to Union lines. They would never return. Slaves still at their homes would never again accept their status passively. Desperate as the situation obviously was, the Confederate Congress resisted. The bill passed the Senate by only one vote. (The Confederates began to train African-American units, but they never saw battle.)

Late in March 1865, Lee tried to draw Grant into a battle in open country. He had 54,000 men to Grant's 115,000 and was easily pushed back into Richmond. On April 2, knowing that his thirty-seven-mile lines were too much to man (Union lines were fifty-three miles long), Lee abandoned Petersburg and therefore Richmond. His desperate plan was to make a dash west, turn south, resupply in untouched North Carolina, and link up with Johnston for a last stand.

Grant easily prevented Lee's escape. Desertions had reduced the Army of Northern Virginia to 30,000 men, and many were shoeless. On April 9, Lee met Grant at Appomattox Courthouse, Virginia, in, ironically, the home of a man who had moved there from Manassas after the first Battle of Bull Run. To Lee's surprise (he expressed his gratitude), Grant's terms were simple and generous. The Confederates surrendered all equipment and arms except for the officers' revolvers and swords. When Lee pointed out that unlike in the Union army, Confederate cavalry, enlisted men included, personally owned their horses, Grant promptly said they could keep them for plowing. After taking an oath of loyalty to the Union, the southern troops could go home. At Lee's request, Grant provided rations for the Confederates; they were near starvation.

Whatever he may have been thinking, Jefferson Davis ordered Joseph Johnston to fight on. The veteran soldier, who had not fared well by Davis's decisions, knew better. On April 18, he surrendered to Sherman at Durham, North Carolina. The remnants of two smaller Confederate armies gave up over the next several weeks.

THE AMERICAN TRAGEDY

More than a third of the men who served in the two armies died in action or of disease, were wounded, maimed permanently, or captured. In some southern states, more than one-quarter of all the men of military age lay in cemeteries. The depth of the gore can best be understood by comparing the 620,000 dead (360,000 Union, 260,000 Confederate) with the population of the United States in 1860, about 30 million. Considering that half the population was female and 7 or 8 million males were either too old or too young for military service, more than one out of every twenty-five men who were "eligible" to die in the war did. Until the Vietnam

THE ASSASSINATION OF PRESIDENT LINCOLN,
AT FORD'S THEATRE WASHINGTON.D.C.APRIL 14TH 1865.

Booth's murder of Lincoln as drawn up soon after the assassination. Newspapers and magazines were generally uninterested in accuracy in these "instant illustrations," though this representation is confirmed by the eye-witness accounts gathered by investigators.

War of the 1960s and 1970s added its dead to the total, more Americans were killed in the Civil War than in all other American wars combined.

ASSASSINATION

There was one more casualty to be counted. On April 14, a few days after the fall of Richmond, before Johnston's surrender, President Lincoln and his wife attended a play at Ford's Theater in Washington. Shortly after ten o'clock, Lincoln was shot point-blank in the head by a zealous pro-Confederate, **John Wilkes Booth.** Lincoln died early the next morning.

Booth was one of those disturbed characters who pop up periodically to remind us of the role of the irrational in history. An actor with romantic delusions, Booth organized a cabal including one mental defective to avenge the Confederacy by wiping out the leading officials of the Union government.

Don't Swap Horses

Until the end of the nineteenth century, candidates for the presidency did not actively campaign. They did, however, urge on their supporters. In the wartime election of 1864, Lincoln provided his party's slogan by telling the story of the Dutch farmer who said he never swapped horses in the middle of a stream. Indeed, Americans never have changed presidents voluntarily during a war. Even during the unpopular war in Vietnam, it took the retirement of Lyndon B. Johnson in 1968 to put Republican Richard M. Nixon in the White House. With the war still on in 1972, Nixon won reelection by a landslide.

Only he succeeded in his mission, although one of his gang seriously wounded Secretary of State Seward with a knife.

As he escaped the theater, Booth shouted, "*Sic semper tyrannis!*" which means "Thus always to tyrants" and was the motto of the state of Virginia. Booth fled into Virginia; on April 26 he was cornered and killed at Bowling Green. In July four others were hanged for Lincoln's murder, including a woman, Mary Surratt, in whose boardinghouse the plot was hatched. (She was probably innocent of anything more than a vague awareness of the scheme.) But vengeance did not bring the president back, and his loss proved to be inestimable, perhaps more for the South than for the North.

FATHER ABRAHAM

To this day, Lincoln remains a central figure of American history. More books have been written about him than about any other American. He was the American Dream made flesh. He rose from the lowliest frontier origins to become the leader of the nation in its greatest crisis.

Lincoln was not so very popular as a president. The radicals of his own party assailed him because of his reluctance to make war on slavery early in the war, and for his opposition to punishing the South harshly when the war neared its end. Northern Democrats vilified him because the war dragged on for so long. As late as September 1864, because of the casualties of Grant's Richmond campaign, Lincoln expected to lose the November election to George McClellan.

Lincoln weathered McClellan's threat thanks in part to political machinations; he made Nevada a state, gaining three electoral votes, although the territory consisted of little more than a dozen mining camps of uncertain future.

> ### "Union" and "Nation"
>
> Before 1861 "United States" was grammatically plural; since 1865 it has been singular. That is, before the Civil War, one said, "The United States *are* . . ." Since then we have said, "The United States *is* . . ."
>
> Lincoln quietly charted the transformation in his speeches. In his first inaugural address (March 1861) he used the word *Union* twenty times, *nation* not once. In his first message to Congress (July 1861), he said *Union* forty-nine times and *nation* three times. In the Gettysburg Address, Lincoln never said *Union* but referred to *nation* five times.

States controlled by Republicans permitted soldiers to vote by absentee ballot, a first in American history; four out of five of them voted for Lincoln. Lincoln also appealed to prowar Democrats by dropping the name "Republican" and calling himself the Union party candidate. For vice president he chose a Democrat from Tennessee, Andrew Johnson, hoping to win votes from Unionist Democrats in the border states.

But Lincoln did not win the election of 1864 because of political ploys. He won because Sherman had captured Atlanta and it was obvious that the Confederacy was doomed. Lincoln had won the respect of a majority of the people of the North by the example of his dogged will, personal humility, and eloquent humanitarianism. In a speech dedicating a national cemetery at Gettysburg in November 1863, he stated American ideals more beautifully (and succinctly) than anyone had done since Jefferson's preamble to the Declaration of Independence. His second inaugural address, delivered in Washington a month before Lee's surrender, was simultaneously a literary masterpiece, a signal to southerners that they could lay down their arms without fear of retribution, and a plea to northerners for a compassionate settlement of the national trauma. "With malice toward none," he concluded, "with charity for all; with firmness in the right, as God gives us to see the right, let us strive on to finish the work we are in."

CONSEQUENCES OF THE CIVIL WAR

The triumph of the Union guaranteed several fundamental changes in the nature of the American republic. The inseparability of the states was established beyond argument. The theories of John C. Calhoun, so compelling in the abstract, were buried without honor. If the United States was ever a federation of sovereign states, it was not so any longer. It was a nation, one and indivisible. Southern politicians have called themselves "states' righters" since the Civil War. But never after 1865 would any of them suggest that a state could leave the Union if its people disapproved of a national policy.

A NEW POLITICAL MAJORITY

The political dominance of the South was dead. Since the founding of the republic, southerners had played a role in the government of the country out of proportion to their numbers. Eight of the fifteen presidents who preceded Lincoln came from slave states. At least two of the seven northerners who held the office—Pierce and Buchanan—were cowed or persuaded by southern political power to serve the interests of slavery. After Lincoln and Andrew Johnson, no citizen of a former Confederate state would occupy the White House until Lyndon B. Johnson in 1963, and he was more westerner than southerner.

Southerners had dominated Congress through a combination of the extra members that the three-fifths compromise gave slave states, political skill, and an on-again-off-again agrarian alliance with western farmers. In making good on the threat to secede, the southern bloc lost everything but its leaders' political savvy. The Democratic party remained a major force in New York, Connecticut, New Jersey, and the agricultural Midwest. But the Republicans held the edge everywhere else above the Mason–Dixon line. Never again would an agrarian coalition dominate the federal government.

In its place, northeastern industrial and financial interests came to the fore. Businessmen had been late in joining the antislavery coalition. To bankers, great merchants, and factory owners, the Republican party was of interest more because of its economic policies than because of its opposition to slavery. With the war concluded, the "special interests" held a strong position within the party and could exploit the emotional attachment of most northern voters to keep the "Grand Old Party" in power.

NEW ECONOMIC POLICIES

During the war, the Republican Congress enacted a number of laws that would have been defeated had southerners been in their seats and voting. In July 1862, about the time of Antietam, both houses approved the Pacific Railways Act. As modified later in the war, this act gave 6,400 square miles of the public domain to two private companies, the Union Pacific and the Central Pacific railroads. These corporations were authorized to sell the land and use the proceeds to construct a transcontinental railway, the ultimate internal improvement. In 1864, while Grant slogged it out with Lee before Richmond, Congress gave the Northern Pacific Railroad an even more generous subsidy. These acts revolutionized the traditional relationship between private enterprise and the federal government.

The tariff was another issue on which southern agricultural interests had repeatedly frustrated the manufacturers of the Northeast. Since 1832, with few exceptions, the Democratic party drove the taxes on imported goods ever downward. The last tariff before the war, passed in 1857 with the support of southern congressmen, set rates lower than they had been since the War of 1812.

In March 1861, even before secession was complete, the Republican Congress rushed through the Morrill Tariff, which pushed up import duties. In 1862 and 1864, rates went even higher. By 1867 the average tax on imported goods stood at 47 percent, about the same as set by the act of 1828 that the southerners had called the Tariff of Abominations and that Calhoun called fit grounds for secession.

The South had long frustrated the desire of northern financial interests for a centralized banking system. Opposition to a national bank was one of the foundation stones of the old Democratic party. During the war, with no southern congressmen in Washington and with the necessity of financing the Union army looming over Congress, New York's bankers had their way.

FINANCING THE WAR

The Union financed the war in three ways: by heavy taxation, by printing paper money, and by borrowing—that is, selling bonds abroad and to private investors in the United States. The principal taxes were the tariff, an excise on luxury goods, and an income tax. By the end of the war, the income tax provided about 20 percent of the government's revenue.

The government authorized the printing of $450 million in paper money. These bills were not redeemable in gold. Popularly known as "greenbacks" because they were printed on one side in green ink, like modern money, they had value because the federal government declared they must be accepted in the payment of debts. When the fighting went badly for the North, the greenbacks were traded at a discount. By 1865 a greenback with a face value of $1 was worth only 67 cents in gold. This inflation was minuscule compared with inflation in the Confederacy, where government printing presses ran amok. By 1864 a citizen of Richmond paid $25 for a pound of butter and $50 for a breakfast. By 1865 prices were even higher; many southern merchants accepted only gold or Union currency, including greenbacks!

The banking interests of the North were uncomfortable with the greenbacks. However, they profited nicely from the government's large-scale borrowing. By the end of the war, the federal government owed its own citizens and some foreigners almost $3 billion, about $75 for every person in the country. Much of this debt was held by the banks. Moreover, big financial houses like Jay Cooke's in Philadelphia reaped huge profits in commissions for selling the bonds.

FREE LAND

Another momentous innovation of the Civil War years was the **Homestead Act.** Before the war, southern fear of new free states in the territories paralyzed every attempt to liberalize the means by which the federal government disposed of its western lands. In May 1862 the system was overhauled. The Homestead Act provided that every head of family who was a citizen or who intended to become a citizen could receive 160 acres of the public domain. There was a small filing fee, and homesteaders were required to live for five years on the land that the government gave them. Or after six months on the land, they could buy it outright for $1.25 per acre.

A few months after approving the Homestead Act, Congress passed the Morrill Act. This law granted each loyal state

Family Circle

In Washington, slavery was abolished by congressional act, with slave owners compensated for their financial loss. One of the largest payments, and surely the oddest, was to Robert Gunnell, an African American who received $300 each for his wife, children, and grandchildren—eighteen people in all. Gunnell had owned them as slaves, believing it was the safest status for members of his family. They made him $5,400 richer.

30,000 acres for each representative and senator that state sent to Congress. The states were to use the money they made from the sale of these lands to found agricultural and mechanical colleges. In subsequent years the founding of sixty-nine land-grant colleges greatly expanded educational opportunities, particularly in the West.

Again, it was a free-spending policy that parsimonious southern politicians would never have accepted, and the revolutionary infusion of government wealth into the economy spawned an age of unduplicated expansion—and corruption.

FREE PEOPLE

No consequence of the Civil War was as basic as the abolition of slavery. In a sense, the peculiar institution was doomed when the first shell exploded over Fort Sumter. As Congressman **Benjamin E. Wade** of Ohio told southerners in 1861, "The first blast of civil war is the death warrant of your institution." As an immoral institution, slavery might well have survived indefinitely; immoral institutions do. By the middle of the nineteenth century, however, slavery was also hopelessly archaic. The ultimate irony of wars that are fought to preserve outdated institutions is that war itself is the most powerful of revolutionary forces. Precariously founded institutions such as slavery rarely survive the disruptions of large-scale armed conflict.

Some 150,000 African Americans, some free northerners, most of them runaway slaves, served in the Union army. They were less interested in preserving the Union than in freeing all slaves. Their bravery won the admiration of many northerners. Lincoln confessed his surprise that blacks made such excellent soldiers, and he seems to have been revising the racist views that he shared with most white Americans.

For a time, at least, so did Union soldiers. Fighting to free human beings, a positive goal, was better for morale than fighting to prevent secession, a negative aim at best. By 1864, as they marched into battle, Union regiments sang "John Brown's Body," an abolitionist hymn, and Julia Ward Howe's more poetic "Battle Hymn of the Republic":

> As He died to make men holy,
> Let us die to make men free.

Because the Emancipation Proclamation did not free all slaves, in February 1865 radical Republicans in Congress proposed, with Lincoln's support, the Thirteenth Amendment to

By the end of the war 150,000 African Americans had donned Union uniforms, serving both in units doing menial labor (where some officers wanted to keep them) and in some of the fiercest assaults of 1864. In several instances Confederate soldiers murdered black prisoners. In the last month of the war the Confederacy began to train black soldiers, but it was too late to make up for the decimation of the southern armies.

the Constitution. It provided that "neither slavery nor involuntary servitude, except as a punishment for crime . . . shall exist within the United States." Most of the northern states ratified it within a few months. Once the peculiar institution was destroyed in the United States, only Brazil, Cuba and Puerto Rico, Muslim lands, and undeveloped parts of the world continued to condone the holding of human beings in bondage.

FURTHER READING

General David F. Berenger et al., *Why the South Lost the Civil War,* 1986; James McPherson, *Ordeal by Fire: The Civil War and Reconstruction,* 1981; David J. Eicher, *The Longest Night: A Military History of the Civil War,* 2001; Edward Hagerman, *The American Civil War and the Origins of Modern Warfare,* 1988; Herman Hattaway and Archer Jones, *How the North Won: A Military History of the Civil War,* 1980; Ivan Musicant, *Divided Waters: The Naval History of the Civil War,* 1995; Geoffrey C. Ward, *The Civil War,* 1999.

Combat Lauren M. Cook, *They Fought Like Demons: Women Soldiers in the American Civil War,* 2002; Joseph Glathaar, *Forged in Battle: The Civil War Alliance of Black Soldiers and White Officers,* 1990; Elizabeth Leonard, *All the Daring of the Soldier: Women in the*

Civil War Armies, 1999; Gerald E. Linderman, *The Experience of Combat in the Civil War,* 1987; Richard M. McMurry, *Two Great Rebel Armies,* 1989; James M. McPherson, *For Cause and Comrades: Why Men Fought in the Civil War,* 1997; J. Tracy Power, *Lee's Miserables: Life in the Army of Northern Virginia from the Wilderness to Appomattox,* 1998.

The Generals Gabor Borit, *Lincoln's Generals,* 1994; Joseph G. Glathaar, *Partners in Command: The Relationships Between Leaders in the Civil War,* 1993; Gilbert E. Govan and James Livingood, *General Joseph E. Johnston, CSA,* 1993; William Marvel, *Burnside,* 1991; William S. McFeeley, *Grant,* 1981; Richard M. McMurry, *John Bell Hood and the War for Southern Independence,* 1982; Alan Nolan, *Lee Considered: General Robert E. Lee and Civil War History,* 1991;

Charles B. Royster, *The Destructive War: William Tecumseh Sherman, Stonewall Jackson, and the Americans,* 1991; Brooks D. Simpson, *Ulysses S. Grant,* 2000; Jean E. Smith, *Grant,* 2001; Craig L. Symonds, *Joseph E. Johnston: A Civil War Biography,* 1993.

Lincoln Lawanda Cox, *Lincoln and Black Freedom,* 1981; Philip S. Palaudan, *The Presidency of Abraham Lincoln,* 1994; Garry Wills, *Lincoln at Gettysburg: The Words that Remade America,* 1992.

Politics and Society North Jean Baker, *Affairs of Party: The Political Culture of the Northern Democrats in the Mid-Nineteenth Century,* 1983; Iver Bernstein, *The New York City Draft Riots,* 1990; E. D. Fite, *Social and Industrial Conditions in the North during the Civil War,* 1976; J. Matthew Gallman, *The North Fights the War: The Home Front,* 1994; James W. Geary, *We Need Men: The Union Draft in the Civil War,* 1991; Elizabeth D. Leonard, *Yankee Women: Gender Battles in the Civil War,* 1994; Philip S. Palaudan, *"A People's Contest": The Union and the Civil War, 1861–1865,* 1988; James A. Rawley, *The Politics of Union,* 1974; Joel Silber, *A Respectable Minority: The Democratic Party in the Civil War Era,* 1977.

Politics and Society South Stephen Ash, *When the Invaders Came: Conflict and Chaos in the Occupied South,* 1996; Michael B. Ballard, *A Long Shadow: Jefferson Davis and the Final Days of the Confederacy,* 1997; William Blair, *Virginia's Private War: Feeding Body and Soul in the Confederacy, 1861–1865,* 1998; Drew Gilpin Faust, *Mothers of Invention: Women of the Slaveholding South in the American Civil War,* 1996; Gary W. Gallagher, *The Confederate War,* 1997; Emory M. Thomas, *The Confederate Nation, 1861–1865,* 1979, and *The Confederacy as a Revolutionary Experience,* 1991.

KEY TERMS

The following terms are covered in this chapter and can also be found in the list of Key Terms at the back of the book.

Benjamin F. Wade	**John Wilkes Booth**
Homestead Act	**Pickett's Charge**

"Rock of Chickamauga"	**The Wilderness**
"Sherman bow ties"	

ONLINE SOURCES GUIDE

Use this listing to find online documents, images, interactive maps, simulations, and other resources related to this chapter:

American History Resource Center
http://history.wadsworth.com/rc/us

Selected Documents
The Emancipation Proclamation (1863)
The Gettysburg Address (1863)
Resolutions from the 1864 Republican national convention

Selected Images
Confederate dead in Virginia
Ulysses S. Grant

Thomas Jonathan "Stonewall" Jackson
Robert E. Lee
Rose O'Neal Greenhow, a Confederate spy
Dead at Chancellorsville (VA), May 1863
Pickett's Charge at the Battle of Gettysburg, July 1863
African-American recruiting poster
Fourth U.S. Colored Infantry E Company

Interactive Time Line (with online readings)
Driving Old Dixie Down: General Grant's War of Attrition, 1863–1865

Discovery

How were more parts of society affected by the Civil War than in previous wars?

In thinking about this question, begin by breaking it down into the components shown below. A discussion of the significance of each component should appear in your answer.

Government and Law: For this exercise, read the document excerpts "President Abraham Lincoln Calls in the Troops, 1861" and "Proclamation of April 17, 1861." What justification does Lincoln have for raising troops? What justification does Davis have for raising troops? Whose is the better justification? What do each of these proclamations suggest the war is about?

President Abraham Lincoln Calls in the Troops, 1861

By The President of the United States.
    A PROCLAMATION.

Whereas the laws of the United States have been for some time past and now are opposed and the execution thereof obstructed in the States of South Carolina, Georgia, Alabama, Florida, Mississippi, Louisiana, and Texas by combinations too powerful to be suppressed by the ordinary course of judicial proceedings or by the powers vested in the marshals by law:

Now, therefore, I, Abraham Lincoln, President of the United States, in virtue of the power in me vested by the Constitution and the laws, have thought fit to call forth, and hereby do call forth, the militia of the several States of the Union to the aggregate number of 75,000, in order to suppress said combinations and to cause the laws to be duly executed.

The details for this object will be immediately communicated to the State authorities through the War Department.

I appeal to all loyal citizens to favor, facilitate, and aid this effort to maintain the honor, the integrity, and the existence of our National Union and the perpetuity of popular government and to redress wrongs already long enough endured.

I deem it proper to say that the first service assigned to the forces hereby called forth will probably be to repossess the forts, places, and property which have been seized from the Union; and in every event the utmost care will be observed, consistently with the objects aforesaid, to avoid any devastation, any destruction of or interference with property, or any disturbance of peaceful citizens in any part of the country.

And I hereby command the persons composing the combinations aforesaid to disperse and retire peaceably to their respective abodes within twenty days from this date.

Deeming that the present condition of public affairs presents an extraordinary occasion, I do hereby, in virtue of the power in me vested by the Constitution, convene both Houses of Congress. Senators and Representatives are therefore summoned to assemble at their respective chambers at 12 o'clock noon on Thursday, the 4th of July next, then and there to consider and determine such measures as, in their wisdom, the public safety and interest may seem to demand.

In witness whereof I have hereunto set my hand and caused the seal of the United States to be affixed.

Done at the city of Washington, this 15th day of April, A.D. 1861, and of the Independence of the United States the eighty-fifth.

By the President:

ABRAHAM LINCOLN

Proclamation of April 17, 1861 the President of the Confederate States

Whereas, Abraham Lincoln, the President of the United States has, by proclamation, announced the intention of invading this Confederacy with an armed force for the purpose of capturing its fortresses, and thereby subverting its independence and subjecting the free people thereof to the dominion of a foreign power; and, whereas, it has thus become the duty of this government to repel the threatened invasion, and to defend the rights and liberties of the people by all the means which the laws of nations and the usages of civilized warfare place at its disposal;

Now, therefore, I, Jefferson Davis, President of the Confederate States of America, do issue this my proclamation, inviting all those who may desire, by service in private armed vessels on the high seas, to aid this government in resisting so wanton and wicked an aggression, to make application for commissions or letters of marque and reprisal to be issued under the seal of these Confederate States.

Warfare: For this exercise, read the document excerpt "Aftermath of Destruction" and look at the photo of Richmond in ruins in Chapter 25 (p. 409). Note the devastation of the war in the photograph and the description. Was this extent of destruction necessary? Why or why not? Was the Union the only army responsible for the devastation? What kinds of changes might be required following this kind of devastation? Might it provide for renewal? How so?

The Aftermath of Destruction at a Town Near Washington, D.C., 1864

THE REBEL INVASION

A Visit to the Front lines of Battlefield.
[From the Washington Chronicle, July 14]

I proceeded north of Fort Stevens on the seventh street road half-a-mile, when I came to the ruins of the residence of Mr. Lay of the city post office, which was destroyed day before yesterday by shell from Fort Stevens to prevent the sharp shooters from occupying it. A little north of this depleted stop are the ruins of the residence of Mr. Carberry, which was also destroyed by our cannonball. Near this place I came upon the new made grave of an unknown cavalry man. Still further north and a mile from Fort Stevens, I came to a fence thrown across the road, and occupied as a breastwork by the rebels the day previous. Here were marks of hard fighting; Union and rebel muskets, broken and unbroken, and thrown aside by their owners, hay piled in a heap by the way; while hats, caps, haversacks, pouches, and thousands of cartridge sand bullets were scattered here and there on both sides of the rebel breastworks and among the rifle pits dug by the Union soldiers in a field near by. Every rail on the fence and the tree show well the work which has been done the last few hours in that vicinity. While I was looking on the scene a squad of Union Calvary passed on the way from the front, escorting [?] rebel captures, covered with dust and apparently worn out with constant traveling and hard

service. I proceeded on my way, and visited the residences of Dr. S. Heath and Captain Richardson—Here was a scary picture. Hearing of the approach of the rebels on Monday morning, they removed the female members of their families to the fort, and before they could return the rebels had possession of the premises. Everything about the place is scattered in great confusion. What clothing could be made use of the rebels exchanged for their less attractive suits. The building is badly shattered by our artillery fire. Eight common balls or shells had passed through one side to the other and the doors, windows, and side boards are filled with bullet marks. In the field south of this house are the graves of eleven rebel dead, and in a corn field on the opposite side in [?] the way fifteen other rebel soldiers rest from their destructive work. In a grove on the opposite from Mr. Blair's residence, was found a book (the eighth volume Byron's works) tacked by a rebels, which I have brought with me, and transcribes the following inscription, while which is written on a fly-leaf:

NEAR WASHINGTON, JULY 12, 1864
Now, Uncle Abe, you had better be quiet the balance of your administration. We only come near your town this time just to show what we could do—but if you go on in your mad career we will come again soon, and then you had better stand from under.
Yours, respectfully,
The Worst Reb you ever saw.
FIFTY-EIGHT VIRGINIA INFANTRY.

To read extended versions of the documents, visit the companion Web site http://history.wadsworth.com/americanpast8e; click on "Discovery Sources."

CHAPTER 25

Aftermath

Reconstructing the Union; Failing the Freedmen 1865–1877

National Archives

You say you have emancipated us. You have; and I thank you for it. But what is your emancipation? ... When you turned us loose, you gave us no acres. You turned us loose to the skies, to the storm, to the whirlwind, and, worst of all, you turned us loose to the wrath of our infuriated masters.

Frederick Douglass

When the guns fell silent in 1865, some southern cities—Vicksburg, Atlanta, Columbia, Richmond—were flattened, eerie wastelands of charred timbers, rubble, and free-standing chimneys. Few of the South's railroads could be operated for more than a few miles. Bridges were gone. River commerce had dwindled to a trickle; the only new boats were from the North. Commercial ties with Europe—and with the North—had been snapped. All the South's banks were ruined.

Even the cultivation of the soil had been disrupted. Thousands of small farms owned by the men who served in the Confederate ranks lay fallow. Plantation owners who fled when Union armies advanced discovered that weeds and brambles were more destructive conquerors than Yankees. Many who had labored in their fields for them, the former slaves, were likely to be gone. When southern blacks were told they were free men and women, the first impulse of many was to test their freedom by walking off, even if they had no destination in mind. Ex-slaves who stayed in the only home they had ever known wondered if the crop they were planting that spring belonged to them or to their old master.

THE RECONSTRUCTION CRISIS

In view of the desolation, *Reconstruction* seems the appropriate word for America's postwar era. In fact, as the word was understood in 1865 and 1866 and for another decade, "Reconstruction" had nothing to do with laying bricks, rehabilitating railroads, or recovering fields. Reconstruction referred to the political procedure by which the eleven rebel states were restored to "a normal constitutional relationship" with the federal government. It was the Union, that great abstraction over which so many had died, that was rebuilt.

Blood was shed during the Reconstruction era too, but little glory was won. Few political reputations—northern, southern, white, black, Republican, Democratic—emerged from Reconstruction unstained. Perhaps Abraham Lincoln

National Archives

Richmond in ruins, more from a fire that got out of control than from bombardment. Atlanta looked worse. The Shenandoah Valley and northeastern Georgia were laid waste. Even areas of the South untouched by war were impoverished, dwellings and fields neglected. This was the condition of many of the states that had to be reconstructed.

had been sainted only because he did not survive the war. Indeed, the Reconstruction procedure Lincoln proposed as early as 1863 was repudiated by Congress, which surely would have fought him over it had he lived and tried to push it through. His successor, Andrew Johnson, adopted Lincoln's Reconstruction plans, and Congress ruined him.

Lincoln foresaw the serious problems that faced him. He described as "pernicious" the constitutional hair-splitting with which both sides began to debate the nation's Reconstruction policy. But when Richmond fell and Lee surrendered, he had offered no alternative to his 1863 plan.

LINCOLN VERSUS CONGRESS

By December 1863, Union armies occupied large chunks of the Confederacy. Ultimate victory in the war, while not yet in the bag, was a reasonable expectation. To provide for the rapid reconciliation of North and South—Lincoln's postwar priority—he proclaimed that as soon as 10 percent of the eligible voters in a former Confederate state took an oath of allegiance to the Union, the people of that state could write a new state constitution, organize a government, and elect representatives to Congress. Immediately, southern states that were mostly occupied—Tennessee, Arkansas, and Louisiana—complied.

But Congress refused to recognize them as Union states, returning them to military command. Republican congressmen had been alarmed from the start of the war by Lincoln's unilateral expansion of presidential powers. No president, not even Andrew Jackson (still vilified by Republicans), had exercised as much authority as Lincoln did. During a war that threatened to destroy the Union, congressmen swallowed their anxieties. But Reconstruction was a postwar issue, and Lincoln's 1863 proposal did not involve Congress. That would not do, particularly inasmuch as Lincoln spoke of prompt elections of senators and representatives; Congress was keenly sensitive to its right to judge the credentials of men who showed up claiming to be duly elected members. That was no pernicious abstraction!

THE WADE–DAVIS BILL

The radicals were a minority of the congressional Republicans in 1864. But they were vociferous and persuasive, and they had additional reasons to reject Lincoln's proposal. They were abolitionists who blamed the slavocracy, the South's great planters, for causing the terrible war. They were determined that the slavocrats be punished—if not hanged then gelded politically. To ensure that the reconstructed southern states be governed differently than they had been before the war, they insisted that the *freedmen,* as the emancipated slaves were called, participate in southern government. (The word freed*men* referred to women—and children, for that matter—not just to adult males; it would not have occurred to Americans of 1865 to speak of "freedpeople" or "freedpersons.")

So in July 1864 Congress enacted the **Wade–Davis Bill.** It provided that only after *50 percent* of the eligible voters of a former Confederate state swore loyalty could the Reconstruction process begin. And Congress—not the president!—would decide when the southern states were again part of the Union. Wade–Davis did not include a comprehensive procedure for Reconstruction. Mainly, it was enacted to slow down a process that, to the radical Republicans, Lincoln seemed to be hell-bent on hastening. If Congress was just buying time, it won the skirmish with the president.

Lincoln killed Wade–Davis with a **pocket veto,** which did not require him to explain his reasons for rejecting it in a veto message that would likely exacerbate the dispute. During the final months of his life, he dropped hints that he would compromise with Congress. He even reached out to the radicals (whom he had never much liked) by saying he had no objection to giving the right to vote to blacks who were "very intelligent and those who have fought gallantly in our ranks." He urged the military governor of Louisiana whom he had appointed to extend suffrage to some blacks. And there things stood when John Wilkes Booth sent history on an unanticipated course.

LINCOLN'S GOALS

Why did Lincoln dodge radical demands that the **freedmen** be granted civil rights equal to those of whites? First, his highest postwar priority was the reconciliation of northern and southern whites, no little thing given the bitterness of the war. He made his intentions eloquently clear in his second inaugural address a few weeks before he was shot. "With malice toward none, with charity for all, . . . let us strive on to finish the work we are in, to bind up the nation's wounds, . . . to do all which may achieve and cherish a just and lasting peace among ourselves."

For Lincoln, the interests of the freedmen were secondary to the interests of American whites, if that. If white southerners' insistence that they would never accept blacks as equals prevented reconciliation with the Union, Lincoln was willing to give way. Radical Senator Ben Wade said that Lincoln's views on black people "could only come of one who was born of poor white trash and educated in a slave state." This was as unfair as it was ugly. Lincoln's racial attitudes changed during the war, slowly and ambivalently. Again, he dodged making any strong statements for which he would be held accountable. But he was impressed by African-American bravery in battle.

As ever, Lincoln the politician was flexible: "Saying that Reconstruction will be accepted if presented in a specified way, it is not said that it will never be accepted in any other way." He was telling the radicals that nothing about Reconstruction, including the future status of the freedmen, was final.

Still, for Lincoln, it all kept coming back to what was best for the goal of sectional reconciliation.

Reconstruction 1863–1877

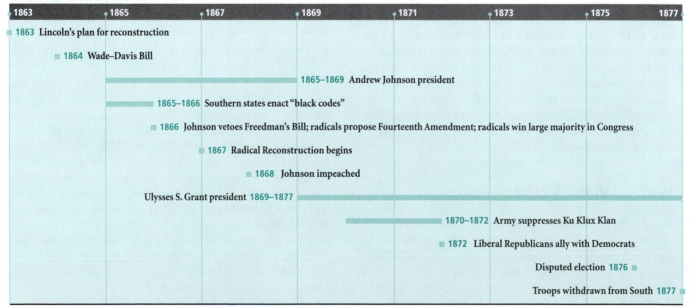

| 1863 | 1865 | 1867 | 1869 | 1871 | 1873 | 1875 | 1877 |

1863 Lincoln's plan for reconstruction

1864 Wade–Davis Bill

1865–1869 Andrew Johnson president

1865–1866 Southern states enact "black codes"

1866 Johnson vetoes Freedman's Bill; radicals propose Fourteenth Amendment; radicals win large majority in Congress

1867 Radical Reconstruction begins

1868 Johnson impeached

Ulysses S. Grant president 1869–1877

1870–1872 Army suppresses Ku Klux Klan

1872 Liberal Republicans ally with Democrats

Disputed election 1876

Troops withdrawn from South 1877

STUBBORN ANDREW JOHNSON

After April 15, 1865, it did not matter what Lincoln thought, and Andrew Johnson was not a flexible politician. Nor had his own "white trash" views on race undergone any changes during the war.

Johnson grew up in stultifying frontier poverty in Tennessee. Unlike Lincoln, who taught himself to read as a boy, Johnson was an illiterate adult when he asked a schoolteacher in Greenville to teach him how to read and write. She did, and married him too, and encouraged her husband to go into politics. Johnson won elective office on every level from town councilman to congressman to senator. He owned a few slaves, but he hated the secessionist cotton planters of western Tennessee. He was the only southern senator to refuse to walk out of Congress in 1861; he called for a ruthless war on the rebels and, when they were defeated, not reconciliation but punishment, the gallows for Jefferson Davis. Lincoln appointed him governor of occupied Tennessee and chose him to run for vice president in 1864 in the hope of winning the votes of other southern Unionists.

Johnson's political experience was extensive, but his personality was ill suited to national politics. Whereas Lincoln was sure of what he could accomplish, Johnson was unsubtle, insensitive, willful, and stubborn. He got off to an unlucky start as vice president. Near collapse with a bad cold on inauguration day, he bolted several glasses of brandy and was visibly drunk when he took the oath of office. Fortunately, only a few people were present, and Lincoln told aides that Johnson was not to speak at the public ceremony outside the Capitol.

Johnson was not, in fact, a "problem drinker." Inauguration day was a fluke. And nothing was made of his gaffe at the time because the likeliest group to jump on Lincoln's vice president, the radical Republicans, rather liked Johnson; they liked him much more than they liked Lincoln because of Johnson's repeated calls for punishing leading rebels. As military governor of Tennessee he had approved some confiscations of rebel estates.

But the radicals misread Johnson's anti-Confederate ardor. Emancipation pleased him only because it hit at the wealth and power of the great planters, not because he thought slavery was a wicked institution or cared about how blacks were treated. Before he was president, there was no call for him to express his views on race or, for that matter, about the differences between Lincoln and Congress on Reconstruction policy.

JOHNSON: THEY ARE ALREADY STATES

In fact, Johnson ignored Lincoln's hints that he would discuss Reconstruction with congressional Republicans. With insignificant changes, he made Lincoln's presidential Reconstruction program of 1863 his own program. Reconciliation would be quick; the president, not Congress, would oversee the procedure and decide when the rebel states were readmitted to the Union. Johnson did not consult with congressional leaders before announcing his plan.

Johnson was a pretty fair student of the Constitution. To him, as to Daniel Webster, the Union of states was permanent. Constitutionally, the Union *could not* be dissolved; states *could not* secede. There had indeed been a rebellion, a war, and an entity known as the Confederate States of America. But, said Johnson, individuals had rebelled, fought against the U.S. government, and created the Confederacy. The states of Virginia, Alabama, and the rest had not seceded because that was constitutionally impossible. Virginia and the rest were still states, constitutional components of the Union. Seating their duly elected representatives in Congress was a purely administrative matter, which made it the responsibility of the executive branch of the government. It was simple and obvious to him.

REBEL CONGRESSMEN, PARDONS, AND BLACK CODES

There was nothing wrong with Johnson's constitutional reasoning. In 1861 every Unionist had said what he said in 1865. Johnson's problem was his refusal to see beyond constitutional propriety to the messy world of human feelings, hatred, resentment, and flesh and blood—especially blood. To real people, what the Preamble to the Constitution, John Marshall, and Daniel Webster might say about Virginia and the rest meant far less in 1865 than the fact that in four years of a war begun by southerners, more than half a million people had been killed.

Now, under Johnson's Reconstruction rules, the white people of the rebel states quickly wrote state constitutions and elected congressmen and senators—including four Confederate generals, six members of Jefferson Davis's cabinet, and as senator from Georgia, the Confederate vice president, Alexander H. Stephens. This did not sit well with northerners, some of whom were still buying tombstones for their menfolk.

Johnson's pardons did not improve the mood in the North. Some Confederate leaders had to be pardoned, of course. Lincoln, in the interests of reconciliation, would surely have pardoned many respected (and cooperative) rebel leaders soon after the war ended. But Johnson was manic in the matter. Before the end of 1865 he signed pardons for 13,000 Confederates, restoring their civil rights. That was a rate of 2,000 per month; few who applied were denied. What was Johnson thinking? Reconciliation required the goodwill of northerners too.

Few white northerners believed in the intrinsic equality of the races. Probably only a minority of congressional radicals did; the same Congress that wrote the Fourteenth Amendment guaranteeing equal civil rights to all voted to segregate schools by race in the District of Columbia. Nevertheless, the war had been fought to abolish slavery, and the *black codes* enacted by the Johnson-approved southern state governments seemed, to many people, to reintroduce slavery without using the word. Indeed, South Carolina refused to repeal its ordinance of secession, and Mississippi refused to ratify the Thirteenth Amendment; Alabama rejected part of it (a neat trick in that its guts consist of thirty-two words).

The **black codes** of some states made it illegal for African Americans to live in towns and cities, a backhanded way of keeping them in the fields. In no state were blacks allowed to vote or to bear arms. South Carolina said that African Americans could not sell goods! Mississippi required freedmen to sign twelve-month labor contracts before January 10 of each year. Those who did not could be arrested, with their labor for the year sold to the highest bidder in a manner strongly reminiscent of the slave auction. Dependent children could be forced to work. Blacks who reneged on their contracts were not paid for the work they already had performed. Mississippi even made it a crime for blacks to insult white people or make insulting "gestures."

THE RADICALS: THE STATES HAVE FORFEITED THEIR RIGHTS

The radical Republicans knew that Johnson's Reconstruction plan and the southern response to it were unpopular in the North. But that did not mean that a majority of northern voters would look favorably on their plan to grant full civil rights to the freedmen. Sixteen of twenty-three Union states did not allow blacks to vote. The radicals needed to win majority support, particularly from the Republicans in Congress who considered themselves moderates.

Different radicals offered different constitutional justifications for rejecting Johnson's stalled Reconstruction program and supporting Congress's right to oversee the process. It

Thaddeus Stevens of Pennsylvania, a longtime abolitionist, was the leader of the Radical Republicans in the House of Representatives. Proslavery southern extremists hated him; a Confederate raiding party went out of its way to burn a factory he owned. He hoped to establish complete civil equality for blacks in both north and south, but settled for less.

North Wind Picture Archives

might be more accurate to say that they offered different terminologies.

Thaddeus Stevens of Pennsylvania, the radical leader in the House, said that the Confederate states had committed "state suicide" when they seceded. They were not, in 1865, alive. Therefore, it was within the power of Congress alone to admit them as states when they were "reborn." Charles Sumner, a prominent Senate radical, said that the former southern states were "conquered provinces." Their constitutional status was identical to that of territories seized from Mexico in 1848. Congress (not the president) had admitted California as a state in 1850; Congress would admit the former Confederate states when Congress approved of the state constitutions they wrote. Another Republican, Samuel Shellabarger of Ohio, came up with language that was more persuasive to moderates sitting on the fence: when the rebel states seceded, they "forfeited" the rights given states by the Constitution.

Congress's Joint Committee on Reconstruction settled on a plausible formula: "The States lately in rebellion were, at the close of the war, disorganized communities, without civil government, and without constitutions or other forms, by virtue of which political relations could legally exist between them and the federal government." This provided all but a few Republicans loyal to Johnson with grounds for refusing to seat the southerners who came to Washington as the elected representatives of the rebel states.

RADICAL GOALS AND MOTIVES

The radicals were motivated by ideals, passions, and hard-headed politics. Most of them had been abolitionists, morally repelled by the institution of slavery. Thaddeus Stevens, Ben Wade, Charles Sumner, and others believed in racial equality and were determined, if they could carry the day, that African Americans would enjoy full civil rights. Stevens, Wade, and George W. Julian hated the slavocracy, the great planter elite that they blamed for the war.

The planters' power had been maimed by the abolition of slavery, but they still owned the land. Julian proposed to confiscate the estates of the planters, particularly those who had been active Confederates, high-ranking army officers, and government officials. He had a good precedent to point at: the confiscation of Loyalist estates after the War for Independence. Not only would confiscation punish the rebels and destroy their economic power at a strike; but by dividing the plantations into forty-acre farms to be granted to the freedmen, the government would give southern blacks the economic independence that, in the Jeffersonian tradition, was essential to good citizenship.

The radicals had frankly partisan motives too. The Republican party was a sectional party. In 1860, the last election before the rebellion, the southern states did not bother to list Republican candidates on ballots. To the radicals, if the party did not establish itself in the South, it was doomed to be defeated at the polls. The party's precarious political situation was worse in 1865 than it had been before the war when Democrats controlled the Senate and the Republicans held only a slender majority in the House. With slavery gone, the number of southern representatives would increase. The three-fifths compromise was dead. Where slave states had counted three-fifths of the slaves in calculating the number of their congressmen, they were now entitled to count the entire population at face value.

There were white southern Republicans in 1865: Whig Unionists who had sat out the war and small-scale farmers in the mountain counties of Kentucky, Tennessee, Virginia, and North Carolina who had opposed secession. Many of them had fought in Union armies, and they no more wanted to see the return to power of the secessionist Democrats than the radicals did. But white Republicans were a minority in every state, a tiny minority in the cotton South. If the party was to compete with the Democrats in the former Confederacy, it was necessary to ensure that the freedmen voted. Thaddeus Stevens put no pressure on moderate Republicans to work for African-American suffrage in the North, where the idea was not popular. But if southern blacks did not vote, he argued, the Republican party was a dead duck. "I am for Negro suffrage in every rebel state," he told Congress (specifying *rebel states*). "If it be just, it should not be denied; if it be necessary, it should be adopted; if it be a punishment to traitors, they deserve it."

1866: THE CRITICAL YEAR

Stevens and the other radicals had to be accommodating with the moderate Republicans. This was difficult for natural antagonists like Ben Wade. But the radicals were few. If they were to see their programs effected, they had to win over Republicans who were not as sure as they were that the freedmen had to have full citizenship.

Luckily for them, President Johnson was uncompromising. He pushed the Republican moderates into the radicals' arms by trying to destroy a constructive federal agency that was averting starvation and social chaos in the South and, then, by writing off the moderate Republicans and turning to the hated Democrats, including southern Democrats, for political support.

THE FREEDMEN'S BUREAU

The former slaves responded to freedom in different ways. Some, who were bewildered by the announcement or who had been treated decently by their masters, stayed put. Promised wages when their masters found money, they worked in the fields much as they always had (no longer worrying about the blacksnake whip). Other freed slaves took to the roads. Some heard rumors that every slave family would be granted "forty acres and a mule," and they searched for the Union officer who would provide the coveted farm. Some wanderers gathered in ramshackle camps that were often disorderly. Gangs of discharged Confederate soldiers, trudging sometimes hundreds of miles toward their homes, clogged the roads too. There were plenty of racial incidents.

Congress saw more problems coming and acted to avert chaos. In March 1865 Congress established the Bureau of Refugees, Freedmen, and Abandoned Land, to be administered by the army commanded by General O. O. Howard.

Howard's most pressing task was relief: avoiding mass starvation in the South. Just in 1865, the **Freedman's Bureau** distributed rations to 150,000 people, about a third of them whites. When Congress decided not to confiscate land on a large scale, Bureau agents negotiated labor contracts between destitute former slaves and landowners. Because there was little coin in the South and southern banknotes were worthless, many of these arrangements were not unlike what some black codes prescribed. They were sharecropping arrangements: the actual field workers and the landowners taking shares of the crop in varying proportions.

The Bureau set up medical facilities for the inevitable health problems. (Again, whites were served as well as freedmen.) Ultimately the Bureau built and staffed forty-six hospitals and treated more than 400,000 cases of illness and injury.

With the freedmen, the most popular Bureau program was its school system. Freedom released a craving for education among blacks, adults as well as children. Appleton and Company, a publishing house, sold a million copies annually of Noah Webster's *Elementary Spelling Book*—the "Blue-Backed Speller" from which American schoolchildren learned to read for forty years. In 1866 sales jumped to 1.5 million, the 50 percent increase due to sales to freedmen. Teachers from the North, mostly white women, opened multigrade "one-room schoolhouses" throughout the South. Many of the teachers later reminisced that never before or after had they such dedicated pupils.

OPEN CONFLICT

In 1865 Congress gave the Freedmen's Bureau a year to do its job. The assumption was that, by then, reconstructed state governments would take over the schools, hospitals, and Bureau-run institutions. In February 1866, however, Reconstruction was at a standstill. Congress refused to recognize Johnson's state governments but had itself certified none. The South was still occupied territory. So Congress extended the life of the Freedman's Bureau for two years.

Johnson vetoed the bill, insisting that the former rebel states had constitutional governments. A month later, he vetoed another bill that granted citizenship to the freedmen. The Constitution, he said, gave the states the power to decide the terms of citizenship within their borders. Once again he

Discouraging Rebellion

A now forgotten but, at the time, significant provision of the Fourteenth Amendment forbade the former Confederate states to repay "any debt or obligation incurred in aid of insurrection or rebellion against the United States." By punishing banks and individuals, including Europeans and European banks, that had loaned money to the rebel states (the Confederacy no longer existed), the amendment put potential underwriters of future rebellions on notice that such loans had consequences.

The Valentine Museum

The Freedmen's Bureau was the federal government's response to the old proslavery argument that freeing the slaves in the South would cause serious social and economic problems. The Bureau confronted many of those problems, from starvation to African-American illiteracy, with remarkable success. Former slaves gratefully remembered Bureau schools, so great was their hunger to learn. Many Freedmen's Bureau schools were run by northern white women; this class has (far right) a black teacher, probably a northerner.

had the better constitutional argument, and he might have won the political contest had northerners not been appalled by some of the black codes and massive mob attacks on freedmen in several southern cities, including New Orleans.

In June 1866, perceiving the shift in mood in their favor, radical Republicans, now joined by moderates, drew up a constitutional amendment on which to base congressional Reconstruction policy (and to answer Johnson's point about citizenship). The long, complex Fourteenth Amendment banned from federal and state office all high-ranking Confederates unless they were pardoned by Congress. The amendment also established, for the first time, national citizenship. It guaranteed that all "citizens of the United States and of the State wherein they reside" would be treated equally under the laws of all the states.

If ratified, the Fourteenth Amendment would prevent the southern states from passing laws like the black codes. However, the radicals were taking a big chance. The Fourteenth Amendment would also cancel northern state laws that discriminated against blacks. In that aspect of the amendment Johnson saw his opportunity. Calculating that many northerners, particularly in the Midwest, would rather have ex-Confederates in Washington than grant equal rights to African Americans, he decided to campaign personally against the radicals in the 1866 congressional election.

THE RADICAL TRIUMPH

The first step was to organize a new political party. Just as Lincoln did not want to run as a Republican in 1864, Johnson did not want to be labeled a Democrat in 1866. On his behalf, Secretary of State Seward, a few Republican senators, the governor of Massachusetts, and some prominent Democrats held a "National Union party" convention in Philadelphia. Their message was sectional reconciliation. As a symbol, the convention opened with a procession of northern and southern Johnson men in pairs, a southerner and a northerner, marching arm in arm.

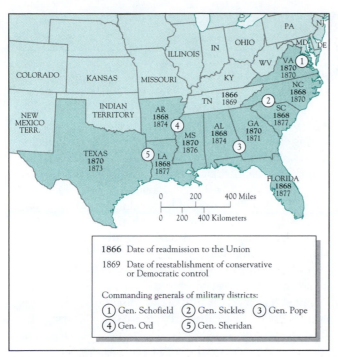

MAP 25:1 Radical Reconstruction

The radicals partitioned the Confederacy into five military districts of manageable size. The Union army supervised the establishment of state governments that guaranteed equal civil rights to freedmen, whence each state was readmitted to the Union (with Republican-dominated governments). Tennessee was not included in the program. Occupied for much of the war by the Union army, Tennessee had a reconstructed state government by 1866 thanks, ironically, to its wartime governor, Andrew Johnson, who, as president, opposed radical Reconstruction.

Unhappily for Johnson, the first couple on the floor was South Carolina Governor James L. Orr, a huge, fleshy man, and Massachusetts Governor John A. Andrew, a little fellow with a way of looking intimidated. When Orr seemed to drag the mousy Andrew down the length of the hall, the radicals had a field day. It would have been worse in the age of television, or even when newspapers were able to reproduce photographs. But Republican cartoonists filled the gap: the National Union party was a rebel's party with northern flunkeys.

In the fall, Johnson himself ensured defeat. He toured the Midwest on what he called a "swing around the circle," delivering dozens of blistering speeches denouncing the Republicans. No president had ever politicked so personally, not even when seeking election for himself. To make things worse, Johnson had learned his oratorical technique in the rough-and-tumble, stump-speaking tradition of eastern Tennessee. Voters there liked a hot debate between politicians scorching each other and ridiculing hecklers—when the issue at stake was selecting the next county sheriff. But the style was disconcerting when the president of the United States snapped at the bait radical hecklers waved in front of him. Drunk again, the radicals said with mock sadness, reminding voters of Johnson's inauguration as vice president.

The result was a landslide. Most of Johnson's candidates were defeated. The Republican party, now firmly in radical

hands, controlled more than two-thirds of the seats in both houses of Congress, enough to override every veto Johnson handed them.

RADICAL RECONSTRUCTION

The radical Reconstruction program was adopted in a series of laws passed by the Fortieth Congress in 1867. They dissolved Johnson's southern state governments and partitioned the Confederacy into five military provinces, each commanded by a major general. The army would maintain order while voters were registered: blacks and those whites not disenfranchised by the Fourteenth Amendment. The constitutional conventions these voters elected were required to ratify the Thirteenth and Fourteenth Amendments and to give the vote to adult black males. After Congress approved their constitutions, the reconstructed states would be admitted to the Union and their senators and representatives to Congress.

RADICALS IN CONTROL

Tennessee complied immediately; the state was never really affected by radical Reconstruction. In 1868, as a result of a large freedman vote, six more states were readmitted. Alabama,

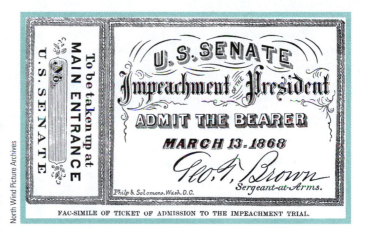

A ticket to the impeachment trial of President Johnson. It was the high point of Washington's social season with the chief justice presiding, the entire Senate sitting as jury, and leading House radicals as prosecutors. The president, however, did not attend; he was acquitted by one vote.

Impeached Presidents

Andrew Johnson was impeached—that is, accused by the House of Representatives of offenses grave enough to warrant his removal from office. Impeachment is the equivalent of indictment in criminal law. At his trial—the Senate is the "jury"—Johnson was acquitted by one vote and remained in office.

President William Clinton was impeached for perjury and obstruction of justice in 1999. He too was acquitted. Articles of impeachment were drawn up against President Richard M. Nixon for lying to Congress in 1974. When impeachment and conviction seemed likely, he resigned the presidency.

Gullah

A *dialect* is a regional variety of a language that is distinctive because of words unique to it, or different rules of grammar, or pronunciation—or a combination of the three. The nonstandard speech of many African Americans today is a dialect.

A *pidgin* is a simplified language that is consciously invented by different peoples in close contact who do not understand each other. Pidgins have evolved everywhere in the world where two different peoples have traded with one another. (The word *pidgin* was how Chinese merchants in South Asia pronounced "business.") Pidgins are usually based on one dominant language, but they reduce its grammar to basics for easy learning and instant communication on a narrow range of subjects such as business. Several English-based, French-based, and Portuguese-based pidgins are spoken by hundreds of thousands of people today. The "Hawaiian accent" is a remnant of what was once a pidgin.

When people adopt a pidgin as their language, elaborating on it so they can speak about a broad range of subjects, linguists call it a *creole*. Creoles sometimes become full-blown languages; Jamaican English, a creole, may be in the process of becoming a language independent of English.

Uncountable creoles developed among the first Africans in America. Their masters spoke English. The other slaves with whom they worked and lived spoke languages just as incomprehensible. So the first generation created a pidgin so they could understand overseers and fellow slaves. Their children—second-generation African Americans—had no use for their parents' mother tongues (who else spoke them?) and they knew more English than their parents had. They transformed the pidgin into a fuller creole.

Almost all slave creoles died out after emancipation. African Americans began to move around the country during Reconstruction and found their localized creoles useless. However, on the "sea islands" off the coast of South Carolina, Georgia, and far northern Florida, Gullah, sometimes called Geechee, flourished and survives to this day. It is still the language of home, church, and social occasions for at least a hundred thousand people. At last count, between 5,000 and 8,000 mostly elderly sea islanders spoke only Gullah.

Because Gullah is not a written language, its history is something of a mystery. Even the origin of the name is disputed. The most obvious explanation is that Gullah is a corruption of Angola, which makes sense. During the final years of the legal African slave trade, 1803–1807, sea island planters imported 24,000 Africans; 60 percent of them were from Angola (present-day Angola and Congo). However, there is some reason to believe that the word *Gullah* was in use by 1750, before Angolans had been imported in great numbers. Some linguists think it derives from Gola, the name of a tribe that lived on the border of modern Liberia and Sierra Leone. Sea island planters favored Africans from that region because they were skilled rice growers. Similarities between Gullah and a creole still spoken in Sierra Leone, Krio, are so striking that Gullah may have first emerged not on the sea islands but in Africa. Another school of linguists sees strong Jamaican and Barbadian creole influences, which is plausible: most slaves destined for North America were "seasoned" on those islands.

Arkansas, Florida, Louisiana, North Carolina, and South Carolina all sent Republican delegations, including some black congressmen, to Washington. In the remaining four states—Georgia, Mississippi, Texas, and Virginia—whites obstructed every attempt to set up a government in which blacks participated. The military continued to govern there until 1870.

In the meantime, Congress effectively took charge of the federal government. Johnson was reduced to vetoing every radical bill and watching as his vetoes were overridden. Congress even took partial control of the army away from Johnson, then struck at his control of his own cabinet. The Tenure of Office Act forbade the president to remove any appointed official who had been confirmed by the Senate without the Senate's approval of his dismissal.

It was obvious to all what was coming. The radicals wanted Johnson to violate the Tenure of Office Act so they could impeach him. Johnson knew it, and in part because of his constitutional scruples, he meant to violate it, certain that it was an infringement on the independence of the executive branch of the government. Moreover, his secretary of war inherited from Lincoln, Edwin P. Stanton, had allied with the radicals. He was, in effect, a not very well-disguised spy within the cabinet. In February 1868 Johnson fired Stanton. The House of Representatives passed articles of impeachment. The chief justice, Salmon B. Chase, sat as judge at the trial. The Senate was the jury. Conviction—and removal of Johnson from office—required a two-thirds vote. Four-fifths of the senators were Republicans. All but a few had dependably voted the radical line. The radicals were confident.

THE IMPEACHMENT TRIAL

All but two of the eleven articles of impeachment dealt with the Tenure of Office Act. As expected, Johnson's defenders argued that even if the act was constitutional, which was

Gullah is quite different from the "southern accent" and from "African American dialect." Its sounds are soft and it is spoken rapidly, not drawled. Well over 90 percent of its vocabulary is English, but pronunciation differs so radically from any other English pronunciation that outsiders cannot understand much more than the shortest, simplest statements. Spelled out phonetically, however, Gullah is easily deciphered. Here is the first sentence of the Lord's Prayer in Gullah:

> Ow'urr Farruh, hu aht in Heh'um, hallowed be dy name, dy kingdom come, dy wil be done on ut as it done in heh'um.

Linguists have traced hundreds of Gullah words, especially the names given to Gullah children, to Mandinka, Yoruba, Iwo, and Ibo, all Nigerian languages. Probably they were introduced to the language by slaves from that country, who were numerous.

How did Gullah thrive when other slave creoles died out? Cultural continuity is part of the reason. Before 1800, when the Angolans began to arrive, most sea island slaves' African roots were in a rather limited area of Sierra Leone. The isolation of the sea islands cut the Gullahs off from mixing with mainland slaves, reinforcing their sense of cohesion. Their creole was adequate for all their communications. Whites were few on the islands. Wealthy planters lived in Charleston. Many plantations were supervised by black slave drivers and sometimes, even at the top, by black plantation managers. When the Civil War began, there were more than 33,000 blacks in the Beaufort district of South Carolina, and 6,700 whites. When Union troops occupied the islands early in the war, virtually every white

southerner fled. By 1870, 90 percent of St. Helena Island's population was black.

Because of their isolation, the Gullahs were generally more self-sufficient than most mainland slaves—and likely more confident in themselves. When the Union army put up confiscated sea island plantations for sale, an astonishing number of Gullahs had enough money to buy farms in small parcels, sometimes just ten acres. By 1870 seven of ten Gullah families owned their homes and farms.

African religious practices survived on the sea islands even after the Gullahs became Methodists or Baptists in the early nineteenth century. White missionaries were frustrated to distraction, even anger, when islanders explained that, while a dead person's "soul" went to live with God in heaven, his "spirit" or ghost continued to roam the islands, sometimes helping live descendants, sometimes doing them mischief. Only a century later was it learned that Gullah spirits had West African origins. The word *voodoo* entered the American language through the Gullahs, although on the sea islands it simply meant "magic" with none of the sinister connotations of West Indian voodoo as sensationalized in movies.

African folktales survived longer and closer to the originals on the sea islands than they did elsewhere in the South. Joel Chandler Harris, the white journalist who collected the B'rer Rabbit and other slave stories (now known to have African origins) found the sea islands his most productive hunting grounds. In 1925 DuBose Heyward wrote a play, *Porgy,* better known as the opera based on it, *Porgy and Bess.* It was set among Gullahs who, after the Civil War, moved to Charleston.

---

dubious, it did not apply to Johnson's dismissal of Stanton because Johnson had not appointed him; Lincoln had. It was a good argument, enough to win the day had the issue been a legal one rather than political. The other two articles condemned Johnson for disrespect of Congress, which was silly. Johnson had indeed insulted Congress: he had neglected only obscenities in the words with which he described congressional radicals. The president's defenders replied that pointed and vulgar language did not qualify as one of the "high crimes and misdemeanors" the Constitution stipulates as grounds for impeachment.

The radicals needed 36 senators' votes to remove Johnson from office. No more than 18 could vote to acquit. The tally was 35 to 19 for conviction. Johnson remained president by a single vote.

Actually, it was not that close. The radicals' case was so flimsy and motivated by such sordid politics that at least six Republican senators who otherwise voted for radical pro-

grams were privately disgusted. Each agreed privately that if his vote was needed to acquit, he would vote for acquittal. However, they were practical politicians. If their votes were not essential to win acquittal, they would vote to convict so as to maintain their good standing in the party. It was 1868, an election year. The Republican candidate was General Grant, and he was a sure winner. The "secret six" wanted to enjoy the advantages of belonging to the majority party with a friendly president.

Events proved they had good reasons to vote their careers rather than their consciences. The Republican from Kansas who provided Johnson's margin of victory was kicked out of the party and lost when he ran for reelection.

THE FIFTEENTH AMENDMENT

In the 1868 electoral vote, Grant easily defeated New York Governor Horatio Seymour, 214 to 80. However, the popular vote was very close; Grant won several states' electoral votes

Birth of a Legend

The legend of a South "prostrate in the dust" during Reconstruction had its origins during the Reconstruction era. In 1874 journalist James S. Pike wrote of "the spectacle of a society suddenly turned bottomside up. . . . In the place of this old aristocratic society stands the rude form of the most ignorant democracy that mankind ever saw, invested with the functions of government. It is the dregs of the population habilitated in the robes of their intelligent predecessors, and asserting over them the rule of ignorance and corruption, through the inexorable machinery of a majority of numbers. It is barbarism overwhelming civilization by physical force."

by a whisker. In fact, only a minority of white voters chose Grant. His nationwide plurality was 300,000; he got 500,000 black votes in the southern states. Grant lost New York, the largest state, by a thin margin. Had all blacks been able to vote in New York (a few could, under special circumstances), Grant would have carried the state easily. Grant won Indiana by a handful of votes; had African Americans been able to vote in Indiana, Grant would have won by a landslide.

Thaddeus Stevens had argued in 1865 that the Republican party's future depended on the freedmen voting in the southern states. The results of the 1868 election showed that the party's edge in some northern states depended on black men voting there.

Consequently, the Republicans drafted a third "**Civil War Amendment.**" The Fifteenth Amendment forbade states to deny the vote to any person on the basis of "race, color, or previous condition of servitude." Because Republican governments favorable to blacks still controlled most southern states, the amendment was easily ratified.

GRANT AND THE RECONSTRUCTED STATES

At 46 years of age, Ulysses S. Grant was the youngest president yet. A military man most of his adult life, he had never expressed much interest in politics. Certainly he never expressed any strong feelings about slavery or abolition; nor had he shown any particular hostility to or sympathy toward African Americans.

Grant had admired Lincoln and was loyal to him. One of Grant's more attractive personal traits was his loyalty to those who stood by him; after Shiloh and through the carnage before Richmond, Lincoln did just that. But Lincoln was four years dead, and Lincoln's wartime critics, the radicals, were calling the shots for the Republican party that honored Grant by making him president. In things political, Grant deferred to them. Circumstances, not conviction, made him the defender of radical Reconstruction.

The southern states readmitted under the radical program elected Republican majorities in their legislatures and sent mostly Republicans to Congress. In some states, where black people were a majority of the population or nearly so— South Carolina, Mississippi, Louisiana—Republican domination was a matter of course. In other southern states, a bloc

African-American vote plus white Republicans plus the demoralization of Democrats under military occupation, and some intimidation of whites by the army, put Republicans in power.

Blacks were the backbone of the southern party, providing 80 percent of Republican votes. But white men ran the party. No African American was elected governor in any state; there were only two black senators, Blanche K. Bruce and Hiram Revels, both from Mississippi. There were fewer than twenty black Republican congressmen. Indeed, Blacks filled only a fifth of appointed jobs, mostly low-level ones, although the size of the African-American vote justified four times as many. The "black rule" of which Democrats spoke was a myth.

CORRUPTION

Who were the white Republicans in the South? Some were former Whigs who had opposed secession. In the mountain counties, particularly in Tennessee, a majority of ordinary whites voted Republican. A few prominent Confederates decided that any political future they had lay with the Republicans. Democrats called them "scalawags"—scoundrels, reprobates—they betrayed the white race to ignorant, savage former slaves. Northern Republicans who moved South after the war for political purposes or to invest in the redevelopment of the shattered economy, likely to be a high-profit enterprise, were known as "carpetbaggers." Supposedly they had arrived in the South so poor they could fit everything they owned in a carpetbag, the cheapest sort of suitcase; but they were soon rich from looting southern state treasuries along with their scalawag friends and their black stooges.

Lowlife carpetbaggers could be found on the lower levels of the Republican party. But the dozen or so carpetbaggers who rose to high political office were men with money that the South sorely needed. The real "crime" of Reconstruction was the fact that African Americans had a say in government.

There was plenty of corruption, as there inevitably is when governments spend a lot of money quickly. The Republican legislatures voted huge appropriations for legitimate, even essential programs that the prewar southern legislatures had ignored. There was not a single statewide public school system in any former Confederate state until Reconstruction. The first free schools for white as well as black southern children were founded by the Republican legislatures. Programs for relief of the destitute and institutions for the handicapped and the insane were few in the prewar South.

Start-up costs for such institutions were immense, and politicians, all the way to the top, dipped into the flow of money to fill their own purses. The Republican governor of Louisiana, Henry C. Warmoth, banked $100,000 during a year when his salary was $8,000. Favored state contractors padded their bills obscenely and bribed state officials not to examine their invoices closely. In 1869 the state of Florida spent as much on printing as had been spent on every function of the state's government in 1860. The Democrats liked to zero in on petty but open and ludicrous corruption, as when former slaves in the South Carolina legislature appropriated $1,000 to one of their number who had lost that sum at the racetrack.

There was nothing unique to southern Republicans or African Americans in such thievery. The 1860s and 1870s were an era of corruption throughout American society. Civil War contractors had cheated the government. The crooked "Tweed Ring" that looted New York City was Democratic. The champion crooks of the nineteenth-century South were not Reconstruction Republicans but post-Reconstruction Democrats. After a "black Republican" administration in Mississippi ran a nearly corruption-free regime for six years, the first Democratic treasurer of the state absconded with $415,000. This paled compared to the swag E. A. Burke, the first post-Reconstruction treasurer of Louisiana, took with him to Honduras in 1890: $1,777,000.

THE REDEEMERS AND THE KLAN

Nevertheless, political corruption was an effective issue for Democrats out to defeat Republicans at the polls. They persuaded whites who had voted Republican to switch to the Democrats as the only way to avoid ruinous taxes. Race was an even more effective issue. The spectacle of former slaves who had said "yes sir" and "no sir" abjectly to every white man now dressing in frock coats and cravats, making laws, and drinking in hotel bars infuriated many whites. Democratic politicians called themselves "redeemers." They would redeem the prostrate South from thieving **carpetbaggers and scalawags** and redeem white southerners from the degradation the "Damn Yankees" were forcing upon them.

In states where a more or less solid white vote could be mobilized for the Democrats, the solidly Republican black vote could be overcome. Virginia was "redeemed" immediately, North Carolina and Georgia after a brief campaign. Elsewhere, redeemers brought economic pressure on blacks to stay home on election day. Most southern blacks survived as tenant farmers; in only a few small areas, such as the sea islands of South Carolina and Georgia, did a substantial number of black farmers own land. Tenants with families to support were inclined to value their leased cabins and acreage more highly than voting when their landlords told them it was one or the other.

Blacks determined to exercise their rights were met with violence. In 1866 General Nathan Bedford Forrest of Tennessee founded the Ku Klux Klan as a social club for Confederate veterans. Like other men's lodges, the Klan was replete with hocus-pocus, including the wearing of white robes and titles like Kleagle and Grand Wizard. In 1868, with the triumph of the radical Republicans in Congress, the Klan was politicized. Similar organizations, such as the Knights of the White Camellia and dozens of local groups, were formed. Masked and riding only at night to avoid Union army attachments, Klan-type organizations harassed, terrorized, whipped, and murdered not only politically active African Americans but also blacks who were said to be "impudent" or refused to work for whites. The Klan hit the South like a tornado. The federal government estimated that the Klan

The Granger Collection, New York

Ku Klux Klan night riders shoot up the house of an African American who voted or, possibly, merely offended whites by insisting on his dignity as a free man. At the peak of Klan violence in 1868 and 1869, it is estimated that Klan-like terrorists murdered an average of two people a day, almost all of them blacks.

The Grant Scandals

In 1872 newspapers exposed a massive fraud in the construction of the Union Pacific Railroad. Union Pacific officials created a dummy corporation, the Crédit Mobilier, to construct the line on contract. The Crédit Mobilier then overcharged the Union Pacific as much as $20 million. When rumors of the scam prompted talk of a congressional investigation, the Union Pacific sold stock at a big discount to key politicians to quash the investigation. Grant knew nothing of it. But his vice president, Schuyler Colfax, was in the fix up to his neck.

Grant's secretary of war, William W. Belknap, pocketed bribes from a federal contractor who supplied western army units and Indian tribes with goods due them under the terms of treaties with the government. Belknap then shut his eyes when the company delivered less than the contracts required. He was caught red-handed and resigned, but Grant refused to prosecute him. Officials in the Treasury Department, in cahoots with the president's personal secretary, Orville Babcock, provided excise tax stamps to whiskey distillers at a discount. In effect, they stole the stamps as a clerk in a store might steal cigars. No one was punished.

---

murdered 700 in 1868, all but a few of them blacks. The next year was worse.

And it worked. Rather than invite a Klan visit, African Americans in increasing numbers stopped voting. In 1870 and 1871 Congress passed two Ku Klux Acts, which made it a federal offense "to go in disguise upon the public highway . . . with intent to . . . injure, oppress, threaten, or intimidate [citizens] and to prevent them from enjoying their constitutional rights." The laws were effective. The Union army harassed known or suspected Klansmen and destroyed many "Klaverns." Between 1870 and 1872 Texas arrested 6,000 Klansmen. Still, the greatest single Klan atrocity occurred in April 1873 when 100 blacks were killed.

By then five former rebel states were in redeemer hands, and the Republicans faced powerful Democratic opposition in the others. Just as important, northern support for radical Reconstruction was in rapid decline.

GRANT'S TROUBLED ADMINISTRATION

Grant was lionized after Appomattox. He was showered with gifts, including cold cash. New York City's present to him of $100,000 was the biggest. Wealthy businessmen and bankers, knowing he would be president, treated him well. The Illinois shopkeeper and soldier in dusty, rumpled uniform who whittled sticks during battles was dumbstruck. He took zestfully to the high life, from dining on fancy food to wearing silk top hats and well-tailored suits of the finest fabrics.

The celebrity and money came too fast to a man who had struggled to pay the bills for thirty years—and to his wife Julia Grant, who had struggled to keep a family together. The Grants never quite grasped the fact that their benefactors were not so much appreciating them as they were paying in advance for future favors. There is no evidence that corruption tainted Grant personally. But his administration was shot through with it, and his sense of loyalty was so strong that he never punished or even shunned those of his "friends" who were exposed as crooks.

BLACK FRIDAY: A REPUTATION TARNISHED

Most of the thievery that discredited Grant's presidency was exposed only late in his eight years as president. But there was an odor of corruption in Washington from the start. Henry Adams, the fourth-generation scion of the distinguished Massachusetts family, smelled it in 1869 when, returning from a sojourn in Europe, he visited the city, in part to inquire how the Grant administration might wish to use his services. Adams virtually fled Washington, writing that the capital was filled with men of shady character chasing the fast buck and, to all appearances, catching it. Another writer described the Grant years as "the great barbecue" with the government "supplying the beef."

Grant got off to a bad start as president. He made the mistake of accepting an invitation to visit the yacht of James "Jubilee Jim" Fisk, not a social occasion one could enjoy inconspicuously. Fisk and his associate, Jay Gould, who was also aboard, were already disreputable financial schemers. In the "Erie War" the previous year (see Chapter 27), they had tried to bilk railroader Cornelius Vanderbilt of hundreds of thousands of dollars in a stock fraud. The final acts of the battle were played out in public, chronicled in detail in the newspapers. At one point, to avoid arrest, Gould and Fisk fled New York to New Jersey and holed up in a hotel guarded by underworld toughs.

Their purpose in entertaining Grant on a yacht was that there he would be seen. Gould and Fisk created the illusion that they had a privileged relationship with the president while they secretly schemed with Grant's brother-in-law, Abel R. Corbin. The stakes were high: Gould and Fisk planned to corner the nation's gold supply. Success depended on the federal government keeping its gold holdings—the largest in the country—off the open market. Corbin assured them that, as a trusted relative, he would ensure that Grant would do just that.

The stage set, Gould and Fisk bought up gold futures, commitments to buy gold at an agreed price at a specified future date. By snapping up every future on the market, Gould and Fisk sent the price of gold soaring. By September 1869 it was selling for $162 an ounce. By taking delivery of gold futures they had purchased at $20, $30, $40 less per ounce, they would make a killing in an instant.

Corbin kept the pressure on Grant, but treasury officials, realizing what was happening, persuaded Grant that he would look very bad indeed if he took no action. On their advice, he dumped $4 million of the government's gold on the market on Friday, September 24—**Black Friday.**

Culver Pictures, Inc.

Horace Greeley was one of the country's most influential editors in a day when, with newspapers the sole source of information for common people, editors were powerful political figures. But he was a terrible choice as a presidential candidate. He had backed almost every reform and dabbled in almost every fad, many of them objects of popular ridicule, for forty years. Even if all the corruption in Grant's administration had been known in 1872, it is unlikely Greeley could have defeated General Grant.

The price of gold collapsed. Gould did not make as much money as he had hoped, but he made plenty. Without informing his partner, he had already sold out. Nor did Fisk lose; he simply refused to honor his future commitments and hired thugs to intimidate those with whom he had signed contracts. But businessmen who had purchased gold at bloated prices to pay debts and wages were ruined; thousands of employees of bankrupt companies lost their jobs. And the luster of a great general's reputation was tarnished before he had been president for eight months.

THE ELECTION OF 1872

By 1872 some Republicans like Henry Adams's father, Charles Francis Adams; Senators Carl Schurz of Missouri, Lyman Trumbull of Illinois, and Charles Sumner of Massachusetts; and crusading editors **Horace Greeley** of the *New York Tribune* and E. L. Godkin of *The Nation* concluded that, with Grant's acquiescence, thieves were taking over the party.

They were even more disgusted by the well-publicized thievery in the southern state governments that, they believed, stayed in power only because of Grant's support. Some of them—Sumner was an exception—concluded that the whole idea of entrusting poor and ignorant blacks with the vote was a mistake. Better to allow the redeemers, Democrats that they were, to take over and run clean governments. The dissidents formed the Liberal Republican party and said they would oppose Grant in the presidential election of 1872. Their convention nominated Horace Greeley to run against him.

It was an unwise choice. Greeley was a lifelong eccentric and looked it. During his 61 years he had clambered at least briefly aboard every reform movement and fad that had marched down the street, not only abolitionism and women's rights, but vegetarianism, spiritualism, and phrenology (reading a person's character in the bumps on his or her head). His appearance invited ridicule. He looked like a crackpot with his round, pink face, close-set, beady eyes, and a wispy white fringe of chin whiskers. He wore an ankle-length white overcoat on the hottest days and carried a brightly colored umbrella on the driest. Pro-Grant cartoonists had an easy time making fun of him.

Greeley also seemed to be a poor choice because, on their own, the Liberal Republicans had no chance of winning the election. They needed the support of both northern and southern Democrats. The Horace Greeley of 1872 might call for North and South to "clasp hands across the bloody chasm" and denounce carpetbaggers as "stealing and plucking, many of them with both arms around Negroes, and their hands in their rear pockets." The Horace Greeley of 1841–1869 had roasted northern Democrats daily in the *Tribune* and vilified southern Democrats for their espousal of slavery and rebellion.

Nevertheless, the Democrats nominated Greeley. If the Liberal Republicans could not hope to win without the Democrats, the Democrats could not hope to win without the Liberal Republicans. The ratification of the Fifteenth Amendment in 1870 had added tens of thousands of blacks—all Republicans, and *not* Liberals—to the voters' lists.

In fact, the mismatched two-party coalition could not win anyway. With half the southern states still governed by Republicans, and Grant still a hero in the North despite rumors of scandals, the president won 56 percent of the popular vote and a crushing 286 to 66 victory in the electoral college.

THE TWILIGHT OF RECONSTRUCTION

Poor Greeley died weeks after the election. One by one, dragging their feet, the other Liberals returned to the Republican party. Grant would be gone after the election of 1876, they figured. Perhaps the party would learn its lesson and nominate a reformer. In fact, the exposure of several scandals during Grant's second term guaranteed just that.

Except for Sumner, who was pushing for a federal civil rights law when he died in 1874 (it was enacted in 1875

The Civil Rights Act of 1875

In 1875, the twilight of Reconstruction, Congress enacted the Civil Rights Act. It outlawed racial discrimination in public facilities such as hotels and theaters, and forbade the exclusion of blacks from juries. Another provision forbidding racially segregated schools, which had been in Charles Sumner's draft of the bill, was not included. Although the law was not as thoroughgoing as the historic Civil Rights Act of 1964, its purposes were identical.

The 1875 law had no effect on racial discrimination. Rutherford B. Hayes, president in 1877 because he acquiesced in white Democratic control of the South, did not enforce it. In 1883 a number of lawsuits calling for its enforcement reached the Supreme Court. In the civil rights cases, with only one dissenting vote, the Court ruled the act unconstitutional because it outlawed *social* discrimination, which was beyond the power of Congress. The dissenting justice was John Marshall Harlan, who also stood alone in defending equal rights for blacks in

the more famous case of *Plessy v. Ferguson* in 1896.

In Congress, the last gasp of Republican support for African-American rights was the Force Bill of 1890, designed to guarantee southern blacks the right to vote. (It was the equivalent of the Voting Rights Act of 1965.) The House approved the Force Bill, but it failed passage in the Senate when Republican senators from silver-producing states voted against it in return for southern Democratic support of a law propping up the price of silver.

thanks to the regular Grant Republicans in Congress), the Liberals of 1872 were not unhappy when, at the end of 1874, redeemers in Texas, Arkansas, and Mississippi wrested those states back to the Democratic party. By 1876 radical Republicans were in power only in South Carolina, Florida, and Louisiana.

THE DISPUTED ELECTION

The Democratic candidate in 1876, New York Governor Samuel J. Tilden, said he would withdraw the troops from those three states, which would reduce the numbers of black voters there and end Reconstruction. The Republican candidate, Governor Rutherford B. Hayes of Ohio, ran on a platform that guaranteed African Americans rights in the South but weakly. Personally, Hayes was well known to be skeptical of black capabilities, and he was a personal friend of several white southern politicians. Both candidates were honest government reformers. Tilden had helped destroy the Tweed Ring in New York. As governor, Hayes had run a squeaky-clean administration.

When the votes were counted, Hayes's personal opinions about the wisdom of Reconstruction seemed beside the point. Tilden won the popular vote handily, and he appeared to have won the electoral college 204 to 165. However, Tilden's count included the electoral votes of South Carolina, Florida, and Louisiana, where Republicans still controlled the state governments. On telegraphed instructions from Republican party leaders in New York, officials in those three states declared that Hayes had carried their states. According to this set of returns, Hayes eked out a 185 to 184 electoral vote victory.

It was not that easy. When the returns reached Washington, there were two sets of them from each of the three disputed states—one set for Tilden and one for Hayes. Because the Constitution did not provide for such an occurrence, a special commission was established to decide which returns were valid. Five members of each house of Congress and five members of the Supreme Court sat on the panel. Seven of them

were Republicans; seven were Democrats; one, David Davis of Illinois, a Supreme Court justice and once Abraham Lincoln's law partner, was known as an independent. No one else was interested in determining the case on its merits; each commissioner intended to vote for his party's candidate, no matter what documents were set before him. The burden of naming the next president of the United States fell on David Davis.

He did not like the setup. No matter how conscientious and honest Davis was—and he had a good reputation—half the country would call for his scalp. Davis prevailed on friends in Illinois to get him off the hook by naming him to a Senate seat that was vacant. He resigned from the Court and, thereby, from the commission. His replacement was a Republican justice, and the stage was set for the Republicans to steal the election.

THE COMPROMISE OF 1877

The commission voted on strict party lines, eight to seven, to accept the Hayes returns from Louisiana, Florida, and South Carolina—giving Rutherford B. Hayes the presidency by a single electoral vote. Had that been all there was to it, there might well have been violence. At a series of meetings, however, prominent northern and southern politicians and businessmen came to an informal agreement with highly placed southern Republicans with redeemer connections.

The "Compromise of 1877" involved several commitments, not all of them honored, for northern investments in the South. Also not honored was a vague agreement on the part of conservative southerners to build a white Republican party in the South based on the economic and social views that they shared with northern conservatives.

As for the disputed election, Hayes would move into the White House without resistance by either northern or southern Democrats. In return, he would withdraw the troops from South Carolina, Florida, and Louisiana, thus allowing the Democratic party in these states to oust the Republicans and eliminate African-American political power. Those parts of the compromise were honored.

FURTHER READING

General Eric Foner, *Reconstruction: America's Unfinished Revolution,* 1988, and *A Short History of Reconstruction,* 1990; James McPherson, *Ordeal by Fire: The Civil War and Reconstruction,* 1982; Michael Perman, *Emancipation and Reconstruction, 1862–1879,* 2003.

African Americans after Slavery Herman Belz, *Emancipation and Equal Rights,* 1978; Eric Foner, *Nothing but Freedom,* 1983; Leon F. Litwack, *Been in the Storm So Long,* 1979; William McFeeley, *Frederick Douglass,* 1991; James McPherson, *The Struggle for Equality,* 1964; Harold O. Rabnowitz, *Southern Black Leaders of the Reconstruction Era,* 1982; Daniel Sowll, *Rebuilding Zion: The Religious Reconstruction of the South, 1863–1877,* 1998; Joel Williamson, *The Crucible: Black–White Relations in the American South since Emancipation,* 1984.

The Freedmen's Bureau Barry A. Craven, *The Freeman's Bureau and Black Texas,* 1992; Jacqueline Jones, *Soldiers of Light and Love: Northern Teachers and Georgia Blacks,* 1980; Peter Kolchin, *First Freedom,* 1972; Robert C. Morris, *Reading, 'Riting, and Reconstruction: The Education of Freedmen in the South, 1861–1870,* 1981; Donald Nieman, *To Set the Law in Motion: The Freedman's Bureau and the Legal Rights of Blacks, 1865–1868,* 1979.

Politics Michael L. Benedict, *The Impeachment and Trial of Andrew Johnson,* 1973; Dan Carter, *When the War Was Over: The Failure of Self-Reconstruction in the South, 1865–1867,* 1985; LaWanda Cox, *Lincoln and Black Freedom: A Study in Presidential Leadership,* 1981; Laura F. Edwards, *Gendered Strife and Confusions: The Political Culture of Reconstruction,* 1997; Dewey Grantham, *Life and Death of the Solid South,* 1988; Peyton McCrary, *Abraham Lincoln and Reconstruction,* 1978; Roy Morris, *Fraud of the Century: Rutherford B. Hayes, Samuel Tilden, and the Stolen Election of 1876,* 2003; Otto H. Olson, *Reconstruction and Redemption in the South,* 1980; Michael Perman, *The Road to Redemption: Southern Politics 1868–1879,* 1984; George C. Rable, *But There Was No Peace: The Role of Violence in the Politics of Reconstruction,* 1984; L. Seip, *The South Returns to Congress,* 1983; Brooks D. Simpson, *The Reconstruction Presidents,* 1998; Jean E. Smith, *Grant,* 2001; Xi Wang, *The Trial of Democracy: Black Suffrage and Northern Republicans, 1860–1910,* 1997.

The Southern Economy Richard N. Current, *Those Terrible Carpetbaggers,* 1988; Michael Goray, *A Ruined Land: The End of the Civil War,* 1999; Lawrence Powell, *New Masters: Northern Planters during the Civil War and Reconstruction,* 1980; Roger L. Ransom and Richard Sutch, *One Kind of Freedom: The Economic Consequences of Emancipation,* 1977; James Roark, *Masters without Slaves: Southern Planters in the Civil War and Reconstruction,* 1977; Gavin Wright, *Old South, New South: Revolutions in the Southern Economy since the Civil War,* 1986.

KEY TERMS

The following terms are covered in this chapter and can also be found in the list of Key Terms at the back of the book.

black codes	"Civil War Amendment"	Horace Greeley	Wade–Davis Bill
Black Friday	freedmen	pocket veto	
carpetbaggers and scalawags	Freedmen's Bureau		

ONLINE SOURCES GUIDE

Use this listing to find online documents, images, interactive maps, simulations, and other resources related to this chapter:

American History Resource Center
http://history.wadsworth.com/rc/us

Selected Images
Union troops parade in Washington, 1865
Depiction of Andrew Johnson as unsympathetic to South
Black codes

Freedmen in Richmond, Virginia, 1865
Burning of a freedmen's school, 1866

Interactive Time Line (with online readings)
Aftermath: The Reconstruction of the Union, 1865–1877

Discovery

Evaluate the success with which African Americans were integrated into American society during Reconstruction.

In thinking about this question, begin by breaking it down into the components shown below. A discussion of the significance of each component should appear in your answer.

Culture and Society: For this exercise, read the document excerpt "Race Relations in Georgia and South Carolina, ca. 1871" and look at the illustration of "Ku Klux Klan night riders." How do the two accounts of race relations in Georgia and South Carolina differ? What is the basic fear that is expressed here? In the second account, why is the author perplexed by some of their actions? Does he appear to be justifying slavery at all? How so? Do the fears expressed in these accounts explain the illustration? What arguments might southerners make to justify their violent actions toward African Americans? How might this affect race relations in the South for years to come?

Race Relations in Georgia and South Carolina, ca. 1871

From *Testimony Taken by the Joint Select Committee to Inquire Into the Condition of Affairs in the Late Insurrectionary States.*

1) Statement of C. W. Howard [a Georgia editor]

The negroes show their inherent vices, . . . indolence, theft, and sensuality. Before the war closed, when it was thought that the negroes would be emancipated, all of us apprehended a repetition of the scenes of San Domingo; but nothing of the kind has occurred. The negroes have been quiet and orderly, under very strong temptations to be otherwise; temptations not originating with themselves, but with a class of very bad men who came among them, and who endeavored to foster ill blood between the races for their own aggrandizement. But those men had little brains and less principle, and the negroes soon saw through them. If they had been like members of the *internationale*, or of the *commune*,— earnest fanatics—I think they would have done much harm; but I think their power is very much at an end, and the result has been very different from what we feared. The negroes have been orderly and quiet, for the main part, to a wonderful degree. On the other hand, the conduct of the

whites has been very different from what experience and analogy might have induced us to expect. Those people suddenly having been liberated, given the power to vote, to sit upon juries, and to hold office, it was very natural to suppose that the whites, as a mass, would have a feeling of the strongest animosity toward them. But it has not been so; and, as a general rule (of course there are exceptional cases) the two races, in their intercourse with each other, have acted in a manner which no former experience would have led us to anticipate. I think that the negroes generally are going to their old masters, and their old masters are treating them with kindness and even-handed justice. . . .

2) Statement of Alexander P. Wylie [a newspaper writer from South Carolina who claims he was a Unionist before and during the war. He describes a group of blacks organizing themselves after they had had a violent clash with the Ku Klux Klan]

[The negroes] came on down to Chester, warning the negroes to come; that the fight was to commence; sending runners to various quarters. On Monday morning I went up; it was the first I heard of it. They were then encamped in the borders of the town, within the corporation, a few hundred yards from the court-house, picketing the roads, preventing people from going in and out in that direction.

Question. How many were there at the time?

Answer. Something like a hundred, I think.

Question. Fully armed?

Answer. All armed with muskets.

Question. Proceed.

Answer. It created great excitement. . . . There is a negro company there at Chester Village of about one hundred, commandeered by a mulatto, John Lee. . . . There were negro women there, I know two; one of them has been treated most kindly throughout her life by an old aunt of mine; she raised the cry, "Now is the time to burn," and a night or two after that the fire was set. She cried out, "Now is the time to burn." A number did that. I recollect one girl there who had been treated just as a white girl—a bright mulatto, and still living with her old owner to this day. No person suspected such a feeling in her. And she said that she would delight in . . . to be in hell, to have a churn-paddle, and churn the whites to all eternity.

The Granger Collection, New York

Ku Klux Klan Night Riders

To read extended versions of the documents, visit the companion Web site http://history.wadsworth.com/americanpast8e; click on "Discovery Sources."

Appendix

* *

The Declaration of Independence

The Constitution of the United States
of America

Admission of States

Population of the United States

Presidential Elections

Justices of the U.S. Supreme Court

The Declaration of Independence
The Unanimous Declaration of the Thirteen United States of America

When in the Course of human events it becomes necessary for one people to dissolve the political bands which have connected them with another, and to assume among the Powers of the earth, the separate and equal station to which the Laws of Nature and of Nature's God entitle them, a decent respect to the opinions of mankind requires that they should declare the causes which impel them to the separation.

We hold these truths to be self-evident, that all men are created equal, that they are endowed by their Creator with certain unalienable Rights, that among these are Life, Liberty and the pursuit of Happiness. That to secure these rights, Governments are instituted among Men, deriving their just Powers from the consent of the governed. That whenever any Form of Government becomes destructive of these ends, it is the Right of the People to alter or to abolish it, and to institute new Government, laying its foundation on such principles and organizing its Powers in such form, as to them shall seem most likely to effect their Safety and Happiness. Prudence, indeed, will dictate that Governments long established should not be changed for light and transient causes; and accordingly all experience hath shewn, that mankind are more disposed to suffer, while evils are sufferable, than to right themselves by abolishing the forms to which they are accustomed. But when a long train of abuses and usurpations, pursuing invariably the same Object evinces a design to reduce them under absolute Despotism, it is their right, it is their duty, to throw off such Government, and to provide new Guards for their future security. Such has been the patient sufferance of these Colonies; and such is now the necessity which constrains them to alter their former Systems of Government. The history of the present King of Great Britain is a history of repeated injuries and usurpations, all having in direct object the establishment of an absolute Tyranny over these States. To prove this, let Facts be submitted to a candid world.

He has refused his Assent to Laws, the most wholesome and necessary for the public good.

He has forbidden his Governors to pass Laws of immediate and pressing importance, unless suspended in their operation till his Assent should be obtained; and when so suspended, he has utterly neglected to attend to them.

He has refused to pass other Laws for the accommodation of large districts of people, unless those people would relinquish the right of Representation in the Legislature, a right inestimable to them and formidable to tyrants only.

He has called together legislative bodies at places unusual, uncomfortable, and distant from the depository of their Public Records, for the sole Purpose of fatiguing them into compliance with his measures.

He has dissolved Representative Houses repeatedly, for opposing with manly firmness his invasions on the rights of the People.

He has refused for a long time, after such dissolutions, to cause others to be elected; whereby the Legislative Powers, incapable of Annihilation, have returned to the People at large for their exercise; the State remaining in the mean time exposed to all the dangers of invasion from without, and convulsions within.

He has endeavoured to prevent the Population of these States; for that purpose obstructing the Laws for Naturalization of Foreigners; refusing to pass others to encourage their migrations hither, and raising the conditions of new Appropriations of Lands.

He has obstructed the Administration of Justice, by refusing his Assent to Laws for establishing Judiciary Powers.

He has made Judges dependent on his Will alone, for the tenure of their offices, and the amount and payment of their salaries.

He has erected a multitude of New Offices, and sent hither swarms of Officers to harass our People, and eat out their substance.

He has kept among us, in times of peace, Standing Armies without the Consent of our legislatures.

He has affected to render the Military independent of and superior to the Civil Power.

He has combined with others to subject us to a jurisdiction foreign to our constitution, and unacknowledged by our laws; giving his Assent to their Acts of pretended Legislation:

For Quartering large bodies of armed troops among us:

For protecting them, by a mock Trial, from Punishment for any Murders which they should commit on the Inhabitants of these States:

For cutting off our Trade with all parts of the world:

For imposing Taxes on us without our Consent:

For depriving us in many cases, of the benefits of Trial by Jury:

For transporting us beyond Seas to be tried for pretended offences:

For abolishing the free System of English Laws in a neighbouring Province, establishing therein an Arbitrary government, and enlarging its Boundaries so as to render it at once an example and fit instrument for introducing the same absolute rule into these Colonies:

For taking away our Charters, abolishing our most valuable Laws, and altering fundamentally the Forms of our Governments:

Text is reprinted from the facsimile of the engrossed copy in the National Archives. The original spelling, capitalization, and punctuation have been retained. Paragraphing has been added.

For suspending our own Legislatures, and declaring themselves invested with Power to legislate for us in all cases whatsoever.

He has abdicated Government here, by declaring us out of his Protection, and waging War against us.

He has plundered our seas, ravaged our Coasts, burnt our towns, and destroyed the lives of our people.

He is at this time transporting large Armies of foreign Mercenaries to compleat the works of death, desolation and tyranny, already begun with circumstances of Cruelty and perfidy scarcely paralleled in the most barbarous ages, and totally unworthy the Head of a civilized nation.

He has constrained our fellow Citizens taken Captive on the high Seas to bear Arms against their Country, to become the executioners of their friends and Brethren, or to fall themselves by their Hands.

He has excited domestic insurrections amongst us, and has endeavoured to bring on the inhabitants of our frontiers, the merciless Indian Savages, whose known rule of warfare, is an undistinguished destruction of all ages, sexes and conditions.

In every stage of these Oppressions We have Petitioned for Redress in the most humble terms: Our repeated Petitions have been answered only by repeated injury. A Prince, whose character is thus marked by every act which may define a Tyrant, is unfit to be the ruler of a free People.

Nor have We been wanting in attentions to our British brethren. We have warned them from time to time of attempts by their legislature to extend an unwarrantable jurisdiction over us. We have reminded them of the circumstances of our emigration and settlement here. We have appealed to their native justice and magnanimity, and we have conjured them by the ties of our common kindred to disavow thee usurpations, which, would inevitably interrupt our connections and correspondence. They too have been deaf to the voice of justice and of consanguinity. We must, therefore, acquiesce in the necessity, which denounces our Separation, and hold them, as we hold the rest of mankind, Enemies in War, in Peace Friends.

WE, THEREFORE, the Representatives of the UNITED STATES OF AMERICA, in General Congress, Assembled, appealing to the Supreme Judge of the world for the rectitude of our intentions, do, in the Name, and by Authority of the good People of these Colonies, solemnly publish and declare, That these United Colonies are, and of Right ought to be FREE AND INDEPENDENT STATES; that they are Absolved from all Allegiance to the British Crown, and that all political connection between them and the State of Great Britain, is and ought to be totally dissolved; and that, as Free and Independent States, they have full Power to levy War, conclude Peace, contract Alliances, establish Commerce, and to do all other Acts and Things which Independent States may of right do. And for the support of this Declaration, with a firm reliance on the protection of divine Providence, we mutually pledge to each other our Lives, our Fortunes and our sacred Honor.

THE CONSTITUTION OF THE UNITED STATES OF AMERICA

We the People of the United States, in Order to form a more perfect Union, establish Justice, insure domestic Tranquility, provide for the common defence, promote the general Welfare, and secure the Blessings of Liberty to ourselves and our Posterity, do ordain and establish this Constitution for the United States of America.

Article. I.

SECTION. 1. All legislative Powers herein granted shall be vested in a Congress of the United States, which shall consist of a Senate and House of Representatives.

SECTION. 2. The House of Representatives shall be composed of Members chosen every second Year by the People of the several States, and the Electors in each State shall have the Qualifications requisite for Electors of the most numerous Branch of the State Legislature.

No Person shall be a Representative who shall not have attained to the Age of twenty five Years, and been seven Years a Citizen of the United States, and who shall not, when elected, be an Inhabitant of that State in which he shall be chosen.

Representatives and direct Taxes[1] shall be apportioned among the several States which may be included within this Union, according to their respective Numbers, which shall be determined by adding to the whole Number of free Persons, including those bound to Service for a Term of Years, and excluding Indians not taxed, three fifths of all other Persons.[2] The actual Enumeration shall be made within three Years after the first Meeting of the Congress of the United States, and within every subsequent Term of ten Years, in such Manner as they shall by Law direct. The Number of Representatives shall not exceed one for every thirty Thousand, but each State shall have at Least one Representative; and until such enumeration shall be made, the State of New Hampshire shall be entitled to chuse three; Massachusetts eight; Rhode Island and Providence Plantations one; Connecticut five; New York six; New Jersey four; Pennsylvania eight; Delaware one; Maryland six; Virginia ten; North Carolina five; South Carolina five; and Georgia three.

When vacancies happen in the Representation from any State, the Executive Authority thereof shall issue Writs of Election to fill such Vacancies.

The House of Representatives shall chuse their Speaker and other Officers; and shall have the sole Power of Impeachment.

SECTION. 3. The Senate of the United States shall be composed of two Senators from each State, chosen by the Legislature thereof, for six Years; and each Senator shall have one Vote.[3]

Immediately after they shall be assembled in Consequence of the first Election, they shall be divided as equally as may be into three Classes. The Seats of the Senators of the first Class shall be vacated at the Expiration of the second Year, of the second Class at the Expiration of the fourth Year, and of the third Class at the Expiration of the sixth Year, so that one third may be chosen every second Year; and if Vacancies happen by Resignation, or otherwise, during the Recess of the Legislature of any State, the Executive thereof may make temporary Appointments until the next Meeting of the Legislature, which shall then fill such Vacancies.[4]

No Person shall be a Senator who shall not have attained to the Age of thirty Years, and been nine Years a Citizen of the United States, and who shall not, when elected, be an Inhabitant of that State for which he shall be chosen.

The Vice President of the United States shall be President of the Senate, but shall have no Vote, unless they be equally divided.

The Senate shall chuse their other Officers, and also a President pro tempore, in the Absence of the Vice President, or when he shall exercise the Office of President of the United States.

The Senate shall have the sole Power to try all Impeachments. When sitting for that Purpose, they shall be on Oath or Affirmation. When the President of the United States is tried, the Chief Justice shall preside: And no Person shall be convicted without the Concurrence of two thirds of the Members present.

Judgment in Cases of Impeachment shall not extend further than to removal from Office, and disqualification to hold and enjoy any Office of honor, Trust or Profit under the United States: but the Party convicted shall nevertheless be liable and subject to Indictment, Trial, Judgment and Punishment, according to Law.

SECTION. 4. The Times, Places and Manner of holding Elections for Senators and Representatives, shall be prescribed in each State by the Legislature thereof, but the Congress may at any time by Law make or alter such Regulation, except as to the Places of chusing Senators.

The Congress shall assemble at least once in every Year, and such Meeting shall be on the first Monday in December, unless they shall by Law appoint a different Day.[5]

SECTION. 5. Each House shall be the Judge of the Elections, Returns and Qualifications of its own Members, and a

---

Text is from the engrossed copy in the National Archives. Original spelling, capitalization, and punctuation have been retained.

[1]Modified by the Sixteenth Amendment.

[2]Replaced by the Fourteenth Amendment.

[3]Superseded by the Seventeenth Amendment.

[4]Modified by the Seventeenth Amendment.

[5]Superseded by the Twentieth Amendment.

Majority of each shall constitute a Quorum to do Business; but a smaller Number may adjourn from day to day, and may be authorized to compel the Attendance of absent Members, in such Manner, and under such Penalties as each House may provide.

Each House may determine the Rules of its Proceedings, punish its Members for disorderly Behaviour, and, with the Concurrence of two thirds, expel a Member.

Each House shall keep a Journal of its Proceedings, and from time to time publish the same, excepting such Parts as may in their Judgment require Secrecy; and the Yeas and Nays of the Members of either House on any question shall, at the Desire of one fifth of those Present, be entered on the Journal.

Neither House, during the Session of Congress, shall, without the Consent of the other, adjourn for more than three days, nor to any other Place than that in which the two Houses shall be sitting.

SECTION. 6. The Senators and Representatives shall receive a Compensation for their Services, to be ascertained by Law, and paid out of the Treasury of the United States. They shall in all Cases, except Treason, Felony and Breach of the Peace, be privileged from Arrest during their Attendance at the Session of their respective Houses, and in going to and returning from the same; and for any Speech or Debate in either House, they shall not be questioned in any other Place.

No Senator or Representative shall, during the Time for which he was elected, be appointed to any civil Office under the Authority of the United States, which shall have been created, or the Emoluments whereof shall have been encreased during such time; and no Person holding any Office under the United States, shall be a Member of either House during his Continuance in Office.

SECTION. 7. All Bills for raising Revenue shall originate in the House of Representatives; but the Senate may propose or concur with Amendments as on other Bills.

Every Bill which shall have passed the House of Representatives and the Senate shall, before it become a Law, be presented to the President of the United States; If he approve he shall sign it, but if not he shall return it, with his Objections to that House in which it shall have originated, who shall enter the Objections at large on their Journal, and proceed to reconsider it. If after such Reconsideration two thirds of that House shall agree to pass the Bill, it shall be sent, together with the Objections, to the other House, by which it shall likewise be reconsidered, and if approved by two thirds of that House, it shall become a Law. But in all such Cases the Votes of both Houses shall be determined by yeas and Nays, and the Names of the Persons voting for and against the Bill shall be entered on the Journal of each House respectively. If any Bill shall not be returned by the President within ten Days (Sundays excepted) after it shall have been presented to him, the Same shall be a Law, in like Manner as if he had signed it, unless the Congress by their Adjournment prevent its Return, in which Case it shall not be a Law.

Every Order, Resolution, or Vote to which the Concurrence of the Senate and House of Representatives may be necessary (except on a question of Adjournment) shall be presented to the President of the United States; and before the Same shall take Effect, shall be approved by him, or being disapproved by him shall be repassed by two thirds of the Senate and House of Representatives, according to the Rules and Limitations prescribed in the Case of a Bill.

SECTION. 8. The Congress shall have power To lay and collect Taxes, Duties, Imposts and Excises, to pay the Debts and provide for the common Defence and general Welfare of the United States; but all Duties, Imposts and Excises shall be uniform throughout the United States;

To borrow Money on the credit of the United States;

To regulate Commerce with foreign Nations, and among the several States, and with the Indian Tribes;

To establish an uniform Rule of Naturalization, and uniform Laws on the subject of Bankruptcies throughout the United States;

To coin Money, regulate the Value thereof, and of foreign Coin, and fix the Standard of Weights and Measures;

To provide for the Punishment of counterfeiting the Securities and current Coin of the United States;

To establish Post Offices and post Roads;

To promote the Progress of Science and useful Arts, by securing for limited Times to Authors and Inventors the exclusive Right to their respective Writings and Discoveries;

To constitute Tribunals inferior to the Supreme Court;

To define and punish Piracies and Felonies committed on the high Seas, and Offences against the Law of Nations;

To declare War, grant Letters of Marque and Reprisal, and make Rules concerning Captures on Land and Water;

To raise and support Armies, but no Appropriation of Money to that Use shall be for a longer Term than two Years;

To provide and maintain a Navy;

To make Rules for the Government and Regulation of the land and naval Forces;

To provide for calling forth the Militia to execute the Laws of the Union, suppress Insurrections and repel Invasions;

To provide for organizing, arming, and disciplining, the Militia, and for governing such Part of them as may be employed in the Service of the United States, reserving to the States respectively, the Appointment of the Officers, and the Authority of training the Militia according to the discipline prescribed by Congress;

To exercise exclusive Legislation in all Cases whatsoever, over such District (not exceeding ten Miles square) as may, by Cession of particular States, and the Acceptance of Congress, become the Seat of the Government of the United States, and to exercise like Authority over all Places purchased by the Consent of the Legislature of the State in which the Same shall be, for the Erection of Forts, Magazines, Arsenals, dock-Yards, and other needful Buildings;—And

To make all Laws which shall be necessary and proper for carrying into Execution the foregoing Powers, and all other Powers vested by this Constitution in the Government of the United States, or in any Department or Officer thereof.

SECTION. 9. The Migration or Importation of such Persons as any of the States now existing shall think proper to admit, shall not be prohibited by the Congress prior to the Year one thousand eight hundred and eight, but a Tax or duty may be imposed on such Importation, not exceeding ten dollars for each Person.

The Privilege of the Writ of Habeas Corpus shall not be suspended, unless when in Cases of Rebellion or Invasion the public Safety may require it.

No Bill of Attainder or ex post facto Law shall be passed.

No Capitation, or other direct, Tax shall be laid, unless in Proportion to the Census or Enumeration herein before directed to be taken.

No Tax or Duty shall be laid on Articles exported from any State.

No Preference shall be given by any Regulation of Commerce or Revenue to the Ports of one State over those of another: nor shall Vessels bound to, or from, one State, be obliged to enter, clear, or pay Duties in another.

No Money shall be drawn from the Treasury, but in Consequence of Appropriations made by Law, and a regular Statement and Account of the Receipts and Expenditures of all public Money shall be published from time to time.

No Title of Nobility shall be granted by the United States: And no Person holding any Office of Profit or Trust under them, shall, without the Consent of the Congress, accept of any present, Emolument, Office, or Title, of any kind whatever, from any King, Prince, or foreign State.

SECTION. 10. No State shall enter into any Treaty, Alliance, or Confederation; grant Letters of Marque and Reprisal; coin Money; emit Bills of Credit; make any Thing but gold and silver Coin a Tender in Payment of Debts; pass any Bill of Attainder, ex post facto Law, or Law impairing the Obligation of Contracts, or grant any Title of Nobility.

No State shall, without the Consent of the Congress, lay any Imposts or Duties on Imports or Exports, except what may be absolutely necessary for executing its inspection Laws: and the net Produce of all Duties and Imposts, laid by any State on Imports or Exports, shall be for the Use of the Treasury of the United States; and all such Laws shall be subject to the Revision and Controul of the Congress.

No State shall, without the Consent of Congress, lay any Duty of Tonnage, keep Troops, or Ships of War in time of Peace, enter into any Agreement or Compact with another State, or with a foreign Power, or engage in War, unless actually invaded, or in such imminent Danger as will not admit of delay.

Article. II.

SECTION. 1. The executive Power shall be vested in a President of the United States of America. He shall hold his Office during the Term of four Years, and, together with the Vice President, chosen for the same Term, be elected, as follows:

Each State shall appoint, in such Manner as the Legislature thereof may direct, a Number of Electors, equal to the whole Number of Senators and Representatives to which the State may be entitled in the Congress: but no Senator or Representative, or Person holding an Office of Trust or Profit under the United States, shall be appointed an Elector.

The Electors shall meet in their respective States, and vote by Ballot for two Persons, of whom one at least shall not be an Inhabitant of the same State with themselves. And they shall make a List of all the Persons voted for, and of the Number of Votes for each; which List they shall sign and certify, and transmit sealed to the Seat of the Government of the United States, directed to the President of the Senate. The President of the Senate shall, in the Presence of the Senate and House of Representatives, open all the Certificates, and the Votes shall then be counted. The Person having the greatest Number of Votes shall be the President, if such Number be a Majority of the whole Number of Electors appointed; and if there be more than one who have such Majority, and have an equal Number of Votes, then the House of Representatives shall immediately chuse by Ballot one of them for President; and if no Person have a Majority, then from the five highest on the List the said House shall in like Manner chuse the President. But in chusing the President, the Votes shall be taken by States, the Representation from each State having one Vote; A quorum for this Purpose shall consist of a Member or Members from two thirds of the States, and a Majority of all the States shall be necessary to a Choice. In every Case, after the Choice of the President, the Person having the greatest Number of Votes of the Electors shall be the Vice President. But if there should remain two or more who have equal Votes, the Senate shall chuse from them by Ballot the Vice President.[6]

The Congress may determine the Time of chusing the Electors, and the Day on which they shall give their Votes; which Day shall be the same throughout the United States.

No Person except a natural born Citizen, or a Citizen of the United States, at the time of the Adoption of this Constitution, shall be eligible to the Office of President, neither shall any Person be eligible to that Office who shall not have attained to the Age of thirty five Years, and been fourteen Years a Resident within the United States.

In Case of the Removal of the President from Office, or of his Death, Resignation, or Inability to discharge the Powers and Duties of the said Office, the Same shall devolve on the Vice President, and the Congress may by Law provide for the Case of Removal, Death, Resignation or Inability, both of the President and Vice President, declaring what Officer shall then act as President, and such Officer shall act accordingly, until the Disability be removed, or a President shall be elected.[7]

The President shall, at stated Times, receive for his Services, a Compensation, which shall neither be increased nor diminished during the Period for which he shall have been elected, and he shall not receive within that Period any other Emolument from the United States, or any of them.

Before he enter on the Execution of his Office, he shall take the following Oath or Affirmation:—"I do solemnly swear (or affirm) that I will faithfully execute the Office of President of the United States, and will to the best of my Ability, preserve, protect and defend the Constitution of the United States."

---

[6]Superseded by the Twelfth Amendment.
[7]Modified by the Twenty-fifth Amendment.

SECTION. 2. The President shall be Commander in Chief of the Army and Navy of the United States, and of the Militia of the several States, when called into the actual Service of the United States; he may require the Opinion, in writing, of the principal Officer in each of the executive Departments, upon any Subject relating to the Duties of their respective Offices, and he shall have Power to grant Reprieves and Pardons for Offences against the United States, except in Cases of Impeachment.

He shall have Power, by and with the Advice and Consent of the Senate, to make Treaties, provided two thirds of the Senators present concur; and he shall nominate, and by and with the Advice and Consent of the Senate, shall appoint Ambassadors, other public Ministers and Consuls, Judges of the supreme Court, and all other Officers of the United States, whose Appointments are not herein otherwise provided for, and which shall be established by Law; but the Congress may by Law vest the Appointment of such inferior Officers, as they think proper, in the President alone, in the Courts of Law, or in the Heads of Departments.

The President shall have Power to fill up all Vacancies that may happen during the Recess of the Senate, by granting Commissions which shall expire at the End of their next Session.

SECTION. 3. He shall from time to time give the Congress Information of the State of the Union, and recommend to their Consideration such Measures as he shall judge necessary and expedient; he may, on extraordinary Occasions, convene both Houses, or either of them, and in Case of Disagreement between them, with Respect to the Time of Adjournment, he may adjourn them to such Time as he shall think proper; he shall receive Ambassadors and other public Ministers; he shall take Care that the Laws be faithfully executed, and shall Commission all the Officers of the United States.

SECTION. 4. The President, Vice President and all civil Officers of the United States, shall be removed from Office on Impeachment for, and Conviction of, Treason, Bribery, or other high Crimes and Misdemeanors.

Article. III.

SECTION. 1. The judicial Power of the United States, shall be vested in one supreme Court, and in such inferior Courts as the Congress may from time to time ordain and establish. The Judges, both of the supreme and inferior Courts, shall hold their Offices during good Behaviour, and shall, at stated Times, receive for their Services, a Compensation, which shall not be diminished during their Continuance in Office.

SECTION. 2. The judicial Power shall extend to all Cases, in Law and Equity, arising under this Constitution, the Laws of the United States, and Treaties made, or which shall be made, under their Authority;—to all Cases affecting Ambassadors, other public Ministers and Consuls;—to all Cases of admiralty and maritime Jurisdiction;—to Controversies to which the United States shall be a Party;—to Controversies between two or more States;—between a State and Citizens of another State;[8]—between Citizens of different States,—between Citizens of the same State claiming Lands under Grants of different States, and between a State, or the Citizens thereof, and foreign States, Citizens or Subjects.

In all Cases affecting Ambassadors, other public Ministers and Consuls, and those in which a State shall be Party, the supreme Court shall have original Jurisdiction. In all the other Cases before mentioned, the supreme Court shall have appellate Jurisdiction, both as to Law and Fact, with such Exceptions, and under such Regulations as the Congress shall make.

The Trial of all Crimes, except in Cases of Impeachment, shall be by Jury; and such Trial shall be held in the State where the said Crimes shall have been committed; but when not committed within any State, the Trial shall be at such Place or Places as the Congress may by Law have directed.

SECTION. 3. Treason against the United States, shall consist only in levying War against them, or in adhering to their Enemies, giving them Aid and Comfort. No Person shall be convicted of Treason unless on the Testimony of two Witnesses to the same overt Act, or on Confession in open Court.

The Congress shall have Power to declare the Punishment of Treason, but no Attainder of Treason shall work Corruption of Blood, or Forfeiture except during the Life of the Person attainted.

Article. IV.

SECTION. 1. Full Faith and Credit shall be given in each State to the public Acts, Records, and judicial Proceedings of every other State. And the Congress may by general Laws prescribe the Manner in which such Acts, Records and Proceedings shall be proved, and the Effect thereof.

SECTION. 2. The Citizens of each State shall be entitled to all Privileges and Immunities of Citizens in the several States.

A Person charged in any State with Treason, Felony, or other Crime, who shall flee from Justice, and be found in another State, shall on Demand of the executive Authority of the State from which he fled, be delivered up, to be removed to the State having Jurisdiction of the Crime.

No Person held to Service or Labour in one State, under the Laws thereof, escaping into another, shall, in Consequence of any Law or Regulation therein, be discharged from such Service or Labour, but shall be delivered up on Claim of the Party to whom such Service or Labour may be due.

SECTION. 3. New States may be admitted by the Congress into this Union; but no new State shall be formed or erected within the Jurisdiction of any other State, nor any State be formed by the Junction of two or more States, or Parts of States, without the Consent of the Legislatures of the States concerned as well as of the Congress.

The Congress shall have Power to dispose of and make all needful Rules and Regulations respecting the Territory or other Property belonging to the United States; and nothing in this Constitution shall be so construed as to Prejudice any Claims of the United States, or of any particular State.

---

[8]Modified by the Eleventh Amendment.

SECTION. 4. The United States shall guarantee to every State in this Union a Republican Form of Government, and shall protect each of them against Invasion; and on Application of the Legislature, or of the Executive (when the Legislature cannot be convened) against domestic Violence.

Article. V.

The Congress, whenever two thirds of both Houses shall deem it necessary, shall propose Amendments to this Constitution, or, on the Application of the Legislatures of two thirds of the several States, shall call a Convention for proposing Amendments, which, in either Case, shall be valid to all Intents and Purposes, as Part of this Constitution, when ratified by the Legislatures of three fourths of the several States, or by Conventions in three fourths thereof, as the one or the other Mode of Ratification may be proposed by the Congress; Provided that no Amendment which may be made prior to the Year One thousand eight hundred and eight shall in any Manner affect the first and fourth Clauses in the Ninth Section of the first Article; and that no State, without its Consent, shall be deprived of its equal Suffrage in the Senate.

Article. VI.

All Debts contracted and Engagements entered into, before the Adoption of this Constitution, shall be as valid against the United States under this Constitution, as under the Confederation.

This Constitution, and the Laws of the United States which shall be made in Pursuance thereof; and all Treaties made, or which shall be made, under the Authority of the United States, shall be the supreme Law of the Land; and the Judges in every State shall be bound thereby, any Thing in the Constitution or Laws of any State to the Contrary notwithstanding.

The Senators and Representatives before mentioned, and the Members of the several State Legislatures, and all executive and judicial Officers, both of the United States and of the several States, shall be bound by Oath or Affirmation, to support this Constitution; but no religious Test shall ever be required as a Qualification to any Office or public Trust under the United States.

Article. VII.

The Ratification of the Conventions of nine States, shall be sufficient for the Establishment of this Constitution between the States so ratifying the Same.
Done in Convention by the Unanimous Consent of the States present the Seventeenth Day of September in the Year of our Lord one thousand seven hundred and Eighty seven and of the Independence of the United States of America the Twelfth. **In witness** whereof We have hereunto subscribed our Names,
Articles in Addition to, and Amendment of, the Constitution of the United States of America, Proposed by Congress, and Ratified by the Legislatures of the Several States, Pursuant to the Fifth Article of the Original Constitution.

Amendment I[9]

Congress shall make no law respecting an establishment of religion, or prohibiting the free exercise thereof; or abridging the freedom of speech, or of the press; or the right of the people peaceably to assemble, and to petition the Government for a redress of grievances.

Amendment II

A well regulated Militia, being necessary to the security of a free State, the right of the people to keep and bear Arms shall not be infringed.

Amendment III

No Soldier shall, in time of peace, be quartered in any house, without the consent of the Owner, nor in time of war, but in a manner to be prescribed by law.

Amendment IV

The right of the people to be secure in their persons, houses, papers, and effects, against unreasonable searches and seizures, shall not be violated, and no Warrants shall issue, but upon probable cause, supported by Oath or affirmation, and particularly describing the place to be searched, and the persons or things to be seized.

Amendment V

No person shall be held to answer for a capital or otherwise infamous crime, unless on a presentment or indictment of a Grand Jury, except in cases arising in the land or naval forces, or in the Militia, when in actual service in time of War or public danger; nor shall any person be subject for the same offence to be twice put in jeopardy of life or limb; nor shall be compelled in any criminal case to be a witness against himself, nor be deprived of life, liberty, or property, without due process of law; nor shall private property be taken for public use, without just compensation.

Amendment VI

In all criminal prosecutions, the accused shall enjoy the right to a speedy and public trial, by an impartial jury of the State and district wherein the crime shall have been committed, which district shall have been previously ascertained by law, and to be informed of the nature and cause of the accusation; to be confronted with the witnesses against him; to have compulsory process for obtaining witnesses in his favor, and to have the Assistance of Counsel for his defence.

Amendment VII

In suits at common law, where the value in controversy shall exceed twenty dollars, the right of trial by jury shall be preserved, and no fact tried by a jury, shall be otherwise reexamined in any Court of the United States, than according to the rules of the common law.

---

[9]The first ten amendments were passed by Congress September 25, 1789. They were ratified by three-fourths of the states December 15, 1791.

Amendment VIII

Excessive bail shall not be required, nor excessive fines imposed, nor cruel and unusual punishments inflicted.

Amendment IX

The enumeration in the Constitution, of certain rights, shall not be construed to deny or disparage others retained by the people.

Amendment X

The powers not delegated to the United States by the Constitution; nor prohibited by it to the States, are reserved to the States respectively, or to the people.

Amendment XI[10]

The Judicial power of the United States shall not be construed to extend to any suit in law or equity, commenced or prosecuted against one of the United States by Citizens of another State, or by Citizens or Subjects of any Foreign State.

Amendment XII[11]

The Electors shall meet in their respective States and vote by ballot for President and Vice-President, one of whom, at least, shall not be an inhabitant of the same State with themselves; they shall name in their ballots the person voted for as President, and in distinct ballots the person voted for as Vice-President, and they shall make distinct lists of all persons voted for as President, and of all persons voted for as Vice-President, and of the number of votes for each, which lists they shall sign and certify, and transmit sealed to the seat of the government of the United States, directed to the President of the Senate;—The President of the Senate shall, in the presence of the Senate and House of Representatives, open all the certificates and the votes shall then be counted;—The person having the greatest number of votes for President, shall be the President, if such number be a majority of the whole number of Electors appointed; and if no person have such majority, then from the persons having the highest numbers not exceeding three on the list of those voted for as President, the House of Representatives shall choose immediately, by ballot, the President. But in choosing the President, the votes shall be taken by states, the representation from each state having one vote; a quorum for this purpose shall consist of a member or members from two-thirds of the states, and a majority of all the states shall be necessary to a choice. And if the House of Representatives shall not choose a President whenever the right of choice shall devolve upon them, before the fourth day of March next following, then the Vice-President shall act as President, as in the case of the death or other constitutional disability of the President.—The person having the greatest number of votes as Vice-President, shall be the Vice-President, if such number be a majority of the whole number of Electors appointed, and if no person have a majority, then from the two highest numbers on the list, the Senate shall choose the Vice-President; a quorum for the purpose shall consist of two-thirds of the whole number of Senators, and a majority of the whole number shall be necessary to a choice. But no person constitutionally ineligible to the office of President shall be eligible to that of Vice-President of the United States.

Amendment XIII[12]

SECTION. 1. Neither slavery nor involuntary servitude, except as a punishment for crime whereof the party shall have been duly convicted, shall exist within the United States, or any place subject to their jurisdiction.

SECTION. 2. Congress shall have power to enforce this article by appropriate legislation.

Amendment XIV[13]

SECTION. 1. All persons born or naturalized in the United States, and subject to the jurisdiction thereof, are citizens of the United States and of the State wherein they reside. No State shall make or enforce any law which shall abridge the privileges or immunities of citizens of the United States; nor shall any State deprive any person of life, liberty, or property, without due process of law; nor deny to any person within its jurisdiction the equal protection of the laws.

SECTION. 2. Representatives shall be apportioned among the several States according to their respective numbers, counting the whole number of persons in each State, excluding Indians not taxed. But when the right to vote at any election for the choice of electors for President and Vice-President of the United States, Representatives in Congress, the Executive and Judicial officers of a State, or the members of the Legislature thereof, is denied to any of the male inhabitants of such State, being twenty-one years of age, and citizens of the United States, or in any way abridged, except for participation in rebellion, or other crime, the basis of representation therein shall be reduced in the proportion which the number of such male citizens shall bear to the whole number of male citizens twenty-one years of age in such State.

SECTION. 3. No person shall be a Senator or Representative in Congress, or elector of President and Vice-President, or hold any office, civil or military, under the United States, or under any State, who, having previously taken an oath, as a member of Congress, or as an officer of the United States, or as a member of any State legislature, or as an executive or judicial officer of any State, to support the Constitution of the United States, shall have engaged in insurrection or rebellion against the same, or given aid or comfort to the enemies thereof. But Congress may by a vote of two-thirds of each House, remove such disability.

SECTION. 4. The validity of the public debt of the United States, authorized by law, including debts incurred for

---

[10]Passed March 4, 1794. Ratified January 23, 1795.

[11]Passed December 9, 1803. Ratified June 15, 1804.

[12]Passed January 31, 1865. Ratified December 6, 1865.

[13]Passed June 13, 1866. Ratified July 9, 1868.

payment of pensions and bounties for services in suppressing insurrection or rebellion, shall not be questioned. But neither the United States nor any State shall assume or pay any debt or obligation incurred in aid of insurrection or rebellion against the United States, or any claim for the loss or emancipation of any slave; but all such debts, obligations, and claims shall be held illegal and void.

SECTION. 5. The Congress shall have the power to enforce, by appropriate legislation, the provisions of this article.

Amendment XV[14]

SECTION. 1. The right of citizens of the United States to vote shall not be denied or abridged by the United States or by any State on account of race, color, or previous conditions of servitude—

SECTION. 2. The Congress shall have power to enforce this article by appropriate legislation.

Amendment XVI

The Congress shall have power to lay and collect taxes on incomes, from whatever source derived, without apportionment among the several States, and without regard to any census or enumeration.

Amendment XVII[15]

The Senate of the United States shall be composed of two Senators from each State, elected by the people thereof, for six years; and each Senator shall have one vote. The electors in each State shall have the qualifications requisite for electors of the most numerous branch of the State legislatures.

When vacancies happen in the representation of any State in the Senate, the executive authority of such State shall issue writs of election to fill such vacancies: Provided, That the legislature of any State may empower the executive thereof to make temporary appointments until the people fill the vacancies by election as the legislature may direct.

This amendment shall not be so construed as to affect the election or term of any Senator chosen before it becomes valid as part of the Constitution.

Amendment XVIII[16]

SECTION. 1. After one year from the ratification of this article the manufacture, sale, or transportation of intoxicating liquors within, the importation thereof into, or the exportation thereof from the United States and all territory subject to the jurisdiction thereof for beverage purposes is hereby prohibited.

SECTION. 2. The Congress and the several States shall have concurrent power to enforce this article by appropriate legislation.

SECTION. 3. This article shall be inoperative unless it shall have been ratified as an amendment to the Constitution by the legislatures of the several States, as provided in the Constitution, within seven years from the date of the submission hereof to the States by the Congress.

Amendment XIX[17]

The right of citizens of the United States to vote shall not be denied or abridged by the United States or by any State on account of sex.

Congress shall have power to enforce this article by appropriate legislation.

Amendment XX[18]

SECTION. 1. The terms of the President and Vice-President shall end at noon on the 20th day of January, and the terms of Senators and Representatives at noon on the 3d day of January, of the years in which such terms would have ended if this article had not been ratified; and the terms of their successors shall then begin.

SECTION. 2. The Congress shall assemble at least once in every year, and such meeting shall begin at noon on the 3d day of January, unless they shall by law appoint a different day.

SECTION. 3. If, at the time fixed for the beginning of the term of the President, the President elect shall have died the Vice-President elect shall become President. If a President shall not have been chosen before the time fixed for the beginning of his term, or if the President elect shall have failed to qualify, then the Vice-President elect shall act as President until a President shall have qualified; and the Congress may by law provide for the case wherein neither a President elect nor a Vice-President elect shall have qualified, declaring who shall then act as President, or the manner in which one who is to act shall be selected, and such person shall act accordingly until a President or Vice-President shall have qualified.

SECTION. 4. The Congress may by law provide for the case of the death of any of the persons from whom the House of Representatives may choose a President whenever the right of choice shall have devolved upon them, and for the case of the death of any of the persons from whom the Senate may choose a Vice-President whenever the right of choice shall have devolved upon them.

SECTION. 5. Sections 1 and 2 shall take effect on the 15th day of October following the ratification of this article.

SECTION. 6. This article shall be inoperative unless it shall have been ratified as an amendment to the Constitution by the legislatures of three-fourths of the several States within seven years from the date of its submission.

Amendment XXI[19]

SECTION. 1. The eighteenth article of amendment to the Constitution of the United States is hereby repealed.

SECTION. 2. The transportation or importation into any State, Territory, or possession of the United States for delivery or use therein of intoxicating liquors, in violation of the laws thereof, is hereby prohibited.

---

[14]Passed February 26, 1869. Ratified February 2, 1870.

[15]Passed May 13, 1912. Ratified April 8, 1913.

[16]Passed December 18, 1917. Ratified January 16, 1919.

[17]Passed June 4, 1919. Ratified August 18, 1920.

[18]Passed March 2, 1932. Ratified January 23, 1933.

[19]Passed February 20, 1933. Ratified December 5, 1933.

SECTION. 3. This article shall be inoperative unless it shall have been ratified as an amendment to the Constitution by conventions in the several States, as provided in the Constitution, within seven years from the date of the submission hereof to the States by the Congress.

Amendment XXII[20]

No person shall be elected to the office of the President more than twice, and no person who has held the office of President, or acted as President, for more than two years of a term to which some other person was elected President shall be elected to the office of the President more than once.

But this Article shall not apply to any person holding the office of President when this Article was proposed by the Congress, and shall not prevent any person who may be holding the office of President, or acting as President, during the term within which this Article becomes operative from holding the office of President or acting as President during the remainder of such term.

Amendment XXIII[21]

SECTION. 1. The District constituting the seat of Government of the United States shall appoint in such manner as the Congress may direct:

A number of electors of President and Vice President equal to the whole number of Senators and Representatives in Congress to which the District would be entitled if it were a State, but in no event more than the least populous State; they shall be in addition to those appointed by the States, but they shall be considered, for the purposes of the election of President and Vice President, to be electors appointed by the State; and they shall meet in the District and perform such duties as provided by the twelfth article of amendment.

SECTION. 2. The Congress shall have power to enforce this article by appropriate legislation.

Amendment XXIV[22]

SECTION. 1. The right of citizens of the United States to vote in any primary or other election for President or Vice President, or for Senator or Representative in Congress, shall not be denied or abridged by the United States or any State by reason of failure to pay any poll tax or other tax.

SECTION. 2. The Congress shall have power to enforce this article by appropriate legislation.

Amendment XXV[23]

SECTION. 1. In case of the removal of the President from office or of his death or resignation, the Vice President shall become President.

SECTION. 2. Whenever there is a vacancy in the office of the Vice President, the President shall nominate a Vice President who shall take office upon confirmation by a majority vote of both Houses of Congress.

SECTION. 3. Whenever the President transmits to the President pro tempore of the Senate and the Speaker of the House of Representatives his written declaration that he is unable to discharge the powers and duties of his office, and until he transmits them a written declaration to the contrary, such powers and duties shall be discharged by the Vice President as Acting President.

SECTION. 4. Whenever the Vice President and a majority of either the principal officers of the executive department or of such other body as Congress may by law provide, transmit to the President pro tempore of the Senate and the Speaker of the House of Representatives their written declaration that the President is unable to discharge the powers and duties of his office, the Vice President shall immediately assume the powers and duties of the office of Acting President.

Thereafter, when the President transmits to the President pro tempore of the Senate and the Speaker of the House of Representatives his written declaration that no inability exists, he shall resume the powers and duties of his office unless the Vice President and a majority of either the principal officers of the executive department or of such other body as Congress may by law provide, transmit within four days to the President pro tempore of the Senate and the Speaker of the House of Representatives their written declaration that the President is unable to discharge the powers and duties of his office. Thereupon Congress shall decide the issue, assembling within forty-eight hours for that purpose if not in session. If the Congress, within twenty-one days after receipt of the latter written declaration, or, if Congress is not in session, within twenty-one days after Congress is required to assemble, determines by two-thirds vote of both Houses that the President is unable to discharge the powers and duties of his office, the Vice President shall continue to discharge the same as Acting President; otherwise, the President shall resume the powers and duties of his office.

Amendment XXVI[24]

SECTION. 1. The right of citizens of the United States, who are eighteen years of age or older, to vote shall not be denied or abridged by the United States or by any State on account of age.

SECTION. 2. The Congress shall have power to enforce this article by appropriate legislation.

Amendment XXVII[25]

No law, varying the compensation for the service of the Senators and Representatives, shall take effect, until an election of Representatives shall have intervened.

---

[20]Passed March 12, 1947. Ratified March 1, 1951.

[21]Passed June 16, 1960. Ratified April 3, 1961.

[22]Passed August 27, 1962. Ratified January 23, 1964.

[23]Passed July 6, 1965. Ratified February 11, 1967.

[24]Passed March 23, 1971. Ratified July 5, 1971.

[25]Passed September 25, 1989. Ratified May 7, 1992.

Admission of States

Order of admission	State	Date of admission	Order of admission	State	Date of admission
1	Delaware	December 7, 1787	26	Michigan	January 26, 1837
2	Pennsylvania	December 12, 1787	27	Florida	March 3, 1845
3	New Jersey	December 18, 1787	28	Texas	December 29, 1845
4	Georgia	January 2, 1788	29	Iowa	December 28, 1846
5	Connecticut	January 9, 1788	30	Wisconsin	May 29, 1848
6	Massachusetts	February 6, 1788	31	California	September 9, 1850
7	Maryland	April 28, 1788	32	Minnesota	May 11, 1858
8	South Carolina	May 23, 1788	33	Oregon	February 14, 1859
9	New Hampshire	June 21, 1788	34	Kansas	January 29, 1861
10	Virginia	June 25, 1788	35	West Virginia	June 20, 1863
11	New York	July 26, 1788	36	Nevada	October 31, 1864
12	North Carolina	November 21, 1789	37	Nebraska	March 1, 1867
13	Rhode Island	May 29, 1790	38	Colorado	August 1, 1876
14	Vermont	March 4, 1791	39	North Dakota	November 2, 1889
15	Kentucky	June 1, 1792	40	South Dakota	November 2, 1889
16	Tennessee	June 1, 1796	41	Montana	November 8, 1889
17	Ohio	March 1, 1803	42	Washington	November 11, 1889
18	Louisiana	April 30, 1812	43	Idaho	July 3, 1890
19	Indiana	December 11, 1816	44	Wyoming	July 10, 1890
20	Mississippi	December 10, 1817	45	Utah	January 4, 1896
21	Illinois	December 3, 1818	46	Oklahoma	November 16, 1907
22	Alabama	December 14, 1819	47	New Mexico	January 6, 1912
23	Maine	March 15, 1820	48	Arizona	February 14, 1912
24	Missouri	August 10, 1821	49	Alaska	January 3, 1959
25	Arkansas	June 15, 1836	50	Hawaii	August 21, 1959

Population of the United States
(1790–2005)

Year	Total population (in thousands)	Number per square mile of land area (continental United States)	Year	Total population (in thousands)	Number per square mile of land area (continental United States)
1790	3,929	4.5	1829	12,565	
1791	4,056		1830	12,901	7.4
1792	4,194		1831	13,321	
1793	4,332		1832	13,742	
1794	4,469		1833	14,162	
1795	4,607		1834	14,582	
1796	4,745		1835	15,003	
1797	4,883		1836	15,423	
1798	5,021		1837	15,843	
1799	5,159		1838	16,264	
1800	5,297	6.1	1839	16,684	
1801	5,486		1840	17,120	9.8
1802	5,679		1841	17,733	
1803	5,872		1842	18,345	
1804	5,065		1843	18,957	
1805	6,258		1844	19,569	
1806	6,451		1845	20,182	
1807	6,644		1846	20,794	
1808	6,838		1847	21,406	
1809	7,031		1848	22,018	
1810	7,224	4.3	1849	22,631	
1811	7,460		1850	23,261	7.9
1812	7,700		1851	24,086	
1813	7,939		1852	24,911	
1814	8,179		1853	25,736	
1815	8,419		1854	26,561	
1816	8,659		1855	27,386	
1817	8,899		1856	28,212	
1818	9,139		1857	29,037	
1819	9,379		1858	29,862	
1820	9,618	5.6	1859	30,687	
1821	9,939		1860	31,513	10.6
1822	10,268		1861	32,351	
1823	10,596		1862	33,188	
1824	10,924		1863	34,026	
1825	11,252		1864	34,863	
1826	11,580		1865	35,701	
1827	11,909		1866	36,538	
1828	12,237		1867	37,376	

Figures are from *Historical Statistics of the United States, Colonial Times to 1957* (1961), pp. 7, 8; *Statistical Abstract of the United States* (1974), p. 5, Census Bureau for 1974 and 1975; and *Statistical Abstract of the United States* (1988), p. 7.

(continued)

Population of the United States *(continued)* (1790–2005)

Year	Total population (in thousands)	Number per square mile of land area (continental United States)	Year	Total population (in thousands)[1]	Number per square mile of land area (continental United States)
1868	38,213		1907	87,000	
1869	39,051		1908	88,709	
1870	39,905	13.4	1909	90,492	
1871	40,938		1910	92,407	31.0
1872	41,972		1911	93,868	
1873	43,006		1912	95,331	
1874	44,040		1913	97,227	
1875	45,073		1914	99,118	
1876	46,107		1915	100,549	
1877	47,141		1916	101,966	
1878	48,174		1917	103,414	
1879	49,208		1918	104,550	
1880	50,262	16.9	1919	105,063	
1881	51,542		1920	106,466	35.6
1882	52,821		1921	108,541	
1883	54,100		1922	110,055	
1884	55,379		1923	111,950	
1885	56,658		1924	114,113	
1886	57,938		1925	115,832	
1887	59,217		1926	117,399	
1888	60,496		1927	119,038	
1889	61,775		1928	120,501	
1890	63,056	21.2	1929	121,700	
1891	64,361		1930	122,775	41.2
1892	65,666		1931	124,040	
1893	66,970		1932	124,840	
1894	68,275		1933	125,579	
1895	69,580		1934	126,374	
1896	70,885		1935	127,250	
1897	72,189		1936	128,053	
1898	73,494		1937	128,825	
1899	74,799		1938	129,825	
1900	76,094	25.6	1939	130,880	
1901	77,585		1940	131,669	44.2
1902	79,160		1941	133,894	
1903	80,632		1942	135,361	
1904	82,165		1943	137,250	
1905	83,820		1944	138,916	
1906	85,437		1945	140,468	

[1]Figures after 1940 represent total population including armed forces abroad, except in official census years.

(continued)

Population of the United States *(continued)*
(1790–2005)

Year	Total population (in thousands)	Number per square mile of land area (continental United States)	Year	Total population (in thousands)[1]	Number per square mile of land area (continental United States)
1946	141,936		1976	218,035	
1947	144,698		1977	220,239	
1948	147,208		1978	222,585	
1949	149,767		1979	225,055	
1950	150,697	50.7	1980	227,225	64.0
1951	154,878		1981	229,466	
1952	157,553		1982	232,520	
1953	160,184		1983	234,799	
1954	163,026		1984	237,001	
1955	165,931		1985	239,283	
1956	168,903		1986	241,596	
1957	171,984		1987	234,773	
1958	174,882		1988	245,051	
1959	177,830[2]		1989	247,350	
1960	180,671	60.1	1990	250,122	70.3
1961	186,538		1991	254,521	
1962	189,242		1992	245,908	
1963	189,197		1993	257,908	
1964	191,889		1994	261,875	
1965	194,303		1995	263,434	
1966	196,560		1996	266,096	
1967	198,712		1997	267,744	
1968	200,706		1998	270,299	
1969	202,677		1999	274,114	
1970	205,052	57.52	2000	281,400	
1971	207,661		2001	286,909	
1972	209,896		2002	289,947	
1973	211,909		2003	290,850	
1974	213,854		2004	293,656	
1975	215,973		2005	296,410	

[1]Figures after 1940 represent total population including armed forces abroad, except in official census years.

[2]Figures after 1959 include Alaska and Hawaii.

Presidential Elections
(1789–1832)

Year	Number of states	Candidates[1]	Parties	Popular vote	Electoral vote	Percentage of popular vote[2]
1789	11	**George Washington***	**No party designations**		**69**	
		John Adams			34	
		Minor Candidates			35	
1792	15	**George Washington**	**No party designations**		**132**	
		John Adams			77	
		George Clinton			50	
		Minor Candidates			5	
1796	16	**John Adams**	**Federalist**		**71**	
		Thomas Jefferson	Democratic-Republican		68	
		Thomas Pinckney	Federalist		59	
		Aaron Burr	Democratic-Republican		30	
		Minor Candidates			48	
1800	16	**Thomas Jefferson**	**Democratic-Republican**		**73**	
		Aaron Burr	Democratic-Republican		73	
		John Adams	Federalist		65	
		Charles C. Pinckney	Federalist		64	
		John Jay	Federalist		1	
1804	17	**Thomas Jefferson**	**Democratic-Republican**		**162**	
		Charles C. Pinckney	Federalist		14	
1808	17	**James Madison**	**Democratic-Republican**		**122**	
		Charles C. Pinckney	Federalist		47	
		George Clinton	Democratic-Republican		6	
1812	18	**James Madison**	**Democratic-Republican**		**128**	
		DeWitt Clinton	Federalist		89	
1816	19	**James Monroe**	**Democratic-Republican**		**183**	
		Rufus King	Federalist		34	
1820	24	**James Monroe**	**Democratic-Republican**		**231**	
		John Quincy Adams	Independent Republican		1	
1824	24	**John Quincy Adams**	**Democratic-Republican**	**108,740**	**84**	**30.5**
		Andrew Jackson	Democratic-Republican	153,544	99	43.1
		William H. Crawford	Democratic-Republican	46,618	41	13.1
		Henry Clay	Democratic-Republican	47,136	37	13.2
1828	24	**Andrew Jackson**	**Democratic**	**647,286**	**178**	**56.0**
		John Quincy Adams	National Republican	508,064	83	44.0
1832	24	**Andrew Jackson**	**Democratic**	**687,502**	**219**	**55.0**
		Henry Clay	National Republican	530,189	49	42.4
		William Wirt	Anti-Masonic		7	
		John Floyd	National Republican	33,108	11	2.6

[1]Before the passage of the Twelfth Amendment in 1804, the Electoral College voted for two presidential candidates; the runner-up became vice president. Figures are from *Historical Statistics of the United States, Colonial Times to 1957* (1961), pp. 682–83; and the U.S. Department of Justice.

[2]Candidates receiving less than 1 percent of the popular vote have been omitted. For that reason the percentage of popular vote given for any election year may not total 100 percent.

*Note: Boldface indicates the winner of each election.

Presidential Elections
(1836–1888)

Year	Number of states	Candidates	Parties	Popular vote	Electoral vote	Percentage of popular vote[1]
1836	26	**Martin Van Buren**	**Democratic**	**765,483**	**170**	**50.9**
		William H. Harrison	Whig		73	
		Hugh L. White	Whig		26	
		Daniel Webster	Whig	739,795	14	
		W. P. Mangum	Independent		11	
1840	26	**William H. Harrison**	**Whig**	**1,274,624**	**234**	**53.1**
		Martin Van Buren	Democratic	1,127,781	60	46.9
1844	26	**James K. Polk**	**Democratic**	**1,338,464**	**170**	**49.6**
		Henry Clay	Whig	1,300,097	105	48.1
		James G. Birney	Liberty	62,300		2.3
1848	30	**Zachary Taylor**	**Whig**	**1,360,967**	**163**	**47.4**
		Lewis Cass	Democratic	1,222,342	127	42.5
		Martin Van Buren	Free Soil	291,263		10.1
1852	31	**Franklin Pierce**	**Democratic**	**1,601,117**	**254**	**50.9**
		Winfield Scott	Whig	1,385,453	42	44.1
		John P. Hale	Free Soil	155,825		5.0
1856	31	**James Buchanan**	**Democratic**	**1,832,955**	**174**	**45.3**
		John C. Frémont	Republican	1,339,932	114	33.1
		Millard Fillmore	American	871,731	8	21.6
1860	33	**Abraham Lincoln**	**Republican**	**1,865,593**	**180**	**39.8**
		Stephen A. Douglas	Democratic	1,382,713	12	29.5
		John C. Breckinridge	Democratic	848,356	72	18.1
		John Bell	Constitutional Union	592,906	39	12.6
1864	36	**Abraham Lincoln**	**Republican**	**2,206,938**	**212**	**55.0**
		George B. McClellan	Democratic	1,803,787	21	45.0
1868	37	**Ulysses S. Grant**	**Republican**	**3,013,421**	**214**	**52.7**
		Horatio Seymour	Democratic	2,706,829	80	47.3
1872	37	**Ulysses S. Grant**	**Republican**	**3,596,745**	**286**	**55.6**
		Horace Greeley	Democratic	2,843,446	[2]	43.9
1876	38	**Rutherford B. Hayes**	**Republican**	**4,036,572**	**185**	**48.0**
		Samuel J. Tilden	Democratic	4,284,020	184	51.0
1880	38	**James A. Garfield**	**Republican**	**4,453,295**	**214**	**48.5**
		Winfield S. Hancock	Democratic	4,414,082	155	48.1
		James B. Weaver	Greenback-Labor	308,578		3.4
1884	38	**Grover Cleveland**	**Democratic**	**4,879,507**	**219**	**48.5**
		James G. Blaine	Republican	4,850,293	182	48.2
		Benjamin F. Butler	Greenback-Labor	175,370		1.8
		John P. St. John	Prohibition	150,369		1.5
1888	38	**Benjamin Harrison**	**Republican**	**5,477,129**	**233**	**47.9**
		Grover Cleveland	Democratic	5,537,857	168	48.6
		Clinton B. Fisk	Prohibition	249,506		2.2
		Anson J. Streeter	Union Labor	146,935		1.3

[1]Candidates receiving less than 1 percent of the popular vote have been omitted. For that reason the percentage of popular vote given for any election year may not total 100 percent.

[2]Greeley died shortly after the election; the electors supporting him then divided their votes among minor candidates.

Presidential Elections
(1892–1932)

Year	Number of states	Candidates	Parties	Popular vote	Electoral vote	Percentage of popular vote[1]
1892	44	**Grover Cleveland**	**Democratic**	**5,555,426**	**277**	**46.1**
		Benjamin Harrison	Republican	5,182,690	145	43.0
		James B. Weaver	People's	1,029,846	22	8.5
		John Bidwell	Prohibition	264,133		2.2
1896	45	**William McKinley**	**Republican**	**7,102,246**	**271**	**51.1**
		William J. Bryan	Democratic	6,492,559	176	47.7
1900	45	**William McKinley**	**Republican**	**7,218,491**	**292**	**51.7**
		William J. Bryan	Democratic; Populist	6,356,734	155	45.5
		John C. Wooley	Prohibition	208,914		1.5
1904	45	**Theodore Roosevelt**	**Republican**	**7,628,461**	**336**	**57.4**
		Alton B. Parker	Democratic	5,084,223	140	37.6
		Eugene V. Debs	Socialist	402,283		3.0
		Silas C. Swallow	Prohibition	258,536		1.9
1908	46	**William H. Taft**	**Republican**	**7,675,320**	**321**	**51.6**
		William J. Bryan	Democratic	6,412,294	162	43.1
		Eugene V. Debs	Socialist	420,793		2.8
		Eugene W. Chafin	Prohibition	253,840		1.7
1912	48	**Woodrow Wilson**	**Democratic**	**6,296,547**	**435**	**41.9**
		Theodore Roosevelt	Progressive	4,118,571	88	27.4
		William H. Taft	Republican	3,486,720	8	23.2
		Eugene V. Debs	Socialist	900,672		6.0
		Eugene W. Chafin	Prohibition	206,275		1.4
1916	48	**Woodrow Wilson**	**Democratic**	**9,127,695**	**277**	**49.4**
		Charles E. Hughes	Republican	8,533,507	254	46.2
		A. L. Benson	Socialist	585,113		3.2
		J. Frank Hanly	Prohibition	220,506		1.2
1920	48	**Warren G. Harding**	**Republican**	**16,143,407**	**404**	**60.4**
		James N. Cox	Democratic	9,130,328	127	34.2
		Eugene V. Debs	Socialist	919,799		3.4
		P. P. Christensen	Farmer-Labor	265,411		1.0
1924	48	**Calvin Coolidge**	**Republican**	**15,718,211**	**382**	**54.0**
		John W. Davis	Democratic	8,385,283	136	28.8
		Robert M. La Follette	Progressive	4,831,289	13	16.6
1928	48	**Herbert C. Hoover**	**Republican**	**21,391,993**	**444**	**58.2**
		Alfred E. Smith	Democratic	15,016,169	87	40.9
1932	48	**Franklin D. Roosevelt**	**Democratic**	**22,809,638**	**472**	**57.4**
		Herbert C. Hoover	Republican	15,758,901	59	39.7
		Norman Thomas	Socialist	881,951		2.2

[1]Candidates receiving less than 1 percent of the popular vote have been omitted. For that reason the percentage of popular vote given for any election year may not total 100 percent.

Presidential Elections
(1936–2004)

Year	Number of states	Candidates	Parties	Popular vote	Electoral vote	Percentage of popular vote[1]
1936	48	**Franklin D. Roosevelt**	**Democratic**	**27,752,869**	**523**	**60.8**
		Alfred M. Landon	Republican	16,674,665	8	36.5
		William Lemke	Union	882,479		1.9
1940	48	**Franklin D. Roosevelt**	**Democratic**	**27,307,819**	**449**	**54.8**
		Wendell L. Willkie	Republican	22,321,018	82	44.8
1944	48	**Franklin D. Roosevelt**	**Democratic**	**25,606,585**	**432**	**53.5**
		Thomas E. Dewey	Republican	22,014,745	99	46.0
1948	48	**Harry S Truman**	**Democratic**	**24,105,812**	**303**	**49.5**
		Thomas E. Dewey	Republican	21,970,065	189	45.1
		J. Strom Thurmond	States' Rights	1,169,063	39	2.4
		Henry A. Wallace	Progressive	1,157,172		2.4
1952	48	**Dwight D. Eisenhower**	**Republican**	**33,936,234**	**442**	**55.1**
		Adlai E. Stevenson	Democratic	27,314,992	89	44.4
1956	48	**Dwight D. Eisenhower**	**Republican**	**35,590,472**	**457**	**57.6**
		Adlai E. Stevenson	Democratic	26,022,752	73	42.1
1960	50	**John F. Kennedy**	**Democratic**	**34,227,096**	**303**	**49.9**
		Richard M. Nixon	Republican	34,108,546	219	49.6
1964	50	**Lyndon B. Johnson**	**Democratic**	**43,126,506**	**486**	**61.1**
		Barry M. Goldwater	Republican	27,176,799	52	38.5
1968	50	**Richard M. Nixon**	**Republican**	**31,785,480**	**301**	**43.4**
		Hubert H. Humphrey	Democratic	31,275,165	191	42.7
		George C. Wallace	American Independent	9,906,473	46	13.5
1972	50	**Richard M. Nixon**	**Republican**	**47,169,911**	**520**	**60.7**
		George S. McGovern	Democratic	29,170,383	17	37.5
1976	50	**Jimmy Carter**	**Democratic**	**40,827,394**	**297**	**50.0**
		Gerald R. Ford	Republican	39,145,977	240	47.9
1980	50	**Ronald W. Reagan**	**Republican**	**43,899,248**	**489**	**50.8**
		Jimmy Carter	Democratic	35,481,435	49	41.0
		John B. Anderson	Independent	5,719,437		6.6
		Ed Clark	Libertarian	920,859		1.0
1984	50	**Ronald W. Reagan**	**Republican**	**54,281,858**	**525**	**59.2**
		Walter F. Mondale	Democratic	37,457,215	13	40.8
1988	50	**George H. Bush**	**Republican**	**47,917,341**	**426**	**54**
		Michael Dukakis	Democratic	41,013,030	112	46
1992	50	**William Clinton**	**Democratic**	**44,908,254**	**370**	**43.0**
		George H. Bush	Republican	39,102,343	168	37.4
		H. Ross Perot	Independent	19,741,065		18.9
1996	50	**William Clinton**	**Democratic**	**47,402,357**	**379**	**49**
		Robert J. Dole	Republican	39,198,755	159	41
		H. Ross Perot	Reform	8,085,402		8
2000	50	**George W. Bush**	**Republican**	**50,456,062**	**271**	**47.9**
		Albert Gore	Democratic	50,996,582	266	48.4
		Ralph Nader	Green	2,858,843		2.7
2004	50	**George W. Bush**	**Republican**	**60,693,281**	**286**	**52**
		John F. Kerry	Democratic	57,355,978	251	47
		Ralph Nader	Green	240,896		

[1]Candidates receiving less than 1 percent of the popular vote have been omitted. For that reason the percentage of popular vote given for any election year may not total 100 percent.

Justices of the U.S. Supreme Court

Chief Justices appear in bold type

	Term of Service	Years of Service	Appointed by
John Jay	1789–1795	5	Washington
John Rutledge	1789–1791	1	Washington
William Cushing	1789–1810	20	Washington
James Wilson	1789–1798	8	Washington
John Blair	1789–1796	6	Washington
Robert H. Harrison	1789–1790	—	Washington
James Iredell	1790–1799	9	Washington
Thomas Johnson	1791–1793	1	Washington
William Paterson	1793–1806	13	Washington
John Rutledge[1]	1795	—	Washington
Samuel Chase	1796–1811	15	Washington
Oliver Ellsworth	1796–1800	4	Washington
Bushrod Washington	1798–1829	31	J. Adams
Alfred Moore	1799–1804	4	J. Adams
John Marshall	1801–1835	34	J. Adams
William Johnson	1804–1834	30	Jefferson
H. Brockholst Livingston	1806–1823	16	Jefferson
Thomas Todd	1807–1826	18	Jefferson
Joseph Story	1811–1845	33	Madison
Gabriel Duval	1811–1835	24	Madison
Smith Thompson	1823–1843	20	Monroe
Robert Trimble	1826–1828	2	J. Q. Adams
John McLean	1829–1861	32	Jackson
Henry Baldwin	1830–1844	14	Jackson
James M. Wayne	1835–1867	32	Jackson
Roger B. Taney	1836–1864	28	Jackson
Philip P. Barbour	1836–1841	4	Jackson
John Catron	1837–1865	28	Van Buren
John McKinley	1837–1852	15	Van Buren
Peter V. Daniel	1841–1860	19	Van Buren
Samuel Nelson	1845–1872	27	Tyler
Levi Woodbury	1845–1851	5	Polk
Robert C. Grier	1846–1870	23	Polk
Benjamin R. Curtis	1851–1857	6	Fillmore
John A. Campbell	1853–1861	8	Pierce
Nathan Clifford	1858–1881	23	Buchanan
Noah H. Swayne	1862–1881	18	Lincoln
Samuel F. Miller	1862–1890	28	Lincoln
David Davis	1862–1877	14	Lincoln
Stephen J. Field	1863–1897	34	Lincoln
Salmon P. Chase	1864–1873	8	Lincoln
William Strong	1870–1880	10	Grant
Joseph P. Bradley	1870–1892	22	Grant
Ward Hunt	1873–1882	9	Grant

[1]Acting Chief Justice; Senate refused to confirm appointment.

(continued)

Justices of the U.S. Supreme Court (continued)

Chief Justices appear in bold type

	Term of Service	Years of Service	Appointed by
Morrison R. Waite	1874–1888	14	Grant
John M. Harlan	1877–1911	34	Hayes
William B. Woods	1880–1887	7	Hayes
Stanley Matthews	1881–1889	7	Garfield
Horace Gray	1882–1902	20	Arthur
Samuel Blatchford	1882–1893	11	Arthur
Lucius Q. C. Lamar	1888–1893	5	Cleveland
Melville W. Fuller	1888–1910	21	Cleveland
David J. Brewer	1890–1910	20	B. Harrison
Henry B. Brown	1890–1906	16	B. Harrison
George Shiras, Jr.	1892–1903	10	B. Harrison
Howell E. Jackson	1893–1895	2	B. Harrison
Edward D. White	1894–1910	16	Cleveland
Rufus W. Peckham	1895–1909	14	Cleveland
Joseph McKenna	1898–1925	26	McKinley
Oliver W. Holmes, Jr.	1902–1932	30	T. Roosevelt
William R. Day	1903–1922	19	T. Roosevelt
William H. Moody	1906–1910	3	T. Roosevelt
Horace H. Lurton	1910–1914	4	Taft
Charles E. Hughes	1910–1916	5	Taft
Willis Van Devanter	1911–1937	26	Taft
Joseph R. Lamar	1911–1916	5	Taft
Edward D. White	1910–1921	11	Taft
Mahlon Pitney	1912–1922	10	Taft
James C. McReynolds	1914–1941	26	Wilson
Louis D. Brandeis	1916–1939	22	Wilson
John H. Clarke	1916–1922	6	Wilson
William H. Taft	1921–1930	8	Harding
George Sutherland	1922–1938	15	Harding
Pierce Butler	1922–1939	16	Harding
Edward T. Sanford	1923–1930	7	Harding
Harlan F. Stone	1925–1941	16	Coolidge
Charles E. Hughes	1930–1941	11	Hoover
Owen J. Roberts	1930–1945	15	Hoover
Benjamin N. Cardozo	1932–1938	6	Hoover
Hugo L. Black	1937–1971	34	F. Roosevelt
Stanley F. Reed	1938–1957	19	F. Roosevelt
Felix Frankfurter	1939–1962	23	F. Roosevelt
William O. Douglas	1939–1975	36	F. Roosevelt
Frank Murphy	1940–1949	9	F. Roosevelt
Harlan F. Stone	1941–1946	5	F. Roosevelt
James F. Byrnes	1941–1942	1	F. Roosevelt
Robert H. Jackson	1941–1954	13	F. Roosevelt
Wiley B. Rutledge	1943–1949	6	F. Roosevelt

(continued)

Justices of the U.S. Supreme Court *(continued)*

Chief Justices appear in bold type

	Term of Service	Years of Service	Appointed by
Harold H. Burton	1945–1958	13	Truman
Fred M. Vinson	1946–1953	7	Truman
Tom C. Clark	1949–1967	18	Truman
Sherman Minton	1949–1956	7	Truman
Earl Warren	1953–1969	16	Eisenhower
John Marshall Harlan	1955–1971	16	Eisenhower
William J. Brennan, Jr.	1956–1990	34	Eisenhower
Charles E. Whittaker	1957–1962	5	Eisenhower
Potter Stewart	1958–1981	23	Eisenhower
Byron R. White	1962–1993	31	Kennedy
Arthur J. Goldberg	1962–1965	3	Kennedy
Abe Fortas	1965–1969	4	Johnson
Thurgood Marshall	1967–1994	24	Johnson
Warren E. Burger	1969–1986	18	Nixon
Harry A. Blackmun	1970–1994	24	Nixon
Lewis F. Powell, Jr.	1971–1987	15	Nixon
William H. Rehnquist[2]	1971–2005	34	Nixon
John P. Stevens III	1975–	—	Ford
Sandra Day O'Connor	1981–	—	Reagan
Antonin Scalia	1986–	—	Reagan
Anthony M. Kennedy	1988–	—	Reagan
David Souter	1990–	—	G. H. Bush
Clarence Thomas	1991–	—	G. H. Bush
Ruth Bader Ginsburg	1993–	—	Clinton
Stephen G. Breyer	1994–	—	Clinton
John G. Roberts, Jr.	2005–	—	G. W. Bush

[2]Chief Justice from 1986 (Reagan administration).

KEY TERMS

3-D
Short for three-dimensional movies, colloquial reference to one of the gimmicks with which the movie industry responded when television viewing cut sharply into movie attendance. Using two cameras and providing special plastic and cardboard "glasses" to customers, the studios produced a three-dimensional effect much like the stereopticon viewers of the late nineteenth century.

A Century of Dishonor
Influential book published in 1881 by Helen Hunt Jackson. It traced the history of United States treatment of Indians as a series of treaties repeatedly violated not by the tribes but by the U.S. government. Jackson's book contributed to a groundswell of sympathy for Indians in the East that led directly to the Dawes Severalty Act of 1887.

abolition
Declaration of slavery's illegality by the government, as opposed to manumission, which refers to the freeing of individual slaves. In the years after the Revolution, all of the northern states abolished slavery.

Adams, Samuel (1722–1803)
Protest leader in Boston who may have been instrumental in escalating resentment of British policies to full-blown rebellion. He failed to arouse the city after the Boston Massacre but conceived of and organized the Boston Tea Party that led directly to open warfare.

Adams-Oñis Treaty (1819)
A diplomatic triumph for Secretary of State John Quincy Adams. Spain sold Florida to the United States for $5 million. Adams's only concession to Spain was to agree to the Spanish version of the border between Spanish Texas and Louisiana.

Alamo
The name given to an old, largely abandoned mission compound in San Antonio, Texas. (Alamo means "cottonwood tree.") It became the symbol of Texan independence when, in March 1836, Mexican president Santa Anna defeated a handful of defenders there and executed the survivors. Less than two weeks later, Santa Anna massacred other Texas rebels at Goliad, but somehow they are not so well remembered.

Algonkian
Linguists' names to the three major language families of the Eastern Woodlands Indians. There was also a distinct tribe in Canada the French called Algonquin.

America First Committee
Influential organization opposing American intervention in World War II. Motivated by hostility to the Soviet Union, Anglophobia, or the belief that Britain was doomed to lose the war, the Committee opposed President Roosevelt's massive aid to Great Britain until the Japanese attack of Pearl Harbor ended the debate.

American Colonization Society
Founded in 1817 to help free blacks emigrate to West Africa. The society hoped that by answering slave owners' fears of a large free black population in the United States, they would be encouraged to free their slaves. Presidents Madison and Monroe supported it, as did other prominent southerners like John Marshall and Henry Clay.

American Independent party
Third party organized by Alabama Governor George Wallace to contest the 1968 election. Wallace hoped to unite southern whites disturbed by civil rights legislation and northern working-class whites resentful of what they considered special privileges extended to minorities.

American Railway Union
Apparently successful union of railroad workers led by Eugene V. Debs (later the head of the Socialist Party of America). The ARU was destroyed by federal intervention when its members supported strikers at the Pullman Palace Car Company in 1894.

"American style," the
A term used by British military officers, often disdainfully, for the adoption by colonials of Indian methods of making war: concealment, ambush, raids, and undisciplined individual action in battle.

American System
The name Henry Clay gave to his comprehensive Federalist-like program to reconcile the sometimes conflicting economic interests of Northeast, West, and South. Clay's "system" included federally financed internal improvements on a massive scale, a somewhat liberalized federal land policy, a high protective tariff to subsidize the development of manufacturing, and the Second Bank of the United States to moderate the nation's financial institutions.

Amherst, Jeffery (1717–1797)
British general, the commander of troops in North America in the French and Indian War who turned the tide of the war in Britain's favor. Later he refused to command British troops against Americans in the War for Independence.

Anaconda Plan
Name given to the blockade of the Confederacy General Winfield Scott proposed in 1861. Ridiculed at first, the blockade was adopted after the Union defeat at Bull Run. By the end of the war, the blockade had, like the constrictor snake, asphyxiated the southern economy.

annulment
Declaration by a religious or civil authority that an apparent marriage between a man and a woman was, in fact, never a valid marriage, as opposed to a divorce, which dissolves a valid marriage. Roman Catholics were (and are) not permitted to divorce; their marriages can be annulled for one of several specified reasons.

Anti-Masonic party
Founded in 1826 after the murder of a man who had published a book about the Masonic Order's secret rituals, it was a single-issue party aimed at destroying what seemed like the pervasive power of a sinister conspiracy. Briefly, the party had astonishing success, peaking in 1832 when it elected more than fifty congressmen. Most Anti-Masons became Whigs when that party was organized.

Arnold, Benedict (1741–1801)
One of the few well-trained, professional soldiers in the colonies at the outbreak of the Revolution. In 1775, in uneasy cooperation with Vermont militia leader Ethan Allen, he captured Fort Ticonderoga and several other frontier forts from the British. In 1776 he led a poorly planned, provisioned, and executed attack on Montreal and Quebec. A hero of the Battle of Saratoga in 1777, he believed he had been passed over for promotion and attempted to betray West Point to the British. His name became synonymous with "traitor."

assumption
The second part of Secretary of the Treasury Alexander Hamilton's financial (and political) program, the assumption of all state debts by the federal government. Hamilton overcame the opposition of Virginians James Madison and Thomas Jefferson by offering to use his influence to locate the permanent national capital on the Potomac River.

Atlanta Compromise
A "compact" between southern whites and blacks proposed by African-American educator Booker T. Washington in 1895. Blacks would accept social discrimination if they were provided opportunities to improve their economic lot by learning technical skills. Most southern blacks and middle- and upper-class whites supported the Atlanta Compromise. It had no effect on lower-class whites' often violent racism.

baby boom
Term coined to describe the soaring birthrate that began in 1946 when young couples separated by World War II were reunited. Demographers expected the spike in the birthrate to be brief, but births remained high until 1964.

Baker, Ray Stannard (1870–1946)
One of the most responsible investigators (and best writers) among the muckraking

journalists, Baker was critical of the Jim Crow segregation laws that were being enacted across the South at the turn of the century with progressive support. He became a devoted protégé of Woodrow Wilson and wrote an admiring biography of him.

Barbary Pirates
Commerce raiders sanctioned by the rulers of the Barbary States of North Africa (Morocco, Algiers, Tunis, Tripoli). They seized merchants of countries that did not pay an annual tribute. The United States sometimes paid the tribute but several times attempted to end the Barbary Pirate menace by bombarding and raiding their bases.

Bataan Death March
Forced march in 1942 of 10,000 American and Filipino prisoners of the Japanese up the Bataan Peninsula in the Philippines to prison camps in the interior. Japanese contempt for soldiers who surrendered resulted in deliberate starvation, beating, and even murder of the men. About 1,000 men died on the march. Another 5,000 died in the camps before the end of the war. The survivors were living skeletons, like the inmates of Nazi concentration camps.

Battle of Saratoga
On October 17, 1777, after several weeks of battling, British General John Burgoyne surrendered his entire army of redcoats and Hessians to General Horatio Gates near what is now the resort town of Saratoga, New York. Armies did not often surrender in the eighteenth century; they retreated to fight another day. Partly because of his own bad luck and partly because he was not reinforced as he expected, Burgoyne was trapped in the wilderness. The American victory was so momentous it brought France into the war.

Battle of the Bulge
Completely unforeseen German counteroffensive in Belgium in December 1944 aimed at splitting the Allied forces and capturing Antwerp, which was the key port in the Allies' supply line. The attack was initially successful, driving a large "bulge" in Allied lines.

Battle of the Little Big Horn
Greatest single victory by Plains Indians during the wars with the U.S. Cavalry. In June 1876 Colonel George Armstrong Custer led 250 men into a trap set by several thousand Sioux and Cheyenne warriors, who killed every soldier.

Battle of Yorktown
Only the second time during the War of Independence that a British army surrendered. General Charles Cornwallis was trapped on the Yorktown peninsula because three columns of American and French troops moved quickly to cut off any escape by land and a French fleet from the West Indies arrived to prevent British ships from evacuating Cornwallis by sea. The British surrendered in October 1781.

Benton, Thomas Hart (1782–1858)
Senator from Missouri between 1820 and 1851. He was a tireless spokesman on behalf of small family farmers. A personal enemy of Andrew Jackson (they were involved in a gunfight), he reconciled with Jackson when Jackson was elected president in 1828, and was one of his most valuable supporters in Congress.

Beringia
Scientific name (after Danish explorer Vitus Bering) for the "land bridge" between Siberia and Alaska during the last Ice Age over which human beings first crossed to the Americas.

Berkeley, Sir William (1606–1677)
Royal governor of Virginia (1642–1652, 1660–1677), he promoted emigration, particularly among Anglican gentry, and governed Virginia autocratically with the support of the wealthiest planters. Forced to flee a rebellion led by Nathaniel Bacon in 1676, he returned and hanged so many of Bacon's followers that King Charles II removed him from office.

Bessemer process
Technique of making steel from iron cheaply by blasting molten iron so that impurities (except for a precise quantity of carbon) were oxidized. It was developed simultaneously in the 1850s by Henry Bessemer in England and William Kelly in the United States. Although it was universally called the "Bessemer process," the U.S. Patent Office recognized Kelly as the earlier inventor.

Bethune, Mary McLeod (1875–1955)
African-American educator, the daughter of former slaves, she and Eleanor Roosevelt became close personal friends. As head of the Negro Affairs Division of the National Youth Administration, Bethune was the highest-ranking African American in the Roosevelt administration.

Biddle, Nicholas (1786–1844)
President of the Second Bank of the United States between 1823 and 1836. Biddle was a conservative and responsible banker who transformed the B.U.S., after poor beginnings, into a valuable regulatory institution. As a politician, however, Biddle was inept. He boasted not only of his power, but of the mischief he could cause if he chose to act irresponsibly. His arrogance played into the hands of the anti-Bank Jacksonians, who argued that, in a democracy, no private institution should have such power.

black codes
Laws enacted in 1865 by former Confederate states considered by President Johnson to be restored to the Union. Although they varied in details from state to state, all of the black codes reduced African Americans to a social and civil status inferior to that of whites. Northern anger over the black codes contributed to the defeat of Johnson's Reconstruction policies.

Black Friday
September 24, 1869. The price of gold plunged in hours from $162 an ounce to $135 when President Grant dumped $4 million in government gold on the market. Businesses were wiped out by the thousands. Tens of thousands of working people lost their jobs. The panic was brief but serious.

black power
Rallying cry coined by Stokely Carmichael, militant head of the Student Nonviolent Coordinating Committee during the mid-1960s. The slogan was used by diverse groups and individuals and meant many things ranging from black separatism to bloc voting.

Bleeding Kansas
Antislavery northerners' political reference to the violence in Kansas Territory between free-state and slave-state settlers that began in the wake of the Kansas–Nebraska Act of 1854.

bloody shirt
Republican party political appeal to voters of the Civil War generation. When orators "waved the bloody shirt," they reminded voters of the deaths and maimings in the war that was caused by the South, and that the Democratic party was the party of the South.

Blue Eagle
The symbol of the National Recovery Administration (NRA). For a year, during popular enthusiasm for the NRA's close regulation of businesses large and small, the Blue Eagle was ubiquitous in the United States.

blue laws
Laws regulating moral behavior such as activities forbidden on the Lord's Day, Sunday. Every American colony enacted them. The Puritan colonies of Massachusetts and Connecticut had the most comprehensive codes and were most rigorous in enforcing the laws.

Bonus Boys
World War I veterans who, in the summer of 1932, came by the thousands to Washington in an attempt to pressure Congress and the president to give them immediately as a Depression relief measure a bonus of $1,000 due them by law for their military service in 1945. President Hoover ordered General Douglas MacArthur to evict them from government buildings. MacArthur exceeded his instructions and attacked the Bonus Boys' Hooverville. The incident destroyed what was left of Hoover's reputation.

Booth, John Wilkes (1838–1865)
Well-known actor, a fanatical pro-Confederate, Booth organized a conspiracy to kill the leading members of the Lincoln administration after the fall of Richmond. Only he succeeded—in killing President Lincoln.

border ruffians

Name given by abolitionists and Free Soilers to western Missourians who regularly crossed the border into Kansas Territory to vote in territorial elections and bully free-state settlers.

Boulder Dam (Hoover Dam)

Colossal concrete dam on the Colorado River between Arizona and Nevada that is still one of the civil engineering wonders of the century. It is 700 feet high and spans 1,200 feet. The water in Lake Meade behind the dam irrigates farms in three states and Mexico. The power generated by the dam made possible the growth of Las Vegas, Nevada.

"bounty jumpers"

Professional deserters, more a problem in the Union than in the Confederacy. They enlisted in units that paid recruits a cash bounty, quickly deserted, and enlisted, for another bounty, in another unit.

Bourbons

Name given to the Democratic party political bosses of the southern states during the late nineteenth century; "Bourbon" was a reference to the family name of the kings of old-regime France, whose rule was synonymous with extreme conservatism. The Bourbons were displaced in some states in the 1890s by populistic Democrats, who assailed them for neglecting the needs of poor white southerners.

Bradley Martin ball

Extravagant high-society costume ball in New York in January 1897 during the depths of a serious depression, it was denounced as callous by moralists and as foolish by some business leaders, notably the great banker J. P. Morgan.

Brant, Joseph (1742–1807)

A Mohawk (his Iroquois name was Thayendanegea) who was an Anglican and related by marriage to a British official, he convinced most of his tribe to ally with the British against the Revolutionaries. He was the joint commander of a force that was defeated at Fort Stanwix when it tried to join Burgoyne's army at Saratoga.

brinkmanship

"The ability to get to the verge without getting into war" to further American foreign policy goals in the words of its chief exponent, 1950s Secretary of State John Foster Dulles. In the Cold War nuclear standoff the practice of brinkmanship did not allow much margin for miscalculation.

broad construction

A term applied later to Alexander Hamilton's contention that any action not explicitly forbidden to the federal government by the Constitution was constitutional. It became a unifying principle of the Federalist Party. Opposition to broad construction contributed to the emergence of the Jefferson Republican party.

Brown v. School Board of Topeka

Historic unanimous Court decision of 1954 that ruled racially segregated "separate but equal" schools, and by implication other racially discriminatory public institutions, to violate the constitutional rights of African Americans.

Buffalo Soldiers

Plains Indians' name for the African-American soldiers of the Ninth and Tenth Cavalry Regiments. Although other explanations of the name have been suggested, it almost certainly reflected the fact that the soldiers' nappy hair reminded straight-haired Indians of a bison's coat.

burned-over district

The name given to a swath of land across western New York that experienced one religious excitement after another in the 1820s, 1830s, and 1840s. It was a hotbed of religious mania and experimentation. Among the notable people who lived in the "district" were Charles Grandison Finney, William Miller, the Fox sisters, and Joseph Smith.

Calvert, George (1550?–1632)

and Cecilus Calvert (1605?–1675), father and son, the First and Second Lords Baltimore. Favorites at the court, they were Roman Catholic and envisioned their Maryland colony as a refuge for English Catholics, who were persecuted at home. All Christian worship was tolerated in Maryland under the Calverts.

carpetbaggers and scalawags

Derisive terms applied by southern Democrats to northerners who came to the South after the war to loot the defeated states (carpetbaggers) and southerners who betrayed the South and the white race to control the state governments by manipulating black voters (scalawags).

caucus

An Algonkian word adopted by Americans to mean a meeting of like-minded people to plan strategy for a common goal. Between 1804 and 1824 the Republican party named its presidential nominees in a caucus of the party's senators and representatives. (Until 1820 the Federalists did likewise.)

cavaliers

The name assumed by those who supported King Charles I in the English Civil War, it is an Anglicization of the French word for "knight." When they were defeated in the Civil War, many cavaliers of middling rank emigrated to Virginia to form the core of the Tidewater aristocracy.

Centennial Exposition

One of the earliest world's fairs, and the first in the United States, it was held in Philadelphia in 1876 to commemorate 100 years of independence. It is best known because its theme was American industry and technology. The telephone was first demonstrated at this exposition.

Central Powers

The name of the alliance of Germany, Austria–Hungary, and Italy in 1914. (Bulgaria was an associated nation.) The combination was opposed by the Allied Powers of Russia, France, and Britain. Many historians regard the existence of two hostile alliances of powerful countries as an important cause of World War I.

chads

A word known to few people before November 2000 when "chads" became central to determining the winner of the presidential election in Florida and, with Florida, the electoral college. A chad was the tiny piece of perforated paper popped out of punch card ballots used in some Florida election districts. Republicans claimed that if the chad was still clinging to the ballot, the ballot was invalid.

Channing, William Ellery (1780–1842)

Prominent Boston clergyman who, in 1819, denounced the Calvinist (Congregationalist) doctrine of predestination. He was instrumental in the founding of the American Unitarian Association in 1825 and became a moderate advocate of the abolition of slavery.

"China Lobby"

Name given (by its critics) to the not formally organized but active and influential network of prominent Americans who promoted Chiang Kai-shek as a great democratic leader who deserved massive American support in his civil war with the Chinese Communists. The "Lobby" included such people as Joseph Cardinal Spellman, Catholic archbishop of New York, and the publisher of *Time* and *Life* magazines, Henry Luce.

Citizen Genêt (1763–1834)

Edmond Charles Genêt, minister of France during the months President Washington was trying to keep the United States neutral in the war between France and Britain. Genêt commissioned Americans as French privateers, whose capture of British merchant ships caused Washington to order him to leave the country.

"Civil War Amendment"

Between 1804 and 1865, there were no amendments to the Constitution. Three amendments were rapidly ratified in the wake of the Civil War. The Thirteenth (1865) abolished slavery. The Fourteenth (1868) required the states to treat all citizens equally. The Fifteenth (1870) forbade denying the vote to any person on the basis of race, religion, or "previous condition of servitude"— that is, because citizens had been slaves.

Civilian Conservation Corps (CCC)

Created in 1933, the CCC provided jobs in national parks, national forests, and other federally owned lands. After initial anxieties, it was an extremely popular program. By the time it was disbanded in 1942, 500,000 men between the ages of 18 and 25 had passed through it.

civilized tribes," "the

A term applied to the Cherokee, Creek, Choctaw, and Chickasaw peoples of Georgia, Alabama, and Mississippi because they, unlike other tribes, were sedentary, farmed the land, and adopted other aspects of white American culture, including, in the case of the Cherokee, a comprehensive school system and newspapers. Although the civilized tribes disproved the rationale for removal—the incompatibility of white and Indian cultures—they too were forced off their lands.

Clinton, DeWitt (1769–1828)
Nephew of Jefferson's second vice president, Clinton was elected governor of New York in 1817. During the preceding decade he had been the chief promoter of a plan to join the Hudson River and Lake Erie with a canal more than 300 hundred miles long. After twice failing to win federal financial backing, he persuaded the New York legislature to fund "Clinton's Folly," the Erie Canal. The Erie Canal guaranteed that New York City would become—as it has remained—the nation's great metropolis.

Columbian Exchange
Term coined in the late twentieth century to describe the exchange, beginning in 1492, between the "Old World" (Europe, Africa, and Asia) and the "New World" of plants, animals, and micro-organisms previously known to only one of the "worlds."

Columbus, Christopher (1451?–1506)
Italian-born navigator who, in the employ of the queen of Castille (Spain), made a landfall in the Americas in 1492 while searching for a direct sea route to east Asia. He was the discoverer of America who "counted"; the European absorption of the Americas began with his voyage.

Committee on Public Information
Wartime agency headed by a progressive journalist, George Creel, the CPI censored war news in the interests of morale and also emphasized, through propaganda, the importance of universal patriotism, encouraging the suppression of dissent.

Common Sense
Pamphlet written by Thomas Paine and published in January 1776. In splendid prose, Paine vilified George III as a tyrant and condemned the institution of monarchy. It is generally agreed that the pamphlet was the single most persuasive propaganda in the debates of the Revolutionary era. Paine would write several more important works during the late 1700s.

Comstock, Anthony (1844–1915)
Anti-obscenity crusader who sponsored and wrote anti-obscenity laws in New York, Boston, and other cities, and even a federal law forbidding the use of the mails for distributing obscene materials. As a postal inspector, Comstock claimed to have destroyed 160 tons of obscene publications. His definition of obscenity included pamphlets explaining birth control methods. British playwright George Bernard Shaw coined the term "Comstockery" to describe excessive prudery.

Comstock Lode
The richest silver deposit in the United States, discovered—or rather recognized as silver—by gold miners in 1859. The principal town on the Comstock Lode was Virginia City, about midway between Reno and Carson City, Nevada. Virginia City produced silver well into the twentieth century.

conquistadores
Spanish for "conquerors." Beginning with the soldiers of Hernán Cortés, it was the name adopted by the men who won Mexico and Peru for Spain, as well as Spanish explorers who found no great kingdoms to conquer such as Francisco Coronado in the American Southwest.

containment
Name given to American policy toward the Soviet Union inspired by a memorandum by State Department officer George Kennan. Its purpose was to avoid war by measured responses to Soviet actions "containing" further Russian expansion.

copperheads
Strictly speaking, pro-Confederate northerners. However, Republicans used the term loosely to apply to Democrats who favored negotiation with the Confederacy or otherwise criticized Lincoln's policy so as to taint all critics with disloyalty.

Coral Sea
Site, off Australia, of the first great Japanese–American naval battle of World War II in early May 1942. The Japanese won a tactical victory, losing a light carrier but sinking an American fleet carrier. However, Coral Sea was a strategic defeat. Admiral Isoroku Yamamoto had not, as he hoped, cut the American supply line to Australia to force American and Australian troops to abandon Port Moresby in New Guinea.

corporate colony
A colony with a royal charter vesting governing powers in the shareholders of a commercial company. When landowners in corporate colonies became, in effect, the shareholders, corporate colonies were self-governing. Plymouth, Massachusetts Bay, Rhode Island, and Connecticut were such commonwealths for much of their history.

"corrupt bargain"
The charge hurled by Jacksonians at President John Quincy Adams and his secretary of state, Henry Clay, when the House of Representatives chose Adams over General Jackson in the skewed election of 1824. Jacksonians believed or, at least said, that in return for being named secretary of state, Clay used his influence in the House to have Adams chosen over Jackson.

Cortés, Hernán (1485–1547)
Spanish conqueror of Mexico, a bold soldier who combined the military superiority of his soldiers, shrewd diplomacy, and manipulation of the Aztec emperor Moctezuma to conquer the empire for Spain.

cotton diplomacy
Confederate president Jefferson Davis's attempt in 1861 to bring Great Britain into the war on the southern side by creating a shortage of raw cotton on which the British textile industry depended. Davis kept the 1860 crop off the market. The strategy failed.

"cotton Whigs" and "conscience Whigs"
Terms applied during the 1850s to northern Whig politicians who were abolitionists (conscience Whigs) and those who hoped to downplay slavery and the sectional split as political issues because of the importance of southern cotton to northern industry—and because they hoped to avoid the split of the Whig party along sectional lines.

coverture
The English legal principle defining the status, in the law, of married women. When a woman married, her legal person was subsumed into her husband's. She was obligated to obey him; he controlled (although he did not legally own) any property she had held before the marriage.

Coxey, Jacob S. (1854–1951)
Wealthy businessman of Massillon, Ohio, who in 1894 led a march of the unemployed to Washington to petition for inflation of the nation's money supply and a massive public works program to create jobs. Although the march was well publicized for six weeks, Congress and the president ignored Coxey. He was arrested in the capital for a trivial offense.

crafts unions
Labor organizations comprising exclusively skilled workers such as locomotive engineers, carpenters, plumbers, iron molders, and so on. Crafts unions were generally successful in forcing employers to negotiate wages, hours, and job conditions.

Crawford, William F. (1772–1834)
Georgia politician; secretary of the treasury in 1824; considered the Virginia Dynasty candidate when the Republican caucus nominated him to stand for the presidency. His support was mostly restricted to the southern states.

CREEP
Phonetic acronym of the Committee to Reelect the President, President Nixon's campaign organization in 1972. The men caught burglarizing the Democratic party's national headquarters were CREEP employees, a revelation that eventually led to the president's downfall.

Crime of '73," "the
Name given to the Demonetization Act of 1873 by advocates of bimetallism, money redeemable in either gold or silver coin. The Demonetization Act, which terminated silver coinage, was motivated by the fact that national silver production was low in 1873 and the market price of the metal so high that few producers were presenting it to the U.S. mint at the government's submarket buying price. It was called a "crime" only several years later, when silver production had soared and the price of silver had declined.

dark horse candidate
A major party's candidate for the presidency who had not been considered a possible

nominee, but who was selected by the party when it was unable to agree on serious contenders. In 1844 James K. Polk of Tennessee was the Democratic party's dark horse candidate when delegates who favored the annexation of Texas refused to accept Martin Van Buren, the party's most prominent leader. In 1883 the Republicans chose a dark horse candidate, James A. Garfield, when the convention deadlocked among three nominees who were bitterly opposed to one another.

de Champlain, Samuel (1570?–1635)
Founder of Quebec and, thereby, of the French empire in North America. He was the first governor of New France (Canada).

de Gardoqui, Diego
A Spanish diplomat who tried to divide the commercial northern states from the agricultural states by proposing to the Confederation Congress that Spain would open her colonies to American merchants if the United States gave up its treaty rights to navigate the Mississippi River. Northerners wanted to accept the offer; southerners and westerners threatened to break up the Confederation if the deal was made. The Mississippi was vital to them.

debt bondage
The plight of many southern tenant farmers, both black and white, in the final decades of the nineteenth century and well into the twentieth. Because of declining cotton and corn prices, tenants found themselves in debt to merchants (who were often their landlords) even after selling the year's crop, and therefore unable to terminate their tenancies. Debt put them in bondage.

Declaratory Act
Enacted by Parliament in March 1766, on the same day the Stamp Act was repealed, it stated Parliament's constitutional right to tax colonials. It was both a face-saving action and an assertion of a principle on which a large majority of members of Parliament agreed.

Democratic-Republicans
(and National-Republicans)
In 1828 there was just one political party, the Republicans. There were, however, two factions. Andrew Jackson's backers, with John C. Calhoun and Martin Van Buren, Jackson's southern and northern lieutenants, called themselves Democratic-Republicans. They were, by their own definition, the party of democracy. John Quincy Adams's supporters—his chief lieutenant was Henry Clay—called themselves National-Republicans to emphasize both Adams's and Clay's commitment to energetic national government. The Democratic-Republicans became the Democratic Party. The National-Republicans later became Whigs.

détente
The Nixon–Kissinger policy toward the Soviet Union and China: a realistic recognition that maintaining Cold War hostility indefinitely meant risking nuclear war and, in the meantime, involved the great powers in expensive, self-destructive limited wars, like the war in Vietnam. Détente did not end the Cold War as Nixon and Kissinger had hoped. Soviet leader Leonid Breszhnev and presidents Jimmy Carter and Ronald Reagan scuttled it.

Dillinger, John (1903–1934)
One of several midwestern bank robbers of the Great Depression who became something of a popular hero, in part because he cultivated a Robin Hood image, "robbing the rich and giving to the poor."

dime novels
Brief, cheaply produced, sensationalistic adventure books of the late nineteenth century often about western heroes, sometimes real people like James B. "Wild Bill" Hickok and William F. "Buffalo Bill" Cody. They were aimed at adolescent boys but were read by a great many adults and, certainly, adolescent girls too.

discretionary income
An individual's or household's income in excess of what is needed for necessities— "spending money." Traditional American culture prescribed that such money be saved or invested. In the 1920s people were encouraged to spend it on consumer goods. A considerable rise in discretionary income during and after World War II was the key to the consumption that has driven the American economy since.

dot.coms
Colloquial term for Internet companies that attracted billions in investment during a speculative mania in the late 1990s. A majority of them collapsed, many disappearing completely, in 2000–2001, wiping out the money invested in them.

"doughface"
Contemptuous name applied by antislavery northerners to northern Democrats who supported the South in sectional issues: "a northern man with southern principles." The implication was that they kneaded their faces, like dough, to appear to be one thing before northerners and another before southerners. Presidents Pierce and Buchanan were doughfaces; the greatest of the doughfaces was Stephen A. Douglas, and his attempt to mollify sectionalists in North and South was his undoing.

Douglas, Stephen A. (1813–1861)
Perhaps the most capable Democratic politician of the 1850s, he would certainly have been a more constructive president than either Franklin Pierce or James Buchanan, both of whom the party chose in preference to him. Determined to soothe sectional animosities, Douglas aggravated them so badly with his Kansas–Nebraska Act of 1854 that, even in 1860, when he might well have won the presidential election, southern Democrats rejected him and split the party.

Drake, Francis (1540?–1596)
English adventurer, commander of the second voyage around the world, the greatest of the "sea dogs." His seizures of Spanish ships and raids of Spanish seaports were so bold and damaging that the Spanish invested him with diabolical powers. He was a major figure in organizing England's defense against the Spanish Armada.

DuBois, W. E. B. (1868–1963)
African-American scholar and civil rights activist, he opposed Booker T. Washington's "Atlanta Compromise," instead urging blacks to demand full civil rights. DuBois believed that the future of African Americans depended on the creation of an educated elite, "the talented tenth." He was for many years editor of the *Crisis,* the journal of the National Association for the Advancement of Colored People.

"dumbbell" tenement
Winning design in a competition to find a healthful apartment building affordable by the poor. James E. Ware's dumbbell, so-called because of its shape from above, provided a window for every apartment. Unfortunately, when dumbbell tenements were constructed next to one another, the ventilation shaft between them was so narrow as to defeat the purpose of the design.

durante vita
Latin, a legal term meaning "throughout life." In Maryland and Virginia during the 1650s and 1660s, it was applied to Africans in servitude, explicitly defining them, on the basis of their race, as slaves.

Dust Bowl
A broad belt in the heart of the country extending from the Dakotas to Texas where, in 1935, after a prolonged drought, winds whipped the powdery topsoil into the air, where it was so dense that visibility in the worst-hit areas was reduced to ten feet for days at a time. The worst part of the Dust Bowl was in northern Texas and western Oklahoma.

dynamic conservatism
Dwight D. Eisenhower's "philosophy" of government in 1953. The words had little meaning; Eisenhower was a pragmatic president without an ideology who meant only to scale back the size of the government the New Deal and World War II had created.

East India Company
Trading corporation organized in 1600 much like the Virginia and Plymouth companies that founded the first English colonies in North America. Unlike them, the East India Company succeeded and, by 1773, was governing much of the Indian subcontinent. Parliament's Tea Act, which led to rebellion in the American colonies, was enacted to help the East India Company out of serious financial difficulties.

Eaton, Peggy (O'Neill)
The wife of Jackson's Secretary of War, John Eaton, whose reputation for sexual license caused her social ostracism by the wives of the members of Jackson's cabinet. The tempest in Washington society virtually immobilized

the administration and threatened to shatter the recently built Democratic party coalition. In providing Jackson with a way out of the mess that offended no one, Martin Van Buren won the president's favor and, in time, Jackson's selection of him as his successor.

Eighteenth Amendment
The Prohibition amendment that forbade the manufacture, sale, transportation, and importation of intoxicating liquors in the United States.

El
Short for "elevated," or elevated railway; a solution to rapid, long-distance transportation in big cities. Pulled by steam locomotives in the nineteenth century, the passenger trains ran on iron and steel structures along principal streets, leaving the roadways below to pedestrians and horses and wagons. They were too expensive for all but the largest cities such as New York, Chicago, and Philadelphia.

Elizabeth (1533–1603, reigned 1558–1603)
Queen of England during the era in which England, previously a nation of secondary importance in Europe, began its rise to the rank of the world's great powers. The first English attempts to found colonies in North America occurred during the "Elizabethan Age."

Emancipation Proclamation
Presidential order of September 22, 1862, stating that all slaves in territory controlled by rebels as of January 1, 1863, were henceforth free under American law. Lincoln hoped the proclamation might induce Confederates to make peace before 1863 as their best chance to retain their slaves.

enclosure movement
The practice of landowners in England from the sixteenth through the eighteenth centuries of enclosing with hedges fields previously devoted to crops, thus converting them into pasture for sheep. Farmers were thrown off the land that once supported them and formed a large impoverished class from which many settlers of the colonies were drawn.

Enlightenment
Term applied to the emergence of rationalism among educated Europeans and colonials in the late seventeenth and eighteenth centuries, and the decline of traditional nonrational religious beliefs among them.

enumerated articles
Colonial exports that could be shipped only to England even if their ultimate destinations were elsewhere. They were the colonies' most valuable and most easily sold produce: tobacco, cotton, sugar.

factory system
Manufacturing goods by machinery in watermill-powered (later steam-powered) factories by employees working full-time for wages. It replaced the "putting out system," hand manufacture at home, usually part-time

as a supplement to farming and paid for by the "piece," the amount produced. The invention of powered machinery that replaced dozens, even hundreds of home workers made "cottage industry" obsolete in most kinds of manufacture.

farmers' Alliances
Farmers organizations of the 1880s, originally nonpolitical but, by 1890, active proponents of several reforms. There were three Alliances with more than a million members each: a "Colored Farmers" Alliance and a white organization in the South, and a white Alliance in the West.

favorite son
Candidate for a party's presidential nomination who is not a serious contender but who is nominated by a state as a personal honor or as a compromise possibility in a convention that deadlocks between two (or more) serious candidates. A favorite son candidate differs from a dark horse candidate in that the former's name is put into nomination from the start of a convention. Franklin Pierce was a favorite son candidate to whom the Democrats turned in 1852.

Federal Reserve System
Created in 1913, it was a network of regional Federal Reserve Banks governed by a board of directors, most of whom were named by the president, with the power to regulate the money supply by setting the interest rates at which state banks borrowed money. The Federal Reserve was designed to give the government a say in banking decisions previously in the hands of the great New York private banks like J. P. Morgan. The Federal Reserve was a partial return to what Hamilton had envisioned in the Bank of the United States.

Field, Cyrus (1819–1892)
Successful self-made businessman (a paper manufacturer) who became obsessed with the idea of telegraphically linking the United States and Europe by means of a transatlantic cable. He sank his fortune and other large investments into several attempts between 1857 and 1866, succeeding in the latter year.

"Fifty-Four Forty or Fight!"
A popular slogan in 1845, this referred to the northern boundary of the Oregon Country (the southern boundary of Russian Alaska) at 54° 40' north latitude. If Great Britain did not yield the whole of Oregon, the United States would go to war. President Polk used the patriotic hysteria behind the slogan but had no intention of going to war with Britain in an attempt to win the northern part of Oregon (now British Columbia), where there was no American presence worth mentioning. He persuaded the British to divide the Oregon Country at the Webster–Ashburton line, 49° north latitude, which is the present Canadian–American border.

fire-eaters
A name applied to young southern politicians of the 1850s for whom the defense of slavery

and the denunciation of antislavery northerners (in inflammatory words) was the heart of their politics. Commonly, they threatened secession from the Union when they believed slavery was threatened or the honor of white southerners insulted.

Fiske, John (1842–1901)
A Harvard historian who was the leading exponent of social Darwinism, the philosophy of Herbert Spencer, in the United States. Spencer's interest was in relationships within a society. He coined the phrase *survival of the fittest,* justifying as natural the fact that some grew extremely wealthy while masses languished in poverty. Fiske applied this harsh principle to relations among the peoples—the "races"—of the world. That the white race dominated other races, he said, was not unjust or immoral, but the natural outcome of white superiority.

Fitzhugh, George (1806–1881)
Southern lawyer whose books combined praise of slavery as a benign institution and condemnation of the materialism of the North with its exploitation of free wage workers. He was a major proponent of the "positive good" proslavery argument.

Five Nations
Another name for the Iroquois Confederation of New York; the nations were the Mohawk, Senecas, Onandagas, Oneidas, and Cayugas. During the seventeenth century they were invaluable allies of the English colonies against the French.

flexible response
The Kennedy administration's alternative to the Eisenhower–Dulles Soviet policy of brinkmanship and "massive retaliation." The United States would respond to Soviet (or Chinese) provocations not with empty threats of all-out war but in proportion to the seriousness of the provocations, openly or covertly.

Florida land boom
Runaway speculation of the mid-1920s in land on Florida's Atlantic shore, especially in Miami Beach. Land prices reached absurd levels and then collapsed suddenly, wiping out millions of dollars. Despite the hard-hitting lesson in the inevitable consequences of irrational speculation, hundreds of thousands of Americans immediately began to speculate in stocks.

Fort Ross
Russian stockade and village built on the Pacific Ocean deep within Spanish Alta California in 1812. Russian expansion far to the south of Alaska worried John Quincy Adams. Fort Ross was a major reason for the proclamation of the Monroe Doctrine. The Russians hoped to supply Alaska with foodstuffs produced at Fort Ross. In 1839 they found another source of supply and abandoned the fort.

Foster, Stephen Collins (1826–1864)
The first writer of popular songs to be recognized as an individual. Despite the

fact that he endlessly polished his lyrics before publishing his songs, Foster was a prolific musician and writer. He wrote many kinds of music, including genteel "parlor songs" for middle-class families. However, he was best known for songs, some in dialect, written for minstrel shows, which he insisted should not be called "Ethiopian songs," which he regarded as demeaning. Foster meant to humanize African-American slaves and their relationships.

Fourteen Points, the
President Woodrow Wilson's list of American goals in the treaties that would end World War I. Most points were specific but expressed Wilson's ideals of national self-determination, freedom of the seas, and an organization of nations that would prevent future wars.

freedmen
Former slaves who were freed by the Emancipation Proclamation and the Thirteenth Amendment. The term referred to all former slaves—children and women as well as men.

Freedmen's Bureau
Federal agency administered by the army, established in March 1865. Its purpose was to provide food, clothing, and medical treatment to former slaves and white refugees and to supervise the distribution of small farms carved out of abandoned and confiscated lands. President Johnson's July 1866 veto of a bill extending the life of the Freedmen's Bureau transformed the tension between the president and congressional Republicans into open political conflict.

Freeman, Elizabeth
A slave in Massachusetts called "Mumber" or "Mumbet" who sued her master for her freedom on the grounds that the state constitution declared that "all men are born free and equal." She won her case; the judges freed all slaves in Massachusetts.

Freeport Doctrine
Propounded by Stephen A. Douglas in a debate with Abraham Lincoln at Freeport, Illinois. Although the *Dred Scott* decision said that territorial legislatures could not prohibit slavery, Douglas argued that a territory could keep slave owners out by failing to enact laws protecting property rights in slaves.

Friedan, Betty (1921–)
Author of *The Feminine Mystique,* published in 1963. It was scathingly critical of the social and cultural role assigned to middle-class women in the 1950s: lively housewife–mother and sexually attractive helpmate to her husband. Friedan became famous overnight and in 1966 was one of the founders of the National Organization of Women, which spearheaded the new feminism of the later twentieth century.

Fugitive Slave Act
One of the provisions of the North–South Compromise of 1850, it was designed to foil the underground railroad by which 1,000 to 1,500 slaves were escaping their masters each year. Antislavery northern state judges who had frustrated attempts to return runaway slaves were bypassed by the creation of federal commissioners who ruled on the claims of slave owners and slave catchers and assisted them. Northerners who aided runaway slaves were fined and jailed. The Fugitive Slave Act of 1850 meant that it was not enough for runaway slaves to escape to a free state; they had to get beyond the reach of American law, to Canada.

funding
The foundation of Hamilton's financial plan for the new government: the federal government would establish its credit by repaying the Confederation debt in full at face value. Speaker of the House James Madison opposed rewarding speculators by paying them on a par with payments to patriots who had lent the government money during the Revolution. But Hamilton won in Congress.

G.I.s
The name for themselves adopted by World War II soldiers. It referred to "government issue," the bureaucratic term for uniforms and other equipment handed out to recruits. It was the equivalent of the World War I term "doughboy."

"gag rule"
Derogatory term for a rule adopted by the House of Representatives in 1836 to table—that is, not to consider—abolitionist petitions presented to Congress. Congressman John Quincy Adams, while finding the abolitionists disruptive, insisted they had a right to be heard and eloquently fought against the gag rule.

Gage, General Thomas (1721–1787)
Commander of the British army in America named royal governor of Massachusetts in 1774 in the wake of the Boston Tea Party and the Coercive (Intolerable) Acts. Tragically for Gage, who was married to an American woman and sympathetic to Americans (he had lived in the colonies since 1763), it fell to him to administer policies that led to rebellion. His troops called him "Tommy the Old Woman" because of his reluctance to take aggressive action against the rebels, which was a reflection of his hopes that the dispute could be resolved without war.

GAR
The Grand Army of the Republic, a Union veterans' association (the equivalent of the Veterans of Foreign Wars today), founded in 1866, was a social organization and officially nonpolitical. In fact, it was a Republican party auxiliary, promoting pensions for veterans, a Republican issue. Its membership peaked in 1900 at 400,000.

Garvey, Marcus (1887–1940)
A Jamaica-born journalist who opened the United Negro Improvement Association (UNIA) in New York in 1916. He called for separation of the black and white races and a black "return" to Africa. Garvey was quite popular among African Americans in New York and other northern cities; but in 1923 the federal government imprisoned him for mail fraud, and the UNIA fell apart.

Gaspée
A royal schooner stationed in Narraganset Bay to collect customs and catch smugglers. When chasing suspected smugglers in 1772, the *Gaspée* ran aground. At night, it was boarded by colonials and burned, an act of rebellion. An intensive investigation failed to turn up a single witness willing to incriminate any of the arsonists.

Geneva Accords
International agreement of 1954 on the future of newly independent Vietnam. For two years the Communist-dominated Viet Minh would administer the northern half of the country, anti-Communist nationalists the south. In 1956 a democratic election would establish the nation's permanent government. The elections were never held when, with American backing, South Vietnam refused to participate.

ghettos
In its most common American usage, urban ethnic neighborhoods inhabited largely by members of a single national, cultural, or linguistic group. The original ghetto, in Venice, Italy, was the part of the city in which Jews were required to reside.

Gibson girl
The "ideal woman" of the 1890s, both in the fashions she wore and in her active lifestyle. The confident, glamorous Gibson girl was named after an illustrator, Charles Dana Gibson, who drew her in various situations for virtually all the prestigious magazines of the period. The most famous real Gibson girl was President Theodore Roosevelt's daughter, Alice.

gold standard
A currency in which paper money is redeemable on demand for gold coin or bullion. The value of gold standard money is stable because the amount of gold in existence does not decrease and rarely increases quickly. The United States went "on the gold standard" in 1873 when money ceased to be based on silver as well as gold. American money ceased being redeemable in gold in 1933.

Good Neighbor policy
American diplomatic policy in Latin America, instituted by President Hoover and adopted by Franklin D. Roosevelt, that reversed thirty years of gunboat diplomacy (military intervention) and dollar diplomacy (financial bullying). Hoover and FDR respected the sovereignty of the Latin American republics and dealt with them as equal states.

graduation
A reform of federal land law associated with Senator Thomas Hart Benton of Missouri, graduation provided that federal land unsold after auction be offered at half the minimum per acre price and, later, at one-quarter of the

minimum. It was designed to make federal land affordable to a larger number of people.

grandfather clause
A device employed by several southern states to ensure that race-neutral disqualifications from the right to vote such as literacy tests applied only to African Americans. If a man's grandfather had voted before 1867, he was exempt from the obligation to prove his literacy. Because the laws clearly disqualified blacks, none of whose grandfathers could vote before 1867, the Supreme Court ruled grandfather clauses unconstitutional in 1915.

Grange
Popular reference to the Patrons of Husbandry, a farmer's organization founded after the Civil War to provide social and cultural diversions to farm families. (Local lodges of the patrons were called "granges," an old word for farmhouse.) During the 1870s, the Grange was politically active in a campaign to regulate railroad freight and storage rates.

Great Awakening
A widespread revival of religious piety in the colonies during the mid-eighteenth century. It split old denominations like the Congregationalists, Presbyterians, and Anglicans and promoted new ones, the Methodists and Baptists.

"Great Communicator"
Nickname attached to Ronald Reagan, president from 1981 to 1989, for his skill, honed by a career as a film actor, of persuading Americans to support him. The nickname was a play on Henry Clay's the "Great Compromiser." Reagan's critics called him the "Teflon president" because none of the many scandals of his administration "stuck" to him.

"Great Disappointment"
On March 21, 1844, thousands or hundreds of William Miller's followers—reports vary widely—gathered on hilltops or in churches in upstate New York to await the Second Coming of Christ, which Miller had predicted would occur on that day. When it did not occur, the Millerites called the day the "Great Disappointment." There was a second disappointment in October.

Great Society
President Lyndon B. Johnson's name for the reform legislation he pushed through Congress before and especially after his landslide victory in the election of 1964. Many of its social programs failed to accomplish Johnson's hopes. The Great Society was expensive, although it was the addition to them of the costs of the war in Vietnam that caused the government's fiscal crisis of the 1970s.

Greeley, Horace (1811–1872)
Founder of the *New York Tribune,* Greeley promoted free public education, temperance, and abolition. He was a founder of the Republican party, and during the last years of the Civil War, he was a radical who criticized Lincoln. By 1872 he had lost faith in radical

Reconstruction and ran for president as the Liberal Republican and Democratic parties' candidate.

Green Berets
Officially known as "Special Forces," they were members of elite units in the U.S. Army specially trained in anti-guerrilla warfare in the Third World. The Green Berets were a favored project of President John F. Kennedy, who placed great importance on countering Soviet-inspired insurrections in undeveloped nations.

Green Mountain Boys
Informal militia in "Vermont," mountainous forestland claimed by the colonies of Massachusetts, New Hampshire, and New York. The leader of the militia, Ethan Allen, insisted that Vermont was independent of all. In 1775, along with militia from Massachusetts, the Green Mountain Boys forced the surrender of the British garrison at Fort Ticonderoga.

greenbacks
Colloquial term for paper money issued by the federal government during the Civil War; the backs of the bills were printed in green ink. Greenbacks were not redeemable in gold and fluctuated in value. During the 1860s and 1870s, their continuance divided gold standard conservatives and inflationists, especially farmers, who wanted to keep the greenbacks in circulation.

Grenada
Tiny Caribbean island republic occupied by American troops in 1983 when its Cuban-backed "Marxist" government collapsed. President Reagan justified the invasion because of the presence of Cuban troops, who turned out to be construction workers too old for military service.

Grenville, George (1712–1770)
First Lord of the Treasury who sponsored the Sugar Act of 1764 and the Stamp Act of 1765, taxes on the colonies that resulted in the first protests that led to the American Declaration of Independence.

Grimké, Sarah and Angelina (1792–1873) and (1805–1879)
Daughters of a distinguished and wealthy South Carolina planter and slave owner. They became abolitionists, and then, despite their social standing, they were harassed violently, so they moved to the North. Both were active members of the American Anti-Slavery Society. Angelina married abolitionist orator Theodore Dwight Weld.

Gulf of Tonkin Resolution
Legal basis for the American war in Vietnam, it gave the president authority to take whatever measures he thought necessary to defend against attacks on American armed forces. It was named for an incident in the Gulf of Tonkin in August 1964 when North Vietnamese patrol boats were said to have fired on American destroyers.

Gunsmoke
The most popular and longest-lasting of the more than forty "westerns" introduced by the

television networks during the mid-1950s. At the peak of the mania, a third of television time in the evening was dedicated to shows set in the "Wild West." *Gunsmoke* had 635 half-hour episodes, a record for television production that lasted until the late 1990s.

"Half-Breeds" ("Stalwarts")
Two bitterly opposed factions of the Republican party during the 1870s and early 1880s. The Stalwarts, led by Senator Roscoe Conkling of New York, unabashedly defended the spoils system; "stalwart" workers for the party should be rewarded with government jobs. The Half-Breeds, led by Senator James B. Blaine of Maine, flirted with the civil service reform movement but, in reality, used the patronage as cynically as the Stalwarts did.

Hanna, Mark (1837–1904)
Cleveland industrial and an associate of John D. Rockefeller, he was, as early as the 1880s, impressed by William McKinley and determined to make him president. McKinley's lack of intellectual luster and his close relationship with Hanna persuaded many that Hanna manipulated McKinley as if he were a puppet. In fact, the two men seem to have had a friendship of equals.

Harlan, John Marshall (1833–1911)
Long-serving justice of the Supreme Court who was the sole dissenter in *Plessy* v. *Ferguson* (1896), which approved "separate but equal" public accommodations for blacks and whites: segregation. In an eloquent dissent, Harlan, a southerner who had owned slaves as a young man, wrote that separate facilities for blacks were inherently equal because they were "badges" of inferiority.

headright system
Device meant to encourage emigration to Virginia. An emigrant was granted fifty acres of land for every person (per head) whose costs of transportation to Virginia he paid: himself, members of his family, other free people, and servants.

Henry the Navigator (1394–1460)
Portuguese prince who devoted his life to organizing expeditions of discovery into the Atlantic and to the south of Portugal along the western coast of Africa. He also encouraged improvements in ship design and navigational instruments.

Henry, Patrick (1736–1799)
Virginia lawyer who rose to prominence as a protestor in the 1760s and 1770s as a fiery anti-British orator. Henry remained in politics after independence but lost his following due in part to his inconsistency.

Hiawatha (1520?–?)
Poet Henry Wadsworth Longfellow's spelling of the name of a sixteenth-century Iroquois who devoted his life—successfully—to eliminating war among the five Iroquois tribes of New York and establishing a confederacy for the resolution of intertribal disputes.

hidalgo
Spanish for low-ranking noble. Many Spaniards who were not of noble blood claimed to be hidalgos, demanded the rights accorded nobility, and affected aristocratic manners and pretensions.

Homestead
The largest factory in the world when it was constructed in the 1870s outside Pittsburgh, Pennsylvania. Homestead was the centerpiece of Andrew Carnegie's steel manufacturing empire and the site of a violent strike in 1892.

Homestead Act
Adopted by Congress in May 1862, it gave 160 acres of federal land free to any citizen or immigrant intending to become a citizen who agreed to build a dwelling, live on the land, and cultivate it.

Hooverizing
Slang term during World War I (and for some years thereafter) meaning economizing. Herbert C. Hoover, wartime Food Administrator, issued one voluntary program after another for economizing on food production.

Hoovervilles
The humorous but bitter name—a dig at President Herbert Hoover—given to ramshackle shantytowns built on vacant lots in cities during the early Depression by unemployed people who lost their homes. In New York City a huge, sprawling Hooverville was built in Central Park.

Howard University
Founded in 1867 and named for the white general who headed the Freedman's Bureau, O. O. Howard, this was the most prestigious and probably the best African-American university in the country. No longer a blacks-only institution, it remains reputed for excellence.

Huguenots
French Protestants similar to the English Puritans; their religious beliefs were similar to those of England's Puritans. They were a minority in France troublesome to the Crown until one of them became king as Henri IV. He became a Catholic but, in 1598, issued an edict giving the Huguenots limited toleration and political rights. When toleration was revoked in 1685, most of them left France.

Hundred Hours War
President George H. W. Bush's name for the astonishingly rapid destruction of the much-vaunted Iraqi army in 1991 when the United States expelled Iraq from oil-rich Kuwait. The president was disappointed in the aftermath of the brilliant military campaign. He expected the obviously discredited Saddam Hussein to be overthrown by Iraqis, but he was not.

Hutchinson, Anne (1591–1643)
Extraordinary Massachusetts woman who confounded the governors of the colony by challenging orthodox religious teachings and the seventeenth-century assumption that religious doctrine was for women to accept and not to ponder. She was banished to Rhode Island but relocated in New Netherlands, where she was killed by Indians.

I-beam girder
Steel girder, so-called because it was shaped like an "I" in cross-section. Perfected by William L. Jenney in 1885, it made possible the construction of skyscrapers because the weight of the tall buildings was borne by a riveted internal skeleton rather than thick stone foundations and walls.

IBM cards
Properly known as "Hollerith cards" after their inventor, they were most Americans' introduction to the computer. Data were fed into early computers on the cards (slightly larger than a dollar bill) in which clerks punched holes representing names, addresses, and courses in which students wished to register; or, a step forward, students and applicants and examinees for a job blacked in "machine-readable" boxes on the cards. The computer did the rest.

impressment
The eighteenth- and nineteenth-century term for what we would call conscription or the draft. Impressment was forced military service. During the 1790s and early 1800s, British impressment of seamen on American ships into the Royal Navy (the British claimed they were British subjects and therefore subject to impressment) contributed to the growth of demands that the United States go to war to defend the country's honor and independence.

indentured servants
The principal source of labor in the colonies during the seventeenth century, and a major source in the northern colonies during the eighteenth century. In return for passage to America and some other compensation, poor men and women, mostly English during the 1600s, bound themselves to work for a master for three to seven years. Their contract was called an "Indenture."

Indian Reorganization Act
Law of 1934 allowing Indian tribes to form corporations that could take control of lands previously allotted to individual Indians, a system that had resulted in the loss of much of the land reserved for Indians in 1884. The Reorganization Act encouraged traditional Indian religions, crafts, and customs.

Industrial Workers of the World
Revolutionary labor union founded in 1905, it opposed the American Federation of Labor's insistence on admitting only skilled workers. Instead the IWW admitted all workers and organized them in "industrial unions" that included all workers in an industry. Members were known as "Wobblies," a name they accepted.

initiative
A progressive political reform at the state or municipal level. A means by which voters can bypass elected legislators who fail to enact a popularly supported law, it provides that if a specified number of signatures on a petition are certified, the measure on the petition will be presented to voters in a referendum. If it wins a majority, the measure becomes law regardless of the legislature's or governor's inaction.

Insurgents
The name given to progressive Republican congressmen, mostly from the Midwest, who angered President Taft by voting with Democrats in the House of Representatives to reduce the powers of the reactionary House Speaker, Joseph Cannon. Taft denied campaign funds to the Insurgents in the midterm election of 1910. Two years later, the Insurgents deserted the Republican party to support Progressive party candidate Theodore Roosevelt in the presidential election.

Inter Caetera
A papal bull (proclamation by the pope binding on Catholics) of 1493 in which Pope Alexander VI divided all the world's land not in the possession of a Christian ruler between Spain and Portugal.

interchangeable parts
Mass-produced castings of small metal parts so nearly identical that they could be used interchangeably: one of the foundations of the industrial economy. Eli Whitney demonstrated gun locks made of interchangeable parts before Congress. He was awarded a contract for 10,000 muskets. His process proved to be not up to the job, but the technology was perfected by others.

internal improvements
What today would be called "public works." Internal improvements were government-financed (sometimes government-owned) construction projects designed to boost the economy. They included harbor improvements, dredging rivers for navigation, and roads. The greatest and most famous federally financed internal improvement of the early nineteenth century was the National Road.

Interstate Commerce Commission (ICC)
The first permanent federal regulatory commission, established by Congress in 1887 in response to demands for the regulation of railroads. The ICC was ineffective in its early years not because of lack of authority but because most commissioners were closely tied to the nation's great railroad companies.

Interstate Highway Act
Congressional act of 1956 appropriating $1 billion a year—by 1960 $2.9 billion—to construct limited-access, fast highways connecting major cities and, eventually, ringing cities. The act was justified by fiscal conservatives as essential to national defense.

Iran–Contra affair
Secret arrangement engineered by top officials in the Reagan administration to aid pro-American rebels in Nicaragua (the "contras") in violation of the Boland Act.

Missiles were sold to the Khomeini government in Iran, which had abetted the long captivity of American hostages with some of the profits given to the contras. If President Reagan was aware of the transaction, he was guilty of a federal crime. If he was not, high-ranking members of his administration were making policy without his knowledge.

Iroquois
Linguists' names to the three major language families of the Eastern Woodlands Indians. There was also a distinct tribe in Canada the French called Algonquin.

Jay Cooke and Company
The largest and most prestigious investment bank in the United States during the 1860s and early 1870s, it was the federal government's borrowing agency during the Civil War. When the bank failed in 1873, it caused a panic that led to a serious depression.

jayhawkers
Armed free-state irregulars in eastern Kansas in the middle and late 1850s, the equivalent of the proslavery border ruffians from Missouri.

Jesuits
Priests belonging to the Society of Jesus, a well-educated, disciplined, militant, flexible order devoted to missionary work. Jesuits were the most important religious order in New France. They were extremely successful in winning Indians to Roman Catholicism.

John Birch Society
Right-wing extremist organization founded by candy manufacturer Robert Welch. Members believed an international Communist conspiracy had infiltrated and controlled American education, churches, and the federal government. It was influential in the Republican party during the mid-1960s.

John Brown's Raid
Seizure of the federal arsenal at Harper's Ferry, Virginia, by a small band of men led by abolitionist John Brown in the fall of 1989. Brown's tiny army was killed or captured within a few days, but the threat of a slave rebellion Brown intended to start convinced many southerners that abolitionists, abetted by the Republican party, threatened their personal safety.

"Johnny Reb" (and "Billy Yank")
The name Union soldiers chose to personalize Confederate soldiers, the equivalent of Johnny Reb's "Billy Yank."

joint occupation
After Spain and Russia abandoned their claims to the Oregon Country (the present states of Oregon and Washington, the Idaho panhandle, and the Canadian province of British Columbia), the United States and Great Britain agreed to a "joint occupation" of the area. This put other nations on notice that their claims in Oregon would be resisted. However, by granting the few transient British and American nationals there equal rights and protection, joint occupation avoided an Anglo–American conflict. By the mid-1840s, a large American population in the south part of the Oregon Country made the unusual device obsolete.

Jomini, Antoine-Henri (1779–1869)
Swiss general whose treatise on battlefield tactics, *The Art of War,* was translated into English and adapted into a book widely read at West Point. To some extent, every Union and Confederate officer with formal military training had been educated in Jomini's school.

judicial review
The Supreme Court's power, now accepted without question, to declare an act of Congress signed by the president unconstitutional, therefore invalidating it. There is no mention of such a power in the Constitution, although the principle was well known. The Supreme Court asserted its right to invalidate acts of Congress in *Marbury* v. *Madison,* 1803.

King Caucus
The term coined in 1824 to denigrate the caucus or meeting of Republican senators and representatives to select the party's presidential candidate. 1824 was the final year the caucus met.

King George III (1738–1820, reigned 1760–1820)
King of Great Britain during the crisis that led to the American War of Independence and the Revolution itself. He was somewhat unfairly made the scapegoat of American grievances. His reign was longer than that of any other British monarch except Queen Victoria, although he was helplessly insane during the final decades of his life.

king's friends," "the
The name given the Parliamentary faction bound by patronage to George III. Unlike his predecessors, George I and George II, who favored the "Whigs" who had put them on the throne, George III favored the "Tories" who supported greater royal participation in government.

kitchen debate
Propaganda stunt well-planned and executed by Vice President Nixon on a visit to the Soviet Union in 1959. At an exposition, in front of a mockup of a well-equipped modern American kitchen, Nixon engaged Soviet Premier Khruschev in a comparison of the American and Russian standards of living that Nixon could not lose.

"Know-Nothing" party
Derisive name for the American party of the 1850s, an anti-immigration and anti-Catholic movement that won control of several states between 1852 and 1854, electing forty-three members of Congress.

Kultur
The German word for "culture." German nationalists spoke much of the virtues, even the superiority, of German culture. Anti-German propagandists exploited popular revulsion toward the harsh German occupation of Belgium and what seemed to some the immorality of submarine warfare to describe *Kultur,* using the alien and vaguely menacing German spelling and pronunciation, as meaning brutality and savagery.

land grant universities
The Morrill Act of 1862 gave state governments federal lands—30,000 acres for each member of Congress—which were to be used to finance public universities. They were required to have agricultural and mechanical courses of study and military science, but were permitted to add other programs that the states chose. The sixty-nine schools eventually founded under the Morrill Act are known as land grant universities. Eventually 17 million acres were distributed to the states in aid of education.

Landon, Alfred M. (1887–1987)
Governor of Kansas and the Republican presidential nominee in 1936. Landon was a former Bull Moose Progressive and considered himself a liberal. The Republican party chose him to dodge the label "economic royalists" that FDR had pinned on them. Landon won the electoral votes of only two states.

League of Nations
The international organization founded in the Treaty of Versailles that would, President Wilson hoped, avert future wars by providing a permanent assembly in which differences between nations would be peacefully resolved. Opposition to the League was widespread in the United States, which was never a member.

Lecompton Constitution
Proposed Kansas state constitution, making Kansas a slave state, submitted to Congress in the fall of 1857. Congress rejected the Lecompton Constitution because Stephen A. Douglas and other northern Democrats joined Republicans in insisting that it be ratified by a territorywide referendum.

Levittown
Name of several American cities built after World War II by William Levitt in response to the severe housing shortage.

liberty ships
Freight-carrying vessels mass-produced during World War II. They were fragile but quickly and cheaply made. About 2,700 of them were built between 1941 and 1945. At the end of the war, several new ones were finished every day.

Liliuokalani (Lydia Kamekeha, 1838–1917)
During the long reign as king of Hawaii by her pro-American brother, David Kalakaua, Liliuokalani, like him, was an ally of the small white American oligarchy that dominated the islands. However, when she became queen in 1891, she revoked the constitution that gave the Hawaiian Americans their power and proclaimed that only native Hawaiians could

vote. She was immediately overthrown, and seven years later, the United States annexed Hawaii.

Looking Backward

A novel by Edward Bellamy published in 1888, it depicted twenty-first century America as a utopia made possible by democratic socialism, which Bellamy called "Nationalism." The novel inspired the creation of mostly middle-class "Nationalist Clubs." Bellamy himself joined the Populist party, founded in 1892, but was disillusioned when, four years later, the Populists abandoned their reform program.

Louisbourg

A French fortress on Cape Breton Island (northern Nova Scotia). The French were the masters of fortification architecture, and they considered Louisbourg impregnable. It was a haven for French privateers who harassed New England fishermen and merchant ships. An army of New Englanders captured the fortress at a great cost in lives in 1745. British peacemakers returned it to France, causing considerable resentment in New England.

Lusitania

A British transatlantic liner torpedoed and sunk by a German submarine off the coast of Ireland in May 1915. Some 1,200 of 2,000 people aboard were killed, 139 Americans among them. A wave of anti-German anger swept the United States because the ship ostensibly carried only passengers. (In fact, there were munitions aboard.)

machine gun

The most significant of many weapons first used on a massive scale between European powers during World War I. The machine gun, at relatively little cost, increased a soldier's firepower from 50 to 100 times. Its impact ended the era of the infantry (and cavalry) charge.

Mainline Canal, the

The most ambitious of the canals built in imitation of the Erie Canal's astonishing success, Pennsylvania's Mainline Canal was specifically designed to restore Philadelphia as a legitimate competitor of New York City as an exporter of western produce and a supplier of manufactures to the West. It was longer than the Erie and traversed far more difficult terrain, which was its undoing. There were 174 locks on the Mainline Canal compared to the Erie's 84.

Mandan

Unique Plains Indian tribe in that, in addition to hunting bison, Mandan were also farmers and lived in substantial dwellings in fixed villages. They had been hospitable to whites since they provided winter quarters for the Lewis and Clark expedition. The Mandan were destroyed as a tribe by smallpox and by the enmity of the Sioux, who repeatedly attacked them.

Manhattan Project

Code name for the huge, expensive, secret development of the first atomic bomb. It began in three locations in 1939 with hundreds of scientists, few of whom knew the purpose of the specialized research to which each was assigned. The bomb was intended for Germany, which, President Roosevelt feared, might be first to develop an atomic bomb. Germany was defeated before the bomb was finished, but the only two in existence (one was exploded in a test) were dropped on Japan, ending the war.

"Manifest Destiny"

Clearly obvious destiny, a phrase coined by Democratic party journalist John L. O'Sullivan in a newspaper article favoring the annexation of Texas in 1845. It was, he wrote, America's "manifest destiny to overspread the continent." The phrase caught on as a slogan during the Mexican War and became part of American political language.

Mann Act (1911)

Federal law making it a crime to transport a woman across state lines for prostitution or "other immoral purposes." Ostensibly aimed at organized "white slavery," entrapment of girls into unchasteness and, therefore, prostitution by seduction or rape, most Mann Act defendants were men who crossed a state line accompanied by women with whom they had consensual sexual relations with no money changing hands.

manumission

The legal freeing of a slave by an owner, a synonym for *emancipation*, manumission was a legal procedure regulated by states. During the 1780s and for several decades thereafter, with slavery in widespread disrepute, southern states made manumission easy.

Marquette, Jacques (1637–1675) and Louis Joliet, sometimes Jolliet (1645–1700)

A Jesuit priest and trapper who found the portage connecting the Great Lakes and the Mississippi River system, descended the Mississippi to the mouth of the Arkansas River, and concluded that the Mississippi emptied into the Gulf of Mexico, not the Pacific. Their discoveries laid the groundwork for the expansion of the French Empire.

Marshall Plan

American program, announced in 1947, for financial aid to European nations where World War II had so destroyed the economy that rapid recovery was impossible without outside assistance. It was designed to head off the social turmoil that might bring Communists to power.

McCarthyism

Named for Senator Joseph McCarthy of Wisconsin who, in the early 1950s, used the effective technique, the term refers to the silencing of critics and the intimidation of potential critics by accusing all opponents of being secret Communists, "fellow travelers"(non-Communists who backed the party lines), or "comsymps" (Communist sympathizers). McCarthy included even General George C. Marshall in this category.

mercantilism

The name later given to the philosophy that dominated English economic policy beginning in the seventeenth century. Mercantilists held that the government should closely regulate a nation's economic activity, particularly in encouraging trade, to increase the flow of wealth, in the form of gold and silver coin, into the nation.

mercenary

Soldier who fights for whoever will pay him rather than for king, country, religion, or any other such cause. Armies of the sixteenth century (and through the eighteenth) were comprised largely of mercenary soldiers.

merchants-adventurers companies

Enterprises involved in foreign trade owned not by an individual but by several, sometimes numerous shareholders, who shared the costs of investment, the risk, and any profits. They were chartered by the king and given special privileges to encourage investment. The companies that founded the earliest English colonies were patterned on the merchants-adventurers companies.

Merrimack

The world's first ironclad warship, a ram, introduced by the Confederate navy in March 1862 to break the blockade of the Chesapeake Bay by wooden vessels. The *Merrimack* was effective but was immediately neutralized by a Union ironclad, the *Monitor*, which fought her to a draw.

Mesoamerica

Mexico and Central America, the land mass between North and South America. (In Greek *meso* means "between.") It was the home of one of the two advanced civilizations that originated in the Western Hemisphere.

Metacomet (?–1676)

Wampanoag chief known to New Englanders as "King Philip." In 1675 he formed the first pan-Indian anti-white alliance in American history, winning the cooperation of tribes that were ancestral enemies. Briefly successful, King Philip's rebellion was crushed; he was killed, his head impaled on a stake in Boston.

metes and bounds

Legal description of property lines that refers to other properties and roads and to natural features of the land such as watercourses, outcroppings of rock, even trees. Of European origin, the metes and bounds system was adopted by the colonies and even used in lands sold in Kentucky during the 1780s after the system had been abandoned in the Northwest Territory.

Millerites

Followers of William Miller, who preached that the end of the world—the Second Coming of Christ—would come in 1843 or 1844. When his prophecy proved faulty, remnants of the Millerites regrouped as the Seventh Day Adventists.

minié balls

Despite the word *ball*, conical bullets favored by both northern and southern infantry during the Civil War because of the more disabling wound they produced.

minstrel show

Minstrel is a medieval word meaning a traveling musician. In the United States beginning in the 1840s, the word was applied specifically to a formulaic stage show featuring white performers in "blackface" makeup pretending to be plantation slaves who sang, danced, parried humorously with one another, and performed comic skits. Minstrel shows remained popular throughout the nineteenth century.

missile gap

Disparity between the number of intercontinental ballistic missiles in the American and Russian nuclear arsenals unfavorable to the United States. It was a theme of John F. Kennedy's campaign for the presidency in 1960. The "gap" did not exist, but President Eisenhower could not respond without revealing how many missiles the United States had and how many American intelligence believed the Soviets possessed.

Missouri Compromise (1820)

Engineered by Henry Clay to end an angry North–South sectional split over the application for statehood, with slavery, of Missouri Territory. Missouri was admitted as a slave state, Maine as a free state so that the numbers of slave and free states remained equal. The compromise forbade future slave states in territory north of 36° 30' north latitude, placating antislavery northerners.

Mitchell, John (1870–1919)

A coal miner at the age of 12, he was president of the United Mineworkers Union before he was 30, increasing its membership from 40,000 to 200,000. He became extremely popular as the moderate head of the union during the bitter anthracite miners' strike of 1902, which ended in a victory for the workers. Later he became a vice president of the American Federation of Labor. Mitchell was not the stainless hero many believed him to be. Late in his career he was beset by well-founded rumors that he took payoffs from mine owners to settle disputes.

Moctezuma II, sometimes Montezuma (1480?–1520, reigned 1503–1520)

Emperor of the Aztecs. His bewilderment at the appearance of Cortés with his army and his indecisiveness were key elements in the extraordinary Spanish conquest of Mexico.

"Monkey Trial"

Trial in Dayton, Tennessee, in 1925. John Scopes was prosecuted for violating a state law prohibiting the teaching of Darwin's theory of evolution in public schools. The trial was sensational news nationally because of the participation of celebrities such as William Jennings Bryan and attorney Clarence Darrow.

Monroe Doctrine

Proclaimed by President Monroe in 1823 (although he did not use that name), its significant provision was that the United States declared the Western Hemisphere closed to further colonization and restoration of imperial authority. In diplomatic but unambivalent language, Monroe stated that any such European actions would be regarded as an act of war against the United States.

Moral Majority

Political action committee organized in 1980 by the Rev. Jerry Falwell to work for the presidential campaign of Republican nominee Ronald Reagan. Falwell blamed liberal Democratic politicians and courts for the decay of traditional moral standards and an increasing crime rate.

"moral suasionists"

The temperance movement of the early nineteenth century split early on how to fight the evil of drunkenness. Moral suasionists said that drinking, in moderation or at all, was the individual's moral decision. Their program was to encourage people to drink moderately or preferably to swear off drinking "T-totally." Legal suasionists insisted on removing the possibility of drinking by forbidding the manufacture and sale of alcoholic beverages.

"more bang for a buck"

Flippant description of President Eisenhower's policy of sharply reducing federal expenditures on the traditional army and navy in favor of spending on the production of nuclear weapons and the planes and missiles to deliver them, a less expensive defense program.

muckrakers

Journalists specializing in exposés of corruption in business and politics or examining social evils such as racial discrimination or child labor practices. They were given the name by President Theodore Roosevelt because they "raked muck" looking for stories. The term was taken from a well-known religious book of the Reformation period, John Bunyan's *Pilgrim's Progress*.

mugwumps

Derogatory name given to Republican reformers, mostly genteel New Yorkers, who supported Democratic presidential candidate Grover Cleveland in 1884 because of his honest record. "*Mugwump*" was said to be an Algonkian Indian word meaning "big shot."

Muir, John (1838–1914)

Born in Scotland, raised in Wisconsin, Muir suffered an accident that injured his eyesight but sent him on a 1,000-mile hiking trip when he became enamored of wilderness. Success as a fruit grower and marriage to a well-to-do woman allowed Muir to devote himself full-time to exploration of the Sierra Nevada and remote parts of Alaska. He was instrumental in protecting California's Yosemite Valley as the second national park in 1890. Two years later he founded the Sierra Club, still the nation's largest and most influential preservationist organization.

Muskogean

Linguists' names to the three major language families of the Eastern Woodlands Indians. There was also a distinct tribe in Canada the French called Algonquin.

NAFTA

The North American Free Trade Area Treaty, signed by Canada, the United States, and Mexico in 1994. Patterned on the European Common Market, which had been an economic boon for western Europe, NAFTA provided for the elimination of trade barriers among the three North American countries over a period of fifteen years.

National Road

Also called the Cumberland Road after its eastern terminus, Cumberland, Maryland, the head of navigation on the Potomac River. Originally it ran to Wheeling (then in Virginia, now West Virginia) on the Ohio River. Henry Clay of Kentucky promoted its extension to Vandalia, Illinois, which provided cross-country transportation to parts of Ohio, Indiana, and Illinois that did not have easy access to the Ohio River. Eventually the road continued to the Mississippi opposite St. Louis.

Nauvoo

City in western Illinois that, during several years in the 1840s as the home of Joseph Smith and the Mormons, was the largest city in the state. Nauvoo prospered, but after Joseph Smith was murdered by a mob in 1844, Brigham Young led the Mormons to the Great Salt Lake basin.

Navigation Acts

Parliamentary acts (1660–1663) regulating colonial trade so that it benefited the mother country. For example, all trade had to be carried in English or colonial-owned ships manned by English or colonial sailors.

New Deal

The slogan of the Democratic party's presidential campaign coined by candidate Franklin D. Roosevelt when he dramatically flew to Chicago after his nomination to address the nominating convention. He pledged himself to a "New Deal for the American people."

"New Democrat"

Designation adopted by a number of rising young Democratic politicians after the Reagan–Republican election sweep of 1980. With the label of "liberal" in bad odor, the New Democrats supported black civil rights and liberal positions such as abortion on demand but appealed to tax-conscious voters by promising responsible, frugal spending policies. The most successful of the New Democrats was Bill Clinton of Arkansas.

"New Era"

Slogan coined by apologists for the Coolidge years, 1923–1929, when (they said) business culture, endorsed and abetted by the federal government, had ushered in permanent and ever-increasing prosperity. The New Era ended with the stock market crash of October 1929.

New Federalism
Nixon's slogan (which never caught on) for his policy of distributing to the states federal money to finance Great Society programs. It was a meaningless sop to anti–Great Society Republicans. It did not reduce Lyndon Johnson's welfare state legislation and actually increased the size of government bureaucracies.

new immigrants
A term coined during the 1890s to distinguish the immigrants of that period, mostly from southern and eastern Europe, from the "old immigrants" of the years preceding 1880, most of whom were British, Irish, and German. Many Americans believed that the new immigrants could not be assimilated.

New Nationalism
The name Theodore Roosevelt gave to the far-reaching program of progressive reform he outlined at Osawatomie, Kansas in 1910. Roosevelt revived the program and the name in his Bull Moose party candidacy for the presidency in 1912. His Democratic opponent in the election (and the victor), Woodrow Wilson, called his much less ambitious program the New Freedom.

"NINA"
Abbreviation found in "help wanted" advertisements in newspapers, on shop windows, and at factory gates during the later nineteenth century. It meant "no Irish need apply," reflecting hostility toward Irish Americans during the period.

"nine old men"
President Franklin D. Roosevelt's ill-advised term in 1937 for the nine justices of the Supreme Court after they invalidated, by narrow margins, several key New Deal laws. Roosevelt wanted to add justices to the Court to ensure a pro–New Deal majority. For the first time in his presidency, public opinion was against him, and he backed off.

normalcy
Word popularized during the presidential campaign of 1920 by Republican candidate Warren G. Harding. Harding used the term instead of *normality* in the speechwriter's text because, to him, *normality* implied mental health. The word was widely ridiculed.

Northern Securities Case (1904)
The Northern Securities Company was a holding company designed by banker J. P. Morgan. Its purpose was to end ruinous competition of three major northwestern railroads. Theodore Roosevelt earned the nickname the "trustbuster" when his administration convinced the Supreme Court that the company was a monopoly illegally in restraint of trade. The company was dismantled.

Northwest Ordinances
A series of laws enacted by the Confederation Congress between 1784 and 1787 that provided for the creation of future states in the Northwest Territory: lands west of Pennsylvania and north of the Ohio River. Slavery was forbidden in the Northwest Territory so as to reserve the land for family farmers.

O'Connor, Sandra Day (1930–)
First woman to sit on the Supreme Court. She was appointed by President Reagan in 1981 because he expected her to be a solid conservative vote on the Court and, no doubt, to annoy feminists, most of whom were Democrats. O'Connor was an undistinguished justice; her conservatism was cautious, never shrill like some other Republican-named justices of the era. She retired, pending appointment of a replacement, in 2005.

Okies
Name given to the thousands of Dust Bowl refugees (not all from Oklahoma) who migrated west to California, mostly by automobile, along U.S. Highway 66. Originally the term was derogatory, signifying dirt-poor, ignorant yokels; but after a few years, the "Okies" themselves, taking pride in overcoming disaster, adopted it fondly.

Omaha Convention
1892 convention of the newly founded Populist party in Omaha, Nebraska. Its platform called for comprehensive political, economic, and social reforms.

Omnibus Bill
Henry Clay's name for the law he drafted to resolve the sectional crisis of 1850 with compromise between militantly proslavery southern congressmen and antislavery northerners, both abolitionists and Free Soilers. In this context omnibus means "including all"; Clay's bill addressed all differences between proslavery and antislavery Americans and required each side to make concessions. In the end, all of Clay's proposals were adopted, but not as a single act of Congress. Zealots of both sides voted against the Omnibus Bill because they refused to concede some questions for the sake of a compromise.

OPEC
Acronym for Organization of Petroleum Exporting Nations, a cartel formed behind Saudi Arabian leadership in 1960 but not effective until the 1970s. OPEC's mostly undeveloped countries had large oil reserves and cooperated in reducing production, thereby raising the price of oil. During the early 1970s OPEC's production cuts caused severe gasoline shortages in the United States.

Open Door
The name given to an international China policy defined in a series of "Open Door notes" that Secretary of State John Hay circulated among the imperial powers to sign. The Open Door policy guaranteed that China would not be carved into colonies and that all nations would have the right to trade everywhere in the country. The British, who had devised the policy to avoid an imperialist scramble such as the one that carved up Africa, gladly signed Hay's notes. Germany and Japan disliked the policy but were pressured to sign.

Operation Overlord
Name of the project—unprecedented in scale—of assembling the massive force of soldiers, weaponry, and a transport fleet for the invasion of western Europe in World War II. Overlord culminated in D-Day, June 6, 1944, on the beaches of Normandy. It was headed from its inception in June 1942 by Dwight D. Eisenhower, whose command of the complex secret operation and conciliatory management of difficult subordinates was masterful.

Orphan Boy
A Mississippi steamboat, undistinguished among the hundreds of paddle-wheelers on the river when it was built in 1841 except that, with 40 tons of cargo aboard, it floated in water just two feet deep. That was the record. Most designers settled for a draft of four feet and much more tonnage in cargo.

Ostend Manifesto
Declaration signed in Ostend, Belgium in 1854 by the American ministers to Spain, France, and Britain. It recommended to President Pierce that the United States should offer to buy Cuba from Spain for $120 million and, if Spain should refuse, take Cuba by force.

outer perimeter
First Japanese strategic object in World War II, to establish a ring of strong defensive positions from the mid-Pacific south and west to New Guinea (even northern Australia) and in southeast Asia, thus preventing the United States from attacking closer to Japan than 2,000–3,000 miles.

Pacific Railway Act
Congressional legislation of 1862 authorizing the first transcontinental railroad, it set the pattern for western railway construction by subsidizing (with land grants, loans, and other financial guarantees) private companies to build and own the lines.

paddyrollers
Southern dialect for patrollers: armed and mounted bands of white men, sometimes volunteers, sometimes hired by the county, who rode the roads and plantations of the South by night looking for slaves who were abroad. With broad legal powers, the usually rough men were known for their brutality, feared, and hated.

Paleo-Indians
literally "old Indians" (*paleo* is Greek for "old"); anthropologists' term for the ancestors of the native Americans whom Europeans called "Indians."

Palmer, A. Mitchell (1872–1936)
Attorney General under Woodrow Wilson who, during Wilson's convalescence in 1919, tried to win support for his presidential ambitions by launching a series of raids on

radical and, particularly, communist offices and meeting places.

Patton, George W. (1885–1945)
Commander of the Seventh and later the Third Army in Europe in World War II, he was probably the best American battlefield commander. He understood as early as World War I that the tank and mobility held the key to future wars. He was killed in an automobile accident shortly after the war ended. There was no role for him in Cold War America except that of shrill dissident.

"peculiar institution"
Term by which white southerners referred to slavery. It was a euphemistic alternative to saying the word *slavery,* just as eighteenth-century slave owners had called their slaves "servants" and nineteenth-century planters often called their slaves "my people." However, it was also a pointed reference to the fact that although slavery was not unique to the South by the fourth decade of the century, it was almost unique, distinct and particular to the American South.

Pendleton Act
Federal law of 1883, enacted in the wake of Garfield's assassination, it established the Civil Service Commission, which administered examinations to applicants for some government jobs so that appointments were made on the basis of merit rather than party affiliation. By 1900 almost half of all government employees were protected from dismissal for political reasons.

Penn, William (1644–1718)
Heir of a wealthy English family who became the leading member of the Society of Friends (Quakers) and consecrated his land grant in America (Pennsylvania) to Quaker principles, including religious toleration.

Pennsylvania System
An early but quickly abandoned prison reform: all inmates lived in solitary confinement in individual cells. The hope was that long meditation on their crimes would result in individual reform; it was a method of punishing crime rooted in the evangelical belief in personal redemption. However, the Pennsylvania System was expensive, and mental breakdowns among convicts were frequent. More successful was the Auburn System, in which convicts were together for work and meals (although rarely permitted to converse).

Perot, Ross (1930–)
Erratic, self-made Texas millionaire and philanthropist who declared himself an independent candidate for president in 1992 during a television interview. His announcement caused a groundswell of support among people, mostly described as conservatives, who put him on the ballot in almost all fifty states. Perot drew 19 percent of the popular vote and would probably have drawn more had he not briefly withdrawn from the campaign alleging personal attacks on his daughter.

Perry, Oliver Hazard (1785–1819)
American naval officer who, with a fleet of ten vessels, hurriedly and poorly built on the banks of Lake Erie, and defeated and captured a superior British fleet in the Battle of Lake Erie. By eliminating further British threats on the lake, Perry's victory compensated for serious American setbacks on land, restoring the war on the Canadian border to a deadlock.

pet banks
The Whigs' name for the state banks in which, after they lost the Bank War with Jackson, the president deposited government revenues. Many of the pet banks proved irresponsible when sums of money previously unimaginable were given to them. Their freewheeling "wildcat" loans contributed to a repeat of the Panic of 1819 and, after Van Buren's inauguration in 1837, a serious depression.

petite guerre
French for "little war," roughly the equivalent of the English term "American style." Petite guerre consisted of sudden surprise attacks on outlying New England villages and towns, destruction of them, and quick withdrawal. Attacks were usually supervised by French officers but carried out by Indians.

Pickett's Charge
The Confederate frontal assault on the Union center across open country on the third day of the Battle of Gettysburg in July 1863. It was a blunder. Lee attacked the Union army at its strongest point.

pig iron
The form in which manufacturers of steel and finished iron goods purchased iron from iron smelters. The ingots were called "pigs" because of their rounded shape, like a pig at rest.

Pike, Zebulon (1779–1813)
Army officer who, on orders from Louisiana Governor James Wilkinson in 1806, explored the southern part of the Louisiana Purchase and into Spanish Mexico. Pike's party traveled 4,000 miles; but the expedition was not as celebrated as Lewis and Clark's, probably because, in part, President Jefferson suspected Pike was involved in the "Burr Conspiracy." He was not.

Pilgrims
Term applied to the small sect of Separatist Puritans by one of their leaders, William Bradford. They were Calvinists but insisted on separating from the Church of England; they were the dominant people in the Plymouth colony, founded in 1620.

Pinkertons
Employees of the Pinkerton Detective Agency. Originally a company that provided bodyguards and criminal investigators, the agency was best known in the late nineteenth century for helping employers destroy labor unions among their workers.

Pitt, William the elder (1708–1778)
Energetic and effective head of the British government during the French and Indian War. Pitt designed the policy of concentrating British military might in North America.

placer mining
The method of mining employed by the men who flocked to California in the great gold rush of 1949 and for several years thereafter. Placer gold was pure gold mixed with sand, earth, and gravel of river beds. Extracting it was an entirely mechanical process—washing it from the worthless dirt called "tailings"; no chemicals or expensive heavy machines were necessary. The Forty-Niners shoveled the gravel into a wooden box or trough with riffles at the bottom to catch the heavy gold while a constant stream of water floated the lighter sand and clay away. As long as the placer deposits held out, a poor man was at no disadvantage. Anyone willing to work could mine placer gold.

Plymouth Company (and London Company)
Commercial companies—early corporations—chartered by the Crown in 1606 and granted land in North America where they were authorized to found colonies. The London Company founded Jamestown, Virginia, in 1607, the Plymouth Company Plymouth Plantation in Massachusetts in 1620.

pocket veto
Article 1, Section 7, of the Constitution provides that a bill approved by Congress becomes a law ten days after the president receives it (or sooner if he signs it) unless he vetoes the bill, explaining his objections to it. However, if Congress "prevents" the president's return of an unsigned bill by adjourning within ten days of sending it to the president, the bill fails to become law, and the president is not required to write a veto message. This is called a "pocket veto."

Pontiac (1720?–1769)
Chief of the Ottawas, a loyal ally of the French during the French and Indian War. Like King Philip before him and Tecumseh after, he led a multitribal uprising against the British in 1763 aimed at driving them out of what is now Ohio, Indiana, Michigan, and Illinois. His warriors captured ten of twelve British forts; they were defeated at the battle of Bushy Run.

popular sovereignty
Strictly defined, rule by the majority of people. In politics after 1854, the term referred to the principle of the Kansas–Nebraska Act that a majority of the settlers of Kansas (and other territories) would decide by majority vote whether they would enter the Union as slave states or as free states.

"positive good"
Catchword applied to the aggressive defense of slavery that was a response to the abolitionist movement during the 1830s. Most white southerners had considered slavery at best a necessary evil saddled on the South by history. After 1830, proslavery Americans ceased to be defensive and

maintained that slavery was a positive good for both whites and blacks.

preemption
Sometimes called "squatter's rights," it was a proposed reform of federal land law that allowed squatters, people who had improved federal land before it was offered for sale, to buy what were their homes at the minimum per acre price. Preemption was designed to prevent speculators from outbidding actual settlers for land they had improved.

Proclamation of 1763
Shaken by the unforeseen Indian uprising led by Pontiac, the king and Parliament forbade colonials to settle west of the Appalachian ridge that separates the watersheds of streams flowing into the Atlantic and those emptying into the Ohio and Mississippi rivers. It was intended to allow a cooling-off of relations with the Indians, most of whom had been allies of the French.

proprietary colony
A colony owned by a man or group of men who were given large American land grants and the right to govern them by the king. Most of the colonies were, at least briefly, proprietary colonies. The two most successful were Maryland, owned by the Calvert family, and Pennsylvania, owned by the Penns.

Puritans
The name given to and accepted by English Calvinist Protestants; the word referred to their determination to purify the Church of England of Roman Catholic rituals and practices. Puritan emigrants peopled much of New England.

Quebec Act
Parliamentary act of 1774 regarded by some colonists as one of the Coercive (Intolerable) Acts designed to punish Massachusetts. It gave official status to the French language and Roman Catholic religion in Quebec and extended the boundaries of the province to the Ohio River, which incorporated into the province the country over which Britain and the colonies had fought France in the French and Indian War.

Queen Isabella (1451–1504, reigned 1475–1504)
Queen of Castille (Spain), known as "Isabella the Catholic" for her piety; she sponsored and partly financed Christopher Columbus's historic explorations.

"QWERTY"
The arrangement of keys on the keyboard of the first successful typewriter, it remains the arrangement of computers today. The configuration of letters was dictated by the fact that the strikers on manual typewriters were mechanically operated. To avoid jamming, Sholes kept the strikers of the most frequently used letters at a distance from one another.

recall
A progressive political reform at the state or municipal level, often coupled with the initiative. The recall enables voters to remove an elected official from office before his or her term has expired. As soon as a sufficient number of signatures on a petition to recall an official are certified, the question is put to voters in a referendum. If a majority votes to recall, the official is removed from office.

rectangular survey
The innovative system of land survey adopted by the Confederation Congress for the Northwest Territory. It impressed a gridiron pattern on the Territory before opening the land to sales. The rectangular survey was later adopted to other territories acquired by the United States from France and Mexico.

Red Scare
Term first applied to the post–World War I era when Attorney General A. Mitchell Palmer encouraged widespread fear that Communists seriously threatened American institutions and stability. The second Red Scare was during the Korean War, when Republicans, particularly Senator Joseph McCarthy of Wisconsin, convinced many Americans that the federal government was honeycombed with Communist subversives.

referendum
A popular election not to choose among candidates for a public office but to approve or disapprove a measure such as legislation put on the ballot by initiative, an official up for recall, or an amendment to a state constitutional or municipal charter.

Regulators
Back country farmers in the Carolinas who resented the neglect of their interests by the North and South Carolina colonial governments. They created their own illegal county governments and collected taxes, which they refused to send to the colonial capitals. The Regulators were defeated in the Battle of Alamance in 1771.

removal
The Indian policy of the federal government and most western state governments between the 1810s and the 1840s. Because Indian communal culture, based largely on hunting, was incompatible with American individualism and agriculture, Congress, the presidents, and state legislatures signed treaties, one by one, with the eastern tribes in which the Indians agreed to remove to west of the Mississippi, usually to Indian Territory (present-day Oklahoma), giving up their claims to land east of the river.

Revere, Paul (1735–1818)
Boston silversmith and leader of the city's Sons of Liberty. His engraving of the Boston Massacre of 1770 misrepresented the British soldiers as aggressively attacking Bostonians. In 1774, on horseback, Revere rushed the militant Suffolk Resolves from Boston to Philadelphia where the First Continental Congress was meeting. The next spring, he made the shorter but more famous "Midnight Ride of Paul Revere," dashing into the Massachusetts countryside to warn rebellious farmers that British troops were marching to Concord to seize colonial arms stored there.

revisionists
Historians of World War I who claimed that underlying the stated reasons for American intervention in World War I was the fact that American financiers and munitions makers had so great a stake in a British victory that they maneuvered the United States into the war.

rider
Legislator's term for a (usually unrelated) clause that is attached to a bill already under consideration in Congress or in a state assembly. The proponent of the rider avoids the risk of having a committee prevent it from reaching the floor. By attaching it as an "amendment" to a bill that Congress cannot easily vote down, such as an appropriations bill, those who dislike the rider will—it is hoped—have to hold their noses and vote for it.

"Rock of Chickamauga"
Nickname given to Civil War General George H. Thomas for preventing a rout of Union troops at Chickamauga by holding his line like a "rock." Thomas was a Virginian but refused to join the Confederacy.

Rogers, Will (1879–1935)
The most popular humorist of the 1920s and early 1930s. Originally a rope trick performer in vaudeville, Rogers's running patter, sharply witty but delivered in a folksy Oklahoma drawl, and his engaging smile made him a national favorite on the stage, on radio, and in films. Part Cherokee, Rogers boasted of his Indian heritage. He was highly political and actively praised President Roosevelt.

Rough Riders
The informal name given to a volunteer cavalry unit of the Spanish–American War associated with future president Theodore Roosevelt (although he was actually second in command). The name was stolen from Buffalo Bill's *Wild West* show. Many of the Rough Riders were showpeople, athletes, and cowboys. By exaggerating the Rough Riders' role in capturing San Juan Hill outside Santiago de Cuba, Roosevelt made his name a household word.

round robin
A petition on which signers wrote their names not below the text of their demands, but in the margins around the text. The message was that there was no single instigator or leader of the movement, but that all signed it as equals.

royal colony
A colony administered by the Crown. No colonies were founded as royal colonies. However, all were "royalized," taken over by the monarch, before the War for Independence except Rhode Island, Connecticut, Maryland, and Pennsylvania.

Sacco and Vanzetti
Italian immigrant anarchists arrested for armed robbery and murder in 1920,

convicted for the crime, and sentenced to death. They became the focus of an international protest movement based on the belief that they were innocent and were being railroaded because they were Italian immigrants and political radicals. Sacco and Vanzetti were electrocuted in 1927.

safety bicycle
Invented late in the 1880s (by whom is disputed), it replaced the dangerous big-wheel "bone crusher" and in the 1890s made bicycling, already a popular recreation among young men, a national mania. In essentials, the design of the safety bicycle is identical to bicycles today. Its most important social consequence was its attractiveness to women, who defied the convention that women should be physically inactive; young women became as avid bicyclists as young men.

salutary neglect
Salutary means "healthy," "wholesome." The term refers to the colonial policy of British Prime Minister Robert Walpole: so long as the colonies were profitable to British manufacturers and merchants, it would be folly to antagonize colonials by close political control and even strict enforcement of trade laws the colonials violated.

Samuel Gompers (1850–1924)
Principal founder of the American Federation of Labor and its annually elected president from 1886 to 1924. Gompers believed in organizing only skilled workers and in working for "bread and butter" goals: high wages and shorter hours. He opposed ultimate utopian goals.

Santa Fe Trail
Trail between Independence, Missouri and Santa Fe in Mexico (now New Mexico) blazed by William Becknell, a trader, in 1821. For fourteen years, wagon convoys of increasing size carried American goods over the trail, exchanging them for furs, silver, and gold. The Santa Fe Trail tied Santa Fe more closely economically to the United States than to Mexico.

Schlieffen Plan
Secret German military plan to resolve Germany's problem in facing powerful enemies in both the east (Russia) and the west (France). First proposed in 1905 and often amended, the plan called for an all-out attack on France, forcing France (and possibly Britain) out of the war before Germans moved east to fight Russia.

Scotch-Irish
Protestant Irish from Northern Ireland (Ulster) whose ancestors were lowlands Scots settled in Ireland on lands confiscated from Catholic Irish. They had been a combative people in Scotland and Ireland; they remained so in North America, where they were the largest single immigrant group in the eighteenth century. Most settled on the frontier and were the vanguard of expansion into Indian lands.

sea dogs
The name adopted by intensely Spain-hating English seafarers, mostly from Devonshire in

the southwest, who, during Elizabeth I's reign, raided and looted Spanish ships and ports when, officially, England and Spain were at peace.

Second American Party System
Between the mid-1790s and about 1816, the Federalists and the Jefferson Republicans competed for power in the United States. The Federalists disintegrated after the War of 1812 and, until 1824, the Republicans were effectively the only American party. In 1824 the Republicans shattered. Beginning in 1828 the Democratic-Republicans, later the Democratic party, cohered under the leadership of Andrew Jackson. In 1834 the Whig party was organized in opposition to the Democrats. This second party system survived until the 1850s, when the Whig party fell apart. The emergence of a new Republican party, which included former Whigs, marked the beginning of the third party system that survives today.

Second Continental Congress
Meeting of delegates from the thirteen colonies, convened in 1775, which dispatched George Washington to take command of rebellious militiamen in Massachusetts and, in July 1776, adopted the Declaration of Independence. The Congress was the governing body of the "United States" throughout the War for Independence.

Section 7(a)
The section of the National Industrial Recovery Act of 1933 that obligated employers to bargain with labor unions approved by a majority of employees. When the Supreme Court declared the NRA unconstitutional, Congress reenacted Section 7(a) as the Wagner Act of 1935.

Serra, Junípero (1713–1784)
A Franciscan missionary in Mexico who, between 1769 and 1784, founded nine missions in California between San Diego and San Francisco. The missions were self-sufficient Indian communities governed by priests like Serra. Eventually, missions were built within a (long) day's walk of one another so that travelers along the *camino real* never had to sleep outdoors.

settlement house
An immigrant aid institutions, founded in immigrant neighborhoods during the final decades of the nineteenth century, that provided charity but also educational and recreational programs. The most famous one was Hull House, founded by Jane Addams in Chicago.

Seven Sisters
Seven elite women's colleges in the Northeast, most founded in the late nineteenth century. Named after the Pleiades, seven sisters of Greek mythology—and a constellation—they were the social equivalent and, at the turn of the century, probably the educational equals of the Ivy League colleges. Four of the Sisters were in Massachusetts (Mount Holyoke, Radcliffe, Smith, and Wellesley); two were in New York

(Barnard and Vassar); and one was in Pennsylvania (Bryn Mawr).

sharecroppers
Tenant farmers who, in return for use of the land, a cabin, a mule and plow, and seed, gave the proceeds from the sale of (usually) half of the crop to the owner of the land. Sharecropping developed in the South in response to the fact that landowners needed people to work the land and former slaves needed a means of making a living and a place to live.

Shays' Rebellion
Armed uprising of several thousand farmers in western Massachusetts led by Daniel Shays. They resented the state's taxation policies, which favored mercantile interests in Boston, and Boston's political domination of the state. The rebellion was easily suppressed; but the fact that it started at all sufficiently alarmed conservatives that they welcomed the proposal to meet and strengthen United States government.

Sherman Antitrust Act
Congressional legislation of 1890, it forbade business combinations (monopolies and near-monopolies) "in restraint of trade"— that is, combinations designed to eliminate competition. It was ineffective during the 1890s because the attorneys general of the decade were unsympathetic with its purposes and the courts hostile.

Sherman bow ties
The name given by General Sherman's soldiers in Georgia to sections of rail that they heated over fires of railroad ties and bent into the shape of bow ties around telegraph poles. "Sherman bow ties" symbolized of the totality of the destruction the army wreaked in Georgia.

siglo de oro
Spanish for "golden century." It refers to the 1500s when American gold and silver made Spain by far the richest, most powerful, and most feared country in Europe.

"single tax"
The brainchild and rallying cry of a movement inspired by Henry George's book, *Progress and Poverty*, published in 1879. George's proposed "single tax" was to be levied on "unearned increment"—income from mere ownership of property, such as rents, which owed nothing to enterprise or ingenuity.

slave driver
Term applied to a supervisor of slaves— an overseer—who was himself a slave. In African-American folklore after the Civil War, slave drivers were more brutal than white overseers or masters. Frederick Douglass said as much in his autobiography. The personal exemption from heavy labor being a slave driver entailed, and other privileges, were apt to encourage such behavior.

"slavocracy"
A word contrived by antislavery Republicans as an equivalent of *democracy* or *aristocracy*, meaning rule by the "slave power."

Smith, Al (Alfred E. Smith, 1873–1944)
Popular and successful reform governor of New York through most of the 1920s, he was the Democratic presidential candidate in 1928. Smith lost, mainly because it was a time of prosperity. But because of anti-Catholicism he also failed to carry eight southern states that were dependably Democratic: Smith was a Roman Catholic.

social Darwinism
Philosophy or "ideology" of the late nineteenth century that justified great wealth, even when made by ruthless and unethical means, by defining economic life in terms associated with the Darwinian theory of evolution: "survival of the fittest" and "law of the jungle."

Social Security
The name given to the federal program that, beginning in 1935, provided pensions for the elderly. Federal old age pensions were not in the New Deal's original plans; the Democratic party established Social Security because of the popularity of an unrealistic pension plan advocated by Dr. Francis Townsend of California.

Specie Circular
President Jackson's 1836 directive to the Treasury Department to accept only specie (gold and silver coin) in payment for federal lands. Jackson's purpose was to halt a runaway inflation in paper money issued by state banks, a crisis for which he was in part responsible. With only about one gold dollar for every ten paper dollars in circulation, the Specie Circular caused a rash of bank failures and, a year later, a serious depression.

Spillane, Mickey (1918–)
Author of the "Mike Hammer" crime novels popular during the 1950s; by 1956 all seven of Spillane's books were on the list of the ten best-selling books of all time. Private detective Mike Hammer was brutal, in fact murderous; Spillane also pushed laws proscribing the description of sexual activities to the era's limits.

Spirit of St. Louis
Name of the plane specifically designed by Charles A. Lindbergh and others for a single flight: the first solo crossing of the Atlantic by air, which Lindbergh completed in 1927 in the greatest occasion of popular hysteria in a decade in which there were many.

"spoils system"
The view that government jobs should be used by the party in control to reward those who supported the party and worked for its success in elections. Government jobs were the "spoils" of political war. A Jackson supporter, William Marcy, put it bluntly in 1829: "To the victor belongs the spoils." In introducing the spoils system to the federal government in 1829, Jackson broke with the tradition—an ideal rather than, necessarily, the reality—that the people best qualified to do a government job should be appointed to it.

stagflation
Term coined during the presidency of Gerald Ford to describe an unprecedented economic phenomenon: simultaneous inflation and recession (stagnation). Previously inflation had characterized an overheated economy, and prices had fallen during recessions.

"Stalwarts" (and "Half-Breeds")
Two bitterly opposed factions of the Republican party during the 1870s and early 1880s. The Stalwarts, led by Senator Roscoe Conkling of New York, unabashedly defended the spoils system; "stalwart" workers for the party should be rewarded with government jobs. The Half-Breeds, led by Senator James B. Blaine of Maine, flirted with the civil service reform movement but, in reality, used the patronage as cynically as the Stalwarts did.

Stamp Act of 1765
Second attempt by Parliament to tax the colonies. It was met with violent protest and the Stamp Act Congress, a concerted action by delegates from nine colonies. The Stamp Act was repealed before it went into effect.

Stanton, Elizabeth Cady (1815–1902)
One of the founders of American feminism, she resented the disabilities she suffered because of her sex from girlhood. In 1840, on her wedding trip to Europe, she and several other women were denied the right to sit on the floor of an antislavery convention. From then on, while raising seven children, Stanton devoted her life to winning the vote and professional opportunities for women and reforming divorce laws.

Starr Report
Report of a committee chaired by Kenneth Starr ostensibly investigating the Clintons' involvement in dubious finances in Arkansas. Finding nothing incriminating, the committee investigated Clinton's sexual relationship with a young White House intern, Monica Lewinski. Starr tricked Clinton into lying under oath, then presented physical evidence proving his perjury. The Starr Report led directly to Clinton's impeachment in 1998.

Stimson Doctrine
American proclamation in 1931 (erroneously attributed to Secretary of State Henry L. Stimson; it was President Hoover's decision) that the United States would recognize no territorial changes accomplished by armed aggression. It was a response to the Japanese detachment of Manchuria from China.

Stono
A plantation in South Carolina that was the center of a slave rebellion in 1739. The slaves, some of them Roman Catholics from the Congo, hoped to escape to Spanish Florida, where, outside St. Augustine, there was a fortified village of runaway black slaves.

strict construction
The counterpart to "broad construction" argued in Washington's cabinet by Secretary of State Thomas Jefferson. Jefferson said that the Bank of the United States Hamilton proposed was unconstitutional because the Constitution did not specifically allow Congress to create such an institution. Jefferson's strict construction of the Constitution was a foundation of his commitment to small, weak government.

subtreasury system
After the demise of the Second Bank of the United States in 1836 and President Jackson's unsuccessful experiment depositing federal funds in state banks, the "pet banks," President Martin Van Buren in 1837 attempted to disassociate the government from banking by establishing "subtreasuries," essentially government vaults in which all federal monies would be stored. The system was never really functional because the government ran a deficit each year of Van Buren's presidency.

Suffolk Resolves
A series of resolutions drafted in Boston (Suffolk County, Massachusetts) in 1774 and carried to the First Continental Congress in Philadelphia where they were adopted. The Suffolk Resolves were assertive without being rebellious in their opposition to the Intolerable Acts; they helped to steer the colonial protest movement toward defiance of the king and Parliament.

Sugar Act (1764)
Parliamentary legislation that lowered the duty on molasses imported from outside the empire but also provided for enforcement by vice-admiralty courts, which were without juries. It was the first attempt to tax the colonies that was roundly protested.

supply-side (economics)
Name given to a federal economic policy formulated by Arthur Laffer and adopted by the Reagan administration. Cutting taxes the wealthy paid would increase the nation's supply of goods and services; unemployment would be reduced by the growing economy; the distribution of wealth—each person's share—would take care of itself. "Reaganomics," as critics called the president's policy, was an updating of the "trickle down" theories of Andrew Mellon, secretary of the treasury during the 1920s.

sweatshop
Name applied to hand manufacturing in private apartments, it was the bulwark of the needle trades (finishing men's and women's garments with buttonholes and the like). The sweatshop was the urban equivalent of the traditional "putting-out" system.

swing states
States in which the Democratic and Republican parties were about equal in strength during the late nineteenth century and that could, therefore, "swing" either way in presidential elections. The most important swing state was New York, with 35–36 electoral votes. Only in 1876 did the victorious presidential candidate fail to carry New York, and that contest is known as the "stolen election."

tabloids
Strictly speaking, newspapers printed in a new format introduced during the 1920s.

Their pages were half the size of traditional newspapers and turned like the pages of a book rather than unfolding. They were convenient for urban readers who commuted in crowded trolleys and subways. In practice, tabloids emphasized sensational scandals over conventional news.

Taft, William Howard (1857–1930)
The twenty-seventh president of the United States, he was unfairly maligned as a reactionary (and has been since by some historians). In fact, Taft was an able functionary with a phlegmatic judicial temperament—which he knew. He did not want to be president and hated being president. He wanted to be a judge, and fortune smiled on him. In 1921 the Chief Justice of the Supreme Court died just a few months after his successor would have been named by the Democratic Wilson. But a Republican was president, and he gave Taft the job that he had wanted for fifteen years.

Tammany Hall
A social club that became the Democratic party's political machine in New York City. Into the 1920s, Tammany Hall ran New York City except for brief interludes when reformers won elections by protesting Tammany's corruption.

Tenochtitlán
Capital of the Aztec empire, a large, sophisticated, and well-defended city surrounded by Lake Texcoco in the valley of Mexico, the site of present-day Mexico City. The Aztecs called themselves the Mexica.

Tenskwatawa (1770?–1834?)
Also known as "The Prophet," a Shawnee visionary, brother to the great chief Tecumseh, who, with great success, preached a revival of traditional Indian ways to the Indians of the Northwest Territory. He founded "Orphet's Town," or Tippecanoe, in northern Indiana. In 1811, ignoring the instructions of the absent Tecumseh, he ordered an attack on a force led by William Henry Harrison that ended in a devastating defeat for the Indians and the destruction of Tippecanoe. The Prophet moved to Missouri and Kansas and continued to preach his message with less success.

The Burr Conspiracy
In 1805 and 1806 Aaron Burr, his political career ruined, traveled down the Mississippi with an Irish adventurer from Ohio, meeting confidentially with several prominent westerners, including Andrew Jackson of Tennessee and, in New Orleans, the governor of the Louisiana Territory, James Wilkinson. Most historians suspect he planned to establish a new country in Mexican Texas, possibly including parts of Louisiana. Wilkinson accused him of treason; Burr was tried but acquitted.

The Hundred Days
Term coined in the summer of 1933 for the first three and a half months of the Roosevelt administration, when FDR deluged Congress with bills to relieve those hit hardest by the Depression, to stimulate economic recovery, and to reform the abuses the New Dealers believed caused the Great Depression.

The Influence of Sea Power upon History
A book by American navy captain (later admiral) Alfred T. Mahan, published in 1890. Mahan wrote that no nation could be great unless it had an industrious foreign trade protected by a powerful navy. His persuasiveness made the book a best seller and influential for many years on European leaders like the emperor of Germany and Winston Churchill of Great Britain as well as on Americans. Mahan's theories convinced Congress to build a modern navy; the need of steam-powered ships for coaling stations throughout the world contributed to the American turn to imperialism during the 1890s.

The Man in the Gray Flannel Suit
Novel of 1955 by Sloan Wilson that, despite its critique of suburban life and middle-class ambition to accumulate material goods, was a best seller among people like the characters of the novel. Its popularity indicated to some social critics that apparently placid Americans were discontented with their lot.

The Man Nobody Knows
Best-selling book by advertising company executive Bruce Barton, published in 1925. It depicted Jesus as a business executive (and advertising man). Rather than being condemned as blasphemous, Barton's bizarre portrayal of Jesus was accepted in the business culture of the Coolidge era.

The Wilderness
Heavily wooded country west of Chancellorsville, Virginia, where General Grant began his assault on Richmond in early May 1864; 30,000 soldiers were killed, wounded, or captured in two days, 18,000 of them Union troops.

three-fifths compromise
The most artificially contrived provision of the Constitution of 1787, it averted a northern state–southern state split by providing that slaves (numerous only in the South) be counted as three-fifths of a person in the apportionment of each state's tax burden and representation in Congress.

Tidewater
Land bordering the broad, slow-moving tidal rivers of the Chesapeake Bay; the most valuable land in Virginia and Maryland because at high tide seagoing ships could tie up directly at plantations. The "Tidewater aristocracy" became Virginia's ruling class.

time zones
A part of everyone's life today, the four times zones of the contiguous United States were proposed in 1870 and adopted by the federal government in 1883. Previously, time was a local concern, set by town and city governments. Unsurprisingly, even in adjacent cities, "the right time" was different. Once railroads, which ran "by the clock," extended 1,000 miles and more, efficiency and safety demanded uniform time nationally.

"Tippecanoe and Tyler Too"
The Whigs' euphonious campaign slogan in 1840. Tippecanoe referred to William Henry Harrison's victory over the Indians of the Old Northwest almost thirty years previously. The Whigs unembarrassingly imitated the Democrats' celebration of Jackson as the "hero of New Orleans." Vice presidential candidate John Tyler had little following outside Virginia, but "Tyler Too" rhymed nicely. (Tippecanoe and Tyler Too did not carry Virginia.)

Townshend Duties
Parliamentary taxes on various colonial luxury imports. All were abolished after an effective colonial boycott except the duty on tea.

Treaty of Ghent (1814)
Anglo–American treaty ending the War of 1812, negotiated in Ghent (now Belgium) by John Quincy Adams, Albert Gallatin, Henry Clay, and several other commissioners. The talks dragged on because the British insisted on establishing an Indian buffer state between the United States and Canada. In the end, both sides agreed to end the war on the status quo antebellum—that is, with nothing changed from what it had been before the war.

Treaty of San Lorenzo (Pinckney's Treaty)
Treaty with Spain in 1795. Spain gave up claims to disputed territory (most of present-day Alabama and Mississippi) and, more important at the time, agreed to allow Americans in the West to export their crops through New Orleans, then a Spanish city.

Treaty of Washington (1921)
Post–World War I naval disarmament treaty engineered by Secretary of State Charles Evans Hughes. The United States, Great Britain, Japan, France, and Italy agreed to limit the size of their navies in proportion to their defensive needs.

trickle down
Phrase coined by Andrew Mellon, secretary of the treasury during the 1920s, to justify cutting taxes for the rich and increasing the tax burden on the middle and working classes. When the wealthy invested their windfalls, Mellon argued, prosperity would "trickle down" to all.

Truman Doctrine
The government's policy to resist Soviet-backed attempts to overthrow anti-Communist governments with massive financial and military aid.

Twain, Mark (Samuel Langhorne Clemens, 1835–1910)
Probably the single most popular American writer of the late nineteenth century, best known for *The Adventures of Huckleberry Finn*, simultaneously a boy's adventure story, a critique of racism, and a satire of antebellum southerners. Twain was a prolific writer for newspapers and magazines as well as in

books; he was also a successful and hilarious lecturer in great demand in Europe as well as at home.

Twelfth Amendment (1804)

After the original method of electing the president and vice president resulted in a president and vice president of different political parties in 1796, and, in 1800, a tie that gave the choice of president to the defeated political party, it was clear that the Constitution needed to be amended. The Twelfth Amendment provided that presidential electors separately designate their choice for president and their choice for vice president, a system that is still in effect.

U.S. English

A propaganda organization and political lobby of the 1990s dedicated to winning a constitutional amendment stating that English was the official language of the United States. Members of the organization feared that the concentration of Spanish-speaking immigrants in the Southwest would result in the loss of the politically and culturally unifying power of a single national language.

Uncle Tom's Cabin

Novel by Harriet Beecher Stowe, published in 1852. It was undoubtedly the most effective antislavery propaganda ever published. "Uncle Tom" is a kindly, religious slave who, in being passed from owner to owner, experiences both the worst and the best of southern slave owners. Stowe based his experiences on actual events she gleaned from newspapers. When assailed by southerners for distorting reality, she published a "key" to her novel, containing references documenting every significant event in the book.

underground railroad

Informal term for networks of white and black abolitionists in the northern states who helped fugitive slaves win their freedom by hiding them from authorities; providing food, shelter, and money; and passing them on to the next "conductor" on the line. Few conductors were able to stay on the job for many years because once they were identified, they were harassed by officials and professional slave catchers.

"unrestricted submarine warfare"

Name given to Germany's total exploitation of the U-boat, a weapon on which it held a monopoly. It meant attacking, without warning, all ships of every type engaged in trade with Great Britain. Because it violated the American principle of complete freedom of the seas for neutral vessels, Germany's resumption of the policy as of February 1, 1916, ensured American intervention on the side of the Allies.

Valentine's Day Massacre

The February 1929 murder of seven rival gang members by gunmen employed by Chicago bootlegger Al Capone. Although there had been hundreds of "gangland murders" in Chicago, the massacre aroused so much anger that authorities became much

more serious in their attempts to bring Capone down.

vertical integration

A means of dominating an industry, used most famously by steelmaker Andrew Carnegie; it involved getting control of sufficient sources of raw materials to provide for a company's needs (in Carnegie's case, iron and coal mines) and transportation (Great Lakes ore boats and a railroad from Lake Erie to the Carnegie mill near Pittsburgh). Through cost cutting at every step of the business, Carnegie's selling price was far lower than that of competitors who dealt with independent mines and railroads.

Vesey, Denmark (1767?–1822)

A free black carpenter and Methodist preacher in Charleston, Vesey organized an abortive slave rebellion in 1822. He had been a seaman as a boy and intended for the rebel slaves to seize ships and sail for Haiti. An informer betrayed the conspiracy, and Vesey and other ringleaders were hanged.

Vespucci, Amerigo (1451–1512)

Italian explorer who made two of the earliest European voyages to the Western Hemisphere (possibly several more). He was first to recognize that the lands Columbus discovered were not "the Indies" but were a "New World," previously unknown to Europe. A German mapmaker mistakenly believed Vespucci had discovered this New World and named it "America," the Latin form of his name.

vice-admiralty courts

Courts originally restricted to special litigations in which decisions were rendered by judges without juries. George Grenville tried to transfer the cases of accused violators of the Sugar Act and Stamp Act to these courts because colonial juries, especially in smuggling cases in New England, frequently ignored overwhelming evidence of guilt and acquitted their neighbors.

victory gardens

Small family gardens, dubbed "victory gardens" when the federal government promoted them as a contribution to the war effort during World War II. By 1945, 20.5 million families were tending them; in that year between 30 and 40 percent of the nation's vegetable production was home-grown.

Vietnamization

President Nixon's policy of replacing American combat troops in Vietnam with South Vietnamese troops. In part, his program was designed to halt the increasing opposition to the war among working people who were sustaining the high casualties of the war.

Villa, Pancho (1877–1923)

The name under which Doroteo Arango, a Mexican revolutionary soldier and sometimes bandit, was first romanticized, then execrated in the United States. Villa's calculated murder of American engineers and

raid of Columbus, New Mexico, a border town, prompted Woodrow Wilson to send the U.S. Army to find and capture him in 1916. Villa eluded the expedition.

Virginia Dynasty

Four of the first five presidents were Virginians; thus, sometimes sarcastically, politicians alluded to a dynastic succession in the presidency. Even in 1824 two of the four candidates for the presidency, Crawford and Clay, were Virginia-born.

virtual representation

British constitutional principle that members of the House of Commons represented not only the people of the district from which they were elected, but all British subjects.

Wade, Benjamin F. (1800–1878)

Republican senator from Ohio; he was one of the leaders of the radical Republicans who demanded that southern rebels be harshly punished at war's end.

Wade–Davis Bill

Reconstruction plan enacted by Congress in July 1864 to counter Lincoln's proclamation setting terms by which the former Confederate states would be readmitted to the Union. It differed from Lincoln's plan in requiring 50 percent rather than 10 percent of a state's voters to take an oath of loyalty to the Union; and Congress, not the president, would direct the Reconstruction process.

"War Hawks"

Ultranationalistic members of the Congress, mostly westerners and southerners, all under 40 and Jefferson Republicans, many just elected to Congress for the first time, whose calls for war against Britain to defend American honor pressured President Madison in 1812 into asking for a declaration of war that he had worked to avoid.

War Industries Board

World War I superagency headed by financier Bernard Baruch and entrusted with coordinating production of industries vital to the war effort.

Watergate

Name of a luxury apartment and office complex in Washington where, in 1972, the Democratic party had its headquarters. When burglars in the office were arrested, a long, complex sequence of revelations tied the crime and an attempt to cover it up to President Nixon. The "Watergate scandal" was the cause of his disgrace and resignation in 1974.

Wayne, "Mad Anthony" (1745–1796)

Got his nickname because of his reckless bravery during the Revolution when he fought at Quebec, Brandywine—he captured Stony Point on the Hudson River, a major victory over the British—and in the South against Cornwallis. In 1794 he defeated the twice victorious Indians of the Northwest Territory at the Battle of Fallen Timbers.

Webster, Daniel (1782–1852)

Massachusetts Whig politician, usually considered the greatest orator in an age of great orators. In a Senate debate with Robert Hayne over the doctrine of nullification in 1830, Webster made an eloquent plea for the Union against state sovereignty as the wellspring of American liberty.

"wets"

The name applied during the 1920s to people who opposed Prohibition and called for its repeal. Supporters of Prohibition were known as "drys."

Whiskey Rebellion

Uprising of farmers in western Pennsylvania protesting the federal excise tax of 7 cents on a gallon of whiskey, practically their only export to the East. Determined to demonstrate the authority of the federal government, Washington led a large army toward the rebellious area to suppress the rebels. The rebellion fell apart before force was necessary.

Whitman, Marcus and Narcissa

(1802–1847) and (1808–1847)
Presbyterian missionaries in the Oregon Country; along with another couple, the Whitmans went overland to the Oregon Country in 1836. (The two wives were the first women to cross the North American continent since Sacajawea with the Lewis and Clark party.) The Whitmans' mission at Walla Walla was spectacularly unsuccessful, in part because of the couple's disdainful attitude toward the Indian culture. When a measles epidemic devastated the local Indians in 1847, they murdered the Whitmans and twelve other whites.

Williams, Roger (1603?–1683)

A learned, cantankerous minister, an early emigrant to Massachusetts Bay who quarreled with the governors of the colony, was banished, and founded the town of Providence, which became the core of the Rhode Island colony. Williams insisted that religious belief was an individual choice and responsibility; Rhode Island tolerated all forms of worship.

Wilmot Proviso

A rider attached to an army appropriations bill in 1846, at the beginning of the war with Mexico, by Congressman David Wilmot, providing that "neither slavery nor involuntary servitude shall ever exist" in any lands taken from Mexico. The House of Representatives approved it and attached the Wilmot Proviso to fifty bills during and after the war. Each time, the proviso was removed in the Senate. The Wilmot Proviso inspired the formation of the Free Soil party.

Winthrop, John (1588–1649)

Prominent English Puritan who elected to emigrate to America rather than live in a country he believed sinful and a target of divine wrath. He was governor of the Massachusetts Bay colony ten of the colony's first twenty years and a major force in shaping the colony's character.

Wirt, William (1772–1834)

One of the best lawyers of his era, he argued 174 cases before the Supreme Court. Attorney general between 1817 and 1829, he strengthened the office. His patriotic and adulatory biography of Patrick Henry, published in 1817, made a Revolutionary War hero of the orator.

Wisconsin idea

The name given to the close partnership between the state government and state university in Wisconsin, initiated by the progressive Republican governor Robert M. La Follette early in the twentieth century. For example, the university's agricultural school not only educated future farmers but provided agents to visit farmers and advise them on agricultural problems.

WMD

Weapons of mass destruction. George W. Bush's claim that Saddam Hussein possessed chemical, biological, and possibly nuclear weapons with which he planned to launch a massive terrorist war was his chief justification for invading Iraq. No WMD were found after a year of searching. The revelation of the poor intelligence on which the president acted (or his outright lie) contributed to the sharp drop in his popularity in mid-2005.

Wolfe, General James (1727–1759)

British general who commanded the successful capture of Quebec in 1759. He was killed in the battle.

Worcester v. Georgia (1832)

When the state of Georgia arrested a Congregationalist minister for living among the Cherokee Indians without a state license to do so, the minister sued on the grounds that Georgia laws did not apply to Cherokee treaty lands. By a 5–1 vote, the Supreme Court found in Worcester's favor: the Cherokee nation's treaty with the United States took precedence over state laws. Georgia ignored the decision, and President Jackson refused to enforce the Court's decision.

Works Progress Administration (WPA)

The New Deal's broadest jobs program. The WPA not only provided money for construction projects but hired unemployed writers, scholars, actors, painters, and sculptors. Popular with the intelligentsia, the WPA was vilified by conservatives because many of its productions had a leftist political slant.

X, Y, Z Affair, the

X, Y, and Z were code names for three French diplomats who told Americans seeking to negotiate a treaty that talks could begin only after the United States made a loan to France and paid a large bribe to the French foreign minister. Indignation in the United States made President Adams briefly popular as he prepared to defend the nation's honor in a war with the French.

Zimmerman telegram

Diplomatic note wired to Mexico by German Foreign Minister Arthur Zimmerman, proposing that if the United States declared war on Germany, Mexico should attack the United States to keep the American army home. At the end of the war, Mexico would be rewarded by the return of the "lost provinces" of New Mexico and Arizona. The telegram was intercepted by the British and divulged to the United States to encourage American intervention in the war.

Photo Credits

INDEX

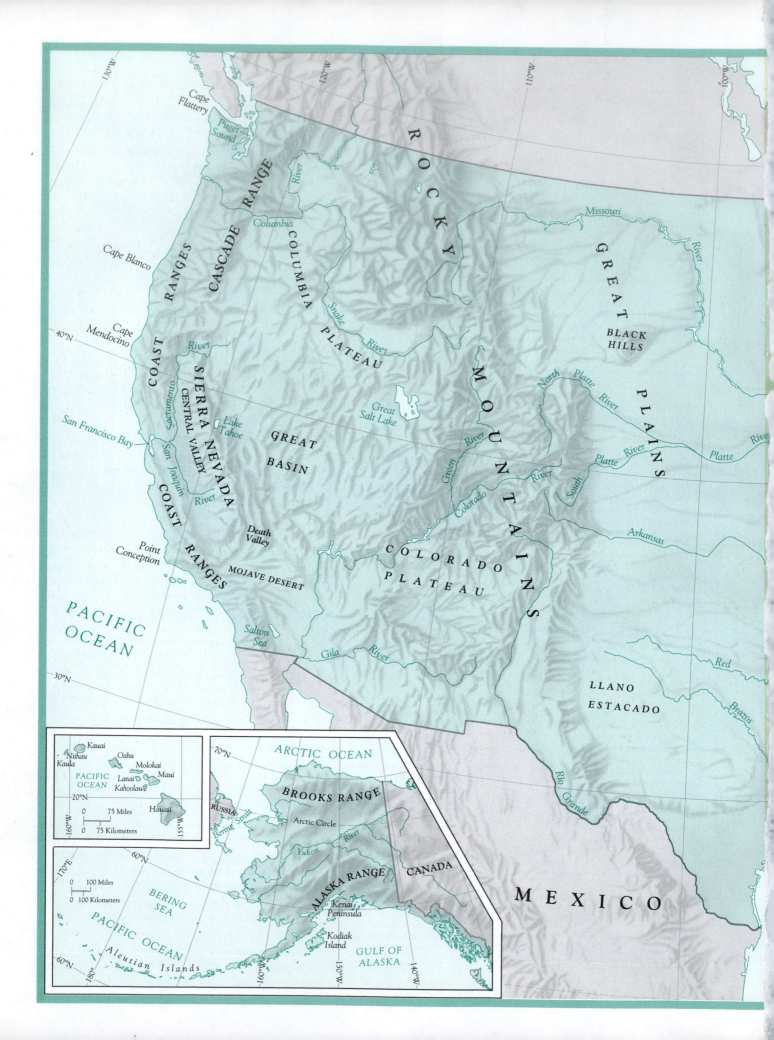

ROCKY
CASCADE RANGE
COAST RANGES
COLUMBIA PLATEAU
GREAT PLAINS
M O U N T A I N S
SIERRA NEVADA
CENTRAL VALLEY
GREAT BASIN
COAST RANGES
COLORADO PLATEAU
MOJAVE DESERT
LLANO ESTACADO
BLACK HILLS

Cape Flattery
Puget Sound
Columbia River
Cape Blanco
Snake River
Missouri River
Cape Mendocino
40°N
River
Great Salt Lake
North Platte River
San Francisco Bay
Sacramento
Lake Tahoe
Green River
Platte River
Platte
San Joaquin River
Colorado River
South Platte River
Arkansas
Point Conception
Death Valley
PACIFIC OCEAN
Salton Sea
30°N
Gila River
Red
Brazos
Rio Grande
M E X I C O

180°W
170°W
110°W
100°W

PACIFIC OCEAN
Kauai
Niihau
Kaula
Oahu
Molokai
Lanai
Kahoolawe
Maui
Hawaii
20°N
0   75 Miles
0   75 Kilometers
160°W
155°W

ARCTIC OCEAN
70°N
BROOKS RANGE
RUSSIA
Arctic Circle
Bering Strait
Yukon River
ALASKA RANGE
CANADA
Kenai Peninsula
60°N
BERING SEA
Kodiak Island
PACIFIC OCEAN
Aleutian Islands
GULF OF ALASKA
170°E
180°
100°W
150°W
140°W
0   100 Miles
0   100 Kilometers